THE OXFORD HANDBOOK OF

MARTIN LUTHER'S THEOLOGY

THE OXFORD HANDBOOK OF

MARTIN LUTHER'S THEOLOGY

Edited by

ROBERT KOLB

IRENE DINGEL

and

L'UBOMÍR BATKA

OXFORD

UNIVERSITY PRESS

OXFORD
UNIVERSITY PRESS

Great Clarendon Street, Oxford, OX2 6DP,
United Kingdom

Oxford University Press is a department of the University of Oxford.
It furthers the University's objective of excellence in research, scholarship,
and education by publishing worldwide. Oxford is a registered trade mark of
Oxford University Press in the UK and in certain other countries

Published in the United States of America by Oxford University Press
198 Madison Avenue, New York, NY 10016, United States of America

British Library Cataloguing in Publication Data
Data available

Library of Congress Cataloging in Publication Data
Data available

ISBN 978–0–19–960470–8 (Hbk.)
ISBN 978–0–19–876647–6 (Pbk.)

CONTENTS

PART V LUTHER'S VIEW OF SANCTIFIED LIVING

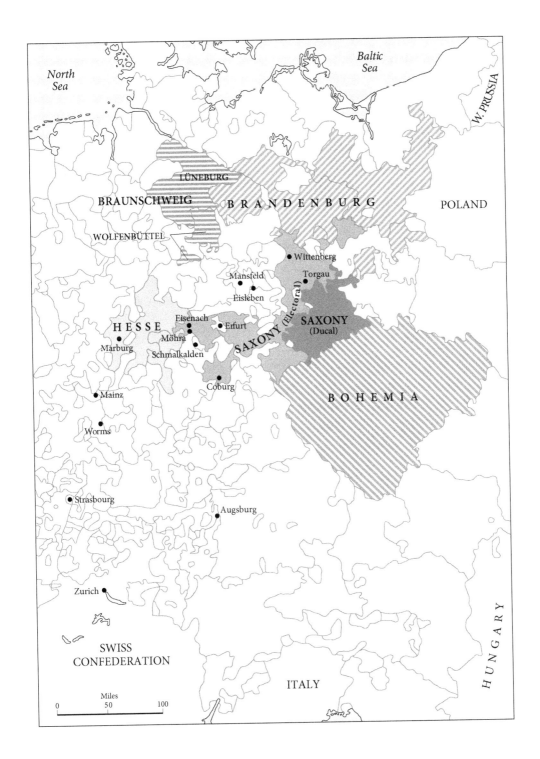

North
Sea

Baltic
Sea

W. PRUSSIA

LÜNEBURG

BRAUNSCHWEIG

BRANDENBURG

POLAND

WOLFENBÜTTEL

• Wittenberg

Mansfeld
•

Torgau
•

• Eisleben

Eisenach
•

HESSE

Möhra
•

• Erfurt

SAXONY (Electoral)

SAXONY
(Ducal)

Marburg
•

Schmalkalden
•

Coburg
•

• Mainz

BOHEMIA

Worms
•

• Strasbourg

Augsburg
•

Zurich •

SWISS
CONFEDERATION

HUNGARY

ITALY

Miles

0   50   100

LIST OF ABBREVIATIONS

Ap	Apology of the Augsburg Confession
AWA	*Archiv zur Weimarer Ausgabe.* Cölogne: Bohlau, 1981
BC	*The Book of Concord.* Robert Kolb and Timothy J. Wengert (ed.). Minneapolis: Fortress, 2000
BSLK	*Die Bekenntnisschriften der evangelisch-lutherischen Kirche.* 11. ed. Göttingen: Vandenhoeck & Ruprecht, 1992
CA	Augsburg Confession
CP	Church Postil
CR	*Corpus Reformatorum* [1–25]. *Philippi Melanthonis Opera quae supersunt omnia.* C. G. Bretschneider and H. E. Bindweil (ed.). Halle and Braunschweig: Schwetschke, 1834–60
CR Z	*Corpus Reformatorum* [88–101] *Huldrych Zwingli Werke.* Berlin: Schwetschke/ Leipzig: Heinsius Nachfolger 1905–63
CR/CO	*Corpus Reformatorum, Calvini Opera.* G. Baum, E. Cunitz, and E. Reuss (ed.). Braunschweig: Schwetschke, 1863–1900
FC	Formula of Concord
Ep	Epitome
SD	Solid Declaration
LCC	Library of Christian Classics. Philadelphia: Westminster, 1953–65
LSA	*Martin Luther. Studienausgabe.* 6. vols. Hans-Ulrich Delius (ed.). Berlin/Leipzig: Evangelische Verlagsanstalt, 1979–99
LW	*Luther's Works.* Saint Louis/Philadelphia: Concordia/ Fortress, 1958–86
MBWR/MBWT	*Melanchthons Briefwechsel.* Heinz Scheible (ed.). Stuttgart-Bad Cannstatt: fromann-holzbog, 1977–; R = Register volumes, T = Texte volumes
MSA	*Melanchthons Werke in Auswahl* [Studienausgabe]. Robert Stupperich (ed.). 7 vols. Gütersloh: Gerd Mohn, 1951–75
WA	*D. Martin Luthers Werke.* Weimar: Böhlau, 1883–1993
Br	*Briefe*
DB	*Deutsche Bibel*
TR	*Tischreden*

LIST OF CONTRIBUTORS

Kenneth G. Appold, James Hastings Nichols Professor of Reformation History, Princeton Theological Seminary, Princeton, USA

Matthieu Arnold, Professor of Modern and Contemporary Christianity, Faculty of Protestant Theology, University of Strasbourg, Strasbourg, France

Heinrich Assel, Professor of Systematic Theology, Ernst Moritz Arndt University, Greifswald, Germany

Ľubomír Batka, Dean of the Lutheran Theological Faculty, Docent of Systematic Theology, Comenius University, Bratislava, Slovakia

Nestor Luiz João Beck, Professor and dean emeritus, Universidade Luterana do Brasil (ULBRA), Canoas, Brazil

Theo M. M. A. C. Bell, Lecturer emeritus, Faculteit Katholieke Theologie, University of Tilburg, Tilburg, The Netherlands

Thomas A. Brady, Jr., Peder Sather Professor emeritus of History, University of California–Berkeley, USA

Christoph Burger, Professor of Church History emeritus, Faculty of Theology, The Free University, Amsterdam, The Netherlands

Amy Nelson Burnett, Paula and D. B. Varner Professor of History, University of Nebraska/Lincoln, Lincoln, USA

David P. Daniel, Docent emeritus of Church History, Lutheran Theological Faculty, Comenius University, Bratislava, Slovakia

Theodor Dieter, Director and Research Professor, Centre of Ecumenical Studies, Strasbourg, France

Irene Dingel, Director of the Leibniz Institute of European History (Department of Western Church History), Mainz, and Professor of Church History and History of Dogma in the Evangelical Theological Faculty, Johann Gutenberg University, Mainz, Germany

Mary Jane Haemig, Professor of Church History, Luther Seminary, Saint Paul, USA

Erik Herrmann, Associate Professor of Historical Theology, Concordia Seminary, Saint Louis, USA

Paul R. Hinlicky, Professor of Lutheran Studies, Roanoke College, Salem, USA; Professor of Systematic Theology, Institute of Lutheran Theology; Docent, Evangelical Theological Faculty, Comenius University, Bratislava, Slovakia

Gordon A. Jensen, Academic Dean, William Hordern Professor of Theology, Lutheran Theological Seminary, Saskatoon, Canada

Robert Kolb, Professor of Systematic Theology emeritus, Concordia Seminary, Saint Louis, USA

Volker Leppin, Professor of Church History (Medieval and Reformation), Evangelical Theological Faculty, Eberhard-Karls University of Tübingen, Tübingen, Germany

Carter Lindberg, Professor of Church History emeritus, Boston University School of Theology, Boston, USA

Pilgrim W. K. Lo, Professor of Systematic and Historical Theology, Lutheran Theological Seminary, Hong Kong, China

Johannes von Lüpke, Professor of Systematic Theology, Kirchliche Hochschule Wuppertal/Bethel, Wuppertal, Germany

Mark Mattes, Professor of Theology and Philosophy, Grand View University, Des Moines, USA

Charlotte Methuen, Senior Lecturer in Church History, University of Glasgow, UK

Gregory Miller, Professor of History, Malone College, Canton, USA

Gerhard Müller, Landesbishop emeritus, The Evangelical-Lutheran Church of Braunschweig; Professor of Historical Theology Emeritus, Friedrich-Alexander University of Erlangen, Erlangen, Germany

Tom Joseph Omolo, Professor of Systematic Theology, Neema Lutheran College, Matongo, Kenya

Steven Paulson, Professor of Systematic Theology, Luther Seminary, Saint Paul, USA

J. Paul Rajashekar, Luther D. Reed Professor of Systematic Theology, The Lutheran Theological Seminary at Philadelphia, Philadelphia, USA

Ricardo Rieth, Professor of Church History and Dean, Universidade Luterana do Brasil (ULBRA), Canoas, Brazil

Ronald K. Rittgers, Erich Markel Chair in German Reformation Studies, Professor of History and Theology, Valparaiso University, Valparaiso, USA

Robert Rosin, Professor of Historical Theology, Concordia Seminary, Saint Louis, USA

Risto Saarinen, Professor of Ecumenics, Faculty of Theology, University of Helsinki, Helsinki, Finland

Johannes Schwanke, Professor of Systematic Theology, Staatsunabhängige Theologische Hochschule, Basel, Switzerland

Jeffrey G. Silcock, Associate Dean for Research, Lecturer in Theology, Australian Lutheran College, Adelaide, Australia

Notger Slenczka, Professor of Systematic Theology (Dogmatics), Theological Faculty, Humboldt University, Berlin, Germany

†**Heribert Smolinsky**, Formerly Professor of Medieval and Modern Church History, Institute for Biblical and Historical Theology, Albert-Ludwigs University of Freiburg, Freiburg/Br., Germany

Jane E. Strohl, Professor of Reformation History and Theology, Pacific Lutheran Theological Seminary, Berkeley, USA

Mark Thompson, Principal and Professor of Systematic Theology, Moore Theological College, Sydney, Australia

Jonathan Trigg, Independent scholar, London, UK

Anna Vind, Professor of Church History, Faculty of Theology, University of Copenhagen, Copenhagen, Denmark

Timothy J. Wengert, Ministerium of Pennsylvania Professor of Reformation History, Lutheran Theological Seminary at Philadelphia, Philadelphia, USA

Martin Wernisch, Docent, Protestant Theological Faculty, Charles University, Prague, Czech Republic

Vítor Westhelle, Professor of Systematic Theology, Lutheran School of Theology, Chicago, USA

Eike Wolgast, Professor of Medieval and Modern History, Ruprecht-Karls University of Heidelberg, Heidelberg, Germany

INTRODUCTION

L'UBOMÍR BATKA, IRENE DINGEL, AND ROBERT KOLB

THE 17 December 2011, issue of *The Economist* dedicated an article to Martin Luther, specifically to 'how Luther went viral', noting his role in the first major public relations event in European history, with his massive campaign for reform through a variety of print media. In 2011 a poll of some 13,000 non-German Europeans placed 'Luther's Reformation' third on a list of 'the most important historical events that you associate with Germany'. Luther himself was placed fourth, after Goethe, Chancellor Merkel, and Einstein, on a list of 'the most important Germans' (*Forschung & Lehre* 2011: 764). No other event and no other person from more than two centuries ago surfaced in the consciousness of those Europeans. Such a list is just as arbitrary and subjective as the decision of editors of *Life* magazine to judge Luther as the third most important figure of the millennium in 2000 or the vote conducted by a German television network three years later that found Germans regarding Luther as the second most important person in their history.[1]

Nonetheless, because of his actions in 1517 Protestant Christians around the world have chosen 2017 as the year in which they will mark the five-hundredth anniversary of 'the Reformation'. For widely varying theological schools of thought it is Luther's public call for consideration of reform that sets the date for the beginning of all ecclesiastical reform of the early modern period. With Augustine, Anselm, Thomas Aquinas, and Schleiermacher, Martin Luther remains among the most widely read and influential Christian thinkers to this day. *The Oxford Handbook of Martin Luther's Theology* offers students and scholars a springboard for delving into the Wittenberg reformer's thinking and the scholarly interaction with his writings.

This Handbook differs from other similar works on Luther in that it restricts its focus to Luther's thought and does not attempt, apart from the initial essay, to offer a guide for studying his career, significant and fascinating as it is. Much research has been dedicated to exploring the details of his development and the roles he played in society and church, often seeking answers to his precise place in the course of German

---

[1] See <http://www.german.about.com/cs/culture/a/bestger.htm>.

and European history. Such questions remain important and deserve study, but particularly in Africa, Asia, and Latin America, where new interest in Luther is stirring, it is his thought and its potential application to twenty-first-century questions that challenges and intrigues increasing numbers of thinkers, Christian and non-Christian alike. As with other such handbooks or 'companions' designed to aid newcomers to a field of research, essayists were asked to offer a survey of their subject to provide orientation to central questions in studies of Luther's way of thinking and past or current treatment of these areas or aspects of his thinking and its impact on the world. This volume is intended to serve those seeking orientation to the vast palette of Luther scholarship. The authors have striven to set Luther's thought in its historical context and to make it clear which challenges and which concerns shaped his thinking as he strove to make use of his intellectual inheritance and to bring new insights to the people of his culture. Six foci help readers enter into his way of thinking: (1) his grounding in the thinking of his day, (2) his own hermeneutical principles for his way of interpreting and applying Scripture, (3) his theological emphases, (4) his views of various aspects of Christian living, (5) his use of specific genres and the role they played in shaping his thought, and (6) the various ways in which his thought interacted with contemporaries and has been interpreted in the centuries since his death.

Luther research has experienced changes in agenda and concern in the last generation as the 'Luther Renaissance' of the early and middle decades of the twentieth century ran its course (Stayer 2000: 3–47). Readers will notice in these essays that some topics have commanded more interest in recent years than others as the conversation among those who study the reformer's thought has gone on. Two pairs of essays focus on two recent debates among scholars: Luther's relationship to the Middle Ages and his teaching on the justification of sinners in God's sight.

As with all other thinkers, Luther developed his theology within the framework of his own education and the discussions and practices of his teachers, at home, in the monastery, at the university, through publications of those who had preceded him as well as personal contacts with older contemporaries. The first section of this volume seeks to provide glimpses into the contexts in which his conception of God and creation took root and sprouted, with essays on the scholastic and the monastic mystical theologies of his time as well as his relationship to earlier reform movements, particularly that around Jan Hus. As a professor of the Bible the influences of traditional streams of medieval Scriptural interpretation as well as that of the ancient Church Fathers shaped his thought. These influences combined with insights and tools he took from contemporary humanistic scholarship. Because one issue under debate in the early twenty-first century is the extent to which Luther's thought is marked by continuity with the past and to what extent he broke with the past and introduced new methods and content to the practice of theology and the proclamation of the Christian gospel, we have invited two scholars to sketch the concerns of this discussion.

The fundamental frameworks from which thinkers of all kinds proceed are vital for the final form of their thought. This *Handbook*'s second section examines fields of hermeneutical presuppositions that guided Luther and shaped the way in which he formulated the biblical message and conveyed his ideas. Along with essays on his under-standing of history and of language stand examinations of his 'theology of the cross' and his distinctions of law and gospel, two components of being human, and the two realms or spheres in which human beings live as well as freedom and bondage. These essays comment on the ways in which Luther's foundational principles of interpreting God and the human condition took shape in the development of his theology.

The third section of the *Handbook* presents essays on eleven vital topics of his teaching which he constructed for his preaching, catechesis, exegetical lectures, and pastoral care. Among these doctrinal topics justification by grace through faith commands a good deal of attention. Because another of the most animated debates of the past half-century in Luther studies has concerned the proper understanding of the justification of sinners in relation-ship to God, we have invited two scholars to sketch two approaches to interpreting Luther's conception of God's restoration of human righteousness or fundamental human identity.

Although Luther is often seen as a theologian who concentrated on the relationship of God with sinful human beings and particularly on his efforts to save them through the incarnation of the second person of the Trinity and Jesus' suffering, death, and resurrec-tion, his ethical thought also had a significant impact on the society of his own and later times. His concept of the Christian's callings in daily life and his interpretation of God's commandments for everyday living not only helped shape public life in his own period but still command serious attention and elaboration today. Seven scholars introduce readers to aspects of his understanding of how human beings should behave in relation-ship to each other within the contexts of their callings in obedience to God's commands. In this section Luther's treatment of Jews and Turks is addressed, and along with that essay another exploring the possibilities which his legacy offers for twenty-first-century inter-religious dialogue.

Relatively little has been written in the past about the influence the various genre of writing which he used moulded Luther's thought. This *Handbook* features experimental engagements with four of the literary forms—his exegesis, preaching, and catechesis; his works on pastoral care; his polemics; and his translations. He employed each of these and other genres as well to accomplish various tasks in his service to the church and the world around it, and each shaped his thinking in specific ways.

All thinkers who remain in conversation with people of their own or later eras are conveyed to a wider public on the basis of their interaction with those who disagree with them, those who agree with them, and those who interpret their thought, whether posi-tively or negatively, to that wider audience. Essays in the final section of the *Handbook* assess how Luther's ideas grew within the context of his home at the University of Wittenberg and how his thought was received and processed by contemporary Roman Catholics and Protestants of other traditions and how his exchanges with his contem-poraries shaped his own thinking. Other essays investigate how later generations con-strued and altered his thinking for use in their own times and situations, from the Late Reformation and Protestant Orthodoxy, through Pietism and the Enlightenment, into the nineteenth and twentieth centuries. Covering these last two centuries are essays on Protestant, Roman Catholic, and Marxist interpretation of Luther as well as on his continuing influence in Protestant circles and in general in Asia, Africa, and Latin America.

This *Handbook* differs from other similar works on Luther also in its approach to selection of authors. It incorporates three generations of scholars, those reaping the harvest of a long career, those engaged in the midst of their academic service, and those beginning to publish the results of their initial ventures into the reformer's mind. Our authors come from sixteen countries. That Europeans and North Americans continue to predominate in the field of Luther research will probably not be the case in another generation, as African, Asian, and Latin American scholars join those from Europe, North America, and Australia in interpreting Luther's insights anew from their specific perspectives. Representatives from several disciplines take part in the discussion of Luther, including musicologists, art historians, linguistic and literary scholars, doctrinal or systematic theologians, church historians, and secular historians. Scholars from the last three disciplines have contributed to this volume.

A Finnish theologian with rich experience teaching in China has written that Luther 'holds great potential to impact Chinese Christian thought, and he remains a model of social reform [in China]', a 'source of inspiration for Chinese theologians and scholars who are creating, in their own cultural contexts, new ways of constructing an authentic Chinese Christian theology' (Ruokanen 2008: 171). This author also noted that in 2007 new Chinese history textbooks for all universities in the People's Republic discussed Luther as one of the hundred most influential personalities of history, a forerunner of the modernization of human society. In this case China represents thinkers throughout the Global South or Majority World. Continuing interest in Luther's way of thinking within Western Europe and North America also make such a *Handbook* necessary. Its editors hope that it will serve its purpose of aiding those who turn to the Wittenberg reformer for conversation in the midst of their specific contexts and will assist them in translating his thought from his own culture, long-since disappeared, into the developing societies of the twenty-first century. Only in this way will he be taken seriously as the figure in history he was.

REFERENCES

'Beethoven, Goethe, Gutenberg: Ergebnisse einer Umfrage des Goethe-Instituts'. *Forschung & Lehre 10/11* (2011): 764–5.
'How Luther Went Viral'. *The Economist*, 17 December 2011, 93–5.
Ruokanen, Miikka (2008). 'Luther and China'. *Dialog 47*: 167–71.
Stayer, James (2000). *Martin Luther, German Saviour: German Evangelical Theological Factions and the Interpretation of Luther, 1917–1933*. Montreal: McGill-Queen's University Press.

PART I

LUTHER'S LIFE

CHAPTER 1

....

LUTHER'S LIFE

....

CHARLOTTE METHUEN

I. FROM CHILDHOOD TO PROFESSOR OF THEOLOGY

....

MARTIN Luther's life began and ended in the town of Eisleben in Saxony. He was born there on 10 November, almost certainly in 1483, possibly in 1482 (Brecht 1985–93: 1.1), to Hans Ludher (c.1459–1530), the second son of a family which owned a farm in Möhra, near Eisenach in Thuringia, and Margarethe Lindemann (c.1460–1531), daughter of a well-respected and well-established Eisenach family. Martin's cousins included 'two pastors, two lawyers, a physician, two schoolmasters, a university docent, and three public officials' (Siggins 1978: 142). The baby was baptized the next day, on Saint Martin's Day, and given the name of the saint. Soon afterwards, the family moved to Mansfeld where Hans Ludher became involved in copper mining as a smelter. By 1491, perhaps supported by his wife's family, he was one of the committee of four which represented the interests of the Mansfeld mining community to the city council (Siggins 1978: 143; Brecht 1985–93: 1.4).

Luther received his initial schooling in Mansfeld, where he attended the *Trivialschule* or elementary school from the age of about seven. Here he would have learned the classical *trivium*: grammar, rhetoric, and logic, all taught in Latin. At twelve or thirteen he was sent to Magdeburg, where he boarded with a group of Brothers of the Common Life and attended the cathedral school. A year later, probably in 1498, he moved to Eisenach and attended Saint George's parish school (Brecht 1985–93: 1.16, 20). In Magdeburg and Eisenach Luther was probably introduced to the modern piety or *devotio moderna* and met members of religious orders. However, his father's plans for him were clear: Martin was to proceed to university, attain his *magister artium* (Master of Arts), and study law.

In spring 1501 Luther signed the matriculation book at the University of Erfurt: *Martinus ludher ex mansfelt*. Erfurt had been founded in 1392, the fifth German university after Prague, Vienna, Heidelberg, and Cologne. About 230 students matriculated in Luther's year. He was introduced by his teachers to the *via moderna* ('modern way'), or nominalist school, of philosophy, but almost certainly also encountered some of the new humanist ideas (Brecht 1985–93: 1.28, 32–44). In 1502 Luther was awarded his BA and in January 1505 his MA, placed second in his class of seventeen (Beutel 2003: 4). Luther was later to be critical of the medieval system of education. However, there can be no doubt that Luther's own education equipped him well: he acquired good Latin, a love of Latin poetry, and an appreciation of the importance of careful definition and logical argument, all of which would stand him in good stead as a teacher of Bible and theology.

For the twenty-one-year-old Luther, however, the study of theology was not an option. In May 1505 he began his studies at Erfurt's Faculty of Law. From the start he seems to have had doubts about this choice, and it may have been now that he first started to study the Bible in earnest (Brecht 1985–93: 1.47–8). In early July 1505, returning from a visit to Mansfeld, he narrowly escaped being struck by lightning, praying to Saint Anne, the mother of the Virgin Mary: 'Help me, and I will become a monk.' Despite the disapproval of his father, by 17 July Luther had applied to enter the Erfurt house of the observant Augustinian hermits (Brecht 1985–93: 1.48–50).

Throughout his monastic life Luther dedicated himself to keeping the rule: prayer, fasting, regular self-examination, and confession to a superior were an integral part of his life. It was not until 1520 that he gave up praying the full office (Brecht 1985–93: 1.64–5). Despite his efforts—and both Luther and his superiors remembered him as extremely conscientious—Luther could not attain security about his own salvation. In 1506 his superiors instructed him to prepare for ordination to the priesthood; he was ordained deacon probably on 27 February 1507 and priested on 3 April the same year. As part of his preparation he read the *Explication of the Canon of the Mass* by Gabriel Biel (1415–95), published in 1499, and the *Rosetum* of Jean Mauburne, which emphasized the importance of a correct manner of celebration and the need for the priest to be at one with God. These works did nothing to alleviate Luther's sense of inadequacy and unworthiness. His first mass on 2 May 1507 was difficult (Brecht 1985–93: 1.72–3). Over the years that followed, his fears and uncertainties—his *Anfechtungen* or *tentationes* (temptations)—continued to shake his understanding of how salvation might be achieved.

During his novitiate Luther embarked on a careful study of Scripture, in accordance with the instructions of Johann von Staupitz (1465–1524), Vicar General of the Augustinians in Germany and Professor for the Bible at the University of Wittenberg, who had emphasised study of the Bible in the Augustinian monasteries. He encouraged Luther to study theology (Brecht 1985–93: 1.84–6). As he advanced, Luther was made responsible for teaching philosophy to students in his Augustinian house. He studied scholastic philosophy and theology, regretting the distraction from his engagement with Scripture. He seems to have been a successful teacher; in autumn 1508 was sent to the University of Wittenberg. There he shared responsibility for teaching philosophy, particularly Aristotle's *Nichomachean Ethics*, while continuing with his own studies. In March 1509 he was awarded his *baccalaureus biblicus* (bachelor of the Bible), which qualified him to lecture on the Bible, and later that year in Erfurt his *baccalaureus sententiarius* (bachelor of the Sentences), which equipped him to teach Peter Lombard's *Sentences*, the standard medieval theological textbook (Brecht 1985–93: 1.92–3).

Before he began teaching, Luther travelled to Rome. The Augustinian order was divided over the reforms proposed by Staupitz, and in 1510 Luther was sent to put the case of the reform movement. In Rome he was struck both by the amazing range of possibilities—holy places, pilgrimages, relics, masses, and especially the churches—offered to the pilgrim, but also by the extravagant and corrupt pomp which surrounded the papal court (Brecht 1985–93: 1.98–105). Whilst he was there, the split within the Augustinian order saw Luther's friend Johannes Lang transferred from Erfurt to Wittenberg; when Luther returned to Germany, he too was sent to Wittenberg.

There he oversaw the training of Augustinian novices, preached in the monastery, and studied for his doctorate in theology. He was awarded his doctoral degree in October 1512, taking an oath 'not to advance any idle and foreign teachings which were condemned by the church and offensive to pious ears' (Brecht 1985–93: 1.125–7; quote 126). Staupitz nominated Luther to the professorship of the Bible; in autumn 1513 Luther began teaching. His appointment marked the beginning of a long association between Luther, the University of Wittenberg, and three successive Electors of Saxony: first Frederick, 'the Wise' (1463–1525), the founder of the University of Wittenberg; from 1525 Frederick's brother John 'the Steadfast' or 'the Constant' (1468–1532); and finally, from 1532, John's son John Frederick 'the Magnanimous' (1503–54).

Luther began by lecturing on the Psalms. In 1515 he started to lecture on Romans, turning to Galatians in 1516 and to Hebrews in 1517, returning to the Psalms from 1518 (Brecht 1985–93: 1.129). Luther's lectures show how his ideas about faith, works, law, free will, and justification developed, and how he was reading and interpreting Scripture. From 1514 he was also appointed by the council to preach in the town church, generally on the gospels in the morning and on the epistles in the afternoon (Brecht 1985–93: 1.150–5), engaging with the biblical text in both German and Latin, addressing both students and the people of Wittenberg. He was influenced by his reading of Johannes Tauler (*c.*1300–61) and other German mystical writers. His initial, incomplete edition of the *Theologia Deutsch*, or *German Theology*, was published in 1516, erroneously ascribed to Tauler. Luther's introduction to the complete edition, published in 1518, highlighted the significance of this work for him: 'I thank God that I have found and heard my God in the German tongue, as neither I nor [the scholastic theologians] have yet found him in the Latin, Greek, or Hebrew tongue' (WA1.379).

By 1516 Luther was beginning to express his concern at the misunderstanding and abuse of indulgences in his sermons, and to engage more deeply with questions of free will, grace, and salvation in his lectures; in late 1516 he presided over a disputation on the extent of free will (WA1.145–151; Brecht 1985–93: 1.166–7). He was also preparing a German commentary on the penitential psalms (6, 32, 38, 51, 102, 130, and 143), intended 'not for well educated Nurembergers, but for raw Saxons' (WABr1.93). This was printed in Wittenberg in the spring of 1517 and reprinted at Leipzig within the year. In May Luther wrote to Johannes Lang, by now the prior of his former house in Erfurt, that 'our theology and Saint Augustine are progressing well…Indeed no one can expect to have any students if he does not want to teach this theology, that is, lecture on the Bible or on Saint Augustine or another teacher of ecclesiastical eminence' (WABr 1.99; LW48.42). That summer, Luther disputed in the university against scholastic theology (WA1.224–228; LW31.9–16; Brecht 1985–93: 1.172). His reputation as a critic of scholastic theology was growing.

II. The Indulgence Crisis and its Repercussions

Indulgences enabled Christians to replace a personal or direct form of penance with an action, offered to the church for some worthy cause, often taking the form of a financial contribution. Pope Boniface VIII issued the first jubilee indulgence in 1300; it proved very profitable. The underlying theology, based on a treatise by Alexander Hales, was laid out in the Bull *Unigenitus*, proclaimed by Pope Clement VI in 1343: through his death Christ had given to the church a great treasure of merit, which had been further increased by the good deeds of Mary, the saints, and all the elect, and which could be dispensed by Peter and Peter's successors—the popes—to the faithful. By the mid-fifteenth century indulgences could be acquired not only to benefit the soul of the giver but also for the souls of relatives or friends, as Pope Sixtus IV made explicit in the Bull *Salvator Noster*, proclaimed in August 1476 (Rupp and Drewery 1970: 14). By the late fifteenth century indulgences had become a major source of income for the church. Papal permission could be given to bishops, dioceses, or even cities to have a campaign preached locally, retaining a portion of the profits and passing the rest to Rome. Thus, in the late fifteenth century Strasbourg's city council was granted permission to preach an indulgence to raise funds to build a hospice for the sick. When Pope Julius II issued a jubilee indulgence in 1507 to fund the rebuilding of St Peter's basilica in classical style, this was nothing new. However, it was this indulgence, renewed by Pope Leo X in 1513 and 1515, which would spark the Reformation.

In 1514 Albrecht of Brandenburg (1490–1545) was elected archbishop of Mainz, a post he held alongside his offices as archbishop of Magdeburg and administrator of the diocese of Halberstadt. The cost of incurring a third major office put him heavily in debt, and in 1515 Leo X's renewal of the jubilee indulgence presented a possible solution: the preaching of an indulgence. Albrecht appointed the Dominican Johannes Tetzel, an experienced preacher of indulgences, to lead the campaign in Magdeburg (Brecht 1985–93: 1.180–3). Tetzel's emotive preaching left no doubt about what could be expected: 'Don't you hear the voices of your wailing dead parents and others, who say, "Have mercy upon me, have mercy upon me, because we are in severe punishment and pain. From this you could redeem us with a small alms, and yet you do not want to do so"?' (Lindberg 2000: 31). Luther criticized such promises in his Ninety-five Theses against indulgences: 'They preach only human doctrines who say that as soon as the money clinks into the money chest, the soul flies out of purgatory' (thesis 27; WA1.234; LW31.28). In the course of 1517 Tetzel preached the indulgence across much of the arch-diocese of Magdeburg (Brecht 1985–93: 1.183). Elector Frederick, however, refused to allow the papal indulgence to be preached in his territory. He had an extensive relic col-lection, housed in Wittenberg's castle church and opened twice each year, on the second Sunday after Easter and on All Saints' Day; he therefore had little interest in allowing any competition into Electoral Saxony. However, their ruler's lack of interest did not stop the burghers of Wittenberg crossing the river Elbe to secure themselves the papal indulgence.

Contemporary woodcuts show indulgence preachers displaying the papal arms prom-inently before the cross and setting up tables to count the money offered by the faith-ful (Brecht 1985–93: 1.181); these images originated with opponents to the indulgence trade and alluded to (Mk 11:15–9, Mt 21:12–7, Lk 19:45–8, Jn 2:13–6) the money-changers in the temple. In a series of sermons in spring 1517 Luther criticized the preaching of indulgences as a desecration of the gospel because it gave those who responded a false sense of security (Brecht 1985–93: 1.186–90). He was convinced that contrition must imply change of life. Although he probably did not yet hold the doctrine of justifica-tion by grace through faith alone, he certainly believed that it was faith and the active love of neighbour, rather than any tasks or payments set by the church, which opened the way to salvation. Luther knew the humanist correction to the Latin translation of Matthew 4:17, which argued that the Greek was more correctly translated 'Repent!' than 'Do penance!' The task of the believer was not to undertake acts of penance but to live a life of repentance. This was the content of the first of the Ninety-five Theses which he drew up for a proposed *Disputation on the Value of Indulgences*. On 31 October 1517 he sent these, with a covering letter, to Albrecht of Mainz (WABr1.110–112; LW49.45–49; Brecht 1985–93: 1.190–2). He probably wrote also to his diocesan bishop, among others. Whether Luther also nailed the theses to the door of Wittenberg's castle church is not clear: it would have been normal practice to publicize disputation theses there, but it would also have been usual to wait for a reply from those invited to participate.

It was entirely within Luther's rights as a professor to call for such a disputation; in fact a formal academic disputation on Luther's Ninety-five Theses never took place. Albrecht did not receive Luther's letter until late November. He referred Luther's the-ses to the University of Mainz for an opinion and sent a copy to Rome. Meanwhile the theses were spreading fast; they had been printed, in Latin and in a German translation by the Nuremberg councillor Caspar Nützel, in Nuremberg, Leipzig, Basel, and per-haps Augsburg. By February 1518 voices in Rome were demanding that his order should silence Luther (Brecht 1985–93: 1.204–6).

Recognizing the importance of explaining his ideas, Luther wrote a *Sermon on Indulgences and Grace* in German (WA1.243–246). It was published in March 1518, with editions printed in Wittenberg, Leipzig, Nuremberg, and Augsburg. Around the same time—in preparation for Lent—Luther's *Short Explanation of the Ten Commandments* also appeared; here he sought to explore what it meant to make one's whole life one of repentance (WA1.250–256). Luther also engaged Tetzel, who had published a set of counter-theses defending indulgences. Johannes Eck (1486–1543), professor of theology at Ingolstadt and a papal legate, soon emerged as an opponent (Brecht 1985–93: 1.206–13).

His order now offered Luther a platform. Staupitz appointed Luther to preside over the disputations at the General Congregation of the German Augustinians, to be held in Heidelberg in April 1518 (Brecht 1985–93: 1.211–16). There Luther defended twenty-eight theological theses and twelve philosophical theses before an audience which included the future reformers Martin Bucer (1491–1551) and Johannes Brenz (1499–1570), arguing that without grace, the human will could not choose good, and suggesting that all theology must be grounded in the cross. 'The law says, "do this", and it is never done', he concluded: 'Grace says, "believe in this", and everything is already done' (thesis 26; WA1.354; LW31.41). Some characteristic themes of his theology were emerging. He returned to Wittenberg to a phase of intense writing.

In August 1518 Luther received a summons to Rome to respond to an accusation of heresy. Luther wrote to George Spalatin in Augsburg, asking that he use his influence to have the case heard before German judges (WABr1.188; LW48.72). Elector Frederick now intervened. As an imperial elector, at a time when no one could know how long the elderly Emperor Maximilian (1459–1519) would live, Frederick had considerable influence. He chose to use it to assert his own authority against that of both the pope and the emperor by protecting Luther. Frederick negotiated with Cardinal Thomas Cajetan, the papal legate, that Luther should be questioned on German territory, and in October 1518 Cajetan summoned Luther to Augsburg (Brecht 1985–93: 1.248–50). In their three-day encounter Luther argued that the selling of indulgences had no basis in Scripture, and that to suggest that the pope controlled access to the treasure of the church—that is, to merit and grace—was also unbiblical. Cajetan condemned Luther's questioning of papal authority and instructed Frederick that he should be given up to Rome (Brecht 1985–93: 1.260–1). With Luther already back in Wittenberg, Frederick once again refused, requiring instead that Luther should be tried by theologians and scholars with good scriptural knowledge, not by canon lawyers (Brecht 1985–93: 1.264).

III. Leipzig and the Process against Luther

In Augsburg, Staupitz had released Luther from his vows of obedience, leaving him free to defend his views, but depriving him of the order's protection. Luther was now dependent on the support of Elector Frederick, without which he would almost certainly have shared the fate of Jan Hus (c.1369–1415), the Bohemian reformer burnt at the stake at the Council of Constance a century earlier. After Augsburg Luther must have been acutely aware that this fate could become his at any time. At the behest of Karl von Miltitz, the pope's chamberlain, Luther agreed to keep silent while negotiations took place with the pope; in February 1519 he published a conciliatory *Instruction on Several Articles which*

are Ascribed and Assigned to him by his Detractors (WA2.69–73; Brecht 1985–93: 1.265–
73). He initiated reforms to the curriculum of the University of Wittenberg, decreasing
the influence of Aristotelian logic and physics and emphasizing the classical languages,
Latin, Greek, and Hebrew. He was aided by the newly appointed professor of Greek,
Philip Melanchthon (1497–1560), who arrived in Wittenberg in August 1518 aged just
twenty-one, and who would become one of Luther's closest friends and staunchest supporters (Brecht 1985–93: 1.275–82; Scheible 1997: 28–34).

In summer 1518 Luther's colleague at Wittenberg, Andreas Bodenstein von Karlstadt
(*c*.1486–1581), wrote against Johannes Eck in defence of Luther's theology. Eck called for
a public disputation, which eventually took place in Leipzig in summer 1519. Eck had
engaged to dispute on free will with Karlstadt, but he insisted that Luther be required to
attend and debate the questions of papal supremacy (Brecht 1985–93: 1.299–306). While
the imperial election was taking place in Augsburg, electing the young Habsburg king
Charles of Spain emperor on 28 June, Luther was in Leipzig. In the second phase of the
disputation Luther presented views on ecclesiastical authority which, as Eck pointed
out, were similar to those for which Hus had been condemned at Constance. Luther
riposted that his view was based on Scripture and that the condemnation of Hus indicated that not only the pope, but also councils could err (Brecht 1985–93: 1.319–22). With
this explicit and public denial of the authority of the medieval church and its institutions, the debate had moved into a new arena. Luther's criticism of the practice of indulgences, which in the Ninety-five Theses had been carefully phrased so as to suggest that
pope and Curia were unaware of what was going on, had given way to an explicit questioning of papal authority.

Against the backdrop of the growing conflict with Rome, Luther composed a series of
devotional works. 1519 saw the publication of short catechetical works in German on the
Lord's Prayer, confession, baptism, and the Lord's Supper, as well as his Galatians commentary, based on the lectures he had given in 1516. Particularly the catechetical works
gained a wide circulation; they later formed the basis of his catechisms (1529). Meanwhile,
Froben in Basel had printed Luther's collected works; they were condemned by theologians at the University of Cologne in August 1519. In early 1520 the Louvain theologians followed suit (Brecht 1985–93: 1.338–41). Luther was disgusted that the rejection of his views
did not call on Scripture and resented being branded a heretic. In 1520, as the process in
Rome moved towards Luther's condemnation, he explored the implications of his insights
in a series of works, including his three so-called Reformation treatises. The first, published in German in August, was *To the Christian Nobility of the Germany Nation, on the
Improvement of the Christian Estate* (WA6.404–469; LW44.123–217), a call to the German
rulers to reform the church if the church would not reform itself. The second, written
in Latin, printed in October, was *On the Babylonian Captivity of the Church: A Prelude*
(WA6.497–573; LW36.11–127), an exposition of the sacraments which redefined their
number, first to three—Lord's Supper, baptism, and penance—and then to two—Lord's
Supper and baptism. The third, *On the Freedom of the Christian*, or *On Christian Freedom*,
written in Latin and dedicated to Pope Leo X in a perhaps somewhat spurious attempt
to appease him, was published in November, with a German translation following

almost immediately (German text: WA7.20–38; Latin text: WA7.49–73: ET of the Latin text: LW31.333–379); this was Luther's first extended discussion of the doctrine of justification by faith. The first and third of these treatises were to become two of the most popular and influential of Luther's works.

Exsurge Domine—Arise, O Lord—the papal bull condemning Luther and his teachings, was promulgated in Rome on 15 June 1520 (Brecht 1985–93: 1.391–5). It threatened Luther with excommunication if he did not recant within sixty days. Although it was proclaimed across Germany by Johannes Eck and at the imperial court by the papal legate Jerome Aleander (1480–1542), and Luther's supporters published it in Saxony to increase his popularity, the bull did not actually reach Luther in Wittenberg until October. Once more, Elector Frederick supported Luther. In Cologne, after the imperial coronation, he conferred with Aleander, requiring that Luther be tried by 'reasonable, educated, pious, and irreproachable judges' in Germany (Brecht 1985–93: 1.418). Frederick suggested that Luther should appear before the next imperial diet, in Worms (Brecht 1985–93: 1.421). Scarcely was Frederick back in Wittenberg, when on 10 December Luther publicly burned the bull, together with his copy of Canon Law, and published a treatise proclaiming that he had done so (WA7.161–182; LW31.383–395; Brecht 1985–93: 1.423–6). On 3 January 1521 Leo X issued the bull *Decet Romanum*, formally excommunicating Luther.

IV. THE DIET OF WORMS

The Diet of Worms had been scheduled for Epiphany (6 January) 1521, in recognition that the new emperor was three times king: of the united Spain, of Naples, and of the Germans. It finally opened on 28 January. The imperial diet was the primary organ of imperial rule within the Holy Roman Empire; laws proposed by this particular diet were intended to give more power to the German princes and reduce the power struggles between them and the emperor. Most of the German rulers, both secular and ecclesiastical, attended. Church interests were well represented, for the emperor had the right to fill any senior diocesan or cathedral post within the Empire which fell vacant during his first year of office. Merchants gathered in Worms, hoping to attract the custom of the princes and their retinues. Allowing Luther to speak publicly at Worms, his opponents feared, would offer him the chance of expounding his ideas to a broad and possibly susceptible audience. He was summoned to appear in a closed session towards the end of the diet.

Luther probably set out for Worms on 2 April. He was welcomed enthusiastically on his way, preaching to crowds in Erfurt, Gotha, and Eisenach, and arrived in Worms on 16 April to considerable acclaim (Brecht 1985–93: 1.448–52). He was instructed to appear before the diet the following afternoon. Luther was questioned by Johann von Eck, a senior priest in Trier and representative of the Archbishop of Trier (not the Johannes Eck against whom Luther had disputed in Leipzig). Von Eck asked Luther whether a pile of some twenty-five works were his, and whether he would stand by what he had written in them. Luther's legal representative, Jerome Schurff (1481–1554), professor of Canon Law at Wittenberg, demanded that the titles be read out. Luther agreed that he was the author. On the second point, Luther requested time to answer. After consultation von Eck responded that although the emperor was surprised that Luther did not have an answer prepared, he might have a day to consider (Brecht 1985–93: 1.452–5).

Luther withdrew and spent much of the night in prayer and consultation. The next morning he had his answer ready (WA7.832–838; LW32.109–113; Brecht 1985–93: 1.456–62). He apologized for any breach of court etiquette and again declared himself to be the author of the works he had been shown. On the question of whether he stood by their contents, he observed that his books were of different kinds.

> In some I have dealt with religious faith and morals so simply and evangelically that my very antagonists are compelled to confess that these books are useful, harmless, and fit to be read by all Christians....If I were to start revoking them, what should I be doing?

A second group of writings consisted of polemic against 'the papacy and the doctrine of the papists' who had 'laid waste all Christendom, body and soul', and had been particularly destructive to the German nation. 'If I revoke these books, all I shall achieve is to add strength to tyranny', Luther said. A third class had been written against individuals. Luther conceded that he had sometimes been 'more acrimonious than befits my religion or my calling', but to revoke what he had said would be to accede to their opinions. Von Eck replied that Luther should not question the teachings of the church. Moreover, he was not answering the question: would he revoke his writings, or would he not? Luther's answer was unequivocal:

> Unless I am convinced by the testimony of Scripture or plain reason (for I believe neither in pope nor councils alone since it is agreed that they have often erred and contradicted themselves), I am bound by the Scriptures I have quoted, and my conscience is captive to the Word of God. I neither can nor will retract anything, for it is neither safe nor honest to go against one's conscience. Amen.

It is almost certain that Luther did not actually say: 'Here I stand—I cannot do otherwise', although that was certainly the implication of his words. As he left the room, he was heard to say, 'I am finished'. Like Hus to the Council of Constance, Luther had come to the Diet of Worms under a month's guarantee of safe passage. Unlike Hus, Luther's safe passage was honoured. After some days of fruitless negotiation with representatives of the imperial estates (Brecht 1985–93: 1.464–70), Luther left Worms on 26 April.

On 8 May Luther was placed under imperial ban. On 25 May, as the diet drew to a close, Charles V issued the Edict of Worms, condemning Luther and calling for his execution, condemning any who offered him hospitality, shelter, or support; and demanding the burning of his books (Brecht 1985–93: 1.473–6). From now on, Luther would live without legal protection; it would generally be impossible for him to leave the territories of Electoral Saxony.

V. THE WARTBURG AND REFORMATION IN WITTENBERG

Luther had been instructed not to preach. However, on his return journey from Worms to Wittenberg, he found himself being entreated to do so. In Hersfeld he accepted the invitation of the abbot and the town council and gave a sermon although he warned that the town might lose its imperial privileges. In Eisenach he was again asked to preach although he told Spalatin that the 'fearful parish priest' had 'protested before me in the presence of a notary and witnesses. Yet he humbly apologized for the necessity of doing so, pleading fear of his tyrants' (WABr2.338; LW48.226). Luther spent that night with relatives in nearby Möhra. The next morning, on 4 May, he was apprehended by Elector Frederick's soldiers and carried off to Frederick's stronghold, the Wartburg near Eisenach (Brecht 1985–93: 1.470–2). The abduction, of which Luther had advance knowledge, was intended to protect him from the consequences of the Edict of Worms.

Luther remained in the Wartburg for nearly a year, abandoning his monk's tonsure by growing his hair and his beard, and passing as a knight, Junker Jörg (Brecht 1985–93: 2.1). He wrote against the theologians at Leuven and Paris—*Against Latomus* (WA8.43–128; LW32.137–261) and *A Judgment of the Theologians at Paris* (WA8.267–312)—composed a rejection of auricular confession (WA8.138–186), a treatise on the misuse of the mass (WA8.481–563; LW36.133–230), and a critical assessment of monastic life and particularly religious vows (WA8.573–669). He published expositions of the gospels and epistles, and model sermons or 'Postils' for Advent and Christmas (WA10.1). He translated the New Testament into German. Published in September 1522, the 'September Testament' used the second edition of Erasmus' new Latin translation of the New Testament and edition of the Greek text, the *Novum Instrumentum*, with which Luther had been familiar since the publication of the first edition in 1516 (Brecht 1985–93: 2.46–53). Luther's German Bible translation would become perhaps his most significant and best-known legacy, important both for the theological accents of his translation and for its influence on the German language.

Frederick the Wise had ensured Luther's safety, but his absence in Wittenberg left a vacuum. Melanchthon assumed some measure of theological leadership, in late 1521 publishing the first edition of his *Loci Communes*, or *Commonplaces*, a theological work which was the first systematic presentation of Luther's reforming theology. Karlstadt took a more practical approach. After the Diet of Worms he, together with the Wittenberg humanists Martin Reinhardt and Matthias Gabler, had been invited by King Christian II of Denmark to Copenhagen to teach Luther's ideas there. Considerable unrest ensued, due largely to the unpopularity of the king, and Karlstadt left after only a month, leaving Gabler and Reinhardt to continue the work (Grell 1992: 96). Back in Wittenberg, Karlstadt worked with Melanchthon and the town council to introduce reforms based on Luther's teachings. One of Luther's brother-friars, Gabriel Zwilling, introduced changes into the monastery: in September or October the traditional celebration of the mass was discontinued and a simplified version substituted, still in Latin, with the congregation receiving communion in both kinds (that is, the wine as well as the bread). Luther's *The Misuse of the Mass* supported this development. Zwilling also began to remove images from the church. However, when Karlstadt sought to extend these reforms to the town church, unrest ensued. In early December Luther made a secret visit to see for himself (Brecht 1985–93: 2.25–30).

Luther returned to the Wartburg pronouncing himself content with the situation in Wittenberg. However, tensions were rising: matters soon came to a head. On Christmas Day 1521 Karlstadt conducted the service in Wittenberg's church in German instead of Latin, wearing his academic gown, and encouraged the congregation to receive communion in both kinds whether or not they had made their confession or kept their fast. Karlstadt also announced his engagement to Anna von Mochau; they were married on 19 January, demonstrating Karlstadt's rejection of priestly celibacy (Brecht 1985–93: 2.34). By mid-January Karlstadt had stopped hearing private confessions, had ceased to elevate the host during celebrations of the Lord's Supper, had rejected the rules about fasting, and was encouraging the removal of images and statues from Wittenberg's churches. Together with the city council, he worked to draft a church order for Wittenberg, dissolving confraternities and other lay orders, and setting up a poor chest to benefit from the proceeds (Brecht 1985–93: 2.38–40).

Matters were further complicated by a group of radical 'prophets' who had been expelled from nearby Zwickau and been led to Wittenberg by their leader, Thomas Müntzer (c.1489–1525). Like Karlstadt, Müntzer and his followers questioned the validity of infant baptism. Unlike Luther, they believed that the Lord's Supper had a symbolic character. Frederick, who, despite his support for Luther, was not enthusiastic about the evangelical theology, was already dismayed by the disorder in the Wittenberg church. He was even more horrified by the teachings of the Zwickau prophets and forbade any further changes in Wittenberg.

Luther was convinced that practical reforms to the life of the church must have the agreement of the local rulers, both princes and magistrates, and that matters had moved too quickly in Wittenberg. In response to an appeal from the town council, and against Frederick's will, he returned in early March 1522 (Brecht 1985–93: 2.42–4). Donning his monk's habit once more, he preached a series of sermons highlighting the needs of those with 'weak consciences', who needed further teaching, recommending the reversal of many of the changes which Karlstadt had introduced, and reinstating the mass in Latin, while retaining communion in both kinds. Luther wished the Reformation in Wittenberg to take an orderly course with the support of the Elector.

In 1523, Luther produced a series of works relating to the proper conduct of worship, including a simplified order of 'mass and communion for the church at Wittenberg', still in Latin (WA12.205–220; LW53.19–40; Brecht 1985–93: 2.122–6), and a German baptismal liturgy, which retained several medieval rituals, including exorcism, anointing, and clothing the child in white (WA12.42–48; LW53.96–103; Brecht 1985–93: 2.121–2). Further liturgical reform did not prove possible until after Frederick's death in 1525; his brother, John, who succeeded him, was more sympathetic to Luther's ideas and consequently to liturgical change. Luther turned instead to writing hymns to popularize his theology. By 1524 he had composed over twenty of the forty hymns he would write during his career although not yet 'A Mighty Fortress is our God', which appeared in 1529 (Brecht 1985–93: 2.129–35). Luther understood music and singing as gifts of God, rightly used in praising God and proclaiming God's saving work of grace. His hymns became one of the central means of spreading his theology to a largely illiterate population. However, education was also important to Luther: with Melanchthon's support he encouraged the improvement of schools and education, writing in 1524 to remind city councils of their responsibilities to establish and sustain Christian education (Brecht 1985–93: 2.138–42). Melanchthon's continuing efforts towards the reform of schools and universities were to earn him the title 'Educator of Germany'—*Praeceptor Germaniae*—by the end of his life. He recognized that if the Reformation were to take hold, preachers and teachers must be educated in Luther's theology, and educate others in their turn.

VI. DEFINING THE REFORMATION

Events in Wittenberg during the winter of 1521/22 had highlighted fundamental differences among those who sought to take Scripture as their only authority. Such debates between Luther and other theologians were both to define and split the emerging Protestant movement. The period from 1524 until 1530 was marked by controversy.

The Zwickau prophets read Scripture but trusted in the direct inspiration of the Holy Spirit, and they seemed to Luther to introduce an ethical rigour which mirrored the theology of works which he rejected. He had similar concerns about Karlstadt's theology (Brecht 1985–93: 2.57–72). Both were expelled from Wittenberg in 1522; Müntzer began espousing the cause of the peasants who were protesting at their lack of political representation and the erosion of such freedoms as they had. Peasant revolts (the *Bauernkriege*) had broken out across the German lands from the end of the fifteenth century, but in the mid-1520s, following legal reforms in the Empire, they took on new urgency (Blickle 1998: 94–116, 162–77). Convinced that the Scriptures preached Christian freedom and equality, Müntzer became a leader of the peasants in Thuringia, and in September 1524 was the main author of the Mühlhausen Articles. He was executed after the disastrous defeat at the battle of Mühlhausen in 1525 (Brecht 1985–93: 2.146–57, 172–4, 184–5; Goertz 1993: 159–91).

Luther's first reaction was a treatise admonishing both rulers and peasants to peace and emphasizing their respective responsibilities and duties (WA18.291–334; LW46.17–43; Brecht 1985–93: 2.174–8). However, when violence mounted and he realized that the peasants' actions and arguments were being attributed to the influence of his theology,

Luther was incensed. His treatise *Against the Murderous and Thieving Hordes of Farmers* (WA18.357–361; LW46.49–55) was a heated and intemperate attack; it was unfortunate that its publication coincided with the massacre of a large group of rebels by the princes. This intervention placed Luther firmly on the side of the princes and magistrates who upheld the already-existing social order. Luther's reading of the gospel might be radical in its rejection of distinctions between the spiritual and the temporal, but it did not imply the entire reordering of society.

In 1525 Luther's conflict with Erasmus also came to a head. Their differences centred on the question of whether or not the human will could play a part in choosing salvation. Erasmus had long been deeply—and wittily—critical of the extravagant lifestyles of some bishops and abbots, of the bickering between monastic orders, and of the abuse of relics, pilgrimages, indulgences, fasting, monastic vows, and the invocation of saints. His satirical *In Praise of Folly* (1509) was widely read and highly influential; his editions of the Church Fathers made their thought accessible to the sixteenth-century theologians; his revised Latin translation of the New Testament with an edition of the Greek text informed the critique of late-medieval theology as well as the new vernacular translations, including Luther's. Their contemporaries initially saw Luther as developing the ideas which Erasmus had begun: Erasmus, it was said, laid the egg which Luther had hatched. Erasmus himself disagreed, commenting, 'I laid a hen's egg: Luther hatched a bird of quite a different breed'.

Erasmus had become increasingly disturbed by Luther's theology: his understanding of the interpretation of Scripture, which in Erasmus' view was overly simplistic; his rejection of the authority of the church and tradition, which Erasmus believed to be disrespectful to the theological consensus; and his theology of human nature, which ran contrary to Erasmus' understanding of the value of human will and human reason. However, he feared that Luther's detractors 'will not rest until they have overthrown all knowledge of languages and all humane studies'. Erasmus was particularly concerned that Luther's approach would end by splitting the church rather than reforming it (Augustijn 1991: 125–45; quote 123).

In autumn 1524 Erasmus published a treatise *On Free Will* (ET: LCC 17.35–97; Brecht 1985–93: 2.220-3), which presented the case, both biblical and theological, for some cooperation of the human free will in salvation. Luther did not respond immediately. He may have been reluctant to enter into disagreement with Erasmus, but he was also taken up with the spreading social unrest across the German lands; in Wittenberg he was dealing with the aftermath of the death of Elector Frederick in May. In June he married the former nun Katharina von Bora (1499–1552). He finally responded in late 1525 with *On Bound Choice*. Luther argued that predestination to election must be the inevitable consequence of the doctrine of justification by faith—only God can choose who is saved—and recommended that Erasmus restrict himself to his excellent editorial work rather than meddling with theology (WA18.600–787; LW33.15–295; Brecht 1985–93: 2.225–32). Erasmus was annoyed by what seemed to him Luther's failure to engage with his arguments; he was also infuriated by the continued association of his own ideas with Luther's. As he had feared, 'Erasmian' and 'Lutheran' were coming to be used as opprobrious synonyms by opponents of reform, especially in Spain and Italy. This association acknowledged Erasmus' considerable influence on many reformers, including not only Luther but also Philip Melanchthon, Huldrych Zwingli (1484–1531), and later John Calvin (1509–64); it also reflected a growing suspicion of Erasmus' work among members of the Roman ecclesiastical hierarchy. Erasmus died in 1536; in 1541 his works were placed on the Index of Forbidden Books in Rome.

A further conflict developed around the Reformation understanding of the sacraments. This dispute would split the movement. In 1520 Luther had redefined the number and meaning of the sacraments, affirming baptism and the Lord's Supper, but rejecting the remaining five medieval sacraments: penance (which he had initially retained), confirmation, extreme unction, marriage, and ordination. The conflict with Karlstadt and Müntzer had shown differences in understanding of both baptism and the Lord's Supper. By 1524 Zwingli, reformer in Zürich, had begun to articulate a theology of the Lord's Supper which Luther associated with Karlstadt's: the Lord's Supper, argued Zwingli, was a symbolic meal which recalled to believers' minds the death of Christ on the cross; it was a thanksgiving for Christ's work of salvation; and it brought together the people of God as a community in which Christ was spiritually present. The bread and wine were symbols of Christ's presence in the minds and hearts of believers; however, for Zwingli they did not actually become Christ's body and blood (Stephens 1986: 218–59). Zwingli was convinced from his reading of Augustine that this was how the Lord's Supper had been understood in the early church.

In 1526 Luther wrote a treatise condemning Karlstadt's views on the Lord's Supper: *The Sacrament of the Body and Blood of Christ, against the Fanatics* (WA19.482–593; LW36.335–361). Zwingli swiftly responded with an explication of his own position, *A Clear Instruction Concerning Christ's Supper* (CR91.789–862; LCC24.185–238), followed the next year by his *Friendly Exegesis* (CR92.562–758; Zwingli 1984: 2.233–369) in which he laid out his problems with Luther's position. Luther's reply affirmed *That these words 'This is my body' still stand firm against the fanatics* (WA23.64–283; LW37.13–151), to which Zwingli responded with a treatise arguing *That these words 'This is my body' will always have their old meaning* (CR92.805–977). Their battle continued with Luther's *Confession Concerning the Lord's Supper* (WA26.261–509; LW.37.161–372) and Zwingli's rejection of it (CR93,2.29–248) in conjunction with the Basel reformer Johannes Oecolampadius (1482–1531). The conflict between Luther and Zwingli divided the fledgling reform movement at a moment when its political unity had become desperately important.

VII. REFORM AND REFORMATION IN THE GERMAN EMPIRE

Luther's ideas gained wide acclaim even by 1521, but popular acceptance of his ideas did not inevitably lead to changes in ecclesiastical practices and structures.

Political interests were crucial if the Reformation was to be implemented. Introducing the Reformation involved changes to church life: replacement of the Latin mass by a simplified liturgy, administration of communion in both kinds, encouragement of vernacular preaching, discontinuation of pilgrimages and processions, rejection of distinctive clerical dress, recognition that clergy might marry, and renunciation of the diocesan bishop's authority. Monasteries and convents were closed, social welfare systems established, and ecclesiastical funds diverted to pay preachers, support the poor, improve education, and fulfil local needs (such as the repairing of roads, bridges, or city defences). These measures were usually authorized—and often initiated—by the local prince or city council.

Although Luther was unable to travel outside Saxony, he strongly supported the introduction of the Reformation elsewhere. In 1517 Wenzelaus Linck (1483–1547), the dean of Wittenberg's theology faculty, was sent to Nuremberg as the Augustinian preacher and popularized Luther's ideas there. When in 1521, two of Nuremberg's prominent citizens, Willibald Pirckheimer (1470–1530) and Lazarus Spengler (1479–1534), spoke out in favour of Luther's writings and were censured by the church authorities, the city council sought—not entirely successfully—to protect them. The way was paved for Nuremberg to become an early convert to the Reformation. By 1523 some priests had married, the Lord's Supper was being offered in both kinds, and the poor chest had been introduced, the Reformation was only formally introduced by the city council in 1525. In Strasbourg the poor chest was introduced after the formal adoption of the German mass in 1524; in Ulm a majority of citizens seems to have accepted the teachings of either Luther or Zwingli while continuing to attend the Latin mass. In Wittenberg, the full practical consequences of Luther's theology were eventually introduced only after the death of Elector Frederick; Luther's 'German Mass' did not appear until late 1525 or even early 1526.

Some towns and parishes moved to ban the Latin mass as the first step towards reform. In 1522, not long after Karlstadt's abortive attempts at sustained reform in Wittenberg at Christmas 1521, Kaspar Kreutz introduced a German evangelical mass in Nördlingen, in southern Germany. In 1524 the mass began to be celebrated in German at Worms and at Strasbourg: Müntzer introduced a German evangelical mass in Allstedt although Luther rejected his theological stance. The introduction of vernacular liturgy or other reforms thus did not always imply acceptance of Luther's theology although it did usually indicate an interest in biblical reform. In Livonia the enthusiasm for the new teachings was accompanied by a frenzy of destruction of images which was far from the kind of orderly reforms which Luther favoured. The young Landgrave Philip of Hesse (1504–67), who in 1524 was the first of the German princes to introduce the Reformation into his territory, was more attracted by the principle of *sola scriptura* (by Scripture alone) than by the doctrine of justification by faith alone; he also found Zwingli's theology of the Lord's Supper more convincing than Luther's (Schneider-Ludorff 2006: 307, 309–11). Wittenberg theologians also assisted the spread of the Reformation. Melanchthon advised on many reforms, and Johannes Bugenhagen (1485–1558), professor and pastor of Wittenberg's town church, went on to assist in the introduction of the Reformation in Braunschweig, Hamburg, Hildesheim, Lübeck, and other locales.

Territories and imperial cities which introduced the Reformation were making political statements in their defiance of the Edict of Worms. Other German rulers could and did react against them. In 1524 a synod of southern German rulers and bishops in Regensburg approved ecclesiastical reforms while agreeing to oppose Luther's teachings; in 1525 Duke George of Saxony (1471–1539), cousin of Elector Frederick and his successor John, founded a union of north German rulers to withstand both the demands of the peasants and Luther's teachings. The following year Philip of Hesse and John of Saxony drew up the Treaty of Gotha-Torgau establishing an alliance with a number of other north German states and cities, including Anhalt, Braunschweig-Lüneburg, Magdeburg, and Mansfeld. John also signed a treaty with Prussia.

In 1526 an imperial diet took place at Speyer. The emperor was at war with France and at odds with Rome, a conflict which would end with the Sack of Rome in May 1527, and he needed military support. Rather than reinforcing the Edict of Worms, he proposed an Edict of Toleration, requiring princes and magistrates to 'behave themselves in their several provinces' such that 'they may be able to render an account of their doings both to God and the emperor'. In practice, this allowed each ruler to determine the religious allegiance of their territory and created space for the Reformation to expand.

By 1529 a brief period of peace with France had allowed the emperor to turn his attention to matters within the Empire. The imperial diet that year, again in Speyer, revoked the Edict of Toleration, calling for an ecclesiastical council to establish unity in religion; changes which had been introduced might be retained, but no new changes should be allowed. The gospel should be preached 'according to the teachings of the church'; the Latin mass must be allowed everywhere; and those who denied the presence of Christ in the Lord's Supper or rejected infant baptism should be banished.

The diet's decision provoked a Protest from fourteen imperial cities (Nuremberg, Strasbourg, Ulm, Constance, Reutlingen, Windsheim, Lindau, Kempten, Memmingen, Nördlingen, Heilbronn, Isny, St Gall, and Weissenburg; Frankfurt and Cologne initially signed but withdrew before the Protest was published) and five territories (Electoral Saxony, Hesse, Brandenburg-Ansbach, Braunschweig-Lüneburg, and Anhalt). Drafted with the support of several leading theologians, including Melanchthon, Simon Grynaeus (1493–1541) from Basel, and Erhard Schnepf (1495–1558), Philip of Hesse's court preacher, the Protest stated that its signatories were being asked 'to deny our Lord Jesus Christ, to reject His Holy Word', and called for agreement about 'what is meant by the true and holy church'. The Protest was presented to the diet but was ignored. The protesting rulers—from now on known as 'Protestants'—met to draw up a treaty. When representatives from Zürich indicated that they too would like to join, Wittenberg drew back, protesting that Zwingli's theology was opposed to Luther's.

This was a disaster for the political unity of the Protestants. Philip of Hesse, acutely aware of the strategic advantage of including Zürich, invited Luther and Zwingli to Marburg to settle their differences. In October 1529 Luther and Zwingli, accompanied by their supporters, met. They agreed on fourteen theological points, but noted 'we have not reached an agreement as to whether the true body and blood of Christ are bodily present in the bread and wine' (WA30,3.170; LW38.88). After Marburg the Protestants found themselves in two camps, with Luther, Wittenberg, and many of the German territories and cities on one side, and Zwingli in Zürich, together with the other Swiss cities and, at least initially, Martin Bucer in Strasbourg, on the other.

In the years that followed Bucer, Melanchthon, and Calvin would seek to resolve these differences, with little to show for their efforts. The Lutherans and the Reformed (as the reformers of Switzerland and the Rhineland came to be known), developed into separate confessions who did not receive the Lord's Supper from each other. It was not until 1973, with the Leuenberg Concord, that European Lutheran and Reformed churches entered into a formal theological relationship of communion.

VIII. The Diet of Augsburg and the Augsburg Confession

Relationships between the Protestant princes and territories and the emperor continued to deteriorate. When in June 1530 the next imperial diet was convened at Augsburg, the emperor had two priorities: repelling the Turks, who had besieged Vienna in autumn 1529 and were still in possession of substantial territories in Hungary, and solving the religious tensions within the Empire. He requested the major protagonists to present statements of faith at the diet. Unable to attend, Luther remained in Coburg, more than 150 miles away, where he was kept in touch with the proceedings by letter, and received visitors. Melanchthon was charged with presenting Wittenberg's position; he drafted the *Augsburg Confession* or *Confessio Augustana*. It presented Luther's theology and the fruits of the experience of introducing the Reformation into Saxony. Bucer presented the *Confession of the Four Cities* or *Confessio tetrapolitana* on behalf of Strasbourg, Memmingen, Lindau, and Constance, and Zwingli brought his *Account of Faith*, or *Ratio Fidei*. Eck and a group of papal theologians responded to Melanchthon's confession with the *Papal Confutation*, or *Confutatio Pontificia*, read to the assembly before the emperor. Melanchthon responded with his *Apology* or *Apologia* in 1531.

The emperor found none of the Protestant statements acceptable. Relationships deteriorated further. Early in 1531 John of Saxony and Philip of Hesse established the Smalcald League of the Protestant princes and territories, a defensive alliance should the emperor attack its members. In 1535 it was agreed that membership of the League should be open to those who subscribed to the Augsburg Confession. In an attempt to give the League a stronger theological basis, Luther subsequently drafted articles which were presented to the assembly held at Smalcald in 1537 and subscribed by most of the theologians present, but not officially adopted by the League (Brecht 1985–93: 3.191–3). Melanchthon adapted the *Augsburg Confession* in 1540 for negotiations with Roman Catholic theologians ordered by Emperor Charles, producing the so-called *variata* version. In 1555, following nearly a decade of conflict within the Empire, the Augsburg Confession was anchored in the Peace of Augsburg, making it legal for princes who subscribed to the Confession to use it to define the church in their territories. Dispute ensued over which version of the *Augustana* was meant. Other theological positions had no legal standing in the Empire; the Reformed confessions based on the work of Heinrich Bullinger (1504–75) in Zürich and Calvin in Geneva would not achieve legal recognition until the end of the Thirty Years War in 1648. The original edition of the *Augsburg Confession* finally became the defining statement of what it meant to be Lutheran.

IX. FAMILY LIFE

In June 1525 Luther had married Katharina von Bora, who had arrived in Wittenberg after fleeing with eight other nuns from her convent in Nimbschen at Easter 1523. Luther originally thought that Katharina might be a suitable wife for his colleague Nicolaus von Amsdorf (1483–1565), but Katharina had other ideas; Luther conceded that given the strength of his arguments for clerical marriage, he should 'set an example' (Hahn and Mügge 1999: 20; Brecht 1985–93: 2.195–7). His marriage had a confessional aspect which was common to many reformers, and indeed their wives (Methuen 2010: 713–15). The couple's financial resources were limited, but Katharina—Katy—proved herself an able financial manager. It was to prove a happy and successful marriage. Their first child, Johannes, was born to Luther and Katharina on 7 June 1526: 'it is a great miracle when a woman is made pregnant by a man', Luther commented in the eucharistic treatise he was writing at the time (WA19.490; LW36.341). Hans, as he was known, had five siblings: Elisabeth, born 10 December 1527, who died on 3 August 1528, causing Luther a depth of sorrow which surprised him (WABr4.511; Brecht 1985–93: 2.204); Magdalena, who was born on 4 May 1529—Luther discussed her weaning with Argula von Grumbach when she visited him during the Diet of Augsburg (WABr5.347–348)— and deeply grieved Luther by her death on 20 September 1542 at thirteen (Brecht 1985–93: 3.237); Martin, born on 9 November 1531; Paul, born on 28 January 1533; and Margarete, born on 17 December 1534. Katharina was certainly pregnant again at least once after Margarete's birth, for in 1540 she became very ill after a miscarriage and took many weeks to recover (Brecht 1985–93: 3.235).

Katharina and Luther lived in the former Augustinian monastery in Wittenberg, which provided a home for their own family and the children of two of Luther's sisters as well as lodging for students, paying guests, and other visitors. Katharina managed the household, oversaw the orchards, brewed beer, and latterly ran the farm at Zöllsdorf which she and Luther bought in 1540. She engaged with Luther and their guests in their discussions at table, and when he was away, Luther frequently included in his letters messages to be passed on to his colleagues. Luther's references to her—'Mrs Doctor', 'the preacher', 'Lord Katy' (WABr9.168; WABr10.205; WABr11.149; WABr7.91)—indicate affectionate respect if also a touch of irony. His life with Katharina provided a stable context within which Luther could exercise his ministry.

X. POLITICAL NEGOTIATIONS AND THE LAST YEARS

During the 1530s and 1540s Luther was able to consolidate his ideas. His complete German translation of the Bible was published in 1534. Work on revising the translation would continue for the rest of his life: the last complete edition to appear during his lifetime was printed in 1545. As Luther's ideas spread, political and theological allegiances shifted and changed. In 1536 Luther and the theologians in Strasbourg reached an agreement on the Lord's Supper, the Wittenberg Concord (Brecht 1985–93: 3.42–51). Luther advised on religious colloquies held at Hagenau, Worms, and Regensburg in 1540 and 1541 although he did not expect much of them; he rejected the statement on justification agreed at Regensburg by Melanchthon and Cardinal Gasparo Contarini (1483–1542). Throughout these years Luther continued to teach at the university and to preach in Wittenberg's parish church. As confessional allegiance became an increasingly political matter, he worked to negotiate peace between opposing parties. His advice was not always wise; his support for Philip of Hesse's bigamous marriage in 1540 proved politically inept (Brecht 1985–93: 3.205–15; Schneider-Ludorff 2006: 310). He wrote some important works, particularly his monumental *On the Councils and the Church* (WA50.509–653; LW41.9–179). However, in his last years Luther also wrote some of the most polemical of his writings, notoriously against the Jews (culminating in *On the Jews and their Lies* in 1542 [WA53.417–552; LW47.137–306; Brecht 1985–93: 3.337–51]), and against the pope (*Against the Roman Papacy, an Institution of the Devil* [WA54.206–299; LW41.263–376; Brecht 1985–93: 3.359–64], published in 1545).

Despite complaining of feeling old and tired, Luther continued to involve himself in political and theological disputes. In autumn 1545 and again in January 1546 he travelled to Eisleben, to assist the local rulers in reaching a settlement of a family quarrel. Towards the end of January he became ill. He died in Eisleben on 18 February 1546 (Brecht 1985–93: 3.369–77).

Almost immediately the fragile balance of power between Electoral Saxony and Ducal Saxony tipped into open conflict. Emperor Charles V finally could attempt to execute the condemnations of the Edict of Worms (1521). His war against John Frederick of Saxony and Philip of Hesse succeeded with the help of John Frederick's cousin and Philip's son-in-law, Moritz of Saxony. In the subsequent negotiations Moritz gained the electoral title, and John Frederick was forced to cede substantial territories, including Wittenberg. In 1548 Charles V imposed the Augsburg 'Interim', intended as a temporary measure until the Council of Trent, called by Pope Paul III, which had held its first sessions between 1545 and 1547, could bring about a religious settlement. The Interim outlawed all Protestant practices except clerical marriage and communion in both kinds; resistance to it demonstrated just how successfully the Reformation had established itself in many areas. The Interim proved unenforceable, and war once more broke out. In 1555 the Peace of Augsburg established the principle of *cuius regio eius religio*: the ruler's faith determined the people's faith. So long as the ruler was not a bishop, he might dictate whether religion in his territory should be defined by the Augsburg Confession or by the pope. Imperial cities must make provision for both forms of religion. The faith of Luther as stated in the Augsburg Confession had achieved legal status in the Empire.

But what was that faith? The period from 1549 until 1574 was characterized by a series of controversies over the proper interpretation of Luther's teachings and over the influence of Melanchthon's theology. Theologians argued about how to define 'neutral matters neither defined nor prohibited in Scripture' or *adiaphora*; about the proper understanding of justification; about the role of good works in salvation; about the Lord's Supper; about the question of whether human beings can cooperate in salvation; and about whether the Law applied to those who were justified. It would be another twenty years before a further definitive statement of faith was drafted: the Formula of Concord (1577). By then, under the influence of Germany's political leaders and a new generation of theologians, Luther's reforming theology had become a new confession: Lutheranism.

REFERENCES

Augustijn, Cornelis (1991). *Erasmus: His Life, Works and Influence*. Toronto: University of Toronto Press.

Beutel, Albrecht (2003). 'Luther's Life'. In *The Cambridge Companion to Martin Luther*, ed. Donald K. McKim. Cambridge: Cambridge University Press, 3–19.

Blickle, Peter (1998). *From the Communal Reformation to the Revolution of the Common Man*. Leiden: Brill.

Brecht, Martin (1985–93). *Martin Luther*. Vol. 1: *His Road to Reformation, 1483–1521*; vol. 2: *Shaping and Defining the Reformation, 1521–1532*; vol. 3: *The Preservation of the Church, 1532–1546*. Philadelphia: Fortress Press.

Goertz, Hans-Jürgen (1993). *Thomas Müntzer: Apocalyptic Mystic and Revolutionary*. Edinburgh: Clark.

Grell, Ole Peter (1992). 'Scandinavia'. In *The Early Reformation in Europe*, ed. Andrew Pettegree. Cambridge: Cambridge University Press, 94–119.

Hahn, Udo and Marlies Mügge (1999). *Katharina von Bora. Die Frau an Luthers Seite*. Stuttgart: Quell.

Lindberg, Carter (2000). *The European Reformations Sourcebook*. Oxford: Blackwell.

Methuen, Charlotte (2010). 'Preaching the Gospel through Love of Neighbour: The Ministry of Katharina Schütz Zell'. *Journal of Ecclesiastical History* 61: 707–28.

—— (2011). *Luther and Calvin: Religious Revolutionaries*. Oxford: Lion.

Rupp, E. Gordon and Benjamin Drewery (1970). *Martin Luther* (Documents of Modern History). London: Arnold.

Scheible, Heinz (1997). *Melanchthon. Eine Biographie*. Munich: Beck.

Schneider-Ludorff, Gury (2006). 'Philipp of Hesse as an Example of Princely Reformation: A Contribution to Reformation Studies'. *Reformation and Renaissance Review* 8: 301–19.

Siggins, Ian (1978). 'Luther's Mother Margarethe'. *Harvard Theological Review* 71: 125–50.

Stephens, W. Peter (1986). *The Theology of Huldrych Zwingli*. Oxford: Clarendon Press.

Zwingli, Ulrich (1984). *Huldrych Zwingli Writings*, ed. and trans. H. Wayne Pipkin, 2 vols. Allison Park, PA: Pickwick.

PART II

THE MEDIEVAL BACKGROUND AND ORIGINS OF LUTHER'S THOUGHT

CHAPTER 2

....

LUTHER AS LATE MEDIEVAL THEOLOGIAN

His Positive and Negative Use of Nominalism and Realism

....

THEODOR DIETER

I. INTRODUCTION

....

UNDERSTANDING Luther as late medieval theologian is anything but obvious since he has very often been seen as the founder of a totally new theological era. But Luther grew up, was educated, and lived in a late medieval context; thus he had to relate to it by receiving, rejecting, or transforming doctrines, ideas, theological and philosophical methods, practices, and institutions of the time.

With respect to this complex relationship it is appropriate to perceive him as a late medieval theologian. This chapter explains this conclusion by analysing Luther's 'positive or negative use of nominalism and realism', i.e., by describing Luther's relationship to scholastic theologies and philosophies. In doing so, we should be aware that there was another important stream of theology in the Middle Ages beside scholastic theology, namely monastic theology going back to patristic times and culminating in Bernard of Clairvaux. Luther was a monk (more precisely, a friar) for twenty years, in the formative period of his theology and even during the beginning of the Reformation. Some of his divergences from scholastic theology can be traced to the monastic theology that he received, appropriated, and transformed in a creative way (Köpf 1999). In order to give a comprehensive view of Luther as late medieval theologian, we should also take into consideration what Luther received and appropriated from mystical theology (Leppin 2007), 'Frömmigkeitstheologie' (Hamm 1982), and what has been called the 'Transformation of Academic Theology for Lay People' (Burger 1986). Since another chapter in this volume focuses on Luther's relation to the monastic tradition, we will limit ourselves to his use of nominalism and realism here.

What are 'nominalism' and 'realism'? In a narrow sense both are distinguished by giving opposite answers to the question of whether universals have an extra-mental reality or not—the first one denying it, the second affirming it.[1] The universals controversy in the West arose during the twelfth century and was revived in a new way in the fourteenth century. Since the early fourteenth century, the term *modernus* no longer denoted a contemporary; rather, it indicated a new method as opposed to an old one, especially in the interpretation of Aristotle's works. In the fifteenth century the terms *moderni, nominales*, and *terministae* were used more or less synonymously. Luther was familiar with the *Wegestreit* (battle between the two 'ways' of practising philosophy, the so-called *via moderna* and *via antiqua*) that developed in the course of the fifteenth century. Both ways identified their positions not by referring to contemporary authors, but by drawing on authors from earlier centuries as authorities for interpreting the works of Aristotle and doing philosophy. The *Wegestreit* originally had its *Sitz im Leben* in the faculty of arts but had significant consequences for the higher faculties, especially for theology. Thus, in 1474 the French King Louis XI banished the nominalists at the university of Paris in order to safeguard the true faith. He applauded the doctrine of the *doctores reales* as the standard to be followed and mentioned as normative figures Aristotle, Averroes, Albert the Great, Thomas Aquinas, Bonaventure, and John Duns Scotus, while he forbade the study of the writings of thinkers like William of Ockham, Gregory of Rimini, John Buridan, Pierre d'Ailly, Marsilius of Inghen, and others.

The *via moderna* was not simply nominalism, and nominalism should not be identified too quickly with Ockhamism, especially since recent research has cast doubts on whether it is adequate at all to speak of 'Ockhamism'. The protagonists who have been summarized under this label were creative and independent thinkers. But in the conflict between the 'ways' Ockham served as champion and figurehead of the *via moderna* since the reading of his writings was forbidden in Paris in 1339. He was accused of heresy at the papal court in Avignon, and he was involved in a sharp conflict with the pope, which made him suspect. Conversely, since John Wyclif, a protagonist of realism, was condemned several times for holding heretical ideas concerning the Eucharist and ecclesial hierarchy, that fact could be used as leverage in the struggle against realism. In any case, both realists and nominalists considered each other's view of universals to be wrong—and the wrong understanding could only lead to heresy. Thus the relation between philosophy and theology was the underlying agenda in the conflict between the 'ways'. While the *via antiqua* insisted on a close connection between the arts faculty and the theological faculty, interpreting Aristotle as consonant with faith, the *via moderna* emphasized the differences between natural insight (Aristotle) and supernatural faith, and pointed to tensions and contradiction between them.

[1] Luther described the difference in the Table Talk (WATR5,653,1–18) this way: Does 'humanity' (*humanitas*) refer to a common humanity in all human beings (Thomas Aquinas) or do the words 'man' and 'humanity' refer to all individual human beings (Ockham)?

With these reservations in mind, some tenets of 'nominalism' can be described in brief. Denying the extra-mental reality of universals meant focusing on individual things, but this did not imply that concepts in the intellect are merely arbitrary. On the contrary, they contain a clear relation to the world of things. In order to clarify this relation, one should (a) undertake careful semantic analyses to see how words function in a sentence (*supposition*) and (b) analyse how the cognition of individuals is possible and how to reach general propositions. In epistemology, challenges in the quest for certainty led to the development of concepts of intuitive and abstractive cognition. The requirement of evidence for scientific propositions had far-reaching consequences, especially in theology. Since semantic and logical analyses played a very important role for nominalists, and since they said that a person knows only propositions, realists accused them of destroying the sciences and proclaimed: 'We go right to the things, not caring about the terms.' In retrospect, it is clear that claiming individual things to be the only real things led nominalists like Buridan to become precursors of the empirical sciences. As a consequence of the condemnations of 219 articles by Bishop Tempier of Paris in 1277, theologians had to avoid any hint of necessitarianism in their writings. Thus they emphasized the contingency of all created things and the freedom of God by using the distinction between the absolute and ordained power of God. While it has often been said that this distinction was a hallmark of nominalism, it was in fact much older than the fourteenth century and had been used by Thomas Aquinas and Duns Scotus, too. Nevertheless, nominalists used it much more often. The absolute power of God referred to the whole range of possibilities that God possesses, which are only limited by the principle of contradiction. But God has established structures and rules in the physical world as well as in the realm of grace (his *pactum*) to which he has committed himself so that human beings can rely on them. Reference to the absolute power of God meant for Ockham emphasizing the possibility that God could have committed himself to a different order, so the given order is not necessary but contingent. But Ockham did not think of two different powers for God's action (some other theologians understood the distinction in this way). Even though God can act differently from his established order (for example, in miracles), his order is nevertheless reliable. Of course, God is able to achieve without secondary causes what he normally causes together through them (Courtenay 1990, 2008).

Nineteenth- and twentieth-century researchers who took Thomism as their yardstick perceived nominalism very negatively: as a regrettable dissolution of the synthesis of philosophy and theology achieved in Thomas Aquinas—as scepticism, fideism, and voluntarism. Luther, who several times claimed to belong to the Ockhamist 'sect', was seen by many as the nadir of a long movement of decline. Others who appreciated Luther's criticism of Ockhamism agreed that he had good reasons for his criticism of the theology of his time, but they argued that he had struggled with a non-Catholic Catholicism and so was not able to restore true Catholicism in its full and proper shape. For more than half of a century, extensive research has developed a much more differentiated and positive view of nominalism, especially of Ockham and other 'Ockhamists'. Most researchers no longer feel themselves obligated to evaluate the orthodoxy or heresy of people like Ockham; rather, they see these philosophers and theologians as participants in a long process of discussing problems, checking solutions, identifying weaknesses and short-comings in previous theories, and trying to overcome them.

Luther was educated in Erfurt in the *via moderna* (1501–5). In 1497 Jodocus Trutvetter and Bartholomäus Arnoldi of Usingen, who later became Luther's philosophical teachers, used a Quodlibet disputation to give the arts faculty a clearly 'modern' profile. They argued that in the whole universe there are only singular, absolute, permanent entities, namely sub-stance and quality. Only categorical terms of substance and quality refer to things in the world. The 'principle of economy'—no plurality is to be accepted unless there is a necessity for it—was for them the basic principle of the 'modern way'. They regarded Ockham as the 'venerable beginner of the *via moderna*', but they were critical of him in several respects. In fact, a critical attitude against all authorities was characteristic of their approach. They ridi-culed those who said that Aristotle had never contradicted the Christian faith and empha-sized that theology deals with the highest truths according to which all other truth claims have to be measured. What contradicts the Catholic truth was understood to be false and erroneous. Nevertheless, the clear awareness of the differences between theology and phi-losophy did not lead to a separation between them. Years later Luther stated that Trutvetter was the first of all from whom he had learned that only the Holy Scriptures deserve trust while all other books deserve critical judgement (WABr1.171,72–73). Gabriel Biel, who became Luther's main source for scholastic theology, offered his commentary on Lombard's *Sentences* as an abbreviated version of Ockham's commentary (*Collectorium*) with a good number of modifications. Through Biel, Ockham's theology became the epitome of nomi-nalist theology.

Here we will pursue Luther's *use* of nominalism and realism but not the *influence* of these intellectual movements on Luther. Asking for the influence of particular ideas on people does not help to explain why these ideas became convincing for some people but not for others. It is more useful to ask how a thinker receives certain ideas and which reasons he gives for agreeing or disagreeing with them. Where Luther and nominalism are concerned, we will have to deal with two different forms of use. In the first kind Luther explicitly indi-cates that he refers to a certain thinker or scholastic theoretical element. As long as he does not do this only in passing, we will be able to analyse his use of that element. Second, we may wonder in many other cases whether he is silently making use of certain scholastic elements. We can find many conjectures and speculations about this in the secondary lit-erature. But in a great number of texts it is very difficult to decide since certain similarities between particular thoughts in Luther and in one of the scholastic theologies do not alone provide enough evidence to assert unambiguously that Luther is using those elements. Luther could have developed a certain idea from another starting point and with differ-ent argumentation. Or a certain element may not be so specific that one can identify it as belonging to this or that school only. Thus we will mainly focus on texts in which Luther himself makes clear that he is drawing on a scholastic idea.[2]

---

[2] This chapter focuses much more on Luther's use of nominalism than on his relation to realism since Luther learnt more from and struggled much more with nominalist theologians than with the others.

Luther mentions several times that he belonged to the 'party of the Ockhamists' (WA6.600,11) or the terminists (WATR5.653,1–2). 'Ockham, my master, was the greatest logician' (WATR2.516,6), 'the most prudent and learned' (WATR1.137,11); 'with his mind he defeated all and confuted all other "ways"' (WATR4.679,24–25). He called Trutvetter 'the prince of the logicians of our time' (WA Br 1; 150,21f) while he criticized Aquinas as being responsible for the domination of Aristotle in theology (WA8.127,20). 'In the whole of Thomas there is not a single word that promotes confidence in Christ' (WATR2.193,5f). In many cases, such sayings do not offer much precise information about the contents and arguments that were at stake. A better source for identifying Luther's use of medieval philosophical and theological traditions is his marginal notes on Peter Lombard's *Sentences* (AWA9.251–560).[3] Luther lectured on this basic textbook of medieval theology from autumn 1509 until probably summer 1511, excepting the time of his trip to Rome. Luther did not comment constantly, the notes are often short and thus difficult to interpret, and on many topics he later changed his mind; thus we will focus on only one theme that also appears in Luther's last disputation: the use of semantic analysis and logic in Trinitarian theology.

II. DISPUTATION AGAINST SCHOLASTIC THEOLOGY (1517)

To know how Luther himself understood his relation to various scholastic theologians, his later so-called *Disputation against Scholastic Theology* (WA1.224–228; LW31.9–16; Grane 1962; Dieter 2001: 80–107.175–93) is quite revealing. In it Luther offers 97 theses, many of which announce against whom they are directed: a common saying or opinion of the scholastics (10); the understanding of many (2) or some (1); philosophers, moral teachers, and recent logicians (5); Duns Scotus (3), Cardinal Pierre d'Ailly (4), Ockham (2), and Gabriel Biel (13).[4] Luther's relationship to scholastic theologians as it is presented in this disputation is merely negative or critical. Nevertheless, Luther distinguishes between criticisms that are directed against all scholastics and others that are only aimed at individual theologians identified by name. All of these latter theologians belong to the *via moderna* (with the exception of Duns Scotus). Gabriel Biel is Luther's

---

Since 'nominalism' is used with many different meanings, it is necessary to focus on how Luther deals with certain elements of thought that can be described as 'nominalist'. Hence this chapter does not aim at a comprehensive overview but only at the analysis of certain important topics.

   [3] See also Luther's comments on works of Anselm of Canterbury, Bonaventure, Augustine, and Ockham in 'Erfurter Annotationen 1509–1510/11' (AWA9) and his marginal notes on Biel's *Collectorium* and *Canonis Missae Expositio* (WA59.25–53).

   [4] In a few cases, two or three theologians are mentioned together ('against Scotus, Gabriel', 'against the Cardinal, Gabriel', 'against Ockham, the Cardinal, Gabriel'). They are counted here individually.

main target in this disputation. Luther's theses refer to and are centred on a small text of the third book of Biel's *Collectorium* of about four (!) pages in the printed version (Biel 1979: 503–7). This clearly indicates that the problem discussed by Biel at this place is absolutely fundamental for the reformer. It is the *dubium*: 'Whether the human will of the pilgrim is able to love God above all by its own natural capacities and thus fulfil the love commandment' (Biel 1979: 503).

Biel offers five propositions that explain aspects of the positive answer he gives to this question. Luther deals with four propositions picking up several arguments that Biel offers in favour of them. Forty-one theses directly discuss the propositions, 36 theses deal with the topic in a wider sense, and 15 theses mainly express criticisms of Aristotle (theses 39 to 42 on his moral theory, theses 43 to 44 on the theologian's alleged need to study Aristotle, theses 45 to 53 mainly on the role of Aristotle's logic in theology).

We no longer have the proofs for the theses of this disputation, as we do for the theses of the 'Heidelberg Disputation', but we can find the basis for them in Luther writings and lectures during the same period. By quoting several propositions of Biel's, Luther makes it clear that he intends to comment directly on them. At the same time Luther's criticisms come from very different presuppositions than Biel's and other scholastics', so we can sometimes get the impression that Luther has missed the point. But the fact that Luther organized a scholastic disputation means that he presupposed a common starting point and was able to demonstrate why he decided to go in a different direction.

The common starting point is the conviction that the law of God is summarized in the commandment to love God (Mt 22:37–8). But how is this commandment to be understood? Biel identifies four aspects to how God is to be loved: with one's whole heart (that is: with one's will), with one's whole mind (that is: with one's intellect), with one's whole soul (that is: with one's whole sensitive power), and with one's whole strength (that is: with the moving power of the limbs of the body that allow for external actions). To love God means to love him with all that is in us. Nothing should be in us that is not directed to God. After these explanations, it is highly astonishing that Biel concludes with the sentence that this understanding of the love commandment is equivalent to the phrase 'to love God above all' (*diligere Deum super omnia*), since *diligere* is an act of the will that does *not* include the whole person (Biel 1979: 490–1, 483–4).

Here is the point of divergence, and it is crucial to realize this in order to understand Luther's specific approach properly. He takes seriously that, according to the biblical commandment, God expects a wholehearted and comprehensive dedication of the person to him and not only an act of the human will (including its external execution, of course), so that any unwillingness or reluctance that resists the inner will to love God amounts to a transgression of God's law (WA1.368,10–20; 367,15–368,3; LW31.60–62). Luther calls the scholastic theologians who claim that human beings by their own powers can love God above all 'stulti' [stupid] and 'Sawtheologen' [sow theologians], and he requires them to prove that they are without concupiscence—for only then can they claim to love God above all (WA56.274,11–275,16; LW25.261–262). Obviously, Luther has a different understanding of 'love of God' and 'will' here than Biel. Luther's argument creates a complex situation. On the one hand, when Luther denies the human capacity to love God above all, he presupposes *his* understanding of the biblical love commandment as requiring full and perfect dedication of the whole person to God. Biel would agree with Luther that such love is not in the natural power of human beings but would disagree with him that God requires such love as fulfilment of the law.

On the other hand, Luther takes seriously Biel's claim that love of God as an act of the human will is the fulfilment of the divine commandment. But since the doctrine of grace teaches that the fulfilment of God's law is not possible without grace, Luther draws the consequence that the freedom of the will (in this respect) does not exist. Drawing this consequence clearly presupposes that the law of God is to be fulfilled by an act of the will. But, as we have seen, Luther denied this. Thus Luther could have argued that even if a person loved God with her will, this act of the will alone would not meet what God requires since there is a difference between a moral and a theological or spiritual understanding of the fulfilment of the law. In a series of theses in the *Disputation against Scholastic Theology* Luther makes this point. For example, Biel argues against the proposition 'The law must be fulfilled in the grace of God': if this were true, it would follow that one would sin by not killing, not committing adultery, etc. But Luther denies that this is the correct conclusion to draw. Rather, we should infer that apart from grace a person who does not kill, commit adultery, and so forth sins all the same since she does not fulfil the law spiritually. 'Spiritually that person does not kill, does not commit adultery, does not steal when he neither becomes angry nor lusts' (theses 61–4, WA1.227,12–18; LW31.13 [translation altered]).

From this perspective Luther's main emphases in the disputation should be understood through his own words in thesis 18: 'To love God above all things by nature is a fictitious term.' The corresponding positive claim is: 'An act of friendship is done, not according to nature, but according to prevenient grace' (thesis 20). This is explicitly said against Biel, who had attributed this act to nature but stated that whenever such an act is realized, at the very same instant God gives his grace, so that such an act is never without grace and infused love. Biel connects the act of love of God by nature with the infusion of grace by referring to biblical statements like Zechariah 1:3 ('Return to me, [...] and I will return to you'). Luther rejected attribution of the first to nature and the second to grace as Pelagianism (theses 26–8).[5] Biel presupposes the nominalist principle that 'God does not deny his grace to someone (B) who does what is in his or her power (A)'. The early Luther himself shared this logic, 'If A, then B' (WA4.261,39–262,17; LW11: 396–7), with the important difference that 'A' for him was a work of prevenient grace and later the self-accusation of a person, according to 1 Corinthians 11:31. But for the scholastics, that rule itself was an expression of grace since God in his freedom cannot be forced to accept any created entity—not even an act of loving God. Only because God has freely determined himself to accept certain created realities can human beings expect such

---

[5] Interestingly, Thomas Aquinas interpreted Zech. 1:3 through Jer. 31:18 and Lam. 5:21 (*Summa Theologiae* I/II, qu. 109, art. 6 ad 1)—contrary to Biel.

acceptation on account of God's commitment (*pactum*). Even though Luther shared this concept of the *pactum* at the beginning, step by step he rebuilt it by changing what 'A' meant. At the end of this process he overcame the whole structure by replacing the *pactum* with the *promissio*—the promise that creates what it says and requires special faith in this precise promise.

It is very revealing how Luther used the phrase 'by the absolute power of God' (thesis 55). Biel stated that by the absolute power of God it could happen that a morally good act could remain without grace since the phrase 'morally good act (of loving God) without grace' does not include a self-contradiction, and God is free to react or not to any created reality by giving or denying his grace. Luther, on the contrary, did not ask whether an act of loving God is accepted by God. Rather, he insisted that such love of God cannot come into being without grace; therefore, 'loving God without grace' is a contradiction in terms and not possible even under God's absolute power. Luther's use of this term shows how deeply his way of thinking was different from the nominalists' since he did not reflect on what God *could* do without reference to his created order. Rather he focuses on what God *does* (God's ordered power) in view of human sinfulness.[6]

Luther's difference from the nominalists on the subject of God's acceptation of sinners becomes clear in his opposition to the distinction between the fulfilment of the law according to its content—assumed to be possible by nature—and its fulfilment according to the intention of the lawgiver—meaning that the law has to be fulfilled in grace because only then is it meritorious according to the ordered power of God. This distinction was meant as protection against Pelagianism, so that human beings would not be able to think that they could fulfil the law by their own power (Biel 1979: 507). It is most revealing that for Luther the consequence of this thought would be: if the law is fulfilled according to its content by nature, it is fulfilled—simply—without grace (theses 58–60). The nominalist idea of God's free acceptation and thus the necessity of grace is simply excluded by Luther in his discussion of Pelagianism. Luther does not think along the lines of divine acceptation. The same criticism is operative when Luther speaks of 'that damned word "formed" [by charity]' (WA56.337,18; LW25: 325) that is often quoted and misunderstood. Luther has most often been understood as emphasizing that grace remains completely outside of the person. Just the opposite is the case here: Luther criticizes scholastics like Pierre d'Ailly and Biel in that for them grace does not significantly alter the person; it only changes the meritorious character of what people can in principle achieve by their natural powers.

The main target of Luther's criticism is Biel together with Ockham and Pierre d'Ailly, especially their understanding of grace and free will. Thomas Aquinas is not mentioned in this disputation though he is included in a few general accusations. Later, in his discussions with Thomists in the indulgence debate, Luther was challenged to reflect more on Thomas and his authority, but it is still not clear what Luther knew of him (despite

---

[6] See also thesis 56 (explicitly against Ockham): 'God cannot accept man without his justifying grace.'

Janz 1989), and—with a few exceptions—we do not have detailed arguments that allow for describing his 'use' of Thomas' thoughts. The more general theses in the disputation that are directed against 'all' include the problem of the compatibility of theology and philosophy, especially Aristotle, and the necessity of philosophy, mainly logic, for theology. They seem to struggle primarily with what is called 'institutional Aristotelianism' (Dieter 2001: 14–18). Elements of what he denied at this time will be found in Luther's later works. Involved in many controversies, Luther used some of the philosophical tools he had learnt, mainly semantic analysis and logic, to explain and defend his positions.

III. Logic and Trinitarian Theology

Peter Lombard and especially his commentators dealt with the problem of logic in Trinitarian theology in their discussions of a topic that seems very strange to us, namely the question whether one can say that the divine essence generates the Son or the essence. Peter denied this; his position was confirmed against the criticism of Joachim of Fiore by the canon *Firmiter* during the Fourth Lateran Council (1215). But in his marginal notes Luther was not satisfied with this, arguing that the two following propositions are quite similar: 'The divine essence generates God' and 'God generates God'. While the latter proposition was accepted by Peter in a previous section in line with the Creed (it confesses that Jesus Christ is 'God from God, light from light'), the first proposition was denied. But Luther contested that there is a basic difference between both propositions since the subject terms (God, essence) in both of them could be used either relatively / personally (*relative / personaliter*—directly referring to the persons of the Trinity) or essentially / substantially (*essentialiter / substantialiter*—directly referring to the essence of the Trinity). Understood essentially, both propositions are wrong, but understood relatively, both are true. Thus according to Luther, the truth values of these sentences depend on whether 'God' or '(divine) essence' are used in one or the other way (AWA9.284,11–14). Interestingly, Luther continued by saying that Peter Lombard's arguments for his position were not conclusive but what the Holy Spirit said was true and apparently the Spirit had spoken through the Lateran Council (AWA9.284,15–17).

Luther found this argument in a commentary on the *Sentences* by the nominalist theologian Pierre d'Ailly (cf. AWA9.284–285, n. 3) and summarized it in a few sentences in his marginal notes. D'Ailly referred to Augustine's distinction of two ways of using the names for God. Luther, too, commented on the respective passages of Augustine's *De trinitate* (AWA9,583,15–29). Luther used this distinction also in a Christmas sermon in 1514 (WA1.20,1–22,21). He wished his audience to understand the first sentences of the Gospel of John: 'In the beginning was the Word, and the Word was with God, and God was the Word.' Astonishingly, this led Luther to discuss logical problems in that sermon. One could argue: 'This divine essence is the Father (1). This divine essence is the Son (2). Thus: The Son is the Father (3)'. This syllogism is formally correct, and its two premises are materially correct, but the conclusion is wrong, according to the Christian faith. This created a very unfortunate alternative for medieval thinkers: either the Christian faith is irrational, or the universality of syllogistic conclusions has to be denied. There was a debate of two hundred years refining the requirements for a formally correct syllogism. Pierre d'Ailly proposed rules for identifying the correct supposition of the respective terms so that fallacies could be avoided. Luther claimed to have found a better way to overcome the problem and to reconcile the truth of the Trinitarian dogma with the syllogistic rules. He phrased the inference this way: 'Whatever God is, is the Father' (1), 'The Son is God' (2), thus: 'The Son is the Father'. Luther identified the mistake as the fallacy of equivocation, which means that in proposition (1), 'God' is used as a term of essence (*terminus essentialis*), while in proposition (2) 'God' is used as a term of person (*terminus personalis*). Thus the middle term 'God' is not used in a univocal way. Later, Luther will say that the 'thing itself'—the Triune God—is equivocal. Thus it is no wonder that fallacies occur when terms that refer to God enter into a syllogism.

In the *Disputation against Scholastic Theology* Luther presented five theses dealing with logic in theology. He criticized Pierre d'Ailly for assuming that syllogistic forms were valid in Trinitarian doctrine. For Luther, this doctrine does not contradict the syllogistic rules. The issue is that they cannot be applied because the 'thing' is equivocal, and in fact Peter's rules should identify and exclude equivocations. The very few syllogisms in this field are pretty trivial. Luther received the semantic tools of coping with the problem from Pierre d'Ailly but criticized him in the course of his career, yet in his last disputation Luther called him 'the most learned of the scholastics' (WA39,2.288,21). In this disputation of 1544 he presented the same constellation of persons and positions as in his early marginal notes: Peter Lombard denying that the divine essence generated or was generated, the criticism of Joachim of Fiore, the canon *Firmiter* affirming Peter's position, the distinction between the twofold use of terms in divine matters (absolutely—relatively), the reference to Augustine, and mentioning Pierre d'Ailly as, so to speak, witness for his position. Nevertheless, there was a difference, namely that that decision of the Fourth Lateran Council no longer had any authority for Luther so that he did not present his understanding in a subjunctive form as in 1509 or as Peter did ('if the church had not decided differently') but in an affirmative one (White 1994: 181–230; Dieter 2001: 378–430).

IV. DE SERVO ARBITRIO

In *On Bound Choice* Luther distinguishes between 'God or the will of God as preached, revealed, offered and worshiped, and [...] as he is not preached, not revealed, not offered, not worshiped' (WA18.685,3–5; LW33.139). Luther is challenged to develop this distinction by the fact that, on the one hand, we read in Ezekiel (18:23): 'As I live, says the Lord, I desire not the death of a sinner, but rather that he should turn and live', but, on the other hand, we observe that there are many human beings who simply reject God's offer. In order to cope with this situation,

Luther presents two ways of speaking of God, namely with respect to God revealed and to God hidden. God 'does not will the death of a sinner, according to his word; but he wills it according to that inscrutable will of his' (WA18.685,28–29; LW33.140). This distinction resembles structurally the distinction between the absolute and ordained power of God in scholasticism. But Luther does not refer to this scholastic topic; rather, he claims that his distinction is based on the Apostle Paul (for example, Romans 9:19–21). In fact, he explicitly rejects the absolute–ordained distinction together with the distinction between the necessity of the consequence and the necessity of the consequent, both seen as means to escape the painful offence by the awareness that we live under necessity (WA18.719,12–19; LW33.190). While in scholastic doctrine the term 'absolute power' denominates the whole range of the possibilities of God for which the principle of contradiction allows and that which God normally does not realize but could do and from time to time does do, in Luther the hidden God is continuously active. He 'works life, death, and all in all' (WA18.685,22–23; LW33.140). 'By the omnipotence of God, however, I do not mean the potentiality by which he could do many things which he does not, but the active power by which he potently works all in all' (WA18.718,28–30; LW33.189). While the scholastics used the concept of the absolute power of God to safeguard the non-necessity of all that exists and happens outside of God, Luther emphasizes the necessity of all because of God's working all in all. Thus Luther's distinction between the hidden and revealed God and the scholastic distinction between the absolute and ordained power are totally different.

Luther closely connects his distinction with the problem of 'whether God foreknows anything contingently, and whether we do everything of necessity' (WA18.614,27–28; LW33.36). In doing so, he takes up a problem that was discussed by scholastic theologians and philosophers for centuries. God is omniscient, he cannot be deceived, his knowledge is immutable, and since he is a necessary being, his knowledge is necessary, too. Nevertheless, the problem is whether God who knows all and everything knows contingent entities and events as contingent or whether the necessity that he knows everything has the consequence that everything that he knows is itself necessary. In this case, free will would not exist. Scholastic theologians made many and very different attempts to avoid this consequence and demonstrate that God's necessary knowledge is compatible with the contingency of the created world and with free will. Luther in fact broke with this tradition arguing: (a) God's will is immutable: thus his foreknowledge is immutable, too, and (b) if his foreknowledge is immutable, then 'God foreknows necessarily' (WA18.615,26–8; LW33.37).

> If he foreknows as he wills, then his will is eternal and unchanging (because his nature is so), and if he wills as he foreknows, then his knowledge is eternal and unchanging (because his nature is so). From this it follows irrefutably that everything we do, everything that happens, even if it seems to us to happen mutably and contingently, happens in fact nonetheless necessarily and immutably if you have regard to the will of God.
>
> (WA18.615,29–33; LW33.37–38)

The scholastics 'admit that everything happens necessarily, though by the necessity of consequence (as they say) and not by the necessity of the consequent' (WA18.616,14–15; LW33.39–40). Luther explains 'necessity of consequence' this way: 'If God wills anything, it is necessary for the thing to come to pass, but it is not necessary that the thing which comes to pass should exist; for God alone exists necessarily, and it is possible for everything else not to exist if God so wills' (WA18.617,2–5; LW33.40) 'Necessity of the consequent' would mean absolute necessity. Since Luther dismisses the scholastic distinction between God's absolute and ordained power, he seems to think that God does not will contingently but necessarily, even though free from any external determination. 'Necessity of the consequence' means the necessary relation between A and B ('if A, then B') while both the antecedent A and the consequent B are not necessary as such. But when Luther claims that the antecedent A (God's will or God's foreknowledge) is necessary, then also the consequent B is necessary, so that the distinction between the two types of necessity appears as a vain scholastic subtlety.

Luther does not develop his argument in detail; thus many presuppositions that are implied in it remain hidden. It is difficult to imagine how Luther could substantiate his claim that 'free choice is plainly a divine term' (WA18.636,28; LW33.68) as long as he states that 'it remains a fact that everything that comes into being does so necessarily, if the action of God is necessary' (WA18.617,9–10; LW33.40). It is also difficult to see how the statement that everything happens by necessity is compatible with the so-called political use of the law—its use in governing the relations of human beings with each other for which freedom of the will is presupposed. Luther's argument against free will from the omniscience and omnipotence of God is a metaphysical argument in spite of the added biblical references. It is in principle different from his theological argument referring to the doctrine of grace except that both meet in the denial of the freedom of the will. We can deny that metaphysical argument while wholeheartedly embracing Luther's doctrine of grace. It is revealing that the metaphysical problem and the arguments that Luther dealt with were also discussed in medieval Jewish and Islamic theology and philosophy.

V. Christology

Luther's Christology is much richer and more comprehensive than it is presented in the disputations 'The Word Became Flesh' (1539) and 'The Divinity and Humanity of Christ' (1540). Nevertheless, the problem of the relationship of his Christology to Ockhamism is raised especially with respect to these disputations. One opinion perceives Luther as a sharp critic of Ockhamist Christology, contesting that the proposition 'God is man' can be understood so 'that the human nature is maintained or supposited by the divine nature, or the divine *suppositum*' (WA39,2.95,34–35). Luther criticizes that the *moderni* do not allow for propositions like 'The Son of Mary is the creator of the world', denying that God and man are 'one thing'. They interpret the sentence 'God is man' in such a way that 'man' refers to the 'Son of God maintaining the human nature'. This amounts to the proposition 'God is the Son of God maintaining the human nature' (WABr9.444,51–445,74). Luther on the contrary emphasizes the unity of both natures in the one person of Christ. He explains this by applying the 'communication of properties' (*communicatio idiomatum*) in his understanding: what is said about Christ as man is also said about Christ as God. Thus one can say: 'This man has created the world' and 'this God suffered' (Schwarz 1966). Another study interprets Luther differently:

> Thus, all in all, Luther's Christology is extremely Ockhamist. It is characterized by an insistence on the basic features of Ockhamist Christology: the emphasis on the unity of the person, Christ; the consequent difference between the terms 'human nature' and 'man', when applied to the man Jesus; the stress on the *communicatio*, as being a very direct consequence of the unity of the person of Christ (together with Ockhamist semantics); and the resolution of the seeming paradoxes that arise from the *communicatio*, as being a product of the fallacy of *simpliciter* and *secundum quid*. (White 1994: 297)

the latter phrases distinguishing whether a proposition about Christ is said with explicit reference to him as God or as human being, or whether such a reference is not made.

VI. Physics: Motion

'[A]s has often been said, to make progress is nothing else than always to begin' (WA4.350,14–15; LW11.477). This sentence has many times been quoted and understood as if Luther in principle denied that any progress in Christian life could happen. He seemed to perceive the Christian as a Sisyphus who would always be put back to the very starting point of his existence no matter which steps he might have taken. But if one sees Ockham's understanding of motion as the background, it becomes clear that the sentence quoted is just the definition of the motion of the Christian existence. Instead of denying progress, Luther challenges the Christian not to stop making progress.

With respect to justification, scholastic theologians distinguished two different motions: (a) the motion from sin to grace that happens in an instant. It is an alteration; there is 'either a justified person or a sinner', and (b) the motion in which grace increases that is understood in analogy to the process of intensification of a quality. Luther learned to understand that even though there is an either–or of being under grace or not being under grace, sin is not expelled in an instant. Thus the concept of grace as a quality is not appropriate in describing existence under grace.

While Aristotle defines motion by using the concepts of 'actuality' and 'potentiality', it is characteristic for Ockham to analyse motion by making a cut at any point in the motion, defining this point by the affirmation of A and the negations of $B_{1,2}$.... The object in motion has reached A but not yet $B_{1,2}$... Luther superimposed those two motions on each other and tried to describe the existence of the Christian by means of Ockham's theory of motion. According to the Bible, Christians go from clarity to clarity (2 Cor. 3:18) while the form of this clarity is the same. Luther interpreted just this motion of the growth of the righteous in such a way that at any moment the person is understood both as righteous (with respect to the very first starting point [sin], from which she moved away, and any previous point of the motion) and as sinner (with respect to any future point of motion and the final goal of being righteous totally without any remaining sin); thus any moment of the motion of growth is understood *at the same time* as the alteration from unrighteousness to righteousness—in opposition to Ockham's understanding, which had distinguished two types of motion.

> [E]very righteousness for the present moment is sin with regard to that which must be added in the next moment [...] Hence he who in the present moment trusts that he is righteous and stands in that opinion has already lost righteousness, as it is clear likewise in motion: That which is the goal in the present moment is the starting point in the next moment. But the starting point is sin, from which we must always be going; and the goal is righteousness, to which we must always be going.
>
> (WA4.364,15–23; LW11.496)

This does not of course mean that the Christian is half justified and half a sinner. The Christian is righteous. Luther used Ockham's concept of motion in order to have a model for describing Christian existence under grace not by the concept of quality but of: the *simul* of being righteous and sinner while *semper* (continuously) going from justification to justification in struggling with sin and growing in grace (Dieter 2001: 276–346).

VII. THE LORD'S SUPPER

Discussing the Lord's Supper in *The Babylonian Captivity of the Church*, Luther identified three captivities to which the sacrament had been subjected. The second is that it had become an article of faith that in the consecration of bread and wine the substance of bread and wine is transformed into the substance of the body and blood of Christ while the accidents of the bread (size, taste, weight, etc.) remain (WA6.508,1–512,6; LW36.28–35). Luther used several nominalist ideas in criticizing the theory of transubstantiation. He reported that as a student he was challenged to critical reflection when he read how Pierre d'Ailly applied the principle of economy in comparing the theory of transubstantiation with the theory of consubstantiation, arguing that the latter needed fewer miracles in order to be explained, so this theory should be preferred—if the church had not decided differently at the Fourth Lateran Council (1215). Many late medieval theologians were convinced that neither Scripture nor reason allow for preferring the theory of transubstantiation. Only later that decision lost its binding force for Luther when he—mistakenly—thought that it was the Thomistic, that is, the Aristotelian church that made the decision. Then Luther could follow his better insight, as he saw it (WA6.508,7–26; LW36.28–29).

In discussing an argument that Thomas Aquinas had brought forward in favour of transubstantiation, Luther—without mentioning names—drew on the criticism of it by Duns Scotus, Ockham, Biel, and others. Thomas had argued that in order to avoid idolatry in adoring the consecrated host, transubstantiation must have happened so that there is no longer bread. But the critics—and Luther followed them—objected that this would also require that the accidents would have to disappear, which is obviously not the case (WA6.509,35–510,3; LW36.31–32).

Luther used nominalist ideas, too, in criticizing another aspect (WA6.510,9–24; LW36.32). The basic problem of transubstantiation is that the being of accidents is a being-in (a substance), but after transubstantiation the substance of the bread is no longer there. For Thomas, quantity functioned as the foundation for the other accidents of the bread. This presupposes that quantity can be separated from substance. That is precisely what most nominalists denied. Trutvetter and Usingen had argued in 1497 that there are only two categories (substance and quality) whose terms directly refer to real things. If Thomas nevertheless took quantity as the entity in which the other accidents have their being-in, then God must create this quantity anew since it cannot be separated from substance. This is a clear criticism of a position of Thomas (without mentioning him) from a nominalist point of view.

Luther discussed a further argument that could be presented in favour of transubstantiation (WA6.510,25–511,12; LW36.33–34). It is the understanding of the proposition that the subject term and the predicate term must *supposit* for or refer to the same single thing in order for the proposition to be true. Thus the sentence 'this is my body' is true only if 'this' refers to the body of Christ. Thus transubstantiation seems to be necessary. Luther attributes this understanding of the proposition to Aristotle, but it is clearly nominalist. In his later debate with Zwingli (1526) Luther identifies this problem as the problem of the *praedicatio identica* (WA26.437,30–445,17, LW37.295–303). He argues that one can either understand the subject term from the predicate term (transubstantiation) or the predicate term from the subject term (Wyclif). In the debate with the Swiss reformer he uses the rhetorical concept of synecdoche in order to describe the relationship between the body of Christ and the bread in the Lord's Supper that is more than simply consubstantiation. This requires that the sentence 'This is my body' has to be analysed first grammatically before it can be interpreted logically. Then no logical conflict will appear. Thus, Luther's criticism of the second captivity of the sacrament of the altar drew heavily on late medieval criticism of Thomas' theory with the important difference that Luther let that criticism become effective since he no longer felt bound by the decision of 1215.

In his debate with Zwingli on the Lord's Supper, Luther reviewed the argument that Christ's body sitting at the right hand of God cannot be at the same time on Eucharistic tables (Hilgenfeld 1971: 183–232). He clearly identified the burden of proof in this debate, claiming that Zwingli had to prove that even for God in his omnipotence there is only one way in which Christ's body can be present in a certain place. Luther conversely demonstrated that there are more types of local presence. For this purpose, he explicitly referred back to the late scholastic distinction between three different types of local presence: local or circumscriptive, definitive, and repletive. Luther could find these types for example in Usingen's textbook on *Physics* or in Biel's *Collectorium*.

Luther described the first type so that 'an object is circumscriptively or locally in a place, i.e. in a circumscribed manner, if the space and the object occupying it exactly correspond and fit into the same measurements, such as wine or water in a cask' (WA26.327,23–25; LW37.215). Secondly, 'an object is in a place definitively, i.e. in an uncircumscribed manner, if the object or body is not palpably in one place and is not measurable according to the dimensions of the place where it is but can occupy either more room or less' (WA26.327,33–328,20; LW37.215). The object has no quantitative dimensions while being present in a certain place. This is what Luther was interested in, while the scholastics added that such an object as a whole is in a whole certain place and in each of its parts (for example, the rational soul in the body) and that it is naturally not in another place at the same time (for example, an angel). Therefore, when they understand the local presence of Christ's body on the Eucharistic tables in this definitive way, they must see it as happening supernaturally. Luther reflects on the omnipotence of God, too, not as limited by the principle of contradiction but as testified by Scripture. The resurrected Christ going through the stones of his grave or through walls of houses was a good example for this type of local presence. Thus Zwingli's presupposition was refuted. It is interesting that Luther did not consider God's power by asking what God could do. Instead, he asked what God has done according to the testimony of Scripture and everyday experience. The third type of local presence belongs to God alone: he 'is simultaneously present in all places whole and entire, and fills all places, yet without being measured or circumscribed by any place' (WA26.329,27–30; LW37.216).

Luther used several elements of nominalist theology and philosophy as supporting tools in the debate on the Lord's Supper with his opponents, but they were not fundamental for his own position.

VIII. Double Truth?

In the disputation 'The Word Was Made Flesh' (1539), Luther criticized the Sorbonne: 'The Sorbonne, the mother of errors, very badly posited [*definivit*] that the same thing is true in philosophy and theology' (WA39,2.3,7–8). This thesis has been taken by some as an indication that Luther held the so-called 'doctrine of the double truth'. The concept of the double truth is mentioned in the Prologue of the Bishop of Paris, Stephan Tempier, to the text of his condemnation of 219 theses in 1277: some members of the faculty of arts say that something is true according to philosophy but not according to the Catholic faith, as if two contrary truths existed and as if a truth in the writings of some damned pagan people stood against the truth of Holy Scripture. In accord with this, Luther's teacher Usingen stated in his textbook on *Physics* that the principles of natural reason do not contradict theological principles and truths, and therefore what is true in theology is also true in philosophy.

But Luther did not have the doctrine of the double truth in mind (Hägglund 1955). He emphasized that every truth agrees with every truth—that is, every true proposition agrees with every true proposition (WA39,2.3,1–2). Nevertheless, there are different areas of truth, such that a proposition that is true in one area does not necessarily make sense in another. Luther offers many examples (WA39,2.5,13–36). 'Humidity moistens' is true in the area of air, but obviously 'heretical' in the area of fire. One may hang a weight from a material point—this is true, but if we are referring to a mathematical point or line, then this would not be true (WA39,2.5,29–30.15–16). One may consider different arts and their respective works and see that the same proposition is never true in all of them. This is even more the case with the relation of philosophical and theological propositions. Luther thus argues that the realm of objects of philosophy differs in character from the realm of objects of theology.

Luther often used tools of nominalist philosophy, mainly semantic analysis and logic, in order to express his doctrine, to defend it against criticism, and to defeat opposing teachings. In criticizing positions of the *via antiqua*, mainly of Thomas Aquinas, he followed partly the lines of the nominalist criticism of that way. Nevertheless, in theology his main criticism was directed against theologians like Biel, Pierre d'Ailly, and Ockham. Even though he shared for some time the theory of the *pactum*, he changed and finally overcame this model of nominalist thinking. He developed quite a different understanding of loving God, of will, and of law, and from this understanding he denied the freedom of the will and the possibility of fulfilling God's law by natural powers, thus developing a new understanding of grace. He used the distinction between God's absolute and ordained power in a way very different from the nominalists, and he cannot be understood in the line of their theology of divine acceptation. It does not make much sense to call Luther a nominalist since 'nominalism' has so many meanings and aspects. But it is important for a better understanding of Luther to identify elements that can be called 'nominalist' and then carefully to analyse how Luther used and modified them.

References

Biel, Gabriel (1979). *Gabrielis Biel Collectorium circa quattuor libros Sententiarum, Liber tertius*, ed. Wilfried Werbeck and Udo Hofmann. Tübingen: Mohr/Siebeck.

Burger, Christoph (1986). *Aedificatio, fructus, utilitas. Johannes Gerson als Professor der Theologie und Kanzler der Universität Paris*. Tübingen: Mohr/Siebeck.

Dieter, Theodor (2001). *Der junge Luther und Aristoteles. Historisch-systematische Untersuchungen zum Verhältnis von Theologie und Philosophie*. Berlin and New York: de Gruyter.

Grane, Leif (1962). *Contra Gabrielem. Luthers Auseinandersetzung mit Gabriel Biel in der Disputatio Contra Scholasticam Theologiam 1517*. Copenhagen: Gyldendal.

Hägglund, Bengt (1955). *Theologie und Philosophie bei Luther und in der occamistischen Tradition. Luthers Stellung zu der Theorie von der doppelten Wahrheit*. Lund: Gleerup.

Hamm, Bernd (1982). *Frömmigkeitstheologie am Anfang des 16. Jahrhunderts. Studien zu Johannes von Paltz und seinem Umkreis.* Tübingen: Mohr/Siebeck.

Hilgenfeld, Hartmut (1971). *Mittelalterlich-traditionelle Elemente in Luthers Abendmahlsschriften.* Zürich: Theologischer Verlag Zürich.

Janz, Denis R. (1989). *Luther on Thomas Aquinas: The Angelic Doctor in the Thought of the Reformer.* Stuttgart: Steiner.

Köpf, Ulrich (ed.) (1999). 'Monastische Tradition bei Martin Luther'. In *Christoph Markschies and Michael Trowitzsch. Luther zwischen den Zeiten.* Tübingen: Mohr/Siebeck, 17–35.

Leppin, Volker (2007). 'Transformationen spätmittelalterliche Mystik bei Luther'. In *Gottes Nähe unmittelbar erfahren. Mytik im Mittelalter und bei Martin Luther,* ed. Volker Leppin and Bernd Hamm. Tübingen: Mohr/Siebeck, 165–86.

Schwarz, Reinhard (1966). 'Gott ist Mensch. Zur Lehre von der Person Christi bei den Ockhamisten und bei Luther'. *Zeitschrift für Theologie und Kirche* 63: 289–351.

White, Graham (1994). *Luther as Nominalist: A Study of the Logical Methods Used in Martin Luther's Disputations in the Light of their Medieval Background.* Helsinki: Luther-Agricola-Society.

Suggested Reading

Courtenay, W. J. (1990). *Capacity and Volition: A History of the Distinction of Absolute and Ordained Power.* Bergamo: Pierluigi Lubrina Editore.

—— (2008). *Ockham and Ockhamism: Studies in the Dissemination and Impact of His Thought.* Leiden and Boston: Brill.

Oberman, Heiko A. (1963). *The Harvest of Medieval Theology: Gabriel Biel and Late Medieval Nominalism.* Cambridge, MA: Harvard University Press.

CHAPTER 3

LUTHER'S ROOTS IN MONASTIC-MYSTICAL PIETY

VOLKER LEPPIN

I. THE CURRENT STATE OF RESEARCH

THE term 'mysticism' appeared first the eighteenth century in the graphic arts and has also been used to describe certain forms of piety. A single, precise definition has never been found. This phenomenon becomes more comprehensible when 'mysticism' is understood as a religious mindset that presupposes God's transcendence over against believing human beings as a fact of experience and then strives to overcome this transcendence at least momentarily in the present. Thus, the transcendental becomes immanent—at least for a moment—and thereby suspends the believer's this-worldly limitations through special ecstatic experiences, or through certain exercises (although neither is necessary). Mysticism, or mystical influence, cannot therefore be linked to any particular patterns of behaviour, or to some qualitatively explicable particular form of piety. Nor is the definition—inaccessible to historical investigation—that stipulates certain prior experiences very helpful. The earlier 'definitions of the essence' of mysticism have very little current potential or practical use. However, due to the influence of literary criticism on research into mysticism, it has become beneficial to delineate the influence of mysticism through literary contexts. There, where authors are being read productively on the subject of transcendence breaking into the present, people are participating in mystical discourse.

This tradition of mysticism, or mystic spirituality, was able to take on distinct forms in various temporal and social contexts although these forms are difficult to categorize. Erich Vogelsang's (1937) categorization of Areopagitic, Roman, and German mysticism, despite its frequent use in current Luther research, can no longer be considered appropriate, due simply to the diversity of criteria used for such categorization, and especially to those national labels, 'Roman' and 'German'. They reveal its historical origin. Vogelsang wrote in the context of his direct and indirect engagement with Alfred Rosenberg, the most important National Socialist ideologue. It reflects the fact that many theologians of a German-Christian bent attempted to adapt the subject of 'Luther and mysticism' to National Socialist ideology during the Third Reich. In his *Mythus des 20. Jahrhunderts* Rosenberg had integrated pseudo-mystical elements into his worldview.

This misuse of the concept 'Luther and mysticism' caused evangelical Luther research in Germany since the Second World War largely to avoid the subject. However, its international relevance persisted, due particularly to the 1966 International Congress for Luther Research, papers by Erwin Iserloh (1985) and Heiko Augustinus Oberman (1986), as well as research by Steven Ozment (1969) and Theo Bell. Bell (1993) has drawn renewed attention to the immense importance of Bernard of Clairvaux for Luther. Since the 1970s, however, the importance of mysticism has been increasingly discussed, also within the German-speaking world (Zur Mühlen 1972, 2003; Köpf 1984, 1989). In recent years focus has fallen once again on the vernacular literature of the upper Rhine. It serves as an important bridge enabling investigation of medieval experience and spirituality as critical formative influences on Luther's theological development and reminds historians that Luther had lived as a monk for two decades and for more than one decade had been thoroughly integrated within a monastic-mystic environment with its unique conceptual patterns. Even his account of *Anfechtung* during this time rests on a mystical concept that Luther used his whole life to describe spiritual crises.

II. Mystical Literature as a Deepening of the Monastic Spirituality of Humility

When Luther entered the monastery in 1505, he came into a world of monastic spirituality for which mystical theology was a natural form of piety. Though later recollections should be treated cautiously, they reveal that the study of mystical authors belonged from early on to the daily routine of monastic life. According to the epilogue of *Epistola Theologorum Parisiensium*, apparently written by Luther, he had learned already as a young man that Hilary, Jerome, Augustine, and Bernard became theologians without reading Aristotle (WA60.125,40–44). This is significant because it shows how Luther himself drew a line of continuity from ancient and medieval authorities to later fundamental insights and because it indicates an early familiarity with precisely these forms. Besides Bernard, Luther was also familiar with Bonaventure, or at least works ascribed to him, from early on. Since 2009 the long unknown annotations to these works have become accessible in published form (AWA9.89–147). They probably date back to autumn 1509, before his lectures on Lombard's *Sentences*. These annotations give a relatively early indication that Luther had come into contact with one of the most popular and widely read mystical works of the late Middle Ages, enriched with countless pseude-pigrapha and used in numerous contexts for spiritual stimulus. Luther's marginal notes, markings, and underlinings document a meticulous reading, in which Luther stressed those things which were able to invigorate his own life's journey, for instance, the praise of poverty (AWA9.100,21–22) or an emphasis on the medical profession as *status perfectior* compared with other professions (AWA9.103,3–4). Luther also found reinforcement here for the biblical orientation of his piety, for example, when he highlighted the words of Richard of Saint Victor: 'every truth not confirmed by the authority of the Scriptures is suspect' (AWA9.106,14–15) in a statement on the canonization of Bonaventure, or when he drew a comparison between Holy Scripture and heaven in a brief marginal note (AWA9.142,10). His underlining emphasizes references to Christ, for example, of a formula that would become critical for Luther's thinking later, 'daily Christ is mystically sacrificed for us' (AWA9.108,29). This sentence occurs in a tract dealing with preparation for mass: instructed in mystic literature, Luther was engaging in a spiritualization of sacramental piety and an expansion of sacramental piety into the daily life of the sinner. Rather than revealing a piety characterized by particular phenomena, these all reinforced a general monastic spirituality, an orientation to a universally viable piety reflected in the remark: 'holiness and religion are the same thing' [*sanctitas et religio non different*] (AWA9.105,2). This rather prevalent way of reading mystical texts corresponded to a widespread approach reflecting not least Bonaventure's *Opuscula Parva*, as Luther had them. They contained many instructions for a virtuous life. Luther's own situation shaped his use of such expressions to relativize scholastic theology (AWA9.129,5–7). It is here, as well as in Luther's participation in humanistic discourse, that the rudiments of his dissociation with the scholastic theology he had encountered should be understood. This break became more and more noticeable in his teaching and ultimately led to his *Disputatio contra scholasticam theologiam*. His annotations of Bonaventure show that his abandoning scholasticism, manifest later, had begun in its academic form even before he began lecturing on Lombard's *Sentences*.

Because no edition of Bonaventure existed until 2009, his significance for Luther has not yet been adequately explored in current scholarship. It could be said that Bonaventure is the key to Luther's understanding of Bernard of Clairvaux. On the title page and the inner face of the anterior cover page of the *Opuscula Anselmi* (which was also earlier read and annotated), Luther cited a large excerpt from the Pseudo-Bonaventure (AWA9.8, n. 7; 11, nn. 11–12) that he had read. Even if this does not explain all references to Bernard during this time, it highlights the fact that Luther encountered Bernard through, or at least in considerable unanimity with, Bonaventure. How strongly these theologians formed a unit for Luther may be seen in his statement in 1542: 'Bernhard truly loved Christ's incarnation, as did Bonaventure. All praise to both because of this article' (WA43.581,11–12; LW5.221). In past years scholarship has taken up in particular this very significant thread of Bernard reception. In the process research has not only underscored the reformer's enduring affinity to the Cistercian abbot, as indicated in this citation, but it has also assessed Bernard's role in Luther's theological development. Melanchthon's account in his preface to the second volume of Luther's

Latin works—though notoriously fraught with faulty information—shows how close this association was for contemporaries. According to Melanchthon, an old man consoled Luther in the monastery by referring to a quotation from Bernard; this initially directed Luther to Paul and the righteousness that comes through faith (CR6.158). Even if the passage cited here is from Romans 3:28 and not 1:17, and notwithstanding the validity of the story itself, it does show that for contemporaries the mystic influence was closely connected to the reformational discovery. In fact, the two were closely associated, as Zur Mühlen demonstrated, namely, that Luther's lectures on Romans went hand in hand with reading mystical works.

The intensive reading of Bernard which Luther pursued is reflected earlier in the *Dictata super Psalterium*. There Bernard attains special significance for Luther as a teacher of souls, who writes about temptations that may befall the human being (WA4.74,21–30; LW11.223) and leads the way to features of passion-mysticism: 'According to Bernard the soul does not rest apart from Christ's wounds' (WA3.640,40). Luther then seized upon a unique accent of Bernardine mysticism, essentially a suffering-mysticism, in that for Bernard the entire life of Christ appeared as suffering. At the same time this intensified a spirituality which Luther encountered in other ways as well in his Order. According to a later recollection, Staupitz was the one who directed him to the wounds of Christ (WATR2.112,9–16, §1490). His dedicatory letter to the *Resolutions* of 1518 documents in other ways as well Staupitz's close association with mystical theology in the context of Luther's theological development. Without this influence of mysticism this would be impossible to imagine.

This is also reflected in the close link between Luther's mystical reading and his interpretation of Paul in the Romans lectures. His *scholion* on Romans 8:16 features the most elaborate Bernard quotation in Luther's entire work, a detailed explanation of the Holy Spirit's activity from Bernard's '*Sermo in festo annuntiationis*' (WA56.369–70). Within this quotation is, moreover, a quotation from Romans 3:28, where Bernard conspicuously adds a '*gratis*' into the quotation: 'If the Apostle thinks the human being is justified *by grace* through faith' [*Sic enim arbitratur Apostolus iustificari hominem gratis per fidem*]. Luther, for his part, does not include this addition in his quotation of Paul.

Luther's use of Bernard may not, of course, be reduced to purely positive reception. Rather, the transformation of Bernardine thought includes a tacit revision. Certainly, Bernard's own assertion here includes an indication that all *merita* are due to God alone. Yet Luther uses precisely this place to digress briefly from the quotation, whereby, in mystical manner, he stresses the vanity of human attempts to perform good works in God's sight. This connection between Bernardine and Pauline thought, reported by Melanchthon, may thus be thoroughly reconstructed from the perspective of the history of theology as well. This passage may indeed be interpreted as antecedent to the *pro me*, the mystical background of which may be verified beyond Luther's underlining in the *Opuscula Parva Bonaventurae*. Bernard emphasized that mere faith in the fact that God alone achieves merits is not enough, but that the believer must also verify this for himself as a gift of the Holy Spirit. Thus, Bernard rejects a mere *fides historica* without concrete relation to the reality of the believer's salvation as insufficient.

A similar ambivalence between continuity and innovation in Luther's use of Bernard is also found in the concept of *humilitas*. Ernst Bizer's seminal studies demonstrate this to have been crucial for the theology of Luther's lectures until 1518 (Bizer 1966). Thus, one can speak of Luther's distinctive *humilitas* theology. The monastic background of this concept is obvious. Just as obvious is the fact that Bernard also uses the concept of *humilitas* repeatedly. The concept of a *humilitas* theology, therefore, may also be understood and used as a paraphrase for the predominantly monastic character of Luther's early theology. Yet, Bizer's further suggestion that Luther suddenly abandoned this *humilitas* theology in favour of justification, which became decisive after autumn 1518, becomes problematic in view of Luther's continued use of mystical authors. Completely independent of the disputed question of the date of Luther's reformational insight, it is striking that Luther, even from an unambiguously reformational point of view, can quote Bernard in support of *humilitas*. In the *Operationes in psalmos*, on Psalm 21:22, he introduced a distinction between *humilitas* and *humiliatio* (WA5,656,28–30) with express reference to Bernard in order to emphasize divine activity. Yet, here again, citing Bernard does not mean complete dependence on him; Luther did not adopt Bernard's idea that *humiliatio* produced by coercion should be transformed into a voluntary *humilitas* as a presupposition for justification. Luther's relationship with mystical authors, therefore, remains productive and transformative even after the new reformational approach appeared. Luther's association with mysticism cannot be treated simply in terms of the 'pre-Reformation–Reformation' schema and then forced into a pre-Reformation period. Instead, its enduring impact must be taken into account. Bernard's inspiration extended even to the core of the Heidelberg Disputation. While Luther does not cite Bernard explicitly in theses 19 and 20, nonetheless, by distinguishing between the theologian who wishes to catch sight of the invisible things of God by means of earthly inferences and the theologian for whom God becomes visible through his passion (LSA 1.215,10–13), he incorporates an idea that repeatedly occurs in Bernard, according to which the invisible God took the incarnation—and thus, according to Bernard, the beginning of suffering—upon himself because he wanted to become visible to human beings (Bernard 1994: 118,21–26). Hence, the echo of Bernard's mystical theology resonates in the theses that laid the groundwork for the distinction, so essential to Luther, between *theologus gloriae* and *theologus crucis* (thesis 21).

The most obvious and well-known effect of Bernardine theology, however, is found in the image of the bride in Luther's *Freedom of the Christian*. The popular notion that the soul is united with Christ the Bridegroom (WA7.25,28, cf. LW31.351) was obviously inherited from the mystical interpretation of the Song of Songs. Luther began to use it in this form from Bernard, who based all of his sermons on the Song of Songs upon the master narrative of the events transpiring between Christ and the individual soul. This connection to Bernard, of course, has more to do with its structure and content than with citations that can be analysed philologically. Luther does not explicitly attribute the image of the bride to Bernard. Indeed, considering the immediate context of his life, he could just as well have learned and adopted it from Staupitz, who had used the image of a spiritual marriage in his *Libellus de praedestinatione* c. 9. However this image may have come to Luther specifically, he seized upon it in a work intended to unfold a summary of the Christian life at a point intended to illustrate clearly what may be epitomized as the doctrine of justification. Hence, it takes a central place in his thinking, again making it clear that reformational insight and mystical piety are not to be considered as antitheses, but as mutually corroborative fundamental insights into Christian existence, even if Augustinian–Pauline terminology gradually overrode the mystical in the course of Luther's life. Yet, as the above-quoted citation from 1542 shows, this did not, from Luther's perspective, negate his concurrence with Bernard.

III. Mystical Liminal Experiences

Luther did not have the same kind of continuing positive relationship with Dionysius the Areopagite, the pseudonymous *Corpus Dionysiacum*, as he did with Bernard. On the contrary, after initial enthusiasm he turned away from the speculative theology of the *Corpus Dionysiacum*. At first, however, this enthusiasm reached deep into his ordinary world. Luther later recalled: 'Even I was in that school, where I thought I was among the angelic choirs though I had rather fallen among the devils' [*Nam fui et ego in ista schola, ubi putavi me esse inter choros Angelorum, cumtamen inter Diabolos potius sim versatus*] (WA40,3.657,35–36), clearly referring to the hierarchical division of the spiritual realm in the *Corpus Dionysiacum*. Even while he was expositing Lombard's *Sentences*, Luther was aware of the relevant Dionysian text, *De caelesti hierarchia*, and its discussion of the *ordines angelorum* (AWA9.425,10). At least in his monastic piety, Luther was temporarily concerned with ecstatic experiences characteristic of a certain type of mysticism. Thus, in a similar vein he recalled in a Pentecost sermon from 1523: 'I saw many monks and clerics who were uncertain while I was being taken up into the third heaven' [*Multos vidi monachos et clericos, qui incerti sunt, et ego semel raptus fui in 3um celum*] (WA11.117,35–36).

His extremely negative devaluation of such behaviour, whereby he speaks of a *versatio inter Diabolos*, comes (retrospectively, of course) from the perspective of having become a reformer. But this also demonstrates that for the young Luther ecstatic experiences represented merely an intermediary stage and carried very little weight compared to an emphasis on *humilitas* and its associated penitential piety. For a while, this existential dimension coalesced with his reception of theological ideas from the *Corpus Dionysiacum*. Thus, in the *Dictata super psalterium* on Psalm 65 (64 Vulgate), Luther drew explicitly on the *theologia negativa*, which was mediated to the medieval tradition of the West through the *Corpus Dionysiacum*. He described, in terms strikingly parallel to his own apparent practical experience, how it induces silence '*in raptu et extasi*'. This, and not the affirmative theology practised by *nostri theologi*, was supposed to make a true theologian (WA3.372,13–27; LW13.313). Considering this assertion in connection with other ways by which he absorbed mystical elements, it becomes clear that at this relatively early time Luther saw little difference among the various sources of mystical thought. His opposition to the vacuous nature of the disputation in favour of mysticism was reflected also in his underlinings in Bonaventure (AWA9.129,5–7), where the antithesis is not the *raptus*, of course, but the *ars amandi* [art of loving]. Likewise, an emphasis on a mystical, as opposed to a scholastic, brand of theology can be delineated as Bernard reception even in the Heidelberg Disputation. Thus, for Luther, around 1515, the *Corpus Dionysiacum* is still in perfect agreement with other sources of mystical spirituality.

This positive relationship soon dissolved. The beginning of his abandonment of the *Corpus Dionysiacum* becomes clear in his Romans lectures. In his exegesis of Romans 5:2 Luther expands on the point that access to the Father comes only through Christ: 'This also applies to mystical theology and the struggle in inner darkness which omit all images of Christ's suffering' (WA56.299,27–300,1, cf. LW25.287). Although he did not yet counter Dionysius explicitly, Luther clearly understood the discrepancy here between a speculative-ecstatic mysticism of Dionysian imprint and Bernard's Christologically mediated passion-mysticism. Since these lectures are chronologically correlated with his reading of Tauler, one would expect to find in them the impetus for Luther's new orientation. However, in content, Luther became acquainted in Bernard with what decisively facilitated his critique of a misguided Dionysian mysticism. In his *Operationes in psalmos* he turned what he had learned from Bernard against the Dionysian-oriented mysticism, which he decried as pure deception: 'One may not identify himself as a mystical theologian because he reads, understands and teaches or imagines he can understand and teach. One becomes a theologian by living, rather by dying and being condemned, not by understanding, reading, or speculating' (WA.5,163,27–29). The front had shifted. The *Corpus Dionysiacum*, having landed on the wrong side, now belonged with scholastic theology. This changed nothing concerning his altogether positive reception of other forms of mysticism. His strong emphasis on dying refers now more clearly than ever to the newly developed mystical sources in Tauler and the *Theologia Deutsch*.

IV. The Mystical Piety of Penance as Impulse towards Theological Re-orientation

Striking and critical for the reception of mysticism in the Reformation was Wittenberg's becoming a veritable centre for Tauler reading by the beginning of the sixteenth century (Otto 2003). Besides Luther, Amsdorf and Karlstadt devoted themselves to the work of this fourteenth-century mystic, which by this time was available in several printed editions. Also handed down under Tauler's name were several sermons by Eckhart, which, moreover, were fraught with problems because several of Eckhart's key statements had been condemned in 1329 by the bull *In agro dominico*. Together with Eckhart and Heinrich Seuse, Tauler formed a circle of preachers of 'German mysticism', today described geographically as 'upper-Rhenish mysticism'. Luther encountered these preachers while lecturing on Romans, probably in early 1515, and was enthusiastic about them. This is confirmed in a letter to Spalatin on 14 December 1516: Luther, in almost sacramental terms, recommended Tauler's sermons (WABr1.79,58–64).

Luther's experience as he read can be traced through marginal notes, contained in a volume of the Ratschulbibliothek in Zwickau. As with his notes on Bonaventure, these marginal notes do not lend themselves easily to qualitative analysis. But there are some significant clues. In the margins Luther writes, 'Note this' (WA9.104,11), referring to a passage where Tauler invited readers to bring their own deep remorse directly to God, especially because one runs the risk of forgetting which sins to confess by the time one gets to confession. Thus, Tauler's concern here is for the inculcation of *contritio cordis*— indeed such that it came at the expense of the other elements of penance. The *confessio oris*, at any rate, was declared secondary; the same held for the *satisfactio operis*, at least in the sense performing the requirements of penance. This aspect of Luther's reading of Tauler, where the sacrament was undermined, intensified all the more through the reflections that followed, in which Tauler expressly demanded that his hearers not run immediately to their confessor when they were experiencing such inner remorse. Here Luther commented, 'most useful advice' [*utilissimum consilium*] (WA9.104,12).

This is by no means an inconsequential remark. Rather, it concerns a central element of Luther's development. This becomes clear when, a few lines before this recommendation by Tauler, one reads: 'Dis ensol nut sin ines tages und des anderen nut: es sol sin alle tage, ane underlos solt du din selbs war nehmen' (Tauler 1910: 355,31f). Here Tauler pointed to a conception of penance that would not limit it to confession to a priest but instead make it a foundational event of the Christian life, as it appears later in the first of Luther's theses against indulgences: 'When our Lord and master Jesus Christ said, "Repent", he wanted the entire life of the faithful to be a life of repentance' (WA1.233,10–11; LW31.25). Tauler paved the way for this concept of penance, as he did for Luther's second thesis, against limiting penance to the confession of sins to the priest: 'this word cannot be understood as referring to the sacrament of penance, that is, confession and satisfaction, as administered by the clergy' (WA1.233,12–13; LW31.25).

Consideration of that context helps clarify the looming conflict over indulgences. Late medieval theological thinking concerning penance, like many other polarities that characterized the late Middle Ages, recognized one more internal, another more external, orientation. The latter belongs to a piety characterized by various kinds of quantification, the most serious consequence of which occurred in the piety associated with indulgences, in which acts of penance could be measured, calculated, and even purchased. The former, inward element, on the other hand, had its home especially in mysticism and in reform piety as they found expression, for example, in the *Devotio moderna*. This tradition of internalized penitential piety clearly influenced Luther; he became acquainted with it within a mystical context, that is, in a theological domain where he considered himself to be at one with numerous authors. He intended to learn a kind of theology that was superior to scholasticism, and with this inward-looking concept of penance he clearly combated forms of externalization.

Hence, his protest against indulgences did not emerge as a wholesale battle against late medieval piety, but rather as a protest against one form of late medieval piety on the basis of his legacy from another form. A letter to Staupitz on 31 March 1518, less than half a year after the theses were published, shows how close this link is between mystical persuasion and the beginning stages of his protest against indulgences: 'I really followed Tauler's theology and his booklet, which you gave me recently, printed by our Christian, Aurifaber' (WABr1.160,8–9). This not only demonstrates conscious agreement with Tauler but also refers to yet another source of mystical spirituality in Luther's development.

The booklet mentioned was the *Theologia deutsch*. The context of Luther's study of mysticism includes the publication of this mystical text, dating from the mid-fourteenth century, his first venture into publishing. In 1516 he issued an incomplete version, in 1518 the complete work. In undertaking this edition, he continued a process already begun, which emerged in theses 19–21 of the Heidelberg Disputation, regarding mystical theology as authentic theology and setting it off against other forms of theology. Hence, in the preface to the complete edition of 1518—and with outright national overtones—he wrote:

> Let anyone who wishes read this little book and then let him say whether our theology is new or old, for this book is not new. Some may say as previously that we are German theologians. We can let that be. I thank God that I hear and find my God in the German tongue, for they and I have not found him in Latin, Greek, or Hebrew. God grant that this booklet become better known. Then we will find that German theologians are without doubt the best theologians. Amen. (WA1.379,5–12; LW31.75)

What moved Luther decisively in this text was its conception of repentance. Luther had already made this clear in the first edition of 1516. It is entitled 'A spiritual, noble booklet on the correct distinction and understanding of what the new and old person is. What Adam's child and God's child is. How Adam must die in us and Christian arise' [Ein geistlich, edles Buchlein von rechter underscheid und vorstand, was der alt und neu mensche sei. Was Adams und was Gottes kind sei. Und wie Adam inn uns sterben unnd Christus ersteen soll] (WA1.153). This wording explains not only how the experience of life and death came to be stressed in his confrontation with the *Corpus Dionysiacum*. Even its significance Luther learned from the tradition of Tauler and the *Theologia deutsch*. Again it was deeply tied to their understanding of repentance. In the *Theologia deutsch*, especially in chapters 15–16 (according to modern enumeration), the death of the Old Adam and the resurrection of Christ in us are described in terms of a renunciation of sin, expressed with the verb 'bussen' ('to do penance') (*Franckforter*, 91,28. 32; 92,35). When this is read together with the title page, which simply stresses the process of dying, it becomes clear that at the centre of Luther's struggle with mysticism during this time was something of a penitential process—with a profound existential dimension and with little to do with sacramental performance. Indeed, such a concentration on penance theology implied, as with Tauler, a critical turning-point. Luther's readings involved those theological elements, in which this concept of remorse over sin was developed in such a way that the sacrament of penance administered by the church could be made obsolete.

Mystical theology influenced Luther significantly from 1515 onward. That is clear from the development of his own theology, with its own emphases (Luther even explains that he came across no other book, 'next to the Bible and Saint Augustine', from which he had learned more than the *Theologia deutsch* [WA1,378.21–23; LW31.75]), the issuance of his edition of *Theologia deutsch*, and the development of the theses against indulgences. Based on his own account, one might even say that his encounter with mysticism produced a sort of conversion experience. The dedicatory letter to Staupitz in the *Resolutiones* to his *Theses against Indulgences* suggests as much. While he does not mention Tauler here explicitly, it is rather likely, given its content and temporal sequence, that he is drawing on his reading of Tauler:

> I remember, Reverend Father, that during your most delightful and helpful talks, through which the Lord Jesus wonderfully consoled me, you sometimes mentioned the term 'penance'. I was then distressed by my conscience and the tortures of those whose endless and insupportable commands teach the so-called method of confession. Therefore, I accepted you as a messenger from heaven when you said that penance is genuine only if it begins with love for righteousness and God and that what they consider the final stage and completion is in reality the very beginning of penance.
>
> Your word pierced me like the sharp arrow of the Mighty One. Thus I began to compare your statements with Scripture passages which speak of penance. Behold, what a most delightful pastime. Words came from everywhere smiling and assenting to your advice. What had been the most bitter word, 'penance', now sounded sweeter and lovelier than all others. God's commands become sweet when we learn them not from books but from wounds of our sweetest Savior. (WA1.525,4–23; LW48.65–66)

The letter further reveals that the event that Luther is recalling here had to have taken place some time before his reading of Erasmus' *Novum Instrumentum*. This recollection would thus point to 1515 at the very latest and therefore to that year in which Luther began his reading of Tauler. But more than anything, it points to a new understanding of penance, *poenitentia*.

As just explained, this understanding of penance was indeed the main subject in Luther's reading of Tauler as well as of the *Theologia deutsch*. Thus, in terms of both its temporal sequence and content, this comment points to Luther's reception of Tauler and suggests noteworthy connections. Staupitz opens the way to Tauler—this also explains why in Wittenberg of all places Tauler was read with such intensity—and it is here that Luther discovers a key to unlock the entire Bible, and hence all of theology. As his marginal notes to Bonaventure show, Luther did not regard mysticism and the Bible as mutually exclusive, but complementary. Moreover, a look at his reference to the 'wounds of the sweetest Christ' [*vulnera dulcissimi Christi*] reveals a metaphorical context of the passion and wounds of Christ, which played a huge role for Bernard. Here everything came together that had appeared significant in Luther's mystical tendencies in a larger context which Luther described as a revelation. Every element of his discovery of *iustitia*, as he recalled in 1545 (WA54.186; LW34.336), is found here too. Just as Luther later compared his discovery of *iustitia* with entering into paradise, he speaks here of a transcendental voice from heaven. In both cases a new understanding of a single word—here *poenitentia*, there *iustitia*—opens up the entire Scriptures for him. What is more, in both cases he uses the word *dulcis*, characteristic for mystical settings. All of these observations make it possible to speak of a 'mystical discovery', whereby attempting to pinpoint it in time would be just as futile as in the case of his discovery of *iustitia*. In both cases Luther compresses a longer lasting development anecdotally, albeit retrospectively, into a single momentary occurrence.

More important than attempting to find the exact date of this inner development, however, is the observation that still in autumn 1518 Luther linked the mystical message of *poenitentia* with a critical change in his life. Indeed, already in the *Resolutiones* this increasingly overlaps with Pauline concepts of justification. In fact, Luther's marginal notes on Tauler indicate that, and for what reason, he was particularly receptive to this kind of theology. On the margin of his edition of Tauler he wrote: 'Therefore all salvation is resignation of the will in all things so that he may teach both of spiritual and temporal things. And pure faith in God' (WA9.102,34–36). The entire salvation event is compressed to naked faith in God. This is not yet the doctrine of justification as Luther would later develop it, but it shows where he was able to connect it with mystical aspects of his thought.

Luther's study of mysticism thus led him to central tenets of his later theology. But he was only able to develop this one stage after another. It is not in direct continuity with mysticism, and it makes little sense to debate whether or not Luther was a mystic. In the sense of the literary definition of mysticism explained at the beginning of this chapter, Luther was someone who, having been influenced by mysticism, grasped it and transformed it. It would be inadequate though to view Luther's association with mysticism as merely an intermediary stage or interpret the echoes of mysticism in the *Freedom of the Christian* as mere mystical dress for authentic justification theology. Both approaches weaken mysticism's significance for him. Luther's engagement with mysticism gave him the decisive impulse to turn away from those models of theology that did not accord with the content of mystical experience. In so doing, he made careful selections within the range of mystical theology and decided to continue to employ its forms when he saw their potential for a theology that accorded with Christ.

To this end, he availed himself of the traditions of Bonaventure and Bernard, but especially of the upper-Rhenish mysticism that fit closely with the reality of his life as a friar. Out of these traditions he formed a larger picture capable of grasping this new conviction in words. He never completely broke with mysticism though he did repeatedly distance himself from certain of its forms and excesses. From the Areopagite he distanced himself already early on. Through the years he also had to distance himself from various conclusions of mysticism that threatened to obscure the basic insights of reformational teaching. In Karlstadt and Müntzer Luther perceived a kind of mystic reception in which an appeal to the Holy Spirit was actually supposed to procure a free course for their own spirit—what Luther described as '*Schwärmertum*'. Against this he held ever more firmly to the '*extra nos*' character of God's Word. This '*extra nos*', as Zur Mühlen (1972) has shown, had a mystical history, too, and it was developed by Luther in an effort to come to terms with the roots of mysticism. Then it could foster assurance rather than an excessive inwardness, as was often the case with mysticism. Thus, Luther's increasing scepticism, indeed animosity, towards certain strands of mystic reception and towards the *Corpus Dionysiacum* should not be understood as a rejection of all other forms of mystical piety. The heritage of mysticism continued to shape Luther's theology in various configurations of transformation, not least in his theology of the Word. Also the dialectical relationship of law and gospel reflected corresponding dialectical relationships between dying and rising found in mysticism.

Thus, Luther's relationship to mysticism cannot easily be characterized. Inasmuch as Luther converted mysticism into new, transformed configurations, he did not simply continue it, nor did he break with it. He gave it a new configuration within the context of a new theology. In this sense his work is an independent contribution to mystical discourse.

Translated by David Preus

REFERENCES

Bell, Theo (1993). *Divus Bernhardus. Bernhard von Clairvaux in Martin Luthers Schriften.* Mainz: Zabern.

Bernard of Clairvaux (1994). *Bernhard von Clairvaux, Sämtliche Werke. Lateinisch / deutsch*, ed. Bernard B. Winkler. Vol. 5. Innsbruck: Tyrolia.

Bizer, Ernst (1966). *Fides ex auditu. Eine Untersuchung über die Gerechtigkeit Gottes durch Martin Luther*, 3rd edn. Neukirchen: Neukirchener Verlag.

Hinten, Wolfgang von (ed.) (1982). *Der Franckforter (Theologia Deutsch)*. Munich: Artemis.

Iserloh, Erwin (1985). 'Luther und die Mystik'. In Iserloh, *Kirche—Ereignis und Institution. Aufsätze und Vorträge*. Bd. 2. Münster: Aschendorff, 88–106.

Köpf, Ulrich (1984). ' Martin Luther als Mönch'. *Luther* 55: 66–84.

—— (1999). 'Monastische Traditionen bei Martin Luther'. In *Luther—zwischen den Zeiten. Eine Jenaer Ringvorlesung*, ed. Christoph Markschies and Michael Trowitzsch. Tübingen: Mohr/Siebeck, 17–35.

Oberman, Heiko Augustinus (1986). ' Simul gemitus et raptus: Luther und die Mystik'. In Oberman, *Reformation. Von Wittenberg nach Genf*. Göttingen: Vandenhoeck & Ruprecht, 45–89.

Otto, Henrik (2003). *Vor- und frühreformatorische Tauler-Rezeption. Annotationen in Drucken des späten 15. und frühen 16. Jahrhunderts*. Gütersloh: Gütersloher Verlagshaus.

Ozment, Steven Edgar (1969). *Homo Spiritualis: A Comparative Study of the Anthropology of Johannes Tauler, Jean Gerson and Martin Luther in the Context of their Theological Thought*. Leiden: Brill.

Tauler, Johannes (1910). *Die Predigten Taulers aus der Engelberger und der Freiburger Handschrift sowie aus Schmidts Abschriften der ehemaligen Straßburger Handschriften*, ed. Ferdinand. Berlin: Weidmann.

Vogelsang, Erich (1937). 'Luther und die Mystik'. *Lutherjahrbuch* 19: 32–54.

Zur Mühlen, Karl-Heinz (1972). *Nos Extra Nos. Luthers Theologie zwischen Mystik und Scholastik*. Tübingen: Mohr/Siebeck.

—— (2003). 'Mystische Erfahrung und Wort Gottes bei Martin Luther'. In *Mystik. Religion der Zukunft—Zukunft der Religion?* ed. Johannes Schilling. Leipzig: Evangelische Verlagsanstalt, 45–66.

SUGGESTED READING

Hamm, Berndt and Volker Leppin (eds.) (2007). *Gottes Nähe unmittelbar erfahren. Mystik im Mittelalter und bei Martin Luther*. Tübingen: Mohr/Siebeck.

Leppin, Volker (2002). ' " Omnem vitam fidelium penitentiam esse voluit". Zur Aufnahme mystischer Traditionen in Luthers erster Ablaßthese'. *Archiv für Reformationsgeschichte* 93: 7–25.

—— (2005). 'In Rosenbergs Schatten. Zur Lutherdeutung Erich Vogelsangs'. *Theologische Zeitschrift* 61: 132–42.

Lohse, Bernhard (1994). 'Luther und Bernhard von Clairvaux'. In *Bernhard von Clairvaux. Rezeption und Wirkung im Mittelalter und in der Neuzeit*, ed. Kaspar Elm. Wiesbaden: Harrasowitz, 271–301.

CHAPTER 4

....

LUTHER AND MEDIEVAL REFORM MOVEMENTS, PARTICULARLY THE HUSSITES

....

MARTIN WERNISCH

THE earliest Protestant historiography established the tradition of looking for Luther's precursors on the basis of Reformation theologies of history. Under the influence of Romanticism these trailblazers were called 'reformers before the Reformation' (Ullmann 1841/2). However, this emphasis produced a reaction, and positivistic historiography minimized the role of Luther's predecessors. These historians contended that among Luther's medieval teachers, people who held recognized positions in church and society predominated over opposition figures; and when Luther crossed the boundaries of the Middle Ages, he moved away from both groups. This stance characterized—but was gradually intensified by—research during the twentieth century (Oberman's work in general, esp. 1966, 1986).

When Luther broke out of the bounds within which his instructors had moved, he needed to give assurance that he was not a heresiarch, advancing what no Christian anywhere had ever believed. Therefore, he welcomed every indication left by credible figures who had advocated similar views. For example, he appreciated learning of the work of Johann Wessel Gansfort and Johann Pupper of Goch. In 1522 he published their texts with emphatic commendations that correspond to conclusions by researchers who hold that these men's viewpoints were relatively close to the reformer's. Yet the story actually ends with these initial observations (WA10,2.316–317,329–330). Evidently, these thinkers did not suggest anything to Luther that was not already clear to him. Even worse: under Wessel's influence Honius' Epistle on the Lord's Supper became a trigger for catastrophic disputes. Thus, the praise soon ceased. The result was not much different from the case of Savonarola, a predecessor about whom Luther had strong reservations (WA12.248). Thus, the continuing attention that Luther devoted to John Hus is all the more striking, but not necessarily easier to explain. The polyphony of existing interpretations suggests the opposite. A sound assessment must be based on a careful classification of a plethora of scattered statements by Luther.

Initially, it is necessary to take a chronological perspective because Luther's statements reflect a dramatic development. He had known of the Prague master from his youth. However, a negative preconception defined Luther's initial position. During his first encounter with Hus' sermons in a monastery library, the reformer sought proof of the legitimacy of denunciations of Hus in those texts. When instead they fostered doubt, Luther reacted emotionally and fled from them (WA50.37,12–39,14).

Luther preferred to break away 'safely', guided by those who were engaged in confuting the early reformers. With their assistance he studied a specific offshoot of the Hussite movement, the Bohemian [Czech] Brethren, to whom he referred with the common, heresy-laden label, *Pighardi*. In the 1510s he presented the 'Bohemians' as prime examples of heretics. He still regarded them as such in his theses against indulgences, where he demanded that arguments against their objections be strong—not a fictitious 'abundance of merits' that would prove the church wrong (WA1.608,28–35; LW31.217).

Discrediting the view of opponents by identifying them with a previously condemned heresy was one of the polemicists' best-loved weapons. His opponents quickly began to look for affinities that he had not yet acknowledged. In the Leipzig Disputation (1519) Johann Eck, the most significant among Luther's critics, drove him to unambiguous statements in which he took the side of heresiarchs, following whose condemnation it should no longer have been possible to reject obedience to the pope as a requirement for salvation. Here Luther fought a battle that was even more difficult internally than externally. However, he acquitted himself honourably. Convinced that there is no power in the church that should be permitted to dispute the articles of faith offered by biblical revelation, Luther found a superior witness in Hus, not only against the pope, but even against the council to whose authority he had previously appealed (WA59.433–605).

The reversal that occurred at Leipzig could not have been easy for the Saxon prince-elector, whose ancestors had acquired that title during the battle against the Hussites. Thus, it is not surprising that letters from Prague (accompanied by Hus' book, *De ecclesia*), in which Prague Utraquists acknowledged their new alliance, remained buried at the electoral chancellery for months (WABr1.417–420, cf. 1.514,27–32). At the beginning of 1520 his prince may have still had this scandal in mind when he asked Luther to try to teach the gospel without unnecessary conflicts with the bishops.

The reformer responded to this appeal with the letter in which his affirmation of Hus crested (WABr2.41–2). Spreading the message for which Christ had to die does not happen without conflicts. Hus was burned at the stake for publicly preaching the gospel. However, Luther recognized, he himself had actually done nothing different. He began unwittingly; nevertheless, it is true: 'We are all Hussites without knowing it!'

This exceptionally pointed statement was bound to attract attention. A number of interpreters have tried to safeguard Luther's originality by questioning his judgement. It is said that Luther overestimated Hus because he did not quite understand Hus or even himself. Such an approach is unwarranted. The reformer's view of Hus did not change significantly after this point. It may have become differentiated, but it is not appropriate to speak of a 'cooling off' of his admiration for Hus. Indeed, declarations of love for Hus were not missing from the older Luther's writings (1540; WATR4.581, §4922).

If in this letter Luther said that he supported 'all' of Hus, he primarily had in mind Hus' dispute with the heavy-handed, arbitrary 'church *magisterium*', and in relationship to the articles repudiated by the council, Luther's statement is accurate. If in Leipzig Luther declared some of these to be 'properly Christian', he subsequently revised that publicly: all of them are (WA7.135,11–136,19; LW32.82–83). In the same context another motif of the letter recurs: It is even possible to identify the most important teachers of ancient times—Augustine, Paul, and Christ himself—as Hussites. The Hussite articles are in harmony with their teachings (WA6.588,4–592,4).

When Luther read *De ecclesia* sometime before writing his letter, he could confirm certain of the tenets that the concise version of Hus' articles foreshadowed. That context substantiated the articles' salutary intention (WA5.451,29–452,9). The ecclesiology of both reformers was based on the principle that Christ is the sole head of the church and that its organization should foster God's Word, not obstruct it. Later, Luther explicitly referred to Hus' argument that the rock on which Christ promised to build the church was not Peter's person but his faith, and to Hus' definition of the church as 'the number of the predestined' and a 'spiritual congregation' (cf. WA18.657,21–26, further WA5.451,29–452, esp. 451,31–33).

Of course, the two authors are far from being in complete agreement. Luther continued to remould the ideas that he had adopted. A simple historical reconstruction of Hus' thoughts did not interest him. Nor did he expect the two perspectives to be identical. From the first time he read Hus' book, Luther acknowledged that Hus was a scholar who should not be disregarded as a theologian (WABr2.72,9–11). Yet, although Hus was able to see further than his opponents, the early fifteenth-century scholarly environment affected his thinking. Therefore, Luther's high estimation of Hus in no way precluded a strong critique.

In general, Luther characterized Hus' teachings as being unduly under the sway of Thomism. Among several inadequacies, Luther stressed that Hus (like others in his time) failed to diverge from the scholastic distinction of commandments and *consilia*, which precluded a proper distinction between gospel and law (WA40,3.666,36–667,4). This discovery that Hus had missed such a key reformational insight confused modern scholars insofar as they frequently viewed it as a revocation of Luther's previous affirmations of Hus. However, Luther did not take that course. He qualified the significance of the Prague master only to the extent that Hus accomplished 'less as a beginner' (WA7.135,30–33), like John the Baptist, who also did not lose his place in the new covenant when the Messiah surpassed him. In his own time Hus 'mastered more than the whole world' (WATR4.581–582, §4922). Luther saw that what he perceived to be especially important was his own special contribution, and he realized that one could not expect this from his theological predecessor. Luther devised a vivid aphorism to clarify the historical developments that distinguished Hus' time from his: In his struggle against the papacy Hus took as his starting point a way of life that clearly was ungodly, while

Luther concentrated on the hidden core of ungodliness in false doctrine (WATR3.306, §3403a–b). When he noted that he frequently was incorrectly identified as Hussite, he wished only to prevent an oversimplified explanation of the origin of the Lutheran 'heresy' and thereby disregard his own mission, which was a hundred times more dangerous to them (WA7.135,23–136,11).

'So much more is seen in full light'. Yet, the fact that Hus attempted his struggle in the twilight was part of his greatness. If others downplayed Hus, Luther recalled what a relief it was that he himself could set out on a path which Hus had already broken. While Hus had assailed a fully empowered enemy, Luther confronted an already weakened foe (WATR2.348–349, §2177a–b). Above all, Luther perceived Hus to be a prophetic figure (WA50.39,9–11) who had carried out the initial breakthrough that he extended. Luther retained undimmed respect for Hus as a 'holy martyr' (WA53.167). In dying, Hus had definitively transcended his constraints. His Christ-like martyrdom demonstrated that Hus had practised a justifying faith (WATR3.92, §2926a–b). Therefore, Luther could forgive his shortcomings with regard to the doctrine of justification. Luther reminded his more demanding followers that they had not faced the test that Hus had withstood in such an exemplary way.

Dying in faith played an essential role in Luther's approach to history. Luther would only be a heresiarch if he established a new church. Yet he could not revive the original church if it had perished in the mean time. He ascertained that during the time of papal rule, witnesses to Christianity's health could best be identified by the one to whom they called—and what they invoked—during their final hour (WA18.650,23–651,30; LW33.36–87).

Hus did not serve as Luther's only example of such figures, yet he was referred to remarkably often. Various people could have taken precedence over him with regard to particular details. However, Luther could esteem Hus as an academician, preacher, and critic of papal policy who successfully liberated the church from Rome on the basis of the authority of the gospel. Therefore, the reformer also spoke of Hus' historical primacy. At the same time, Luther had to value the fact that his predecessor accepted, rather than sought, confrontation. His description of Hus' departure from earlier misconceptions highlighted the dynamics in which conflict introduced new elements to, and accelerated the development of, Hus' thinking. Of course, at a critical moment this conflict also cut that short. However, it did not halt the impact of Hus' message.

The way in which the violent measures of Hus' judges 'missed the mark' fascinated Luther. The seed that had been forced underground had sprouted (WATR5.182, §5485). 'The gospel that we now have had been born of Hus' blood' (WA25.124,7–8). An epochal rupture had occurred. However, Luther did not perceive that in purely this-worldly terms. He described it in apocalyptic hues, using the motif of the Antichrist, who was identified with the pope. Today, this motif frequently is downplayed because it cannot be easily applied in a positive way and is likely to cause offence in this ecumenical era. Yet, this motif had considerable significance for Luther. Indeed, when the Reformation came into earth-shaking tension with the universality of the church, such apocalyptic imagery provided an eschatological vanishing point which helped that movement reorient itself and facilitated decision-making. Hus initiated the identification of the Antichrist although he was not its only source. At the end of 1518 Luther privately disclosed his first suspicion that the Antichrist had taken control of the curia (WABR1.270,9–14, cf. Hendrix 1981: 44–70). However, that premonition needed time to ripen. Reflection on apocalyptic motifs increased when Luther got his hands on pertinent Czech literature (WABr1.597,22–24) and gained new intensity when Luther referred to Hus as an early, enlightened witness to the pope's identity as Antichrist. That which he had conjectured breached the surface. Not until June 1520 and, for the time being, only in conditional terms, Luther moved toward Hus' conclusion: if the pope really wanted to hold sway over Scripture, he would meet the Scripture's own definition of the Antichrist (WA6.322,2–22; LW39.101–102). However, Luther was already convinced that this was happening. Thus, he was prepared to react boldly even if, in the end, that meant excommunication. In 1526 Luther still gave Hus credit for being the 'first' to call the pope the Antichrist (WA19.333,12–14).

To summarize: Both by what he achieved and what he failed to accomplish, Hus helped Luther establish his own place in history. Luther's chronology of world history most clearly defined Hus' role as an orientation point. There, Luther placed himself between the 'one who was martyred by Satan's council' and the hopeful prospect of the end of the ages (WA53.167–71).

Sometimes Luther mentioned Hus in the same breath with John Wycliffe, but not with the same respect. The more abrasive radicality of the Oxford master did not evoke respect. Regarding the Lord's Supper, Wycliffe anticipated Luther's antagonists, who, due to their logical abstractions, did not do justice to the concrete nature of language, and therefore, smothered the truth of Christ's real presence in the sacrament with the doctrine of transubstantiation (WA26.437,30–445,17; LW37.294–303). However, on at least one point Wycliffe's provocative formulation of a concept corresponded to Luther's viewpoint. He used one of Wycliffe's repudiated articles about 'absolute necessity' as an argument against the postulate that sinners exercise freedom of choice vis-à-vis God (WA7.146,6). Erasmus subsequently reproached Luther for being in league with marginal eccentrics. He replied that until recently he had supported the official majority, but now he could not help but realize that the minority position of the Bible and Augustine is more characteristic of Christ's witnesses (WA18.639,13–642,16).

Luther was not familiar with Wycliffe's own writings, but he did acquire a Lollard commentary on the Apocalypse and published it in 1528 to support his interpretation of the Antichrist. Once again, he associated that with John Hus and Jerome of Prague (WA26.123,2–24), passing over other figures in Hussite history in silence. Nevertheless, Luther was interested in heirs of Hus who were his contemporaries; he quickly stopped suspecting them of heresy and regarding them as schismatics. He adopted the Utraquists' dominant argument as his own: because Christ had expressly instituted communion 'in both kinds', the church did not have the right to deny the chalice to any believer (WA6.503,9–504,25).

Proposals about ways to overcome the consequences of division accompanied this change in perspective. The first, more concise of these was in his appeal *To The Christian Nobility* (WA6.454,17–457,27; LW44.295–200), the second and more detailed in his *De instituendis ministris ecclesiae* of 1523 (WA12.169–96; LW40.7–44). This prescription, intended to help the Utraquists end their plight of half-hearted dependence on Rome, simultaneously represents Luther's most thoroughgoing treatise on the universal priesthood of all believers. From the very beginning he saw this principle as a consequence of the Hussite article on the freedom to preach God's Word (WA8.425,7–38). He subsequently applied this tenet to individual parishes, but now he had to deal with the problems of the entire regional Czech church. Consequently, he drew up a multi-step model, which started in local parishes and culminated in the election of a joint superior.

Luther also allowed for the more realistic option of choosing an administrator from the ranks of existing priests. He even successfully recommended his Czech mediator as a candidate. However, Luther was mistaken about him. After several months the reforms that had been initiated foundered. The Utraquist church thus assimilated Luther's initiatives at a much slower pace than was originally anticipated. Parallel discussions with the Bohemian Brethren went better despite the fact that Luther considered them to be heretics longer than the Utraquists. If, owing to their origin, he regarded the Brethren as sectarians, he was not entirely mistaken. However, he eventually realized that their original split from the world enabled the Brethren to cross the Rubicon at which the Utraquists had hesitated.

His *Open Letter to the Nobility* urged the inclusion of the *Pighardi* (for whom he soon began to prefer the more neutral term, 'Waldensians') in conciliatory talks. Despite that, he still was not sure if they espoused Christ's substantial presence in the Lord's Supper although he was no longer convinced of the opposite. Therefore, he suggested two alternatives: if the Brethren could defend their orthodoxy, they should be accepted back under the archbishop; if not, for the time being they should continue to stand aside and be instructed in the truth.

The impetus for this change of position may have come from more meticulous, independent reading. It was also fed by personal contacts. At the very beginning Luther met with the most open Bohemian Brethren, who sought him out at their own initiative. The patience with which the reformer took up the manifold difficulties of rapprochement best accounts for this instance of mutual trust. These difficulties were due to the fact that during the first phase of the official contacts, people who were willing to learn from Luther could not play a major role. Lucas of Prague, already an old man, remained the main conversation partner. Lucas did not hesitate to enlighten the Saxon reformer like an older brother in a way that sometimes was rather provincial, even comical. In response, Luther graciously acknowledged that Lucas was his older brother and magnanimously declared that 'nowhere in the world is there such purity of the gospel' as among the Brethren (WABr2.573,17). Nevertheless, this assessment did not mean that Luther did not have anything to criticize about the Unity. Although in Lucas' time the Brethren were beginning to become more open than they had been to the need for higher education and to greater emphasis on justification by faith, they remained in midcourse and needed an impetus for further development.

For Luther's part, the most consequential document from those discussions was a work from 1523 entitled *The Adoration of the Sacrament* (WA11.431–456; LW3.275–305).

Lucas' concerns determined the title although Luther mainly expected him to provide a clearer explication of how the Brethren understood Christ's presence 'beneath the sacrament'. When that was not forthcoming, Luther set forth what he considered to be essential in this regard, supporting the concept of 'true presence' with unprecedented force. For the first time he had to defend the words of institution against a 'symbolic' interpretation. He acquainted himself anew with a principle in Honius' Epistle that could dismantle all the key affirmations of faith, and the comparison stood the Brethren in good stead. Although they emphasized that Christ's body is present 'spiritually', they also envisaged its reality.

The difficulties reaching an understanding with the Brethren also benefited Luther. Until that time, hardly anyone else had compelled Luther to wrack his brains over the intellectual patterns of a subtle doctrine of the Lord's Supper from a different conceptual tradition. Responding to previous discussions of Wycliffe and Hus, the Brethren's doctrine had attained a complicated structure that was prepared to accept emphases from both sides of subsequent eucharistic disputes among 'Protest-ants'. Although Luther could look favourably upon their positions, formulations later to be used by Reformed theologians were also anticipated here. During the 1530s Luther still complained about how hard it was to understand Brethren teachings (WATR2.413–414, §2309a–b). However, these discussions helped Luther clarify his own position in a timely way before the invectives of the 'sacramentarians' began.

Something similar occurred with regard to baptism. The Brethren alarmed Luther with their approach to the baptism of children, carried out under the assumption that it would become operative in the future. Reflecting on this incongruity, Luther was strengthened in his conviction about its full validity (especially about *fides infantium*, WA17,2.81,8–82,21). Therefore, he had arguments ready against the later Anabaptists (WA26.167,16–18).

The Brethren's contribution to Luther's doctrine of the Lord's Supper also had a more positive, and perhaps more direct, impact. In a message to Strasbourg in 1524—when the Reformation's fateful internal conflict was already smouldering—Luther recalled having encountered a repudiation of sacramental transfiguration twice before in forms superior to those expressed in Karlstadt. Even so, in the end, he was not persuaded although he had also experienced profound doubts five years earlier (WA15.394,12–20). Czech sources are ranked highly among the resources that can be associated with statements that Luther made in 1519 and 1520.

Luther apparently overcame the temptations mentioned in his *Sermon on the Sacrament of Christ's Body* (1519) by simply removing the definition of Christ's presence from the rational sphere (WA2.749,23–750,3; LW35.60–61). This fully corresponded to the position expressed against the Brethren, who had startled him with their heretical doctrine about the sacrament (WA6.80,24–81,9; LW36.28–35). However, by 1520 he had arrived at a more differentiated stance. He acknowledged that strong arguments of absurdity and uselessness could legitimately be applied against the purely human speculation represented by the doctrine of transubstantiation without it being necessary to give up Christ's real presence (WA6.508,27–512,6)! This turning point correlated with Luther's view of the Brethren, with his proposal that they be 'reintegrated', insofar as Luther correctly understood that their belief was actually similar to his current understanding because the presence of the body and blood of Christ—not a conjecture of Thomas or the pope—is the article of faith (WA6.456,31–457,12; LW44.198–199). The concurrence of these two views is all the more significant because a brief repudiation of transubstantiation in a statement about the Brethren preceded treatises on this theme.

At the time Luther shared the Brethren's stress on the spiritual benefits of the sacrament. This emphasis was so strong that the question of the real presence all but receded into the shadows. Consequently, the *Adoration of the Sacrament* had to use a different word. Undoubtedly, that resulted from a mutually profitable exchange between Lucas and Luther. It thus is possible to see how amiably this issue was addressed—in contrast to Luther's repudiation of later opponents. Of course, the Brethren never attacked Luther the way that those antagonists did. On the contrary, they began to draw a line against spiritualistic extremes even before the reformer's friends replaced Lucas as the head of the Unity of Brethren and began to develop confessional documents for the Brethren based on Luther's paradigm. During that era, for example in 1538, Luther was able to declare that the two folds had become one (WA50.380,25–29).

Opportunities for further research into particular details are emerging. Compared with Luther, there continues to be an imbalance in accessibility to, and elaboration on, writings by other Reformation figures. Presently, some of the existing literature is trapped in languages that are not widely known. Nevertheless, it appears that the balance is improving because, among other things, much of the ideological ballast that encumbered this area earlier has disappeared.

(Translated by Joyce J. Michael)

REFERENCES

Hendrix, Scott H. (1981). *Luther and the Papacy: Stages in a Reformation Conflict*. Philadelphia: Fortress.

Oberman, Heiko A. (1986). *Dawn of the Reformation*. Edinburgh: Clark.

—— (1966). *Forerunners of the Reformation: The Shape of Late Medieval Thought*. New York: Holt.

—— (1999). 'Hus and Luther: Prophets of a Radical Reformation'. In *The Contentious Triangle*, ed. Rodney L. Petersen and Calvin A. Pater. Kirksville: Thomas Jefferson University Press, 135–66.

Ullmann, Carl (1841/2). *Refomatoren vor der Reformation, vornehmlich in Deutschland und den Niederlanden*. 2 vols. Hamburg: Perthes. English translation: *Reformers before the Reformation, principally in Germany and the Netherlands*. Edinburgh: Clark, 1855.

SUGGESTED READING

Batka, L'ubomír (2009). 'Jan Hus' Theology in a Lutheran Context'. *Lutheran Quarterly* 23: 1–28.

Daniel, David P. (1988). 'A Spiritual Condominium: Luther's Views on Priesthood and Ministry with Some Structural Implications'. *Concordia Journal* 14: 266–82.

Molnár, Amedeo (1983). 'Luthers Beziehungen zu den Böhmischen Brüdern'. In *Leben und Werk Martin Luthers von 1526 bis 1546*, ed. Helmar Junghans. Göttingen: Vandenhoek & Ruprecht, 627–39.

Peschke, Erhard (1981). *Kirche und Welt in der Theologie der Böhmischen Brüder: Vom Mittelalter zur Reformation*. Berlin: Evangelische Verlagsanstalt.

....

CHAPTER 5

LUTHER'S ABSORPTION OF MEDIEVAL BIBLICAL INTERPRETATION AND HIS USE OF THE CHURCH FATHERS

....

ERIK HERRMANN

I. INTRODUCTION

....

ON the morning of 19 October 1512, a young Martin Luther entered the castle church in Wittenberg and solemnly pledged his faithfulness to the duties and responsibilities of a teacher of the church (Scheel 1930: 548–66; Brecht 1985: 125–8). Upon receiving the marks of his office—the doctoral ring and cap, and the Bible—he was presented to the assembly as the church's newest *doctor in biblia*, a teacher of the sacred Scriptures. Two days later he was inducted into the faculty senate of the University, assuming the faculty chair as *lectura in biblia* and swearing to promote the theology faculty and uphold its statutes.

The scene is neither unusual nor striking. Luther's pledges and professional responsibilities were typical of a faculty in the medieval university. His title and lecture chair, '*in biblia*', was entirely traditional and reflected the professed task of all professors of theology: to exposit the Scriptures (Köpf 2002: 81–2). Though the University of Wittenberg was new and somewhat eclectic in its approach to academic methods, the faculty statutes were quite conventional, the prescribed task of theology defined as the 'explanation of the Sacred Scripture...the interpretation of the Divine Law, and the instruction on the Book of Life' (Friedensburg 1926: 1.32). Such is the context in which Luther began his career as an exegete of Scripture.

Any consideration of Luther's relationship to the history of Western biblical interpretation must first acknowledge that his institutional and vocational framework remained deeply connected to the medieval tradition. Certainly, Luther endeavoured to reform the institutional framework, to reshape curriculum and methods. But this was a conscientious expression of his vocation as a sworn *doctor in biblia*, not a repudiation of it (Harran 1985). Even his dramatic moment at the Diet of Worms echoed those early vows as he again publicly declared his commitment to the testimony of the Scriptures and his 'captivity' to the Word of God. The intensity with which Luther concentrated on the Scriptures was perhaps extraordinary, punctuated in no small measure by his own spiritual struggles. Yet the context of his exegetical efforts—even after being thrust into the public—remained indebted to the traditional contours of his vocation in the university.

Such observations are not meant to place Luther in one period over against another—medieval versus modern. Initial attempts to examine Luther's exegesis often sought to discover in Luther a harbinger of modern exegetical methods (Meissinger 1911: 36–7: cf. Bauer 1928: 14–44, 145–52; Holl 1932; Vogelsang 1929; Seeberg 1934; Hahn 1934; Ebeling 1942, 1971; Preus 1969). More recent efforts have looked to correct this tendency by leaning hard in the opposite direction, emphasizing Luther's solidarity with the past (Hagen 1993; Mattox 2002; Hiebsch 2002). However, this latter approach can create difficulty accounting for what made Luther's exegesis so striking and revolutionary for his contemporaries. Perhaps it is best to consider Luther the exegete as a man 'between the times'. Luther's well-known criticisms of the medieval exegetical tradition—for example, its obsessive and reckless use of allegory, or its interpretation of the Pauline *iustitia Dei* —suggest a sharp rupture with the past. However, his indebtedness to traditional sources, methods, and interpretations throughout his career is likewise demonstrable.

Luther's reception of the medieval exegetical tradition is therefore complex. He is both deeply influenced by it and also a creative and critical force *within* it. Often heard within Luther studies, the language of sharp discontinuity, of a radical 'break' with the tradition, can be misleading. First, it implies that the exegetical tradition of the West is monolithic, a relatively uniform and static phenomenon. This is not the case. While there are many shared features that arguably warrant the use of the term 'tradition' in the singular, there are also a variety of emphases and conflicts within it. When Luther read the medieval or patristic commentaries, he encountered a polyphony of voices, sometimes building on one another, at other times revising or critiquing each other.

Second, Luther worked within a framework of inherited questions and problems in the history of exegesis that he did not reject out of hand. Even when his creativity took him in important new directions that put him at odds with the exegetical tradition, Luther's continued engagement with his patristic and medieval predecessors exhibits the ongoing relevance of the tradition for his biblical interpretation.

Finally, Luther shared a range of assumptions about the nature and function of the biblical text, including the necessity of piety and faith for its proper interpretation. As with the majority of the tradition, the science of theology and exegesis was not to be severed from the subjective experience of redemption. The impact of one upon the other was inevitable. No meaningful division between the monastic daily office, the lecture hall, or the pulpit existed for Luther (Steinmetz 1980b).

The most intense interaction with the exegetical tradition occurs in the earlier writings of Luther, especially his early lectures at the University of Wittenberg. In the context of these first lectures one observes most clearly Luther's deep indebtedness to the tradition and his remarkable creativity. These lectures also represent some of Luther's most crucial moments in his theological development. However one evaluates Luther's later recollections on this process, he is quite clear that it is within the context of his early exegetical efforts that definitive theological insights emerged. For these reasons, the following observations will emphasize these writings, with some indication given to Luther's later attitudes, especially in his continued use of traditional exegetical sources.

II. Luther's Reception of Traditional Exegetical Sources

Understanding Luther's relationship to the Western exegetical tradition begins with identification of his sources. Exegetical texts were not the only sources that influenced Luther's interpretation of Scripture. Writings dealing with monastic life and piety were part of the prescribed readings in Luther's monastery. The collected sermons of Bernard of Clairvaux were in the library of the Erfurt Augustinians; Luther's familiarity with them is evident early on (Matsuura 1984; Kusukawa 1995; Schulz 1995). Texts of scholastic theology, especially commentaries on the *Sentences* of Peter Lombard, were also available to Luther and central to his university studies.

Luther's choice of sources for his biblical interpretation reflects both his reliance on the exegetical tradition as well as the direction of his particular theological interests. For instance, during his first lectures on the Psalms (1513–15) Luther utilized a broad range of works. He regularly consulted the *Glossa Ordinaria*, the *Postilla* of Nicholas of Lyra, and the *Postilla* of Hugh of St Cher—three standard works of medieval commentary—as well as the Psalms commentaries of Augustine, Cassiodorus, Faber Stapulensis, and Johannes of Turrecremata (WA55,1.xxv, n. 2). For his lectures on Romans (1515–16) and Galatians (1516–17), commentaries of Jerome and Ambrosiaster and Augustine's anti-Pelagian treatises stood out. For his lectures on Hebrews (1517–18) John Chrysostom's commentary was most important. Although explicit reference to his sources became less frequent in his later lectures, throughout them all a variety of medieval and patristic writings were ever in arm's reach. Among the more significant sources that Luther used are those discussed here.

II.1. The Vulgate Bible

The central, foundational text for both the medieval exegetical tradition and Luther was, of course, the Bible, in particular the Latin Vulgate. Its text remained relatively fluid throughout the Middle Ages. Even among printed editions, variations remained as the increased interest in philology yielded additional corrections, annotations, and emendations. Especially the works of humanists in the fifteenth and sixteenth centuries contributed to a new surge of instability of its text. Critical editions of the Bible like Lorenzo Valla's *Collatio Novi Testamenti* (1452) and *In Latinam Novi Testamenti Interpretationem Annotationes* (1505), or Erasmus' *Novum Instrumentum* (1516), introduced a level of textual flux heretofore unknown since the Vulgate's inception. Luther embraced this development, at times making his own changes to the text for his lectures on the basis of recent scholarship (Volz 1957; Ebeling, 'Luthers Psalterdruck vom Jahre 1513', 1971: 1.69–131; on Luther's knowledge and use of Hebrew in his early lectures see Raeder 1961, 1967). Yet arguably Luther's greatest contribution to this phenomenon was as a translator, changing the shape of the biblical text in the history of its interpretation with the magisterial *Biblia deutsch*.

II.2. *Glossa ordinaria*

If the *versio vulgata* was the standard biblical text of the Middle Ages, then the *Glossa ordinaria*— as its name implies—was the standard biblical commentary. The history of the *Gloss* is complex and still imperfectly known, though much of the scholarly consensus attributes its inception to the circle gathered around Anselm at the cathedral school of Laon in the twelfth century (Smalley 1978: 46–66; Gibson 1992; Froehlich 1993: 192–96; Smith 2009; Froehlich 2010: III.1–19). Drawing from earlier collections and *apparatus* from the eleventh century, Anselm, with his fellow *magistri*, gathered together comments for lectures on the Scriptures, many from the Fathers. These 'glosses' were eventually transcribed on the same page as the biblical text, woven in between it and encompassing it in the margins. Others, including Anselm's brother Ralph, Gilbert de la Porrée, and Peter Lombard, made additions and emendations, eventually providing commentary for every book, indeed every chapter of the Bible. Soon the *Gloss* became the standard exegetical tool for scholars as well as preachers (Froehlich 2010: IV.1–21). As a product of interpretative trends in the Middle Ages, an instrument for the transmission of the early Fathers, and a vehicle for exegetical consensus, it is difficult to imagine a more important work than the *Glossa ordinaria* for the history of exegesis.

Luther's familiarity with and use of the *Gloss* was extensive (Froehlich 2009). It is likely that the edition used was one of the impressions from the Basel printers, Johann Froben and Johannes Petri, an edition that had added Nicholas of Lyra's *Postilla* and *Additiones* alongside the printed *Gloss* (Froehlich 2009: 34–5; cf. 1993: 12–26 and 1999). While this was probably Luther's main text during his cursory lectures on the Bible in

1509 as a *baccalaureus biblicus*, the earliest evidence of its use is found in Luther's marginal comments to Lombard's *Sentences*, which he lectured on from 1509–10 (e.g., his comments on book III, dist. 23, c. 1–3, on Romans 1:17, WA9.90,10–11). He consulted the *Gloss* throughout his entire career but used it most extensively in his earlier lectures where he even followed its format, having copies of the biblical text printed for his students with wide margins and interlinear spaces to make room for his own glosses and comments.

The extent of the influence of the *Gloss* on Luther is not always easy to determine, masked by the common practice of reproducing its interpretation without comment or attribution, especially in cases of positive appropriation. But as a rule criticism is usually louder than compliments, and so we are more accustomed to reading Luther's negative comments about the *Gloss*. His objections are sometimes limited to particular passages and interpretations: in other instances he expresses frustration with the entire text as having little grasp of the whole of Scripture, suspicious of its scholastic provenance; one report alleges that Luther even thought that Thomas Aquinas was the author of the *Gloss* (WA48.691,18, §7118). More often Luther's reservation over the *Gloss* had to do with the authority ascribed to it and the neglect of the Scriptures that could result (WA15.38–41): any 'gloss' is merely a human opinion and comment in contrast to the authority and reliability of God's Word (Froehlich 2009: 41–3). In spite of his dismissive remarks, there are no indications that Luther ever left the *Gloss* on the shelf. Whether resource or foil, the *Gloss* remained one of the principal vehicles for Luther's absorption of the Western exegetical tradition.

II.3. Nicholas of Lyra

Very popular by Luther's time, Nicholas of Lyra's *Postilla litteralis super Biblia* (1322–31) has the distinction of being the first printed commentary on the entire Bible (Rome, 1471–2), preceding even the printing of the *Glossa ordinaria*. Numerous editions were published during the end of the fifteenth and the beginning of the sixteenth century (Lyra 1487; Gosselin 1970). With its singular focus on the literal sense of the Scriptures and knowledge of the Hebrew text, Lyra was arguably the definitive biblical commentary of its day.

Nicholas (*c.*1240–1349), a Franciscan, studied with the Jewish rabbis of Évreux. Such study of Hebrew and other Jewish sources, though uncommon, had some precedent already among the twelfth-century Victorines, with a growing interest among thirteenth- and fourteenth-century Franciscan biblical scholars (Smalley 1978; Hailperin 1963; Bunte 1994; on this tradition of Hebrew study, Klepper 2000). For Lyra, familiarity with the *hebraica veritas* was an indispensable means towards understanding the literal sense of the Old Testament. For this reason, Lyra tells his readers that he will consult not only catholic doctors but Hebrew teachers as well, and he specifically praises 'Rabbi Solomon' (Rabbi Solomon ben Isaac, aka 'Rashi', 1040–1105) as one who focuses on the literal sense of the Scriptures (Lyra 1487: Prologue). This *sensus litteralis* was, at least in theory, regarded by the tradition as the foundation of all doctrine as well as all other (mystical) interpretations, and Lyra was determined to restore its exposition to its proper place of prominence. According to Lyra, the literal sense of the text is the meaning originally intended by its author, accessible through an understanding of the historical context. Lyra not only recognized that such authorial intent could include figurative, parabolic, and even allegorical forms, but also—because God is the true cause and author—meaning could extend beyond the context of the human author across the biblical canon (Minnis 1984). Thus with the *causa/auctor* of the text being *duplex*, Lyra advances a *duplex sensus litteralis*, a 'double-literal sense' that embraces the original context of the Old Testament prophet and its Christological meaning. Lyra was also well aware of the traditional four-fold sense of Scripture even if he did not engage it fully in his own work. His tropological or moral interpretation of the text (*Postilla mystica seu moralis*, 1339) was often printed with his literal exposition but proved far less influential.

By Luther's time, editions of Lyra were almost universally printed with the *Additiones*, a set of subsequent commentary on Lyra's *Postilla*. The first set were by the Spanish bishop, Paul of Burgos (c.1351–1435), a converted Jewish rabbi, who was often critical of Lyra's over-dependence on rabbinic interpretations. This was followed by the *Defensarium* or *Responsiones* of the Franciscan Matthias Döring (c.1390–1469), who sharply countered much of Burgos' comment.

As with the *Glossa ordinaria*, Luther consulted Lyra's *Postilla* regularly throughout his career. Its primary importance for Luther was as an exegetical *Hilfsmittel*, a scholarly tool that gave one a better understanding of the 'historical sense' of the text, a sense of the underlying Hebrew of the Old Testament, and the rabbinic tradition. Most of Luther's positive comments on Lyra pertain to this (e.g., WATR1.44.31; WATR4.426; WA48.691). Yet for all of Lyra's unique contributions toward understanding the literal sense of the text, his overall interpretation of the Scriptures is often unremarkable, in continuity with much of medieval tradition, especially in the Pauline corpus, where much of Luther's more significant exegetical insights sharply diverged from the tradition, including Lyra. That, along with Luther's standing criticism of Lyra's hermeneutic of the 'double-literal sense' make the famous dictum, *Si Lyra non lyrasset, Lutherus non saltasset*—'if Lyra had not played his lyre, Luther would not have danced'[1]—an exaggeration if not a *dictio absurde* (Smalley 1978: xxxii), the positive influences notwithstanding.

II.4. Faber Stapulensis

At first blush Faber Stapulensis (Jacques Lefèvre d'Etaples, c.1455–1536), an older contemporary of Luther, seems out of place in a list of Luther's medieval and patristic

---

[1] The provenance of this saying is uncertain. However, it is undoubtedly an adaption of an earlier, more general remark of praise for Lyra as mentioned already in Gregor Reisch's *Margarita philosophica* in 1508: 'Si Lyra non lyrasset, nemo doctorum in Bibliam saltasset'.

exegetical sources. A French humanist, Faber was an important representative and advocate of the new learning, the *studia humanitatis*. His exegetical works exhibit his philological interests and expertise, and his efforts were highly regarded by many of his fellow humanists. His *Quincuplex Psalterium* (1509) was an exercise of textual criticism for the Psalms as was his commentary on the Pauline epistles (1512) (Payne 1974; Feld 1982; Massaut 1983; de Savignac 1984; Backus 2009). Luther's eager use of Faber's commentaries for his early lectures is one of the more obvious examples of the reformer's debt to Renaissance humanism (WA4.461–526; cf. Hahn 1938).

However, Faber's hermeneutical approach to the Scriptures reflects attitudes toward the biblical text consistent with developments in late medieval views of the Bible. His particular rejection of the traditional four-fold method of exegesis for the sake of a single, spiritual-literal (Christological) sense is idiosyncratic, but it grows out of the broader trends among medieval scholars who increasingly associated the spiritual meaning of the Scriptures with its literal sense (Smalley 1978: 83–4; Minnis 1984; Ocker 2002; on Faber's Christological hermeneutic, see Bedouelle 1978). Luther's deep sympathy for Faber's hermeneutical approach represents another aspect of medieval biblical interpretation that found a home in Luther's own efforts.

II.5. The Fathers

Even with the unique contribution and creativity of the individual exegete, medieval biblical interpretation was in large measure a particular use of the Church Fathers. As such, commentaries were some of the most influential channels of patristic thought. For instance, commentaries in the Carolingian period were more often exegetical *florilegia* —an assemblage of patristic comment—than original interpretations. Such selection and juxtaposition of sources gave the impression of a consensus among the Fathers that added to the authoritative weight of their interpretations (Chazelle and Edwards 2003). Likewise, the *Glossa ordinaria*, which eventually displaced the Carolingian commentaries, had a similar effect. Unfortunately, with exegetical conclusions excerpted from their original contexts, the chain of quotations in such commentaries provided a convenient but fragmented picture of the patristic reading of Scripture.

Though other collections of patristic authors were produced throughout the Middle Ages, no complete editions of the Fathers were published for broad availability until the advent of the printing press. The confluence of this new technology and the new scholarly interests of the Renaissance gave expression to an enthusiasm for ancient sources that also included hopes for a new era of theological clarity and piety (Spitz 1963). The Basel printer Johann Amerbach (c.1440–1513) longed to publish complete editions of the four doctors of the Western church. In 1492 he published an edition of Ambrose, followed by Augustine's complete *Opera* in 1506. The works of Jerome, begun in 1507, were not completed until after his death, published by Johann Froben (1460–1527) in nine folio volumes in 1516.

Many other collections followed, with Froben and others printing new editions of Cyprian, Tertullian, Hilary of Poitiers, and John Chrysostom. With complete editions of the Fathers now widely accessible, their writings took up a new, formative role in the history of biblical interpretation.

The timing for the appearance of many of these works could hardly have been more opportune for Luther's own lecture activity. Already in his early lectures, Luther consulted the newly printed writings of Jerome, Augustine, 'Ambrosiaster' (whose commentaries on the Pauline epistles were included in the *Opera* of Ambrose), and Chrysostom (Schulze 1997; plus studies in Grane et al. 1993, 1998). As he worked with this new transmission of the patristic tradition, fresh tensions emerged for Luther, not only between the early church and the more recent medieval and scholastic tradition—a tension that the humanists would also stress—but also among the Fathers themselves. For Luther, this tension was most acute between the writings of Jerome and Augustine. Almost immediately after the publication of Jerome's works, Luther noted the dissonance, expressing to his friend, Georg Spalatin, his preference for Augustine over Jerome (WABr1.69–71, §27, 19 October 1516). Even so, Jerome consistently remained along with Augustine Luther's most important and oft-cited patristic source throughout his career of biblical interpretation.

By Luther's day the perception of Jerome had begun to shift from the austere saint of asceticism to the erudite scholar beloved by the humanists (Rice 1985; Hamm 1990). Luther shared a similar appreciation, deeply admiring Jerome's immense learning, and the breadth of his biblical scholarship and commentary. Still, Luther's well-known censure of Jerome often overshadows this appreciation: 'There is certainly more erudition in Aesop than in the whole of Jerome'; 'he has not even a word to say about faith and the doctrine of true religion'; 'it is a wonder that in so many [of his] books there is not a word about Christ'; 'God forgive [Jerome] for all the harm he has done through his doctrine' (WATR 1.194, §445; 1.106, §253; 1.194, §455; 1.194, §445). However, Luther's exegetical activity reveals a more ambivalent relationship. In the Pauline lectures especially, Luther fluctuates between admiring Jerome's commentary and disappointment on key exegetical points (WA57,2.2,15; WA57,2.26,20–24). Luther's initial annotations to Jerome's *Opera* are filled with praise, especially for his letters against the Pelagians (Brecht and Peters 2000; cf. Lössl 2009). But in 1519 he sharply confronted Jerome's 'narrow' interpretation of Paul's teaching on the law that only sheltered the scholastics' 'modern Pelagianism' (WA2.489,17–18, 492,10–11, 515,25–26, 495,31). Jerome's reception was further complicated by his extensive use of Origen in his own commentaries (Schatkin 1970), an association that Luther rarely regarded as felicitous. He advised judicious engagement of his commentaries rather than blind adherence (WA2.508,16–21). In short, Luther used Jerome critically but continuously, sometimes disparagingly but never dismissively: 'I cannot think of a doctor whom I have come to detest so much, and yet I have loved him and read him with the utmost ardor!' (WATR1.194, §445).

Like Jerome, Augustine's influence on Luther was both considerable and complex. On the one hand, Augustine's tremendous importance for the entire Western tradition—as well as for Luther himself—is indisputable. The question is rarely *whether* Augustine is influential, but *which* Augustine is so. The prolific North African exhibits an evolution and diversity of thought that permitted diverse if not divergent interpretations throughout the Middle Ages. The label 'Augustinian' is similarly ambiguous, signifying a variety of trends and associations throughout the medieval and Reformation periods (Steinmetz 1973). One particularly fruitful area of research has focused on the role that Augustine's writings played within the Augustinian Order during the later Middle Ages. Whether such reception constituted a distinct, late medieval 'school' continues to be debated; nevertheless, this line of inquiry has notably advanced our appreciation for the renewed study of Augustine after 1300 (Trapp 1956; Zumkeller 1964; Courtenay 1987; Saak 2001). The suggestion that Luther's reception of Augustine is indebted to such a distinct 'Augustinian Renaissance' has been more controversial and difficult to substantiate (suggested initially by Stange 1902, 1900; building on Trapp and Zumkeller: Oberman 1974, 1975, 1981; cf. Grane 1968; Steinmetz 1973; Bienert 1989). Certain is the distinctive if not decisive role that Augustine played in Luther's early biblical interpretation, especially for Paul's writings. This is arguably his chief import. For Luther, Augustine is the apostle's '*interpres fidelissimus*'—his most faithful interpreter (WA1.353,12–14).

Luther was surely familiar with some of Augustine's writings early on through the *studium generale* of the Erfurt monastery, but his more systematic study of Augustine apparently began in autumn 1509, coinciding with his lectures on Lombard's *Sentences* (WA9.28–94, cf. Delius 1984: 6; Delius 1987: 244–5). By the time of his first Psalms lectures (the *Dictata super psalterium*), his respect for Augustine was considerable; he consulted Augustine's *Ennarationes in Psalmos* frequently over the next two years. Absent, however, was any meaningful familiarity with Augustine's writings against the Pelagians. Though Luther wrestled with themes that were central to the concern of the anti-Pelagian writings (e.g., letter and spirit, justice and justification, the law of the Old Testament and the gospel of the New Testament), these texts leave virtually no mark on the lectures. In 1515, however, this changed dramatically. Beginning new lectures, on Paul's epistle to the Romans, Luther began citing Augustine's anti-Pelagian writings extensively. He also consulted Augustine's earlier commentary on Romans, but clearly Luther found the later writings far more perceptive and reliable for interpreting Paul (Demmer 1968: 237–42; Grane 1972, 1973, 1975).

This shift in exegetical sources is perhaps the single most significant moment in Luther's theological development. In the convergence of Paul and the anti-Pelagian Augustine Luther first perceived with clarity the deep rift that stood between what he believed to be the correct understanding of the Scriptures and the scholastic theology in which he was trained (Schulze 1997: 578; Grane 1999). Not simply a matter of ancients versus moderns, Luther set Augustine against *Aristotle*, defining the problem as a fundamental incompatibility of theological method (e.g., WA56.172,5–11, 273,6–9, 350,23–24, 354,14–15). Augustine, Luther contended, tracked closely with Paul's unique mode of theological argumentation—the *modus loquendi Apostoli* or *modus loquendi theologicus*. The scholastics, however, imposed an alien philosophical framework on Paul—a *modus Aristotelis* or *modus methaphysicus*, thereby violating the apostle's message (WA56.334–335 [Rom. 7:1–2]; *Scholion*, cf. WABr1.150,24–25, §61). This conflict of theological and exegetical sources and methods in which the anti-Pelagian Augustine emerges as the predominant interpretative authority determined the course of Luther's initial reform efforts, e.g., the disputation of his student Bartholomäus Bernhardi (1516) and his own programmatic disputations (1517–18) (WA1.142–151,221–228,350–374). Thus, Luther wrote his former colleague, Johannes Lang (May 1517):

> Our theology and Saint Augustine are advancing as hoped and reign in our university by God's help. Aristotle declines gradually and is heading toward complete ruin in short order. It is remarkable how the lectures on the *Sentences* are disdained; there is no one that can expect to have any students unless they profess this theology, that is, the Bible or Saint Augustine, or some other teacher of ecclesiastical authority. (WABr1.99,8–13, §41, 18 May 1517)

The enormous importance that Luther ascribed to Augustine as an exegete and theologian does not, however, preclude criticism of this church father. Luther regarded Augustine as a theological touchstone and teacher yet always a Student of the Scriptures. Luther felt little tension between his respect for the sanctity of the Fathers and his acknowledgement of their fallibility. Subject to the same mistakes and oversights as anyone, their authority was always conditioned by the quality of their exegesis: 'Let me not put my trust in Augustine; let us listen to the Scriptures' (WA7.142,30–31).

III. LUTHER'S RECEPTION OF TRADITIONAL EXEGETICAL METHODS

Luther's regular use of patristic and medieval sources gives some indication of his relationship to the exegetical tradition. Yet perhaps the more crucial question concerns exegetical methods. Ever since Karl Holl's groundbreaking essay, the emergence of Luther's 'hermeneutic' has dominated much of the literature on the subject, casting his relationship to the tradition in largely antagonistic terms (see p. 72 above; cf. Kolb 2009: 42–71). But the question of exegetical 'method' is really a broader one that encompasses the range of presuppositions and practices that shape one's approach to the Bible (Froehlich 1995: 144–6). In this wider context Luther's relationship to the tradition is again rather complex.

In Luther's particular context both the obligations of his doctorate and life in the cloister informed his reading and interpretation. Such confluence of the scholarly, pastoral, and personal use of the Scriptures reflects not only a common medieval setting for biblical interpretation but also the very traditional assumption that such activities belonged together: Peter Cantor described theology as a building with *lectio* as the foundation, *disputatio* as the walls, and *praedicatio* as the roof (PL 205, 25AB). One's exegetical method was conceived as intensely intellectual and scientific as well as intensely spiritual. To separate biblical interpretation from piety would have been both strange and troubling.

Within this context Luther's approach to the Scriptures was also decidedly more monastic than scholastic. From his earliest lectures he was preoccupied with themes of monastic culture (e.g., *humilitas, accusatio sui, poenitentia*) rather than problems more in line with the scholastic *quaestio* (Schwarz 1985: 210): 'The important word is no longer *quaeritur*, but *desideratur*; no longer *sciendum* but *experiendum*.' Luther's well-known recipe for the practice of theology, *oratio, meditatio, tentatio* (see Leclercq 1982: 5 and chapters 11, 32), echoed the monastic exegetical practice of *lectio divina* (WA50.659,3–4). In a similar use of traditional language Luther urged the kind of reading of Scripture that 'gets at the flesh of the nut'—a reading that moves beyond the words on the page and the events of ancient history toward a present, existential history with the living Christ (WABr1.17,39–44, §5; WA55,1.8,29–34; on previous usage of this metaphor, cf. de Lubac 2000: 165; Ocker 2002: 91). Some practices accomplished this better than others; important for Luther's theological development is his coming to terms with the various attempts to solve this hermeneutical problem.

The Christological reading of Scripture is the common starting point for all patristic and medieval biblical interpretation. Precisely how this was to be carried out, however, varied throughout the tradition. In this regard, it was the Old Testament that exhibited the most pronounced problem as Marcion's rejection of it indicated. But most followed a more moderate solution, underscoring the figural nature of salvation history, in which the New Testament was foreshadowed throughout the events of the Old. There Christ lay hidden under the veil of figures, types, and prophecies, like a kernel enclosed within its shell. Thus, the Old Testament text was not what it seemed, even as a seed looks little like the tree that eventually emerges from it. The Scriptures' true sense lay in its future fulfilment and could be only understood properly from that vantage point.

Still, the relevance of the Scriptures did not immediately impress itself on the Christian. Even when read as subtly signifying the events surrounding Christ, its distance from the Christian begged for a deeper significance, moving beyond the particularities of history to things more universal. Origen offered the most compelling, influential solution to this problem, stressing Paul's language of the 'letter' and the 'spirit' (2 Cor. 3:6) as key. For Origen, the Scriptures were analogous to a living person, possessing both a corporal and a spiritual nature, a literal and spiritual sense. Shaped by the Neoplatonic ethos that aligned the body and its lower appetites with the higher spiritual and rational faculties of human nature, Origen argued that the Scriptures were to be read as moving the Christian from the physical and temporal concerns of the literal sense to the spiritual and eternal things of Christ. The literal sense was thus necessary but also penultimate. However, if clinging to the literal sense when reason or charity demanded its rejection, Paul's dictum 'the letter kills' serves as a warning. In either case, the Christian relevance of the Scriptures was achieved by quickly moving past the original context of the ancient author to a spiritual significance that more readily speaks to Christian doctrine and devotion.

The medieval tradition embraced both Origen's schema of spiritual meaning and the figural/typological structure of sacred history as part of conventional reading and inter- preting practices. Following John Cassian (c.360–435), medieval exegetes commonly spoke of a four-fold sense of the Scriptures, sometimes referred to metaphorically as the 'Quadriga'. According to this four-fold structure, the Old Testament letter is fulfilled in Christ and the church (*allegory*), exhibited in the life of the present believer (*tropol- ogy*), and consummated in its fullness on the Last Day (*anagogy*). Thus, the movement from the literal sense of Scripture to its spiritual meaning mirrored the progression of salvation history from the Old to the New Testament, paralleling one's moral progress from the temporal, carnal life to the inner, spiritual, and heavenly virtues directed to eternal life.

Luther knew such methods well, incorporating many aspects of this tradition even as he struggled to clarify his own approach to the text. So, for example, in his first lec- tures on the Psalms, the four-fold sense of the Scriptures was particularly prominent; while he exhibited a certain originality in its appropriation, his use of the *Quadriga* was largely conventional. Luther also worked with the traditional assumption that the Psalms of David were prophetic utterances about Christ. His insistence that this prophetic-Christological meaning was the *literal sense* of the Psalms is perhaps a more curious position. Some scholars have even suggested that it represents a critical step toward a fundamentally new hermeneutic (Hahn 1934, 1938; Ebeling 1942; but cf. Preus 1969). But here too Luther echoed recent trends in biblical exegesis. Late medieval sen- sitivity to questions of poetics and prophecy, of genre and authorial intent resulted in a shift toward an increasingly 'fat' literal sense; meaning that was traditionally ascribed to one of the three spiritual senses was now being attributed to the *sensus literalis* (Spitz 1963), as seen in both Nicholas of Lyra's 'double literal sense' and in Faber Stapulensis' single literal-spiritual sense. In the first Psalms lectures Luther was more inclined to side with Faber over against Lyra.[2] While this 'spirituality of the letter' continued to remain important for Luther, read within the context of late medieval exegesis, it was not particularly novel.

Often the search for the point of Luther's critique of the exegetical tradition has focused on his use or non-use of allegory and the four-fold sense of Scriptures. Those who have argued that Luther's theological breakthrough entailed the rejection of alle- gory must admit that he continued to use it in varying degrees throughout his life. On the other hand, those who have argued for Luther's strong affinity to the traditional method have difficulty explaining Luther's harsh words against allegory. Unfortunately, this line of inquiry tends to impose a modern suspicion of textual multivalence on a period that was not overly concerned with such matters.

---

[2] WA55,1.6,25–26; cf. WA4.476,11–20. Ebeling's interpretation of the 'double *Quadriga*', from the preface of the *Dictata* (Ebeling 1971: 1.51–3), remains strangely disconnected from its anti-Lyra intent, see Herrmann 2005: 76–80.

Luther did, in fact, grow ambivalent toward the traditional four-fold approach to the Bible, but not because it made the Scriptures say too much. For Luther it did not say enough. He acknowledged that such traditional reading practices may indeed find Christ in the Scriptures, but ultimately neither the *Quadriga* nor a 'prophetic-literal' sense could offer clear guidance for the *meaning* and *significance* of Christ for the reader (WATR1.136,14–15, §335; Preus 1969: 153–4). This was the heart of Luther's hermeneutical problem: When suffering from a 'bruised conscience', who is Christ *pro me*—'for me?': the teacher of mysteries, the giver of a new law, the exemplar of humility or some other virtue, the coming judge? At best, the traditional approach begged this deeper question; at its worst, it complicated and compounded the problem. Eventually, Luther came to understand that the key to finding the true significance of Christ—his meaning in salvation history and his relevance for the individual—was not a matter of literal versus spiritual interpretation but learning to distinguish law from gospel (Ebeling 1971: 1.42–3; Herrmann 2005: 147–93; cf. WA7.502,34–35, WATR5.210,6–7, §5518). The development of this new approach to Scripture entailed the confluence of a number of insights over a period of several years, one of which involved his sudden, decisive turn to Augustine's anti-Pelagian writings in his first lectures on Paul.

The traditional methods that Luther inherited proposed a solution to the Christian appropriation of the Scriptures through a framework of *graduated continuity*—the continuity of prophecy to fulfilment, and the movement from literal to spiritual meanings. Yet precisely for this reason it was unable to deal with the radical *discontinuity* suggested in Paul's writings between adherence to the law and faith in the promises of Christ. Luther grappled with Paul and had a personal stake in trying to understand this relationship of law and faith as expressed in Paul's doctrine of justification and the 'righteousness of God'. The tradition's efforts to bring the gospel into correlation with the law as the law's allegorical or spiritual interpretation just complicated and confused Paul's meaning for Luther. In the traditional framework the gospel's righteousness of faith was only a deeper, inner righteousness of the law—a spiritual Law of Christ perfecting the more carnal Law of Moses. As such, the righteousness of the gospel was both a gift and a standard; it was the provision for a new possibility of righteousness but also the measure of its final realization in the judgement of the Last Day (Oberman 1966).

In the midst of his confusion, Luther found Augustine's writings against the Pelagians a helpful corrective. On the one hand, Augustine was conventional in that, like Origen, he recognized polysemy in the Scriptures, distinguishing between the literal meaning and the various figurative and spiritual meanings that could be drawn from the text. However, regarding the Pauline distinction of 'letter' and 'spirit', Augustine introduced a different interpretation. Here he argued that Paul's killing 'letter' and quickening 'spirit' was not the distinction between the literal and spiritual senses, but rather law and grace. Specifically, 'letter' was the law of the Old Testament experienced before the bestowal of grace as an impossible moral imperative, while 'spirit' referred to the grace of the Holy Spirit and the gift of love that made it possible to fulfil the law's demands (cf. Augustine, *De spiritu et littera*; *De doctrina christiana*, III, xxxiii, 46, following Tyconius' *Liber Regularum*).

Because Augustine still conceived of this distinction in largely salvation-historical terms, it remained relatively compatible with the traditional approach to the hermeneutical problem. In fact, Augustine did not seem to have any inkling that his particular interpretation of letter and spirit had hermeneutical consequences at all (*De doctrina christiana*, III, xxxiii, 46; cf. Ebeling 1971: 1.12–17). But in Luther's hands Augustine's distinction became dislodged from its salvation-historical moorings and transformed into a new basis for interpreting the Scriptures (Herrmann 2005: 147–93). Luther's understanding of 'letter' and 'spirit' was now conceived as the recurring theme of law and gospel, God's encounter with his people throughout both the Old and New Testaments—uprooting that he might plant, condemning that he might have mercy, killing that he might make alive—all expressed paradigmatically in the death and resurrection of Christ. In this way Luther conceived a new framework for the Christological relevance of the entire Bible. Allegories could be retained for illustrative use, but no longer were they essential for getting at 'the flesh of the nut'.

This was arguably one of Luther's most creative adaptations of traditional methods as he reoriented Augustine's interpretation of Paul to the hermeneutical problem that Origen and others had tried to address. In doing so, he found himself at once a debtor to the exegetical tradition and its critic. Luther's originality was thoroughly infused with a particular stream of patristic biblical interpretation, informed by questions and problems developed throughout the Middle Ages. It is perhaps for this reason that trajectories of Luther's recasting of method received such wide acceptance among his contemporaries. A mere novelty might excite a few, but Luther's new approach to the Scriptures emerged within the perennial problems of biblical interpretation and piety, thus making a powerful claim for both its relevance and catholicity.

IV. 'Tasting the Brook to Drink from the Spring'

IV.1. Luther and the History of Biblical Interpretation

Interest in the history of exegesis, a wide-ranging field of research with much potential for Luther scholarship, has surged in recent years (though its focus seems more concerned with bridging the perceived disconnect between exegesis and theology rather than its contribution to our understanding of church history) (Cahill 2000; Mayeski 2001; *Journal of Theological Interpretation*). It has been over sixty years since Gerhard Ebeling called upon church historians to take up the history of exegesis as an essential framework for their work. As a Luther scholar, he offered a few examples from Luther's first lectures on the Psalms, suggesting a method for understanding Luther within the history of biblical interpretation and its reception (Ebeling 1947; cf.

Ebeling 1971: 1.132–95, 196–220). Initially received with enthusiasm, Ebeling's invitation has elicited only slow progress due to various frustrations over methodology and the availability of sources (de Boor 1972; Froehlich 1978, 1995). However, an important handful of Luther and Reformation scholars have made significant advances in this field of biblical exegesis and its history, enlarging and nuancing our understanding of Luther's relationship to his predecessors and contemporaries (Hagen 1974; Steinmetz 1980a; Kolb 1990, 1993; Rosin 1997; Mattox 2002; cf. Muller in Muller and Thompson 1996: 3–7). Moreover, such studies on the history of exegesis have contributed to the larger discipline by bringing the biblical text on to the stage of historical influences alongside the more common *longue durée* of social, political, and economic history. Rather than a waxen nose ever giving way to other forces and philosophies, the biblical text itself is recognized as having shaped and constrained theologians and institutions. Biblical texts *make history*, they do not just *have* one (Froehlich 1978).

Certainly this is true in the case of Luther. To be sure, the inherited tradition influenced how he read the Bible. Yet his absorption of the exegetical tradition was also conditioned and mediated by the very Scriptures that helped give the tradition its shape and language. Thus, Luther's criticism of trends in the scholastic tradition was a critique primarily along these lines—that the language of the Scriptures had sadly become less formative than the language of Aristotle and the dialectical inventions of recent theologians. For this reason Luther preferred the early Fathers and those who read the sacred texts *sans* the 'Philosopher'. Here he saw himself as one siding with the majority against the minority, the patristic and monastic reading over against 'our teachers'. Yet the abandonment of the biblical *modus loquendi* was a line of critique that could extend beyond the scholastics to the Fathers and the whole exegetical tradition as he encountered it, as his eclectic use of the tradition and his explicit reflections on this experience demonstrate. Thus in 1539, having recounted how he 'worked on the letter to the Hebrews with Saint Chrysostom's glosses, the letter to Titus and the letter to the Galatians with the help of Saint Jerome, Genesis with the help of Saint Ambrose and Saint Augustine, the Psalter with all the writers available', Luther reflects on an image that he attributes to Bernard of Clairvaux:

> [Saint Bernard] regards the holy fathers highly, but does not heed all their sayings, explaining why in the following parable: He would rather drink from the spring itself than from the brook, as do all men, who once they have a chance to drink from the spring forget about the brook, unless they use the brook to lead them to the spring. Thus Scripture, too, must remain master and judge, for when we follow the brooks too far, they lead us too far away from the spring, and lose both their taste and nourishment, until they lose themselves in the salty sea. (WA50.519,33–520,10)

The expressed theological primacy of the Scriptures over other received authorities and opinions is a well-known feature of Luther's thought. Unlike other *auctoritas*, its authority is not derived but always remains normative. But there is also a sense in which the necessary priority of the biblical text simply strikes Luther as a matter of proper perspective and method. The image of the wellspring and its tributaries inspires commitments of theology and piety, but it is a historical metaphor too, and one that found frequent expression in the humanist cry *ad fontes*—'back to the sources!' Thus, we arrive at another fundamental feature of Luther the exegete: the comingling of Renaissance currents with the other brooks and streams that fed Luther's labours with the Bible and the course of the Reformation (Spitz 1974).

References

Backus, Irena (2009). 'Jacques Lefèvre d'Etaples: A Humanist or a Reformist View of Paul and His Theology?' In *A Companion to Paul in the Reformation*, ed. R. Ward Holder. Leiden: Brill, 61–90.

Bauer, Karl (1928). *Die Wittenberger Universitätstheologie und die Anfänge der Deutschen Reformation*. Tübingen: Mohr/Siebeck.

Bedouelle, Guy (1978). 'La lecture christologique du psautier dans le Quincuplex Psalterium de Lefèvre d'Etaples'. In *Histoire de l'exégèse au XVIe siècle*, ed. Olivier Fatio. Geneva: Droz, 133–43.

Bienert, Wolfgang (1989). '"Im Zweifel näher bei Augustin"?—Zum patristischen Hintergrund der Theologie Luthers'. In *Oecumenica et Patristica*, ed. Damaskinos Papandreeou et al. Stuttgart: Kohlhammer, 179–81.

Brecht, Martin (1985). *Martin Luther: His Road to Reformation, 1483–1521*, trans. James L. Schaaf. Minneapolis: Fortress.

Brecht, Martin and Christian Peters (eds.) (2000). *Martin Luther. Annotierungen zu den Werken des Hieronymus*, AWA 8. Köln: Böhlau.

Bunte, Wolfgang (1994). *Rabbinische Traditionen bei Nikolaus von Lyra*. Frankfurt am Main: Lang.

Cahill, Michael (2000). 'The History of Exegesis and Our Theological Future'. *Theological Studies* 61: 332–47.

Chazelle, Celia and Burton Van Name Edwards (eds.) (2003). *The Study of the Bible in the Carolingian Era*. Turnhout: Brepols.

Courtenay, William J. (1987). *Schools and Scholars in Fourteenth Century England*. Princeton: Princeton University Press.

de Boor, Friedrich (1972). 'Kirchengeschichte oder Auslegungsgeschichte'. *Theologische Literaturzeitung* 97: 401–14.

de Lubac, Henri (2000). *Medieval Exegesis: The Four Senses of Scripture*, trans. E. M Macierowski, Vol. 2. Grand Rapids, MI: Eerdmans.

de Savignac, Jean (1984). 'Commentaires de Lefèvre d'Etaples sur certains textes de Paul'. *Etudes Théologiques et Religieuses* 59: 301–16.

Delius, Hans-Ulrich (1984). *Augustin als Quelle Luthers: Eine Materialsammlung*. Berlin: Evangelische Verlagsanstalt.

—— (1987). 'Zu Luthers Augustinrezeption'. In *Congresso Internazionale su S. Agostino nel XVI Centenario della Conversione*, III, Studia Ephemeridis 'Augustinianum'. Rome: Institutum Patristicum 'Augustinianum', 26: 244–5.

Demmer, Dorothea (1968). *Lutherus Interpres. Der theologische Neuansatz in seiner Römerbriefexegese*. Wittenberg: Luther Verlag.

Ebeling, Gerhard (1942). *Evangelische Evangelienauslegung. Eine Untersuchung zu Luthers Hermeneutik*. Munich: Kaiser.

—— (1947). *Kirchengeschichte als Geschichte der Auslegung der Heiligen Schrift*. Tübingen: Mohr/Siebeck.

—— (1971). *Lutherstudien*, Vol. 1. Tübingen: Mohr/Siebeck.

Feld, Helmut (1982). 'Die Wiedergeburt des Paulinismus im europäischen Humanismus'. *Catholica* 36: 294–327.

Friedensburg, Walter (1926). *Urkundenbuch der Universität Wittenberg*, Vol. 1. Magdeburg: Holtermann.

Froehlich, Karlfried (1978). 'Church History and the Bible'. *Princeton Seminary Bulletin* N.S. 2: 213–24.

—— (1993). 'Walafrid Strabo and the *Glossa Ordinaria*: The Making of a Myth'. *Studia Patristica* 28: 192–6.

—— (1995). 'The Significance of Medieval Biblical Interpretation'. *Lutheran Quarterly* 9: 139–50.

—— (1999). 'The Fate of the *Glossa Ordinaria* in the Sixteenth Century'. In *Die Patristik in der Bibelexegese des 16. Jahrhunderts*, ed. David Steinmetz. Wiesbaden: Harrassowitz, 19–48.

—— (2009). 'Martin Luther and the *Glossa Ordinaria*'. *Lutheran Quarterly* 23: 29–48.

—— (2010). *Biblical Interpretation from the Church Fathers to the Reformation*. Aldershot: Ashgate.

Gibson, Margaret T. (1992). 'The Place of the *Glossa ordinaria* in Medieval Exegesis'. In *Ad Litteram: Authoritative Texts and their Medieval Readers*, ed. M. D. Jordan and K. Emery. Notre Dame: University of Notre Dame Press, 5–27.

Gosselin, Edward (1970). 'A Listing of the Printed Editions of Nicolaus de Lyra'. *Traditio* 26: 399–426.

Grane, Leif (1968). 'Gregor von Rimini und Luthers Leipziger Disputation'. *Studia Theologica* 22: 29–49.

—— (1972). 'Augustins "Expositio quarundam propositionum ex epistola ad Romanos" in Luthers Römerbriefvorlesung'. *Zeitschrift für Theologie und Kirche* 69: 304–30.

—— (1973). 'Divus Paulus et S. Augustinus, interpres eius fidelissimus'. In *Festschrift für Ernst Fuchs*, ed. Gerhard Ebeling, Eberhard Jüngel, and Gerd Schunack. Tübingen: Mohr/Siebeck, 133–46.

—— (1975). *Modus Loquendi Theologicus. Luthers Kampf um die Erneuerung der Theologie 1515–1518*. Leiden: Brill.

Grane, Leif (1999). 'Luther und das Luthertum'. In *Reformationsstudien: Beiträge zu Luther und zu Dänischen Reformation*, ed. Rolf Decot. Mainz: Zabern, 117–26.

Grane, Leif, Alfred Schindler, and Markus Wriedt (eds.) (1993). *Auctoritas Patrum: zur Rezeption der Kirchenväter im 15. und 16. Jahrhundert*. Mainz: Zabern.

—— —— (eds.) (1998). *Auctoritas Patrum II: Neue Beiträge zur Rezeption der Kirchenväter im 15. und 16. Jahrhundert*. Mainz: Zabern.

Hagen, Kenneth (1974). *A Theology of Testament in the Young Luther: 'The Lectures on Hebrews'*. Leiden: Brill.

—— (1993). *Luther's Approach to Scripture as Seen in His 'Commentaries' on Galatians 1519–1538*. Tübingen: Mohr/Siebeck.

Hahn, Fritz (1934). 'Luthers Auslegungsgrundsätze und ihre theologischen Voraussetzungen'. *Zeitschrift für systematische Theologie* 12: 165–218.

—— (1938). 'Faber Stapulensis und Luther'. *Zeitschrift für Kirchengeschichte* 57: 356–432.

Hailperin, Herman (1963). *Rashi and the Christian Scholars*. Pittsburgh: University of Pittsburgh Press.

Hamm, Berndt (1990). 'Hieronymus—Begeisterung und Augustinismus vor der Reformation'. In *Augustine, the Harvest, and Theology (1300–1650): Essays Dedicated to Heiko Augustinus Oberman in Honor of his Sixtieth Birthday*, ed. Kenneth Hagen. Leiden: Brill, 127–233.

Harran, Marilyn (1985). 'Luther as Professor'. In *Luther and Learning*, ed. Harran. Selinsgrove: Susquehanna University Press, 29–51.

Herrmann, Erik (2005). '"Why then the Law?" Salvation History and the Law in Martin Luther's Interpretation of Galatians 1513–1522'. Ph.D. dissertation, Concordia Seminary, Saint Louis.

Hiebsch, Sabina (2002). *Figura Ecclesiae: Lea und Rachel in Martin Luthers Genesispredigten*. Münster: LIT.

Holl, Karl (1932). 'Luthers Bedeutung für den Fortschritt der Auslegungskunst (1921)'. In *Gesammelte Aufsätze zur Kirchengeschichte*, Vol. 1. Tübingen: Mohr/Siebeck, 544–82.

Klepper, Deeana Copeland (2000). 'Nicholas of Lyra and Franciscan Interest in Hebrew Scholarship'. In *Nicholas of Lyra: The Senses of Scripture*, ed. Philip D. W. Krey and Lesley Smith. Leiden: Brill, 289–311.

Kolb, Robert (1990). 'Sixteenth-Century Lutheran Commentary on Genesis and the Genesis Commentary of Martin Luther'. In *Théorie et pratique de l'exégèse, Actes du troisième colloque international sur l'histoire de l'exégèse biblique au XVIe siècle*, ed. Irena Backus and Francis Higman. Geneva: Droz, 243–58.

—— (1993). 'The Influence of Luther's Galatians Commentary of 1535 on Later Sixteenth-Century Lutheran Commentaries on Galatians'. *Archiv für Reformationsgeschichte* 84: 156–84.

—— (2009). *Martin Luther: Confessor of the Faith*. Oxford: Oxford University Press.

Köpf, Ulrich (2002). 'Martin Luthers theologischer Lehrstuhl'. In *Die theologische Fakultät Wittenberg 1502–1602*, ed. Irene Dingel and Günter Wartenberg. Leipzig: Evangelische Verlagsanstalt, 71–86.

Kusukawa, Sachiko (1995). *A Wittenberg University Library Catalog of 1536*. Binghamton: Medieval and Renaissance Texts and Studies.

Leclercq, Jean (1982). *The Love of Learning and the Desire for God*. New York: Fordham University Press.

Lössl, Josef (2009). 'Martin Luther's Jerome: New Evidence for a Changing Attitude'. In *Jerome of Stridon: His Life, Writings, and Legacy*, ed. Andrew Cain and Josef Lössl. Aldershot: Ashgate, 237–51.

Massaut, Jean P. (1983). 'Lefèvre d'Etaples et l'exégèse au 16e siècle'. *Revue d'Histoire Ecclesiastique* 78: 73–8.

Matsuura, Jun (1984). 'Restbestände aus der Bibliothek des Erfurter Augustinerklosters zu Luthers Zeit und bisher unbekannte eigenhändige Notizen Luthers: Ein Bericht'. In *Lutheriana: Zum 500. Geburtstag Martin Luthers von den Mitarbeitern der Weimarer Ausgabe*. Köln: Böhlau, AWA 5, 315–32.

Mattox, Mickey (2002). *Defender of the Most Holy Matriarchs: Martin Luther's Interpretation of the Women of Genesis in the Enarrationes in Genesin, 1535–1545*. Leiden: Brill.

Mayeski, Marie Anne (2001). 'Quaestio Disputata: Catholic Theology and the History of Exegesis'. *Theological Studies* 62: 140–5.

Meissinger, K. A. (1911). *Luthers Exegese in der Frühzeit*. Leipzig: M. Heinsius Nachfloger.

Minnis, Alastair J. (1984). *Medieval Theory of Authorship: Scholastic Literary Attitudes in the Later Middle Ages*. London: Scholar Press.

Muller, Richard A. and John L. Thompson (eds.) (1996). *Biblical Interpretation in the Era of the Reformation*. Grand Rapids, MI: Eerdmans.

Nicholas of Lyra (1487). *Biblia cum postillis...* Nürnberg: Koberger.

Oberman, Heiko (1966). 'Iustitia Christi and Iustitia Dei: Luther and the Scholastic Doctrines of Justification'. *Harvard Theological Review* 59: 1–26.

—— (1974). 'Headwaters of the Reformation: Initia Lutheri—Initia Reformationis'. In *Luther and the Dawn of the Modern Era: Papers for the Fourth International Congress for Luther Research*, ed. Oberman. Leiden: Brill, 40–88.

—— (1975). '"Tuus sum, salvum me fac!" Augustinréveil zwischen Renaissance und Reformation'. In *Scientia Augustiniana*, ed. C. P. Mayer and W. Eckermann. Würzburg: Augustinus-Verlag, 349–93.

—— (1981). *Masters of the Reformation: The Emergence of a New Intellectual Climate in Europe*, trans. Dennis Martin. Cambridge: Cambridge University Press.

Ocker, Christopher (2002). *Biblical Poetics before Humanism and Reformation*. Cambridge: Cambridge University Press.

Payne, John (1974). 'Erasmus and Lefèvre d'Etaples as Interpreters of Paul'. *Archiv für Reformationsgeschichte* 66: 54–83.

Preus, James S. (1969). *From Shadow to Promise: Old Testament Interpretation from Augustine to the Young Luther*. Cambridge, MA: Harvard University Press.

Raeder, Siegfried (1961). *Das Hebraische bei Luther untersucht bis zum Ende der ersten Psalmenvorlesung*. Tubingen: Mohr/Siebeck.

—— (1967). *Die Benutzung des masoretischen Textes bei Luther in der Zeit zwischen der ersten und zweiten Psalmenvorlesung, 1515–1518*. Tübingen: Mohr/Siebeck.

Rice, Eugene (1985). *Saint Jerome in the Renaissance*. Baltimore: Johns Hopkins University Press.

Rosin, Robert (1997). *Reformers, the Preacher and Scepticism: Luther, Brenz, Melanchthon and Ecclesiastes*. Mainz: Zabern.

Saak, Eric Lelan (2001). 'The Reception of Augustine in the Later Middle Ages'. In *The Reception of the Church Fathers in the West*, Vol. 1, ed. Irena Backus. Leiden: Brill, 367–404.

Schatkin, Margaret (1970). 'The Influence of Origen upon St. Jerome's Commentary on Galatians'. *Vigiliae Christianae* 24: 49–58.

Scheel, Otto (1930). *Martin Luther: vom Katholizimus zur Reformation*, Vol. 2. Tübingen: Mohr/Siebeck.

Schulz, Erika (1995). 'Bücher aus den beiden Wittenberger Klosterbibliotheken in der Bibliothek des Evangelischen Predigerseminars'. In *700 Jahre Wittenberg*, ed. Stefan Oehmig. Weimar: Böhlau, 519–34.

Schulze, Manfred (1997). 'Martin Luther and the Church Fathers'. In *The Reception of the Church Fathers in the West*, Vol. 2, ed. Irena Backus. Leiden: Brill, 573–626.

Schwarz, Reinhard (1985). 'Luthers unveräußerte Erbschaft an der monastischen Theologie'. In *Kloster Amelungsborn 1135–1985*, ed. Gerhard Ruhbach and Kurt Schmidt-Clausen. Amelungsborn: Klosterverwaltung, 209–32.

Seeberg, Erich (1934). 'Die Anfänge der Theologie Luthers'. *Zeitschrift für Kirchengeschichte* 53: 229–41.

Smalley, Beryl (1978). *The Study of the Bible in the Middle Ages*. Notre Dame: University of Notre Dame Press.

Smith, Lesley (2009). *The Glossa Ordinaria: The Making of a Medieval Bible Commentary.* Leiden: Brill.

Spitz, Lewis W. (1963). *The Religious Renaissance of the German Humanists.* Cambridge, MA: Harvard University Press.

—— (1974). 'Headwaters of the Reformation: Studia Humanitatis, Luther Senior, et Initia Reformationis'. In *Luther and the Dawn of the Modern Era*, ed. Heiko A. Oberman. Leiden: Brill, 89–116.

Stange, Carl (1900). 'Über Luthers Beziehungen zur Theologie seines Ordens'. *Neue Kirchliche Zeitschrift* 11: 574–95.

—— (1902). 'Luther über Gregor von Rimini'. *Neue Kirchliche Zeitschrift* 13: 721–7.

Steinmetz, David C. (1973). 'Luther and the Late Medieval Augustinians: Another Look'. *Concordia Theological Monthly* 44: 245–60.

—— (1980a). *Luther and Staupitz: An Essay in the Intellectual Origins of the Protestant Reformation.* Durham: Duke University Press.

—— (1980b). 'The Superiority of Pre-Critical Exegesis'. *Theology Today* 37: 27–38.

Trapp, Damasus (1956). 'Augustinian Theology of the 14th Century: Notes on Editions, Marginalia, Opinions and Book-Lore'. *Augustiniana* 6: 146–274.

Vogelsang, Erich (1929). *Die Anfänge von Luthers Christologie nach der ersten Psalmenvorlesung.* Berlin/Leipzig: de Gruyter.

Volz, Hans (1957). 'Luthers Arbeit am lateinischen Psalter'. *Archiv für Reformationsgeschichte* 48: 11–56.

Zumkeller, Adolar (1964). 'Die Augustinerschule des Mittelalters: Vertreter und Philosophisch-Theologische Lehre'. *Analecta Augustiniana* 27: 167–262.

CHAPTER 6

....

HUMANISM, LUTHER, AND THE WITTENBERG REFORMATION

....

ROBERT ROSIN

WITHIN days of their release, Martin Luther's Ninety-five Theses captured wide attention, sparking comment pro and con far beyond the academic circle for which they were intended. The natural, all-too-human desire to find a way to stand before a righteous God with one's own righteousness had driven Luther into the monastery. *Desperatio monachos facit*—'Desperation makes monks' went the saying Luther knew full well from personal experience. Indeed, the quest for certainty in salvation was no mere academic exercise, even if Luther had proposed an academic debate with his propositions on the church door. In university circles, sparring over theses was the traditional way of putting ideas to the test, running them through the gauntlet of dialectic and logic where syllogisms might expose fatal flaws and pare down rough edges to arrive at a polished answer—the truth of the matter.

Academic debates happened all the time without drawing attention beyond local university circles. Yet Luther could hardly have been surprised that his proposals on such a charged issue as the promotion and sale of indulgences would attract more than casual notice beyond little Wittenberg. After all, the Christian's eternal good was at stake, but so, too, were the financial interests of powerful people, extending to Rome itself. The theses went viral, the debate expanded, and Luther soon was known for more than simply attacking the pope's crown and the monks' belly.

But another set of theses authored by Luther a month before the famous Ninety-five arguably carried even more weight in the long run. In September 1517 Luther penned his 'Ninety-seven Theses', his 'Disputation Concerning Scholastic Theology', which struck at the heart of how theology was done in his day. If Luther were correct, if he could weigh in and win the day against the 'schoolmen', theology would not be the same. There was no doubt Luther stood squarely in opposition to the scholastic approach, and he knew it: 'It is an error to say that no one becomes a theologian without Aristotle. This counters what is commonly said. Moreover, no one becomes a theologian unless it is without

Aristotle....In short, all Aristotle is to theology as darkness is to light'. With those blunt assertions Luther headed in a radically different direction not simply in terms of the theological content but more importantly in terms of method (WA1:221–8, LW31.9–16, theses 43–4, 50). It is difficult to overestimate just how significant this step was. Within their own circle scholastics might argue over how to view reality or how to construct their philosophical frameworks, some using the *via antiqua* and others the *via moderna*. But regardless of whether one adopted the 'old way' of looking at things as a moderate realist in the camp of Thomas Aquinas, or opted for the 'new way' of the nominalist perspective that Luther himself had learned, the scholastics all agreed that the problems they sought to solve must be approached using the tools of dialectic and syllogistic logic. Tradition demanded that theology be run through that matrix. Luther's assertions sprang from different roots and rested on a different frame (Grane 1962 traces Luther's significant departure in theological sources and content). This new approach not only would bring about a personal breakthrough for Luther but would fuel wider change, with Wittenberg emerging as a leader in evangelical educational and theological reform.

The Reformation has been explained from various angles—top down, bottom up, the action of great men, the product of the people, and more. It has been portrayed as the well-intended yet wrongly directed reaction to latter-day scholasticism, or as the harvest of medieval theology in its autumn years,[1] as a revolution that is theological, political, economic, cultural—or all of the above (Dickens and Tonkin 1986 provides orientation). Understandably, there is a ring of truth in any number of approaches, for the Reformation was part of real life, full of complexities, with big ideas, mixed motives, and ragged edges. Still, amid worthy competing voices, one helpful way to understand Luther and Wittenberg's reform is as the product of theology rethought in light of educational and cultural contributions made by Renaissance humanism.[2]

'No humanism, no Reformation', Bernd Moeller declared (1972: 36). That might be reworked to say 'no Renaissance education, no Reformation', for while the 'New Learning' of the *studia humanitatis*, the 'study of man', had an impact in various directions, the educational angle made the difference for Luther and Wittenberg, providing tools and attitudes to study texts with new eyes, with a new approach or method. As the century wore on, the Reformation returned the favour. Mindful of the debt owed this New Learning, the Reformation incorporated humanism into its schools in appropriate ways on various levels and continued to lean on this revival of the balanced liberal arts well into the seventeenth century.

The Roman church did much the same, finding value in humanism in an effort to undergird its own theological positions and to promote its own understanding of reform. Not only was Rome interested in humanism in its own right, but the success

---

[1] The view that the Reformation was well-intended but misguided was suggested by Lortz (1939); see Chapter 44. An alternative approach that sees late medieval nominalism yielding good seed to sprout again in the Reformation came with Oberman (1963).

[2] On the contrast offered by linking Reformation to the scholasticism of the day or to the new educational thrust, see the exchange of ideas in Oberman (1974a) and Spitz (1974).

achieved by the Evangelical movement's use of humanism was also incentive to keep pace (D'Amico 1983; Stinger 1985/1998; Trinkaus 1970). However, Rome would come to different conclusions and finish with a different product, so to speak, because it coupled humanism with assumptions and theological underpinnings different from those held by Luther and the Wittenberg reform (Trinkaus 1983: 3.341–463).

In time, humanism branched off in different directions—into natural science, for example—while still continuing to undergird theology. Yet the Reformation did not shy away from scholarly exploration or from defending that 'New Learning' to which it owed much. Nor was the Reformation averse to continuing to use parts of the old approach to theology that as a whole it found problematic. Much of the old way of talking and even thinking remained when humanism arrived; the vocabulary and the organization continued to be employed by the Reformation. Those elements stayed not so much out of inertia but because these hold-over ideas, language, and thought patterns were deemed to be not a problem but rather still valid for theology. No point reinventing the wheel so long as it aligned with the new approach. Reformers did not necessarily think about this. They simply continued to use some of the old because it gave them no trouble. At the same time, what finally mattered to the theological reform that emerged was not how much of the old was retained, but what of the new was introduced. That took them in a much different direction (see Chapter 5).

Wittenberg benefitted from the rebirth of classical learning that found a place in the culture of the German lands and wider Europe (Spitz 1975). The Renaissance had grown since the mid-fourteenth century with roots in Francesco Petrarch's discovery of Cicero with his classical Latin and a greater classical spirit. As the movement was translated across the Alps into the septentrional climes, early proponents of the new learning began to plough a new course.[3] Itinerant intellectuals such as Peter Luder and Rudolf Agricola, early fathers of the movement, inspired others first to do more of the same while perfecting the basics, and then to branch out. So Conrad Celtis, Johannes Reuchlin, Ulrich von Hutten, Mutianus Rufus, Willibald Pirckheimer, and others refined the poetry, plunged into the ancient languages, fired up German identity with a kind of nationalistic fervour, and generally set the stage for an even greater push that eventually came to the university scene. Rulers employed the literati to embellish their correspondence and legal work, giving statecraft a certain flair (Gilmore 1963). Histories were written to stir allegiance and kindle virtues useful for good government. The universities lagged for a time before opening up to humanism. Scholasticism held sway in the curriculum, and the schoolmen understandably showed little interest in sharing their virtual monopoly on method. Still, humanists could be found in the wider university communities such as Heidelberg or Erfurt, ready and willing to teach, though kept out of the normal academic flow. At times when humanists actually were engaged as instructors, they found

---

[3] Septentrional refers to 'seven oxen' (*septen + triones*) of the ox cart constellation in the northern sky, perhaps better known as *ursa major*, the 'big bear' or the Big Dipper. So 'septentrional' was simply a way of referring to that which is 'of the north', saying it with a flourish to show off one's learning.

themselves saddled with a prescribed text and notes to present rather than being left to think things through their own way.

What was this humanism that the scholastics resisted and that helped the Reformation? 'Humanism' has been applied to at least three major intellectual movements. The first was the revival of classical learning in the Renaissance–Reformation era that explored human potential. The second came in the nineteenth century, epitomized by Wilhelm von Humboldt's optimism that went beyond merely highlighting human ability to promoting an upward trajectory for humankind, a view then recast as 'progressive humanism' by Marxist or collectivist socialism. In the twentieth century, such philosophers as Bertrand Russell and Corliss Lamont championed a third sort of humanism seen in the Humanist Manifesto, coupling an anthropocentric focus with an intentional rejection of religion (Buck 1987).

Humanists of the first sort would have been amazed at the twentieth-century variety. The Renaissance devotees of the *studia humanitatis* certainly focused on human potential, but they sought no divorce from God. They did not jettison Christianity for some wider universalism. Instead, their wordplay was yet another way to show off their learning, entertaining their circle with clever in-house talk.

Still, to reprise Tertullian's query, 'What does Athens have to do with Jerusalem?' the answer is 'plenty'. Humanism sought the revival of classical antiquity according to its form and norm along with its underlying spirit (Joachimsen 1930: 419–20). This interest in both content and approach proved valuable in the long run as humanists, who were also Christian, focused on human nature and the human potential they believed must be there in light of men and women being the foremost creatures of God. After all, Genesis focuses in detail on human creation after all else was done, highlighting a unique design created in God's image and likeness (Trinkaus 1970 illustrates that Italian humanist approaches to theology differed significantly from scholasticism). Differences over anthropology—how deep was the fall into sin, how much could one still do, and to what extent was divine grace needed to attain that goal?—arose naturally when other assumptions or points of view complicated the varied picture offered by humanists, some of whom favoured the evangelical Reformation, while others stood by Rome. If nothing else, such questions about human possibility underscored a need to support education and to revisit especially the biblical texts to find answers.

While Renaissance humanism took various directions, its interests arose from a basic interest in reviving the classical liberal arts. The analytical and communication skills of the *trivium*—grammar, logic, and rhetoric—and the fundamental way then to understand the world around through the quadrivium—mathematics, geometry, astronomy, and music—remained in the curriculum. But the balance had been lost with all the attention paid to logic since the medieval revival of Aristotle. Renaissance humanism sought to restore a balance. While logic still had its place, logic by itself, no matter how complex, could prove to be thin stuff compared to the richer, more varied understanding of life that the *studia humanitatis* claimed to offer. A start on that restoration grew from interest in the core of grammar (or language), poetry, rhetoric, history, and moral philosophy (Kristeller 1955). These were developed, incorporated, and adapted as generations changed, and they especially helped the evangelical Reformation that employed these tools in various ways.[4] Grammar and language, for example, meant more than writing good Latin. A working ability in Greek and Hebrew was an obvious plus with the Reformation emphasis on *sola scriptura*. But beyond reading texts in the original, grammar also laid a foundation for good communication, for clear and winsome prose aimed at setting forth the message based on the biblical texts. Language also might be stretched to include literacy, important for the baptized people of God using the Scriptures in their role as the universal priesthood of believers.

Poetry touched the affective side of human nature as lyrics both appealed to minds and strummed heartstrings as well. After all, man does not live by syllogistic logic alone. Poetry's rhythm and rhyme helped teach theology through hymns sung stanza by stanza. Rhetoric sought to persuade through well-constructed discourse, important for the pulpit and valuable for educational and polemical literature, so that the Reformation's short and snappy appeals could be more valuable than tomes of logical argument, no matter how carefully constructed. Luther famously commented that the church was not a 'pen house' but a 'mouth house', putting a premium on communication, with theology understood as present-tense engagement rather than as truths from bygone days kept now in books on shelves. Of course, while Luther emphasized the *verbum evangelii vocale*, the spoken word of the gospel, that cast no aspersions on books. Rather in Luther's mind, the printing press was God's gift to extend the reach of grammar, poetry, and rhetoric (Eisenstein 1979: 374). Of course, for Luther and his circle, all this was complicated by fallen human nature. No appeal, no matter how persuasive, changed human hearts without the Holy Spirit working in and through the vocabulary. Still, the preacher bore the responsibility to communicate as best he could.

History, another core subject, had once been used simply as illustration in support of rhetoric. But the humanists felt a gulf between antiquity and their own era. History laid bare past human actions for good or ill, and while some eras were admired more than others, history taught the impossibility of freezing time and the necessity of taking up the tasks in one's own age. The long view of history lay behind Luther's comparison of the gospel to a *Platzregen*, a spot downpour from a raincloud moving here and there. *Carpe diem*: take advantage while there is time. And so historians, Luther would write, were most useful people, and their accounts were 'precious things' for what they taught about life as God works out his purposes (WA50.383, LW34.275).

Moral philosophy put history's lessons into practice. For all the past might teach, life is not just recycled. History may not repeat itself, but it surely rhymes (attributed to Mark Twain). An honest look makes clear that life is not neat and clean but rather is rife with ragged edges and must engage its present-tense challenges in its own right. To

---

[4] Spitz (1963). The varied use made of humanism by the thinkers Spitz includes is striking, particularly Luther at the end, who certainly shares interests with the others but also displays a different spirit, not focusing on humanism in its own right but for the value it brought to the theological enterprise, a tool to unpack the Scriptures.

that end, the liberal arts that groomed talent and liberated human potential put people in good stead—at least as ready as they can be to take up responsibilities and tasks laid upon them. Moral philosophy addressed life's ethical challenges.

All this—grammar, poetry, rhetoric, history, moral philosophy—was to be done with flair, with elegance, with an eye toward aesthetics (Gray 1963). Presentation mattered in its own right, beyond just the arriving at results. Perhaps this point helps most in deciding whether Luther was truly a humanist. On one hand, he enjoyed and employed the common conventions shared by devotees of the New Learning. For example, humanists would classicize mundane family names: Schwartzerd became Melanchthon. From 1517 to 1519 Luther, who had already changed the family 'Luder' to a more Latin-like 'Luther', referred to himself as *Eleutherius*, a Greek-rooted play on his name meaning the liberated one or one who frees—perhaps to 1 Corinthians 9:19 or John 8:32 and the effect of the gospel that Luther, in good humanist fashion, termed *eruditio divina* (Moeller and Stackmann 1981). But if being a humanist meant appreciating and finishing with some fine piece of learning or elegant writing for its own sake, then no matter how beautiful, count Luther out. Luther is a biblical theologian who benefitted from and was influenced by the New Learning, seeing humanism as a tool to unlock that *eruditio divina* in order to hear *Deus loquens*, God clearly and directly addressing the reader-believer with divine truth that made free.

How Luther first became interested in humanism and the world of the classics is not certain. The moment when things clicked in Luther's mind may be even less certain than dating the Tower Experience although this is not for lack of effort from well-versed scholars (Junghans 1985). But the New Learning had made enough of an impression on Luther, so that while he gave up law studies, he took Plautus and Vergil with him into the cloister. Then Luther, along with his Augustinian friend Johannes Lang, first took up Greek, and in 1509 Luther began to teach himself Hebrew with Johannes Reuchlin's new grammar. In contrast, Luther seemed to find his one-semester stint leading Wittenberg students through Peter Lombard's *Sentences* a frustrating experience. Beyond simply disagreeing with some of the positions of earlier scholastics, Luther complained about the 'rancid rules of the logicians', an argument with method (WA9.47,6; Baylor 1977). Apparently his interest in an alternative to scholasticism was growing.

Luther soft-pedalled his own learning, calling himself a bumpkin (*rusticus*). It is true that his Latin lagged behind a colleague's such as Melanchthon. But Luther certainly knew classical sources. Gordon Rupp noted that Luther's *De servo arbitrio* actually has more classical allusions than did Erasmus's *De libero arbitrio* (Luther 1969: 28–31). Erasmus wanted to impress and probably intimidate with his learning. Luther did not care, but he knew that Erasmus would see all Luther had included without literary boasting. Yet in 1524 in *To the Councilmen of All Cities in Germany That They Establish and Maintain Christian Schools*, Luther bemoaned not having read more poets and historians during his earlier school years, while being required to read 'the devil's manure, philosophers, and sophists' instead (WA15.46,19–21, LW45.370). Luther must have compensated for what seemed to him to be a late start. Melanchthon, after Luther's death, noted that Luther had read widely in the ancients including Cicero, Vergil, Livy, and more. The classical references Luther made on the fly in his Table Talk, with its causal, non-scripted remarks in on-the-spot conversation, are impressive. Despite his antipathy for Aristotle when it came to theology, Luther frequently cited the Stagarite (still often critically) along with Cicero and Vergil, as well as Terence, Horace, Plato, Quintilian, Homer, and Ovid. Others mentioned include Aesop, Plautus, Herodotus, Juvenal, Xenophon, Suetonius, Aeschylus, Felix, Caesar, Pliny, Tacitus, Demosthenes, Polycrates, Plutarch, Sulpicius, Parmenides, Zeno, and more, classical figures who were being published in the Empire during the first decades of the sixteenth century. Whether Luther gathered these by reading or from contact with friends, the fact remains that he found them useful, voices from the past to enlighten the present (begin with Schmidt 1883).

Luther was well beyond name dropping and dabbling when it came to history. He knew the writings of Lorenzo Valla and appreciated them not only for their style but also for the material they offered. His reading of Valla's critique of the Donation of Constantine in a 1520 edition from humanist Ulrich von Hutten helped accelerate Luther's move away from the papacy (Fried 2007: 31). In 1537 Luther unleashed his own blast against the forgery. Humanist interest in history fuelled nationalism. Tacitus, for example, stirred German pride that helped rally people behind Luther, the German Hercules (Hans Holbein's famous woodcut portrays Luther as Hercules, dispatching the Cologne Dominican and inquisitor Jacob von Hoogstraten, having already slain Aristotle, Thomas Aquinas, William of Occam, and Peter Lombard, who lay at his feet). Historians were, as noted, useful people in Luther's eyes, a way to understand life as a kind of divine drama with God acting behind and through characters great and small, all God's masks (*larvae Dei*) as God accomplishes divine purposes. Thus, the past perhaps sheds light on present problems, hinting at the divine impetus otherwise hidden. So, thought Luther, God gives the East over to the Turks to bring language teachers to the West (which actually was happening well before Luther's comment). Mistaken notions aside, Luther had a lively interest in history, influenced most by Melanchthon, who lectured on world history and wrote prefaces for others, as did Luther, right up to the end of his life. Luther's prefaces included those to Spalatin's *Magnifice consolatoria exempla et sententiae ex passionibus sanctorum*, Robert Barnes' *Vitae Romanorum Pontificum*; *Historia Galeatii Capellae* (1539), and Georg Major's *Vitae patrum* (1544) and *Papstreue Hadrian IV. und Alexandrus III. gegen Kaiser Friedrich Barbarossa* (1545) (Spitz 1997). History also fuelled the national spirit hailed by the likes of Conrad Celtis and Ulrich von Hutten, no small thing for Luther's Reformation facing Rome. Tacitus in particular was useful for documenting the slide of Rome in the face of the Germans who, though lacking high culture, excelled in the basic virtues that sustained them (Holborn 1937; Spitz 1957: 93–105; Borchardt 1972).

Another gift from the past was the classical languages. Luther admired the ancients' skills, even though they humbled him, reducing him to a stammer (Schmidt 1883: 14). In *To the Councilmen of All Cities in Germany*, Luther urged the study not only of the languages per se, but also the ideas in the ancient texts. He preferred Cicero to Aristotle, finding Cicero a more valuable commentator on life's challenges addressed in moral philosophy. Even texts that might pose problems for theology—for example, Cicero's

De natura deorum and speculation about God's existence—were important to consider, and Cicero understood life's vanity as in Ecclesiastes. There was no avoiding such issues. Rather address them, and what better way than through the ancient texts, challenging yet elegant. Luther found plenty of elegant writers to cite in letters and the classroom (understandably) and even in sermons. Quintilian was a particular favourite. Pliny the Younger and Varro provided information on a range of topics. Ovid and Horace were used multiple times. When a Silesian schoolmaster was criticized for having students read Terence, Luther urged the teacher to continue, despite Terence raising eyebrows with some of his language and material. Better to address such matters in school with guidance for real life (WATR1.430–1, §867). Luther himself was not shy about reading Lucretius and Lucan, finding the sceptics at least honest in their criticism (Schmidt 1883: 58). Still, in the end, more widely useful advice might come from Aesop, and so Luther himself did an edition for schools (WABr5.309; Springer 2011).

This sampling, hardly exhaustive, ought to make plain that while Luther was fundamentally a biblical theologian, he hardly operated in a cultural vacuum. In fact, he drew freely and widely from the Renaissance revival of the liberal arts, using the efforts at educational liberation not simply for theology, but for the intellect and character they would develop. The *studia humanitatis* was of value to Luther. Simply put, it opened up life. With Luther at Wittenberg, it helped open the life of the mind and fuel the Reformation.

In 1502 Saxon Elector Frederick's new university opened and offered the usual academic fare from both Thomist and Occamist perspectives. Some early statute revisions based on Tübingen as a model, and a tilt toward the *via moderna* marked by the arrival of Luther's old Erfurt teacher Joducus Trutfetter, are nothing out of the ordinary. But from the start Wittenberg had the real possibility to be different. Frederick's charter opened the door to 'poetry and the other arts' (Blaschka 1952: 84; Grossman 1975: 36–75; Junghans 1985: 56–62). Scholastics would have to compete for their place in the university as was clear from the beginning. The first rector, Martin Pollich von Mellerstadt, was amenable to humanism. Poet Hermann von dem Bosche came as the first professor of rhetoric while Nicholas Marschalk handled Greek and perhaps some Hebrew. When Marschalk left in 1505, Hermann Trebelius carried on. Languages were a start although it would take some time to approach exegesis through the lens of linguistic or literary study because of scholastic resistance. Law studies had an Italian accent with the 1506 coming of Christoph Scheurl from Bologna. He soon moved on, but others were attracted to the fledgling school (Junghans 1985: 56–9).

Wittenberg's 1507 *Rotolus doctorum* records early faculty and their course offerings. Humanist Balthasar Phachus, for example, taught rhetoric and poetry, treating such texts as the Aeneid. Other New Learning proponents included Georg Daripinus, Andreas Meinhardus, Kilian Reuther, Otto Beckmann in medicine, and Christian Beyer in law. Humanists often moved on quickly, lured to greener grass and other sodalities of scholars. In theology Johannes von Staupitz was not a humanist, but he tolerated them as did others brought in for that faculty.

Beyond the manpower, Wittenberg offered courses with a humanist flavour (Friedensburg 1926: 14–17). Instead of the traditional *Doctrinale* of Alexander de Villa

Dei, Simon Steyn used Johannes Verulanus' new text (edited by Johannes Crispus) for Latin grammar. Kilian Reuther used a new edition of Aristotle's *De Anima* although he kept Aquinas's commentary. Did the humanist Reuther know he could push only so far (Bauch 1897: 323–5; Nauert 1973; Grossmann 1975: 73–5)? Hebrew seemed to be available but on a small scale (Bauch 1904: 22–4). Greek was tutored privately by Andreas Karlstadt and Johannes Lang (Grossmann 1975: 48–53). Scholastics understandably resisted. After all, teaching positions were at stake. But scholasticism and humanism certainly did not lock horns in orchestrated efforts to squeeze each other out. The picture is more one of coexisting in an uneven truce, still divided over educational method and goals (Ozment 1979; Overfield 1984). Things were stewing in Wittenberg, but humanism needed help from within to sink permanent roots and recast the curriculum.

Luther was that catalyst. By the time Luther finished his doctorate (1512) and joined the theological faculty (1512), humanism had become part of his theological framework with the languages. As a professor he was obligated to contribute to the growing body of exegetical knowledge, but new to the task, he had nothing in the files, so to speak. Pressed to produce, Luther found value in the writings of Faber Stapulensis, a French humanist, whose ideas on Psalms and various epistles Luther found helpful and a relief from scholastic logic. More help came in a better text: Erasmus's New Testament in both Greek and Latin. While change does not come overnight, from early on it is evident that Luther was doing something different. With Romans in mid-decade, he realized he had hit on another method (Grane 1975, 1985). More than classroom material, the results were helping Luther sort through his own issues while finding that loving God so long sought after. More, what about others like him in the classroom and congregations beyond? This was no mere academic exercise, and Luther worked to bring more of humanism's tools to the university.

Luther found a sympathetic ear in Georg Spalatin, a university acquaintance become advisor to Elector Frederick. Spalatin helped build the library in Wittenberg, adding classic, patristic, and contemporary humanist works (Friedensburg 1917: 153–4; cf. Erasmus 1910: 2.415–18; Kusukawa 1995). Frederick relied on Spalatin to keep current on university developments, and in Spalatin, the university in turn had a friend with influence (Friedensburg 1917: 42–159; Höss 1956). A 1517 visitation gave Luther and colleagues an opening to lobby for reducing the scholastic presence even more, while favouring the humanist liberal arts emphasis that also helped evangelical theology (Friedensburg 1926: 74–81, 83–7). As a result, Aristotle's logic, physics, and metaphysics were studied 'according to new translations', and there were new offerings in Quintilian (a humanist favourite) and in Latin, Greek, and Hebrew (Friedensburg 1926: 85–6). More changes would come in following years, but Luther was confident Wittenberg was on a new course (WABr1.153–4).

Among the more important changes in 1518 was the start of a university-sanctioned *Pädagogium* for language training, and new faculty positions were created for teaching Greek and Hebrew. Melanchthon filled the Greek post, and Matthaeus Aurogallus eventually came for Hebrew. Melanchthon's inaugural lecture made plain not only where his sympathies lay but also that the elector had made a good choice. Wittenberg became the first university to have the languages as an official part of the arts curriculum.

Momentum continued in 1519. The faculty called for an end to lectures in Thomism and a reduction in other scholastic fare, while introducing more courses on Ovid, Pliny, and Quintilian, along with more on the languages (WABr1.195–7). With other academic suitors likely to come calling on Melanchthon, the elector gave him a raise, and Spalatin reported on this to Frederick in glowing terms (Friedensburg 1926: 89–90).

Introducing new courses proved easier than eliminating the old, but gradually the scholastic offerings were deemphasized and removed. For example, the study of Thomist philosophy was retained not simply from tradition. It had to be mastered for baccalaureate and masters' degrees. On the other hand, Luther pressed to drop Peter Lombard as a basic text and to teach instead from the Scriptures and the Fathers (WABr1.381–4). Because the path to degrees was bound so closely to certain traditional topics and approaches, it was important, if the new curriculum was to succeed, that humanist-oriented offerings also be accepted. Luther discussed that with Spalatin (WABr1.195–6). The change in course offerings meant there was some faculty shuffling. For example, when Bartholomaeus Bernhardi shifted from the arts faculty to theology, Luther argued that there was no need to continue Thomist lectures on logic because Scotist logic was also taught and would be sufficient. Cutting perceived redundancy would both weaken Aristotle and make available other offerings in new subjects. When Frederick first hesitated at the suggestion, Luther and others reiterated their argument, noting also that the money saved by cutting duplicate offerings could be used to raise Melanchthon's salary, making sure he would not be tempted to move elsewhere (WABr1.262–3, 325–6, 349–50; Friedensburg 1926: 89).

As the Reformation continued to heat up after 1519, other pressing issues often demanded the attention and energy of Luther and his colleagues, but curriculum concerns were never far from sight. The details of still more changes proposed by Melanchthon in summer 1520 are somewhat vague although it seems he wanted Aristotle studied directly from the texts without a Thomist or Scotist filter. When Luther was hidden away in the Wartburg after the 1521 Diet of Worms, Melanchthon continued to press for change.

On his way back from Worms, Elector Frederick went by way of Wittenberg to see for himself what was developing. His visit prompted more discussion between Spalatin and the faculty, led especially by Melanchthon and Rector Peter Lupinus. That in turn brought Frederick's general directive in summer 1521 charging the rector to work with Melanchthon, Nikolaus von Amsdorf, and Christian Beyer to introduce workable changes from their reform proposals. This resulted in still more deemphasizing of Aristotle and generally furthered humanist-oriented studies. The students had already gone on record in a sense some months earlier when it came to the canon law, as they used the volumes to stoke the flames of their December 1520 bonfire outside Wittenberg's Elster Gate. Now the university administration had its say when the endowment that had supported the teaching of canon law was redirected to strengthen biblical studies (Friedensburg 1926: 118–19, 1917: 131–5).

Although the course was set and would remain, the focus on humanism, Luther, and Wittenberg's university reform did not end in 1521. Remnants of the old programme hung on, while other changes would be introduced for some years to come, though not at the same pace or with the same dramatic results. At least one important older element—disputation—would return in the 1530s. This was not because the reforms had failed. Rather disputation was needed, not simply to grant academic degrees but also as a kind of apologetic self-defence, so Wittenberg's alumni could hold their own with others groomed in syllogistic hair-splitting. Nevertheless, after Frederick visited in 1521, endorsed the changes to date, and then gave instructions to proceed with more of the same, Wittenberg permanently had turned a corner. When it began, many might have expected Wittenberg to be yet another in the line of late medieval universities following a traditional pattern, but Wittenberg soon became a rallying point for humanists, an experiment in the New Learning applied in a university setting, and a focal point for evangelical theology produced by the new tools and approach.

While Luther was no humanist per se, he clearly understood the value of the tools provided and the view of life the *studia humanitatis* offered to people created in the divine image. Where once Luther sought to flee the world for what he thought would have been the shelter of the cloister to find certainty of salvation, instead he returned to embrace life in this world, living as part of God's created order, mindful of the sin that by nature still remained while filled with joy for the message of salvation by grace and faith alone for Christ's sake. It was life in the First Article of the Creed lived in the confidence in the Second Article as God sustained him in the Third—a living confession of the creedal faith that reflected the biblical message that humanism had helped Luther unpack. And it was lifelong learning right to the end. Luther's deathbed confession was evangelical theology pure and simple. Then found tucked away was a scrap with the last lines he had penned:

> No one who has not been a shepherd or a peasant for five years can understand Vergil in his *Bucolics* and *Georgics*. I maintain that no one can understand Cicero in his letters unless he has been involved in efforts to govern the state for twenty years. And let no one who has not guided congregations with the prophets for a hundred years believe he has tasted Holy Scripture thoroughly. Because of this the miracle is tremendous in John the Baptist, in Christ, and in the apostles. Lay not your hand on this divine *Aeneid*, but bow before it and adore its every trace. We are beggars. This is true! (WATR5.318, LW54.476)

Scripture as the divine *Aeneid*—the story of the journey not of Aeneas to a new city that would become Rome, but of Christians through life to a golden city, the Heavenly Jerusalem already founded, finished, and waiting. It was all important to read the signposts correctly—where one had been, is now, and is heading—so exegesis mattered greatly for the result it produced, and that is why Luther insisted that Wittenberg's approach in the 1510s had to change. 'Reformation' is used now to mean a larger movement or era. Luther first spoke of 'Reformation' in a narrower sense though he realized the implications of what was afoot. As he wrote to his old professor Joducus Trutfetter, 'I believe simply that it is impossible to reform the church if the canons, the decretals, the scholastic theology, the philosophy, and the logic as they are now are not uprooted and another study installed' (WABr1, §74). Luther and Wittenberg did just that.

REFERENCES

Bauch, Gustav (1904). 'Die Einführung des Hebräischen in Wittenberg mit Berücksichtigung der Vorgeschichte des Studiums der Sprache in Deutschland'. *Monatsschrift für Geschichte und Wissenschaft des Judentums* 48: 22–32, 77–86, 145–60, 214–23, 283–99, 328–40, 461–90.

—— (1897). 'Wittenberg und die Scholastik'. *Neues Archiv für Sächsische Geschichte und Altertumskunde* 18: 285–339.

Baylor, Michael G. (1977). *Action and Person: Conscience in the Late Scholasticism and the Young Luther.* Leiden: Brill.

Blaschka, Anton (1952). 'Der Stiftsbrief Maximilians I. und das Patent Friedrichs des Weisen zur Gründung der Wittenberger Universität'. In *450 Jahre Martin-Luther-Universität Halle-Wittenberg, vol. 1: Wittenberg 1502–1817*, ed. Leo Stern et al. Halle: Martin-Luther-Universität, 69–85.

Borchardt, Frank L. (1972). *German Antiquity in Renaissance Myth.* Baltimore: Johns Hopkins University Press.

Buck, August (1987). *Humanismus: seine Europäische Entwicklung in Dokumenten und Darstellung.* Freiburg im Breisgau: Alber.

D'Amico, John F. (1983). *Renaissance Humanism in Papal Rome: Humanism and Churchmen in the Eve of the Reformation.* Baltimore: Johns Hopkins University Press.

Dickens, Arthur Geoffrey and John M. Tonkin (1986). *The Reformation in Historical Thought.* Oxford: Blackwell.

Eisenstein, Elizabeth (1979). *The Printing Press as an Agent of Change.* Cambridge: Cambridge University Press.

Erasmus, Desiderius (1910). *Opus epistolarum, vol. 2: 1514–1517*, ed. P. S. Allen. Oxford: Oxford University Press.

Fried, Johannes (2007). *Donation of Constantine and Constitutum Constantini: The Misinterpretation of a Fiction and Its Original Meaning.* Berlin: Mouton de Gruyter.

Friedensburg, Walter (1917). *Geschichte der Universität Wittenberg.* Halle: Niemeyer.

—— (ed.) (1926). *Urkundenbuch der Universität Wittenberg.* Magdeburg: Holtermann.

Gilmore, Myron (1963). *Humanists and Jurists: Six Studies in the Renaissance.* Cambridge: Belknap.

Grane, Leif (1962). *Contra Gabrielem: Luthers Auseinandersetzung mit Gabriel Biel in der Disputatio Contra Scholasticam Theologiam 1517.* Copenhagen: Gyldendal.

—— (1975). *Modus loquendi theologicus: Luthers Kampf um die Erneuerung der Theologie (1515–1518).* Leiden: Brill.

—— (1985). 'Luther and Scholasticism'. In *Luther and Learning: The Wittenberg University Symposium*, ed. Marilyn J. Harran. Selinsgrove: Susquehanna University Press, 52–68.

Gray, Hannah Holborn (1963). 'Renaissance Humanism: The Pursuit of Eloquence'. *Journal of the History of Ideas* 25: 497–514.

Grossmann, Maria (1975). *Humanism in Wittenberg, 1485–1517.* Nieuwkoop: De Graaf.

Höss, Irmgard (1956). *Georg Spalatin, 1484–1545: Ein Leben in der Zeit des Humanismus und der Reformation.* Weimar: Böhlau.

Holborn, Hajo (1937). *Ulrich von Hutten and the German Reformation*, trans. Roland H. Bainton. New Haven: Yale University Press.

Joachimsen, Paul (1930). 'Der Humanismus und die Entwicklung des deutschen Geistes', *Deutsche Vierteljahrsschrift für Literaturwissenschaft und Geistesgeschichte* 8: 419–80.

Junghans, Helmar (1985). *Der junge Luther und die Humanisten*. Göttingen: Vandenhoeck & Ruprecht.

Kristeller, Paul (1955). *Renaissance Thought: The Classic, Scholastic and Humanist Strains*. New York: Harper & Row.

Kusukawa, Sachiko (1995). *A Wittenberg University Library Catalogue of 1536*. Binghamton, NY: Medieval & Renaissance Texts & Studies.

Lortz, Josef (1939/1968). *Die Reformation in Deutschland*, 2 vols. Freiburg im Breisgau: Herder. English translation: *The Reformation in Germany*, trans. Ronald Walls. New York: Herder.

Luther, Martin (1969). *Luther and Erasmus: Free Will and Salvation*, ed. E. Gordon Rupp and Philip S. Watson. Philadelphia: Westminster.

Moeller, Bernd (1972). 'The German Humanists and the Beginnings of the Reformation'. In *Imperial Cities and the Reformation: Three Essays*, ed. and trans. H. C. Erik Midelfort and Mark U. Edwards, Jr. Philadelphia: Fortress.

Moeller, Bernd and Karl Stackmann (1981). 'Luder-Luther-Eleuterius: Erwägungen zu Luthers Namen'. *Nachrichten der Akademie der Wissenschaften in Göttingen I. Philologisch-Historische Klasse* 7: 171–203.

Nauert, Charles G., Jr (1973). 'The Clash of Humanists and Scholastics: An Approach to Pre-Reformation Controversies'. *Sixteenth Century Journal* 4: 1–18.

Oberman, Heiko A (1963). *The Harvest of Medieval Theology: Gabriel Biel and Late Medieval Nominalism*. Cambridge, MA: Harvard University Press.

—— (ed.) (1974a). *Luther and the Dawn of the Modern Era: Papers for the Fourth International Congress for Luther Research*. Leiden: Brill.

—— (1974b). 'Headwaters of the Reformation: Initia Lutheri—Initia Reformationis'. In Oberman (1974a), 40–88.

Overfield, James (1984). *Humanism and Scholasticism in Late Medieval Germany*. Princeton: Princeton University Press.

Ozment, Steven E. (1979). 'Humanism, Scholasticism, and the Intellectual Origins of the Reformation'. In *Continuity and Discontinuity in Church History: Essays Presented to George Huntston Williams on the Occasion of his 65th Birthday*, ed. Forrester Church and Timothy George. Leiden: Brill, 133–49.

Schmidt, Oswald Gottlob (1883). *Luthers Bekanntschaft mit den alten Klassikern: Ein Beitrag zur Lutherforschung*. Leipzig: Veit.

Spitz, Lewis W. (1957). *Conrad Celtis: The German Arch-Humanist*. Cambridge, MA: Harvard University Press.

—— (1963). *The Religious Renaissance of the German Humanists*. Cambridge, MA: Harvard University Press.

—— (1974). 'Headwaters of the Reformation: Studia Humanitatis, Luther Senior, et Initia Reformationis'. In Oberman (1974a), 89–116.

—— (1975). 'The Course of German Humanism'. In *Itinerarium Italicum: The Profile of the Italian Renaissance in the Mirror of Its European Transformations*, ed. Heiko A. Oberman and Thomas A. Brady, Jr. Leiden: Brill, 371–436.

Spitz, Lewis W. (1997). 'Luther's View of History: A Theological Use of the Past'. In Lewis W. Spitz, *The Reformation: Education and History*. Aldershot and Brookfield, VT: Ashgate/ Variorum, 139–54.

Springer, Carl (2011). *Luther's Aesop*. Kirksville: Truman State University Press.

Stinger, Charles L. (1985/1998). *The Renaissance in Rome*. Bloomington: Indiana University Press.

Trinkaus, Charles (1970). *In Our Image and Likeness: Humanity and Divinity in Italian Humanist Thought*. 2 vols. Chicago: University of Chicago Press.

—— (1983). *The Scope of Renaissance Humanism*. Ann Arbor: University of Michigan Press.

CHAPTER 7

LUTHER'S TRANSFORMATION OF MEDIEVAL THOUGHT

Discontinuity and Continuity

GERHARD MÜLLER

LUTHER did not regard himself as a heretic who rejected the teaching of the church. Rather, he had sworn in his doctoral oath of 1512 to defend authentic preaching (Scheurl 1963). However, he complied with his oath according to his convictions (Lohse 1997: 109–13). The ancient church dogmas he never questioned (Markschies 1999). Nevertheless, he felt compelled to distance himself from certain teachings and practices adopted in the high and late Middle Ages, not through innovation, but by returning to the Bible and the Church Fathers, with noticeable influences from mysticism or from theologians like Bernard of Clairvaux (Köpf 1991, 2008). Therefore, his concept of 'Re-Formatio' must be earnestly explored.

I. STATUS OF RESEARCH

In 1958 Ernst Bizer declared that Luther's 'discovery of the righteousness of God' compelled him to break from his previous teaching. He abandoned his earlier 'theology of humility' and recognized that the righteousness of God is 'given through the Word' (Bizer 1958). Thereby, he is said to have abandoned much of what the Western church had taught. Gerhard Ebeling, however, highlighted his many connections to late medieval scholasticism (Ebeling 1962). Scholars therefore re-edited Luther's Psalms lectures from 1513–15 in order to assess his connections to and modifications of the medieval legacy (WA55, an uncompleted project). But the evaluation of what he took from the past and what he transformed remains controversial.

Karl-Heinz zur Mühlen demonstrated the significance of mysticism for the young Luther. This traditional element did not disappear from Luther's piety and teaching (zur Mühlen 1972; Müller 2000). In contrast, Oswald Bayer emphasized Luther's concept of God's promise, incorporating Bizer's perspective: it is not a matter of what human beings do but what God does: The understanding of the reality of creation as a gift [of God] stands in sharp contrast to a widespread late medieval opinion Luther encountered (Bayer 2009: 90–93). In contrast, Volker Leppin accentuates Luther's personal history and several late medieval traditions as seedbeds of Luther's thought and behaviour (Leppin 2006). Berndt Hamm makes a similar claim, highlighting the particular personal dynamics that generated Luther's thought and work (Hamm 1993). Matthias Haudel defines the distinction: 'as opposed to the tendencies of the Middle Ages toward juridification and moralizing ethics, reconciliation [was placed] explicitly in the... penetrating light of *biblical Heilsgeschichte*' (Haudel 2010: 300).

II. DISCONTINUITIES

II.1. Rejection of Scholasticism

In his theses 'Against Scholastic Theology' (4 September 1517) Luther delivered an all-out attack on an important part of the tradition of the Western church (WA1.224–228; LW31.9–16). In ninety-seven theses he assaulted all scholastic theologians—especially moral theologians—including Gabriel Biel, William of Occam, Duns Scotus, and Pierre d'Ailly. The influence of Aristotle on theology concerned him most. This had been the important advance in the Middle Ages: with Aristotle's help theologians thought they could solve many theological problems. Philosophy should be the handmaiden of theology (Dieter 2001). Luther thought it had become queen over God's teaching. He demanded freedom from these shackles.

'Nearly the entire, wicked ethic of Aristotle [is] hostile toward grace.' Luther substituted a different understanding of God's grace than the scholastics held: 'It is a fallacy (to think) that the teaching of Aristotle concerning happiness does not conflict with catholic teaching' (WA1.226,10–13; LW31.12). Luther placed himself squarely in the 'catholic' tradition. His opposition to Aristotle culminated in the theses: 'It is a fallacy to say that without Aristotle one cannot become a theologian... On the contrary, one only becomes a theologian without Aristotle... In short, the entirety of Aristotle relates to theology as darkness toward light' (WA1.226,14–26; LW31.14).[1]

[1.] Leppin (2006: 132) compares this to Heidelberg thesis 29 (1518): 'Whoever wishes to do philosophy with Aristotle without harming themselves must necessarily first become completely foolish in Christ' (WA1.355,2–3).

Scholasticism's great 'advance' was, in Luther's mind, a grandiose journey down the wrong path. A new direction was needed. His attack aimed at the entire discipline of philosophy. Luther emphatically refused to turn to Plato despite fifteenth-century revivals of Platonic thought (Garfagnini 1994). His concern was simple: 'It is impossible by any means to fulfil the law without the grace of God.' Luther also interpreted the law of God differently from the scholastics (Grosse 2010): 'God's grace brings about the fulfilment of righteousness exorbitantly through Jesus Christ because he abolished the law' (WA1.227,23,33–4). To a new understanding of grace and law was added a new understanding of righteousness. God's grace is clearly superior to the law and to human righteousness. In his afterword Luther declared adamantly: 'In all this we wish to say nothing, and we believe that we have said nothing, that was not in conformity with the Christian church and the church's teachings' (WA1.228,34–36; LW31:16). Can this standard assertion of that time be so brazenly asserted after Luther's renunciation of scholasticism? From this point forward, Luther grounded himself on the Holy Scriptures, Augustinian theology, and the remaining Church Fathers, presuming thereby to be 'catholic'.

With this assault the professor entered into new terrain. His theological teachers in Erfurt completely rejected him, but in Wittenberg and Nuremberg his remarks were welcomed (WA1.221–222). Christoph Scheurl wrote from Nuremberg that the local 'Staupizianer' approved of him. Scheurl did not begin this letter with the usual greeting but with the words: 'To restore the theology of Christ and to walk in his law' (WABr1.115,1–116,7; 3 November 1517). For Scheurl another type of theology, established by Christ and thus biblical, had emerged, and this theology had to produce a new ethics.

In *To the Christian Nobility of the German Nation* (1520) Luther demanded 'a good, vigorous reform' of the universities. That meant that those books of Aristotle which were considered his best should no longer be studied, his physics, metaphysics, psychology (Luther regarded Aristotle's *De anima* as his 'best book' [that is, Aristotle at his most 'Aristotelian']), and ethics because in them nothing proper was taught, neither concerning natural nor spiritual matters. On the other hand, his works on logic, rhetoric, and poetics were approved (WA1.457,7,28–458,29; LW44.200–201). Here Luther was unable to get his way. Occasionally he himself freely put Aristotle to use (Andreatta 1998). Besides, Philip Melanchthon fostered continued consideration of Aristotle in Wittenberg theology (Müller 1981; Kuropka 2002). Nevertheless, Luther turned away from scholastic methodology and stayed away throughout his life.

II.2. The Modification of Piety

As a priest Luther had experienced that indulgences made many complacent. People assumed that by paying for indulgences they were exempt from all punishment for their sins, and free from all guilt before God. Luther reacted against this. One root cause for the Reformation lay in his concern for proper pastoral care (Barth 2009). This becomes clear in Luther's 'Theses on the power of indulgences' from 1517. Luther argued that heaven exists where there is 'certainty' of salvation. This is not dependent on human action but 'entirely on God's decision' (WA1.234,7–8,31–32; LW31.27–28). One must not do everything that is in him, as some medieval theologians taught, but one must realize that he is completely dependent on the 'pronouncement, the assurance, of the forgiveness of sins' (WA1.235,12–13; LW31.29), which is only possible through 'the merits of Christ' (WA1.236,14–15; LW31.30). This 'true, proper treasure of the church' must replace every human invention. This treasure is nothing other than 'the most holy gospel of the glory and grace of God' (WA1.236,22–23; LW31.31). Christians should be urged 'to follow their head, Christ, through punishments, death, and hell'. They should not rely on a mere feeling of security (WA1.238,18–21; LW31.33). Purgatory must not frighten them any longer because Christ's cross frees believers from anxiety and anguish.

Although Luther and others had expressed such criticism earlier, his Ninety-five Theses aroused a remarkable amount of attention (Winterhager 1999: 12–21), prompting Luther to explain his thoughts more precisely in 1518–19 through many German treatises, among them one on the Lord's Supper, defining it as communion [*Gemeinschaft*] with Christ and all his saints, a sign that the believers were one body with the Son of God (WA2.743,7–22; LW35.50–51), divinely given to strengthen and exhort his own against the sin that lingers after baptism (WA2.744,19–26; LW35.53). The Lord's Supper was 'a sacrament of love'; as we receive God's love, we should show his love 'to those in need' (WA2.745,7–9,17–18,25–27; LW35.56). Many masses were celebrated, but the example of Christ was not placed before the eyes of the congregation. Instead, preachers presented various works and ways on how to live well (WA2.747,7–9; LW35.56): 'When love does not grow daily and thus transform a person so that he joins most intimately with every person, then the fruit and significance of this sacrament is not present' (WA2.748,3–5; LW35.58). Such superficial piety does not recognize that Christ joins with us in the Lord's Supper 'until he destroys sin in us entirely and makes us like him on the Last Day'. Above all, faith is necessary so that a gracious exchange 'of our sins and sufferings with Christ's righteousness' takes place (WA2.749,3–5,31–35; LW35.59–60). Luther warned that faith can completely perish through false certainty (WA2.752,2; LW35.63). The Lord's Supper is for people 'a ford, a bridge, a door, a ship, a stretcher, in which and through which we navigate from this world into eternal life' (WA2.753,17–19; LW35.66; Barth 2009: 350–5 speaks of 'the therapeutic function of the Supper'). A new piety was emerging.

The reformer saw the sacramental piety of his time grounded in the false theology of recent centuries (WA2.754,19–758,6; LW35.67–73). He called for the lay chalice and declared that a council should renew this practice (WA2.742,24–29; LW35.50) since the risk of infection was not as great as many thought 'because the people seldom' commune. Christ enjoined both forms for the entire community despite his awareness of this danger (WA2.743,3–6; LW35.50). With this claim he rejected the decision of the Council of Constance forbidding communion under both kinds (15 June 1415). Contradicting a council was dangerous because he could no longer appeal to infallible decisions of councils. That this question was a hotly disputed topic becomes apparent from the reaction Luther received. This demand quickly elicited criticism from many sides. In this treatise's second edition, he added an appendix because of it, in which he substantiated his understanding with strong words (WA2.758,8–24; LW35.73).

Still in 1519 Luther spoke out on usury and preparing for death (WA6.3–8,36–60; WA2.685–697; LW42.99–115), continuing what he deemed to be the proper legacy of the Christian tradition. In 1919 Holl labelled this the 'new construction of morality' (Holl 1923: 155–287). Thereby, he narrowed the focus of Luther's concern in a neo-Kantian fashion but based his interpretation on the reformer's direct application of the New Testament. It led Luther to call for changes in teaching and in the entire life of the church. Admittedly, he did not achieve these ambitious goals; his preface to the *German Mass* (1526) states he still was not seeing people who wanted to be serious Christians (WA19.75,3–30; LW53.64). However, he attempted to change the church's trajectory by pointing to Jesus' work of salvation and its consequences for all the baptized.

II.3. The Rupture of the System

The initiative for rupture originated from Rome: Christoph Volkmar has labelled it 'the rupture of the system' [*Systembruch*]. Already in late 1517 Cardinal Albrecht of Brandenburg sent the theses on indulgences, which Luther had sent him, with additional writings of the Wittenberg theologian, to the papal Curia (Müller 1989: 88). An exchange between Cardinal Cajetan and Luther in 1518 brought no agreement (Müller 1989: 82–3). The bull threatening excommunication, *Exsurge Domine* (15 June 1520; it had been published officially in Rome on 24 July 1520; Müller 1989: 86), was the result, but the Wittenberg theologian was not intimidated; on 10 December 1520, he burned it in Wittenberg (Brecht 1981: 403–4). The rupture became certain, however, through the bull of excommunication, *Decet Romanum Pontificem* (3 January 1521; Müller 1989: 88). Luther and his followers were barred from the fellowship of the western church (Fabisch 1991).

Already in 1520 the reformer demarcated himself sharply from Rome. He urged the emperor and the secular nobility in Germany to reform the church since the bishops were not in a position to do so. He sought to break down three 'walls' by which popes had tried to establish their claims to power. They distinguished between spiritual and secular people and claimed a higher authority for the ordained. Against this, Luther argued that everyone baptized is ordained as a 'priest, bishop, and pope' (WA6.408,11–12; LW44.129; cf. 6.405,9–411,7; LW44.123–133). This repudiated the hierarchy of the Roman church while according highest worth to all the baptized, destroying the existing foundation of the church wherever the Bible was so understood. As another 'wall' the professor identified the contention that only clergy may interpret Scripture and the pope cannot err in matters of faith (WA6.411,3–412,38; LW44.133–136). The third fortification of Roman supremacy lay in the claim that only the pope can convene a council (WA6.413,1–415,6; LW44.136–139). The professor declared that if necessary a secular noble can convene a 'proper, free council' (WA6.413,29; LW44.137). This was a bold attack on positions which the Roman Curia had constructed in recent decades, though not always successfully. Secular authorities also believed that God had called them to such tasks and they were responsible to him. Therefore, Rome had not always been able to attain its political rights above all others.

In twenty-seven points Luther commented on various issues in need of reform, including papal privileges and the large Roman Curia, which he suggested should be reduced to 1 per cent of its size (WA6.417,22–24; LW44.142–143). He demanded reform of the cloisters, the priesthood, including abolition of compulsory celibacy (WA6.440,19–28; LW44.175) and marriage laws (WA6.446,27–447,16; LW44.183–184). He strongly criticized pilgrimages, popular though they were, and proposed that the pope should stop canonizing saints (WA6.447,18–448,25; LW44.185–187). People deserved to suffer all these abuses because they 'despised [God's] holy Word of baptismal grace' (WA6.450,18; LW44.189). Luther thought that begging could be prevented by caring for the poor at home (WA6.450,22–451,19; LW44.189–191). In addition, he condemned papal meddling in secular politics (WA6.454,6–14; LW44.194–195; cf. Schneider 2011: 116–19, on Pope Julius II). The church's treatment of the Hussites needed to be considered anew (WA6.454,12–457,27; LW44.195–200). Finally, he demanded a reform of the university. He offered proposals for the reform of all faculties except the medical faculty, which he left for the 'physicians' (WA6.459,1; LW44.202). In both his last points he placed secular and ecclesiastical abuses together, putting blame also on the secular nobility for not doing everything that was necessary in his opinion, for example the abolition of brothels and the proper treatment of sexuality. Here, he asked, are we not 'all baptized for chastity?' (WA6.467,18–19; LW44.214–215).

Had the emperor and the German nobility adopted these proposals as their own, then the church in Germany would have become still more independent from Rome than the French church. But neither the emperor nor the majority of the German nobility was ready in 1520/1521 to adopt these positions. They realized that here a rupture in the system was being proposed because Luther had defined the status of being God's child on the basis of baptism as the highest status among human beings. In so doing, not only did he diminish the papal honour but also the honour of many others whose worth rested solely upon their offices, which were less important for Luther than the gift appropriated through baptism. This treatise let people recognize 'the entire breadth of the ecclesiastical and political consequences of Luther's theology' (Köpf 2010: 23). After Luther and his followers had been excluded from the church's means of grace, the Wittenberg theologian attacked this verdict and declared the papal bull to be a work of the Antichrist (WA6.597–617; Hendrix 1981; Müller 1989: 388–416). Thereby, the bridge to Latin Christendom was demolished. Luther did not see himself as an innovator, but as one who was fighting abuses, instructing the people, and asserting again the true but partially suppressed Christian message (Lohse 1997: 107–13, on Luther's sense of his own mission).

II.4. Rejection of Medieval and Late Medieval Conciliar Decisions

In 1439 the Council in Florence established seven rites as sacraments: baptism, confirmation, Eucharist, penance, Last Rites, ordination, and marriage (Denzinger 254–9, §698–702). In *On the Babylonian Captivity of the Church* (1520) Luther attacked this definition, declaring that only baptism, penance, and the Lord's Supper were sacraments. He actually wanted to speak instead about the single sacrament and the three sacramental signs (WA6.501,33–38; LW36.18). He felt compelled to enter this battle (WA6.502,5; LW36.19), expressing his position on the basis of Scripture without any qualms. The sacraments, as components of the new covenant (WA6.550,34–35; LW36.92), had to have been instituted by Christ himself and accompanied by an external sign. Therefore, prayer, for example, could not be designated as a sacrament (WA6.571,35–572,11; LW36.123–124). Thirdly, each sacrament has a particular divine promise of forgiveness of sins. On the basis of this definition, only the three mentioned sacraments remained for Luther. He wrestled with the definition of confession and absolution as a sacrament (WA6.552,28–31; LW36.95).

Luther dealt with the Eucharist in detail. First, he criticized depriving the unordained of the chalice as contradicting Scripture (WA6.502,18–503,29; LW36.20–21). Not Bohemians and Greeks but 'you Romans are the heretics and godless schismatics' (WA6.505,18–24; LW36.24). This, the 'first captivity' of the sacrament, affects 'its substance, its integrity' (WA6.507,6–7; LW36.25). No mere outward formality, this issue concerned the fullness of Christ's gift, which was being withheld from believers. The sacrament's second 'prison' was the teaching of transubstantiation. In the Lord's Supper a transformation of the elements into Christ's body and blood does not take place. Rather, his body and blood are really present under bread and wine. Luther grounded this position upon the words of institution and additionally with a Christological argument. As divinity and humanity come together in the person of Christ—Christ is not only God nor only human—so it is also in the Lord's Supper (WA6.508,2–512,6; LW36.28–35, against the Fourth Lateran Council, Denzinger 200, §430). The third 'prison', according to Luther, is the assertion that the mass is a good work, which can be credited to others (WA6.512,7–526,33; LW36.35–57). Against this doctrine Luther contended that the Lord's Supper is the last will and testament of Jesus. Therefore, it depends on the one bequeathing, what is bequeathed, and the heirs who receive it. In the Lord's Supper Jesus pledges that he will die to attain the forgiveness of sins for sinners. This is the inheritance; those who believe this promise are his heirs (WA6.513,6–514,10; LW36.37–38). Only faith in the divine promise counts as worthy preparation and legitimate use of this sacrament. The power of the mass lies 'in the words of Christ, through which he testifies that the forgiveness of sins is granted to all who believe that his body is given and his blood is shed for them' (WA6.517,22–23,34–35; LW36.43). Luther urged all with 'sorrowful, depressed, confused, ashamed, and erring consciences' to receive the sacrament. He urged this 'because the word of the divine promise in this sacrament grants the forgiveness of sins, which certainly applies to everyone who is agonized by the sting or allure of sin'. The word of this divine promise is 'the only medicine' for all sins. Indeed, trust belongs in the action of the healing God: 'Faith alone is precisely peace for the conscience' (WA6.526,22–30; LW36.57). To this end Luther encouraged every believer to receive the sacrament not as an obligation but in gratitude for this liberating gift of God.

The remaining six topics are treated much more briefly. Baptism delivers 'death and resurrection, that is, full and complete righteousness' (WA6.534,3–4; LW36.67–68). Here,

however, faith in the word of promise, namely the promised salvation, is also necessary (WA6.534,1–16, 527,33–4; LW36.67–68, 58–59). Papal laws had allowed baptism to
be nearly forgotten (WA6.537,32–538,3, 541,28–542,38; LW36.73, 79–81). Luther advocated infant baptism (WA6.538,4–25; LW36.73–74). He demanded that all human vows
must take second place behind this sacrament (WA6.538,26–541,17; LW36.74–78). In 1521
Luther said that monastic vows subordinate God's direction for human life to their own
way of living (WA8.573–669). Up to that point, only a papal dispensation could free one
from monastic vows. The reformer explained that penance had been effectively eliminated under the papacy because it was currently taught that remorse was more important than faith (WA6.543,12–13; LW36.81). Furthermore, confession and the penalties
imposed by the church had become 'excellent tools to use for the benefit and the power' of
the church (WA6.545,35–36; LW36.85). Confession and absolution too must be directed
toward faith so that ample comfort is experienced anew by those who properly receive
this sacrament (WA6. 543,5–27; LW36.81–82). Confirmation, marriage, ordination, and
Last Rites were not recognized as sacraments because they were not instituted by Christ
and do not offer the particular promise of forgiveness (WA6.549,20–571,23; LW36.91–
123). Luther rejected ordination as a sacrament most strongly, considering it to be an
invention of the church (WA6.560,20–21; LW36.106–107). In discussing the priesthood
of the baptized, he insisted that all who have been called to proclaim God's Word are to
preach that Word faithfully. This ministry does not depend on an 'ordination', which is
only 'a rite for the selection of a preacher in the church' (WA6.564,6–17; LW36.111–113).

These critical comments not only rejected decisions by councils but also attacked
the church in which these decisions had met approval. Thus, he deepened the chasm
between the church and himself since these issues concerned both academic teachings
and piety. Some of Luther's demands aimed at significant change in the church's life.

III. Future Tasks

Although Luther accepted the theological decisions of the first millennium, his criticism of the church's teaching and life was nonetheless so drastic that the church could
not tolerate him in its ranks. On what was his criticism based? Was it a cultural discrepancy that stood in the way of mutual understanding and mutual agreement? Why
did so many remain faithful to the old beliefs? Political reasons may have played a role,
but certainly not in all cases. The theological controversies which emerged from reform
were not conducive to agreement but further deepened the chasms. In addition, the theological work that went on in Rome has not received the attention it deserves (Müller
1999: 87–105). More intense research on individual persons and problems is needed
(Volkmar 2008). Furthermore, Luther's congruity with the church of his time and his
distancing himself from it must be evaluated anew.

Translated by Theodore J. Hopkins.

REFERENCES

Andreatta, Eugenio (1998). 'Aristoteles als literarische Quelle Martin Luthers'. *Lutherjahrbuch* 65: 45–52.

Barth, Hans-Martin (2009). *Die Theologie Martin Luthers. Eine kritische Würdigung*. Gütersloh: Gütersloher Verlagshaus.

Bayer, Oswald (1989). *Promissio. Geschichte der reformatorischen Wende in Luthers Theologie*, 2nd edn. Darmstadt: Wissenschaftliche Buchgesellschaft.

—— (2009). 'Ethik der Gabe'. In *Angeklagt und anerkannt. Luthers Rechtfertigungslehre in gegenwärtiger Verantwortung*, ed. Hans-Christian Knuth. Erlangen: Martin-Luther-Verlag, 45–52.

Bizer, Ernst (1958). *Fides ex auditu. Eine Untersuchung über die Entdeckung der Gerechtigkeit Gottes durch Martin Luther*. Neukirchen: Neukirchener Verlag.

Brecht, Martin (1981). *Martin Luther. Sein Weg zur Reformation 1483–1521*. Stuttgart: Calwer-Verlag.

Denzinger, Heinrich (1991). *Kompendium der Glaubensbekenntnisse und kirchlichen Lehrentscheidungen*, ed. Peter Hünermann. 37 ed. Freiburg im Breisgau: Herder.

Denzinger, Heinrich, ed. (2009). *Enchiridion symbolorum definitinionum et declarationum de rebus fidei et morum*, ed. Peter Hünermann 42. Ed., Freiburg im Breisgau: Herder.

Dieter, Theodor (2001). *Der junge Luther und Aristoteles*. Berlin: de Gruyter.

Ebeling, Gerhard (1962). *Evangelische Evangelienauslegung. Eine Untersuchung zu Luthers Hermeneutik*. Darmstadt: Wissenschaftliche Buchgesellschaft.

Fabisch, Peter (ed.) (1991). *Dokumente zur Causa Lutheri*. Münster: Aschendorff.

Garfagnini, Gian Carlo (1994). 'Art. Pico della Mirandola'. *TRE* 24: 602–6.

Grosse, Sven (2010). 'Heilsgewissheit des Glaubens. Die Entwicklung der Auffassungen des jungen Luther von Gewissheit und Ungewissheit des Heils'. *Lutherjahrbuch* 77: 41–63.

Hamm, Berndt (1993). 'Von der spätmittelalterlichen reformatio zur Reformation: der Prozeß normativer Zentrierung von Religion und Gesellschaft'. *Archiv für Reformationsgeschichte* 84: 7–82.

Haudel, Matthias (2010). 'Das evangelische Buß-, Beicht- und Versöhnungsverständnis in ökumenischer Perspektive'. *Kerygma und Dogma* 56: 299–321.

Hendrix, Scott H. (1981). *Luther and the Papacy, Stages in a Reformation Conflict*. Philadelphia: Fortress.

Holl, Karl (1923). *Gesammelte Aufsätze zur Kirchengeschichte*, 3rd edn. Tübingen: Mohr/Siebeck.

Köpf, Ulrich (1991). 'Bernhard von Clairvaux im Werk Martin Luthers. Bemerkungen zur neueren Forschung'. *Rottenburger Jahrbuch für Kirchengeschichte* 18: 225–33.

—— (2008). 'Wurzeln reformatorischen Denkens in der monastischen Theologie Bernhards von Clairvaux'. In *Reformation und Mönchtum. Aspekte eines Verhältnisses über Luther hinaus*, ed. Athina Lexutt et al. Tübingen: Mohr/Siebeck, 29–56.

—— (2010). 'Der Reformator Philipp Melanchthon'. In *Philipp Melanchthon*, ed. Friedrich Schweitzer, Sönke Lorenz, and Ernst Seidel. Neukirchen: Neukirchener Verlag, 11–26.

Kuropka, Nicole (2002). *Philipp Melanchthon: Wissenschaft und Gesellschaft, Ein Gelehrter im Dienst der Kirche*. Tübingen: Mohr/Siebeck.

Leppin, Volker (2006). *Martin Luther*. Darmstadt: Wissenschaftliche Buchgesellschaft.

Lohse, Bernhard (1997). *Martin Luther. Eine Einführung in sein Leben und sein Werk*, 3rd edn. Munich: Beck.

Markschies, Christoph (1999). 'Luther und die altkirchliche Trinitätstheologie'. In *Luther—zwischen den Zeiten*, ed. Christoph Markschies and Michael Trowitzsch. Tübingen: Mohr/Siebeck, 37–85.

Müller, Gerhard (1981). 'Die Aristoteles-Rezeption im deutschen Protestantismus'. In *Die Rezeption der Antike. Zum Problem der Kontinuität zwischen Mittelalter und Renaissance*, ed. August Buck. Hamburg: Hauswedell, 55–70.

—— (1989). *Causa Reformationis. Beiträge zur Reformationsgeschichte und zur Theologie Martin Luthers*. Gütersloh: Gütersloher Verlagshaus.

—— (1999). 'Luthers Lehre im Urteil der römische-katholischen Kirche'. In *Luther—zwischen den Zeiten*, ed. Christoph Markschies and Michael Trowitzsch. Tübingen: Mohr/Siebeck, 87–105.

—— (2000). *Die Mystik oder das Wort?* Stuttgart: Steiner.

Scheurl, Siegfried Freiherr von (1963). 'Martin Luthers Doktoreid'. *Zeitschrift für bayerische Kirchengeschichte* 32: 45–52.

Schneider, Hans (2011). 'Martin Luthers Reise nach Rom, neu datiert und neu gedeutet'. In *Studien zur Wissenschafts- und Religionsgeschichte*, Akademie der Wissenschaften zu Göttingen, ed. Werner Lehfeldt. Berlin: de Gruyter, 1–157.

Volkmar, Christoph (2008). *Reform statt Reformation. Die Kirchenpolitik Herzog Georgs von Sachsen 1488–1525*. Tübingen: Mohr/Siebeck.

Winterhager, Wilhelm Ernst (1999). 'Ablaßkritik als Indikator historischen Wandels vor 1517'. *Archiv für Reformationsgeschichte* 90: 7–71.

zur Mühlen, Karl-Heinz (1972). *Nos extra nos. Luthers Theologie zwischen Mystik und Scholastik*. Tübingen: Mohr/Siebeck.

....

CHAPTER 8

LUTHER'S TRANSFORMATION OF MEDIEVAL THOUGHT

Continuity and Discontinuity

....

VOLKER LEPPIN

ANSWERING the question of Martin Luther's continuity with the Middle Ages involves substantial questions of definition. Whenever such continuity is strongly emphasized, one must ask whether the significance of the reformational discovery is being given its due, and thus whether there were legitimate grounds for the emergence of the Evangelical confession of the faith. Whenever the break with the Middle Ages is strongly accented, the risk arises that theological convictions regarding important elements of Protestantism determine the explanation of historical events.

The historical conception of Matthias Flacius long dominated the Lutheran understanding of the Middle Ages, essentially the same image drawn centuries before the Reformation by those who like him saw themselves as combatants against the oppressive rule of the Antichrist. Heidelberg professor Carl Christian Ullmann's *Reformatoren vor der Reformation* (1841–2) is also indebted—in modern scholarly form—to this conception. Ullmann highlighted certain individuals within the panorama of medieval thinking and interpreted them only from the perspective of the Reformation. His basic assumption posited a sharp divide between Luther and the Middle Ages.

Karl Holl gave this conceptualization a definite contour. His highlighting the doctrine of justification as the genuine centre of reformational discovery (in an essay of 1917 contained in Holl 1948: 1–90) not only asserted a central point of doctrine as the essence of Lutheran theology; he also drew a sharp line between the Reformation and the Middle Ages. Heiko Augustinus Oberman (1965) stimulated essentially new aspects of this discussion in the 1960s with studies of the impact of scholastic theology on Luther. He also pointed to the importance of mysticism in this context, suggestions developed especially by Steven Ozment (1969). Even if the details of these interpretations remain matters of considerable dispute, they had made one thing abundantly clear: Luther's intellectual biography cannot be understood correctly apart from the fact that, during the important years of his education, he operated—he lived, thought, and even carved out his career as professor and monk—within the medieval church. No matter when one dates Luther's turning to his reformational insights, one is dealing here with an educated man in his thirties, whose formative years of intellectual influence lay behind him. Alongside specific arguments that emphasize the breach between the Reformation and the Middle Ages, most recent debate has focused on the question of which theoretical concepts are appropriate for clarifying the complex relationship of continuity and innovation. Berndt Hamm has opted for a model describing this as 'emergence' (Hamm and Welker 2008), which has the advantage of delineating a gradual growth while also taking sudden jolts in the process into account. Comparable to this model, borrowed from the natural sciences, the simple term 'transformation' seems more suitable for explaining different facets of development since, at its root, this term presumes the interaction between continuity and novelty. Where something is transformed, it remains to some degree and yet at the same time is converted into a different state or form. It may assume various manifestations, ranging from unbroken continuity to complex recombination.

I. Unbroken Continuity

A wealth of evidence in Luther's writings demonstrates natural continuities. This holds not only for general statements that Staupitz had 'initiated our teaching' (WATR1.245,11–12, §52), but also for very concrete contexts where Luther evinces in himself the effects of Staupitz's pastoral care. From the Coburg on 19 June 1530 Luther wrote a poignant letter of consolation to Hieronymus Weller, who was suffering *tristia spiritu*. As consolation, he referred to his own experience. In such situations, Luther explained, Staupitz had told him that such trials are necessary and useful (WABr5.519,30–32, §1670). The consolation he received from his confessor in the monastery became paradigmatic for the kind of consolation that would characterize the Reformation. Indeed, a reference from the same context in which Staupitz told him that God still had great things in store for him underscores this continuity in a quasi-prophetic way, just as the *vaticinium Staupitii* concerning Luther's future greatness is an integral part of the Table Talk. Furthermore, there are often expressions of his everyday piety, in which Luther quite deliberately maintains continuity with his origins. The reformer, some time after becoming a father, used the catechism to instruct his own children, describing it as what he, too, had learned as a child (his own *'puerilis doctrina'*, WATR1.30,27, §81). In this connection he pointed out that learning the parts of the catechism was a late medieval tradition that he himself had adapted in his own catechisms.

Direct continuities also have implications for the more central areas of Luther's work. Thus, for all the differences from late medieval translations of the Bible in his translation, even here it is possible to see a transformation, which does not have a specific reformational, but rather humanistic, form. As is well known, Erasmus, in his *Paraclesis to the New Testament* (1516), formulated a fiery appeal for translation of the Bible into the vernacular. His work with the ancient languages makes it clear that the next stage of this demand was abandoning translation from the Vulgate for translation from the original languages. Against this background Luther's Bible translation remains a bold linguistic accomplishment, programmatic and at the same time fulfilment of a humanist programme formulated before the Reformation.

Such continuities were not limited to this early phase. Even in the intra-Protestant disputes over infant baptism, Luther very naturally used an argument for continuity, thus showing clearly how determined he was to continue good traditions. In his book *Concerning Rebaptism, To Two Pastors* (1528), he explained without second thoughts:

> Were infant baptism wrong, God would certainly not have permitted it to continue so long, nor let it become so universally and thoroughly established in all Christendom; it would have sometime gone down in disgrace. (WA 26.167,23–26; LW 40.255)

Knowing that there was no positive proof for infant baptism in Scripture, Luther argued on the basis of its long recognition by the church as a valid form of the sacrament and defended this aspect of the primary sacrament of Christianity with its actual continuity even in the medieval papal church. Indeed, he used this as an argument against those who thought otherwise.

II. Apparent Continuity

Methodologically, consideration of Luther's continuity with the Middle Ages must always account as well for ideas that may contain parallels without demonstrating any direct lines of continuity. Thus, Helmar Junghans (2001) has noted that Luther's doctrine of the two realms reveals striking similarities to certain models of the relationship between emperor and pope as they were developed during the fourteenth century. He referred particularly to William of Ockham, who in several publications, especially the *Breviloquium* and the *Dialogus*, had developed a theory according to which imperial power is derived not from ecclesiastical authority, but arises from two sources. After God cursed Eve, and thus established a basic dominion, concrete forms of government were created by human deliberation and agreement.

In fact, one can see here similarities in Luther, where he accounts for governmental authorities with the premise that they are needed to fight sin. Of course, the differences should not be overlooked, either. Luther's doctrine of the two kingdoms is intricately bound up with the doctrine of two realms, and therefore with the doctrine of law and gospel, which is not found in Ockham in this particular context. Luther's knowledge of Ockham's political writings was minimal as well. For Luther, Ockham was relevant chiefly as an author of scholarly theological publications. As such Luther had perceived him primarily through the mediation of Gabriel Biel. That he became more intensely interested in writings from Occam's church-political phase after 1324, or had ever even taken notice of them, cannot be substantiated.

These apparent continuities are found not only in this context but also in the doctrine of justification. In the fourteenth century Thomas Bradwardine had used the formulation 'by faith alone' to describe the justification of sinners (*De causa Dei* l.1, c. 43). This does not, however, prove any connection to Luther, nor would it be appropriate to identify this squarely with Luther's doctrine of justification since the central theological position which Luther assigned to this teaching is missing in Bradwardine. The case of Bradwardine's contemporary, Gregory of Rimini, is a little more complex. Rimini developed a strong doctrine of predestination and saw predestination as embracing the call of the human being, justification, and glorification (*vocatio, iustificatio,* and *glorificatio*). All of these were purely the effects of God's grace, and they countered original sin in human beings in that, although original sin in its essence indeed remained, human beings no longer stood under its condemnation. When these phrases are read from a sixteenth-century standpoint, they sound much like *simul iustus et peccator*— so much, in fact, that researchers, especially Oberman, searched for connections with Luther, plausible especially since Gregory himself was an Augustinian monk. Although it cannot be confirmed that Wittenberg adopted its own *via Gregorii*, the widespread critique of Oberman's theory that Luther cited Gregory for the first time in 1519 must be revised in light of Jun Matsuura's new edition of the Erfurt 'Annotations', which underlines the likelihood that Luther had knowledge of Gregory even during his time in Erfurt (AWA9.696.12–14). Nonetheless, since the evidence at hand is scarcely sufficient to maintain an extensive influence of Gregory on Luther, these suggestions attest for the time being to parallels, rather than continuities, of intellectual lines. On the other hand, this conclusion should not be underestimated, for it reveals the range of potentially plausible ideas into which Luther's new theology came. Some of the ideas he represented could just as well have been thought or spoken of in a similar manner earlier, and it was not until the confessional boundaries emerged that this or that statement could be attributed to the respective camps of Reformation or Roman Catholicism.

III. Enlarging Social Horizons

The picture is different in regard to Luther's extension of medieval patterns for living and social order as the Reformation developed. Bernd Moeller (1998) interpreted the Reformation, to use Johannes Schilling's formulation, as a 'new monasticism'. Max Weber's idea of Protestantism as 'inner-worldly asceticism' partially anticipated this observation although his judgement focused more on Calvinism than Lutheranism. The extension of the monastic ethos into the actual practice of the daily life of the people became concrete when one considers how, for instance, according to the Freedom of the Christian the inner person should gain the upper hand over the outer. These words of counsel, which Luther does not give to monks but to all believers, sound just like an ascetic mastery of self. To address the core message of the Reformation more acutely: the doctrine of justification offered the immediate access to God that previously had been limited to mystically gifted individuals living the monastic life, to all believers.

Combined with this doctrine is another more radical extension of social values: the genesis of the idea of the universal priesthood. It took the attribution of the priesthood away from those ordained or consecrated for holy service and transferred it to all the baptized:

> Whoever crawls out of baptism can boast that he has already been consecrated a priest, bishop, and pope... It follows from this argument that there is truly no essential difference among laity, priest, prince, bishop, as they say, in terms of responsibility or assignment, and in terms of their place in society.
>
> (WA6.408,11f. 26–28; cf. LW 44.128)

But precisely in separating the priesthood from the sacrament of ordination was Luther able to draw on a medieval tradition with which he had been acquainted, at least in principle, since 1515 through his reading of Johannes Tauler. Tauler declared in a sermon: 'This godly person is an inward person, who should be a priest' (Tauler 1910: 164,34–165,1). Thus, on a metaphorical level, the status of the mystical life—among both men and women—was elevated, and the clerical hierarchy, at least in terms of the respect accorded it, was significantly reduced. Nonetheless, priesthood remained in a monastic context and was referred to a particular way of life. It was precisely here that Luther's transformation constituted an expansion of the social horizon. Inasmuch as for him all who have crawled out of the baptismal font have been consecrated priests and bishops, he was redefining a clear designation that lost its nature as a distinguishing mark within Christian society, transferring all people, as a matter of principle, into the status of priest. The continuity in this abolition of the special place of the ordained priesthood is just as clear as the explosive force that lay in the very nature of this transformation. The conception of the universal priesthood, cited from Luther's *Open Letter to the German Nobility*, served in this concrete literary context to encourage the nobility in Germany to take responsibility for the destiny of the church. This idea, too, had been discussed in the Middle Ages, again by Ockham, who, in the face of papal failings at his time, considered the emperor a legitimate agent for church reform. With Luther this consideration—now a specific transformation of what had been a mystical expression—acquired a force of its own, which was then put into reformational practice. At this point it is still possible to detect a rather substantial continuity that was decisive for the translation of reformational theology into reformational action and perhaps represents the actual key to this process.

IV. Reformational Breakthrough

The element of discontinuity within continuity becomes clearer in those transform-ative processes in which Luther draws on late medieval traditions and, on the basis of his reformational theology, breaks with them in such a way that they are placed into a new context. This is particularly evident in the transformation of concepts from late medieval mysticism into the teaching of law and gospel. This underly-ing transformative process is particularly evident in those statements of Luther according to which the law prepares the soil for the gospel, e.g., in his church postils of 1522:

> Second, God's design in the law is to enable the human being to know himself; to per-ceive the false and unjustified state of his heart and how far he is from God and how utterly his nature amounts to nothing, so that he disdain his own honourable way of living and recognize it is nothing in comparison to what belongs to the fulfilling of the law. So humbled, he may creep to the cross, immerse himself in Christ, for his grace, and give up on himself and place all his comfort on Christ.
>
> (WA10,1.1.455,5–11; CP6.272)

This is a synopsis of Augustine's statement in *De spiritu et littera*: 'the law is given that we may seek grace; grace is given that we may fulfil the law' (*Lex ergo data est, ut gratia quaereretur, gratia data est, ut lex inpleretur*) (CSEL60.187,22 3). But the sharpness with which Luther in his church postils addresses the vanity of human deeds as the objective of the preaching of the law points to a broader background. According to his later Antinomian Disputations, the objective of the law is *despera-tio* (WA39,1.50,36–37, 40,1.368, 12.32–33). This term points to a continuity with the late medieval theology of penance; in fact, Luther could describe *desperatio* in the Heidelberg Disputation as God's *opus alienum* (WA1.357,6–8). In the *Resolutiones* to his disputation against indulgences, written around the same time as the Heidelberg Disputation, Luther uses this term to signify a true *contritio cordis* (WA1.540,23–25). Once again, this concept has a solid place in mystical theology, and especially in Johann Tauler:

> Die dirte porte von disen daz ist ein war wesenlicher ruwe der súnden. Welicher ist daz? Das ist ein gantz war abeker von allem dem daz nút luter Got enist oder des Got nút ein ware sache enist, und ein war gantz zuoker zuo Gotte mit allem dem daz man ist. (Tauler 1910: 36, 10–14)

Luther had more than merely a general awareness of this concept; indeed, continuity with such reflections can be linked directly to his own reading experiences. In his copy of Tauler's sermons he made a brief marginal note: '*Hoc* nota tibi', in a place where con-trition is described in terms of recognizing one's own nothingness:

...so ile und tring dich in Got als swintlich das dir die sunde zemole enphallent, ob du der mitte zuo der bichte kumest, das du ir nut enwissest ze sagende. Dis ensol dich nut entsetzen; es enist dir nut uf gevallen ze schaden, sunder zuo eine bekent- nisse dines nichtes und zuo einer versmehunge din selbes in einer gelossenheit, nut in einer swermuotikeit. (Tauler 1910: 355.36–356,2; cf. WA9.104,11–14)

This is even more radical than Luther's words cited above on the effect of the law, and precisely in this it is possible to trace a specific way in which Luther transformed earlier ideas. Quite early Luther manifested a high regard for the element of remorse in the medi- eval practice of penance. His reading of Tauler deepened, perhaps even to some extent prompted, this tendency. With an increasing emphasis on the Word as God's means of salvation, however, Luther breached these insights of penance-theology with a theology centred on God's Word and described remorse as something produced by the law.

Still more striking is the fact that Luther not only borrowed this idea from mystical thought but also adopted the dialectical structure mentioned above, according to which the law leads to the destruction of the self, and the gospel of Christ raises up the believer again. Even in mysticism the detrimental effect of penance is only a first step—a prere- quisite to the crucial second step. Tauler explains:

und daz ist alleine der kerne und daz marg des ruwen; und dan mit einer versaster getrúwunge versinken in das minnenkliche luter guot das Got ist, und an ime und in ime iemer zuo blibende und anzuohangende mit minnen und mit luterre meinunge in eime vollen bereiten willen, den liebsten willen Gottes zuo tuonde also verre also er mag. (Tauler 1910: 36.14–18)

Thus, there is a striking parallel between Luther's doctrine of law and gospel and the mystical description of the way of salvation. The gracious acts of God follow upon a destructive annihilation of the human self and a person's own stubbornness, and this sequence is by no means coincidental but so designed by God. Yet, in contrast to the par- allel found in the doctrine of the two realms, for which (see above) no literary continuity was discovered, one may trace the genesis of the doctrine of law and gospel in this con- text, piece by piece, out of mystical teaching—albeit not in such a way that it represents a simple linear development. Rather, the continuity persists through a breakthrough, the roots of which lie in Luther's new emphasis on the Word of God. Here, a gradual transformation took place towards a new configuration of basic theological coordinates. More explicitly than the mystics, Luther attributed the negative precursory aspect of the destruction of reliance on human effort to God, or to his external Word. This changed the mode of transformation, but it did not erase the underlying continuity as such.

V. COMPLEX RECOMBINATIONS

From what has just been explained, it is clear that the phenomenon of the transforma- tion Luther wrought cannot, as a general rule, be described in linear fashion. Were this the case, then attempts to set Luther apart from the Middle Ages, some quite radical, would be altogether unthinkable, with their plausibility stemming from the particular emphasis they give to the innovative elements present in every transformation. There are therefore elements in which Luther's continuity with the Middle Ages comprises a number of aspects, which enable explanations of what is new in his thought only in the context of medieval settings. Particularly complex is the question of the central teaching of Luther's theology: the doctrine of justification, Holl's mark distinguishing Luther from the past (Holl 1948). Here an emphasis on continuity cannot mean that Luther's reformational insights are equated simply with elements he inherited from the tradition. That would make the historic event just as incomprehensible as would an emphasis on innovation in his thought which ignored elements of continuity altogether.

Besides the simple parallels within the doctrine of justification mentioned above, there are definitely powerful elements of genuine continuity as well. These continuities do not suggest that Luther's own discoveries, based on his reading of Augustine and Paul, have less significance for the development of justification. They do aid understanding of the horizon of plausibility against which Luther was able to discover what he discovered in these widely read authors.

Crucial for this discovery was the influence of scholasticism on Luther. Particularly Werner Dettloff (1963), who studied the subject in the context of discussion within the monastic orders, especially the Franciscans, has shown that the *via moderna* developed the concept that persons could be accepted by God directly, without sacramental preparation. The doctrine of God's power formed the background for this idea. While God had established a certain order of salvation according to his 'ordained or ordered' power, de potentia ordinata, upon which human beings could also depend in the ordinary performance of the sacraments, he also wielded the ability by his absolute power, *de potentia absoluta*, to act in ways that did not correspond to the ordinary course of events but broke through them. In this way God was also able to call Paul, for instance, despite the fact that the future apostle did not have a previous disposition towards the gospel. Such reflections, which Luther took from Gabriel Biel, could be interpreted and used in more than one way, possibly leading to Pelagian-sounding phrases intimating that sinners are justified 'by exercising purely natural powers', *ex puris naturalibus*, yet potentially highlighting grace.

Decisive for the further formulation of Luther's doctrine of grace was another current of the tradition, mysticism. Critical for understanding how he came to the doctrine of justification is the idea of 'nearby grace' (Hamm 2004), whereby Christ draws close to a person in a manner that overcomes the common medieval gradualism, thus creating a new immediacy. This immediatization creates a relationship with God which no longer depends strictly on intermediary channels such as the clergy, giving rise to formulations in which Luther's message of justification almost seems to have been formed at this earlier stage. For example, Tauler explained that human beings receive salvation 'no more by human works or merit but by pure grace and by the merits of our Lord Jesus Christ' (Tauler 1910: 123, 7–8). Although this statement may appear to be isolated, it is nevertheless far more significant than the formulas cited above from Bradwardine and Gregory. In the case of Luther's extensive reception of Tauler, therefore, also a real continuity is evident. Just how important these mystical influences were for Luther, can be felt in the *Freedom of the Christian*: 'Not only does faith give so much that the soul becomes one with the divine Word, but also it unites the soul with Christ, as a bride with her bridegroom' (WA7.25,26–28; cf. translation from the Latin, LW31.351).

It is so obvious that this image of the bride and groom is rooted in the mystical theology of Bernard of Clairvaux, and then mediated to Luther through Staupitz, that it would require some effort to deny the strong line of continuity which this manner of speaking about justification shows. As a matter of fact, Luther's doctrine of justification does not simply correspond to medieval models, but it stands in continuity with medieval traditions insofar as Luther refined, sorted out, and converted them into a new complex overall structure.

Luther's complex relation to the late Middle Ages cannot be grasped by a simple yes or no to the question of continuity. Different modes of transformation pertain to very different domains of his thought and activity, which could be comprehended here only by means of particular elements and examples. Each has its own context: the continuation of catechetical teaching had a much different function for Protestant self-understanding than the genesis of the doctrine of justification. Both these examples demonstrate that only a finely tuned consideration of the many strands of continuity in which Luther lived and thought will make his own completed transformations understandable. Only then will it be possible to recognize what in him is actually new.

Translated by David Preus

REFERENCES

Dettloff, Werner (1963). *Die Entwicklung der Akzeptations- und Verdienstlehre von Duns Scotus bis Luther*. Münster: Aschendorff.

Hamm, Berndt (2004). *The Reformation of Faith in the Context of Late Medieval Theology and Piety: Essays*, ed. Robert J. Bast. Leiden: Brill.

Hamm, Berndt and Michael Welker (2008). *Die Reformation. Potentiale der Freiheit*. Tübingen: Mohr/Siebeck.

Holl, Karl (1948). *Gesammelte Aufsätze zur Kirchengeschichte*. Bd. 1: *Luther 7*. Tübingen: Mohr/Siebeck.

Junghans, Helmar (2001). 'Das mittelalterlicher Vorbild für Luthers Lehre von den beiden Reichen'. In Junghans, *Spätmittelalter, Luthers Reformation, Kirche in Sachsen. Ausgewählte Aufsätze*, ed. Michael Beyer and Günther Wartenberg. Leipzig: Evangelische Verlagsanstalt, 11–30.

Moeller, Bernd (1998). 'Die frühe Reformation in Deutschland als neues Mönchtum'. In *Die frühe Reformation in Deutschland als Umbruch*, ed. Moeller. Gütersloh: Gütersloher Verlagshaus, 76–91.

Oberman, Heiko Augustinus (1965). *Der Herbst der mittelalterlichen Theologie*. Zürich: EVZ-Verlag. English translation: *The Harvest of Medieval Theology*. Cambridge, MA: Harvard University Press, 1963.

Ozment, Steven Edgar (1969). *Homo spiritualis: A Comparative Study of the Anthropology of Johannes Tauler, Jean Gerson and Martin Luther in the Context of their Theological Thought*. Leiden: Brill.

Tauler, Johannes (1910). *Die Predigten Taulers aus der Engelberger und der Freiburger Handschriften sowie aus Schmidts Abschriften der ehemaligen Straßburger Handschriften*, ed. Ferdinand Vetter. Berlin: Weidmann.

Ullmann, Carl (1841–2). *Reformatoren vor der Reformation*, 2 vols. Hamburg: Perthes.

SUGGESTED READING

Bizer, Ernst (1966). *Fides ex auditu. Eine Untersuchung über die Gerechtigkeit Gottes durch Martin Luther*, 3rd edn. Neukirchen: Neukirchener Verlag.

Hamm, Berndt, Bernd Moeller, and Dorothea Wendebourg (1995). *Reformationstheorien. Ein kirchenhistorischer Disput über Einheit und Vielfalt der Reformation*. Göttingen: Vandenhoeck & Ruprecht.

Junghans, Helmar (1985). *Der junge Luther und die Humanisten*. Göttingen: Vandenhoeck & Ruprecht.

Leppin, Volker (2008). *Die Wittenberger Reformation und der Prozess der Transformation kultureller zu institutionellen Polaritäten*. Stuttgart and Leipzig: Verlag der Sächsischen Akademie der Wissenschaften.

—— (2010). 'Luther's Transformation of Late Medieval Mysticism'. *Lutheran Forum* 44: 25–9.

McGrath, Alister (1987). *The Intellectual Origins of the European Reformation*. Oxford: Blackwell.

Oberman, Heiko Augustinus (ed.) (1974). 'Headwaters of the Reformation. Initia Lutheri—Initia Reformationis'. In *Luther and the Dawn of the Modern Era: Papers for the Fourth International Congress for Luther Research*. Leiden: Brill, 40–88.

—— (1981), *Gregor von Rimini. Werk und Wirkung bis zur Reformation*. Berlin: de Gruyter.

Oberman, Heiko Augustinus and Frank A. James (eds.) (1991). *Via Augustini: Augustine in the Later Middle Ages, Renaissance and Reformation. Essays in Honour of Damasus Trapp*. Leiden: Brill.

Saak, Eric Leeland (2002). *High Way to Heaven. The Augustinian Platform between Reform and Reformation 1292–1524*. Leiden: Brill.

Steinmetz, David C. (1980). *Luther and Staupitz: An Essay in the Intellectual Origins of the Protestant Reformation*. Durham: Duke University Press.

PART III

THE HERMENEUTICAL PRINCIPLES THAT GUIDED LUTHER'S TEACHING AND PREACHING

CHAPTER 9

....

LUTHER ON GOD AND HISTORY

....

MARK THOMPSON

I. 'This Governance of God'

....

THE remembrance of past events supplies faith with comfort and nourishment (WATR 1: 545.14–15, §1077). Five hundred years on, we are used to seeing Martin Luther as a man who made history. The tremendous reforming power unleashed in the course of his teaching, preaching, and writing in the mid-1510s transformed Europe. His stand against the papacy and the empire inspired and continues to inspire generations of Christians. Its repercussions in time reached as far as Australia, literally on the other side of the world. Of course, Luther, like all caught up in the middle of such events, could not know that his legacy would endure. It all seemed so fragile at the time, under assault from all sides. Indeed, only a matter of months after his death the Catholic emperor's soldiers marched through the streets of Wittenberg, and Luther's wife Katherine had to flee. Nevertheless, for all the uncertainty about the immediate future, Luther spoke and wrote from within a series of firm convictions about the time in which he lived and the nature of history itself. These were most certainly sixteenth-century convictions, shaped in large measure by the approach of Augustine. The revolution in historiography associated with von Ranke and others was still three hundred years in the future. In contrast, Luther's method was 'pre-modern and uncritical' (though at points, such as his evaluation of the *Donatio Constantini*, a humanist concern for verification via primary sources opens up other possibilities) (Wriedt 1996: 45). What is more, his convictions about history were inextricably tied to wider, more explicitly theological considerations.

II. Scholarly Interest in Luther's Understanding of History

Luther's historical perspective has come under scrutiny from historians and theologians alike in recent decades. This research has largely built upon work done early in the twentieth century by Walther Köhler, Hanns Lilje, and Hans H. Pflanz. Köhler demonstrated Luther's familiarity with key historical sources from the patristic and medieval periods. In preparing to defend his theses Luther expressed, in accord with Augustine, Aquinas, and others, a conviction that world history is a divine phenomenon (Köhler 1900). Lilje highlighted the influence of Renaissance humanism on Luther's appeal to history, his use of apocalyptic imagery, and his sense that the Ottoman threat in Europe was a sign that the end is near (Lilje 1932). Pflanz drew attention to Luther's discussion of the two kingdoms in *On Bound Choice*—history is played out in a conflict between the kingdom of God and the kingdom of Satan (WA18.743.29–744,2; LW33.227; Pflanz 1939: 17–19).

However, contemporary interest in Luther's concept of history is most often traced to the work of Heinrich Bornkamm. Bornkamm treated the subject amidst a collection of essays entitled *Luther's World of Thought* (1958) and in *Luther and the Old Testament* (1960). He observed that Luther interpreted all history in a thoroughly theological manner: 'faith inquires into the invisible background of historical space' (Bornkamm 1958: 202). With the sharpened eyes of faith Luther saw in that space 'an incessant struggle between divine and satanic powers' played out through 'three essential factors that shape history: the nation, the law and the great men' (Bornkamm 1958: 202, 196). He contrasted the nation with the 'mob', the law with violence, and great men with those who ape them. Luther, Bornkamm insisted, was confident that God administers history with an absolute and yet ultimately inscrutable sovereignty: 'all events of history, all men of history, and all forces of history are masks of God who works all in all' (Bornkamm 1958: 203). On both the large and the small scale, God is at work both to effect salvation and to exercise judgement. Yet even in the midst of exacting judgement, God does not withdraw his gifts from the world (Bornkamm 1985: 211). In this way, the history of the nations and the history of faith are not two distinct and distant things. Mercy and judgement form an invisible whole.

> History, as God's field, is in none of its traits profane or irrelevant to either him or us. Rather, it is in its whole development judgment history [*Zornesgeschichte*] and salvation history [*Heilsgeschichte*], always full of decision, threat, and grace.
>
> (Bornkamm 1969: 64)

Bornkamm addressed the First International Congress on Luther Research in 1956, calling for a continuation of the research begun in Köhler's work. Heinz Zahrnt had already published his classic monograph, insisting that Luther really only knew one kind of history, sacred history, since God's rule extends over every area of life. For Luther, 'final expectation and political self-statement', eschatology and history, are not mutually exclusive but are carried by each other (Zahrnt 1952: 18, 21, 133).

John Headley responded to Bornkamm's challenge in 1963 with *Luther's View of Church History*. Headley introduced a number of important distinctions made by Luther into the discussion, namely those between God's nature and his activity, between the preached God and the hidden God, and between the absolute and the ordained power of God. 'Second only to the recognition of the sole effectiveness of God in history, is the idea of the divine concealment for the understanding of history' (Headley 1963: 4). Serving this basic idea is Luther's conception of the two kingdoms—the kingdom of God's right hand and the kingdom of God's left hand:

> With the categories of the two kingdoms, Luther is able to accent the redemptive nature of God's action in time and to emphasize history as an exercise in faith far more effectively than he could with the categories of Creation...Wherever in the world the work of Christ is effective through the instrument of the Word, there world history assumes the character of redemptive history. (Headley 1963: 17)

While Luther's understanding of history displayed certain similarities with that of Augustine, important distinctions are discernible:

> Unlike Augustine, Luther lived and thought in the shadow of the impending end of this historical course; his eschatology reflected that of the New Testament. Secondly, the themes of this history for Luther were faith and unbelief. These themes do not pertain to Augustine in the same way...Finally, the Church was fully and really present for Luther from the beginning of time and was not [simply] prefigured before Christ's birth. (Headley 1963: 267)

One of the most significant interpretations of Luther's life and theology in the last quarter of the twentieth century remains Heiko Oberman's *Luther: Man between God and the Devil* (1989). Oberman stressed the deeply eschatological character of Luther's understanding of history. Human history is the arena of the struggle against the enemies of the gospel, 'for where God is at work—in man and in human history—the Devil, the spirit of negation, is never far away' (Oberman 1989: 12). Adapting Augustine and Bernard, Luther saw three epochs of history: the time of the persecutors, the time of the heretics, and the time of the destroyers (Oberman 1989: 270). Yet he was no Chiliast, seeking to transform society in preparation for the millennium. He believed that an intensification of opposition to the gospel would precede the great final-day Reformation. In his second series of Psalms lectures, Luther saw only an eschatological resolution to this struggle: 'Thus the only thing that can comfort you in this last stage is the Day of Judgement and your faith that the Lord rules in Eternity—ultimately all the godless will vanish' (AWA2.615.1–3).

Winfried Vogel picked up this and similar insights into Luther's thinking about history (1986). He drew attention to the way in which, during a sermon on Luke 21 preached on 5 December 1529 (WA29.617–624), Luther felt free to apply the apocalyptic language of Scripture to current events:

> The darkening of the sun, for example, means that Christ's light does not shine in Christendom any more and that the gospel is not being preached. The falling of the stars is the loss of faith on the part of those who want to become monks or priests in order to earn their salvation. Christ, Luther says, is the Sun, the church is the moon, and the Christians are the stars. The rush and brawl of water and wind is the discord of the world, and the lack of discipline that has gained so much ground. The term 'the day breaks' means that the gospel will 'rise' and be preached in anticipation of the last day! (Vogel 1986: 255)

Luther was not comfortable with attempts to be more specific. On the basis of Matthew 24:36 he rejected contemporary Johannes Stöffler's 1499 prediction of an eschatological flood in 1524 and Michael Stiefel's attempt to set the time of the Second Coming for 8 a.m. on 19 October 1533 (WABr6.462–463; Vogel 1986: 256–7; Luther to Stiefel, 26 June 1533). Nevertheless, Luther supported his own sense of the imminence of the end with some calculations of his own. In 1541 he produced his *Reckoning of the Years of the World* (*Supputatio annorum mundi* WA53.22–172), a chronological table in which he mapped out the expected six thousand years of the earth's history culminating in or around the year 1540. The final sixth millennium would not be completed in full, on analogy with the uncompleted three days between the crucifixion and resurrection (WA53.171; Vogel 1986: 257–8).

Lewis Spitz examined Luther's developing interest in history, perhaps stemming from his work in preparation for the Leipzig Disputation in July 1519. Just a few years later he lamented that he did not know more about history.

> How I regret now that I did not read more poets and historians, and that no one taught me them! Instead, I was obliged to read at great cost, toil and detriment to myself, that devil's dung, the philosophers and sophists, from which I have all I can do to purge myself.
>
> (*To the councilmen of all cities in Germany that they establish Christian schools* 1524, WA15.46,18–21; LW34:370)

Luther appears to have made up for that lack in the years that followed. Ancient writers were cited frequently in his table-talk; he wrote an attack upon the *Donatio Constantini* in 1537 (WA50.69–89), discussed Tacitus at length with Melanchthon on a journey to Torgau in 1537, and wrote a number of significant prefaces to historical works (Spitz 1989: 140–1).

The first decade of the twenty-first century witnessed the publication of several important studies of Luther's approach to history. Otto Hermann Pesch contrasted Luther's eschatological treatment, based on a conviction of the imminent end, with Aquinas' more cyclical understanding of history based on a particular concept of creation (Pesch 2000: 136). Pesch observed that Luther habitually illustrated biblical assertions with historical examples, yet spoke of the way God's work was hidden from human beings. Luther's famous sense of obligation as an appointed doctor within the church was tied to his view of the moment of history in which he stood: he was obligated 'to strengthen his sisters and brothers in the last fight against the temptations of the Antichrist' (Pesch 2000: 135–6).

Particularly significant is Wieland Kastning's penetrating and insightful study. Luther came to value history not simply as a source for sermon illustration but also for attaining general wisdom, though he acknowledged important limits here and the necessity of assistance from the Holy Spirit (Kastning 2008: 30–2). An appeal to history did not, however, exist in isolation or independence from the appeal to Scripture. So at Leipzig Luther described history as 'the mother of truth' (*mater veritatis*)—intriguingly distinguishing between Bartolomeo Platina's histories and history itself—while later he distinguished between the *a priori* function of Scripture and the *a posteriori* function of history when it came to engaging with the papacy (Kastning 2008: 36–8; cf. *Disputatio I. Eccii et M. Lutheri Lipsiae habita*, 1519, WA2.289,13–14; 'Vorrede zu R. Barus, Vitae Romanorum pontificum', 1536, WA50.5,26–28; cf. Oberman 1989: 259). Underlying these convictions, Kastning suggests, was Luther's perception of an eschatological unfolding of the unity of reality: it is only as we endure the vacillations of affirmation and negation, affliction and comfort, wrath and grace, the silence of God and the event of his Word, that we gain even the most tentative grasp of what is real and what ultimately is the object of faith (Kastning 2008: 16).

How is God's work in history to be related to his saving work? Volker Leppin explores this connection, drawing attention to the 'anthropological counterparts' through which God accomplishes his purposes in history. Luther could speak of Alexander the Great and Hannibal as masks (*larvae*) of God, and of the papacy since Gregory I as the Antichrist (Leppin 2009: 606, 604). He also understood the Turks (Islam) as the fleshly counterpart of the papacy as the spiritual anti-Christ, appealing to biblical texts such as Matthew 7 and 24 and Ezekiel 38. On the other hand, he expected something different from the Jews. His own early attempts to evangelize Jews whom he encountered were fuelled by his expectation that there would be an end-time turning of the Jews en masse to Christ (Leppin 2009: 605).

Scholarly interest in Luther's approach to history shows no signs of abating. Making sense of what is going on around us is as urgent a Christian enterprise as ever and Luther's perspective, as one caught up in the middle of tumultuous events which appeared to defy resolution, promises insight into our own situation some five hundred years later.

III. LUTHER'S KNOWLEDGE OF HISTORY

In 1536 Luther admitted he had not known much history when he first engaged the theologians of Rome:

> At first I was not very skilled in history. I attacked the papacy *a priori* (as they say), from Holy Scripture. Gladly, others now confirm my results *a posteriori*, from history. (WA50.5,26–28)

He had earlier written to the councilmen of the German cities encouraging them to set up schools where, among other things, history could be taught. Here he set out the benefits as he saw them of the study of history:

> But if children were instructed and trained in schools, or wherever learned and well-trained schoolmasters and schoolmistresses were available to teach the languages, the other arts, and history, they would then hear of the doings and sayings of the entire world, and how things went with various cities, kingdoms, princes, men and women. Thus, they could in a short time set before themselves as in a mirror the character, life, counsels, and purposes—successful and unsuccessful—of the whole world from the beginning, on the basis of which they could then draw the proper inferences and in the fear of God take their own place in the stream of human events. In addition, they could gain from history the knowledge and understanding of what to seek and what to avoid in this outward life, and be able to advise and direct others accordingly. (WA15.45,12–22; LW45.368–369)

Luther quickly sought to overcome his own ignorance of history. In preparation for the Leipzig Disputation (1519) he studied Rufinus' Latin translation of Eusebius' *Church History*. When Eck sought to associate Luther's ideas with those of the condemned heretic Jan Hus, he found Luther had a rather more extensive knowledge of the issues surrounding the Council of Constance than he had anticipated (Brecht 1985: 317–22). The necessity of debate and particularly of countering the appeal to history by his opponents led Luther to appreciate the usefulness of history as confirmatory evidence. However, as his statement at Worms made clear, he did not regard arguments from history as a substitute for an appeal to his final authority, Holy Scripture. The line of dependence ran in one direction only. For Luther '[t]he authority and veracity of history as a knowledge derive from its agreement with Scripture' (Headley 1963: 44).

In later life Luther enjoyed engaging his colleagues and students in discussion about the great histories of the past, with which he was becoming increasingly familiar. Sometimes his comments were critical, as when in his lectures on Genesis in 1542 he remarked on their lack of glory of God's Word: 'Indeed, what is history without the Word of God?' (WA43.672,17; LW5.353). At other times he could consider them remarkably truthful, as when Tacitus observed that the German people were drunkards (*Wider

Hans Wurst, 1541, WA51.548,27–31; LW41.239; there he also demonstrated knowledge of Suetonius' work, WA51.553,11–13; LW41.244). He could even anticipate contemporary historical concerns, at least in part, as, for example, when he observed that Livy had written the Roman view of history and not that of Carthage or of the other nations which had been conquered (Spitz 1989: 142).

In later life Luther wrote prefaces to a number of contemporary pieces of historical work. The best known of these historical pieces was Galeatius Capella's *Commentarii…de rebus gestis pro restitutione Francisci II, Mediolanensium Ducis* (1538). Luther's preface contained a number of important comments on the importance of history:

> For since histories describe nothing else than God's work, that is, grace and wrath, it is only right that one should believe them, as though they were in the Bible. They should therefore indeed be written with the very greatest diligence, honesty and truthfulness. (WA50.383,17–384,9; LW34.277–278)

IV. LUTHER'S THEOLOGICAL FRAMEWORK FOR UNDERSTANDING HISTORY

Luther's developing understanding of history was bound to be, like his understanding of everything else in life, deeply theological. He made the point quite fulsomely in the preface to Capella's history:

> Upon thorough reflection one finds that almost all laws, art, good counsel, warning, threatening, terrifying, comforting, strengthening, instruction, prudence, wisdom, discretion, and all virtues well up out of the narratives and histories as from a living fountain. It all adds up to this: histories are nothing else than a demonstration, recollection, and sign of divine action and judgment, how He upholds, rules, obstructs, prospers, punishes, and honors the world, and especially men, each according to his just desert, evil or good. And although there are many who do not acknowledge God or esteem him, they must nevertheless come up against the examples and histories and be afraid lest they fare like those individuals whom the histories portray.
>
> (WA50.385,15–18; LW34: 275–276)

Luther's commitment to viewing all reality as God's creation kept him from treating human history in isolation from God's rule and purpose. This 'unity of reality' is ultimately only eschatologically manifest, yet it nevertheless underlies what remains quite diverse and diffuse in our experience of history (Kastning 2008: 16). History, like everything else in the natural world, is a vehicle for the accomplishment of God's purpose, even if the precise correlation remains hidden from us. Certainly Luther was confident enough to identify the papacy as the Antichrist and the Islamic threat in eastern Europe as the work of Satan (1529, WA1.354,17–20).

Yet Luther also understood these challenges as acts of divine judgement. God too was active in what was happening around him. He could even see the exposure of the wickedness of the papacy in his own time and the Edict of Worms in 1521 as concrete evidence that God's wrath was imminent (Kastning 2008: 386–7). In history there is a coordination of the purpose of the Creator and the processes within creation. Nevertheless, care was needed at this point, for while God in his activity is ubiquitous, he remains hidden except to the eye of faith.

At this point Luther's understanding of history intersects with his well-known theology of the cross. In the Heidelberg Disputation (1518) God's powerful salvation, effected through the apparent weakness of the cross, provides a pattern for God's immanent involvement in all of human history.

> 19. That person does not deserve to be called a theologian who looks upon the invisible things of God as though they were clearly perceptible in those things which actually happened;
> 20. he deserves to be called a theologian, however, who comprehends the visible and manifest things of God seen through suffering and the cross.
>
> (WA1.354,17–20; LW31.40)

While God is at work in all things, his work and its purpose are not equally discernible in all things. Luther could distinguish between primary and secondary causes in the world (1532, on Psalm 127:1, WA40,3.211,22–23). He could also distinguish between God's 'strange' or 'alien' work of judging, condemning, and punishing and God's 'natural' or 'proper' work of forgiving, justifying, and saving, a distinction which could be correlated with Luther's immensely important understanding of law and gospel (1534, on Psalm 90, WA40,3.584,29–585,16; LW13.135; Disputatio prima contra Antinomos, 1537, WA39,1.1–6). However, each of these distinctions is built upon an even deeper conviction that in the world God often acts 'under the form of the contrary' (sub contraria specie). This is an insight that emerged as early as his Romans lectures in 1515–16.

> Thus 'the kingdom of heaven is like a treasure hidden in a field'. The field is dirty in contrast to the treasure; while the one is trodden underfoot, the other is picked up. And yet the field hides the treasure. So also 'our life is hid with Christ in God', that is, in the negation of all things which can be felt, held, and comprehended by our reason. So also our wisdom and righteousness are not at all apparent to us but are hidden with Christ in God. But what does appear is that which is contrary to these things... (WA56.393,3–9; LW25.383)

> And thus just as the wisdom of God is hidden under the appearance of stupidity, and truth under the form of lying—for so the Word of God, as often as it comes, comes in a form contrary to our own thinking [...], so also the will of God, although it is truly

and naturally 'good and acceptable and perfect', yet it is so hidden under the disguise of the evil, the displeasing, and the hopeless, that to our will and good intention, so to speak, it seems to be nothing but a most evil and most hopeless thing and in no way the will of God, but rather the will of the devil . . .

(WA56.446,31–33, 447,3–7; LW25.438–439)

This insight is nowhere more critical than in Luther's explanation of the way in which God's omnipotence is not compromised by the activity of Satan and of sinful people in the world. He explained this at length to Erasmus in *On Bound Choice*:

Now, Satan and man, having fallen from God and been deserted by God, cannot will good, that is, things which please God or which God wills; but instead they are continually turned in the direction of their own desires, so that they are unable not to seek the things of self. This will and nature of theirs, therefore, which is averse from God, is not something non-existent. For Satan and ungodly man are not non-existent or possessed of no nature or will, although their nature is corrupt and averse from God. That remnant of nature, therefore, as we call it, in the ungodly man and Satan, as being the creature and work of God, is no less subject to divine omnipotence and activity than all other creatures and works of God.

Since, then, God moves and actuates all in all, he necessarily moves and acts also in Satan and ungodly man. But he acts in them as they are and as he finds them; that is to say, since they are averse and evil, and caught up in the movement of this divine omnipotence, they do nothing but averse and evil things [. . .] Here you see that when God works in and through evil men, evil things are done, and yet God cannot act evilly although he does evil through evil men, because one who is himself good cannot act evilly; yet he uses evil instruments that cannot escape the sway and motion of his omnipotence . . .

The omnipotence of God makes it impossible for the ungodly to evade the motion and action of God, for he is necessarily subject to it and obeys it. But his corruption or aversion from God makes it impossible for him to be moved and carried along with good effect. God cannot lay aside his omnipotence on account of man's aversion, and ungodly man cannot alter his aversion.

(WA18:709,12–24, 709,28–31, 710,3–7; LW33.175–177)

This is the explanation of both everyday events and great moments in history. The great men of history operate as 'masks' of God. Lecturing on Genesis 13 Luther explained:

Hannibal thinks that he is conquering the Romans by reason of the great courage and the extraordinary diligence he possesses. Alexander has greater gifts, which enable him to be successful in all his undertakings. But these are 'masks'. They are the only things we see. But God's control, by which governments are either strengthened or overturned, we do not see. (WA42.507,16–19; LW2.342)

God's omnipotence does not jeopardize the reality of historical existence precisely because of God's self-concealment and this idea of the 'masks of God' (*larva Dei*) (Headley 1963: 4, 6).

Such an understanding gives pride of place to faith, if history is to be seen for all that it in fact is. Indeed, as Headley observed, at certain points it becomes clear that faith and unbelief are the twin themes of history as far as Luther is concerned:

> Faith and unbelief—these are the great themes of Church history. And at the vortex is the Word, this veritable attack of God upon world history. The Word that constitutes the Church as a community of believers is the same Word that impels this terrible struggle. The arena of its redemptive action is the entire world; the fruit of its redemptive action is the Church—neither physically demonstrable nor triumphant, but crucified, dispossessed, hidden. (Headley 1963: 55)

Not only is faith played out against its opposite in history; faith is critical to understanding history, especially that history joined to the Word as sacred history. Luther made this clear in his preface to Menius' commentary on 1 Samuel:

> …you will see these same stories [*historias*] through the use of faith to be reborn as if by a certain baptism and to be made new for us in our age, yes even to live forever and to serve usefully with splendid and most clear examples of faith for the purpose of edifying, urging, instructing, and consoling—in short, for all that Paul attributes to the word of faith. For what is a sacred story [*historia sacra*] but the visible word of faith or work of faith, because it teaches us the same by deed and by work that Scripture otherwise gives by word and by proclamation? (WA30,3.539,31–540,1)

Faith enables God's child to make sense of what otherwise defies understanding. So Luther's meditation on the progress of Jacob towards Bethel and in particular the way 'a terror from God fell upon the cities that were around them, so that they did not pursue the sons of Jacob' (Gen. 35:5), brought faith, the doctrine of creation, and world history into the closest relationship.

> The Holy Spirit reminds us by this example that we should learn the doctrine of creation correctly, namely, that all things are in God's hand, and that we should accustom and encourage ourselves to confident trust in our Creator, which, to be sure, is still very small and weak in us. For if we firmly concluded that God is our Creator, we would certainly believe that He has heaven and earth in His hands [...] The providence and government of God shines forth also in the histories of the heathen. Hannibal could have gained possession of Rome without any trouble and difficulty after slaying the warlike leaders and armies of the Romans. But he was checked by God [...] For it is God who takes away the spirit of princes and is terrible to the kings of the earth. With a single word or nod he shatters the spirits of the great warriors Pyrrhus, Hannibal, etc. This is the true knowledge and faith regarding creation, and

this lesson should be carefully meditated and practiced so that we stir ourselves up to pray and to believe. (WA44.180,10–15, 181,7–10, 181,17–22; LW6.242–244)

As always with Luther, God's Word makes the difference, generating faith and giving it direction. God's Word enables the believer to see God's hand at work in the world. The most mundane matters are given importance when God's Word is attached to them and then they far outstrip the magnificent 'histories of the heathen' in glory and in useful-ness. So Luther saw value in the incident of Leah, Rachel, and the mandrakes which Reuben had found in the field (Gen. 30:14–16), a value which outweighed the work of Virgil, Homer, and Livy (WA43.672.13–16; LW6.353):

> For this reason these histories are called sacred and are common to all men who have the Word of God and in whom God works, and does so with good pleasure, with His mercy, and with His grace. He does not deal in this way with Alexander, Scipio, Cicero, Hannibal, etc. Therefore we should rejoice and be grateful and happy to find rest in God's good pleasure, and we should bear with equanimity whatever troubles confront us. And no matter how unimportant, servile, wom-anish, and full of wretchedness our works are, we should nevertheless add this title: THE WORD OF GOD, because of which everything we do becomes glorious and will remain forever, while, on the other hand, the histories of the world are eternally wretched. (WA43.672,40–673,7; LW5.354)

Undergirding all of this was the deeply eschatological frame of Luther's understanding—not only eschatological, of course, but apocalyptic. He had a keen sense of living in the last days of a cosmic battle between the gospel of Christ and the lies of the Devil, between Christ's people and the Antichrist. The public revelation of the papacy's opposition to the gospel, the Edict of Worms, the rise of heretics, anarchy and revolt, and the advance of the Turk into central Europe all confirmed this assessment in Luther's mind. Yet it was betrayal and false teaching in the church which stood out as most significant. Again in lecturing on Genesis, Luther saw a clear parallel between his own time and that of Noah:

> The Flood came, not because the Cainite race had become corrupt, but because the race of the righteous who had believed God, obeyed His Word, and observed true worship had fallen into idolatry, disobedience of parents, sensual pleasures, and the practice of oppression. Similarly, the coming of the Last Day will be hastened, not because the heathen, the Turks, and the Jews are ungodly, but because through the pope and the fanatics the church itself has become filled with error and because even those who occupy the leading positions in the church are licentious, lustful, and tyrannical. (WA42.270,15–21; LW2.12)

In Kastning's words:

> When apocalyptic expectation is recognised as the constant in Luther's theological assessment of his time, its oscillation between announcements of wrath and grace are variations on one and the same fundamental insight: Luther understood that time

later known as the Reformation as a temporally limited interim before the return of Christ, in which God once again in unprecedented clarity reveals the gospel as a call to the last gathering and conversion. (Kastning 2008: 386)

In this context Luther's self-understanding, a topic of immense scholarly interest in the last century or so, receives its most important contours (Kolb 1999). Much is often made of the way Luther's contemporaries identified him as the 'Elijah of the Last Days' (Oberman 1989: 8). Luther laid no claim to be a prophet. He had been reluctantly drawn into this business, made a doctor of the church not by his own design but in obedience to the instruction of Staupitz and others, and forced to speak out because of that denial of truth he heard all around him:

> They accuse me of claiming that I alone am everybody's teacher. My answer is that I have not done this since I am always inclined to crawl into a corner. But my enemies have dragged me into the open through cunning and force to win glory and honor at my expense. Now that the game is going against them, they consider me guilty of vainglory. And even if it were true that I had set myself up all alone, that would be no excuse for their conduct. Who knows? God may have called me and raised me up. They ought to be afraid lest they despise God in me [...] I do not claim to be a prophet, but I do say that the more they scorn me and the higher they regard themselves, the more reason they have to fear that I may be a prophet [...] And even if I am not a prophet, as far as I am concerned I am sure that the Word of God is with me and not with them, for I have the Scriptures on my side and they have only their own doctrine. This gives me courage, so that the more they despise me and persecute me, the less I fear them. (1521, WA7.311,10–22, 313,17–19, 313,21–25; LW32.8, 9–10)

While the connections with Elijah are obvious and there is some evidence Luther made the connection himself at points, more often he saw the parallels between his own situation and that of Noah, preaching to a world on the brink of judgement which very largely refused to listen (Holl 1968: 19; Parsons 2001 develops this in detail). This was not just the ageing Luther expressing his frustration at the lack of responsiveness of his contemporaries. Yet not surprisingly the thought surfaces most extensively in his commentary on Genesis. Throughout his discussion of Genesis 6 he drew comparisons between Noah's situation and his own. For instance:

> When all these people became corrupt, Noah alone remained steadfast, a truly amazing man [...] There is, therefore, no doubt that the perverse generation hated him intensely and harassed him in various ways while exposing him to ridicule: 'Is it you alone who is wise? Is it you alone who pleases God? Are all the rest of us in error? Shall we all be condemned? Is it you alone who is not in error? Is it you alone who will not be condemned?' [...] The wretched papists assail us today with this one argument, saying: 'Do you think that all the fathers were in error?'
>
> (WA42.300,21, 23–27, 31–32; LW2.54–55)

Luther could identify with Noah while clearly recognizing the difference between them. Nevertheless, his understanding of what God had done once in human history, made possible by God's Word which drew attention to this history's proper meaning, shaped not only his perspective on his own world but on his personal identity.

V. LUTHER AND THE USE OF HISTORY

We have already identified numerous examples of the way in which Luther made use of historical information in illustrating theological truth taught in Scripture. He did not see this as in any way compromising the unique and final authority of Scripture. Put the other way around, 'absolute biblical authority never meant that Luther excluded a wide variety of other authors from his quiver of citable authorities so long as they confirmed what he believed stands in Scripture' (Kolb 2012: xiii). Sometimes this appeal to history and retelling its story arose within his exposition of Scripture. At other times the retelling of world history stood more on its own, only theologically interpreted. Nevertheless, Luther saw a value to the study of history that went beyond sermon illustrations or ammunition for his debates against his opponents. He encouraged those responsible for government in Germany to establish schools and include history in the curriculum. He encouraged his students to see how the lessons of Scripture are played out as lessons of history.

> These past twenty years we have undertaken many measures against the Turk, but without success. Why? Our sins have stirred up the wrath of God against us. Since He, therefore, wished to lay a punishment on us, He armed our enemies, the Turks, with anger and cruelty against us. But to us He sent fear, so that it is rightly thrown up to us that we have forgotten our valour and have degenerated from our ancestors. (On Psalm 2, 1532, WA40,2.232,30–34; LW12.34)

Of particular interest as an example of Luther's use of history is his *Reckoning of the Years of the World* from 1541. It remains true that Luther himself did not take this work too seriously, regarding it merely as a useful device rather than as a way of predicting the date of Jesus' return (Spitz 1989: 150). He explained its purpose in the introduction:

> This calculation of the years was prepared for my own use, not to be a chronicle or history but so that I might have before my eyes a kind of table of the times and years handed down in Scripture and so that I might recall the number of years the patriarchs, judges, kings and princes lived or ruled or over how long a period of time one succeeded from another. (WA53.22,11–18)

It was not an entirely novel enterprise. Luther modified Melanchthon's reworking of Carion's *Chronicon* (the original had been published in German in 1532 and translated into Latin in 1537) and endorsed the Jewish calculation of the history of the world spanning 6,000 years, based on the week of creation:

Six thousand years stands the world.
   Two thousand empty.
   Two thousand the Law.
   Two thousand the Messiah.
   These are the six days of the week in the sight of God. The seventh day is the eternal Sabbath. (WA53.22,2–7)

Nevertheless, the *Reckoning* goes its own way at various points, as what is essentially an annotated timeline unfolds. Luther divided the millennia somewhat idiosyncratically and even then sat quite loose on these calculations. However, this work did confirm him in his conviction that the Last Day was imminent. By his calculations the earth was 5,500 years old in 1540 and on a parallel with the shortened three days between the crucifixion and the resurrection, Luther did not expect the sixth millennium to be completed (WA53.171). So once again Luther's engagement with history serves his theological concerns: there is an urgency to the gospel work he is engaged in since it will soon be followed by the return of Christ and the day of judgement.

VI. FOLLOWING LUTHER'S TRAJECTORY

Luther fascinates as one who took history seriously, whether it was biblical history, 'the histories of the pagans', or the history of his own time. He brought an acute awareness of God's intimate yet hidden involvement in the world to his reflection on each type of history. His conviction that world events are not irrelevant to God's purpose but the very means by which that purpose is accomplished was tied to his understanding that all things exist as God's creation. The apocalyptic character of his engagement with world history was born of intense sensitivity to the battle between faith and unbelief in the world, between God's purpose and Satan's schemes. His willingness to identify himself and others as heralds of grace, the papacy as the Antichrist, and the Islamic military threat of the sixteenth century as an act of divine judgement, all flow out of his theology of the cross and a particular understanding of the distinction between God's proper work and his strange work.

Luther would call those who follow the path he trod to engage the wider movement of God's purposes as well as look for his providential rule in domestic and seemingly trivial matters. The truth taught in the Scriptures is being played out on the stage of human history, but this is only seen by those who turn to history with the eyes of faith. Ultimately, though, this governance of God can only resolve into the public vindication of Christ and those who are his, just as on that day all resistance and opposition will be overcome. In the meantime Luther encouraged the study of history, as he did when writing to the councilmen of Germany in 1524.

In Luther's ideal library there would be a judicious selection of books, giving pride of place to Holy Scripture, but including the best commentaries, language texts, books on the liberal arts and law and medicine. But 'among the foremost', he insisted, 'would be the chronicles and histories, in whatever languages they are to be had'. He explained why:

> For they are a wonderful help in understanding and guiding the course of events, and especially for observing the marvellous works of God.
>
> (1524, WA15.52,1–14; LW45.376)

REFERENCES

Bornkamm, Heinrich (1958). *Luther's World of Thought*. German original 1947; trans. Martin H. Bertram. Saint Louis: Concordia.

—— (1969). *Luther and the Old Testament*. German original 1948; trans. Eric W. and Ruth C. Gritsch. Philadelphia: Fortress.

Brecht, Martin (1985). *Martin Luther: His Road to Reformation 1483–1521*. German original 1981; trans. J. L. Schaaf. Philadelphia: Fortress.

Headley, John M. (1963). *Luther's View of Church History*. New Haven: Yale University Press.

Holl, Karl (1968). 'Martin Luther on Martin Luther'. In *Interpreters of Luther*, ed. Jaroslav Pelikan. Philadelphia: Fortress, 9–34.

Kastning, Wieland (2008). *Morgenröte künftigen Lebens; das reformatorische Evangelium als Neubestimmung der Geschichte: Untersuchungen zu Martin Luthers Geschichts- und Wirklichkeitsverständnis*. Göttingen: Vandenhoeck & Ruprecht.

Köhler, Walther (1900). *Luther und die Kirchengeschichte nach seinen Schriften, zunächst bis 1521*. Erlangen: Junge.

Kolb, Robert (1999). *Martin Luther as Prophet, Teacher, and Hero. Images of the Reformer, 1520–1620*. Grand Rapids: Baker.

—— (2012). *Luther and the Stories of God. Biblical Narratives as a Foundation for Christian Living*. Grand Rapids: Baker Academic.

Leppin, Volker (2009). '"In diesen letzten Zeiten": Gottes Geschichtswirken und Gottes Heilswirken bei Martin Luther'. In *Heil und Geschichte*, ed. Jörg Frey, Stefan Krauter, and Hermann Lichtenberger. Tübingen: Mohr/Siebeck, 597–607.

Lilje, Hanns (1932). *Luthers Geschichtsanschauung*. Berlin: Furche.

Oberman, Heiko Augustinus (1989). *Luther: Man between God and the Devil*. German original 1982. New Haven: Yale University Press.

Parsons, Michael (2001). 'The Apocalyptic Luther: His Noahic Self-Understanding'. *Journal of the Evangelical Theological Society* 44: 627–45.

Pesch, Otto Hermann (2000). '"Behold, I am doing a new thing" [Is. 43:19]? History of Salvation and Historic Moments of Transition in Thomas Aquinas and Martin Luther'. *Science et Esprit* 53: 123–42.

Pflanz, Hans H. (1939). *Geschichte und Eschatologie bei Martin Luther*. Stuttgart: Kohlhammer.

Spitz, Lewis W. (1989). 'Luther's View of History: A Theological Use of the Past'. In *Light for our World: Essays Commemorating the 150th Anniversary of Concordia Seminary*, ed. John W. Klotz. Saint Louis: Concordia, 139–54.

Vogel, Winfried (1986). 'The Eschatological Theology of Martin Luther. Part I: Luther's Basic Concepts'. *Andrews University Seminary Studies* 24: 249–64.

Wriedt, Markus (1996). 'Luther's Concept of History and the Formation of an Evangelical Identity'. In *Protestant History and Identity in Sixteenth-Century Europe. Vol. 1: The Medieval Inheritance*, ed. Bruce Gordon. Aldershot: Ashgate, 31–45.

Zahrnt, Heinz (1952). *Luther deutet Geschichte: Erfolg und Mißerfolg im Licht des Evangeliums*. Munich: Müller.

CHAPTER 10

··

LUTHER'S USE OF LANGUAGE

··

JOHANNES VON LÜPKE

I. INTRODUCTION

···

MARTIN Luther's way of using language forms a connecting thread running through the variety of tasks which he undertook as exegete, translator, preacher, pastor, theological teacher, poet, and author. The author Luther was essentially a linguistic theorist, not only in the sense that he continually thought about language but especially because his thinking was based in language and took its specific form linguistically. His theology is therefore certainly also linguistic *theory*; it contains insights into the significance of language from both theological and anthropological points of view. But it is primarily and totally linguistic practice. Luther put language to work; it is the instrument and constituting element of writing (Brecht 1990). Simultaneously, his creative foundation lies in language, the source which made his cognitive process possible and set its standard. His use of language shaped his theology and his thinking in general. When he specifically reflected on language, he did so in order to experiment with the proper linguistic usage.

In seeking to characterize Luther's use of language, the question of its norm arises. Precisely that is the task of grammar, when, on the one hand, it conforms to current usage and tries to describe it as precisely as possible, in order to, on the other hand, regulate proper speaking. *Modus loquendi* (the way language is spoken) and *norma loquendi* (the norm for speaking) are intimately bound together (WA26.38,12–14; LW28.265: '*In rebus omnibus est spectandum modus loquendi. Grammatica debet tradere normam loquendi*'). 'The natural way of speaking is empress; it trumps all subtle, quibbling, sophistic formulations' (WA18.180,17–18; LW40.190). This principle applies to translation, both to the expression in the language of the source from which translation is made and the language into which it is being translated insofar as the word is to become its vernacular equivalent (on Luther's use of his own mother tongue, early modern high German in a specifically Thuringian-Saxon variety, cf. Wolf 1980, 1996). In both cases the norm for linguistic usage becomes clear in its exercise and practice. It is not externally imposed upon language according to the ideas or laws of reason apart from use of the language but rather developed out of its use. When Luther assigns grammar an important, practically defining, significance for theology (WA6.29,7–8: 'Inter omnes scientias humanitus inventas precipue est ad propaganda theologiam utilis grammatica') and speaks programmatically of a theological grammar, this conception takes on descriptive and prescriptive implications (e.g., WA40,1.418,21–33; LW16.267).

As a theological grammar Luther's use of language rests on the specific tradition of the Bible's language. It intends to capture biblical usage, translate it into given 'vernaculars', and display it anew in proclamation. Precisely for this purpose it made use of general linguistic theory, as it had taken form in the canon of disciplines in the liberal arts bequeathed by the ancients. As defined by the linguistic concept derived from Plato (Kratylos 388a), language is an organon, an instrument, which can serve various purposes in conveying information and making distinctions, expressing subjective feeling and also requirements and arrangements for common action. Under this aspect ancient rhetoric (Aristotle, Cicero, and Quintilian) distinguished various genre of speech. Luther had a good command of this rhetorical tradition since Melanchthon had adapted and intensively cultivated it at the University of Wittenberg (De rhetorica libri tres, 1519; Institutiones rhetoricae, 1521). The reformational programme of education continued to be bound to the curriculum of the liberal arts insofar as it accorded the three linguistically grounded disciplines—grammar, dialectic, and rhetoric—foundational significance for the study of theology. Even if Luther had rejected Aristotle's metaphysic and ethics, he could nonetheless recommend further use of his 'books on Logic, Rhetoric, and Poetics' (WA6.458,26–28; LW44.201–202). In connection with learning Hebrew, Greek, and Latin, university study of grammar, dialectic, and rhetoric served the purpose of learning the language of Holy Scripture in its own logic and form and opening it up for preaching.

II. Instructions for Theological Linguistic Usage: *Oratio, Meditatio*, and *Tentatio*

Luther's esteem for language and linguistic disciplines was ultimately grounded in the fact that the subject of theology is comprehended in language. Knowledge of God becomes concrete through hearing and understanding God's Word in human language. The almost axiomatic presupposition of Luther's theology presumed that God lets himself be 'publicly heard' and 'in our human language' offers 'to be our God' (WA38.365,16–17; LW43.200). The basic rules which Luther formulated for studying theology are thus essentially instructions for proper use of language (cf. WA50.657–661; Bayer 1994: 55–106). God is recognized when human beings call on him in prayer (oratio), meditate on his Word, as recorded in Holy Scripture (meditatio), and rely on his truth despite conflicting experiences (*tentatio*). Engaging the Word embraces and per-meates all of life. Since Luther conceived of theological study under these three rules, he simultaneously clung to experiences which demonstrate that this Word really is true in engaging the biblical Word. The norm, expressed in the form of rules, is grounded in the authority of the Bible, in its own efficacy. Luther found especially the Psalter, most espe-cially Psalm 119, had coined this trio of *oratio, meditatio*, and *tentatio*. Just as these rules arise from the daily engagement with the psalms in monastic prayer-life, so they aim at fostering use of the biblical Word, now indeed in the boundless, contradictory experi-ence of life outside the monastery.

Together these rules form something like instructions for how to use the Word. The actions and attitudes they recommend are so presented that in using the Word its own power and truth can unfold. Prayer aims at having the person oriented towards 'the true master of Scripture' (WA50.659,16; LW34.286), letting the author of Scripture himself speak, instead of exalting one's own reason as 'master'. Talking with God means first: hear-ing God's Word in the form of his promise (*promissio*) and his command (*praeceptum*) and responding as it were, 'handing [the Word] over', back to him (WA34,1.381,20–21: '*Do ist nicht uff andacht noch verdinst, sed in promissione herendum: ich secz dyr, liber her, deyn wort fur und nicht meyn verdinst*'; cf. WA34,1.380,24–25: '*Hoc sit fundamen-tum: Promissio et praeceptum*'). When human beings fix their faith on the promise, they may rely on it and be certain that God hears their prayers. Using the Word means also God's attributes, as in the Lord's Prayer, when we claim God's name, kingdom, and will as they become effective and begin to work for us, 'that all that God is must serve our use' and that also 'what otherwise must be done without us may also be done in us' (BSLK 670,43–45, 678,10–11; BC 445, 449). In the language of prayer the exchange between God and human being takes place in the greatest depth and breadth imaginable, embracing everything divine and everything human. Trusting in God's generosity, people spread out 'their apron' in prayer in order to 'receive much' (BSLK 668,38–40; BC 444).

Even if prayer is intended to cause human beings to speak the concerns of their inmost heart, this communication remains bound to the 'external Word', set down in the written Word placed in Scripture and continually encountered anew in oral proclama-tion. In this connection Luther understood 'meditation' chiefly as dealing with the *ver-bum externum*: 'not only in the heart, but also externally' one should 'continually goad and massage [*treiben und reiben*], read and reread, the oral speech and written words in the book, with diligent attention and reflection on what the Holy Spirit means by them' (WA50.659,22–25; LW34.289).

God's Word is intended to be 'physically heard and handled' (WA28.75,32), that is, first, it is intended to be comprehended through the use of physical powers, particularly the capacity of the senses and of the human voice, as a Word which puts a total claim on human beings and motivates them. External activity, such as reading it aloud, repeating it, and also singing it, is necessary for the Word to enter the heart and create living faith there. This is Luther's foundational insight that he especially aimed at the *Schwärmer*: it is the '*lingua externa*' (concrete language) which creates '*fidem in cor*' (faith in the heart) (WA46.422,1). In this physical use of language human beings conform to the Holy Spirit's use of language, as he expressed himself in the letters of Scripture and embodied himself in them, so to speak (Ringleben 2010: 292, can speak of an 'incarnational move' here insofar as 'the spiritual substance of Holy Scripture and thus the divine essence in the sensual appearance of what is written' is 'fully present in the externality of the literal wording').

The concept of the 'external' or 'physical Word' is thus to be understood theologically as well: God's Spirit is a spirit who expresses himself and is only comprehensible in words. 'Nowhere' can he 'be found more present and more alive than in the holy letters themselves, which he has written' (WA7.97,2–3: 'spiritus nusquam praesentius et vivacius quam in ipsis sacris suis, quas scripsit, literis inveniri potent'). Luther's understanding and practice of meditation is decisively determined by this theological insight. Precisely because the Holy Spirit is present in his writings as author and thus binds himself to their wording, the human spirit is to cling firmly to this form of language in order to focus one's own thoughts and submit to the discipline of the Holy Spirit's school. In short: Luther's concern is to let reason be driven by various emotions of the heart and continually surrender its own fantasies to what the Holy Spirit dictated. Since it clings to the written letters, it lets the author speak again and again and lets the Word work on it—to its innermost part. In this respect, meditation with its attachment to the Word it receives leads to a peculiar experience of freedom: 'as soon as I take a psalm or passage of Scripture in hand, light is shining and my heart burns, so that I gain a new confidence and feeling' (WA28.76,19–21).

The experience gained in meditating on the words of Scripture proves itself in the midst of contradictory experiences, which Luther designated 'Anfechtung' (tentatio, spiritual struggles). For him this was a 'touchstone, which not only teaches you to know and understand but also to experience how right, how true, how sweet, how lovely, how powerful, how comforting God's Word is, wisdom above all wisdom' (WA50.660,1–4; LW34.286–287; cf. WA24.576,5–12). Also this third rule is intended to be understood as instruction for using God's Word. It is the same 'substance', which in the practice of meditation serves as the foundation and support of faith. It reveals its capacity to support and its great worth in its withstanding contradictory experiences under the powers of sin and death and can triumph over them (precisely this Luther presumed to gain from the text's literal sense: in it alone is the 'entire substance of faith and Christian theology' ('tota fidei et theologiae Christianae substantia') and 'it alone stands firm in distress and conflict, conquers hell's gates with sin and death, and triumphs to the praise and glory of God'. Practising faith consists in ascribing the greater power in the battle of the powers to the Word, finally almighty power over every other power.

III. GOD'S WORD AS THE SUBJECT OF THEOLOGY

In spiritual struggles, that is, in the conflict of differing experiences, the subject of theology becomes clear: God's Word as being in its substantial sense. The attributes of the metaphysical doctrine of God, e.g., immortality, eternality, omnipotence, refer to something here which belongs more on the side of the merely accidental, relational, according to the metaphysical doctrine of God. When God shares himself linguistically in the word of promise, the Word, comprehended in sensory experience as a transitory phenomenon, assumes a reality that is 'greater than heaven and earth' (WA40,1.596,6–7; LW26.391: '*maior quam coelo et terra*'; cf. Ringleben 2010: 612–15 ['*promissio infinita*], and WA40,3.61,15–23). '*In sensu finitissima et quasi centrum*' (in the most finite sense yet as if the centre) (WA40,1.596,8; LW26.391), the Word of *promissio* as the Word of eternal God has a significance that cannot be fathomed. What intensifies at the point of the promise and appears to evaporate bears, as *verbum centrale* (the central word), a reality of immeasurable extent, a '*maxima et infinita sphera*' (WA40,1.596,21; LW26.391). This coincidence of the finite and infinite, temporal and eternal, the created and the creative in the Word certainly exceeds normal benchmarks of sensual experience and reason. The standard according to which one may judge in this case exists in the Word itself and its judgement (cf. WA40,3.22–23: '*hoc faciendum est, ut non iudicemus secundum hoc, quod sentimus, sed secundum quod pronunciat et iudicat verbum seu ipse Deus in verbo suo*'). It is only to be found in faith just as only in faith is the Word of promise seen as supportive, reliable, and in this sense true.

By concentrating the subject of theology on the point of the promising Word (cf. esp. Bayer 1971, 2003, ³2007) and finding there its Archimedean point, which supports everything and around which everything turns, the system of categories changed under which the reality of all things—of God, human beings, and the world—is understood. A new definition of ontology took form, and within it decisively a new understanding of substance and relationship. Through the Word God supports all things (Heb. 1:3), which means: all things exist in and through the Word. Luther understood 'substance' as that which bestows existence and in which things 'subsist' (fundamental is WA55,2.388–389, 137–165 [WA3.419,25–420,13], esp. lines 145–146: '*Sic enim dicitur omne illud, per quod quisque [in sua vita] subsistit*'; cf. Joest 1967: 238–42). Luther's anthropology makes this clear: what the human being is essentially must be understood from that which carries him in faith and renews him. The same is true of the church insofar as it 'subsists' in God's Word. Only through God's Word does it come into existence; alone in it can it exist (WA1.13,38–39: '*Stat fixa sententia, ecclesiam non nasci nec subsistere in natura sua, nisi verbo Dei*', cf. WA30,2.650,19–21). When in this context Luther uses the concept of substance, it is precisely not ascribed to the nature of human beings or the church, but to the external foundation of what constitutes them. This does not refer to what a created object has in itself or what it can do by itself, but rather to that power upon which it depends and which it cannot hang on to itself. Compared to a 'substance', which Luther deemed God's Word to be, all the substantial things ascribed to human beings, such as reason, amount to nothing (WA18.784,17–27; LW33.290). As little as they can claim things as their own and retain things on their own, so much these things have the character of gifts and so much is the essence of the whole human being dependent on receiving—that means essentially on faith. Being is thus essentially interpreted as being in relationship.

Being in relationship is not only a matter of viewing created being. Simultaneously, the Word in which all creatures subsist says—as God's Word—something about God himself. God expresses himself in his Word. That is true in Christology and in the theology of creation, inasmuch as the Word, which in Jesus Christ became human, is identical with the Word through which and in which all things were created and are preserved. That and how God relates to his creatures characterizes him essentially. He is 'an eternal source... which pours out pure goodness, from which all that is and is called good, flows' (BSLK 565,41–566,2; BC 389). He is 'a God, who has given himself completely to us with everything he is and has' (WA26.505,38–39; LW37.366). The concept of substance is therefore theologically not at all to be understood as if God were without relationship, complete in and of himself. That is precisely what Luther saw as the chief error of a metaphysical doctrine of God, as decisively shaped by Aristotle. Against it Luther posited a basic rule of theological dialectic: 'God is not to be sought under the category of substance but under the category of relationship' ('*Deum quaerendum esse non in praedicamento substantiae, sed relationis*', cf. Johann Gerhard's formulation, *Loci theologici*, prooemium de natura theologiae, Gerhard 1863: 28, cf. WA40,2.354,3–4, 421,6–7 (22–24) [LW12.376–377], 40,3.62,38–63,20, 334,23–6, WA42.634,20–22, 635,19, WA46.337,4–5 [27–28]). While the 'Aristotelian or philosophical God', which Luther simultaneously identifies as the God of Jews, Turks, and papists, is not at all in relationship with us and reveals himself therefore as a 'totally miserable essence' (*miserrimum ens*) (WATR1.73, §155), Holy Scripture presents the God who 'is God for us because he gives us his Epiphany, his appearance... and speaks with us' (WA43.240,29–32). God's being is not to be sought outside his way of appearing to us; rather we are to perceive in phenomena God's being for us. In what he says we simultaneously find the communication of what he essentially is. He is essentially '*deus verbosus*' (WA39,2.194–5; LW34.316; Ringleben [2010: passim] assesses Luther's entire theology under this leitmotif), a God who talks with his creatures constantly and 'in everyday language' so they 'are incessantly driven and directed by the Word' (WA24.38,9–10).

It is clear that his use of language shaped Luther's theology in its entirety and that it is the subject of his theology. One misses this if one thinks that it is possible to abstract theology from its mediation through language. It makes sense, however, when theology takes God at his word and develops itself consistently as linguistic theory. A closer look at specific topics reveals how Luther's theology developed as linguistic theory.

IV. LANGUAGE AS A TOPIC OF THEOLOGICAL ANTHROPOLOGY

If God speaks to us 'in our human language' (WA38.365,16–17; LW43.200), the language he uses must be interpreted with reference to its significance for human existence.

Under the various human capabilities and gifts the highest place is ascribed to the ability to speak, the specific characteristic distinguishing humans from other living beings. Language is the quintessence of living as human beings: 'compared to a speaking person, a person without words is nothing more than half-dead, and there is no more powerful or noble human activity than speaking since human beings are distinguished from other animals most decisively by speaking' (WADB10,1.100,10–13; LW35.254; cf. WA29.349,31–350,13, 350,2–4). Thus, language enters the theological definition of being human precisely where reason stands in the philosophical definition. Human beings are linguistic beings; even their reason is dependent on language. More precisely, it is the emotions of the heart which move human beings in their speaking and then in their thinking. From this angle Luther corrected the philosophical definition: the human being is an 'animal rationale habens cor fingens' (a rational animal with a creative heart) (WA42.348,38; LW1.124).

Characteristic for Luther's understanding of human language is the implied close connection between language and heart. The proximity of language to the heart means first: the heart and the emotions working in it express themselves in language: 'the first things to burst forth and emerge from the heart are words' (BSLK 572,30–31; BC 392). In words one recognizes what is in the human heart; its innermost state appears externally through language. That is seen in the psalms, which let us see into the saints' hearts. With a proverbial expression Luther can say, 'speech is the image or portrait of the heart' (WA10,1,1.187,15–16, cf. WA18.604,10–11, LW35.255, LW33.12; Seneca ep. 115,2). Luther's translation of Matthew 12:34 has become proverbial: 'what fills the heart goes through the mouth'. This emphasizes the dependence on linguistic expressions of that which moves human beings in the depths of the heart and what eludes their rational definition of themselves. In this regard human beings do not have control of themselves but are at the mercy of the emotions of the heart in thinking, speaking, and acting. However, it must also be remembered that the heart never completely and purely enters into human speech (Beutel 1991: 184–8).

Secondly, inversely, words impact and change the state of the heart. In the relationship of heart and language not only bondage and impotence are experienced. Instead, the power of language can reveal itself as a power of freedom. The Word bestows freedom. If the Word is thus the foundation of freedom, it is presumed that it will be perceived in faith as God's Word. More precisely, in the gospel the human soul attains freedom (WA7.22,3–14, cf. LW31.345). Its 'virtues' are ascribed to the soul so that 'a true child of God comes into existence through God's Word, holy, righteous, true, peaceful, free, filled with all good' (WA7.24,24–27, cf. LW31.349). To believe the gospel as God's Word means trusting in its efficacy. This faith is practised in the Christian's continuous engagement with the Word, 'forming it within oneself' (WA7.23,7–9) and thus relying on its forming power. 'When I grasp the Word through faith, it makes a new heart and new thoughts in me (through the Holy Spirit working through it)' (WA45.654,15–17).

The efficacy of the Word in the human heart is theologically grounded on the power of the Holy Spirit. He uses human language to create faith in the heart (WA46.422,1). That is indeed possible only because and insofar as this instrument itself has both spiritual and physical elements. Just as the human being as a whole 'consists of flesh and a living soul', so language represents simultaneously, as physical and spiritual capabilities, the whole person. Luther paid particular attention precisely to the corporeal phenomena, the organs of the tongue and voice, to find in them the creaturely expression of the 'unfathomable wisdom of God' (WA50.370,31). Articulation takes place through the tongue's and throat's movements, when words are heard not only as acoustic phenomena but also as meaningful expressions. This eludes rational explanation as a 'wondrous work and skill' (WA50.370,18–30; cf. WA47.25,18–21, and Ringleben 2010: 456–60; Emrich 2010, esp. 69–71).

Even if the linguistic *commercium* of body and soul constitutes an insolvable mystery, it can be cultivated. Precisely therein lies the importance of rhetoric as one of the classical liberal arts. It is responsible for the art of speaking well ('*ars bene dicendi*') in distinction to grammar, the theory of speaking correctly ('*scientia recte loquendi*') and dialectic, of defining and distinguishing ('*recte definire et dividere*') in the sense of explaining 'what the subject is about' (Ringleben 2010: 367, in the context of his helpful discussion of the *trivium*, 352–70; cf. Ebeling 1971: 150–83; on rhetoric, Maaser 1999: esp. 124–90). For Luther, to speak 'well' meant using language so that it moves the human being in the heart. Rhetoric is here understood concisely as 'rhetoric of the heart' (Stolt 2000: esp. 42–61). While dialectic as theory simply reaches the *intellectus*, rhetoric is concerned with the emotions, particularly the powers of the will, which define the human being as a whole. To influence and alter them, a language is needed which affects human beings sensually and addresses them in their ability to imagine concrete images. In short, it needs a language which utilizes poetic qualities. From this angle Luther can appreciate particularly the language of the psalms. The title of Psalm 122 ('I rejoice') indicates that this psalm is a 'song and poem of the best and greatest poet' (WA40,3.74,3–4; other examples, Ringleben 2010: 360–4). The rhetoric of the Holy Spirit reaches its goal in the joy of the heart. The gospel as a message which brings joy is thus seen as the master work of rhetoric understood theologically. This goes beyond dialectic but remains dependent upon it. In the relationship of these two disciplines the relationship of law and gospel becomes clear, according to Luther: 'The decalogue is the dialectic of the gospel and the gospel is the rhetoric of the decalogue' (WABr5.409,28–29). In the decalogue the proper relationship of God and human beings is presented clearly; in the gospel the human being is placed into the proper relationship to God. Precisely that happens above all in oral speech, through which Christ 'comes to you or you are brought to him' (WA10,1,1.13,21–22; LW35.121).

V. GOD IN THE WORD

The language in which the human heart expresses itself and in which it is addressed, is from a theological point of view simultaneously the medium in which God comes to human beings. God is therefore not only the author of the Word that is efficacious in human hearts; he is actually present himself in the Word. As Luther shows particularly in his interpretation of the prologue to John's gospel, God and the Word are to be thought of as a unity with a distinction within itself (cf. Beutel 1991; on Christology particularly, also Bayer and Gleede 2007). The Word that in Christ became human is essentially God. And God's essence lies completely in his Word. While human speech is always 'only referential or as a sign' (WA10,1,1.188,10), which refers to the reality at its base and distinguishes itself as a deficient mode of the presentation or appearance of the speaker himself, the divine Word is characterized by the speaker's very presence. It is 'not a mere wind or echo, but it brings with it the entire essence of the divine nature' (WA10,1,1.186,15–16). Jesus Christ is God's image, not in the sense of a copy of one to be sought somewhere else but in such a way that the Godhead enters him completely and can be found in him. 'The divine nature' is so 'formed... that it enters completely this image and is the image itself, and its lustre... enters essentially into its appearance' (WA10,1,1.186,17–20). In this context Luther can speak of a 'real appearance' (WA10,1,1.157,20–21; Church Postil 1522; Hebrews 1:1–12). 'The image and the one whose image it is' are here 'of one essence' (WA10,1,1.156,11). As God appears here, as he lets himself be heard and seen in Jesus Christ, he actually *is*. What the Word means *is* truly here 'in sign or word' (WA10,1,1.187,6). This theological understanding of language is sharply distinct from creaturely language and its philosophical concept: 'The philosophical sign presents an absent object; the theological sign presents an object that is present' (WATR4.666,8–9, §5104, 1540: '*Signum philosophicum est nota absentis rei, signum theologicum est nota praesentis rei*'; Bayer ³2007: 48 sees in this insight 'that the linguistic sign is already the subject matter of... Luther's great hermeneutic, in the strict sense his reformational discovery').

If the entire divine nature enters this Word, that means that it essentially occupies God's place. Luther explained John 1:1 ('in the beginning was the Word, and the Word was with God, and God was the Word'): 'in God a conversation or Word exists which embraces God totally and is God himself'. It is a word 'which is therefore great, as God is, yes, this very Word is God himself' (WA46.546.23–24, 29–30; LW22.12). God's being is thus to be thought of as bound to the Word, as a communicative being. And vice versa, the Word delivers the divine being. If this Word, which in Jesus Christ became human, 'embraces God's entire essence and nature completely in itself' (WA10,1,1.155,21, Church Postil 1522, Hebrews 1:1–12), then all of God's attributes apply to it, including those which distinguish God categorically from his creatures. Especially the attribute of omnipotence distinguishes this Word from all human words. It is a creative word, of which Psalm 33:9 says, 'when he speaks, it happens'. Precisely this word is so tightly and inseparably bound to a human being in Jesus Christ that it is fully present and efficacious in him. John the Evangelist 'does not want to treat God's divine, almighty, eternal Word—or speak of him—any other way than in flesh and blood, which has gone to earth' (WA10,1,1.202,9–11). In Christ's person 'the highest omnipotence and the greatest impotence meet and commune with each other' (WA47.214,7–8, on John 3/4, 1538–40, LW22.509).

VI. Using God's Creative Word: Hermeneutical Consequences

Luther explored the mystery of Christ's person under the concept of the *communicatio idiomatum*, the mutual exchange of divine and human attributes. From that vantage point the way God's Word functions in its universal dimensions and especially its relationship to Holy Scripture become clear. Here lies the key to Luther's theology of creation, his biblical hermeneutic, and not the least his understanding of the sacraments (Steiger 1996). Analogous to the communicative unity of God and human being in Jesus Christ, the essential concept of 'condescension' defines the other forms of God's Word as well. Since God involves himself in his creation, he 'empties' himself of his power and lets creatures share in his power at the same time. To perceive God conveyed through the senses and in language certainly requires a particular way of dealing with language. The question is: how can and should a human being use language in order to unfold God's action and his presence? Which language is particularly fitting to bring him into this conversation?

We presume the insight that the words of Holy Scripture may be 'used' in a two-fold sense: first, they are used by human authors and recipients; second, by God, who employs human words in order to inscribe them as 'living words' on the hearts of the faithful (WA55,2.244,125–128 [WA3.256,9–11]). The word is to be 'always in use, in movement, in flight, so that the Lord himself is always arousing and motivating faith in us' (WA5.505,29–34). When Luther persistently demands that attention be paid to the *usus loquendi* of Scripture (e.g., WA2.424,16–17, WA18.700,33–35, WA26.444,37–38: '*auff die sprache sehen, was da fur eine weise, brauch und gewonheit ist zu reden*'), he is not only concerned about explaining what individual words mean but especially about recognizing what they cause to happen. Every language has its own particular 'usage', that is, words are used differently and assume different meanings in specific contexts (e.g., WA19.357,16–358,8). Simultaneously each unfolds its particular power in its respective applications and contexts. It is essential in interpretation to understand linguistic usage and to preserve it in translation. This usage embraces both clarity in reference to the subject and simultaneously 'power, energy, and efficacy' (WA13.242,16–17) in being shaped by the subject itself. Semantics (*significatio*) and pragmatics (*potestas*) belong inseparably together here (cf. WA26.273,25–26; LW37.172–173; connections to the linguistic philosophy of Ludwig Wittgenstein emerge at this point, cf. Illge 2008).

The significance of the biblical writings is not exhausted by their reporting historical facts. With the subject matter (*res*) they convey its use (*usus rerum*) (WA5.543,13–14: '*non solum res, sed et usum rerum exprimit*'). The decisive question concerns the 'use of the Word, not only its history'; the question is, 'how one should use the gospel and for what is it useful and what can it do' (WA9.630,28–30). Its proper use is faith, which accepts the history as history which happened 'for us'. Especially the gospels tell the story of Jesus and intend to be so understood that today's reader and hearer are taken into it. Thus, its use consists in making the reality which it relates efficacious and applicable for us today (cf. WA9.630,14–22). In this sense the biblical words and the narrative which they convey possess a sacramental quality (cf. WA9.440,3–4: 'omnia verba, omnes historie Euangelice sunt sacramenta quedam, hoc est sacra signa, per que in credentibus dues efficit, quicquid ille historie designant'; on the 'sacramental word', cf. Ringleben 2010: 144–69). Thus, the faith which they produce is simultaneously the condition for discerning them properly: 'you must let these words address you, you, you, and cling to them, believe without any doubt that it happens to you as they say' (WA10,1,2,2.25,16–17).

In faith human beings experience the Word delivered in Scripture as a message directed to them and receive it as a promise. They participate in the reality promised only when they place themselves in the Word. The gift-bestowing Word of the Lord's Supper, 'this is my body, given FOR YOU', includes the invitation, 'ponder, and include yourself in that "YOU" so that he is not talking with you in vain' (BSLK 720,42–721,2; BC 473). Enfolding oneself in that Word is an act of humility, which Luther in an elegant observation on the grammar of Holy Scripture could compare with the grammatical practice of declining: the first person pronoun is moved from the nominative into the genitive, dative, and accusative (cf. WA48.203, §273; Luther joins the conjugation of the noun deus to the declination of the personal pronoun). The concept 'God' translates itself into the verbum in the sense of a verb; on the interpretation of this observation, which contains a theological grammar in nuce: von Lüpke 1992, esp. 238–41). The subject moves itself from the position it had claimed, with the ability to govern its own life, into the position of belonging to another, of receiving and being talked to by another. The same movement may be intended when Luther on various occasions urges 'crawling' into the Word (WA32.98,17–20, WA10,1,1.193,11–16: 'hallt dich an diße gotliche wort, da kreuch eyn und bleyb drynnen wie eyn Haß ynn seiner steynritzen'). Just as God's Word confronts us in simple, lowly, inconspicuous human language—with rhetorical terminology, in genus humile (Stolt 2000: 64–70)—so it points human beings downward, where they may do nothing of themselves but receive everything from God.

The locale of the Word, which human beings enter in faith, turns out to be the locale of the new creation, figuratively speaking: the Word is the uterus in which human beings are 'conceived, carried, and born' (WA10,1,1.232,13–15, see Beutel 1991: 227–8, 421; cf. WA40,1,597,6–7). Here stress falls on the present tense: in and through the Word human beings are placed into the process of creation taking place now. They perceive themselves continually renewed as God's children. They are and remain humans in process, without ever being released from being situated in God's creative Word: 'as we have been in the Word, so we must return to the Word when we stop being, when we listen to it. We were in the Word before we were human. John drives us into the Word, teaching... as they will eternally remain in the Word' (WA45.392,9–15; cf. WA44.270,13–14: 'Ex verbo conditi sumus, in verbum opportet nos reverti').

This trifling, weak Word that sinners disregard becomes their 'door', so to speak, when it addresses and moves them in faith. It opens access to primary and ultimate things and thus has fundamental significance (WA7.97,26–29; LW28.352). As creative Word, it reveals itself not least by renewing the human language into which it enters. As the

Holy Spirit uses language as author of Holy Scripture, he simultaneously introduces new linguistic usage. This new linguistic usage arises from the union of God and human being in Jesus Christ. In him, that is, in the communication of God and human being, which is the mystery of the essence of his person (*communicatio idiomatum*), new relationships are created, which subject all that exists to new definition. All words take on new meaning when referred to him, presupposing his presence (WA39,2.94,17–18; cf. WA39,2.30,19). That involves not only new designations for what exists, which retains its characteristics. Rather, the relationship with Christ adds something essential to creatures. By the power of the Word they are more and different than what they had taken themselves to be, what they appeared to be. When Luther appropriates rhetorical figures of speech such as metaphor and synecdoche, as he does especially in his doctrine of the sacraments, he continually stresses their reality. He is concerned with transformations and associations which take place in the reality of the creation. It is renewed because it is placed in a network of new relationships: God in Jesus Christ enters this reality and makes himself present sacramentally. Thus the Lord's Supper is a 'creative word that combines the elements with Christ's body'; the 'is' creates 'a new reality' (Ringleben 2010; more detailed: Ringleben 1997 and 2003).

In the tension between ancient biblical language and the reality of full communion with God that has not yet been fully realized, Luther believed that the task of theology is that of linguistic theory, which claims to take over all traditional forms of linguistics and renew them. By referring to the Bible's linguistic world, in the school of the Holy Spirit and with his rhetoric, theology learns and teaches simultaneously a 'new dialectic' and a 'new grammar' (WA39,2.304,6–8) and is intent on distinguishing God and human being from each other in the medium of language and on bringing them together in an eternal, continuous new conversation.

References

Bayer, Oswald (1971–2/1989). *Promissio. Geschichte der reformatorischen Wende in Luthers Theologie*. Göttingen: Vandenhoeck & Ruprecht.

—— (1994). *Theologie*. Gütersloh: Gütersloher Verlagshaus.

—— (2003/2007). *Martin Luthers Theologie. Eine Vergegenwärtigung*. Tübingen: Mohr/Siebeck.

Bayer, Oswald and Benjamin Gleede (eds.) (2007). *Creator est Creatura. Luthers Christologie als Lehre von der Idiomenkommunikation*. Berlin and New York: de Gruyter.

Beutel, Albrecht (1991). *In dem Anfang war das Wort. Studien zu Luthers Sprachverständnis*. Tübingen: Mohr/Siebeck.

Brecht, Martin (1990). *Luther als Schriftsteller. Zeugnisse seines dichterischen Gestaltens*. Stuttgart: Calwer Verlag.

Ebeling, Gerhard (1971). *Einführung in theologische Sprachlehre*. Tübingen: Mohr/Siebeck.

Emrich, Britta (2010). 'Lebendige Stimme. Zu Wesen und Bedeutung der menschlichen Stimme nach Martin Luther'. *Luther* 81: 69–89.

Gerhard, Johann (1863). *Loci theologici*, ed. Eduard Preuss. Berlin: Schlawitz.

Illge, Hannes (2008). *Gewissheit durch das Wort. Eine sprachphilosophische Untersuchung von Luthers fundamentaltheologischer Einsicht.* Frankfurt am Main: Lang.

Joest, Wilfried (1967). *Ontologie der Person bei Luther.* Göttingen: Vandenhoeck & Ruprecht.

Maaser, Wolfgang (1999). *Die schöpferische Kraft des Wortes. Die Bedeutung der Rhetorik für Luthers Schöpfungs- und Ethikverständnis.* Neukirchen-Vluyn: Neukirchener Verlag.

Ringleben, Joachim (1997). 'Luther zur Metapher'. *Zeitschrift für Theologie und Kirche* 94: 336–69.

—— (2003). 'Metapher und Eschatologie bei Luther'. *Zeitschrift für Theologie und Kirche* 100: 222–39.

—— (2010). *Gott im Wort. Luthers Theologie von der Sprache her.* Tübingen: Mohr/Siebeck.

Steiger, Johann Anselm (1996). 'Die communicatio idiomatum als Achse und Motor der Theologie Luthers. Der "fröhliche Wechsel" als hermeneutischer Schlüssel zu Abendmahlslehre, Anthropologie, Seelsorge, Naturtheologie, Rhetorik und Humor'. *Neue Zeitschrift für systematische Theologie und Religionsphilosophie* 38: 1–28.

Stolt, Birgit (2000). *Martin Luthers Rhetorik des Herzens.* Tübingen: Mohr/Siebeck.

von Lüpke, Johannes (1992). 'Theologie als "Grammatik zur Sprache der heiligen Schrift". Eine Studie zu Luthers Theologieverständnis', *Neue Zeitschrift für systematische Theologie und Religionsphilosophie* 34: 227–50.

Wolf, Herbert (1980). *Martin Luther. Eine Einführung in germanistische Luther-Studien.* Stuttgart: Metzler.

—— (ed.) (1996). *Luthers Deutsch. Sprachliche Leistung und Wirkung.* Frankfurt am Main: Lang.

SUGGESTED READING

Bielfeldt, Dennis (2002). 'Luther on Language'. *Lutheran Quarterly* 16: 195–220.

Bielfeldt, Dennis, Mickey L. Mattox, and Paul Hinlicky (2008). *The Substance of the Faith: Luther's Doctrinal Theology for Today.* Minneapolis: Fortress.

Stolt, Birgit (1989). 'Lieblichkeit und Zier, Ungestüm und Donner. Martin Luther im Spiegel seiner Sprache'. *Zeitschrift für Theologie und Kirche* 86: 282–305.

Streiff, Stefan (1993). *'Novis linguis loqui'. Martin Luthers Disputation über Joh 1,14 'verbum caro factum est' aus dem Jahr 1539.* Göttingen: Vandenhoeck & Ruprecht.

von Lüpke, Johannes (2009). 'Gott in seinem Wort wahrnehmen. Überlegungen zu einem nach-metaphysischen Gottesverständnis im Anschluss an Anselm von Canterbury und Martin Luther'. In *Phänomenologie und Theologie*, ed. Klaus Held und Thomas Söding. Freiburg im Br.: Herder, 74–105.

CHAPTER 11

....

LUTHER'S
THEOLOGIA CRUCIS

....

VÍTOR WESTHELLE

I. THEOLOGY OF THE CROSS: AN IRONIC
EPISTEMIC MOVE

....

CRUX *sola est nostra theologia*, 'the cross alone is our theology' wrote Luther in *Operationes in Psalmos* of 1519–21 (WA5.176,32–33). This short definition comes in the aftermath of his Heidelberg Disputation of 1518. In the Heidelberg Disputation Luther, with alacrity and precision, presents the much celebrated distinction between the *theologia gloriae* and *theologia crucis*, or as Luther most often preferred to phrase it, the distinction between the *theologian* of glory (*theologus gloriae*) and the *theologian* of the cross (*theologus crucis*): 'A theologian of glory calls evil good and good evil. A theologian of the cross calls the thing what it actually is' (*Theologus gloriae dicit malum bonum et bonum malum, Theologus crucis dicit id quod res est.* [thesis 21], WA1.354,21–22; LW31.40). Gerhard Forde called attention to Luther's preferred choice of words and points to the subject of doing theology instead of being the object of the discourse: 'Luther does not talk about theology in the abstract but rather about the different kinds of theologians and what they do, and the way they operate' (Forde 1997: 11). This distinction became the sharpest expression of Luther's rejection of the dominant canons of rationality that have been accepted as ancillary partners of theology (*ancillae theologiae*) guiding and ordering the theological discourse (Bayer 2007: esp. 16–32). Such a rupture with dominant ways of thinking or speculation was kindled by Luther's discovery of the epistemological implications of the scandal of having a crucified God. 'Calling the thing what it is' takes away from theology the pretence of saving God from death and humiliation. This epistemological gesture of Luther was eclipsed during Protestant Orthodoxy but somehow resurfaced with the emergence of pietism and its emphasis on *praxis* and not *theoria*.[1] Later came the devastating effects of the Enlightenment and its criticism of the traditional pillars that supposedly sustained the Christian church rationally.[2] For the theologian of the cross, reason does not sustain that which faith alone maintains, which again raised the question of the relationship between theology and the philosophy of science (Bayer 2007: 74–82). A window for reconsideration of the importance of Luther's insights was open, but the opportunity was not seized.

The theses of the Heidelberg Disputation, the *locus classicus* for the *theologia crucis*, conclude with an often overlooked section on philosophy, which explains what those accepted canons were for the contemporary reader. The frequent polemical references to Aristotle (in all but three of the twelve theses) are figurative expressions or metonymies for speculative and rational theological constructs in general. Medieval standards for theology began with general philosophical assumptions—most often appealing to Aristotle—to establish the premises of natural revelation before special revelation could be presented. However, Luther is sardonic in these philosophical theses. If the present-day reader were to take them up first, it would be clear that the philosophical theses provide the background for his basic argument in the theological theses. The fact that he places them at the end is an ironic subversion on the part of the reformer.

The Disputation opens with two seminal concepts that were to inform Luther's theology throughout his life: law and work. These categories also function in the later Luther as synecdoches for two of the earthly spheres, or orders of creation, for which humans are responsible and 'cooperators with God' (as he eloquently phrased it earlier in the *On Bound Choice* [WA18.754,14–16; LW33.243]): *oeconomia* and *politia*. In these orders philosophy and science—even Aristotle's—have something to contribute. Luther agreed that the hegemonic modes of rationality are not necessarily opposed to theology but definitely are distinct fora (*sunt diversa non contraria* [WA39,2.26,29–31,11–18,31,17–25; LW38.259]). However, his earlier work of radically distinguishing them was the necessary and opportune move to bring an epistemic change to the way theology was being done. Luther's theological manifesto was indeed 'only the cross is our theology' even as it did not exhaust the scope of what he had to say.

It was Martin Heidegger, in *Being and Time*, that brought Luther's epistemologically novel approach into the limelight. In the introduction of his opus he writes:

> *Theology* is seeking a more primordial interpretation of man's Being toward God, prescribed by the meaning of faith itself and remaining within it. It is slowly beginning to understand once more Luther's insight that the 'foundation' on which its

---

[1] See, e.g., Spener 1964: 95: 'it is by no means enough to have knowledge of the Christian faith, for Christianity consists rather of practice'. Luther is quoted more than any other author and always with reverence and affection, even if it certainly misses Luther's worldliness and the recognition of the *vita passiva* for the reception of faith.

[2] See the classic essay by Gotthold Ephraim Lessing, 'On the Proof of the Spirit and of Power' with his famous thesis: 'accidental truths of history can never become the proof of necessary truths of reason'. In Lessing 1957: 53.

system of dogma rests has not arisen from an inquiry in which faith is primary, and that conceptually this 'foundation' not only is inadequate for the problematic of theology, but conceals and distorts it. (Heidegger 1962: 30)

For Luther the concealment and distortion was manifest in the ways in which the cross and the contradictions it entails were veiled and domesticated. The theology of the cross is a *habitus*, a way of accepting contradictions. The very expression the*ology* of the cross is thus an oxymoron, for the cross does not fit into a logical scheme, a 'foundation'. It implies an ironic epistemic move (cf. Solberg 1997: 95–139; Kolb 2005: 3 and also p. 148 discussing a passage in *On Bound Choice* regarding the necessary weakness of human knowledge in the understanding of the Word of God [WA18.659,28–33; LW33.99–100]).

II. TWO INTERPRETATIVE TENDENCIES

Luther used the expression 'theology of the cross' (*theologia crucis*) for the first time in his lectures on the epistle to the Hebrews of 1517–18. The context in which it emerged is precisely the one that stresses the unresolvable paradoxes. In this lecture he wrote:

> Frequently in the Scriptures there are two opposite ideas side by side. For example, judgment and righteousness, wrath and grace, death and life, evil and good. This is what is referred to in the phrase...'And alien work is done by him so that he might affect his proper work' [Is 28:21]...Here we find the Theology of the Cross, or, as the apostle expresses it: 'The word of the cross is a stumbling block to the Jews, and foolishness to the Gentiles' [1 Cor 1:18, 23], because it is utterly hidden from their eyes.
>
> (WA57,3.79,2–80,11; cited in Prenter 1971: 1–2)

Luther's resolve to keep the irresolution that the cross entails is directed to the two dominant 'solutions' he inherited from the models of atonement developed in medieval theology. These are represented by Anselm's 'satisfaction' model and by the 'moral influence' theory suggested by Abelard. Both options—one emphasizing the objective dimension of the cross event as working out the redemptive work of Christ and the other the subjective affection of a radically loving gesture—worked out the contradiction into a resolution. One tends toward a sacramental emphasis, working *ex opere operato*, while the other emphasizes the cross as an exemplary token. Neither is to be excluded, *exemplum et sacramentum* (WA5.639,32–34. WA2.501,34–37; LW27.238. See also Bayer 1971: 78–100; Blaumeiser 1995: 368–82), God's favour and God's gift. Luther's retention of the paradox, his decisive avoidance of 'closure', keeps the focus on a cross that we simultaneously behold and endure.

Danish theologian Regin Prenter put this very sharply when discussing Luther's theology of the cross in relation to the two dominant schools of theology in Germany, at the time the hegemonic centre of Protestant theology. These schools were easily recognized by the names Rudolf Bultmann and Karl Barth. Prenter's evaluation of these two main theological currents when he originally wrote his essay (Prenter 1959) is worth looking into. The first was a theology of the cross without the Word, while the latter was a theology of the Word without the cross. He concludes his essay with these words, referring to Barth and Bultmann respectively:

> But a cross which is either only objective (outside of us) or only subjective (personal to us) is not the cross of Christ which is the means of our salvation. The deep truth of Luther's theology of the cross is that it views the cross on Golgotha and the cross which is laid upon us as *one* and the same. Is there no wisdom in this old truth for our own teaching and life? (Prenter 1959: 18)

For Prenter 'the cross we are called to bear is in a mysterious way identical with the cross of Christ' (Prenter 1959: 13). This brings to the fore a pertinent point in Luther's use of the cross-motif. The reformer normally equated the cross of Christ and (human) suffering and often used cross and (human) suffering interchangeably. However, even as this equation avoids the pitfalls of the objective Anselmian or the subjective Abelardian types, it can easily equalize suffering across the board, which Luther himself could be accused of, particularly in the crucial year of 1525, with the tragic events that culminated in the Peasant Revolt (Ruge-Jones 2008: 152–9). However, the suffering he equated with the cross is not a state of mind but a physical and concrete condition in which not all participate in the same way. In the commentary on the *Magnificat* (1521) he became very explicit:

> You must feel the pinch of poverty in the midst of your hunger and learn by experience what hunger and poverty are, with no provision on hand and no help in yourself or any other man, but in God only; so that the work may be God's alone and impossible to be done by any other. You must not only think and speak of a low estate but actually come to be in a low estate and caught in it.
>
> (WA7.593,30–594,3; LW21.347–348)

Prenter is the first to acknowledge that 'Luther is not speaking here about spiritual hunger and thirst, but about actual physical hunger and thirst' (Prenter 1959: 17). But then he immediately asks the pertinent question that a sensitive privileged person would ask: 'Can we go along with all this? And if not, must we then not admit that Luther's theology of the cross is not relevant for us? I will not go so far as to say that Luther's theology of the cross is completely irrelevant to us' (Prenter 1959: 17). And why is it not *completely* irrelevant? Because we still experience 'the reality of guilt and death'. At the end of his otherwise enlightening analysis Prenter still fell back into a sacramental interpretation of the vicarious suffering of Christ.

Another attempt to avoid the objective–subjective pitfall in discussing the theology of the cross can be found, for example, in the work of Jon Sobrino, a Jesuit theologian from El Salvador. He is a Spaniard who followed Luther's counsel to feel himself 'the pinch of poverty' and went to work in Central America. He confesses his preference for the 'Lutheran' option for a theology of the cross that is not caught in metaphysical theodicies, or in atonement theories (Sobrino 1993: 235). Like Prenter he does combine the particularity of the cross of Jesus with the suffering of daily life but does not equate them. Rather, Sobrino speaks of an 'analogous' relation between the cross that Christ endured and the 'crucified people...the ones who most abundantly and cruelly "fill up in their flesh what is lacking in Christ's passion". They are the Suffering Servant and they are the Crucified Christ today' (Sobrino 1993: 271). Sobrino's merit is to recognize the particularities of sufferings and their social locations. They cannot be equated but only analogically related. He avoids the sacramentally vicarious interpretation and says that 'the only suffering that has meaning is the suffering for the sake of struggling against suffering' (Sobrino 1993: 241). He attributes this approach to Dorothee Soelle (1975). Here is where the cross of Christ becomes an exemplary case. The one who so suffers becomes also a redemptive agent. But how can the victim's struggle become redeeming for herself if it brings her end? Even as Prenter leaned toward a sacramental view, Sobrino governs his use of the motif only from the exemplary interpretation.

These two options in the interpretation of the theology of the cross have been already detected in a different context by the influential work of Walther von Loewenich, *Luther's Theology of the Cross* (1976). But Loewenich's theological frame is more related to the doctrine of justification than to atonement theories. In the introduction of the first German edition of this book (1929) von Loewenich gave the reason for the stance he took:

> In current research it is generally regarded as settled that Luther's theology of the cross must be understood as his pre-Reformation theology.... Otto Ritschl gave the clearest expression to this view.... Ritschl claims that the theology of the cross bears a typically monkish stamp and thereby proves to be only a preliminary stage of the real Luther. (von Loewenich 1976: 12)

Von Loewenich's interpretation of the theology of the cross severs any relation between the theology of the cross and mysticism and locates it as the core of Luther's Reformation theology; it was not a relic of ingrained monkish life. But with this he also reveals that his programmatic move was predicated on a particular contextual cleavage in post-First World War Germany and the strong emergence of the 'neo-orthodox' movement that rejected all but the supremacy of the *verbum externum*, the word that does not indwell in creation, it is *extra nos*. In his 'Addendum' to the fourth edition some three decades later he offers a careful yet candid acknowledgement:

> I continue to maintain that Luther's theology of the cross and the German mysticism of the Middle Ages are basic conceptions that diverge. But I have made this difference too pointed in a systematic way, and turned it into an absolute antithesis for the sake of the conclusion. With that I paid my tribute to the dominant theological view of the time. (von Loewenich 1976: 221–2)

This discussion and the ensuing tendencies are indeed very contextually bound. Consequently present Luther research is ploughing its way to some implication of how to read the theology of the cross in the context of the debate over Luther's understanding of justification. The debate ranges from a *forensic* understanding of it that emphasizes the priority of the external Word, received in faith, as an act of imputation of a benefit (*favor*) in declaring the sinner righteous, and the *indwelling* of Christ through faith (*theosis*) in which Christ is received as gift (*donum*) (Braaten and Jenson 1998, cf. on the specific relationship of *theosis* to Luther's *theologia crucis*, Peura 1994: 175–94).

The emergence of the cross-motif in Luther's early theology and his interpretation of the righteousness of God, the Reformation's breakthrough, go hand in hand. The distinction between *theologia gloriae* and *theologia crucis* is connected with the 'new definition of righteousness' (WA31,2.439,19–20; LW17.230), as the reformer enticingly phrased it. And it is so because it distinguishes *active* speculation from the purely 'pathic experience', a simple and utterly *receptive* disposition (*vita passiva*) that alone makes a theologian (*Sola experientia facit theologum*, WATR1.16,13, §46; LW54.7). In this context, the attempt to frame Luther's theology in general, and his theology of the cross in particular, regardless of its merits, might be misguided if the paradigms offered and employed are the ones that have dominated the Western academic world since the nineteenth century, or as von Loewenich aptly phrased it in his 'confession', in 'the dominant theological view of the time'.

III. A New Definition of Justice (Righteousness)

The doctrine of justification and the theology of the cross are distinct but symmetrically complementary perspectives through which Luther unfolds all the further aspects of his theological work, as the two focal points of an ellipsis. Already for the early Luther, *iustitia dei* required a rupture with human rationality defined by the *economic* principle of fair exchange, 'I give so that you give back' (*do ut des*), and the *juridical* retributive principle of giving to each his due (*suum cuique*) (WA31,2.439,5–7; LW17.229). These principles found their way into Anselm's celebrated question: *Cur Deus Homo?* (Wherefore God became human?). Not long after Anselm's argument became public, Abelard responded carrying the premise of Anselm to its logical absurdity. If God's son had to die to pay for human sin, who is to pay for killing the son of God? Abelard abandoned the question of justice altogether and gave prominence to God's love that does not need to comply with juridical principles. But for Luther the question of justice could not be evaded. What tormented him was the classical and hegemonic definition of it as controlled by human reason. That was his theological struggle in the years that led to the inception of the theology of the cross as it was explicitly named between 1517 and 1518 (on this development, see McGrath 1985: esp. 95–147).

A decade later, Luther carefully elaborated the meaning and magnitude of this discovery. In his 1528 lectures on Isaiah, he provided this definition: 'Behold the new definition of justice [*definitionem novam iusticiae*]: justice is the knowledge of Christ [*iusticia est cognitio Christi*]' (WA31,2.439,19–20; LW17.230). The expression *cognitio Christi* must be understood as a double genitive: We need to know about Christ, but equally have the mind of Christ in us. In other words, this knowledge is not only historical but also existential, Christ in our stead and we in the stead of Christ in his relationship to the Father.

Luther used Isaiah 53, the song of the Suffering Servant, as the springboard for his explication and employs the expression 'wonderful exchange' (*mirabilem mutationem*). Such exchange is marvellous in that it nullifies what human reason's definition of justice, at its best, attributes also to God: *suum cuique*. He goes on to explicitly state: 'The sophists say that righteousness is the fixed will to render to each his own' (*Iusticia est constans voluntas renddendi cuique, quod suum est*, WA31,2.439,5–6; LW 17.229).

IV. THE HIDDENNESS OF GOD

Jesus on the cross was not the Anselmian settling of accounts. He was God as a gift in a sacrificial act of revelation that at the same time discloses the human condition and God's hidden identification with it. Both entail an ironic severance with the predominant mode of rationality based on analogical reasoning, in ordered discourses, and systems of speculative accomplishments. In the early Luther these ordered discourses fall into two broad categories, law and work, which are metonymies for the two estates (*Stände*), *politia* and *oeconomia*, that he develops positively as orders of creation alongside *ecclesia* (cf. Ch. 25 in this volume). They are good and necessary but not of the essence for the theological endeavour *stricto sensu*. They are God's masks (*larvae*). God is only revealed there where the Word became flesh and took the decisive consequences of embodiment: death, and death on a cross as an executed criminal. In this revelation *sub contrariis*, 'under its opposite', God is ultimately revealed as the Word incarnate, taking the ultimate consequences of creation, sin, decay, and death. For that very reason it defies the *logos* of this world and its regimes of the acceptable truth.[3] But it begs the question of how this could be revelation. This led Luther to make a sharp distinction between God in God-self, God's aseity, and God revealed in the Word, the 'preached God': 'God must be left to himself in his own majesty … it is no business of ours. … [we must make] the distinction between God preached and God hidden, that is, between the Word of God and God himself' (WA18.685,14–27; LW33.139–140).

What needs to be kept in mind is that when Luther speaks of the hiddenness of God two senses are implied. One says that God is hidden *sub contraria specie* as in

---

[3] In Dietrich Bonhoeffer's early lectures on Christology he captured Luther's point: 'Christ is the Counter-Logos. Classification is no longer a possibility, because the existence of this logos spells the end of the human logos' (1978: 30).

the cross, in suffering, and death. Yet another sense implied is of a God hidden even behind the Word. Early in the twentieth century von Loewenich and Paul Althaus already detected this double sense which is elucidated in "To the Unknown God', an essay by Brian Gerrish (1973; cf. von Loewenich 1976: 221, the correction in the 'Addendum' to the fourth edition). God is both hidden *in* and *behind* the cross (McGrath criticizes this 'ambivalence': 164–5). The crucial passage in Luther comes from *On Bound Choice*, where he has a lengthy discussion on the 'distinction between the Word of God and God himself', who 'is not to be inquired into, but reverently adored, as by far the most awe-inspiring secret of Divine Majesty, reserved for himself alone and forbidden to us' (WA18.285,25–31; LW33.139–140). To use the expression of Rudolf Otto, the divine is at the same time *fascinans* and *tremendum*; it makes us wonder in devotion and tremble at what may come. David Tracy offers a pertinent comment:

> All Christian theology today needs to read Luther again for rethinking both Hiddenness I and II in God: Hiddenness I for facing the central christological insight that God is understood in Christ *sub contrariis* in and through Christ's cross and, in the light of that cross, in and through the suffering caused by all violence throughout history; and Hiddenness II to allow one to admit the fearsomeness of God that Luther, in his volcanic religious experiences as well as in his commentaries on Genesis and Isaiah, makes available to all serious readers of the complexity and ambiguity of the full biblical portrait of God. It is Luther (here quite different from even Augustine and Pascal) who will not hesitate to reflect on what the ancient Greek tragedians named 'fate'. (Tracy 1996: 11)

Again in his argument against Erasmus in *On Bound Choice*, Luther, in defending the clarity of Scripture (*claritas scripturae*), says that whatever is not revealed in it and pointing to Christ belongs to a mystery that we cannot explain or dare to speculate about; the Scriptures are enough (*sola scriptura*); not that by them we will be appeased and satisfied but because with them we will be nourished to continue to wonder the mystery (WA18.631,37–632,2; LW33.60). He refuses to venture into the territory that explores God's intent or election and predestination. This territory remains uncharted. 'Let God be God' is a daunting affirmation of this (WA10,1,1.24,4–11; CP7.117; cf. Kolb 2005: 32–4). But it is better to admit that there is an inscrutable shadow-side to God than the other options available. It is simply a descriptive statement of our finite experience, and of the very finitude of our reason. If it is blasphemy, it is Job's; this is the one God who is great enough to take it. In Luther's words, it is 'to flee from and find refuge in God against God' (*ad deum contra deum confungere*, WA5.204,26–27).

Theology is properly done *in usu passionis*, at the foot of the cross. It demands a suspension of all human endeavours and, particularly, those that pertain to theological and systematic constructions. Therefore, Luther never adopted or developed the models of atonement competing at his time but instead pointed to the cross rather as an epistemological cipher that destabilizes all theological discourse and theoretical, or speculative, achievements so that the Word of God can be heard.[4] Luther widely used the expression, 'theologian of the cross', and less frequently referred to 'theology of the cross'. This points to his resistance to reify theological discourse but rather to regard it as *usus*, an experience, an attitude (*animus*), or a disposition (*habitus*) toward the reception of God's free grace. When the expression *theologia crucis* is used, it should be primarily understood as a subjective genitive: it is from the standpoint of the cross that theology itself is possible.

The theology of the cross is the doctrine of justification and vice versa. Justification accomplishes its work by killing all that pertains to human efforts and accomplishments (*vita activa*) (WA5.165,33–37; see Bayer 2007: 106–14; Westhelle 2010a); the cross represents the reality of Jesus' passion in surrendering to God, and is also the symbol[5] for all human suffering insofar as it is an experience of the human participation in the same pathos where God, as *deus absconditus*, ubiquitously meets us. Cross and suffering as pathos becomes the key to divine revelation under its opposite (*sub contraria specie*). In consequence, revelation under its opposite entails the double meaning referred to earlier: it denotes the cross of Christ as God's solidarity with humanity and is conveyed by the Word of God (revelation hidden in the cross), but it also denotes the human suffering that the Word does not decode or explain (revelation hidden behind the cross). God's hidden revelation appears not only in the word of the cross but also beyond and behind it. In biblical terms the difference between the two encompasses the spectrum of the passion narrative of Mark's Gospel and the book of Job.

V. Developing Further Theological Consequences

Although Luther's most celebrated works on *theologia crucis* are dated from the early Reformation through 1525, the basic theme receives renewed treatment in various later works, both in continuity with the early work (cf., e.g., Kolb 2010), but also in applying it to other theological loci. If explicit references to the theology of the cross dwindle, what the reformer does is to elaborate some of the theological consequences and hermeneutical implications of the insights evoked by the theology of the cross.

In the *Confession Concerning Christ's Supper* of 1528 (WA26.326,29–327,23; LW37.214–215, quoted in Formula of Concord, Solid Declaration VII.94–103, BSLK 1006–8; BC

---

[4] Aulén 1961: 101–22 argues that although atonement was not a central topic for the early Reformation, Luther, contrary to many of his followers and interpreters, aligned himself at least implicitly with the 'classical type' used during the Patristic period departing decisively from the Anselmian ('Latin') type.

[5] Symbol is here used in its strong Tillichian sense as that which points to a reality in which it *participates*. See Tillich 1951: 177: 'The concept of participation has many functions. A symbol participates in the reality it symbolizes; the knower participates in the known; . . . the Christian participates in the New Being as it is manifest in Jesus the Christ.'

609–11) Luther presented three modes of Christ's presence. After describing the first ('circumscribed corporeal', i.e., the historical Jesus), and the second ('incomprehensible, spiritual', as in the sacrament of the altar), he went on to describe the 'divine heavenly, exalted mode'. According to this mode one 'must place the existence of Christ, which constitutes him as one person with God, far, far beyond things created, as far as God transcends them; and, on the other hand, place it as deep in and as near as God is in them'. This presence needs to be material, enfleshed in the finitude of matter to its most radical consequences and depth, even in death itself 'otherwise our faith is false' (WA26.336,15–18; LW37.223, see Anthony 2010). Dying is the ultimate form of pathos, of radical receptivity that excludes any juridical (law) or economic (work) negotiation. This explains why, for Luther, the theology of the cross essentially links the passion of Christ with human suffering as we saw above (Prenter 1971: 4). All suffering is an experience of *passio*, of receptivity that makes any human effort to administer it a failure. The cross of Jesus and suffering are essentially identical because the cross of the historical Jesus is identified with the human situation as the condition for the reception of grace and the annulment of law and work. In the cross, death and gift coincide. And implicit in this 'third mode' is something that still needs further development (but see Gregersen 2009). What is the implication of this to all things created, including the whole planetary environment, if God is in Christ there in the depth of all suffering, immersed in what Luther once called 'the majesty of matter'?

If in the *Confession* of 1528 Luther takes the insight of the theology of the cross and applies it to Christology and particularly to his interpretation of Chalcedon (cf. Westhelle 2010a), in the preface to the publication of his German texts from 1539 (WA50.659.3–660,16; LW34.287; cf. Bayer 2007: 42–65), Luther takes the methodological consequences of doing theology at the foot of the cross. There he describes what makes a preacher and a theologian. During the Middle Ages theologizing was largely accepted as comprising three steps: *lectio*, *oratio*, and *contemplatio*. Luther changes the order of the first two. He starts with *oratio* and then moves to *meditatio* (which includes *lectio*). But what is more significant and relevant for our topic: he totally changes the last step from *contemplatio* to *tentatio*. His choice of inserting these terms in Latin in the midst of a German text underscores his intention of making clear where the difference lay between his way of doing theology and the dominant one in the Middle Ages. The radical difference finds itself in the explanation where he presents his choice for a German translation: 'Third, there is *tentatio*, *Anfechtung*. This is the touchstone that teaches you not only to know and understand, but also to experience how right, how true, how sweet, how lovely, how mighty, how comforting God's Word is, wisdom beyond all wisdom.' *Anfechtung* means being in trial, probation, and tribulation, spiritual or otherwise. This is the 'touchstone' because you cannot do theology without *experiencing* cross and suffering and persecution. Prayer and meditation ought to lead to *Anfechtung* only so we may know that the Devil and his minions are indeed being confronted.

In the later Luther, cross and suffering made their appearance very explicitly in his discussion of the church in *On the Councils and the Church*, of 1539 (WA50.628,35–643,52; LW34.148–166). In this text he expanded his earlier (1519) minimalist definition of the church comprising alone the gathering around Word and sacrament (WA2.754,9–16; LW35.67, used by Melanchthon in the Augsburg Confession article VII and by Calvin in *Institutes* IV.I,9). In the 1539 text Luther enumerated seven marks or holy possessions. The first four are encompassed in Word and Sacrament (Word, Baptism, Lord's Supper, Confession and Forgiveness, which is the daily return to Baptism). Then he adds two, Ministry and Public Worship, which are indirectly implied in the church as a community gathered around Word and Sacrament. Yet a seventh mark is definitely added: cross and suffering, which is his application of the consequences of the theology of the cross to ecclesiology. This is significant insofar as not only the individual Christian, but the social collectivity of the community is in itself, as community, suffering affliction and persecution (*tentatio, Anfechtung*), which therefore also makes the church a space for a revelatory event.

Hence regardless whether it is the individual, the theologian in her vocation, the church, or the world, the cross remains as the theological criterion *sine qua non: crux probat omnia* (WA5.179,31).

REFERENCES

Anthony, Neal J. (2010). *Cross Narratives: Martin Luther's Christology and the Location of Redemption*. Eugene, OR: Pickwick.

Aulén, Gustaf (1961). *Christus Victor: An Historical Study of the Three Main Types of the Idea of Atonement*, trans. A. G. Hebart. New York: Macmillan.

Bandt, Hellmut (1958). *Luthers Lehre vom verborgenen Gott. Eine Untersuchung zu dem offenbarungsgeschichtlichen Ansatz seiner Theologie*. Berlin: Evangelische Verlagsanstalt.

Bayer, Oswald (1971). *Promissio: Geschichte der reformatorischen Wende in Luthers Theologie*. Göttingen: Vandenhoeck & Ruprecht.

—— (2007). *Theology the Lutheran Way*, trans. Jeffrey G. Silcock and Mark C. Mattes. Grand Rapids, MI: Eerdmans.

Blaumeiser, Hubertus (1995). *Martin Luthers Kreuzestheologie. Schlüssel zu seiner Deutung von Mensch und Wirklichkeit. Eine Untersuchung anhand der Operationes in Psalmos (1519–21)*. Paderborn: Bonifatius.

Bonhoeffer, Dietrich (1978). *Christ the Center*, trans. Edwin H. Robertson. San Francisco: Harper & Row.

Braaten, Carl E. and Robert W. Jenson (eds.) (1998). *Union with Christ: The New Finnish Interpretation of Luther*. Grand Rapids, MI: Eerdmans.

Forde, Gerhard O. (1997). *On Being a Theologian of the Cross: Reflections on Luther's Heidelberg Disputation, 1518*. Grand Rapids, MI: Eerdmans.

Gerrish, Brian A. (1973). 'To the Unknown God: Luther and Calvin on the Hiddenness of God'. *Journal of Religion* 53: 263–92.

Gregersen, Niels Henrik (2009). 'Deep Incarnation: The Logos Became Flesh'. In *Transformative Theological Perspectives*, ed. Karen L. Bloomquist. Minneapolis: Lutheran University Press, 167–81.

Heidegger, Martin (1962). *Being and Time*, trans. John Macquarrie and Edward Robinson. New York: Harper & Row.

Kolb, Robert (2005). *Bound Choice, Election, and Wittenberg Theological Method: From Martin Luther to the Formula of Concord*. Grand Rapids, MI: Eerdmans.

—— (2010). 'Luther's Theology of the Cross Fifteen Years after Heidelberg: Luther's Lectures on the Psalms of Ascent'. *Journal of Ecclesiastical History* 61: 69–85.

Lessing, Gotthold Ephraim (1957). *Lessing's Theological Writings*, trans. and ed. Henry Chadwick. Stanford: Stanford University Press.

Loewenich, Walther von (1976). *Luther's Theology of the Cross*, trans. Herbert J. A. Bouman. Minneapolis: Augsburg.

McGrath, Alister E. (1985). *Luther's Theology of the Cross: Martin Luther's Theological Breakthrough*. Oxford: Blackwell.

Peura, Simo (1994). *Mehr als ein Mensch? Die Vergöttlichung als Thema der Theologie Martin Luthers von 1513 bis 1519*. Mainz: von Zabern.

Prenter, Regin (1959). 'Zur Theologie des Kreuzes bei Luther'. *Lutherische Rundschau: Zeitschrift des lutherischen Weltbundes* 1959/60: 270–83.

Prenter, Regin (1971). *Luther's Theology of the Cross*. Philadelphia: Fortress.

Ruge-Jones, Philip (2008). *Cross in Tensions: Luther's Theology of the Cross as Theologico-social Critique*. Eugene, OR: Pickwick.

Sobrino, Jon (1993). *Jesus the Liberator*. Maryknoll, NY: Orbis.

Soelle, Dorothee (1975). *Suffering*, trans. Everett R. Kalin. Philadelphia: Fortress.

Solberg, Mary (1997). *Compelling Knowledge: A Feminist Proposal for an Epistemology of the Cross*. New York: SUNY.

Spener, Philip Jacob (1964). *Pia Desideria*, trans. Theodore G. Tappert. Philadelphia: Fortress.

Tillich, Paul (1951). *Systematic Theology I*. Chicago: University of Chicago Press.

Tracy, David (1996). 'The Hidden God: The Divine Other of Liberation'. *Cross Currents* 46: 11.

Vercruysse, J. E. (1976). 'Luther's Theology of the Cross at the Time of the Heidelberg Disputation'. *Gregorianum* 57: 523–38.

Wengert, Timothy J. (2002). '"Peace, Peace . . . Cross, Cross": Reflections on How Martin Luther Relates the Theology of the Cross to Suffering'. *Theology Today* 59: 190–205.

Westhelle, Vítor (2006). *The Scandalous God: The Use and Abuse of the Cross*. Minneapolis: Fortress.

—— (2010a) 'Hybridity and Luther's Reading of Chalcedon'. In *Gudstankens aktualitet. Bidrag om teologiens opgave og indhold og protestantismens indre spaending: Festskrift til Peter Widmann*, ed. Else Marie Wiberg Pedersen, Bo Kristian Holm, and Andres-Christian Jacobsen. Copenhagen: ANIS, 233–54.

—— (2010b). 'Justification as Death and Gift'. *Lutheran Quarterly* 24: 249–62.

CHAPTER 12

··

LUTHER'S HERMENEUTICS
OF DISTINCTIONS

Law and Gospel, Two Kinds of
Righteousness, Two Realms, Freedom and
Bondage

··

ROBERT KOLB

MARTIN Luther's impact on church and society has arisen from a variety of causes. His contribution to Christian theological discussion and much of his influence on societal theory over the centuries rests upon his profound redefinition of the essence of the Christian faith and life (and thus of what it means to be human). Medieval religion on the popular level conceived of the relationship of God and human creatures fundamentally in terms of the human approach to God through ritual actions, in the liturgy and in a range of ritual practices that permeated daily life. Alongside this popular perception the clergy conceived of the bond that holds the church together as, above all, a hierarchical system, with the pope as the vicar of Christ at its head. Luther repudiated both fundamental conceptions. Throughout his career he frequently criticized an understanding of sacramental ritual as effective *ex opere operato*, understood to deliver grace to the faithful simply on the basis of their performance of and participation in the rite rather than through faith. He repeatedly challenged the claims of the hierarchy to special powers in dispensing grace and governing the church.

Reformers of all stripes asserted that these conceptions reflected more the pagan rhythms of the pre-Christian past than the biblical presentation of God's interaction with human creatures (Hendrix 2004: 1–35). The Wittenberg theologians joined significant late medieval thinkers in stressing the need for inward devotion to God and criticizing this use of external religious actions to seek God's favour (see chapters 3, 4). Luther and his colleagues strove rather to cultivate reliance on God's grace, his promise that creates trust in him, for gaining spiritual benefits, a view anticipated by some late

medieval thinkers as well. Luther rejected the papal claim to divinely established authority and power over the church integral to the papal system of governing the church. He
accorded pastors only the power to exercise God's Word publicly, power conveyed to all
God's people in oral, written, and sacramental forms of the Word.

Thus, Luther transformed the core definition of what it means to be Christian into a
relationship based essentially on God's approach to sinful human beings, in his Word. It
is his creative and re-creative instrument, whereby he brought the universe into being
(Gen. 1) and through which he changes the identity of sinners, making them his children by giving them trust in Christ and his atoning work in dying and rising.

This focus on God as a God in conversation and community with his people led
Luther to frame his thinking with three fundamental distinctions as he approached
Scripture and assessed human life: what God says to his human creatures (law and gospel), what it means to be human (two kinds of righteousness), and the spheres or dimensions in which human life is lived (two realms). He further presumed that Christ has
liberated believers from all that restricts the proper exercise of their humanity, freeing
them to live genuinely human lives, praising God and loving and serving other creatures, human and non-human. In different ways each distinction discloses Luther's
understanding that God is almighty Creator and Re-creator, alone responsible for all
that exists, including the reborn sinner who trusts in him, and that at the same time God
holds human creatures totally responsible for being the persons he made them to be.
He held these two axioms in tension without trying to resolve them into a harmonious
synthesis (Kolb 2012: 1–27).

I. The Proper Distinction of Law
and Gospel

Luther did not know that he was devising hermeneutical principles for generations to
come, so he was not always careful or consistent in his use of terminology that became
critical for his practice of theology. He also admitted that 'law' and 'gospel' have various meanings in Scripture; his own usage of the terms reflects this variety. But when he
defined 'law' and 'gospel' in distinction to each other, he emphasized the importance of
differentiating God's Word as it conveys his re-creative power through forgiveness of
sins, which claims sinners as his own children, rendering them righteous in his sight,
from the commands that express his expectations for their performance as his children.
'Gospel' in this sense speaks of God's gift, his actions, particularly in justifying rebellious
creatures through Christ's atoning work, restoring them to trust in him; 'law' speaks of
what their Creator designed human creatures to do, a design that finds sinners always
falling short and reaping condemnation.

Luther's use of this distinction illustrates how pastoral considerations governed his
thinking. He believed that pastoral care and consolation depend on distinguishing

the divine words which set forth what God expects human creatures to do, placing the burden of performance on them, from his words that create trust and thus restore the relationship for which he created human beings, through Christ's assuming the burden of their sin in his death and resurrection. This gospel also embraced the Holy Spirit's creation and maintenance of faith. Yet changing situations around the reformer led him to emphasize different aspects of each and of their relationship to each other as specific situations arose. The medieval Catholic accent on human works and their role in attaining grace and/or salvation provided a constant background to Luther's practice. Nonetheless, his assessment of the need of those whom he was addressing in specific situations for the call to repentance, the consolation of God's promise in Christ, or basic instruction in proper obedience to the Creator altered the tone, balance, and urgency of his exercise of the distinction. Genre also shaped his use of the distinction, as he preached to the Wittenberg inhabitants, addressed learned theologians of the Roman party, or sketched catechetical instruction for the public (Heintze 1958 treats Luther's homiletical application of the distinction).

At the end of Luther's life Melanchthon reflected the older colleague's guiding conviction for the practice of theology when he counted the proper distinction of law and gospel as his most important achievement (CR6.155–70; cf. CR11.726–34). In the 1510s this distinction had slowly taken form and rose in prominence in Luther's engagement with the biblical text (Herrmann 2005: 67–193). It remained part of the presuppositional framework for his application of Scripture to hearers' and readers' lives, but he treated the practice of the distinction as a topic in itself only twice in print. Both originally sermons, designed to aid Wittenberg hearers, he intended the published versions to aid village pastors, not as a technical theological examination but a guide to their own composition of sermons for calling their hearers to repentance and conveying to them forgiveness and life in Christ. The first (preached 1532) (WA36.8–42) reflected the struggle in the early 1530s with medieval concepts of grace won through human contribution and Luther's rejection of the legalism of the Schwärmer, e.g., Thomas Müntzer. The sermon shows the practical application of Luther's counterpoint to both, expressed in his Galatians lectures (1531), which also contain rich exposition and use of the distinction. The second (1537) entered the public discussion of the alleged 'antinomianism' of his former disciple Johann Agricola in the late 1530s (WA45.145–156). Both sermons defined law and gospel in much the same ways, but the former focused on the unconditional nature of God's gift of salvation through trust in Christ, the latter on the need for believers to hear the law as a call to repentance and instruction in Christian living.

Indeed, in every sermon Luther addressed the law to rebellious sinners, the gospel to troubled, despairing sinners (WA36.22,28–23,13, 41,13–14, 30–32), reflecting his belief that all theology delivers God's action to his people in their existential situation, either in their defiant rebellion against God or in their anguished disquiet under his judgement, whether understood explicitly or only implicitly. Thus, strictly speaking, in the existential context of fallen human experience, God's providential goodness in creating and providing for his creatures is not part of the gospel despairing sinners must hear.

Nonetheless, Luther frequently included it in his proclamation of the good news Jesus brings his people.

In 1521 he wrote, 'almost all Scripture and the understanding of all theology depends on the proper understanding of law and gospel' (WA7.502,34–35). In context the law had to come first, diagnosis before cure, as he noted in his catechetical *Prayerbook* of 1522 (WA10,2.376,19–377,13; LW43.13). Luther gave his students the elemental orientation for ministry as he began his Galatians lectures (1531): 'There are two words. One, the teaching of the law, must terrify, humiliate, distress.... Without this distinction we cannot preserve our theology. Christ is hidden, and no one can be given consolation' (WA40,1.44,5, 45,8). 'Whoever knows well how to distinguish gospel from law should thank God and know that he is a real theologian' (WA40,1.207,1–4; LW26.115). 'This is the distinction of law and gospel. Through the law a demand is made for what we should do. It presses for our activity for God and the neighbour. In the gospel we are required to receive a gift.... The gospel is pure gift, freely bestowed, salvation' (WA36.14,22–32, cf. 36.31,33–32,25). The two dare never be separated but must be strictly distinguished, for they are words from God of a different nature, with different impacts. Luther often used the analogy of killing and making alive, eliminating the identity of the sinner before God, changing that identity into his child (e.g., WA1.356,33–357.17; LW31.44; WA1.540,7–14; LW31.99). 'I destroy the one I am to help. The one I want to quicken, save, enrich, and make pious, I mortify, reject, impoverish, and reduce to nothing' (WA2.128,29–31; LW42.79).

In 1521 Luther introduced priests who were using his first postil for training in his way of preaching to his developing definition of gospel. He anchored it in Jesus Christ, in his death and resurrection (Kolb 2011). 'Gospel is and should be nothing else than a discourse or story about Christ... that he is the Son of God and became human for us, died, and was raised, that he has been established as Lord over all things' (WA10,1,1.13,3–6; LW35.117–118). In this treatise he defined 'law or commandment' as that which 'requires deeds of us'—in contrast to 'divine promises in which God promises, offers, and gives us all his possessions and benefits in Christ' (WA10,1,1.13,1–6; LW35.120). The nature of the gospel as a promise of forgiveness and new life became the heart of Luther's operative application of the benefits won by Christ for sinners through his death and resurrection (Bayer 1971). In Augustinian fashion he presented Christ as blessing, gift, or 'sacrament' and Christ as example. The chief message presents him as gift, a 'present God has given you' and 'the foundation and chief blessing of your salvation', but that led inevitably to taking 'him as your example, giving yourself in service to your neighbour just as you see that Christ has given himself for you', with the result that faith and love fulfil God's commands (WA10,1,1.11,12–13,2; LW 35.119–120).

When sinners view obedience to the law as a means by which they may merit salvation, Luther squared it off against the gospel, for then it either leads to idolatry (trust in one's own efforts) or crushes the sinner under the weight of its accusation or demand. In that case the gospel liberates the repentant person from the law's weight, consoling the anxious conscience. Faith receives a message from heaven, so that 'the law cannot make its demands on the troubled heart any longer; it has tortured and smothered us enough and must now yield to the gospel, which God's grace and mercy gives us' (WA36.22,18–21). The gospel concentrates the believer's attention on Christ, 'your treasure, your gift, your help, comfort, and saviour'. In critical situations the heart cannot distinguish promise and command, giving and requiring. When the conscience is hit head-on and feels its sin, and death is pressing, with war, pestilence, poverty, shame, and the like, the law says, 'You are lost. I demand this and that from you, but you have not done it and cannot do it.' When this happens, the law terrifies people to death, stomps on them, and they must despair. 'Whoever can make the distinction in this situation, make it! For here this distinguishing is absolutely necessary!' Implied here is an expansion of the negative impact of the law on those living outside God's design for life. All life's disruptions—war, pestilence, poverty, shame—can become voices of the law. They may not accuse, but they crush by making clear the dependence of victims of other people's sins or natural evils on something beyond the false gods on which they had been relying.

In the face of all voices of the law Christ helps sinners in two ways, Luther concludes. First, he takes their part against God's judgement upon them and serves as 'the cloak that is thrown over our shame—...because he has taken our sin and shame upon himself—but in God's sight he is the mercy seat, without sin and shame, pure virtue and honour. Like a brooding hen he spreads his wings over us to protect us from the hawk, that is, the devil with the sin and death that he causes. God has forgiven this sin for Christ's sake'. Second, Luther continued, 'he wants to give us the Holy Spirit and the strength to begin to love God and keep his commandments. When Christ demanded that the man give up everything to follow him (Matt. 19:16–25), he was saying that keeping God's commandments involves knowing and having Christ' (WA45.153,15–154,36).

Luther's definition of 'gospel' is less problematic for modern scholars than his understanding of God's law. The former remained much the same after 1520 although his imaginative application of biblical models and metaphors led to sprightly variation in his proclamation (Siggins 1970: esp. 108–43). 'The gospel or faith is something that does not demand our works or tell us what to do, but tells us to receive, to accept a gift, so that we are passive, that is, that God promises and says to you: "this and that I impart to you. You can do nothing for it; you have done nothing for it, but it is my doing"' (WA36.14,22–26). Luther based the 'gospel' on Christ's atoning work in his death and resurrection (Kolb 2011), not fitting neatly into Gustaf Aulén's atonement 'motifs' (1961) but using elements of both Christ's resurrection victory over all his people's enemies and his substitutionary satisfaction of the law's demand for the death of the sinner with his own death. Christ's entire work leads to the justification of sinners. Luther's gospel also embraced the work of the Holy Spirit which conveys the benefits of Christ through oral, written, and sacramental forms of this Word of forgiveness and new life based on his death and resurrection (chapters 17–20). Variations on these themes graced his preaching and lecturing. While scholars have argued about where the emphasis in Luther's proclamation of the atonement lay, disputes have been less pointed than those over the law.

Luther viewed the law as God's design for human life and therefore often praised it as the Creator's good gift, necessary for instruction of Christians. Nonetheless, sinners' existential encounters with the law always place their actions, and thus, their being, under its evaluation. Ultimately, whatever else the law may do to a person, it 'lays guilt upon me. I have not done this or that, I am unrighteous and a sinner in God's record of guilt. It is a word which puts my guilt on my account' (WA36.17,23–24, cf. 36.1–35). Such encounters are eschatological: the law either demands obedience or places sinners under judgement and pays them sin's wages, death (Rom. 6:23a). Christ fulfilled the law in place of sinners by dying under the law's condemnation (WA39,1.47,23–24, thesis 51; 49,14–17, theses 12–13; 50,18–21, theses 33–34; 52,18–19, thesis 74; 84,14–15, thesis 7; Peters 1981: 30–8) since the change of the sinner's identity to that of child of God involves the elimination of sin as well as the restoration of righteousness (Kolb 2011).

As God's design for living, the law functions in two ways, Luther wished to tell the papally called council (Smalcald Articles, III.ii, BSLK 436–7; BC 311–12). First, its purpose is to curb sin. In doing so it brings the blessing of social order (through threat of punishment or promise of reward). However, its curbing also produces rebels who simply want to defy God, and it produces false saints who try to use it to merit salvation. Its foremost function or power, however, reveals sin, original sin and its fruits. It evaluates sinners' actions, imprisoning them or crushing them like a hammer on a rock (Jer. 23:29) (WA40,1.517,10–518,6; cf. BSLK 436–7; BC 312). It demands their perfect obedience, beginning with trust in God (WA36.13,25–27, 30,19–35).

The heart of the law lay for Luther in the first commandment, which his *Small Catechism* explained as God's will that his human creatures 'fear, love, and trust in him above all things' (BSLK 507; BC 351; cf. WA36.8,14–10,18, 25,1–34, 28,12–36, 33–38). The law reveals 'what the human being is, what he was, and what he will become once more'. Its first prescriptive is ' "You shall love God with your whole heart".… You had this treasure in paradise and were created so that you could love God with your whole heart. You have lost that and must return to it. Otherwise, you cannot come into God's kingdom' (WA45.146,25–31). God's commands begin with the heart of humanity, the relationship of love and trust between God and creature. Out of that ultimate trust in him proceed all the deeds performed by human beings. Believers should reject all that distracts them from trusting and serving God, even commands of governmental or ecclesiastical authorities (WA36.20,3–21,22,39,9–40,23).

However, Luther also viewed God's design for human life expressed in his law as an aid for the believer's decision-making moved by the gospel. Luther repeatedly makes clear that the gospel liberates human creatures from the coercion and judgement of the law but not from God's design and plan for human living as the law reveals it: 'we must keep the Ten Commandments still, but we know when to keep them in their proper place' (WA36.18,6–7,14–16,29–31). Without ever adopting Melanchthon's term 'third use of the law', Luther frequently used God's commands for instructing his hearers in godly, upright living. Already in his Wartburg postil (1521–2) his concern for instructing people in the fruits of faith, proper godly behaviour in accord with God's commands, became clear and remained clear till the end of his life. In 1535 he wrote, 'I think of each commandment as, first, instruction, which is really what it is intended to be, and consider what the Lord God demands of me so earnestly. Second, I turn it into a thanksgiving; third, a confession; and fourth, a prayer' (WA38.365,1–4).

His instructive use emerged often in his Genesis lectures.

> Even though God demands our virtues and does not want us to be addicted to the lusts of the flesh but earnestly charges us not only to hold them in check but to slay them completely, yet our virtues cannot help us before God's judgment... The chief and most important part of teaching is the promise... Afterwards there is the law also. For God does not only promise but also gives orders and commands. The law covers your accommodating your will to what God commands.
>
> (WA42.564,27–29, 565,5–8, 12–18, 21–23; LW3.22–23)

'The law must not be cast aside because of the promise of grace but must be taught in order that discipline and instruction concerning good works may be retained and we may be taught to know and humble ourselves after we have sinned', so that people may 'govern and direct their conduct in a godly and prudent manner according to the norm of the law' (WA44.703,30–40; LW8.170–171).

An extensive discussion of the relation of God's expectation that his human creatures trust him above all else, expressed in a command, and his promise that bestows the gift of the trust that fulfils this impossible command apart from any human effort took place in the second quarter of the twentieth century (Heintze 1958: 121–7). It highlighted the interaction of God's total responsibility with the responsibility integral to humanness. Heintze argued that Luther's use of the law in all its aspects aimed at human good and thus should be subsumed under the gospel (Heintze 1958: 257ff.), thus missing the key point that law and gospel presume two different actors and two different kinds of human action: trust in response to the gospel, involving no human act of will but created by the Holy Spirit, and obedience to the law, which human thinking and willing produces (see Schloemann's critique, 1961: 36–42).

Luther's distinction of law and gospel has provoked a number of significant debates in the past two centuries. Gerhard Forde traced them to J. C. K. von Hofmann's attempt to relate Luther's thought to the modern world by rejecting the 'Anselmic' view of Christ's atoning work as substitutionary and satisfying the law's demand and the associated understanding of God's law as an 'ontological-static' given almost independent of God himself. Von Hofmann's 'salvation-history' programme for the revival of Lutheran thought attracted sharp critique from others in the Lutheran confessional revival, especially F. A. Philippi and Theodosius Harnack. Harnack criticized Albrecht Ritschl's dismissal of the concept of God's wrath and regarded von Hofmann's focus on the emergence of the new humanity through salvation-history as deficient, misguided, and wrong (Heintze 1958: 11–29; Schultz 1958: 86–193; Forde 1969: 3–134).

Karl Barth's rejection of the Lutheran law/gospel distinction and his insistence that God's law is fundamentally a word of grace led to a significant re-examination of the subject within Lutheranism, particularly focused on Luther's views of 'natural law' and of the third use of the law. This debate suffered in part from a lack of one agreed-upon definition of that third use, in part from a failure to recognize the nature of Luther's Ockhamistic view of the law as God's creation, tool, and his own design for humanity which he faithfully keeps in force. Critiques of various worth and perspective emerged in the 1930s–60s (Forde 1969: 137–233, Kinder and Haendler 1986), from, among others, Werner Elert (1948, 1962: 17–176), Helmut Thielicke (1948), Wilfried Joest (1951), Gustaf Wingren (1958: 310–22), Hans Joachim Iwand (1959), and Gerhard Ebeling (1970: 110–40). Althaus counselled substituting 'command' for God's positive instruction for living (1966a); others favoured the Pauline term '*paranesis*'. Whether labelled 'law' or not, discussion of God's expectations for human attitudes and actions continues to put the burden on the human being, and the proclaimer's intended 'use' often fails to have that intended impact or function in the hearer or reader. God's expectations remain God's expectations for his people's performance, whether called 'law', 'command', or 'gospel imperative'.

The nature of Luther's view of natural law and the extent to which he held to such a view has occasioned discussion (Lau 1933: esp. 42–4; Heintze 1958: 198–208; Heckel 2010: esp. 43–80). While he could defend his ethical statements by appealing to Scripture, later works continued to echo his position laid down in his *How Christians Should Regard Moses* (1525): Moses was the intermediary who delivered the law written also into Gentiles' hearts to Israel; therefore, his expression of this law retains validity only insofar as it agrees with the New Testament and natural law. 'I keep the commandments which Moses gave not because Moses gave them but because they have been implanted in me by nature, and Moses agrees precisely with nature' (WA16.380–23–5; LW 35.168; cf. his Genesis lectures [1545]; WA44.704.13–42; LW8.171–172; cf. Lau 1933: 42–4 and Heckel 2010).

Standard treatments of Luther's theology include summaries of the current state of the debate; the distinction permeates their entire analyses as well (Althaus 1966b: 251–73; Lohse 1999: 267–76; Barth 2009: 230–52; Bayer 2008: 58–66; Kolb 2009: 50–5). The many extensive examinations of Luther's distinction of law and gospel often tell more about their authors than the object of their research, for this distinction is always an exercise in the practical application of the biblical text to contemporaries' lives. Systematic theologians will continue to adapt the distinction to the ever-widening variety of contexts in which they work. Those contexts today include cultures with little sense of a personal God or of individual human responsibility, so vital for Luther's way of distinguishing the two. Nonetheless, contemporary Christian conversation can profit much from both his multi-faceted view of how Christ's death and resurrection relate to people in many situations and his conviction that the law functions in various ways to reveal the absence of the Creator in people's lives, not only in transgression of his commands and resulting guilt or shame. Historians need to deepen our understanding of Luther's own practice by repeating Heintze's kind of analysis (based on sermons on the first commandment, the Sermon on the Mount, and Christ's passion) in a larger assortment of Luther's preached and published sermons—two distinct genres even though the former (available second-hand from student notes) often were edited into the latter (processed by the third hand of the editor). All who engage Luther are irresistibly drawn into the magnetic field at the heart of his practice of theology, ensuring that the distinction of law and gospel will be debated wherever his works are read.

II. THE DISTINCTION OF TWO KINDS OF HUMAN RIGHTEOUSNESS

Luther spoke of God's action in its essential, verbal forms by distinguishing law and gospel. His view of what it means to be human took form in his distinction of 'two kinds of righteousness', two distinct aspects that constitute the human being. Related but not identical to law and gospel, this distinction provides the foundation for his explaining the human creature's relationship to God and to all God's other creatures, particularly other human beings.

Luther believed that Aristotle had misled Christians into thinking that human righteousness could be defined as performance of eternal law, obedient adherence to its commands. In 1518 he tested this conviction, distinguishing three aspects of humanity that were right or righteousness—the way God designed them to be—in their specific roles or contexts. His *Treatise on Three Kinds of Righteousness* (WA2.43–47) contrasted each with kinds of sin. Criminal sin, manifest evil, punishable by civil authorities, is the opposite of what Luther later called 'civil righteousness', behaviour that makes for orderly society and praise from others. A year later this kind of righteousness faded into the performance of good deeds by Christians because outwardly they may look quite similar and because all his readers were baptized Christians. At the heart of human sinfulness stands a second kind of sin, 'essential, inborn, original sin', inherited, corrupting all newborns and all their thoughts and deeds. At the heart of the humanity God created is the righteousness that is 'inborn, essential, original, from outside, the righteousness of Christ' (*iustitia aliena*, not best translated 'alien righteousness' but 'righteousness given from outside ourselves'). The third kind of sin, 'actual sin', the product of original sin, emerges in thoughts and deeds that human beings commit themselves. 'The righteousness produced within us' (*iustitia propria*, not best translated 'proper righteousness') takes form in what believers do in obedience to God's commands on the basis of their faith.

In 1519 Luther wrote in greater detail on *Two Kinds of Righteousness* (WA2.145–152; LW31.297–306), contrasting the righteousness of faith (*iustitia aliena*) with the righteousness of self-mortification and its product and necessary complement, love for the neighbour (*iustitia propria*). He turned finally to the terms passive and active righteousness and labelled this distinction 'our theology' in 1531: 'we teach a precise distinction between these two kinds of righteousness, the active and the passive, so that morality and faith, works and grace, secular society and religion may not be confused. Both are necessary, but both must be kept within their limits' (WA40,1.45,24–27; LW26.7; see Kolb and Arand 2008: 21–128).

'Righteousness', Luther recognized, 'is of many kinds', political, ceremonial, moral. In their specific purposes and places all identify human beings as truly human. 'Over and above there is the righteousness of faith' (WA40,1.40,16–27; LW26.4), 'this most excellent righteousness, the righteousness of faith, which God imputes to us through Christ without works' as a 'merely passive righteousness'. 'For here we work nothing, render nothing to God; we only receive and permit someone else to work in us, namely, God' (WA40,1.41,15 26; LW26.4 5).

Luther used the analogy of earth's needing the gift of rain to produce its fruit as an example of the nature of this passive righteousness found in the gift of trusting in God's re-creative action in Christ as the basis for human action. He did not specifically use the illustration of the distinction between the gift of life and identity given a child by the parents who conceive and give birth to him or her, on the one hand, and the actions of the child which fulfil its nature as a human being. Nonetheless, the language of parent and child filled his treatment of Christian existence. The two aspects of human existence consist of (1) the righteousness or identity that is given by whatever becomes 'god' for a person through ultimate trust, and (2) the forms of righteous performance and the identities that stem from the expectations of that 'god' for performance, actions corresponding to divine commands (LC, BSLK 560–3, 386–8).

Thus,

> the righteousness of the law...has to do with earthly things; by it we perform good works. But as the earth does not bring forth fruit unless it has been first watered and made fruitful from above...so also by the righteousness of the law we do nothing even when we do much; we do not fulfil the law even when we fulfil it. Without any merit or any work of our own, we must first become righteous by Christian righteousness...This righteousness is heavenly and passive....We do not perform it; we accept it by faith through which we ascend beyond all laws and works...for this righteousness means to do nothing, share nothing, and know nothing about the law or about works but to know and believe only this: that Christ has gone to the Father...that he is our high priest, interceding for us and reigning over us and in us through grace. (WA40,1.46,20–47,21; LW26.8)

Therefore, Luther asserted, 'I do not seek active righteousness. I ought to have and perform it; but I declare that even if I did have and perform it, I cannot trust in it or stand up before the judgement of God on the basis of it. Thus I put myself beyond all active righteousness, all righteousness of my own or of the divine law, and I embrace only the passive righteousness which is the righteousness of grace, mercy, and the forgiveness of sins' (WA40,1.42,26–43,15; LW26.6). Throughout, Luther tied the gift of passive righteousness for sinners to Christ; God had bestowed it in his creative act upon Adam and Eve at creation, but it returns to those who have rejected God only through Christ's death and resurrection (WA46.44,34–45,3; LW24.347; WA40,1.250,10–13; LW26.143; WA 40,1.300,15–22; LW26.179).

As an anthropological presupposition the distinction of two kinds of righteousness reinforces the distinction of law and gospel by emphasizing that the gospel alone establishes the core identity or righteousness of believers and moves them to produce the fruits of faith; the law prescribes and evaluates the human reaction to God. This reaction takes shape in faith, directing praise to God, and love to other creatures, human and otherwise. Thus, this anthropology lies at the heart of Luther's understanding of God's justification of sinners through the unconditional gifts of forgiveness and new life in Christ and of his sanctification of believers as he leads them into performing God's commands in relation to both him and all his creatures.

Scholars investigating Luther's thought have treated this distinction, though often without highlighting it (but see Althaus 1966b: 224–50; Ebeling 1970 122–4; Iwand 2008; Kolb and Arand 2008: 21–128). With mounting interest in theological exploration of what it means to be human, this way of discussing human identity and human responsibility will undoubtedly command more attention in the future.

III. The Distinction of Two Kingdoms and Two Realms

Luther employed the language of 'kingdoms' (*Reich*) in at least three different ways, never as a systematic 'doctrinal topic' but rather as framework or presupposition for viewing human life. Rarely he applied the label '*Reich*' to institutions of church and secular government, somewhat parallel to some medieval variations of Augustine's two cities framework (on how Luther digested and transformed medieval theories in accord with his distinction of law and gospel, see Mantey 2005). Much more frequently he used the terminology to designate God's rule in conflict with Satan's rule (see chapters 9, 24) and for the two spheres or dimensions of life in which God rules and Satan tries to subvert human faithfulness. These spheres are also labelled 'governments' (*Regiment*), 'right-hand' and 'left-hand' or 'heavenly' and 'earthly', referring to the vertical dimension of life, the relationship of human creature with the Creator, and the horizontal, the relationship with other creatures, human and non-human (Lau 1933, Cranz 1959, Bornkamm 1966, and Frostin 1994 can serve as introductions to the countless studies of the subject). The third category did not become a dogmatic topic in Lutheran theology and found use only indirectly until revived in the nineteenth century, in the service of two agendas. One served German political interests, at its furthest from Luther's intent, dividing Christian life into one sphere relating to God, the other under supervision of secular government (Duchrow 1970; Duchrow and Huber 1976: 19–140). The other used it to clarify the correlation of faith and works, of God's justification of sinners and their subsequent sanctified life of new obedience, focusing on carrying out God's command in the walks of life with which God had structured human life (see chapters 25–30, esp. 28).

Though often equated with law and gospel and active and passive righteousness respectively (Luther, too, obscured the distinction among these distinctions), Luther is clearest when we note that both the horizontal and the vertical dimensions of life are the spheres in which both law and gospel operate and both aspects of humanity function. In the relationship with God (Luther's heavenly realm) the gospel creates or establishes the relationship, but the first three commandments describe what believers do in practising the relationship of trust and praise. Passive righteousness constitutes this relationship, but active righteousness obeys the law that defines humanity as above all trusting God and then praising him. The believer's passive righteousness and the gospel provide motivation for living in proper relationships with God's creatures (Luther's earthly realm), and the law guides the actions produced by that motivation, directing decisions on how to be righteous towards other creatures actively.

Although Luther and Calvin are often depicted as having radically different concepts of the Christian in relation to society, David van Drunen has argued most plausibly that Luther's uses of 'two kingdoms' terminology found rather significant echoes in Calvin's thought (Van Drunen 2010).

Closely related to the distinction of the two realms in Luther's biblical exposition was his adaptation of medieval social theory, which distinguished three fundamental human situations, the household (which Luther divided into family life and economic activities), the society or governmental structures, and the church (see chapter 25). It should be noted that while the church's activities create and sustain the vertical dimension of life, the church operates in the 'left-handed realm' as an institution.

Several critical issues raised surrounding the distinction of the two realms have attracted attention, often leading to scholars becoming lost in the 'labyrinths' of this concept created by problems of their own eras. Particularly prominent has been the use of Luther to justify the autonomy of the secular sphere from God's law, an idea contrary to his thinking and his practice (Duchrow and Huber 1976). The two realms have also figured significantly in the discussion of the callings or vocations of Christians to serve God in all areas of life, and to do so according to the standards of 'civil righteousness' or 'natural law' (see esp. Wingren 1957: 162–212).

In the midst of social turmoil in various parts of the world, focus on Luther's contributions to thinking about the conflict of the kingdoms of God and Satan on the battlefields of God's two realms, in the vertical and horizontal dimensions of life, became prominent in discussions among Lutherans on topics of concern particularly in the Majority World in the 1960s–90s (e.g., Dalferth 1996; Schwambach 2004). As with the other two distinctions Luther's perceptions of how both God's Word and human experience in these two dimensions of life function offer raw material for thinking through the human dilemma and human potential in twenty-first-century frameworks.

IV. Freedom and Bondage

In *On Bound Choice* (1525) Luther contrasted the bondage of the human will with the will liberated by the Holy Spirit through faith (see chapter 15). Five years earlier he had used the language of freedom and bondage to sketch the heart of his message, God's justifying act that liberated sinners from the oppression of sin, and God's sanctifying action that set these liberated believers into a life lived for others. Referring not to the will alone but to the whole person who trusts in Christ, this treatise, *On Christian Liberty*, presented the hermeneutical distinction of freedom and bondage that contrasted the freedom *from* the believer's oppressors—sin, death, Devil, the law's accusation, God's wrath upon sin, and other such enemies—with the believer's freedom *for* the true exercise of humanity in love and service towards God and other creatures, which Luther termed 'being bound' to the neighbour in 1520 (German WA7.20–38; Latin WA7.42–78; LW333–377; Luther 2008). This distinction continued to guide Luther's exposition of the complementary nature of justification and sanctification throughout his life.

Luther's definition of 'freedom' has often been misunderstood, fitted against its grain into later definitions, especially in Western cultures with 'Enlightened' concepts of individuality and liberty (Zeeden 1950–2: 1.227–350; Brecht 1995). In the past century some, such as Marxist philosopher Herbert Marcuse, have deplored Luther's concept of 'freedom' for its distance from modern uses of the term and its quietism; their arguments have been subjected to theological criticism on several grounds, including their failure to recognize why Luther rejected Aristotle's anthropology (see ch. 15) and how Luther weaves an anthropology of the whole person into his concept (e.g. Bayer 1970; Jüngel 2008: 50–6).

'Freedom' was not a frequently used term in Luther's era but had been employed to express the rights of the German nation in dealing with Rome; the possible impact of humanism is important in this discussion as well (Schmidt 2010: 8–23). Luther articulated the 'rights' of the faithful by asserting that the 'Spirit of freedom' (2 Cor. 3:17) gives Christians 'the power to test and judge what is right or wrong in matters of faith' (WA6.412,20–31; LW44.135). He proclaimed freedom to monastics who wished to escape the monastery so that they might learn how they could do that in good conscience, 'with God's approval and without danger, and how they may use such freedom in a disciplined and Christian way' (WA10,2.72,17–20; LW35.131–132). Such freedom for making godly decisions within the larger structure of God's plan for human life remained part of Luther's understanding of Christian existence throughout his career.

In 1520, however, Luther's 'freedom' announced the existential liberation of believers from sin, liberation accomplished by Christ in dying 'for' sin and rising 'for' the restoration of passive righteousness in God's sight (Rom. 4:25; Kolb 2011). The treatise also insisted on the practice of active righteousness towards others since believers experience freedom from the need to be 'curved in upon oneself', the defensiveness inevitable when sinners rely on their own efforts to secure life. In his assessment of his book in writing the open letter which accompanied it when he sent it to Pope Leo X, he claimed 'this little treatise... contains the whole of Christian life in brief form'. Eberhard Jüngel noted how elements of Luther's *theologia crucis*, his description of salvation as the joyous exchange of Christ's righteousness and the sinner's sin, and the exercise of active righteousness are integral to his concept of freedom from all that is hostile to believers and their freedom to act as truly human beings in being bound to serve others (Jüngel 2008: 29–50, 56–87).

Luther placed the argument regarding Christian freedom in the context of medieval anthropological discussions of the 'inner' and 'outer' person but broke from the Platonic and Aristotelian framework that determined its earlier usage. No longer was the 'inner' person the soul or spirit that longed for God while the 'outer' person pursued 'fleshly' desires, 'inner' or 'spiritual' referred to the trust in God that shaped all of life; the 'fleshly' was all that strove against that trust, putting faith in someone or something else, including one's own efforts (Jüngel 2008: 56–68; Muhlhan 2012: 63–96). Freedom from all that is hostile to being truly human comes through Christ's embrace of the sinner, whom he takes as his bride in a 'joyous exchange' (*fröhliche Wechsel*), in which his righteousness becomes the sinner's and the sinner's sin becomes Christ's. In adapting this medieval bridal imagery, Luther used a metaphor in which the 'union' of the two is defined by each person's retaining his or her distinct characteristics. This reinforces what Jüngel sees as a basic presupposition of *On Christian Liberty*: 'we are to be human, not God… This is the summa' (1988: 19–27).

In 1520 Luther asserted that trust in Christ grasps his liberating work in dying to eliminate sinners' transgressions and rising to restore them to righteousness in God's sight (WA7.51,27–53,33; LW31.346–350). 'Freedom' takes concrete personal form in the lordship and servanthood created by this trust. It makes believers lord over the hostile foes that arise out of or in connection with their sins, including Satan, God's wrath and his law's condemnation, their guilt and death, while this trust simultaneously binds them to the freedom to love as God designed them to love. 'Lordship is a state of being that exists as genuine effectual promise; it is not an obtainable civic/social state of being in a temporal sense, but is manifest in the believer as the overcoming of sin' (Muhlhan 2012: 86). Brett Muhlhan (2012: 49–62) correctly demonstrates the baptismal context of this conclusion (although Luther does not develop the baptismal foundation of his argument here, relying on his earlier argument in *The Babylonian Captivity of the Church*), demonstrating the plausibility of Jonathan Trigg's assertion that Luther's 'doctrine of justification by faith is intimately related to—indeed even predicated upon—[his] understanding of the abiding covenant of baptism' (1994: 2). This justifying, liberating action of God, grasped in faith, frees believers from the tyranny of securing their own salvation and being in bondage of false opinions about their own merit, which drive them into concern primarily about themselves (WA7.70,14–27; LW31.372–373). Christ's liberation from the bondage to contributing to one's own salvation frees believers for true love towards others. Muhlhan (2012: 22–40) rightly observes the treatises' polemic against works-righteousness of every kind.

Luther knew the difference between his kind of freedom and political freedom. Eleven years later, lecturing on Galatians 5:1, he commented that believers stand fast 'not in the freedom for which the Roman emperor has liberated us but in the freedom for which Christ has liberated us' since 'Christ has freed us not from some human servitude or the power of tyrants but from God's eternal wrath. Where? In the conscience…. This freedom is magnificently perfect and incomprehensible' (WA40,2.2,28–29,3,20–30). Having escaped from the lordship of the law, sin, and death, believers recognize the servitude to the neighbour which liberated humanity entails (WA40,2.64.15–19). In the pursuit of the exercise of freedom in love for others believers are engaged in eschatological struggle against their own desires, Luther emphasized in 1520, so that they may 'bring the body into subjection in order to more sincerely and freely serve others', as Christ did (Phil. 2:7) even though these works do not gain merit in God's sight since he has already justified them (WA7.64,15–23; LW31.364–365; cf. WA7.65,26–36; LW31.366).

Luther's distinction of freedom from evil and bondage to love and service for others remained a theme in his writings even though the explicit terminology and contrast were not used, as Muhlhan (2012: 155–233) has demonstrated. The description of Christ's deliverance of sinners from the fetters of evil continued to shape Luther's proclamation of the gospel throughout his career (Rieske-Braun 1999). In his *Large Catechism* he wrote that 'the one who has given himself completely to us, withholding nothing' has come to those whom 'the devil had led into disobedience, sin, death, and all misfortune' and who had 'no resources, no help, no comfort' and 'lay under God's wrath and displeasure'; he has 'snatched us, poor lost creatures, from the jaws of hell, won us, made us free, and restored us to the Father's favour and grace' (BSLK 651–653; BC 434–435). This liberation meant, in the *Small Catechism*'s words, 'that I may belong to him, live under him in his reign, and serve him in eternal righteousness, innocence, and blessedness' (BSLK 511; BC 355). That was, for Luther, 'the whole of Christian life in brief form'.

V. Conclusion

In these four distinctions Luther captured the contradictions and complementarities of human life and moved from his study of Scripture into pastoral proclamation and care by being able to distinguish elements in God's message for humanity and aspects of human nature and experience. Fundamental to understanding Scripture, he taught, was the distinction of God's design for human performance from God's pardoning, liberating, and re-creating action that transformed sinners into his children. Equally fundamental were the distinctions between the passive, receptive aspect of humanity and the active, performing aspects of being human and the distinction between the two dimensions of human life, in relationship to God and in relationship to his creation. Embracing these distinctions was his distinction between the freedom God grants through Christ from all evils, the enemies of human creatures, and the freedom for living the truly human life, being bound to the neighbour. These distinctions guided Luther's study and preaching of God's Word and his application of it to the lives of his hearers and readers.

References

Althaus, Paul (1966a). *The Divine Command: A New Perspective on Law and Gospel*, trans. Franklin Sherman. Philadelphia: Fortress.
—— (1966b). *The Theology of Martin Luther*, trans. Robert C. Schultz. Philadelphia: Fortress.
Aulén, Gustaf (1961). *Christus Victor: An Historical Study of the Three Main Types of the Idea of Atonement*, trans. A. G. Hebart. New York: Macmillan.

Barth, Hans-Martin (2009). *Die Theologie Martin Luthers, eine kritische Würdigung.* Gütersloh: Gütersloher Verlagshaus.

Bayer, Oswald (1970). 'Marcuses Kritik an Luthers Freiheitsbegriff'. *Zeitschrift für Theologie und Kirche* 67: 453–78.

—— (1971). *Promissio. Geschichte der reformatorischen Wende in Luthers Theologie.* Göttingen: Vandenhoeck & Ruprecht.

—— (2008). *Martin Luther's Theology: A Contemporary Interpretation,* trans. Thomas H. Trapp. Grand Rapids, MI: Eerdmans.

Bornkamm, Heinrich (1966). *Luther's Doctrine of the Two Kingdoms in the Context of his Theology,* trans. Karl H. Hertz. Philadelphia: Fortress.

Brecht, Martin (1995). 'Die Rezeption von Luthers Freiheitsverständnis in der frühen Neuzeit'. *Lutherjahrbuch* 62: 121–51.

Cranz, F. Edward (1959). *An Essay on the Development of Luther's Thought on Justice, Law, and Society.* Cambridge, MA: Harvard University Press.

Dalferth, Silfredo Bernardo (1996). *Die Zweireichelehre Martin Luthers im Dialog mit der Befreiungstheologie Leonardo Boffs.* Frankfurt am Main: Lang.

Duchrow, Ulrich (1970). *Christenheit und Weltverantwortung. Traditionsgeschichte und systematische Struktur der Zweireichelehre.* Stuttgart: Klett.

Duchrow, Ulrich and Wolfgang Huber (1976). *Die Ambivalenz der Zweireichelehre in lutherischen Kirchen des 20. Jahrhundert.* Gütersloh: Mohn.

Ebeling, Gerhard (1970). *Luther: An Introduction to His Thought.* Philadelphia: Fortress.

Elert, Werner (1948). *Zwischen Gnade und Ungnade.* Munich: Evangelicher Presseverband.

—— (1962). *The Structure of Lutheranism,* trans. Walter A. Hansen. Saint Louis: Concordia.

Forde, Gerhard (1969). *The Law–Gospel Debate: An Interpretation of Its Historical Development.* Minneapolis: Augsburg.

Frostin, Per (1994). *Luther's Two Kingdoms Doctrine.* Lund: Lund University Press.

Heckel, Johannes (2010). *Lex charitatis* [1973]. English translation: *Lex Caritatis: A Juristic Disquisition on Law in the Theology of Martin Luther,* trans. Gottfried G. Krodel. Grand Rapids, MI: Eerdmans.

Heintze, Gerhard (1958). *Luthers Predigt von Gesetz und Evangelium.* Munich: Kaiser.

Hendrix, Scott (2004). *Recultivating the Vineyard: The Reformation Agendas of Christianization.* Louisville: Westminster John Knox.

Herrmann, Erik (2005). '"Why Then the Law?" Salvation History and the Law in Martin Luther's Interpretation of Galatians 1513–1522'. Ph.D. dissertation, Concordia Seminary, Saint Louis.

Iwand, Hans Joachim (1959). *Um den Rechten Glauben.* Munich: Kaiser.

—— (2008). *The Righteousness of Faith,* trans. Randi H. Lundell. Eugene, OR: Wipf & Stock.

Joest, Wilfried (1951). *Gesetz und Freiheit. Das Problem des tertius usus legis bei Luther und die neutestamtentliche Parainese.* Göttingen: Vandenhoeck & Ruprecht.

Jüngel, Eberhard (2008). *The Freedom of a Christian. Luther's Significance for Contemporary Theology,* trans. Roy A. Harrisville. Minneapolis: Fortress. German original: *Zur Freiheit eines Christenmenschen. Eine Erinnerung an Luthers Schrift.* Munich: Kaiser, 1991.

Kinder, Ernst and Klaus Haendler (1986). *Gesetz und Evangelium. Beiträge zur gegenwärtigen theologischen Diskussion.* Darmstadt: Wissenschaftliche Buchgesellschaft.

Kolb, Robert (2009). *Martin Luther: Confessor of the Faith.* Oxford: Oxford University Press.

—— (2011). 'Resurrection and Justification: Luther's Use of Romans 4:25'. *Lutherjahrbuch* 78: 39–60.

Kolb, Robert (2012). *Luther and the Stories of God: Biblical Narratives as a Foundation for Christian Living*. Grand Rapids, MI: Baker.

Kolb, Robert and Charles P. Arand (2008). *The Genius of Luther's Theology: A Wittenberg Way of Thinking for the Contemporary Church*. Grand Rapids, MI: Baker.

Lau, Franz (1933). *'Äußerliche Ordnung' und 'Weltlich Ding' in Luthers Theologie*. Göttingen: Vandenhoeck & Ruprecht.

Lohse, Bernhard (1999). *Martin Luther's Theology*, trans. Roy Harrisville. Minneapolis: Fortress.

Luther, Martin (2008). *The Freedom of a Christian*, trans. Mark D. Tranvik. Minneapolis: Fortress.

Mantey, Volker (2005). *Zwei Schwerter—Zwei Reiche. Martin Luthers Zwei-Reiche-Lehre vor ihrem spätmittelalterlichen Hintergrund*. Tübingen: Mohr/Siebeck.

Muhlhan, Brett (2012). *Being Shaped by Freedom: An Examination of Luther's Development of Christian Liberty, 1520–1525*. Portland, OR: Pickwick.

Peters, Albrecht (1981). *Gesetz und Evangelium*. Gütersloh: Mohn.

Rieske-Braun, Uwe (1999). *Duellum mirabile. Studien zum Kampfmotiv in Martin Luthers Theologie*. Göttingen: Vandenhoeck & Ruprecht.

Schloemann, Martin (1961). *Natürliches und Gesetz bei Luther. Eine Studie zur Frage nach der Einheit der Gesetzesauffassung Luthers...*. Berlin: Töpelmann.

Schmidt, Georg (2010). 'Luthers Freiheitsvorstellungen in ihrem sozialen und rhetorischen Kontext (1517–1521)'. In *Martin Luther—Biographie und Theologie*, ed. Dietrich Korsch and Volker Leppin. Tübingen: Mohr/Siebeck, 9–30.

Schultz, Robert (1958). *Gesetz und Evangelium in der Lutherischen Theologie des 19. Jahrhunderts*. Berlin: Lutherisches Verlagshaus.

Schwambach, Claus (2004). *Rechtfertigungsgeschehen und Befreiungsprozess. Die Eschatologien von Martin Luther und Leonardo Boff im kritischen Gespräch*. Göttingen: Vandenhoeck & Ruprecht.

Siggins, Ian D. Kingston (1970). *Martin Luther's Doctrine of Christ*. New Haven: Yale University Press.

Thielicke, Helmut (1948). 'Zur Frage Gesetz und Evangelium, eine Auseinandersetzung mit Karl Barth'. In Thielicke, *Auf dem Grunde der Apostel und Propheten*. Stuttgart: Quell-Verlag.

Trigg, Jonathan (1994). *Baptism in the Theology of Martin Luther*. Leiden: Brill.

Van Drunen, David (2010). *Natural Law and the Two Kingdoms: A Study in the Development of Reformed Social Thought*. Grand Rapids, MI: Eerdmans.

Wingren, Gustaf (1957). *Luther on Vocation*, trans. Carl C. Rasmussen. Philadelphia: Muhlenberg.

—— (1958). *Theology in Conflict*, trans. Eric H. Wahlstrom. Philadelphia: Muhlenberg.

Zeeden, Ernst Walter (1950–2). *Martin Luther und die Reformation im Urteil des deutschen Luthertums*. Freiburg/Br: Herder.

PART IV

LUTHER'S TREATMENT OF THE TRADITIONAL TOPICS OF WESTERN CHRISTIAN THEOLOGY

CHAPTER 13

LUTHER'S DOCTRINE OF GOD

STEVEN PAULSON

MARTIN Luther was an orthodox teacher of the Catholic doctrine of God according to the two majestic articles of the Trinity and incarnation. He consistently taught 'that Father, Son, and Holy Spirit, three distinct persons in one divine essence and nature, is one God, who created heaven and earth', 'that neither the Father or the Holy Spirit, but the Son, became a human being', and that the Father's only begotten Son is one person with two natures, divine and human, that are not confused or separated (SA I; BSLK 414; BC 300).

Yet Luther taught these doctrines in a free fashion according to the chief article, that Jesus Christ, our God and Lord, 'was handed over to death for our trespasses and was raised for our justification' (Rom. 4:25). This made his doctrine of God startlingly fresh and useful in evangelical proclamation, while he was actively borrowing language from his predecessors: 'On this article stands all that we teach and practice against the pope, the devil, and the world. Therefore we must be quite certain and have no doubt about it' (SA II.i.5; BSLK 416; BC 301).

I. GOD AND JUSTIFICATION

The article of justification takes the whole of theology (*summa*) to be composed of two parts: (1) the Justifying God and (2) 'I, the sinner' (Psalm 51 [1538]; WA40.2:328:17–18; LW12.311). In the first, Luther asserted that God is not a goal, but is the most active God (*actuosissimus deus*), who never ceases to justify. The Justifying God reversed the normal pattern of considering God as one and three (*de deo uno* and *de deo trino*) under the category of God as the Greatest Good (*summum bonum*), to which humans are attracted as their final goal. Lombard began with Augustine's distinction between what humans use in order to attain their goal in life, and what they should enjoy as that goal (*usus* and *frui*): 'the more we enjoy him already in this life, even if through a glass darkly, the more tolerably do we endure our pilgrimage, and the more ardently do we desire to come to its end' (Lombard 2007: 8, citing Augustine, *De doctrina Christiana* 1.30.31).

Instead, God became for Luther first and finally the One Who Gives, the subject of justification. As Luther described his own discovery of the gospel, 'the righteousness of God is that by which the righteous lives by a gift of God, namely by faith...the passive righteousness with which the merciful God justifies us by faith' (Preface to Latin Works [1545], WA54.186,3–13; LW34.337).

God is the one who gives. What he gives is not an effect of a cause, but himself, and the preached word is the way he bestows this gift upon creatures. The second part of theology, 'I, the sinner', names the one to whom God gives himself. God's active justification is given freely while sinners are yet ungodly—the passive righteousness of receiving rather than achieving.

In justifying a sinner, this God does not one but two works in his words: the first puts to death, and the second raises up. The first is an *alien* work, divine nevertheless, and the second is God's *proper* work: 'Strange is his deed, alien his work!' (Isa. 28:21), which leads to the prophecy uttered in fear of the God of Israel, who would use Cyrus as a messiah: 'truly thou art a God who hides himself' (Isa. 45:15). There Luther found the basic distinction between God who hides himself (desiring the death of the sinner in an awful wrath), and the same God who does not desire the death of a sinner (Ezek. 18), but reveals his merciful, loving heart in raising the dead as from the valley of dry bones (Ezek. 37).

Audaciously, Luther applied the distinction between law and gospel to God, wherein the distinction ceased being merely epistemological or exegetical, and became the basic criterion of theology: 'When I discovered the distinction of law and gospel, I made the breakthrough' (WATR5.210, 12–16; LW54.442–443). This led to Luther's new approach in the doctrine of God in *On Bound Choice* (1525). The only way to understand the God who justifies is constantly to distinguish God as unpreached, naked, feared, from God as preached, clothed in his words, and trusted. Without the distinction of 'preached and unpreached' there is no trustworthy understanding of God, sinful human beings, or their relation in justification. A theologian is deceived 'by not making any distinction between God preached and God hidden, that is, between the Word of God and God himself' (WA18.685,25–27, cf. 684,26–688,26; LW33.138–144).

Luther struggled with the common religious assumption that God and the law were one in essence (thus the *summum bonum*). In that case, God would be justified in using the law to condemn the unjust. But Luther then paid attention to the context, in which he saw that Habakkuk was giving a promise, not a command. This then opened the broader argument of Paul in Romans 3:4 and Psalm 51:4: 'That you may be justified in your words'.

God in his absolute being, without words or proclamation, *is* righteous in himself, but this poses a terrible threat to the unrighteous, inspiring fear instead of faith. So God *becomes* the God who seeks to be justified by the unrighteous in his words, a great vulnerability in which God stoops low in order to give sinners faith: 'If you believe in the revealed God and accept his Word, then he will also gradually reveal the hidden God to you' (WA43.460,26 28; LW5.46).

Luther then identified the particular word of promise, distinguished from commands or threats, in which God could be infallibly trusted. All Scripture then became the book of commands and promises instead of an allegory that guided the religious on their quest for the good. God ceased being equivalent with law and became a lawless God who gives apart from merit, so that God's primary attribute was no longer *goodness* that makes him desirable to humans as their distant goal but *faithfulness* that comes near while we are yet ungodly.

Luther spoke personally, intimately, of God who seeks justification in his words of promise since God's heart is not given in the law. This broke the old equation between God and law, especially regarding righteousness, and paired God in essence (now heart) with the forgiveness of sins. This unleashed a new speech for God in Luther that was intimate, playful, and joyous (cf. his hymn 'Dear Christians One and All Rejoice' [1523]; Leaver 2007: 161–2; WA35.435–437; LW53.294–51).

Luther described the effect this theology has on sinners: 'It is our business, however, to pay attention to the Word and leave that inscrutable will alone, for we must be guided by the Word and not by that inscrutable will' (*On Bound Choice*, WA18.685,29–30; LW33.140). Thus, once this distinction is made, theology teaches the practice of how one flees from the unpreached God to the preached one. Therefore, theology never takes place in a vacuum or neutral place, but does its work under the duress of the cosmic struggle between God and the Devil over the faith of sinners and so the fate of the world itself. There is no way of grasping God as he is, in the heart, without the life and death struggle to find a gracious God. Thus, theology must be the practice of becoming a theologian of the cross, as Luther explained to Erasmus: 'Those, however, who have not yet experienced the office of the law, and neither recognize sin nor feel death, have no use for the mercy promised by that Word' ['I desire not the death of a sinner'] (WA18.684.30–32; LW33.138).

Luther's doctrine of God distinguishes whether one is dealing with God in his Word or outside his Word, in Christ or outside Christ, clothed or naked. Only in this way can theology actually reach its proper goal, which is a confession of faith in IMMANUEL deep in the flesh, a most thoroughgoing interplay among the doctrines of incarnation, Trinity, and justification (cross) that confesses: 'apart from this man there is no God' (*Confession concerning Christ's Supper* [1528], WA26.332,19–20; LW37.218). This confession is, on the one hand, a plaintive plea that sinners have no other place to go to find a gracious God than the man Jesus; but on the other hand, it is the joyous shout of the redeemed from the depths of hell, who have finally found their Creator where that God wanted to be found. Luther's contribution to the doctrine of God hinges upon his confession that 'this man Jesus' is alone God, who had come to favour the ungodly in a strange election that directly contradicts the law's judgement of unrighteousness.

That God elects at all is unsettling to those seeking their Greatest Good, but election is revolting when it occurs apart from the law so that the sinful and unclean are chosen entirely without works—simply by the arrival of Christ with the forgiveness of sin. It was revolting to Luther himself, until 'it opened the door to heaven' and IMMANUEL alone was his God (Preface to Latin Works, WA54.179–187: LW34.327–328).

II. God Unpreached

Luther arranged names of God, qualities and characteristics of God, proofs for God's existence, natural knowledge, revelation, and any other topics in theology according to whether God was preached and offered, or naked, absolute, and unpreached. Therefore, Christian teaching on God, the Father almighty, is not good news until we are given to confess Christ alone as our Lord.

This also means that theologians cannot disguise themselves as rationally neutral in relation to this God, but are hostile, in rebellious opposition, so that their attempts to prove God's existence, the necessity of the cross, or the triune nature of God's being are distorted. They are theologians of the cross, not of glory (Heidelberg Theses, 1518, WA1.353,1–354,36; LW31.39–45). Once Luther made this distinction traditional pillars in the doctrine of God began to fall.

First is the assumption that God is the great object of desire's love (among humans certainly, and quite possibly all created things)—including Augustine's 'my heart is restless till it rests in thee, O Lord'. Both Platonic and Aristotelian approaches to the doctrine of God ended with Luther. In their place was put the counter-intuitive assertion that God is and works one way through a preacher, and contrariwise without any preacher.

The second traditional pillar to fall was the *opinio legis*, the desire to wed God with law. It does not matter whether equating God and law was done aesthetically as the beauty of order, or morally as the highest example and final judge, or rationally as the perfect mind. Luther learned from Paul that God gives and uses the law, but not for righteousness. For good or ill to sinners, God operates outside the law. A lawless God who is not preached is experienced as a sheer, abstract horror no different than the Devil. But as preached, lawless God is sheer bliss since this God does not merely give rewards for merit but reconciles the world to himself through his Son (2 Cor. 5:18).

Then fell a third pillar that required God to be changeless or merely reactionary to human effort. This opened Luther's way for God not merely to be adaptive to time as with Darwin or the German speculative philosophy or Process theology, but actually to enter sinful creation so deeply that he not only united himself to sinful flesh, but died. Such a statement is true only when preached; otherwise it is plainly false in the 'absolute' sense. Luther's is a radical argument for understanding God's entry into time and space that effects everything from the teaching of the sacraments to what happened to God in Christ's crucifixion: 'The course of the world... is God's mask in which he hides himself, reigns and busies himself so wonderfully in the world' (Psalm 127 [1524], WA15.373,7).

The fact that God is invisible is universally known, but Luther treated God's hiddenness actively, and in two dialectically opposed ways as preached or unpreached.

Hiddenness ceased being an attribute of God, and so a reference to the limit of human reason. It became an act of God: God hides, he is not merely hidden. The unpreached God actively hides precisely so that he will never be found. Luther then took up what it meant for God to arrive in his Word and to hide in the cross and proclamation precisely so that he may be found—not to kill but give life. But to the lights of nature (reason) and even of grace (revelation), this first form of hiding is entirely irrational and seems to destroy any grounding for faith. Only days after Moses was called and ordained by God to preach to Pharaoh (in order to shut his ears!), 'while they were at a lodging place on the way, the Lord met him and tried to kill him' (Ex. 4:24). Luther concluded that God actively hides even from those who seek him in the struggle for life against death and refuses to be found outside his words. To reason this is abhorrent since it destroys the attempt to equate God with the law. Luther's theological description of the way God hides has subsequently inspired fear and loathing. Two basic attempts have historically been made to tame it.

The first thinks of hiddenness merely as the subjective limit of human knowledge, and so an epistemological matter. Thus, instead of knowledge of the thing itself, we must confine ourselves to practical, moral, and aesthetic knowledge. This was used by eighteenth- and nineteenth-century Lutheran neo-Kantians to reject metaphysics and pursue theology as the expression of the subject's faith. Presently there is a backlash against both the loss of history in Kantian versions of Luther's theology and the turn to the subject, and so also the way that theologians like Albrecht Ritschl, Karl Holl, and even Erlangen theology spoke of divine hiddenness by concentrating on the subject of faith.

The other attempt to tame Luther's hidden God asserts an underlying metaphysics, usually 'triune', that assures us that God's essence is mercy even when we do not experience it, so that the single attribute of divine love unites and explains all those acts of God that appear evil. Even Lundensian theologians like Gusaf Aulén and Anders Nygren used hiddenness as God's 'holiness', or transcendence, in the form of a 'background' to God's single essence of love. Only in revelation would this monism of being appear hidden under the form of its opposite, the cross, and so it has become common to limit God's hiddenness to that under the sign of God's opposite alone (Aulén 1948; Nygren 1953). God's love as an eternal law is taken to refer to an ontological state of affairs within the 'inner' God before and outside time. But Luther refused to make God at heart into the law, the Greatest Good, or love-in-essence without the proper distinction. Therefore, God refuses to be found outside his words, and so hides in absolute, abstract majesty and silence from which sinners must flee. The first reaction to God is fear and flight that ends in death, as God himself demands it.

Luther handles natural knowledge of God apart from the attempt to prove that the transcendent distance between Creator and creatures is so great that natural knowledge fails (Barth), or that the immanent connection between them is so great (Spinoza) that even sin cannot overcome it. Luther was not interested in seeking potential in the person for 'knowing' God, but was interested in God deeply present in all creation: 'God is present in death or hell, both of which are more horrible and foul than either a pit or a sewer... a godly mind not only says that he is in those places, but must by necessity learn and know that he is there' (WA18.623,14–17; LW33.47). In fact, knowledge of God before the preacher arrives is so easily accessible to 'I, the sinner' that it leaves no recourse but despair. Luther rejected ontological knowledge through nature in terms of a human capacity for seeking the divine, but he recognized natural knowledge legally, in terms of God's relation to the law and judgement. Luther joined two key assertions of Paul in Romans: 'For what can be known about God is plain to them... seen through the things he has made' (1:19–20), and 'Gentiles, who do not possess the law... show that what the law requires is written on their hearts...' (2:14–15).

Luther saw the import of the relationship of God and law in the nominalism of his day (whether God is free in relation to his own law); yet, his real interest was not whether God had absolute power in relation to the law but determined by ordained power to rule according to that very law. That was to think only of God unpreached; instead, Luther sought God's freedom from the law *as God preached*, and there he rejected nominalism's doctrine of God altogether. In the preached God, Luther asserted that Christ is the end of the law: 'Christ fulfilled the whole law. For he is the end (*finis*) of the law (Rom. 10:4), not only of the ceremonial laws or the judicial laws, but also of the Decalogue itself, in this life through the remission of sins which the gospel offers to all who believe in him; in the life eternal, however, also formally' (Second Antinomian Disputation, 1538, WA39,1.453,9–12; Sonntag 2008). Thus, even the eternal law that applies in all places and times is historicized as something 'behind' God, who has become justified in his words. Thus, the law itself must be distinguished as 'before Christ' and 'after Christ'—the first to be fulfilled (in the damned), and the second 'as fulfilled in the blessed' (WA39,1.349,39–350,6; Sonntag 2008: 141). God not only is lawless in himself; he specifically becomes lawless in his words of remission of sins for the justification of sinners.

The result was that God's essence and his majestic attributes, like omnipresence, were handled in two opposite ways and in a most active sense. Upon addressing Jonah's question, 'Whither shall I go from thy Spirit?' Luther explains that 'God has two kinds of essence, or presence—the one is natural, the other spiritual' (1526, WA19.197,18–19; LW19.44). Naturally God is present everywhere, as in Isaiah 66:1, 'Heaven is my throne, and the earth is my footstool', and so God is also present even in hell, death, and sin as in Psalm 139:8, 'If I make my bed in Sheol, Thou art there'. In this way there is no escape from God or his wrath. However, Luther noted, 'God is present spiritually only where he is spiritually known'. God is *naturally* everywhere; *spiritually* he is present only 'wherever his Word, faith, Spirit and worship are'. Consequently, reason confines God to one place or another which it calls 'holy' as a means of absenting God.

Luther believed reason is profound and often accurate about God. He gave much more credit to it than scholastic theologies which treated natural knowledge as partial, and so in need of revelation to be completed or purified. For Luther, nature does not need this kind of perfecting since reason is 'an extremely bright light'. Most importantly, nature knows that 'God is a being who is able to deliver from every evil' (WA19.206,12–30; LW19.54). This is better knowledge than simply that God exists (hence Luther does not bother with such arguments that depend upon shallow cause and effect), or that

God has eternal attributes, or even that God is the highest good. Reason actually knows that 'all good things come from God', and it senses that there is a God in times of trouble who can actually deliver from evil. The *Large Catechism* described what it means to 'have a god', as 'that One to whom the frightened run and seek help in time of desperate need' (BSLK 560; BC 386,1–2).

But Luther notes two deadly defects in nature—not defects of knowledge but of faith. First, reason knows that God is able to help and that God is essentially kind, but its knowledge lacks the true thing: it knows God's omnipotence in general, but does not know if God 'is willing to do this also for us'. It cannot apply the pronoun 'for you' to itself, so it reasons that God is indeed essentially gracious, but because the law stands between creatures and Creator, God is not inclined to use his mercy *for me*. Only a preacher remedies that situation.

A second defect of reason proves fatal: 'Reason is unable to identify God properly.' It knows that (1) there is a God, (2) this God has a law, and (3) this God judges according to the law (WA40,1.607,28–609,14; LW26.399), but it makes the fatal mistake of equating God with that law. Luther said that this is like recognizing someone's face but not remembering the person's name or knowing what he has in his mind. It cannot pick God out from among the legal forms which reason has a sense for, such as money, the self, or a god who rewards good deeds. While its knowledge is significant, reason nevertheless produces idols and fails. Reason's faith remains general.

So, Luther concluded: 'as you believe, so you have him' (*creatrix divinitatis*—a creator of divinity). This is not to say, as Feuerbach did, that humans make God by projection of their innards because there is nothing else there. It is that the faith of the heart makes its God from the law, and so misidentifies God. If God is not grasped as he wants to be in the preached word of promise apart from law, then necessarily God will be your God unpreached as wrath and death.

Reason is good at fleeing this angry God, but does not know where to go: 'nature cannot surmount the obstacle posed by this wrath, it cannot subdue this feeling and make its way to God against God and pray to him, while regarding him its enemy' (Jonah lectures, WA19.223,12–17; LW19.72). An omnipotence of the unpreached God is wrath and inspires only fear and flight. The omnipotence of the preached God, however, is life itself because there God's all-working power is concentrated in the one necessary attribute of God: *faithfulness* to the promise made in Christ, 'who made heaven, earth, the sea, and all that is in them, who keeps faith foremost' (Ps. 146:6; WADB10,1.96,4–9).

For this reason Luther thought the Christian's greatest comfort was precisely the all-working power of God, or predestination. A silent God is sheer absoluteness—without an absolution (Forde 1990: 30–4). Reason finds abhorrent the notion that God chooses (foreknows and ordains) outside the law. Since this God is omnipotent, this predestination must naturally occur outside time, in God's eternity. This leaves no room for free will.

Luther did not disagree with any of reason's necessary conclusions about God, fate, or bondage of the will. But God's prior destination properly belongs not with maintaining the perfection of the law but with promising to justify the ungodly. From the beginning

God has wanted to justify by preaching. Reason does not know this since it seeks God in the law, apart from the person of his Son Jesus Christ.

The relation of God and evil is an endless conundrum to human reason because nature assumes the free will, but Luther addressed this conundrum at the end of *On Bound Choice* in terms of three 'lights' (WA18.784,35–785,38; LW33.291–292). One is never free from this struggle while there is no preacher: 'God cannot lay aside his omnipotence on account of man's aversion, and ungodly man cannot alter his aversion' (WA18.710,6–7; LW33.177). The 'light of nature' cannot cut the Gordian knot of God and evil, and so despairs, either by abandoning theology altogether for atheism, or making evil into a non-being that God nevertheless uses for his own good purpose. Then a new light, the 'light of grace' shines and immediately there is a preached answer to the question of reason: God has conquered evil in his Son Jesus Christ, by dying (or losing to it) and proceeding to create a new kingdom in which is no evil, ruled by a new Lord without the law. The attempt of reason to distinguish between God and evil is then abandoned, indeed, even when in the middle of attack, one cannot distinguish God, evil, or Devil. So it was for the Syro-phoencian woman begging for scraps from Jesus' table (Mk. 7), and indeed for Christ himself hanging upon the cross: 'My God, my God why have you forsaken me?' (Mk. 15:34). Instead, one learns to flee from this God—to the preached God in Christ, whose crucifixion reveals the proper issue. Not 'What is the origin of evil?' But 'What is the end of evil?' For the end of evil is also the end of the law and the unpreached, silent God.

Thus, in what Luther calls the eschatological 'light of glory', when evil itself is defeated and the old sinners no longer live, God will be seen as the destroyer of evil. In the midst of the life-and-death struggle this is not yet clear, but there is comfort in knowing that feeling (glory) will catch up with hearing (grace) in the end.

III. THE PREACHED GOD

For Luther's doctrine of the Trinity we turn from the unpreached God to the preached God. Much of the preached God is addressed doctrinally in Christology and Pneumatology, but here we take up Luther's distinction between God in himself, and *for you*: 'But he is there for you when he applies his Word and binds himself to it and promises: you are to find me here' (WA23.150,13–17; LW37.68). This reveals the second divine hiding in which God actively wants to be found—in Christ, and him crucified—justified in his words.

Most theologians choose between God's transcendence and God's immanence; Luther did not: 'For as in his own nature God is immense, incomprehensible, and infinite, so to man's nature he is intolerable. Therefore if you want to be safe and out of danger to your conscience and your salvation, put a check on this speculative spirit.' That check is to begin the doctrine of God 'where Christ began—in the Virgin's womb, in the manger, and at his mother's breasts' (WA40,1.77,28–29).

The influence of Kantian dualism made Luther's doctrine of the Trinity appear to come 'to rest as an erratic boulder' (Elert 1962: 217) since God was effectively removed from history, and theology was reduced to morality, with God as the highest exemplar of duty. The response of German idealism brought God back into history, so that for Hegel history itself became, 'theodicy, a justification of God...thus the evil in the world was to be comprehended and the thinking mind reconciled with it' (Hegel 1953: 18). Justifying God in his own words went by the wayside. A combination of these approaches was attempted in the following century with Karl Barth's emphasis on providential transcendence. This had the effect of establishing a triune ontology as the theoretical framework for Luther's doctrine of God instead of the distinction of unpreached and preached God.[1] In recent theology this has given precedence to the inner triune being over the economic, even while equating the two according to 'Rahner's rule'. This line of thought makes special use of Luther's graduate disputations at the University of Wittenberg to view Luther in the light of nominalism that takes the essence of God simply as a reference to the three persons and perceives proclamation as an existentialist reference akin to the theology of Rudolf Bultmann, especially via Gerhard Ebeling (White 1994: 230; Helmer 1999).

Luther was indeed interested in using the syllogism in graduate disputations, but he assumed the basic distinction of God unpreached and preached in doing so. It is the same in theology to say 'The Father always "generated" or "generates" the Son...although it is certain in divinity, since he is eternity itself, there is no place in grammar or philosophy where past, present, and future is the same' (Theses 20 and 24 from his disputation for Erasmus Alber, 24 August 1543, WA 39,2.254,21–22,30–32; see Bielfeldt et al. 2008: 194). Luther was aware that doctrines of the Trinity do not themselves keep from being as cold as ice when they follow Aristotle and Epicurus in making distinctions of infinite and finite (God contemplating himself), or when they merely distinguish the immanent and economic. It is true that the Father always speaks, *and* the Word he speaks never was once when he was not, and the Holy Spirit always hears even within the 'inner' Trinity prior to any external word that creates what it says. But God does not seek to be justified in this; indeed, he cannot be. For sinners it is a crushing blow to have God eternally and universally speaking, but not for their own sake. For this reason, God the Father speaks to his incarnate Son standing in the water of the Jordan being baptized by John, and the Holy Spirit descends as a dove, so that those who are near (and even Christ himself) can hear externally the very words God has said internally from before the beginning: 'This is my Son, with whom I am well pleased' (1546, WA20.217–232; LW58.357–369).

The general discussion of God that precedes the Trinity has an important place in the current interest in Luther's teaching on the religions and mission to those who have no preacher, along with the problem of atheism's unfaith. Without this preceding general discussion, Trinity becomes a speculation that forces sinners to seek God's essence in

---

[1] Many followed in Barth's train, notably Wolfhart Pannenberg, Robert Jenson, Eberhard Jüngel, and in a new vein, Tuomo Mannermaa 1989.

love apart from any speaking to them in particular. Luther scholarship needs to address current theologies of love and Oswald Bayer's admonition: 'It is one of the grandiose blunders of the more recent history of both philosophy and theology that the attempt has been made to conceptualize this almighty nature theologically as trinitarian' (Bayer 2008: 339). Only after dealing with God in the 'general', absolute, unpreached sense, did Luther deal with the Trinity as the preached God: 'I hear that there is one essence and three persons. As for what goes on there, one simply has to remain silent and believe God, who put himself on show in his Word to be known by us' (Disputation of Georg Major, WA39,2.384,15–22; White 1994: 228).

The preached God concerns the first article of the Apostles Creed: that we believe God is the Father, almighty, who created the heavens and the earth. Luther expounds upon this teaching of God in his *Large Catechism*. That God is the *Father* means that he is the Father of Christ, not begotten but begetting. Just so, he is given to faith as our heavenly Father—despite our own sin—in the promise like that given to Abraham, bestowed by Christ when he taught his disciples to 'pray like this, "Our Father, who art in heaven"' (Mt. 6: 9). By this means God's name is given so that 'I, the sinner' have access to the Justifying God in prayer. The chief attribute of this Father is that he is almighty, in that none can overturn his will as it pertains to election and the faithfulness to the promise. God's proper work is to create; the almighty Father does this through speaking, whether at the beginning: 'and God said, "Let there be Light," and there was light (Gen. 1), or at the end, "Abraham believed God makes the dead live and calls into being that which does not exist" (Rom. 4:17)'. Thus, creation by God in his words is *creatio ex nihilo*, even in the form that fosters and preserves life in the old world, called *creatio continua*.

However, God's name as Father, his almighty attribute of faithfulness, and his work as our own creator are all believed, and so prior to faith's birth, they have a direct counterpart in unbelief. Before 'Father', 'almighty', and 'create' (as noun, adjective, and verb) give freedom to sinners, they first come as oppressive and accusing realities of a God who stands in opposition. Father comes first as 'patriarchal', almighty as 'fate', and creation is felt not as life but temporality, finitude and death. With this insight Luther comes into contact with current theologies of liberation, but not without the proper distinction of God with and without Christ/Word.

Luther laid out his final teaching of God preached in his *Confession* of 1528: 'This is the three persons and one God, who has given himself absolutely and completely, along with all that he is and has' (WA26.505,38–506,12; LW37.366; cf. this translation in Bayer 2008: 99). God actively gives. What God gives is no less than himself, which for Luther defines a sacrament as God's self-giving. God's sacramental self-giving is not a mere part of divinity, but it is divinity whole and complete. Luther never preached two or three gods or powers; he was not a Manichaean or anti-Trinitarian. The one God seeks justification in his words because he is wholly and completely given there, but to faith alone—not for sight/feeling.

Therefore God gives all he is, which is first and foremost his favour (*favor dei*) or heart, and thus follows all that he has as gift (*donum*). The giving is 'to us' in God's words—which are never less than works of creation—and so Luther added, 'heaven and earth and all creatures'. God does not want to be found behind or above his created things where he is without any word (especially not in the speculative question, why?), but he wants to be found in such things as a peach stone, where he gives himself in the form of a promise: 'you may eat freely from every tree of the garden...' (Gen. 2:16). In this way all creatures were meant to serve and benefit us, explaining the meaning of the image of God and the gift of dominion.

'But this gift has been darkened and has become useless through the fall of Adam.' Adam's fall, original sin, was not to trust God's Word put in the things he made. Adam did not want to find God in the peach but sought him naked in majesty outside the created things, without words of promise. Yet God refuses to vacate these created things, so that he continues to give himself in creatures, but hides in (not above or behind) them as in a mask (*larvae dei*). Consequently, when sinners are awakened to God's wrath, they fear God's presence in the most insignificant created thing, like the rustling of a leaf (Lev. 26:36), and creation narrows into a prison of death (WA49.136,16–21).

> For this reason, at a later time, the Son gave himself to us as well.... The Son also gave himself to us, including his works, cross, wisdom, by which the Father created all through the Son, and his own righteousness—which reconciled us with the Father. God does not want to be found in anything without his Son, through whom all things are made.... This is how I will do so: 'From an unrevealed God I will become a revealed God. Nevertheless, I will remain the same God. I will be made flesh'... (WA43.459,24–25; LW5.45)

But we did not want him there either, putting Christ on the cross because we did not want to hear what he had to say as he hung upon the cross. Yet God refuses to be found anywhere else, though he is deeply hidden in the sign of his direct opposite—suffering, death, curse—more deeply hidden within Christ's cross than ever in the peach. Since we did not want the Father in created things, the Son gave the Father to us again by giving us his own self as the only begotten Son. 'At a later time' does not refer to Christ's origin but to his incarnation; nor does it refer to the ancient heresy of monarchian modalism, or historical phases of revelation, but it is God giving himself a second time, by which Christ manages to give to sinners the Father whom they wilfully do not desire. Grace gives Christ with all his benefits, and Christ gives the Father to sinners (with all his gifts), despite themselves.

Luther dwelt at greatest length, however, on the third article, and so the Holy Spirit—because it is necessary to proclaim the doctrine of the Trinity: 'But because this grace could not benefit anyone if it would stay hidden away very secretly and could not come to us; therefore the Holy Spirit comes and gives himself completely to us as well.'

The chief article, justification, requires a preacher. The Holy Spirit sends such preachers so that grace is not so deeply hidden that we never find Christ hidden in the repulsive cross. Without the Son, we never use the gift of the Father, and without the Holy Spirit, we cannot grasp the Son. 'He teaches us how to recognize such a wonderful blessing of Christ, which is shown to us, helps us to receive it and to hold onto it, shows how to use it profitably and how to give it to others, to multiply it and to advance it.' This is what is meant by God establishing the office of proclamation in the world. By it we receive the promise and give it to others exponentially. Indeed, God did not want sinners to grasp the Son without the Holy Spirit. That would be to grasp the cross without its being preached for you, thus becoming merely a negative theology of glory.

So he gave himself in the Holy Spirit through preaching, and thus the sacraments, or means of grace. But bound sinners did not want him there either, rejecting the preacher and this Word. However, God refuses to be found anywhere else and finally breaks through to create faith *ex nihilo*: hence the Spirit in particular is *Creator Spiritus* (Prenter 1953). The Spirit's is a new creation ('once again alive and righteous') that, unlike the old creation, will never be destroyed. So it lives without death and outside the law.

Even the Spirit, however, is not removed from the act of God hiding, and so has an alien work that is the destruction of the old: the written law kills; the Spirit gives life (2 Cor. 3:6), so Luther concludes that the Holy Spirit 'works the suffering of Christ in us', which is to put sinners to death, 'and lets it serve to give everlasting bliss', which is the new life. The Holy Spirit does these two works, as Luther noted in his First Antinomian Disputation: 'This illustrates the simile concerning the uncreated and incarnate Word...when the Holy Spirit is God in his nature, then he is the Author of the law, without whom the law does not convict of sin. When he, however, is the Gift through Christ, then he is our Vivifier and Sanctifier' (WA29,1.370,24–27; Sonntag 2008: 91).

Therefore, the preached God is the almighty Father, who created the heavens and the earth, *ex nihilo*, by his Word (*verbum*), not once, but continually through his offices or estates (*Stände*) of family, church, and government. This God is One being, three persons, by whom we receive everything for life. We receive the Father in creation (never without the Son and Holy Spirit), the Son Jesus Christ crucified for our sakes, and the Holy Spirit in the preaching of Him. Adam and Eve rebelled against God by searching for better words behind the things of creation, apart from their preacher. Seeking to be their own gods, they fell under the dominion of Satan. In this created world God gives his law, not to bestow freedom but to remove the free will for our safety and as a mirror that judges us. God rules the old creation through the law that preserves and fosters life; God rules the new life by the gospel alone, and in both worlds opposes death, sin, and the Devil. The law, though holy and good for preserving creation, does not, however, save rebels; only Christ does that—by faith alone. How is this faith given? The Holy Spirit sends a preacher to end the old life and to bring the good news of Christ's resurrection, whose promise creates anew, raising from the dead. When the Holy Spirit creates faith, where and when it pleases, the Spirit does so *ex nihilo*, by the Word of promise (*promissio*), not once but continually, using the means of word and sacrament. When the preached God arrives, he seeks to be justified in his words, which means to say the 'Amen' to God's justification of the sinner, apart from the law, so that faith confesses that it has no other God than 'this man, Jesus Christ'.

REFERENCES

Aulén, Gustaf (1948). *The Faith of the Christian Church*, trans. Eric H. Wahlstrom and G. Everett Arden. Philadelphia: Muhlenberg.

Bayer, Oswald (2008). *Martin Luther's Theology: A Contemporary Interpretation*, trans. Thomas H. Trapp. Grand Rapids, MI: Eerdmans.

Bielfeldt, Dennis, Mickey L. Mattox, and Paul R. Hinlicky (2008). *The Substance of Faith*. Minneapolis: Fortress.

Elert, Werner (1962). *The Structure of Lutheranism*, vol. I, trans. Walter A Hansen. Saint Louis: Concordia.

Forde, Gerhard (1990). *Theology is for Proclamation*. Minneapolis: Fortress.

Hegel, G. W. F. (1953). *Reason in History*, trans. Robert S. Hartman. Indianapolis: Bobbs-Merrill.

Helmer, Christine (1999). *The Trinity and Martin Luther: A Study on the Relationship between Genre, Language and the Trinity in Luther's Works (1523–1546)*. Mainz: Zabern.

Leaver, Robin A. (2007). *Luther's Liturgical Music: Principles and Implications*. Grand Rapids, MI: Eerdmans.

Lombard, Peter (2007). *The Sentences*, trans. Giulio Silano. Toronto: Pontifical Institute of Mediaeval Studies.

Mannermaa, Tuomo (1989). *Der im Glauben gegenwärtige Christus*. Hannover: Lutherisches Verlagshaus.

Nygren, Anders (1953). *Agape and Eros*, trans. Philip S. Watson. Philadelphia: Westminster.

Prenter, Regin (1953). *Spiritus Creator*, trans. John M. Jensen. Philadelphia: Muhlenberg.

Sonntag, Holger (ed. and trans.) (2008). *Solus Decalogus est Aeternus: Martin Luther's Complete Antinomian Theses and Disputations*. Minneapolis: Lutheran Press.

White, Graham (1994). *Luther as Nominalist*. Helsinki: Luther-Agricola Society.

SUGGESTED READING

Althaus, Paul (1966). *The Theology of Martin Luther*, trans. Robert C. Schultz. Philadelphia: Fortress.

Bayer, Oswald (2007). *Theology the Lutheran Way*, ed. and trans. Jeffrey G. Silcock and Mark C. Mattes. Grand Rapids, MI: Eerdmans.

Bornkamm, Heinrich (1958). *Luther's World of Thought*, trans. Martin H. Bertram. Saint Louis: Concordia.

Brosché, Fredrik (1978). *Luther on Predestination: The Antinomy and the Unity between Love and Wrath in Luther's Concept of God*. Stockholm: Almqvist & Wiksell.

Dillenberger, John (1953). *God Hidden and Revealed: The Interpretation of Luther's Deus Absconditus and its Significance for Religious Thought*. Philadelphia: Muhlenberg.

Ebeling, Gerhard (1970). *Luther: An Introduction to His Thought*, trans. R. A. Wilson. Philadelphia: Fortress.

Forde, Gerhard (1997). *On Being a Theologian of the Cross*. Grand Rapids, MI: Eerdmans.

Gerrish, Brian A. (1973). '"To the Unknown God": Luther and Calvin on the Hiddenness of God'. *The Journal of Religion* 53: 263–92.

Harnack, Theodosius (1927), *Luthers Theologie mit besonderer Beziehung auf seine Versöhnungs-und Erlösungslehre, Erste Abteilung: Luthers theologische Grundanschauungen, Neue Ausgabe.* Munich: Kaiser.

Hinlicky, Paul R. (2010). *Luther and the Beloved Community: A Path for Christian Theology after Christendom.* Grand Rapids, MI: Eerdmans.

Hirsch, Emanuel (1930). *Luthers Gottesanschauung.* Leipzig: Dörffling und Franke.

Ickert, Scott S. (1993). 'Luther on the Timelessness of God', *Lutheran Quarterly* 7: 45–66.

Iwand, Hans Joachim (1974). *Luther's Theologie,* ed. Johann Haar. Munich: Kaiser.

Jüngel, Eberhard (1995). 'The Revelation of the Hiddenness of God'. In *Theological Essays,* trans. Arnold Neufeldt-Fast and J. B. Webster. Edinburgh: T&T Clark.

Kolb, Robert and Charles P. Arand (2008). *The Genius of Luther's Theology.* Grand Rapids, MI: Baker Academic.

Loewenich, Walter von (1976). *Luther's Theology of the Cross,* trans. Herbert J. A. Bouman. Minneapolis: Augsburg.

Lohse, Bernhard (1999). *Martin Luther's Theology: Its Historical and Systematic Development,* ed. and trans. Roy A. Harrisville. Minneapolis: Fortress.

McSorely, Harry J. (1968). *Luther: Right or Wrong? An Ecumenical Theological Study of Luther's Major Work, The Bondage of the Will.* New York: Newman Press.

Otto, Rudolph (1925). *The Idea of the Holy.* London: Oxford University Press.

Paulson, Steven (2004). *Luther for Armchair Theologians.* Louisville: Westminster/John Knox Press.

Reinhuber, Thomas (2000). *Kämpfender Glaube: Studien zum Luthers Bekenntnis am Ende von De servo arbitrio.* Berlin: de Gruyter.

Schwanke, Johannes (2004). *Creatio ex nihilo. Luthers Lehre von der Schöpfung aus dem Nichts in der Grossen Genesisvorlesung (1535–1545).* Berlin: de Gruyter, 2004.

Schwarzwäller, Klaus (1969). *Sibboleth: Die Interpretation von Luthers Schrift De servo arbitrio seit Theodosius Harnack. Ein systematisch-kritischer Überblick.* Munich: Kaiser.

Steinmetz, David C. (1986). *Luther in Context.* Bloomington: Indiana University Press.

CHAPTER 14

LUTHER'S THEOLOGY OF CREATION

JOHANNES SCHWANKE

LUTHER's theology of creation is not limited to a mere description of what happened 'in the beginning', nor is it restricted to some initial and selective point of life. Instead, creation is the principal and permanent feature of God's action, something happening constantly and taking place in a threefold way: by creation, preservation, and re-creation.

Equally, Luther's theology of creation describes God's sovereignty. For Luther creation always is a 'creation out of nothing'. This means: God acts purely out of freedom and love and not because of any obligation. Therefore, creation, preservation, and re-creation happen 'purely because of fatherly, divine goodness and mercy without any merit and worthiness in me'. Every calculating *do ut des*—I give to you so that you give to me—comes here to an end. Creation, preservation, and re-creation are not earned by one's own virtue but given *sola gratia*—by grace alone (cf. 1 Cor. 4:7).

I. CREATION

I.1. Created Individuality

The starting point and core of Luther's theology of creation is his famous explanation of the first article in the *Small Catechism*:

> I believe that God has created me together with all creatures, has given me body and soul, eyes, ears, and all body parts, reason and all senses and still preserves [them]; in addition, clothing and shoes, food and drink, house and home, wife and child, fields, cattle and all goods, provides me richly and daily with all necessities and sustenance for this body and life, protects me against all danger, and guards and protects

me from all evil—and all that purely because of fatherly, divine goodness and mercy without any merit and worthiness in me. (BSLK 510–11, BC 354; cf. Ps. 139:14)

Luther's reflection on creation begins with his own being created: 'I believe that God created me together with all creatures.' This means that God's creation is no collective, abstract, or technical occurrence, but something profoundly personal: The 'I' who speaks, the human being who is endowed with individuality, perceives himself in his individuality to be created by God and praises him, according to this faith, as his own creator. David Löfgren thus summarizes the matter: 'Luther's theology of creation does not begin with the representation of the creator, but with the concretely created' (Löfgren 1960: 21). Indeed, with the concretely created instance of my own person and world. The relevance of the creator is grounded in the relevance of this creator to *me*.

Luther wants to prevent the submersion of the individual in the entire context of creation: as a creature the individual stands alone before God, is personally addressed by God, and must also give a personal answer to this same God. He writes in his lectures on Genesis, 'If you look at my person, I am something new, because sixty years ago I was nothing. Such is the judgement of the world. But God's judgement is different; for in God's sight I was begotten and multiplied immediately when the world began, because God's words "Let Us make man" created me too. Whatever God wanted to create, he created then when he spoke. [...] God, through his Word, extends his activity from the beginning of the world to its end' (WA42.57,34–58,2; LW1.76).

For Luther, general cosmological genesis, as well as the general genesis of various creatures, are ultimately of secondary importance. Instead, the starting point and centre of his doctrine of creation is the creation of himself as a creature who is a person in his own right. Likewise, his personal environment is the effective sphere of divine creativity (WA42.23,16–18; WA42.25,1; LW1.29–30, 33). Therefore, one must first grasp the personal element of creation before the global aspect of the created world can come into view.

I.2. Primordial History as Present History

As Luther sees himself in his individuality as created, addressed, and desired by God, the history of creation can be nothing else than present history. For Luther, creation is not something past, but something present; he therefore interprets primordial history as a history of the present. Consequently, neither is God's creative activity bound to particular periods of life.

Luther was firmly convinced of the historicity of Adam and Eve (WA42.71,15–17; LW1.93); he offers no statement concerning the relationship between a theology of creation and natural science—simply because this question was of no relevance during his time. Nevertheless, Luther is reluctant to interpret primordial biblical history merely as the beginning of things, as the *initium* but rather insists that its meaning be understood in terms of a *principium*. The Vulgata as well translates 'In the beginning' (Gen. 1:1) with 'in principio', not with 'in initio'; while '*initium*', means a beginning, which, once started, stays in the past and has no further influence, '*principium*' is a beginning which stays relevant for what it initiated. Luther does not allow himself to be distanced from God's creative work by any isolated, past original history, by any 'beginning of things', but instead sees himself placed in the most radical fashion in the creative event of primordial history, which he interprets as a history of the present. Luther's personal and present environment is the effective sphere of divine creativity. It is not Adam who is ultimately relevant here, but Luther. In an interlacing of times, past, present, and future come together in a single moment; pervading time, God's living creative Word is without end and remains ever 'effective' to this very day, is *verbum efficax* (WA42.40,32–33, 39; LW1.53).

I.3. Life as God's Gift and the Mediation of Creatures

Although Luther takes his own person as the point of departure of his doctrine of creation, his personality and individuality nevertheless does not stand by itself, nor does it originate from an isolated dialogue with God: Human life—indeed, life as such—is nonetheless bound up in the greater context of creation and Luther does not conceal the individual's responsibility for the greater household of creation. The fact that God 'has created me' cannot be divorced from the 'together with all creatures'. Luther therefore condemns a false pride coming out of this special human position towards the rest of creatures (WA45.15,7–21). Instead, one must give serious consideration to one's fellow humans, animals, and plants.

The reason for Luther's attention towards other creatures is that God's action as creator can only be perceived through the mediation of creatures. We know God's life-giving and life-promising gift in no other way but primarily through the actions and attentions of our own parents, to whom we were born. Luther's high regard for marriage as a 'nursery' (WA42.178,31–33; LW1.240) as well as a 'fountain' (WA42.579,9–10; LW3.44) of all walks of life is founded precisely in this life-giving and life-preserving communication between man and woman, parents and child, God and human beings. God speaks, creates, i.e., he does not act in the abstract, not in the nude, as it were, but rather binds his activity to creaturely events.

The beginning of human life is mediated, that is to say, it is bound to procreation through one's parents and to birth itself through one's mother. This beginning is determined equally by both the sovereign action of the creator, in which a human being is miraculously presented with life, and utterly human sexual activity. Human creation is grounded in the harmony of divine and human action: on the one hand, in the encounter of God and human being, creator and creature; on the other hand, in the encounter of man and woman, body and soul, and flesh and spirit. Both, the divine act of creation and the human act of love, joined together, simultaneously mark the beginning of life.

This care remains hidden from the infant, is given without being earned, makes its life possible, and allows it to grow and learn. We were taken care of long before we could take care of ourselves; our existence was desired by others long before we ourselves desired it. Before a human being can say 'I', he or she is already addressed by the divine and human 'you' (WA43.480,40–481,2; LW5.75). Observing creation, we see unconditional giving.

Perceiving creation begins with an awareness of one's own limits and everyday dependence on God's giving. Directly linked with this insight are other creatures around us as well as the environment in which we live.

I.4. Creation as Communication

For Luther, the creation and development of human life is not a technical-mechanical production but is embedded in an organic dialogue in which the creator's Word, the answer of the creature, and even the protest of the creature all have their place. This organic communication (cf. also Ps. 19:2) is not determined by fixed laws but remains in its dialogical character something living, sensual, and even resistant.

The encounter and union of two different things in a creative act is constitutive of human life, of any life. Human life owes itself to a fundamental communicative event, which marks the beginning of human life—indeed, of any life whatsoever—and makes it possible in the first place. The constituent duality is thereby not cancelled out, however, but remains an integral part of the creative union. Creation must be understood as a communicative act in two respects: For the theologian Luther, the communicative basic axiom is already present in God's call to himself: 'Let us make man', and in his performative Word 'Let there be light'. Creation thus is not effected monologically but dialogically. For the modern scientist, this communicative basic axiom of the creation event is realized in and through the free genetic exchange of information which forms the necessary presupposition for the fusion of two cells. This exchange of information is a communicative event which is indispensable for the natural reproduction of life. No one can reproduce all by himself. One cannot reproduce without communicating; there are always two elements involved, and it is the exchange of information involved in this communication which makes evolution possible. In this way all creation fulfils God's demand: 'be fruitful and multiply' in terms of a communicative, information-exchanging act of creation. This creative communication, moreover, will turn out to be characterized by freedom. That is to say: the biological partner and also the creature that comes into being are not subjected to one's own dictatorial determination but retains his or her own rights.

God's creative Word grants human beings freedom and dignity; it respects human opposition and otherness; it listens to the human response, which is precisely no mere echo to God's own Word. Instead, God's Word gives human beings time for response.

God addresses human beings in a creative and dialogical manner but places them under no dictatorship; God is a poet, not a dictator.

Humans, instead, are in danger of opting for the monologue. The mirror in which Narcissus receives the answer of his own echo can be taken to present a symbol of our times. By opting for monologue, Narcissus refuses to encounter the other. His creative, other-related communication breaks off, or rather submits to a will that focuses exclusively on its own reflection. The warning against self-reflective self-absorption and a monologuing existence, which the ancients connected with this myth, has been confirmed in a surprisingly literal way. Creating a reflection of the human self through cloning seems within reach. After all, everything alien, new, or different presents an initial irritation and feeds the desire to restrict oneself to the known. We flirt with the comfortable resonance of what is our own, with what our echo repeats to us. Both in view of bioethics and in view of social ethics in general, the story of Narcissus and Echo is a heuristic for our way of dealing with each other, a symbol of universal human self-love. Based on Luther's understanding of God's creation, it can be said that God's creation corrects the human desire to only accept what is similar to our own being and to decline the life of those who do not fit into our own biological, social, and economic standards.

The human being must remain communicative and not become stingy and self-referential. Whoever fails to serve the other, centring upon nothing but himself, will die, along with his possessions. Human dominance and the human address to the creature are in that case not creative but deadly—as *incurvatio in seipsum*. If human dignity, as built in the image of God, ceases to be based in God's address to human beings, which extends without exception to all humans and awards them a principal authorization to live, other criteria will gain prevalence. Contingent preferences then lead to a selective communication that affects especially the beginning and end of life. As a consequence, the life and the space of human action linked with it, which God has unconditionally granted to human beings, can then no longer be recognized as a gift. Both life and life-space are then perceived as a possession which must be defended, refused, or distributed in view of expected benefits. The passing on of the life one has received and of the opportunities for its development then no longer happen unconditionally, but conditionally.

Christian teaching about creation has to listen to Luther and resist any attempt to let merely human sympathies or personal preferences govern the way in which God's gift of participation in his procreative work is received. God's address to human beings, and his award of life to them, happened, in Luther's words, irrespective of any human 'merit and worthiness'. Accordingly, for example, no handicap or dementia may compromise our readiness to address all humans as humans, and to do so with the presumption of full personhood. The human being's inviolable dignity must be recognized in all; it cannot be deserved, and therefore can also not be lost. It has been awarded us and can therefore not be denied us. It is, as it were, a *character indelebilis*.

II. Preservation

II.1. God's Continuing Presence

For Luther, creation is never independent from God. Therefore, nothing can exist without God's sustenance and preservation. Luther denies a deistic belief, which implies that God would leave his creation. Instead, this created world neither exists nor works like a wound-up clock, which, once set in motion, can then be left to its own devices. For Luther, creation remains vitally dependent on its creator, as the creature itself has no self-sustaining power. Even the most simple biological or natural event, no matter how 'automatic' and 'natural' it appears, is for Luther a miracle because it would not take place without God's creative Word, without his giving and sustaining (WA42.261,1–8; LW1.355). This means, a miracle is not bound to the extraordinary but is foremost found in the most common and simple events. Admittedly, human cooperation in biological or other events is necessary, but this human cooperation is strictly bound to God's operation, his work and his giving. This unconditional giving receives its meaning primarily in the present. God does not just create but also sustains and preserves his creation; this preservation is never suspended, not even in sin.

Luther also denies the hubristic idea as if it now was the task of humans to solely take care of the creation. Even if creation seems to exist independently and seems to multiply itself without any supernatural help, for Luther creation stays dependent on God and cannot exist without his sustenance. God remains with his creation, is effective in it, continually allows new animals and human beings to be born, continually grants new beginnings, and in this way preserves creation (WA42.57,22–24; LW1.75). God's *conservatio*, his sustaining of creation, is, for Luther, a sign of his abiding goodness as the creator: 'We Christians know that for God creating and preserving are identical' (WA43.233,24–25; LW4.136), the one cannot be without the other; both are and remain indivisibly bound to one another (WA43.200,15–16; LW4.90).

II.2. The Necessity of Preservation in the Face of Evil

The necessity of God's preservation of creation is not self-evident: Why does God's work need special protection and sustenance? This points to the fact that creation is in danger, that evil exists. The world is God's creation and at the same time God's enemy; it cheats and is cheated; it is in danger and is a danger (WA17,1.318,11.2; WATR2.327,3).

Just as Luther's reflections on creation begin with the creation of himself, sin as well is nothing collective, abstract, or technical, but something profoundly personal: It is *I* who have sinned (2 Sam. 12:7: '*You* are the man!'). And just as creation is not so much something past, but something present, the Fall as well is something which daily takes place in every life. Sin means not to trust God's promises but to ask: Did God really say this? (WA42.118,11–32; LW1.157; cf. Gen. 3:1). It means to be narcissistically curved back in on oneself (*incurvatio in se ipsum*; WA3.212,36; LW25.345, 25,258,27–28 and 25.304,2–305,6), cutting one's ties with God, with life and with others. But to be sure: just as every creature cannot call itself into existence but is dependent on God's will and action, every creature as well cannot move in the opposite direction and annihilate itself. Even suicide (cf. Jer. 20:9 and 14–18; Job 3:3–19) will not disconnect from God's power and care. God remains the creator and sustainer of everyone: comforting a despondent heart is for Luther the resurrection of a corpse (WA44.546,24–25; LW7.332).

This overall dependence of creation on the creator, of course, poses the question whether God himself is also the source of evil. Here, Luther emphasizes that God is good, that the Devil is not only the personification of evil but also its source (WA50.473,34–37; WA40,1.94–96; WA13.89,1–3); a difference between the two is that the Devil cannot create (WA16.130,6–12; cf. the Hebrew word 'bara', to 'create', which is only used for God's creating).

Despite sin, God remains the creator and sustainer. Although God is not the creator of the fallen creature, the fallen creature fully remains God's creation.

II.3. The Realm of Preservation: The Three Estates of Church, Household, and State

For Luther, God's preservation takes place in the three estates, walks of life, or hierarchies: church, household, and state (WA42.516,33–35; LW2.356). They 'are to be found in and remain in every kingdom, as far as the world extends, and will last until the world comes to an end' (WA31,1.410,16–17; cf. LW13.369). Here, God and humans cooperate in various ways. Humans, while cooperating, receive a share of God's strength and power; nevertheless, God remains the only originator.

These three estates are three fundamental realms of life, in which God's promise and Word of creation organizes human life. Luther summarizes these estates in his interpretation of Genesis 2:16–17. 'In this text we find the establishment [*institutio*] of the church, before the household and the state existed. A church is thus established [here] that has no walls or any kind of external features, set in the broadest and most pleasant space. After the church was instituted, then the household was established as well. So the temple comes before the house, just as it is also placed on a higher level. There was no state before there was sin, since it was not yet necessary. The state is the necessary means for dealing with the depraved condition of nature' (WA42.79,3–14; 42.22,17–32; LW1.103–104, 1.115, and 1.131).

In his social and ethical decisions Luther does not so much orient himself around the classic teaching of the two kingdoms of God's rule and the Devil's, but instead, he puts these three estates in the centre of his thinking. Luther's great contribution to Christian ethics, therefore, is that he does not limit God's presence to a sacred realm, but sees God's presence in all of creation: in church, household, and state. And if *all* of creation is *God's* creation, there is no separation of holy and profane any more. Instead, there are a variety of realms in which every human—i.e. also every non-Christian—is called. The three estates, church, household, and state, describe the human being's relationship to God, to himself, and to the world.

These three forms of life can be described as follows:

(a) *The Church.* The church is the first and fundamental estate. For Luther, it is established in Genesis 2:16–17, when God addresses the human being by allowing him to eat from all trees of the garden except from one. This divine address and the expectation of the human answer set the basic framework in which church and religion operate. As it is an order of creation (WA42.78,26–41, 42.80,41–81,14; LW1.103, 106), this church includes all human beings and all religions. All human beings hear God's address, and all must answer to it. One must add that this church no longer actually exists because it has been corrupted by human sin.

(b) *The Household.* The household is the second estate; it is sometimes also referred to as 'economy'. The household is established in Genesis 1:28–9, when God enables fellowship and posterity by saying, 'Be fruitful and multiply'. Luther sees this estate as the relationship between parents and children, between husband and wife, between human beings and their field of work. It is the interrelationship of the human being with nature, the daily acquisition of his means of sustenance, his daily bread.

(c) *The State.* The third estate as the political or stately realm is not one of creation. Instead, it is an order made necessary because of the Fall. It is established in Genesis 1:28–9, where God gives dominion over the earth and in Genesis 3:16–24, where life after the Fall is newly ordered. This estate is easily underestimated and frequently considered 'unspiritual'. But Luther points out that its main task is to battle against sin (WA42.79,8–11; LW1.103). It establishes peace and preserves order when human society is in danger of falling apart or countries start battling against others. For Luther, in the end it establishes peace, so that religion can prosper and the gospel can be preached without interruption.

God's Word of Institution. Each estate is established by God's Word. Although all three realms may seem simple and unspectacular, their simple human deeds are sanctified by God's life-giving and life-promising address. These realms and estates are sanctified because they are established by God's Word and will to unite his work with the work of creatures. Luther points out, 'God could gather a church without the Word, manage the state without a government, produce children without parents [...]; but he commands us and wants us to preach and to pray, and everyone to do his duty in his station' (WA43.391,3–6; LW4.354). Nevertheless, the holiness of these three estates is not openly visible. It only becomes visible when one looks for God's Word, with which he established these institutions.

The importance of God's Word becomes clear when Luther observes the duties of normal life: A maid cleaning the floor or parents cleaning nappies are considered as engaging in something unglorious. But Luther points out that these trivial tasks are highly honoured by God because God himself has installed these tasks by his Word of institution (WA10,2.295–297). God hides himself under the trivial outside form of the estates, just as if he wore a simple coat of a beggar (WA43.140,27; LW4.7), because God wants to show human beings the weight of his Word: The importance of God's works is not visible from the outside but is recognizable merely through his Word of institution (WA43.138,30–31; LW4.4).

God's Word of institution becomes Luther's most important criterion: It sanctifies the estates and gives the human being his place in them (WA42.517,12–18; LW2.356). Luther's discovery of the world as God's gift makes him see the world not as something 'worldly', but as something spiritual. Everything that human beings are and have are God's gifts (WA42.544,27–28,265,39–41; LW2.393,5) which are to be used (WA42.497,7–9; LW2.329). Luther sees even money as a positive gift from God and declines to follow a Franciscan ideal of poverty (WA42.496,17–18,495,24–25; LW2.328,327).

II.4. The Shaping of the Given World

The formation of the world happens when human beings use what God has given to them. They should not harden themselves to these gifts of life from God and withdraw themselves from it. Instead, these promised domains and estates of life are given in order to be filled out and shaped. To deny that human beings are called to give shape to the world is to deny life itself. Luther sees human beings as duty bound to make use of the gifts and domains that have been placed at their disposal.

For Luther, the government and rule of human beings is grounded in the fact that God does not keep the power of creation for himself: The ability to communicate, to engage with others, to have and establish fellowship, and thereby to create something new, is also given to human beings. As a God who shares himself with his creatures without reservation, God gives human beings a share in the divine attributes, makes them able to speak (WATR1.565,22–24; WATR4.546,11–13). Along with this capacity for language, human beings are also given the gift of verbal power: Adam's governance and rule is manifested in the naming of the animals (WA42.90,14–20; LW1.119). With this gift of God's participation and the resulting participation of the human being, a marvellous cooperation of divine and human energies takes place in the strictest sense: God gives himself into human hands, into human mouths, gives human beings divine creative attributes, and therewith a share in God's own work.

Luther distinguishes himself sharply from monks who have left the world and in doing so failed to perceive their commission to give shape to the world. They spurn the tasks given with their stations in life precisely because they do not heed God's Word of institution and therewith the God who entrusted human beings with this task, however miserable and lowly it may seem. Luther writes: 'Hence when a maid milks the cows or a hired man hoes the field—provided that they are believers, namely, that they conclude that this kind of life is pleasing to God and was instituted by God—they serve God more than all the monks and nuns' (WA43.106,2–6; LW3.321).

For Luther, the free gift of the world through God's promise, 'You may have dominion!', does not mean that our fellow creatures are commodities for consumption. Instead, to rule means: 'Rule, so that everything blooms.'

III. RE-CREATION

III.1. Justification as Creation 'Ex Nihilo'

For Luther re-creation is of the same order as creation. The human being—just as in creation and preservation—receives here as well, as Luther shows in various examples, for instance, by the justification by faith and the baptism of infants.

Analogous to the Word of God, which in the beginning created everything out of darkness, now the Holy Spirit speaks into the dark human heart the words 'there shall be light' and thereby creates a new creature. This 'new', spiritually re-created human being is last but not least 'new' because it receives a new way of perceiving God, the world, and its own life. God is the one who 'gives life to the dead and calls into existence the things that do not exist' (Rom. 4:17) and who in the same way 'justifies the ungodly' (Rom. 4:5). Creation and re-creation are categorical gifts. God's giving takes place sola gratia, 'without any merit and worthiness on my part'. With this formula from his Small Catechism Luther identifies the doctrine of creation with the doctrine of justification.

This especially becomes clear in Luther's famous confession:

> We believe in God, who is an almighty creator, who makes everything out of nothing, who makes out of evil good, out of the hopeless and lost redemption and salvation. Just as Paul writes in Romans 4:17, 'He who creates new things out of nothing' and 2 Corinthians 4:6, 'God, who said, light shall shine out of darkness'. This means: Not out of a gleaming coal a little spark, but 'out of the darkness light'; also out of death life, out of sin righteousness, out of the slavery of the devil and hell heaven and the liberty of the children of God. (WA44.607,33–39; LW8.39)

III.2. The New World

The bodily re-creation of God's creature is a miracle which is still to come. Even if death and decay threaten to be the last and definitive word, Luther encourages every creature to trust precisely that sovereign creator, who once created heaven and earth out of nothing. For Luther, no Christians should be confused or frightened by their own death, the destruction of their own personal cosmos and existence, and the darkness and apparent annihilation. Instead, they should trust in God, the creator of all things, who has promised to bring the dead back to life and to bring about a new world. Yes, as surely as God created the world in the beginning, he will re-create it with all its people in a new world.

Trusting this creator, death seems like a little nap or like a birth into a new world. Luther writes, 'We are to sleep, until he [sc. Christ] comes and knocks on the little grave and says: "Doctor Martin, arise!" Then I will come to life in an instant and will be happy with him forever' (WA37.151,8). Luther can also speak of death as a cradle, in which one is put like a little child and where one sleeps until the resurrection (WA43.360,42–361,1; LW4.313). Even further: For Luther, death is a kind of birth and life is like being in a uterus, not knowing what will come in the future life after death. 'So little the children in their mother's womb know of their birth, so little we know of the eternal life to come' (WATR3.276,26–27, §3339). Luther hereby links God's sovereignty in creation, conservation, and resurrection to the human passivity in birth, to death and resurrection, and to the human ignorance of knowing what will come. Man is totally dependent on God. God is the 'creator out of nothing' and the human being is 'nothing' because he is nothing without God and his unfailing love as the motive of all creation (cf. 1 Cor. 13:2).

This means for Luther that God the creator, preserver, and re-creator calls life into existence, preserves and protects all beings, justifies the ungodly, resurrects the dead, and will create a new world according to his promise. He was, is, and remains the sovereign creator of everything.

Reference

Löfgren, David (1960). *Die Theologie der Schöpfung bei Luther*. Göttingen: Vandenhoeck & Ruprecht.

Suggested Reading

Bayer, Oswald (2008). *Martin Luther's Theology: A Contemporary Interpretation*, trans. Thomas H. Trapp. Grand Rapids, MI: Eerdmans.

Schwanke, Johannes (2004). *Creatio ex nihilo. Luthers Lehre von der Schöpfung aus dem Nichts in der großen Genesisvorlesung (1535–1545)*. Berlin: de Gruyter.

von Lüpke, Johannes (1999). 'Schöpfer/Schöpfung VII. Reformation bis Neuzeit'. *TRE* 30: 305–26.

CHAPTER 15

LUTHER'S ANTHROPOLOGY

NOTGER SLENCZKA

LUTHER'S understanding of what it means to be human is best viewed in its particularity against the background of classical scholastic anthropologies, which he had learned in the course of his theological study and found wanting (section I). His engagement with these anthropologies even as he began his theological work led to a redefinition of the basis of his understanding of humanity (section II); its developed form appears in his *Disputatio de homine* (1536, 'On the Human Being') (section III). There the foundational principles of his anthropology appear, which will be expounded in the following in several steps (sections IV–VII). The question of the freedom of the will was the anthropological doctrine which Luther most emphasized (section VIII). The essay concludes with the presentation of Luther's method in treating anthropology (section IX).

I. Luther's Scholastic Background

1. The pre-Reformational scholarly understanding of humanity with which Luther came in contact during his theological study arose, first, from commentary on Aristotle, particularly *De Anima* (*On the Soul*), and second, from the commentary of Peter Lombard's *Sentences*, since the thirteenth century also influenced by Aristotelian interpretations.

1.1. Reduced to their essentials (overlooking some far-reaching differences), these pre-Reformational positions adopted a hylomorphic taxonomy of body and soul. Nearly all high- and late-scholastic teachers assumed the definition of the human soul as '*forma corporis vivere potentis*' (the form of body capable of living, cf. *De anima* II,1.412.a,27–8) even if the question of the unity of the form, the soul, was debated. The Dominican school, influenced by Thomas, predominantly presumed the unity of the form of the soul in its various capabilities (*nutritive, sensory, intellectual/rational*) (Thomas, *STh* I q 76 a 3 and 4). The larger part of the Franciscan school, in contrast, held more or less radically the thesis that these capabilities constitute different parts of the soul (Oberman 1965: 57–9; Wilhelm of Occam; Leff 1975: 547–8; Bonaventura; John Duns Scotus).

1.2. While Aristotle analysed the capabilities of the soul (especially mobility, and sensory and intellectual capabilities) in *De anima*, the centre of his ethics focused on the task created by the inherent connection of *animalitas* and *rationalitas* in human beings: controlling the *animalitas* (especially the drives integral to human bodily existence, shared with animals) by the *rationalitas* (what characterizes human beings as spiritual beings, associated with angels [and God]) (Nicomachean Ethics = EthNic, I, esp. 13). This rendered his ethics an ethics of virtue. Virtues are the acquired dispositions (or capabilities) of the soul which enable human beings to do what is right when they are drawn by their drives, which sometimes tend toward extremes. These dispositions (justice, courage, etc.), Aristotle taught, are acquired by practice: the designation of a person e.g. as 'righteous' (capable and willing to distribute what one has) is not earned by someone who accidentally distributes what is good in a proper way, but by someone who as a result of a long practice does so gladly and with ease in varying situations (EthNic II,1).

1.3. Aristotle's ethic of virtue is placed in the context of a theory of the highest, life-determining good, which Aristotle saw in the *eudaimonia* (satisfaction), when human striving reaches its goal by finding lasting rest. Aristotle sketched various successful ways of living which could be oriented by different objectives, all with a view toward the goal of satisfaction (EthNic I,3): one can seek this rest either in bodily pleasure or civic honours, but also in philosophy, understood as viewing God as the goal toward which the entire cosmos strives (cf. Augustine, *De doctrina Christiana* III,3–IV,4). Variations of this concept, which Plato had previously formulated as the question of the goal or meaning of human living, occur in most views held in late antiquity.

1.4. In a context of Neoplatonic cosmology, it was Augustine who transferred the legacy of the ethics of happiness from antiquity to medieval theological reflection. Augustine enriched this ethics of happiness, particularly through the distinction of what is essentially and originally designed to be used ('*uti*') as means to an end (for him: everything created) from what is to be enjoyed as an end in itself, that is, only God himself ('*frui*') (Augustine, *De doctrina Christiana* III,3–IV,4). Augustine combined this design with a doctrine of sin: perverting their original motivation into *superbia* (pride) or *amor sui* (self-love), human beings enjoy what is designed to be used and use God for their own purposes (Augustine, *De civitate Dei* XIV, XIII,32).

1.5. Summarizing the Augustinian theological tradition, Peter Lombard's *Sententiae* (= *Sent*), on which also Luther wrote a commentary, treated anthropological conceptions in the doctrine of creation and the exposition of virtues, which Lombard placed in the context of Christology (*Sent* III). There he discussed human beings as created for the purpose of finding their happiness in God ('*fruitio Dei*'—striving toward the vision of God), as the guilt-ridden but inescapable failure to live according to this purpose, and as the reorientation of the human life to God as its goal. This reorientation manifests itself in the soul in virtues (faith, love, hope), which are produced by grace, the latter being a quality of the soul which is derived from Christ and mediated to human beings through the sacraments.

1.6. Aristotelian anthropology fit relatively easily into this concept because, as mentioned above, its hylomorphism originally belonged in this context of the question posed by late antiquity regarding the goal and purpose of human life, which had shaped the ecclesiastical-theological tradition based on Augustine; the Christian authors of late antiquity and the Middle Ages read biblical eschatology within this framework. At the same time it was clear that in this context the questions of the essence and the design of human beings are inseparably connected. At its foundation this anthropology was conceived soteriologically.

II. Luther's Redefinition of Humanity

2. Luther's understanding of humanity assumed this foundation, which he learned at the latest in lecturing on Lombard's *Sentences*, part of his required academic course of studies, which embraced past treatments of this work, especially within the Franciscan school.

2.1. Indeed, two further sources influenced Luther: the anthropology of the Psalms and of the New Testament epistles on which he lectured on the one hand, and on the other hand his interest in pastoral care, whetted by his own personal experience, focused on of the sacrament of penance. The two are closely connected since Luther read the psalms and the pious subjective experience reflected in the Pauline epistles as a model of self-understanding for his contemporaries who wrestled with spiritual problems and hoped for forgiveness in the sacrament of penance. This penitential context was, of course, familiar to scholastic authors but seldom won from them a genuinely scholarly biblical commentary with Luther's emotional intensity, which practically had the character of pastoral instruction or, later, a sermon. The scholarly reflection on the sacrament of penance had its place much more in the handbooks for hearing confession and the corresponding literature oriented toward the practice of this sacrament (e.g. Raymund of Penaforte, *Summa poenitentiae*, 1238).

2.2. In contrast, Luther's lectures offer readers no real anthropology, no scholarly reflection on the sacrament of penance. Instead, already his first Psalms lectures, which remained pre-Reformational in treating penance, offered instructions for self-reflection, directed by Christ's example, pursuing insight into a person's own *humilitas* (humility), appropriating Christ's *affectus* (emotions) produced by his self-humiliation as, Luther says, the Psalms express it (Ebeling 1971: 1–68). Luther presented, e.g. in interpreting Psalm 1 or 69, a contact point in which the hearer was grasped in his inner being by what he saw in others, the saints and Christ. Luther interpreted Psalm 69 in its literal sense as a lament of Christ descending into hell, as the Creed confesses. This lament, Luther asserted, embraced the saints, who re-enact Christ's descent into hell and his ascension from hell to God's right hand by meditating in their own *affectus* (emotional state) on their fallenness in sin and on their misfortune: 'By their emotional state, all saints die with the Lord and descend to hell with him. In the same way, they rise with him and ascend to heaven and send the gifts of the Spirit to others. All this, I say, is to be understood tropologically [not a literal interpretation]. For they die [not literally; Notger Slenczka] but emotionally and as far as the desire and purpose to commit sin is concerned. Similarly, they descend into hell as they feel the punishment of hell [*quoad affectum penarum*]. Thus, all the prayers of the psalms which are uttered in the person of Christ as being in hell, are also uttered in the person of the saints, as descending into hell by their affects with mind and heart' (Dictata on the Psalms, WA3.431,40–432,7, LW10.372). Luther directed his hearers to recognize themselves as sinners, aiming to make them people who appropriate the *affectus* of Christ and of the saints as their own. Decisive in this is precisely that Luther offers these thoughts in the framework of expositing a psalm of lament (Ps. 69), interpreting it literally as Christ's own words, commenting on his own descent into hell. More precisely, Christ speaking the psalm expresses the emotions which accompanied his descent into hell. Luther's interpretation aims at awaking these emotions in his hearers, who were to use the self-reflection sketched there in Luther's commentary on the psalm as their own, incorporating themselves not simply into the events of Christ's death and descent into hell but into Christ's experience, his emotions, expressed in the words of the psalm. Hearers did not really receive an interpretation of the psalm but rather were incorporated into the subjective situation and its inner conditions which the psalm narrates. The *humilitas* (humility) so experienced, in which the hearer is aware that he is lacking *bonitas* (goodness) completely, is in itself the manner in which the hearer distinguishes goodness from himself and thus God becomes present as the *omnitudo bonitatis* (the perfect fullness of goodness).

2.3. This peculiar way of thinking—the presence of Goodness itself, that is, the presence of God, is possible only where the one praying sees himself as fully lacking the good—permeates Luther's early comments on what it means to be human (Slenczka 2009). It demonstrates, first, that and how for Luther the experience of spiritual struggle accessible in the Psalms became a means of interpreting his own existence. Second, it makes clear that Luther discussed the essence of being human fundamentally within the framework of understanding a problem that Luther research labels 'relational', in the sense that for Luther this essence must be understood in terms of human standing *coram Deo* (in relationship to God) (Ebeling 1971: 280–309; Bayer 2003: 140–59; Härle 2005: 87–8). By this, all scholastic definitions are categorized as reflection on the essence of human beings *coram hominibus* (from a human perspective) (cf. *Disputatio de homine*, WA39,1.175–7, LW34.137–40).

2.4. The particulars of Luther's anthropology are formed by his reshaping the traditional categories of 'inner' and 'outer' (the inner and outer person, *caro* [flesh] and *spiritus* [spirit]) as he wrote his great Reformational treatises (1520) (Hirsch 1954: 117–21; Joest 1967: 163–233). On the one hand, the relevant passages reveal the origin of these categories in a dualistic body-soul (*On the Freedom of a Christian*; WA7.21,18–22,22) or triadic body-soul-spirit distinction (*The Magnificat*; WA7.550,23–34); on the other hand, Luther connected the received anthropological definitions with the relevant observation that the Pauline distinction of *pneuma* or *spiritus* (spirit) and *sarx* or *caro* (flesh) is not a distinction within a person but rather one which defines the entire person in relationship to God (e.g. Rom. 8:1–17). On this basis he identified what determines being human in terms of 'spirit' or 'the inner person' as faith's relationship with God, thus defining 'spirit' specifically as 'heart' or 'conscience', the location of the human being's relationship with God (*The Magnificat*; WA7.550,25–34; LW21.303). At this point faith means that human beings base themselves and their entire life with all its aptitudes and capacities on God in utter trust in the gospel's promise, thereby being 'spiritual' in the Pauline sense (Slenczka 2007a). Or they refuse this promise and hang their heart on another factor that determines their humanity, making these factors into their own god. Such people are 'fleshly'. 'Spirit' and 'flesh' are thus not primarily designations for parts or abilities of a human being but characterize 'the entire person'—all his aptitudes and capacities—in relationship to God (cf. *De servo arbitrio*, WA18.733–44; LW33.212–29).

2.5. This gives the traditional definition of 'sin' new connotations as well. Obviously, Luther, too, associated the term 'sin' with the carnal orientation of human beings to 'the world', and obviously the Augustinian understanding of sin, oriented around sexuality, persisted in his writings. It is also obvious that the doctrine of sin in Augustine and Augustinianism is not simply inimical to the body but also that Augustine and the tradition he launched emphasized that *concupiscentia* (desire) was essentially understood in the contrast of *amor sui* (love of self) and *amor Dei* (love of God) (*De civitate dei* XIV.XIII,32). Nonetheless, Luther brought a new emphasis into focus: faith, understood as absolute trust in God and as 'grounding oneself' in God or 'clinging' to him (cf. the exposition of the first commandment in the Large Catechism), determines human life and thus presents a criterion from Christian revelation for distinguishing sin and sinlessness. Sinlessness is not attained in the ideal of monastic abandonment of the world and love for God expressed only by abandoning it; rather sinlessness is attained when unconditional trust in God governs one's entire relationship with the world (1520, WA7.24,22–27,9; cf. LW31.349–52). On the other hand, the real, central sin is unbelief in the sense of not trusting, for it is faith understood as trust which ascribes to God all positive predicates, in that it expects all things from him (WA7.25,5–25; cf. LW31.350–1; Romans lectures, WA56.234; LW25.219; cf. *De servo arbitrio*, 1525, 782,13–24; LW33.288; Galatians Commentary, 1535, WA40,1.360; LW26.226–7). This matches Luther's perception of the Decalogue's central and fundamental demand, which 'governs' all other commands, the first commandment, which he explained as the command that aims to cultivate this faith and is fulfilled in faith. According to this understanding sin's core lies in offense against the first commandment, so understood (cf. e.g. *On Good Works*, 1520, WA6.204,13–216,39; LW44.23–39; Large Catechism, BSLK 560; BC386–7).

2.6. The decisive insight in this anthropology lies in its defining the realm of the 'spirit' or the 'heart' or 'conscience' as initially not an anthropological given which then secondarily relates to God by means of faith. Rather, there is only one way in which human beings exist, by being in relationship with another person than the self, by means of 'relying' (*sich verlassen*). Thus, human existence is grounded in someone other than oneself. Also the sinner, who is not grounded by means of a trusting faith in God, Luther maintains, relies on someone or something outside himself and places the burden of expectation of being stabilized either on himself—on his 'works', expecting to be justified by them—or on temporal things, expecting them to stabilize life, an expectation they cannot fulfil (Joest 1967: 233–320). To be precise: every doctrine of creation, also those of the pre-Reformation period, holds that human creatures are externally constituted and grounded inescapably in someone outside themselves. But, according to Luther, this does not simply describe an objective view of the human life as being constituted by another person or by God, but is a manner of self-awareness—not simply being constituted but being aware of being constituted (Slenczka 2007b); and the interest in these subjective implications is the decisive insight which connects Luther with modern theology, e.g. Schleiermacher (cf. section 5).

III. The *Disputatio de Homine*

3. Luther summarized his anthropological insights in his *Disputatio de homine* (WA39,1.175–80; LW34.137–44; cf. Ebeling 1977), which he composed in the context of the renewal of the disputation as an instructional form, at the same time and with the same subject as his disputation on Romans 3:28. The thematic focus of this disputation, at least at first glance, concerns the relationship of philosophical and theological anthropology. Theses 1–19 develop the insights on being human which philosophy provides, theses 20–40 the theological definition of being human. Theses 1–19 contain a definition (1–3), the attestation of human excellence in comparison to the rest of creation (4–9), and the attestation of the insufficiency of this definition (10–19). The second part, on the theological definition, offers first such a definition (20–3), deduces from that fallenness in sin, even of the highest human abilities (24–5), and thus demarcates this position from Pelagian positions (26–31), concluding with a kind of 'eschatological definition'. The fundamental views and guiding characteristics of the mature Luther's anthropology emerge: their content (3.1) and their significance (3.2).

3.1. The decisive distinction of the two approaches to being human—philosophical and theological—consists in philosophy's definition of the human creature as '*animal rationale, sensitivum, corporeum*' (a living being equipped with reason, perception, and a body). That means: it identifies human beings as only mortal, earthly beings (thesis 3). Indeed, philosophy catches a glimpse of the *forma* that even after the Fall distinguishes human beings from animals (theses 4–9) and of the similarity of this *forma* to God (thesis 4, cf. 8). Using Aristotle's doctrine of the four factors or causes, Luther held that these philosophical insights are limited by the fact that philosophy recognizes only the *causa materialis* (the body) and—to some extent—the *causa formalis* (the soul) of human beings, but not the *causa efficiens* (God) and the *causa finalis* (eternal life, thesis 13, cf. 10). Only theology defines 'the entire and perfect human being' (thesis 20) by seeing human beings '*in fonte ipso, qui Deus est*' (in their source, which is God) (thesis 17). The point of this definition (21–3) lies in its placing the elements of humanity which the philosophical definition grasped— in Luther's view—into the context of the salvation-historical grand narrative, where its significance can be found. Thus, at its centre stands the insight that human beings—even the '*pulcherrima illa et excellentissima res*' (the most beautiful and magnificent thing) (thesis 24), reason—lie under sin and in the devil's power. From this flow theses 26–31; in the style of canonical condemnations they demarcate this teaching from Pelagian positions, which ascribe to reason the capability to do good, the ability to attain salvation. Over against that presumption of philosophy, Luther himself used Romans 3:28, '*hominem iustificari fide*' (the human being is justified by faith) as the comprehensive definition of being human (thesis 32). It is comprehensive because here justification is not characterized as a human activity but as something done to the human being (thesis 33). This establishes, Luther says, at the same time that the human being—and indeed the all capacities of the human being and every human being—is a sinner apart from this 'being justified' (theses 33–4). According to Luther's concluding theses, this definition places the insights available to philosophy in proper place, so that the '*homo huius vitae*' (the human being of this life) which philosophy recognizes (thesis 35, cf. 19), is merely '*materia*' (passive potential for being formed) for the future form of life ('*ad gloriosam futuram suam formam*', thesis 36): the restoration of God's image.

3.2. Systematizing these theses results in several anthropological axioms.

3.2.1. First, the axiom that the human being has no proper understanding of himself (thesis 17). In the 1530s Luther emphasized that fundamental conviction repeatedly, e.g. in the Smalcald Articles (BSLK 434,8–12; BC 311). The insight into the completely lost condition of human beings under sin is not accessible to them apart from the proclamation of the gospel. That is anthropologically relevant because it makes clear that according to Luther sin is not something that human beings can make the object of their own reflection, but is rather something that continually and simultaneously determines their reflection on themselves and, as a result of this condition, distorts it. The self-understanding of human beings, which believes that they are capable of superb ethical performance and that their freedom to perform in this superb manner is relevant for salvation, is in itself the expression of human sin. This mistaken self-understanding is according to Luther inseparable from the conditions of sin.

This human 'overestimation of oneself' is grounded in the capabilities of reason, which do distinguish human beings from all other living creations even 'after the Fall'; the structure of 'sin' emerges in that human beings make something of this distinguishing fact—which is valid in relationship to the world, which is lower than the human being—in their relationship to God.

3.2.2. Second, the foundation of true knowledge of the human self is theology, and first of all in the narrative context of the history of salvation between creation, fall, and redemption, which in a second step Luther focused on the message of justification '*fides absque operibus*' (by faith apart from works). Soteriology is the origin of true anthropology according to Luther. This has three further implications: first, this reveals the fact that human beings are externally constituted; this takes form in the passive '*iustificari*' (to be justified over against justifying oneself). Second, this passivity also takes form in the concept of '*fides*' (faith) as the basis of justification, expressly in distinction from works: '*fides*' is clearly to be defined in such a way that it is not a work. Third, that means that faith is defined as the counterpart of the *passivum divinum* of '*justificari*'—'to be justified'.

3.2.3. Finally, the fact that human beings receive their existence from someone outside themselves corresponds to the affirmation that human beings in themselves can be seen correctly only in someone other than themselves. Human beings do not know themselves directly but only by knowing their foundation and the fact that they are defined through this foundation (theses 17, 21–3). Human beings are not only given their existence from outside themselves, but they can view themselves properly only through this external foundation, in which they have their existence. Again, this shows that 'receiving existence from another' and the insight into this being externally constituted cannot really be separated from each other but are one and the same idea. Receiving one's existence from outside oneself consists in being aware of this being constituted by something other than oneself.

3.2.4. This reception of human existence is not only to be understood as being grounded in someone else (God), but simultaneously has its own unique understanding of time (theses 35–40): the essence of being human is not a given in the present but places the present in relation to the past—the original image of God—and in relation to the future, in which this human essence will be restored. When human beings '*huius vitae*' (in this life) are defined as '*materia ad gloriosam futuram suam formam*' (matter [pointing to] a glorious future form), by '*materia*' ('matter'), a concept has been chosen which in the context of Aristotelian Hylomorphism expresses the pure passivity of being defined by another (i.e. the essential form). The notion of passivity is repeated here since Luther expressly places the human being as '*materia*' parallel to the condition of reality 'before creation' (thesis 37). This parallel of creation and redemption—purely passive createdness and a corresponding purely passive redemption and justification—constitutes a fundamental theme in Luther's anthropology (*De servo arbitrio*, WA18.753,39–754,17; LW33.242–3; *Disputatio de fide*, theses 65–71, WA39,1.48,14–30; LW34.113–14).

3.3. Luther's foundational thesis posited that a correct anthropology has its basis in the doctrine of justification or in the salvation-historical narrative context of creation, fall, and redemption. The act of justification, in which Luther summarized (thesis 32) this narrative, is simultaneously the anthropological application of this narrative of the history of salvation to the individual. Since Luther grounds his anthropology on salvation history or on the act of justification, his anthropological insights cannot be synthesized in a systematic topic '*De homine*', which would describe the essence of humanity as something that is the basis of the history of salvation or of the biographical event of justification. There is no essence of humanity beyond the history of salvation or beyond the event of justification. Rather, human existence arises only from this narrative and from what is determined by its application to the individual's biography. That means that there is one anthropology from the perspective of being sinful and another from the perspective of faith. Again, the conclusions of the competing perspective are seen differently from the perspective of faith: the excellence of humanity according to philosophy, seen from the perspective of faith, is the mistaken self-understanding of the sinner. This complex relationship must be treated, beginning with Luther's specific understanding of justification, expanding on aspects of the *Disputatio de homine* sketched above (3.2.2, cf. section IV). Thereafter, the sinful human existence must be assessed precisely (as treated in 3.2.1, cf. section V). The context of justifying faith and Luther's concept of God receive brief treatment (cf. section VI). Finally, the essence of being human, as presumed and presented in the contrast between justification and sin, is discussed, and with that Luther's affirmation that reason is in fact, indisputably, a distinguishing mark of humanity is clarified (VII).

IV. Union with Christ

4. The 'Finnish' Luther research initiated by Tuomo Mannermaa (1989, cf. Peura 1994) deserves credit for pointing out that Luther's concept of justification is closely connected to the theme of '*unio cum Christo*' (union with Christ): faith justifies because through it Christ is present in the believer and belongs to the believer.

4.1. This theme, which actually stands at the centre of the 1531 Galatians lectures, can be traced back to the first sermons ascribed to Luther and is also at the centre of the programmatic writings of 1520, especially *On Christian Liberty*. There Luther affirms that faith justifies because it binds the soul like a bride to Christ, with the result that all that Christ is and has belongs to the soul, while he assumes all the soul's negative qualities (WA7.25,26–26,12; cf. LW31.351; cf. *Sermon on the Sacrament*, 1519, WA2.742–758; LW35.49–73). The result is that believers are righteous through the righteousness of Christ; through Christ's wisdom the believer is wise, etc. (Ein kleyn Unterricht, Kirchenpostille, WA 10,1,1.10–12). The Finnish Luther researchers are concerned that this righteousness not be a 'merely' ascribed or imputed righteousness but a righteousness in which Christ is present in believers in a 'real-ontological' manner (Mannermaa 1989; Peura 1994, 1999). This clearly contradicts the observation above, that an essential feature of Luther's anthropology is the conclusion that human beings are centred outside themselves: that they have their existence given from outside themselves, that life has its centre in the divine act of imputation and in the human being's 'understanding himself' in this way (cf. Saarinen 1989). A model of believers' sharing Christ's attributes and participating in Christ replaces the concept of the creation of the human being from outside the self. This model seems to have the advantage of freeing the justification of sinners on the basis of Christ's righteousness from the appearance of being a purely 'synthetic' judgement, that in no way launches a transformation in the subject and its way of life: 'real-ontologically', participation in the righteousness of Christ who dwells in believers is in itself the effect of being saved that produces changes.

4.2. Indeed this reference to the '*unio cum Christo*' (union with Christ) does not make clear why Luther insists that it is precisely faith in which Christ is present and why precisely faith connects the soul with Christ and vice versa. A more careful look at the passages in which Luther presents justification according to this model of '*unio cum Christo*' makes it clear that Luther clearly presumes that the *unio cum Christo* becomes real through the person's new understanding of self through the consoling word of the person of Christ: 'Faith must be taught correctly, namely that by it you are so glued to Christ that he and you are as one person, which cannot be separated but remains attached to him forever and declares, "I am [like] Christ," and in turn Christ says, "I am [as] this sinner who is attached to me and I to him." We are bound through faith in one flesh and bone…so that this faith couples Christ and me more intimately than a husband is coupled to his wife' (WA40,1.285,28–286,17; LW26.168). The presence of Jesus' person in faith is therefore realized by the human being appropriating another person in that he understands himself in a new and different way. Faith is an act of 'appropriation' or of 'taking hold of': 'fides apprehensiva' (appropriating faith) (cf. Luther's theses De Fide, 1–25, WA39,1.44,4–46,10). Christ's presence is thus not a physical presence of Christ 'located within' the believer, but a presence which has its foundation in, and consists of, the believer's identification of Christ with himself and vice versa, the recognition that his own existence (sin) has been appropriated and borne by Christ:

> Thus, when speaking of Christian righteousness, the person [i.e. the concept that indicates independence of being] must be laid aside. When I cling to my own person and speak of it, then this person, whether I want this or not, becomes an actor, who is subject to the law. But here it is necessary that Christ and my conscience become one body, so that [looking at myself in my conscience] I see nothing else than the crucified and risen Christ.
> (Galatians commentary, 1535, WA40,1.282,18,22; from German translation by Notger Slenczka; cf. LW26.166)

4.3. With this more precise definition it becomes clearer than in the presentation in the Disputatio de homine in which sense human beings are externally constituted: this does not take place in some kind of relationship based on physical dependence, and it does not take place by having another person located within one's own person and present in that way, however one might imagine that. Rather, being constituted 'externally' takes place 'in faith', that is, when the person of Jesus of Nazareth, which is distinct from the believer, is grasped as the grounding of one's own understanding of self and appropriates his person in this way. The believer 'knows himself' as another person, and faith is nothing else than this knowledge of self as another person—cf. the quotation above: 'by it [i.e. faith] you are so glued to Christ that he and you are as one person, which cannot be separated but remains attached to him forever and declares, "I am [like] Christ."' These are peculiar expressions: faith is 'extra se' (outside the self) or faith is the event that 'ponit nos extra nos' (places us outside ourselves) (WA40,1.589,8/25–6; LW26.387; zur Mühlen 1972). This 'being outside' remains not merely outside but rather is appropriated, indeed in faith, in an act of consciousness, or more precisely, in an act of self-consciousness mediated by the integration of this other person.

4.4. At the same time this makes clear that the determination of the human being's location in time—that the present tense of human existence is 'materia Dei ad futurae formae suae vitam'—understands faith as 'being grounded' in another person, which includes reaching for completion, in which the temporal difference between what is determined and what determines—*materia* and *forma*—is brought together and fused. Luther clearly presumed that the unity of sinners and Christ, constituted through faith, will be completed eschatologically in a *unio cum Christo*—a union with Christ. This idea presupposes the concept that the future gradually permeates the present. In this way Luther raises the subject of the ethical transformation of the Christian life and connects it with justification '*sola fide*'. This is seen in the *Disputatio de homine* (thesis 39) or in the expression in *On Christian Liberty* that the unity with Christ in faith is reflected ethically in the Christian's becoming 'a Christ' for the neighbour (WA7.35,20–36,10, 38,6–12).

4.5. Altogether, the person's being grounded outside the self—the unity with Christ that consists of faith in the promise of the person of Jesus—is analogous to the unity of divinity and humanity in the person of Jesus of Nazareth and the communication of attributes based on this unity (the mutual sharing of characteristics of his humanity with God and of his divinity with the human being, which expresses itself respectively in the definitions of God and of being human). A presentation on Luther's anthropology can only hint at this. This analogy points to the fact that the external constitution of humanity represents a key concept in Luther's theology that would allow us to sketch a kind of 'ontology of the gospel' in Luther (see on the implementation of this idea, Baur 1993, Steiger 1996, Slenczka 2012; cf. Joest 1967).

V. Luther's Understanding of Sin

5. The description of the way in which human beings understand themselves apart from justification identifies them as beings which do not perceive themselves and their lost condition accurately.

5.1. Luther asserted that the sinner's inability to recognize sinfulness in himself is not an incidental element in this sinfulness, as if the question of what is actually sin in the human essence can be answered quite apart from this assertion. Rather, it is this inability to know oneself correctly that is the determining factor in sin itself. Sin is precisely the will's desire to be grounded not extrinsically but rather to understand the self without reference to the origin and goal of human life, purely from that which is visible and accessible in the present state of human beings. Sin is unbelief as the inability and refusal to find oneself only in reaching out to another.

5.2. Presuming the starting point of Luther's thinking in the context of the sacrament of penance, this desire manifests itself first in his attempt to use an ethical life as the means to establish the ultimate worth of his own life, which is proclaimed in the definitive verdict of what is therefore called the 'last' judgement. Like his scholastic teachers, Luther had absorbed the Aristotelian ethic of virtue, which leads to regarding virtue as the result of the appropriate actions. Thus, it focuses the virtue of being righteous on human action and places this concept of virtue within the framework of the Christian expectation of divine judgement. Therefore, Luther understood this idea as the demand to attain the affirmation of human righteousness in God's judgement by accumulating meritorious works (cf. *Against Scholastic Theology*, theses 40–4, WA1.226,1–31; LW31.11–13). Luther pointed out that such an attempt is doomed to failure because what is meritorious in such deeds, or in the remorse over past deeds, is not decided at the level of properly performing acts but at the level of the attitude motivating these actions—deeds and remorse have to be motivated by love toward God. This motivation is not under human control, so that at this level, we therefore can never find security about the last judgement. Individuals can govern their own actions, but not the joyful disposition toward God's will required for the actions to be truly good (theses 13–30, WA1.224,28–225,30, LW31.10–11). According to Luther, it is essential and inescapable for human beings apart from faith in the gospel that they try to constitute themselves and in this way find stability in the face of the divine demand that human beings account for themselves—and inescapably they fail in this attempt.

5.3. This in turn implies that human beings are inescapably placed in a situation of having to give account, which Luther consigned to the concept of law, contending that the Decalogue, the Sermon on the Mount, and the command to love God and neighbour determined its content. However, the experience of the demand to give account of oneself is not dependent on the explicit proclamation of the law's normative content. The dispute around Johannes Agricola's rejection of the proclamation of the law in the church elicited Luther's explicit formulation of the proposition that there is no escape from the situation determined by the law even if the law is not proclaimed in preaching: the existential experience of the obligation to give account of oneself and the question of the worth of one's own life arise initially not out of the explicit proclamation of the law and are not connected to any specific content. Instead, this question determines the course of human life as long as it does not find its answer in faith in Christ. The law is not, as Johannes Agricola thought (according to Luther's interpretation, *Antinomian Disputations* I, theses 7–12, WA39,1.342,24–343,6), a past period of salvation history that the coming of the gospel ended. Instead, Luther held it to be the ongoing experience of human beings apart from Christ (*Antinomian Disputations* II, theses 47–8, WA39,1, 350,3–6,39–40,352,3–6). The conscience or heart, that is, the innermost part of the human being (thesis 40), is, Luther asserted, the location where the experience actually takes place, an experience that is, objectified, externalized by the concept of a law proclaimed at the Sinai and by the concept of a divine judgement:

Just as they stand in judgment before themselves while their conscience testifies and their thoughts accuse them or excuse them, so they will also be judged by God on the evidence of the same witness. For they do not judge themselves on the basis of other people's judgments on them or on the basis of the words of those who praise or criticize them, but rather on the basis of their innermost thoughts, which are so deep in their hearts that their souls cannot escape from these thoughts and get away from them, nor can they silence them, as they can silence human judgments and words. Therefore God, too, will judge all people according to them and will reveal our innermost thoughts, so that there is no possibility to flee further inside, to a more private hiding place. These thoughts will of necessity be revealed and open before the eyes of everyone, as if God wanted to say: 'See, it is not I who am judging you, but I merely agree with your own judgment about yourself and acknowledge this judgment. If you cannot judge differently concerning the witness of your own thoughts and conscience, neither can I. Therefore, on the basis of the witness of your own thoughts and your own conscience, you are worthy of either heaven or hell.'

(*Romans Lectures*, 1516/1516, WA56.203,27–204,2; LW25.187–8)

The inescapability of the demand to give account of oneself cannot be removed by neglecting the proclamation of the law of Moses, as Agricola demanded. The impossibility of escaping this experience of God stems from the law's presence in the innermost part of human beings (conscience, heart), and reveals itself in their relationship to themselves in so far as it is not silenced by the gospel, where they find rest.

5.4. With this Luther presumes that human beings experience the law's demand for an account always in sensing the difference between demand and performance. The law appears as a burden, as slavery, continually causing anxiety, making demands as it insists on being fulfilled. It does not let the human being find rest. An inescapable demand exists in the relationship of human beings to themselves, and they must regard its fulfilment as that which gives them worth. Here Luther distinguished three ways or postures with which human beings relate to the law's voice within them. The posture of ignorance suppresses it or does not listen to it. In the posture of '*superbia*' (pride) people regard the law as something they can fulfil and deal with it on the basis of this presumption; this is a condition in which they deceive themselves and become obdurate. It slips into '*desperatio*' (despair) when they realize that the demand to give account of oneself does not expect only the fulfilling of the law in external actions but the harmony of the human will with God's will in this demand. This harmony does not exist when human beings experience the demand for an accounting and realize the gap between demand and performance.

5.5. It is clear that this 'experience of the law' is the salvation-historical or religious-biographical concretization of what Luther had described in the *Disputatio de homine* as the human self-deception that is inseparable from the essence of sin. For in all three forms of relating to the law, sin, which determines who the human being is, remains hidden since sinners do not understand that they are in need of redemption; in all three forms sinners hold that they are, in principle, able to fulfil the law according to the letter and the spirit. Sinners see reason, which distinguishes them from other forms of life, as the foundation for complying with the demand within themselves. It is precisely this 'knowing oneself as not needing redemption' which, Luther holds, constitutes the core of sin. He often interpreted this as offense against the first, and thus the chief, commandment: the human creature who does not see himself as needing redemption is the human being who 'wants to be God himself' (*Against Scholastic Theology*, thesis 17, WA1.225,1–2; theses 94–7, WA1.228,28–33; LW31.10, 15).

VI. JUSTIFICATION AND FAITH

6. In this situation it is the gospel which overcomes the fundamental posture of sinners and lets them view what sin is 'in its depths' (Smalcald Articles, BSLK 434; BC 311). Simultaneously, it breaks through the sinner's self-deception. According to Luther, the gospel is the assurance of what Jesus Christ accomplished in his suffering, cross, and resurrection, which serves as the foundation of the sinner's own life, the basis of his own identity. This acknowledgement of Christ and of the God who is acting in him as the origin of all the good that human beings produce is both the acknowledgement that in the human being himself there is no good, and the acknowledgment of God as the 'summum bonum' ('the origin and source of all good', as in BSLK 560; BC 386–7; WA40,1.360; LW26.226–7). Faith is precisely this fundamental posture of grateful reception which acknowledges the giver. It overcomes and conquers the posture and roots of sin, the refusal to recognize oneself as dependent. Simultaneously, it recognizes and confesses God 'as God', as the giver of all good, by that fulfilling the first commandment without compulsion.

VII. REASON IN THE SINNER

7. The narrative that takes shape in salvation history and the existential biography, where, Luther held, the essence of being human becomes clear, would be incomplete if it were not also clear that even in the state of sinfulness reason retains the dignity and majesty it had apart from faith, before it came to believe in Christ.

7.1. Following late scholastic theology as well as Augustine, Luther distinguished the spheres of reality which are subordinate to human beings (the inanimate and the animate, mobile world of matter, plants, and animals) and those which are above them (the reality of the angels and God). This distinction is presumed when Luther labels reason as the chief and best thing in comparison with 'ceteris rebus huius vitae' (the other things of this life) (Disputatio de homine, theses 4, 6). It singles out the human being as a being equipped with a sense of orientation and competence for action. It is the origin of 'quidquid in hac vita sapientiae, potentiae, virtutis et gloriae ab hominibus possidetur' (what human beings possess in wisdom, power, virtue, and glory) (thesis 5). This position of prime importance, which human beings, specifically reason, have through the comparison with things and animals not gifted with reason (thesis 1), is, Luther held, confirmed by the commission to exercise dominion in Genesis 1:28 (thesis 7, 8).

7.2. Luther never raised doubts about this designation of reason as that which takes control of theoretical and practical reality. It fits into the narrative of creation, sin, and grace, in which the essence of being human is presented in two ways: first, Luther viewed reason as the mechanism which human beings retain under sin and which orients them to the common good, so that sin's effects, which make them egocentric, adverse to the common life, are not removed but are limited. This means that it is not, e.g., the Decalogue or the Sermon on the Mount which gives people their ethical orientation but 'the law written in the heart', which according to Luther agrees in principle with the Decalogue.

7.3. Luther presumed that all human beings have assigned tasks which place them in the role of serving and caring for other people.

7.3.1. In this he took over the pre-Reformational ethic of (social) standing and bound these estates together with the motif of 'calling' (German 'Beruf' which nowadays means a job or a profession, but echoes the original being called to do something [by God]). These orders through which God established structures for life—marriage, relationships to parents and to governmental authority—are not a matter of choice: human beings find themselves in them, and for Luther they are confirmed and sanctioned by Scripture. Specifically the fourth and sixth commandments are for Luther, like the biblical paranetic statements and, of course, Romans 13:1–7, instruction for the orders and (social) standings which determine and orient life. The allusion to the orders established for human life is, on the one hand, a reference to a specific form in which human beings encounter God's commandment *in concreto* and how these commands make themselves clear to people. On the other hand, they serve to set boundaries for human action and simultaneously to open up possibilities for action: Luther contrasts this order that has always been in place, in which human life has been situated and in which God's commandments function, with the esteem accorded to a life oriented by the 'evangelical counsels'—chastity, obedience, poverty. God's established order functions as the counterpoint to the esteem these deeds had in medieval society, which threatened to become rivals to the God-given orders for life. All human beings, even Christians, are obligated to these orders established by God rather than to special ascetic feats. The orders are not a matter of personal choice.

7.3.2. However, for Christians, these orders become opportunities for service, for participation in the freedom of Jesus Christ, who humbled himself to perform such service. For Christians the orders are fields of activity in which, free of self-interest, they serve the neighbour, whom they are to protect, each in his situation, from the results of sin (*On Christian Liberty*, 1520, WA7.20–38; LW31.333–77; *Whether Soldiers, Too, Can Be Saved*, 1526, WA19.623–62; LW46.93–137; cf. Slenczka 2008). Also punishment by governmental authorities for transgressions of the law is, Luther holds, an exercise of the service of love for the neighbour: Christians recognize that sin can be removed only through the action of the Holy Spirit and that human life together dare not presume that members of society are sinless and free of self-interest. Instead, human communal life is only possible when the preservation of the common life over individual self-interest—by the threat of punishment—is effectively practised. Practising freedom from self-interest, which faith makes possible, understands relationships with others that are part of the design of the orders as the form of love and thus of service to the neighbour and the community. For Luther these orders arise not from the special revelations to Christians or from biblical directives; instead, they are fundamentally accessible to all people through reason and are universally experienced as obligations. This demonstrates Luther's proximity to forms of argumentation based on natural law. His continual reference to the biblical basis of such orders serves to confirm and give positive sanction to the orders, at times also to explain their original purpose, but this is not constitutive for the orders or the fact that human beings are obligated to live within them. Here, the ability of human reason to recognize, establish, and preserve social order proves to continue also under the conditions of sin.

7.3.3. Luther's refusal to sketch a specifically Christian ethic or to call upon Scripture as the foundation for specifically Christian guidelines for society figured in his dispute with the 'left wing of the Reformation' (which called upon Scripture and the 'sola Scriptura' principle) and the social utopias it produced. Instead, he set reason—precisely not Scripture—as the source, norm, and fundamental criterion of proper ethical demands; even the prescriptions of the Old Testament must demonstrate that they are correct and valid according to this norm. Their authority to impose obligations on human beings is decided by their conformity to the law written in the heart of the Christian (WA16.380,17–28; LW35.168). Even governmental authority is not categorically obligated to act according to the Decalogue but rather must make decisions that are just in particular situations and directed by the 'bonum commune' (the common good) (On Temporal Authority, WA11.271,27–273,25,276,6–26; LW45.118–20; On Good Works, WA6,260,24–261,19; LW44.94–5).

8. Scholastic theology had inherited the question of whether, and in what sense, human beings exercise a free will from Augustine and his dispute with Pelagius and the Semi-Pelagians.

8.1. In the theological and philosophical discussions of High Scholasticism this question had two foci. Comment on the ninth chapter of Aristotle's Peri Hermeneias (On Interpretation) provided one location for the discussion of the compatibility of this freedom with God's predestination. It treats to what extent statements on future, contingent events can be regarded as true. If sentences referring to future, contingent events can already be true in the present (e.g. Peter is predestined to salvation), the event is no longer contingent, but is necessary. Combining commentaries on chapter 9 of Peri Hermeneias with the content of Christian soteriology profoundly complicates the question, and it becomes a field on which considerable acumen must come into play (cf. e.g. William of Occam, Tractatus de praedestinatione, 2007).

For here—the second focus for discussing the problem of the free will in pre-reformation scholasticism—the theological question emerges in the framework of soteriology whether, and if 'yes' then 'what', human beings contribute to attaining salvation (Oberman 1965: 113–75). In so far as the final attainment of salvation is the result of divine predestination, through which God saves human beings without their doing anything, as Augustine in his later years maintained, the attainment of human salvation loses every trace of contingence and is dependent—in so far as salvation is dependent on human beings fulfilling certain conditions (e.g. faith or contritio, remorse)—on these conditions taking place necessarily in human lives. If Peter is predestined by God to salvation and salvation has the condition of merits or contrition or faith, then necessarily Peter is led by God to fulfilling these conditions; on the other hand, how is someone who is not predestined as Peter is, and therefore is not led by God to gain merits or to believe, to be held responsible for something he not only did not do but was unable to do? The concern is, on the one hand, maintaining the necessity of grace in appropriating salvation, which dare not be attained through human performance; on the other hand, maintaining the guilt of sin and thus the righteousness of God. His righteousness is guaranteed only when human salvation is not fully in God's hands since that would ascribe the corruption of sinners to God. Therefore, acquiring salvation had to presume some merit on the human side, to distinguish those who share in salvation from those who are finally condemned as sinners. Not the least, the transforming power of grace and the new orientation for living appropriate to the state of salvation had to be emphasized.

In the context of the interpretation of the sacrament of penance, pastoral interests shaped the concerns of theologians, who sought to keep the conditions for receiving grace demanded from the will manageable. Thus, they offered interpretations that would not destroy the certainty of the person seeking grace. In the framework of the theology of penance the description of the 'materia' of the sacrament served this end. The valid forgiveness and the restoration of a state of grace would be created by the promise pronounced in absolution if, and only if, the penitent meets the requirements of *confessio oris* ([complete] oral confession of sins), *satisfactio operis* (satisfaction for the temporal results of sin), and especially the *contritio cordis* (abhorrence of the deeds already committed, motivated by love for God and his will—not by fear of punishment). The definitions of these presuppositions ('*facere quod in se est*', to do what is possible) was originally and actually conceived as assurance that imposed limits on the scrupulosity of penitents. In fact—and not only for Luther—they produced a far reaching insecurity over the fulfilling of these presuppositions and thus over the validity of the absolution.

The mainstream of high and late scholastic theological tradition was interested in finding a formula to connect a fundamental freedom of the will with the exclusive efficacy of grace. Attempts to describe the conditions of receiving grace in a way that its undisputed exclusive efficacy did not destroy the necessity of human merit included the distinction of the *necessitas consequentis* (the necessity of the result of God's predestination) from the *necessitas consequentiae* (the inner necessity of that which results) and properly relating primary and secondary causes (the will that is renewed, empowered, and continually supported by grace attains merits, but only by grace).

8.2. Since his *Disputation on the Powers and Will of the Human Being Apart from Grace* (1516, conclusion 2, corollary I), particularly in the Heidelberg Disputation (1518), Luther advanced the thesis that the will apart from grace is not free in relationship to sin but is a freely willing slave. The 'free will' after the fall into sin is a '*res…de solo titulo*' (a mere verbal claim) (Heidelberg Disputation, thesis 13). Luther followed the later Augustine fully: in the question of human salvation the will is totally passive; God alone is at work. Erasmus addressed this topic by contending that at this point Luther had gone too far and here agreement could be attained, if not with Luther, at least with his comrades. His chief argument was, on the one hand, that Scripture relates ethical directives to salvation, reflecting his theological interest in the ethical impact of Christian proclamation; on the other hand, his interest focused on the implications of a strictly predestination soteriology for the image of God. God's actions in punishing sin had to correspond to the actions of their human object. If the sinner had no possibility for another decision, God would be punishing sin, which he had caused in the human being or at least could have, but had not, prevented.

8.3. Luther's argument for the bondage of the human will is dependent, first, as in the 'Disputatio de homine', on the conviction that human beings are not justified by works but only by Christ and thus by faith, understood as the opposite of works: the posture of passivity and receptivity. Every concession to the freedom of the human will tended to ascribe to the will and not to God's grace the decisive contribution to salvation. This tarnished God's, Christ's, honour (De servo arbitrio, WA18.729,19–730,19,676,10–15; LW33.206–7, 125). Luther disputed the position held by all schools of thought at his time, that sin does not completely destroy the human being's highest faculties, reason and the will's freedom of choice, but only weakens them (on Psalm 51, 1532/1538, WA40,2.313–470; LW12.303–410). He did so precisely with the argument that, first, on its own, reason cannot view itself clearly, and second, human beings are indeed capable of determining that they will do what is commanded but are incapable of determining that they want to obey the commandment and freely consent to God's will: 'Through the fall the will, understanding, and all natural powers are destroyed, so that the human being is no longer whole but rather is turned in upon himself by sin... that he no longer recognizes God, does not love him, but instead flees from him, fears him, and thinks that he is not God, that is, that he is merciful and good, but rather a judge and tyrant' (WA40,2.323,32–324,19; LW12.308–9). Under this premise Luther understood Scripture's commands not, like Erasmus, as a testimony of human capability but, according to Romans 3:20, as the proclamation of the law in its usus elenchticus (the accusing or crushing function of the law): its goal is to convince human beings of their inability to will and to do God's will (WA18.673,34–674,4,676,28–677,36,679,13–19,695,2–7; LW33.121,126–8,130, 154). This deduction of anthropological insights from the context of salvation history corresponds to Luther's grounding the exclusive efficacy of God in salvation and the bondage of the human will that accompanies it as a necessary element of his concept of God, according to which God's sovereignty rules out the possibility of his reacting to previously performed human actions, which would mean that something outside God controlled and governed him (WA18.706,8–24,718,1–719,3; LW33.171,188–90).

8.4. With this concept of God Luther left behind his soteriological argument in its narrower sense. That is interesting because it shows that his thesis on the bondage of the human will goes farther than the soteriological argument: on the one hand, Luther limits the bondage of will to the relationship to God and the question of how salvation is attained. In regard to salvation the human will is bound while in all other aspects of human action it is free and accountable (Disputatio de homine, theses 4–9; see section 3). That naturally implies that ethical activity in the world—in so far as it is not borne and reliably accompanied by faith in God—has no effect on a person's salvation. But on the other hand, some of Luther's formulations show that he sees human bondage as a more universal theological and anthropological phenomenon, so that the human will is bound not only in relationship to salvation but in every other aspect as well (WA18.615,31–617,22,709,5–35,719,20–35; LW33.37–41,175–6,191). This is interesting because already in 1516 (WA1.147,38–148,12) but also in *De servo arbitrio* Luther set this conclusion over against the assertion that the will is bound in the sense of 'being compelled' (e.g. WA18.720,32–5; LW33.192–3). He presumes apparently that willing must be free in the sense of 'not being compelled'—otherwise, it would not be what one wills but what one must do. Willing excludes necessity. Precisely this free willing, Luther writes, is bound in the sense that human beings do not control the direction of this willing (Slenczka 2010). The one who wills does not govern his will. The will thus does not face the alternative of sin and grace but rather—without distracting from its character as a will—is determined by it without recourse, inevitably. Being bound by sin means being a sinner freely, but without the capability to govern this direction of will. This makes it clear that sin is for Luther a form of willing, an inevitable disposition of the act of willing; nonetheless, the act of willing that is not under the control of the person who is willing. Sin is an inevitable act of freedom. This insight of Luther has implications because it not only proceeds from theological premises but because it leads to understanding the power of the will not on the basis of the phenomenon of decision-making and demonstrates that 'willing' does not take place in a situation which is not predetermined in terms of alternatives, in which a choice of alternatives happens freely. Instead 'willing' always is determined in one way or another, but this determination of will is not under human control. This aspect of Luther's doctrine of the bound will is not specifically theological, but rather corresponds to what actually happens: every act of willing is free; otherwise it would be a coercion. But every act of willing is always determined, has a direction which, as the act of willing is performed (as the person does something willing and gladly), is not under the person's control. The deeds of a person are under its command—but it is impossible to govern oneself in whether one gladly does something or begrudgingly. Human beings can indeed ponder and question their willing but cannot determine it or decide about it. That human beings do not have control over their lives in this freedom is a general and generally plausible insight because it corresponds to human experience. That human will—as will—is free, and that notwithstanding that human beings are not able to govern this freedom (to determine what to do gladly or loathingly) is not only a theological insight derived from soteriology but an insight that corresponds to common human self-awareness. Implicit in Luther's position is that human beings are always, inevitably, so constituted that they want to be God themselves and do not want to recognize that they are grounded in another (*Against Scholastic Theology*, theses 86–7 and 16–17, WA1.228,13–15, 225,1–4)—they are bound to freely wanting to be God.

9. Luther viewed human beings as beings who live according to their essence when through the gospel of Christ they are grounded outside of their own self. That means that human beings who live apart from Christ are out of tune with their own design. Neither theoretically nor by the exercise of their own will can they 'get behind appearances' and understand themselves or 'determine their own lives'. Luther's anthropology thus has aspects which can be used for constructing theory and can lead into further understanding of what it means to be human. That is particularly true of his

observations on the bound will. But it is also clear that Luther was not interested in the possibilities for constructing theory. Precisely compared with contemporary scholarly theological anthropologies, a completely different atmosphere for understanding humanity materializes here. Luther's anthropology is not concerned with the synthetic potential which Aristotelian texts certainly have but rather with the experience of the self and therefore with finding a proper, truly human way of life. He focuses on the specific experiences of the demand to account for oneself (law) and of redemption by being externally constituted (gospel). For him what being human really is emerges out of these elements. The sources of his anthropology are not, however, theological axioms or biblical dicta, or rather, they are such only in so far as they interpret his own experience or can be translated into his own experience—in other words, in so far as he recognizes in them his own spiritual struggles and can use them to overcome these struggles. This anthropology has—like all theology—its source in experience, Luther contended, and it aims toward interpreting and arousing experience. It is a matter not of recognizing (*cognoscere*) the state of sinfulness and the redemptive force of the gospel, but of feeling (*sentire*) it, as he writes in his commentary on Psalm 90:

> This knowledge of sin, moreover, is not some sort of speculation or an idea which the mind thinks up for itself. It is a true feeling, a true experience, a hard-fought struggle of the heart, as [David] testifies when he says, 'I know my transgressions', that is I feel and experience them... In theology this is the essence of being human. The theologian's goal is that human beings become aware of their nature, corrupted by sins. When that happens, despair follows, casting them into hell... When the spirit feels that, the second part of this knowledge must follow, which is not speculative but completely practical and emotional. People hear and learn what grace and justification are, what God's plan for the human being who has fallen into hell is, namely that he has decided to restore him through Christ, etc. Here the miserable spirit is restored and on the basis of this teaching of grace affirms with joy, 'even if I am in myself a sinner, in Christ I am no sinner'... This is the twofold theological recognition which David conveys in this psalm, so that the psalm aims to foster the human being's theological apprehension: so that no one speculates about [God's] majesty, what God might do, how powerful he is, and likewise not about being human, how much human beings are masters of their own concerns, as a lawyer does, or over the sick, as a physician does, but over the human being as sinner. For the real subject of theology is the human being, accused of sin and lost, and God, the one who justifies and rescues the sinful human being. (WA40,2.326,34–328,18; LW12.310–11)

References

Baur, Jörg (1993). *Luthers klassische Erben*. Tübingen: Mohr/Siebeck.

Bayer, Oswald (2003). *Martin Luthers Theologie. Eine Vergegenwärtigung*. Tübingen: Mohr/Siebeck.

Ebeling, Gerhard (1971). 'Die Anfänge von Luthers Hermeneutik' (1951). In G. Ebeling, *Lutherstudien, I*. Tübingen: Mohr/Siebeck, 1–68.

Ebeling, Gerhard (ed.) (1977). 'Disputatio de homine'. In *Lutherstudien*, II, 1 and 2. Tübingen: Mohr/Siebeck.

Härle, Wilfried (2005). *Menschsein in Beziehungen. Studien zur Rechtfertigungslehre und Anthropologie*. Tübingen: Mohr Siebeck.

Hirsch, Emanuel (ed.) (1954). *Drei Kapitel zu Luthers Lehre vom Gewissen*. In *Lutherstudien I*. Gütersloh: Gütersloher Verlagshaus.

Joest, Wilfried (1967). *Ontologie der Person bei Luther*. Göttingen: Vandenhoeck & Ruprecht.

Leff, Gordon (1975). *William of Occam: The Metamorphosis of Scholastic Discourse*. Manchester: Manchester University Press.

Mannermaa, Tuomo (1989). *Der im Glauben gegenwärtige Christus. Rechtfertigung und Vergottung. Zum ökumenischen Dialog*. Hannover: Lutherisches Verlagshaus.

Mühlen, Karl-Heinz zur (1972). *Nos extra nos. Luthers Theologie zwischen Mystik und Scholastik*. Tübingen: Mohr/Siebeck.

Oberman, Heiko (1965). *Spätscholastik und Reformation*. Vol. I: *Der Herbst der mittelalterlichen Theologie*. Zurich: Theologisches Verlagshaus (= *The Harvest of Medieval Theology: Gabriel Biel and Late Medieval Nominalism*. Cambridge, MA: Harvard University Press, 1963).

Occam, William of (2007). *Tractatus de praedestinatione, de praescientia Dei respectu futurorum contingentium*, lat.-fr., ed. and trans. Cyrille Michon. Paris: Librairie philosophique J. Vrin.

Peura, Simo (1994). *Mehr als ein Mensch? Die Vergöttlichung als Thema der Theologie Martin Luthers von 1513 bis 1519*. Mainz: Zabern.

—— (1999). 'Luthers Verständnis der Rechtfertigung: forensisch oder effektiv?'. In *Recent Research on Martin Luther*, ed. Evangelical Theological Faculty Bratislava. Bratislava: Evangelical Faculty, 34–57.

Saarinen, Risto (1989). *Gottes Wirken auf uns. Die transzendentale Deutung des Gegenwart-Christi-Motivs in der Lutherforschung*. Wiesbaden: Steiner.

Slenczka, Notger (2007a). '"Allein durch den Glauben". Antwort auf die Frage eines mittelalterlichen Mönchs oder Angebot zum Umgang mit einem Problem jedes Menschen?'. In *Luther und das monastische Erbe*, ed. Christoph Bultmann et al. Tübingen: Mohr/Siebeck, 291–315.

—— (2007b). 'Das Kreuz mit dem Ich. Theologia crucis als Gestalt der Selbstdeutung'. In *Kreuzestheologie: kontrovers und erhellend*, ed. Klaus Grünwaldt and Udo Hahn. Hannover: Lutherisches Verlagshaus, 99–116.

—— (2008). 'Gott und das Böse. Die Lehre von der Obrigkeit und von den zwei Reichen bei Luther'. *Luther* 79: 75–94.

—— (2009). 'Fides creatrix divinitatis. Zu einer These Luthers und zugleich zum Verhältnis von Theologie und Glaube'. In *Denkraum Katechismus. Festgabe für Oswald Bayer zum 70. Geburtstag*, ed. Johannes von Lüpke and Edgar Thaidigsmann. Tübingen: Mohr/Siebeck, 171–95.

—— (2010). 'Von der Freiheit des unfreien Willens. Bemerkungen aus theologischer Perspektive'. In *Freiheit—Natur—Religion. Studien zur Sozialethik*, ed. Christian Spieß. Paderborn: Schönigh, 51–84.

—— (2012). '"In ipsa fide Christus adest—im Glauben selbst ist Christus da". (Luther) als Grundlage einer evangelischen Lehre vom Abendmahl und von der Realpräsenz Christi'. In *Abendmahl*, ed. Hermut Löhrt. Tübingen: Mohr/Siebeck, 137–93.

Steiger, Johann Anselm (1996). 'Die communicatio idiomatum als Achse und Motor der Theologie Luthers. Der "fröhliche Wechsel" als hermeneutischer Schlüssel zu Abendmahlslehre, Anthropologie, Seelsorge, Naturtheologie, Rhetorik und Humor'. *Neue Zeitschrift für Systematische Theologie und Religionsphilosophie* 38: 1–28.

CHAPTER 16

LUTHER'S TEACHING ON SIN AND EVIL

L'UBOMÍR BATKA

I. INTRODUCTION

LUTHER's theology does not centre solely on one topic. He was convinced that Christian doctrine as a whole was explicitly or implicitly revealed in the Scriptures. The doctrine of justification depends on the doctrine of sin and cannot be separated from the doctrines of Trinity and Christology. Therefore, the proper understanding of sin enables a person to become a good theologian, and a good reader and hearer of Holy Scripture (WA44.507,15–19; LW7.280). Only 'sinful and guilty man, subjected to the death and sin', as Luther stated in his famous 'Lecture on Psalm 51' in 1532, can be justified and saved.

Gerhard Ebeling's apposite statement that 'not every talk about God is theology' can be rephrased as 'not every talk about God and man is theology' because in Luther's definition of the 'subject matter of Theology', the 'divine and truly theological wisdom' is—different than Aquinas' (Pesch 1982: 246), or later Calvin's (Ebeling 1971: 255–72)—human beings 'guilty of sin and subject to perdition and God who is the Justifier and Redeemer of man' (WA40,2.328,17–18; LW12.311; Bayer 2008: 37–42). German theologian Christof Gestrich is right in suggesting that in order to do justice to Luther's theology of sin, it would be better to use the term *hamartolology*—a doctrine of the sinful human person—and not *hamartiology*, a doctrine of sin (Gestrich 1989: 218). Characterizing humans as essentially guilty and condemned, and God as Justifier and Saviour, is fundamental, although not new, for Luther: he adopted Paul's (Rom. 5:18), and Augustine's (*De spiritu et litera*, 9.VI) formulation. Nor is the form of Luther's definition new. He followed the medieval scholarly methodology of seeking an ideal definition in the form of one sentence with subject and predicate. What was new was the particular widening of the object of theology to God and humanity, and both particular predicates related to each other. The simultaneous importance of both parts for a brief and profound definition of the theology as such: that was an original contribution of Luther.

This essay aims to show why Luther could say that every human (cf. Ps. 111:16; Job 14:4; Rom. 3:19; Rom. 5:12) is utterly in need of the 'New Adam' (Rom. 5:15) acting decisively for his salvation. This is demonstrated in his explanation of the Creed's second article in the *Small Catechism* (1529): 'Jesus Christ, true God…and also true human being…has redeemed me, a lost and condemned human being. He has purchased and freed me from all sins, from death, and from the power of the devil' (BSLK 511; BC 355,4). In the first step this essay defines the sources relevant to this topic and examines Luther's terminology. Subsequently, the essence of sin, the origin of sin, and the effect of sin on human beings are treated. In conclusion, the question of the essence of perdition will be raised. Death did not concern Luther as limitation of created life, nor as mortality of the body. The key problem of human beings is the evil of perdition resulting from their sinfulness.

II. SOURCES AND TERMINOLOGY

Luther did not write a specific treatise solely on sin or evil. But there are very few treatises where the topic of sin does not appear. The significance of Luther's view of sin for all of his theology was emphasized in the first half of the last century by Erich Seeberg (Seeberg 1950: 103–13). Certainly, it was not Luther's psychology or the medieval perpetual cycle of sin, confession, and penance that led him to the strong emphasis on sin. His immersion in biblical language led him to the wide spectrum of broken human relationships to God. Besides classical passages like Genesis 2–3, Genesis 8, Psalms 32 and 51, Matthew 7:17–19, and 12:33, and Romans 1–7, the list gradually widened to include Exodus 34:6–7, 1 Kings 8:46, 2, Chronicles 6:36, Ecclesiastes 7:21, Job 7:20, 9:2, 9:15, 27:6, and 1:8, Psalms 31:6, 142:2, 129:8, and 71:14, Isaiah 64:6, Jeremiah 30:11, 1 Timothy 1:15, Romans 7:19, Philippians 3:13, James 3:2, 1 John 1:8 and 5:18, Revelation 22 (WA56.287,25–288,32; LW25.275–276). Looking at this rather untypical selection, the criticism of Luther's hermeneutical imposition upon the text of 'the radical understanding of sin and justification by faith', and his 'lack of appropriate distance from the text', as posed for example by C. Clifton Black (1985: 345), might appear appropriate. Indeed, a text like Psalm 51 was, according to Luther, a superb source for the doctrine of original sin, and not only as an example for Christian conduct, as with Augustine (*Enarratio in Psalm LI*). He described the content of the psalm in his *Summaries of the Psalms* (1531): 'It is the best doctrinal psalm, in which David properly teaches what sin is, whence it comes, what it damages, how we become free of it. For in this psalm, like nowhere else, sin is so clearly shown to be inherited and with us from birth' (WA38.36,25–28). But to do justice to Luther, it must be said that in accordance with his definition of the subject matter of theology, he was explaining Psalm 51 in accordance with Romans 3 (WA4.497,32–498,3; WA40,2.366,30–31; LW12.338; WADB7.14,24–33; WATR3.217,16–20). In Luther's view, it was Paul who hermeneutically connected the biblical passages in the New and Old Testaments and developed a soteriological and anthropological unity (Stolle 2002: 201–2).

Luther used both German and Latin terminology. After he started to expound the Hebrew text in his first lectures on Psalms (1513), he relied on the work of the German humanist Johannes Reuchlin, *Septem psalmi poenitentiales hebraici cum grammatica translatione latina* (1512). Luther's first serious theological inquiry related to the doctrine of sin was his work on the distinction in Hebrew terminology (Raeder 1967: 12–16), which continued into his lectures on Romans (1515–16) (WA56.284,4–5; LW25.271). His exposition of *Seven Penitential Psalms* (1517) not only offered the first German translation of the text but deepened and clarified his theological convictions regarding the biblical view of sin. After his second lecture on Psalms (the *Operationes*, 1521), Luther's use of 'sin'-related terminology translated from Hebrew, appears stable and methodical. Luther understood the Hebrew word '*pęscha*' (פשע) as crude evil deeds and transgressions of the law and translated it into German as '*Sünde*', '*Ungerechtigkeit*', and '*Übertreter*'. However, in his revision of the German translation of *Seven Penitential Psalms* (1525), as already in the German *Prayerbook* (1522), Luther changed the translation consistently to '*Übertretung*' (WA18.499,30; LW14.166). For Luther, the second Hebrew word '*aon*' (עון) corresponds to Latin '*iniquitas*' and German '*Ungerechtigkeit*', meaning the lack of righteousness *coram deo*. A significant and noteworthy change occurred in 1525, when he started to use the German word '*Missetat*' (WA18.499,37; LW14.167), primarily in the sense of actual sin. To the Hebrew term '*hattaa*' (חטא), which expressed the fundamentally wrong attitude in departing from God and inclining to evil, Luther gradually ascribed 'original sin', '*Erbsünde*'. Finally, he interpreted the Hebrew word '*rascha*' (רשע) as rude Godlessness, as pride and a lack of fear of God, an active self-confidence of one's own righteousness and denial of sin. He definitely decided this stood for the German word '*Übel*' (evil) (WA18.500,24; LW14.169). This shows again that Luther's understanding of sin was formed primarily by biblical usage (Bayer 2008: 181–2).

Generally, Luther used the term sin (*peccatum*) and distinguished between original sin (*peccatum originale*) (WA31,1.539,12; WA40,2.84,11; WA44.506,10–12; LW7.278) and a transgression of the law of God, which is actual sin (*peccatum actuale/peccata actualia*) (WA56.271,6; LW25.259; WA44.507,30; LW7.280). Luther talked about *peccatum originis* (*Ursünde*) when speaking of the first sin of Adam and Eve in Paradise (WA44.508,8; LW7.281; WADB3.52,2–8). The term *Erbsünde* can be translated as 'inherited sin' (*peccatum hereditare*) and expresses the notion of the whole of the human race submerged in sin. Especially from 1517 on, a development can be observed in Luther's doctrine on sin. As Luther moved toward reformational theology, his concept of original sin increasingly deepened. The German term *Sünde* moved steadily away from the description of the 'actual sin' towards the meaning of 'original sin'. Generally speaking, for Luther, the notion of original sin expresses the notion of the sinful state in its universal, total, and radical aspect. Therefore, we often find Luther's synonymous terms like *universale peccatum, generale peccatum*, or more precisely *totum peccatum*, and—a term not used among Scholastics—*peccatum radicale*, root sin (Ebeling 1985: 78).

III. The Essence of Sin

III.1. Unrighteousness

A typical medieval framework for any hamartiological doctrine was based on the Pauline distinction between 'flesh' and 'spirit'. In the Augustinian school it was generally accepted that after the fall into sin, a person is born as a carnal human being and needs grace (*gratia*) to achieve virtue (*virtus*) and goodness (*bonitas*). The loss of the obedience of the flesh (the lower powers) to the spirit (higher powers of the soul) was perceived as a punishment for Adam's sin. In medieval times this perception became accepted in all theological schools (Köster 1979: 125–40).

Luther upheld the perception of the powers of the soul until his first translation of the *Seven Penitential Psalms* (1517, WA1.190,7,10)—something he changed in both instances in the revision of 1525 (WA18.503; LW14.171)—and distinguished between three powers of the soul: intellect (*intellectus*), will (*voluntas*), and memory (*memoria*). Reinhard Schwarz aptly summarized Luther's early position: the intellect is a power of knowledge and can achieve the virtue of wisdom (*sapientia*) and the theological virtue of faith (*fides*). The will leads to the virtue of goodness (*bonitas*) and the theological virtue of love (*caritas*). The memory has the power of preserving and keeping, leading to the virtue of power (*potentia*), and to the theological virtue of hope (*spes*) (Schwarz 1962: 98–117). Analogically, as early as in his first lectures on Psalms and until the first semester of his lectures on Romans, Luther held the conviction that the consequence of original sin weakened all three powers of the soul (WA3.285,17), so that the capacity of reason turned to ignorance (*caecitas, ignorantia*), the capacity of will turned into wickedness (*malitia, concupiscentia*), and finally the power of memory diminished to weakness (*infirmitas, instabilitas*) (WA4.496,28–29). This lack of spiritual powers sets every human under God's judgement since:

> the ungodly and proud man is, first of all, the excuser and defender, and the justifier and saviour of himself. . . . But in case someone does not yet understand that no one is righteous before God, who alone is justified, the following expresses it more clearly: Behold, I was conceived in iniquity (v. 6). . . . For we are still unrighteous and unworthy before God, so that whatever we can do is nothing before him.
>
> (WA3.288,37–289,1; LW10.236)

Luther understood unrighteousness primarily as the turn to created things and the lack of love for God; he differentiated it from sin: 'iniquity is that by which a person is turned toward the creature because he prefers its love to the love of God, and that is evil; sin, however, is that by which a person is turned away from God, which is to transgress the commandment and law of God' (WA3.174,33–35). This Augustinian concept of God as *summum bonum* and *summum ens* enabled Luther to grasp sin primarily as a *peccatum omissionis*. Such aversion from God and his good will turns the human will into nothingness (*nihil*)—a conceptually important term in Luther's early stages, as Sameli Juntunen has shown in his profound study (Juntunen 1996: 201–62). This is not a neutral state but rather a condition of tension and enmity, where the sinner makes God a liar and deprives him of the opportunity to make the sinner righteous:

> For there is an unending controversy about all these things between God and proud men...for God in his mercy desires...all men for the very reason that they are liars, unrighteous, foolish, weak, sinful men to be made truthful, righteousness, wise, strong, and innocent through his truthfulness, righteousness, wisdom, strength, and innocence, and thus to be freed from lying, unrighteousness, foolishness, weakness, and sin, in order that his truthfulness, righteousness, wisdom, strength, and innocence may be glorified and commended in them and by them.
>
> (WA56.216,27–33; LW25.202)

In his early stage Luther spoke about inclination toward evil resting in the weakened powers as an 'evil movement' (*motus mali*) of the will giving way to other sins (WA3.292,33–36; LW10.242). Gradually, Luther deepened his understanding of the inclination toward evil as a corruption of nature, and not only as its weakening. In his sermon on Christ's Circumcision of 1 January 1517 Luther spoke in relation to Psalm 51:5 about universal '*malum originale*', which leads to many other evil desires, creating anger, pride, luxury, and greed (WA1.121,26–27). Quite often at this stage his enumeration leaned on the medieval catalogue of seven mortal sins, which create total separation from God and give rise to many subsequent sins. Progressively up to 1517, pride became the most important mortal sin in Luther's view. Just before Easter 1518, Luther published *A Brief Explanation of the Decalogue* in order to create a new book for preparation for penance. To each commandment of the Decalogue Luther ascribed a particular mortal sin. Pride is included in the first two commandments, lust and gluttony in the sixth, wrath and envy in the fifth, sloth in the third, and greed in every commandment (WA1.254,4–6). Luther still used this distinction known to his contemporaries but simultaneously moved the emphasis to egocentrically selfish love and contempt for God and neighbour as the result of original sin (WA1.254,10–14). However, as Luther's theology developed, he ceased to use this distinction entirely. Once the forgiveness of sins was no longer dependent on the enumeration of all sins, the differentiation between *peccatum veniale* and *peccatum mortale* lost its meaning, as for example in his *Sermo de poenitentia* (1518, WA1.322,33–36). In 1519, in his *Eine kurze Unterweisung, wie man beichten soll*, Luther gave clear advice to confess only known mortal sins that trouble the conscience in full awareness that even good deeds, without God's mercy, are only deadly deeds (WA2.60,6–16). In his further development Luther rejected the vice catalogues like the famous *Hortulus animae*, saying that Psalms, the Decalogue, or even the Lord's Prayer are enough to examine one's own heart, as he demonstrated in his *Sermon von dem Sakrament der Buße* (1519, WA2.59,26–27) or later in his *Preface to the Prayerbook* (1522, WA10,2.377,4–6; LW43.14). The effect of this new position is visualized vividly in the famous painting from Lucas Cranach in the Lutherhaus in

Wittenberg; the painting depicts the transgression of the Decalogue and not just the seven mortal sins. At this point in time, Luther was already firmly convinced that the true nature of sin is to be found entirely in original sin and not in a mortal sin of *peccatum actuale*. For Luther, the law declares every sin a mortal sin. The true deadly sin is the denial of one (WA2.60,19f.) and in neglecting the fact that under God's judgement nothing can help to gain life and escape death (WA2.60,16–19).

III.2. Concupiscence

An important development in Luther's thought can be observed during his lectures on Romans. A letter to Spalatin from 19 October 1516 records his new discovery caused by reading a volume of Augustine's anti-Pelagian writings in Amerbach's reprint from 1506 (WABR1.70,9–12; LW48.24; Grane 1975: 32–5). From this point on, Luther's main focus shifted to the effect of aversion to God, which, as an active act of will in reality and not just as a possibility, led people to turn to created things. Luther defined the primary effect as being bent toward oneself (*incurvatio in se ipsum*) (WA56.304,29–305,1; LW25.291; cf. WA56.365,5; LW25.345). Contrary to the nominalist hamartiology, in which the 'tinder of sin' (*fomes peccati*), as consequence of original sin, was generally understood as punishment for the loss of original righteousness but not as sin itself (Oberman 1983: 120–45), Luther's deepened understanding regarded this as too little. A clear reference to a passage from Augustine's *Contra Julianum* effectively demonstrates this change with a related corollary:

> Therefore, actual sin (as the theologians call it) is, strictly speaking, the work and fruit of sin, and sin itself is that passion (tinder) and concupiscence, or that inclination toward evil and resistance against the good which is meant in the statement, 'I had not known that concupiscence is sin' [...] so sin is the turning away from the good and the turning toward evil, and the works of sin are the fruit of sin [...].
>
> (WA56.271,6–15; LW25.259)

Luther accepted Augustine's understanding of concupiscence as every impulse of the spirit to love oneself, one's own neighbour, or a part of one's own body, because of itself and not because of God as *summum bonum*. This shift had tremendous implications leading to critical objections against scholastic theology, questioning the scholastic understanding of sacramental grace, justification, and virtues and, of course, radicalizing the teaching about original sin.

If the tinder of sin represents only the material principle of sin, as such, however, without guilt, and the formal principle is only the lack of original righteousness and some sort of weakness caused by the loss of primary grace, then the sacramental infusion of grace in baptism restores new righteousness to a person. To become a sinner means to let the tinder 'enflame' through external temptations and thus to fall into sinful deeds (*peccata actualia*).

Luther, however, disagreed, convinced that Church Fathers such as Ambrose and Augustine were on his side. In accordance with Augustine's psychological explanation (WA56.275,5–8; LW25.262) he interpreted all bodily desires as proof for the active dominion of concupiscence over the sinner's will. If one is honest, his own experience proves that human sin comes from inside, and the rather neutral tinder has to be an active act of concupiscence. From 1515 on, Luther became firmly convinced—contrary to the preceding tradition and contrary to his own position about the privation of the qualities of will, reason, and memory (WA56.312.6–10; LW25.299)—that concupiscence in human beings is sin. It is such a profound 'sickness of nature' (WA 56.283,15; LW25.270), desiring only evil, 'the loathing of the good; the disdain for light and wisdom but fondness for error and darkness; the avoidance and contempt of good works but an eagerness for doing evil' (WA56.312,10–13; LW25.299) that it cannot be 'washed away' even in baptism. Concupiscence remains in the sinner even after baptism: as the 'Hydra, that extremely stubborn monster', concupiscence is original sin (WA56.312,4–16; LW25.299). Luther claimed that Augustine was on his side in regard to the concupiscence remaining in a baptized person. The guilt of the sin is forgiven in baptism (*in reatu*), but in reality it remains even after baptism (*in actu*) (WA56.273,10–274,1; LW25.261). In fact, Augustine's passages relate to concupiscence but not to original sin itself (*Contra Julianum* II:III.5). It would not be correct to say that Luther was mistaken on this issue. Again, decisive was the Pauline connection in Romans 4:7 with Psalm 32:1, which contains the Hebrew terms '*aon*' and '*hattaa*': 'Blessed are those whose transgression is forgiven, whose sin is covered.' Luther, influenced by the Augustinian talk regarding the non-imputation of sin, interpreted the verse as non-imputation of original sin (*hattaa*). The conclusion was clear: concupiscence remains after baptism; original sin is 'covered' and 'non-imputed as sin': ergo, concupiscence is original sin. 'The second word, sin as *hattaa* and practically everywhere interpreted as sin, I take to refer to the root sin in us or to concupiscence [desire] for evil' (WA56.277,11–13; LW25.264; Pesch 1967: 93–7). This position became the *cantus firmus* of Luther's theology. He continued reading Augustine and became firmly convinced that he was right. Regardless of its condemnation by Leo X in *Exsurge Domine* 1520 (cf. WA7.103,9–111,11), he never gave up this position. Luther elaborated further on his understanding by turning his attention to Galatians 5:16–21 and Romans 7:7–20 as, for example, in his *Against Latomus* (1521, WA8.36–128; LW32.133–260). In the final part of his reply to one of his best opponents (in Luther's eyes), he summarized the core of the problem in a precise statement:

> Paul calls that which remains after baptism sin; the fathers call it a weakness and imperfection, rather than sin. Here we stand at the parting of the ways. I follow Paul, and you the fathers—with the exception of Augustine, who generally calls it by the blunt names of fault and iniquity. (WA8.101,34–40; LW 32.220)

Worth mentioning in this regard is Luther's *Disputatio de iustificatione* (1536), with its emphasis on the active drive of original sin as concupiscence toward evil (WA39,1.116,14–118,12; LW34.184–187).

Already in his Romans lectures, the consequences were clear. Original sin is so radical that human beings are always (*semper*)—up to death—unable to find good. As a consequence Luther had to reject the scholastic notion of *syntheresis*—the small but steady and inextinguishable—inclination to good, which made possible the premise on which the medieval praxis of penance was based, namely the necessity of striving to do good (*facere quod in se est*) (WA56.289,27–28; LW25.277; cf. WA40,1.291,29–292,17; LW26.172–173). Even the minutest motion of the soul is lacking the love to God from all powers (WA56.275,19–22; LW25.262). The 'semper' aspect of sin did not allow the possibility of differentiation between the fulfilment of commandments according to the substance of the deed (*quoad substantiam facti*) or according to the intention of the giver of the commandment (*ad intentionem praecipientis*) (WA56.279,13–16; LW25.279; cf. WA40,1.227,21–228,26; LW26.128–129). The double Commandment of Love (Deut. 6:5–9; Matt. 22:37–40) cannot be fulfilled (Dieter 2001: 80–106). Regardless of the self-perception of Duns Scotus or Gabriel Biel as being orthodox, in Luther's eyes, as he wrote in October 1516, their theology led to neo-Pelagian conclusions (WABR1.66,32–35; WA56.502,32–503,5; LW25.497).

It is no exaggeration to say that here rests the foundation for Luther's more profound criticism of scholastic theology, similar to his 'On capabilities of man's will without the grace' (1516), saying clearly that without grace human will is enslaved to sin (WA1.147,38–148,33). This argument reappeared in his sharp criticism of scholastic theology in his *Disputatio contra scholasticam theologiam* (1517), later in his *Heidelberg Disputation* (1518, esp. thesis 13, WA1.360,5–12; LW31.48–49), and in the *De servo arbitrio* (1525).

The reason for this radical understanding of sin is expressed in *Against Latomus*. Making sin great is inseparably connected with exalting God's grace and salvation in Christ (WA8.108,112,113; LW32.230,236,240). For Luther, there is an either/or, either a pure love for God, or sinful concupiscence. Already, the aversion to God's commandment and the lack of love for it hinders the sinner from fulfilling the law. The one excludes the other; therefore, even the best deeds stand *coram deo* as mortal sin. In this case, as Theodor Dieter pointedly demonstrates, the question arises: what does that imply for the believer's righteousness that needs to be understood in simultaneity with sinfulness? And how can a Christian believe he is under God's grace when there is no habitual quality in his heart, not to mention even a natural capability (Dieter 2001: 303–4)? One of the most distinctive polarities of Luther's theology, expressed in the formula *simul justus et peccator*, does not mean partly sinner and partly saint, but rather must be grasped in the new dynamic of the *semper-* movement from sin to righteousness that begins every moment anew and continues without end until death (Dieter 2001: 313–17).

III.3. Unbelief

Luther's usage of the term *peccatum radicale*, which appeared in his thought already during his Romans lectures, needs special consideration. Gradually, it became a genuine part of Luther's Reformation theology. It sprang out from the parable of a tree bearing good and bad fruit in Matthew 7:17 and 12:33. The parable, understood in the hamartiological sense, is speaking implicitly about the deep-rooted sin in human hearts. In its illustrative power the term offers generally understandable conclusions and is pedagogically effective.

By using it, Luther was able to reverse the association of righteousness with righteous deeds, countering the influence of Aristotle's ethics, as Luther clearly explained in a letter from October 1516: 'For we are not, as Aristotle believes, made righteous by the doing of righteous deeds, unless we deceive ourselves; but rather—if I may say so—in becoming and being righteous people we do righteous deeds. First, it is necessary that the person be changed, then the deeds [will follow]' (WABR1.70,29–32; LW48.25). Put symbolically, the tree is first, then comes the fruit (WA40,2.433,19–22; LW12.385). In a hamartiological context this diminishes the importance of sinful acts and raises the importance of original sin. Bad fruit from a tree is only a 'visible proof' that the tree is bad.

Secondly, this narrative imagery asserts that the quality of fruit corresponds to the sort of tree which produces it: like tree, like fruit. Luther's *Sermon on Three Kinds of Righteousness* (1518) expresses this clearly. Listing major biblical passages like Psalm 51, Matthew 7 and 12, and Romans 5, Luther explained that out of the 'three kinds of sin', it is 'the second kind' of sin, original sin—as 'essential, inborn, alien sin' that causes all unrighteousness and merits condemnation of the human essence and its human works—which 'renders all prior righteousness to be nothing, evil, and cursed'. 'Either make the tree good and its fruits good, or the tree evil and its fruits evil' (WA2.44,14–21).

Thirdly, describing original sin as 'root sin' makes it clear that the real problem of human beings rests under the surface, like the root of a tree. The true essence of sin cannot rest in the wickedness of deeds, but in the person. This should not be misunderstood 'substantially', as if the evil nature of human beings as created is responsible for sin. Luther's position drives one to Augustine's premise: 'If sin be natural, it is not sin at all' (*De civitate Dei*, 9.15), and his understanding of sin was based on the relationship of human beings to God expressed in its fundamental form as faith. 'For Luther the concept of sin was constantly oriented toward God—not toward an impersonal law that was transgressed' (Elert 1962: 30). From 1517 on, Luther was absolutely clear: The principal attitude toward God is human belief or unbelief: 'the greatest sin' is 'the sin of unbelief' (WA18.782,13; LW29.182). In his *Brief Explanation of the Decalogue*, Luther stated, as Gregory of Rimini before him: 'All sons of Adam are idolaters and guilty of the first commandment' (WA1.399,11).

In his treatise *On the Freedom of a Christian* (1520) Luther moved to more explicit comprehension of unbelief. In the context of evangelically defined soteriology (WA7.32,5–22; LW31.361) Luther asked aptly: 'what rebellion, what unbelief, what insult is greater than not believing in his [God's] promise?' (WA7.54.11–12; LW31.350). Luther talked about faith created by the Word of Christ, by his gospel (*promissio*), proclaiming the merciful act of justification and salvation in Christ incarnate so that the essence of original sin can be grasped; 'nothing makes a man good except faith, or evil except unbelief' (WA7.33,10–12; LW31.361; Bayer 2008: 179–80). Instead of thinking in substantial categories (*praedicamento substantiae*), Luther's mature theology embraced relational categories (*praedicamento relationis*, WA40,2.354,2–5). Original sin is primarily a broken relationship with God that is deep-rooted in the human heart from the very beginning of life (WADB7.6,32–8,2; LW35.369). The corruption of sin is so deep that a person cannot create his own faith; it has to be received from outside as a *recreatio ex nihilo* (Schwanke 2004: 11–12). Referring to the above-mentioned definition of the subject matter of theology, it is obvious that for Luther a meaningful discussion of human original sin is possible only by relating the human being to Christ, and not speaking about human beings, or even God, alone. Early in his lecturing career Luther understood the lack of belief as active resistance against the judgement of God: in other words, the law's judgement that a person is a sinner (Bayer 1989: 153). From 1519, in light of his newly developed reformational teaching, his understanding of unbelief deepened. It became an active resistance against the gospel, blasphemy against Christ, a refusal of grace, an abomination of the promise. Luther stated this clearly in his preface to Romans (1522), 'the Scriptures look especially into the heart and single out the root and source of all sin, which is unbelief in the inmost heart' (WADB7.6,32–34; LW35.369; Batka 2007: 224–9). This view did not change during Luther's later years. An excellent example is offered in *Disputatio de iustificatione* (1536, WA39,1.78–126; LW34.145–196).

Finally, it should be said that during the period of the formation of confessions of faith we find explicit passages that bring together the understanding of original sin as concupiscence and simultaneously the understanding that by nature man cannot possess 'true fear of God and true faith in God' (BSLK 53; BC 38). For example, Luther's *Explanation of Psalm 51* (1532) for Elector Johann states:

> Even if I, David, am righteous before the world, in your sight, I am a great sinner because you are true and you will find sin in me. Even if I would not be an adulterer, which I am, nonetheless, my heart is... full of infidelity, concupiscence, lack of fear of God and trust in God. (WA31,1.539,23–27)

Luther's aim was to show the deep-rooted and radical sinful corruption (radicality) of all human powers (totality) and all people (universality) before God and his judgement (cf. WA40,1.231,30–32; LW26.131), causing guilt on the human side. Luther's definition of the *subiectum theologiae* was not based on subjective guilt (*culpa*), but rather on the perception of an objective guilt as perceived in the juridical language talking about a status (*reatus*). Guilt as a relational term results from a twisted relationship; it means an 'injury of personal connection' between human beings and God. Is it not problematic to claim a connection between original sin and personal guilt? This seems unjust and irrational. How can all human beings be affected by the sin that occurred in a different lifetime?

IV. The Origin of Sin

Questions regarding why God permitted the Fall of human beings are only curious speculations, according to Luther. An extensive discussion on this topic in his Genesis lecture (1535–45) is rather an exception (WA42.41–176; LW1.54–236; Ebeling 1985: 78; worth reading is the whole passage from Gen. 2:15 to Gen. 3:24 in WA42.77,21–176,17; LW1.101–236). More useful is ruminating about what God does to accomplish human beings' justification and salvation:

> Therefore, learn carefully the article about original sin. And you should not argue about why God has permitted what people with an inquisitive bent are accustomed to inquire into. No, you should rather ask how we are rescued and freed from this evil and know that God speaks with us to arouse us to acknowledge it. When it has been acknowledged, he says: 'Your sins are forgiven you; take heart, my son (cf. Matt. 9:2) because I have given my Son as a Lamb that is spotless from the beginning'.
>
> (WA44.507,37–42; LW7.281)

Obviously, Luther never questioned the biblical narrative of Adam and Eve; he took Genesis in a literal sense as fact of history, nicely expressed, for example, in his *Confession concerning Christ's Supper* (1528):

> For I confess and am able to prove from Scripture that all have descended from one man, Adam, and from this man, through their birth, they acquire and inherit the fall, guilt and sin, which the same Adam, through the wickedness of the devil, committed in paradise; and thus all people along with him are born, live, and die altogether in sin. (WA26.502,25–30; LW37.362)

Precisely for this reason it is important to say that the reformer did not develop his teaching on original sin from some sort of 'original state theology', as some scholars contend (Gross 1972: 34). In his early years Luther shared Augustine's perception of original sin as pride: 'But the sores are pride and the inborn sickness and remains of original sin' (WA3.215,27–28; LW10.178 [Ps. 38:6]). As his theology developed into a new understanding of law and gospel, Luther's understanding of original sin changed as well; it led to the rejection of scholastic teaching about the supralapsarian gift of grace as *donum superadditum*, which created the original human righteousness. Human righteousness rested, so Luther thought, in faith that trusts the Word of God. Luther understood the first Word of God to human beings as a promise, clearly shown in his *The Babylonian*

Captivity of the Church (1520): 'For God does not deal, nor has ever dealt, with man otherwise than through a word of promise, as I have said. We in turn cannot deal with God otherwise than through faith in the Word of his promise' (WA6.516,30–32; LW36.42).

The first temptation to sin, according to Luther, was not the sin of *luxuria*, as generally thought. It was the questioning of the Word of God through another word. Original sin should be understood as distrust of God's promise and trust in another word that is not from God. It was a false faith leading to sinful acts. 'As, therefore, faith alone makes a person righteous and brings the Spirit and pleasure in good outward works, so unbelief alone commits sin and brings forth the fleshly pleasure in bad outward works, as happened to Adam and Eve in paradise, Genesis 3', as Luther said in his preface to Romans (1522, WADB7.6,34–8,2; LW35.369). This line of argument appeared again in the Smalcald Articles and was elaborated in a general statement about original sin as spiritual 'enthusiasm' that led to disobedience toward God: 'This is all the old devil and old snake, who also turned Adam and Eve into enthusiasts and led them from the external Word of God to "spirituality" and their own presumption although he even accomplished this by means of other, external words' (BSLK 454; BC 322). God's speaking opened room for communication. Original righteousness could rest only in the 'category of relationship', in the same way as the righteousness of justified man is a *iustitia passiva* (Kolb 1999: 463). In it, a person finds his 'true essence': likewise 'in unbelief, in sin [he finds] his empty essence, a terrible state of affairs' (Bayer 2008: 180).

Luther's understanding of the original state can be summarized as follows: human beings are 'righteous' *coram deo* always, as in the beginning, only through faith (WA40,2.323,30–324,19; LW12.308–309). There is nothing else that made and makes them 'unrighteous', only disbelief in God's promise. Every suggestion that Luther did not have a historic perception of Adam and Eve is anachronistic. Adam, Eve, or, for example, King David or Job, were for Luther historical persons, but simultaneously human 'types' in general. Adam lost his righteousness through sin. David was conceived with it from his birth. Job suffered under God's wrath. Their status *coram deo* is the same. That leads to the question of how sin could be transmitted, according to Luther.

Theories of human conception called Traducianism and Creationism were well known to Luther. At the beginning of his career his position was closer to Creationism, as taught by Peter Lombard. Later—different from Melanchthon—his position came closer to Traducianism, as for example, in his Genesis lectures or disputations (Althaus 1966: 160; Ebeling 1982: 46–58). The term *peccatum hereditare* may lead to the notion that people inherit the *peccatum actuale* of Adam as something foreign to them, or that it is an issue of biological transference (through sexual intercourse).

The metaphor of a bad tree bearing evil fruit explains Luther's position suitably. If the tree does not become bad on the basis of its bad fruit, and the tree is bad before it starts bearing fruit, then the quality of the tree must be a given at the earliest point of its existence. In the realm of human life this is conception. The central biblical passage, Psalm 51:5, 'in sin did my mother conceive me', evokes the understanding that the child inherited the sin of the mother. Luther clearly opposed such an understanding. In his translation of this passage in his new edition of the *Explanation of the Seven Penitential Psalms*

(1525) Luther deliberately avoided the translation 'evil act' and instead used 'behold, I was brought forth in iniquity' (WA18.501,29; LW14.169). Since original sin corrupted all human powers, even conception is not without sin; however, conception is not sin or evil as such (WA40,2.380,25–33; LW12.347–348, cf. WA37.55,38–56,2).

All passages where Luther spoke about 'sinful seed' from which the sinner grows must be understood in a similar fashion. The seed is corrupted but not evil. Instructive is a passage in the records of work on the revisions of the translation of the Bible (1531) in relation to Psalm 51:7 with its vivid image of a plant bearing new seeds of grain, which propagate a new generation (WADB3.52,2–8; cf. WA40,1.223,31–35; LW26.126). It is helpful because it makes clear that those seeds bring forth just the same kind of grain and nothing else. Luther's intention is in line with Job 14:4; from a sinner can be born nothing else than another sinner. Terms like 'evil seed' and 'sinful seed' express the idea of the 'next generation', that is, the 'following generation', as in his *Magnificat* (1521):

> The Latin phrase 'all generations' I have rendered in German with 'children's children', although literally it means 'all generations'.... They understand the word 'generations' of the totality of humankind, whereas its meaning here is rather the line of natural descent, as father, son, grandson, and so on, each member being called a generation. The Virgin Mary means to say simply that her praise will be sung from one generation to another, so that there will never be a time when she will not be praised.
>
> (WA7.570,8–18; LW21.324; cf. WADB8.12,26–29; LW35.237)

This expresses the idea of a connection between all people in one generation and simultaneously the connection of all generations of people through the *peccatum radicale*. The phrase 'conceived and born in sin' (*in peccatis coceptus et natus*) became a *cantus firmus* in Luther's homiletical, catechetical, and pastoral language, of course, with the conclusion that everything that follows is equally affected by the sin (WA40,2.380,11–381,4; LW12.347–348). From a theological point of view the passivity in the process of being conceived is not secondary: The passivity of being born into sin is equal to the passivity of becoming righteous.

Finally, Luther's main concern in the whole discussion about the inheritance of sin is to make clear that by conception every person has received original sin with his nature, and it has become an absolutely personal sin, unlike in scholasticism, where personal sin could be only *pecccatum actuale* (Ebeling 1985: 82–8). Even if a person was passive in the moment of conception and *peccatum radicale* was something foreign, it became a sin that belonged to his person. Precisely this individual aspect stands over some sort of generalizations regarding the sinful and damned clump of humanity (*massa perditionis*), and it became characteristic for Luther's doctrine of original sin. The whole intention of Psalm 51:5 rests in making clear that it is not the sin of the begetting mother, nor the sin of Adam, but my own sin, with which I was born. From his early lectures on Romans (WA56.286,14–16; LW25.273) to his mature reformational works, Luther wanted to make clear—again in the analogy from Matthew 12—that just as each tree has its own root, so each person has his own original sin. Original sin is therefore not a non-personal enslaving power, nor, as it appears in recent years, some sort of 'structural sin'. Worth mentioning here is Luther's famous statement in his *Confession* of 1528, 'I—I myself—I was conceived in sin, and in sin did my mother bear me' (WA26.503,14–15; LW37.363; cf. Bayer 2008: 192–3). In this way, paradoxically, Luther's teaching on original sin unites the universal, total, and radical with the personal and individual moment, enclosing the full responsibility of human beings *coram deo*. Just as the root rests under the surface, so original sin is not apparent at the first glance; naturally, the human being does not perceive himself as a sinner. Only the word of law can show how deep human sin is. Due to this corruption the sinner might see the evil act but does not understand its connection to original sin.

V. THE EFFECT OF SIN

Luther's use of the biblical image of an evil tree bearing evil fruits (Matt. 7 and 12) painted the image of *peccatum radicale* as perpetual persistence of sin during one's entire lifetime (*peccatum perpetuum*). A tree can only live as long as it is connected to its roots. On the other hand, as long as the tree lives, it is not without fruit. There is not a single original sinner who would be able to avoid *peccata actualia* during his lifetime.

Luther expressed this situation profoundly in his definition of the subject matter of theology (*homo reus et perditus*). The second characteristic of humanity defined this 'guilty person' as subjected to perdition, which as the *terminus technicus* implies, is not only eternal death (WA26.502,29; LW37.362; cf. WA39,1.86,10–11; LW34.156) but everything that destroys human beings (WA56.313,6–10; LW25.300) and consequently leads to damnation. The corruption of reason (*ratio/intellectus*), of the will (*voluntas*), and of the bodily capacities (*corporalia*)—in the *Dictata* this was the memory (*memoria*)—necessarily leads to human rebellion against God: 'Original sin itself, therefore, leaves free choice with no capacity to do anything but sin and be damned' (WA18.773,17; LW33.272).

The deep-rootedness of sin does not stop at a neutral point of moral indifference but creates evil as it leads to animosity and destruction (WA18.755,23–37; LW33.245). Luther's comparison of the human will to a 'beast of burden', ridden either by God or by Satan (WA18.635,17–22; LW33.65), often earns criticism. But it must be seen as a consequence of the exclusive power of original sin to destroy the sinner temporarily and eternally; 'outside of Christ there is nothing but Satan, apart from grace nothing but wrath, apart from light only darkness, apart from the way only error, apart from the truth only a lie, apart from life only death' (WA18.779,19–21; LW33.282; cf. WA26.503,19–20; LW37.363). This is the main point of the Scripture, and Luther is a master in expressing things in antithetical pairs. By sharp contrast, he demonstrates that perdition is not what the sinner will be at one time; perdition is all around us and presently, as an inescapable 'subjection to Satan, ungodliness, error, darkness, sin, death, and the wrath of God' (WA18.782,22–23; LW33.287). At this point the sinner is no longer only an agent of evil. The evil of perdition makes him suffer under its destructive power. A sinner oppressing others becomes a sinner being oppressed; sin tragically destroys the human being who is actively participating in it. Indeed, it is a battle within one's self and a battle over one's self.

V.1. Actual Sins

In this context Luther offers a noteworthy example in the story of King David, using his crime with Bathsheba and all the subsequent consequences as examples of the typical traits of every act of sin. David's sin 'doubled' rapidly, so that in the end David had transgressed all Ten Commandments (WA40,2.319,32–320,25; LW12.306). *Peccata actualia* compared to bad fruits of a bad tree are manifold, gross, and subtle, and they serve as the basis for recognizing the fundamental radical nature of original sin, 'for the tree must come before the fruit, as Christ also says in Matthew 12(:33)' (WA40,2.433,20–22; LW12.385).

In accordance with Luther's understanding of original sin, unbelief is the worst sin of all. Therefore, in David's case, the real offence rests in the fact that this pious king—unmentioned, for example, in the *Dictata* (WA3.175,20–22), but clearly seen in the *Ennaratio* (WA 40,2.320,20–24; LW12.306)—gave reason for blasphemy against God (2 Sam. 12:14). Ernst Kinder correctly observed that the '*committing* of sin' follows always from '*being* a sinner' (Kinder 1959: 37). Evil fruits of the bad tree include broken relationships to creation and oneself, ingratitude for what one has, refusal to give anything to others, and curving everything in upon oneself, pursuing selfish desires. Obviously, this fundamental sinful predicament should not be taken too narrowly as talking only about human moral capabilities. Respectively, arguing from the position of twofold righteousness, the possibility of achieving righteousness in the realm of *civilis* shall not become relative (Kolb 1999: 449–66); however, 'this righteousness is valid only before men' (Althaus 1966: 143).

On the other hand, it is more than logical that the denial of sin leads to self-righteousness, refusal to repent, and rejection of God's justification, but also to denying God's promises regarding salvation. The oppressive slavery that imposes perdition is an evil punishment when the human being is left alone to the power of damaging sin with the full consent of divine judgement.

V.2. The Wrath of God

As opposed to God's love, his justice rewards the good or punishes the evil (Ruth 2:12, 2 Sam. 3:39, Ps. 94:1, Rom, 12:19, Heb. 10:30). God's judgement reveals unbelief and all (hidden) sins and strikes sinners as enemies of God through the 'hammer and thunder' of divine law, 'pounding the wrath of God into a person and threatening him with death' (WA40,1.260,15–24; LW26.150; Rieske-Braun 1999: 66–89). Once a person is confronted with the weight of his own sinfulness, it is impossible to stand firm against God's judgement:

> So the law reveals a twofold evil, one inward and the other outward. The first, which we inflict on ourselves, is sin and the corruption of nature; the second, which God inflicts, is wrath, death, and being accursed. These are, if you wish, guilt and penalty... In accordance with the Scripture, we should speak fully and bluntly of sin—or guilt, or inward evil—as a universal corruption of nature in all parts: an evil which inclines us to evil from our youth on. (WA8.104,22–29; LW32.224–225)

The judgement of God revealing divine anger changes human self-perception as well as the perception of the world around us: 'all creatures seem to be nothing but God and the wrath of God even though it is only a rustling leaf, as Moses says in Leviticus 16' (WA19.226,14–15; LW19.75; cf. WA31,1.147,10; WA5.212,38–213,2). The 'wrath of God' as vengeance and punishment (cf. Rom. 6:23 and Rom. 8:2) creates fear and leads to hell (Dietz 2009). Disregarding all naturalistic and vivid pictures of hell, Luther's theological insights are very important: Hell is basically a place where there is no Word of God. Therefore, it is an empty, faithless, sinful, and evil place, and as such it can be the world around us, or it can be even our own conscience (Slenczka 2005: 443; Althaus 1966: 169–78). Hell is an evil place where not only the soul but also the body can suffer and death seems to be the only salvation.

Death is not a natural occurrence in human life. Undoubtedly, for Luther, the corruption of the *corporalia* in original sin causes death. 'Scripture teaches us that our death and dying do not come naturally but are the fruit and punishment of our father Adam's sin' (WA36.557,10 22). At the height of his career, in the *Exposition of Psalm 90*, Luther dealt with the topic of God's wrath and death as tyranny which cause profound despair in the sinner (Elert 1962: 27–8).

V.3. The Devil

The Devil represents the ultimate power of evil's tyranny over the sinner. The concept of the Devil, Satan, and Antichrist belong to the core of Luther's theological language and personal conviction, expressed by combining biblical, theological, traditional, and popular themes (Althaus 1966: 161–8) from a wide range of contexts. It would be an oversimplification to describe Luther's conviction only as a medieval phenomenon. Even if the statement of Heiko Oberman about 'new faith in the Devil' as 'an integral part of the Reformation discovery' appears to be exaggerated, in his biography of Luther he correctly says that:

> Luther's world of thought is wholly distorted and apologetically misconstrued if his conception of the Devil is dismissed as a medieval phenomenon and only his faith in Christ is retained as relevant or as the only decisive factor. Christ and the Devil were equally real to him: one was the perpetual intercessor for Christianity, the other a menace to mankind till the end. To argue that Luther never overcame

the medieval belief in the Devil says far too little; he even intensified it and lent
to it additional urgency: Christ and Satan wage a cosmic war for mastery over
Church and world. (Oberman 1989: 104)

Even in such harsh passages of Luther, where the description of almighty God in
his terrifying hiddenness (*deus absconditus*) comes close to the impression that the
Devil is only his mask (as elaborated by Oswald Bayer 2008: 201–6), or in linking the
thought of *deus absconditus* with the 'theology of the cross' (Loewenich 1954: 22–54),
Luther was not primarily interested in terrifying the sinner. His concern was pastoral;
he wanted to comfort believers, making it clear that Devil is not God. The Devil is the
hybris and the spirit of negation; his goal—to put it in a way that synthesizes Luther's
countless statements about the Devil—as an enemy of God the Creator, Saviour,
Sanctifier, is to pervert God's work in the human creature and world (cf. Reinhuber
2000: 56–62).

   Luther never doubted that God the Father was not the creator and cause of sin and
evil. Sin brings forth evil. Satan did not sin from the beginning of his existence (John
8:44, 1 John 3:8, Ezra 28:15) but from the beginning of his deviation from the truth
(WA42.113,39–40; LW1.151). His evilness rests not in the lack of something, but rather
it is a total denial and perverse rage against God, his Word, and therefore all his work.
The Devil betrays God and 'corrupts the Word of God in order by this means to lead
the innocent human being into sin and death' (WA42.113,8–10; LW1.150; WA37.152,33–
153,3). By leading people away from God's Word the evil spirit managed to bring all
the consequences of evil upon them. 'I say that the spiritual endowments are not
sound but corrupt, in fact, totally extinguished through sin in man and in the devil.
Thus, there is nothing but a depraved intellect and a will that is hostile and opposed to
God's will—a will that thinks nothing except what is against God' (WA40,1.293,24–28;
LW26.174).

   In Luther's vivid imagery the evil spirit appeared commonly as a '*Poltergeist*', using
witchcraft (WA40,1.313,24–322,22; LW26.189–197; Haustein 1990: 68–122), blinding
eyes and creating illusions, but not changing the object itself (WA40,1.314,25–315,18;
LW26.190–191). The mind of the Devil is ruled and led by fear, anger, pleasure, and
other vices; it therefore can be described as a 'clever spirit' only in the sense that he uses
his reason solely to lie, cheat, and harm others. As a pure evildoer and saboteur, the
Devil 'has a thousand dangerous tricks' (WA40,1.321,17; LW26.196). The continuous
battle against God's creation leads to unhappiness, shame, sickness, calamity, troubles,
and cruelty.

> But we are all subject to the devil, both in regard to our bodies and in regard to our
> material possessions. We are guests in the world, of which he is the ruler and the god.
> Therefore, the bread we eat, the drinks we drink, the clothes we wear—in fact, the
> air and everything we live on in the flesh—are under his reign. Through the witches,
> therefore, he is able to do harm to children, to give them heart trouble, to blind them,
> to steal them, or even to remove a child completely and put himself into the cradle in
> place of the stolen child. (WA40,1.314,17–22; LW26.190; cf. WA37.153,4–7)

Despite the raging battle, Satan is always 'God's Satan'. God lets evil things happen; the Devil injures people, or even destroys them, but all his acts are only possible with God's permission (WA40,1.314,15–17; LW26.190). In this way the creation is subjected to futility, since it is a consequence of sin and fallenness, as instruments that God allowed although they do not belong to nature. The awareness of the Devil's threat (present or apocalyptic) might cause terror and fear, but it is not so much the notion of what the Devil can do, as what Christ's judgement means when a soul is damned. It should not be the Devil who inspires horror in the viewer, but the anguish over the notion of what it means to damned and cast off by God. It should become clear that only God can protect against evil. The only way to drive away the Devil is through faith in Christ.

For Luther, it is clear that the evil spirit cannot desire anything else but to want to get it all. He wants to exalt himself 'above Christ' (WA42.18,33–35; LW1.23). As the enemy of Christ, his primary weapon is talk, and his principal tool is a lie. He wants to, by all means necessary, overturn Christ's gospel through slandering, accusing, cursing, lying, and mocking his victims (WA53.511,28–34; LW47.254; WA33.306,28; LW23.293). In his language Luther did not hesitate to reply with words of contempt, preaching the Word of the gospel, knowing the source of his strength:

> Mr. Devil, do not rage so. Just take it easy! For there is One who is called Christ. In him I believe. He has abrogated the law, damned sin, abolished death, and destroyed hell. And he is your devil, you devil, because he has captured and conquered you, so that you cannot harm me any longer nor anyone else who believes in him.
>
> (WA40,1.276,27–32; LW26.162)

The raging of the Devil also affects the Holy Spirit's work. The ultimate evil spirit uses his reason to persecute and aims his will toward the destruction of Christ's church. A very strong motif in Luther's theology throughout his career was the motif of the Devil's tempting God's people and even Jesus himself, trying to lead them away from the true doctrine. The Devil becomes the source of heresies, perverting the truth, aping the sacraments, turning true worship into idolatry, polluting purity, poisoning relationships, altering works through his word internally. In this case Luther would not depict a figure of an evil spirit since in this case he is best represented through human figures—in most cases Luther's opponents. The Devil has many faces: Pickards, the pope, the papacy, 'enthusiasts', Anabaptists, Black Magic, the Jews, the Turks, pagans, even philosophy and false theology (Hendrix 1974: 243–83; Rupp 1983: 255–73). Luther's theological presupposition was that the evil spirit can be everywhere, and nobody is safe from him if left without God's Word.

The importance of talking about evil in Luther's theology appears in its demonstration that evil is much more than inconsequential. Luther was not looking for an insight into evil but wanted to teach people how to escape evil and get rid of it. Instead of speculating about the origin of evil, Luther was instead looking at the reality of the victory over evil. In the case of sin, as in death, the only help against perdition is the gospel of Christ. It is God's Word that creates the world, righteousness, and new life. It is God's

Word that protects the world, humanity, and the church against sin and evil, against their pernicious assaults and rage. God's justifying work gives salvation and supports the order and stability of the spiritual and political realms.

VI. CONCLUSION

Luther departed from scholastic theology's rather neutral assessment of original sin. He wanted to make it absolutely clear that the whole life of a Christian should stand under the light of the knowledge of sin and the mercy of God. Luther deepened the meaning of original sin through his definition of *peccatum radicale*. The biblical picture of an evil tree bearing evil fruit can be used as a metaphor for the fundamental corruption of the essence of the tree. Even if the original sin remains hidden to the eye of natural man, throughout life, it is not possible to separate from it, even in the life of baptized and believing Christians. It encompasses the whole human life from the beginning in its total, universal, and radical aspects. As the result of sin, evil has simultaneously a tragic dimension in making the evildoer into a victim. Luther's notion of sin and evil is thoroughly consistent with his orientation around the doctrine of the Word of God, defining the origin of sin and evil in unbelief in the gospel. Luther makes it clear that thinking about sin and evil belongs to the subject of theology and that critical thinking about sin is still necessary.

REFERENCES

Althaus, Paul (1966). *The Theology of Martin Luther*, trans. Robert C. Schultz. Philadelphia: Fortress.

Augustine (1957). *Contra Julianum*. In *Saint Augustine. Against Julian*, ed. Matthew Schumacher. New York: Fathers of the Church.

—— (1995). *Civitate dei and De spiritu et litera*. In *Augustine: Anti-Pelagian Writings*, ed. Philip Schaff. NPNF 2. Peabody: Hendrickson.

—— (1995). *Enarratio in Psalm LI*. In *Expositions on the book of Psalms*, ed. A. C. Coxe. NPNF 8. Peabody: Hendrickson.

Batka, Ľubomír (2007). *Peccatum radicale. Eine Studie zu Luthers Erbsündenverständnis in Psalm 51*. Frankfurt am Main: Lang.

Bayer, Oswald (1989). *Promissio. Geschichte der reformatorischen Wende in Luthers Theologie*, 2nd edn. Darmstadt: Wissenschaftliche Buchgesellschaft.

—— (2008). *Martin Luther's Theology: A Contemporary Interpretation*, trans. Thomas H. Trapp. Grand Rapids, MI: Eerdmans.

Black, C. Clifton II (1985). 'Unity and Diversity in Luther's Biblical Exegesis: Psalm 51 as a Test-Case'. *Scottish Journal of Theology* 38: 325–45.

Dieter, Theodor (2001). *Der junge Luther und Aristoteles. Historisch-systematische Untersuchungen zum Verhältnis von Theologie und Philosophie*. Berlin: de Gruyter.

Dietz, Thorsten (2009). *Der Begriff der Furcht bei Luther*. Tübingen: Mohr/Siebeck.

Ebeling, Gerhard (1971). *Lutherstudien*. Vol. 1. Tübingen: Mohr/Siebeck.

—— (1982). *Lutherstudien. 2. Disputatio de homine, 2. Teil (Die philosophische Definition des Menschen. Kommentar zu These 1–19)*. Tübingen: Mohr/Siebeck.

—— (1985). *Lutherstudien 3. Begriffsuntersuchungen. Textinterpretationen. Wirkungsgeschichtliches*. Tübingen: Mohr/Siebeck.

Elert, Werner (1962). *The Structure of Lutheranism I*, trans. Walter A. Hansen. Saint Louis: Concordia.

Gestrich, Christof (1989). *Die Wiederkehr des Glanzes in der Welt. Die christliche Lehre von der Sünde und ihrer Vergebung in gegenwärtiger Verantwortung*. Tübingen: Mohr/Siebeck.

Grane, Leif (1975). *Modus loquendi theologicus. Luthers Kampf um die Erneuerung der Theologie (1515–1518)*. Leiden: Brill.

Gross, Julius (1972). *Geschichte des Erbsündendogmas. 4, Entwicklungsgeschichte des Erbsündendogmas seit der Reformation*. Munich: Reinhardt.

Haustein, Jörg (1990). *Martin Luthers Stellung zu Zauber und Hexenwesen*. Stuttgart: Kohlhammer.

Hendrix, Scott (1974). *Ecclesia in Via: Ecclesiological Developments in the Medieval Psalms Exegesis and the Dictata super Psalterium (1513–1515) of Martin Luther*. Leiden: Brill.

Juntunen, Sameli (1996). *Der Begriff des Nichts bei Luther in den Jahren von 1510 bis 1523*. Helsinki: Luther-Agricola-Gesellschaft.

Kinder, Ernst (1959). *Die Erbsünde*. Stuttgart: Schwabenverlag.

Kolb, Robert (1999). 'Luther on the Two Kinds of Righteousness: Reflections on His Two-Dimensional Definition of Humanity at the Heart of His Theology'. *Lutheran Quarterly* 13: 449–66.

Köster, Heinrich (1979). *Handbuch der Dogmengeschichte 2*, Faszikel 3b. Freiburg/Br: Herder.

Loewenich, Walther von (1954). *Luthers theologia crucis*, 4th edn. Munich: Kaiser.

Oberman, Heiko Augustinus (1983). *The Harvest of Medieval Theology: Gabriel Biel and Late Medieval Nominalism*. Durham: Labyrinth.

—— (1989). *Luther: Man between God and the Devil*. New Haven: Yale University Press.

Pesch, O. Hermann (1967). *Theologie der Rechtfertigung bei Martin Luther und Thomas von Aquin. Versuch eines systematisch-theologischen Dialogs*. Mainz: Matthias-Grünewald.

—— (1982). *Hinführung zu Luther*. Mainz: Matthias-Grünewald.

Raeder, Siegfried (1967). *Die Benutzung des masoretischen Textes bei Luther in der Zeit zwischen der ersten und zweiten Psalmenvorlesung (1515–1518)*. Tübingen: Mohr/Siebeck.

Reinhuber, Thomas (2000). *Kämpfender Glaube. Studien zu Luthers Bekenntnis am Ende vom De servo arbitrio*. Berlin: de Gruyter.

Rieske-Braun, Uwe (1999). *Duellum mirabile. Studien zum Kampfmotiv in Martin Luthers Theologie*. Göttingen: Vandenhoeck & Ruprecht.

Rupp, E. Gordon (1983). 'Luther against "The Turk, the Pope, and the Devil"'. In *Seven-Headed Luther*, ed. Philip Newman Brooks. Oxford: Clarendon Press, 255–73.

Schwanke, Johannes (2004). *Creatio ex nihilo. Luthers Lehre von der Schöpfung aus dem Nichts in der Großen Genesisvorlesung (1535–1545)*. Berlin: de Gruyter.

Schwarz, Reinhard (1962). *Fides, spes und caritas beim jungen Luther unter besonderer Berücksichtigung der mittelalterlichen Tradition*. Berlin: de Gruyter.

Seeberg, Erich (1950). *Luther's Theologie in ihren Grundzügen*, 2nd edn. Stuttgart: Kohlhammer.

Slenczka, Notger (2005). 'Christliche Hoffnung'. In *Luther Handbuch*, ed. Albrecht Beutel. Tübingen: Mohr/Siebeck, 435–43.

Stolle, Volker (2002). *Luther und Paulus. Die exegetischen und hermeneutischen Grundlagen der lutherischen Rechtfertigungslehre im Paulinismus Luthers*. Leipzig: Evangelische Verlagsanstalt.

SUGGESTED READING

Althaus, Paul (1966). *The Theology of Martin Luther*, trans. Robert. C. Schultz. Philadelphia: Fortress.

Bayer, Oswald (2007). *Theology the Lutheran Way*, trans. Jeffrey Silcock and Mark Mattes. Grand Rapids, MI: Eerdmans.

Lohse, Bernhard (1999). *Martin Luther's Theology: Its Historical and Systematic Development*, ed. and trans. Roy Harrisville. Minneapolis: Fortress.

CHAPTER 17

JUSTIFICATION BY FAITH

The View of the Mannermaa School

RISTO SAARINEN

TUOMO Mannermaa's view of Christ present in faith as the central tenet of Luther's teaching on justification has been extensively discussed in Reformation studies. This essay first presents Mannermaa's own contribution. Second, it portrays some of the most important historical findings and claims of his pupils. Third, it describes the ecumenical dimension of this school. Fourth, it reviews some historical contexts on which the discussion has focused. Fifth, it outlines some new frontiers. While the first and second sections are concerned with Luther's own view, the fourth and fifth sections situate Luther's doctrine of justification into some broader historical and theological contexts. As the presentation adopts the perspective of a 'school', many other non-controversial topics remain beyond its scope.

I. MANNERMAA'S CONTRIBUTION

Tuomo Mannermaa presents his view in *Der im Glauben gegenwärtige Christus* (1989, ET: 2005, 2010). Mannermaa summarizes Luther's doctrine of justification as follows:

> According to Luther, justification is not merely a new ethical or juridical relation between God and a human being. When a human being believes in Christ, Christ is present, in the very fullness of his divine and human nature, in that faith itself. Luther understands the presence of Christ in such a concrete way that, according to his view, Christ and the Christian become 'one person'. In this 'happy exchange', the human being becomes a partaker of God's attributes. The attributes that Luther mentions most often are 'life', 'righteousness', 'wisdom', 'salvation' ('blessedness'), 'power', 'joy', 'courage', 'new understanding', and 'love'.
>
> (Mannermaa 2005: 87–8; discussing Luther's *Galatians Commentary*, WA40)

Mannermaa is critical of a merely forensic view of justification in traditional Lutheran theology and defends an effective view, in which Christ represents both God's favour and God's gift to humans. The criticized view, typical of later Lutheranism, deviates from Luther's own intentions. In Mannermaa's view:

> justification and the real presence of God in faith are in danger of being separated by the one-sidedly forensic doctrine of justification adopted by the Formula Concordiae and most of subsequent Lutheranism. In Luther's theology, however, both these motifs are completely united in the person of Christ. Christ is both the *favor* and the *donum*, without separation or confusion. . . . Christ (both his person and work), who is present in faith, *is* identical with the righteousness of faith.
>
> (Manermaa 2005: 5; discussing the *Galatians Commentary*, WA40)

This emphasis on an effective view of justification continues one German line of discussion, initiated by Karl Holl and continued by Wolfhart Pannenberg and many others, concerning the anticipatory and transformatory nature of God's act of justification. More original is Mannermaa's claim that he considers Christ's presence as 'ontological reality' (2005: 8) and Christian holiness as 'essential, ontological relationship with God' (2005: 88). In his German publications Mannermaa speaks of the 'real-ontic character' (1989: 189) of Christ's presence. For many Protestant theologians these features sound too philosophical and too Roman Catholic.

Mannermaa's most original and most debated contribution to Luther studies concerns his thesis that effective justification can be considered as a Western counterpart to the Eastern view of salvation as deification or theosis. 'The concept of *deificatio* is at the very heart of the Reformer's doctrine of justification' (2005: 46, referring to WA40,1.20, 29); 'the presence of Christ means a particular kind of divinization of Christians' (2010: 64, referring to WA10,1,2.168,5–11 and WA1.28,39–41). For many, such statements lean towards a pantheistic mysticism that abolishes the fundamental difference between God and creation. Mannermaa notes, however, such statements are not entirely without precedents in Protestant theology, citing Regin Prenter and Georg Kretschmar on Luther's use of deification terminology (2005: 7).

In some later articles Mannermaa counters the criticism that his concepts of ontology and essence lead to a predominantly philosophical view of being, arguing that Luther's 'ontology is a theological one, even though he uses philosophical terminology in expressing what he intends to say' (1998: 12); it employs Trinitarian concepts which are genuinely theological (1993). Mannermaa also emphasizes that the concept of theosis should not lead into a theology of glory:

> Luther's concept of theosis, then, is understood correctly only in connection with his theology of the cross. The participation that is a real part of his theology is hidden under its opposite, the *passio* through which one is emptied. It is not grasped in rational knowledge but only in faith, and the grasp that faith has of it in this life is still

only the beginning of a much greater participation that awaits in eschatological ful-filment. (Mannermaa 1998: 10; referring to WA1.20–29)

II. Historical Findings and Claims in the Mannermaa School

Although Mannermaa did not publish new major books or entirely new research ideas after 1989, he remained the central figure of a large group of Luther scholars in Helsinki, which included Risto Saarinen (1989), Simo Peura (1994), Sammeli Juntunen (1996), Antti Raunio (2001), and Pekka Kärkkäinen (2005). A number of other Finnish scholars, most notably Juhani Forsberg (1984), Eeva Martikainen (1992), and Eero Huovinen (1997) also employ Mannermaa's views in their mono-graphs on Luther's theology.

Among these studies Simo Peura's *Mehr als ein Mensch?* (1994) has received most attention since it tackles the issue of deification in Luther's theology. Luther knows the verbal forms *deifico*, *vergotten*, and *durchgotten*, employing them 32 times (as listed in Peura 1987: 172). Compared to many other topics, this is not a big amount, and one aspect of the debate concerns the relative importance of such fairly rare expressions. Peura, however, builds his discussion predominantly around the concepts of participation and transformation which characterize the reality of new righteousness in a Christian. He also pays attention to biblical passages like Psalm 82:6 and 2 Peter 1:4, which have tradi-tionally been employed in the context of deification. Peura concludes that Luther under-stands the effective justification ontologically although his concepts differed from those of the metaphysics of scholasticism (1994: 213, 220, 295–302, discussing Luther's *Lectures on Romans*, WA56, and *Operationes in Psalmos*, WA5).

Antti Raunio (2001) investigates the theological content of the so-called Golden Rule (Matt. 7:12) in Luther. While much of traditional Scandinavian Luther research has emphasized the role of natural law as a valid principle of social ethics and civil use of the law, Raunio argues that the use of the Golden Rule as the law of neighbourly love is not limited to these natural and civil spheres. For Luther, the Golden Rule is also and primarily a rule of divine love which descends to humans. In his incarnation and salvific work Christ becomes a paradigm of the Golden Rule. Luther further urges Christians to act as 'Christs' to one another, performing acts that imitate divine love. To do this, faith and not only natural reason is needed. In this manner, the Golden Rule becomes a genuinely theological principle which moves beyond the natural and civil sphere (2001: 200–4, 331–3, discussing *Lectures on Romans*, WA56, and *Sermo de duplici iustitia*, WA2.145–152). Raunio both continues the expression of effective justification in terms of love and connects faith and love more intimately than has been the case in earlier Scandinavian Luther research.

Pekka Kärkkäinen (2005) investigates Luther's Trinitarian terminology with special regard to the Holy Spirit. Kärkkäinen shows on the one hand that Luther's Trinitarian language is deeply rooted in the theological tradition. At the same time, Luther embeds some of his own insights into a Trinitarian framework. For instance, he emphasizes that the sending of the Spirit occurs through faith so that Christian love emerges through this faith. Motivated by biblical passages like Galatians 3:7 and 4:6, Luther connects faith and Holy Spirit so intimately that the promise of faith also implies the sending of the Spirit. This means that the Christian existence in faith contains the effective grace and love in the Spirit which God sends through faith. Given this, Luther's theology of faith witnesses to a Trinitarian structure: we are justified because of the work of Christ, and when faith receives this gospel, God also sends the Spirit through this very faith (Kärkkäinen 2005: 105–7, 112, discussing especially Luther's *First Galatians Lectures*, WA2).

The so-called 'Mannermaa school' bears typical traces of a theological school: a central figure and several pupils who apply the ideas of their mentor to new thematic areas and problems. At least the following claims concerning justification by faith have been presented as regulative ideas for the Mannermaa school:

(1) Forensic and effective or 'transformatory' affirmations of justification are both necessary in thinking and speaking about justification. A stronger version of this (1b) says that these affirmations are 'fully convertible' or that 'grace and gift presuppose each other' (Peura 1998: 56; Marshall 2002: 20–1).

(2) Justification brings about a 'real-ontic' unity between Christ and Christian in faith. This inhabitation and participation can sometimes be called deification. It is a union with Christ in which participating persons are not abolished; this union is theological rather than philosophical (Bielfeldt 1997: 92–5).

(3) Ancient and medieval concepts of salvation are more adequate in describing this union with Christ than modern terminologies. When modernity bypassed the ontological understanding of righteousness, it reduced important aspects of faith to 'volitional obedience'. Modern Protestant doctrines of forensic justification may even be 'on the verge of making this righteousness fictional' (Braaten and Jenson 1998, ix; Jenson 1999: 294).

Especially with regard to (3), one may speak of a certain duality inherent in the Mannermaa school. On the one hand, the works mentioned above claim to be historically adequate research which aims at outlining Luther's own view and avoiding anachronisms. Not infrequently, this historical approach makes a claim of continuity with ancient and medieval tradition, implying a break with Enlightenment vocabularies. On the other hand, the Mannermaa school is also a systematic-theological project which aims at producing a concept of Lutheranism which can be fruitful in church life. Ecumenism in particular has been a test case of the systematic-theological project.

III. THE ECUMENICAL DIMENSION

Since 1976 Mannermaa developed his approach in the ecumenical dialogue between the Finnish Evangelical Lutheran Church and the Moscow Patriarchate. Although other Finns first found Mannermaa's ideas problematic, they soon gained acceptance and were expressed in the joint theses of this dialogue (Saarinen 1997: 38–54). Later, other Lutheran–Orthodox conversations also applied the view of Christ's presence in faith to claim that Lutheranism can approach the Orthodox view of theosis. For instance, the Council of the German Protestant Church (EKD) holds in its statement of 1999 that a German Protestant–Romanian Orthodox text outlining this view can be regarded as an expression of correct doctrine (Koppe 1999: 149). The global Lutheran–Orthodox Joint Commission stated in 1998 that 'Lutherans, together with the Orthodox, affirm that salvation is a real participation by grace in the nature of God as St. Peter writes, "that we may be partakers of the divine nature"' (Gros 2007: 21).

The effective and transformatory understanding of justification by faith has also been affirmed in Lutheran–Roman Catholic ecumenism. Catholic Luther scholars, in particular Peter Manns, like Mannermaa, emphasized Luther's continuity with ancient Christian tradition, arguing that modern Protestant scholarship had obscured Luther's Catholic roots. Manns' posthumous piece (Manns and Vinke 1997) in the Mannermaa Festschrift (Bayer et al. 1997) reports of a joint plan of Mannermaa and Manns to write a theology of Luther from a Catholic and ecumenical perspective. Extensive Catholic evaluations of the Mannermaa school have been published by Hubertus Blaumeiser (1995: 217–31), who shows in which ways the language of participation and theosis is connected with a theology of the cross; Reinhard Messner (1996), who considers the ecclesiological implications of Mannermaa's approach; and Angelo Maffeis (2004: 29–57), who demonstrates that the Mannermaa school reorients Lutheran theology and ecumenism towards positions understandable for Catholics.

During the 1990s Mannermaa's approach was frequently discussed in the context of the Catholic–Lutheran *Joint Declaration on the Doctrine of Justification* (JDDJ: Gros 2000: 566–82). Referring to Mannermaa's approach, Wolfhart Pannenberg (1993: 242–53) asserts that both Luther and the Council of Trent proceed from the view that the being of the faithful in Christ is decisive in justification. A proper understanding of the believer's communion with Christ enables an ecumenical alleviation of the confessional differences regarding justification. Peura (1998: 64) criticizes the first version of JDDJ because of its lack of the dimension of 'union with Christ'. The later versions of JDDJ express this dimension stronger, saying, for example, that 'persons are by faith united with Christ, who in his person is our righteousness (1 Cor. 1:30): both the forgiveness of sin and the saving presence of God himself' (Gros 2000: 570).

While this statement cannot be only credited to the influence of the Mannermaa school, some theologians who were critical of the JDDJ interpret it in this manner. Dorothea Wendebourg (1998: 158–9, 164) considers that the differences between earlier and later versions of the JDDJ are due to the interpretation presented by Mannermaa and his pupils, of whom Huovinen and Peura participated in the drafting of JDDJ. Particularly interesting in this regard is the understanding of the Lutheran view of 'justified and sinner at the same time'. During the last steps of the JDDJ process Cardinal Joseph Ratzinger (1999) considered that there cannot be such dualism in any objective sense: if the persons are not made righteous, they are not justified. In keeping with this consideration, the so-called Annex to the JDDJ says that the justified are 'truly and inwardly renewed' and 'do not remain sinners in this sense'. However, they remain sinners in the sense that they have sinned (Gros 2000: 580). Whether the emphasis on true renewal is due to the Mannermaa school or not, it was perceived as such by Protestant critics.

IV. Historical Contexts: Word and Faith, Osianderism, Faith and Love

Next to the ecumenically minded Catholics, the most important academic support for the Mannermaa school comes from the 'Evangelical Catholic' wing of American Lutheranism. Especially the volume *Union with Christ*, edited by Carl Braaten and Robert Jenson (1998), as well as several other publications of Jenson have contributed to Mannermaa's impact in the English-speaking world. Jenson's creative development of Mannermaa's views has led, for instance, to an ontological reaffirmation of hearing:

> We are justified by faith because faith is intent listening to the gospel, because the gospel communicates God's 'good things' and because in hearkening we are shaped to what we hear.... God's 'good things' are God himself; God is his own Word; therefore the 'good things' in God's word are God himself; and therefore what we 'have' as we hear that Word is God himself. (Jenson 2003: 283–4)

Here Jenson makes visible one historical context in Mannermaa's approach that has been discussed critically in theological scholarship. Lutheran theology has often considered that the constitutive relationship of Word and faith does not need any ontological dimension to establish the Christian existence. If this existence needs ontological grounding, the Word of God may lose something of its constitutive importance. Jenson solves this problem by identifying the Word with Christ and God's reality. Unlike Jenson, William W. Schumacher (2010: 137) maintains that the centrality of the Word in Luther's theology does not allow for mystical and ontological dimensions. When the Mannermaa school bypasses this centrality of the Word, they cannot see that 'God's word of promise.... is more "real" than any description of reality' (Jüngel 1999: 181). Eberhard Jüngel considers, in contrast, that Mannermaa's thesis on the presence of Christ in faith can be truthfully approached from the perspective of the creative Word of God: when this word imports the righteousness of God to the human person, it does not remain merely external but is received in the intimate inner sphere of human being.

The ontological dimension can also be questioned historically through relying on the sufficiency of purely forensic justification in Luther's theology. Kurt E. Marquart (2000: 204) defends 'the absolute priority of imputation and its exclusive sway in justification'. For this reason, he finds Mannermaa's ontological interpretations problematic although he appreciates Mannermaa's appeal to the ancient church. For Reinhard Flogaus (1997: 338–42), Mannermaa's view of justification comes close to Osianderism, according to whom the presence of God in Christians amounts to a participation in the majestic divine essence. Peura (1996) locates the crucial difference to Osiander in Luther's view that the faithful Christian participates in the humanity and cross of Christ. Pannenberg (1993: 255) considers that while Luther teaches the indwelling of Christ as consequence of justification, Osiander regards this indwelling as the ground of justification.

The historical dimension of Osianderism and Lutheran orthodoxy has prompted many new studies. Theodor Mahlmann (1996) shows how early Lutheranism could conceive strictly orthodox forms of union with Christ in its theological reflection. Georg Kretschmar (1990) and Karsten Lehmkühler (2004) outline the broad reception history of theosis and the indwelling of God in post-Reformation theology. The theology of Andreas Osiander has also been re-evaluated: Rainer Hauke (1999) and Anna Briskina (2005) find that Osiander preserves and develops important insights of Luther's view of justification. Olli-Pekka Vainio (2008: 95–118) has recently published a Finnish re-evaluation of Osiander's view of justification, coming closer to Hauke's and Briskina's positive assessments.

Several studies contextualize the insights of the Mannermaa school with particular focus on the relationship of faith and love. Bo Kristian Holm (2006: 162–3) analyses the concept of gift in Luther, showing that its social and communicative dimensions are as significant as the ontological aspects emphasized by Mannermaa. Holm pleads for a 'divine sociality' in which God's gift establishes the possibility of Christian neighbourly love (2006: 186–90). Following Raunio, Werner Jeanrond (2010: 100–1) argues that Luther's approach to love has enormous implications for the theology of love because, 'in a way, one could say that in Luther's thinking love has become a Christian possession'. As Catholic theologian, Jeanrond has mixed feelings about Luther's aim to 'distinguish *Christian* love from other forms of love'.

While the studies of Holm and Jeanrond proceed significantly beyond the original ideas of the Mannermaa school, they manage to connect these ideas with some very vital historical contexts of Luther's doctrine of justification, especially the context of neighbourly love. 'Justification by faith' needs to be connected with the emergence of love as fruit of faith. The terminology of gift, divine sociality, and the Golden Rule establishes this connection in ways that steer a middle course between problematic synergism and loveless quietism.

V. New Frontiers: Later Lutheranism, Gift, and Passivity

Two new volumes update the current discussion around the Mannermaa school. Olli-Pekka Vainio's *Justification and Participation in Christ* (2008) re-evaluates Luther's relationship to his colleagues and later Lutheran reformers. While Mannermaa tends to postulate a gap between Luther and his later followers, Vainio attempts to see common features. He shows in which ways Christ's presence remains a significant tenet of justification by faith in sixteenth-century Lutheranism. The volume *Engaging Luther*, edited by Vainio (2010), is a textbook which applies the Finnish paradigm to new areas, for instance, music and the role of the Virgin Mary, in Luther's thinking.

In his introduction to this volume Risto Saarinen (2010a: 23–4) returns to the relationship of God's favour and gift in Luther's view of justification. He argues that grace and gift cannot be fully convertible, as the theological concept of gift presupposes God's favourable or beneficial agency, but not vice versa. Although the benevolent attitude and agency of God are often factually accompanied with a theological gift, this is by no means already presupposed in the concept of favour or benevolence. Because of this asymmetry between favour and gift at the conceptual level, Saarinen considers that there is a certain conceptual priority of favour over the gift. In terms of our above-mentioned list of the regulative ideas of the Mannermaa school, such a position approves (1), (2), and (3) without adopting the stronger variant (1b).

In another recent article, Saarinen (2010b) discusses the passivity of the human person in justification. He approves Holm's contention (2006) that justification needs be seen in the context of giving and receiving God's benevolent gift. While Holm emphasizes the reciprocal elements involved in the social reality of gifts, Saarinen aims at safeguarding the passivity of the recipient. Referring to the use of 'receive' (*accipere*) in contexts regulating the proper giving and receiving of favours (*beneficia*), Saarinen pleads for a strongly asymmetric mutuality: targeted intentional giving of gifts and services is typically encountered and received with faintly intentional or even non-intentional passivity. Continuing such use of *accipere* and *beneficia*, Luther can meaningfully speak of a purely passive reception of God's grace in faith. This passivity does not, however, express fatalism, but it remains compatible with the recipient's inherent freedom as person. A deeper theological understanding of giving and receiving *beneficia* can thus elucidate the difficult issues of freedom and bondage in Luther's theology. More work in this direction is necessary before the picture of justification by faith in the Mannermaa school can be completed.

References

Bayer, Oswald et al. (eds.) (1997). *Caritas Dei: Beiträge zum Verständnis Luthers und der gegenwärtigen Ökumene. Festschrift für Tuomo Mannermaa zum 60. Geburtstag.* Helsinki: Luther-Agricola Society.

Bielfeldt, Dennis (1997). 'The Ontology of Deification'. In *Caritas Dei: Beiträge zum Verständnis Luthers und der gegenwärtigen Ökumene. Festschrift für Tuomo Mannermaa zum 60. Geburtstag*, ed. Oswald Bayer et al. Helsinki: Luther-Agricola Society, 90–113.

Blaumeiser, Hubertus (1995). *Martin Luthers Kreuzestheologie*. Paderborn: Bonifatius.

Braaten, Carl and Robert Jenson (eds.) (1998). *Union with Christ: The New Finnish Interpretation of Luther*. Grand Rapids, MI: Eerdmans.

Briskina, Anna (2005). *Philipp Melanchthon und Andreas Osiander im Ringen um die Rechtfertigungslehre*. Frankfurt am Main: Lang.

Flogaus, Reinhard (1997). *Theosis bei Palamas und Luther*. Göttingen: Vandenhoeck & Ruprecht.

Forsberg, Juhani (1984). *Das Abrahambild in der Theologie Luthers. Pater fidei sanctissimus*. Wiesbaden: Steiner.

Gros, Jeffrey et al. (eds.) (2000). *Growth in Agreement 2*. Geneva: World Council of Churches.

—— (eds.) (2007). *Growth in Agreement 3*. Geneva: World Council of Churches.

Hauke, Rainer (1999). *Gott haben—um Gottes Willen. Andreas Osianders Theosisgedanke und die Diskussion um die Grundlagen der evangelisch verstandenen Rechtfertigung*. Frankfurt am Main: Lang.

Holm, Bo Kristian (2006). *Gabe und Geben bei Luther*. Berlin: de Gruyter.

Huovinen, Eero (1997). *Fides infantium. Martin Luthers Lehre vom Kinderglauben*. Mainz: Zabern.

Jeanrond, Werner G. (2010). *A Theology of Love*. London: T&T Clark.

Jenson, Robert W. (1999). *Systematic Theology*, vol. 2. Oxford: Oxford University Press.

—— (2003). 'Luther's Contemporary Theological Significance'. In *The Cambridge Companion to Martin Luther*, ed. Donald K. McKim. Cambridge: Cambridge University Press, 272–88.

Jüngel, Eberhard (1999). *Das Evangelium von der Rechtfertigung des Gottlosen als Zentrum des christlichen Glaubens*. Tübingen: Mohr/Siebeck.

Juntunen, Sammeli (1996). *Der Begriff des Nichts bei Luther in den Jahren von 1510 bis 1523*. Helsinki: Luther-Agricola Society.

Kärkkäinen, Pekka (2005). *Luthers trinitarische Theologie des Heiligen Geistes*. Mainz: Zabern.

Koppe, Rolf (ed.) (1999). *Gemeinschaft der Heiligen. Theologische Gespräche der EKD mit der Rumänischen Orthodoxen Kirche*. Hermannsburg: Missionshandlung.

Kretschmar, Georg (1990). 'Die Rezeption der orthodoxen Vergöttlichungslehre in der protestantischen Theologie'. In *Luther und Theosis*, ed. Simo Peura and Antti Raunio. Helsinki: Luther-Agricola Society, 61–80.

Lehmkühler, Karsten (2004). *Inhabitatio. Die Einwohnung Gottes im Menschen*. Göttingen: Vandenhoeck & Ruprecht.

Maffeis, Angelo (2004). *Teologie della Riforma*. Brescia: Morcelliana.

Mahlmann, Theodor (1996). 'Die Stellung der Unio cum Christo in der lutherischen Theologie des 17. Jahrhunderts'. In *Unio*, ed. Matti Repo and Rainer Vinke. Helsinki: Luther-Agricola Society, 72–199.

Mannermaa, Tuomo (1989). *Der im Glauben gegenwärtige Christus. Rechtfertigung und Vergottung*. Hannover: Lutherisches Verlagshaus.

—— (1993). 'Hat Luther eine trinitarische Ontologie?' In *Luther und Ontologie*, ed. Anja Ghiselli et al. Helsinki: Luther-Agricola Society, 9–27.

—— (1998). 'Why Is Luther so Fascinating?' In *Union with Christ: The New Finnish Interpretation of Luther*, ed. Carl Braaten and Robert Jenson. Grand Rapids, MI: Eerdmans, 1–20.

—— (2005). *Christ Present in Faith: Luther's View of Justification*. Minneapolis: Fortress.

—— (2010). *Two Kinds of Love: Martin Luther's Religious World*. Minneapolis: Fortress.

Manns, Peter and Rainer Vinke (1997). 'Martin Luther als Theologe der Liebe'. In *Caritas Dei. Beiträge zum Verständnis Luthers und der gegenwärtigen Ökumene. Festschrift für Tuomo Mannermaa zum 60. Geburtstag*, ed. Oswald Bayer et al. Helsinki: Luther-Agricola Society, 265–86.

Marquart, Kurt E. (2000). 'Luther and Theosis'. *Concordia Theological Quarterly* 64: 182–205.

Marshall, Bruce (2002). 'Justification as Deification and Declaration'. *International Journal of Systematic Theology* 4: 1–28.

Martikainen, Eeva (1992). *Doctrina. Studien zu Luthers Begriff der Lehre*. Helsinki: Luther-Agricola Society.

Messner, Reinhard (1996). 'Rechtfertigung und Vergöttlichung—und die Kirche'. *Zeitschrift für Katholische Theologie* 118: 23–35.

Pannenberg, Wolfhart (1993). *Systematische Theologie 3*. Göttingen: Vandenhoeck & Ruprecht.

Peura, Simo (1987). 'Der Vergöttlichungsgedanke in Luthers Theologie 1517–1519'. In *Thesaurus Lutheri*, ed. Tuomo Mannermaa et al. Helsinki: Luther-Agricola Society, 171–84.

—— (1994). *Mehr als ein Mensch? Die Vergöttlichung als Thema der Theologie Martin Luthers von 1513 bis 1519*. Mainz: Zabern.

—— (1996). 'Gott und Mensch in der Unio. Die Unterschiede im Rechtfertigungsverständnis bei Osiander und Luther'. In *Unio*, ed. Matti Repo and Rainer Vinke. Helsinki: Luther-Agricola Society, 33–61.

—— (1998). 'Christ as Favor and Gift: The Challenge of Luther's Understanding of Justification'. In *Union with Christ: The New Finnish Interpretation of Luther*, ed. Carl Braaten and Robert Jenson. Grand Rapids, MI: Eerdmans, 42–69.

Raunio, Antti (2001). *Summe des christlichen Lebens. Die 'Goldene Regel' als Gesetz der Liebe in der Theologie Martin Luthers von 1510 bis 1527*. Mainz: Zabern.

Ratzinger, Joseph (1999). 'Das Geheimnis und das Wirken der Gnade'. *30 Tage* 6/7, July.

Repo, Matti and Rainer Vinke (eds.) (1996). *Unio*. Helsinki: Luther-Agricola Society.

Saarinen, Risto (1989). *Gottes Wirken auf uns. Die transzendentale Deutung des Gegenwart-Christi-Motivs in der Lutherforschung*. Wiesbaden: Steiner.

—— (1997). *Faith and Holiness: Lutheran–Orthodox Dialogue 1959–1994*. Göttingen: Vandenhoeck & Ruprecht.

—— (2010a). 'Finnish Luther Studies: A Story and a Program'. In *Engaging Luther: A (New) Theological Assessment*, ed. Olli-Pekka Vainio. Eugene, OR: Cascade, 1–26.

—— (2010b). 'The Language of Giving in Theology'. *Neue Zeitschrift für Systematische Theologie und Religionsphilosophie* 52: 268–301.

Schumacher, William (2010). *Who Do I Say That You Are? Anthropology and the Theology of Theosis in the Finnish School of Tuomo Mannermaa*. Eugene, OR: Wipf & Stock.

Vainio, Olli-Pekka (2008). *Justification and Participation in Christ: The Development of the Lutheran Doctrine of Justification from Luther to the Formula of Concord (1580)*. Leiden: Brill.

—— (ed.) (2010). *Engaging Luther: A (New) Theological Assessment*. Eugene, OR: Cascade.

Wendebourg, Dorothea (1998). 'Zur Entstehungsgeschichte der "Gemeinsamen Erklärung"'. *Zeitschrift für Theologie und Kirche, Beiheft* 10: 140–206.

CHAPTER 18

LUTHER ON JUSTIFICATION AS FORENSIC AND EFFECTIVE

MARK MATTES

In light of Pope Paul III's call in June 1536 for a general council of the church to address concerns raised by the Protestant princes, the Saxon elector John Frederick requested a maturing Luther to provide a doctrinal 'last will and testament', a definitive statement of his teachings. Luther responded with the Smalcald Articles (1537) and testified to his stance on the article of justification, 'How a Person is Justified and Concerning Good Works'. Luther writes, 'I cannot change at all what I have consistently taught about this until now, namely, that "through faith" (as Saint Peter says) we receive a different, new, clean heart and that, for the sake of Christ our mediator, God will and does regard us as completely righteous and holy. Although sin in the flesh is still not completely gone or dead, God will nevertheless not count it or consider it' (BSLK 460; BC 325,1).

I. JUSTIFIED BY FAITH IN GOD'S PROMISE

William Russell notes, 'The new emphasis in Luther's theology, which was counter to the prevailing theology of the time, is that there was nothing done by the guilty party that earns or even contributes to this forgiveness. This was God in Christ's gratuitous work, performed and offered to the world as a gift.' In this definitive statement the overall shape of Luther's own exposition of his view of the article of justification is 'forensic' (Russell 1995: 78). That is, God evaluates sinners by means of an alien, external righteousness—that of Christ—which offers a change of status before God, who evaluates, 'reckons', sinners not on the basis of their merit but instead on the righteousness of Christ, our 'mediator'. Luther's testimony in the Smalcald Articles parallels his earlier defence of the article of justification in *On Bound Choice* (1525), where he argued that the righteousness of faith does not depend 'on any works, but [instead] on God's favourable regard and his "reckoning" on the basis of grace' (WA18.772,11–12; LW33.271).

For over a century Luther scholars have tended to disassociate Luther from a forensic approach to the article of justification, regarding it as 'implausible, cold, impersonal, and arbitrary' (Clark 2006: 272), a 'legal fiction', needing ethical or ontological supplementation or warrant. Justification could not be God's simple declaration of a sinner as righteous for Jesus' sake. Instead, such judgement must be based on an analytic judgement of sinners as being made righteous. In this view, sinners must first become intrinsically and properly righteous before God analytically judges them to be righteous. In contrast, the forensic approach makes a synthetic evaluation since sinners are judged to be righteous for the sake of another, Jesus Christ, whose righteousness is distributed to them freely. In order to safeguard Luther from the accusation of justification as a legal fiction, the 'forensic' approach to justification is attributed to Melanchthon, whose views are then played off against Luther's—even in the face of the evidence that Luther held a forensic approach and that he and Melanchthon were theological partners. However, Luther's forensic approach of necessity conveys a specific effect since the justifying word is a verdict which simultaneously kills sinners and makes them alive. The justifying verdict is a performative word which does what it says and says what it does (Bayer 2007: 128–34; cf. Kolb and Arand 2008: 129–159, 175–203).

The attempt to pit a forensic approach to justification, 'being declared righteous', against an 'effective' approach, 'being made righteous', simply does not apply to Luther. Scholars who reject or undermine Luther's distinctively forensic approach to justification fail to take Luther's view of language into account; he believed that words actually alter and create reality, that is, that words can make being, even *ex nihilo*, similar to God's creative word that originates the world. Justification by faith alone, in which God creates new creatures out of the nothingness of sin, parallels Luther's doctrine of creation, in which God creates and preserves all things out of nothingness. The Smalcald Articles state that faith in Christ alters not only the status but also the nature of believers: they receive 'different, new, clean' hearts. God not only imputes a sinner's faith in Christ as righteousness, but such faith embraces Christ, who renews us within (BSLK 460; BC 325,1). The *Small Catechism* says it pithily: 'Where there is forgiveness of sins [forensic justification], there is also life and salvation [effective justification]' (BSLK 520; BC 362,5–6). Pitting forensic against effective justification was certainly not an issue between Luther and Melanchthon, usually mistakenly identified as the culprit who, in contrast to Luther, hawked the forensic approach.

For Luther the article of justification seeks to describe how God remakes sinners to be people of faith. An 'effective' dimension to justification is inescapable, crucial, and decisive for Luther. However, this effective dimension of justification, like the forensic dimension, is something we passively undergo or receive (Forde 2004). Perhaps not too surprising for those who worship a crucified Jew, it takes the form or shape of death and resurrection—exactly what Christians claim to receive in the sacrament of holy baptism.

Robert Kolb grounds Luther's view of justification in the etymology of the German word *rechtfertigen*:

> 'Justify' or 'render righteous'—meant 'to do justice to': that is, to inflict punishment, 'judicially' on the basis of a conviction, and thus to execute the law's demands, or 'to conduct a legal process as an activity of a judge', 'to execute, to kill'. From early on, Luther spoke of God's killing and making alive as he described justification, for he presumed that sinners must die (Rom. 6:23a) and be resurrected to life in Christ. (Kolb 2009: 126)

Luther noted that we are humanized by God's judgement that evaluates us as sinners. On Psalm 5:3 Luther wrote, 'Through the kingdom of his [Christ's] humanity, or (as the apostle says) through the kingdom of his flesh, occurring in faith, he conforms us to himself and crucifies us, by making out of unhappy and arrogant gods true human beings, i.e., miserable ones and sinners' (WA5.128,39–129,4). Luther's insight is that outside of sheer trust in God's mercy, doing virtuous acts or loving deeds, so valued by late medieval piety and theology as a basis for earning merit, is tantamount to self-righteousness.

Luther's discovery, based on his study of Paul—in contrast to scholastic theology—is that there are *two* kinds of righteousness, active and passive (Kolb and Arand 2008: 21–128). Before God (*coram deo*) we are rendered passive, suffer the death of the old being, so that God might be allowed to be our God and to redeem us in Christ. Before the world (*coram mundo*), faith lends itself to good works, to actively help our neighbours and the world, similar to how good fruit flourishes on a good tree.

> This is our theology, by which we teach a precise distinction between these two kinds of righteousness, the active and the passive, so that morality and faith, works and grace, secular society and religion may not be confused.... Christian righteousness applies to the new man, and the righteousness of the law applies to the old man....(Lectures on Galatians [1535], WA40,1.45,24–28; LW26:7)

II. PAST AND CURRENT MISPERCEPTIONS

The impact of Luther's view of justification for theology and wider culture did not have the theological impact one might have hoped. Instead, Luther's theological heirs tended to weld the doctrine of justification by faith alone onto an anthropology inspired by philosophical and humanistic concerns that affirmed the free choice of the will, a position antithetical to Luther's position of the human before God (*coram deo*) (Forde 1993). In essence, the Lutheran movement failed to construct an anthropology compatible with Luther's view of justification—a sad state, given that Luther himself believed that justification by faith alone was definitive of humanity (WA39,1.176,33–35; LW34.139). Increasingly, Enlightenment figures defined freedom as autonomy, which Immanuel Kant saw as a rational exercise in choice when an agent implements the 'categorical imperative'—acting on principles which have universal and necessary applicability.

Albrecht Ritschl sought to apply Luther's teachings to nineteenth-century theological concerns, appropriating Luther's views of forgiveness within an ellipsis bounded by the twin points of forgiveness and ethical responsibilities. Nevertheless, especially as noticed by Theodosius Harnack,

> Ritschl had abridged or completely overlooked basic elements of Luther's theology. Among these were the ideas of the wrath of God, judgment, the dialectical distinction between the law and the gospel, as well as Luther's more radical statements about sin and grace. Ritschl took concepts that were really theological concepts for Luther and redefined them in terms of inner freedom and of ethics. (Lohse 1980: 220)

In contrast, Harnack revived the centrality of law—accusation—and gospel—regeneration—in Luther's interpretation (Lohse 1980: 221). Adolph von Harnack revived an ethicizing approach to Luther and claimed that for Luther justification is 'being righteous and becoming righteous' (Harnack 1903: 7,208). Similarly, Karl Holl tended to situate Luther's work within an ethical framework. For Holl, Luther's is 'a religion of conscience' (Holl 1977: 48–61), one which 'included the element of "duty" (*Pflicht*)' (Lohse 1980: 225). Holl tended to blur the distinction between Luther's earlier pre-Protestant views from his later, more mature views. 'Thus, according to Holl, as with Ritschl and von Harnack, Luther made no sharp distinction between being made righteous and being declared righteous. That distinction belonged to orthodoxy' (Clark 2006: 278). Nineteenth- and early twentieth-century Luther studies tended to revamp Luther's view of justification in terms of Kantian approaches to ethics, accentuating human autonomy, the separation of metaphysics from ethics, and the quest for a 'kingdom of ends', in which agents honour the autonomy of their peers.

More recently, a school of Luther studies has developed around the thinking of Tuomo Mannermaa. Guided by concerns for ecumenical relations with Eastern Orthodox church bodies, Mannermaa has aimed to present Luther's view of justification as properly divinization or *theosis*. In this perspective, a purely forensic view of justification falls short of the meaning of salvation for Luther, which Mannermaa regards as participation in God's very nature itself (Mannermaa 2005: 22). For Mannermaa, when Luther speaks of grace as *favor*, Luther never disassociates or separates God's forgiveness from the gift of divine indwelling. Indeed, both *favor* and *donum* [gift] form an inseparable unity in the person of Christ, who through faith is really, ontically present. Hence, in Mannermaa, the Lutheran Confessions' perspective of a forensic justification is fundamentally at odds with Luther himself. This school accentuates Luther's view of Christ as the 'form' of faith in the *Galatians Commentary* (1531) (Mannermaa 2005: 39). The difference between Luther and his Roman Catholic opponents is over whether or not it is love which establishes 'formal righteousness' (the Roman Catholic position) or Christ himself united with the believer through faith (Luther).

This view has been criticized by a number of scholars (e.g., Schwarzwäller 1995: esp. 146–8; Schumacher 2010). In responding to Mannermaa Timo Laato indicates that throughout Luther's writings, especially the *Galatians Commentary* (1531), Christ's atoning work in 'salvation history' precedes faith. Indeed, because Christ is the object of faith (God's *favor*), he is present in faith as *donum*. Hence, for Luther, salvation is based not on the indwelling Christ who deifies, but forensically on Christ who died for us (Laato 2008: 338). Indeed, Mannermaa's view leads to an unnecessary dilemma: *favor* is construed as objective while *donum* is somehow subjective. The truth, instead, is that we are dealing with a two-fold objectivity. A spoken, 'external word', which is God's *favor* in the form of a *gift*, grounded *both* in the objectivity of the cross and the proclamation to sinners as a benefit that requires such distribution, imparts both death and life to its hearers. Just as God's will is an active word ordering creation in Genesis, God's *favor* here is not a possession or essence of God's own, but *is* precisely the *gift*, applied to the unrighteous while and as they are unrighteous. Only on account of this truly objective foundation of imputation as forgiveness for Jesus' sake is the gift (*donum*) of the present Christ preached and so given—not to the old creature as old, but to the new creature as the act of new creation itself. Undoubtedly, Luther affirmed that

> faith brings the believer into union with Christ and through that union Christ communicates not just the benefit of justification but himself. Nevertheless, it is equally clear that for Luther the Christian is justified on the basis of nothing else but Christ's imputed righteousness. He made a logical distinction between these aspects of union with Christ while not divorcing them.
>
> (Clark 2006: 292; cf. WA2.503,20–505,2; LW27.241)

III. Justification in Historical Context

Luther developed his views on justification in the context of late medieval scholasticism, particularly the theology of Gabriel Biel. The most important theological agenda of the young Luther (1513–21) was the nature of God's righteousness. Luther came to believe that righteousness is of two kinds, an active and a passive, and not merely one, as the tradition previously had assumed. The medieval tradition assumed only an active righteousness, that is, that we are saved by developing our potential to become God-like, although most theologians taught that grace must initiate the *viator* or pilgrim on the journey towards the beatific vision, in which one becomes a *comprehensor*, finding ultimate favour in God in heaven.

There was a broad consensus in medieval views of justification:

> One is ordinarily justified because and to the degree that one is intrinsically sanctified, whether as a necessity because of the divine nature (as in realism) or as a consequence of an apparently arbitrary divine will (as in voluntarism), whether from a strongly predestinarian standpoint (e.g., Bradwardine) or a Pelagianizing approach (e.g., Ockham). Justification was a process begun at baptism and ordinarily concluded only at the judgment. This process was described in different ways with

differing degrees of emphasis on the nature and role of human cooperation, but, in virtually every pre-Reformation scheme, God is said to have taken the initiative (*gratia praeveniens*) to infuse within the sinner divine grace. By all accounts, the sinner was obligated to cooperate with that grace toward final justification.

(Clark 2006: 285)

Medieval views all affirmed that while initially alien or external to the believer righteousness must become proper to the believer through works of love. Faith itself along with love and hope was one of the three theological virtues.

Specifically, Gabriel Biel balanced God's initiative for salvation with human cooperation 'by insisting that "out of purely natural powers" (*ex puris naturalibus*) sinners could "do what is in them" (*facere quod in se est*). By doing their best they could win "congruent merit", a worthiness or righteousness before God that is not truly worthy, but nonetheless accepted by God as the basis for receiving his grace' (Kolb 2009: 32). This account is unable to offer a standard in which one can know or be certain that one has indeed done one's best. This led Luther to scour the Scriptures, where, in his intense study of Paul and the Psalms, he believed he had discovered a passive righteousness, salvation through trusting God's word of promise of forgiveness, imparting a new status and, thereby, a new nature, a 'clean heart', for the believer.

Such insights led Luther to an unthinkable move for the scholastic theologians: distinguishing law from gospel. In this distinction, the law is not a manual that presents the steps to travel to eternal life, but is instead a tormentor attacking any self-righteousness one seeks to bring before God. The gospel is not 'new law', but is instead a gift-word of promise that assures terrified consciences of God's mercy given only to sinners, a word which quickens the dead to new life. Luther's discovery of a passive righteousness allowed him to reframe his concept of active righteousness. Brian Gerrish notes that

the believer does not earn this divine imputation with his faith, neither is there any legal fiction: God counts the confidence of the heart as 'right' because that is what it is. Its rightness lives in the fact that faith, for its part, does not make God an idol but takes him for exactly what *he* is: the author and giver of every good, the precise counterpart of the believer's confidence. In a sense faith, by believing, is the 'creator of divinity' in us: it lets God be God. (Gerrish 1982: 86)

Since righteousness can no longer be configured as works that help us merit righteousness before God, but trust alone right-wises the sinner, works take on a new meaning. God needs no works—the neighbour, however, does.

As Luther came to see it, the problem with sinners, old beings, is their inability to trust God to be God for them, provide for and take care of them. Instead, old beings prefer to be 'god' for themselves. This old being cannot be reformed. Indeed, the best that humanity has to offer—religion—simply aggravates the worst self-righteousness in old beings, as Luther himself experienced as a friar within the monastery. We sinners need to become new beings. This happens only by God's re-creative Word. God's foren-sic word of judgement, which in fact kills old beings, is given in tandem with the word of absolution: your sins are forgiven you, for Jesus' sake. God's Word does not merely pro-vide information about God, the world, or the self, or establish directives for our actions. Such information is encapsulated in God's law, whether heard in Scripture, sermon, or nature. Only the gospel-promise can still its accusation of sinners.

In the word of absolution God embraces the sinner, who in faith is reborn.

> That the linguistic sign is itself the reality, that it represents not an absent but a pre-sent reality, was Luther's great hermeneutical discovery, his 'reformation discovery' in the strict sense. He made it first (1518) in reflection on the sacrament of pen-ance...the word of absolution is a speech-act that first establishes a state of affairs, first creates a relationship. (Bayer 2003: 76)

Hence, Luther notes, 'grace actually means God's favour, or the good will which in himself he bears toward us, by which he is disposed to give us Christ and pour into us the Holy Spirit with his gifts...the gifts and the Spirit increase in us every day, but they are not yet perfect since there remain in us the evil desires and sins that war against the Spirit' (*Prefaces to the New Testament*, WADB7.8/9,10–16; LW35.369; cf. Kolb 2009: 108–9). Appealing to Gerhard Forde, Kolb recognized that attempts to pit effective justification against forensic, whether in the Holl school or the Mannermaa school, 'are both historically inaccurate and theologically unnecessary' since in Forde's words (Forde 1982: 36), 'the more "forensic" Luther's teaching becomes (especially in preaching), the more "effective" it is, because nothing can be more real than that which God's Word declares' (Kolb 2009: 128). With respect to the article of justifica-tion, preaching which distinguishes law and gospel is the most important practice in the church's life.

IV. New Frontiers for Research

Justification gives rise to several new avenues for research. Three are presented here. First, the question naturally arises: Is the doctrine of justification a meta-doc-trine which we can use to evaluate all other doctrines? (Jenson 2010). If justifica-tion by faith alone is singled out as the foremost criterion of truth in theology, as opposed to those perspectives in which justification is simply one doctrine among many, then it positions all other doctrines. For Luther, justification *is* a meta-doc-trine. In his 1530 exposition of Psalm 117, Luther writes, 'If this one teaching [on jus-tification] stands in its purity, then Christendom will also remain pure and good, undivided and unseparated; for this alone, and nothing else, makes and maintains Christendom' (WA31.255,5–8; LW14.37). There are objections to justification as a meta-doctrine: Since the Bible uses numerous metaphors to indicate salvation, why should the forensic one be singled out as definitive? Defenders of Luther's view are quick to note that this matter boils down to whether or not the gospel as scripturally understood is indeed promise. If it is, then the centrality accorded the article of justification in Luther's view is justified.

Second, the *Joint Declaration on the Doctrine of Justification* between the Roman Catholic church and member churches of the Lutheran World Federation, a document attempting reconciliation between Catholics and Lutherans, declares that 'the doctrine of justification...is more than just one part of Christian doctrine. It stands as an essential relation to all truths of faith, which are to be seen as internally related to each other' (*Joint Declaration* 2000: 16). As Gordon Jenson notes, 'While giving it an important place in the pantheon of doctrines, it [the *Joint Declaration*] does not make it the article by which the church stands and falls' (2010: 30; cf. Dingel 2001). Since that is the case, it would seem that the *Joint Declaration* as an attempt at compromise simply fails to convey the radicality of Luther's perspective. However, well after a decade, it is now apparent that the *Joint Declaration* has made virtually no difference in the life of Roman Catholics or Lutherans, especially given that grass-roots ecumenism was quite alive and well prior to its adoption.

Third, the most important research for the future in light of Luther's view of justification is the attempt to understand human nature in terms of passive and active righteousness. In that view, the being of the human, at the core, *is* faith (whether that be in God or an idol). But this insight has yet to impact theology and the wider academy.

V. CONCLUSION

Luther's approach to the article of justification is forensic; sinners are imputed the righteousness of Christ, are forgiven for Jesus' sake. Nevertheless, his view of justification is also 'effective', not in that God analytically evaluates our ethical behaviour of becoming righteous or our ontological union with Christ, but in that we are killed by the law, which accuses sinners to death, and raised by the gospel promise, which grants forgiveness, life, and salvation. All of human life is restored in the Word that re-establishes our creatureliness before God. For Luther, God became human just so that we through faith might ourselves become human, in opposition to the self-deification or control that all sinners arrogate to themselves, either through self-righteousness attendant to piety or prodigality. For Luther we live trusting in God's providence, free from self-centred incurvation, open to nature as creation, that is, God's address to us, and in service to our neighbour. Given that our secular age is in no less a quest for a divine-like control over nature and the world, Luther's is a message that is most relevant and welcome.

REFERENCES

Bayer, Oswald (2007). *Theology the Lutheran Way*, trans. Jeffrey Silcock and Mark Mattes. Grand Rapids, MI: Eerdmans.

Clark, R. Scott (2006). 'Iustitia Imputata Christi: Alien or Proper to Luther's Doctrine of Justification?' *Concordia Theological Quarterly* 70: 269–310.

Dingel, Irene (2001). 'The Debate over Justification in Ecumenical Dialogue'. *Lutheran Quarterly* 15: 293–316.

Forde, Gerhard (1982). *Justification by Faith: A Matter of Death and Life*. Philadelphia: Fortress.

—— (1993). 'Lutheranism'. In *The Blackwell Encyclopedia of Modern Christian Thought*, ed. Alister E. McGrath. Oxford: Blackwell, 354–8.

—— (2004). 'Forensic Justification and the Christian Life: Triumph or Tragedy?' In *A More Radical Gospel: Essays on Eschatology, Authority, Atonement, and Ecumenism*, ed. Mark Mattes and Steven Paulson. Grand Rapids, MI: Eerdmans, 114–36.

Gerrish, Brian (1982). 'By Faith Alone: Medium and Message in Luther's Gospel'. In *The Old Protestantism and the New: Essays on the Reformation Heritage*. Edinburgh: T&T Clark, 66–89.

Harnack, Adolf von (1903). *History of Dogma*, trans. Neil Buchanan. Boston: Little, Brown.

Holl, Karl (1977). *What Did Luther Understand by Religion?* ed. James Luther Adams and Walter F. Beuse, trans. Fred W. Meuser and Walter R. Wietzke. Philadelphia: Fortress.

Jenson, Gordon (2010). 'Is the Doctrine of Justification a Meta-Doctrine in Lutheran Thinking?' In *Lutherans and Theological Method: Perennial Questions and Contemporary Challenges*, ed. David Ratke. Minneapolis: Fortress, 27–41.

Joint declaration on the Doctrine of Justification (2000). Grand Rapids, MI: Eerdmans.

Kolb, Robert (2009). *Martin Luther: Confessor of the Faith*. Oxford: Oxford University Press.

Laato, Timo (2008). 'Justification: The Stumbling Block of the Finnish Luther School'. *Concordia Theological Quarterly* 72: 327–46.

Lohse, Bernhard (1980). *Martin Luther: An Introduction to His Life and Work*, trans. Robert C. Schulz. Philadelphia: Fortress.

Mannermaa, Tuomo (2005). *Christ Present in Faith: Luther's View of Justification*, trans. Kirsi Stjerna. Minneapolis: Fortress.

Russell, William R. (1995). *The Schmalkald Articles: Luther's Theological Testament*. Minneapolis: Fortress.

Schumacher, William (2010). *Who Do I Say that You Are? Anthropology and the Theology of Theosis in the Finnish School of Tuomo Mannermaa*. Eugene, OR: Wipf & Stock.

Schwarzwäller, Klaus (1995). 'Verantwortung des Glaubens. Freiheit und Liebe nach der Dekalogauslegung Martin Luthers'. In *Freiheit als Liebe bei/Freedom as Love in Martin Luther*, ed. Dennis D. Bielfeldt and Klaus Schwarzwäller. Frankfurt am Main: Lang, 133–58.

SUGGESTED READING

Bayer, Oswald (2003). *Living By Faith: Justification and Sanctification*, trans. Geoffrey Bromiley. Grand Rapids, MI: Eerdmans.

—— (2008). *Martin Luther's Theology: A Contemporary Interpretation*, trans. Thomas Trapp. Grand Rapids, MI: Eerdmans.

Forde, Gerhard (2007). *The Preached God: Proclamation in Word and Sacrament*, ed. Mark Mattes and Steven Paulson. Grand Rapids, MI: Eerdmans.

Iwand, Hans J. (1982). *The Righteousness of Faith According to Luther*, trans. Randi H. Lundell. Eugene, OR: Wipf & Stock.

Kolb, Robert (2004). 'Contemporary Lutheran Understandings of the Doctrine of Justification: A Selective Glimpse'. In *Justification: What's at Stake in the Current Debate?* ed. Mark Husbands and Daniel Treier. Downers Grove: Intervarsity, 153–76.

Kolb, Robert and Charles P. Arand (2008). *The Genius of Luther's Theology: A Wittenberg Way of Thinking for the Contemporary Church*. Grand Rapids, MI: Baker Academic.

Mattes, Mark (2004). *The Role of Justification in Contemporary Theology*. Grand Rapids, MI: Eerdmans.

Paulson, Steven (2006). 'The Augustinian Imperfection: Faith, Christ, and Imputation and Its Role in the Ecumenical Discussion of Justification'. In *The Gospel of Justification in Christ: Where Does the Church Stand Today?* ed. Wayne Stumme. Grand Rapids, MI: Eerdmans, 104–24.

CHAPTER 19

LUTHER ON CHRIST'S PERSON AND WORK

MATTHIEU ARNOLD

I. THE CURRENT STATE OF SCHOLARLY RESEARCH

RESEARCH on Luther's Christology has concentrated, notably in the second half of the nineteenth century and in several twentieth-century works, on the manner in which he understood the work of salvation by Christ (see the excellent summary in Rieske-Braun 1999: 23–65). For some scholars, such as Karl Holl, Christ played only a secondary role in Luther's thought. For Johann Christian Konrad von Hofman (1882–5) Luther spoke far more of the salvation acquired by Christ at the expense of death-dealing powers (the Devil, sin, death) than of reconciliation with God. According to Hofmann, who developed this thesis in several other works (Hoffman 1857–9), there is no trace in Luther's work of the theory of Anselm of Canterbury: Luther does not present God as a judge who punishes, nor Jesus Christ as the person who is judged in the place of human beings, because, for Luther, God's principal characteristic is love.

In response to the initial writings of Hofmann, Gottfried Thomasius (1857a, 1857b) and Theodosius Harnack maintained, on the contrary, the proximity of Luther's thought and Anselm's. The debate with Hofmann led Theodosius Harnack to rediscover the extent to which Luther took the wrath of God against human sin seriously (1862/86): for Harnack, the wrath of God is a fundamental point in theology *and* in Luther's experience. Harnack postulates an agreement between the ideas of Luther and Anselm on the subject: in order to wipe clean human error and still the anger of God, reconciliation can only take place through the vicarious satisfaction offered by Christ.

Between the publishing of the volumes by Thomasius and Harnack's *Luthers Theologie*, the liberal theologian Albrecht Ritschl wrote a detailed study of the relation between justification and reconciliation (1870–4). For Ritschl, in Luther's soteriology, the theory of Jesus Christ's combat against the powers of evil was more important than the notion of a substitutionary death (cf. Anselm). Ritschl defended, along with Abelard, the idea that it is humankind who needs to be reconciled with God; indeed he wondered if the mythological motif of Christ's combat against the forces of evil was reconcilable with Luther's reformational discovery: was it not rather, said Ritschl, a relic of medieval theology which Luther did not quite manage to set aside?

The next work to command wide readership which argued for the importance of this 'dualist combat theme' in Luther appeared in 1930 (Aulén 1931, 1930); it made this theme the centre of Luther's theology and even of the history of Christian doctrine. For Gustaf Aulén Luther revivified this theme of the early church, God's personal combat, in direct opposition to Anselm's ideas and those of later scholasticism. Against Theodosius Harnack, Aulén maintained that the idea of the anger of God—which is certainly present in Luther—does not in fact reflect the essence of God to the same extent as his love. The success of Aulén's theory did not prevent Paul Althaus (1962) from reaffirming with Anselm the predominance of Christ's struggle against the *anger* of God: it is God who, through his wrath, gives the powers against whom Christ fights their power.

So for Theodosius Harnack and for Althaus, Luther *combined* the Anselmian motif of reconciliation (the dominant theme in his thought) with the patristic motif of combat (a secondary theme in his thought), whereas for Ritschl and Aulén, among others, Luther moved beyond Anselm's theory by reformulating the ancient idea of the *duellum mirabile*. They contended that the theory of combat is not reconcilable with the theory of satisfaction.

In 1974 Theobald Beer placed the accent on the theme of the 'joyful bargain' (*fröhlicher Wechsel, admirabile commercium*), which Luther developed principally in his treatise *On the Freedom of the Christian* (1520). Beer held that this theme was the heart of Luther's Christology, arguing that he developed conceptions of salvation and reconciliation which are not only in tension but even incompatible and contradictory. Unfortunately, the criticism levelled against Beer seems justified: that his work amasses quotations without providing adequate contextual, historical, and literary analysis.

But Beer was not alone in privileging a systematic, theoretical approach to Luther's Christology: this approach was equally followed by Theodosius Harnack and by those who disagreed with him, including Paul Althaus. None of these scholars really took any account of the different historical contexts and the various literary genres in which Luther wrote. Erich Seeberg (1937) presented the development of Luther's Christology in three major stages; but not until the work of Ian D. K. Siggins (1970) and above all of Marc Lienhard (1973) were there sophisticated studies of Luther's Christology with a clear historical perspective. On the one hand, Lienhard proved the central place of Christology in the theology of Luther; on the other, he studied the diverse influences which were brought to bear on this Christology, together with its development, in particular following the quarrel with Zwingli over the Lord's Supper in 1527–8. Lienhard presented the journey of Luther's Christological ideas throughout his life, from the early writings before 1517 to his commentary on Isaiah 53 of 1544.

II. LUTHER'S CHRISTOLOGY

II.1. A Central Theological Theme used throughout Luther's Works

In the preface to his *Commentary on the Epistle to the Galatians* (1531), Luther insisted on the importance of Jesus Christ in his theology: 'There reigns in my heart a single fact: faith in Christ. It is from there that all my theological meditation flows; it is through there that this meditation goes to and fro, flowing in and out day and night like the tides; without this fact, from so high, so broad and so deep a wisdom, I would not have managed to seize more than a few delicate and meagre beginnings of crumbs' (WA40.1.33,7–11). Unlike Anselm of Canterbury, for example, Luther did not, strictly speaking, publish a treatise on Christology. However, Christology is still found right at the centre of his theology, linked with justification by faith alone. In his life and thought Luther passed from a terrifying vision of Christ as judge to a comforting and reassuring vision of God who saves humanity in Christ and who declares humanity justified on the basis of the righteousness of another (*iustitia aliena*), namely, of Christ. In addition, as we shall see shortly, his Christology is closely linked to his soteriology: the person and work of Christ save Luther from death, from sin, and from the Devil, and amount to the only comfort in the face of the temptations of these malevolent powers.

Luther's Christology does not constitute a dogmatic system. As in other areas of his theology, when he spoke of the person and work of Christ, Luther did not intend to offer an exhaustive system, outlining all of Christology, nor to do the work of a dogmatician. Luther did not expound the work of Christ with the same breadth as Calvin in Book II of his *Institution de la religion chrestienne*. Even so, as Lienhard has underscored, 'it is a real Christology, that is to say a coherent collection of themes concerning the action of God and man in Jesus Christ, as well as the salvation brought to man' (Lienhard 1973: 402).

More than being expressed in a specific work, Luther's Christology is deployed across all the literary genres which he used: university lectures and disputations, his translation of the Bible and prefaces to the biblical books, treatises, sermons, catechisms, hymns, letters, table talk, and even his polemical writings. To present Luther's Christology, we have to employ the widest range of his works possible, throughout his life: in terms of his Christology, it would be an especially grave error to neglect the writings of the 'later Luther' after 1525 (see esp. Lienhard 1983: 1.77–92, 2.748–55). This attention to chronology is necessary because Luther's Christology witnesses to his development across the course of time, as we can illustrate with the theme of Christ as example (*exemplum*). In his *Sermon on Preparing for Death* (1519), Luther speaks of Christ as an example, notably at paragraph 14: Christ was confronted with the same desperate temptations as we are, but he triumphed over them by remaining connected to the will of God (see WA2.691,23–692,16; LW42.107–108). In his *Brief Instruction on What We Must Seek in the Gospels* (1522) Luther discusses Christ as example and sacrament: the purpose of the gospels is not only to detail the life of Christ, but—for the believer, at least—to enable him to possess the work of Christ for himself. It is for the believer that Christ acts and suffers (see WA10.1,1.11,12–18; LW35.119). If Luther takes up Augustine's phrase 'exemplum et sacramentum' (cf. *De Trinitate* IV.3), which is based mainly on John 13:15 and 1 Peter 2:21, it is in order to show that the Christ given to the believer implies an ethical transformation in the believer's life: Jesus Christ is for humankind a sacrament inasmuch as he is the human being's righteousness before God; Jesus Christ is an example for humankind insofar as he calls humanity to follow him in service of the neighbour. But, as Lienhard has shown, from 1525 on Luther began to be more cautious about the theme of Christ-as-example (Lienhard 1991: 255). It is clear that Luther insisted on the fact that Christ can only be an example *after* having been a sacrament, 'gift and present': Christ must first act in us in order for us to follow in his way.

We can also observe that, during the quarrel about indulgences (1517–21), which had definite consequences for Luther's conception of the papacy and the church, he stressed—against the traditional church—the theme of Christ as the head and master of the church and the believer (cf. e.g., *On the Papacy of Rome*, 1520, WA6.285–324; LW39.55–104). This theme was subsequently relegated to the background: as we shall see below, when Luther speaks in his catechisms of Christ as *Herr* [Lord], he stresses Christ's saving work and its benefit to believers.

Some other developments are best understood as Luther marshalling arguments (in German: *Entfaltung*) rather than making modifications (German: *Entwicklung*) in the evolution of his Christology: during public controversies, Luther found himself obliged to develop arguments which he had never needed to deploy before, without actually altering his ideas. This is the case, for example, as we shall see below, on the question of the two natures of Christ, linked to the controversies amongst Protestants concerning the Lord's Supper.

II.2. The Context: Theology and Piety at the End of the Middle Ages

When he wrote works which looked back to his younger days, such as the preface to his collected writings of 1545, where Luther presents the theology and piety which he had known during his youth, he paints a picture of an aloof and frightening God. But does this reminiscing actually correspond to reality? Some recent studies, such as those of Berndt Hamm and Volker Leppin (Leppin 2006; Hamm 2010), have seen a more nuanced approach in Luther on this point: his terrifying depictions were written side by side with more reassuring images, which were influenced largely by his reflections on the incarnation. The popular piety of the Late Middle Ages certainly taught a God as severe as he was distant, and preaching stressed the judgement of God. But in the same epoch, the teaching that Christ was humanity's advocate before God was equally popular, and the passion of Christ, everywhere present in religious imagery of the Late Middle Ages, shaped a piety marked by human emotion (Hamm 2010: 465). This nearness of the

Christ of grace—whereas before the second half of the fifteenth century he had been depicted as the sovereign and judge of the world—influenced literary and pictorial representations of God the Father, including the popular images of the *artes moriendi*: God himself overcomes the distance which separates him from human beings and allows humanity to appreciate his merciful and saving presence (Hamm 2010: 467–71). In these images of the last third of the fifteenth century, widely distributed through the printing press, Christ is to be found, accompanied by God the Father and Saint Mary, at people's deathbeds. Thus, even before Luther some theologians were stressing the 'nearness of the grace' of God revealed in Jesus Christ, and Luther's Christology does not mark a rupture with the theological currents which preceded it: through their insistence on the nearness of Christ and through their quest for assurance of grace and salvation, medieval ideas ended up paving the way to Luther.

It is true nonetheless that other theologians of the '*Spätmittelalter*' continued to downplay a message of an intimate and merciful God and to prefer an insistence on a salvation that was very hard to obtain, limited to the most virtuous, and so but rarely won (Hamm 2000, 2004). It is equally true that late medieval theology and piety did not set human effort and divine grace in opposition, but on the contrary underlined the *cooperation* of the individual in his salvation: along the ascending path leading to heaven and salvation, the human being received help from God, Father, Son, and Holy Spirit. It is also true that artistic depictions of the Late Middle Ages propagated a sort of 'digital' piety in the way that they allied the grace of Christ to human effort: hence praying in front of an image of the Christ of sorrows was worth as many days' indulgence to the believer as the wounds of Christ themselves (Hamm 2010: 479–81, 484). The imitation of Christ was conceived as the performance of specific numbers of works of satisfaction (which abolished post-mortem punishment) and works of merit (which received a post-mortem reward). Against this conception Luther exalted spontaneous and free works, which flowed from faith in the salvation accomplished by Jesus Christ.

In addition, as we shall see below, Luther's Christology is not solely rooted in late medieval Christology; indeed, Luther represents a break with the Late Middle Ages to some extent. Luther's Christology cannot simply be identified with the Late Middle Ages—otherwise, the traditional remedies which Johannes von Staupitz had proposed to him in the monastery (WATR1.59,7–60,12, §137) would have been accepted by Luther as sufficient. Luther was, of course, influenced by Augustine, Bernard of Clairvaux, and by late medieval piety and theology, which stressed the suffering Christ. In his Christological reflections, as for the rest of his theology, Luther borrowed from all these traditions, mixing them and interpreting them in his own personal fashion. Thus, breaking with those who had gone before him, when he discussed salvation, Luther diminished the active imitation of Christ by the believer in order to concentrate more on the triumphant power of Christ. Indeed, Luther's *Lectures on the Epistle to the Romans* (1515–16, WA56.3–154; LWW 25), especially on chapters 12 to 15, freely adopted the language of 'Christ as example', who leads the believer into the land of love and service (see the comment on 15:3–4). But even while developing these points, Luther did not actually adopt a spirituality of the imitation of Christ. We scarcely need to remind ourselves, too, that Luther was influenced by numerous, different, and varied New Testament Christological affirmations. Thus, Hebrews 9:29 enabled him to speak of Christ as mediator and as 'High Priest, destroyer of sin and author of justice and salvation' (WA57.3.54,14–15). Luther often used Hebrews 6:20 to assign the roles of high priest and intercessor to Christ. For Regin Prenter, Colossians 2:9 and John 14:9 express the entirety of Luther's Christology (Prenter 1953: 267).

II.3. The Person of Christ: The Trinity and the Question of the Two Natures

It is difficult, indeed impossible, clearly to distinguish the person and the work of Christ in Luther: for him, Christology and soteriology are indissoluble—'Christology has soteriology as its aim; soteriology is based in Christology' (Lohse 1999: 223). For Luther, in effect, we cannot truly know Jesus Christ except from his work, in particular from his work for each human being. It is therefore within the framework of his soteriological perspective that Luther writes on the person of Christ and expresses his faithfulness to the tradition of the church: 'The devil can have no peace when our beloved Christ is preached according to the Apostles' Creed, that is, that God and man, he died and was raised for us' ('Es hat der Teuffel keinen friede können haben, wo der liebe Christus gepredigt wird nach dem ersten Symbolo, das er sey Gott und mensch fur uns gestorben und erstanden') (*Sermon on the Creed*, 1538, WA50.268,15–18; LW34.209).

Luther insisted both on the true divinity of Christ, guarantee of salvation (if he was only human, Christ could not save us), and on the reality of his humanity, his submission to the law, his suffering and his solidarity with others. Luther wrote, in whole or in part, several works on this theme. In 1540 he disputed the ideas of Caspar von Schwenckfeld in his *On the Divinity and Humanity of Christ* (*De divinitate et humanitate Christi*, WA39.2.93–96). He had previously discussed the two natures of Christ in a disputation on John 1:14 in 1539 (WA39.2.3–33) and in the parts of *On the Councils and the Churches* (1539, WA50.509–653; LW41.9–178) which addressed dogmatic topics. His later writings against the Jews (see especially *The Last Words of David*, 1543, WA54.28–100; LW15.267–352 and *The Jews and their Lies*, 1543, WA53.417–552; LW47.137–306) amount to a defence of the divine nature of Christ, of the virginity of Mary, and of the Trinity, which Luther criticized the Jews for denying.

But it was mainly the debate with Zwingli on the subject of the presence of Christ in the Lord's Supper which led Luther most seriously to explore the question of the two natures of Christ, a topic which he had already raised in *On the Babylonian Captivity of the Church* (1520, WA6.511,34–39; LW36.35). After 1520, and even more so after the eucharistic controversy with Zwingli, Luther was preoccupied with the question of the two natures of Christ: it was controversy over the Lord's Supper which led him to write on the question of the two natures. In the Alexandrian tradition Luther affirmed the unity of the person of Christ as man and God together. Again in line with the Alexandrian tradition, he affirmed the kenosis of Christ (Phil. 2:5–6), but with a personal twist: for Luther, it is not the eternal Christ who divests himself of the trappings of divinity at the incarnation; it is rather through the course of his life, in a continuous process and not in a single event, that Christ incarnate refuses to employ 'against us' his divine properties, and so allows himself to be subject to all evil (see, e.g., *Sermon on Two Kinds of Righteousness*, 1519, WA2.148,2–18; LW31.301; Arnold 2013). Whereas for the Church Fathers and for medieval theologians, Christ's sufferings on the cross were physical in nature, Luther held that Jesus Christ also felt himself abandoned and condemned by God, undergoing, in spite of his innocence, all the force of the anger of God. It was important for Luther that it was not just a man who died on the cross, but God himself; without this, salvation—of which God is the author and originator—would not be assured. So for Luther, God died on the cross, but, because of his very divinity, death cannot overcome him (see WA26.319,33–40; LW37.209–10). That said, if Luther stressed this teaching in his *Confession Concerning Christ's Supper* (1528), in other contexts he qualified his position, in a sermon of 1537:

> He was indeed forsaken by God, not that the divinity was separated from the humanity, for divinity and humanity in this person, who is Christ, God's Son, Mary's son, are so united that into eternity they cannot be separated or divided, but it appears so, and whoever reads this, would like to say, 'Here there is no God but simply a human being, and that a person despondent and despairing'. The humanity is left alone, and the devil had free access to Christ, and the divinity had withdrawn its power and left the humanity to fight alone. (WA45.239,32–40)

Does this amount to saying, as Lohse held, that Luther does not follow through the consequences of underlining the unity of the divinity and humanity of Christ (Lohse 1999: 230)? Various theologians, especially Roman Catholic, such as Yves Congar (1964), have criticized Luther for distancing himself from the traditional doctrine of the two natures of Christ and for failing to distinguish sufficiently between the different persons of the Trinity. Earlier, Karl Holl had spoken of Luther's 'modalist tendencies' and had accused him of subordinationism (Holl 1932: 1.72). Lienhard rejected these criticisms, as well as the criticism that Luther concentrates too much on soteriology to develop an advanced Christology in the sense of an ontological reflection on Jesus Christ.[1]

In fact, Luther speaks of the immanent Trinity and not only of the economic Trinity. He clearly distinguishes the persons of the Trinity, aligning himself with the Augustinian doctrine taken up by Thomas Aquinas and Peter Lombard:

---

[1] 'Parce qu'il insiste beaucoup sur l'œuvre du Christ, Luther a été amené à préciser sa façon de comprendre la personne du Christ et il a redécouvert ainsi sur la base de cette œuvre le sens profond de la christologie traditionnelle.' ('Because he insisted strongly on the work of Christ, Luther was led to develop precisely his way of understanding the person of Christ, and in this way he rediscovered on the basis of this effort the deep meanings of traditional Christology' Lienhard 1973: 378.)

What distinguishes the Father is that he is the Father and that he does not have the divine nature of the Son nor of anyone else [...]. What distinguishes the Son is that he is the Son and that he does not possess his divine nature of himself or of anyone else except of the Father alone, for he is begotten of the Father from all eternity [...]. What distinguishes the Holy Spirit from the Father and from the Son is that he is the Holy Spirit who proceeds (*ausgehet*) from all eternity from the Father and the Son.

> (*The Last Words of David*, 1543, WA54.58,19–23,25–26; LW15.303. See
> WA54.64,27–31; LW15.310, where Luther uses Chalcedon in underscoring
> that we must neither confuse [*nicht gemenget*] the persons nor divide [*nicht*
> *zertrennet*] the essence [*Wesen*] of the one God)

As for his interpretation of the doctrine of the two natures, Luther made it serve his soteriology, as we see in the *Heidelberg Disputation* (1518), *On Bound Choice* (1525), and the *Lectures on Genesis* (1535–45). In his interpretations of the Creed and in his catechisms, Luther grounded the identity of Jesus Christ as Lord in his two natures, even if the Apostles' Creed is silent on the matter. Luther combined the three topics of the two natures, the lordship of Christ, and salvation (cf. Lohse 1999: 221):

> I believe that Jesus Christ, true God, begotten of the Father in eternity and also a true human being, born of the Virgin Mary is my LORD. He has redeemed me, a lost and condemned human being. He has purchased and freed me from all sins, from death, and from the power of the devil, not with gold or silver but with his holy, precious blood and with his innocent suffering and death. He has done all this in order that I may belong to him, live under him in his kingdom, and serve him in eternal righteousness, innocence, and blessedness, just as he his risen from the dead and lives and rules eternally. This is most certainly true.
>
> (SC Creed, second article, BSLK 511; BC 355).

Against Zwingli Luther insisted on the unity of the person of Christ. At the same time, he was careful not to muddle the two natures together: 'We do not say that divinity is humanity, or that the divine nature is the human nature, which would be confusing the natures into one essence. Rather, we merge the two distinct natures into a single person, and say: God is man and man is God. We in turn raise a hue and cry against them for separating the person of Christ as though there were two persons' (WA26.324,1–7; LW37.212). So Luther wanted to remain faithful to the affirmations of the Council of Chalcedon, which taught that the two natures were not to be conjoined, separated, divided, or blended together.

In the controversy concerning the real presence of Christ in the Lord's Supper, Zwingli's argument was based on the ascension of Christ: ever since Christ was raised to the Father's right hand, he could not be physically present elsewhere. Luther replied that Christ's resurrection and ascension do not imply a physical presence at the right hand of the Father in a physical location above the earth because this phrase signifies Christ's dominion and omnipresence: 'The right hand of God is not a specific location where a body must or could exist. It is the omnipotent power of God which can at the same time be nowhere and everywhere' (WA23.133,19–22; LW37.57). For Luther, to deny the efficacy of the flesh of Christ in the Lord's Supper is the same as denying the incarnation, which itself is not confined to the past. It is for this reason that Luther held to the ubiquity of the humanity of Christ (and therefore of his body and blood) to the same extent as the ubiquity of his divine nature. Luther also found it important to emphasize, against Zwingli, that the omnipotence of God and his incarnation are not contradictory: it is precisely in the incarnation that God reveals his omnipotence: 'Nothing is so small that God is not smaller. Nothing is so large that God is not greater. Nothing is so short, that God is not shorter. Nothing is so long that God is not longer. Nothing is so wide that God is not wider. Nothing is so narrow that God is not narrower' (*Confession Concerning Christ's Supper*, 1528, WA26.339,34–42; LW 37.228). To justify this contention, Luther made the distinction—with the nominalist tradition—between different types of presence in a given object in a given location. He borrowed from William of Ockham and Gabriel Biel the distinction between, on the one hand, the localized presence of an object (*circumscriptive in loco*); that is, 'the space and the body which is in it are in unison, joined together and are measured reciprocally', and, on the other, the quality of being '*diffinitive in loco*', 'in an unmeasurable way, when the thing or the body cannot be apprehended and is unmeasurable in the space which encloses it, but can occupy space to varying degrees' (see WA26. 327,20–33; LW37.214–215): for example, the wine is in the barrel *circumscriptive in loco*, whereas the soul is in the body *diffinitive in loco*. Luther based the notion of the omnipresence/ubiquity of Christ's human nature on the unity between the two natures of Christ and the 'communication of attributes'. For Lienhard, this communication of attributes is one of the absolutely key concepts in Luther's thought after 1530.[2] For Luther, the properties of the two natures must all be attributed in the same way to the whole person of Christ (see WA45.301,21–25). Here, as Kjell Ove Nilsson has shown, Luther was less concerned about metaphysical properties (for example, changelessness) than about properties which bear on the work of Christ (especially reconciliation and the forgiveness of sin) (Nilsson 1966).

In his theory of 'ubiquity' (a term which Luther himself did not use) Luther extended the traditional doctrine of the two natures. But problems arise when Luther seems to hold a ubiquity in Jesus from the incarnation on—that is, before the resurrection and ascension—and as a divine property somehow communicated to the humanity of Christ. Luther went further than the traditional understanding of the communication of attributes (which attributes to the entire person what belongs to just one of his natures): he defended the idea of a communication of attributes between the two natures themselves. In this way the human nature of Christ can be omnipresent; and, inversely, the divine nature of Christ participates in his human frailty: in Jesus Christ, it is God who suffers and dies on the cross. For Luther, the creating Word is equally the crucified. For Lienhard, Luther's language sometimes lacks formal rigour: he holds that, in spite of his protestations to the contrary, Luther sailed perilously close to

---

[2] Oswald Bayer goes further in affirming that all Luther's Christology is precisely 'doctrine of the communication of attributes (*Idiomenkommunikationslehre*)' (Bayer 2003: 77).

monophysitism (Lienhard 1973: 351, 357). Oswald Bayer disputes this idea: '[...] how-ever, in Christ there was no monophysite mixture' according to Luther (Bayer 2003: 69). Lienhard further states that the doctrine of the ubiquity of Christ's human nature brings Luther close to docetism as well as being 'scarcely faithful to biblical perspectives'. These parts of Luther's scheme seem 'an illegitimate divinisation of the man Jesus' (Lienhard 1973: 359, 386). The question of Luther's fidelity to the affirmations of the Bible and the ancient church is therefore open, and the responses to this question vary according to whichever of Luther's writings are being cited. In any case, it is beyond doubt that Luther united the two natures of Christ more than Ockham or Biel had.

It is interesting to compare the hyperbolical arguments of Luther's writings against Zwingli with the developments which Luther presents a decade later in *On the Councils and the Church* (1539), a treatise which has the traditional church as its tar-get: Luther demonstrates the incomplete character of the Christian doctrine promul-gated in the various councils of the early church. The Council of Nicaea understood the divinity of Christ solely in terms of his essential unity with the Father. The Council of Constantinople proclaimed the divinity of the Holy Spirit. The Council of Ephesus insisted on the singularity of Christ's person. The Council of Chalcedon discussed Christ's two natures. Luther assented to the teaching of all these councils, but he con-tended that, even taken together, the councils 'deliver too little'. Only the teaching of the Scriptures is complete (WA50.618,30–35; LW47.73). We can further observe that, in his later theological disputes, as studied by Axel Schmidt (1990), Luther remained steadfastly within the framework of traditional Christology: he held to a Christ of two natures, fully God and fully man; he stressed the communication of attributes and rejected Nestorian and Arian ideas.

II.4. The Work of Christ: Salvation, the Reconciliation of Man and God, and the Liberation from Evil Powers

For Luther, the doctrine of the two natures of Christ is closely linked to his soteriology. The idea that the presence of God is only saving to mankind when it is linked to the humanity of Jesus Christ is central to Luther's theology (Lohse 1999: 231). Luther's most systematic writings, such as the *Large Catechism* (1529) or the *Smalcald Articles* (1538, esp. BSLK 414–16; BC 300–1), speak first and foremost of the person of Christ, in accord-ance with Christian creeds, and then of Christ's work. But the two are closely linked: if, like Anselm, Luther insisted on the innocence of Christ, linked to his virginal concep-tion (cf. WA26.501,28–29; LW37.362), this is the case in order to guarantee the salvation he obtained on the cross. In numerous writings, including lectures and sermons, Luther revealed himself as the heir of the Western Christian tradition: the 'Latin' doctrine of the atonement, which dominated Western theology into reformational orthodoxy, sees in Christ primarily the God-*man*, 'who laid the holy wrath of the heavenly Father to rest as our substitute and reconciled us with God [...] As the human being who is identi-cal with God moves to the centre as the subject of the satisfaction, and God the Father appears more as the one who receives the sin offering' (Peters 1991: 130). This tradition understood the salvation wrought by Christ principally as a reconciliation with God, and sin as human error, and the rupture between mankind and God as a quasi-legal affair. This doctrinal project is particularly apparent in the theory enunciated by Anselm of Canterbury in his *Cur Deus Homo?* Basing his interpretation chiefly on Galatians 3:13 and Philippians 2:9, Luther used Anselm's concept of the satisfaction wrought by Jesus in receiving, albeit as an innocent person, the punishment which humanity deserved for its sin; Christ, by his obedience, reconciled humankind with God, who allocates to humanity the righteousness of Christ (or for Anselm, the merit of Christ). But we need also to highlight the differences between Luther and Anselm, whom Luther hardly ever quoted after 1518. For Luther, the work of Christ is not only the work of his human nature (Anselm), but also the work of his divine nature. Moreover, Luther went further than Anselm, for whom Christ on the cross did not experience God's anger (Lienhard 1973: 193). For Anselm, the cross served mainly to re-establish a right by the death of the Son; for Luther, it serves rather to appease the anger of God.

In its commentary on the Creed, Luther's *Large Catechism* covers briefly the reconciliation with God which Christ accomplishes ('he has obtained satisfaction for me and paid what I owed' [BSLK 654; BC 435]). It insists more, however, on the fact that Christ has saved humankind from the evil powers which oppressed us: 'I believe that Jesus Christ, the true Son of God, has become my Lord.' But what does 'become a Lord' mean? It means that 'he has delivered me from sin, from the devil, from death and from all misery' (SC Creed, BSLK 511; BC 355). The fact is that Luther, alongside the Latin tradition, allied himself with the early Greek ecclesiastical tradition, which understood the work of Christ's salvation as a redemption, a liberation. This tradition developed the idea of the combat in which Christ must engage against evil powers, and which he wins: Jesus Christ triumphs over sin and death, which had attempted to engulf him, and devours them himself. He frees humanity from all servitude to these evil powers.

As Uwe Rieske-Braun (1999) has shown, we would be wrong to place in opposition (as certain theologians did in previous centuries: see section I above) the two ways in which Luther understood the salvation of Christ: he used the Greek idea of the combat of Christ and the Latin doctrine of satisfaction very current at the end of the Middle Ages, either alternating or combining them. But he never placed them in opposition. For Luther, salvation is at the same time a triumph over sin (together with reconciliation with God) and a triumph over the forces of evil, even if—as his catechisms reveal—the accent is on the second theme (Lienhard 1973: 158; Peters 1991: 139). Luther often linked the triumph over the powers of evil to the motif of a ransom paid to Satan, whom Jesus thus deceives. Augustine had already defended (*De trinitate* XIII, 15) the idea that Christ had overcome Satan by shedding his sinless blood for the sins of humankind. For Gregory the Great and Leo the Great, Satan had allowed himself to be had because he had not been able to master the soul which Christ had given him as a ransom, a soul indissolubly linked to Christ's divinity. Luther picked up this theme of Satan cheated and trapped, especially in his famous hymn which relates the history of salvation 'Dear Christians, One and All,

Rejoice': 'He led his fight secretly / he took on my poor appearance / [because] he wanted to catch the devil' (WA35.424,22–24; LW53.220; cf. WA10.3,25–26). There Luther took up the image of Augustine and Gregory of Nyssa, Christ as a 'lure' and a 'bait' to trap Satan. The famous Easter hymn *Christus lag in Todesbanden* ('Christ lay in the chains of death') depicts the victory of Christ in terms of his 'devouring' and 'swallowing up' death (WA35.444,6–12; LW53.257).

In medieval tradition there existed, beyond reconciliation and redemption, a third way of understanding salvation. This third scheme, proposed by Abelard and picked up by Albrecht Ritschl in the nineteenth century, explores the idea that it is not God who needs to be reconciled with humanity, but humanity which needs to be reconciled with God. According to this concept, the work of salvation consists in what Jesus Christ reveals to humankind of the love of God; in return, Christ triggers the love of human beings for God. Luther did not reproduce this idea in its entirety, but he shared with it the notion that the work of Christ consists (additionally) in revealing the love of God to human beings. In any case, even when Luther uses somewhat Anselmian language, he makes the love of God the primary reality, as attested by the fact that the Father has set his Son on earth: it is not the acts of Christ on the cross which 'merit' the love of God; this love of God precedes the cross.

II.5. The Relation between Christ and the Believer

For Luther, Christ's work of salvation accomplished for humankind's benefit is useless unless it is proclaimed and unless the believer is attached to it by faith. Christ must be preached and the gospel is driven home: 'There is one gospel, just as there is one Christ. The gospel is not and cannot be anything else except the preaching of Christ, Son of God and of David, true God and true man, who by his death and resurrection, has conquered sin, death and hell for us and for all who believe in him' (cf. WADB6.6,22–28; LW35.360). In the spirit of Johannes Tauler and of the marital mysticism of Bernard of Clairvaux, Luther speaks of the union of the individual and Christ. Several times, he uses the image of marriage between the believer and Christ, with the 'joyful exchange' which follows for the believer. This theme of the joyful exchange reaches right back to the early church; it appears again in the Middle Ages, often combined with theories of satisfaction. In *The Freedom of a Christian* (1520) Luther, relying on Ephesians 5:21–33 and Hosea 11, grounded the 'joyful exchange' on the fact that Christ is 'God and man, who has never sinned':

> Here we have a most pleasing vision not only of a blessed struggle and victory and salvation and redemption. Christ is God and man in one person. He has neither sinned nor died, and he is not condemned; his righteousness, life, and salvation are unconquerable, eternal, omnipotent. By the wedding ring of faith he shares in the sins, death, and pains of hell which are his bride's. As a matter of fact, he makes them

his own and acts as if they were his own and as if he himself had sinned; he suffered, died, and descended into hell that he might overcome them all. Now since it was such a one who did all this, and death and hell could not swallow him up, these were necessarily swallowed up by him in a mighty duel. (WA7.25,34–26,1; LW31.351–352)

That said, even if Luther used traditional imagery and terminology, he rejected the mystical concept of a fusion of persons. For him, this joyful exchange more implies a whole community and an exchange of goods between persons. The union of the Christian to Christ is not mystical in type; it comes from the faith which 'unites the soul to Christ as a bride is united to her bridegroom' (WA7.54,31–32; LW31.351). To link the believer to Christ as Saviour, neither mysticism nor theological speculation is of use, but the action of the Holy Spirit, through the public means of preaching and sacrament (BSLK 713; LW 469–470).

The word of preaching links the believer to Christ, and the Holy Spirit gives faith in Christ. It is the gospel which explains the meaning of the incarnation and the work of Christ on the cross (see WA10.1,2.7,7–9. Sermons CP, 6:14 sermon for Advent 1, at Rom. 1:2). This preaching gives rise not only to objective knowledge of Christ but to faith in him, 'so that he might not only be Christ, but your Christ and my Christ', Luther insisted in The Freedom of a Christian (WA7.58,38–59,6; LW 31.357). Karin Bornkamm (1998) observes that the two ministries of Christ which Luther discusses in this treatise are closely linked to God's Word: the ministry of king, by which Christ who reigns by the Word conveys, through the gospel, salvation to the believer; the ministry of priest, through which Christ intercedes for the believer before God (see also Ebeling 1985: 157–80). For Luther, the cross is proclaimed by the Word and 'dispensed' by the sacraments (see WA26.296,31–297,9; LW37.193). It is the Word which acts by saying, 'This is for you, take it, receive it', Luther writes in his treatise Against the Heavenly Prophets (1525; WA18.203,23–24; LW40.213). 'He who believes in Christ and is attached to his Word possesses [Christ] with all his gifts, and so masters sin, death, the devil and hell', affirms Luther (Sermons on 1 Peter, 1523, WA12.284,18–20; LW30.29). This affirmation of a mastery over sin shows that, for Luther, belief in Christ has ethical consequences: along with union with Christ, achieved in the Word and through faith, new life is given to the believer. But can we, for all this, agree with the Finnish School, for whom Luther was speaking here of a divinization of humankind ('theosis') (see Ch. 17 in this volume)? With many scholars, we are of the opinion that we need to be cautious with the idea that theosis held great sway with Luther: the sources are too few to support the theory of the Finnish School (see Ch. 18 in this volume). Even so, the Finnish School had the merit of reminding us that for Luther, union with Christ has ethical consequences.

II.6. Jesus Christ, Sovereign and Lord of History

Next to the salvation worked by Jesus, Luther never forgot to speak of Christ the Creator (and so the Pre-existent Christ, WA10.1,1.149,2, Sermons CP, 6.171) and Christ the Lord. The theme of the sovereignty of Christ reveals itself very clearly in Luther's correspondence—a source generally neglected in studies on his Christology. For Luther, Christ does not only reign in the hearts of believers; we await the day when Christ will reign over the whole world, when he returns in judgement. Even today he is Lord, even if only believers can grasp this.

Certainly, Luther's correspondence, with his letters of comfort (*Trostbriefe*), consistently confirms that God's comforting presence is close to us in Jesus Christ (Mennecke-Haustein 1989; Arnold 1996: 515–90; Ebeling 1997). Nowhere is Christ as present and close as in the hundred or so letters which Luther wrote to the sick, bereaved, and persecuted, and to people suffering from 'spiritual sadness': Jesus Christ constitutes the heart of the comfort offered by Luther in these letters, and it is Jesus Christ who is the herald and mediator of this same comfort, thanks to his redemptive death. In Luther's letters on preparation for death, Jesus Christ appears as the conqueror of death: In a letter to his dying mother, he wrote, 'He says, "Be of courage, for I have overcome the world" [John 16:33]. If he has conquered the world, he has surely also conquered the prince of this world with all his power. But what is this power, if not death itself, through which the devil has submitted us to himself and taken us prisoner because of our sin?' (WABr6.104,32–35, §1820). When Luther wrote to those persecuted for their faith, Jesus Christ was presented as their companion and support: '[…] remember that you do not suffer alone, for he is with you, the one who says: "I am with him in tribulation; because he has hoped in me, I will free him, I will protect him because he has known my name" [Psalm 91:14–15]' (WABr3.238,22–239,25, §707, to the Augustinian monk Lambert Thorn, 19 January 1524; see also WABr4.205,10–13, §1107: '[…] per virtutem Christi, qui tecum est in carcere, erit etiam in tribulatione quacunque, sicut promittit fideliter et suaviter, dicens: "Cum ipso sum in tribulatione"' [WABr4.205,10–13]). To the sick and bereaved, whose sufferings Luther did not underestimate, he recalled the lesson of 2 Corinthians 12:9, that 'the power of Christ is fulfilled in [human] weakness' (WABr7.336,15–17, §2279). The cross shows above all to the bereaved that, in spite of appearances, the will of God is loving, gracious, and grace-filled (Arnold 1996: 545–6). To victims of 'spiritual sadness', Luther wrote, exhorting them to pray to God to protect them from the temptations of the devil 'through the Lord Christ' (WABr9.44,9–10, §3441). 'Spit on the devil and say, "Have I sinned? Well! So I have sinned, and I am sorry. Christ has taken all the sins of the whole world away […]; so it is certain that my sins have been taken away too"' (WABr10,239,13–16, §3837). Luther reminded all his correspondents who doubted the grace of God how much the Son reveals the true face of the Father:

> Among all God's commandments, the greatest is that we must model ourselves on his beloved Son, our Saviour Jesus Christ. He must be each day the most beautiful mirror of our hearts, in which we can see how much God loves us, and how greatly, as a good God, he has taken care of us in giving us his Son. It is right there, right there I say, that we truly learn to understand predestination, and nowhere else. (WABr12.136,41–46, §4224a, cf. WABr11.166,14–16, §4144)

'I know of no other God in heaven or on earth than the one who speaks and acts towards me as I see him in Christ' (WA45.517,10–11).

At the same time, alongside the comforting nearness of Christ, Luther's correspondence stressed Christ's lordship over the world. When, in thousands of letters, Luther spoke to his correspondents of weighty political events, religious questions, or even unusual phenomena or events, he put them all in relation to the sovereignty of Christ. When these events are positive (e.g., the expansion of the Reformation), Luther attributed them to the work of the Lord (Arnold 1996: 152–60); when they are negative (the persecution of Protestants, his own illnesses, etc.), Luther confessed, or appealed through prayer, to the victory and lordship of Christ, who reigns even at the present moment: 'The one we preach, confess, and adore sits at the right hand of God the Father. He himself will see how to scatter and confound the designs and fervour of his enemies, as Psalm 2 teaches us' (WABr10.526,3–5, §3967, cf. Arnold 1996: 164–73). Luther's prayers are particularly ardent in the 1540s, when his Christology is strongly marked by eschatology: in a world hastening to its own ruin, the coming of Christ alone at the 'dear final day' (*lieber jüngster Tag*) will bring deliverance to believers (Lienhard 1973; Arnold 1996: 165–6).

In these ways then, Luther does not underestimate the 'beyond us' of the reality of Christ, even if Christ's work is effected 'for us' and through faith is to be found 'in us'.

II.7. The Reception of Luther's Christology by the First Adherents of the Reformation

Martin Luther transmitted to his wide readership from the 1520s the extremely reassuring and comforting vision of Christ which he had finally grasped: Jesus Christ is not a terrifying judge, but our advocate with the Father; he is the very expression of the Father's mercy. The *Flugschriften* in favour of the Reformation of 1521–2 witness to Luther's influence: the uneducated laity, as well as the lettered clergy, understood the saving action of Jesus Christ through pure grace. They equally understood that all they had to do was to receive this salvation through faith, and they did not forget the ethical consequences of their union with Christ through faith.

Some authors of *Flugschriften* deemed the birth of Jesus Christ 'the eternal day of salvation' ('ayn Ewyger Tag Des Haylss') (Urbanus Rhegius, *Ein Sermon von dem dritten Gebot. Wie man christlich feiern soll*, 1522, in Hohenberger 1996: 385). '[…] let us believe in Christ alone, for he is the rock from which milk and honey flow, as Moses said' (Deut. 32:13), confessed Sergeant Wolfgang Zierer, from Salzburg, who insists on the sufficient grace of Christ (*Ein Christenlich Gesprech / von ainem Waldbru(o)der / vnd ainem waysen*, 1522, in Hohenberger 1996: 261). Another soldier, Haug Marschalck, the son of shop owners from Memmingen, extended this message by developing the double commandment of love (for God and for neighbour), a commandment which can only be accomplished in the imitation of Christ. Only a strong faith, rooted in Christ, is of use for salvation, and this faith implies consequences for our love of neighbour. For Marschalck, who repeated the marital metaphor employed by Luther, the Christian is capable of acting altruistically because he benefits him-self from the 'joyful exchange' (*fröhlicher Wechsel*) (...*Spyegel der Blinden*, 1522, in Hohenberger 1996: 264).

Another significant witness confirms this positive reception of Luther's conception of Jesus Christ: Katharina Zell-Schütz (1498–1562), wife of the Strasbourg reformer Matthew Zell and a figure central for the Reformation in Strasbourg. In an autobio-graphical passage in her correspondence with Ludwig Rabus, Katharina related how Luther had enabled her to surmount her spiritual crisis:

> God had pity on us and on many [other] people; he rose up and sent the most dear and now blessed Dr Martin Luther. By his words and writings, this man painted a picture for me and for others of the Lord Jesus Christ so admirable [den Herren Jesum Christum so lieblich fürschrieben] that I believed myself drawn up from the bowels of the earth and led on earth, or rather, drawn up from a horrible and bit-ter hell in order to be placed in the Kingdom of Heaven, sweet and dear. (*Ein Brieff an die gantze Burgerschafft der Statt Straßburg...Betreffend Herr Ludwigen Rabus...*, 1557, in Schütz-Zell 1999: 2.171, cf. her letter to Kaspar Schwenckfeld, 19 October 1553: '[...] thereafter he freed me from my fear and sent me and many poor, troubled consciences the dear and (I hope) now blessed Martin Luther, who showed me my error and pointed me to Christ, in whom I was to find rest', Schütz-Zell 1999: 2.145)

These statements bear witness that the Christological message of Luther formed for his readership a huge novelty and a powerful comfort.

III. CURRENT RESEARCH PRIORITIES

Since the fundamental synthesis by Marc Lienhard of the stages and themes of Luther's Christology across his work, various important studies have analysed more limited por-tions of Luther's work: academic debates (Schmidt 1990), hymns (Veit 1986; Burba 1956), letters (Arnold 1996: 2005) sermons (Asendorf 1988), or Luther's exegesis of a particular biblical text, such as Psalm 22 (Wolff 2005). Other books have discussed Christological themes across the corpus of Luther's writings: the *duellum mirabile* (Rieske-Braun 1999), Christ's ministries (Bornkamm 1998). Without fundamentally upsetting the image given by Lienhard, these studies have clarified his conclusions and sometimes softened his stance. Perhaps the time has come for a new synthesis, which takes account of what the past four decades of Luther studies has brought to the table, not only the develop-ments within Luther's thought, but also the variations and nuances consequent to the literary genre in use.

Without doubt, such a synthesis would have to highlight the importance of Luther's writings on the Jews and Muslims, about which our understanding has recently been improved (see Ehmann 2008). If Luther's Christological reflections are undertaken primarily in an internal Christian perspective, the importance of the work and the person of Christ for Luther is not without consequence for the way in which he studies other religions, especially when they dispute the divinity of Christ. It is the case that, contrary to Christologies which have been, since the final third of the twentieth century, inclusive and in which the love of God is not 'used up' in Jesus Christ as the Christian tradition has understood him (Hick 1982; Samartha 1990), Luther, as we have seen, holds to an exclusivist position, according to which God allows himself to be known totally in the Jesus Christ revealed in the gospels.

Thus, when Luther rebuffed the supplication of Josel de Rosheim in favour of his fellow Jews in Saxony, he justified his position in these terms:

> 'I have also read your rabbis [...]. But they can do no more than cry that [Jesus Christ] was a Jew crucified and condemned. However, all your ancestors have never left a saint or a prophet without condemning him, stoning him, and making a martyr out of him. They too had to be condemned, these saints and prophets, if your opinion is correct that Jesus of Nazareth had to be crucified and condemned by you the Jews [...]. (WABr8.90,34–41; 91,56–60, §3157)

When Luther asked the magistrates of Basel for permission to allow an edition of the Qu'ran to be printed by Johannes Oporinus, it is again concern for the honour of Christ which is most important for him:

> What has pushed me is that we will never know how the more to displease Muhammad and the Turks, nor how to do them more wrong [...] than by unveiling the Qu'ran to Christians, that they can see what a damnable, ignominious, and hopeless book it is. [...] That is why, dear and kind lords, I ask you in a friendly and Christian spirit not to prevent the publication of this book, for the honour of Christ, for the good of believers, for the harm of the Turks, and for the grief of the devil.
>
> (27 October 1542, WABr10.162,32–38,48–51, §3892; cf. WABr8.225,9–11, §3230: 'At Christus memor sit pauperum suorum et ostendat aliquando virtutem suam in hostem superbum et crudelissimum Mahumeten, Amen'; WABr8.225,9–11)

In this age of interreligious dialogue, a historical and theological study of Luther's Christology in these texts seems indispensable.

It would further be of great use, following the works of Marc Lienhard (1991: 109) and Uwe Rieske-Braun (1999: 258), no longer to separate the cross and resurrection in Luther's message: for too long, research has preferred Luther's 'theology of the cross' (*theologia crucis*), but Luther's Christology is equally a Christology of the resurrection. In dividing the cross and the resurrection, we run the major risk of breathing new life into the suffering, sentimental piety which Luther precisely went out of his way to combat.

REFERENCES

Allgaier, Walter (1996). '"Der fröhliche Wechsel" bei Martin Luther. Eine Untersuchung zu Christologie und Soteriologie bei Luther unter besonderer Berücksichtigung der Schriften bis 1521', Thesis in Theology, University of Erlangen-Nürnberg.

Althaus, Paul (1962). *Die Theologie Martin Luthers. Gütersloh*, 5th edn., 1980. English translation: *The Theology of Martin Luther*, trans. Robert C. Schultz. Philadelphia: Fortress, 1966.

Arnold, Matthieu (1996). *La Correspondance de Luther. Étude historique, littéraire et théologique*. Mainz: von Zabern.

—— (2004). 'Des bienfaits du Repas de Dieu, reçu dans la foi. Quelques sermons de Martin Luther sur l'institution de la Cène'. In *Le Repas de Dieu / Das Mahl Gottes*, ed. Christian Grappe. Tübingen: Mohr/Siebeck, 325–42.

—— (2005). 'La christologie de Martin Luther d'après sa correspondance'. *Revue d'Histoire et de Philosophie religieuses* 85: 151–69.

—— (2013). 'Philippiens 2, 5(6)–11 dans l'exégèse des Réformateurs du XVI siècle'. In *Philippiens 2, 5–11. La kénose du Christ*, ed. Matthieu Arnold, Gilbert Daher, Annie Noblesse-Rocher. Paris: Chef, 115–26.

Asendorf, Ulrich (1988). *Die Theologie Luthers nach seinen Predigten*. Göttingen: Vandenhoek & Ruprecht.

Aulén, Gustaf (1930). *Das christliche Gottesbild in Vergangenheit und Gegenwart*. Gütersloh: Bertelsmann. English translation: *Christus Victor*. London: SPCK, 1931.

Bayer, Oswald (2003). 'Das Wort ward Fleisch. Luthers Christologie als Lehre von der Idiomenkommunikation'. In *Jesus Christus—Gott für uns*, ed. Friedrich-Otto Scharbau. Erlangen: Martin-Luther-Verlag, 58–101.

Beer, Theobald (1974). *Der fröhliche Wechsel und Streit. Grundzüge der Theologie Martin Luthers*, 2 vols. Leipzig: St.-Benno-Verlag. 2nd. rev. edn.: Einsiedeln: Johannes-Verlag, 1980.

Bornkamm, Karin (1998). *Christus—König und Priester, Das Amt Christi bei Luther im Verhältnis zur Vor- und Nachgeschichte*. Tübingen: Mohr/Siebeck.

Burba, Klaus (1956). *Die Christologie in Luthers Liedern*. Gütersloh: Bertelsmann.

Congar, Yves (1964). 'Regard et réflexions sur la christologie de Luther'. In Congar, *Chrétiens en dialogue*. Paris: Cerf, 453–89.

Ebeling, Gerhard (1985). 'Die königlich-priesterliche Freiheit'. In Ebeling, *Lutherstudien, t. III*. Tübingen: Mohr/Siebeck.

—— (1997). *Luthers Seelsorge Theologie in der Vielfalt der Lebenssituationen an seinen Briefen dargestellt*. Tübingen: Mohr/Siebeck.

Ehmann, Johannes (2008). *Luther, Türken und Islam*. Gütersloh: Gütersloher Verlagshaus.

Hamm, Berndt (2000). 'Between Severity and Mercy. Three Models of Pre-Reformation Urban Reform Preaching: Savonarola—Staupitz—Geiler'. In *Continuity and Change: The Harvest of Late Medieval and Reformation History*, ed. Robert J. Bast and Andrew C. Gow. Leiden: Brill, 321–58.

—— (2004). 'Die "nahe Gnade"—innovative Züge der spätmittelalterlichen Theologie und Frömmigkeit'. In *'Herbst des Mittelalters'? Fragen zur Bewertung des 14. und 15. Jahrhunderts*, ed. Jan A. Aertsen and Martin Pickavé. Berlin: de Gruyter, 541–57.

—— (2010). 'Der Weg zum Himmel und die nahe Gnade. Neue Formen der spätmittelalterlichen Frömmigkeit am Beispiel Ulms und des Mediums Einblattdruck'. In *Between Lay Piety and Academic Theology: Studies Presented to Christoph Burger on the Occasion of his 65th Birthday*, ed. Ulrike Hascher-Burger, August den Hollander, and Wim Janse. Leiden: Brill, 453–96.

Harnack, Theodosius (1862/1886). *Luthers Theologie mit besonderer Beziehung auf seine Versöhnungs- und Erlösungslehre*, 2 vols. Erlangen: Blaesing. 2nd edn. Munich: Kaiser, 1927.

Hick, John (1982). *God Has Many Names*. Philadelphia: Westminster, 1982.

Hoffman, Johann Christian Konrad von (1857–9). *Schutzschriften...Christi Versöhnungswerk betreffend...* Nördlingen: Beck.

—— (1882–5). *Der Schriftbeweis. Ein theologischer Versuch*, 2 vols. Nördlingen: Beck.

Hohenberger, Thomas (1996). *Lutherische Rechtfertigungslehre in den reformatorischen Flugschriften der Jahre 1521–22*. Tübingen: Mohr/Siebeck.

Holl, Karl (1932). *Gesammelte Aufsätze*, t. I, 6. Tübingen: Mohr/Siebeck.

Leppin, Volker (2006). *Martin Luther*. Darmstadt: Wissenschaftliche Buchgesellschaft.

Lienhard, Marc (1973). *Luther, témoin de Jésus-Christ. Les étapes et les thèmes de la christologie du réformateur*. Paris: Cerf. German translation: *Luthers Christologische Zeugnis*. Berlin: Evangelisches Verlagsanstalt, 1980. English translation: *Martin Luther's Witness to Jesus Christ*. Minneapolis: Augsburg, 1982.

—— (1983). 'Luthers Christuszeugnis'. In *Leben und Werk Martin Luthers von 1526 bis 1546*, ed. Helmar Junghans. Göttingen: Vandenhoeck & Ruprecht, 1.77–92, 2.748–55.

—— (1991). *Au cœur de la foi de Luther: Jésus-Christ*. Paris: Desclée.

Lohse, Bernhard (1995). *Luthers Theologie in ihrer historischen Entwicklung und in ihrem systematischen Zusammenhang*. Göttingen: Vandenhoeck & Ruprecht. English translation: *Martin Luther's Theology*, trans. Roy Harrisville. Minneapolis: Fortress, 1999.

Mennecke-Haustein, Ute (1989). *Luthers Trostbriefe*. Gütersloh: Mohn.

Nilsson, Kjell Ove (1996). *Simul. Das Miteinander von Göttlichem und Menschlichem in Luthers Theologie*. Göttingen: Vandenhoeck & Ruprecht.

Peters, Albrecht (1991). *Kommentar zu Luthers Katechismen. Bd. 2: Der Glaube—Das Apostolikum*, ed. Gottfried Seebaß. Göttingen: Vandenhoeck & Ruprecht.

Prenter, Regin (1953). *Spiritus Creator*, trans. John M. Jensen. Minneapolis: Augsburg.

Rieske-Braun, Uwe (1999). *Duellum mirabile. Studien zum Kampfmotiv in Martin Luthers Theologie*. Göttingen: Vandenhoeck & Ruprecht.

Ritschl, Albrecht (1870–4). *Die christliche Lehre von der Rechtfertigung und Versöhnung*, 3 vols. Bonn: Marcus.

Samartha, Stanley J. (1990). *One Christ, Many Religions*. Maryknoll, NY: Orbis.

Schmidt, Axel (1990). *Die Christologie in Martin Luthers späten Disputationen*, St. Ottilien: EOS-Verlag.

Schütz-Zell, Katharina (1999). *The Writings*, ed. Elsie Anne McKee. Leiden: Brill.

Schwarz, Reinhard (1966). 'Gott ist Mensch. Zur Lehre von der Person Christi bei den Ockhamisten und bei Luther'. *Zeitschrift für Theologie und Kirche* 63: 289–351.

Seeberg, Erich (1937). *Luthers Theologie*, vol. 2: *Christus. Wirklichkeit und Urbild*. Stuttgart: Kohlhammer.

Siggins, Ian D. Kingston (1970). *Martin Luther's Doctrine of Christ*. New Haven: Yale University Press.

Thomasius, Gottfried (1857a). *Christi Person und Werk. Darstellung der evangelisch-lutherischen Dogmatik vom Mittelpunkte der Christologie aus*, t. II, *Die Person des Mittlers*. Erlangen: Blaesing.

——(1857b). *Das Bekenntniss der lutherischen Kirche von der Versöhnung und die Versöhnungslehre D. Chr. K. v. Hofmann's. Mit einem Nachwort von D. Th. Harnack*. Erlangen: Blaesing.

Veit, Patrice (1986). *Das Kirchenlied in der Reformation Martin Luthers. Eine thematische und semantische Untersuchung*. Stuttgart: Steiner.

Wolff, Jens (2005). *Metapher und Kreuz. Studien zu Luthers Christusbild*. Tübingen: Mohr/Siebeck.

CHAPTER 20

···

LUTHER ON THE HOLY SPIRIT AND HIS USE OF GOD'S WORD

···

JEFFREY G. SILCOCK

THIS chapter begins by noting a few milestones in Luther research on the Holy Spirit before turning to a discussion of the topic itself. The major part of the chapter focuses on the Spirit's work in and through the Word in its three-fold form as written, proclaimed, and sacramentally enacted. The indivisibility of the Word and the Spirit is explored at some length because of its importance for Luther's understanding of the Spirit. A discussion of the role of the Spirit in sanctification (under the heading: good works or the fruits of faith) completes the treatment of the work of the Spirit in Luther's theology. The chapter concludes with a section devoted to the person of the Holy Spirit within the context of Trinitarian theology. The location of this section at the end of the chapter reflects the epistemological fact that we can only know the person of the Spirit through his work.

I. MILESTONES IN LUTHER RESEARCH

Research into Luther's understanding of the Holy Spirit begins at the turn of the last century with the publication of Rudolf Otto's book *Die Anschauung vom heiligen Geiste bei Luther* in 1898. Working predominantly with a Ritschlian interpretation of Christianity, he concludes that the Holy Spirit has no vital significance for Luther's theology and prefers to understand the work of the Spirit psychologically. In fact, Otto could not even say that Luther upholds the tradition of the church in teaching that the Holy Spirit is the third person of the Trinity. Otto's contemporary Erich Seeberg sums up Luther's basic approach to the Spirit with the words: 'The eternal is present in the finite' (Seeberg

1940: 52–3). Seeberg, however, is not particularly interested in the classical questions of Trinitarian theology, for example the distinction between the three persons of the Godhead. He also holds that Luther ascribes no importance to the immanent Trinity, that God is God in himself, but puts all the emphasis on the economic Trinity, that God is God in his saving work in the Son and in the Spirit in the economy of salvation.

Regin Prenter's 1946 dissertation *Spiritus Creator* (English: 1953; German: 1954) is the most comprehensive presentation of Luther's pneumatology in the twentieth century. Prenter begins his book with the assertion that 'the concept of the Holy Spirit completely dominates Luther's theology' (Prenter 1953: ix). His emphasis on Luther's pneumatic realism is a necessary corrective to the earlier research of Otto and Seeberg, which sees Luther's thought very much in line with the psychological and moral spiritualism of the modern age. Prenter, however, claims that Luther has no 'doctrine' of the Spirit in the sense of a rationally consistent theory that is beyond question. In fact, he holds that Luther's testimony to the Spirit contains a 'hiatus' in his treatment of predestination (Prenter 1953: 196 passim). Prenter claims to be following Luther in refusing to rationalize these tensions or to smooth them out to form a logically coherent system. Commendable as that may be, it is just here, with the assertion of a 'hiatus' in Luther's theology of the Spirit, that Prenter betrays his Barthian influence. He uses this putative *diastasis* to undermine the certainty that God's Spirit has bound himself to his appointed means and does not fail to act through them. He goes beyond the traditional *topos* of divine freedom, which Luther never denies, when he stresses the disjunction in Luther between *gratia* and *donum*. The fact that the Spirit may not always create faith in those who hear the Word is another matter.

The most recent piece of Luther research on the Holy Spirit is the 2005 dissertation by the Finnish scholar Pekka Kärkkäinen, which focuses specifically on Luther's Trinitarian theology of the Holy Spirit (*Luthers Trinitarische Theologie des Heiligen Geistes*). He notes that Luther is the first theologian to treat the Spirit in Trinitarian fashion in the sense that he recognizes that the Holy Spirit is the Spirit of the Father as well as of the Son. The work concentrates on Luther's Trinitarian theology of the Spirit between 1520 and 1546; the author explores the rich variety of ways in which Luther speaks of the Spirit in sermons as well as academic writings and disputations (Kärkkäinen 2005: 195–7).

II. THE WORK OF THE HOLY SPIRIT

Luther's treatment of the work of the Holy Spirit covers all items mentioned in the Third Article of the Apostles' Creed: the holy catholic church, the forgiveness of sins, the resurrection of the body, and the life everlasting. These are all God's work, carried out by the holy and life-giving Spirit, whom Luther calls the 'sanctifier' because he alone is holy and sanctifies all who have faith in Christ (BSLK 653–4; BC 435). Luther's exposition of this article in *The Large Catechism* is a 'thick' description, which, by comparison with much contemporary Western theology, is pneumatologically rich. This is one of the main primary sources for Luther's thought on the person and work of the Spirit. Space does not permit a discussion of all the items covered by the Third Article. The emphasis will be on the Word and the Spirit, and the linkage between them, understood from a Trinitarian perspective, for this is the *novum* of Luther's theology, which comes out vividly in his fight against the unbridled enthusiasm (*Schwärmerei*) of the spiritualists or 'heavenly prophets' of his day.

In his treatise *Against the Heavenly Prophets* (1525), Luther makes a vital distinction between salvation *won* and salvation *distributed*. Christ won forgiveness for all on the cross, but he did not distribute it on the cross. Rather, he distributes it here and now through the proclaimed gospel and the enacted sacraments. It is Christ's work on the cross that acquired salvation *for* us, and Christ's work through the Word and the sacraments that distributes it *to* us, and creates and sustains faith *in* us (WA18.203,27–38; LW40.213–214). Again, in the same vein, the reformer maintains that Christ on the cross and all his suffering would be useless to us if we did not have the Word that announces it and brings it to us as a gift (WA18.202,34–203,2; LW40.213). Although in the treatise Luther does not expressly name the Spirit as the one who delivers the gift of salvation through the Word and the sacraments, he does make this explicit in *The Large Catechism*. There he says that God caused the Word to be published and proclaimed, in which he has given the Holy Spirit to offer and apply to us the treasure of Christ's redemptive work on the cross (BSLK 654; BC 436). This 'word-event' is central to Luther's hermeneutic of contemporaneity, for, in a prophetic sense, he bridges Lessing's great ditch of history or the Kantian gap with 'the living Spirit-filled Word which both brings God's power and presence into the present as well as draws the reader into the experience of the text' (Maschke et al. 2001: 182).

II.1. The Church and the Means of the Spirit

The Holy Spirit not only brings Christ out of the past into our present through the Word; the Spirit also brings us to Christ. Thus, Luther says in *The Large Catechism* that the Spirit 'first leads us into his holy community, placing us in the church's lap, where he preaches to us and brings us to Christ' (BSLK 654; BC 435–6). Since the Spirit leads us to Christ by first bringing us into the holy community, the Spirit, Christ, and the church are inseparably united. Luther, therefore, comes full circle when he maintains that 'where Christ is not preached, there is no Holy Spirit to create, call, and gather the Christian church, apart from which no one can come to the Lord Christ' (BSLK 655; BC 436). In other words, the oral Word of the gospel is essential to the church. This agrees with Luther's most concise definition of the church, given in the context of a doctoral disputation (1542): *ubi verbum, ibi ecclesia*—where the Word is, there is the church (WA39,2.176,8–9). For God's Word is efficacious and cannot be without God's people, and conversely, God's people cannot exist without God's Word (*On the Councils and the Church*, 1539, WA50.628,29–630,2; LW41:148–150). Thus, the church is a 'creature of the gospel' (*Explanations of the Disputation Concerning the Value of Indulgences*, 1519, WA2.430,6–7). Everything that Luther says about the church can be deduced from this axiom.

Luther has an unshakeable confidence in the power of God's Word, the principal means of the Spirit. In contrast to Catholic understanding, pneumatology for Luther is the framework for ecclesiology and not vice versa. Where the Spirit is, there is the church. But he does not say that where the church is, there is the Spirit. The Spirit is bound to the Word so that the Spirit is present where the Word is preached. This conviction, which in Latin would read *ubi verbum, ibi Spiritus Sanctus*, is consonant with Luther's basic axiom, *ubi verbum, ibi ecclesia*.

The church is not only called into existence by the Spirit through the Word. It also has the task of handing on the Word. The fundamental form of the means of the Spirit is the oral Word of the gospel, by which the forgiveness of sins is preached to the whole world. The proclamation of the gospel in the divine service (*Gottesdienst*) is a continuation of Jesus' own preaching, for Christ himself speaks to the church today through the proclaimed Word by the power of the Spirit. Luther says in a sermon on the gospel of John (1537), 'God has decreed that no one can or will believe or receive the Holy Spirit without that gospel which is preached or taught by word of mouth' (WA46.582,17–19; LW22.54).

Luther agrees with the patristic tradition that God himself is the active subject in the divine service. The apostles and pastors are nothing but instruments through which Christ brings the gospel from the Father to us. Thus, when Christians receive the absolution, hear a sermon, or receive the sacrament, they can say, 'Today I beheld God's Word and work. Yes, I saw and heard God himself preaching and baptising.' Luther says, 'To be sure, the tongue, the voice, the hands, etc., are those of a human being; but the Word and the ministry are really those of the Divine Majesty himself' (WA45.521; LW24.67; cf. WATR3.669–674, §3868).

Luther does not attempt to explain, on the basis of predestination or human logic, why the proclaimed Word sometimes meets with unbelief. He simply acknowledges it to be a mystery which we will not understand this side of the grave. The important thing that Luther emphasizes is that when the Word is not heard with faith, this does not mean that the Spirit is absent or the Word ineffective. Thus, he says in his preaching on John's gospel (1538), 'The fact that all do not believe the Word, or come to believe and to receive the Holy Spirit, through the Word, does not detract from the efficacy of the gospel' (WA46.582,40–583,9; LW22.55). The preacher is simply the mouthpiece of God and has no control over how the Word is received. We cannot say why the Spirit works efficaciously in some and not in others, why some believe the gospel while others reject it. Our task, Luther says, is to remain faithful in preaching and hearing and to leave the rest to God; for 'he will move hearts as he wills' (WA 39,1,370,10–11).

III. WORD AND SPIRIT

Luther's understanding of the work of the Holy Spirit was developed principally in his dispute with the spiritualists or enthusiasts (*Schwärmer*), the 'radical' reformers from the 'left wing' of the Reformation, e.g., Thomas Müntzer, Andreas Bodenstein von

Karlstadt, and the Zwickau prophets, who wanted to bring the Reformation about by force (the law), which was entirely contrary to Luther's confessional principle: not with human power but by the Word (*sine vi humana, sed verbo*). Müntzer and his followers were far more politically motivated than Luther and took a leading role in the Peasants' Revolt. Luther called him a murderer, and Müntzer in turn condemned Luther as 'the spiritless, soft-living flesh at Wittenberg'. In Luther's estimate Müntzer's preaching was fanatical (*schwärmerisch*), for he held that God's Word works immediately in the human heart through inner illumination and visions given by the Holy Spirit, without any external means. He denounced the spiritualists as false prophets in a letter to Melanchthon dated 13 January 1522 where he remarked that they know of no suffering and cross, but only of glory and triumph (WABr2.423, §449; LW38.366).

One of the most misunderstood aspects of Luther's teaching about the Word and the Spirit is his unrelenting insistence that the Spirit does not speak or act apart from the Word. That is, God does not speak to us in a direct, unmediated way as in certain forms of mysticism. The classical statement on the inseparability of the Word and the Spirit appears in the *Smalcald Articles* (1537) where, *contra* the spiritualists and enthusiasts, Luther boldly asserts that 'it must be firmly maintained that God gives no one his Spirit or grace apart from the external Word which goes before' (WA50.245,6–7; BC 322). He consistently stresses this indivisible nexus between Word and Spirit. The biblical basis for this is Psalms 33:6: 'By the word of the Lord the heavens were made, and all their host by the breath of his mouth.' Here clearly word and breath/spirit (*ruah*) are set in parallel. Since God breathes out (his Spirit) to speak, it is impossible to separate the Word he speaks from the Spirit by which he speaks. As Luther says in a sermon of 1521, anyone who refuses to hear the voice gets nothing out of the breath either (WA9.632,6–8).

Luther's insistence on the inseparability of the Word and the Spirit is misunderstood when it is taken to mean a limitation of God's sovereign freedom. Luther's intention rather is to stress God's reliable promise to be present where he says he will be present. To say that God does not act salvifically apart from the means of grace is not an attempt to bind God but a recognition that God binds us to the means of grace. God can and does work outside the means of the Spirit, most obviously in the realm of creation, but also in the church. Luther is not saying categorically that God cannot act outside the means of the Spirit, but that outside these appointed means, we cannot be sure whether it is the triune God or something else. Even if it is God, outside the means of grace I cannot be sure whether God is present there for me in grace or against me in judgement. Luther holds that I can only be certain that God is there—and there for me (*pro me*)—if I seek him in the places he promises to be found. Luther knows that God is present everywhere in the universe through his Spirit, but God does not want me to look for him everywhere. 'Seek him rather where the Word is, and there you will lay hold of him in the right way' (WA19.492,22–24; LW36.342). When we seek him in the places where he wants to be found, we can be sure that he will be present for us in grace. The crucial point is that we do not bind God, but God binds us to the means of the Spirit while remaining free himself. The reason he binds us is that he wants us to seek him where he has promised to be found: in his holy Word and sacraments.

Luther's mature theology of grace is perhaps nowhere more powerfully expressed than in his treatise *Against the Heavenly Prophets*, where he polemicizes against Karlstadt, Müntzer, and the other 'new prophets' who play the Spirit off against the external means of grace by denigrating the oral Word of the gospel and the humble elements of water, bread, and wine used in the sacraments. In a key passage Luther sums up his polemic against Karlstadt in these words: 'With all his mouthing of the words, "Spirit, Spirit, Spirit," he tears down the bridge, the path, the way, the ladder, and all the means by which the Spirit comes to you' (WA18.137,12–19; LW40.147).

Luther holds that God deals with us in two ways: inwardly and outwardly—inwardly, by means of faith and other spiritual gifts; outwardly, through the gospel, baptism, and the sacrament of the altar, through which, as through means or instruments, the Holy Spirit comes to us. But the relationship between these two ways is crucial. Luther argues, *contra* Karlstadt and the spiritualists, that, according to the order established by God, the external mode comes first and forms the basis for the internal mode (WA18.136,9–15; LW40.146). The direction, therefore, of the divinely established *ordo* is from heaven to earth, from God to his creation, from outside to inside, and not the reverse. But the heavenly prophets 'reverse this order' and preach their own enthusiasm in place of the divine Spirit, who works in the heart from outside through the gospel (WA18.137,20–138,2; LW40.146–147). He maintains that 'Dr. Karlstadt and these spirits replace the highest with the lowest, the best with the least, the first with the last. Yet he wants to be considered the greatest spirit of all—he who has devoured the Holy Spirit feathers and all' (WA18.66,18–21; LW40.83).

Neo-Protestantism has fundamentally misunderstood Luther's emphasis on the indispensability of the external Word, which is enacted in the sermon and the sacrament. Modern subjectivity, under the influence of Hegel, sees these external things as nothing more than mere starting points for higher forms of spirituality, which are completely free of such primitive devices as the external means of grace and depend solely on the mind. Hegel posits a fundamental disjunction between the infinite and the finite so that, on the one hand, true spirituality is completely non-material and, on the other, finite, material things such as water, bread, and wine, cannot mediate the presence of the infinite God. Modern Protestantism in the Enlightenment tradition, aided and abetted by a postmodern neo-gnosticism, will inevitably privilege pure inwardness over externality because of its inability to conceive of the interpenetration of the spiritual and the material (Bayer 2008: 249–53).

The fundamental failure of modern Protestantism to understand Luther at this point is rooted in its failure to understand his crucial emphasis on the *communicatio idiomatum* (communication of attributes). This axiom, which is central to both the theology of Johann Hamann and his contemporary interpreter, Oswald Bayer, posits that the physical and spiritual, although opposites, not only coexist but also mutually interpenetrate, in a *coincidentia oppositorum* (Bayer 2012: 14,80–81,105,170,215). Asendorf (2004) notes that Luther cites Mary as the quintessential, anti-spiritualistic paradigm because in her body, the spiritual and the temporal, true deity and true humanity, are joined together through the Word, and this is precisely the work of the Holy Spirit: to bring heaven and earth together, as happens also in the Lord's Supper, where heaven comes down to earth and earth is taken up into heaven (Maschke et al. 2001: 12–16).

We said earlier that Luther's understanding of the work of the Spirit was developed primarily in his dispute with the *Schwärmer* of his day. Simeon Zahl suggests that Luther's pneumatology has been somewhat 'underexplored' in Luther studies (Zahl 2010: 174). Luther is not shy when it comes to speaking of the experience of the Spirit. The problem for him is 'unmediated experience', for when Luther speaks of experience he normally takes it to mean the experience of God's Word. Zahl suggests that an area of research that Luther scholarship might profitably consider is a re-examination of Luther's insistence on the *verbum externum* but this time in collaboration with the best recent scholarship from the charismatic and Pentecostal tradition, which is keen on exploring an affective pneumatology or pneumatology of experience that takes cognisance of Luther's strictures against an unmediated personal experience of the Spirit (Zahl 2010: 1–30, 158–94).

III.1. The Oral Word

If the oral Word is the primary means of the Spirit, then to speak of the Word *and* the sacraments could give the impression that the sacraments are an 'addition' to the Word and not really necessary. Some modern Protestants will ask why we even need the sacraments and what they could possibly offer that we do not already receive through the Word since both convey the same grace, the same salvation, and the same Spirit. Prenter is correct in holding that the *et* connecting the *verbum* and *sacramenta* is a true *et*, not a *sive*. 'The Reformation knows no *verbum*, no sermon, except in indissoluble connection with the Sacraments, and no Sacraments independent of the sermon' (Prenter 1965: 132). A rejection of the sacraments, therefore, is tantamount to a rejection of the gospel. The sacraments are needed to prevent the gospel from being turned into an ideology just as much as the gospel is needed to prevent the sacraments from being understood as magical rites. The oral Word of the gospel interprets the sacraments, and the sacraments enact the gospel.

Central to Luther's theology of proclamation is his distinction between law and gospel. To make a proper distinction between these two parts of God's Word is, for him, the great art of the true theologian. The law says: Do this. The gospel (speaking the words of Christ) says: I have done it for you. Luther's great evangelical insight is that Christ, who is the chief content of the Bible, is essentially the saviour of sinners, not a lawgiver or preacher of the law. Yet he can also preach the law, and he does so far more radically than Moses ever did, as we see from parts of the Sermon on the Mount (Matt. 5:21–48) (WA32.354,31–407,4; LW21.67–129). Luther calls this his 'alien work' (*opus alienum*), while his 'proper work' (*opus proprium*), the work for which he was sent (John 3:16–17), is his gospel work: to forgive sins and comfort troubled consciences (Althaus 1966: 251–66; Lohse 1999: 267–73; Bayer 2008: 58–64; Bayer 2009).

There is a parallel here between the work of Christ and the work of the Holy Spirit since the Spirit continues the work of Christ in the church today. The Spirit, like Christ, also has his alien (law) work, which is meant to prepare the heart for his proper (gospel) work. Luther asserts in his *First Disputation against the Antinomians* (1537) that when the Spirit speaks through the written code of the law, he is acting in his divine majesty and not as saviour, so that the Word he speaks is the Word of the eternal and omni¬potent God, which is a fire in the conscience. But when the Spirit is wrapped in tongues and spiritual gifts (Acts 2) and speaks through the gospel, he is called gift because he sanctifies and makes alive (WA39.1,370,18–371,1; cf. 39.1,17–20). In his treatise *On Bound Choice* (1525) Luther argues against Erasmus that God acts paradoxically in a way that human reason will never comprehend, for 'God kills in order to make alive' (WA18.633,9–10; LW33.62); he kills the sinful flesh through the law in order to bring the saint to life through the gospel. This dynamic of the crucifixion of the old and the resurrection of the new is enacted by the Spirit throughout the life of the baptized, for this side of heaven Christians remain saints and sinners at the same time (Rom. 7:15–25). The task of the law, therefore, is to bring people to the point where they are receptive to hearing the gospel.

Luther maintains in his *Lectures on Galatians* (1535) that the law's function is not only to disclose sin but also to drive us to Christ. The law, however, cannot do this by itself but only through the power of the Spirit, and then only in conjunction with the gospel (WA40,1.489,27–490,24; LW26.315–316). Luther insists that the law, in its accusing role, can never convey the Spirit as gift, for this happens only through the gospel. After the law exposes sin and accuses the conscience, the Spirit, working through the gospel, presses the law into the service of the gospel and makes it lead the penitent to Christ (WA40,1.529,15–532,36; LW26.345–7; on Gal. 3:24). Luther sets this out clearly in his *Second and Third Disputation against the Antinomians* (1538), where he says emphatically that *paedagogus in Christum* is 'a word of consolation, and the most proper and delight¬ful defini¬tion of the Law' (WA39,1.441,11–12, 532,9–539,2, 542,3–543,3).

Notwithstanding this positive definition of the law, its main tenor in Luther's theology seems to be overwhelmingly negative. This is because so much of what he says about the law is uttered in the context of sin and grace, where the law works antithetically to the gospel. But outside that context Luther speaks very positively about the law and repeatedly says that Christians can delight in it, for it is God's good gift which he originally gave to promote life and human flourishing (cf. Wöhle 1998 passim). The Ten Commandments instruct believers in the good works that are pleasing to God and the Holy Spirit empowers them to do them. Luther demonstrates this in his exposition of the Decalogue in *The Large Catechism* even if he does not expressly mention the Spirit as often as he might.

There can be no doubt that Luther privileges the oral Word over the written Word since for him the Word is first and foremost the *viva vox Dei*. Christ did not commission his apostles to write but to preach. Luther emphasizes in an Advent sermon (1522) that the church is a 'mouth-house, not a pen-house' (WA10,1,2.48,5–6). On the other hand, Luther knows that these two forms of the Word cannot be separated, for the proclaimed Word is grounded in the written Word and needs the written Word as a normative criterion to preserve it from error. The oral Word and the written Word belong together because in and through both the Holy Spirit communicates and mediates Jesus Christ the saviour, who is the chief content of the Bible.

III.2. The Written Word

Luther's key Christological axiom is *Was Christum treibet* (what promotes Christ). Since this highlights the heart of the gospel, it functions as the main criterion of inspiration and canonicity. 'All the genuine sacred books agree on this, that all of them preach and promote [*treiben*] Christ. And that is the true touchstone by which to judge all the books of the Bible: do they promote Christ or not?... Whatever does not teach Christ is not apostolic' (WADB7.384,25–32; LW35.396 alt.). Hermann Sasse regards this thesis as one of Luther's great Reformation discoveries. It clearly states that the church has only one internal criterion for recognizing what is to be accepted as Word of God, namely, the gospel of Christ and the inner testimony of the Holy Spirit (Kadai 1967: 87–8). Even if Luther elevates the material criterion (gospel) in contradistinction to a purely formal way of approaching the authority of Scripture (canon), we need to keep in mind that the Spirit that 'promotes Christ' is always bound to the written words of Scripture. If, as Luther says in his treatise *Avoiding Human Doctrines* (1522), all Scripture points to Christ alone (WA10,2.73,15–17; LW35.132), the King of Scripture (WA40,1.459,16; LW26.295), then this is because the inspired Scriptures themselves are full of the Spirit whose office and function it is to bear witness to Christ (John 14:26).

Hamann remarks that the inspiration of Scripture is just as great an act of abasement and condescension as the creation of the world by the Father and the incarnation of the Son (Betz 2009: 44). In summing up his *London Writings*, he comments, 'It is proper to the unity of divine revelation that the Spirit of GOd [*sic*] should have lowered himself and emptied himself of his majesty through the style of the holy men he inspired, just as the Son of God did by assuming the form of a servant, and just as the entire creation is a work of the greatest humility' (Betz 2009: 118–19). The kenotic condescension of the Spirit in graciously accommodating himself to the human author needs to be matched by a corresponding humility on the part of the reader if the reader is to interpret the Scriptures properly. Indeed, the hermeneutical humility of the reader before the text of the *sacra pagina* is one of the criteria needed by the 'virtuous reader' in order to hear what the Spirit is saying to the church today through the Christian Scriptures.

Apart from a humble, receptive disposition (*vita passiva*), an attentive reading of Scripture also requires the proper tools. Luther breaks with the medieval tradition by giving first place to grammar and rhetoric (in that order) rather than to dialectic (logic and philosophy) in his interpretation of Holy Scripture. But he holds that the Spirit must teach the church a 'new grammar', which is the key to understanding the new language (*nova lingua*) that theology must deploy if it is to be faithful to the divine revelation. Luther develops this at length in his *Disputation Concerning the Divinity and Humanity of Christ* (1540). He argues that it is only according to the grammar of the Spirit that the *coincidentia oppositorum* (coincidence of opposites), which was anathema to Aristotle, can form a valid proposition as in the statements, 'the creator is the creature', 'God is man', 'man is God', 'God dies', and 'the finite can contain the infinite' (WA39,2.104,10–18; 112,15–19 etc.). These formulas, which belong to the new grammar, are the Spirit's gift to the church (WA39,2.104,18–19). They enable theology to speak of the *communicatio idiomatum* (WA39,2.93,5; 111,14–16 etc.) which is impossible for philosophy but crucial for theology.

III.3. The Sacramental Word

Since the Word is the most holy thing on earth, the sacrament is made, blessed, and sanctified by it (WA10,3.70,28–30). This understanding of the constitutive nature of the Word is tied up with Luther's reformational discovery that centres on his understanding of the effective character of God's Word as *promissio*. This *verbum efficax* is, in Austin's language, a performative speech act. Luther comes to this recognition through a careful study of the function of the sacrament of penance in connection with the indulgence controversy (Bayer 1989: 164–202). At first, Luther understands the priestly words of absolution, *Ego te absolvo!* as a declarative act, or, in Austin's words, a constative speech act, which clarifies an existing situation. But once he understands God's *promissio* as the crystallization of the gospel, he realizes that the words of absolution spoken to the penitent do more than describe an existing state of affairs; they establish a new relationship with God and grant the penitent certainty of salvation through the gift of forgiveness and liberation from the grip of sin and a guilty conscience (Bayer 2007: 128–9).

In his battle with the spiritualists, Luther stresses more and more the externality of the sacrament, the very thing that the enthusiasts scorn (BSLK 708–9; BC 467). It is the nature of divine revelation that God comes to us, not as the *Deus nudus*, but clothed in flesh and blood, as in the incarnation, or veiled under the form of ordinary physical elements, as in the sacraments. In his insistence on the indissoluble unity of 'sign' and 'object' (*signum* and *res*), Luther overcomes the false spiritualization that was the fatal weakness of the Augustinian tradition and returns to the sacramental realism (the *est*) of the New Testament. According to Augustine, the sacramental sign (*signum*) points away from itself to an inner or heavenly reality (*res*). However, Luther's decisive hermeneutical insight is that the *signum* points to itself and is itself the *res* (Ringleben 2010: 154–65).

The spiritualists objected to the idea that the Spirit could only be mediated by outward means or signs. They claimed that since visible physical things are fundamentally different from invisible spiritual things, they cannot convey the Spirit or grace. A key text adduced in support of their argument was John 6:63 ('It is the Spirit that gives life. The flesh is useless'), where 'flesh' (*sarx*) stands for everything outward, visible, and physical. In his treatise against the spiritualists, *That These Words of Christ Still Stand Firm*

(1527), Luther argued that where the two words 'flesh' and 'spirit' are placed in opposition to each other in the Scriptures, flesh cannot mean Christ's body but always means the old Adamic flesh that must be opposed by the spirit (Gal. 5:16–25). Furthermore, he asserted emphatically that the Spirit cannot be with us except in material and physical things as in the Word, water, and Christ's body and in his saints on earth (WA23.193,31–33; LW37.95). In a sharp polemic in his *Confession Concerning Christ's Supper* (1528), he asserts that those who want to change God's Word from being something fleshly into being something spiritual end up changing themselves from being spiritual into being fleshly (WA26.466,19–20; LW37.322). In sum, the burden of Luther's argument against the *Schwärmer* is that the gospel, and hence the Lord's Supper, cannot be disconnected from the outward physical means of the Spirit.

The minister is the servant of Christ and the mouthpiece of the Holy Spirit in both the sermon and the sacraments. Luther, therefore, says in *The Babylonian Captivity of the Church* (1520), that we should 'receive baptism at human hands just as if Christ himself, indeed, God himself, were baptizing us with his own hands' (WA6.530,19–31; LW36.62–63; cf. 29,82). He makes the same point in *The Private Mass and the Consecration of Priests* (1533): 'For this reason [Christ] alone is and remains the one true, eternal baptizer who administers his baptism daily through our action or service until the day of judgment' (WA38.239,28–30; LW38.199). So too in the Lord's Supper, it is the minister who recites the words of institution over the gifts, but it is really Christ himself who is speaking. Therefore, in performing this speech act, the minister is standing in the place of Christ (2 Cor. 5:20) and ultimately in the place of the triune God himself.

IV. Good Works or the Fruits of Faith

We saw earlier that Luther insists, against the spiritualists, that the God-ordained order of the Christian life begins with the outward and then moves inwards. They place the mortification of the flesh prior to faith, even prior to the Word, whereas Luther argues that no one can mortify the flesh, bear the cross, and follow the example of Christ by doing good works before they are Christian and have Christ through faith in their heart as an eternal treasure. First, sin is acknowledged and forgiven by means of the Spirit working through law and gospel. Then as the Spirit gives faith where and to whom he wills through the Word, the Christian cooperates with God in the life of sanctification (WA18.139,13–26; LW40.149). Here the sinful flesh is mortified by returning again and again to baptism, and the Holy Spirit empowers the Christian to carry the cross of suffering in a life of discipleship and to be active in love and good works. All this is anchored in baptism and energized by the Spirit as he continues to work through the Word and the Supper to produce in the Christian the fruits of faith. This for Luther is the mark of true progress, yet this *progressus* is never open to empirical verification since, paradoxically, it is always in reverse. Christians progress by continually going back to their baptism and reappropriating its promise every day anew—*semper est in motu et initio*—as Luther says in his *Lectures on the Psalter* (1515–16) (WA3.47,9; LW10.53). Therefore, progress in the Christian life remains hidden (Trigg 2001: 151–73, 204–27). It is marked not by an increasing absence of sin but rather by a deeper awareness of sin and the sufficiency of God's grace. As Luther says in his *On Bound Choice*, 'the church is hidden, the saints are unknown' (WA18.652,23; LW33.89).

At the end of his magisterial tractate *The Freedom of a Christian* (1520), Luther draws attention to the outward orientation of faith which, under the impulse of the Spirit, gives itself in love to the service of the neighbour. He says that Christians do not live in themselves, but in Christ and in their neighbour...They live in Christ through faith and in their neighbour through love. By faith they are caught up beyond themselves into God. By love they descend beneath themselves into their neighbour. Yet they always remain in God and in his love (WA7,38,6–9; LW31.371). Paul speaks of faith as being active in love (Gal. 5:6) and Luther, in his preface to Paul's epistle to the Romans (1546/22), enlarges on this when he says that faith is such a 'living, busy, active, mighty thing' that it is incessantly doing good. It does not ask whether good works are to be done, but before the question is even asked it has already done them, and is constantly doing them (WADB7.10,9–13; LW35.370).

Even if the Christian life, *coram mundo*, is characterized by action, its fundamental orientation *coram Deo* is marked by passivity, for this is consistent with justification by faith and the reception of the Spirit. Strictly speaking, Christians do not 'possess' the Spirit, but the Spirit 'possesses' them. They 'have' the Spirit only insofar as they keep on receiving the Spirit (Eph. 5:18). While the Spirit indwells the baptized through faith, the Spirit may be lost through apostasy. We never have God in our grasp; we never possess the Spirit in a proud or triumphalistic way, but we can only ever receive the Spirit as gift (1 Cor. 4:7). Therefore, the *vita passiva* of faith, which allows God to do his work in us, is the only fitting posture for the reception of the Spirit (*On Good Works*, 1520, WA6,244,3–6; LW44,7).

It is imperative that we 'rest' from our work so that God can do his work in us. This is Luther's interpretation of the Sabbath rest of the third commandment, which he applies to the Christian life and the divine service of worship (*Gottesdienst*). His understanding of prayer and meditation, which also presupposes the basic posture of the *vita passiva*, comes out in his letter to Peter the Master Barber (*A Simple Way to Pray*, 1535), where, among other things, he helps his barber learn how to meditate on the Lord's Prayer by sharing with him his own practice of prayer. He stresses the importance of stillness and receptivity where he is open to God's leading and patiently waits on the Spirit to speak as he meditates on the Word (in this case, the petitions of the Our Father). The following passage provides a glimpse into Luther's world of prayer:

> It may happen occasionally that I may get lost among so many ideas in one petition that I forego the other six. If such an abundance of good thoughts comes to us, we should disregard the other petitions, make room for such thoughts, listen in silence, and under no circumstances obstruct them. The Holy Spirit himself preaches here, and one word of his sermon is far better than a thousand of our prayers. Many times

I have learned more from one prayer than I might have learned from much reading and speculation. (WA38.363,9–16; LW43.198)

The important point to draw from this is that any new insights and ideas that the Spirit gives will not come out of the blue, through unmediated experience, but through prayerful meditation on the Word. (*Oratio* is one of Luther's three 'rules' for the study of theology, along with *meditatio* and *tentatio*, that he gives in his 1539 preface to the Wittenberg edition of his German writings: WA50.659,3–4; LW34.285.) The Holy Spirit in his freedom has bound himself to the letters of the Bible so that any demonstration of the Spirit and power today (1 Cor. 2:4) will happen in no other way than '*in* and *through* the prophetic and apostolic Word that is sure, certain, and utterly reliable' (Bayer 1999: 220).

V. THE PERSON OF THE HOLY SPIRIT

The triune God remains the central mystery of the Christian faith as confessed in the Apostles' Creed and the Nicene-Constantinopolitan Creed (381). Luther sums up the office and work of the Spirit with the following words in his *Confession* of 1528: 'Thirdly, I believe in the Holy Spirit, who is true God with the Father and the Son and who proceeds eternally from the Father and the Son, and yet is a distinct person with respect to his divine being and nature' (WA26.505,29; LW37.365–366).

With the church catholic of all ages, Luther upholds the divinity of the Holy Spirit, but he follows the Western tradition in adopting the *filioque*: that the Spirit proceeds '*ab, ex, de utroque*' (Augustine, *De Trinitate* 15,26,47). In *The Three Symbols* (1538) he confesses that the Holy Spirit proceeds from the Father and is sent by the Son, and yet does not depart from the Godhead, but remains with the Father and the Son in the same Godhead and is one God with both (WA50.274,11–13; cf. LW34.217). Yet he never seems to polemicize against the decision of the Eastern church, recorded by John of Damascus (*De fide orthodoxa* 1.8), that the Spirit proceeds only from the Father and not from the Son, even though he is the Spirit of the Son as well as the Spirit of the Father. In his *Treatise on the Last Words of David* (1543) he uses the language of the Eastern church in affirming that the Father is 'the source or the fountainhead' of the Deity, and that the Son derives his deity from the Father. However, he follows the West in confessing that the Spirit derives his divinity from the Father *and* the Son. This divine order of the begetting (of the Son) and the proceeding (of the Spirit) in the immanent Trinity must be upheld and not muddled or reversed (WA54.64,3–5; LW15.309–310; cf. WA39,2.293,3–5). Just as the Father and the Son are separate persons, and yet each shares the same divine essence, so too does the Spirit. The Spirit proceeds eternally from the Father and the Son (modern ecumenical theology prefers to say 'through' the Son) and yet he also appears physically in the form of a dove, in tongues of fire, in a strong wind, as well as in other ways.

In both forms of proceeding, eternally within the Trinity (*ad intra*) as well as temporally outside the Trinity (*ad extra*), he remains the same Holy Spirit.

This side of the grave God remains hidden from our eyes, and we would know nothing of who he is had he not revealed himself to us. Luther says in his explanation to the Creed that 'in all three articles God himself has revealed and opened to us the most profound depths of his fatherly heart and his pure, unutterable love'. In a classical passage Luther puts it this way: 'We could never come to recognize the Father's favour and grace were it not for the Lord Christ, who is a mirror of the Father's heart. Apart from him we see nothing but an angry and terrible judge. But neither could we know anything of Christ, had it not been revealed by the Holy Spirit' (BSLK 660,38–47; BC 439–40). It is the Spirit who creates access to the Father through Jesus Christ (Eph. 2:18).

Luther accepts the Augustinian distinction between the Spirit as 'person' (*persona*) and the Spirit as 'gift' (*donum*). Thus, in his *First Disputation against the Antinomians* (1537) he says, 'So we distinguish the Holy Spirit as God in his divine nature and essence from the Holy Spirit as he is given to us' (WA39,1.370,12–13). This corresponds to the distinction between God as he is in himself and God as he is through his self-revelation. Luther also takes over the traditional distinction between the inner (immanent) and outer (economic) Trinity. The triune identity of God as three divine persons in one being can only be known from the inner Trinity. God's actions in the world are a unity and cannot be ascribed to specific persons. Here Luther appeals to the rule attributed to Augustine, *opera trinitatis ad extra sunt indivisa*, 'the works of the Trinity toward the outside are indivisible' (WA54.57,35–58,3; cf. LW15.302–309). However, the catechetical sermons on the Trinity, as well as the explanation of the Creed in *The Large Catechism*, show Luther following the traditional practice of assigning principal, but not exclusive, responsibility for the work of sanctification to the Holy Spirit (WA30,1.183,5–7; BC 435–6).

Luther's *Sermon on Trinity Sunday* (1537), where he preaches on Romans 11:33–6, is an important source for his understanding of the person of the Holy Spirit in a Trinitarian context (WA45.89,16–93,33). It stresses that God's inner-Trinitarian essence cannot be inferred from his outer-Trinitarian works (nor, we could add, from the *vestigia trinitatis* within creation and the human soul) but can only be known from revelation. Luther points out that it is specifically the Holy Spirit who reveals the inner-Trinitarian essence by speaking. In this connection, he often quotes Hilary (*De Trinitate*) as saying: 'Who can speak better about God than God himself?' (WA34,1.500,9–10).

The sermon begins with a discussion of how the Holy Spirit comes 'from heaven' to reveal the inner Trinity to Christians. Faced with the unfathomable mystery of God in relation to predestination, Paul asks the question: 'Who has known the mind of the Lord? Or who has been his counsellor?' Luther answers it by pointing to the Spirit in a way that preserves Paul's doxological context. Only the Spirit knows the divine wisdom because only the Spirit knows the mind of God, and so only the Spirit can reveal it to us. As Helmer points out (Helmer 1999: 222–8), Luther weaves into his sermon a homiletical disputation based on Romans 1:18–20, where he argues that our knowledge of God (the inner Trinity) is revealed by the Spirit ('inside-out') and does not have its source in human reason ('outside-in'). He contends that our knowledge of the inner-side of God is not *a posteriori*, it is not an inference drawn by natural reason from empirical observation, but it is *a priori*—however, not in the sense that it is a deduction from some abstract definition of essence, but our knowledge of God comes from the Spirit of God who alone knows the mind of God (1 Cor. 2:11). Paul's doxology, which frames the sermon, is a fitting way to ponder the mystery of the Holy Trinity and the inscrutability of God's ways.

Contemporary theology is again emphasizing a truth that is central to Luther: that the Spirit is the life-giver. When the Third Article confesses that the Spirit is 'the Lord, the giver of life', it is obviously a reference to spiritual life. However, the Spirit is equally the giver of physical life, as when God breathes into Adam the breath (*ruah*) of life (Gen. 2:7). The Holy Spirit, therefore, is the life-giver in the double sense, both physically and spiritually. The Spirit's activity, therefore, cannot be limited to Third Article matters, even if Luther spends most of his time talking about the Holy Spirit in relation to the church and faith. The Spirit's ongoing work in creation and preservation through the life-giving and life-sustaining Word of God is an insight that needs to be further developed as Luther's pneumatology is brought into engagement with theological thought in the twentieth-first century. As he emphasizes in his *Lectures on Genesis* (1535–45), the creative Word, which God the Father continues to speaks over creation in and through the Holy Spirit, remains effective throughout time to this very day (WA42.40,32–33; LW1.54 [on Gen. 1:22]; WA42,17,12–13; LW1.21 [on Gen. 1:5]) (Schwanke 2002: 3).

References

Althaus, Paul (1966). *The Theology of Martin Luther*, trans. Robert C. Schultz. Philadelphia: Fortress.

Asendorf, Ulrich (2004). *Heiliger Geist und Rechtfertigung*. Göttingen: V&R Unipress.

Bayer, Oswald (1989). *Promissio. Geschichte der reformatorischen Wende in Luthers Theologie*, 2nd edn. Darmstadt: Wissenschaftliche Buchgesellschaft.

—— (1999). *Gott als Autor: Zu einer poietologischen Theologie*. Tübingen: Mohr/Siebeck.

—— (2007). *Theology the Lutheran Way*, ed. and trans. Jeffrey G. Silcock and Mark C. Mattes. Grand Rapids, MI: Eerdmans.

—— (2008). *Martin Luther's Theology: A Contemporary Interpretation*, trans. Thomas H. Trapp. Grand Rapids, MI: Eerdmans.

—— (2009). 'Preaching the Word', trans. Jeffrey G. Silcock. *Lutheran Quarterly* 23: 249–69.

—— (2012). *A Contemporary in Dissent: Johann Georg Hamann as Radical Enlightener*, trans. Roy A. Harrisville and Mark C. Mattes. Grand Rapids, MI: Eerdmans.

Betz, John R. (2009). *After Enlightenment: Hamann as Post-Secular Visionary*. Chichester: Wiley-Blackwell.

Helmer, Christine (1999). *The Trinity and Martin Luther: A Study on the Relationship between Genre, Language and the Trinity in Luther's Works (1523–1546)*. Mainz: Zabern.

Kadai, Heino O. (ed.) (1967). *Accents in Luther's Theology: Essays in Commemoration of the 450th Anniversary of the Reformation*. Saint Louis: Concordia.

Kärkkäinen, Pekka (2005). *Luthers Trinitarische Theologie des Heiligen Geistes*. Mainz: Zabern.

Lohse, Bernhard (1999). *Martin Luther's Theology: Its Historical and Systematic Development*, trans. and ed. Roy Harrisville. Minneapolis: Fortress.

Maschke, Timothy, Franz Posset, and Joan Skocir (eds.) (2001). *Ad Fontes Lutheri: Towards the Recovery of the Real Luther. Essays in Honor of Kenneth Hagen's Sixty-Fifth Birthday.* Milwaukee: Marquette University Press.

Otto, Rudolf (1898). *Die Anschauung vom heiligen Geiste bei Luther.* Göttingen: Vandenhoeck & Ruprecht.

Prenter, Regin (1953). *Spiritus Creator*, trans. John M. Jensen. Philadelphia: Fortress.

—— (1965). *The Word and the Spirit: Essays on Inspiration of the Scriptures*, trans. Harris E. Kaasa. Minneapolis: Augsburg.

Ringleben, Joachim (2010). *Gott im Wort: Luthers Theologie von der Sprache her.* Tübingen: Mohr/Siebeck.

Schwanke, Johannes (2002). 'Luther on Creation'. *Lutheran Quarterly* 16: 1–20.

Seeberg, Erich (1940). *Grundzüge der Theologie Luthers.* Stuttgart: Kohlhammer.

Trigg, Jonathan D. (2001). *Baptism in the Theology of Martin Luther.* Leiden: Brill.

Wöhle, Andreas H. (1998). *Luther's Freude an Gottes Gesetz. Eine historische Quellenstudie zur Oszillation des Gesetzesbegriffes Martin Luthers im Licht seiner alttestamentlichen Predigten.* Frankfurt am Main: Haag + Herchen.

Zahl, Simeon (2010). *Pneumatology and Theology of the Cross in the Preaching of Christoph Friedrich Blumhardt: The Holy Spirit between Wittenberg and Azusa Street.* London: T & T Clark.

SUGGESTED READING

Asendorf, Ulrich (1988). *Die Theologie Martin Luthers nach seinen Predigten.* Göttingen: Vandenhoeck & Ruprecht.

Bornkamm, Heinrich (1958). *Luther's World of Thought*, trans. Martin H. Bertram. Saint Louis: Concordia.

Hendrix, Scott (2010). *Martin Luther: A Very Short Introduction.* New York: Oxford University Press.

Kolb, Robert and Charles P. Arand (2008). *The Genius of Luther's Theology: A Wittenberg Way of Thinking for the Contemporary Church.* Grand Rapids, MI: Baker.

Peters, Albrecht (2011). *Commentary on Luther's Catechisms: Creed*, trans. Thomas H. Trapp. Saint Louis: Concordia.

Schlink, Edmund (1961). *Theology of the Lutheran Confessions*, trans. Paul F. Koehneke and Herbert J. A. Bouman. Saint Louis: Concordia.

Vogelsang, Erich (1932). *Der angefochtene Christus bei Luther.* Berlin: de Gruyter.

Watson, Philip S. (1966). *Let God be God: An Interpretation of the Theology of Martin Luther.* Philadelphia: Fortress.

CHAPTER 21

....

LUTHER ON BAPTISM AND PENANCE

....

JONATHAN TRIGG

I. BAPTISM

....

I.1. Context

Baptism was the foundational sacrament in the medieval economy of salvation—yet
the role that it played was essentially a closed one; it was necessary for salvation but
by no means sufficient. The legacy of Augustine's concentration in his debates with the
Pelagians on the negative role of baptism in the removal of original sin was its gradual
reduction to a closed historical event, from which the Christian sets out in need of penance and new sources of grace. If the force of baptism is effectively exhausted in the initial entry into grace and the removal of original sin, it is scarcely surprising that it plays
a limited and essentially static role. The course of Luther's theology, and of what cannot
be separated from his theology—his personal struggle for salvation—can and should be
understood precisely as a rediscovery of the continuing force of baptism in its promise
and power in the life of a Christian.

The more clarity Luther was to achieve in his understanding of this in his struggles, the greater became his anger and grief that Christians should for so long have
been robbed of their freedom and their comfort and of the gospel itself. This gives the
right context for understanding the trajectory of baptism as it appears and functions
in Luther's output over time. It is simply described. In the years before his break with
Rome references to it in his lectures are relatively rare (Jetter 1954; Spinks 2006: 3–4). By
the time of the *Lectures on Genesis* (1535–45) the means of grace in general and baptism
in particular are very much in the foreground; references are frequent, and Luther will
introduce them into contexts where at first sight neither the text nor the subject matter

before him seem to require it (Trigg 1994: 13–15). Between these two end-points we can see a gradual but persistent upward gradient. Why?

The first factor operating in the particular case of baptism stems from its medieval confinement. Although Luther's 'reformation breakthrough' to a new understanding of the righteousness of God, justification, and faith did not at first present itself as a recovery of baptism and baptismal freedom, this connection had certainly been made by the time of the 1520 tract *The Babylonian Captivity of the Church* (WA6.526,34–543,3; LW36.57–81). From 1520 onwards, Luther is increasingly vociferous in his insistence that the ship of baptism remains afloat as the ark of salvation; there has been and will be no 'shipwreck' and thus no need to seek any lifeboat or 'second plank' in substitution.[1] Said another way: grace is indivisible; Luther regarded the supplementation of 'baptismal grace' by means of supplementary or replacement 'graces' available through different sacraments or works not only as unnecessary but impossible: God's grace, given in baptism, is one (Jetter 1954: 230).

The second step upwards in the profile of baptism applies not only to this sacrament but to the means of grace in general. In the 1520s, especially from about 1527, Luther is increasingly aware of his need to contend with new sets of opponents. He sees opponents like Zwingli, and various elements of the 'Radical Reformation', as in varying ways undermining the efficacy and objectivity of the sacraments, even if they do so in the name of faith and the Word. In their magnification of faith and the inward, they despise the commonplace outward—mere water, such as a maid washes with or a cow drinks—and they ignore the fact that God has bound his word of promise and command to that despised outward thing.

It is only once this new set of controversies had had their full impact that Luther's baptismal theology came to its full expression.

I.2. Structure

It is rather easier than might be expected (given his generally polemical, prolix, and unsystematic style) to set out the structure of Luther's baptismal theology. In the *Large Catechism* of 1529[2] he provides a four-fold pattern: (1) the foundation of baptism in the joining of water and the Word (that is, the word of promise and command); (2) the purpose, benefits, and effects of baptism (in effect, salvation); (3) the use of baptism, which can be expressed as the relationship between baptism and faith; and (4) the significance and appropriateness of the sign of baptism, and its right appropriation by the Christian (thus, perhaps, the character it stamps upon the life of a Christian). Most of

---

[1] For example, WA6.529,22–34; LW36.61; references to the 'second plank' ultimately stem from Jerome, *Epist.* 130,9. At first this tradition restricted the restoration of grace after post-baptismal sin to one episode of repentance and absolution.

[2] BSLK 691–707; BC 456–67. The sub-heading 'infant baptism' in this edition rather obscures the structure of Luther's thought; it is to be understood as part of the third section on baptism and faith.

the important issues in Luther's baptismal thought and the apparent difficulties in relating it to his wider theology find their place in this structure, and this essay will follow it. However, although Luther deals in an excursus with infant baptism in the third section as part of his teaching on baptism and faith, and much of the material in this excursus is indeed of direct relevance to his understanding of baptism and faith, his defence of infant baptism itself (5) will require separate treatment.

> 1: Water and the Word. Luther embraces Augustine's formula, *accedat verbum ad elementum et fit sacramentum* (the Word is added to the element and makes a sacrament) as the foundation of his understanding of baptism. Luther's emphatic insistence on the inseparability of Word and water provides him with the answer to those he sees as despising the water as mere water, such as a cow drinks or a maid cooks with (WA51.129,26–36; LW51.376; BSLK 695; BC 459). Luther's understanding of the means of grace through which God chooses to reveal himself will tolerate neither the despising of the appointed externals nor an attempt to seek God apart from them. To treat the water of baptism as mere water is to ignore the Word joined to that water; it leads to an idolatrous attempt to seek God other than where he has chosen to be found, namely concealed under his opposite, hidden under and revealed in something as ordinary and unimpressive as water (e.g., WA42.10,3–10; LW1.11; Trigg 1994: 72–3).

But if the Anabaptists and others despise the water, there are those who commit what may appear to be the opposite error of venerating it apart from the Word. Thus Luther neither tolerates those who ascribe power to the water itself (WA43.387,42–388,6; LW4.349) nor countenances the vain boasting of those who presume on the fact of their baptism without the response of faith (e.g. WA46.707,20–708,9; LW22.197). The two errors are in reality one: they separate what should be joined, water and Word.

Given the polyvalence of 'word' in theological discourse, not least in Luther's, it is important to clarify in what sense it should be taken in this context. In the *Large Catechism* Luther begins with the dominical command in Mt 28:19, and Mk. 16:16 (the latter in effect adds the category of promise to that of command). This is the instituting Word which invests the water of baptism with its dignity and power: 'Baptism is no human plaything but is instituted by God himself... What God instituted and commands cannot be useless' (BSLK 692; BC 457). But if in the catechism Luther is very precise about the Word which is joined to the water, increasingly in his later period there is a marked vigour and fluidity in what Luther says about the Word spoken in baptism. In baptism and the other means of grace we hear God speaking to us, and promising the forgiveness of sins (WA42.514,31–34; LW2.353). We are promised the Kingdom (WA43.204,34–205,2; LW4.96); we are vouchsafed the abiding favour of God (WA44.272,14–30; LW6.364). The conjoining of water and Word establishes the right response of the Christian to his or her baptism—to listen to the Word spoken there, in faith—and this emphasis on listening to what is said to me in my baptism opens the way to a new emphasis on its abiding significance and power in the life of a Christian.

Sometimes the Christian must be like Jacob and actively cling to the promise made in baptism though he or she sees nothing of its fulfilment, as Jacob clung to the promise of his inheritance despite being forced into exile (WA43.568,14 23; LW5.203).

The defining characteristics of Luther's baptismal theology, including those which divided him from his contemporaries, all flow from its foundation in the inseparability of water and Word.

> 2: What baptism does. In the second section of Luther's treatment of baptism in the *Large Catechism*, he asks about its purpose, its gift and its effect. The answer he gives is simple, comprehensive, and unqualified: the gift of baptism is that we should be saved, which is to be 'delivered from sin, death and the Devil and to enter into the kingdom of Christ and live with him forever' (BSLK 695–696; BC 438,25). Elsewhere he speaks of baptism conferring rebirth, incorporation into the Second Adam, holiness, righteousness, wisdom, readmission to paradise, and delivery from the hands of the Devil (WA47.13,13–20; LW22.285; WA33.535,2–537,30; LW23.333–334; WA40,2.381,26–383,17; LW26.241–242; WA31,2.564,9–11; LW17.389: WA43.424,25–32; LW4.401; WA43.526,2–8; LW5.141–142). All this happens 'in the hands of the priest', and there is no reticence in the post-baptismal prayer in Luther's liturgy of 1526; '[almighty God] hath regenerated thee through water and the Holy Ghost' (WA19.541,14–17; LW53.109; cf. WA47.14,24–15,9; LW22.286–287).

However, this unqualified language of baptismal regeneration may mislead. Even within this second section Luther insists upon the need for faith, but faith 'must have something to believe', so it is to 'cling to the water and [believe] it to be Baptism in which there is sheer salvation and life' (BSLK 696; BC 460). If faith is required for the right use of the sacrament, how far can we understand the regeneration of baptism as tied to and completed in the moment of administration? Part of the answer lies in the category of promise; a new identity is received in baptism, yet faith must struggle against appearance to perceive it. But the hidden nature of the new identity bestowed at baptism does not go the whole way to resolve the difficulty; Luther's language requires more subtlety in understanding the connection between the moment when the water is poured and the new birth (and, we might add, understanding the new birth in itself). There are those who have been baptized and yet have no use of their baptism in faith; they may boast of it, but they are Christians in name only (WA46.707,17–708,19; LW22.197–198). Even this qualification, however, does not go far enough—anyone who regards his or her baptism as a closed act, and who presumes upon it, risks failing to see that the word of promise which God continues to speak in baptism continues to demand the response of faith. In other words, despite Luther's unqualified language about the benefits and use of baptism, he cannot be understood as telling the individual baptized Christian that his or her new birth is wholly a past event; at all times it is an event which also lies 'before' us. The significance of baptism, treated in the fourth section in the catechism, makes this clear.

3: Baptism and faith. 'Without faith Baptism is of no use, although in itself it is an infinite, divine treasure.' 'Baptism...is not a work which we do but is a treasure which God gives us and faith grasps', in the same way that Christ on the cross is no work but a treasure offered in the Word and to be received by faith (BSLK 697, 698; BC 460, 461). Luther's persistent adherence to a double principle is clear. First: faith does not create the sacrament, nor does it validate it. Second: the sacrament is of no benefit or use in the absence of faith.

To boast of the outward rite itself, simply to trust in the water poured, is to follow the presumption of Esau (WA43.387,21-388,9; LW4.348–349), whose trust in his primogeniture Luther sees repeated in the church of Rome's boasting of the externalities of baptism and the other means of grace; they do not apprehend them in faith. 'The heart must believe it' (BSLK 698; BC 461). Luther's insistence on the unprofitability of baptism without faith is fully evident in the catechism; and he adheres to it in his latest work (e.g., WA44.713,26–30; LW8.184): 'The Sacrament of the Altar, Baptism, and the Word in the sermon are at hand. But you have as much as you believe' (WA44.719,24–37; LW8.192). However, as his treatment of infant baptism will show, what does and what does not constitute 'faith' in this context requires some refinement.

Well before 1529, Luther is aware that he is fighting on at least two fronts. There were those who insisted on a conveyance of grace simply in the performance of the act; now there are others who so decry the tying of grace to anything external that they charge Luther with reintroducing a works-righteousness in his emphasis on baptism. Baptism is indeed a work—but it is God's work; and thus a treasure whose inherent worth is not compromised by how it is received. In his 1528 treatise *Concerning Rebaptism* Luther uses the image of gold whose worth is not debased merely because of its misuse by a thief; baptism is debased neither by the absence of faith nor by post-baptismal sin (WA26.159,25–161,34; LW40.246–248). The answer to the case of baptism without faith is simple: faith. This is a matter of grounding faith upon its object, and not the other way about. Faith based on the work of God is secure in its foundation, but against the rebaptizers Luther insists that baptism grounded on faith must always be uncertain because the faith of human beings wavers and fails.

Thus Luther's understanding of the means of grace—and perhaps of baptism in particular—is an important clue to his concept of faith, particularly in the later period. It cannot rely on itself, it is directed away from itself to God in Christ; it cannot and need not assess itself—in short we may say that it is unselfconscious.

4: Sign and signification. There is no obvious word or phrase in English to translate *significatio*, which is in effect the subject matter of the final section of Luther's treatment of baptism in the *Large Catechism*. He asks the question, Why this sign of being dipped in the water and drawn out again? If in his second section the reformer is describing the benefit and gift of baptism, which can be summarized as salvation and everything pertaining to it, here there is a narrower concentration on the 'how', or rather upon the stamp which his or her baptism implants upon the life of the one baptized.

The fittingness of being plunged in water is shown in the shape of the life of a Christian, which is 'simply the slaying of the old Adam and the resurrection of the new man, both of which actions must continue in us our whole life long. Thus a Christian life is nothing else than a daily Baptism, once begun and ever continued' (BSLK 704; BC 464–65). Baptism and death are interchangeable terms in Scripture (WA42.369,3–19; LW2.153), and 'in Baptism all Christians begin to die, and they continue to die until they reach the grave' (WA45.506,38–507,12; LW24,50–51). The sign is a double one; as with the drowning so with the lifting up from the water: 'the thing it signifies—the spiritual birth and the increase of grace and righteousness—even though it begins in baptism, lasts until death, indeed, until the Last Day. Only then will that be finished which the lifting up out of baptism signifies', Luther said in his 1519 sermon on baptism (WA2.727,30–728,9; LW35.30).

Regeneration, the new birth, is neither to be divorced from the rite of baptism, nor is its meaning to be exhausted in the moment when the water is poured. Like the salvation which is its gift, the significance of baptism is future as well as past and present. Although Luther is happy to speak of a journey begun in baptism and continued in faith, and speaks of a strengthening of that faith as the journey progresses (e.g., WA45.499,16–27; LW24.42), there is another dynamic in Luther's thought which both qualifies the idea of spiritual progress and forbids the Christian from consigning baptism—act and significance—to the past. Luther in the catechism insists that daily repentance is nothing other than a continual return to baptism (BSLK 706; BC 446), and we should not be surprised that he assumes and requires this continual return to the beginning as at any point in time the Christian cannot examine, assess, or rely upon the results of any progress in the life of the Spirit (Prenter 1953: 97). Reliance upon and glorying in righteousness as a possession is a continual temptation, and Luther clearly assumes that the journey from active to passive righteousness, law to grace, Moses to Christ, is one that will have to be made many times: the continual need to return to the beginning imposes a circular pattern to the life of a Christian (WA40,1.49,24–50,16; LW26.10; Trigg 1994: 169–71).

The Christian is *simul justus et peccator*, at once righteous and a sinner, at all times on (or bisected by) the boundary between the two kingdoms, flesh and spirit. The correlate of this theme in Luther's baptismal theology is the continual and repeated call to hear the word of promise spoken in baptism, and to die the daily death that it signifies. Luther's distinctive emphasis upon the vocation, or vocations, of all Christian people is rooted in this baptismal call to die to self. In the matrix of callings and obligations of daily life at work, in the home, in society, we have the arena in which God brings this baptismal death to pass (WA42.369,3–37 713; LW2.153–155; WA43.672,25–673,36; LW5.354–5).

5: Infant baptism. Luther asks, 'Do children also believe, and is it right to baptize them?' (BSLK 700; BC 462), thus introducing his teaching on infant baptism in the *Large Catechism* with two questions rather than with one. We might conclude that by posing the matter thus, he shows that the possibility—or reality—of infant faith is the foundation of his argument, and some argue that it is indeed the cornerstone of the later Luther's position (Scaer 1999: 147–56). In *Concerning Rebaptism* he appears to be advancing two different arguments about infant faith (WA26.144–174; LW40 241–246). The first is simply that Scripture shows that some children have faith; in telling us that the children offered to idols or slaughtered by Herod were innocent, it implies faith on their part, to which Luther adds the Lord's words about the kingdom belonging to children. Luther's concept of faith is such that children are by no means excluded. But the second argument is dominant; and this is not so much an assertion of the existence of infant faith as a denial that Scripture excludes it. The burden of proof falls on those who base their requirement for rebaptism of those baptized as infants; they cannot prove what they need to prove, namely that infants cannot believe.

But infant faith cannot be the ultimate foundation of Luther's defence of infant baptism, simply because to make faith in *any* way the foundation of baptism runs directly counter to his thinking. Even in *Concerning Rebaptism*, where infant faith is to the fore, Luther uses a variety of defences. Some are idiosyncratic, as when Luther, claiming common ground with the Anabaptists to the extent of agreeing that the pope is the Antichrist, says that as Antichrist reigns in the temple, among holy things, this of itself shows the holiness of that amongst which he has been presiding, including baptism as it has been practised from the beginning. Logically this is an extension of the argument that if baptism as practised since the time of the apostles had not been true baptism, there could have been no church and no giving of the Spirit—there have been both, so the opponents' position is absurd (WA26.168,27–169,2; LW40,1.256–257; Trigg 1994: 99–107, offers a synthesis of Luther's defences). The core of Luther's approach rests in the heart of his understanding of baptism as the Word inseparably joined to the water. Luther can afford to sit light, as it were, to infant faith as a hypothesis, as to the waxing and waning of faith over the course of any life, precisely because he refuses to ground the validity and objectivity of baptism in that faith. In the same way, this denial of faith as foundational frees him at various times to advance the faith of others (*fides aliena*) (BSLK 702; BC 443), and the nature of baptism as a covenant 'with the heathen', from which children must not be excluded (WA26.169,20–35; LW40,1.257–258). Faith is not certain of itself; it attends to God's command and promise, and ultimately to Christ himself.

I.3. Significance

The deep-rooted image of him as above all the man of faith makes Luther's baptismal theology something of a surprise for the new student, who might well share Karl

Barth's puzzlement, in that 'the main themes of [Luther's] theology—law and gospel, justification by faith alone, the freedom of a Christian man, etc.—hardly prepare us for the statement that a small child becomes a Christian in baptism' (Barth 1969. 169). Yet a closer inspection reveals that far from sitting uneasily in the context of his wider thought, Luther's approach to baptism reflects and illuminates many aspects of it. So his insistence that faith does not constitute baptism but receives it preserves that faith from becoming one more exercise in human spirituality to add to all the others, and places the weight entirely on the promise of God. His refusal to allow the denigration of 'mere water' is fully aligned with his theology of the cross, God hidden under the mask of what is his opposite, or under what is despised. His refusal to understand the Christian life as progress onwards and away from the portal of baptism is likewise an expression of Luther's understanding of the Christian as *simul justus et peccator*, righteous and a sinner at the same time, never progressing beyond the need to hear and receive the gracious promise of God in the present moment.

II. PENANCE: THE KEYS, CONFESSION, AND ABSOLUTION

There are two strands in Luther's approach to penance. The first is marked by an intense sensitivity to any assertion that it is a necessary supplement to baptism, or that it is a source of 'replacement grace' to deal with post-baptismal sin. This suspicion is combined with a protest against the ways in which the papacy has limited, burdened, and exploited penance and thus hindered its salutary use as one of the means of grace. Entangled with this is the second strand: Luther's emphatic appreciation of penance as a means of grace.

Luther's vocabulary is fluid: he speaks of the 'Keys', of penance, of forgiveness of the neighbour, of confession and absolution; and these are not readily disentangled from one another. Although when Luther refers to 'the signs' or the means of grace he will typically include 'the Keys' in his list, the others also make their appearance. If the language is fluid, Luther's insistence that the means of grace are in no way to be separated from one another is not. The Keys are not to be considered apart from the ministry of the Word (WA42.636/7; LW3.124); nor is penance to be separated from baptism or the Supper. It is preparation and approach to the Supper, but the foundational link is with the abiding ship of baptism, to which it is a return (Rittgers 2004: 58, 136).

Luther does not achieve consistency concerning whether this is to be considered as a sacrament; in his tract *The Babylonian Captivity of the Church* (1520) he describes it as such, but the *Large Catechism* of 1529 speaks of two sacraments. However the fluidity of Luther's treatment of the God-appointed 'signs' or means of grace remains in that in the section on the Lord's Prayer he interprets the fifth petition as the appropriation of a word of promise: 'forgive, and you shall be forgiven'.

The foundation of Luther's teaching on the sacrament of penance is the same as that of baptism and the Eucharist. It is the divine word of command and promise; and nothing is received other than by faith. Luther appears to allow a much greater fluidity of practice than in the case of baptism, however. Confession of sins may be made to a brother—or sister (WA6.541,1–25; LW36.87)—and the words of pardon and comfort need not always be spoken by a pastor or priest. At one end of the range of Luther's thought on confession and absolution we have his formal instructions to pastors on the ministry of the Keys (e.g., WA26.220,1–19; LW40.296; where it is assumed that pastors will not admit to communion without individual examination beforehand); at the other the simple, yet also sacramental, forgiveness of the neighbour (WA32.424,1–4; LW21.150).

If the Augustinian principle is applied to penance as a sacrament, what is the divine Word joined to the element? And, for that matter, what is the element? In 1519 Luther gives Mt. 16:19 ('whatever you bind on earth shall be bound in heaven...') as the former. The 'element' appears to be the words of absolution spoken by the priest although he also states that an individual Christian—even a woman or a child—can speak these words (WA2.714,3–20, 716,25–35; LW35.9, 12). As in the case of the other sacraments, the worthiness and intention of the minister are not determinative of its validity—the priest's words can be trusted even if he is jesting, or if he himself is under the ban (WA2.717,6–25; LW35.13–14). It is the truth of these words of absolution which have to be apprehended in faith, and faith alone is the mode of appropriating this sacrament. Luther's approach to the three constituent parts of the sacrament distinguished in the tradition—contrition, confession, and satisfaction—is shaped by this principle.

Because faith is the only way of receiving a sacrament, we are free to refrain from assessing the depth of contrition for sin, or the adequacy of the satisfaction offered—to rely on either is beside the point: 'For Christ did not intend to base our comfort, our salvation, our confidence on human words or deeds, but only upon himself, upon his words and deeds' (WA2.714–723; LW35.10). So far as *contrition* is concerned, Luther does not deny the value of true contrition for sins, indeed he is prepared to dissuade people from confession when hatred of sin is feigned rather than genuine (WA6.159,21–35; LW39.30). Yet even if contrition is the inevitable result of attending to God's Word (of command or threat: the law) Luther decries teaching which encourages Christians to rely on that contrition, as indeed he deplores reliance on any aspect of what we would now call 'spirituality'. True contrition is the fruit of faith in the Word (WA6.544,21–545,8; LW36.83–84). Thus understood, contrition is not to be dissociated from faith—and they closely resemble one another in that neither need be, nor indeed should be, self-aware.

Luther accepts and endorses the practice of private *confession* but rails against the restrictions and reservations with which the papacy has hedged it about, including the reservation of certain cases to bishops or to the pope himself, or indeed to priests at all: 'For there is no person to be compared with a Christian brother' (WA6.546,11–17; LW36.86). The Keys belong to the whole church. The application of Luther's theological principles to the way a Christian should approach auricular confession is shown in a 1520 tract, *A Discussion on How Confession should be made* (WA6.157–169; LW39.27–47). Among the recommendations are these (not necessarily in Luther's order): pray for a sense of good intention (=contrition?) if you think you lack it; admit and confess that all you do is tainted by sin, and that full knowledge (and therefore full confession) of sin is impossible; confess those sins of which you are aware, while admitting ignorance; do not be overanxious about categories of sin; and above all, do not trust in your confession but in the merciful forgiveness of God. To avoid this last error, which is the trap of over-scrupulosity, Luther goes so far as to endorse the somewhat surprising advice that on occasion one should go to mass without confession, or when one has been drinking, simply so as to learn to trust in God's mercy and not in one's 'correct confession' (WA6.166,1–30; LW39.40–41).

Luther's view of true *satisfaction* is simply expressed: this is 'the renewal of life'; or, in the words of Jesus to the woman caught in adultery, 'Go and sin no more' (Jn. 8:11). For this true satisfaction the papacy has substituted a catalogue of burdens and tortures, all heaped on 'poor consciences' to the ruin of body and soul (WA6.548,33–549,14; LW36.90). Perversely the Roman church lays invented burdens on sinners while wrongly ignoring the necessary dying to the flesh. Thus in one sense their harshness is to be deplored, while in another they are tricking Christians into the delusion that they need not die the death begun in their baptism—Luther holds to his protest against all the stratagems used to conceal this truth begun as early as 1517 in the Ninety-five Theses: '*Christians are to be exhorted that they be diligent in following Christ, their Head, through penalties, deaths, and hell*.'

But Luther is uncomfortable with the language of satisfaction, however it is interpreted. He insists that the true satisfaction is seen in only one place: 'our Lord Jesus Christ is the one and only Victim with which satisfaction has been made to the wrath of God' (WA44.468,5–16; LW7.227).

The abuse of satisfaction does not exhaust the tyranny of the perversion of the Keys under the papacy, so far as Luther is concerned. He accuses the papacy of having fashioned laws, prohibitions, reservations, and powers for itself; all out of what has been given to the Church to free souls from sin by means of repentance and forgiveness. But his most vehement protest is against penance as 'the second plank' or lifeboat to which one must cling when baptismal grace is lost, a strand in the teaching of the church traceable to Jerome. The unsinkable ark of baptism remains (WA6.529,22–34; LW36.61). Penance cannot be understood other than as a recall to it. This leads us back to what we called the trajectory of baptism and its profile in Luther's thought over time, and in particular why it has become so.

Luther rails against the false comfort offered by the church as a substitute for true penance and a following of Christ 'though penalties, deaths, and hells'. But his fury at what he perceives as the loss of true comfort is still greater, comfort found in the freedom of the sinner justified by God's grace in Christ, the release from all necessity of seeking salvation elsewhere, the Christian's identity as a child of God. Luther increasingly came to express this loss precisely in terms of the loss of baptism; already in *The Babylonian Captivity of the Church* he sees the extinction of the power of baptism amongst adults as the work of Satan (WA6.527,9–22; LW36.57f.). 'The reformation of Luther began at this point; it was Luther who first cracked the basis of the penitential system started by

Hermas, namely the presupposition that baptism is merely a closed historical act and repentance a subsequent act' (Goppelt 1962: 201). Goppelt may be wrong in seeing his refusal to accept a limit or an end to baptism as the starting point for Luther's 'break-through' strictly in terms of the development of his thought over time. We might better understand Luther's insistence on the continuing force of baptism as the consequence of—or, probably better—as an expression of the gospel as he had come to understand it.

The vehemence at the loss of baptism he expresses in *The Babylonian Captivity* and indeed the increasing role it plays in his writings in the years that followed may be taken as a measure of his own bitter experience of this loss and of his various failed attempts to make it good using the means the church offered him.

III. Luther on Baptism: Possible Avenues of Inquiry

III.1. Baptism and the Church: 'Purity' and 'Rightness'

Luther's theology of baptism as of the other means of grace begins with the assertion that God is truly to be encountered there, and that he is calling his church into being where the 'word is heard, where baptism, the sacrament of the altar and absolution are administered' (WA43.596,38–598,6; LW5.244–245). The voice of God is truly heard in baptism; it is never silenced, and does not need human additions to be effective. Individuals differ in their hearing of and response to this Word, and faith must guard against presumption, as for Luther the Christian never graduates from the entry level class; he or she always stands in need of repentance and faith in the promise. The boundary or entry which baptism represents always passes through the Christian in the present moment (in which God speaks his Word); there is always the possibility of following Esau and the false church in a presumptuous reliance on the title deeds, rather than following Jacob and attending to the promise. The boundary between true and false is real, but radically elusive, and one relies on it only to find oneself on the wrong side.

This central assertion about the ministry of Word and sacrament can lead in another direction, however. Luther often supplies adjectives to his declarations about the means of grace: there are plenty of occasions when he speaks of the 'right' teaching of the 'pure' Word and of the 'right' administration and use of the sacraments in a manner thoroughly consonant with Article VII of the Augsburg Confession. For instance: '...the holy sacrament of baptism, wherever it is taught, believed, and administered correctly according to Christ's ordinance' is a mark of the church (WA50.630,21–631,5; LW41.151). Some strands of the Lutheran tradition interpret the qualifying adjectives in a manner which appears to limit their recognition of the unity of the Church, the community of all those under the sign of baptism and addressed by the promise spoken in it.

Which is more fundamental to Luther: his insistence on God's abiding word of promise spoken to all at all times in their baptism, and its sufficiency as a sign that the people of God are gathered to hear it; or his insistence on drawing distinctions between pure and impure, right and corrupted administration and use of baptism and the other means of grace? How does the answer to this question determine the church's understanding and practice of baptism?

III.2. Infant Baptism in a Secular Age

Luther, like his contemporaries, assumed that baptism would be virtually universal. There were the Jews living amongst the Christians, about whom Luther's pronouncements have become notorious. And on the eastern fringes of Europe was the Turk, a potential physical threat, but by no means the most dangerous spiritual one; Luther always looked for these within the company of those who claimed to be the church, as, for instance, one must always look for the papal 'Antichrist' reigning in the midst of holy things rather than anywhere else. In a world where baptism was virtually universal with only these two exceptions, it is unsurprising that Luther and many others found any denial or refusal of infant baptism to be an alarming discomfort, threatening them (in Barth's words) with a form of spiritual agoraphobia.

But now, in a multicultural and increasingly secular world, how Luther's defence of infant baptism is understood will affect its interpretation in a world where baptism is by no means universal. If infant faith is fundamental, what justification could there be for restricting the sacrament to the children of believers? Or does in fact an irreducible covenantal element (perhaps linked to *fides aliena*—the faith of others, parents, godparents, the church) underlie Luther's defence?

REFERENCES

Barth, Karl (1969). *Church Dogmatics*, vol. IV.4, trans. G. W. Bromiley. Edinburgh: Clark.

Goppelt, Leonhardt (1962). 'The Existence of the Church in History according to Apostolic and Early Catholic Thought'. In *Current Issues in New Testament Interpretation: Essays in Honor of Otto A. Piper*, ed. William Klassen and G. F. Snyder. New York: Harper, 193–209.

Jetter, Werner (1954). *Die Taufe beim jungen Luther. Eine Untersuchung über das Werden der reformatorischen Sakraments- und Taufanschaung*. Tübingen: Mohr.

Prenter, Regin (1953). *Spiritus Creator*, trans. John Jensen. Philadelphia: Muhlenberg.

Rittgers, Ronald K. (2004). *The Reformation of the Keys*. Cambridge, MA: Harvard University Press.

Scaer, David (1999). *Baptism*. Confessional Lutheran Dogmatics. St Louis: Luther Academy.

Spinks, Bryan D. (2006). *Reformation and Modern Rituals and Theologies of Baptism: From Luther to Contemporary Practices*. Aldershot: Ashgate.

Trigg, Jonathan (1994). *Baptism in the Theology of Martin Luther*. Leiden: Brill.

CHAPTER 22

LUTHER AND THE
LORD'S SUPPER

GORDON A. JENSEN

I. RECENT SCHOLARSHIP ON LUTHER'S UNDERSTANDING OF THE LORD'S SUPPER

LUTHER studies in the twentieth century explored Luther's understanding of the Lord's Supper in three general ways. One area of research explored the development of his thought; the second focused on Luther's debates with various opponents, while the third focused on particular themes in his theology of the Lord's Supper.

In 1908 Friedrich Gräbke published a study which identified four distinct chronological stages in the development of Luther's theology of the sacrament of the altar. For the most part, Luther scholars have followed these categories. In the first stage Luther focuses on the Word, which gives assurance and forgiveness, while almost ignoring the sacramental elements themselves. In the second stage, beginning in 1525, the body and blood of Christ are seen as the vehicle for forgiveness. In the third stage, beginning in 1526, Luther combines the first two stages so that the body and blood, along with forgiveness, are the focal point. Finally, by Marburg Colloquy of 1529, Luther reaches the final stage, arguing for a sacramental union between Christ, the elements, and the proclamation of the forgiveness of sins.[1] Susi Hausamann (1969) took a different approach by categorizing Luther's theological development based upon his opponents. She proposed three stages: the Traditional, the Anti-Roman, and the Anti-Enthusiast.

Scholarship that has focused on Luther's writings on the Lord's Supper in comparison to his opponents began with the comprehensive studies provided by Ernst Bizer (1962, 1940) and Ernst Sommerlath (1930). The most extensive study in the English language has been that by Hermann Sasse (1959). Carl Wisløff (1964) has traced how

---

[1] For example, Gräbke's four categories are slightly modified by Faulkner (1917) and Quere (1985).

the implications of Luther's reformation theology led him to question the traditional Roman Catholic teachings on the mass. The debate between Karlstadt and Luther has recently been addressed by Amy Nelson Burnett (2011). In his seminal work Walther Köhler (1924/53) compared Luther's and Zwingli's views of the Lord's Supper from theological and political perspectives. This work is important since the political pressure for an agreement by rulers supportive of the Reformation is often overlooked.

After the impasse at the Marburg Colloquy in 1529 and the death of Zwingli in 1531, the Lord's Supper debates no longer occupied centre stage. Nevertheless, conversations between Luther and Bucer continued, leading to the Wittenberg Concord of 1536. The disagreements between Luther and Calvin, while significant for later generations, engaged the second generation of Luther scholars more than Luther himself, and have been explored by Helmut Gollwitzer (1937), Hans Grass (1954), Irene Dingel (1996), and Johannes Hund (2006).

Most studies on Luther's theological understanding of the Lord's Supper have focused on what Luther meant by the term 'real presence'. Along with many of the authors already mentioned, this research has been ably summarized by Albrecht Peters (1966). Finally, the liturgical aspects of Luther's sacramental theology have provided important perspectives in keeping the debates within the context of the worship service. Reinhard Meßner (1989) has written an interesting monograph on Luther's liturgical reforms.

II. Luther's Challenges to the Roman Catholic Position on the Lord's Supper

Luther's initial writings on the Lord's Supper reflect the medieval tradition, including the doctrine of transubstantiation, the sacrifice of the mass, communion in one kind, and the ability of the priest (through ordination) to effect transubstantiation. In 1518 Luther published a *Sermon on the Proper Preparation of the Heart for the Sacramental Reception on the Eucharist* (WA1.329–335), reflecting a pastoral concern that was never far from the surface in all subsequent debates.

Luther's 1519 treatise, *The Blessed Sacrament of the Holy and True Body of Christ and the Brotherhoods* (WA2.742–758; LW35.45–74), reflects his interpretation of Augustine's understanding of the outward sign (*signum*) of bread and wine, which points to the community of believers (*communio*), and the importance of the faith of the believer. At this stage he holds that the spiritual body is more important than the natural body in the sacrament (WA2.752.1–17; LW35.62). While Zwingli also takes this idea from Augustine and develops it in his argument against Luther, Luther works to increasingly connect the two together. Luther's emphasis on faith also led him to question the idea of the sacrament justifying the person by the mere action of the sacrament (*ex opere operato*) since this would contradict the emphasis placed on faith making the sacrament effective

(WA2.751.18–752.3; LW35.63–64; cf. Meinhold 1960). Instead, he highlights the 'action of the one acting' in faith (*opus operantis*).

The shift in Luther's theology of the Supper begins in 1519 with the publication of *The Lord's Supper, A Treatise on the New Testament, that is, the Holy Mass* (WA6.353–378; LW35.79–112). Luther explores the Lord's Supper as a testament or will, given by Christ to the community of believers under the seal, or sign, of the bread and wine.[2] This testament promises forgiveness of sins and is received by faith. This shift in understanding begins to open the floodgates to Luther's critiques of multiple eucharistic practices. His primary theological critique focuses on the sacrifice of the mass, in which people offer something to God. Rather, he argues that as a testament, the Lord's Supper is the gift of promise, given by the testator to the heirs. Luther notes that it is not about a 'benefit received [by God] but a benefit conferred' by God to us (WA6.364.20; LW36.93). God's promises become central, replacing the focus on human works. This focus on God's promise also leads Luther to criticize masses for the dead (as 'works' used to reduce one's time in purgatory), and the practice of priests 'mumbling' the words of institution into the cup (because it prevents the heirs from hearing what is promised to them in the will). Also criticized are the practices of communion in only one kind, treating the sacraments as magic to ward off evil, and the commercialization of the sacrament, whether through private masses or masses for the dead. All of these practices detract from the gift God gives at the table of the Lord. However, while God's promises and actions in the sacrament become more central for Luther at this point, he still emphasizes the faith of believers, ensuring the proper reception of this proclaimed gift from God. Over the next decade, he would work to resolve this tension by focusing on the proclaimed life-giving Word in the sacrament that strengthens and creates faith.

Luther's attack on the doctrine of transubstantiation comes in his 1520 treatise, *The Babylonian Captivity of the Church* (WA6.497–573; LW36.3–236). While he does not reject the idea of transubstantiation itself, since it was an attempt to protect the idea of Christ's real presence in the sacrament, Luther feels that it is not appropriate as doctrine (WA6.508.1–512.6; LW36.28–35). In fact, he considers it an unhelpful human concept lacking a logical foundation (McCue 1968: 413). However, Luther also realized that the idea of transubstantiation was interwoven into the doctrine of the 'real presence', which he did not want to abandon. While transubstantiation and consubstantiation both attempted to explain *how* and in what way the bread and wine become Christ's body and blood by using philosophical categories, in doing so they drew attention away from what is given in the meal: the forgiveness of sins. Yet Luther insisted that forgiveness could only happen if Christ were truly present in the Supper.

The Babylonian Captivity of the Church did not stop with a critique of transubstantiation, however. Luther also decried the practice of withholding the cup from the laity (WA6.502.18–507.33; LW36.20–28), since to do so was to disobey Christ's

---

[2] Reinhard Schwarz (2009) provides an excellent overview of this emphasis on the idea of testament, arguing that this theme remains constant throughout Luther's life.

command of Matthew 26:27 ('Drink of it, all of you'). This practice was considered worse than the doctrine of transubstantiation. Luther also redoubled his attacks on the mass as a sacrifice or good work (WA6.512,7–526,33; LW36.35–57). His emphasis on God and God's Word as the subject rather than the object of the verb/action of the sacrament brought Luther's rediscovered understanding of justification squarely into the heart of the sacramental action. The focus must always be on the benefits God gives, not on what humans offer. Luther would return to this argument again in his treatise *The Misuse of the Mass* of 1521 (WA8.506–537; LW36.162–198), and in the 1523 *The Adoration of the Sacrament* of 1523 (WA11.431–456; LW36.275–305). As he states, 'sacrifice and promise are further apart than sunrise and sunset. A sacrifice is a work in which we present and give to God something of our own. The promise, however, is God's word, which gives to us the grace and mercy of God' (WA8.512.10–19; LW36.169). This becomes the focus of his theology of the Lord's Supper, intimately connected to God's Word of promise.

This emphasis on what Christ gives in the sacrament also allowed Luther to shift the focus away from the priest's actions of consecrating the elements and onto God's activity in the sacrament. Zwingli, Bucer, and others, who placed the emphasis on the faith of the recipients, fell prey to the same error as the Romanists: the vital actions of the sacrament were shifted from God to either the presider's consecrating power or the recipient's ability to properly believe. In both cases God was removed as the subject of the verb/action.

At this stage of development, however, Luther still saw the sacramental elements, which contained Christ's body and blood, as signposts pointing to the gift or promise of the proclaimed Word, to be accepted in faith and, as such, the Lord's Supper itself was not as important as God's Word of promise. They were still treated as separate things. This separation of the elements from the promise began to change, however, as Luther was pushed by the South German and Swiss reformers to clarify what he meant by 'real presence'.

The other writings by Luther on the Lord's Supper in this initial stage[3] were predominantly pastoral. They included reactions to the rapid changes in communion practices in Wittenberg while he was still in the Wartburg castle in late 1521, and clarification over the adoration of the sacrament. While in favour of exercising 'Christian freedom' in these matters, Luther was still concerned with how to best guide his parishioners into healthy practices that better reflected the gospel and God's promises.

---

[3] *Receiving Both Kinds in the Sacrament* (1522, WA10,2.11–41; LW36.231–268) suggests that the needed reform of the mass be introduced slowly. *The Adoration of the Sacrament* (1523, WA11.431–456; LW36.269–305) addressed the Bohemian concerns about the adoration of the sacramental elements, and Hoen's argument that 'this is my body' really means 'this signifies my body'(WA11.434,5–436,9; LW36.279–287). *The Abomination of the Secret Mass* of 1525 (WA18.22–36; LW36.307–328), criticized the practice of the priest whispering the words of institution into the cup since the people then could not hear God's promises proclaimed.

III. The Public Battles with Karlstadt, Zwingli, and Oecolampadius

Between the years 1525 and 1528 Luther's writings on the Lord's Supper shifted from the Roman Catholic abuses to attacks levelled on him by other Protestant reformers. Luther had initially been reluctant to write publicly against the other reformers, sensing that internal disagreements among the reformers would hurt their cause. But after repeated attacks on his position, Luther had had enough. He responded with three major articles: *The Sacrament of the Body and Blood of Christ—Against the Fanatics* (1526, WA19.482–523; LW36.329–361); *That These Words of Christ, 'This is My Body,' etc, Still Stand Firm Against the Fanatics* (1527, WA23.64–283; LW37.3–150); and the *Confession Concerning Christ's Supper* (1528, WA26.261–509; LW37.151–372).

In another treatise of 1526, *Against the Heavenly Prophets in the Matter of Images and Sacraments* (WA18.62–125, 134–214; LW40.73–223), Luther clarified how Christ's forgiveness obtained on the cross was connected to the forgiveness given in the sacrament. Karlstadt had charged Luther with teaching that 'a piece of bread forgives sins' (WA18.201,16–17; LW40.211), when forgiveness comes only on the cross. Luther responded by making the distinction between the obtaining of forgiveness, which was a one-time event, and the distribution of that forgiveness in the sacrament. As Luther states: 'Christ has achieved [forgiveness] on the cross, it is true. But he has not distributed or given it on the cross. He has not won it in the supper or sacrament. There he has distributed and given it through the Word, as also in the gospel, where it is preached' (WA18.203,30–34; LW40.213–214). This distinction is important. Further, Luther's emphasis on the word 'distribute' also served another purpose: it moved the sacramental action away from a focus on how the bread and wine become the body and blood of Christ to the benefit given by Christ. The distribution of forgiveness, rather than the adoration of a transubstantiated host, makes it a means of grace. Christ is truly given and distributed in Christ's own body 'for us and our salvation', as stated in the Nicene Creed (BSLK 26.13–14; BC 23,4).

The main problem addressed in all three of these treatises relates to the 'real presence' of Christ in the Supper. The first argument Luther made for 'real presence' was to counteract the tendency to split the physical from the spiritual presence of Christ. Karlstadt, Zwingli, and Oecolampadius, echoing Cornelius Hoen,[4] had insisted that Christ was only spiritually present in the Lord's Supper,[5] based on their exegeses of John 6:63: 'flesh is of no avail'.[6] Köhler noted that Zwingli could not accept that bodily eating could have

---

[4] Hoen's argument is found in 'A Most Christian Letter', in Oberman 1966: 268–76 and in *Zwinglis Werke*, CR 91.512–19.

[5] Chapter 38, 'Luther and the *Schwärmer*' by Burnett, describes Karlstadt's debates and disagreements with Luther, and therefore this information is not repeated here.

[6] Years earlier, however, Luther had argued that John 6:63 was not about the futility of the physical body in sacraments. He insisted that Christ was speaking about faith in the incarnate Word

a spiritual effect, even if it were Christ's body. In his mind, 'body of Christ' could there-fore refer only to the church, and the blood to Christ's blood shed at Calvary (Köhler 1924: 1.4/3, 4/5). Thus, while Zwingli used John 6:63 to interpret the various accounts of the Lord's Supper, Luther began with the biblical accounts of the Lord's Supper and used them to interpret John 6:63. Further, while Zwingli and Karlstadt argued that since 'the flesh is of no avail', Christ's body in the sacrament was of no avail, Luther insisted that Christ's incarnational presence in the sacrament was different than the meaning of 'flesh' as reliance on created objects,[7] and 'spiritual eating' did not mean the absence of the physical but, rather, eating that which was offered in faith. God's 'Word made flesh' (John 1:14) and faith are now irrevocably connected. Thus, if the physical were of no value, argues Luther, then the incarnation would be of no value (WA23.167,28–204,31; LW37.78–101; WA26.353,18–377,31; LW37.237–251). The incarnation involved both the human and divine, which could not be separated (WA26.332,24–36; LW37.218). But here Luther adds a caveat by clarifying what the 'eating' of Christ's body in the sacrament entails: it is not 'cannibalism'. Instead, Christ's body is given, not 'in the same form or mode but in the same essence or nature' (WA26.299,17–21; LW37.195). Luther felt that he was unfairly accused of eating a baked, roasted, ground-up God (WA23.77,17–21; LW37.22),[8] and of thinking that simply by eating these physical substances, one would automatically receive spiritual benefits (*ex opere operato*). Luther insisted that Christ's flesh is not only of no help to a person, but rather, it was actually poison and death if eaten without faith and the Word (WA26.353,27–354,8; LW37.238). Christ's real presence was not only life-giving—it could also be deadly to body and soul.

Luther's second argument against a 'spiritualized presence' addressed the attempts to separate the bread and wine from the body and blood of Christ. This argument revolved around the words of Jesus, 'This is my body'. Karlstadt had argued that 'this' does not refer to the bread; Zwingli insisted that these words were to be interpreted as 'this [bread] represents my body'; while Oecolampadius interpreted it as, 'This is a figure of my body'. Luther preferred to let the words speak for themselves (WA19.484,13–499,38; LW36.336–346; WA26.263,19–292,23; LW37.164–190). Luther argued that his opponents' arguments were problematic theologically, but that they were also illegitimate on gram-matical grounds (WA23.89,32–114,13; LW37.30–45; WA18.144,16–163,22; LW40.154–173; WA26.298,32–313,32, 383,14–498,13; LW37.195–202). The plain meaning could not be eas-ily dismissed. Christ is truly present in the bread and wine, Luther insists, and this insist-ence on the real presence of Christ forms the foundation of his argument.

The third argument against the 'real presence' in the Supper put forward by Zwingli and the others was the idea that God could not be both at the right hand of God and in the Supper at the same time. Luther responds to this objection with recourse to a

---

(WA6.502,7–28; LW36.19–20), rather than the mere spiritual presence of Christ in the sacrament of the altar.

[7] According to Luther's explanation of the first commandment in the *Large Catechism*, this reliance on anyone or anything other than God was idolatry (BSLK 560,22–24; BC 386,3).

[8] Zwingli had accused the Lutherans of this in his 'Reply to Urban Rhegius', CR 91.934.

possible explanation through the argument that Christ is God and as God everywhere present (later dubbed ubiquity), Christ could be seated at the Father's right hand and yet present on the altar because God's right hand, as a metaphor for his omnipotence, was everywhere (WA26.326.29–327.32; LW37.213–214). The right hand of God was not a place, but wherever God was active in the world. However, in response to Zwingli's claims that this idea of ubiquity would mean that God was in every scrap of bread, Luther also insisted that Christ has promised he would be found specifically in the bread of the sacrament given 'for you' (WA23.151,13–24; LW37.68–69). Any limitations placed on God would cause God to no longer be God.

Most important for Luther, however, was the argument that Christ had promised to be present in the bread and wine. To explain this 'mystery', Luther suggested the idea of a *unio sacramentalis* (sacramental union) between the bread and wine and the body and blood of Christ, but he refused to try to explain *how* that happened. He did not want a doctrine or theory about the Lord's Supper to distract from the benefits of the Lord's Supper. As Sasse (1959: 161) notes, 'even the words, "in the bread", "with the bread", "under the bread"…were never regarded by Luther as more than attempts to express…the great mystery that the bread is the body'. They were all merely prepositions used in an attempt to describe this 'real presence'. When Zwingli pushed him to explain how the bread could be called Christ's body when it remained bread, Luther used the idea of *synecdoche*[9] since it could take seriously the reality both of the body and blood of Christ and of the elements themselves. If people did not like his explanations of 'sacramental union' or 'synecdoche', that was fine with him. They were only terms that tried to explain Christ's forgiving presence in the sacrament. For Luther it was simple: If Christ declared, in his Word, that this was his body and blood, then it must be so. On this confession of faith he rested his case. The bread and wine were not symbols pointing to something: in them Christ is truly present, and one encounters forgiveness of sins, life, and salvation (BSLK 520.28–30; BC 362,5–6) in this same Christ.

IV. LUTHER, BUCER, AND THE 1536 WITTENBERG CONCORD

Following the Marburg Colloquy, conversations continued between Luther and Bucer, encouraged by Melanchthon. In two treatises written in 1534,[10] Bucer revealed that he now accepted Luther's understanding of the 'real presence', not as a mere physical or

---

[9] Sasse (1959: 163) defined *synecdoche* as 'an abbreviated speech in which the containing vessel is mentioned instead of its contents'. He notes that a synecdoche would be to point to a wallet and say, 'here is one hundred dollars'. The wallet is not actually a hundred dollars, but it contains that reality.

[10] Bucer's *Report from Holy Scripture* and *Defense Against Catholic Axiom* are summarized in Greschat 2004: 101–6.

spiritual presence, but in terms of a sacramental presence. Repeatedly, Bucer recalled Luther's use of the term 'sacramental union' to explain that presence. But there were two issues that created tension between them. The first was a discussion over the preposition used to describe the relationship between the bread and the body of Christ. While Luther was flexible on this point (as noted above), Bucer insisted 'with the bread' (*cum pane*) be used because the preposition 'with' placed the bread and wine on a 'parallel' plane to the body and blood, without mixing the two together. It was this preposition that made it into the Wittenberg Concord of May 1536, signed by the Wittenberg and South German theologians.

Luther and Bucer also debated who ate the body of Christ in the meal. Luther's emphasis on the 'real presence' and his interpretation of 1 Corinthians 11:29 led him to argue that whoever partakes of the sacrament eats the body of Christ. The faith of believers, whether they were godly (*pii*) or ungodly (*impiorum*), did not affect what was received. As Peters (1966: 105) succinctly states, 'Luther's statements about Christ's presence in the Supper leave no place for the obedience of faith' as a factor that causes Christ's body and blood to be present—although faith is necessary to receive its benefits. Luther had made this position clear in his *Instructions* to Melanchthon, as he headed to Kassel in December 1534. Luther stated that the sacrament affects all people, not just the pious (WABr12.159,19–20, 44–46). Bucer, however, insisted that the faith of the believer was crucial in the reception of the sacrament to prevent people from thinking that its mere celebration (*ex opere operato*) would be sufficient—a position which the reformers had rejected years earlier. The impasse was resolved when Luther, following a proposal offered by the Wittenberg pastor Bugenhagen, proposed a third category—the 'unworthy' (*indigni*), as noted by Sasse (1959: 309; cf. Bizer 1940: 124 and Köhler 1924/53: 2.320–38). Bucer could accept that the 'unworthy' received the body of Christ in the bread, and Luther felt that all were unworthy since everyone is simultaneously justified and sinner (*simul iustus et peccator*). Thus, the Wittenberg Concord stated that 'the body and blood of the Lord are truly extended also to the unworthy, and that the unworthy receive, where the words of institution of Christ are retained' (WABr12.207,17–20, 209,12–15).[11]

V. CONCLUSION

Luther's writings following the Wittenberg Concord simply repeated the polemical arguments he had put forward earlier. But Luther did not direct all his writings on the sacraments towards his opponents. His *Large* and *Small Catechisms*, later treatises on the Lord's Supper, and even the comments on the Supper in the *Smalcald Articles* reflect his position

---

[11] An English translation of the *Wittenberg Concord* can be found in Pelikan and Hotchkiss 2003: 2.799.

without (generally) the scathing arguments. The sacraments are for the people, 'for the forgiveness of sins, life and salvation' (BSLK520,25–30; BC 362,5–6). This emphasis on what the sacraments 'give' is why the battle over the sacraments was so crucial for him.

In the *Instructions* which Luther gave to Melanchthon in December 1534 before Melanchthon headed to Kassel to prepare the groundwork for the Wittenberg Concord two years later, Luther makes a statement that summarizes his mature theology of the Supper: 'Our opinion is that the body is in such a way with or in the bread that it is truly received with the bread. Whatever the bread suffers or does is also true of the body. Thus, it is rightly said of the body of Christ that it is distributed, given, received, eaten' (WABr12.160,64–67). The focus has shifted from what was transubstantiated to what is distributed and given 'for us'—namely, Christ himself and his forgiveness. As the sacrament is received and eaten, forgiveness, life, and salvation are realized. The sacrament is also given as a gift from God, based on God's Word of promise alone, proclaimed from outside of us (*extra nos*), and not on the faith of the recipient. Thus, for Luther, the sacrament of the altar is nothing less than the life-changing presence and action of God's grace and creating Word for a troubled people.

References

Bizer, Ernst (1962, 1940). *Studien zur Geschichte des Abendmahlsstreits im 16. Jahrhundert.* Darmstadt: Wissenschaftliche Buchgesellschaft.

Burnett, Amy Nelson (2011). *Karlstadt and the Origins of the Eucharistic Controversy: A Study in the Circulation of Ideas.* Oxford: Oxford University Press.

Dingel, Irene (1996). *Concordia controversa. Die öffentlichen Diskussionen um das lutherische Konkordienwerk am Ende des 16. Jahrhunderts.* Gütersloh: Gütersloher Verlagshaus.

Faulkner, John Alfred (1917). 'Luther and the Real Presence'. *The American Journal of Theology* 21: 225–39.

Gollwitzer, Helmut (1937). *Coena Domina. Die altlutherische Abendmahlslehre in ihrer Auseinandersetzung mit dem Calvinismus dargestellt an der lutherischen Frühorthodoxie.* Munich: Kaiser.

Gräbke, Friedrich (1908). *Die Konstruktion der Abendmahlslehre Luthers in ihrer Entwicklung dargestellt.* Leipzig: Deichert.

Grass, Hans (1954). *Die Abendmahlslehre bei Luther und Calvin. Eine kritische Untersuchung.* Gütersloh: Bertelsmann.

Greschat, Martin (2004). *Martin Bucer: A Reformer and His Times*, trans. Stephen E. Buckwalter. Louisville: Westminster John Knox.

Hausamann, Susi (1969). 'Realpräsenz in Luthers Abendmahlslehre'. In *Studien zur Geschichte und Theologie: Festschrift für Ernst Bizer*, ed. L. Abramowksi and J. F. G. Goeters. Neukirchen-Ulm: Neukirchener Verlag, 157–73.

Hund, Johannes (2006). *Das Wort ward Fleisch. Eine systematisch-theologische Untersuchung zur Debatte um die Wittenberger Christologie und Abendmahlslehre in den Jahren 1567 bis 1574.* Göttingen: Vandenhoeck & Ruprecht.

Köhler, Walther (1924/53). *Zwingli und Luther: Ihr Streit über das Abendmahl nach seinen politischen und religiösen Beziehungen*, 2 vols. Gütersloh: Bertelsmann.

McCue, James F. (1968). 'The Doctrine of Transubstantiation from Berengar through Trent: The Point at Issue'. *Harvard Theological Review* 61: 385–430.

Meinhold, Peter (1960). 'Abendmahl und Opfer nach Luther'. In *Abendmahl und Opfer*, ed. Peter Meinhold and Erwin Iserloh. 35–73.

Meßner, Reinhard (1989). *Die Meßreform Martin Luthers und die Eucharistie der Alten Kirche: Ein Beitrag zu einer systematischen Liturgiewissenschaft*. Innsbruck and Vienna: Tyrolia.

Oberman, Heiko A. (1966). *Forerunners of the Reformation: The Shape of Late Medieval Thought*. New York: Holt, Rinehart, and Winston.

Pelikan, Jaroslav and Valerie Hotchkiss (eds.) (2003). 'The Wittenberg Concord'. In *Creeds and Confessions of Faith in the Christian Tradition*. Part Four: *Creeds and Confessions of the Reformation Era*. Vol. 2. New Haven: Yale University Press, 796–801.

Peters, Albrecht (1966). *Realpräsenz. Luthers Zeugnis von Christi Gegenwart im Abendmahl*, 2nd edn. Berlin: Lutherisches Verlagshaus.

Quere, Ralph W. (1985). 'Changes and Constants: Structure in Luther's Understanding of the Real Presence in the 1520s'. *Sixteenth Century Journal* 16: 45–78.

Sasse, Hermann (1959). *This is My Body: Luther's Contention for the Real Presence in the Sacrament of the Altar*. Minneapolis: Augsburg.

Schwarz, Reinhard (2009). 'The Last Supper: The Testament of Jesus'. In *The Pastoral Luther: Essays on Martin Luther's Practical Theology*, ed. Timothy J. Wengert. Grand Rapids, MI: Eerdmans, 198–210.

Wisløff, Carl (1964). *The Gift of Communion: Luther's Controversy with Rome on Eucharistic Sacrifice*, trans. Joseph M. Shaw. Minneapolis: Augsburg.

SUGGESTED READING

Althaus, Paul (1966). *The Theology of Martin Luther*, trans. Robert C. Schultz. Philadelphia: Fortress.

Bizer, Ernst (1955). 'Die Abendmahlslehre in den lutherischen Bekenntnisschriften'. In *Die Abendmahlslehre in den reformatorischen Bekenntnisschriften*, ed. Ernst Bizer and Walter Kreck. Munich: Kaiser, 3–42.

Bornkamm, Heinrich (1983). *Luther in Mid-Career, 1521–1530*. Philadelphia: Fortress.

Brecht, Martin (1990). *Martin Luther. Vol. 2: Shaping and Defining the Reformation, 1521–1532*, trans. James L. Schaaf. Philadelphia: Fortress.

Clark, Francis (1967). *Eucharistic Sacrifice and the Reformation*, 2nd edn. Oxford: Blackwell.

Elert, Werner (1973). *The Lord's Supper Today*, trans. Martin Bertram. Saint Louis: Concordia.

Hazlett, Ian (1975). 'The Development of Martin Bucer's Thinking on the Sacrament of the Lord's Supper in its Historical and Theological Context 1523–1534'. Th.D. Dissertation, University of Münster.

Hendel, Kurt K. (2008). 'Finitum capax infiniti: Luther's Radical Incarnational Perspective'. *Currents in Theology and Mission* 35: 420–33.

Hopf, Friedrich Wilhelm (1937). 'Die Abendmahlslehre der evangelische-lutherischen Kirche'. In *Abendmahlsgemeinschaft?* Munich: Kaiser.

Iserloh, Erwin (1965). 'Sacramentum und Exemplum—Ein augustinisches Thema lutherischer Theologie'. In *Reformata Reformanda. Festschrift für H. Jedin*. Vol. 1, ed. E. Iserloh and K. Repgen. Münster: Aschendorff, 247–64.

Jenson, Robert W. (1978). *Visible Words*. Philadelphia: Fortress.

Kinder, Ernst (1959). 'Die Gegenwart Christi im Abendmahl nach lutherischem Verständnis'. In *Gegenwart Christi*, ed. F. Viering. Göttingen: Vandenhoeck & Ruprecht, 33–65.

—— (1959). '"Realpräsenz" und "Repräsentation"'. *Theologische Literaturzeitung* 84: 882–94.

Peters, Albrecht (1970). 'Das Abendmahl nach Luther'. *Jahrbuch des Evangelischen Bundes* 13: 98–134.

—— (2012) *Baptism and Lord's Supper: Commentary on Luther's Catechisms*. Vol. 4, trans. Thomas H. Trapp. Saint Louis: Concordia.

Raunio, Antti (2009). 'Faith and Christian Living in Luther's Confession Concerning Christ's Supper (1528)'. *Lutherjahrbuch* 76: 19–56.

Sommerlath, Ernst (1930). *Der Sinn des Abendmahls nach Luthers Gedanken 1527–1529*. Leipzig: Dörffling und Franke.

Vajta, Vilmos (1970). 'Evangelium und Sakramente: Entwurf einer Problemstellung'. *Oecumenica* 5: 9–40.

Wengert, Timothy J. (2009). *Martin Luther's Catechisms: Forming the Faith*. Minneapolis: Fortress.

CHAPTER 23

LUTHER ON THE CHURCH

DAVID P. DANIEL

IN his tract *On the Papacy in Rome* (1520) Luther wrote that,

> according to Scripture…Christendom means an assembly of all the people on earth who believe in Christ…This community or assembly means all those who live in true faith, hope and love. Thus the essence, life, and nature of Christendom is not a physical assembly but an assembly of hearts in one faith, as St. Paul says in Ephesians 4 [:5], 'One baptism, one faith, one Lord'…This is what spiritual unity really means, on the basis of which men are called a 'communion of saints'.
>
> (WA6.292.37–293,1; LW39.65)

Nine years later, in his *Large Catechism*, Luther professed:

> I believe that there is on earth a holy little flock and community of pure saints under one head, Christ. It is called together by the Holy Spirit in one faith, mind, and understanding. It possesses a variety of gifts and yet is united in love without sect or schism. Of this community I also am a part and member, a participant and co-partner in all the blessings it possesses. (Creed, BSLK 657; BC 437–8)

In his *On the Councils and the Church* (1539) Luther declares that 'here the creed clearly indicates what the church is, namely, a communion of saints, that is, a crowd or assembly of people who are Christians and holy, which is called a Christian holy assembly, or church' (WA50.624; LW41.143).

For just over three decades, from his first exegetical lectures on the Psalms and Romans (Holl 1921; Fagerberg 1955; Maurer 1958; Hendrix 1974) to his final outbursts against the papacy and false brethren (Edwards 1963; Hendrix 1981: 150–9) Martin Luther was clear both on what the church is not and on what the church is and where it is to be found. Canon law and clergy, ecclesiastical rites and traditions, institutional, administrative and theological structures (Pelikan 1968: 6–8) do not constitute the church. The church is the *communio sanctorum*, the community of believers or saints, whose only head is Christ Jesus. (Althaus 1966: 294–313). It is created and sustained by the proclamation of the gospel of the forgiveness of sins. Wherever this gospel, God's

Word, is preached and believed, there is the church (WA12.191; LW40.37). The church is one, holy, catholic (universal), and apostolic (WA26.506; LW37.367). Apart from the church there is no Christ, no truth, no salvation (WA26.507; LW37.368). It is a spiritual assembly that transcends time and space and is perceived through faith (WADB7.418–420; LW35.410–411). At the same time it is a historical reality, truly present and visible in the world (WA50.629; LW41.149).

Throughout his life Luther utilized much of the terminology of traditional ecclesiology (Lohse 1999: 277). However, he radically redefined its vocabulary, infusing traditional words and concepts with new emphases and connotations in order to convey his conviction of what and where the true church is (Althaus 1966: 288; Lohse 1986: 177). This occurred contemporaneously with the formulation of his new understanding of the relationship between God's righteousness and God's grace (Arts 1972).

Medieval theologians had not developed ecclesiology as a separate theological *locus* (Ginther 2008). Their concerns were primarily the authority of canon law, the sacramental system, the ecclesiastical hierarchy, and the papacy as crucial agents for the preservation of the church's orthodoxy and unity. Their ecclesiology was largely a response to the challenges posed by heresy and schism to the unity of the church and ecclesiastical authority. In general, 'heretics' and 'schismatics' were condemned chiefly because they sought to redefine the character and nature of the 'true' church by emphasizing poverty, moral purity, anti-clericalism, and/or divine election, thus threatening existing ecclesiastical institutions, structures, and traditions (Hendrix 1976). Therefore, medieval churchmen emphasized apostolic succession, the sacraments, and other ecclesiastical structures, including papal primacy, as the chief marks of the catholicity and unity of the church.

Luther's study of Scripture, and specifically his understanding of the gospel, was the lens through which he critically examined how the church actually functioned in society and evaluated the theological arguments it had developed for specific ecclesiastical practices and structures. Luther's studies led him to take a path that diverged from the ecclesiological attitudes of the late medieval church. What was new in Luther's ecclesiology was his point of departure—soteriology and Christology. Luther's understanding of the church is founded upon his conviction that human justification and salvation is solely God's work in Christ (Rupp 1956).

I. Luther's Ecclesiological Themes or Leitmotifs

Lohse (1999: 6–7) and others have noted the integration of historical-genetic and systematic methodologies necessary for the investigation of Luther's ecclesiology. Luther did not formulate a 'programme' of ecclesiastical reformation, nor did he prepare a comprehensive systematic ecclesiology during the three decades of his reform activity. He did not claim scriptural mandates for any particular ecclesiastical structure. His ecclesiological concerns were made manifest in works occasioned by specific controversies or dealing with specific practical pastoral questions as well as by comments scattered throughout his exegetical works (Pelikan 1958), sermons, and correspondence. Although Luther did not stray far from what he found in the Scriptures, it is clear that his understanding of the church was shaped by his reflection upon the nature and function of the gospel and the broadening of his own theological horizon (Beyer 1983: 93). His comments must be understood within their historical contexts since his language, style, and emphases were adapted to respond to specific practical concerns or polemic purposes. It is not sufficient to indicate *what* Luther wrote but to note *when* and to *whom* and for what purpose he prepared his comments. In addition, the 'systematic' structure of Luther's ecclesiology and its functional dynamic can be discerned in the leitmotifs that appear again and again in his works, albeit with subtle or significant changes in emphases.

Luther's ecclesiology is not institutional or structural but soteriological and kerygmatic (Lohse 1999: 278). While Luther uses the broad range of biblical images and metaphors to refer to the church (Klug 1993: 11–12), he frequently refers to it as the *communio sanctorum*, the community of saints or believers in Christ (WA50.624–625; LW41.143), infusing both words, *communio* and *sanctorum*, with new meanings (Althaus 1966: 294–304). It is a Christological community, created, preserved, and united in Christ. God creates this holy people through the proclamation of the forgiveness of sins by the Word of the gospel. His ecclesiology likewise reflects, in its polarities, many of the motifs of what was later called the 'Wittenberg' theology (Kolb and Arand 2008)—God hidden and revealed, the distinction between law and gospel, two kinds of righteousness, two kingdoms or two modes of God's governance, and that a Christian is simultaneously justified and a sinner—to distinguish between the universality and particularity of the church and to explain the relationship, comprehensible by faith, between the reality of the church in the presence of God (*coram deo*) and its concrete, real manifestation in the world (*coram mundo*) (Arand 2008: 162–5).

Among the most significant ecclesiological themes treated again and again in his discussions of what the church is and how it functions in this world are: (1) the church is a community of the saints, a holy people or assembly, who share their faith and gifts; (2) Christ is the only head of the one true church; he alone knows who are his sheep; (3) outside of the church, apart from Christ, there is no salvation;(4) the true church is *coram deo* spiritual, internal transcending time; at the same time it is *coram mundo* in that historical reality, the humanly made external or physical church; (5) the true church in the world is perceived by faith and recognized by its marks or signs, namely the preaching of the gospel of the forgiveness of sins and the sacraments; (6) all Christians by virtue of their baptism and faith are priests (*sacerdotum*), to whom all spiritual authority is given; (7) the priests call those who will serve as their pastors to the divinely established public office of preaching the gospel and administration of the sacraments; (8) by virtue of its repudiation of the gospel and perversion of spiritual authority, the papacy is the Antichrist. In addition, while Luther held that institutional forms and liturgical practices are not divinely mandated, whatever is introduced to the church should promote good order and the gospel.

Luther transformed the understanding of the church by emphasizing that it was not an institution but a community gathered by the Spirit through the gospel of the forgiveness of sins. The chief mark or sign of the church was its possession of and subordination to God's Word. Luther is convinced that the church is not a human work but God's work, who alone creates and sustains his people through his Word (WA50.476; LW47.118). No theological concept was more important for his ecclesiology than his multi-hued understanding of the term 'word'—for Christ, the gospel preached, the sacraments, and Scripture. For Luther the Word is the decisive mark of the church (Althaus 1966: 288–91; Lohse 1999: 278; Kolb and Arand 2008: 129–220). The proclamation of the Word, the gospel of the forgiveness of sins, is the unique, most certain, and most noble sign of the church. It is the true treasure of the church (WA1.237,22–23; LW31.31). The entire life and substance of the church is the Word of God. 'God's Word,' Luther wrote, 'cannot exist without God's people and God's people cannot exist without God's Word' (WA50.629,34–35; LW41.150). In the church 'we teach with the Word, we consecrate with the Word, we bind and absolve sins by the Word, we baptize with the Word, we sacrifice with the Word, we judge all things by the Word' (WA12.181; LW40.23). God's Word, the gospel of the forgiveness of sins, is the golden thread that binds together all of Luther's comments on the church from his earliest lectures on the Psalms until his bitter invectives during his last battles.

II. The Contexts of Luther's Ecclesiological Works

Within the confines of this essay it is possible to deal with the context of only some of the most important of Luther's ecclesiological works, noting the themes that he regularly employed as he discussed the nature and functioning of the church, and finally indicating three major issues debated by interpreters of Luther's ecclesiology.

Luther formulated almost all of the fundamental principles of his theological understanding of the church during his conflict with the hierarchy of the Roman church prior to his appearance at the Diet of Worms in 1521. In his subsequent continuing conflict with Rome, Luther, heretic and outlaw, professor and pastor, had to defend, further clarify, and apply his ecclesiology—both to aid his supporters and to guard against its misappropriation or application by those who advocated other ecclesiastical principles and practices. The emergence of divergent religious parties within the empire focused attention on the question of how the true church of Christ, the *communio sanctorum*, could be recognized in this world. It was this question that propelled Luther on the road to Reformation, resonated like a *basso continuo* throughout his ecclesiological works, and emerged as a crucial issue for theological colloquies, controversy, and confessions for Luther, his contemporaries, and their successors down to the twenty-first century (Avis 1981).

II.1. Luther's Ecclesiology, 1513–17

Five phases can be discerned in Luther's formulation and application of his ecclesiology. The first stage can be considered to have begun with his assumption of the professorship of Bible at Wittenberg in 1513 and to have lasted until the 'posting' of the Ninety-five Theses. It culminated with the publication of these theses concerning indulgences (WA1.233–238; LW31.25–33) and the preparation of his *Explanations of the Ninety-five Theses* (WA1.525–628; LW31.83–252), in which he considered the authority of the pope to have been established not by God but by the church, i.e., by human and not divine authority (WA1.236–237; LW31.234–240). During these four years, in his lectures on Psalms (Holl 1921; Fagerberg 1955; Maurer 1958; Hendrix 1976), Romans, Galatians, and Hebrews (Arts 1972; Hendrix 1981: 18–21) Luther emphasized that the church was a community of holy people in Christ fed by the faithful preaching of the Word. Luther asserted that papal decisions are limited by both councils, canon law, and Scripture, and he repeatedly called for pope and hierarchy to take seriously their pastoral responsibility. However, he did not publicly attack the pope directly. His attack on indulgences was based on his conviction that sacramental penance as practised in the Roman church was quite different from the repentance demanded by Scripture, to which Christian teaching and practice must conform.

II.2. Luther's Ecclesiology, 1518–21

The second and arguably the most creative phase in the development of Luther's ecclesiology began in the spring of 1518 and concluded with Luther's appearance at the Diet of Worms on 16 April 1521. During these three years Luther developed almost all of the major themes of his ecclesiology: the fundamental authority of the Word; Word and sacraments, newly defined, as the key marks of the true church; the rejection of the infallibility of councils and the papacy; the priesthood of all the baptized; the repudiation of sacerdotalism; the denunciation of the papacy for its failure to submit to the authority of the Word and exercise its pastoral role of proclaiming the gospel of the forgiveness of sins; the distinction between the true spiritual church, whose members are known only to God, and the external, physical or visible church that is a *corpus permixtum*, a body comprised of both sinners and saints (Aurelius 1983).

During the spring of 1518, while Luther repudiated scholastics as theologians of glory and postulated a theology of the cross during the Heidelberg disputation, Sylvester Prierias prepared his *Dialogue on the Power of the Pope*. In it Prierias declared infallible the doctrine of the Roman church and papal authority from which even Scripture derived its strength. Anyone who did not accept this, who contradicted the teachings of the church in matters of faith and morals or its practices, is heretical. This tract persuaded Luther that papal authority and scriptural authority were intractably opposed to each other. This conviction was reinforced by his tense sessions with Cardinal Cajetan (Tomasso de Vio) in Augsburg (October 1518), during which the papal legate refused to be swayed by any of Luther's citations from Scripture. It was clear they differed not only on the issue of papal credibility and but also on their understanding of the nature of faith and the essence of the Christian life. Luther rejected Cajetan's demand for his recantation. Although he continued to express respect for the papacy, he was convinced that the hierarchy was not fulfilling its responsibility to feed the people with the Word of Christ (Hendrix 1981: 56–64; Lohse 1986: 45–6).

The various strands of Luther's theological development came together during 1519 as he wrestled with questions of grace, righteousness and good works, and the authority and responsibility of the hierarchy from a scriptural perspective. He also engaged in an intensive study of the councils and church history in the months prior to the Leipzig debate that confirmed his doubts about identifying the church of Christ with the Roman church (Hendrix 1981: 81–5; Lohse 1999: 118–22; Spehr 2010: 115–79). The exchange of theses between Eck, Karlstadt, and Luther culminated in Luther's *Explanation of Proposition Thirteen Concerning the Power of the Pope* (WA2.183–240). The pope did not have authority over Scripture but the Scripture over the popes. Christ had given the keys, the responsibility to preach the gospel of the forgiveness of sins, to the church. To feed Christ's sheep by teaching the Word of God was the chief function of the church and the successors of the apostles. Therefore the church owed its existence solely to Christ, its head, who was present where the gospel was preached and the sacraments rightly administered. The stage was set for the confrontation between Eck and Luther (4–13 July 1519). Prior to Leipzig, Luther had regularly appealed to a consensus of Scripture, councils, Church Fathers, and sound arguments against papal decrees. During the debate he declared that popes, councils, and Church Fathers could err and that Scripture, the Word of God, is above all human words (Hendrix 1981: 88–9). During the debate Luther asserted that some of the articles of Hus and the Bohemians were wrongly condemned at Constance, for they were clearly Christian and evangelical. The stage was set for the ongoing struggle over the papacy and authority within the church and the denunciation of Luther as a heretic.

After Leipzig Luther rapidly broadened his attacks upon the theology and practices of the Roman church as the two themes of scriptural authority and the church as a community of the saints intertwined in his *Treatise on the New Testament* (WA6.353–378; LW35.79–111). In this treatise Luther refers to the universal priesthood of all the baptized for the first time (WA6.370; LW35.100) and declared the pope was a tyrant and Antichrist (WA6.374; LW35.107). Meanwhile, as the Roman Curia prepared Luther's condemnation and issued the bull *Exsurge Domine* (15 June 1520), Luther responded in German to a defence of Eck by the Franciscan Alveld, *On the Papacy at Rome* (26 June, WA6.285–324; LW39.123–217). It is significant because it indicates that his understanding of the church and papacy after Leipzig was in flux. In it Luther held that Christendom or church is spoken of as church in three ways. It is an assembly of all believers in Christ on earth, the communion of saints or spiritual unity, created by the Holy Spirit. It is necessary, Luther wrote, to distinguish between spiritual, internal, essential Christendom and physical external Christendom with its humanly made institutions and orders, including canon law and prelates. The former, the spiritual, is the true church, whose head is Christ alone. It has no need of an earthly head. The latter has a hierarchy that is not created by divine command but is a human arrangement. Luther also indicated a third meaning for the term church: places of worship. Luther maintained that the office of the keys, the power to forgives sins, is a gracious promise given to the whole community of Christendom and noted that he was willing to accept the pope's decrees but only if they conformed to Scripture.

Luther's ecclesiological views coalesced in the late spring and summer of 1520 as is shown by their concrete application in the so-called 'Reformation treatises' published between August and November 1520: *To the Christian Nobility of the German Nation* (completed in June and published on 18 August) (WA6.404–469; LW44.123–217), *The Babylonian Captivity of the Church* (WA6.497–573; LW36.11–126), and *The Freedom of a Christian* (WA7.20–38 German, 7.49–73 Latin; LW31.343–377). In the first, Luther not only attacked hierarchical clericalism and made extensive specific suggestions for ecclesiastical reform to be supervised and implemented by the lay authorities. He provided a theological basis for his suggestions, the priesthood of all believers. All Christians were priests (*sacerdotes*) even if all were not pastors or ministers (*ministri*). The difference between them was in neither status (*Stand*) nor authority but only in function or office (*Amt*). Therefore, secular authorities, because of their authority as priests and the responsibilities of their secular office, were to take in hand the reform of the church (WA6.408; LW44.129). This was a repudiation of a clerical 'spiritual' status that was the source of the three walls impeding reform of the Roman church: (a) that spiritual authorities are superior to secular authorities; (b) that only the pope can authoritatively and inerrantly interpret Scripture; and (c) that papal authority is superior to that of the councils.

Luther attacked the theological foundations of the sacerdotal sacramentalism of the Roman church in his *Babylonian Captivity of the Church* and, redefining the nature of a sacrament, reduced the number of sacraments from seven to three and finally to two within the same tract. While his attacks on the three 'captivities' of the mass—withholding the cup from the laity, the doctrine of transubstantiation, and considering the mass a good work—contained historical inaccuracies, the primary focus of his attack was the rejection of the mass as a sacrificial good work performed by the priest. The sacramental system of the church was rejected because it served as an instrument of papal tyranny. While maintaining the rights of Christians as priests, he underscored the significance of the special public office of the ministry of the Word, of preaching the gospel (WA6.566; LW36.116).

After receiving the bull *Exsurge Domine* in October, Luther was convinced the pope was the Antichrist. However, he still did not attack the pope personally and even addressed a final appeal to him in the *Open Letter to Leo X* that prefaced his tract *On the Freedom of a Christian*. Influenced in part by the efforts of the papal legate, Karl von Miltitz, Luther's letter reiterated the distinction he made between the person of the pope and the office of the papacy, a theme that then remained constant in his criticisms of the papacy (Hendrix 1981: 112–16). In the tract itself, which is an exposition of Christian freedom and responsibility, Luther applies his distinction between the 'inner' and the 'outer' human creature to substantiate his defence of the spiritual liberty of Christians. He likewise clearly distinguishes between the priesthood of believers and the ministry of the Word. 'Although we are all equally priests, we cannot all publicly minister and teach. We ought not do it even if we could' (WA7.58; LW31.356). It was clear that Luther and the papacy had fundamentally disparate understandings of the nature of the church and its spiritual authority. Although Luther had appealed his case to a general council of the church in November, the burning of the papal bull, copies of the decretals, and other 'papist' publications on 10 December 1520 confirms that he had rejected papal authority. Three weeks later, in the bull *Decet Romanum Pontificem* (3 January 1521), Leo X excommunicated Luther. The die was cast for the ongoing struggle between Rome and Luther on what constituted the true church and where it could be found.

II.3. Luther's Ecclesiology, 1521–6

The third phase of Luther's ecclesiological development began after his appearance in Worms (18 April 1521). Although Luther's refusal to recant at Worms was 'pastoral and not political', a protest against an 'unfaithful hierarchy on behalf of the faithful people' (Hendrix 1981: 133–4), it had political as well as ecclesiastical consequences for Luther and his supporters. On the one hand, Luther was convinced that the papacy was a demonic power that represented the Antichrist rather than Christ. In 1521 and 1522 he attacked papal pretensions and the abuse of ecclesiastical office again and again in five treatises responding to attacks made by Augustine Alveld and Jerome Emser.[1] The most important of these treatises is probably the *Answer to the Hyperchristian, Hyperspiritual, and Hyperlearned Book by Goat Emser in Leipzig* (WA7.621–688; LW39.143–224), in which Luther reiterates his argument for the common priesthood of all believers and indicates the exegetical principles from which his concepts of church and ministry had emerged. In his tract of 1522, directed against his old foe, Archbishop Albrecht of Mainz, *Against the Spiritual Estate of the Pope and the Bishops, Falsely So Called* (WA10,2.105–158; LW39.247–299) as in his *Judgment on Monastic Vows* (WA8.573–669; LW44.251–400) Luther rejected holy orders as a sacrament, denied that the clergy comprised a separate spiritual estate within Christendom, condemned the papacy, compulsory

---

[1] E.g., *On the Papacy in Rome Against the Most Celebrated Romanist in Leipzig*, WA6.285–324; LW39.55–104 (countering Alveld), *To the Goat in Leipzig*, WA7.262–265; LW39.111–115 (countering Emser), *Concerning the Answer of the Goat in Leipzig*, WA7.271–283; LW39.121–135. Emser's coat of arms displayed a goat.

monastic vows, the special 'spiritual' character of the clergy, the mass, and indulgences that enslaved the consciences of individuals. Against these he juxtaposed Christian or evangelical freedom that depends solely and completely on Christ, who has freed the conscience from good works through the gospel and teaches reliance only on his mercy. Luther condemned the papacy as Antichrist because it would not fulfil its pastoral responsibility to feed God's people with the gospel of the forgiveness of sins and reform the church and was thus attacking God's kingdom, the church, from within.

Luther was equally harsh upon those reformers whom he perceived as threatening Christian freedom and the power of the gospel with a new legalism that sought to establish communities consisting only of true believers, who questioned the validity of infant baptism and the sacraments, or who supported iconoclasm and disrupted ecclesiastical and civil order. When Karlstadt's rapid introduction of radical changes in liturgy and practice and the appearance of the so-called Zwickau prophets, who claimed new revelations directly from the Holy Spirit, created disorder in Wittenberg, Luther abandoned the fortress Wartburg to return to the city. The eight *Invocavit* sermons preached from 9–16 March 1522 (WA10,3.1–64; LW51.70–100) re-established order in the city and repudiated interpreting and utilizing the gospel as a new law. The sermons reveal Luther's conviction that the Holy Spirit works through the gospel to create faith and transform life. The gospel bestows freedom upon Christians who, however, have the responsibility to show love and concern for the weaker brethren, trusting in the power of the Word in the life of the church. This argument was presaged by his postil on Matthew 11:2–10 prepared in 1521 and published in his *Adventspostille* of 1522, in which he enunciated for the first time his distinction between law and gospel (WA10,1.2.147–70; CP1.87–113). The publications from the early 1520s express Luther's concern that reforms of the liturgy, institutions, and the life of the church be carried out in an orderly and decent manner that respected the weaker brethren as well as the responsibilities of temporal authorities (WA10,3.9,9–13; LW51.73).

As the Reformation spread, Luther received requests from individual communities of Christians for biblical justifications of their right to call their own pastors to preach and administer the sacraments according to the gospel. Among these were the lay leaders of Leisnig in Saxony, to whom Luther sent a short treatise on public worship (WA12.35–37; LW53.11–14), a preface for the reorganization of the common chest of the city (WA12.11–30; LW45.169–194), and the treatise *That a Christian Assembly or Congregation has the Right and Power to Judge Teaching and to Call, Appoint, and Dismiss Teachers, Established and Proven by Scripture* (WA11.408–416; LW39.305–314). In it Luther provided biblical substantiation for his argument that a Christian congregation in possession of the gospel not only has the authority but the duty to depose those who teach and preach contrary to God's Word. They likewise have the duty to call preachers and teachers to administer the Word. Whoever is chosen or called by the congregation thus has the office of preaching, the highest office in Christendom, imposed upon him and deserves respect.

In the same year (1523) Luther sent *Concerning the Ministry* (WA12.169–195; LW40.7–44) to the magistracy of Prague. It succinctly presented the relationship between the priesthood of the baptized and the office of the ministry. It expressed Luther's growing sympathy for the Utraquist Hussites, already shown by his letter to the Czech estates in July 1522 (WA10,2.172–174), in which he urged them not to seek reconciliation with 'Rome' and even suggested that a union of the Utraquists and the Lutherans might be possible if, after patient discussions guided by the gospel, they could find unity in teaching (Pelikan 1964: 124–5). Gallus Cahera, an Utraquist then in Wittenberg, urged Luther to write a tract for the Utraquists, who had difficulty obtaining regularly ordained pastors. Luther reiterated what he had originally set forth in *The Address to the Christian Nobility*, namely, that 'all Christians are priests, all priests are Christians' in equal degree, by virtue of their baptism. As priests, each and every Christian has the full and unfettered right to exercise the functions of the priesthood, that is 'to teach, to preach and proclaim the Word of God, to baptize, to consecrate or administer the Eucharist, to bind and loose sins, to pray for others, to sacrifice, and to judge doctrine'. These are the seven rights and marks of the priesthood, of each and every Christian. The first and foremost of these, however, upon which everything else depends and from which everything else flows, 'is the teaching of the Word of God. For we teach with the Word, we consecrate with the Word, we bind and absolve sins by the Word, we baptize with the Word, we sacrifice with the Word, we judge all things by the Word' (WA12.179,38–180,4; LW40.21).

In this tract Luther clearly distinguishes, however, between the priesthood of the baptized and the pastoral office of the Word. 'No individual can arise by his own authority and arrogate to himself alone what belongs to all' (WA12.189,17–20; LW40.34). 'A priest is not identical with presbyter or minister, for one is born a priest, one is made a minister' (WA12.178,9 10; LW40.18). Therefore, where Christians are without the public ministry of the Word, ministers should be selected from the community of believers, hands laid upon them to certify that they are the community's bishops, ministers, or pastors (WA12.193,33–194,3; LW40.40). When this is done, the people should 'believe beyond a shadow of a doubt that this has been done and accomplished by God' (WA12.191,25–26; LW40.37). While he denies that ordination conveys an indelible character, he affirms that

> ordination indeed was first instituted on the authority of Scripture, and according to the example of and decrees of the Apostle, in order to provide the people with ministers of the Word. The public ministry of the Word...ought to be established by holy ordination as the highest and greatest of the functions of the church, on which the whole power of the church depends since the church is nothing without the Word and everything in it exists by virtue of the Word alone. (WA12.173,2–8; LW40.11)

Moreover, if and when the recommended procedure becomes common, 'then these bishops [pastors] may wish to come together and elect one or more from the number to be their superiors, who would serve them and hold visitations among them...' (WA12.194,14–17; LW40.41) Luther's recommendations were not implemented by the Utraquists, however, due in part to Cahera's inauguration of negotiations with the papal party in Bohemia, his abandonment of Utraquism, and, ultimately, his exile. Luther was greatly disappointed in Cahera and the disruption of relations with the Czech Utraquists (Pelikan 1964: 124–5).

II.4. Luther's Ecclesiology, 1525/6–30

The fourth phase of Luther's ecclesiological development began in 1525 and culminated with the Diet of Augsburg. It was marked by his increased concern about good order and teaching in the church and the need to develop formal procedures or structures that would strengthen the congregations and assure a regular supply of pastoral candidates. It was this concern that led to a change in his ecclesiological emphases. After 1527 he emphasized more frequently the distinction between the priesthood and the ministerial office that exercises spiritual authority publicly (Green 1966). Although he continued to emphasize that all priests individually possessed the same rights, not every individual Christian or priest is prepared to preach and teach. Nor would it be proper for an individual to claim the right to exercise that which is held in common without the consent of the whole body or of the church, such as the celebration of Holy Communion or the calling or deposing of pastors. What God mandated is that the church, the priesthood, the congregation or community, calls suitable candidates to the public office of preaching and teaching the Word (Daniel 1988: 270–6).

Changes in Luther's ecclesiological emphases, though not its substance, resulted from developments that demanded his attention in 1525 and thereafter—his dispute with Erasmus, his controversy with Zwingli, whose influence spread among the upper (southern) German reformers, the challenge of Anabaptism, the social turmoil and political tensions resulting from the uprisings of peasants and miners and the bloody reaction of the landlords, the death of Elector Frederick in May 1525, and the Diet of Speyer in the summer of 1526. The diet approved what was a temporary truce in the enforcement of the Edict of Worms until a general or national council of the church would resolve the ecclesiastical questions. This truce gave the Lutheran princes and cities an opportunity to consolidate their movement.

The consolidation of Lutheranism required the clarification of outstanding theological issues, especially concerning the sacraments and the establishment of a system of designating, theologically equipping, and supervising pastors for local congregations. Three theological challenges confronted the Lutheran movement in this period: Anabaptism, Zwinglianism, and, within the Lutheran camp itself, those who argued against preaching of the law to effect repentance, a prelude to beginnings of the antinomian controversy. These all came to a head in 1528/9 as Luther published three works, *Concerning Rebaptism* (WA26.144–174; LW40.229–262), his *Confession concerning Christ's Supper* (WA26.261–509; LW37.161–372), and his introduction to the *Instructions for the Visitors of Parish Pastors in Electoral Saxony* (WA26.195–240; LW40.269–320). In the first, Luther reiterates his belief that the efficacy of baptism does not depend on the faith of the baptized and defends infant baptism. He also emphasizes that in this world the church is comprised of both saints and sinners and that even if the Antichrist is in the church, it is still the church. Christ preserves true Christianity even under the papacy (WA26.147,13–40; LW40.231–233). In the first two parts of his *Confession concerning Christ's Supper* Luther provides his most detailed explanation of his view of the Lord's Supper and his understanding of the union of the two natures in Christ. The third section is Luther's confession of faith concerning disputed articles, in which he provides a succinct definition of the church and its unity despite diversity:

> I believe that there is one holy Christian church on earth, i.e., the community or number or assembly of all Christians in all the world, the one bride of Christ, and his spiritual body, of which he is the only head. The bishops or priests are not her heads or lords or bridegrooms, but servants, friends, and... superintendents, guardians, or stewards.
>
> (WA26.506,30–35; LW40.367)

His introduction to the visitation articles of 1528 indicated that the disturbing conditions in the church required institutional supervision and argued that, although the elector was not obliged to teach or rule in spiritual affairs, he did have the obligation of a temporal sovereign to secure order when strife or dissension arise. Princes, as Christian brothers acting out of love, could temporarily serve as 'emergency bishops' to provide for the visitation of pastors (Spitz 1953: 134). After 1528 Luther begins to use more frequently the distinction between spiritual and temporal authority and rulers and to propose that superintendents be appointed who would exercise the essential functions of a bishop, namely, to assure the preaching of the gospel and the right administration of the sacraments.

The state of the churches and pastoral care indicated by the visitations of pastors led Luther to place increased emphasis upon the connection between the work of the Holy Spirit and preaching and teaching as the crucial task of the ministerial office. Therefore, during 1528–9 Luther prepared his two catechisms. The *Large* (German) *Catechism* was intended to assist in the instruction of pastors. In his treatment of the third article of the Apostles' Creed he reiterates and expands what was summarized in the *Small Catechism*, namely the connection between the work of the Holy Spirit, the preaching of God's Word, and the unity of the church (LC, Creed 40–8; BSLK 654–6; BC 436–7). Luther again argues that the Greek *ecclesia* means assembly, just as the word *communio* should be understood as meaning a 'community'. Thus, the church is a gathering or community of those made holy by the Spirit. He then confesses 'I believe that there is on earth a holy little flock and community of pure saints under one head, Christ. It is called together by the Holy Spirit in one faith, mind, and understanding. It possesses a variety of gifts, and yet is united in love without sect or schism' (LC, Creed, 51; BSLK 657; BC 437–8).

II.5. Luther's Ecclesiology, 1530–46

During the last fifteen years of his life Luther continued to be concerned with the relationship between the priesthood of the baptized and the ministry. In addition, while accepting the activities of princes as emergency bishops, he sought in vain to develop an episcopacy that would be in conformity with both his understanding of the priesthood and of the pastoral or ministerial office. During this period the question of the unity of the true church in Christ, its characteristics or marks, and its existence as both hidden to the world but manifest in faith came to the foreground.

Luther was concerned about sectarianism and schism and sought to maintain the unity of Christendom, but not at the expense of a true understanding of the gospel. The Diet of Speyer (March–April 1529), which repudiated the recess of the 1526 diet and called for the immediate implementation of the Edict of Worms; the ultimate failure of the colloquy of Marburg (2–3 October 1529) to reconcile the Christological and hermeneutical perspectives of Luther and Zwingli; the recess of the Diet of Augsburg of 1530 that gave the Lutherans until April 1531 to respond to the Catholic Confutation of their Augsburg Confession for presentation to a general council; and the formation of the Lutheran Smalcald League in February 1531 clearly indicate the growth of separate and distinct religious parties in the empire. Luther's *Warning to his Dear Germans* (WA30,3.276–320; LW47.11–55) warned about the possibility of an armed attack on the Lutherans while his *Commentary on the Alleged Imperial Edict* (WA30,3,331–388; LW34.67–104) emphasized that proper doctrine is not determined by councils but by the Holy Spirit and the gospels. Luther's sermons on the gospel of John 6–8 from November 1530 to March 1532 emphasized this as well. These sermons reveal his concern for the growing division in the church but also his conviction that the gospel itself was at stake. He insisted that the gospel must be preached purely and the sacraments administered rightly. In a sermon on John 7 preached on 26 August 1531 Luther declares that there is no question that the church or churches exist:

> We are agreed with the pope that there is a church. We believe that there is assuredly a Christian church... But this is the question at issue, the bone of contention: 'Which is the Christian church?' Likewise, there is no question that there is a saving baptism and a sacrament of the Lord's Supper. The disputed question is: 'Who has the true sacrament?' And 'since the Christian church must preach the true gospel, who possesses it in its purity?' (WA33.455,1–36; LW23.285)

Despite the growing estrangement among the religious parties in the empire, Luther steadfastly maintained his conviction that the church was one despite disagreements among the religious parties. Following the 'ecumenical principle' enunciated in his letter to the Czech estates over a decade earlier and the *satis est* of Augsburg Confession VII, he approved the articles of the Wittenberg Concord agreed to by the southern German and Wittenberg reformers in 1536 (Kittelson and Schurb 1986) and the statements of the Czech Unity of the Brethren (*Unitas Fratrum*), whose confession of 1533 and their *Confessio Bohemiae* of 1535 he had printed in Wittenberg with his own introductions (WA38.78–80; WA50.379–380) even though he did not agree fully with the precise formulations employed in these articles.

In 1536, as the theological conversations of the theologians were being conducted in Wittenberg, Pope Paul III issued a summons for a council to meet in Mantua the following year. Luther had to react. Although he had called into question the authority of councils even in doctrinal matters at Leipzig in 1519 and was convinced that reconciliation with Rome and the papacy was impossible, he had formally appealed his case to a council of the church. Likewise, the imperial diet and even the emperor had indicated that a general council should resolve the religious partisanship in Germany. At the behest of Elector John Frederick he compiled another personal statement on disputed issues for presentation to the council. The draft was discussed with his colleagues and emerged as the *Smalcald Articles* of 1537. Its statements on ordination and the church reiterated even more succinctly what he had already written in his *Confession* on the Lord's Supper of 1528 and the *Large Catechism*, that

> God be praised, a seven-year old child knows what the church is: holy believers and 'the little sheep who hear the voice of the shepherd'. This is why children pray in this way, 'I believe in one holy Christian church'... Its holiness exists in the Word of God and true faith'. (SA 12,2–3; BSLK 459–60; BC 325–5)

But the council was postponed and convened eight years later in Trent.

During this hiatus Luther took the opportunity to complete his most extensive, distinctly ecclesiological work, the historical and theological analysis *On the Councils and the Church* (1539) (WA50.509–653; LW 41.9–178), in which he considered the history and significance of the first four ecumenical councils. He argues that councils cannot establish new articles of faith or mandate good works or ceremonies. However, a council can keep the church from error. It can and must condemn falsehood, that is, whatever is not in accordance with Scripture (WA50.613,27–28, 34–36; LW41.130–131). That is what had happened in the ecumenical councils, each of which had been convened to deal with one chief issue and acted to preserve the gospel itself. The decrees of the genuine councils on these primary concerns remain in force permanently (WA50.563,15–16; LW41.72–73).

But Luther was convinced that a council under papal domination could not reform the church. He suggested it would be possible for the emperor and princes to convoke a general synod for the German lands. Because they are Christians, they have the obligation to convoke a council (WA50.623,5–16; LW39.141–142). In the third section, in words that recall his seven rights or marks of the priesthood in *On the Ministry* (WA12.179,38–180,16; LW40.21) he characterizes the seven principal marks (*notae*), signs, or holy possessions by which the holy Christian people, the true church, is externally recognized, namely (1) the holy Word of God; (2) the holy sacrament of baptism; (3) the holy sacrament of the altar; (4) the office of the keys exercised publicly; (5) that ministers are called and consecrated (for there must be bishops, pastors, or preachers, who publicly and privately administer the previous four holy possessions); (6) prayer, public praise, and thanks to God; (7) the sacred cross, that is, enduring misfortune, persecution, inward and outward suffering for the sake of Christ. Though not distinctively a mark of Christians alone, love for others also marks the church (WA50.628–642; LW41.148–166).

In 1541 as tensions increased in the empire, Luther published *Against Hanswurst* (WA51.469–572; LW41.185–256), his vitriolic, no-linguistic-holds barred attack upon Duke Heinrich of Braunschweig-Wolfenbüttel, an enemy of the Reformation and the Smalcald League. The ecclesiological significance of the tract is Luther's repetition of the distinction between the true ancient church and the false, new, church of the Romanists. In this treatise he list ten marks of the true church: (1) holy baptism; (2) the holy sacrament of the altar; (3) the keys; (4) the office of preaching God's Word; (5) the apostolic confession of faith; (6) the Lord's Prayer; (7) respect for the temporal power; (8) praise and honour for the estate of marriage; (9) the suffering of the true church; (10) the renunciation of revenge or persecution. Luther also suggested that fasting and sober life could be an eleventh mark of the church (WA51.479–487; LW41.194–198).

Luther draws attention to the fact that the true church, although it is a spiritual entity that transcends time and space, is present visibly in the world, even if troubled by discord and sin. It may appear hidden and must bear suffering, but it is also clearly discerned by faith that recognizes the marks of the true church in the living faith of the church. Luther argues, 'we have proved that we are the true, ancient church, one body and one communion of saints with the holy, universal, Christian church.' He challenges the papists to prove that they are true to the Word, for their doctrine and practice, such as indulgences, indicate 'that you are the new false church, which is in everything apostate, separated from the true, ancient church, thus becoming Satan's whore and synagogue' (WA50.487,7–8; LW41.199). Despite its faults, the church of reformers is the true ancient church; while there are true Christians in the Roman church, the papacy has corrupted it by its innovations in doctrine and practice.

Four years later, in the spring 1545 during the political struggle between Emperor Charles V and Pope Paul III, and encouraged by the leaders of the Smalcald League, Luther bitterly repudiates the pope's claim to supreme authority to judge both temporal and religious affairs with vitriolic language in his *Against the Roman Papacy, an Institution of the Devil* (WA54.206–299; LW41.263–376). The work was published on the same day the council convened in Trent. In it he attacked the claim of the papacy to authority over secular rulers, its abuse of ecclesiastical authority, its neglect of its pastoral obligations, and its failure to proclaim the gospel of the forgiveness of sins. The popes claimed the right to judge all but were not to be judged by anyone. For that Luther heaped his scorn upon the papacy. He was convinced that it attempted to hold captive, not just the beloved community of Christ, but the Word itself. This accounts for the language which shows his anger, frustration, and concern for the church (Hendrix 1981: 154–6; Edwards 1963). As his life and struggle for the reform of the church drew to a close, he had to return to the very questions and practices that had led him on the road to Reformation and his understanding of the Christological nature and kerygmatic task of the church.

III. INTERPRETING LUTHER'S ECCLESIOLOGY

Interpretations of Luther's ecclesiology reflect changed vantage points and attitudes that resulted from the formation of distinct confessional or ecclesiastical communities and the transformation of the perception of Christendom during the Reformation era and the centuries that followed. Lutheran Orthodoxy, which fostered corporate confessional identity and consistorial authority, understood and applied Luther's ecclesiology quite differently than did the pietists whose concern was with personal faith, discipline, and public witness. The secularization of society, state supervision of churches, as well as the separation of church and state, Christian denominationalism, neo-confessionalism, and the ecumenical movement focused attention upon fundamental ecclesiological questions. The scholarly 'Luther revival' of the late nineteenth and twentieth centuries was in part a manifestation of a renewed interest in Luther's understanding of church and ministry in a changing world. Much of what was written concerning Luther's ecclesiology did not focus on explicating Luther but sought to apply Luther to support or to combat diverse ecclesiastical or theological concerns (Saarinen 2008). As Lohse cautions, 'there can be no doubt that every description of Luther's theology is at least linked to a given author's often very personal attempt to make a statement...' (Lohse 1999: 4) while those who employ an historical-genetic approach that focuses upon the circumstances of specific works and traces 'the development of various controversies and the sequence of topics in dispute' (Lohse 1999: 7) can overlook elements that 'both sides accepted without question' and the fact that during the sixteenth century there probably was more agreement on the doctrine of the church than is ordinarily recognized (Avis 1981: 215–17; Lohse 1986: 177).

No comprehensive study of Luther's understanding of the nature of the church has yet appeared in print. It is noteworthy that there is little dispute among the interpreters (Klug 1993: 346) concerning Luther's views of its 'quiddity' or 'whatness', and the marks of the church. Likewise, there is little disagreement on Luther's views of the essential functions of the public ministry or its significance for the life of the church. However, there are marked variations in interpretations of the source of the ministry and its relationship to the priesthood of all the baptized or the congregation.

In the first part of his study of Luther's views on pastoral or ministerial office, Wilhelm Brunotte (1959: 9–13) provides a valuable survey of works concerning Luther and the ministry from the mid-nineteenth century to the middle of the twentieth century. Klug provides an English synopsis of Brunotte's historiographical chapter and a précis of his summary of Luther's theology (1993: 346–59). Klug's work is a useful survey of the Lutheran understanding of church and ministry for both laypeople and scholars since it also provides summaries of conversations with nearly three dozen European theologians, historians, and churchmen known for their investigations of Luther and his theology. Taken together, these two works provided a solid introduction to issues that concerned interpreters of Luther's approach to church and ministry up to the mid-twentieth century.

The major focus of debate was the question 'Does the public or special ministry of the Word arise from and draw its authority from the priesthood of all believers or from its divine institution?' 'Is the pastor's authority granted by God from above or delegated to him from below by the congregation?' The debate emerged during the neo-confessional struggles in Germany during the nineteenth century (Fagerberg 1952; Sundberg 1990: 82–6) and pitted the view of Julius Stahl against Johann Höfling. Stahl held that pastors are ministers of the church, called to the office divinely instituted by God and responsible to ecclesiastical authorities. Höfling grounded pastoral authority on the divinely instituted means of grace and held that the pastor conducted the ministerial functions delegated to him by the congregations (Gerrish 1965: 408). Attempts to synthesize their views were made by Adolf von Harless and C. F. W. Walther, who emphasized that the office of the ministry and the priesthood of believers are closely interconnected and that God's exercises his will through the priesthood of believers (Klug 1993: 352; Nichol 1990: 94–6). Brunotte and Lohse support the 'high' divine institutional view of the ministry but maintain the close link between the based general priesthood and the special office. Pauck (1972), Lieberg (1981), and Althaus (1966), on the other hand emphasize that Luther's view of the nature of the Christian ministry is bipolar since it is both an expression of the common priesthood of all believers and is also a divinely appointed office and function. As Althaus writes: 'Luther without hesitation co-ordinates these two derivations of the office of the ministry—the one from "below" and the other from "above". He sees no contradiction in them.' In the first, the office is based 'upon the presupposition of the universal priesthood' while in the second 'he derives it directly from its institution by Christ without reference to the universal priesthood' (Althaus 1966: 324).

A corollary to this debate is the question of Luther's view of ecclesiastical supervision of pastors by bishops. As Lohse (1999: 296) points out, Luther never challenged the office of bishop and considered the bishop's task essentially the same as the pastor's except that he should also care for pastors, a view the reformer set forth in *An Example of How to Consecrate a True Christian Bishop* (WA53.231–260). As Spitz (1953) shows, Luther agreed to the role of the prince as a *Notbischof* only as a temporary measure.

Finally, the basis of Luther's attitude towards the papacy has been analysed by Bizer (1958), Bäumer (1971), and Hendrix (1981). While Bizer stressed the 'discovery' of the authority of God's Word as the key to Luther's hostility towards the papacy, Bäumer saw a two-step shift in Luther's view from 1518 to 1519 that culminated in a deep, personal hatred for the papacy. Hendrix (1981) argues that Luther's attitudes towards the papacy went through several stages and was the result not just of his new understanding of authority but of his conviction that the popes and other ecclesiastical offices had failed in their primary obligation, to feed the people with God's Word.

Luther's ecclesiological concern was to define what and where the true church is and to encourage Christians, individually and collectively, to live transformed by the gospel for one another as the body of Christ in this world. The task for future scholars is to analyse how Luther sought to accomplish this through his preaching and correspondence.

References

Althaus, Paul (1966). *The Theology of Martin Luther*, trans. Robert C. Schultz. Philadelphia: Fortress.

Arand, Charles P. (2008). 'What are Ecclesiologically Challenged Lutherans to Do? Starting Points for a Lutheran Ecclesiology'. *Concordia Journal* 34: 157–71.

Arts, Jan (1972). *Die Lehre Martin Luthers über das Amt in der Kirche. Eine genetisch-systematische Untersuchung seiner Schriften von 1512 bis 1525.* Helsinki: Luther-Agricola Gesellschaft/Hameenlinna.

Aurelius, Carl Axel (1983). *Verborgene Kirche. Luther's Kirchenverständnis in Streitschriften und Exegese 1519/1521.* Hannover: Lutherisches Verlagshaus.

Avis, D. Paul (1981). *The Church in the Theology of the Reformers.* Atlanta: John Knox.

Bäumer, Remigius (1971). *Martin Luther und der Papst.* Münster: Aschendorf.

Beyer, Michael (1983). 'Luthers Ekklesiologie'. In *Leben und Werk Martin Luthers von 1526 bis 1546. Festgabe zu seinem 500. Geburtstag*, ed. Helmar Junghans. Berlin: Evangelische Verlagsanstalt, 1.93–138, 2.55–65.

Bizer, Ernst (1958). *Luther und der Papst.* Munich: Kaiser.

Brunotte, Wilhelm (1959). *Das geistliche Amt bei Luther.* Berlin: Lutherisches Verlagshaus.

Daniel, David P. (1988). 'A Spiritual Condominium: Luther's Views on Priesthood and Ministry with some Structural Implications'. *Concordia Journal* 14: 266–82.

Edwards, Mark U. (1963). *Luther's Last Battles.* Ithaca: Cornell University Press.

Fagerberg, Holsten (1952). *Kirche und Amt in der deutschen konfessionellen Theologie des 19. Jahrhunderts.* Uppsala and Wiesbaden: Almquist & Wiksells.

—— (1955). 'Die Kirche in Luthers Psalmenvorlesungen 1513–1515'. In *Gedenkschrift für D. Werner Elert. Beiträge zur historischen und systematischen Theologie*, ed. Friedrich Hübner, Wilhelm Maurer, and Ernst Kinder. Berlin: Lutherisches Verlag, 109–18.

Gerrish, Brian (1965). 'Priesthood and Ministry in the Theology of Luther'. *Church History* 34: 404–22.

Ginther, James R. (2008). 'The Church in Medieval Theology'. In *The Routledge Companion to the Christian Church*, ed. Gerard Mannion and Lewis Muely. London: Routledge, 18–62.

Green, Lowell C. (1966). 'Change in Luther's Doctrine of the Ministry'. *Lutheran Quarterly* o.s. 18: 173–83.

Hendrix, Scott H. (1974). *Ecclesia in via: Ecclesiological Developments in the Medieval Psalm Exegesis and the Dictata supra Psalterium (1513–1515) of Martin Luther.* Leiden: Brill.

—— (1976). 'In Quest of the Vera Ecclesia: The Crisis of Late Medieval Ecclesiology'. *Viator* 7: 347–78.

—— (1981). *Luther and the Papacy: Stages in a Reformation Conflict.* Philadelphia: Fortress.

Holl, Karl (1921). 'Die Enstehung vom Luthers Kirchenbegriff'. In *Gesammelte Aufsätze zur Kirchengeschichte I.* Tübingen: Mohr/Siebeck, 245–78.

Kittelson, James and Ken Schurb (1986). 'The Curious Histories of the Wittenberg Concord'. *Concordia Theological Quarterly* 50.2: 119–37.

Klug, Eugene F. A. (1993). *Church and Ministry: The Role of Church, Pastor, and People from Luther to Walther.* Saint Louis: Concordia.

Kolb, Robert and Charles P. Arand (2008). *The Genius of Luther's Theology: A Wittenberg Way of Thinking for the Contemporary Church.* Grand Rapids, MI: Baker Academic.

Lieberg, Hellmut (1981). *Luther on the Ministerial Office and Congregational Function*, trans. R. C. Gritsch. Philadelphia: Fortress.

Lohse, Bernhard (1986). *Martin Luther: An Introduction to His Life and Work*. Philadelphia: Fortress.

—— (1999). *Martin Luther's Theology: Its Historical and Systematic Development*, ed. and trans. Roy. A. Harrisville. Minneapolis: Fortress.

Maurer, Wilhelm (1958). 'Kirche und Geschichte nach Luthers Dictata super Psalterium'. In *Lutherforschung heute. Referate und Berichte des 1. Internationalen Lutherforschungskongresses, Aarhus, 18–23 August 1956*, ed. Vilmos Vajta. Berlin: Lutherisches Verlagshaus, 85–101.

Nichol, Todd (1990). 'Ministry and Oversight in American Lutheranism'. In *Called and Ordained: Lutheran Perspectives on the Office of the Ministry*, ed. Todd Nichol and Marc Kolden. Minneapolis: Fortress, 93–113.

Pauck, Wilhelm (1972). 'Luther and the Ministry'. *The Springfielder* 36: 3–11.

Pelikan, Jaroslav (1958). 'Die Kirche nach Luthers Genesisvorlesung'. In *Lutherforschung heute. Referate und Berichte des 1. Internationalen Lutherforschungskongresses, Aarhus, 18–23 August 1956*, ed. Vilmos Vajta. Berlin: Lutherisches Verlagshaus, 102–10.

—— (1964). *Obedient Rebels: Catholic Substance and Protestant Principle in Luther's Reformation*. New York: Harper & Row.

—— (1968). *Spirit Versus Structure: Luther and the Institutions of the Church*. London: Collins.

Rupp, E. Gordon (1956). 'Luther and the Doctrine of the Church'. *Scottish Journal of Theology* 9: 384–92.

Saarinen, Risto (2008). 'Lutheran Ecclesiology'. In *The Routledge Companion to the Christian Church*, ed. Gerard Mannion and Lewis Muely. London: Routledge, 170–86.

Spehr, Christopher (2010). *Luther und das Konzil. Zur Entwicklung eines zentralen Themas in der Reformationszeit*. Tübingen: Mohr/Siebeck.

Spitz, Lewis W. (1953). 'Luther's Ecclesiology and His Concept of the Prince as Notbischof'. *Church History* 22: 113–41.

Sundberg, Walter (1990). 'Ministry in Nineteenth-Century European Lutheranism'. In *Called and Ordained: Lutheran Perspectives on the Office of the Ministry*, ed. Todd Nichol and Marc Kolden. Minneapolis: Fortress, 77–92.

SUGGESTED READING

Arand, Charles P. (2007). 'The Ministry of the Church in the Light of Two Kinds of Righteousness'. *Concordia Journal* 33: 146–65.

Brecht, Martin (ed.) (1990). *Martin Luther und das Bischofsamt*. Stuttgart: Calwer.

Doerne, Martin (1932). 'Gottes Volk und Gottes Wort (zur Einführung in Luthers Theologie der Kirche)'. *Lutherjahrbuch* 14: 61–98.

Elert, Werner (1962). *The Structure of Lutheranism*. Vol. I: *The Theology and Philosophy of Lutheranism especially in the Sixteenth and Seventeenth Centuries*, trans. Walter A. Hansen. Saint Louis: Concordia.

Fischer, Robert (1966). 'Another Look at Luther's Doctrine of the Ministry'. *Lutheran Quarterly* 18: 260–71.

Goebel, Hans Theodor (1990). 'Notae Ecclesiae. Zum Problem der Unterscheidung der wahren Kirche von der falschen'. *Evangelische Theologie* 50: 222–41.

Höhne, Wolfgang (1982). *Luthers Anschauungen über die Kontinuität der Kirche. Eine Studie zu ihrer Einheit, Heiligkeit, Katholizität und Apostolizität*. Berlin: Lutherisches Verlagshaus.

Hok, Gosta (1954). 'Luther's Doctrine of the Priesthood and Ministry in the Theology of Luther'. *Scottish Journal of Theology* 7: 16–40.

Kirchner, Hubert (1983). 'Luther und das Papsttum'. In *Leben und Werk Martin Luthers von 1526 bis 1546. Festgabe zu seinem 500. Geburtstag*, ed. Helmar Junghans. Berlin: Evangelische Verlagsanstalt, 1.441–56; 2.871–4.

Kohlmeyer, E. (1928). 'Die Bedeutung der Kirche für Luther'. *Zeitschrift für Kirchengeschichte* 47, NF 10: 466–511.

Kolb, Robert (1990). 'Ministry in Martin Luther and the Lutheran Confessions'. In *Called and Ordained: Lutheran Perspectives on the Office of the Ministry*, ed. Todd Nichol and Marc Kolden. Minneapolis: Fortress, 49–66.

Krarup, Martin (2007). *Ordination in Wittenberg*. Tübingen: Mohr/Siebeck.

Lönning, Inge (1985) 'Luther und die Kirche. Das blinde Wort und die verborgene Wirklichkeit'. *Lutherjahrbuch* 52: 94–112.

Lutz, Jürgen (1990). *Unio und Communio. Zum Verhältnis von Rechtfertigungslehre und Kirchenverständnis bei Martin Luther. Eine Untersuchung zu ekklesiologisch relevanten Texten der Jahre 1519–1528*. Paderborn: Bonifatius.

Müller, Gerhard (1965). 'Ekklesiologie und Kirchenkritik beim Jungen Luther'. *Neue Zeitschrift für Systematische Theologie und Religionsphilosophie* 7.1: 100–28.

—— (1974). 'Martin Luther und das Papsttum'. In *Das Papsttum in der Diskussion*, ed. Georg Denzler. Regensburg: Pustet, 73–101.

Nichol, Todd and Marc Kolden (eds.) (1990). *Called and Ordained: Lutheran Perspectives on the Office of the Ministry*. Minneapolis: Fortress.

Noll, Mark A. (1978). 'Martin Luther and the Concept of a "True" Church'. *The Evangelical Quarterly* 50.2: 79–85.

Olsson, Herbert (1952). 'The Church's Visibility and Invisibility According to Luther'. In *This is the Church*, ed. Anders Nygren, trans. Carl C. Rasmussen. Philadelphia: Muhlenberg, 226–42.

Pesch, Otto Hermann (1985). 'Luther und die Kirche'. *Lutherjahrbuch* 52: 113–39.

Prenter, Regin (1961). 'Die göttliche Einsetzung des Predigtamtes und das allgemeine Priestertum bein Luther'. *Theologische Literaturzeitung* 86: 321–52.

Tuchel, Klaus (1958). 'Luthers Auffassung vom geistlichen Amt'. *Lutherjahrbuch* 25: 61–98.

CHAPTER 24

LUTHER'S ESCHATOLOGY

JANE E. STROHL

I. INTRODUCTION

IN many ways Luther's eschatology reflects the traditional teaching of his day. One died; one was raised in the body to come before God for final judgement; some were clothed in the grace of Christ and brought to salvation; others perished eternally. In addition to its concern with these last things, eschatology also deals with the fate of the world. Divine judgement does not just fall upon individuals. Kingdoms, peoples, and churches will be called to account for their response to the gospel. These two arenas of eschatology overlap. Christians were dependent upon the civil and religious communities of which they were a part to provide them with right proclamation and practice. For Luther the negligence or corruption of those responsible for their spiritual welfare would serve as no excuse. Luther himself feared the possibility that if he were wrong, he would be responsible for bringing the souls of many to perdition. Moreover, with his understanding of salvation through grace by faith alone, there would be no second chances, no cleansing term in purgatory, when the prayers and works of the living could help secure for the dead safe passage to the heavenly realm.

II. BRIEF HISTORY OF SCHOLARLY DEBATES OVER LUTHER'S ESCHATOLOGY

In the 1920s and 1930s the German scholars Paul Althaus and Carl Stange debated Luther's understanding of the afterlife. Althaus insisted that Luther attributed eternity to both the redeemed and the damned. He cited WA43.481, 32 in support of his position: 'for the one with whom God speaks, whether in wrath or mercy, is certainly undying. The person of God who speaks and the word which he utters demonstrate that we are creatures with whom God wishes to speak unto eternity and in undying fashion.' Thus, the distinction between law and gospel will carry over from this world into the next, with the wrath of God now falling only on the damned and the saving grace of the gospel only on the saved. For Althaus, there will be a preliminary revivification of all the dead effected by the Holy Spirit so that they may face judgement. This is not to be confused with the true resurrection of the redeemed. He speculated that those who spurned God in life will be condemned to bear God's eternal presence while remaining unable to love their Maker and Redeemer (Althaus 1930, 1941; cf. Althaus 1949).

Stange, in contrast, insisted that there can be no eternal divine word of condemnation, for when the sinner has experienced the word of judgement bearing down upon him, he is no longer godless but in the hands of God, who exercises his alien work so as to accomplish his proper work. There is no unending second use of the law. The problem is not God's judgement but God's absence, not God's wrath but God's silence. The ungodly, who are deaf to the law and ignorant of the gospel, live in and for the nothingness of the world, like animals. They endure the fullness of God's wrath without even being conscious of it. Stange insisted that they do not live eternally in the presence of divine condemnation, as Althaus argued. Instead they are obliterated with the earthly things they have loved so well. If you want to know who is in and who is out, just look to see who is not there for the Last Judgement (Stange 1924/5, 1925/6, 1932/3).

Werner Thiede addressed the issue of universalism in Luther's eschatology (1982). Like Althaus and Stange, he demonstrated Luther's avoidance of spatial and temporal conceptions in discussing the state of the departed after death. They rest in the Word of promise, not in some holding tank between heaven and hell. From an earthly perspective there is a troublesome lag between the hour of an individual's death and the dawning of the Last Day, but Luther insists that the soul that goes to sleep in death wakes in its body to the presence of God with no sense of time having passed.

For Stange and Althaus God's salvific will need not be universal to be triumphant. Christ does indeed rule over all, but only for believers is his lordship a blessing. Thiede, however, did not give up the unbelieving for lost. He suggested that Christ, who died for all, will win from all the faith that makes salvation possible. If Christ has defeated death, then it no longer stands as a barrier beyond which there is no hope for the ungodly. This was not the conclusion Luther drew, but Thiede is building on the reformer's belief that no absolute limit can be placed on God's power. Thus, universalism is certainly possible.

When Tiede expressed concern at how little attention has been given to the last things in Luther scholarship, he named Ulrich Asendorf's *Eschatologie bei Luther* (1967) specifically. Asendorf sought to demonstrate that all the important aspects of Luther's thought are explicit in their eschatological orientation. Whether it be soteriology, Christology, or ecclesiology, the overarching eschatological framework serves as the compelling dynamic of the now and the not yet, which accounts for the paradoxical quality of Luther's teaching. Asendorf's analysis makes it clear that one must take account of much more than the destiny of the individual in Luther's eschatology. The process begun by the cross and resurrection of Christ unfolds on several different levels and presses toward distinct resolutions. He also made it clear that theologians who would dwell on the 'now' of the kingdom's in-breaking and thus neglect what is yet to be at the Last Day are not doing Luther's eschatology justice.

III. Luther's Eschatology

Luther believed that in his time the world had reached its final stage. Tired and broken, riddled with contempt for God and arrogant sinning, it practically taunted God to deliver the punishment it deserved. This kind of apocalyptic view is not so much a conclusion drawn from the reality around one as a lens brought to the interpretation of what one sees. In other words, contemporaries of Luther could look at the social dislocations and in particular the condition of the church and conclude that the situation was troubling, as it had always been. Luther, on the other hand, viewed it as terminally toxic. As a consequence, he denounced as demonic whatever he perceived as a threat to the evangelical gospel of free grace and justification by faith.

Early on the pope became for him the Antichrist (Hendrix 1981). The office itself was an abomination. As Luther affirmed, even a good man could not redeem it. The pope called himself the Vicar of Christ, as if the Lord were absent. He usurped Christ's authority and built around himself a fortress of doctrine, binding biblical interpretation and tradition that no one could penetrate. Here, at the church's very heart, the community to which people turned in trust for the gift of saving grace was the abomination of unbelief. Those in authority were content to bring the faithful down to ruin in order to preserve their privileges and wealth. Luther relied on his office as a teacher of the church. He had not, after all, sought the responsibility. The church had imposed it on him, and now he had no choice but to be faithful. He prosecuted a life-long pastoral malpractice suit against the church on behalf of the souls burdened by its demands and driven to despair.

At the time of the Diet of Augsburg in 1530 Luther still held out hope that his countrymen, the German Catholics, would embrace the truth, in distinction from their hardened Italian kin. For security reasons Luther did not attend the Diet, but word came back to him that the evangelical gospel had won the day. The emperor and his allies allowed the Word to be proclaimed for all to hear when the Augsburg Confession was read publicly as part of the proceedings. Reports reached Luther that even among those Catholics who acknowledged the truth of what they heard, there was no inclination to be reformed by it. That, it was said, would require them to give up far too much. After all, Luther was a condemned heretic.

What transpired at Augsburg came under Luther's apocalyptic lens: what he saw was the Devil triumphant. Those who joined the ranks of the evil one became for him both more and less than human (WA30, 3.383). They were not persons guilty of the commonplace weaknesses of sloth, greed, and pride. Their works-righteousness was not reflexive but viciously calculated. They embraced the works and ways of the evil one (WA34,

2.263–264). Consequently, they were no longer in Luther's eyes human beings to be treated with decency under any circumstances but devils to be exposed and destroyed.

For this reason Luther was adamant that at the end of the Augsburg Diet there be no negotiation, no further conversation aimed at achieving a compromise to forestall division. Philip Melanchthon, Luther's colleague and the architect of the Augsburg Confession, perceived the diet as part of a process. For Luther it was the end of Rome's options and of the reformers' relationship to the Catholic Church. It was also the end of God's forbearance. Rome had fallen under final judgement, and the evangelicals had no further obligation to them (WA32.101–102; WA33.131–132). This consignment of his enemies to the Devil was characteristic of Luther. The list included not only Rome but spiritualists, Anabaptists, Zwinglians, Turks, and Jews. Anyone who, in Luther's view, threatened the truth of the gospel, refused to be corrected, and infected others with their false teaching was unconditionally condemned.

Luther insisted that it is not possible to read God's judgements from history precisely. God acts in the world through masks. In addition, the theology of the cross makes vain any attempt to penetrate the mystery of God's working. Nonetheless, Luther does presume to identify final verdicts from God in the fates of his opponents. It is possible to separate the sheep from the goats, and although Luther did not call for the slaughter of the ungodly like the spiritualist Thomas Müntzer, whom he despised, he did insist that they should be abandoned to their fate. There comes a point beyond which there will be no more conversation, no more proclamation to certain stubborn consciences. In the end times one seals one's fate by one's response to the gospel, and there is a point of no return. The word of judgement, terrifying as it would be to many, was for Luther a joyous prospect more than a fearsome one. The petition of the Lord's Prayer would be answered: God's kingdom would come at last and the true church would be victorious.

IV. The Last Things

Although Luther does talk about the Last Judgement coming as a cosmic winnowing of humankind, he is even more concerned with the judgement rendered to each of us in the hour of our death. At the opening of his 1521 Invocavit Sermons Luther stated that everyone must fight his own battle with death and that no one can die for another (WA10,3.1,15–2,3; LW51.70). Just as in Luther's portrayal of communal and universal eschatology, the issue of confessing the faith is paramount, and essential to confession is the experience of what Luther called *Anfechtung*, that is, the assault of temptation, doubt, and despair upon the believer's conscience (WA49.268). Luther portrays the life of faith as a process of what may be called enforced kenosis. The virtuous works and pious aspirations we collect so eagerly must be wrested from our hearts. We cannot be filled with the grace of Christ if we are full of our own righteousness or our own consuming sense of failure.

Life is to be lived in the shadow of death. Evangelical discipleship requires one to live righteously in the world, to serve one's neighbours generously and to accept suffering patiently. One does not seek to transcend such suffering; rather, one sinks deeply into what cannot in truth be avoided. As Luther says, while the believer is in this dark place, it feels like an eternity of misery. Yet it proves to be the forecourt to paradise, for one emerges from the darkness into the fullness of Christ's light. One is not free to choose the crosses one will bear; one has no choice. In sharp opposition to the monastic practice of his day, in which special practices of self-denial were enforced and regarded as meritorious, Luther insisted that life in its natural course would bring more than enough crosses one's way. One does not endure them to win God's favour; one receives them as part of the gift of salvation, a sign of God's paternal care. This regimen of the cross undergirds the confession of the gospel. It challenges the believer to depend on God's promises alone. Over time one's strength increases until, even facing the hidden God, the believer can hold God to God's word, despite what feels like God's indifference or even hostility. For Luther, the story of Jacob wrestling with the angel in Genesis 32 is a prime example of the bold tenacity required of believers, a persistence that borders on defiance. Luther understands the angel to be Christ since Jacob exults that he has striven with God and man. Jacob does not emerge from the encounter unscathed, but he holds on to his opponent, refusing to let go until he receives a blessing. And he gets what he wants (WA 44.103, 22–108, 17; LW 6.138–145).

The final *Anfechtung* is death. For Luther, all the trials that have preceded have been foretastes of this last hour. The harrowing temptation that plagues one in life is now at its most fearsome. One faces the anguish of dying, the painful necessity of letting go of everything and everyone that has shaped one's world, the fear of judgement, the doubt of God's love. Under this kind of pressure it is easy to fall back into old harmful patterns of belief. Rather than surrender completely to God's mercy, that is, to be justified by faith alone, one may turn desperately to self-justification by works. Or the dying person may become consumed by guilt and despair, a particularly virulent form of what Luther calls being turned in on the self (*incurvatus in se*). This is the time to call God to account for the promises of the gospel. The dying rightly cry out, 'But I am baptized' in order to repel the tempter and claim Christ as 'my' Saviour.

For Luther the ultimate test of any proclamation of the gospel is its pastoral effectiveness. It all comes down to its ability to sustain the believer in death. Luther denounced the practice of the church of his day as pastoral fraud. Its insistence on the need for human cooperation in the process of salvation left the dying defenceless against demonic temptation. Works, either one's own or those of the saints, fail as insurance in the face of death. They divert one's attention from the cross to the self, where there is no hope. After all, insisted Luther, the thief executed with Jesus saw nothing but the Lord on the cross and asked humbly for his mercy. He had no opportunity to do good works, yet Jesus received him into his kingdom (WA.37.60).

The role of God in the final hours of the believer's life is an ambiguous one. Here one encounters God both hidden and revealed. Luther insists that the Devil is always God's Devil, and so if he comes to torment the dying, it is ultimately by God's will

(WA31,1.147–148). Thus even in their final moments believers may be challenged to wrestle like Jacob to grasp the revealed God and hold on until that God gives the blessing that will carry them safely into the kingdom. If faith falters, the gospel can be lost, and now there will be no further opportunity for repentance or amendment of life. This moves uncomfortably close to the works-righteousness that Luther denounced vehemently throughout his reforming career. At the end it comes down to the Christian having faith of sufficient strength to withstand the suffering inflicted by the hidden God and to rely on the promises of the God revealed in Jesus Christ. Yet Luther built his understanding of the gospel on the conviction that it is God's faithfulness that secures our salvation, a faithfulness that trumps all human weakness and failure. Although the hidden God might put the dying believer to a dreadful test, one would expect the revealed God to render any negative consequences null and void. Nonetheless, Luther allowed for the possibility that all could be lost at the end. While proclaiming faith to be a gift, Luther still held the dying person responsible for remaining constant in the conviction that he is saved by grace alone (WA37.456). When one is tempted so cruelly in one's last hours, it is not clear whether one clings to God's promise or is held by it. Is the final confession on our lips our victory or God's gift?

In the many letters of consolation Luther wrote to the bereaved, he regularly urged them to take comfort in the fact that their loved ones had died confessing their faith in Christ and claiming Christ's saving work as 'pro me', that is, true not in general but specifically for this person in the throes of death. Such a confession guaranteed a safe journey through the dark, narrow passage of the grave into the wide and luminous realm of resurrected life. Given his conviction that the world was hurtling into chaos and destined for a violent end under God's judgement, Luther could also tell grieving parents and spouses that the ones who died prematurely were blessed. It was a sign of God's favour that they were taken from a world so lost in shameless sinning before they could be infected by its toxins (WABr8.485; cf. Mennecke-Haustein 1989; Leroux 2007).

Luther's beliefs about death were put to the test with the sudden death of his daughter Magdalena in 1542 at the age of 13. At first the consolations he had offered to others, the assurance of Christ's victory over the grave, and the relief of knowing that his child was beyond the reach of worldly harm, proved insufficient. In a letter to a friend he readily acknowledged the majesty of Christ's death to which no other death can compare. But he went on to say that he and his wife bore in themselves a mortal wound. The victory of the Saviour cannot drive out their deep sorrow, for all Luther can see is his cherished daughter's face. With time, however, Luther found consolation in the beliefs he offered to others. He emphasized the fact that Magdalena died full of faith in Christ; he recognized her early death as a timely rescue from a dangerous world (WABr10.169). Finally, he came to regard what was at first a faith-shaking tragedy as a sign of God's favour. 'It is astonishing how much the death of my Magdalene torments me, whom I simply cannot forget. But I am completely certain that she is in the place of consolation and eternal life, and that God has thereby given me a great sign of His love, in that He has in my lifetime taken my flesh up into His lap' (WABr11.113).

Luther also believes it possible for the dying to pass from this life without the danger of virulent temptation. Rather, a life of courageous confession has already inflicted the terrors of death repeatedly. When it comes time for the body to perish, those who have witnessed faithfully to the gospel at all costs will make the transition from this world to the next gently. Death has become a little sleep from which they shall wake when the Lord comes and knocks upon the door of their resting place. A striking example of this is Luther's attitude toward Elector Johann, the Saxon ruler who attended the 1530 Diet of Augsburg. He earned the title 'the Steadfast', because of his bold stance before his Catholic opponents and the emperor, even though the possibility that war would result was very real. At his death Luther comforted the mourning Saxons with the assurance that the elector had already died at Augsburg, when he withstood the temptation to compromise his confession. As a consequence, he passed from this world to the next like a sleeping child, with neither pain nor fear. Luther concluded the sermon by exhorting the Saxons to imitate their prince in steadfast confession, so that they too may experience the same kind of gentle death. In other words, at the last hour the hidden God stays hidden and the peace of the God revealed in Christ prevails. However death comes, it is finally the answer to the lifelong prayer of the believer, 'Lead us not into temptation but deliver us from evil.' Through it we are released from sin's affliction and earthly care. The freedom of the Christian is made complete (WA36.244, 28–254, 34; LW51.237–238).

According to Luther, we are bitterly estranged from God because of sin. His theology, with its emphasis on the uses of the law, free grace, and the right relationship between faith and works, addresses this issue. But there is also the problem that we die. With the defeat of sin must come the unconditional victory of life. When discussing the third article of the Creed in his *Small Catechism* Luther makes the progression clear: 'Daily in this Christian church the Holy Spirit abundantly forgives all sins—mine and those of all believers. On the Last Day the Holy Spirit will raise me and all the dead and will give to me and all believers in Christ eternal life. This is most certainly true' (BSLK 512; BC 356). The promise of the resurrection is already known in the Old Testament. Adam and Eve hear it in God's declaration to the serpent (WA42.143, 38–147, 39; LW1.191–198). Abraham, when he receives the command to sacrifice Isaac, is adamant that even were his son burnt to cinders, still he would live. God had promised that Isaac would be the source of many descendants. Even death could not make that promise null and void (WA43.218, 6–222, 23; LW4.115–121).

Paul's remarks concerning physical and spiritual bodies led Luther to reflect on the nature of the resurrection life in his sermons on 1 Corinthians 15 (WA49.395–441, 727–780). He envisions a new world in which sexual distinctions among persons will remain but all differentiations according to office and rank will be done away with. Marriage and other socially institutionalized relationships belong to the old order and have no place in the new. In this life we are obliged to seek the support we need from a variety of sources. We require a preacher for some things, a doctor, a parent, and a governing authority for others. In the resurrected life, however, God will be all in all for every one of us. There will be no need for physical nourishment or medicine, no need for the law because there will be no sin to curb. A resurrected humanity will no longer need to encounter God hidden under word and sacrament as here on earth, for they will be able to see God face-to-face.

Luther insists that resurrection is corporeal. Both soul and body receive the sacraments, and thus, both are destined for eternal life. When Paul says flesh and blood cannot inherit the kingdom of God, Luther understands him to mean humanity as first created, not after the fall. The human of dust is made from and for the earth. This body is unfit by nature for heaven, the soul by the corruption of sin. Luther understands the spiritual body that is raised up to be a real body of some kind of flesh and blood yet possessed of extraordinary powers. Nothing that it desires to do will be impossible for it. It can move from earth to the heights of heaven in a moment, play with a mountain as a child does with a ball, or command a tree to bear silver leaves and golden apples. Luther allows that although all will be equal before God in grace and heavenly nature, their glory will differ according to their works in this life. Sarah or Rachel will be something special before other women, and St Peter will stand out among the ranks of the saved.

V. CONCLUSION

The eschatological force of Luther's theology is clear. Although he abided by the Lord's caution that the exact time of the end was known only to the Father, Luther was confident that the world was writing the last chapter of its history. It was a moment of ultimate decision for individuals, communities, and kingdoms. The gospel had emerged in a clarity unparalleled since the time of the apostles. One could, as Luther put it, buy while the market was hot, or watch the gospel slip away forever. There would be no second chances. This sense of urgency lay behind the ferocity and at times brutality of Luther's offensive against anyone who, in his judgement, threatened the gospel of free grace. Clearly the Devil was assuming many forms, from the outrageous papal Antichrist to the morally irreproachable Turk. He was confident that the veil between God's kingdom and the earthly realm was lifting, that it was possible to begin separating the sheep from the goats. The great paradoxes that characterized the Christian's life—simultaneously saint and sinner, the Word of God as law and gospel, discipleship lived in two distinct realms—were about to be resolved. The tension of managing the seemingly incompatible was soon to end. With the coming of the Lord the believer would become wholly saint; law and gospel would be heard as one Word; and the kingdom of God would be undivided. Luther is credited with saying that if he knew the world would end tomorrow, he would go out and plant an apple tree today. In no way was he dismissive of life in this world. Indeed, he criticized monastic life (and Anabaptist practice) for withdrawing from the challenges of the world and insisting instead on a sanctified lifestyle that hovered between heaven and earth. For Luther disciples remain in the midst of the sinful world, serving the neighbour with no regard to amassing personal righteousness. We marry and raise the next generation of children. We buy property and build houses and save for the retirement we expect to enjoy. We fight for the poor believing that their future can be different. Still, there is no escaping the clouds of divine judgement moving in upon us.

The ongoing challenge of Luther's eschatological views falls upon the heirs of the Lutheran tradition more than upon Luther scholars. This tradition continues today to proclaim the gospel as God's freely given promise of mercy and abundant life through Jesus Christ, a gift that is ours for the taking by faith. Lutheran proclamation directs itself to those on the margins—the burdened consciences, the unbelieving, the despairing—and is confident of its power to break human bondage to sin of all kinds. And following Luther's diagnosis that works-righteousness is the first and last sin, Lutheran practice strives to uproot the human penchant for legalism. However, in the more than five hundred years since the Reformation, the intense eschatological framework, in which all of Luther's central doctrines took shape, has been lost. Theologians need to explore the implications of that for their own traditions as communities seek to embody the eschatology of Scripture today.

REFERENCES

Althaus, Paul (1930). *Unsterblichkeit und ewiges Sterben bei Luther. Zur Auseinander-setzung mit Carl Stange.* Gütersloh: Bertelsmann.

—— (1941). 'Luthers Gedanken über die letzten Dinge'. *Lutherjahrbuch* 23: 9–34.

—— (1949). *Die Letzten Dinge. Lehrbuch der Eschatologie,* 5th edn. Gütersloh: Bertelsmann.

Hendrix, Scott (1981). *Luther and the Papacy: Stages in a Reformation Conflict.* Philadelphia: Fortress.

Leroux, Neil R. (2007). *Martin Luther as Comforter: Writings on Death.* Leiden: Brill.

Mennecke-Haustein, Ute (1989). *Luthers Trostbriefe.* Gütersloh: Mohn.

Stange, Carl (1924/5). 'Die Unsterblichkeit der Seele'. *Zeitschrift für systematische Theologie* 2: 431–63.

—— (1925/6). 'Zur Auslegung der Aussagen Luthers über die Unsterblichkeit der Seele'. *Zeitschrift für systematische Theologie* 3: 735–84.

—— (1932/3). 'Luthers Gedanken über Tod, Gericht und ewiges Leben'. *Zeitschrift für systematische Theologie* 10: 490–513.

Thiede, Werner (1982). 'Luthers individuelle Eschatologie'. *Lutherjahrbuch* 49: 7–49.

Asendorf, Ulrich (1967). *Eschatologie bei Luther.* Göttingen: Vandenhoeck & Ruprecht.

—— (1971). *Gekreuzigt und Auferstanden. Luthers Herausforderung an die moderne Christologie.* Hamburg: Lutherisches Verlagshaus.

Baldwin, John T. (1995). 'Luther's Eschatological Appraisal of the Turkish Threat in *Eine Heerpredigt wider den Türken*'. *Andrews University Seminary Studies* 33: 185–202.

Edwards, Mark U., Jr. (1983). *Luther's Last Battles: Politics and Polemics, 1531–46.* Ithaca: Cornell University Press.

Headley, John M. (1963). *Luther's View of Church History.* New Haven: Yale University Press.

Lindberg, Carter (2000): 'Eschatology and Fanaticism in the Reformation Era: Luther and the Anabaptists'. *Concordia Theological Quarterly* 64: 259–78.

Modalsli, Ole (1983). 'Luther über die Letzten Dinge'. In *Leben und Werk Martin Luthers von 1526 bis 1546. Festgabe zu seinem 500. Geburtstag,* ed. Helmar Junghans. Göttingen: Vandenhoeck & Ruprecht, 1.331–45.

Oberman, Heiko (1989). *Luther: Man Between God and the Devil*, trans. Eileen Walliser Schwarzbart. New Haven: Yale University Press.

Pesch, Otto Hermann (1988). 'Im Angesicht des barmherzigen Richters. Lebenszeit, Tod und jüngster Tag in der Theologie Martin Luthers'. *Vierteljahresschrift für ökumenische Theologie* 42: 245–73.

Scaer, David P. (1983a). 'The Concept of Anfechtung in Luther's Thought'. *Concordia Theological Quarterly* 47: 15–30.

—— (1983b). 'Luther's Concept of the Resurrection in his Commentary on 1 Corinthians 15'. *Concordia Theological Quarterly* 47: 209–24.

Vogel, Winfried (1986). 'The Eschatological Theology of Martin Luther. Part I: Luther's Basic Concepts'. *Andrews University Seminary Studies* 24: 249–64.

—— (1987). 'The Eschatological Theology of Martin Luther: Luther's Exposition of Daniel and Revelation'. *Andrews University Seminary Studies* 25: 183–99.

PART V

LUTHER'S VIEW OF SANCTIFIED LIVING

CHAPTER 25

THE FRAMEWORK FOR CHRISTIAN LIVING

Luther on the Christian's Callings

JANE E. STROHL

See, according to this rule the good things we have from God should flow from one person to the other and be common to all, so that everyone should 'put on' his neighbour and so conduct himself toward him as if he himself were in the other's place. From Christ the good things have flowed and are flowing into us. He has so 'put on' us and acted for us as if he had been what we are. From us they flow on to those who have need of them, so that I should lay before God my faith and my righteousness that they may cover and intercede for the sins of my neighbour which I take upon myself, and so labour and serve in them as if they were my very own. This is what Christ did for us. This is true love and the genuine rule of a Christian life. Love is true and genuine where there is true and genuine faith. Hence the Apostle says of love in I Corinthians 13 that 'it does not seek its own'.

We conclude, therefore, that a Christian lives not in himself, but in Christ and in his neighbour. Otherwise he is not a Christian. He lives in Christ through faith, in his neighbour through love. By faith he is caught up beyond himself into God. By love he descends beneath himself into his neighbour. (*The Freedom of a Christian* (1520), WA7.69,1–16; LW31.371)

LUTHER was frustrated throughout his career by people's failure to understand his teaching on good works. Although accused of doing away with them, Luther insisted that his purpose was to do away with false understandings about good works, two very different things. For what reason is the old Adam drowned so that the new Adam might emerge from the waters of baptism, cleansed and refreshed, if not for the work of loving one's neighbours? For Luther, it is not as if the justified believer has a choice in the matter. The grace of Christ forgives sins and opens hearts, into which the Holy Spirit pours its love, and love is not passive. It creates eyes to see the needs of others previously ignored. It creates ears to hear cries for help and to hear them as addressed to us rather than dismiss them as someone else's responsibility.

The criticism confronting Luther was twofold. First of all, if works were not required to receive forgiveness, then people simply would not do them. If you did not lean on the sinner, she would just do the minimum necessary to obtain God's grace. Moreover, what would be the point of doing good works after justification?

On the other hand, even allowing that good works might follow reconciliation with God rather than prepare for it, Luther's portrayal of this discipleship as the necessary result of a free and transformed human nature seems to jump the eschatological gun. In class one day a Lutheran seminarian made this dilemma very clear. She was part of a team of students who regularly visited residents in a local nursing home. One of the people assigned to her was a cantankerous woman whose charism for complaining was unparalleled. The student freely admitted that she disliked visiting the old lady, whose ill temper was toxic. 'What Luther is saying is ridiculous,' she concluded. 'I don't go there because I can't imagine anything I would rather do.' In the conversation that followed, two critical pieces of Lutheran self-identity came into play: *simul iustus et peccator* and vocation. One thing the class agreed upon was that the way their classmate felt about her service did not determine the goodness of the work. She may have resented every minute of a visit, but still she went. The nursing home resident had needs to be filled and this young woman took responsibility to fill them. There were plenty of people in the community who would have shared her distaste for geriatric unhappiness, but with this difference: their selfishness would have been enough to keep them from going to the nursing home. And the needs of the elderly woman, whose laundry and shopping were taken care of, who was read to and prayed with, were met. Her caregiver's struggle with hypocrisy was of no importance to her. This is a fine example of Luther's brilliant insight into the perversity of sin. Though people are generally loathe to confess their wrongdoing, here was a young woman insisting on her impure intentions to discredit God's use of her as an agent of new life. This is *incurvatus in se* at its most convoluted!

Luther assumed the medieval analysis of the structure of society which divided human life together into three 'estates' (German: Stand, Latin: status), perhaps better labelled 'walks of life' or 'situations'. These *Stände* included *ecclesia*, the *Lehrstand* (church, the teaching estate), *politia*, the *Wehrstand* (society or secular government, the defending estate), and *oeconomia*, the *Nährstand* (the household, which embraced both family life and economic life, the nourishing estate). This medieval view normally consigned each individual to one of these estates. In each, individuals would exercise an 'office' (German: *Amt*, Latin: *officium*). The offices of the estates consisted of formal societal roles and the functions belonging to those roles. The *ecclesia*, particularly the monastic life, held preference and priority in this medieval schema.

Luther took vocabulary used in the medieval conception for the monastic way of life alone—the office as a calling, a *vocation*—and turned it into the designation for the Christian's recognition that God calls and places all his people into their earthly responsibilities. Luther finally came to teach that every individual participates in all of these walks of life and that whoever exercises these responsibilities in faith according to God's commands is pleasing God (although this obedience justifies no one). Luther continued to designate the three walks of life in the traditional way, but, for instance, in the 'Household Chart of Christian Callings' in his Small Catechism (BSLK 523–7; BC 365–7) he distinguished economic and family aspects of the household.

Vocation is the link that joins faith to works. It is the arena in which the believer experiences the law in all three of its uses and where the transformative power of grace takes root and bears fruit. Luther vehemently rejected the distinction made by the medieval church between spiritual vocations and worldly ones (Wengert 2007). Insisting that whoever emerged from the waters of baptism was the equal of priest, bishop, and pope, Luther did away with the superiority accorded to the spiritual estate or walk of life by the church. Rejecting the idea that vows of poverty, chastity, and obedience placed one in a state of holiness beyond that of baptism, Luther insisted upon a priesthood of all believers established by the sacrament. Everyone who received it was empowered and enjoined by the Holy Spirit to proclaim the gospel to others, to forgive their sins in the name of Jesus Christ, and to offer prayers on their behalf. Baptism was the only indelible mark the Christian required. To try to root priesthood in some other divine command was blasphemous. To claim that the only true spiritual office was sacerdotal priesthood was a lie. In Luther's judgement the hierarchy of the institutional church was founded on these self-serving falsehoods, which denied people a right understanding of the power of God's grace in their own lives (*On Monastic Vows*, 1522, WA8.573–669; LW 44.251–400; cf. Wengert 2007).

One is not saved by one's works, and so the nature of one's worldly employment is of no importance when it comes to justification. Christ died for pig farmers and politicians as well as popes, and they all receive his saving grace in the same way. The choice of earthly vocation remains free. One is to make the best use of one's talents and interests in response to the world's needs. For Luther no work was too insignificant to meet those criteria (with the exception of the dishonourable and sinful, pimps, scam artists, and popes, for example). So the scullery maid, who spent long hours scouring pots, had just as much reason for satisfaction with her labours as the physician employing her would with the professional services he rendered. Both worked in faith, honestly and industriously, kept the needs of others uppermost, and thereby glorified God. Their integrity was an important witness to the world. Others would see their good works and give glory to God.

The chief exception to Luther's understanding of vocation as adiaphoron is monastic life, previously the most honoured of options. The church enshrined this, in Luther's view, egregious form of works righteousness as a superior spiritual estate and thereby devastated countless consciences. Luther was outraged by what he saw as abusive behaviour when the church lured young people into monastic life before they were mature enough to make an informed commitment. Celibacy was a divine gift, and a rare one at that, never a human choice. Yet once the vow was made, there was no escape. Thereafter the monk was forced to live with a tormented conscience.

Luther denounced the celibate life as unnatural; God created human beings for marriage and family. Vocation is as much about one's relationships as it is about one's work in the world. Parent, child, friend, citizen, volunteer, congregation member—it is through these commonplace connections that our discipleship takes shape and God moulds us in the ways of mercy and love.

In his 1952 study (translated 1957) *Luther on Vocation*, the enduring classic on this subject, Gustaf Wingren points out that disciples do not live in a closed moral system. One does not have to reinvent the wheel in the face of every ethical challenge, but neither can one be content with the hallowed responses of the past. For Luther, imitation is the result of deficient ethical earnestness and unabashed narcissism. Wingren writes:

> The motive of imitation is not to serve others and to lose oneself, but to be just as holy as somebody else one knows. In imitation one's aim is steadily centred in oneself. The object sought is one's own achievement of personality; and one's spiritual condition is not the fountain of one's action but the objective of it. (Wingren 1957: 181–2)

Our vocations serve as God's masks. They are the structures that secure the earthly order and the engines of its transformation as well. We must use our vocations creatively but also cautiously, for the devil is quick to hijack them to serve his purposes. The Christian must act shrewdly, sometimes floating like a butterfly, sometimes stinging like a bee, if he is to keep the enemy at bay.

Vocation is defining of the Christian life and yet is temporal in its duration. According to Wingren, when the reign of God is fulfilled, when we escape our simul status and become wholly saint, we will have no further need of vocation. Still, it is hard to see how our vocations would vanish completely. We may no longer labour in them, but the person who is raised from the dead into eternal life has been formed by them and the relationships they create. In some sense we can never exist apart from them.

In the left-hand realm under the first use of the law, vocation provides the foundation for an ordered community. Parents raise godly and obedient children, provide for their education, and determine their futures in accordance with their abilities and the needs of the wider community. Civic officials care for the poor. Judges preserve equity. Even the violence of executioners and soldiers has its place as legitimate service to the neighbour. Moreover, this social structure comprised of distinct yet interconnected responsibilities embraces Christians and non-Christians alike.

For Christians, however, vocation is not just about its civil use. Wingren shows that vocation also carries out the purpose of the law in its second use. The responsibilities are crushing, the failures humiliating, and the weary person falls into rebellion and courts despair. Moreover, sinful pride can root itself deeply in the accomplishments of vocation. Time and again we are reminded that our works are not the source of our being or worth. Of course, God is pleased by good parenting, but good parenting is the fruit of God's grace, not its cause. When one is overwhelmed, when one's best efforts to keep one's children safe fail, it is then that one realizes the necessity and constancy of God's mercy.

There has always been debate whether or not there is a third use of the law in Luther's theology. Without settling that question one way or the other, one can say, as Wingren does, that there is a sanctifying use of vocation for Luther. Without in any way violating the principle of justification by faith apart from the works of the law, Luther does see the transforming power of the Spirit working through vocation. Here the new Adam emerges, even as the old must be drowned daily by the limits and demands vocation imposes. We do not become something that we are not already—parent, child, pastor, day labourer, senator—yet behold we are made new, disciples of justice and vessels of grace.

Through vocation God defines and establishes life in both the created and redeemed realms. Whatever our callings may be, commonplace or exalted, they are all open to the service of the neighbour and transparent to the working of God's Spirit. The apex of vocation for Luther cannot be the monastery, a place apart, but must be the public community with its many paths, all potentially leading to the glory of God and the wellbeing of the creation.

References

Wengert, Timothy J. (2007). "'Per mutuum colloquium et consolationem fratrum'": Monastische Zügen in Luthers ökumenischer Theologie'. In *Luther und das monastische Erbe*, ed. Christoph Bultmann, Volker Leppin, and Andreas Lindner. Tübingen: Mohr/ Siebeck, 207–20.

Wingren, Gustaf (1957). *Luther on Vocation*, trans. Carl C. Rasmussen. Philadelphia: Muhlenberg.

Further Reading

Benne, Robert (2001). *Ordinary Saints, an Introduction to the Christian Life*. Eugene: Wipf & Stock.

Benne, Robert (1995). *The Paradoxical Vision: A Public Theology for the Twenty-First Century*. Minneapolis: Fortress.

Stegmann, Andreas (2012a). 'Bibliographie zur Ethik Martin Luthers'. *Lutherjahrbuch* 79: 305–42.

Stegmann, Andreas (2012b). 'Die Geschichte der Erforschung von Martin Luthers Ethik'. *Lutherjahrbuch* 79: 211–303.

CHAPTER 26

....

LUTHER ON MARRIAGE, SEXUALITY, AND THE FAMILY

....

JANE E. STROHL

... for God has created man and woman so that they are to come together
with pleasure, willingly and gladly with all their hearts. And bridal love or
the will to marry is a natural thing, implanted and inspired by God. This
is the reason bridal love is so highly praised in the Scriptures and is often
cited as an example of Christ and his church.

(WA30,3.236,9–14; LW46.304)

To be sure, when I consider marriage, only the flesh seems to be there. Yet my
father must have slept with my mother and made love to her, and they were
nevertheless godly people. All the patriarchs and prophets did likewise. The
longing of a man for a woman is God's creation—that is to say, when nature
is sound, not when it's corrupted as it is among Italians and Turks.

(WATR2.167,3–7, §1659)

LUTHER'S early reflections on marriage concentrate on its importance as a defence
against lust and as a safe channel for the expression of human sexuality. His
anti-monastic polemic is constant.[1] He distinguishes sharply between the true charism of chastity and what he denounces as the sham, brutally imposed celibacy of the
monastic life. If God favours a person with the former, there is reason for rejoicing, not
because it exempts one from the whole difficult business of sexual relationships but
because, as Paul points out, it frees one from the entanglements of marriage for unin-
terrupted service and worship of God. Luther insists, however, that one cannot by one's
own efforts generate such a calling; it comes only as a divine gift and quite rarely at that.
Those who take upon themselves vows of celibacy that they prove unable to keep had far
better marry, thereby honouring their created nature and corralling their sinful needs.

---

[1] Roman Catholic teaching with regard to the social and spiritual good of marriage and the sanctity of
procreation mirrored Protestant positions in many respects. What is offensive to Luther is the hypocrisy
of honouring marriage while relegating it to a status far inferior to that of monastic celibacy.

Christians remain male and female like other people and have the same innate desire to reproduce their kind. Despite the sin that infects the longing of male and female for one another, it remains in God's eyes a good part of the creation.

The view of marriage as the antidote to sin predominates in Luther's early years. Over time, however, Luther also speaks of marriage as a divine calling. It is no longer chiefly about what marriage prevents; it is about what it allows to happen in terms of obedience to God and service to the neighbour. Despite Luther's praise of the celibate state—in contrast to the monastic regime—one ultimately comes away with the impression that the entanglements and challenges of married life generate the discipleship that is most pleasing to God. Luther emphasizes the holiness of the married estate, but he insists that it is a civil ordinance established as part of God's rule of creation. Marriage and attendant concerns—betrothals, divorce—should be handled exclusively by the temporal authorities.

For Luther the vocation of husband or wife is inseparable from that of parent, and ultimately he holds the latter to be the more important. There is for Luther no greater blessing than the birth of children into a family and no weightier responsibility for husband and wife than becoming effective parents. The parent–child relationship is also one of love. Yet here is a stern affection that must instil fear and exact obedience to be appropriately loving, for its purpose is to produce responsible citizens and faithful disciples.

This essay discusses Luther's primary writings on marital matters in chronological order. It will then look at divorce and some aspects of the parent–child relationship and conclude with an exploration of Luther's portrayal of the patriarchs and matriarchs as married couples.

I. THE EARLY WRITINGS

In his *A Sermon on the Estate of Marriage* (1519) Luther begins by emphasizing the unique nature of marriage, which God grants only to human beings and not to any of the other animals. The importance of this relationship to God is evident in the care God takes in creating Eve for Adam. Luther then distinguishes among three kinds of love: false love, natural love, and married love. False love is self-serving and uses the desired object to satisfy its own appetites. In reality, false love is greed and covetousness posing as love. Natural love is that which binds us to parents, siblings, friends, and family members. The third form, married love, is or should be the greatest and purest of all loves. It trumps the claims of natural love since husband and wife leave father and mother to be joined to one another and create a new family. It seeks nothing other than the self of the beloved.

Luther qualifies this praise with the observation that since the Fall such love is no longer pure. It has been corrupted by the presence of false love, that is, the drive to use the other as the means to satisfy one's own desires. Such love is about the self, not the beloved. Luther then concludes that marriage now can be little more than a prophylactic measure against lust.

At this point he still considers marriage to be a sacrament. Because it signifies the sacred reality of Christ's union with the church, a married man should perform his conjugal duty without the fear of the wicked lust of the flesh that inevitably afflicts him in this most intimate of acts. The taint of lust is also counteracted by the covenant of fidelity that constitutes marriage. Because the couple stays within the limits of their committed relationship, God defends them from the sin of illicit desire. Moreover, within these confines husband and wife are allowed some degree of freedom in their sexual lives:

> In this way God sees to it that the flesh is subdued so as not to rage wherever and however it pleases, and the faithfulness that has been pledged permits even more occasion than is necessary for the begetting of children. But of course, a man has to control himself and not make a filthy sow's sty of his marriage.
>
> (WA2.169,3–7; LW44.11)

The third way in which marriage undermines the damning power of lust is by producing children. However, Luther insists, birth within the bonds of matrimony is only the beginning. Even heathens produce offspring. Christians must raise their children to a life of godliness. Maintaining the covenant of marriage becomes almost a secondary concern.

The following year, 1520, in *The Babylonian Captivity of the Church*, Luther rejects the sacramental status of marriage. He argues that marriage does not impart saving grace and has no divinely instituted sign although it is a divine institution. Since marriage has existed from the beginning of the world and is found among all peoples, not just Christians, there is no reason to regard it as a sacrament of the gospel under the governance of the church.

II. Rejection of Monasticism

Luther's *The Judgment on Monastic Vows* (1521) is an unconditional denunciation of the monastic practice of his day and in particular of the mandatory vow of celibacy. He argues that there is no biblical warrant for the imposition of this discipline. Jesus only discusses it with reference to eunuchs; he neither invites nor calls his hearers to take it up. The same, writes Luther, is true of Paul.

He insists once again that true celibacy is a divine gift, not a human accomplishment. To demand it is a form of works righteousness and a violation of Christian freedom. Most monastics have tormented consciences because they have vowed to do that which they cannot. They are denied the proper outlet for their sexual nature in marriage, and so, argues Luther, they inevitably fall into rampant lust and hypocrisy. Moreover, their celibacy serves no one but themselves; it has nothing to do with the worship of the Lord or the love of the neighbour. Indeed, it excuses them from the very works of mercy Christ has enjoined upon all believers.

Luther concludes the treatise with some comments on marriage. He acknowledges that the married person, because of care for the family and involvement in worldly matters, has less time to tend to the Word of God than does the true celibate. Commenting on Isaiah 56: 4–5, on the gift of being a eunuch, Luther acknowledges that virginity and chastity are greater works and greater gifts than marriage. We know too, he writes, that in our Father's house are many mansions and that one star differs from another in brightness. 'But in relation to the true God and the eunuchs there is no name other than the one we all enjoy, and that name is Christ' (WA8.653,16–17; LW44.375). Marriage does not come across here as a way of life with the potential for joy. It is not for the faint of heart, but its hardships are far preferable to the tormented conscience of the person unable to keep a vow of chastity. Besides, connubial endurance has biblical precedent:

> We do not advocate marriage as an easy way out, nor do we hold out any promises that it will be such. We want it to be permitted, to be a matter of option, so that the man who is able may be continent for as long as he wants. We want the conscience to be free from offense, not from marriage. How much happier a state of affairs it is to tolerate a marriage irksome twice over than to be tortured by the constant pangs of conscience! This kind of trouble has been laid on us by God, and all the holy patriarchs have borne it.
>
> (WA8.665,27–32; LW44.395)

In this treatise Luther does not celebrate married life. It is marked by the cross of Christ, but the light of its grace is less radiant than that of the truly celibate, the eunuch for the kingdom of heaven. Over time, however, Luther comes to see in the life of the family within the community of its neighbours not an arena of potential distraction from the Word of God but the primary setting for experiencing and enacting the gospel.

III. THE ESTATE OF MARRIAGE, 1522

The Estate of Marriage (1522) opens with a statement of reluctance on Luther's part to get further involved with the subject of marriage. He fears that there will be no end to the works imposed by the church that make it difficult for couples to marry; they are in any case illegitimate and abusive.[2] Moreover, following the letter of even sound civil

---

[2] Luther discusses at length eighteen impediments which were recognized as grounds for preventing or dissolving a marriage. These include issues of consanguinity, relationship through marriage, impotence, prior betrothal, coercion, etc. Of the eighteen Luther recognizes only the fourteenth, 'unfitness for marriage', i.e. impotence, as a valid ground for ending a marriage. Otherwise, these restrictions represent for him an illegitimate interference with the freedom of a Christian. He concludes: 'It is a dirty rotten business that a bishop should forbid me a wife or specify the times when I may marry, or that a blind and dumb person should not be allowed to enter into wedlock. So much then for this foolishness...' (WA10,2.287,8–11; LW45.30).

law in marital matters may be inadequate for the accomplishment of God's will and the spiritual health of the believer. In such cases of emergency Luther feels compelled to speak out on behalf of troubled consciences caught in conflict. It is here that the created order of marriage spills over into the realm of law and gospel, where the peace of the conscience before God is of paramount concern.

While upholding the principle of Christian freedom, that a person may marry or not, depending on his or her abilities and inclinations, Luther does insist on a certain natural necessity that drives the human being to mate. 'Be fruitful and multiply', he writes, is more than a command; it is a divine ordinance that human beings dare not hinder or ignore. He compares it to such natural instinctual acts as sleeping and waking, eating and drinking, and the emptying of bladder and bowels. God does not command people to be man or woman but creates them as one or the other. Neither does God command human beings to multiply but forms them so that they are driven to do so. Therefore, celibacy is a vain attempt to reverse the tide and a dishonouring of God's created order.

In the second part of *The Estate of Marriage* Luther discusses divorce, which will be treated below. The final section of the treatise is devoted to the topic of how to live a Christian and godly life in marriage. Luther is a realist. He points out that to honour marriage as a holy estate is something quite different from merely being married. Family life is inevitably fraught with conflict and full of drudgery and hardship. Without the eyes of vocation, that is all one will see. The person who knows herself called to this spouse and this home, however, will be strengthened by the assurance that all that she does and all that she suffers is pleasing to God. Moreover, she will find in her marriage delight, love, and joy without end. The devil has a vested interest in defaming marriage, and so men and women must be on their guard lest they be lured into denigrating one another and rejecting the call to the married estate.

IV. I CORINTHIANS 7 ON SEXUAL RELATIONS (1523)

Marriage is embraced by the law of love, which requires a person to put the neighbour's need before his or her own desire. Consequently, the partners surrender their bodies to each other. When lust assaults one partner, the other is to minister to him or her, and the commitment to offer oneself to one's spouse is indissoluble. The boundaries are clearly drawn; you cannot give yourself to another; your body is no longer yours to give.

Luther is of the opinion that Christians should discipline themselves and conduct their sexual lives with moderation. However, he is adamant that no rules should be imposed on sexual activity, limiting the times and conditions in which intercourse is permissible. How, he asks, can anyone forbid me access to the body that God has decreed should be given to me? Citing the saying, 'Whoever is too passionate in love-making commits adultery against his own wife', Luther rejects the idea as impossible

('*Wer zu hitzig ist ynn der liebe, der ist an seynem eygen weybe eyn ehebrecher. Aber eyn heyde hats geredt, darumb acht ich seyn nicht, und sage, es sey nicht war*', WA12.101,30; LW 28.13). Sex within marriage, as St Paul writes, is given as a defence against lust and unchastity. Under no circumstances should it be restricted and the couple left vulnerable to temptation, except by common agreement of the couple in order to devote themselves to prayer and fasting. Yet even these acts of devotion must yield to conjugal demand. 'Now prayer is a most precious good work, but it must give way to what seems a base thing. The law of love, by which they are bound, brings this about' (WA12.103,6–9; LW 28.14).

V. THE SERMON ON THE MOUNT (1532)

Luther discusses the issue of licit and illicit desire at greater length in his study of Matthew 5:27–30. The temptation of lust is impossible to avoid. Men and women will be thrown together in society. Moreover, it is pleasing to God that men look at women, talk, laugh, and have a good time with them. People are supposed to fall in love so that they will wed. After that, safeguarding love and desire is crucial to sustaining the marriage:

> Without it there is trouble: from the flesh because a person soon gets tired of marriage and refuses to bear the daily discomfort that comes with it; and from the devil, who cannot stand the sight of a married couple treating each other with genuine love and who will not rest until he has given them an occasion for impatience, conflict, hate, and bitterness. Therefore, it is an art both necessary and difficult, and one peculiarly Christian, this art of loving one's husband or wife properly, of bearing the other's faults and all the accidents and troubles. At first everything goes all right, so that, as the saying goes, they are ready to eat each other up for love. But when their curiosity has been satisfied, then the devil comes along to create boredom in you, to rob you of your desire in his direction, and to excite it unduly in another direction.
>
> (WA32.374,1–11; LW 21.89)

Luther takes the reality of lust and the temptation to adultery quite seriously, but he is no alarmist. A man may look at another woman, but he must not look at her the way he should look only at his wife. It is not difficult to tell the difference. Such temptation will inevitably befall us. It comes with being social creatures, gifted with the capacity for passion and affection and blinded by the love of self. It is impossible for us to keep sinful thoughts from occurring; just do not let them take root, cautions Luther. Of course, lustful thought is sin, but no one lives in the flesh without a great many sins. The best protection against adultery is, as Luther says in the Large Catechism (1529), to remind oneself that one's wife is God's special gift and that she alone has the surpassing beauty of God's Word to adorn her. With that, no other woman's allure can compare.

The passage from Matthew 5 with which Luther is working here deals specifically with the sin of adultery. He sees unfaithfulness at work among married couples in other ways as well. There will be dissension and distrust; angry words get spoken; feelings cut deep. The one you share bed and board with will sometimes seem like your worst enemy:

> Husband and wife can become alienated from no one else as readily as from each other. All it takes is one little word, spoken in passing or jokingly, which pierces the heart and cannot be forgotten. And thereafter they both brew pure poison and bitterness in their souls. (WA34.61,25–9)

Your eyes may not be turning toward a new sexual partner, but when your heart is closed to the one you have married, then you are breaking the sixth commandment. You need to pay heed once again to the Word of grace shining through your marriage.

VI. DIVORCE

Luther recognizes the need for divorce in a sinful society and regards its regulation as a matter for the civil authority. At the same time he wants Christians to do their best to exceed secular expectations and hold their marriages to a higher spiritual standard. In *The Estate of Marriage* (1522) Luther identifies three legitimate grounds for marital dissolution: inability to fulfil one's conjugal duty (impotence or frigidity) so that one's spouse is deprived of children; adultery; and refusal to fulfil one's conjugal duty or to live with one's spouse. The resistance of the partner in the last case may well become the cause of the other's fall. Luther suggests that he or she be called to public accountability, and if that does not shame the errant spouse into cooperation, divorce is appropriate. The issue here is one of fraud.

Luther makes it clear, however, that this does not apply to a couple where one partner is unable to meet his or her conjugal responsibilities because of infirmity. Indeed, caring for an invalid spouse is an extraordinary spiritual discipline. He assures readers that God is far too faithful to deprive a person of his spouse through illness without simultaneously subduing his carnal desire.

Luther discusses one additional situation that does not fit under the three major headings with which he began. This is the case of what today we would call 'irreconcilable differences': where husband and wife cannot get along for some reason other than the matter of the conjugal duty: '... certain strange, stubborn, and obstinate people, who have no capacity for toleration and are not suited for married life at all, should be permitted to get a divorce. ... Frequently something must be tolerated, even though it is not a good thing to do, to prevent something worse from happening' (WA32.377,37–378,3; LW21.94).

Luther knows that people can be dangerously deluded. There is no getting around the tedium of daily life, the predictable burdens of family and the aggravations imposed by the outside world. One just has to deal with them. Still, many think they can escape the disappointments, most readily by transferring their affections to a new spouse. However, if you cannot see the hand of God at work in your life in the first place, then it will continue to founder, no matter how you try to spice up the domestic scene. Luther's response to such people is unsparing: get real, grow up, work at your marriage—vocations require effort, after all—remember what the forgiveness of sins is all about, and pray.

Adultery is legitimate grounds for divorce, for the adulterer has in truth already dissolved the marriage by his actions. Luther hopes that the other partner, although set completely free, will nonetheless choose to reconcile. He recognizes, however, that there may be no hope for improvement and a renewal of spousal fidelity, and then the partners must go their separate ways, with only the innocent party free to marry again. The other issue Luther raises here is that of abandonment. He is outraged by the man who takes off, leaving his family to fend for itself and expecting it to take him back whenever he chooses to return. Luther judges such a person to be worse than an unbeliever and less tolerable than an adulterer. He recommends that the authorities issue a summons, and if the offender does not respond within the stated time, that the wife be set completely free. Luther's indignation is evident; the person who would default not just on his commitment to his spouse but on his obligations to his children is beneath contempt.

VII. Parents and Children

As has already been noted Luther extols the vocation of marriage chiefly because it produces family life.

> But the greatest good in married life, that which makes all suffering and labour worthwhile, is that God grants offspring and commands that they be brought up to worship and serve him. In all the world this is the noblest and most precious work because to God there can be nothing dearer than the salvation of souls. Now since we are all duty bound to suffer death, if need be, that we might bring a single soul to God, you can see how rich the estate of marriage is in good works. God has entrusted to its bosom souls begotten of its own body, on whom it can lavish all manner of Christian works. Most certainly father and mother are apostles, bishops, and priests to their children, for it is they who make them acquainted with the gospel. In short, there is no greater or nobler authority on earth than that of parents over their children, for this authority is both spiritual and temporal.
>
> (WA10,2.301,16–27, LW45.46)

Parental responsibility to serve one's children as 'their apostle and bishop' consists of four crucial duties: to provide the sacrament of baptism for infants, to form children in the true faith as they mature, to attend to their education for vocation, and to provide them with a suitable spouse in a timely fashion, that is, before the force of their natural sexual instincts puts them at risk of sin. For the purposes of this article, we will focus on the last of the four.

In 1524 Luther wrote a brief piece entitled *That Parents Should Neither Compel Nor Hinder the Marriage of Their Children, and That Children Should Not Become Engaged Without Their Parents' Consent*. Luther reminds readers that God has established parental authority to build up, not destroy. It has strict limits; it cannot go so far as to inflict damage on the child, especially not on his or her conscience. Thus, a father violates his sacred trust and acts against God when he forces his child into a marriage without love. Luther allows that interference with a relationship to a particular person can be justified, but it is a gross sin to prevent the child from marrying altogether and force him or her into a life of celibacy. If a father fails to help his child make a suitable match, he again defaults on his parental responsibility. In such a case, if the child has sought the father's assistance in vain, the child may proceed as if the father or guardian were dead and make his or her own marital arrangements.

Luther is equally concerned about the conduct of children in the process of betrothal and marriage. He is adamant that no union should be based on a secret engagement. Clearly, the easiest way around parental objections or interference was to join oneself to another without their knowledge. Protestant and Roman teaching held the free mutual consent of the parties in an exchange of vows to constitute a marriage. However, Luther did not acknowledge the validity of freely exchanged promises between two parties of legally marriageable age if they were made without public witnesses or parental consent, whereas Roman canon law did recognize such unions. Luther objected on four grounds: (1) that such commitments led too easily to conflicts of conscience; (2) that marriage is critical to the life and health of the community and therefore should be contracted publicly before one's neighbours and with the recognition of secular authorities; (3) that a betrothal contracted without the approval of one's parents violates the fourth commandment; and (4) that no word of God is proclaimed over the couple's action and consequently God has not joined them together. The bride, says Luther, has only the fine words and promise of her seducer to go by, and on these she dare not rely.

Luther also condemns children who, presuming on the fact that they should not be forced into marriage, resist a union that is honourable and desirable. It is their duty to abandon what Luther calls their 'foolish young love' and honour their family's judgement. Parents, however, can only go so far in leading a child to wisdom. Once they offer their counsel, their consciences are clear. If children reject their considered opinion and persist in their intention to make a match to which their parents object, the parents are free to leave them to their own devices, commit the matter to God, and consider their parental obligation met.

VIII. The Patriarchs and Matriarchs as Married Couples

Luther makes creative use of biblical narratives to support his arguments concerning the holy status of marriage and family life. Husbands and wives do not figure significantly as

actors in the New Testament, but the stories of the Old Testament patriarchs and matriarchs provide him with rich material. Indeed, Luther expands with relish on what he
finds there, decking these figures out with a full range of emotions and domestic virtues.
Given the promise made to Abraham that God would make of him a great nation, these
couples are deeply concerned with childbearing. Luther comments that it is hard for
us to imagine the anguish and shame caused by barrenness in their time. Indeed, the
worst stresses fall on these marriages when infertility becomes an issue. Consequently,
the greatest manifestation of God's goodness is the opening of the womb, so that the
childless woman is able to take her place in the line of those carrying God's promises to
future generations.

When commenting on the creation story in his lectures on Genesis (1535), Luther
notes that with the work of the fifth day God not only 'saw that it was good', God also
'blessed them'. Only with the fifth day does God bring living things into being, and the
blessing given to them and not to the inanimate part of the creation has to do with their
distinctive method of reproduction: 'But here there is procreation from a living body
into a living body. This, therefore, is a new work, that a living body grows and multi-
plies out of its own body' (WA42.39,37–9; LW1.53). This capacity to bear live young is
the effect of the Word making fruitful the common act of reproduction (WA42.40,5–12;
LW1.53).

When discussing Adam and Eve, Luther understands Genesis 2:18, 'Then the Lord
God said, 'It is not good that the man should be alone', to be concerned with what he
calls the common good of the species rather than the personal good of Adam. The other
created living beings had companions with whom they could mate, but 'so far Adam
was alone; he still had no partner for that magnificent work of begetting and preserving
his kind' (WA42.87,36–8; LW1.116). He required Eve so that he could fulfil his duty to be
fruitful and multiply. It is only after the Fall that he has need of her to ward off the sin of
illicit desire.[3] The animals, Luther notes, do not have to contend with lust, but neither do
they have the kind of spiritual, affective relationship that comes with human marriage.
Luther laments the damage done to the intimacy between husband and wife by the loss
of innocence. Delight gives way to shame and resentment.

God tells the woman, 'I will greatly multiply your pain in childbearing, in pain you
shall bring forth children, yet your desire shall be for your husband, and he shall rule
over you' (Gen. 3:16). In this Luther hears as much good news as bad. Yes, the flesh will
suffer, but God does not repudiate Eve. Nor is she deprived of the blessing of procreation
or separated from her husband to live in solitude. Most of all, in keeping what Luther

---

[3] Luther speaks from the male perspective: woman is man's defence against lust. The following is
typical: 'In Paradise woman would have been a help for a duty only. But now she is also, and for the
greater part at that, an antidote and a medicine; we can hardly speak of her without a feeling of shame,
and surely we cannot make use of her without shame' (WA42.89,34–7; LW1.118). Considering the
universal nature of the Fall, it is a given that women too are plagued with selfish, raging desire that
threatens to use rather than honour the partner in every respect of a relationship. Eve also needs Adam to
be able to subject lust to love.

calls the glory of motherhood, she also has the assurance that the Seed who will crush the head of her betrayer will come from her. The discomfort of pregnancy and the danger of childbirth pale in comparison, concludes Luther. Then he writes:

> Without a doubt, therefore, Eve had a heart full of joy even in an obviously sad situation. Perhaps she gave comfort to Adam saying: 'I have sinned. But see what a merciful God we have. How many privileges, both temporal and spiritual, he is leaving for us sinners! Therefore, we women should bear the hardship and wretchedness of conceiving, of giving birth, and of obeying you husbands. His is a fatherly anger, because this stands: that the head of our enemy will be crushed, and that after the death of our flesh we shall be raised to a new and eternal life through our Redeemer. These abundant good things and endless kindnesses far surpass whatever curse and punishments our father has inflicted on us. These and similar conversations Adam and Eve undoubtedly carried on in order to mitigate their temporal adversities.
>
> (WA42.148,35–149,5; LW1.99)

Adam and Eve, caught in sin and facing the trauma of life in the post-Fall world, represent marriage at its best. The couple accepts the arduous work that lies before them as God's charge, and they stand together as companions, sharing words of comfort and faith. Clearly, there is more going on in the relationship than merely the containment of lust and the raising of children.

Abraham and Sarah serve Luther as a model for the discipleship of Christian couples first and foremost because of their faith. Both these elderly people give up the home they know to answer God's call to go forth to a strange land. When promised the birth of a child at their advanced ages, they are shocked but confident of God's truthfulness. Luther also praises their daily discipleship because of the commonplace duties and normal domestic tedium it entails. He contrasts this in most pejorative terms to the idle, inflated 'spiritual' life of the monastics and assures his readers that the menial tasks that occupy Sarah and Abraham, done as they are in faith, are more precious than any trumped-up work of holiness and celibacy. When, Luther says, you are confident of doing full justice to your calling and of having no need to pray 'forgive us our trespasses' because of negligence, dissatisfaction, or impatience, then feel free to go into the desert and busy yourself with showy works of piety.

Luther finds in Sarah a treasury of housewifely virtues. He makes much of the fact that when the three guests inquire as to Sarah's whereabouts, Abraham answers, 'She is in the tent' (Gen. 18: 1–16). Women, writes Luther, are given to a certain levity and indecent curiosity. They either run around or hang out conspicuously at their doors to pick up the latest gossip. Such women on the loose are susceptible to moral laxity. Sarah, however, is right where she belongs within their home, leaving her husband and his guests in peace while she prepares the meal and manages the household.

Yet one should note that Sarah is not always so amiable and modest. Luther maintains that in the matter of Hagar and Ishmael, Abraham is lax in protecting the promise made to him and Sarah concerning their descendants. He loves the slave woman and their son with a natural affection and does not see their impudence. Sarah is the one who obliges him to expel them lest Ishmael presume on his primogeniture at Isaac's expense. Although Luther is at some pains to protect Sarah's wifely modesty, stating that she humbly implores but does not command Abraham, he simultaneously recognizes the reality of dissension, hot anger, and quarrelling in their marriage and by extension in every marriage. This is one of the spiritual disciplines of the 'secular' life, which outstrips any monastic practice. In this instance Sarah, by fulfilling her worldly responsibilities as wife and mother, acts as the unlikely but indispensable champion of the Word. Through bearing Isaac and protecting his position as heir to the promise, she becomes the mother of the faithful.[4]

Luther's commentary on the courtship of Jacob and Rachel offers interesting observations on the realities of physical attraction. Reflecting on Jacob's infatuation with Rachel and indifference to Leah, Luther offers the opinion that ugly women are usually the more fertile. By rights, men should love women for the sake of procreation; they should not be swayed by appearance. However, God indulges the male's preference for beautiful women to help sweeten the conjugal pot. Because of original sin man's sexual urges are unpredictable and urgent. He needs to marry and stay married despite the hardships, and if it takes feminine beauty to get the deed done, so be it.

Luther speaks of Jacob the suitor with fond amusement. According to his calculations the patriarch is 84 years old, but in the presence of this beautiful girl he is rejuvenated. Luther praises Jacob's extraordinary chastity, some 68 years until now, but continence is destined to end in marriage. This is not a surrender to carnal necessity but a venture into love from the very start, when the patriarch kisses Rachel at the well:

> Other histories about very great events—about the burning of Sodom, about the sacrifice of Isaac—[the Holy Spirit] has described with very few words and has summed up in barely five or six verses. But when he comes to these sordid, carnal and foolish matters, he is wordy beyond measure, in order that we may know that the Lord takes pleasure in those who fear him. For if we believe and are sure of the freely offered mercy of God, we should not doubt that everything we do pleases God very much and that he has numbered even the hairs of our head, yes, that the kisses and embraces are pleasing to him, likewise the removal of that stone. All these things are recounted in this passage as very great and extraordinary works in the eyes of God and the angels. God could not forget them but wanted them recorded for our instruction and consolation. (WA43.624,12–22; LW5.283)

Luther does not dismiss the ardour and delight of new love as frivolous. They will not sustain a couple through the challenges of years of married life, but such enchantment is a very fine place to start.

---

[4] One finds a similar dilemma in the narrative of Isaac and Rebekah, when the wife transgresses the bounds of propriety and obedience to her husband in order to preserve the divine promise. In this case Rebekah disguises Jacob as Esau so that he might secure the paternal blessing due the firstborn, despite the aged Isaac's stated intent of bestowing it on Esau.

IX. Conclusion

God has formed human beings to want what God wants: that we leave our parents and cleave to our spouses; that we be fruitful and multiply. God does not call a person to marriage in general. God calls you to be married to a particular person. The word of divine command and favour is spoken over this union. It is absolutely clear that here is the spouse you are to have and no other. The certain boundary will frustrate couples at times, but its clarity is also a kindness. Husband and wife can persevere in the demanding work of marriage, confident that their efforts are pleasing to God, their failures forgiven, and their commitment to one another enduringly blessed.

In a fallen world marriage is a crucial weapon in the ongoing battle against sin even though, as Luther observes, strong marriages become particular objects of the devil's venom. However, marriage is not a sacramental means of grace. No one is saved by matrimony. Marital status is an adiaphoron. One can wed or not as one pleases; in terms of salvation it is of no importance to God. On the other hand, marriage and family are of utmost importance in the earthly realm, not just as the bedrock of the civil order, but as the most efficient school of Christian discipleship. Wife, husband, mother, father—these are for Luther the foundational Christian vocations. They are essential to the formation of the vast majority of believers on earth, but they are apparently not a foretaste of the life to come, where they will neither marry nor be given in marriage.

RECOMMENDED READINGS

Hendrix, Scott (ed.) (2008). *Masculinity in the Reformation*. Kirksville: Truman State University Press.

Karent-Nunn, Susan and Merry Wiesner-Hanks (2003). *Luther on Women: A Sourcebook*. Cambridge: Cambridge University Press.

Lazareth, William H. (1960). *Luther on the Christian Home: An Application of the Social Ethics of the Reformation*. Philadelphia: Muhlenberg.

Mattox, Mickey Leland (2003). *'Defender of the Most Holy Matriarchs': Martin Luther's Interpretation of the Women of Genesis in the 'Enarrationes in Genesin', 1535–45*. Leiden: Brill.

Treu, Martin (1999a). 'Die Frau an Luthers Seite: Katharina von Bora—Leben und Werk'. *Luther* 70: 10–29.

Treu, Martin (1999b). *Katharina von Bora, die Lutherin. Aufsätze anläßlich ihrer 500. Geburtstages*. Wittenberg: Stiftung Luther-Gedenkstätten in Sachsen-Anhalt.

CHAPTER 27

....

LUTHER'S TREATMENT OF ECONOMIC LIFE

....

RICARDO RIETH

I. THE STATE OF RESEARCH

....

SYSTEMATIC discussion of Luther's economic thought began in the nineteenth century. Among economic historians, especially important were the contributions of representatives of the socialist school and the economic historicism in Germany. Karl Marx called Luther 'the oldest German political economist'. He studied the economic views of the reformer, partly motivated by Friedrich Engels. Engels had briefly suggested an ideological connection between Luther and the classical bourgeois political economic theories by calling its founding theoretician, Adam Smith, the 'Luther of economics'. Marx argued for this emphasis on Luther in the history of political economics in several writings. He believed that Luther recognized the difference between lending and buying and demonstrated that usury was present in both. Marx used his understanding of Luther's views to call attention to how capital accumulated by usury caused the ruination of the bourgeois, peasants, artisans, knights, nobles, and princes. Usury initiated both the concentration of property and the exploitation of working conditions, i.e., the ruination of those working under previous working conditions.

Representatives of nineteenth-century economic historicism evaluated Luther's views completely differently from Marx. Their evaluation set the course of future research, which partly ignored Marx's interpretation and partly found it indefensible. For Wilhelm Roscher (1874), in some questions of economics where canon law seemed to agree with the Bible, Luther led a reaction, which retreated from modern progress to the strictures of canon law. He had little conception of the productivity of capital and emphasized the possibility of loss when a person uses capital. Luther's exaggeration of the importance of agriculture compared to trade could not be said to be organized as a system nor was it a forerunner of François Quesnay's physiocracy since in that regard Luther maintained instead the medieval point of view.

However, Luther only seldom avoided finding the appropriate mean between extremes in economic questions. He sharply distinguished between ideal and reality. He was far from either the monastic deprecation of goods or an epicurean exaggeration of their importance. In this regard he railed against both the Fuggers' practices and communism. Luther enthusiastically greeted the growth of population because he really lived in a time striving for progress, in which rapid expansion of the possibilities for prospering precluded any fear of over-population. He saw great benefits in the division of labour and regarded the social structure of the 'estates' as an organic whole. Roscher found strange Luther's conviction that the common worker's wage was the standard for setting prices although Adam Smith later adopted it.

The judgement of representatives of economic historicism that Luther's economic views belonged to the medieval world largely determined later research in the history of economics. Obviously, at specific points differences among various economic historians must be recognized. In general, they emphasized Luther's defence of the right of private property—together with the rejection of the 'communism' of his time—which was said to have shaped the central—already bourgeois—character of the reformer's work and his promotion of a new understanding of work. This understanding, combating begging, together with Luther's ideals which were clearly shaped by monasticism, created the presuppositions for the possibility of an increase in productivity in the economic realm. Within this conception the otherwise backward Luther played a role as a pioneer of the future economic breakthrough that took place in the second half of the nineteenth century in Germany with the industrial revolution. He lived in an age in which the conditions for the implementation of his ideas were not present.

How can such different, contradictory assessments of Luther's economic thought be evaluated? Certainly these scholars took fundamentally different approaches to evaluating Luther's contribution. Marx emphasized the reformer's way of thinking, his methodological observations: through the ways in which he discussed the problem alongside his way of finding the appropriate answer, Luther grasped the fundamental elements of capitalist economics. Roscher and his successors, on the other hand, focused on individual economic problems. Thus, they found Luther to be a backward, medieval thinker, who did not comprehend the fundamental and irreversible economic revolution of his time.

Theological research which tried to investigate Luther's thought on economic topics accented his ethical perspective on economics. This approach usually assumed the view of economic historicism, according to which Luther remained trapped in ancient and medieval ways of thinking. Since the end of the 1970s theological research has concentrated more on the role of the Sermon on the Mount in Luther's statements on economic topics. Usually these authors based their study on the challenge of the theological reflection which contemporary economic problems required, especially in view of the gap between poor and rich nations, the unjust trade relationships among them, and the growing foreign debt of the poor. Gerta Scharffenorth tried with the aid of Luther's

economic statements in his interpretation of the Sermon on the Mount to organize
elements of a theory for ethical evaluation. Against many Lutheran ethical systems of
the nineteenth and twentieth centuries Scharffenorth (1982) maintained that Luther
emphasized the significance of the Sermon on the Mount for answering questions of
how to use material blessings, i.e., natural resources and human products from them,
as gifts of the Creator. Her investigation of Luther's approach constructed four steps of
ethical evaluation: first, he identified the problem and described it on the basis of his
analysis; then he applied to the problem statements from the gospels concerning temporal blessings—especially Matthew 5:40–2; third, he confronted the accepted normative bases of action in such cases with fundamental biblical commands; and finally, he
reviewed the questions to guarantee the possibility of independent, free decisions by
one's conscience.

Hans-Jürgen Prien (1992) analysed Luther's writings on economic ethics in their
contexts and compared them in order to answer the question to what extent his
social-economic analysis was appropriate. He also differentiated between Luther's fundamental ethical orientation and concrete orientation for action. Ethics as the sanctification of the justified always meant for Luther bearing the cross, together with love
for the neighbour. Luther established the connection of ethics in this sense to Christian
freedom in *On Christian Liberty* (1520). Prien wanted to test to what extent he held to
his fundamental ethical approach. Prien shared Scharffenorth's interpretation, stressing
repeatedly that Luther's ethical argumentation presumed Jesus' directives in the Sermon
on the Mount, which he summarized in three steps: suffering, giving, and lending. Prien
described how Luther assessed the validity of the Sermon on the Mount in the economic
realm and placed it into the context of natural law and the Golden Rule: Luther's ethic
was based on an understanding of the Sermon that was determined by the distinction
of law and gospel. The Sermon served not only as evangelical paranese but also as the
absolute accusing force of the law for all Christians. The Sermon dare not be adulterated
legalistically; however, as a programme for action, to be enforced by the first use of the
law, it had a political use. However, this does not produce an inevitable tension between
the Sermon's demands on the person as Christian, as an individual, and his actions in
office and calling because the demands of the Sermon (in the form of the new interpretation of natural law in the Golden Rule) more precisely place a demand on governmental authorities as well.

According to Prien, from a socio-economic point of view Luther's battle against
usury was not completely credible. It resulted from insufficient analysis of the situation, complicated by the transitional nature of his time. In addition, Luther's argument
was essentially weakened by his failure to clearly differentiate charitable and commercial, financial, lending or credit for consumption and production. Even when he began
to recognize productive credit, he remained trapped in agricultural ways of thought.
Evaluation of Luther's economic and social ethical axioms revealed that he clearly
rejected independent rules for economics. He designed the foundations of an economy
without credit on the basis of the ideals of the Sermon on the Mount. His thoughts on
possession of temporal goods defended their function for the community, not for their

disposition by individuals. Prien concluded that a strong point in Luther's ethic was his consistent consideration of justice in each case: he did not understand justice to be a strict, normative application of the law but rather correctly understood principles.

Theological interpretations of Luther's ideas on economics assumed the viewpoint of the economic historians. Marx inaugurated a tradition of evaluating Luther positively as one who clearly saw the developments produced by the procedures of early capitalistic relationships in his time. The reception of the historicist school viewed his concrete observations on economic topics as backward-looking. Research by economic historians and sociologists of religion sketched a picture of Luther determined only incidentally by theological principles.

Research by church historians and historians of theology emphasized social-ethical elements but assumed the ideas of the historicist school. That is also true for research in the 'Luther renaissance'. The negative evaluation of Marx's ideas was reinforced by presenting Luther as a champion of private property although that topic played no central role in his statements, so Marx did not discuss it. A weakness with this research generally lay in its narrow focus on Luther's writings on usury and trade from 1519/20, 1524, and 1540. The central role of the Sermon on the Mount for Luther's thinking was largely ignored and emerged only since the 1980s.

II. BIBLICAL INTERPRETATION AND CRITICISM OF THE ECONOMY

If Luther reflected the social and economic problems of his own milieu, he usually treated them in a particular manner. His so-called 'writings on usury', like the *Open Letter to the German Nobility*, and his writings on schools, his interpretation of the Sermon on the Mount and the Decalogue, and other treatises, lectures, and sermons, typically began by identifying and describing the problem to be addressed. In this context one must observe his consistent appeal to historical experience and his intensive observation and treatment of the reality of daily life, as seen in his countless sermons and table-talks. He placed his observations of problems in the context of applicable statements of Holy Scripture. After performing these two fundamental steps, he rendered his own judgement, in which he offered criticism by confronting the arguments for unjust conduct, or for an unfair structure in the social context, with basic biblical commands. Depending on whom he was addressing, whether governmental authorities who had to recognize their responsibility in governing the world, or the faithful in their estates and calling, he directed them to what he believed to be possibilities for proper action.

Luther did not work systematically on a general analysis of contemporary economic reality. His reflections were instead practical advice and rules for various aspects of economic life—especially questions of finance, policies for setting prices and wages, and provision of goods—reflections of a biblical interpreter and pastoral care-giver, who highly prized observing the realities around him and demanded taking seriously the Christian responsibility for improving those realities.

In no way did Luther regard the Christian's activities in the economic realm as independent of the life of faith. Everything a Christian undertook and accomplished happened within the framework of his service to God. The goods so acquired were to be seen as God's blessings and to be used according to the law of love.

However, reality revealed that most people act according to another principle, not in exercising Christian responsibility. In his lectures on Romans Luther dealt with the interpretation of Faber Stapulensis on Romans 13:1, where he speaks of a two-fold power—established and not established. Luther did not like this interpretation because no power in community life is without divine authorization. In reality, this power is simply viewed and exercised in an unauthorized way. Goods do not lose their goodness through wrong use; if that were the case, money, for example, would rot when stolen. With this example Luther placed economic factors on the same level with the political in regard to *potestas* (power). Unauthorized striving for the power ordained by God and administering this power in unauthorized ways create room for greed in dealing with goods.

The seventh commandment was an important text for dealing with the basics of economics in his time. In 1518 he spoke of four offences against this commandment: stealing, violent appropriation of the neighbour's possessions, usury, and deception in trade (WA1.499,7–505,31). Theological reflection, Luther believed, was the appropriate basis for evaluating such deeds. When jurists speak of five different forms of theft—*furtum simplex, sacrilegium, peculatus, abigeatus, plagiatus*—they understand the seventh commandment merely on the basis of external works. Theologically, it is a mistake to limit our understanding to that of the jurists. Even desiring the goods of others transgresses this commandment in God's sight. Indeed, when there is no sense of 'yours-and-mine', justice disappears automatically.

In the course of his Genesis lectures Luther often made axiomatic comments on economic matters, indeed often more extensively than in other biblical lectures. On the basis of Genesis 1:28 (WA42.53,31–55,27; LW1.71–73) he said that human beings in their fallen nature have no idea of how to deal with other creatures as they had in their perfect condition before the fall into sin. Adam and Eve used other creatures differently than people in Luther's time. They did not, for example, eat the meat of animals. They needed neither clothing nor money when they possessed lordship over all things. Without the fall into sin, greed would not have determined human dealings with other creatures, and the creatures would have simply served holy pleasures and the appreciation of God. Greed ruins the common good.

Regarding Genesis 47:3 (WA44.658,15–42; LW8.108) Luther discussed God's punishment on Egypt, turning it into a desert (Ps. 107:33–4) after Joseph—'a real political leader and theologian'—had administered everything with great insight and faith. Similar things took place in Italy and Thuringia. Earlier Thuringia (Luther's birthplace) had had the most fertile land compared to other German territories. However, by Luther's time Thuringian peasants had to work seven years to produce the same quantity harvested earlier in three years. When God punishes a territory, not only its inhabitants suffer; God even takes away the earth's fertility. Such ecological catastrophes arise from human depravity, especially in the form of usury, when people risk everything to exploit and rob regions, reducing them to desperation.

Luther was conscious of the tensions and contradictions on the economic level between human beings or interest groups of various social levels or within one estate. Already in his lectures on Romans he called attention to the fight between Bishop Wilhelm von Honstein and the city of Strasbourg in the affair of the canon Hepp von Kirchberg. In this lecture he mentioned the disputes of the time between representatives of the higher nobility and the peasants because the nobility seized lands that really belonged to the community (WA56.479,11–15; LW25.471–472). Luther dealt with economic disputes among townspeople. In a letter of 1525 he addressed the mayor and council of Nuremberg because of the theft of parts of his translation of the Bible from Wittenberg print shops by printers who resettled in Nuremberg (WABr3.577–578). Such printers impeded the spread of the gospel.

Luther clearly saw that the rules for existing economic relationships were being increasingly determined by non-local factors, often outside the territory of the government of a region. Precisely where the interdependence and internationalizing of economics corresponded to the disadvantage and exploitation of specific groups and communities in the social structure, he saw injustice at work. For exactly this reason he criticized the large merchant companies and monopolies harshly. As a result of usury, he observed, the person who had lived earlier an entire year for one hundred Gulden, needed in 1540 at least twice as much per year. Although those practising usury lived in Leipzig, Augsburg, and Frankfurt am Main, the impact of their usury could be seen in the marketplace of Wittenberg and in his own kitchen.

Since selfish economic actions always produce an unjust division of goods in society, it is clear that affluence always produces a rise in prices and an increase in hunger. Thus, in 1531 Luther believed that God blesses by giving abundant goods, but that people ruin this blessing. For the same reason he sombrely concluded that by the end of his life usury would have destroyed the German lands. Seneca's opinion that vice becomes habit applied particularly to German territories.

III. USURY

Luther's understanding of the meaning of 'usury' was broad. Usury in its wider sense meant for him not only demanding interest as a return for lending money—according to the philosophical and theological tradition 'usury' in the narrower sense—but also every rise in prices and every exploitation of an emergency by retaining or buying up goods. Thus, in his treatise on usury to pastors (1540, WA51.331–424) Luther called all who demanded five per cent or more as interest on borrowed money 'usurers' (WA51.332,32–333,21). They were 'idolatrous servants of greed or Mammon' and would lose their salvation if they did not repent. In this treatise usury also included setting prices for a product to be sold above its real worth. Many passages in this treatise do speak clearly of usury in the narrower sense.

Taking interest was an explosive issue. The canonical prohibition of interest was still in force although economic developments—particularly in foreign trade—had led to a rapid spread and intensification of banking and financial dealings. Theologians obviously had to think about credit transactions—and economic topics in general—in this era, in which an exchange economy was being transformed increasingly into a money economy.

At the beginning of the sixteenth century the efforts of Johann Eck to give this question more attention won high regard. Eck's teacher in Tübingen, Konrad Summenhart, and before him, Gabriel Biel, had tried to redefine the concept of 'usury', as understood in the ecclesiastical tradition, in relationship to credit transactions. Especially Summenhart emphasized the intention of the one lending money, which could not be publicly identified. Outwardly, a partnership between lender and debtor without risk could not be distinguished from the sin of usury although in fact it is thoroughly legitimate as a financial agreement between partners since both participate in funding it. Nonetheless, such agreements should be avoided in order to prevent confusing the conscience of the neighbour who because of lack of knowledge regards such an agreement as usury. In this way Summenhart showed his pastoral intention to unburden the conscience of those participating in transactions of credit without justifying it in the context of public life.

Eck extended his teacher's conception but with the difference that he set aside the argument of the offence to others. In cases of charging interest he believed that good intentions, not culpable intent, should be presumed of those involved. In 1514 he suggested a three-stage agreement, which entailed no usury. First, both parties should conclude an initial understanding establishing the partnership; then a second understanding—five per cent interest—which specified that the amount be invested without excluding risk. Finally, a third agreement establishes the right to a possible, but only potential, gain, above the five per cent.

On 15 July 1515 Eck held a disputation over taking interest in Bologna, defending his thesis, as he reported, with great success. Humanists, especially from the Nuremberg circle, criticized his view. His departure from ancient and patristic positions on this question, but also his close connection to the Fugger family, formed the basis for critique of Eck's pastoral efforts. The Ingolstadt professor did have connections to the Fugger bank through Konrad Peutinger (despite lack of proof, many presumed that Jakob Fugger had brought Eck to his position). His first opportunity to debate the question of interest came in the Carmelite convent in Augsburg, which had connections to the Fuggers. In October 1514 direct confrontation between the humanists and Eck occurred when the chancellor of the university of Ingolstadt, Bishop Gabriel von Eyb of Eichstatt, refused permission for the disputation on the topic which Eck wished to hold in Ingolstadt. The Fuggers financed his journey with a delegation to Bologna in 1515.

Luther knew this debate over transactions of credit. In his polemic against Eck, however, he never mentioned the matter explicitly. Luther condemned the Fuggers' economic dominance and their profits through machinations with ecclesiastical property but never mentioned Eck in this context. Nevertheless, his strong emphasis on the determining role of self-interest in trade and finance suggests that he never would have found Eck's foundational presupposition regarding good intentions of business partners theologically justifiable.

Luther's experience in his and Melanchthon's exchange with the Basel-born former Dominican court preacher in Eisenach, Jakob Strauß, in 1523/4 influenced his view of taking interest. In contrast to Eck, who discussed the question from the standpoint of the lender, Strauß, influenced by the devastating situation of many in Eisenach, like Luther, took the perspective of the debtors. In 1523 he presented his views in fifty-one theses and maintained that the opinion of popes and councils could never trump God's own commands. Deuteronomy 15:2 and Luke 6:35 served as the biblical basis of his view of the proper conduct of Christians in taking interest. Strauß equated 'interest' and 'usury'. Usury offends love of neighbour and God's command by its very nature and is therefore a grave public sin. The thesis that most definitely elicited critique, which Luther later attacked, was thesis 17: 'damned and departed from the faith is he who in his poverty agrees to pay interest to the rich'.

Strauß's views spread quickly and were adopted and immediately put into practice by many. Among those Strauß condemned were representatives of ecclesiastical institutions which owed their existence to regular reception of interest and were affected by the implementation of his ideas. A majority of the Eisenach town council and Duke John appeared to be on his side. Allegedly, the electoral prince, John Frederick, had Chancellor Gregor Brück (both rejected Strauß's opinion) request Luther's opinion. He responded to the theses in October 1523 (WABr3.176–177, 178–179). Although he favoured abolition of usurious transactions, he found Strauß's action hasty. Particularly the idea that paying interest was a sin was for him indefensible. The question was complicated. He made no conclusive suggestion, but he found following Strauß's procedure ill-advised.

In early June 1524 Strauß moderated his position in another treatise. Debtors should not contribute to the injustice of paying interest by submitting to such agreements. This put the Mosaic regulations regarding the Sabbath year and Jubilee year into practice, clearly borrowing from Luther's *Sermon on Usury* of 1520 (WA6.36–60). Strauß rejected John Frederick's suggestion to discuss the question with Luther and Melanchthon in Wittenberg. He preferred a public discussion. In the context of a memorandum on Strauß's statements, John Frederick asked whether a prince might permit credit transactions; Luther advocated new regulations in this case. Since this matter concerned a widespread practice, debtors should meet their obligations to pay; governmental authorities could not justify refusing to pay. Interest rates should never be higher than five per cent. Even after his moderation of his ideas on interest in his second treatise, Strauß appeared to Luther to be guilty of arousing the population to revolt. Without doubt this controversy decisively influenced Luther's treatise *On Trade and Usury* (1524, WA15.293–313; LW45.245–310).

Luther himself condemned, with few exceptions, all forms of credit transactions. His treatise on usury of 1540 characterized them as 'wanton, greed-driven, unnecessary usury' because they always were associated with sin and never contributed to the community's welfare. The same treatise criticized the excuse of many that five, six, or ten per cent interest, which the lender would receive from one hundred Gulden, was merely a gift from the debtor, a sign of gratitude. Luther regarded this as an attempt of the 'greedy belly' to disguise profit and usury as a gift. It was the sacrifice of 'the needy in their neediness' that produced profit and usury.

Luther criticized above all other kinds of credit transactions the *Zinskauf*, a form designed to avoid the canonical prohibition of interest. This loan was disguised as a sale. In exchange for money from his possession of property the lender received a part of the produce which the lender gained from his work on the property—the so-called *Zins*. In the form of a 'sale of interest for repurchase' the debtor took on the obligation of paying a certain amount beyond the money lent, which the lender 'bought'. In a series of sermons on the Decalogue published in 1518 Luther commented on papal intentions to permit this transaction (*contractus redemptionis*). It intended (1) to create the possibility of survival for the elderly, children, and the sick; (2) to offer servants of the Word—clergy, prelates, and priests; and (3) servants of the community—princes, counsellors, civic leaders—a form of income so they could spend the necessary time in fulfilling official duties. Actually, Luther maintained, they simply served selfish interests. Most wanted to increase their profits through interest and attain material security without work or risk (WA1.505,15–31).

He instructed the elders supervising the common chest in Leisnig to examine precisely whether property and funds assembled by the former ecclesiastical institutions dedicated to the community's welfare had their roots in the 'sale of interest for repurchase' (1523). If so, that was sufficient grounds in itself to reject the practice. His theological convictions led Luther to reject the possibility of lending money for interest as an economic activity for believers. For him this was simply a way for disadvantaged people—e.g., widows or the sick—to gain support without working. Any other lending of money for interest was a matter of greed (WA12.11,7–15,31, 17,30–20,4; LW45.169–176, 178–182).

The massive spread of the practice of the *Zinskauf* demonstrated to Luther how greatly people had disregarded the evangelical teaching regarding their possessions. If Christ's commands to 'let go' of property, to give and lend (Matt. 5:40–2), were followed more closely, the practice would not be so widespread. Luther observed that interest was being demanded for tiny sums, which exceeded the amount lent. Alongside criticism of the *Zinskauf* as a disguise of usury, the Wittenberg reformer also treated the security lenders sought through this practice. Luther thought that it closely resembled usury and was in opposition to God, love, and natural law since the lender sought to take advantage of others in the midst of difficulties. That demonstrated the injustice of the lender's concentrating only on securing his own payments and property rather than on the neighbour's welfare.

Luther also protested against other forms of dealing with financial indebtedness. In a letter to Gregor Brück, 2 January 1540 (WABr9.3), he demanded consistent governmental measures against the practice of *Einreiten*, a practice in which the debtor who did not satisfy obligations to a lender had to receive and host the lender's guests. Normally, this brought total ruin upon the debtor, who could neither pay his initial debt nor afford expenditures for such provision. Luther thought that the princes were obligated to stop the practice or they would be participating in injustice and bore responsibility for the harm it did. Luther expressed regret that people were devouring and ruining each other.

Monks in the Augustinian monastery in Wittenberg were partially supported by receiving interest for money it had lent, a common practice among monasteries. With the introduction of the Reformation these debtors felt justified in not meeting their obligations. In May 1522 the monastery's debtors were no longer paying interest. To buy malt for brewing beer the prior Eberhard Brisger incurred debts, for which Luther was guarantor. The monastery had to pay twenty Gulden annually to Christoph Blanck, a canon of the All Saints foundation in Wittenberg but had no money to do so because its own income from interest was not being collected. In November 1523 Luther asked the elector to issue a command to Christoph of Bressen, who owed the monastery ninety Gulden in interest, to pay (WABr3.196–197). Luther said that he was the last monk in the monastery; Brisger was about to marry. Since the monastery later would belong to the elector, Luther requested that this income pay his salary. Luther's demand was in accord with his recommendation for the care of monks from monasteries that were being abandoned in his 'Preface to the Common Chest' (WA12.13,8–14; LW45.172).

Later Luther commented on his personal relationship to the financial structures. In a letter of 1 February 1527 (WABr4.164–5) he answered Brisger, who asked for a loan of eight Gulden. Luther described his financial position in detail. He was much in debt because of his costly household and was surprised at the amount of Brisger's debts. It was only right that Brisger regretted his wrong step in going into debt and accepted it as a test from God since then God would not abandon him in such a situation. Because of his own carelessness, Luther admitted, he himself was indebted to several people for almost one hundred Gulden. But this was his punishment, from which he hoped the Lord would free him. Lukas Cranach and Christian Döring had even forbidden him to assume the function of a guarantor for the common chest. In order to lend Brisger the sum he wanted, Luther could pawn some objects of value, as he had already done with three goblets for fifty Gulden and another for twelve. That was nothing more than giving alms from another's property. He was ready to speak with others who might be able to help Brisger. From Luther's standpoint his decision could not be condemned as miserliness (*parcitas*) because he was himself generous with money borrowed from others.

IV. COMMERCE

Often Luther commented on commerce in the context of interpreting the seventh commandment. In 1518 he called deception in commerce the fourth transgression of this commandment. In *On Good Works* (1520) he strengthened his position on economic wrongdoing as a sin against this commandment and listed individual machinations, such as greed, usury, over-pricing, taking advantage of others, and using adulterated wares, deceptive measurements, and deceptive weights (WA6.261,31–262,13, 270,25–272,4; LW44.95–96, 106–108).

In *On Trade and Usury* (1524, WA15.293–313; LW45.245–310) Luther described in great detail each of these offences against God's will and the law of love. Theodor Strohm (1985) summarized them: (1) everyone sells at the best possible price and pays no attention to determining price by the amount of work and risk that have been invested; (2) personal guarantees are created which have to produce serfdom and speculatively intervene in God's right to exercise his providential lordship; (3) lending money, goods, or tools with a demand for more or better in return, is usury and is 'condemned by all standards of justice'. All who take five, six, or more per cent for money lent are usurers.

From these three sources arise many other evils, for example: (1) selling goods at interest rather than for cash to attain greater profits; (2) holding back goods (drying up the market) to drive up profits, earning profit from the neighbour's hardship; (3) buying up goods to be able to dictate prices (monopolies); (4) dumping in order to dominate the market; (5) selling goods one does not have on promise of future delivery at prices above what they will cost; (6) using accumulated capital to buy up goods at a price under market value from someone pressed by creditors who has insufficient capital; (7) determining prices by a cartel; (8) paying less than normal prices to those in tight situations for goods sold at market value; (9) risk-free investment at guaranteed interest rates; and (10) manipulation of goods for sale ('putting the most attractive product on top') (WA15.305,1–311,7; LW45.261–269).

Luther wrote in his *Annotations on Deuteronomy* (25:13) on the topic of altering agreements in business dealings (WA14.719,11–16; LW9.249). The seller should deliver good wares appropriate to the price paid by the buyer. Luther emphasized this because unbelievable carelessness and deception take place through the adulteration, alteration, and mingling of various qualities of goods. He compared the oppressors of the poor with the merchants of his time. The prophet criticized hatred for religious festivals—because no commerce should be conducted on those days—retention of grain, shaving the amount of products, raising prices, altering scales, and selling chaff as grain (Amos 8:4–6, WA13.197,36–198,16; LW18.181). Luther regarded raising prices by means of planned scarcity of foodstuffs as grounds to call those who caused such situations robbers and murderers.

Luther thought that the chief rule for merchants was selling goods at the highest price possible. The principle of service to the neighbour was ignored, and prices were established to burden or even damage other people. Neither the labour invested by merchants nor the quality of the goods nor the risk of sale and transport played a role in setting prices. They were deterred only by selfish exploitation of others in their need. Luther thought a Christian's practice of commerce should be oriented to the need of others. The distinction between this and the general practices of merchants at his time was that the latter wanted to enrich themselves by profiting from others' dependence on material goods. They did not pursue the goal of helping the needy get out of their situation through their commerce.

Luther was convinced that money signified something other than a means of payment and exchange for many merchants. Especially Jesus' Sermon on the Mount (Matt. 6:20–1) and daily experience revealed to what extent people sought to use money not as a means to gain what is necessary for human needs; they sought money as an object that had value in and of itself. Continual, increasing accumulation had become necessary for survival. Behind this practice was the idea that merchants had created their own possessions. Therefore, they justified raising prices and manipulating the market for their advantage.

Luther conceded that the calculation of just prices was not easy because of the nature of commerce. Especially for merchants that meant that in their calling they experienced continuous struggle with their own consciences, as he indicated in a letter to Spalatin on 12 February 1544 (WABr10.532). Spalatin had asked Luther about Christian merchants' setting of the price of grain. Luther did not solve the problem with an exact answer because differences in the kind of grain, time, persons, places, situations, and individual cases all played a role. The individual's conscience should answer the question in accord with natural law (Matt. 7:12). Individuals with good consciences also consider Bible texts, Proverbs 11:26 and Amos 5. Since Spalatin wanted to know how righteous people (de bonis) should set prices, neither passage really addressed the question. Finally, regarding such uncertain matters, not regulated by law, each person should find his own proper answer.

Most merchants ignored the gospel's requirements—especially love for the neighbour—in their business dealings, according to Luther, so that he had no great hopes of essentially improving unjust relationships in economic and social structures. Nevertheless, that was no ground for abandoning the prophetic task of reproving greed. Luther felt obligated to uncover various forms of commercial deception, especially when merchants claimed Christian, biblical motives to cover their criminal machinations. He mentioned contributions to the church from unjust profits and the excuses connected to them. Merchants could not justify their 'commercial greed' (kauffgeytz) with the model of Joseph (Gen. 41:36, WA15.305,31–307,10; LW45.262–264). Joseph sought human survival and Egypt's continuing existence by accumulating foodstuffs. Contemporary merchants, on the other hand, were seeking their own advantage without noting whether that contributed to the ruination of the population.

Commercial companies were to be condemned as 'simply legal monopolies'. For Luther, rise in prices could have natural causes, but sometimes individuals or groups intentionally raised prices to attain more profits. He focused most intensively on the latter kind. In a letter of 9 April 1539 to Elector John Frederick he mentioned rising prices that year and the past year; this had happened not because of lack of goods but because of the influences of rich nobles (*Junker*). Luther accused them of buying up all the grain to be able to speculate in grain. A natural cause of rising prices was the extreme growth of the population, which produces hard times and finally starvation. Hard times produce 'rogues' (*Buben*) who 'become greedy'. He preferred, he said, plague to hard times since with fewer people providing food would be easier. Theologically, hard times played a large role in God's punishment of the population, for Luther. If a community was unwilling to give for schools and churches because greed and worry about food dominated their thinking, they deserved catastrophes such as hard times (WABr8.404–405).

V. Current Relevance of Luther's Thinking

The discussion of whether Luther's economic thought marks him as a medieval or a modern thinker in regard to current economic questions often takes precedence in both economic and social histories and theological research. This question, probably shaped by ideas of progress, which dominated scholarship for a long time, must be placed in context. Luther discussed the problems of his time as an interpreter of Scripture in order to criticize and combat injustice. He wanted to attain concrete 'improvement' and never asked whether his actions and positions would limit certain developments or whether the basis of his actions was backward. His realistic and neither sceptical nor negative conviction that the world was otherwise running itself cannot necessarily be called 'medieval'. Particularly today Luther's convictions have great relevance: increasingly humanity feels challenged to surrender its goal of creating a 'modern' world, identified as 'prosperous', for posterity and instead to try to leave posterity anything at all.

References

Prien, Hans-Jürgen (1992). *Luthers Wirtschaftsethik*. Göttingen: Vandenhoeck & Ruprecht.

Roscher, Wilhelm (1874). *Geschichte der National-Oekonomik in Deutschland*. 2 vols. Munich: Oldenbourg.

Scharffenorth, Gerta (1982). *Den Glauben ins Leben ziehen.... Studien zu Luthers Theologie*. Munich: Kaiser.

Strohm, Theodor (1985). 'Luthers Wirtschafts- und Sozialethik'. In *Leben und Werk Martin Luthers von 1526 bis 1546*, 2nd edn., ed. Helmar Junghans. Berlin: Evangelische Verlagsanstalt, 205–23.

Suggested Reading

Barge, Hermann (1951). *Luther und der Frühkapitalismus*. Gütersloh: Mohn.

Junghans, Helmar (2001). *Spätmittelalter, Luthers Reformation, Kirche in Sachsen. Ausgewählte Aufsätze*, ed. Michael Beyer and Günther Wartenberg. Leipzig: Evangelische Verlagsanstalt.

Hendrix, Scott H. (2004). *Recultivating the Vineyard: The Reformation Agendas of Christianization*. Louisville: Westminster/John Knox.

Lindberg, Carter (1993). *Beyond Charity: Reformation Initiatives for the Poor*. Minneapolis: Fortress.

Lehmann, Hermann (1986). 'Luthers Platz in der Geschichte der politischen Ökonomie'. In *Martin Luther. Leben, Werk, Wirkung*, ed. Günther Vogler. Berlin: Akademie-Verlag, 279–94.

Oberman, Heiko Augustinus (1977). *Werden und Wertung der Reformation. Vom Wegestreit zum Glaubenskampf*. Tübingen: Mohr/Siebeck.

Pawlas, Andreas (2000). *Die lutherische Berufs- und Wirtschaftsethik. Eine Einführung*. Neukirchen-Vluyn: Neukirchener Verlag.

Rieth, Ricardo (1996). *'Habsucht' bei Martin Luther. Ökonomisches und theologisches Denken, Tradition und soziale Wirklichkeit im Zeitalter der Reformation*. Weimar: Böhlau.

Wengert, Timothy J. (ed.) (2004). *Harvesting Martin Luther's Reflections on Theology, Ethics and the Church*. Grand Rapids, MI: Eerdmans.

CHAPTER 28

LUTHER'S TREATMENT OF POLITICAL AND SOCIETAL LIFE

EIKE WOLGAST

I. LUTHER'S SELF-UNDERSTANDING

LUTHER was a theologian and considered himself only a theologian, legitimized by his office as professor and as doctor of Holy Scripture. His perception of politics and society had its foundation in the Bible, and his advice on political and social questions was consistently oriented toward the principle of *sola scriptura* (Wolgast 1977; Kunst 1979; Estes 2005; Beutel 2005; Kohnle 2005a; Stümke 2007). He claimed to be a *Seelsorger* and thereby claimed spiritual guardianship when asked about current critical or fundamental problems as an adviser or took a public position on his own: 'It is not fitting for me to say more than to show all what their responsibility is and to inform their consciences' (1529, WA30,2.129,24–25). Luther understood his guardianship comprehensively: 'my teaching office extends so far that it addresses princes just as much as peasants' (1525, WA18.393,22–23).

Luther's judgements concerning politics and society and his recommendations always arose within an eschatological context. He interpreted the conflicts of his time as the incursion of apocalyptic powers into God's creation. The pope, evangelical opponents (e.g. *Schwärmer* [enthusiasts] and 'Sacramentarians'), and the Turks were manifestations of this end-time threat, which human action can only counteract in limited and temporary fashion: 'Things are not in our hands, but in God's' (1532, WA20.47,15). As he saw his reforming work threatened ever more strongly in the last years of his life, Luther hoped for God's immediate and final intervention into a situation which was becoming indefensible from a human perspective: 'Come, beloved last day' (1540, WABr9.175,17). Certainly, Luther's expectation of the end as imminent did not amount to resigned passivity, to mere waiting and taking it as it comes; rather, he required a person to be most active as a *cooperator Dei*.

II. Two Kingdoms/Governments [*Reiche/Regimente*] as a Political Organizing Principle

In order to describe the conditions under which Christians live in the world, Luther utilized two traditional schemes: the concept of the two kingdoms or governments of God and the concept of the three estates. Luther dislodged both schemes from their places in Late Antiquity and the Middle Ages and used them flexibly. The term 'doctrine' is too rigid and is only used in the following for the sake of brevity.

The two kingdoms doctrine underwent a two-fold development with Luther. First, it became dualistic in the eschatological dimension of antagonistic conflict between God's kingdom (*regnum Dei*) and the Devil's kingdom (*regnum diaboli*). Second, it became binary in juxtaposing two equally significant types of God's governance (from the vast literature on 'two kingdoms' in Luther, see especially Törnvall 1947; Lau 1952; Bornkamm 1960; Schrey 1969; Heckel 1973; Duchrow 1983; Gänssler 1983; Anselm 2004; Mantey 2005; Stümke 2007).

The concrete plane on which Christian life in this world takes place is the juxtaposition of two realms. God reigns directly through the preaching of the gospel in the spiritual realm (*regnum spirituale*) and indirectly through governmental action in the secular realm (*regnum mundanum* or *corporale*). Luther explained his concept of the two kingdoms/governments or realms in many writings; most importantly *Temporal Authority: To What Extent It Should Be Obeyed* (1523, WA11.245–281; LW45.81–129) and *Whether Soldiers, Too, Can Be Saved* (1526, WA19.623–662; LW46.93–137). God has 'erected two different governments among people: one spiritual, governed by his Word, without the sword, through which people become pious [good] and just so that they obtain eternal life with its righteousness.... The other is the secular government ruled by the sword, so that whoever will not become pious and just through the Word to eternal life, nevertheless will be compelled through the secular government to be pious and just before the world' (WA19.629,17–24; LW46.99). In the first realm the reward is eternal life; in the other, the rewards are secular goods: peace, order, and justice.

Both governments extend over true Christians, hypocrites, and non-Christians. Luther was realistic in his presumptions: 'Most are and remain unchristian even if they are all, at the same time, baptized people who are called Christians' (1523, WA11.251,36–37). To the kingdom of God and the spiritual realm belong 'all true believers who are in Christ and under Christ' (WA11.249,26–27). For them the sword and the secular kingdom are unnecessary; if there were only true Christians, governing authorities and force would not be required. These Christians, however, are also part of the world. In the conceptualization of the dialectical 'simul' (Nilsson 1966; Wolgast 1977: 33–40), which Luther liked to use, the apparently insoluble differences were overcome 'at the same time'. Christians are not only justified but at the same time also sinners (simul iustus et peccator), and in these two identities they stand under the dominion of the secular government. In fact, when receiving an office as ruler, one becomes a citizen of both worlds, a Christian person and a secular person, a 'duplex persona, fidelis et politicus' (Törnvall 1947: 166–84).

Luther often placed the functions and attributes of God's two kingdoms in opposition, whereby the fundamental equality of both realms was effectively abolished by the higher significance of the spiritual realm: faith versus external order, introduction to eternal life through preaching versus enforcement of an ordered and peaceful life in the world through the ruling authorities, obedience toward God's Word versus obedience toward the governmental mandate of the sword, the equality of Christians versus the inequality of subjects. The representative of the spiritual realm is the preacher; the representative of the secular realm is the prince. Luther understood the state's power (secular authority, magistratus) personally, not institutionally, on the basis of his realm of experience and understanding of the imperial constitution. For him, the ruling authority was the emperor (magistratus superior); beneath him were the princes and municipal councils of 'free cities' (magistratus inferior); then with a lower political rank were all with authority over others. Governing authority was legitimated biblically by appeal to the loci classici: Romans 13:1 and 1 Peter 2:13. This was an infralapsarian arrangement of necessity; its existence was required by the Fall in order to maintain the external order of the world against the consequences of sin.

For Luther the secular government's jurisdiction extended over all areas that did not directly touch the individual's faith and conscience; consequently, it extended over all political and societal circumstances. Governmental authority is responsible for the common good (bonum commune), for preserving or restoring peace and justice: 'Temporal peace is the greatest good on earth; in this, all other temporal goods are also included' (1530, WA30,2.538,18–20). War was only permitted when conducted as a defensive war, which applied, for example, to the Turkish war (Ehmann 2008).

In addition to preserving peace and justice, care for the physical well-being of their subjects also belonged to the domestic task of the government (in sixteenth-century terminology 'policey'). With the stabilization of the reforming movement through the organized implementation of the Reformation in a territory or imperial city and through the associated emergence of the evangelical territorial church with large numbers of—at least nominal ('those weak in faith')—supporters of the new confession, the secular authorities assumed an additional responsibility beyond their previous tasks in the view of the Wittenberg reformers: care for religion (cura religionis). Indeed, the spiritual government, including preachers, remained responsible for the faith, but the evangelical authorities now undertook, besides the traditional protection of the second table of the Decalogue, protection of the first table too (custodia utriusque tabulae). In doing so, the office of the sword did not obtain authorization to suppress religious differences and thus to regulate the consciences of its subjects. In such cases, the authorities would have interfered with the spiritual realm, making themselves guilty of confusing who has rightful authority (*confusio regnorum*), which Luther often criticized. In the context of preserving peace and caring for the common good, however, the ruling authorities definitely had the obligation to establish ecclesiastical and religious external conformity: 'Our princes do not compel faith and the gospel, but they restrict external abominations' (1525, WABr3.616,28–29, 432,12–433,18). Every visible manifestation of differing conceptions of religion was understood as blasphemy that threatened the common good. In such situations rulers could claim to be within their jurisdiction. They did not punish aberrant beliefs, but they did, however, punish external manifestations of deviance. Certainly, this theoretically clear, and for Luther distinctly clear, division of tasks between both realms belied sixteenth-century reality because, with the virtual identification of the civic community and the ecclesial community, most failures to participate in religious rites and ceremonies were already regarded as a disturbance of the public order, a breach of civic norms. The religious conformity demanded and compelled by the governing authorities for those who were part of the civic community certainly violated the consciences of religious dissenters. They only had the choice to refuse conformity, which in Luther's view the authorities could legitimately suppress, or practising a clandestine faith while feigning conformity, even if this was incompatible with their consciences.

Luther regarded the divine legitimacy of the secular authorities derived from his concept of the two kingdoms and governments as one of his major achievements: 'After having written so superbly and usefully on secular authority, as no other teacher has done since the apostolic period (it was then Saint Augustine), I am permitted to boast with good conscience and with the testimony of the world' (1529, WA30,2.110,1–4). Luther's doctrine of ruling authority granted the secular power independence from the spiritual power and granted it equal divine legitimacy. However, both realms were bound equally to God's directives; the secular power was also God's servant.

Despite the equal status of both realms as institutions of God, the *regnum corporale* occupied for Luther a distinctly lesser position than the *regnum spirituale* since its agents were devoted to secular matters. The sword as an instrument of God's indirect action possesses a lesser dignity than the Word, just as faith possesses a greater dignity than reason. The office of secular authority is 'the highest worship to God and the most necessary office on earth', but it is much less than the preaching office (1530, WA31,1.198,24–25).

Governmental duties can be exercised by non-Christians as well as Christians. Faith is not constitutive for their proper administration, but faith facilitates—through knowledge of God's institution of both realms and the definition of their duties—the exercise of governmental functions. The Christian acts in political office as a *persona duplex*. As *persona privata/fidelis* he is obligated to non-violence and must suffer injustice if it is inflicted upon him. As *persona publica/politica* he must, out of love for neighbour, help another who is unable to help himself and demands help; the Christian must act to fend off any injustice threatening or suffered by that person. The structures of the *simul* and the dual personality as a Christian person and a secular person demand that the Christian official give exact consideration and thoroughly examine his conscience with every challenge to action. If injustice is directed against him as an individual, he is challenged as a Christian person; if injustice is directed against him as an office-holder with a responsibility for others, he is obligated as a secular person to use force when other means do not provide a remedy to the problem. Since the conscience has to make the final decision, guided by the norm of love for the neighbour, the Christian is—according to Luther—better suited than the non-Christian to exercise governmental functions. Nevertheless, Luther knew that his vision of Christian office-holders seldom corresponded to reality. His criticism was relentless: since the beginning of the world, it is 'indeed a rare bird who is a prudent prince and still rarer a pious prince. They are generally the greatest fools or the worst rogues on earth' (1523, WA11.267,30–32).

As hearers of God's Word are subordinated to preachers in the spiritual realm, so subjects are subordinated to the governing authority in the secular realm. The subjects' obligation to obedience was strong since Luther equated obedience to the ruling authority with obedience to God. This conviction evoked Luther's own actions when at the end of 1520 he was asked whether he would follow an imperial summons to Worms; he explained, 'I do not doubt that if the emperor calls me, I am called by God' (1520, WABr2.242,10–11). Christians render obedience for the sake of non-Christians, thus manifesting love for the neighbour. Non-Christians are compelled to obey; Christians do so willingly.

Nevertheless, for Luther obedience to the government is not unconditional or unlimited. The limit to obedience is reached when the authorities encroach upon the spiritual regiment and want to coerce the consciences of their subjects. Mandates which 'force [subjects] against God's commands or inhibit them from following these commands' (1520, WA6.265,16–17) may not be obeyed since the soul belongs to God and not to any secular authority. In conflicts between obedience to God's commands and obedience to governmental laws, Matthew 22:21 and, above all, Acts 5:29 (*clausula Petri*) apply. Whether such a conflict exists must be decided in each case, carefully considering all circumstances, and it cannot result in a general termination of obedience. Above all, however, disobedience that appeals to the *clausula Petri* may not express itself in violence. The refusing subject must, instead, confront the injustice of the ruling authorities in verbal protest with the confession of the truth—in the hope of better insight on the ruler's part. If this insight fails to materialize, the consequences of the verbal protest are to be accepted: 'Suffering injustice corrupts no one in his soul; it improves the soul, even if it diminishes the body and possessions' (1520, WA6.259,16–17). The decision to utilize the *clausula Petri* can be made only by the individual conscience and never collectively. For Luther, therefore, there is only an individual disobedience.

III. The Three Estates [*Stände*] as Organizing Principle of Society

Alongside his concept of the two kingdoms/governments, Luther placed the three estates [*Stände*] (*status, ordines*, later also hierarchies, *regimina*), first in 1519, then continually after 1528 (cf. Elert 1932: 49–65; Maurer 1970; Schwarz 1978; Bayer 1984; Schwarz 1984; Brady 1985; Schorn-Schütte 1996: 416–33; Schorn-Schütte 1998; Stümke 2007: 126–53). Together with the concept of the two kingdoms, the three estates were intended to set the societal order in place, to determine and assign individuals to their place in this order. Luther adopted the medieval notion of the three estates with each distinct description of a function: to pray (clergy), to protect (nobility), to labour (peasant and craftsman). Corresponding to these functions, the social world consists of the ecclesiastical estate (*ecclesia*), the political estate (*politia*), and the economic estate (*oeconomia*) (WA6.428,7–9). Here the first estate occupied an elite position, distinguished fundamentally from both lay estates by its task of mediating salvation, especially through vicarious prayer.

Luther broke away from the traditional scheme of *ecclesia, politia*, and *oeconomia* by assigning their activities different values. He fashioned new assignments ('spheres of life', *genera vitae* (Schwarz 1984: 79)) in addition to new values. With the teaching of the common priesthood of the baptized, he destroyed the previously privileged position of the church; in particular, he denied that monasticism was a fundamental order of its own. Furthermore, he defined the *oeconomia* anew as household [*Hausstand*] and marriage [*Ehestand*]. Although previous hierarchies had defined the estate of labourer primarily in terms of Genesis 3:19, as a curse, Luther explained it as the most important estate on earth. Like marriage, it gained dignity as the grower, provider, and sustainer of all estates, and it stood under the protective shield of the fourth commandment. In addition, clergy and nobles belonged to the *oeconomia* as husbands and fathers while nobles and manual labourers—through the common priesthood—were both part of the *ecclesia* as believers. Likewise, the *politia* in Luther's definition expanded to include all subjects under authority. Logically, every person belonged thus to every estate.

All three estates are effective in the world as 'three visible governments' (1539, WA47.853,36); they are 'modes of social relationships' (Brady 1985: 203), which in principle have the same value. Belonging to a particular estate 'as such confers no ethical quality at all' (Elert 1932: 51). Therefore, for Luther each profession was valued equally before God. Different activities, if conducted in love for one's neighbour, attain the same honour before God and before the world. Despite this fundamental equality of work among the estates, Luther nevertheless made definite gradations since he was not at all consistent in distinguishing *ecclesia* as one of the three estates from the *regnum spirituale* of the two-kingdom doctrine. The *ordo ecclesiasticus* differed from both other estates in its different missions in such a way as it acted like the other orders in this world; however, it was not oriented toward a this-worldly goal but toward an other-worldly goal. 'The highest thing in the world is to preach and to absolve' (1539, WA47.854,5). 'Therefore, we distinguish types of labour according to the proper proportion: the labour of the household is good; political activity better; ecclesiastical the best' (1535/45, WA42.159,17–18).

In the Smalcald Articles Luther said, 'In this [article] there is enough doctrine for the life of the church. But, in politics and economics the law is sufficient for us to support ourselves' (1538, WA50.192,6–10, correctly read in Luther 1992: 351). In the same way Luther structured his last writing of February 1546 according to the three estates as spheres of life. Five years as a shepherd or peasant are necessary in order to understand Virgil's *Bucolics* or *Georgics* (*oeconomia*). One had to live twenty years as a citizen in an ordered political community to comprehend Cicero in his letters (*politia*). One had to have governed communities with the prophets for one hundred years, however, in order to merely approach apprehending the Holy Scripture (WA48.241).

As in the two kingdoms doctrine, Luther pointed out the discrepancy between theory and praxis in the three estates doctrine. In each estate abuse is practised by people not acting according to the law of love but according to self-interest. Within all of the estates, however, there is 'a good group [of people]...the chosen children of God and all saints on earth, who are authentic Christians' (1530, WA31,1.87,26–28). For their sake God preserves the three estates and thereby the world; abuse does not cast doubt upon the three-estate system as such.

The fact that the estates are divinely instituted also is clear to Luther from the warfare the forces hostile to God lead against them. The Devil places himself within the two realms to oppose God's rule; within the three estates, he mobilizes heretics, fanatics, hypocrites, false prophets, and false teachers against the church. Insurgents, rebels, corrupt advisers, and sycophants work against the political government; disobedient children, unfaithful servants, and corrupt heads of households sabotage the *oeconomia*. Luther's understanding of society was static. All should remain in the estates to which God assigned them. Luther lamented the common dissatisfaction with one's respective social and material situation and the striving toward a better position. At the same time, however, he usually approved when it happened 'that a person climbed through all estates to the top' (1533, WA37.170,34–35).

Compared to the reality of his time, Luther's social model appeared archaic. He devalued businessmen and merchants compared to peasants, and he made his assessments with reference to the order of creation: 'I know this well that much would be godlier if agrarian work increased and mercantile work decreased' (1520, WA6.466,40–41). The conduct of townspeople could not be legitimated biblically. Love of neighbour was not the impetus for the work of businessmen and merchants; greed was. In contrast, agriculture had biblical sanction; farming was a godly work. Nevertheless, the term farmer [*Bauer*] also had an almost negative connotation with Luther on a consistent basis; '*rusticus*' [farmer/peasant] for him was not only synonymous with rudeness, illiteracy, and unwillingness to learn, but also with arrogance, greed, and usury. Above all, he reproached the peasants for leading unchurchly lives, for thinking very little of their pastors and depriving them of their income (Rieth 1996: 195–8; Kohnle 2005b).

IV. Luther's Conduct in Concrete Crises

Unbeknownst to the wider public, Luther took sides during a local crisis for the ruling party for the first time in 1520. During student riots in Wittenberg he delivered a sermon 'commending the power committed to the magistrates by God's institution, lest all things be ravaged by rebellions' (WABr2.144,9; Bubenheimer 1985; Kruse 2002: 279–385). Already in this relatively minor occurrence he followed his inclination to interpret events apocalyptically. In the turmoil with the students, which had nothing to do with ecclesiastical concerns, he saw the Devil's work trying to discredit the preaching of the gospel, and he set the events in Wittenberg parallel to his battles in the previous years. In light of the 'Wittenberg Unrest' of 1521/2, which touched far greater portions of the population and in terms of content was more significant than the student uprising, Luther wrote at the end of 1521 *A Faithful Admonition To All Christians To Be On Guard Against Unrest and Revolt*; a little more than a year later he followed with *On Secular Authority*. Both treatises were designed to invite people to obedience but were also intended to demonstrate the boundaries of obedience and to warn against violence.

In the beginning of 1523, the Saxon elector Friedrich asked the Wittenberg theologians to produce a memorandum on the right to armed resistance when one is attacked due to faith. Luther's report gave a negative answer to the implicit question; he emphasized that faith is always an individual decision and accordingly the question can be answered only by the individual person. If Christians are persecuted due to their faith, they are not permitted to fight back and may utilize no protection by their political authority. The prince too, in his capacity as a Christian, had to be willing to accept religious persecution without resisting with force (WABr12.35–45; Wolgast 1977: 101–8). Luther did not apply the separation of the two persons to the case of the right to resist in 1523.

The greatest challenge to Luther's ideas about society, which tested the consistency of his teaching on authority, was the Peasants' War of 1525 (Greschat 1965; Kolb 1978; Maron 1980; Brecht 1986: 172–93). The peasants in southwest Germany cited Luther as an authority, and he assumed this role in a certain way: he understood his writings as an instruction for Christians in both parties: how they should conduct themselves in accordance with the Bible. He definitely sympathized with the substance of the social protest as it had found expression in the *Twelve Articles of the Peasantry*. He confronted the lords in his *Admonition to Peace on the Twelve Articles of the Peasantry in Swabia*, stating that among the Twelve Articles were 'several so proper and fair that they dishonour you all before God and the world...For secular authority has not been instituted to exploit subjects and display malice toward them, but to provide benefits and the very best for them' (1525, WA18.298,21–22, 299,4–6). Luther still, however, withdrew transcendent protection from the peasants: it was inacceptable that they justified their claims with divine right and invoked the Bible. In this approach Luther saw *confusio regnorum*, and it always terrified him, when the *regnum spirituale* was used for secular purposes. The freedom of Christians in faith may not be identified with political or social freedom. Appeal to divine right in order to legitimate material demands and political rights violated the second commandment; in fact, the designation of the peasant coalition as 'the Christian assembly' already misused God's name. Furthermore, he warned them against assuming the role of judge in their own affairs. Matthew 26:52 opposed the use of force: 'But what do you [the peasants] think Christ will say to this, that you display his name…when you are actually so far from it, indeed you dreadfully transgress his law?' (1525, WA18.307,31–34). Luther demanded that Christians should be willing to suffer, not be inclined to fight. For him the Christian's right consists not in receiving justice at all costs, and certainly not as retribution, but in suffering. Even if the Twelve Articles agreed with natural law, Christian law required patience and prayer as a remedy, not particular action aimed at the violent destruction of the command–obedience relationship sanctioned by God.

The direct experience with the rebellious peasants in Thüringen together with the activity of Thomas Müntzer and his indignation over the peasants apparently not accepting his *Admonition to Peace* drove Luther to add an appendix to a reprinting of his treatise, which then was also printed separately: *Against the Robbing and Murderous Hordes of Peasants*. In his introduction to the Treaty of Weingarten Luther had recently stated that the peasants had 'no lawful concern at all' since they were defying political authority. This attack on God's order and the peasants' violation against the right to property nevertheless were surpassed from Luther's point of view when they 'created such raging uproar and dreadful immorality under the Christian name and the pretence of the gospel' (WA18.342,28, 343,2–4). In *Against the Hordes* Luther addressed only Christian authorities to inform them of their obligation in the eschatological crisis: 'Any minute the destruction of the world is to be expected' (WA18.361,34–35, 397,8–10). He denied that the insurgents were Christians and only saw them as instruments of the Devil. In this situation any authority that took its duty to God seriously had to react with extreme severity. The Christian prince is God's deputy [*Amtmann*] according to Romans 13:4. 'Where he can punish and does not do so, whether it is murder or bloodshed, he is thus guilty of all murder and evil that the knaves perpetrated.…In addition, forbearance and mercy do not apply here. This is the time of wrath and the sword and not the time of grace' (WA18.360,5–7, 10–11). Luther did not accept the argument that there were many among the rebels who were coerced into involvement by the actions of others. For him, the joint liability of the insurgents was all that counted; in any case, the lords were not obligated to differentiate.

Luther's demonization of the rebellious peasants reveals the problematic consequences of his biblical-theological construct of the relationship between the ruling authority and the subject. Even contemporaries sympathetic to the Reformation were critical of Luther, especially since the element of mercy was missing when Luther applied his doctrine of the governing authorities.

The consequences of the Peasants' War were historically important for Luther's understanding of the world and the society. Theoretically, he adhered to his previous premises and postulates. In practice, however, he changed his point of view. In 1523 he had postulated that a community of responsible Christians may 'judge all doctrine and call, appoint, and dismiss all teachers' (1523, WA11.408–416). In 1525 he evaluated the first of the Twelve Articles, which proclaimed the free choosing and dismissal of pastors by the community, positively—if no claim to divine right was made. If the governing authority did not wish to fulfil the completely legitimate request of the community, the peasants were not permitted to insist on their alleged right, but they should pay clerics themselves and, if necessary, leave the area during persecution (WA18.325,1–15). The experience of the Peasants' War cemented Luther's distrust of the 'common man'—*Herr Omnes*—and caused a certain break with the ideas of communalism and self-determination (Wolgast 2006). After 1526 he appealed more firmly than before to secular governing authorities: they should promote and defend preaching of the gospel in the interest of domestic peace instead of passively tolerating it and hence relinquishing the decision-making to the community, as they had done before. However, more than just the growing mistrust in the 'common man's' power of judgement prompted the modification of his position. After the change of government in Saxony in 1525, Luther for the first time experienced an openly evangelical government with the elector Johann.

In the decade 1529–39 Luther had to examine the coherence of his previous political theology in the context of positive law and the imperial constitution. For the first time since the Peasants' War, in 1529 he grappled with the relationship of command and obedience between secular authorities and subjects, now concretely between emperor and prince. Luther addressed the question of a pre-emptive war already in 1528 in the context of the so-called Pack Affairs, rejecting pre-emptive war because such a war, based on autonomous human judgement, would anticipate God's activity. In this concrete situation he requested waiting, but he agreed that the evangelical princes could meet in preparation in order to react to an assault. Any such preparation, however, should not lead to reliance on one's own strength instead of God's help. In this case, too, the dialectic of the '*simul*' applied: God wishes 'to think, speak, and accomplish without our strength and council and still to work through our fists, tongues, and hearts as through instruments of the divine wisdom and power' (1528, WABr4.435,1–3; Wolgast 1977: 114–25). One can achieve success only in cooperating with God (*cooperatio Dei*), which is then God's success, not the human being's. In this context the important political differentiation between confidence (in God's help) and use (of the means provided by God) first emerged in Luther's thought. He later claimed this to be the only suitable attitude with regard to the political–military alliance: 'Confidence and use are two different things; confidence pertains to God alone; use pertains to the creature' (1530, WA31,1.114,31–32).

The issue of resisting attack for the sake of the faith did not present itself to Luther in 1528 since it was an *inter pares* conflict between imperial princes of the same rank. In this situation the cause of the war was not important for Luther, but whether it was a defensive war. However, after further modifications of religious and ecclesiastical life had been forbidden by the end of the second Imperial Diet of Speyer in 1529, an entirely new context arose: now the emperor was one of the parties in the conflict. Despite the threatening new situation, Luther firmly denied that the evangelical princes and imperial cities were entitled to forge an alliance directed against the emperor for the defence of their faith (Wolgast 1977: 125–65; Böttcher 1991: 40–72). In his memoranda he only considered the personal dimension; he started from the real Christian (*vere Christianus*) as responding and affected object, without considering the altered situation from the early days of the Reformation: the evangelical territory with large numbers of the weak in faith and the emerging new church organization. The main obstacle for a princely right of resistance against the emperor arose from Luther's understanding of the imperial constitution (Günter 1976). He assumed a basic command–obedience relationship between the emperor and the imperial states. In relation to the emperor as the sovereign (*magistratus superior*), the prince lost all official power as a lower authority (*magistratus inferior*). According to Luther's vision, each prince had received his office from the emperor, and he possessed no independent legitimation. At the command of the emperor, a prince, who was usually a *persona publica*, became a *persona privata*, turning into a mere subject (*mere subditus*) without any office, who had to accept persecution for the sake of his faith. At no level of political relationships did Luther acknowledge autonomous intermediate powers between the one who gives commands and the one who obeys, including the relationship between emperor and prince. The prince–emperor relationship, according to Luther's vision, corresponded to the one between the mayor of Torgau and the elector of Saxony. As the official powers of the mayor ceased to exist in front of the elector, so the official powers of the elector ceased to exist in relationship to the emperor. Luther's view of dependent relationships may be displayed as follows:

Responsibility as a *persona privata* (without an office)		Dominion as a *persona publica* (governing authority)
Before God	Emperor (*magistratus superior*)	Over Princes and Subjects
Before the Emperor	Prince (*magistratus inferior*)	Over Subjects
Before the Prince	Subject (*mere subditus*)	

   Luther's conception of the command–obedience relationship and his definition of governing authorities was not undisputed among the Wittenberg theologians. In 1529 Johannes Bugenhagen, referring to 1 Samuel 15:23, advocated that a governing authority which persistently and pervasively exceeds its powers forfeits its office, deposes itself by its misconduct, and hence has lost its claim to obedience (Wolgast 1977: 135–9; Wolgast 1984). In Luther's view, however, such an authority can be overthrown only by God, either by God's direct action or by God's heroic men (*viri heroici*) (Wolgast 1977: 30–2), who obtain their commission from God apart from the structure of justice and law. Removal of governing authorities was certainly also possible for Luther if positive law contained rules for the removal. Thus, according to the imperial constitution the emperor could be deposed by the vote of all the electors who had chosen him. How such a measure was to align with their status as subjects and their duty of obedience, Luther left as an open question. Regarding the political alliance of evangelical princes, he posed the issue in 1529/30 in the same way that he had with the Pack Affairs: it is best to have no alliance; in any case, one must never place one's trust in it.

On the question of the politicians themselves, Luther as always answered according to a Christian concept of action that held the individual responsible: in instances of conflict, 'each person [should] stand for himself and maintain the faith, abandoning body and life if necessary'. No Christian, including a Christian prince, may obey commands of the emperor that violate the conscience but must refuse to obey, invoking Acts 5:29, testifying in verbal protest for the sake of the truth. Then, they are to suffer the consequences without resisting, following Christ's example (1530, WABr5.258–261).

Luther's opposition to a right of resistance was not initially debated by jurists and politicians since Charles V convened an imperial diet in order to ease the situation. In contrast to the expectations of the evangelical party, however, the decisions of the Augsburg Diet in 1530 created a new threat on a separate issue since the evangelicals were commanded to revoke all previous changes they had made. Hence, discussions about the alliance and the right of resistance began again in the evangelical camp. In October 1530 jurists and statesmen from Saxony and Hesse instructed the Wittenberg theologians in Torgau on the legal status of the princes according to the imperial constitution ('Torgauer Wende', the turn at Torgau) (Wolgast 1977: 173–85; Kunst 1979: 242–7; Böttcher 1991: 147–56). Luther had to acknowledge, although reluctantly, that his identification of emperor and prince with ruling authority and subject did not apply constitutionally, but that a mutual obligation (*obligatio mutua*) existed between the emperor and the imperial estates that substantiated a consensual rule in the realm. If he did not satisfy his obligations, the emperor himself had awarded the princes a right of resistance. Furthermore, the princes possessed an independent, hereditary legitimation for their rule, which did not originate from the emperor but existed autochthonously. Moreover, natural law applied in the *regnum corporale*, namely the legal dictum: force may be answered with force (*vim vi repellere licet*).

On the basis of this instruction in law, Luther explained the entire complex of resistance as a question of positive law, for which theologians had no competence according to the allocation of responsibilities in the two realms doctrine. Their task was merely to urge obedience to the laws; they possessed as little of a substantive right to examine this topic as they had to stipulate to the cobbler the substance of the rules of his craft (WATR1.40,22–43,6, §109). With this concession to the legal and political realities, however, Luther still proceeded from the premise that secular law could not violate the rules of human coexistence contained in the gospel. Nevertheless, he did not formulate this caveat explicitly. Therefore, the so-called Torgauer Wende actually granted theology-free space in which proper behaviour before the emperor who had breached the law and persecuted the faith was determined by jurists and statesmen instead of theologians. Fundamentally, Luther adhered to the Christian duty of suffering as a *persona privata*, but he relinquished to jurists the decision whether secular law and the imperial constitution conferred the quality of a *persona publica* on a prince during conflict with the emperor.

Until the Torgauer Wende Luther had directed his advice, intended as pastor though with political impact, to princes as Christians. Since Torgau, Luther identified the prince as a *politica persona* and when acting as prince, he is not acting as 'Christian'

(1531, WABr6.17,10). By virtue of his character as a *persona publica*, the prince had to protect and defend his subjects who were weak in their faith when they demanded it in exchange for their obedience and taxes. Luther, however, never truly accepted the conclusions of the constitutional argument, despite his understanding the legal realities, because they contradicted his world-view with its clear picture of a higher order and a lower order without any authority between them. Nevertheless, he did not openly challenge or revoke the theological concession of Torgau, but in future conflicts Luther, above all, advised waiting and recommended a policy of temporizing in order not to forestall God but to give him time to act.

Luther agreed with the jurists in 1530 that only the princes and city councils could be bearers of the right of resistance since, as imperial estates, they were ruling authorities. In contrast, ordinary subjects and office-holders with only a local sphere of influence were not permitted resistance during conflict with the authority of the imperial estates. Thus, the rebellious peasants from 1525 remained illegitimate even in retrospect. However, only in the crisis of 1538–9 did Luther abandon this limitation of the right of resistance to the imperial estates. After preliminary reflections, he prepared theses for a circular disputation on Matthew 19:21 (May 1539); with these he wished to clarify correct Christian behaviour in the case of religious persecution by the pope (1539, WA39,2.39–44, 52–91; WABr8.366–368; Wolgast 1977: 243–50). In this context he drew upon his understanding of tyranny, the doctrine of the three estates, and the line of argumentation of 'Caesar as the soldier of the pope' (*Caesar miles Papae*). As the basis of his argumentation Luther utilized the ancient and medieval doctrine of the tyrant. A heathen tyrant (*tyrannus gentilis*) was to be tolerated if he persecuted the faith because he did not know better. Under such a tyrant Christians must accept martyrdom, as at the time of Diocletian. Different action was necessary if the pope violently opposed the gospel because he did so under the pretence of acting as a Christian though he was leading souls deliberately into perdition. Luther denied that the pope's actions and those of his minions possessed the character of a ruling authority's actions, and he even denied the emperor's authority when he acted as a 'soldier of the pope'. If the pope usurped the name and authority of a Christian ruling authority, he exposed himself as an anti-Christian pseudo-tyrant, mixing both kingdoms and placing himself outside of the three estates. In this context, Luther amassed different formulas of exclusion: 'new and unique monster', 'a thing without parallel', 'a wild beast and devastator of everything', a werewolf, and thus outside of every divine, natural, and human law. Against a tyrant who knew better yet still persecuted Christians under the appearance of being Christian, every individual (*singuli et soli*)—even one who held no office and had received no command from the ruling authority—was obligated to provide armed resistance. For Luther, this was an exceptional situation with an eschatological background, analogous to his assessment of the events in 1525. If the princes failed or, like the emperor, set themselves on the pope's side, the soul-killer, 'a popular action' must take place, even 'through sedition'. Each person was challenged to decide in his own conscience whether his ruling authority had changed into a helper of the apocalyptic tyrant and must be opposed in a popular revolt. According to the nature of the matter, a definition of such an emergency situation was impossible. Therefore, after 1539 Luther no longer pursued the approach of legitimizing the resistance of office-less subjects, especially after the Treaty of Frankfurt defused the political crisis. Instead, he subsequently continued to accept the right of resistance for the imperial princes against the emperor, but he also continued to advise waiting as the best option and continued to warn against depending on an alliance.

Luther's recommendation to the counsellors in 1538, to 'proceed into the darkness with God's grace' (WABr8.235,57) reflects his fundamental position on political planning: trust in God instead of trust in human calculations. For the officials, however, this was not feasible. Hence, the influence of Luther's suggestions in political questions, which was relatively great under the electors Friedrich and Johann, declined noticeably after the Torgauer Wende. Since then, the opinions regarding political questions, which were requested by the government or produced by the theologians, were mostly generated as collective opinions, formulated by Melanchthon, while Luther only sanctioned them with his signature.

V. LUTHER'S POLITICAL IMPACT

Luther's ideas on politics and society gained canonical character after his death. In the process the two kingdoms and three estates teachings lost their openness and flexibility and stiffened into schemata. After his death Luther's reflections on the right of resistance were exploited by the Wittenberg theologians in order to justify Johann Friedrich of Saxony in fending off an attack of the emperor as 'open tyranny and aggressive violence' for the sake of religion (Scheible 1969: 98–100). The Magdeburg theologians in their *Confession* of 1550–1 broadened Luther's concept of resistance when they awarded themselves a right of resistance as a subordinate ruling authority. Furthermore, they argued that 'the least ruling authority', in its character as the magistrate of a territorial city, was obligated to protect the subjects in its domain against a superior authority if this authority persecutes believers and the faith. Every office-holder, regardless of his legal or dependent status or position, became a ruling authority with all rights included for the sake of religion (Kaufmann 2003: 176–98; Rein 2008).

With the expansion of the modern state, the right of resistance for Lutherans was reduced to the clergy's task as watchmen who reveal the misconduct of the ruling authority and calling them to repentance (Schorn-Schütte 1996: 390–416, 433–49). In any case, modern democratic participation entirely abolished the relationship between higher and lower orders and eliminated the command–obedience structure that Luther had made the foundation of his political and social ideas.

Translated by Theodore J. Hopkins

REFERENCES

Anselm, Reiner (2004). 'Art. Zweireichelehre I. Kirchengeschichtlich'. *TRE* 36: 776–84.

Bayer, Oswald (1984). 'Natur und Institution. Eine Besinnung auf Luthers Dreiständelehre'. *Zeitschrift für Theologie und Kirche* 81: 352–82.

Beutel, Albrecht (ed.) (2005). *Luther Handbuch*. Tübingen: Mohr/Siebeck.

Bornkamm, Heinrich (1960). *Luthers Lehre von den zwei Reichen im Zusammenhang seiner Theologie*, 2nd edn. Gütersloh: Mohn.

Böttcher, Diethelm (1991). *Ungehorsam oder Widerstand? Zum Fortleben des mittelalterlichen Widerstandsrechtes in der Reformationszeit (1529–1530)*. Berlin: Duncker & Humblot.

Brady, Thomas A., Jr. (1985). 'Luther and Society: Two Kingdoms or Three Estates? Tradition and Experience in Luther's Social Teaching'. *Lutherjahrbuch* 52: 197–212.

Brecht, Martin (1986). *Martin Luther, Band 2*. Stuttgart: Calwer Verlag.

Bubenheimer, Ulrich (1985). 'Luthers Stellung zum Aufruhr in Wittenberg (1520–1522) und die frühreformatorischen Wurzeln des landesherrlichen Kirchenregiments'. *Zeitschrift für Rechtsgeschichte*, Kanonist. Abt. 71: 147–214.

Duchrow, Ulrich (1983). *Christenheit und Weltverantwortung. Traditionsgeschichte und systematische Struktur der Zweireichelehre*, 2nd edn. Stuttgart: Klett-Cotta.

Ehmann, Johannes (2008). *Luther, Türken und Islam. Eine Untersuchung zum Türken- und Islambild Martin Luthers (1515–1546)*. Gütersloh: Gütersloher Verlagshaus.

Elert, Werner (1932). *Morphologie des Luthertums Bd. 2. Soziallehren und Sozialwirkungen des Luthertums*. Munich: Beck.

Estes, James M. (2005). *Peace, Order and the Glory of God: Secular Authority and the Church in the Thought of Luther and Melanchthon, 1518–1559*. Leiden: Brill.

Gänssler, Hans-Joachim (1983). *Evangelium und weltliches Schwert. Hintergrund, Entstehungsgeschichte und Anlass von Luthers Scheidung zweier Reiche oder Regimente*. Wiesbaden: Steiner.

Greschat, Martin (1965). 'Luthers Haltung im Bauernkrieg'. *Archiv für Reformationsgeschichte* 56: 31–47.

Günter, Wolfgang (1976). *Martin Luthers Vorstellung von der Reichsverfassung*. Münster: Aschendorff.

Heckel, Johannes (1973). *Lex charitatis. Eine juristische Untersuchung über das Recht in der Theologie Martin Luthers*, 2nd edn. Darmstadt: Wissenschaftliche Buchgesellschaft.

Kaufmann, Thomas (2003). *Das Ende der Reformation. Magdeburgs 'Herrgotts Kanzlei' (1548–1551/2)*. Tübingen: Mohr/Siebeck.

Kohnle, Armin (2005a). 'Luther und das Reich'. In *Luther Handbuch*, ed. Albrecht Beutel. Tübingen: Mohr/Siebeck, 196–205.

—— (2005b). 'Luther und die Bauern'. In *Luther Handbuch*, ed. Albrecht Beutel. Tübingen: Mohr/Siebeck, 134–9.

Kolb, Robert (1978). 'The Theologians and the Peasants: Conservative Evangelical Reactions to the German Peasants Revolt'. *Archiv für Reformationsgeschichte* 69: 103–31.

Kruse, Jens-Martin (2002). *Universitätstheologie und Kirchenreform. Die Anfänge der Reformation in Wittenberg 1516–1522*. Mainz: Zabern.

Kunst, Hermann (1979). *Evangelischer Glaube und politische Verantwortung. Martin Luther als politischer Berater seiner Landesherrn und seine Teilnahme an den Fragen des öffentlichen Lebens*. Stuttgart: Evangelisches Verlagswerk.

Lau, Franz (1952). *Luthers Lehre von den beiden Reichen*. Berlin: Evangelische Verlagsanstalt.

Luther, Martin (1992). *Martin Luther. Studienausgabe. Band 5*. ed. Hans-Ulrich Delius. Berlin: Evangelische Verlagsanstalt.

Mantey, Volker (2005). *Zwei Schwerter—Zwei Reiche. Martin Luthers Zwei-Reiche-Lehre vor ihrem spätmittelalterlichen Hintergrund*. Tübingen: Mohr/Siebeck.

Maron, Gottfried (1980). 'Art. Bauernkrieg'. *TRE* 5: 319–38.

Maurer, Wilhelm (1970). *Luthers Lehre von den drei Hierarchien und ihr mittelalterlicher Hintergrund*. Munich: Verlag der Bayerischen Akademie der Wissenschaften.

Nilsson, Kjell Ove (1966). *Simul. Das Miteinander von Göttlichem und Menschlichem in Luthers Theologie*. Göttingen: Vandenhoeck & Ruprecht.

Rein, Nathan (2008). *The Chancery of God: Protestant Priest, Polemic and Propaganda against the Empire, Magdeburg 1546–1551*. Aldershot: Ashgate.

Rieth, Ricardo (1996). *'Habsucht' bei Martin Luther. Ökonomisches und theologisches Denken, Tradition und soziale Wirklichkeit im Zeitalter der Reformation*. Weimar: Böhlau.

Scheible, Heinz (ed.) (1969). *Das Widerstandsrecht als Problem der deutschen Protestanten 1523–1546*. Gütersloh: Mohn.

Schorn-Schütte, Luise (1996). *Evangelische Geistlichkeit in der Frühneuzeit. Deren Anteil an der Entfaltung frühmoderner Staatlichkeit und Gesellschaft*. Gütersloh: Gütersloher Verlagshaus.

—— (1998). 'Die Drei-Stände-Lehre im reformatorischen Umbruch'. In *Die frühe Reformation in Deutschland als Umbruch*, ed. Stephen Buckwalter and Bernd Moeller. Gütersloh: Gütersloher Verlagshaus, 435–61.

Schrey, Horst (ed.) (1969). *Reich Gottes und Welt. Die Lehre Luthers von den zwei Reichen*. Darmstadt: Wissenschaftliche Buchgesellschaft.

Schwarz, Reinhard (1978). 'Luthers Lehre von den drei Ständen und die drei Dimensionen der Ethik'. *Lutherjahrbuch* 45: 15–34.

—— (1984). 'Ecclesia, oeconomia, politia. Sozialgeschichtliche und fundamentalethische Aspekte der protestantischen Drei-Stände-Theorie'. In *Troeltsch-Studien Band 3*, ed. Friedrich Wilhelm Graf. Gütersloh: Mohn, 78–88.

Stümke, Volker (2007). *Das Friedensverständnis Martin Luthers—Grundlagen und Anwendungsbereiche seiner politischen Ethik*. Stuttgart: Kohlhammer.

Törnvall, Gustaf (1947). *Geistliches und weltliches Regiment bei Luther. Studien zu Luthers Weltbild und Gesellschaftsverständnis*. Munich: Kaiser.

Wolgast, Eike (1977). *Die Wittenberger Theologie und die Politik der evangelischen Stände. Studien zu Luthers Gutachten in politischen Fragen*. Gütersloh: Mohn.

—— (1984). 'Bugenhagen in den politischen Krisen seiner Zeit'. In *Johannes Bugenhagen. Gestalt und Wirkung*, ed. Hans-Günter Leder. Berlin: Evangelische Verlagsanstalt, 100–17.

—— (2006). *Der gemeine Mann bei Müntzer—und danach*. Mühlhausen: TMG.

SUGGESTED READINGS

Ebeling, Gerhard (1997). *Luthers Seelsorge. Theologie in der Vielfalt der Lebenssituationen, an seinen Briefen dargestellt*. Tübingen: Mohr/Siebeck.

Edwards, Mark U., Jr. (1975). *Luther and the False Brethren*. Stanford: Stanford University Press.

Friedeburg, Robert von (2002). *Self-Defence and Religious Strife in Early Modern Europe: England and Germany, 1530–1680*. Aldershot: Ashgate.

Henninger, Frederick William, Jr. (1972). 'Luther and the Empire: A Study of the Imperial Ideal in Reformation Politics, 1522–1540'. Ph.D. Dissertation, University of Nebraska.

Herms, Eilert (2005). 'Leben in der Welt'. In *Luther Handbuch*, ed. Albrecht Beutel. Tübingen: Mohr/Siebeck, 423–35.

Iserloh, Erwin and Gerhard Müller (eds.) (1984). *Luther und die politische Welt*. Stuttgart: Steiner Verlag.

Keen, Ralph (1997). *Divine and Human Authority in Reformation Thought: German Theologians on Political Order 1520–1555*. Nieuwkoop: de Graaf.

Wolgast, Eike (1998). 'Melanchthon als politischer Berater'. In *Melanchthon. Zehn Vorträge*, ed. Hanns Christof Brennecke and Walter Sparn. Erlangen: Universitäts-Bund, 179–208.

CHAPTER 29

PIETY, PRAYER, AND WORSHIP IN LUTHER'S VIEW OF DAILY LIFE

CARTER LINDBERG

Piety, prayer, and worship interweave throughout the whole of Luther's theology and life. While Luther's reflections on prayer and worship appear throughout his writings, some tracts focus his reflections and suggest their extraordinary reception. Chief among these are: *An Exposition of the Lord's Prayer for Simple Laymen* (1519; WA2.80–130; LW42.19–81; five editions prepared by John Agricola; then thirteen editions of Luther's revision and a Latin translation by 1520), *Personal Prayer Book* (1522; WA10,2.375–406; LW43.11–45, some forty-eight editions in Luther's lifetime, and at least eleven more by 1600), and *A Simple Way to Pray* (1535; WA38.358–375; LW43.193–211, some twenty-two German editions) and the *Catechisms* (1529; BSLK 499–733; BC 347–480). The continuing popularity of these tracts is evident in their frequent modern publications (see, for example, Russell 2005; Thompson 2000; Beyer 2007; Junghans 2004; Ratzmann 2007; Leaver 2007). Likewise, Luther's views on worship are concentrated in *The Blessed Sacrament of the Holy and True Body of Christ, and Brotherhoods* (1519; WA2.727–737; LW35.49–73, fourteen editions by 1525 and a Latin translation), *A Treatise on the New Testament, That Is, The Holy Mass* (1520; WA6.353–378; LW35.79–111, fourteen editions by 1524), *An Order of Mass and Communion for the Church of Wittenberg* (1523; WA12.205–220; LW53.19–40, Latin with a German translation), and *The German Mass and Order of Service* (1526; WA19.72–113; LW53.61–90).

I. PIETY

Luther anchored piety, prayer, and worship in his understanding that salvation is received not achieved. 'The proclamation of the gospel of justification has decisive significance not only for theological understanding but also for the praxis of piety' (Vajta 1983: 279; cf. Koch 2002: 65: 'Luther's theology is real as prayer, as practiced piety'). He defined theology as 'man guilty of sin and condemned, and God the Justifier and Saviour of man the sinner. Whatever is asked or discussed in theology outside this subject, is error and poison' (Commentary on Psalm 51 [1532], WA40,2.328,17–20; LW12.311). Theology in this sense is not a collection of timeless truths but a lifelong daily drama. 'It is through living, indeed through dying and being damned, that one becomes a theologian, not through understanding, reading, or speculation' (Lectures on the Psalms [1519–21], WA5.163,28–29). Theology is wisdom gained through experience imposed upon us (*sapientia experimentalis*) guided by prayer, meditation, and agonizing struggle (*oratio, meditatio, tentatio*). The *sapientia experimentalis* is not only that of Scripture but also that of God's encounter in prayer, meditation, and daily life. So, for example, becoming a father enabled Luther to view the fatherhood of God with new eyes (Bayer 1988; Stolt 1994; Stolt 2000: 181–4; Bayer 2008: 29–42).

The diffuse terminology for piety covers a wide spectrum ranging from an individual's inner spirituality to communal religious behaviour. The German '*Frömmigkeit*' and its French equivalents of '*piété*', '*dévotion*', and '*religiosité*' comprehend both religious intentions and their realization in daily life (Arnold 2000: 1–2; cf. BC 357, n. 69). For Luther, piety is the consequence of faith and not vice versa (Axmacher 1995: 65–6). It is the answer of the Christian faith to the claim of God—in praise, thanksgiving, and petition, through word and deed (Aarflot 1977: 161–2). 'Luther himself transformed [piety] from a word for general upright and honorable living to a designation for living a life of faith in God which produces love and service to others' (Kolb 2009: 193).

The subject of 'piety' is itself fraught by both late medieval and post-Reformation conceptions that are often read into Luther (Hamm and Leppin 2007). The post-Reformation conception of piety derives from the seventeenth-century movement known as 'Pietism', which stressed devotional reading of the Bible, religious experience, and holiness of life (Lindberg 2005: 1–20), and from the subjective description of religion by liberal theologian Friedrich Schleiermacher (1768–1834) as the feeling of 'absolute dependence'. But if piety is the subjective experience of an individual's absolute dependence upon God, it becomes doubtful as a research project (Molitor 1976: 8–9; Hamm 1977: 467; Drehsen 1995: 56–7; Jaspert 1995: 144–7; Jung 1998: 3–5).

The long history of these post-Reformation views imbued the term piety with a focus on inner religious experience, moralism, and other-worldliness. Meanwhile, the term 'spirituality', once closely linked to Roman Catholic piety, has become widespread and debased into all sorts of claims for an individual's inner development and self-realization (Kittelson 1995; Jung 1998: 5–6; Lienhard 2002: 7–14, 7; Opahle 2005; Wriedt 2006: 94–5; for a positive use of the term 'spirituality', see Krey and Krey 2007). It is not unusual today to hear people protest, 'I'm not religious but I am spiritual'.

In contrast to both medieval and modern spirituality Luther insisted 'that the spiritual life had to be lived in the world...with all of its endless difficulties and frustrations'. 'Lutheran spirituality begins and ends with the celebration of the mundane, the ordinary life as the vehicle for glorifying God' (Hillerbrand 1999: 134, 8, 140; Wriedt 2006: 98–100;

on prayer and vocation, see Wingren 1957: 184–99). Piety is expressed daily in the multifaceted vocation of the Christian. Thus Luther criticized the view that monastic life was the ideal form of piety. 'As Christians we are called to serve God and our neighbour in the context of our daily struggles to fulfil the divine will that we lead a truly human life' (Aarflot 1977: 165; cf. WA10,1.309,14–19; Kolb 2009: 214–18). As Luther once admonished Philip Melanchthon: 'We are to be human beings and not God' (WABr5.415,45; LW49.337). In this perspective piety is only possible through faith; it is not a progressive sanctification but rather a continual new beginning—'to advance is always a matter of beginning anew'—through the mercy of God (Lectures on Romans [1516] WA56.486,7; LW25.478; cf. Hendrix 2004).

In startling departure from both medieval and contemporary understandings of piety, Luther wrote:

> If mercy is this abundant, then there is no holiness in us. Then it is a fictitious expression to speak of a 'holy man', just as it is a fictitious expression to speak of God's falling into sin; for by the nature of things, this cannot be.... Those whom we call 'holy' are made holy by an alien holiness, through Christ, by the holiness of free mercy.... Therefore let us keep quiet about holiness and holy people. We know that those have been made holy who have become conscious sinners instead of unconscious sinners. They do not presume to have any righteousness of their own—for it is nonexistent— but begin to have an enlightened heart.
>
> (Commentary on Psalm 51, WA40,2.347,29–348,27; LW12, 324–325)

Luther wrote to a fellow friar, Georg Spenlein, in 1516, 'Beware of aspiring to such purity that you will not wish to be looked upon as a sinner, or to be one' (WABr1.35.28–29; LW48.12–13; cf. Lindberg 1984, 1999; Bayer 2003).

Sharply put (and reflecting the definition of piety as general uprightness in public behaviour before Luther): 'It is not the proper role of the gospel to make people pious but rather only to make them Christians. To be a Christian is quite simply to be pious. A person may be pious without being Christian' (Sermon on Mt. 9:8–26 [1526], WA10,1,2.430,30–32). Luther continues, noting that Christian piety is 'alien' piety, i.e., a gift from Christ. 'For Christian holiness, or the holiness common to Christendom, is found where the Holy Spirit gives people faith in Christ and thus sanctifies them' (On the Councils and the Church [1539], WA50.626,15; LW41.145). Luther warns against 'too much religion' lest we 'lose Christ' (Commentary on Psalm 51, WA40,2.387,5–6; LW12.352). A person's 'piety' or holiness is no more a personal achievement than is justification (Adventspostil [1522], WA10,1,2.36,4–8; Wunder 1998: 307; Mikoteit 2004: 15).

Mikoteit argues that Luther's discovery of the message of the justification of the sinner by grace alone led him to understand piety in diametrical opposition to every late medieval, pre-Reformation conception of piety (Mikotiet 2004: 46). Rejecting Wunder's thesis (Wunder 1998) that Luther continued to use the late medieval urban bourgeois sense of piety as civic virtue as untenable, he contends that Luther shifted the understanding of piety from an ethical, moralistic realm to 'a pure theological concept', thereby making piety a positive technical term for the doctrine of justification (Mikoteit 2004: 27, 32).

Piety in the Reformation period has until recently been neglected (Drehsen 1995: 48–9; Jaspert 1995: 135; Jung 1998: 19); Lienhard refers to the study of piety as the 'poor relative' in historical research (Lienhard 2002: 7). This neglect may relate to both the elusiveness of piety as an object of historical study and the ambiguity inherent in the Christian life as set forth in Luther's motif of the Christian being simultaneously sinner and righteous. The doctrine of justification by faith is easier to describe than the life that flows from it (Lienhard 2002: 7). Sources for the study of piety in the Reformation period include nearly every type of literary and plastic expression: prayers, hymns, tracts of devotion and edification, sermons, liturgies and rituals, letters of pastoral care and consolation, biblical commentaries, visitation records detailing religious praxis such as frequency of communion, wills and testaments, catechisms, church orders: all set forth programmes of education, social welfare, architecture, and art (Molitor 1976: 11–19; Hamm 1977: 472–3). 'As much as the "theology of piety" was disseminated through texts, it must be understood as a multi—and mass—media event during the era 1400–1520, accompanied as it was by a flood of painted, printed, and plastic images' (Hamm 1977: 472–3).

II. Prayer

There is a vast literature on Luther's view of prayer (Mikoteit 2004: 48–57 reviews twentieth-century research; cf. Schulz 1976, 1984). This is not surprising for, as numerous scholars note: 'The theology of Martin Luther is a theology of prayer'; prayer is 'a constitutive factor for Luther's theology'; a 'pivotal element in Luther's understanding of spirituality' through 'reflection and rumination on the passages of Scripture' (Russell 1999: 293; Bayer 2008: 346, whose final chapter is titled 'Promise and Prayer'; Hillerbrand 1999: 135). Luther's theology is actualized as prayer, as practised piety (Koch 2001: 123; Koch 2002: 65).

In his monastic life Luther experienced prayer and liturgy that were 'closely bound up with the penitential system, not only as satisfaction for sin, but also through the promises of indulgence attached to particular prayers' (Brown 2008: 238). On the one hand, this experience led to his vociferous life-long rejection of medieval prayer books (e.g., *Betbüchlein*, WA 10,2.375,3–15; LW 43.11). On the other hand, Luther's monastic experience of daily meditative prayer on the Psalms was formative for his life-long enthusiasm for the Psalms as model prayers. 'For Luther the image of the Christian life is most clearly expressed in the Psalms. Their blend of joy and pain, lament and praise, characterized for him the Christian life' (Aurelius 2009: 221).

With his rejection of the medieval view of prayers as good works, Luther turned to the Lord's Prayer as *the* model prayer taught by Christ himself. The Lord's Prayer remained the centre of Luther's prayer praxis, to which he occasionally added some Psalms

(Brecht 1998: 269; Dingel 2006: 34–7). Already by 1519 he published his immensely popular *An Exposition of the Lord's Prayer for Simple Laymen*, based upon earlier sermons (WA2.74–130; LW42.15–81; cf. Peters 1992; Dingel 2006: 31–4). The Catechisms continue Luther's earlier writings on prayer structured around the Ten Commandments (revelation of one's sickness), the Creed (where to find the medicine for the sickness), and the Lord's Prayer (the medicine—grace) (*Betbüchlein*, WA10,2.376, 12–377,13; LW43: 13–14; cf. Brown 2008: 238–9; Wengert 2009: 182–4). 'Luther makes all the parts of the catechism into "a garland of four strands", with each part becoming for him a textbook, song book, penitential book, and prayer book' (Bayer 2007: 72). Indeed, he understood the Catechisms as texts to be prayed (Beyer 2007: 40–2).

Haemig summarizes Luther's view of prayer:

> He asserted that Christians pray because God has commanded them to pray and promised to hear them. For this reason, Christians pray to God, not to Mary or the saints. Prayer was the proper response to God; it never originated the relationship with God. Luther rejected the idea that prayer was a good work and rejected practices—such as repetition of prayers and the use of prayers as works of satisfaction—that might lend support to the idea that prayer was a good work. Prayer was not based in the Christian's worthiness to pray. Need drives her to pray, and she brings all her needs to God, trusting God's promise to hear her. As every Christian is a priest, every Christian should pray. One should not trust in others' prayers and should not leave prayer to the clergy. Prayer should come from the heart and be simple.
>
> (Haemig 2004: 524; cf. Peters 1992: 15–39; Lienhard 1997: 97; *Large Catechism*, BSLK 662–90; BC 440–56)

Luther's emphasis upon prayer as God's commandment and promise (e.g., WA27.129,4–5; cf. Vajta 1983: 284; Brecht 1998: 269–70; Bayer 2008: 346–54; Wengert 2009) freed him from the burden of thinking he must be worthy to address God and for his boldness in assaulting God's ears with claims for help in need (Dingel 2006: 39; Haemig 2009). We are to remind God of his promise to hear us (*On Rogationtide Prayer and Procession* [1519], WA2.175,4–18; LW42: 87, sermon on the fifth Sunday after Easter, 1525, WA 10,1.249,26–36, sermon for Reminiscere, Lenten Postil, 1525, WA17,2.203,29–204,6). A startling example of this is his response to the apparent mortal illness of Philip Melanchthon. Striding into the room where Melanchthon had taken to his deathbed, Luther assailed God in an impudent way that was extraordinary even for him: 'Our Lord God had to bear the brunt of this, for I threw my sack before his doors and wearied his ears with all his promises of hearing prayers that I knew from the Holy Scriptures, so that he had to hear me if I were to trust any of his other promises.' Luther then turned his attention to Melanchthon and told him if he did not start eating, he would excommunicate him. Luther later recalled he had 'prayed Philip back to life' (WATR5.244–246, §5565; LW54.453–454; cf. WABr9.168–172; Wartenberg 2008: 122–3; Wengert 2009: 173–4).

In contrast, Luther was also well aware of how easy it is to drift away to other thoughts in the midst of prayer and compared his wandering attention to his dog's rapt attention when begging at the table. 'Oh, if I could only pray the way this dog watches the meat! All his thoughts are concentrated on the piece of meat. Otherwise he has no thought, wish, or hope' (WATR1.115–116, §274; LW54.37–38; cf. WA28.77,12–24; LW69.18–19, WA40,2.33,23–24; LW12.314–315). Hence Luther recognized the value of 'fixed or exemplary texts, which Luther insisted were all but essential to keep the mind from wandering astray' (Brown 2008: 243). Thus the *Small Catechism* includes models of brief morning, evening, and table prayers for daily life (BSLK 521–2; BC 363–4).

Luther's crucial point is that God hears and responds to prayers not because of their intensity nor the worthiness of the one who prays, but because God promises to hear. 'I would not pray if I did not know that I shall be heard' (sermon on the fifth Sunday after Easter, 1538, WA46.383, cf. Brecht 1998: 273; WATR2.628, §2742a, cf. Wengert 2009: 175). Luther's confidence is summarized in his explanation of 'amen' in the *Small* and *Large Catechisms*: 'That I should be certain that such petitions [of the Lord's Prayer] are acceptable to and heard by our Father in heaven, for he himself commanded us to pray like this and has promised to hear us. "Amen, amen" means "Yes, yes, it is going to come about just like this". Those who doubt 'are not looking at God's promise but at their own works and worthiness, and thereby they despise God and accuse him of lying.... Look! God has attached much importance to our being certain so that we do not pray in vain or despise our prayers in any way' (BSLK 515, 690; BC 358, 456).

Prayer is one of the marks of the church (*On the Councils and the Church*, 1539. WA50.641,20–34; LW41.164). Indeed, 'next to the office of preaching, prayer is the highest office in Christianity. In the preaching office God speaks with us, in prayer we speak with him' (Wartenberg 2008: 119).

III. Worship

When we turn to worship (literature review in Schulz 1983) we are once again returned to the core of Luther's piety: justification by grace alone. 'Worship is the place of justification' (Aurelius 2009: 225). Aurelius illustrates the point with reference to Cranach's Wittenberg Altarpiece. The central panel depicts the institution of the Lord's Supper. The side panels depict the layman Melanchthon baptizing a baby and the town pastor Bugenhagen exercising the power of the keys; the predella shows Luther (on the right) in the pulpit pointing to Christ on the cross (in the centre) with a congregation of local citizens (on the left). The round table of the Lord's Supper draws in the congregation in stark contrast to late medieval portrayals of the priest celebrating mass far removed from the people with his back to them. The Lord's Supper is a communion, not a sacrifice.[1] Luther, portrayed as the layman, Junker Georg at the

---

[1] Noble (2009: 106–9) compares the Cranach Altarpiece with the mid-fifteenth-century 'Altarpiece of the Seven Sacraments' by Rogier van der Weyden. 'The interlocking ideas of community identity,

Wartburg, is turning to the congregation as he receives the cup. The Altarpiece expresses 'the distribution of the gospel to the people', for 'where there is the Eucharist, Baptism, and the Word, there is Christ, the remission of sins, and life eternal' (Aurelius 2009: 228, 233; referring to the Smalcald Articles, BSLK 449; BC 319).

As the place of justification, the worship service is where God's promise is audibly declared in the language of the people present. So Luther rejected the Canon of the Mass in terms of both its theology of sacrifice and its separation from the people as the priest silently recited in Latin. God's word of promise must be heard and understood (*A Treatise on the New Testament, That Is, the Holy Mass* [1520], WA6.362,26–35; LW35.90; cf. *The Abomination of the Secret Mass* [1525], WA18.22–36; LW36.307–328). The mass is no longer the offering of the priest to God, but the offering of God to the people through the words of institution. For Luther, the Lord's Supper is God's action that the church can only receive but not initiate. In rejecting all sacrificial language in relation to the Canon of the Mass, and then reducing the relative importance of the memorial view of the Lord's Supper (certainly in the form advocated by other reformers), Luther stressed the Lord's Supper as the gift, the promise, that comes from outside us (*extra nos*) for us (*pro nobis*).[2] The sermon 'is nothing less than an explanation of Christ's words. "What is the whole gospel but an explanation of this testament?" For Luther, the proclamation of the Word, the sermon, logically belonged to the indispensable makeup of a worship service' (Junghans 2004: 211–12, citing WA6.362,26–35, 374,3–4; LW35.90, 106). 'Let everything be done so that the Word may have free course instead of the prattling and rattling that has been the rule up to now. We can spare everything except the Word' (*Concerning the Order of Public Worship*, [1523], WA12.37,26–29; LW53.14). 'Pastors recognized, implicitly and explicitly, that the focus of their faith had shifted from their performance of ritual directed toward God to the conversation initiated by God to which their people and they respond' (Haemig and Kolb 2008: 123; for social-historical readings of the reformation of ritual, see Muir 1997 and Karant-Nunn 1997).

The Lord's Supper 'is rightly called a fountain of love' (*Babylonian Captivity* [1520] WA6.519,25–26; LW36.46) that not only creates the communion of saints through its reception but also is the community's self-offering to each other. The inseparableness of worship and social ethics is apparent already in Luther's 1519 tract addressed to the laity, *The Blessed Sacrament of the Holy and True Body of Christ, and the Brotherhoods*. Here are the foundations for Luther's theological and legislative contributions to social welfare based on his conviction that worship is the foundation for service to others (Lindberg 1993, 1996, 2008). In his 1523 'Preface' to the Leisnig ordinance for community welfare, Luther wrote, 'Now there is no greater service of God [*gottes dienst*, i.e.,

fidelity to scripture, reformers' apostolicity, the Eucharist in both kinds, Christ's physical presence in the Mass, infant baptism and right confession, form a satisfying iconographic and theological gestalt' (Noble 2006: 123).

[2] For a review of the eucharistic controversies, see Lindberg (2010: 99–101, 131–6, 172–87). The argument by some contemporary advocates of an ecumenical liturgical renewal that Luther erred in rejecting the eucharistic prayer is strongly countered by Wendebourg (1998, 2009) and Olson (2007).

worship] than Christian love which helps and serves the needy, as Christ himself will judge and testify at the Last Day' (WA12.13,26–30; LW45.172–173; cf. Junghans 2001: 135). Luther understood worship as the impetus to serve the neighbour. Worship is not 'for the sake of reward, temporal or eternal, but alone to the glory of God and the neighbor's good' (*Concerning the Order of Public Worship* [1523], WA12.36,33–34; LW53.13). Indeed, Luther can characterize Christian daily life as worship (*Gottesdienst*) because to serve the neighbour and thus obey God's commandment is worship. Conversely, Luther viewed monastic contempt for daily life as idolatrous self-chosen works in place of obedience to God's commands. Once again, we see Luther's connection of piety, prayer, and worship to vocation. 'Vocation is the work of faith; vocation is worship in the realm of the world' (Vajta 1952: 314, cf. 21–3, 305–6, 309–14; cf. Lindberg 1993: 100; Lindberg 1996: 251–4).

IV. FRONTIERS FOR FUTURE RESEARCH

The importance of prayer in Luther's theology, his tracts on prayer, and his explications of the Lord's Prayer are well known. What is yet to be exploited 'as a source of prime importance for the comprehension and practice of prayer according to the reformer is his correspondence' (Arnold 2000; Wartenberg 2008: 121).

Another area for continuing research is the influence of Luther's view of prayer upon succeeding generations. The scholarship on prayer among sixteenth-century Lutherans is relatively sparse. The lack of an entry on 'Prayer' in the *Oxford Encyclopedia of the Reformation* indicates that scholars have given little attention to prayer in any group in sixteenth-century Europe. The recent *Luther Handbuch*, edited by Albrecht Beutel, also does not have a specific entry on 'prayer'. Yet the continuing interest among scholars in grass-roots expressions of faith would seem to compel an interest in this common religious practice (Haemig 2004).

'The history of piety is a model example for an interdisciplinary research project' (Molitor 1976: 19–20). Jung states that evangelical piety in the century of the Reformation has hardly been made the subject of research. Such central themes as baptism, worship, house devotions, use of the Bible, and attending the dying are completely lacking in studies of the history of piety (Jung 1998: 19).

Hamm notes that the medieval theology of piety was disseminated not only through texts but also 'by a flood of painted, printed, and plastic images'. 'The [medieval] Christian is expected to ascend to heaven on the ladder of virtue. And the sources convey the common conviction that no-one can be saved without his or her own volition and ability' (Hamm 2004: 23–4, 89). The studies by Noble (2006, 2009) and Aurelius (2009) have focused on Cranach's Wittenberg Altarpiece to discuss Luther's understanding of worship. Another image to explore is the centrality of the ascent motif in medieval piety depicted by 'the ladder to heaven'. In light of Luther's repeated assertions that all who strive to ascend to heaven will only 'break their necks' (sermons on John's Gospel

1–4 [1538], WA47.61, 24–40; sermon on Genesis 28 [1520], WA9.406,17–20), the piety of 'Himmelsleiter' images deserves more attention. To date there is Anders Nygren's classic study from the 1930s (Nygren 1953), and more recently the studies by Gottfried Seebass (1985); Christian Heck (1999); Christoph Weimer (1999); Bonnie Noble (2006, 2009); and Berndt Hamm (2007: esp. 245).

REFERENCES

Aarflot, Andreas (1977). 'Typen Lutherischer Frömmigkeit'. In *Die Evangelisch-Lutherische Kirche: Vergangenheit und Gegenwart*, ed. Vilmos Vajta, 161–79.

Arnold, Matthieu (2000). 'Invitation et initiation à la prière dans les letters de Martin Luther'. *Revue de l'histoire des religions* 217: 345–61.

Aurelius, Carl Axel (2009). 'Gottesdienst als Quelle des christlichen Lebens bei Martin Luther', *Lutherjahrbuch* 76: 221–34.

Axmacher, Elke (1995). 'Fromm aus Glauben—Überlegungen zu einem theologischen Begriff von Frömmigkeit'. In *Frömmigkeit: gelebte Religion als Forschungsaufgabe; interdisziplinäre Studientage*, ed. Bernd Jaspert. Paderborn: Bonifatius, 65–78.

Bayer, Oswald (1988). 'Oratio, Meditatio, Tentatio. Eine Besinnung auf Luthers Theologieverständnis'. *Lutherjahrbuch* 55: 7–59.

—— (2003). *Living by Faith: Justification and Sanctification*, trans. Geoffrey Bromily. Grand Rapids, MI: Eerdmans.

—— (2007). *Theology the Lutheran Way*, ed. and trans. Jeffrey G. Silcock and Mark C. Mattes. Grand Rapids, MI: Eerdmans.

—— (2008). *Martin Luther's Theology: A Contemporary Interpretation*, trans. Thomas H. Trapp. Grand Rapids, MI: Eerdmans.

Beutel, Albrecht (ed.) (2005). *Luther Handbuch*. Tübingen: Mohr/Siebeck.

Beyer, Michael (2007). 'Martin Luthers Betbüchlein'. *Lutherjahrbuch* 74: 29–50.

Brecht, Martin (1998). '"Und willst das Beten von uns han". Zum Gebet und seiner Praxis bei Martin Luther'. In *Die frühe Reformation in Deutschland als Umbruch*, ed. Bernd Moeller and Stephen E. Buckwalter. Gütersloh: Gütersloher Verlagshaus, 268–88.

Brown, Christopher Boyd (2008). 'Devotional Life in Hymns, Liturgy, Music, and Prayer'. In *Lutheran Ecclesiastical Culture, 1550–1675*, ed. Robert Kolb. Leiden and Boston: Brill, 205–58.

Dingel, Irene (2006). '"Dass man Gott immer in den Ohren liege". Das rechte Beten bei Martin Luther'. In *Sehnsüchtig nach Leben. Aufbrüche zu neuer Frömmigkeit*, ed. Peter Freybe. Wittenberg: Drei Kastanien Verlag, 28–49.

Drehsen, Volker (1995). 'Theologische Frömmigkeitsforschung?' In *Frömmigkeit. Gelebte Religion als Forschungsaufgabe; interdisziplinäre Studientage*, ed. Bernd Jaspert. Paderborn: Bonifatius, 45–63.

Haemig, Mary Jane (2004). 'Jehoshaphat and His Prayer among Sixteenth-Century Lutherans'. *Church History* 73: 522–35.

—— (2009). 'Praying as Talking Back to God in Luther's Genesis Lectures'. *Lutheran Quarterly* N.S. 23: 270–95.

Haemig, Mary Jane and Robert Kolb (2008). 'Preaching in Lutheran Pulpits in the Age of Confessionalization'. In *Lutheran Ecclesiastical Culture, 1550–1675*, ed. Robert Kolb. Leiden and Boston: Brill, 117–57.

Hamm, Berndt (1977). 'Frömmigkeit als Gegenstand theologiegeschichtlicher Forschung. Methodisch-historische Überlegungen am Beispiel von Spätmittelalter und Reformation'. *Zeitschrift für Theologie und Kirche* 74: 464–77.

—— (2004). *The Reformation of Faith in the Context of Late Medieval Theology and Piety*, ed. Robert J. Bast. Leiden and Boston: Brill.

—— (2007). 'Wie mystisch war der Glaube Luthers?' In *Gottes Nähe Unmittelbar erfahren: Mystik im Mittelalter und bei Martin Luther*, ed. Berndt Hamm and Volker Leppin. Tübingen: Mohr/ Siebeck, 237–87.

Hamm, Berndt and Volker Leppin (eds.) (2007). *Gottes Nähe Unmittelbar erfahren. Mystik im Mittelalter und bei Martin Luther*. Tübingen: Mohr/Siebeck.

Heck, Christian (1999). *L'échelle céleste dans l'art du moyan âge. Une histoire de la quête du ciel*. Paris: Flammarion.

Hendrix, Scott (2004). 'Martin Luther's Reformation of Spirituality'. In *Harvesting Martin Luther's Reflections on Theology, Ethics, and the Church*, ed. Timothy J. Wengert. Grand Rapids, MI: Eerdmans, 240–60.

Hillerbrand, Hans J. (1999). 'The Road Less Traveled? Reflections on the Enigma of Lutheran Spirituality'. In *Let Christ Be Christ: Theology, Ethics & World Religions in the Two Kingdoms. Essays in Honor of the Sixty-Fifth Birthday of Charles L. Manske*, ed. Daniel M. Harmelink. Huntington Beach: Tentatio Press, 129–40.

Jaspert, Bernd (1995). 'Frömmigkeit und Kirchengeschichte'. In *Frömmigkeit. Gelebte Religion als Forschungsaufgabe; interdisziplinäre Studientage*, ed. Jaspert. Paderborn: Bonifatius, 123–68.

Jung, Martin (1998). *Frömmigkeit und Theologie bei Philipp Melanchthon. Das Gebet im Leben und in der Lehre des Reformators*. Tübingen: Mohr/Siebeck.

Junghans, Helmar (2001). *Spätmittelalter, Luthers Reformation, Kirche in Sachsen. Ausgewählte Aufsätze*, ed. Michael Beyer and Günther Wartenberg. Leipzig: Evangelische Verlagsanstalt.

—— (2004). 'Luther on the Reform of Worship'. In *Harvesting Martin Luther's Reflections on Theology, Ethics, and the Church*, ed. Timothy J. Wengert. Grand Rapids, MI: Eerdmans, 207–25.

Karant-Nunn, Susan (1997). *Reformation of Ritual: An Interpretation of Early Modern Germany*. London and New York: Routledge.

Kittelson, James M. (1995). 'Contemporary Spirituality's Challenge to Sola Gratia'. *Lutheran Quarterly* N.S. 9: 367–90.

Koch, Traugott (2001). *Johann Habermanns 'Betbüchlein' im Zusammenhang seiner Theologie. Eine Studie zur Gebetsliteratur und zur Theologie des Luthertums im 16. Jahrhundert*. Tübingen: Mohr/Siebeck.

—— (2002). 'Luthers reformatorisches Verständnis des Gebets'. In *Das Gebet*, ed. Friedrich-Otto Scharbau. Erlangen: Martin-Luther Verlag, 47–66.

Kolb, Robert (2009). 'Models of the Christian Life in Luther's Genesis Sermons and Lectures'. *Lutherjahrbuch* 76: 193–220.

Krey, Philip D. W. and Peter D. S. Krey (eds.) (2007). *Luther's Spirituality*. New York: Paulist Press.

Leaver, Robin (2007). *Luther's Liturgical Music: Principles and Implications*. Grand Rapids, MI: Eerdmans.

Lienhard, Marc (1997). *La foi vecue. Etudes d'histoire de la spiritualité*. Strasbourg: Associations des Publications de la Faculté de Théologie Protestante.

—— (2002). 'La piété comme objet d'étude de l'historiographie'. In *Frömmigkeit und Spiritualität. Auswirkungen der Reformation im 16. und 17. Jahrhundert*, ed. Matthieu Arnold and Rolf Decot. Mainz: Zabern, 7–14.

Lindberg, Carter (1984). 'Justice and Injustice in Luther's Judgment of Holiness Movements'. In *Luther's Ecumenical Significance*, ed. Peter Manns and Harding Meyer. Philadelphia: Fortress, 161–81.

—— (1993). *Beyond Charity: Reformation Initiatives for the Poor*. Minneapolis: Fortress.

—— (1996). 'Luther's Concept of Offering' *dialog* 35: 251–57.

—— (1999). 'Do Lutherans Shout Justification but Whisper Sanctification?' *Lutheran Quarterly* 13: 1–20.

—— (ed.) (2005). *The Pietist Theologians: An Introduction to Theology in the Seventeenth and Eighteenth Centuries*. Oxford: Blackwell.

—— (2008). 'No Greater Service to God than Christian Love: Insights from Martin Luther'. In *Social Ministry in the Lutheran Tradition*, ed. Foster R. McCurley. Minneapolis: Fortress, 50–68.

—— (2010). *The European Reformations*, 2nd rev. edn. Oxford: Wiley-Blackwell.

Mikoteit, Matthias (2004). *Theologie und Gebet bei Luther. Untersuchungen zur Psalmenvorlesung 1532–1535*. Berlin and New York: de Gruyter.

Molitor, Hansgeorg (1976). 'Frömmigkeit in Spätmittelalter und früher Neuzeit als historische-methodisches Problem'. In *Festgabe für Ernst Walter Zeeden*, ed. Horst Rabe, Hansgeorg Molitor, and Hans-Christoph Rublack. Münster: Aschendorff, 1–20.

Muir, Edward (1997). *Ritual in Early Modern Europe*. Cambridge: Cambridge University Press.

Noble, Bonnie (2006). 'The Wittenberg Altarpiece and the Image of Identity'. *Reformation* 11: 79–129.

—— (2009). *Lucas Cranach the Elder: Art and Devotion of the German Reformation*. Lanham, MD: University Press of America.

Nygren, Anders (1953). *Agape and Eros*, trans. Philip Watson. Philadelphia: Westminster.

Olson, Oliver K. (2007). *Reclaiming the Lutheran Liturgical Heritage*. Minneapolis: ReClaim Resources.

Opahle, Joachim (2005). 'Spiritualität und Zeitgeist. Über die Frömmigkeit der Werbung'. In *Frömmigkeit. Eine verlorene Kunst*, ed. Andreas Hölscher and Anja Middelbeck-Varwick. Münster: Lit Verlag, 142–56.

Peters, Albrecht (1992). *Kommentar zu Luthers Katechismen*. Vol. 3: *Das Vaterunser*, ed. Gottfried Seebass. Göttingen: Vandenhoeck & Ruprecht.

Ratzmann, Wolfgang (2007). 'Danken, loben und bitten in Luthers Deutscher Messe und in heutigen lutherischen Agenden'. *Lutherjahrbuch* 74: 91–112.

Russell, William R. (1999). 'Prayer: The Practical Focus of Luther's Theology'. In *Let Christ Be Christ: Theology, Ethics & World Religions in the Two Kingdoms. Essays in Honor of the Sixty-Fifth Birthday of Charles L. Manske*, ed. Daniel M. Harmelink. Huntington Beach: Tentatio Press, 293–8.

—— (2005). *Praying for Reform: Luther, Prayer, and the Christian Life*. Minneapolis: Fortress.

Schulz, Freder (1976). *Die Gebete Luthers. Edition, Bibliographie und Wirkungsgeschichte*. Gütersloh: Gütersloher Verlagshaus.

—— (1983). 'Der Gottesdienst bei Luther'. In *Leben und Werk Martin Luthers von 1526 bis 1546*, 2 vols., ed. Helmar Junghans. Berlin: Evangelische Verlagsanstalt, 297–302, 811–25.

—— (1984). 'Gebetbücher III: Reformations- und Neuzeit'. *TRE* 12 (1984): 109–19.

Seebass, Gottfried (1985). *Die Himmelsleiter des hl. Bonaventura von Lukas Cranach d. Ä. Zur Reformation eines Holzschnitts*. Heidelberg: Winter.

Stolt, Birgit (1994). 'Luther on God as Father'. *Lutheran Quarterly* 8: 384–95.

—— (2000). *Martin Luther. Rhetorik des Herzens*. Tübingen: Mohr/Siebeck.

Thompson, Marjorie (2000). *A Simple Way to Pray by Martin Luther*. Louisville: Westminster John Knox.

Vajta, Vilmos (1952). *Die Theologie des Gottesdienstes bei Luther*. Stockholm: Svenska Kyrkans Diakonistyrelses Bokförlag.

—— (1983). 'Luther als Beter'. In *Leben und Werk Martin Luthers von 1526 bis 1546*, 2 vols., ed. Helmar Junghans. Berlin: Evangelische Verlagsanstalt, 279–95.

Wartenberg, Günther (2008). 'Martin Luthers Beten für Freunde und gegen Feinde', *Lutherjahrbuch* 75: 113–24.

Weimer, Christoph (1999). *Luther, Cranach und die Bilder. Gesetz und Evangelium—Schlüssel zum reformatorischen Bildgebrauch*. Stuttgart: Calwer.

Wendebourg, Dorothea (1998). 'Luthers Reform der Messe—Bruch oder Kontinuität?' In *Die frühe Reformation in Deutschland als Umbruch*, ed. Bernd Moeller and Stephen E. Buckwalter. Gütersloh: Gütersloher Verlagshaus, 289–306.

—— (2009). *Essen zum Gedächtnis. Der Gedächtnis-Befehl in den Abendmahlstheologien der Reformation*. Tübingen: Mohr/Siebeck.

Wengert, Timothy J. (2009). 'Luther on Prayer in the Large Catechism'. In *The Pastoral Luther: Essays on Martin Luther's Practical Theology*, ed. Wengert. Grand Rapids, MI: Eerdmans, 171–97.

Wingren, Gustaf (1957). *Luther on Vocation*, trans. Carl C. Rasmussen. Philadelphia: Muhlenberg.

Wriedt, Markus (2006). 'Von Kindern und Eltern, Engeln und Teufeln. Reformatorishe Spiritualität und pädagogischer Neubeginn bei Luther'. In *Sehnsüchtig nach Leben. Aufbrüche zu neuer Frömmigkeit*, ed. Peter Freybe. Wittenberg: Drei Kastanien Verlag, 94–119.

Wunder, Heide (1998). '"Iusticia, Teutonica fromkeyt". Theologische Rechtfertigung und bürgerliche Rechtschaffenheit. Ein Beitrag zur Sozial-Geschichte eines theologischen Konzepts'. In *Die frühe Reformation in Deutschland als Umbruch*, ed. Bernd Moeller and Stephen E. Buckwalter. Gütersloh: Gütersloher Verlagshaus, 307–32.

SUGGESTED READING

Arnold, Matthieu (2002). 'Introduction'. In *Frömmigkeit und Spiritualität. Auswirkungen der Reformation im 16. und 17. Jahrhundert*, ed. Matthieu Arnold and Rolf Decot. Mainz: Zabern, 1–5.

Beutel, Albrecht (2006). '"Einswerden mit Christus". Die Aufnahme mystischer Frömmigkeit bei Martin Luther'. In *Sehnsüchtig nach Leben. Aufbrüche zu neuer Frömmigkeit*, ed. Peter Freybe. Wittenberg: Drei Kastanien Verlag, 79–93.

Burger, Christoph (2006). '"Durch Furcht soll Liebe ihren Einzug halten". Spätmittelalterliche Frömmigkeit zwischen Gnade und Furcht'. In *Sehnsüchtig nach Leben. Aufbrüche zu neuer Frömmigkeit*, ed. Peter Freybe. Wittenberg: Drei Kastanien Verlag, 10–27.

Dieter, Theodor (2008). 'Luther as Critic and Advocate of Spirituality'. *Lutheran Forum* (Winter): 34–40.

Drehsen, Volker (2006). "'Wo Gott redet, da wohnt er auch". Konfessionsbilder Lutherischer Frömmigkeit'. In *Sehnsüchtig nach Leben. Aufbrüche zu neuer Frömmigkeit*, ed. Peter Freybe. Wittenberg: Drei Kastanien Verlag, 50–78.

Hamm, Berndt (1982). *Frömmigkeitstheologie am Anfang des 16. Jahrhunderts. Studien zu Johannes von Paltz und seinen Umkreis.* Tübingen: Mohr/Siebeck.

Jung, Martin (1995). 'Bemerkungen zur frömmigkeitsgeschichtlichen Erforschung der Reformationszeit'. In *Frömmigkeit. Gelebte Religion als Forschungsaufgabe; interdisziplinäre Studientage*, ed. Bernd Jaspert. Paderborn: Bonifatius, 93–100.

Junghans, Helmar (2007). 'Gott danken, loben und bitten im Alltag bei Martin Luther'. *Lutherjahrbuch* 74: 51–68.

Scribner, Robert W. (1994). 'Volksglaube und Volksfrömmigkeit. Begriffe und Historiographie'. In *Volksfrömmigkeit in der Frühen Neuzeit*, ed. Hansgeorg Molitor and Heribert Smolinsky. Münster: Aschendorff, 121–38.

Smolinsky, Heribert (1994). 'Volksfrömmigkeit als Thema der neueren Forschung. Beobachtungen und Aspekte'. In *Volksfrömmigkeit in der Frühen Neuzeit*, ed. Hansgeorg Molitor and Heribert Smolinsky. Münster: Aschendorff, 9–16.

Stolt, Birgit (2002). 'Zum Katechismusgebet in Luthers "Betbüchlein" (1522). Pensumaufsagen oder "Gespräch des Herzens mit Gott?"' In *Das Gebet*, ed. Friedrich-Otto Scharbau. Erlangen: Martin-Luther Verlag, 67–83.

Vajta, Vilmos (1977). 'Der Gottesdienst und das sakramentale Leben'. In *Die Evangelisch-Lutherische Kirche: Vergangenheit und Gegenwart*, ed. Vajta. Stuttgart: Evangelisches Verlagswerk, 135–60.

Weimer, Christoph (2009). 'Luther and Cranach on Justification in Word and Image'. In *The Pastoral Luther: Essays on Martin Luther's Practical Theology*, ed. Timothy J. Wengert. Grand Rapids, MI: Eerdmans, 292–309.

CHAPTER 30

....

LUTHER'S VIEWS OF THE JEWS AND TURKS

....

GREGORY MILLER

I. The Social and Theological Significance of Luther's Views

....

INCREASING multicultural contacts as well as contemporary crisis have prompted scholarly interest in the subject of this chapter. In particular, the Nazi regime's use of Luther's anti-Judaic writings and the widely disseminated claim that Luther was a forerunner to the Holocaust has been a significant stimulus for study. An amazing amount of scholarly energy has been dedicated to understanding and explaining (and sometimes attempting to explain away) Luther's horrific anti-Jewish writings. The terrorist attacks against the United States on 11 September 2001 also have prompted a flood of scholarship on the history of relations between the Christian West and the Islamic world. Although occasional scholars over the course of the twentieth century had investigated Luther's responses to the Turks, as they had all other subjects in his corpus of writings, this contemporary crisis has provided stimulus for a renewed investigation of his significance for the history of Christian–Islamic relations.

All of this scholarly interest is welcome. But one should be cautious lest contemporary concerns and post-Enlightenment understandings of religions as mutually exclusive, coherent bodies of belief and practice warp the inquiry from the outset. Luther knew nothing of 'World Religions'. Modern categorization and frameworks would have been incomprehensible to him. This is not to say that a combined discussion of Luther on the Jews and Turks is anachronistic. At least 123 different Luther writings in the *Weimar Ausgabe* mention Jews and Turks together. Thirteen distinct references are made to the Turks in Luther's *On the Jews and their Lies* alone, for example. However, Luther would have found the pairing to be incomplete—not because it did not include Hindus and Buddhists, but because it did not include papists, *Schwärmer*, and other kinds of unbelievers. For Luther, Jews and Turks were part of a larger group of satanically inspired enemies of the people of God. The fundamental division within humankind was between the true church and the false church, true worship and false worship, the people of God and the servants of the Devil. The Turks were not in the same camp as the Jews because they represented World Religions, but because they embodied a works-righteousness which was the greatest enemy of the gospel.

II. PAST SCHOLARSHIP ON THE SUBJECT

There is an enormous literature on the topic of 'Luther and the Jews'. Of particular importance is Heiko Oberman's *The Roots of Anti-Semitism in the Age of Renaissance and Reformation* (1984). Oberman's small book is helpful in placing Luther's writings in the context of medieval Christian beliefs concerning the Jews as well as the controversies surrounding Christian Hebraism. He demonstrated that those often credited with more tolerant positions, such as Reuchlin and Erasmus, could be intensely anti-Jewish even if they did not utilize the extreme rhetoric of Luther. Most important is Oberman's claim that to speak of anti-Semitism in sixteenth-century Germany is an anachronism. Anti-Semitism, the hatred of Jews as an ethnic group, could not exist before the development of modern theories of race. Luther was vehemently anti-Judaic, but understood Jews to be religiously, not ethnically, separate.

Although not a work of sound scholarship, the first widely popularized version of the argument that Luther was a predecessor to National Socialist anti-Semitism was found in William Shirer's *Rise and Fall of the Third Reich* (1960). The history of the subsequent counter-arguments and qualifications are summarized in Siemon-Netto (2007), an important corrective to the common but facile connection made between Luther and Hitler.

Peter von der Osten-Sacken (2002) provides straightforward descriptions of Luther's and others' descriptions with particular regard to the influence of the vehemently anti-Jewish convert Anton Margaritha. The book also extends the discussion to later Lutheran attitudes towards Judaism. Essays edited by Dean Phillip Bell and Stephen G. Burnett (2006) help to establish the broader context for Luther's views of the Jews. Bell and Burnett substantiate the scholarly consensus that Judaism was not at the periphery of Reformation concerns, but because of the Reformation emphasis on Biblicism (and especially the Hebrew language and texts), it was central to religious developments in the sixteenth century.

Literature on Luther and the Turks is less extensive. Norman Daniels (1993) traces the formation of Western European understanding of Islam as it developed during the Middle Ages into a self-contained and perpetuating body of largely erroneous beliefs which enabled the West to demonize and eventually dominate Islamic West Asia. Daniels' monograph is generally seen as the starting place for understanding Western views of Islam at the outset of the Reformation. Other important contextual studies include Hartmut Bobzin (1995); Nancy Bisaha's (2004) examination of understandings of the Turks and the use of images of them in Renaissance literature; and Thomas Burman (2007).

Johannes Ehmann (2008) provides the most thorough analysis of Luther's actual understanding of Islam. Ehmann focuses on an analysis of a relatively neglected work, Luther's translation of a medieval apologetic by Ricoldo di Monte Croce. Ehmann demonstrates how Luther transformed this traditional medieval document to communicate his theological understanding of Islam as well as to (simultaneously) combat the Roman church. The most extensive treatment of the subject in English is Adam Francisco's *Martin Luther and Islam* (2007). A host of shorter articles on Luther and the Turks deal largely with his understanding of Islam and especially his rejection of crusading. Among these are essays by Rudolf Mau (1983), Siegfried Raeder (2003), and Gregory Miller (2004).

III. Luther on the Jews and Turks

Among the prominent beliefs and attitudes in the Christian West concerning the Jews at the outset of the Protestant Reformation were accusations of blood libel (that Jews captured and slaughtered Christian children for their blood), claims of the theft and desecration of the consecrated host, greed, and the poisoning of wells. Little or no attempt was made to gain any accurate understanding of Jewish life and thought. Luther inherited this tradition. However, Luther's anti-Judaism was different than many of his medieval predecessors because it was not primarily driven by these accusations. Luther's engagement with Judaism developed out of a central framework of Reformation theology contrasting flesh with spirit, salvation by works with salvation by faith, and in its application to the Jews, an opposition between synagogue and church. A strong Christological interpretation of the Old Testament was central for Luther, which led him into sharp conflict with what he considered to be the 'rabbis' interpretation'. Unlike some humanists with an interest in Hebrew, Luther had few actual encounters with Jews, but primarily gained his understanding through late medieval commentators on Scripture (especially Nicholas of Lyra and Paul of Burgos—himself a convert from Judaism), Christian humanist works (such as the commentary on Isaiah by Oecolampadius and on the Psalms by Martin Bucer), as well as through polemic writings such as the convert Anton Margaritha's *The Entire Jewish Faith* (1530).

There is tension and apparent self-contradiction in Luther's engagement with Judaism. In biblical exegesis he took full advantage of developments in grammatical understanding of Hebrew language and the literal meaning of the Old Testament which would not have taken place except for Renaissance Christian Hebraism and its engagement with Jewish scholars. He criticized the church for living out a false gospel in front of the Jews, treating them poorly, and reducing the already small chance that they might receive the gospel. This is most famously present in the humane recommendations for treatment of the Jewish communities of Christendom in his 1523 *That Jesus Christ was Born a Jew* (WA11.314–336; LW45.199–229). In terms of secular aspects of life such as place of residence and choice of work, in this writing Luther goes so far as to recommend that Jews be given equal opportunity and be integrated into society with the hope that some would convert.

Nonetheless, from his earliest Psalm lectures through his last writings, Luther included the Jews within the general category of the 'godless' and the 'enemies'. Rabbinic interpretations of Scripture are characterized as a 'killing' of the biblical text (WA4.98,446, 3.586). As early as his glosses and comments on the Psalms (1513–16, WA3 and 4), Luther expresses a form of replacement-theology, that the church replaces Israel as God's chosen people and heir of the Old Testament promises (Hendrix 1974). The primary role of the Jews after the resurrection of Jesus is to serve as an example of punishment for rejecting Christ. Luther identifies this punishment as the Jew's never-ending exile and repression. This theological understanding remained consistent throughout his life. Luther also was hesitant about the traditional Christian expectation of a large-scale conversion of the Jews at the end of time. The return of Jews to the Holy Land was never a part of his eschatological system. In exegesis of Ezekiel 38 and 39 he stated that the 'mountains of Israel' which Gog and Magog will strike at the end of time must be Europe because the Jews 'have no longer any hope of a re-gathering' (WA30,2.225).

Luther's advice for the practical treatment of Jews does seem, however, to have undergone a distinct shift in the late 1520s. Some scholars have speculated that this was the result of an encounter between Luther and representatives of the Jewish community which occurred in 1525/6. Luther's *That Jesus Christ Was Born a Jew* certainly must have encouraged some in the Jewish community to see him as a potential advocate. They must have been sorely disappointed in their face-to-face meeting. Rabbinic representatives were not open to a re-evaluation of scriptural exegesis under Luther's tutelage, nor were they convinced by him that Jesus was Messiah. After the fact, Luther was angry when the rumour was reported to him that the Jews travelling under the safe conduct had actually blasphemed Christ.

Over the next few years his attitude would harden as he heard rumours of Jewish attempts to convert Christians. The tolerance he earlier had advocated in order to encourage conversions of Jews now looked like a foolish concession to an aggressive, satanic enemy. Any tolerance came to be viewed by Luther as a sinful participation in public Jewish blasphemy. The perspective was particularly demonstrated in Luther's answer to the request of Josels von Rosenheim, a recognized representative of German Jews, for support in obtaining safe transit (WABr8.89–91). Although in his response Luther re-stated a commitment to the 'friendly treatment' of the Jews, the '*freundliche Haltung*' turned out to consist of a firm rejection of the request, a stern warning, and a reminder that the Jews lived under the wrath of God.

Luther's denunciation of the Jews reached its height in three 1543 writings, *On the Jews and their Lies* (WA53.417–552; LW47.137–306), *On the Schem Hamphoras and on the Lineage of Christ* (WA53. 610–648), and *On the Last Words of David* (WA54.16–100).

These writings echo the most extreme late medieval anti-Judaic polemic. In the 1520s Luther expressed scepticism about anti-Judaic traditions such as the blood libel, well poisoning, and desecration of the host; these writings, however, contain unrestrained rumour-mongering. The supposed Jewish 'beliefs' Luther attacked in them included: the claim to be God's chosen people, the expectation of a coming messiah who will lead a bloody extermination of Christians, that Jesus was a magician, and that Mary was a whore. In the fever-pitch of Luther's denunciations the presence of Jews becomes a kind of demon possession for which the only answer is an exorcism. Any toleration, like his self-described 'foolish' toleration in *On That Jesus Christ was Born a Jew*, is nothing short of an alliance with the Devil. Luther considered his earlier expressions to be foolish naïveté (WA53.523). Luther's advice to the political authorities, described as a *sharfen Barmherzigkeit* ('sharp mercy' or 'harsh mercy'), advocates a chilling series of violent actions which remind the modern reader of the Nazi *Kristallnacht*: burn their synagogues, destroy their homes, burn the Talmud and Jewish books, ban the rabbis from teaching, take their possessions, make the young Jewish men into slave workers, expel those who refuse to be baptized. He ended his last sermon, preached in Eisleben on 14 February 1546, with a warning against the Jews in which he reiterated his call for conversion or expulsion (WA51.187–194).

These recommendations concerning social policy in regard to the Jews seem to have had little direct social impact, even in Saxony, although they continued to provide a theological framework of interpretation and contributed to fierce anti-Judaism among some Lutheran clergy in the century after Luther's death. Only in the late nineteenth century did his severe anti-Jewish writings have renewed widespread influence, albeit shorn of their original theological context and placed in the framework of developing German anti-Semitism.

In contrast with his understanding of the Jews, Luther's engagement with Islam was driven by the Ottoman advance into central Europe, later interpreted in a fundamentally apocalyptic framework. Luther's original position was that God had permitted the success of the Turks due to Christian unfaithfulness. The Turks were the 'rod of God'. Just as God had allowed the children of Israel's enemies to defeat them in order to draw Israel back, so God was using the Turks to drive Christian repentance. Many lauded his 1518 statement 'to fight against the Turk is to fight against God, who is punishing our sins through them' (WA7.140). Instead of fighting, the first action must be for Christians to genuinely repent. This fundamental understanding of the role of the Turks in salvation history remained consistent throughout Luther's life.

In 1529 the Ottoman armies moved against central Europe in a campaign culminating in the famous siege of Vienna. Although forced to withdraw, Sulaiman gave every indication that the Ottoman armies would be back. These events were a wake-up call concerning the severity of the Turkish threat. Luther reported that the news of the siege actually made him physically ill (WABr5.163). In two major pamphlets, *On War Against the Turks* (1529) (WA30,2.107–148; LW46.161–205) and *Muster Sermon Against the Turks* (1530) (WA30,2.160–197), Luther clarified his position concerning Christian response to the Turks. Some had understood his earlier statements to be advocating non-resistance (see

WA1.535, Luther's explanation to thesis 5). In these pamphlets he strongly emphasized the rejection of the crusade as a blasphemous confusion of spiritual and secular. Christians *as* Christians were not to participate in battle. Ecclesiastical attempts at military leadership angered God. Clergy were to preach and pray. Soldiers even had a right to protest a church-led crusade through disobedience. In *On War Against the Turks* he wrote, 'If I were a soldier and saw in the battlefield a priest's banner or cross, even if it were the very crucifix, I would run away as though the very devil were chasing me!' (WA30,2.115). There was no religious justification for any military action—be it against false Christians, heretics, or Turks. Spiritual enemies must be fought with spiritual weapons. No crusade or holy war was permissible. This represents a significant point of departure from the mainstream of medieval theology. Since Pope Gregory the Great (d. 604), theologians had argued that the coercion of those that held false beliefs was an appropriate cause of war.

Luther's criticism of the crusade mentality did not lead to a disavowal of violence against Turks. The *Muster Sermon* was written specifically to admonish the 'fist' against the Ottomans. For Luther, the war against the Turks was a 'good war'. Fighting is appropriate because it is the duty of legitimate rulers to defend society against the Turks, just as they would oppose all disturbers of the peace.

Eschatology was central in Luther's understanding of place of the Turks in history. He believed that the end of the world was near and thus the Devil was raging with his two weapons: the Antichrist (the papacy) and the Turks. According to Luther, 'The Turks are certainly the last and most furious raging of the devil against Christ...after the Turk comes the judgment' (WA30,2.162). He claimed that Gog and Magog were the biblical designation for the Turks. This was such an important point for him that he published his translation of Ezekiel 38 and 39 as a separate pamphlet, which included an introduction in which he made the connection explicit (WA30,2.223–226). Furthermore, Luther interpreted Revelation 20 to declare that after a thousand years (dated from approximately the rise of Islam), the Devil would gather Gog and Magog (the Turks) to besiege the city of God's people, but they would be destroyed by fire from heaven and cast into eternal damnation. In the end God will rescue his people. The fight against the Turks is the last event in history.

At times Luther could sound positive about the Turks. He publicly called for more accurate information on Islam. His influence was essential in gaining permission for the first printed Qur'an. In his preface to the *Booklet on the Rituals and Customs of the Turks* (1530), he praised Muslims for their piety, especially in comparison with Roman Catholics. He claimed that the discipline of the Turks would shame any papist so much that none would remain in his faith if he were to spend just three days with the Turks (WA30,2.205–208). However, in demonstrating the religious 'superiority' of the Turks over the papists Luther rather was highlighting the meaninglessness of works-righteousness. Islam is so strongly stamped by 'works' that every works-righteousness within or without Christianity could be characterized as 'Turkish'. Thus Luther's interpretation of the religion of the Turks is congruent with his interpretation of Judaism. The foundation of all orthodoxy and the difference between theological truth and falsehood was a correct understanding of the person and work of Jesus. Because of denial of the divinity of Christ, Islamic theology was categorically false.

When we integrate our discussion of Luther's engagement with the Jews with his understanding of the Turks, a point of discontinuity seems immediately to arise. If Luther did not believe that coercion concerning religion was appropriate, why did he advocate violent action of the state against Jews? Did a deep hatred drive him to bypass his theological convictions? The line seems to have been crossed for Luther as a result of what he considered to be public blasphemy. The state's toleration of Jewish blasphemy against Christ, even behind closed doors, amounted to a tacit support of that blasphemy. Left unpunished, this would bring the wrath of God. The elimination of blasphemy was not a matter for ecclesiastical authorities. But ecclesiastical authorities had an obligation to plead with the state to take action for the benefit of society. Did Luther not also consider the Qur'an to be publicly blasphemous? Certainly. But its publication, as long as it was done with the appropriate interpretative framework, was warranted in order to unmask the enemy. If there had been masjids within Saxony, Luther would have just as vociferously argued for their destruction and the expulsion of Muslims. He would have tolerated minarets no more than Torah arks.

IV. Themes for Future Research

One field of exciting recent scholarship on Luther and the Jews has been in the area of Christian Hebraism. Luther's somewhat conflicted relationship with this movement as well as its relationship to the Reformation in general deserves more attention. In addition, studies on the reception history of Luther's writings on the Jews have focused on the later sixteenth century and on the Nazi era. Relatively speaking, intervening periods have not been as thoroughly researched. We need not reiterate the 'lachrymose' view of Jewish history but should recognize the extraordinary range and nature of the contacts between Jews and Christians (real and imagined). We need to fully integrate our understanding of the history of Judaism in Europe with European history and to recognize Jews not simply as peripheral 'others' but as real and important historical actors who both shaped and were shaped by developments in the Protestant Reformation.

In recent decades scholars have recognized the importance of situating early modern Western Europe within the broader geographical context of its world. Important in this is the recognition of the role of the Ottoman Empire in the mental world of early modern Europeans. The Turks are everywhere in the writings of Western Christians in the sixteenth century. Luther and the reception of his ideas need to be brought more completely into this broader context.

Most importantly, we need to move beyond a scholarship which focuses primarily on examining only what Luther and his contemporaries said about the Jews and Muslims, granting posthumous rewards for tolerant ideas and demerits for perceived bigotry. We need a contextual approach which emphasizes why they wrote and how it shaped their world.

REFERENCES

Bell, Dan Phillip and Stephen G. Burnett (eds.) (2006). *Jews, Judaism and the Reformation in Sixteenth-Century Germany*. Leiden: Brill.

Bisaha, Nancy (2004). *Creating East and West: Renaissance Humanists and the Ottoman Turks*. Philadelphia: University of Pennsylvania Press.

Bobzin, Hartmut (1995). *Der Koran im Zeitalter der Reformation. Studien zur Frühgeschichte der Arabistik und Islamkunde in Europa*. Beirut and Stuttgart: Steiner.

Burman, Thomas (2007). *Reading the Qur'an in Latin Christendom, 1140–1560*. Philadelphia: University of Pennsylvania Press.

Daniels, Norman (1993). *Islam and the West: The Making of an Image*, revised edn. Oxford: Oneworld.

Ehmann, Johannes (2008). *Luther, Türken und Islam. Eine Untersuchung zum Türken- und Islambild Martin Luthers (1515–1546)*. Gütersloh: Gütersloher Verlagshaus.

Francisco, Adam (2007). *Martin Luther and Islam: A Study in Sixteenth-Century Polemics and Apologetics*. Leiden: Brill.

Hendrix, Scott (1974). *Ecclesia in via: Ecclesiological Developments in the Medieval Psalms Exegesis and the Dictata (1513–1515) of Martin Luther*. Leiden: Brill.

Mau, Rudolf (1983). 'Luthers Stellung zu den Türken'. In *Leben und Werk Martin Luthers von 1526 bis 1546*, ed. Helmar Junghans, vol. 2. Göttingen: Vandenhoeck & Ruprecht, 647–62.

Miller, Gregory (2004). 'Luther on the Turks and Islam'. In *Harvesting Martin Luther's Reflections on Theology, Ethics, and the Church*, ed. Timothy Wengert. Grand Rapids, MI: Eerdmans, 185–203.

Oberman, Heiko Augustinus (1984). *The Roots of Anti-Semitism in the Age of Renaissance and Reformation*, trans. James Porter. Philadelphia: Fortress.

Osten-Sacken, Peter von der (2002). *Martin Luther und die Juden. Neu untersucht anhand von Anton Margarithas 'Der gantz Jüdisch glaub' 1530/31*. Stuttgart: Kohlhammer.

Raeder, Siegfried (2003). *Der Islam und das Christentum. Eine historische und theologische Einführung*, 2nd edn. Neukirchen: Neukirchener Verlag.

Shirer, William (1960). *The Rise and Fall of the Third Reich*. New York: Simon & Schuster.

Siemon-Netto, Uwe (2007). *The Fabricated Luther: Refuting Nazi Connections and Other Modern Myths*, 2nd edn. Saint Louis: Concordia.

SUGGESTED READING

Bonfil, Robert (1996). 'Aliens Within: The Jews and Anti-Judaism'. In *Handbook of European History 1400–1600: Late Middle Ages, Renaissance and Reformation*, vol. 1, ed. Thomas A. Brady, Jr., Heiko A. Oberman, and James D. Tracy. Grand Rapids, MI: Eerdmans, 263–302.

Edwards, Mark U., Jr. (1983). *Luther's Last Battles: Politics and Polemics, 1531–46*. Ithaca: Cornell University Press.

CHAPTER 31

LUTHER AS A RESOURCE FOR CHRISTIAN DIALOGUE WITH OTHER WORLD RELIGIONS

J. PAUL RAJASHEKAR

MARTIN Luther lived in an age of prejudice where religious tolerance was non-existent, an era of religious disputations, not dialogue; polemics, not politeness; condemnation, not concord. One should not expect, therefore, Luther to be an advocate of interreligious engagement. Luther did, however, engage issues of the religions in his writings but as a medieval theologian in the context of Christendom. He was acquainted with religions of antiquity, classical philosophies, and, more seriously, with Judaism and the Islam of the Ottoman Turks. He was not aware of the full extent of religious diversity in the world, knew little about the 'grace-oriented' religions within Hinduism or Buddhism, and was only vaguely aware of the 'pagans' in the newly rediscovered Americas.

As a reformer of the church, Luther was primarily concerned with issues affecting Christendom. Unlike some of his contemporaries (notably Erasmus), he had little passion for exploring religions and cultures newly discovered through European territorial conquests. The question of salvation of people of other religions was not the focus of his theological discourse. Given his context and the limitations of the medieval world-view that he shared, Luther's 'theology of religions', understandably, was grounded in his biblical and theological convictions. He saw other religions as mirror images of a distorted Catholicism that he viewed as oriented to 'work-righteousness'.

Beyond his encounters with a few contemporary Jews and his knowledge of the Hebrew Scriptures, Luther's assessments of other religions are a priori judgements or postulates of his Christological convictions. His views were gleaned from the scant literature (especially on Islam) available to him, read from an apocalyptic perspective rather than grounded in any meaningful experiential engagement with their beliefs and practices. There is no evidence that he ever met a living Turkish Muslim. Given these limitations, it would seem impossible to find in Luther any relevant insights that can aid Christian engagement with religious pluralism today. This essay attempts to revisit Luther's profound theology and his theological dialectic for clues that can be stretched to their logical conclusion for interreligious engagement today.

The essay, first, provides an overview of Luther's understanding of religions. Second, it cursorily reviews selected literature on how interpreters of Luther have drawn on his insights for interreligious engagement. Building on that analysis, the third section engages in a critical reading of some key theological categories of Luther as a resource for contemporary engagement with religious pluralism today.

I. Luther on Religions

Luther, like most of his medieval contemporaries, was seldom directly concerned with the significance of religious beliefs and practices outside the realm of Christendom, except when they became a political or existential threat. As professor of Hebrew Scriptures, biblical scholar and exegete, he had ample opportunities to address the question of the salvation of those who have died without faith in Christ or continue to live outside the framework of the Christian church. His understanding of religions, however, was profoundly influenced by his reading of Hebrew Scriptures, and his views were coloured by traits of pagan antiquity he found in the Bible. He was drawn to biblical descriptions of idolatry within and outside Israel in the books of the law and prophets more than in the very short references to idolatry in the New Testament (Bornkamm 1969: 46–57). Underneath the varied forms of idolatry and polytheism, Luther did recognize the human longing or a religious need for some abstract notion of God, even a veneration of the divine name in natural religion and in forms of idolatry (WA14.587,16–588,25; LW9.53–54). But without the true knowledge of the divine Word they are nothing but false and fabricated knowledge. Therefore, they are ultimately meaningless idolization of human power (LW19.383,27–385,23; LW19.186–187). Luther forcefully stated his view in *On Bound Choice*:

> Moreover, since Christ is said to be 'the way, the truth, and the life' (John 14:6) and that categorically, so that whatever is not the way, but error, not truth but untruth, not life but death, it follows of necessity that 'free will', in as much as it neither is Christ, nor is in Christ, is fast bound in error, and untruth and death…outside of Christ there is nothing but Satan, outside of grace nothing but wrath, outside of light nothing but darkness, outside of truth nothing but a lie, outside of life nothing but death—were these things not so, what, I ask you would be the use of all the apostolic discourses and, indeed, of the entire Scriptures? (WA18.779,11–32; LW33.281–282)

Notwithstanding his reading of idolatry and paganism as evidenced in the Hebrew Scriptures through the lenses of *extra Christum nulla salus*, Luther was well aware of the wisdom bequeathed by certain noble pagans, especially, Cicero, Plautus, and Virgil.

He often quoted classical writers and admired their wisdom as something bestowed by God, yet he was reluctant to consider them as being among the elect: 'Since the world began, there have always been superior talents, greater learning, and a more intense earnestness among pagans than among Christians and the people of God. It is as Christ himself acknowledges: "the sons of this world are wiser than the sons of light" (Luke 6:18)...Who dare say that not one among them pursued truth with all his heart? Yet we are bound to maintain that not one of them reached it' (WA18.651,7–16; LW33.87), cf. Williams 1969; Grislis 1998). In *A Letter to Hans von Reichenberg* Luther responded to the critical question: 'Whether a person who dies without faith can be saved?' He noted the weight of the question and its implications for God's love and graciousness, especially in light of Saint Paul's claim that 'God desires all people to be saved' (1 Tim. 2:4). His response, however, was unyielding: 'God cannot and will not save anyone without faith....If God were to save anyone without faith, he would be acting contrary to his own words and would give himself the lie; yes, he would deny himself...It is impossible for God to save without faith, as it is impossible for divine truth to lie' (WA10,2.324,19–27; LW43.53–54). Luther consistently used the doctrine of justification as the decisive standard to distinguish between true and false religion. The religions known to him fall into two basic categories: one includes all religions outside the gospel (including the Roman distortion of the gospel and the divinely instituted sacrificial system instituted by Moses); the other includes only the gospel. Therefore, he urged that Christians should distinguish Christ from all religions of the world. Christ is to be placed above Moses. The forgiveness of sins and grace are greater than the whole world's act of worship (WA12.396–397; Althaus 1966: 128).

The insufficiency of all religions apart from Christ was the decisive standard by which Luther evaluated both Judaism and Islam, the two world religions familiar to him. His polemic and vitriolic outbursts against Jews and the uses and abuses of his legacy in the German Nazi and Communist regimes are too well known to be repeated here (Edwards 1983; Halpérin and Sovik 1984; Kremers 1987; Kaufmann 2006; Gritsch 2012). The Jewish rejection of Christ despite the direct testimony to the work of Christ in the Old Testament served as the premise of his anti-Judaism. In this regard Luther's views were no different from that of his contemporaries. In his early writings Luther was more sympathetic toward Jews and advocated a benevolent treatment of them as persecuted people, as 'blood relatives, cousins and brothers of our Lord of Christ', to whom alone God committed the Holy Scriptures, the law and the prophets, among all nations (WA11.315,25–33; LW45.201). His desire to convert the Jews was unsuccessful, however, and he became frustrated with rabbinical Judaism and its exegesis of Hebrew Scriptures. The incompatibility between his theological exegesis of Scripture and that of Talmudic Judaism made him bitter. Thus, in 1542 Luther published the infamous—his longest—writings about Jews, *On the Jews and Their Lies*, wherein he unleashed his anger by justifying burning synagogues and Jewish homes, confiscating and destroying Talmudic writings, forbidding rabbis to teach, forced hard labour for young Jews, and finally, expulsion from the land (WA53.417–552; LW47.137–306). Luther's invective against Jews in this writing is the culmination of his exegetical conflict with Rabbinical Judaism more than an expression of a deep sense of anti-Semitism. Nonetheless, Luther's views on Jews were indefensibly wrong and must be repudiated. He miserably failed to live up to his own theology of justification by grace, to 'let God be God', or to be 'a Christ to the neighbour', so brilliantly articulated in his writings as he consigned the Jews to God's wrath and judgement (Gritsch 2012: 138–42).

In contrast to his views on Jews, Luther's interest and polemic against Islam was prompted by historical circumstances, especially the military threat by the Ottoman Turks (Grislis 1974; Wallmann 1986; Rajashekar 1990; Kandler 1993; Henrich and Boyce 1996; Miller 2000; Rajashekar and Wengert 2002; Francisco 2007; Ehmann 2008). Quite early in his career, Luther's remarks against crusades in the indulgence contro-versy, referring to the Turks as God's rod for the punishment of Christian transgression, was used against him in the papal bull of excommunication. With the military threat of Ottoman Turks in the conquest of Hungary in 1526 and their appearance at the gates of Vienna in 1529, Luther felt compelled to clarify his earlier views on Christian crusades but also to undertake an analysis of the Turkish religion in order to educate his fellow Germans. In his *On War against the Turks* (1529) (WA30,2.107–148; LW46.161–205), he explicitly advocated war against Turks under the leadership of the emperor as part of his divinely bestowed office. The Turks, he argued, as much as they were agents of God's punishment, were also servants of the Devil, a favourite characterization of all his opponents. Luther, however, explicitly opposed all attempts to incite religious war for wrath or revenge, or self-seeking desires for honour, glory, and extension of territory (WA30.2.116,9–120,24, 130,22–34; LW46.170.4, 185–186).

In due course Luther pursued his interest in the Muslim religion by publishing other tracts and sermons, including introductions to Bibliander's Latin edition of the Qur'an and *The Refutation of the Qur'an*, by Brother Richard (Rajashekar 1990: 181–2; Henrich and Boyce 1996: 250–3). In these writings Luther primarily compared the religion of Turks with Christianity, although not systematically, focusing on Turkish morality, customs, and rituals, rather than their religion or their prophet Muhammad. He mis-understood the role of Muhammad in Islam and compared him to Jesus Christ. Not sur-prisingly, Luther found Islam a religion of 'works'. Because of the Muslim denial of the death of Christ and the exaltation of Muhammad over Christ, all of Islam was categori-cally false (WA30,2.122,5–123,18; LW46.176–178). At times, Luther grudgingly did praise the Turks for their piety and their cultural superiority; however, this was done to put down medieval Catholicism and the papists. He read the Qur'an as a collection of laws, not on par with the Bible, but similar to papal decretals, and therefore a 'foul, shameful book' containing only human wisdom without God's Word and spirit (WA30,2.121,30–122,12; LW46.176–177).

In summary, it should be obvious from the preceding analysis that Luther's under-standing of religions is context- and culture-bound. His thought was derived from a deep understanding of Scripture; it served as the primary tool for understanding and interpreting historical realities of his time. He was absolutely certain of the truth and the uniqueness of the Christian claims, based on the Bible and the doctrinal and the Christological assumptions derived from it. Luther, of course, lived in a religiously and culturally circumscribed context faced with external threats from the Turks. In that regard his views on religions were no different from those of most of his contemporaries. He could not go beyond imagining the religious threats from other faiths as instruments of God's wrath and could see no positive value in other religions. His view of history was influenced by his reading of the Book of Daniel, and some eclectic passages about the Antichrist in the New Testament are highly problematic. On the other hand, Luther anticipated the possibility that some day the Christendom he had known would undergo political and religious change. As an apologist for the Christian faith, he wanted his fellow Christians to be prepared to live under a different religious situation. Luther thus displays a pastoral concern for Christians in the event they were subject to Turkish rule and offered advice as how to witness to their faith and practice 'an existentially applied *theologia crucis*' (Barth 2013: 39–49). With that concern in mind, he had hoped to translate the Qur'an into German. For Luther the conversion of Turks seemed impossible. He therefore was content to offer an apologia for the Christian faith over against Islam (Luther's understanding of mission, a topic relevant to this essay, must be passed over here; for a recent study, see Öberg 2007).

II. Interpreters of Luther

Most interpreters of Luther who have maintained their fidelity to his grammar, if not his syntax, have sought to offer nuanced interpretations of his theology of religions so as to accommodate Christian engagement with other faiths. Paul Althaus, for example, attempted to stretch Luther's theology of religions with reference to the concept of 'general revelation' (*Uroffenbarung*) as the middle way between extolling other religions (Ernst Troeltsch) and practical condemnation of them (Karl Barth). 'General revelation', although God's work, is seen as distinct from Christ's revelation. Religions cannot be considered merely as 'works of man', and they remain part of a divine order or God's history with humans. Drawing on Luther's dialectic of law and gospel, Althaus sees a positive relationship between Christianity and other religions, a relationship of cooperation and dialogue. But that general revelation is ultimately insufficient without a salvific revelation (*Heilsoffenbarung*): thus, a positive evaluation of religions is undermined by a negative assessment of their value. God's work among religions of the world provides people with an original understanding of God so that they recognize the reality of God in the revelation of Jesus Christ (Althaus 1952: 17–22; Knitter 1974). Whatever knowledge, wisdom, and civic righteousness to be found among other religions, in the end, turn out to have no salvific significance. Thus Althaus' reconstruction of Luther's theology of religions does not go beyond Luther's own convictions in affirming an exclusivist stance.

Similar reconstructions are proffered by Lutheran theologians like Ratschow, Pannenberg, and Braaten, either adapting or nuancing Luther's theological categories of creation/redemption, God hidden/God revealed, law/gospel, and the like (Ratschow

1967; Pannenberg 1971; Martinson 1987; Rajashekar 1988; Pannenberg 1991: 119–88; Braaten 1992). All such reconstructions take the question of Christian engagement with other religions seriously, and there is a clear acknowledgement of God's mysterious work among the religions of the world; yet a negative accent persists: world religions have no *salvific* content. Pannenberg and Braaten place the theological problematic of other religions in an eschatological perspective, thus avoiding a theological judgement of the validity of the religions and their claims to truth in the present. From this eschatological perspective, 'Christ is the revelation of the eschatological fulfilment of the religions' (Braaten 1992: 80). Pannenberg states that in Christian dialogues with people of other religious traditions, Christians may recognize Christ's face in some who follow other ways of religion. Christians may also recognize the work of God's providence in their lives and the developments of their tradition. But that presence is always ambiguous, and therefore the salvation of people of other faiths is to be decided by God's eschatological judgement (Pannenberg 1990: 103).

Traditional interpreters of Luther's theology have been often concerned to preserve the uniqueness of the Christian faith over against other faiths or any form of pluralistic relativism. Their theological constructions are seldom grounded in dialogical engagement with other faiths though they intend to make room for such engagement within the grammar of the Christian faith. Those who have engaged in dialogical or missionary encounters with other faiths have sought inspiration from other aspects of Luther's theology. His 'theology of the cross' has been a prominent theme and resource in such efforts. A theology of the cross and the insight that God works *sub contrario*—exactly contrary to what people expect of God—can serve as an antidote to 'self-glorifying theologies', forms of Christian absolutism and a crusading church. But Luther was not prepared to explore God's mysterious work in religions and chose to focus on the revealed God on the cross. In the suffering God he discovered God's passionate love for humanity and the world. Kazoh Kitamori, a Japanese theologian, was one of the first to highlight this theme from Luther's *Heidelberg Disputation* (1518). Drawing on Luther's metaphor of 'God fighting with God' at Golgotha, Kitamori articulated a 'theology of the pain of God' that embraces *all* people from the perspective of divine suffering on the cross. The cross therefore is clue for comprehending the essence of God (Kitamori 1965: 21). The internal suffering of God on the cross has been explored by others in various ways not only as a theme for engaging with the suffering and 'crucified people' of the world (Moltmann 1974; Hall 1986) but also as an interreligious theme for engagement with Muslims—who question the very idea of divine suffering—and with Buddhists—whose perception of reality is grounded in *dukkha* (suffering) (Thomsen 1993; Thiemann 2009; Kusawadee 2010). The divine *dukkha* on the cross as a display of *mahakaruna* (the great compassion) of God serves as a point of convergence between Christian faith and Buddhism. Luther's language of 'human nothingness' and his emphasis on the 'freedom of the Christian' are themes that have remarkable similarities with the Buddhist view of 'emptiness' (*sunyata*) and have resonated well in Christian–Buddhist dialogues (Lohse 1986: 173; Chung 2008: 207).

Luther's theology of the cross as an expression of divine embrace of humanity can serve as a fundamental Christian posture of identity, participation, and solidarity with people of other faiths.

III. A Critical Reappraisal of Luther's Theology Religions

Luther's Christologically oriented exegesis and hermeneutics of Scripture invariably led him to take what we today consider 'exclusivist' positions. We find in his theology of religions a total devaluation of other religions, at best expressions of 'works-righteousness', and, at worst, satanic substitutes. His emphasis on the *solas*, '*solus Deus*', '*solus Christus*', '*sola gratia*', '*sola scriptura*', '*solo verbo*', and '*sola fide*', reinforce claims of Christian exclusivism and absoluteness. These exclusive categories unmistakably draw a rigid boundary between believers and outsiders. They do so in the form of a circular argument. In a multi-faith society, a generic affirmation of *God alone* may not meet great resistance (except by atheists!). However, in Luther's hermeneutics, a theocentric view of reality that easily accommodates other religious beliefs in terms of grace and truth is imposed with a decisive limitation in the claim, *Christ alone*. But this *Christ alone* claim does not represent a 'cosmic Christ' or a 'universal logos'. Rather, it points to a historical Jesus Christ. Then again, a mere historical knowledge of Jesus Christ will not suffice, for it must be tied to *faith* in Christ, which in turn comes by the hearing of the Word (*ex auditu*). The *Word alone* is not any word, any good word, not even the words of Scriptures, but a word of promise that points to *grace alone*. The *grace alone* refers back to what God has done in and through *Christ alone*. The intent of the *solas* then is to accentuate the scandal of Christian particularity.

The series of qualifications in Luther's hermeneutic imposes an understanding of the Christian faith as exclusive as possible so that any interreligious engagement with other faiths becomes impossible outside this frame of reference. The *solas* as categories of exclusion, of course, make sense within the framework of *intra*-Christian discourse, but they would be untenable in religiously plural societies, for they preclude possibilities of *extra*-Christian dialogue by erecting a mighty fortress around Christians.

The *solas* in Luther's theology, however, represent only one side of God's engagement in the world. Luther recognized that God's relation with the world is profoundly dialectical. He therefore was careful to make a distinction between 'law' and 'gospel', along with the corresponding distinctions between 'God hidden' and 'God revealed', 'God's left hand' and 'God's right hand', and the 'realm of creation' and 'the realm of redemption', as the two modalities of God's engagement with the world. Interpreters of Luther, as noted earlier, have found these distinctions helpful categories for articulating an inclusive theology of religions. However, Lutheran interpretation of this dialectic stops short of affirming any *salvific values* in the realm of creation. This 'no' to any salvific significance among other religions makes the Lutheran claim to an inclusive theology of religions rather problematic because interreligious dialogue has no theological significance! Beyond addressing issues of practical coexistence, such a dialogue becomes a disguised form of Christian monologue!

But such a conclusion can be avoided if Luther's dialectic is understood differently. The dialectical categories in Luther's thought are primarily *hermeneutical categories*, or *analytic tools*. They serve as windows through which we perceive and analyse religious realities in the world and not as theological truths. They are *not* intended to be categories of theological judgement over against others a priori. Furthermore, for Luther, the dialectic of law and gospel, God's left hand and God's right hand, God hidden and God revealed, and the like, are to be *distinguished* but not *separated*. When they are separated, the logic of the dialectic comes apart. For this reason, he insisted on holding together *simultaneously* (*simul*) two divergent modes of God's activity in the world and of the human condition.

The dialectic of the *simul* is a foundational assumption of Luther's entire theology: God's revelation is *simultaneously* hidden and revealed; God's activity *simultaneously* occurs through the work of God's left hand and right hand; the saving activity of God is *simultaneously* through law and gospel; the Christian is *simultaneously* saint and sinner; Christ is *simultaneously* human and divine; God is *simultaneously* present here and now and not yet, and so on. If the logic of the dialectic is taken seriously, then it pushes us away from an exclusive theology of the *solas* into an inclusive theology of the *simuls* that invites Christian engagement with people of other faiths. The *solas* indeed provide a reference point, proper grounding or anchor, on the one hand; the *simuls*, on the other hand, thrust the Christian into an open stance toward engagement with people of other faiths or no faith. Without the *solas*, our engagement with other faiths becomes ambiguous and lacks any particular content. If the *solas* alone were to prevail, our conversations would become restricted. Therefore, the particularity of the *solas* needs to be tempered by the *simuls* to create an authentic dialogue with others. If the *simuls* alone were the criteria, without the *solas*, Christians would have difficulty in distinguishing the authentic from the spurious, or the divine and the demonic. The *simuls* are grounded in the *solas* and therefore both need each other and must be held together (the interpretations suggested here were originally generated by a Lutheran World Federation study group, cf. Rajashekar 1988, 2009).

Had Luther pursued the implications of the dialectic of the *solas* and the *simuls*, he might have been able to explore the depth and riches of God's activity in the world in a much more positive light, especially among the Jews and Turks. His reluctance to explore the hidden God's activity invariably led him to focus on the revealed God. That God can desire to do anything with the 'left hand' without contradicting what God does with the 'right hand' is a thought that Luther was unwilling to entertain (Barth 2013: 482). The meaning and significance of the law, for Luther, could be understood in its full depth only through the gospel. The 'true function and the chief and proper use of the law is to reveal to man his sin, blindness, misery, wickedness, ignorance, hate and contempt for God, death, hell, judgment, and the well deserved wrath of God'

(WA40,1.480,32–481,25; LW26.309). From this perspective, the law convicts humans and drives them to the promise of grace. In the framework of Christian existence and in Christian preaching and teaching, the dialectic of the law and gospel in Luther's thought is insightful and theologically significant. But when that dialectic is transposed into the context of contemporary religious pluralism, the law and gospel categories become categories of evaluation and judgement over against others and cease to be analytical tools for understanding the religious reality of the world.

Luther's dialectic of the law and gospel and his emphasis on *simul* does provide a basis for a contemporary theology of interreligious engagement. However, his interpretation of the law in its two uses (the social or sustaining function, and the theological or condemning function) focuses on the negative function of the law. The law is a free gift of God; however, understood as natural law or the Decalogue, it is nonetheless an expression of God's loving will for personal relationship with humanity although embedded in the law's outward demands. Even after the Fall, the law functions not only to reveal God's wrath but also God's love (Althaus 1966; Knitter 1974: 85–9). The law is never merely law, for within it, hidden yet unrecognizable, is a gospel. The law then is not devoid of the gospel, just as the gospel is not devoid of the law. The liberating function of the gospel is not free from obedience to the requirements of the law.

The dialectic of law and gospel, properly understood, can avoid a unilateral application of the law in a negative way against religious communities outside the Christian faith simply by virtue of the fact that the gospel of Jesus Christ is not known there, for wherever the law goes, there also goes God's love. If applied as heuristic categories, law and gospel can lead to a discovery of both law and grace in other faiths. The logic of Luther's dialectic of law and gospel therefore suggests a double dialectic that invites a *bona fide* Christian engagement and dialogue with other faiths. One must thus necessarily posit that the God who is at work among Christians is the same God who is also at work among other religions through law and gospel in Christian reckoning. It is part of the biblical testimony that God is active in creation in love, insofar as Christ is the medium of creation. Luther's *simuls* therefore encourage Christians to explore boldly the mysterious ways in which God is present among other people and may even meet Christ among them.

Luther's dialectic of law and gospel is related to his corresponding dialectic of *Deus absconditus* and *Deus revelatus*, categories crucial for an interpretation of Luther's theology of religions. In his debate with Erasmus in *On Bound Choice* Luther may have undermined the *simul* character of the dialectic by implying a dualistic notion of God (Lohse 1986: 169–70; Barth 2013: ch. 6). His unwillingness to appreciate God's mysterious and unfathomable work, *opus alienum* (Isa. 28:21), outside the framework of the Christian faith, forced him to limit his understanding to *opus proprium* in Christ Jesus. Luther no doubt was inclined to see the hidden working of God behind the behaviour of Muslim Turks, and yet he was so convinced that God had decisively revealed himself in Jesus Christ that he could not imagine the hidden work of God outside the framework of the Christian faith, other than as expressions of God's wrath. He could not imagine the mysterious work of *Deus absconditus* in ways that are unfathomable by humans in other religious faiths. He could not conceive of the possibility of a *Deus revelatus* who may take new revelatory forms in other contexts and cultures without denying or contradicting God's revelation in Jesus Christ. Luther's seemingly one-sided interpretation of God's revelation, in effect, undermined the profound tension in the dialectic of the hidden and the revealed God.

In the context of contemporary religious pluralism, where divergent religious claims to truth are a reality, Christians cannot avoid mutual engagement in dialogue. Luther's theology of religions in his dialectic of the *solas* and the *simuls* opens up possibilities for such an engagement with openness while holding on to one's religious claims, for exploring and, perhaps, discovering, the mysterious presence of a *Deus revelatus* in the world of religions. In Christian dialogues with other faiths, Christians may or may not recognize the *Deus revelatus* present in other faiths because the language and the cultural-linguistic idioms in which that revelation and its salvific significance are couched appear alien in Christian hearing. Nonetheless, the claims and beliefs of other faiths represent the *opus alienum* that Christians cannot fully fathom, but they must remain open to hearing such alien witnesses. Luther's dialectic of the law and gospel and of *Deus absconditus* and *Deus revelatus* therefore also serve as rich categories that invite interreligious exploration, not as a priori categories of judgement but rather as categories of exploration a posteriori. If Luther's *solas* represent categories of exclusion, his *simuls* represent categories of inclusion. Holding them together not only encourages interreligious dialogue but also avoids falling into the trap of either religious exclusivism or religious relativism. Had Luther experienced the profound religious diversity and pluralism of today's world, he probably would have recast the nuances of his dialectic differently for a positive engagement with the world's religions.

REFERENCES

Althaus, Paul (1952). *Grundriss der Dogmatik*. Berlin: Evangelische Verlagasanstalt.
—— (1966). *The Theology of Martin Luther*. Minneapolis: Fortress.
Barth, Hans-Martin (2013). *The Theology of Martin Luther: A Critical Assessment*. Minneapolis: Fortress.
Bornkamm, Heinrich (1969). *Luther and the Old Testament*. Minneapolis: Fortress.
Braaten, Carl (1992). *No Other Gospel! Christianity Among the World's Religions*. Minneapolis: Fortress.
Chung, Paul S. (2008). *Martin Luther and Buddhism: Aesthetics of Suffering*. Eugene, OR: Pickwick.
Edwards, Mark U., Jr. (1983). *Luther's Last Battles: Politics and Polemics, 1531–1546*. Ithaca: Cornell University Press.
Ehmann, Johannes (2008). *Luther, Türken und Islam: Eine Untersuchung zum Türken- und Islambild Martin Luthers (1515–1546)*. Gütersloh: Gütersloher Verlagshaus.
Francisco, Adam S. (2007). *Martin Luther and Islam: A Study in Sixteenth-Century Polemics and Apologetics*. Leiden: Brill.

Grislis, Egil (1974). 'Luther and the Turks'. *The Muslim World* 64: 180–93.

—— (1998). 'Martin Luther and the World Religions'. *Word & World* 18: 143–54.

Gritsch, Eric W. (2012). *Martin Luther's Anti-Semitism: Against His Better Judgment*. Grand Rapids, MI: Eerdmans.

Hall, Douglas John (1986). *God and Human Suffering: An Exercise in the Theology of the Cross*. Minneapolis: Augsburg.

Halpérin, Jean and Arne Sovik (eds.) (1984). *Luther, Lutheranism and the Jews*. Geneva: LWF Studies.

Henrich, Sarah and James L. Boyce (1996). 'Martin Luther—Translation of Two Prefaces on Islam'. *Word & World* 16: 250–66.

Kandler, Karl Herman (1993). 'Luther und der Koran'. *Luther* 64: 3–9.

Kaufmann, Thomas (2006). 'Luther and the Jews'. In *Jews, Judaism and the Reformation in Sixteenth-Century Germany*, ed. Dean Bell and Stephen Burnett. Leiden: Brill, 69–104.

Kitamori, Kazoh (1965). *Theology of the Pain of God*. Richmond: John Knox.

Knitter, Paul (1974). *Towards a Protestant Theology of Religions: A Case Study of Paul Althaus and Contemporary Attitudes*. Marburg: Elwert.

Kremers, Heinz (ed.) (1987). *Die Juden und Martin Luther, Martin Luther und die Juden, Geschichte, Wirkungsgeschichte, Herausforderung*, 2nd edn. Neukirchen-Vluyn: Neukirchener Verlag.

Kusawadee, Banjob (2010). *Holy Suffering*. Bangkok: Lutheran Seminary in Thailand.

Lohse, Bernhard (1986). *Martin Luther: An Introduction to His Life and Work*. Philadelphia: Fortress.

Martinson, Paul Varo (1987). *A Theology of World Religions*. Minneapolis: Augsburg.

Miller, Gregory J. (2000). 'Luther on the Turks and Islam'. *Lutheran Quarterly* 14: 79–97.

Moltmann, Jürgen (1974). *The Crucified God: The Cross of Christ as the Foundation and Criticism of Theology*. New York: Harper & Row.

Öberg, Ingemar (2007). *Luther and World Mission: A Historical and Systematic Study*. Saint Louis: Concordia.

Pannenberg, Wolfhart (1971). *Basic Questions in Theology*, vol. 2. Philadelphia: Fortress.

—— (1990). 'Religious Pluralism and Conflicting Truth Claims'. In *Christian Uniqueness Reconsidered: The Myth of a Pluralistic Theology of Religions*, ed. Gavin D'Costa. Maryknoll: Orbis.

—— (1991). *Systematic Theology*, Vol. 1. Grand Rapids, MI: Eerdmans.

Rajashekar, J. Paul (ed.) (1988). *Religious Pluralism and Lutheran Theology*. Geneva: Lutheran World Federation.

—— (1990). 'Luther and Islam: An Asian Perspective'. *Lutherjahrbuch* 57: 174–91.

—— (2009). 'Rethinking Lutheran Engagement with Religious Plurality'. In *Transformative Theological Perspectives*, ed. Karen L. Bloomquist. Minneapolis: Lutheran University Press, 105–16.

Rajashekar, J. Paul and Timothy J. Wengert (2002). 'Martin Luther, Philip Melanchthon and the Publication of the Qur'an'. *Lutheran Quarterly* 16: 221–8.

Ratschow, Carl Heinz (1967). 'Die Religionen und das Christentum'. In *Der christliche Glaube und die Religionen*, ed. Carl Heinz Ratschow. Berlin: Töpelmann.

Thiemann, Ronald F. (2009). 'Luther's Theology of the Cross: Resource for a Theology of Religions'. In *The Global Luther*, ed. Christine Helmer. Minneapolis: Fortress, 228–46.

Thomsen, Mark W. (1993). *The Word and the Way of the Cross*. Chicago: Division for Global Mission, Evangelical Lutheran Church of America.

Wallmann, Johannes (1986). 'Luthers Stellung zu Judentum und Islam'. *Luther* 57: 49–60.

Williams, George H. (1969). 'Erasmus and the Reformers on Non-Christian Religions and *Salus Extra Ecclesiam*'. In *Action and Conviction in Early Modern Europe: Essays in Memory of E. H. Harbison*, ed. Theodore K. Rabb and Jerrold E. Seigel. Princeton: Princeton University Press, 319–70.

PART VI

THE GENRE IN WHICH LUTHER SHAPED HIS THEOLOGY

CHAPTER 32

THE INFLUENCE OF THE GENRES OF EXEGETICAL INSTRUCTION, PREACHING, AND CATECHESIS ON LUTHER

MARY JANE HAEMIG

WHILE much has been written on Luther as professor, preacher, and catechist (teacher), much less consideration has been given to how these tasks shaped his thinking and expression. It is sometimes said that Luther was not a systematic theologian but rather one who responded to occasions. His engagement in exegetical instruction, preaching, and catechesis—activities that consumed much of his adult life—were highly 'occasional' tasks. This chapter explores how Luther's engagement in these key tasks shaped both his theology and its expression.

I. EXEGETICAL INSTRUCTION

Luther resisted his superior Johann von Staupitz's suggestion that he become a doctor of theology and lecturer on the Bible. Perhaps he recognized that this activity would alter his life's path. At the ceremony at which Luther was awarded his doctorate, he had to promise 'not to advance any idle and foreign teachings which were condemned by the church and offensive to pious ears' (Brecht 1985: 1.126). In later years, when the truth of what he taught was challenged—and also his authority to teach it—Luther many times referred to his doctorate and call to teach as giving him the right and duty to teach as he did.

After his promotion to the doctorate Luther began his biblical lectures in October 1512. Lecturing on the Bible was to occupy the rest of his life. Only when he was away from Wittenberg—at the Wartburg (1521–2) and the Coburg (1530)—did he not lecture to students. The necessity of lecturing forced Luther to a continued, deep engagement with the Bible. It forced him to consider questions of the role of tradition, the focus of the Bible, the proper method for studying it, the proper interpretative lens, the activity of the biblical narrative on its hearers, and issues of translation. Lecturing also caused Luther to speak continually of God's works, and this shaped his preaching and catechesis as well.

Throughout his career as university professor, Luther's exegesis took place in conversation with previous exegetes. The form of the university exegetical lecture drove him to consider the place of exegetical tradition (and by extension all tradition) in understanding the Bible. Repeated references to the early Church Fathers as well as to medieval theologians reveal a wide and deep familiarity with and high respect for the exegetical tradition. Luther did not interpret the Bible in a vacuum but recognized the value of previous exegesis.

Luther clearly preferred some exegetes to others. Augustine and Bernard of Clairvaux are cited, often (though not always) with approval (Steinmetz 1986: 12–22). Luther also exhibited a willingness to depart from exegetical tradition. Frequently he criticized previous exegetes and gave his own reading—under the weight of his call. He believed that his qualification and call as a Doctor in Bible gave him not only the right to do this but also the duty.

Luther did not view tradition as having an authority equal to Scripture itself. However, he valued tradition and did not lightly depart from it. This approach to tradition— familiarity and appreciation as well as a willingness to differ when he believed the biblical text demanded a different reading—carried over into other dimensions of Luther's reforming work. In matters of worship, for example he kept traditional forms but implemented change when Scripture demanded it.

Not only in questions of exegeting individual passages, but also in more general questions of focus and approach, Luther showed appreciation for tradition. In common with patristic or medieval exegetes, Luther saw Christ as the centre of Scripture, indeed, of each individual part of Scripture. For Luther the key question was: which Christ? Was it Christ as gift or Christ as example?

Luther arrived at the answer to this question by studying Scripture. His *Preface to the Wittenberg Edition* of his writings (1539) described the correct way of studying the Bible as involving three steps taught by David in Psalm 119: *Oratio–Meditatio–Tentatio*. Regarding *Oratio* (prayer) he advised his readers to 'despair of your reason and understanding' and instead pray to God 'that he through his dear Son may give you his Holy Spirit, who will enlighten you, lead you, and give you understanding' (WA50.659,7–12; LW34.285–286). *Meditatio* meant to meditate not only in the heart but also externally, by actually repeating and comparing oral speech and literal words, 'reading and rereading them with diligent attention and reflection, so that you may see what the Holy Spirit means by them. And take care that you do not grow weary or think that you have done enough when you have read, heard, and spoken them once or twice, and that you then have complete understanding...' (WA50.659,22–27; LW34.286). The third component, *tentatio, Anfechtung*, Luther described as 'the touchstone which teaches you not only to know and understand, but also to experience how right, how true, how sweet, how lovely, how mighty, how comforting God's Word is...' (WA50.660,1–4; LW34.337). In expanding upon this last component, Luther indicated that experience had taught him this:

> For as soon as God's Word takes root and grows in you, the devil will harry you, and will make a real doctor of you, and by his assaults will teach you to seek and love God's Word. I myself...am deeply indebted to my papists that through the devil's raging they have beaten, oppressed, and distressed me so much. That is to say, they have made a fairly good theologian of me, which I would not have become otherwise. (WA50.660,8–14; LW34.286–287)

The rules that Luther recommended for others came out of his own experience and engagement with Scripture. By his own testimony his meditation on it led to what is commonly called his reformational breakthrough (WA54.186,3–13; LW34.337).

Luther had discovered God's engagement with humans embraced not only demand but also gift. He conveyed this insight in his *Brief Instruction on What to Look For and Expect in the Gospels*, the introduction to the Wartburg Postil.

> The chief article and foundation of the gospel is that before you take Christ as an example, you...recognize him as a gift, as a present that God has given you and that is your own. This means that when you see or hear of Christ doing or suffering something, you do not doubt that Christ himself, with his deeds and suffering, belongs to you.... Now when you have Christ as the foundation and chief blessing of your salvation, then the other part follows: that you take him as your example, giving yourself in service to your neighbour just as you see that Christ has given himself for you... Therefore make note of this, that Christ as a gift nourishes your faith and makes you a Christian. But Christ as an example exercises your works. These do not make you a Christian. Actually they come forth from you because you have already been made a Christian...So you see that the gospel is really not a book of laws and commandments which requires deeds of us, but a book of divine promises in which God promises, offers, and gives us all his possessions and benefits in Christ...
>
> (WA10,1,1.11,12–13,6; LW35.119–120)

Luther's hearing of law and promise in Scripture was his key move. While some scholars have stressed his rejection of previous interpretative methods (e.g., the medieval four-fold interpretation of Scripture) and others have pointed out continuities in methodology and approach, these remain secondary to his emphasis on law and promise. Luther heard both law and promise in both the Old and New Testaments. James Samuel Preus finds that in his first Psalms lectures (1513–15) Luther discovered that the goods of the Old Testament were present in 'words and promises'. When Luther awakened to this fact, 'the result was not only the theological recovery of the Old Testament but the eloquent first themes of an emerging Reformation theology' (Preus 1969: 267). The Old Testament was not a shadow of a reality to come, nor a letter opposed to the spirit.

Luther's engagement with exegetical lectures led to insights that fuelled a reformation. Luther knew he could never simply interpret the Bible; rather he sought to let the Bible speak. The Bible always speaks and does something. It drives or leads the hearer through judgement and forgiveness, demand and gift, law and gospel, death and life. Luther understood that the biblical narrative shapes an evangelical identity (Maxfield 2008: 2, cf. 216–21). He grew to appreciate the stories of biblical figures, especially Old Testament stories, because he saw in them examples of the life of faith. These biblical figures teach us what it is to be Christian (Haemig 2009) and what it is to be dead in sin and made alive by a self-giving God. They teach us how to talk to that God and how to receive the assurance of our salvation.

Luther's work on exegetical lectures also contributed to his translations of the Bible. Though he studied the Scriptures in Greek, Hebrew, and Latin, he saw the need for God's Word to speak the people's language in his own time. Though not the first to translate the Bible into German, Luther's translation succeeded where others had not. Luther's deep knowledge of Scripture combined with his knowledge of languages and rhetorical skills to produce a translation superior from scholarly, literary, linguistic, and rhetorical standpoints. It became a key influence on the modern German language. Luther's exegetical studies and instruction shaped both the method and content of his translation. Luther translated from and to what he saw as the central message of the Bible (cf. his defence of his translation of Romans 3:28 in *On Translating* [1530], WA30,2.632–646; LW35.181–202). He recognized that an 'objective' translation or a 'translation without bias' did not exist and so made his standpoint as a translator very clear.

Luther's translating work forced him to consider how best to introduce hearers and readers to the Bible and to each of its books. Convinced that Jerome's prefaces misled people into a false interpretation, he wrote his own. In seeking to introduce people to the Bible, Luther always focused on what was central: Christ's work 'for you', understood through a clear distinction between law and gospel (WADB8.10/11,2–12/13,22; LW35.235–237). Luther's catechisms were also intended to summarize and introduce the Bible. His *Small Catechism* used woodcuts of Bible stories to illustrate individual parts of the catechism; more profoundly, the *Catechism* sought to convey the heart of the biblical message—God's will for human lives, God's deeds on our behalf, and how to talk with God.

Finally, Luther's engagement with Scripture in preparation for exegetical lectures shaped his approach to the Christian life. His method of approaching Scripture—*Oratio, Meditatio,* and *Tentatio*—mirrored his understanding of how the Christian was to approach life. His *Small Catechism* recommended that the Christian begin the day with the sign of the cross and invocation, the Apostles' Creed, Lord's Prayer, a further prayer and hymn and then 'go to your work joyfully'. The words spoken correspond to the *Oratio* and *Meditatio*. Luther knew full well that precisely in vocation the Christian would experience *tentatio*.

II. PREACHING

Luther elevated the prominence of sermon: 'a Christian congregation should never gather together without the preaching of God's Word and prayer' (WA12.35,19–21; LW53.11). He saw the sermon not merely as human words but as the Holy Spirit's instrument, through which it worked both repentance and faith in believers. As such, the sermon was itself sacramental and not subordinate in the worship service to the celebration of the Lord's Supper.

Luther was an active preacher. He preached Sundays on lectionary texts and also weekdays seriatim through biblical books or on the catechism (he described Wittenberg preaching in his *German Mass* [1526], WA19.79,9–80,24; LW53.68–69). Not only did Luther have a theological understanding of the importance of preaching; he also grasped its practical importance for his reforming work. A number of Luther's early sermons, published individually as pamphlets, aided the spread of his ideas (Edwards 1994: esp. 41–56).

Some effects of Luther's engagement as a preacher were identical to or similar to those of his exegetical teaching. The need to preach led Luther to engage the biblical text deeply, to weigh the homiletical tradition, to consider the proper interpretative lens, and to ponder the activity of the biblical narrative on its hearers. Preaching led to focus on central questions. Luther never used a text as a springboard to discuss something unrelated or only tangentially related to it. While early sermons provided verse-by-verse commentary, Luther departed from this method in later years. Increasingly, his focus on a central message meant that he did not consider all parts of a text equally important. Often he found that central message in a single verse and devoted most of his sermon to that. To find the central point, he employed the same hermeneutic he had discovered in his exegetical studies. He interpreted each text from the perspective of what God in Christ was doing, defining those actions in terms of demand and gift, threats and promises, law and gospel. For this reason, it is sometimes said that Luther had only one sermon.

The Lutheran reformers largely kept the lectionary they had received and so preached on the same texts that Roman Catholic priests did (WA19.79,10–12; LW53.68). Luther affirmed the use of the lectionary. One effect (perhaps unintentional) of this decision was that it became clear that the Reformation was not a matter of selecting different biblical texts than those previously used by Roman Catholics. Rather, reformational insights sprang from the same texts from which Roman Catholics preached. The key question was not which texts were selected but rather how they were preached.

In preaching the lectionary Luther was led to consider how those texts related to the church year and the traditional emphases of the seasons. Advent offers an example (Haemig 2002). In common with the homiletical tradition, Luther saw this season as highlighting the various comings—past, present, and future—of Christ to us. Medieval preaching used this season and its texts to emphasize human preparation for those comings. In contrast, Luther stressed what God was doing for us in each coming and markedly de-emphasized preparation. In the Advent 4 sermon on John 1:19–28 in his 1522 Advent postil Luther wrote:

> The way of the Lord, as you have heard, is that he does all things within you, so that all our works are not ours but his, which comes by faith. This, however, is not possible if you desire worthily to prepare yourself by praying, fasting, self-mortification, and your own works, as is now generally and foolishly taught during the time of Advent. A spiritual preparation is meant, consisting in a thoroughgoing knowledge and con- fession of your being unfit, a sinner, poor, damned, and miserable, with all the works you may perform. The more a heart is thus minded, the better it prepares the way of the Lord, although meanwhile possibly drinking fine wines, walking on roses, and not praying a word. (WA10,1,2.199,3–14; CP 1.124)

Luther thought the chief message of the Advent season was what God in Christ had done, is doing, and will do. He rejected any teaching that the season should foster human works of preparation.

Preaching was one factor that encouraged Luther towards reform of the entire wor- ship service. He had to consider the message preached in relation to other parts of the service, and to consider that parts of the medieval mass contradicted the evangelical message (*Formulae missae* [1523], WA12.206,3–22; LW53.20). Preaching also led Luther to consider the need for new evangelical preaching aids. Luther evaluated the popular postils pastors often used to aid lectionary sermon preparation. Luther referred to these derisively and saw clearly that a thoroughgoing reformation of preaching needed new postils. At the Wartburg he produced his first postil of several (Frymire 2010). It elicited a wave of evangelical postils.

Preaching meant that Luther could never be an ivory tower theologian, simply dealing with a monastic or university audience. In Wittenberg he often preached in the town church, confronting ordinary people several times a week. Preaching forced him to see that theology was never simply a theoretical activity. It was meant to have and did have impact on lives. Further, regular preaching to this audience encouraged simplicity of expression—simple illustrations and earthy metaphors. He never tried to display his own learnedness in the pulpit. Such simplicity of expression can also be attributed to other factors, e.g., Luther's upbringing and personal character, but the regular exercise of the preaching office also had its impact.

Not least, regular preaching influenced other aspects of Luther's work: his exege- sis as he considered in his lectures how texts should be preached, and his catechetical preaching, particularly his sermons of 1528, which shaped both his catechisms.

III. Catechesis

Luther never produced a written comprehensive systematic theology such as that pro-duced by Thomas Aquinas or John Calvin. However, a catechetical structure under-girded much or all of what Luther preached and wrote. His consistent use of catechetical forms and material in all sorts of writings, as well as his advocacy of the catechism as a structure for lay piety, indicate its importance as both shape and resource for his theo-logical reflection.

In the late medieval era 'catechism' designated certain texts basic to Christian exist-ence, necessarily explanations of those texts. In this chapter 'catechism' does not refer to a specific catechism (such as Luther's printed 'catechisms') but rather to that basic collection of texts (Ten Commandments, which were added in the late Middle Ages as a confessional aid to the ancient church's core, Apostles' Creed and Lord's Prayer, alongside varying other elements) which formed the core of medieval and Reformation instruction. Given the prominence of preaching the catechism in late medieval reli-gious life, it is reasonable to assume that Luther gained his first familiarity with it while growing up (Robinson 2001). While we do not know which specific catechism or cat-echisms Luther may have learned or heard as a child, he probably experienced these three parts as well as explanations of the sacraments, other confessional aids such as lists of sins, and the rosary. The forty-six chapters of Dietrich Kolde's *A Fruitful Mirror or Small Handbook for Christians* (1480) (Janz 1982: 29–130) offered, for example, sev-eral aids to identify sins: the Ten Commandments, the five commandments of the church, the seven deadly sins, nine alien sins, openly discussed sins and mute sins against nature, sins against the Holy Spirit, and many sins of the tongue. It also con-tained much else, including descriptions of good works, the protective role of Mary, and how one should die.

The catechism decisively influenced Luther's theology and piety. He encouraged the clergy to engage daily with the catechism, citing his own experience of disciplined rep-etition of and meditation on its texts (BSLK 547–48; BC 38–81). His use of the catechism began very early in his career as he preached on parts of the catechism.[1] His frequent use of catechetical structure and content indicates that he worked out his reformational insights in conversation with familiar texts and forms that were some of the oldest used by the church rather than seeking or constructing new texts on which to base his Reformation. His use of the catechism supported this assertion that he was not creating a new religion but rather recovering the true Christian faith.

---

[1] A partial list of these includes 'A Short Explanation of the Ten Commandments' (1518) WA1.250–256,711; 9, 769; 'A Short Form of the Ten Commandments … the Creed, … The Lord's Prayer' (1520), WA7.204–229; 'The Sacrament of Penance' (1519), WA2.714–723: LW35.3–22; 'The Holy and Blessed Sacrament of Baptism' (1519), WA2.727–737; LW35.29–43; 'The Blessed Sacrament of the Holy and True Body of Christ …' (1519) WA2.742–758; LW35,45–73; 'An Exposition of the Lord's Prayer for Simple Laymen' (1519) WA2.80–130; LW42.15–81.

The catechetical genre shaped his theology by (1) forcing focus on what was most important, (2) providing a link to the past and forcing consideration of where Luther's reformatory insights differed from received tradition, (3) encouraging simplicity and brevity, (4) providing structure, and (5) aiding formulation of crucial points. From the received catechetical tradition, Luther retained the three central elements of Ten Commandments, Apostles' Creed, and Lord's Prayer. He saw God's hand in the construction of the catechism from these three parts. In his *Prayer Booklet* (1522) he wrote:

> It was not unintended in God's particular ordering of things that a lowly Christian person who might be unable to read the Bible should nevertheless be obligated to learn and know the Ten Commandments, the Creed, and the Lord's Prayer. Indeed, the total content of Scripture and preaching and everything a Christian needs to know is quite fully and adequately comprehended in these three items. They summarize everything with such brevity and clarity that no one can complain or make any excuse that the things necessary for his salvation are too complicated or difficult for him to remember. (WA10,2.376,12–15)

Sacraments and confession—important elements of late medieval religion—were also part of his catechetical thinking but in the framework of an evangelical understanding.

The catechetical form also helped Luther to consider where and why he differed from tradition. Luther's ordering of the three chief catechetical parts—Ten Commandments, Creed, Lord's Prayer—in his *Gebetbüchlein* (1522) and his Large and Small Catechisms (WA10,2.375–406) and his letter to his barber, *A Simple Way to Pray* (1535) (WA38.358–375; LW43.193–211) differed from the common medieval ordering which placed the Creed first, before Lord's Prayer and the Ten Commandments, since Augustine began with faith (the creed) as knowledge that needed to be joined to hope (the Lord's Prayer) and love (ten commandments) in order to be salvific. Luther's ordering was more amenable to his law–gospel dynamic (Arand 2000: 27–56). Luther chose to explain the Creed in three articles rather than with the medieval twelve-fold format, which split the Creed into 'facts of faith'; he gave his explanations a structure focusing on the work of the Trinitarian God.

Significant also is what Luther omitted when he discussed the catechism. He did not include the 'Hail Mary' in his catechisms. He did include discussion of it in his *Gebetbüchlein* (1522). This perhaps reflected a tension between how Luther ideally saw the catechism (as expressed in his own) and his pastoral inclination to deal with people where they were. Rather than ignore an important component of medieval catechisms and prayerbooks, Luther chose to include it with an evangelical interpretation. While Luther sought actively to change lay piety, he knew he had to deal with the texts and traditions familiar to laypeople.

Use of the catechism encouraged simplicity, brevity, and clarity of both concept and language. Luther and his fellow reformers rejected what they perceived to be a complicated medieval system of belief and church practice, classifying and totting up sins committed and indulgences obtained, as well as complicated academic theologies inaccessible to the ordinary Christian. So, for example, instead of focusing on lists of sins of various types, Luther found the Ten Commandments the right tool to consider both God's will for humankind and our failure to live as commanded. He appreciated the Apostles' Creed for its concise summary of what God does for humans and the Lord's Prayer as setting a paradigm for Christian prayer. When he wrote his *Small Catechism*, he sought to retain its brevity and clarity, composing simple and memorable explanations with clear (and sometimes repetitive) structures.

Luther used catechetical forms and content in many ways and types of writings. His engagement with the catechism provided structure, touchstone, reference point, resource, and purpose for his own theological work. Catechetical forms configured his thinking. In the third part of *Confession Concerning Christ's Supper* (1528) Luther confessed his own faith, structuring this confession with the three articles of the Apostles' Creed (WA26.499–509; LW37.360–372). One can also see a creedal structure in the three sections of the *Smalcald Articles* (BSLK 407–68; BC 297–328).

A single catechetical part could offer both structure and content for different types of works. His *Treatise on Good Works* (1520) (WA6.202–276; LW44.21–114) used the Ten Commandments to structure his discussion of that topic. *On the Councils and the Church* (1539) used the commandments to define what Christian holiness is (WA50.626,15–268,15; LW41.145–148). His pastoral instruction in the *Small Catechism*, as revised in 1531, urges those confessing to 'consider your calling according to the Ten Commandments...' (BSLK 517; BC 360).

Luther's writings drew extensively on catechetical elements for both structure and form; his writings on worship illustrate this. For example, his *Order of Baptism* (1523) (WA12.42–48; LW 53.96–103) used creedal questions and responses. His *Order of Mass and Communion* (1523) (WA12.205–20; LW53.19–40) advocated that people not be admitted to the Lord's Supper 'unless they can give a reason for their faith and can answer questions about what the Lord's Supper is, what its benefits are, and what they expect to derive from it' (WA12.215,21–28; LW53.32). His 'German mass' clearly declared the need for the catechism (WA19.76,1–23; LW53.64–65).

The catechism also helped Luther to formulate and support arguments. Often he referred to or quoted parts of it in support of his point. He frequently quoted the creedal 'I believe in the Holy Christian Church' in discussions of the church. In *To the Christian Nobility* (1520) Luther attacked three walls he said the Roman church had built to protect itself from reform. Luther drew on that creedal statement to help him demolish the second wall, the claim that only the pope may authoritatively interpret Scripture: '...if the article "I believe in one holy Christian church" is correct, then the pope cannot be the only one who is right. Otherwise we would have to confess, "I believe in the pope at Rome"' (WA6.412,11–19; LW44.135). *On the Councils and the Church* (1539) (WA50.624,4–653,15; LW41.143–178) contains a lengthy analysis of this line from the Creed from the third article. The catechism even influenced the shape and content of Luther's polemics. *Against Hanswurst* cited the presence of catechetical elements—baptism, Lord's Supper, keys, the preaching office, the confessing of the Apostles' Creed, and the praying of the Lord's Prayer—as evidence that the evangelicals were indeed the true church (WA51.479,20–482,31; LW41.194–196).

The catechism decisively influenced Luther's efforts to shape lay piety: it shaped his practical reformatory agenda. It provided a simple yet complete understanding of the Christian faith and corrected false understandings; it encouraged theological reflection and freedom rather than uniformity in the practice of faith; it introduced laity to the Bible, and it provided laity with what they needed to exercise the priestly task. Luther came to realize that the catechism defined and shaped Christian existence.

Luther was disgusted that medieval prayerbooks and catechisms—genres that overlapped and were sometimes indistinguishable—sought to shape lay piety in ways inimical to a proper understanding of God's work. In his *Gebetbüchlein* (1522) Luther criticized existing prayerbooks as 'harmful' and declared that 'these books need a basic and thorough reformation if not total extermination' (WA10,2.375,1–15; LW43.11–12). Yet Luther did not throw out catechetical form and content simply because they had been misused. He realized their usefulness in constructing a new lay piety. In the 1520s Luther sought to reform key elements of church practice in order to ensure that they reflected and nurtured an evangelical understanding of the faith. He reformed the worship service, published evangelical hymns, and reformed the system of oversight. He hoped for a new evangelical catechism that would present the Christian faith in a way consistent with his reformatory insights. Though many explanations of the catechism were written in the 1520s (Cohrs 1900–2), none caught on. In the preface to his *Small Catechism* Luther despaired of what he had encountered during his visitations in rural Saxony (BSLK 501–2; BC 347) and recognized that, properly understood, the catechism provided a simple yet complete summary of the Christian faith as a foundation and remedy for this situation. His own catechisms were not his first attempts to reshape lay piety. Certainly his early sermons on various elements of the catechism sought to do this. His *Personal Prayer Book (Gebetbüchlein)* (1522) was a significant and enduringly influential early catechetical attempt, reprinted seventeen times between 1522 and 1525 and at least forty-four times by the end of the century (WA10,2.375–406; LW43.3–45). There he explained why the three chief parts were necessary:

Three things a person must know in order to be saved. First, he must know what to do and what to leave undone. Second, when he realizes that he cannot measure up to what he should do or leave undone, he needs to know where to go to find the strength he requires. Third, he must know how to seek and obtain that strength. It is just like a sick person who first has to determine the nature of his sickness, then find out what to do or to leave undone. After that he has to know where to get the medicine which will help him do or leave undone what is right for a healthy person. Then he has to desire to search for this medicine and to obtain it or have it brought to him.

  Thus, the commandments teach man to recognize his sickness, enabling him to perceive what he must do or refrain from doing, consent to or refuse, and so he will recognize himself to be a sinful and wicked person. The Creed will teach and show him where to find the medicine—grace—which will help him to become devout and keep the commandments. The Creed points him to God and his mercy, given and made plain to him in Christ. Finally, the Lord's Prayer teaches all this, namely, through the fulfilment of God's commandments everything will be given him. In these three are the essentials of the entire Bible. (WA10,2.376,19–377,13; LW43.13–14)

So Luther structured his efforts to shape lay piety accordingly. In the Betbuchlein (1522) he began by explaining what each one meant and including lists detailing how we break each commandment, followed by brief explanations of how to fulfill each commandment. He also explained the three parts of the Creed. Only after these lengthy sections did Luther comment on the Lord's Prayer, devoting a page or two to each petition. While this prayer book contained other texts, it is clear that commandments, Creed, and Lord's Prayer were the focus.

Luther's engagement with the catechetical form and his realization of the need for a good catechism eventually drove him to write his two catechisms in 1529. Much of their texts derived from his catechetical sermons in Wittenberg in 1528. Through both sermon and catechism Luther showed that his concern was not simply conquering lay ignorance of the faith but rather helping people to know enough of their faith that they could actually derive hope and consolation from it.

As in the *Gebetbüchlein*, the catechism provided a structure for prayer life in *Simple Way to Pray for a Good Friend* (1535) (WA38.358–375: LW43.193–211), Peter, his barber. Luther began by advising Peter to recite the Ten Commandments and the Creed (and some words of Paul or Christ or some psalms). Luther explained each petition of the Lord's Prayer but also made clear that these thoughts were not to limit or routinize lay piety:

> You should also know that I do not want you to recite all these words in your prayer. That would make it nothing but idle chatter and prattle, read word for word out of a book as were the rosaries by the laity and the prayers of the priests and monks. Rather, I want your heart to be stirred and guided concerning the thoughts which ought to be comprehended in the Lord's Prayer. These thoughts may be expressed, if your heart is rightly warmed and inclined toward prayer, in many different ways and with more words or fewer. I do not bind myself to such words or syllables, but say my prayers in one fashion today, in another tomorrow, depending upon my mood and feeling. I stay however, as nearly as I can, with the same general thoughts and ideas.
>
> (WA38.362,37–363,9; LW43.198)

As the catechism aroused Luther's theological reflection, so he hoped the catechism would do the same for laypeople. Luther gave Peter a fourfold method for praying the Ten Commandments that encouraged reflection on the multiple meaning of each commandment, as instruction, thanksgiving, confession, and prayer (WA38.365,1–4).

Clearly, Luther did not consider theological reflection the sole preserve of clerics and professors. The catechism enabled the ordinary Christian to think carefully about the faith. Whether expressed in prayerbook, catechism, or letters to friends, Luther sought to shape lay piety using the same structure, the Ten Commandments, the Creed, and the Lord's Prayer.

The catechism aided Luther in his effort to encourage lay engagement with the Bible. In his first series of catechetical sermons in 1528 Luther stated that these first three parts of the catechism contain all of Scripture (WA30,2.2,20–21), comprehending its central message: how God wants us to live, what God has done for us, and how to talk to this God. For Luther, this was the Bible's basic content; knowing these supplied basic orientation for understanding the whole Bible. Luther also stated that after people had learned their catechism, they should be led further into Scripture (WA30,1.27,28–31).

The catechism was also a link to the future Luther envisioned, in which laypersons knew what God was doing for them, derived hope and consolation from that knowledge, were able to confess and defend the faith, and to pass judgement on Christian teaching. Catechetical knowledge led to the office of oversight. In *To the Christian Nobility* he asserted the right of all Christians to interpret Scripture and judge doctrine. He argued that all Christians were priests, and then questioned 'why should we not also have the power to test and judge what is right or wrong in matters of faith?' (WA6.412,20–23; LW44.135; Junghans 1972). Luther concluded 'it is the duty of every Christian to espouse the cause of the faith, to understand and defend it, and to denounce every error' (cf. *Concerning the Ministry* [1523], WA12.169–195; LW40.7–44). Luther's followers emphasized that knowledge of the catechism gave the necessary knowledge to enable laity to judge doctrine (Haemig 2006). As Luther encouraged his students, clergy, and others to study the catechism, he made clear that it defined Christian existence and provided a weapon in the ongoing battle against the Devil and evil (BSLK 548–9; BC 381).

Exegetical instruction, preaching, and catechesis were not simply activities Luther experienced and in which he himself engaged. They were formative influences on his person and work, and he viewed them as having similar impacts on others.

REFERENCES

Arand, Charles (2000). *That I May Be His Own: An Overview of Luther's Catechisms*. Saint Louis: Concordia.

Brecht, Martin (1985–93). *Martin Luther*, 3 vols., trans. James Schaaf. Philadelphia: Fortress.

Cohrs, Ferdinand (1900–2). *Die Evangelischen Katechismusversuche vor Luthers Enchiridion*. 4 vols. Berlin: Hofmann.

Edwards, Mark U., Jr. (1994). *Printing, Propaganda, and Martin Luther*. Berkeley: University of California Press.

Frymire, John M. (2010). *The Primacy of the Postils: Catholics, Protestants, and the Dissemination of Ideas in Early Modern Germany*. Leiden: Brill.

Haemig, Mary Jane (2002). 'Sixteenth-Century Preachers on Advent as a Season of Proclamation or Preparation'. *Lutheran Quarterly* 16: 125–51.

—— (2006). 'Laypeople as Overseers of the Faith: A Reformation Proposal'. *Trinity Seminary Review* 27: 21–7.

—— (2009). 'Prayer as Talking Back to God in Luther's Genesis Lectures'. *Lutheran Quarterly* 23: 270–95.

Janz, Denis (ed.) (1982). *Three Reformation Catechisms: Catholic, Anabaptist, Lutheran*. New York: Mellen.

Junghans, Helmar (1972). 'Der Laie als Richter im Glaubensstreit der Reformationszeit'. *Luther-jahrbuch* 39: 31–54.

Maxfield, John A. (2008). *Luther's Lectures on Genesis and the Formation of Evangelical Identity*. Kirksville: Truman State University Press.

Preus, James Samuel (1969). *From Shadow to Promise: Old Testament Interpretation from Augustine to the Young Luther*. Cambridge, MA: Harvard University Press.

Robinson, Paul (2001). 'Lord, Teach Us to Pray: Preaching the Pater Noster in Germany and Austria, 1100–1500'. Ph.D. Dissertation, University of Chicago.

Steinmetz, David C. (1986). *Luther in Context*. Bloomington: Indiana University Press.

Suggested Reading

Hagen, Kenneth (1993). *Luther's Approach to Scripture as Seen in his 'Commentaries' on Galatians 1519–1538*. Tübingen: Mohr/Siebeck.

—— (1996). 'Omnis homo mendax: Luther on Psalm 116'. In *Biblical Interpretation in the Era of the Reformation*, ed. Richard A. Muller and John L. Thompson. Grand Rapids, MI: Eerdmans, 85–102.

Meuser, Fred W. (1983). *Luther the Preacher*. Minneapolis: Augsburg.

Pelikan, Jaroslav (1959). *Luther the Expositor: Introduction to the Reformer's Exegetical Writings Companion Volume to Luther's Works*. Saint Louis: Concordia.

Peters, Albrecht (1990–4). *Kommentar zu Luthers Katechismen*, 5 vols. Göttingen: Vandenhoeck & Ruprecht.

Wengert, Timothy J. (2009). *Martin Luther's Catechisms: Forming the Faith*. Minneapolis: Fortress.

CHAPTER 33

....

HOW LUTHER'S ENGAGEMENT IN PASTORAL CARE SHAPED HIS THEOLOGY

....

RONALD K. RITTGERS

IT is a commonplace in contemporary Reformation research that Luther's efforts to reform the church began with an attempt to reform the care of souls, above all, the care of his own soul. His desire to find peace and consolation for his own troubled conscience provided the impetus for Luther's initial wrestling with the *cura animarum* [care of souls] of his day. Increasingly convinced that the spiritual assurance he sought could not finally be found in traditional pastoral care, Luther felt compelled to oppose the failings and abuses he saw in this care with all his might. Because he was entrusted with the *cura animarum* himself, and also with the training of future clergy, Luther felt similarly compelled to offer to his contemporaries the alternative remedy for troubled consciences that he was in the process of developing as he lectured his way through the Psalms, portions of the Pauline corpus, and Hebrews. Luther's new soteriology grew directly out of his concern for the care of souls. This concern set Luther on the road to Reformation and occupied a central role in his life and work: '...the care of souls (*cura animarum*)...was the driving force in Luther's personal development and in his career as a friar, professor, theologian, and even reformer' (Kittelson 2003: 261). In both his private and public life, 'Luther was seized with the problem of the *cura animarum*...' (Kittelson 2003: 262, 264). He was ever preoccupied with the human conscience and its need to be instructed and consoled by the Word of God. This central concern shaped his theology in important ways. Borrowing from Berndt Hamm, one can say that Luther's theology was from first to last a *Frömmigkeitstheologie*; that is, similar to figures such as Jean Gerson, Johannes Paltz, and Johannes von Staupitz, Luther's theology was focused on spiritual edification and consolation, not on speculation, and was especially concerned with promoting sound pastoral care and authentic Christian devotion (Hamm 1999: 9–46; Bast 2004: xv,

18–24). Of course, the content of Luther's 'piety-theology' differed in important respects from the theology of Gerson, Paltz, and even Staupitz (Kolb 2009: 39–40), but his driving concerns remained quite similar to theirs.

I. Luther's Engagement in Pastoral Care

Exploring Luther's engagement in pastoral care more precisely begins with his attempt to pastor himself. Several fears provoked the spiritual crisis that gripped his soul in the monastery: fear of death, fear of not being among the elect, and, most profoundly, fear of divine wrath (Lohse 1999: 88–90); this crisis was also caused by 'his native sensitivity' in spiritual matters (Oberman 1992: 180). The result was *tentationes* or *Anfechtungen*, which may be translated as 'agonizing struggles' (Bayer 2008: 20, 21; cf. Beintker 1954). Luther provided a memorable description of his *Anfechtungen* in his *Explanations of the Ninety-Five Theses* (1518). He begins with a reference to the Apostle Paul's account of his ascent to the third heaven in 2 Corinthians 12:2 and continues:

> I myself 'knew a man' who claimed that he had often suffered these punishments, in fact over a very brief period of time. Yet they were so great and so much like hell that no tongue could adequately express them, no pen could describe them, and one who had not experienced them could not believe them. And so great were they that, if they had been sustained or had lasted for half an hour, even for one tenth of an hour, he would have been reduced to ashes. At such a time God seems terribly angry, and with him the whole creation. At such a time there is no flight, no comfort, within or without, but all things accuse. At such a time as that the Psalmist mourns, 'I am cut off from thy sight' [Ps. 31:22]…In this moment (strange to say) the soul cannot believe that it can ever be redeemed other than that the punishment is not yet completely felt. Yet the soul is eternal and is not able to think of itself as being temporal. All that remains is the stark-naked desire for help and a terrible groaning, but it does not know where to turn for help. In this instance the person is stretched out with Christ so that all his bones may be counted, and every corner of the soul is filled with the greatest bitterness, dread, trembling, and sorrow in such a manner that all these last forever. To use an example: If a ball crosses a straight line, any point of the line which is touched bears the whole weight of the ball, yet it does not embrace the whole ball. Just so the soul, at the point where it is touched by a passing eternal flood, feels and imbibes nothing except eternal punishment. Yet the punishment does not remain, for it passes over again. (WA1.557,33–558,12; LW31:129. Cf. *Operationes in Psalmos*, AWA2.366,10–14)

Bernhard Lohse commented that Luther here describes how he, in a sense, experienced the crucifixion of Christ in his own person, and that this experience completely exceeded his own strength—it utterly broke him: 'The figure of the ball has its point in the fact that the experience of suffering exceeds what can be endured'. (Lohse 1999: 90).

The locus of this crushing experience for Luther was his conscience. There he felt the unbearable weight of divine wrath rolling over him. By his own admission, Luther had grown to hate God for the impossible demands of righteousness that the young monk believed God had placed on human beings. Luther says that he 'raged with a fierce and troubled conscience' against the divine Judge in the monastery (WA54.185,21–2, 186,1; LW34.336–7). For Luther the conscience was at once the most important and the most vulnerable part of the human soul. Scholars have made careful studies of how Luther's conception of the conscience differed from late medieval conceptions, showing how he 'ontologically magnified' the conscience, in some cases even using the term to refer to the whole person (Baylor 1977: 205, with discussion of the necessary qualifiers on this judgement, 208–10). Conscience was no longer a derivative and circumscribed capacity of the soul that judged specific actions based on the innate knowledge of moral first principles; now it occupied a much larger space within the soul and spoke with a much louder and more authoritative voice. Conscience accused and judged the whole person, functioning as a kind of inner tribunal, determining whether the person as such was righteous or not before God. This is how the Wittenberg reformer defined conscience in On Monastic Vows (1521):

> For conscience is not the power of acting but the power of judging, which judges about works. Its proper work (as Paul says in Romans 2[:15]) is to accuse or to excuse, to cause one to stand accused or absolved, terrified or secure. Its purpose is not to do, but to speak about what has been done and what should be done, and this judgment makes us stand accused or saved before God.
>
> (WA8.606.32–7; LW44.298, cited in Zachman 1993: 20–1)

Luther could also equate conscience with the heart (cor), thus indicating his conviction that it could both generate and experience a great range of emotions—everything from joy and peace to anxiety and despair (Zachmann 1993: 22).

Luther's resolution of his own spiritual crisis consisted in large part of a radical reorientation of his conscience from human works to the divine Word, a change that provided him with the peace he so desired. Luther believed that the conscience had no connection to the divine: it rendered judgement on the basis of purely empirical evidence that it evaluated in light of its own sense of right and wrong, which was in turn based upon its (deeply flawed) grasp of the natural law and the axiom that sin is to be avoided (Zachman 1993: 21–6; cf. Baylor 1977: 243). The conscience assessed a person's standing before God on the basis of his or her moral acts, and when it found the person's righteousness to be wanting, it became terrified of divine judgement and looked to moral improvement as its only salvation. According to Randall Zachman, Luther came to view this religion of conscience as a theology of glory that sought to understand and appease God on the basis of human abilities alone (Zachman 1993: 36). In its place Luther posited a religion of the cross that required the conscience to forsake its own moral understanding and to be instructed by the Word alone. The Word first crucified the conscience through the demands of law, which were far more exacting than anything the conscience could concoct for itself. Then the Word consoled the conscience by presenting it with the gift of Christ's righteousness that was to be received by faith; this was the only way for the conscience to have peace.

This radical reorientation of the conscience appears especially in Luther's writings during the Indulgence Controversy. For example, in *For the Investigating of Truth and the Consoling of Fearful Consciences* (early summer 1518) he argued that the human conscience or heart—Luther used the terms interchangeably in this treatise—can only find peace if it turns from man-made doctrine to the Word. Luther specifically has in mind the traditional teaching that sinners must achieve a sufficient level of sorrow for sin in order to be absolved from the guilt (*culpa*) of sin, and that they need to atone for the penalty (*poena*) of sin through works of satisfaction. Luther seeks to marginalize *poena*, treating it as a human invention and thus a purely this-worldly affair that in no way affects the soul's standing before God. 'The remission of guilt reconciles a human being to God, the remission of penalty reconciles a human being to a human being, that is, to the church' (WA1.630,9–10, cf. 630,5–6). Luther is primarily interested in the former kind of reconciliation in this treatise because he believes that it alone brings solace to troubled consciences: 'The remission of guilt calms the heart and takes away the greatest of all punishments, namely, the consciousness of sin' (WA1.630,7–8; cf. *Ein Sermon von dem Sakrament der Buße* [1519], WA2.714,14–20). This remission, in turn, depends upon the penitent's faith in the divine Word of promise, here Matthew 16:19, 'whatever you loose on earth will be loosed in heaven. . .'. 'Therefore, it is certain that sins are loosed if you believe they have been loosed because the promise of Christ the Saviour [Matt. 16:19] is certain' (WA1.631,17–18). Above all, the conscience needed certainty, the assurance that sins truly had been forgiven by God—that divine accusation had given way to divine absolution (Bayer 1971: 166, 169, 343, Bayer 2008: 44–58). It could face whatever trial came its way if only it possessed this confidence of absolution (WA1: 630.13–14). According to Luther, basing peace for one's conscience on the strength of one's sorrow for sin is a 'machination of desperation' (*desperationis machina*) and amounts to calling God a liar and oneself a truth-teller (WA1.631.23–8; on the importance of this concept, see Zachman 1993: 5); it amounts to being a theologian of glory instead of a theologian of the cross.

Zachman aptly observes that the battle between a glory-seeking religion of conscience and a Word-trusting religion of the cross persisted throughout the Christian's lifetime; it was not won once for all during some breakthrough experience—this was certainly not true for Luther. He thought that the conscience continually needed to be redirected to the Word and faith, for, as a power of the flesh, the conscience was deeply prone to reject God and his cruciform means of operating in the world (Zachman 1993: 63). Luther's engagement in pastoral care was largely an effort to fight daily this battle in himself and others.

It should be noted that Luther's primary form of pastoral care was preaching, in both the Augustinian church as well as in the city church, serving as pastor in the latter during Bugenhagen's absence (Brecht 1985–93: 1.150–1, 2.284). 'Aside from his preaching, there is relatively little known about Luther's activity in the parish and the congregation. . . Only occasionally do we see anything about Luther's performing pastoral care in the congregation; presumably, this was usually left to the deacons' (Brecht 1985–93: 3.252–3). Still, Luther did perform pastoral care now and again, especially via letter, and his sermons were deeply pastoral in nature.

Veit Dietrich records one such occasion of actual pastoral care involving Luther. In 1533 Luther visited the home of Benedict Paul in order to console the Wittenberg jurist and burgomaster upon the accidental death of his only son. Luther exhorted the grieving man to lift his eyes from the present evil and to focus on the many gifts he had received from God, 'namely, that you have a knowledge of the Word, that you have Christ's favour, and that you have a good conscience' (Tappert 2003: 68; WATR1.474–80, §949). In 1527 Luther wrote a letter to his friend, John Agricola, the Latin school teacher in Eisleben, regarding the well-being of his wife, Elsa, whom Luther had invited to Wittenberg for a time of respite; Elsa was suffering from an unnamed malady. Luther writes to Agricola:

> I have been glad and willing to receive your Elsa here. Her illness is, as you see, more of the soul than of the body. I am comforting her as much as I know to and can... In a word, her illness is not for apothecaries (as they call them), nor is it to be treated with the salves of Hippocrates, but it requires the powerful plasters of the Scriptures and the Word of God. For what does conscience have to do with Hippocrates? Accordingly, I should dissuade you from the use of medicine and recommend the power of God's Word. (Tappert 2003: 83; WABr4.219, 220)

In his Invocavit Sermons (1522) Luther praised the value of private confession—though not the traditional sacrament of penance—because of its ability to apply the Word directly to troubled consciences. Luther said he would command no one to confess their sins to another, but neither would he permit anyone to deprive him or others of this practice, as was then being considered in Wittenberg (WA10,3.61d,32–62d,33; LW51.98–9).

Luther's engagement in pastoral care was first and foremost an engagement in the consolation of troubled consciences with the Word in order to encourage faith and the peace it could bring (Mennecke-Haustein 1989; Ngien 2007).

II. The Shape of Luther's Theology

Luther's engagement in pastoral care thus clearly shaped certain aspects of his theology. Because of the anxiety he believed traditional penitential theology and practice had caused in human consciences (especially his own), and because he could find no biblical support for it, Luther sought to abolish this sacrament, seeing it as an especially pernicious combination of man-made doctrine and works righteousness, even as he worked to retain a non-penitential version of private confession (Rittgers 2004). Penance-based religion had no place in his evangelical theology.

This opposition to traditional sacramental confession also contributed directly to Luther's rejection of the papacy. In *Concerning Confession, Whether the Pope Has the Power to Command It* (1521), Luther accused the pope of using the sacrament of penance to seduce vulnerable consciences away from their Lord through a false gospel of works righteousness. For Luther, God alone was to reign in the human conscience through the Word;

Christ was to be its only Husband. 'Therefore, he [the pope] is the Antichrist, who places himself above God, as Saint Paul says (2 Thess. 2:4), and breaks open the bridal chamber of Christ and makes all Christians souls into whores' (WA8.152,6–8). Because the pope dared to intrude upon the inner sanctum of the conscience, Luther concluded that he was in league with Satan. This connection between Luther's pastoral concern for the conscience and his castigation of papacy is quite important, for he would later say that the identification of the pope as the Antichrist was decisive for his Reformation breakthrough and therefore for the shape of his evangelical theology (WA54.184,2; LW34.334). The pope's alleged seduction of human consciences was not the only ground Luther saw for concluding that the bishop of Rome was demonic, but this pastoral concern clearly played an important role in his fierce opposition to the papacy.

This same concern influenced the law–gospel dialectic that was so central to Luther's theology (Althaus 1966: 251–73; Lohse 1999: 267–76). As we have seen, Luther believed that the conscience rendered judgement on the whole person. Therefore, it was extremely important for the conscience to employ the proper standard as it reached its verdict. For Luther, that standard was the Word, both the law and the gospel. The law-gospel dialectic reflects Luther's conviction as a pastor that the conscience must first be informed by the law and then crucified by the same so that it can be resurrected by the gospel.

The pastoral concerns that informed the law–gospel dialectic emerge especially in Luther's debate with Erasmus on the soteriological status of the human will. The moral injunctions in Scripture, which the famous humanist had invoked to support his case for limited free will, could not be read to imply that human beings could carry out the divine commandments; this was to confuse the imperative with the indicative mood. For Luther, a divine command did not assume a human ability to fulfil it; quite the contrary, the law assumed human moral impotence and sought to expose it (WA18.676,4-684,26, LW33.125-38). Failure to observe this crucial distinction led not only to pride but also to malformed and tormented consciences that sought in vain to obey the law in hopes of pleasing God. Such people lost sight of the true source of consolation, the gospel, which, according to Luther, allowed the sinner to 'be at peace and happy with an untroubled conscience' (WA18.684,3; LW33.137).

Luther's engagement in pastoral care was especially significant for the shape of his Christology and his understanding of the requirements for a true theologian. Lecturing on Psalm 22 (1521) Luther argues for a novel understanding of Christ's suffering on the cross directly informed by his desire to console troubled consciences (cf. Rittgers 2012: 111–24). He maintains that Christ not only took on himself the penalty of human sin on the cross, Christ also took on the effects of human sin—*all* its effects. Luther explains that Christ did not simply suffer death; he also suffered the anxiety that the human conscience feels in the face of death, along with the fear it experiences of being eternally damned and abandoned by God (WA5.603,14–17). Christ actually experienced this anxiety; he was frightened and terrified in all the ways that human beings are. God the Father hid himself from Christ on the cross and Christ's divine nature withdrew from him, leaving him completely alone (see Chapter 19). Thus, when Christ cried out from the cross, 'My God, my God, why have you forsaken me?' (Matt. 27:46; Mark 15:34), he was actually telling the truth, for he had become a sinner, and truly was abandoned by God (WA5.605,34 –606,1; cf. WA5.606.1–2; and a similar emphasis in Luther's Lectures on Genesis, WA43.550,23–42; LW5.177; WA44.523,38–524,9; LW7.302).

Luther conceded in his lectures that not all would understand these things: Scripture has milk for the weak and wine for the strong; this is consolation for the strong, that is, for those who know what it is to be stretched out on the cross with Christ and to have the terrible ball of divine wrath roll over their souls. This wine delivers such people from doubt when they see that Christ suffered the same, and willingly so, taking on what human beings involuntarily inherit by virtue of original sin. Luther argued that those who need such wine will take great encouragement from seeing how Christ triumphed in such weakness, and triumphed for them—for each one individually (WA5.606,2–28).

The close link that Luther here posits between Christ's suffering and the Christian's suffering rests on a traditional theological conviction that he radicalized. Luther maintains that while Christ was sinless, he was still weak because the humanity he assumed was not perfect prelapsarian humanity, but weak and vitiated postlapsarian humanity. Thus, Christ had to contend with every weakness and temptation that afflicts every human being. When he cried out on the cross, 'My God, my God, why have you forsaken me?' this was not blasphemy, but simply the result of Christ's human nature being overwhelmed by his suffering (WA5.605,4, 25–8). There was nothing novel about saying that Christ took on postlapsarian human nature; but Luther stressed as few before him the true depth of the human weakness that Christ assumed and endured.

In the late medieval tradition the Saviour's words of lament and dereliction on the cross had typically been attributed to Christ speaking in the person of the church (in persona ecclesiae) or to Christ referring to his body and the lower parts of his soul (Lienhard 1982: 25, 116). Luther argued for a different interpretation in the Operationes. When the psalmist cries out to God, 'Why are you so far from saving me, from the words of my groaning?' (Vulgate Ps. 21:2; Ps. 22:1b), Luther insisted that Christ spoke these words in reference to his whole human self (WA5.607,8–12). Christ suffered in every part of his human person; he experienced God-forsakenness in his entire human nature. Christ faced God the Father's wrath and despaired in his conscience, just as the Christian does (Lienhard 1982: 115 emphasizes Luther's conviction that Christ was especially afflicted in his conscience on the cross; it was here that he felt the crushing anxiety of the Father's absence and wrath). Christ was afflicted in soul and body, just as the Christian is. Christ, too, experienced Anfechtungen, although to a degree that far outstripped anything known to the Christian. Thus, according to Luther, the Christian could find in Christ a source of empathy and hope in his own afflictions and God-forsakenness, clearly one of the driving concerns in the Wittenberg professor's Christology. Luther was influenced by late medieval mysticism and Passion piety in his emphasis on the humanity and suffering of Christ, but he clearly went beyond both. As Lienhard observed, 'The way in which Luther describes the suffering of Christ on the cross certainly constitutes a break with tradition' (Lienhard 1982: 116; cf. Wolff 2005: 95, 105, 150, 167, 239–40, 260–1). Wolff argues that in contrast to the traditional treatment of Psalm 22:1, Luther's interpretation presented his cry from the cross with incomparably more intensity, for he found in it the greatest soteriological nearness of Christ to the godless. The crucified one resembles every God-forsaken, cursed, damned sinner or blasphemer. Luther later said of this verse, 'I regard them as the greatest words in all of Scripture' (WATR5.188,19–189,3, §5493, cited in Wolff 2005: 167). Luther stresses in the *Operationes* that in Christ the God-forsaken sinner has a Saviour who has taken on himself the full depths of human estrangement from God and overcome it, the very heart of his pastoral theology.

The experience of such estrangement from God played a key role in Luther's understanding of how true Christian theologians were formed. *Tentatio*, agonizing struggle, was essential to the training and spiritual growth of theologians and pastors of the cross, a conviction that grew directly out of Luther's own spiritual struggles and involvement in pastoral care (Nieden 1999: 83–102). This experience was important because it helped evangelical theologians to appreciate the true value of God's Word and its consoling powers. In the preface to the 1539 edition of his German works, Luther lays down three rules for theological study: *oratio, meditatio,* and *tentatio* (prayer, meditation, temptation or agonizing struggle) (WA50.657–61; LW34.283–8). He regarded *tentatio* as the touchstone for learning theology (WA50.660,1–4; LW34.286–7; see Chapters 11 and 32). In a table talk from 1531 Luther asserted, '*sola experientia facit theologum*' (experience alone makes the theologian) (WATR1.16,13; LW54.7, cited in Bayer 2008: 21–2). Luther here refers not to experience as such, but to the experience of agonizing struggle in the context of wrestling with Scripture (2008: 22). Only those who come to God's Word with a troubled conscience can discover and taste its sweet fruit.

Already in his early lectures on the Psalms (1513–15) Luther was referring to the importance of *tentatio* in providing theologians with a 'broad' education that expands their souls and enables them to understand Scripture and life itself properly (WA55,2.55,20–2, 57.5–7; LW10.49). For Luther, Christian theology was a kind of wisdom gained through agonizing struggle and wrestling with Scripture, something he asserted in his marginal notes on Tauler's sermons in 1516, where he referred to theology as a *sapientia experimentalis* (an experiential wisdom) (WA9.28,21, cited in Bayer 2008: 30). The wisdom gained from such struggling and wrestling was to inform and enrich the theologian's (and the Christian's) pastoral care of others (WA12.374,13–14; LW30.119). This had been the pattern in Luther's own life, and he urged it on his students and followers. Thus, Luther's engagement in the *cura animarum* influenced not only the shape of his theology, but also his very understanding of what a theologian is or ought to be.

REFERENCES

Althaus, P. (1966). *The Theology of Martin Luther*, trans. R. C. Schultz. Philadelphia: Fortress.

Bast, R. J. (ed.) (2004). *The Reformation of Faith in the Context of Late Medieval Theology and Piety: Essays by Berndt Hamm*. Leiden: Brill.

Bayer, O. (1971). *Promissio. Geschichte der reformatorischen Wende in Luthers Theologie*. Göttingen: Vandenhoeck and Ruprecht.

—— (2008). *Martin Luther's Theology: A Contemporary Interpretation*, trans. T. H. Trapp. Grand Rapids: Eerdmans.

Baylor, M. G. (1977). *Action and Person: Conscience in Late Scholasticism and the Young Luther*. Leiden: Brill.

Beintker, H. (1954). *Die Überwindung der Anfechtung bei Luther. Eine Studie zu seiner Theologie nach den Operationes in Psalmos, 1519–1521*. Berlin: Evangelische Verlagsansalt.

Brecht, M. (1985–93). *Martin Luther*, trans. J. L. Schaff. Vol. 1: *His Road to Reformation, 1483–1521*. Vol. 2: *Martin Luther: Shaping and Defining the Reformation, 1521–1532*. Vol. 3: *The Preservation of the Church, 1532–1546*. Minneapolis: Fortress.

Hamm, B. (1999). 'Was ist Frömmigkeitstheologie? Überlegungen zum 14. bis 16. Jahrhundert'. In *Praxis Pietatis: Beiträge zu Theologie und Frömmigkeit in der frühen Neuzeit: Wolfgang Sommer zum 60. Geburtstag*, ed. H.-J. Nieden and M. Nieden. Stuttgart: Kohlhammer, 9–45.

Kittelson, J. (2003). 'Luther and Modern Church History'. In *The Cambridge Companion to Martin Luther*, ed. D. K. McKim. Cambridge: Cambridge University Press, 259–71.

Kolb, R. (2009). *Martin Luther, Confessor of the Faith*. Oxford: Oxford University Press.

Lienhard, M. (1982). *Luther: Witness to Jesus Christ*, trans. E. H. Robertson. Minneapolis: Augsburg.

Lohse, B. (1999). *Martin Luther's Theology: Its Historical and Systematic Development*, trans. R. A. Harrisville. Minneapolis: Fortress.

Mennecke-Haustein, U. (1989). *Luthers Trostbriefe*. Gütersloh: Mohn.

Ngien, D. (2007). *Luther as Spiritual Adviser: The Interface of Theology and Piety in the Luther's Devotional Writings*. Waynesboro, GA: Paternoster.

Nieden, M. (1999). 'Anfechtungen als Thema lutherischer Anweisungen zum Theologiestudium'. In *Praxis Pietatis. Beiträge zu Theologie und Frömmigkeit in der Frühen Neuzeit: Wolfgang Sommer zum 60. Geburtstag*, ed. H.-J. Nieden and M. Nieden. Stuttgart: Kohlhammer, 83–102.

Oberman, H. A. (1992). *Luther: Man between God and the Devil*, trans. E. Walliser-Schwarzbart. New York: Image.

Rittgers, R. (2004). *The Reformation of the Keys: Confession, Conscience, and Authority in Sixteenth-Century Germany*. Cambridge, MA: Harvard University Press.

—— (2012). *The Reformation of Suffering: Pastoral Theology and Lay Piety in Late Medieval and Early Modern Germany*. Oxford: Oxford University Press.

Tappert, T. G. (ed., trans.) (2003). *Luther: Letters of Spiritual Counsel*. Vancouver: Regent College.

Wolff, J. (2005). *Metapher und Kreuz: Studien zu Luthers Christusbild*. Tübingen: Mohr/Siebeck.

Zachman, R. C. (1993). *The Assurance of Faith: Conscience in the Theology of Martin Luther and John Calvin*. Minneapolis: Fortress.

CHAPTER 34

LUTHER'S THOUGHT ASSUMED FORM IN POLEMICS

ANNA VIND

'POLEMICS' cannot simply be defined as a specific literary form or as a matter of a certain style: the definition clearly must begin from the theological understanding lying at the root of Luther's polemical activity. He understood himself as a fighter for the Word of God. In a preface from 1529 he wrote, 'I was born to fight with the scalawags and devils and overcome them' (WA30,2.68,12–16). Thus one could say that the genre of polemics describes most of what he wrote; indeed that polemic was at the core of his whole existence. The polemical Luther is not only found in tracts directed at opponents: we also see him in the scholarly exegetical work, in his practice as a disputant at the university, in prefaces, postscripts, letters, sermons, and table-talk. An investigation of his polemics cannot therefore only deal with combative pamphlets and tracts but must take a larger body of texts into account. What follows outlines Luther's self-understanding as a polemicist, the historical context of his polemical activity, his polemical form and style, and finally an example of the influence of his polemics upon theological doctrine, ecclesiastical issues, and pastoral care.

I. LUTHER'S BELLIGERENT SELF-UNDERSTANDING

In his passionate discussion with Erasmus in 1525, Luther said,

> [...] it is the most constant condition for the Word of God that because of it the world is in turmoil [...] The world and its god neither can nor will bear the Word of the true God, and the true God neither can nor will be silent; when these two gods make war on each other, what can then arise other than uproar in the whole world?. (WA18.626,8–10, 22–24; LW33.52)

It is as a part of this apocalyptic situation that he sees himself (see chapters 9 and 24 above): his own role is to fight the good fight for the sake of God's Word, on which he can stand firmly and courageously. This he had already seen as he denounced indulgences; this is what he claimed at Worms in 1521; and this continued to lie at the root of his polemical efforts until the day of his death. This self-understanding as a part of *militia Christi* was not at all unique to Luther, but had its roots in antiquity, in the biblical universe, and in the theological tradition, often with reference to Paul's words in Ephesians 6:11–17 (Stolt 1974: 86ff.).

Luther has often been accused of an arrogant 'I-know-best' attitude, but this does not adequately describe his understanding of himself. He was acutely aware of his own insufficiency and often tried to avoid attracting too much attention to his own person. His courage and ability to stand forward and hold on to his conviction were directed away from himself and rooted in a deep confidence in God's Word. In replying to Erasmus he describes how fearful and anxious it is for him to be in the midst of the turmoil: as he said, he was not made out of stone. But, believing as he did, he had no choice: 'there are no two ways about it' (WA18.625,19–29; LW33.51).

To understand why this reference to his 'belief' is not only some subjective and superior attitude, we must look at his explanations of his interpretation of Scripture and thus of what makes a good theologian. Some of his clearest hermeneutical thought is found in his elaborate answer to the papal bull of 1520, the *Assertio omnium articulorum M. Lutheri per bullam Leonis X. novissimam damnatorum* (WA7.94–151; see Mostert 1998: 9–41).

Here he explains that the *sine qua non* of trying to understand Scripture is to give way to the spirit of the text. Readers need to discard their own expectations and prejudices and leave room for the words on the page. Luther even interchanges the subjects of the interpretation, indicating that for this to happen the active part is not on the human side: it is the spirit of the text which interprets man. The text hits man hard; he is judged, changed; he sees truth and is enlightened. 'Text' here does not mean the Holy Scripture as a book, but the Word of God present in the Bible.

This expulsion of the human spirit and the invasion of the divine spirit, which happens in the meeting between God's Word and man, is not brought about in a moment, but takes place repeatedly during a lifelong 'meditative' preoccupation with the Bible. This Luther describes in an exposition of Psalm 119:

> Second, you should meditate, that is, not only in your heart but also outwardly massage and poke the spoken words and the letters on the page, reading and rereading them carefully, reflecting on what the Holy Spirit meant to say. Take care that you not become weary or think that it is enough when you have read, heard, spoken and understood the text once or twice. That does not produce a particularly good theologian but rather like premature fruit that falls before it is half ripe.
>
> (WA50.659,22–29; LW34.286; see Oswald Bayer's interpretation in
> Ratschow 1994: 83–5)

Numerous examples demonstrate how Luther put this theory into practice. In his discussion with Jacob Latomus, the scholastic theologian from Leuven, one of the few opponents whom he respected, they discuss the interpretation of selected biblical passages. It is peculiar to Luther that on the one hand he is certain that Latomus has not understood that the content of God's Word is God and man in Christ, and thus the notion of sin and grace (WA8.126,21–25; LW32.257), and this basically prevents Latomus from reading Scripture properly. But on the other hand, Luther also displays tentativeness in his own interpretations. He discusses the meaning of the texts back and forth, indicating that he may not have the full, perfect understanding of a given passage. He tries to give concrete guidelines for the exposition, in, for instance, the questions of literal versus figural sense, of meaning, context, genre, and inspiration from previous interpreters. He concludes by pointing to, and praying for, the working of the Holy Spirit (WA8.74,8–15; LW32.182).

This is not the discourse of a know-it-all, but of one who acknowledges the fundamental importance of God's Word and therefore feels his responsibility as a Christian to strive for truth and fight against falsehood. At the same time we see a theologian with a clear perception of the abiding distortion and fallibility—the sinfulness—of all, including himself, so that he constantly makes a strong critical effort to hold on to that very same Word. His polemics are therefore characterized by both persistence and flexibility. If he had not been persistent, the polemical situations would have been less conspicuous; had he been immovable, the ongoing discussions with ever new opponents would not have made him reformulate his position as he did.

II. The Historical Context

Luther's polemical activity has its roots in various historical contexts. Clearly his background as a professor in the medieval university tradition was significant for his combative development. Many of his early decisive polemical texts—his theses on indulgences included—take the form of theses for academic disputation, prompting a scholarly reply. Among the most important disputations from the early years we can mention *Disputatio contra scholasticam theologiam* (1517), *Disputatio pro declaratione virtutis indulgentiarum* (1517), the Heidelberg Disputation (1518), and the Leipzig Disputation (1519). This argumentative genre revived in the 1530s and became the core of some of his late, and sharp, formulations on crucial reformational topics and against specific opponents. Prominent are his different theses against the antinomians (1537–40), the theses *De homine* (1536) and *De fide iustificante* (1543), five series of theses on the interpretation of Romans 3:28, and several theses on Christology (1539/40), the Trinity (1544/5), and ecclesiology (1535/36/42).

The disputation nevertheless did not form the decisive medium for Luther's polemical activity. More important was the influence from the various forms of pamphlets and tracts flowering in both Latin and the vernacular in the late fifteenth and early sixteenth centuries, nourished by the humanist movement and strongly dependent upon the invention of the printing press (Flood 1998). This coincided with manifestations of a growing dissatisfaction with the existing church and society, and together these tendencies slowly brought about what can be described as a breakthrough in the history of literature. The German literary historian Barbara Könneker has labelled 'the discovery of the word as a weapon' and its mobilization for winning over public opinion 'one of most important literary innovations of this age' (Könneker 1975: 8). Among Luther's forerunners here were Sebastian Brant's *Das Narrenschiff* (1494), Thomas Murner's satirical pamphlets, Erasmus' *Encomium Moriae* (1511), as well as the publications of the Reuchlin affair. They all employed literary means—though in different ways—to argue for moral and religious renewal. Especially the Reuchlin affair paved the way for Luther since it was a battle with words characterized by a public religious and social disagreement between the old-school scholastics and the humanist movement. Many influential humanists saw Luther as continuing this fight and stood behind him with literary pamphlets and tracts as soon as he entered the arena.

III. Luther's Polemical Form and Style

The heady atmosphere of liberation and change during these years was of vital importance to the development of the literary polemical forms. In Luther's case he nevertheless restricted himself to the prose genres mentioned in the introduction: his literary polemics are found in scriptural interpretations, tracts and pamphlets, theses, prefaces, postscripts, sermons, and letters. A departure from prose is his occasional employment of pictorial media, in the form of woodcuts, e.g. in the *Passional Christi und Antichristi* (1521) made in cooperation with Lukas Cranach the Elder (Fleming 1973). Luther never touched widespread and popular polemical genres such as dialogues, allegories, didactic poems, rhymed chronicles or visions, let alone dramas and epic tales (Wolf 1980: 130).

When looking at his oeuvre, we see how innovative Luther was inside the genres he chose: he never restricted himself to a specific formal way of writing (see also Brecht 1990). In the case of scriptural interpretation he broke away from the traditional form after a few years, leaving aside the *glossae* and *scholia* and writing his interpretation of the text continuously. Furthermore, he allowed himself to relate his interpretations to current problems, breaking into the exegesis with polemical digressions. This independence of mind reappears in his pamphlets and tracts, where he answers or chooses to ignore opponents at his own convenience. In responding to Jacob Latomus' polemical book mentioned above, which was written in a traditional medieval style, referring to and quoting from Scripture and the Church Fathers at length, Luther simply ignored the model and selected a few central issues in order to cut his way through to what he saw as the core of the discussion. In the debate with Erasmus of Rotterdam he felt more obliged to follow the structure set out in Erasmus' book on the freedom of the will, *De libero arbitrio diatribe sive collatio* (1524), but once *De servo arbitrio* (1525) was written, he never came back to the discussion, despite Erasmus' pursuing it in *Hyperaspistes* (1526–7). For the first and last time he chose to write in a humanist genre quite unusual for him, in his answer to Johannes Cochlaeus: the Latin lampoon *Adversus armatum virum Cokleum* (1523) (see also Stolt 1974: 78–121; Schwitalla 1986).

This literary freedom recurs in Luther's literary polemical style. He always deliberately considered the recipient when choosing how to shape his thoughts: the choice of language, style, and level of argumentation were strongly dependent upon the situation and the person addressed. Comparisons between different texts, between Latin and German versions of the same texts, and diligent analyses of the careful structure of individual works demonstrate this. The picture which emerges is of a versatile stylist, fully alert to what communicates effectively (Stolt 1969, 1974: 31–77). Luther's style ranges from the plain and natural, spiced with ordinary pictures and examples from everyday life, to the well-formed, ornate, and politely humanistic, and on to the ironic, sarcastic, satirical, coarse, and almost abusively rude. Many examples of the last kind must be considered in polemical context; in light of 'the word as weapon'. This stylistic tool has sometimes been read as a sign of mental problems and has led to some scholarly defamation of Luther (e.g., Grisar 1911–12; Reiter 1937/41; Erikson 1958), but other researchers have shown that the eruptive and verbally violent attacks are a natural part of the landscape of sixteenth-century communication. Not merely the outbursts of a rude, simple-minded or mentally ill personality, they were accepted practice (Edwards 1983). This is not to say that Luther was a gentle soul. Occasionally he himself reflected upon his anger, viewing it primarily as effective and restorative: 'anger refreshes all my blood, sharpens my mind, and drives away my temptations' (WATR2.455,33–35, §2410a; cf. Edwards 1983: 6). But even as he sought to justify his actions, he was aware of the negative effect these outbursts had on his contemporaries (WABr2.168,2–6; LW48.179; WA30,3.470; WABr11.71, cf. Edwards 1983: 6).

As sources of the oral and verbal aspects of his polemics the table-talks, sermons and lectures, and the personal letters, should finally be considered. Except for the letters, these sources were not originally literary, but came to be so in time. They demonstrate that for him written polemic was an offshoot of discursive oral activity. In his table-talks, a genre the value of which as a source is somewhat dubious, we get an impression of his discursive range and his willingness to participate in and contribute to multifaceted discussions. Grounded in his high appreciation of the spoken word, this was ultimately connected to his fundamental understanding of God's Word as an oral phenomenon (WA10,1.17, 7–12; LW35.123). In the table-talks he sometimes qualifies his sermons as a 'verbum vocale', through which he could address ordinary people (WATR2.299,16, §2031 and 6.196–197, §6798). His *Invocavit Sermons*, delivered on the occasion of rioting in Wittenberg in 1522, show how he could take the opportunity to show scorn and deliver sharp reprimands to his listeners if necessary. In the copies of his biblical lectures, which were not meant for publication, we find polemical digressions written for oral delivery in the lecture room. Interestingly, these quite harsh passages often do not recur in the corresponding student manuscripts, suggesting that even though Luther sometimes was carried away during his preparation, he may not always have chosen to present the resultant coarse and cutting critique in public (see the well-known anti-scholastic passage in Luther's Lecture on the Romans (1515–16), the corollary to Romans 4:7, WA56.273,3–275,16; LW25.260–262; the passage does not recur in the student manuscript, see WA57.163–166). Finally, the many letters Luther wrote offer further examples of his polemic, e.g., the letters he wrote to Melanchthon from Coburg in 1530 (WABr5.411–413, §1611; cf. Ebeling 1997: 304–11).

IV. THE INFLUENCE OF LUTHER'S POLEMICS UPON THEOLOGICAL DOCTRINE, ECCLESIASTICAL ISSUES, AND PASTORAL CARE

In an index to the Wittenberg edition of Luther's work from 1556, the books are listed in the following order: 'Streitbücher und Schriften wider das Papsttum; die Aufrührer; die Sakramentenschwärmer; die Widertäufer; die Antinomier; die Juden; die Wuecherer; die Türken; Streit, Vermahnung und Warnung an etliche Weltliche Herren' (Schilling 2003: 45). This covers to a great extent the range of opponents and polemical contexts facing Luther during his life. Roughly speaking they can be broken down into four classes: (1) papal opponents, (2) dissenters among his followers, (3) members of foreign religious communities, and (4) political adversaries.

When considering the influence of his polemics upon theological doctrine, ecclesiastical issues, and pastoral care, the premise of this essay should be repeated: Luther saw the defence of the gospel, God's Word, as his primary goal. This is the anchor point and the fundamental incentive in Luther's engagement in all four polemical contexts. To Luther all adversaries—despite their differences—committed the same sin of betrayal of the gospel. Nonetheless, he was aware of his own fallibility and willingly reformulated his own understanding if necessary. In general, he did not go into discussions in order to force anything through; he did so to attain the truth. Along that road he scrutinized his own beliefs in response to the challenges he met.

The *Invocavit* sermons of 1522 offer a good example, incorporating all three dimensions—doctrinal, ecclesiastical, and pastoral issues—in one event. Luther here castigates his own followers, led by Andreas Karlstadt, in Wittenberg for making the same mistake as the Roman church: with their iconoclasm and zeal for rapid change to the traditional mass, they are imposing a new set of rules upon the community in their attempt to secure the victory of the evangelical faith. This new set of rules is no better than the old since no rule compels to faith, rather the reverse. What Luther had been cultivating in his thinking for several years, the freedom of a Christian in faith, was here turned upside down: a new slavery was being imposed in the name of freedom.

The polemical situation of the *Invocavit* sermons influenced theological doctrine by sharpening Luther's understanding of faith. Where, against his papal opponents, he had underlined the relationship between God and man in faith alone, independent of all external authorities, he now emphasized the external Word of God as an anchor of faith in his answer to the reform-minded dissenters since they seemed to be moving towards a more fanatical and exaggeratedly spiritual understanding. This emphasis upon the 'external' or the 'outward' character of the Word is not as clearly expressed in the *Invocavit* sermons (the sixth sermon on the Eucharist contains the clearest emphasis upon faith as God-given, not something coming from man himself, WA10,3.48–54; LW51.92–5) as it is in his later answers to the sacramentarians, but the point lies squarely at the heart of the controversy in 1522.

In its bearing upon ecclesiastical issues, the situation obliged Luther to underline the concepts of gentleness and love in bringing about ecclesiastical renewal, a posture which continued to characterize his later work on reform of the church service. He was not unappreciative of the wish for a wholly new liturgy lying behind events, but he clearly saw the need for caution and the danger of haste. Reforming church life cannot be done overnight since then it risks becoming strange and perhaps repulsive to the believers.

It follows, finally, that Luther's arguments in these sermons are clearly pastoral. More than once he emphasizes the need to take care of those who are weak in faith and to extend brotherly love towards them. Ecclesiastical reforms should be carried out for their benefit, not in order to placate the strong and independent souls. Furthermore, there is a risk that those who seem strong and independent are not in fact on the right track, and thus by revolt, and in disregard of the social order, they may lead the weaker astray.

V. Past Scholarship Regarding the Topic

Luther's polemics have been treated in many different contexts and from different standpoints by Luther researchers within church history and systematic theology, German philologists, literary historians, social historians, and historians of the book. Thus, the definitions of his polemics vary from theological to more formal definitions, the latter relating to polemical genre and styles, and historical definitions viewing Luther as a part of the growing polemical activity in the sixteenth century. The present account of past scholarship does not pretend to be complete, but points to a selection of titles belonging to these different research contexts (for further literature to 1980, see Wolf 1985).

In church history we find two general introductory works on 'Luther als Schriftsteller' by Heinrich Bornkamm (1975) and Martin Brecht (1990), thematizing his self-understanding, his literary genres and style, including his polemics. These works are extended by the paragraph 'Gattungen' in *Lutherhandbuch* (2005). Here 'Streitschriften' are treated separately by Hellmut Zschoch among other genres such as 'Programmschriften', 'lectures', 'disputations', 'sermons', 'letters', and 'table-talks', in which polemic is also found. Zschoch gives a sound introduction to the theological and literary concept of polemics and goes through the most important polemical discussions between Luther and (1) representatives of the papal church and (2) fellow reformatory adversaries. Luther's polemical work is here given a narrower but solid treatment in its own right.

Two monographs on church history which emphasize Luther's polemics should also be mentioned: Edwards (1983) tries to reach a historical understanding of the older Luther and his harsher polemical works, and Kerlen (1976) analyses Luther's specific way of arguing and making assertions in contradistinction to those of Erasmus.

Among systematic theologians Günter Bader's *Assertio* (1985) also deserves attention since, in a rather different way from Kerlen, and with lines back to the 'assertio' tradition in antiquity and premodern times, he tries to shed new light on the meaning and the use of the concept in the dispute between Erasmus and Luther. Armin Buchholz (1993/2007) carefully works his way through Luther's understanding and use of Scripture in the polemical confrontations with Emser, Latomus, Erasmus, Karlstadt, Zwingli, Oecolampadius, and Schwenkfeld.

In the work of German philologists we find substantial research on Luther's polemics, especially Wolf (1980), and the works of the Swedish philologist Birgit Stolt (1974), particularly the section 'Sinnbilder für die Macht und Wirkung der Rede im 16. Jahrhundert', a detailed analysis of the discussion between Emser and Luther.

Literary-historical and historical contributions include the introduction to sixteenth-century reformatory literature by Barbara Könneker (1975), which is indispensable to any reading of Luther's polemics. Likewise, the social historian Miriam Usher Chrisman who, in revealing the place of the book in society, shows the dissemination and the reception of Luther's message and thus contextualizes him in sixteenth-century polemical culture (1982, 1996).

VI. POTENTIAL NEW FRONTIERS FOR RESEARCH AND SCHOLARLY EXCHANGE

In 1975 Heinrich Bornkamm dedicated what he called his 'einführende Skizze' to two researchers, the literary historian Paul Böckmann and the church historian Wilhelm Maurer (Bornkamm 1975: 39). According to Bornkamm, this was obligatory, because a comprehensive literary analysis of Luther requires both German literary scholars and theologians. His point applies to Luther's works in general, and also more narrowly to his polemics. This should be kept in mind when seeking for potential new frontiers for research and scholarly exchange. A glance at past scholarship makes it abundantly clear that the evidently interdisciplinary character of the research task needs to be further strengthened. In so cross-curricular a field of research, more attention to the whole, in its integrity, must be given in order to create a full picture. As the church historian Albrecht Beutel notes, despite exceptions, 'the question is seldom posed to what extent Luther's specific stylistic characteristics also reveal genuine theological foundations' (Beutel 1991: 478).

REFERENCES

Bader, Günter (1985). *Assertio. Drei fortlaufende Lektüren zu Skepsis, Narrheit und Sünde bei Erasmus und Luther.* Tübingen: Mohr.

Beutel, Albrecht (1991). *In dem Anfang war das Wort. Studien zu Luthers Sprachverständnis.* Tübingen: Mohr.

—— (ed.) (2005). *Luther-Handbuch.* Tübingen: Mohr/Siebeck.

Bornkamm, Heinrich (1975). 'Luther als Schriftsteller'. In *Luther. Gestalt und Wirkungen. Gesammelte Aufsätze.* Gütersloh: Mohn, 39–64.

Brecht, Martin (1990). *Luther als Schriftsteller. Zeugnisse seines dichterischens Gestaltens.* Stuttgart: Calwer Verlag.

Buchholz, Armin (1993/2007). *Schrift Gottes im Lehrstreit. Luthers Schriftverständnis und Schriftauslegung in seinen drei großen Lehrstreitigkeiten der Jahre 1521–1528.* Frankfurt am Main|Gießen: Lang|Brunnen.

Chrisman, Miriam Usher (1982). *Lay Culture, Learned Culture 1480–1599.* New Haven: Yale University Press.

—— (1996). *Conflicting Visions of Reform: German Lay Propaganda Pamphlets 1519–1530.* Atlantic Highlands, NJ: Humanities.

Ebeling, Gerhard (1997). *Luthers Seelsorge. Theologie in der Vielfalt der Lebenssituationen an seinen Briefe dargestellt.* Tübingen: Mohr/Siebeck.

Edwards, Mark U. Jr. (1983). *Luther's Last Battles: Politics and Polemics, 1531–46.* Ithaca: Cornell University Press.

Eriksson, Erik (1958). *Young Man Luther.* New York: Norton.

Fleming, Gerald (1973). 'On the Origin of the Passional Christi and Antichristi and Lucas Cranach the Elder's Contribution to Reformation Polemics in the Iconography of the Passional'. *Gutenberg Jahrbuch* 48: 352–68.

Flood, John L. (1998). 'The Book in Reformation Germany'. In *The Reformation and the Book*, ed. Jean-François Gilmont and Karin Maag. Brookfield: Ashgate, 21–103.

Grisar, Hartmut (1911–12). *Luther*, 3 vols. Freiburg im Breisgau: Herder.

Kerlen, Dietrich (1976). *Assertio. Die Entwicklung von Luthers theologischen Anspruch und der Streit mit Erasmus von Rotterdam.* Wiesbaden: Steiner.

Könneker, Barbara (1975). *Die deutscher Literatur der Reformationszeit. Kommentar zu einer Epoche.* Munich: Winkler.

Mostert, Walter (1998). 'Scriptura sacra sui ipsius interpres. Bemerkungen zu Luthers Verhältnis der Heiligen Schrift'. In *Glaube und Hermeneutik*, ed. Pierre Bühler and Gerhard Ebeling. *Gesammelte Aufsätze.* Tübingen: Mohr/Siebeck.

Ratschow, Carl Heinz (ed.) (1994). *Handbuch Systematischer Theologie, Bd. 1: Theologie.* Gütersloh: Gütersloher Verlagshaus.

Reiter, Paul (1937/1941). *Martin Luthers Umwelt, Charakter und Psychose: sowie die Bedeutung dieser Faktoren für seine Entwicklung und Lehre*, 2 vols. Copenhagen: Munksgaard.

Schilling, Johannes (2003). 'Die Abteilung "Schriften" in der Weimarer Lutherausgabe'. In *WA Begleitheft zu den Schriften, Teil 1–5.* Weimar: Böhlau, 25–53.

Schwitalla, Johannes (1986). 'Martin Luthers argumentative Polemik: mündlich und schriftlich'. In *Formen und Formgeschichte des Streitens. Der Literaturstreit*, ed. F. J. Worstbrock and H. Koopmann. Tübingen: Niemeyer, 41–54.

Stolt, Birgit (1969). *Studien zu Luthers Freiheitstraktat mit besonderer Rücksicht auf das Verhältnis der lateinischen und der deutschen Fassung zu einander und die Stilmittel der Rhetorik*. Stockholm: Almqvist & Wiksell.

—— (1974). *Wortkampf. Frühneuhochdeutsche Beispiele zur Rhetorischen Praxis*. Frankfurt: Athäneum.

Wolf, Herbert (1980). *Martin Luther. Eine Einführung in germanistische Luther-Studien*. Stuttgart: Metzler.

—— (1985). *Germanistische Lutherbibliographie. Martin Luthers deutsches Sprachschaffen im Spiegel des internationalen Schrifttums der Jahre 1880–1980*. Heidelberg: Winter.

SUGGESTED READING

Flood, John L. (1996). 'Heinrich VIII. und Martin Luther. Ein europäischer Streit und dessen Niederschlag in Literatur und Publistik'. In *Spannungen und Konflikte menschlichen Zusammenlebens in der deutschen Literatur des Mittelalters*, ed. Kurt Gärtner, Ingrid Kasten, and Frank Shaw. Tübingen: Niemeyer, 3–32.

Grün-Oesterreich, A. and P. L. Oesterreich (1999). 'Dialectica docet, rhetorica movet. Luthers Reformation der Rhetorik'. In *Rhetorica movet: Studies in Historical and Modern Rhetoric in Honour of Heinrich F. Plett*, ed. P. L. Oesterreich and T. O. Sloane. Leiden: Brill, 25–41.

Starke, Elfriede (1983). 'Luthers Beziehungen zu Kunst und Künstlern'. In *Leben und Werk Martin Luthers von 1526 bis 1546. Festgabe zu seinen 500. Geburtstag*, ed. Helmar Junghans. Göttingen: Vandenhoeck and Ruprecht, 531–48.

Walz, Herbert (1988). *Deutsche Literatur der Reformationszeit. Eine Einführung*. Darmstadt: Wissenschaftliches Buchgesellschaft.

CHAPTER 35

....

LUTHER'S THOUGHT TOOK SHAPE IN TRANSLATION OF SCRIPTURE AND HYMNS

....

CHRISTOPH BURGER

THE Christian message creates translations. Its authoritative texts as well as its liturgy, hymns, devotional and instructional writings have almost always moved into vernacular languages throughout the world. Translations shape the delivery of the actual message of Scripture and tradition in the language, culture, and society in which they are rendered; they form the minds of translators as well as users (Sanneh 2009). Martin Luther recognized the necessity for translating the Word of God into the language of the common people, and in carrying out the task himself he moulded new ways of understanding the Christian faith.

I. TRANSLATION OF THE BIBLE

Luther's translation of the Bible is a milestone in the development of Early Modern German, and therefore it has commanded attention from scholars in several fields. The contention that his translation made the language of the Saxon chancellery the normative form of written Early Modern German is no longer accepted. Luther's translation of the Bible did, however, influence many translations in other languages. His text was even used by translators in the Roman Catholic tradition, such as Hieronymus Emser, Johann Dietenberger, and Johann Eck, whose own translations aimed to counterbalance the influence of Luther's work. When Luther started work on his translation, there were already fourteen High German and four Low German Bible translations in existence, published between 1466 and 1522. All these, however, owed more to the Vulgate than did Luther's translation.

Johannes Wallmann (1994) and Katalin Péter (1995) assert, apparently independently of one another, that Luther and the other sixteenth-century reformers were not really interested in putting the vernacular Bible in the hands of lay people; this was more the achievement of pietists. According to Wallmann and Péter, the reformers judged that catechisms were sufficient for lay people. The hypothesis does not seem to have sparked lively debate, either among Reformation historians or specialists in German studies. One can counter, however, that Luther and his Wittenberg colleagues laboured innumerable hours on a translation of the Bible in the vernacular that would be understandable precisely for lay people. The same is true of Zwingli in Zurich. Calvin did not translate the Bible himself, but he did write a foreword to the translation by Pierre Robert Olivetanus. None of these reformers would have invested these efforts if they did not strive to provide lay people with access to the Bible in their own vernacular.

In 1530 Luther stressed that he went to great lengths to ensure that his translation is easy to understand: 'I have constantly tried in translating to produce a pure and clear German, and it has often happened that for two or three or four weeks we have searched and inquired for a single word, and sometimes not even found it then' (*Sendbrief vom Dolmetschen*, 1530; WA30,2.636,15–20; LW35.188; cf. WA30,2.640,1–2; LW35.193). An incident narrated in the court records also belies the assertion that the reformers' translations were not aimed at lay people: somewhere between 1530 and 1535 a man attending a church service in Dikkelvenne (Belgium) held up an open New Testament to his neighbours and said, 'Look, it is written down here, and that is the way it is' (Heijting 1996: 14).

The historical context of Luther's translation involved, first, his use of languages, tools, and helpers. Even while Luther was still in Erfurt, the influence of humanists, especially his fellow Augustinian Johann Lang, stimulated his interest in the biblical texts in the original Hebrew and Greek. In 1516–18 he lectured on the letters to the Romans, Galatians, and Hebrews, making use of the Greek text prepared by Erasmus, his *Novum Instrumentum*. Luther, however, never mastered Greek to the level of his colleague and friend Melanchthon. He therefore did not translate New Testament texts solely on the basis of the Greek text but relied additionally on the Latin translation contained in Erasmus' *Novum Instrumentum* and on the text of the Vulgate, which he knew largely by heart.

In Erfurt Luther acquired a basic knowledge of Hebrew, with the aid of the introduction to this language from Reuchlin's *De rudimentis hebraicis* (first printed 1506). He put this knowledge to good use already in his first series of lectures on the psalms, which he delivered in 1513–5. Nevertheless, in his translations of texts from the Old Testament, his superior familiarity with the Latin language of scholarship initially remained clearly perceptible. The Wittenberg professor of Hebrew Matthäus Aurogallus was a great help to Luther with this language.

From 1531 a 'Collegium Biblicum' in Wittenberg assisted Luther on a regular basis in revising his Bible translation. The group included not only Melanchthon and Aurogallus, but also Caspar Cruciger, Justus Jonas, and Johannes Bugenhagen. In addition to their reflections on exegetical questions, the scholars, who came from different parts of Germany, took pains to ensure that the Bible translation could be understood in the various German language regions.

For each of his first series of lectures at Wittenberg, Luther arranged for a Latin text of the biblical book in question to be printed. He revised the text before printing, taking into account both textual-critical and literary-critical considerations. In these printings room was always reserved for interlinear and marginal glosses. In 1529 he published a revised Vulgate text of the historical books of the Old Testament, as well as of the New Testament (WADB5) and the Psalter (WADB10,2.158–289). The success of the German Bible, translated from the original biblical texts and also used by Luther in his lectures, was probably the reason not to revise the Latin text of the remaining books of the Old Testament immediately.

In 1517 Luther published his translation of 'the seven penitential psalms' with commentary (WA1.154–220). In a letter to Spalatin Luther described the readers he had in mind: 'They are not published for learned men, but for the completely uneducated, of whom I have many to tolerate' ('Sie sind ja nicht für gelehrte Köpfe herausgegeben, sondern für die ganz Ungebildeten, wie ich viele zu ertragen habe'; WABR1.96,14–15). In a letter to Johann Lang of 18 December 1521, Luther announced that he planned to translate the whole Bible into German (WABR2.413,5–9). Luther started translating and explicating Mary's Magnificat (Lk 1:46b–55; cf. Bluhm 1965: 151–66) before he attended the Diet of Worms. He completed this work at the Wartburg (WA7.544–604; LW21.297–358). In September 1522 Luther published his translation of the New Testament, known as the 'Septembertestament'. Luther had produced the translation at the Wartburg in the space of just eleven weeks; upon his return to Wittenberg he revised it with help from his colleagues. In his preface Luther stated that his manner of translating, his prefaces to the biblical books, and his inclusion of marginal glosses were all intended to ensure that 'the simple man' (*der eynfelltige man*) would know the difference between the gospel and the law (WADB6, 2, 2–11; LW35.357). Translations of books of the Old Testament (Genesis to the Song of Songs) followed in 1522–4. Since Luther's health was rather poor and he was burdened with other duties, his translation of the prophetic and apocryphal books proceeded only slowly. The translation of the whole Bible was not completed until 1534. Luther then applied himself to improving his translation. The last Bible translation overseen by Luther himself was published in 1545/6 (see Aland 1996: 41–52, 435–6 on how to find translations of Bible books in WADB).

In his *Letter on Interpreting* (*Sendbrief vom Dolmetschen*, 1530), Luther responded in detail to the reproach that he had inserted 'alone' arbitrarily in his translation of Romans 3; 28. He argued that this insertion was in line with the sense of the text (WA30,2.637,4–19, 641,9–13, 643,1–12; LW35.189, 195, 197–198; see Bluhm 1965: 125–37, 1984: 106–10, 123–4, 148–9).

Luther claimed that if a person wished to translate, he must know a lot of synonyms (WA30,2.639,21–23; LW35.193). A translator should listen attentively to the mother in her home, children on the street, and simple people at the market, and should translate in such a manner that they would be able to understand the translated text (WA30,2.637,19–22; LW35.189). In his *Summaries of the Psalms and Reasons for Their*

Interpretation (*Summarien über die Psalmen und Ursachen des Dolmetschens*, 1531/3; WA38.9–69), too, Luther gave an account of his manner of interpreting. He wrote that it was important to find the appropriate words in the target language for the concepts formulated in the source text. In his epilogue to his translation of the Psalter (1531), Luther wrote that his translation of 1528 had been nearer to the Hebrew original, but the current one did more justice to the German language (WADB10,1.590,39–48). In 1540 Luther stated of his revisions that they had succeeded in removing the impediments to understanding (WATR5.58–59, §5324).

Luther provided aids to understanding the biblical text in his prefaces and marginal glosses. He added prefaces to his translations of the whole Old and New Testament, but also to the individual books of the Bible. They were intended to facilitate access to the biblical texts, to counter perceptions Luther wished to criticize, and to point to the core of the message of the Bible. Especially important here are Luther's extensive prefaces to the Old and the New Testament and to the Letter to the Romans, which Luther considered the principal text of the New Testament ('das rechte Hauptstück des Neuen Testaments', WADB7.26,12–15; LW35.396). Luther regarded the Gospel according to John, the letters of Paul, and the first epistle of Peter as the most important books of the New Testament (WADB6.10,9–19,29–33; LW35.361–362). For him, the main criterion is whether a biblical book centres on Christ (WADB7.384,25–32; LW35.396). This led him to comment very critically at times on the letter of James when comparing it to Paul's and Peter's epistles (WADB6.10,33–35; LW35.362), though in direct comment on James itself he could at the same time write, 'I praise it and consider it a good book because it sets up no human teachings but vigorously promotes God's law' (WABR7.384,3–6; LW35.395,396).

It is no exaggeration to characterize Luther's translation of the Bible as the centre of his theological work and the sum of his theology (see Bluhm 1965: e.g., 3–35 and Bluhm 1984). He himself viewed all his own writings as dispensable if this would mean that the Scriptures would be shown to advantage (WA50.657,2–11; LW34.283). With his translation he made an important contribution to achieving this. It was his most significant work, judging on the basis of the effort made, the intensity of his contribution, the number of print runs, the reception of the work, and the number of colleagues who collaborated with him in order to obtain the most comprehensible and, at the same time, the most beautiful text. In Luther's own lifetime ten complete editions of the Bible and about eighty editions of parts of the Scriptures were published in Wittenberg alone, in other places about 260 editions appeared. The reaction of Pope Paul IV shows that he viewed the Bible in the vernacular as a real threat: in the first index of forbidden books (1559) he prohibited the printing of vernacular translations of the Bible without the permission of the highest agency of the papal curia that protected the doctrine of the faith, in order to safeguard the supervision of the magisterium of the Roman Catholic church.

Desiderata for future research include a complete dictionary of Luther's language as well as an index of Bible passages cited in Luther's works. At present, it is difficult to compare translations of the same biblical verse in works of different kinds written at different points of Luther's life. For example, in *A Sermon on Preparing to Die* (*Ein Sermon von der Bereitung zum Sterben*, 1519), Luther translated John 16:33 as 'In the world (that is also in ourselves) you will have unrest, but in me, peace' ('In der Welt (das ist auch yn unszselb) werdet yhr unruge haben, In mir aber den friden'; WA2.689,22–23; LW42.105). Three years later, in his 'September testament', he wrote. 'in the world you have fear, but be comforted, I have overcome the world' ('ynn der wellt habet yhr angst, aber seyd get-rost, ich habe die welt vbir wunden') (WADB6.394). It would be very fruitful for Luther researchers of various disciplines to have an index of this kind.

II. HYMNS

Current research on Luther's hymn translations has been facilitated by Markus Jenny's edition of Luther's lyrics and melodies (AWA4, 1985); it is much more reliable than the older one in WA35. The editor gives a general introduction and an overview of the sources and then provides a separate introduction for each hymn written by Luther. A chronological synopsis shows when each text was first printed. This edition gives Luther's texts and the melodies to which they were sung during Luther's lifetime.

From 1984 to 2008, the Union of the German Academies of Sciences and Humanities funded the work of the Society for the Scholarly Edition of German Congregational Hymns (Gesellschaft zur wissenschaftlichen Edition des deutschen Kirchenlieds e.V.). Preparatory work had begun already in 1964. Contrary to the original target of editing the melodies and texts of all hymns and chants in German up to 1800, the Society had to confine itself to editing the melodies of German hymns from the invention of printing until about the year 1610. The great enterprise was completed in November 2008 (cf. Hirschmann and Korth 2010). The Archive of Hymnals (Gesangbucharchiv) in Mainz under the direction of Hermann Kurzke, an emeritus professor of German Studies, remains a helpful source for research in the field. The Bibliography of German Hymnals contains over 28,000 titles.

Luther put hymns to work in propagating the message of the Reformation. In 1523 he received reports that two members of his order had been burned at the stake in Brussels, and this prompted him to write his first hymn: 'Ein neues Lied wir heben an' (AWA4.75–76,217–222, no. 18; LW53.214–216). He praised the martyrs for their faith and summoned the faithful to praise God. In 'Nun freut euch, lieben Christen g'mein' (AWA4.56–58,154–159, no. 2), he summarized his conception of redemption through Jesus Christ. Luther wrote both these hymns not for congregational singing but in order to formulate the Reformation message in a short and understandable manner.

Luther's hymns may also have been a reaction to the fact that Thomas Müntzer had already translated Latin hymns into German and composed a liturgy in the vernacular, his *Deutsches Kirchenamt*. Some of Luther's hymns indeed were written for use in the liturgy. 'Jesaja, dem Propheten, das geschah' (Isaiah 6:1–4 rhymed; AWA4.97–99,243–245 no. 26; LW53.882–883) was intended to be sung during the sharing of the bread in the liturgy of the Lord's Supper, in place of the Latin 'Sanctus'. Luther already highlighted the importance of congregational singing in his *Formula missae et communionis* (1523,

WA12.205–220; LW53.19–40) but emphasized it even more strongly in the 'German Mass', his *Ordnung Gottesdiensts in der Gemeinde* (1526, WA19.72–113; LW53.61–90).

Luther gave the vernacular congregational hymn a firm place in the service and full liturgical rights. His understanding of the gospel determined the composition of his lyrics. At the end of 1523 Luther started writing lyrics based on psalms (cf. Hahn 1981: 246–83), beginning with 'Aus tiefer Not schrei ich zu dir' (Psalm 130, AWA4.68–70,188–193 no. 11; LW53.223–224) and 'ES wollt uns Gott genädig sein' (Psalm 67, AWA4.66–68,184–187 no. 10; LW53.234). The best known is probably 'Ein feste Burg ist unser Gott' (AWA4.100–101,247–249; LW53.284–285). Various explanations have been given for who the 'alt böse feind' ('old evil foe') is (cf. Hahn 1981: 267–83). Luther considered it a hymn based on Psalm 46. He devoted two hymn texts to the Ten Commandments (cf. Hahn 1981: 286–8, AWA4.149–153,226–28, nos. 5, 20; LW53.278–279,281), and one to the Lord's Prayer (AWA4.114–6, 295–298; LW53.296–298 no. 35, cf. Hahn 1981: 288).

Seven of Luther's lyrics are totally original (cf. Hahn 1981: 104–73). More often, however, he used and added to existing German texts (cf. Hahn 1981: 174–245), or translated and finished Latin lyrics (cf. Hahn 1981: 289–300). If, for example, one compares the text of the Latin antiphon 'Media vita in morte sumus' with the three verses written by Luther, which centred on Christ, it is clear that Luther has reshaped the text according to his own insights to 'Mitten wir im Leben sind mit dem Tod umfangen' (AWA4,58f.,160–162 no. 3; LW53.275–276).

Already in 1524 a booklet was published containing eight hymns ('Achtliederbuch'), including four lyrics by Luther from single sheet woodcuts. Shortly afterwards, the 'Erfurter Enchiridion' (in which eighteen of the twenty-five hymns were by Luther) and the 'Geistliches Gesangbüchlein' (with twenty-four of the thirty-two texts by Luther) appeared in print. The same year saw the publication of Johann Walter's Hymnbook for Choirs, with a preface by Luther. In 1529 the printer Joseph Klug published a collection of lyrics authorized by Luther himself. More than half of the lyrics were written by Luther. The most beautiful hymnbook produced during Luther's lifetime, edited by the printer Valentin Bapst, also opened with a preface by Luther. Many more hymnbooks including hymns by Luther were printed during his lifetime (see the websites of the projects discussed above).

Luther's musical talents also exhibited themselves in the composition of melodies. The melody for 'Jesaja, dem Propheten, das geschah' came from Luther's hand. His melody for the Lord's Prayer, 'Vater unser im Himmelreich', did not find widespread acceptance.

Desiderata for future research include more cooperation between specialists in musicology, German studies, and church history. Because Luther's are among the best and most influential German hymns, the bibliography published each year in the 'Lutherjahrbuch' cannot register all research publications by the scholars in these fields.

Luther was indeed a creative translator (Bluhm 1965), and the literal work of translating reflected and stood at the heart of his larger theological enterprise, which translated the Christian faith culturally from the Mediterranean world into the parlance of everyday living among the German-speaking faithful (Nestingen 2001).

References

Aland, Kurt (1996). *Hilfsbuch zum Lutherstudium*, 4th edn. Bielefeld: Luther-Verlag.

Bluhm, Heinz (1965). *Martin Luther, Creative Translator*. Saint Louis: Concordia.

—— (1984). *Luther, Translator of Paul: Studies in Romans and Galatians*. Frankfurt am Main: Lang.

Hahn, Gerhard (1981). *Evangelium als literarische Anweisung. Zu Luthers Stellung in der Geschichte des deutschen kirchlichen Liedes*. Munich/Zurich: Artemis.

Heijting, Willem (1996). "Ziet daer staedt ghescreven ende 't' es zo": het boek en de overdracht van ideën bij de eerste Nederlandse evangelisch gezinden'. In *Mensen van de Nieuwe Tijd. Een liber amicorum voor A. Th. van Deursen*. Amsterdam: Bakker, 14–28.

Hirschmann, Wolfgang and Hans-Otto Korth (eds.) (2010). *Das deutsche Kirchenlied. Bilanz und Perspektiven einer Edition*. Kassel: Bärenreiter.

Nestingen, James A. (2001). 'Luther's Cultural Translation of the Catechism'. *Lutheran Quarterly* 15: 440–52.

Péter, Katalin (1999). 'Bibellesen. Ein Programm für jedermann im Ungarn des 16. Jahrhunderts'. In *Iter germanicum. Deutschland und die Reformierte Kirche in Ungarn im 16.–17. Jahrhundert*, ed. András Szabó. Budapest: Kálvin Kiadó, 7– 38 (Hungarian 1995).

Sanneh, Lamin (2009). *Translating the Message: The Missionary Impact on Culture*. Maryknoll, NY: Orbis.

Wallmann, Johannes (1994). 'Was ist Pietismus?' *Pietismus und Neuzeit* 20: 11–27.

Suggested Reading

Brown, Christopher Boyd (2005). *Singing the Gospel: Lutheran Hymns and the Success of the Reformation*. Cambridge, MA: Harvard University Press.

Das deutsche Kirchenlied. Die Melodien aus gedruckten Quellen bis 1610 (1993–2010). Kassel: Bärenreiter.

Hirsch, Emanuel (1928). *Luthers Deutsche Bibel*. Munich: Kaiser.

Hollander, August den (1997). *De Nederlandse bijbelvertalingen 1522–1545*. Nieuwkoop: de Graaf.

Lamberigts, Mathijs and August den Hollander (eds.) (2006). *Lay Bibles in Europe 1450–1800*. Louvain: Leuven University Press.

Leaver, Robin A. (2007). *Luther's Liturgical Music: Principles and Implications*. Grand Rapids, MI: Eerdmans.

Ludolphy, Ingetraut (n.d.). *Epilogue to Martin Luther: Septembertestament 1522. Nachdruck*. Berlin: Witten and Berlin.

Mühlen, Karl-Heinz zur (1978). 'Luthers deutsche Bibelübersetzung als Gemeinschaftswerk'. *Jahrbuch des evangelischen Bibelwerkes* 18: 90–7.

Oettinger, Rebecca Wagner (2001). *Music as Propaganda in the German Reformation*. Aldershot: Ashgate.

Raeder, Siegfried (1961). *Das Hebräische bei Luther, untersucht bis zum Ende der ersten Psalmenvorlesung*. Tübingen: Mohr.

Reu, Johann Michael (1934). *Luther's German Bible*. Columbus: Lutheran Book Concern.

Sauer-Geppert, Waldtraut Ingeborg (1980). 'Bibelübersetzungen III/1, 5. Die Übersetzungen der Reformationszeit'. *TRE* 6: 239–44, 246.

Schilling, Johannes (1993). 'Martin Luthers deutsche Bibel'. In *Die Bibel—Wort der Freiheit. Zwei Passauer Vorträge. Nachrichten und Berichte Universität Passau*, ed. Dietrich Korsch and Johannes Schilling. Berlin: Sonderheft 13, 7–33.

Volz, Hans (1972). *Einleitung zu: D. Martin Luther. Die gantze Heilige Schrifft Deudsch, Wittenberg 1545*, Bd. 1: 33*–144*.

Volz, Hans and Heinz Blanke (eds.) (1972). *D. Martin Luther. Die gantze Heilige Schrift Deudsch. Wittenberg 1545. Letzte zu Luthers Lebzeiten erschienene Ausgabe*. Munich: Rogner/Bernhard.

Walther, Wilhelm (1917). *Luthers Deutsche Bibel*. Berlin: Mittler.

PART VII

THE IMPACT AND RECEPTION OF LUTHER'S THOUGHT IN HISTORY AND IN THE TWENTY-FIRST CENTURY

CHAPTER 36

THE WITTENBERG CIRCLE

TIMOTHY J. WENGERT

SCHOLARS easily err in portraying Martin Luther's life and thought as if he were a rugged individualist, trapped in his personal ivory tower (an early, if flawed, exception is Bauer 1928). Luther rarely if ever thought or acted alone. He never lived as a recluse although early in his career von Staupitz had to dissuade him from becoming a hermit (WA43.667,26–34; cf. Wengert 2007: 247).

As in the late Middle Ages, scholars in Wittenberg worked together, formed alliances, represented schools (*viae*), and found support in past thinkers and current colleagues, thus modelling theological collaboration throughout Luther's career. At an early stage we can mark the influence of especially Johann von Staupitz (Steinmetz 1980; Hamm 2010). In 1512 Luther received his doctorate in theology under the presidency of Andreas Bodenstein von Karlstadt and quickly took his place alongside him and another colleague, the licentiate Nicholas von Amsdorf (Dingel 2008). Indeed, once Luther convinced Karlstadt and Amsdorf (among others) about his new approach to justification by faith, a remarkable level of cooperation set in, shaping theology and, helped by Luther's lifelong supporter and (later) friend, the courtier-priest Georg Spalatin, providing a strong humanist alternative to Wittenberg's late-medieval curriculum (Junghans 1984; Kruse 2002; Scheible 2010: 75–151).

From 1518 to 1525 the University of Wittenberg attracted scholars who supported both its humanism and theology and who stayed for a longer period of time. These included (alongside Karlstadt and Amsdorf), Philip Melanchthon, Justus Jonas, and Johannes Bugenhagen. Later professors of theology with Luther—Caspar Cruciger, Sr. and Georg Major—were students during this important time (Leder 1983).

Scholars have tended to posit an early phase of cooperation among disparate parties, broken by Luther's return from the Wartburg in 1522 and his subsequent feud with Karlstadt.[1] In fact, excepting Karlstadt, the level of cooperation among these very

---

[1] Kruse (2002: 375–89) is among the latest to propagate this myth, insisting that by 1522 Luther's self-anointed role as Wittenberg's prophet and leader of the Reformation left no room for Karlstadt. The very different path taken by Luther's other colleagues and even by Gabriel Zwilling, whom Luther

different figures actually increased during the latter half of the 1520s and into the 1530s. Luther's *Invocavit* sermons from March 1522 marked not an end to cooperation but a new beginning (WA10,3.1–64; LW51.69–100). During Luther's absence at the Wartburg a reform party had developed and had tried to bring about practical changes commensurate with proposals coming especially (but not exclusively) from Luther. Subsequent negotiations with the Saxon court involved the entire company of like-minded colleagues (MBWT 1.445–454, §§211–214, and MBWT 1.107–108, §174, quoted in Scheible 2009: 60–3). By 1524 Karlstadt had left for Orlamünde, Amsdorf had assumed leadership in reforming Magdeburg, and others had left Wittenberg for service elsewhere. Melanchthon, Jonas, and Bugenhagen then formed the core of collaborators with Luther leading Wittenberg reform. Adding Cruciger, Wolgast (2009: 87) labels them 'the circle of five'. Major replaced Jonas in the 1540s.

Melanchthon had experienced a renewed sense of focus as a result of Luther's sermons (MBWT 1.461,12–13, §222; cf. WA10,3.11). Bugenhagen's and Jonas' respect for Luther and Melanchthon also remained unbroken. Thus, Bugenhagen wrote to Spalatin on 27 November 1522 that 'Prophets are those who preach as Martin does and teach as Philip does...' (Vogt 1888: 9, §5; cf. Kolb 2009: 103).

This circle around Luther formed slowly into a team (Kolb 2009: 103–4), based upon their callings at the university. Luther became a professor of theology in 1512, beginning his lectures on the Bible in 1513. In 1518 Melanchthon came to Wittenberg as professor of Greek but quickly earned his bachelor of Bible in 1519, teaching in both the arts and theology faculties throughout his career, a special position made permanent in 1526 (Scheible 1997; Wengert 1999; see also Junghans 2002). In 1521 Jonas was called as provost of the All Saints' foundation and professor of Canon Law. In 1523, two years after arriving in Wittenberg, Bugenhagen became the pastor at Saint Mary's. He received his doctorate in theology in 1533, alongside Caspar Cruciger, Sr., and became a professor first in 1535, although he had been holding lectures on the Bible for over a decade. In 1521 Cruciger arrived in Wittenberg with his parents to escape the plague in Leipzig, where he had witnessed the Leipzig Disputation. He quickly became one of Melanchthon's favourite students. Thought to need some seasoning, he was dispatched to help Amsdorf at Magdeburg's Latin school (where Major also later taught) before returning to Wittenberg in 1528. He lectured on the New Testament until his untimely death in 1548 (Wengert 1989). Major began university studies in the 1520s, serving as a preacher at the Castle church in the 1530s, receiving his doctorate in 1544 (Wengert 1997; Dingel and Wartenberg 2005; on student life in Wittenberg, see Gößner 2003).

---

also mentioned directly in his Invocavit sermons (WA10,3.22,9–10), calls this analysis into question. Karlstadt's own behaviour—leaving his position and attacking ancient beliefs and practices of the church (Christ's presence in the Lord's Supper and infant baptism)—were certainly not conducive to continued collegial cooperation; see Burnett 2011: 32–5.

Book dedications from the early 1520s demonstrate the relationships among this team (WA8.43,2, 7; MBWT 1.292–293, §142; cf. MBW §47, 54, 199, 299; MBW §283, WA2.412–413). A second early indication of collaboration revolved around the publica tion of commentaries on nearly all the New Testament between 1522 and 1524 (Wengert 1987: 31–42, 255–8). As Eike Wolgast notes, the notion of making joint pronouncements had not yet developed at this early phase in their relationship (2009: 92). Thus, in 1523, when asked by Elector Frederick for an opinion on the right of rebellion against a higher authority, Luther, Melanchthon, Amsdorf, and Bugenhagen gave separate replies. By 1525, however, with Amsdorf having left for Magdeburg, the remaining three plus Jonas gave a common reply to a marriage matter in February and to the Ansbach Proposal in September (MBWT 2.253, §377 = WABr3.443–445; MBW §418 = WABr3.568–570). Three areas—marriage law, Reformation politics, and theology—comprised, along with day-to-day university and church matters, the bulk of their close collaboration through-out the 1530s and 1540s. Their theological teamwork is revealed in Luther's relation to each.

I. Luther's Closest Colleagues: Melanchthon, Bugenhagen, and Jonas

In 1538 the Wittenberg printer Hans Lufft published a revised edition of the *Instruction by the Visitors for the Pastors in Electoral Saxony, Now Corrected by Dr. Martin Luther*. The title page displayed a woodcut, first printed in 1533, sharply defining the 'gang of five'. Surrounding a depiction of Christ as Good Shepherd were the coats-of-arms of the five Wittenberg theologians: the rose of Luther, the snake on a pole (John 3:14) of Melanchthon, Jonah being swallowed by a whale for Jonas, David's harp for Bugenhagen, and the dove bearing an olive branch for Cruciger (whose name meant cross-bearer) (Wengert 2010: X.63). This summarized both the collective authority and the collabora-tion of these five men (Wolgast 2009: 95–6). These instructions by the visitors went out under the imprimatur of Wittenberg's theologians. Yet each interacted with Luther and one another in different ways.

The protocols for the Bible translation also indicate their high level of cooperation (WADB3.XV–XVII; Scheible 1997: 145–7). Far from being simply a 'Luther' Bible, this translation represented the collaboration Wittenberg's faculty (Brecht 1990: 46–56). Johannes Mathesius compared Wittenberg's theologians to the skills demanded in the *trivium*: Bugenhagen the grammarian, Melanchthon the dialectician, Jonas the rhetori-cian, and Luther all in one (quoted in Kolb 2009: 103).

In 1546 the three were also centrally involved at Luther's death. Jonas was present in Eisleben and wrote the first report of the reformer's 'blessed departure'. In Wittenberg

Bugenhagen delivered the funeral sermon in German and Melanchthon the funeral oration in Latin.

II. Philip Melanchthon

The relation of Luther and Melanchthon has received more scrutiny than the others. Earlier, scholars had depicted it as friendship, which meant having to explain breaks and disagreements.[2] Except perhaps for the earliest phase of their relationship, where each admired the other's remarkable gifts, they were equal colleagues with diverse talents and, sometimes, diverse theological emphases, who collaborated on a vast array of theological and practical matters. Melanchthon credited Luther with having taught him the gospel; Luther credited Melanchthon with having taught him dialectics! (Scheible 1997: 143; WATR2.556,1–3, §2629a).

For example, in 1519, Erasmus noted in his own translation of the Greek New Testament that the Greek word χαρις, which Jerome translated as *gratia* (grace), should more accurately be translated *favor Dei*. Melanchthon began making this connection already in 1520 and Luther (at Melanchthon's urging?) followed suit in 1521, abandoning for good the medieval ontological understanding of *gratia* for an understanding of grace as mercy (*misericordia*) (Schäfer 1997: 82–5, 97–101).

Luther contributed to Melanchthon's developing theology while at the Wartburg, when Melanchthon was struggling to integrate the humanities and governmental affairs with Wittenberg's gospel. While in 1520 Melanchthon could speak very critically of all use of humanistic studies in theology, by 1523 he had come to a much different conclusion, based upon Luther's answer to a related question from which Melanchthon derived the civil use of the law and the distinction between civil and divine righteousness (MBWT1.304–311, §151; WABr2.356–369; LW48.259–261). Justice and interest in language and knowledge were no longer *ipso facto* at odds with the gospel and justification by faith alone (Wengert 2003). This insight into the two-fold righteousness of God from Luther quickly became the centrepiece of Melanchthon's thought.

Luther and Melanchthon supported one another's work. When Luther's polemics in *On the Bondage of the Will* against Erasmus' 1524 attack, *Discussion of the Free Will*, failed to convince the Dutch humanist but instead led to the latter's two-volume refutation, the *Hyperaspistes*, Melanchthon took up the banner in his *Scholia* on Colossians of 1527 and especially 1528, turning aside Erasmus' approach with an appeal to the two-fold righteousness of God, which allowed freedom in temporal things but not in matters of salvation (Wengert 1998). Luther acknowledged this collaboration in his preface to Justus Jonas' German translation of the *Scholia* (Wengert 1998: 103–4).

---

[2] See Scheible 2009 and Wengert 1999 for this early literature; cf. Zophy 1998. See also Scheible, 'Melanchthon als theologischer Gesprächspartner Luthers', now in Scheible 2010: 1–27.

I was born for this purpose: to fight with the rebels and the devils and to lead the charge. Therefore my books are very stormy and warlike. I have to uproot trunks and stumps, hack at thorns and hedges, and fill in the potholes. So I am the crude woodsman, who has to clear and make the path. But Master Philip comes after me meticulously and quietly, builds and plants, sows and waters happily, according to the talents God has richly given him. (WA30,2.68,12–69,1)

On justification by faith the two reformers wrote a joint letter to Johannes Brenz explaining their common position (MBWT5.104–113, §1151 = WABr6.98–101; cf. Wengert 1999: 68–70); in 1536 Melanchthon also posed to Luther a series of written questions on the topic, the answers to which he carefully kept and used in the later Osiandrian controversy (WABr12.189–196, cf. WATR6.148,29–153,15, §6727, and MBW §6294, par. 10). On the Lord's Supper Luther and Melanchthon both opposed the sacrifice of the mass, communion in one kind, and transubstantiation. They presented a united front against Zwingli and Oecolampadius at the Marburg Colloquy (1529). Moved by the language of the Church Fathers and negotiations with Martin Bucer after the publication of the *Apology* in 1531, Melanchthon's position came to rest in the Wittenberg Concord of 1536 that insisted on Christ's presence in the Sacrament *with* the bread (MBWT7.131–148, §1744). When, in Melanchthon's eyes, Luther departed from this position (cf. the Smalcald Articles), the former refused to budge (Scheible 1997: 163–6; Fraenkel 1961; Wengert 1999: 70–84). In 1542, when a battle royal erupted in Eisleben over what to do with the leftover communion wine, Luther and Melanchthon (being in different cities) offered quite different opinions; it was up to Luther to find a way to reconcile their positions. 'Mr. Philip defines the sacramental action in relation to external things, that is, against shutting [Christ] up [in a tabernacle] and the procession of the Sacrament. He does not divide that action inside itself nor does he define it against itself.'[3] Contemporaries noted their special level of collaboration. In 1545, when Luther threatened not to return to the University of Wittenberg, Elector John Frederick turned to Melanchthon, Bugenhagen, and Major for help (MBWR4:255–256, §3982, dated 5 August 1545 = WABr11.163–164; cf. Brecht 1993: 162–5).

III. JOHANNES BUGENHAGEN

Between Luther and Bugenhagen a different relationship developed (for most recent work on Bugenhagen, see Dingel and Rhein 2011). In 1523 Luther used his influence to assure that the 'Pomeranian' received the position of pastor at Saint Mary's church in

---

[3] WABr10.348,31–33. The word 'inclusio' could also refer to Christ's inclusion in the bread itself. Melanchthon's uses the word in his letter to Vigelius (*CR* 7:877). See Wengert 2001.

Wittenberg (Vogt 1888: 10–14; Brecht 1990: 71–2). As pastor Bugenhagen was Luther's confessor and with Justus Jonas played a crucial role in nursing Luther back to health in 1527, and through other crises as well (Lohrmann 2010a). He shared preaching duties with Luther. Like the other theologians, he was often a guest at the Luthers' house and even gave in his later lectures on Jonah an independent account of Luther's evangelical breakthrough, probably recounting what he had heard at table (Lohrmann 2008).

Luther received pastoral care from Bugenhagen; the Pomeranian learned the gospel from Luther. For example, his 1522–4 lectures on Isaiah contain no direct reference to Luther, yet, on Isaiah 40:2, used the term central to Luther's understanding of Christian freedom, 'foelix vicissitudo' (joyous exchange) (Gummelt 1994: 88). Kötter (1994: 262–99) compares Bugenhagen's 1525 open letter to Hamburg with Luther's *Freedom of a Christian* but mistakenly overemphasizes differences between Luther and Melanchthon and the incompatibility of humanism and Reformation. Bugenhagen shaped his theological programme around Wittenberg's distinction of law and gospel (Gummelt 1994: passim, esp. 138–44). Alongside Luther and Melanchthon, Bugenhagen produced a wide range of biblical commentaries that bear the Wittenberg stamp: attending to the text, distinguishing law and gospel, sorting out the two-fold righteousness (Lohrmann 2010b). Bugenhagen, not Luther, wrote Wittenberg's first response to Zwingli's position on the Lord's Supper.[4]

Most significantly, Bugenhagen reformed churches in other parts of Europe, including Braunschweig, Hamburg, Lübeck, and Denmark. Church orders that he composed there were influenced by his own work in Wittenberg and by Melanchthon and Luther's joint composition in 1528 of *Instruction by the Visitors* (Leder and Buske 1985). Bugenhagen stretched Wittenberg's influence beyond the university into the structure of early evangelical church life. In this Luther's influence pales in comparison (Brecht 1990: 251–92). Moreover, from 1536 Bugenhagen was the General Superintendent for electoral Saxony, a position he continued to hold even through the regime change of 1547, and often signed the ordination certificates for local and foreign students.

IV. JUSTUS JONAS

Jonas' own theological contribution to Wittenberg's team seems minor in comparison to the others: 'Jonas was not a creative thinker' (Kolb 2009: 120). He produced only a handful of exegetical or other theological works (Gummelt 2009: 121–30), all strictly oriented by Luther's theology. His departure for Halle in 1541 even left some questions about his loyalty to the university though not to its theology (Wolgast 2009: 87, 96–100).

---

[4] *Contra Novum Errorem, de Sacramento corporis et sanguinis Domini nostri Iesu Christi epistola Ioannis Bugenhagii Pomerani*; German: *Ein Sendbrieff wider den newen yrthumb bey dem Sacrament des leybs vnd bluts vnsers Herren Jesus Cristi* (Wittenberg: Klug, 1525).

Yet he remained an important part of this tight circle of reformers. His wife's death in childbirth a few years later occasioned moving letters to him from both Luther and Melanchthon, a poignant testimony to their close relation with him (WABr10.226 228; and MBWT11.366–367, §3115; cf. Kawerau, 1964: 2.91–2 [= MBW §3135]).

Jonas, the Erfurt-trained humanist (Junghans 2009), excelled as translator. He contributed enormously both to spreading Wittenberg's ideas beyond the German-speaking realm with translations into Latin and to opening German readers to the highest level of Wittenberg's theological work. He also sharpened or modified the intent of the original author in his translations (Mennecke 2009; the article's narrow scope does not successfully depict the true breadth and complexity of Jonas' translating). His preface to the German translation of *On the Bondage of the Will* states his goals for translating: 'I have rendered this into German . . . so that everyone, but especially the Papists, who have boasted so greatly as if the teaching about works is substantiated by Erasmus's tract, may realize from this clear answer, how their teaching collapses, even when a Demosthenes is defending it' (Kawerau 1964: 1.95).

His Latin renderings of three of Luther's tracts on the Jews: *That Jesus Christ Was Born a Jew* (1523), *Against the Sabbatarians* (1539), and *On the Jews and Their Lies* (1544) also indicate the way his translations clarify and modify Luther's work. In prefaces to these works Jonas showed his independence from Luther's hate-filled tracts by urging a slightly more open approach to the Jewish people (Kawerau 1964: 1.92–3, 322–34; Oberman 1984: 47–9). Jonas also translated crucial writings of Melanchthon: the commentary on Colossians (1529), the *Apology* of the Augsburg Confession (1531), and the second edition of the *Loci communes theologici* (1536).

V. The Students: Cruciger and Major

Luther called Caspar Cruciger, Sr., his Elisha, a moniker more often attributed to Melanchthon (WABr7.329,16–17). After education in Leipzig and Wittenberg and teaching in Magdeburg, he returned to Wittenberg in the late 1520s. On 18 June 1533 he was the first, along with Bugenhagen and Johann Aepinus, to receive a doctorate of theology under Melanchthon's revised theological statutes. Elector John Frederick and other nobles attended the ceremonies; Jonas gave an oration (Brecht 1993: 126–34).

Cruciger, like Jonas, contributed to the Wittenberg circle through translations. He also wrote several biblical commentaries (Wengert 1989, 1992). He signed about half of the theological opinions emanating from Wittenberg during his tenure. Of the 174 opinions written from 1520 to 1560, Melanchthon signed 146, Luther 106, Bugenhagen 100, Jonas 57, Cruciger 54, and Major 31. Cruciger was on the faculty when 107 of the opinions Kohnle identifies were written; Major for 60 (Kohnle 2002). He accompanied Melanchthon to the 1541 Regensburg Colloquy. He was often a guest at Luther's table and was a noted stenographer, probably producing the protocols for one of the most detailed table conversations, held at Cruciger's house on 11 April 1542, where one can easily observe the interactions of Wittenberg's inner circle (WATR5.133–46, §5424/5424a).

Major came to Wittenberg, an impoverished choirboy, at age nine, became preacher at the Castle church (1537), and received his doctorate on 18 December 1544, after a successful defence of theses a week earlier (WA39,2.284–336). He published commentaries on the entire Pauline corpus and both there and in his church postil showed himself completely dependent upon Luther and Melanchthon (Wengert 1997, 2005). In 1546, with hopes fading for rapprochement with Rome, Major was Wittenberg's chief negotiator at the second round of colloquies in Regensburg and thus was away from the university at the time of Luther's death (Dingel 2005).

An important contribution to the Wittenberg circle came in 1531, when he translated Luther's *Small Catechism* into Latin. It was reprinted at least twenty-one times in the sixteenth century. He also translated several of Luther's works on the Psalms and a few minor works of Melanchthon. Before and after his theological trials over the necessity of good works began in the 1550s, he understood himself to be a faithful interpreter of Luther and Melanchthon's theology.

VI. Luther and his Team

Wittenberg's reform involved more than a single charismatic figure. Luther and his colleagues on the Wittenberg faculty, along with other supporters and students, supported one another throughout their lives. This circle functioned as a well-coordinated team in shaping and spreading Wittenberg's message. Luther was first among equals, but Melanchthon's impact should not be underestimated. Without Bugenhagen, Jonas, other colleagues, and those representing the Wittenberg cause in parishes, courts, and schools, Wittenberg's Reformation would have taken a much different form.

References

Bauer, Karl (1928). *Die Wittenberger Universitätstheologie und die Anfänge der Deutschen Reformation*. Tübingen: Mohr/Siebeck.

Brecht, Martin (1990). *Martin Luther: Shaping and Defining the Reformation, 1521–1532*, trans. James Schaaf. Minneapolis: Fortress.

—— (1993). *Martin Luther: The Preservation of the Church, 1532–1546*, trans. James Schaaf. Minneapolis: Fortress.

Burnett, Amy Nelson (2011). *Karlstadt and the Origins of the Eucharistic Controversy: A Study in the Circulation of Ideas*. New York: Oxford University Press.

Dingel, Irene (2005). 'Die Rolle Georg Majors auf dem Regensburger Religionsgespräch von 1546'. In *Georg Major (1502–1574): Ein Theologe der Wittenberger Reformation*, ed. Irene Dingel and Günter Wartenberg. Leipzig: Evangelische Verlagsanstalt, 189–206.

—— (ed.) (2008). *Nikolaus von Amsdorf (1483–1565)*. Leipzig: Evangelische Verlagsanstalt.

Dingel, Irene and Stefan Rhein (eds.) (2011). *Der späte Bugenhagen*. Leipzig: Evangelische Verlagsanstalt.

—— Günter Wartenberg (eds.) (2002). *Die Theologische Fakultät Wittenberg 1502–1602: Beiträge zur 500. Wiederkehr des Gründungsjahres der Leucorea*. Leipzig: Evangelische Verlagsanstalt.

—— (eds.) (2005) *Georg Major (1502–1574): Ein Theologe der Wittenberger Reformation*. Leipzig: Evangelische Verlagsanstalt.

Fraenkel, Peter (1961). 'Ten Questions concerning Melanchthon, the Fathers and the Eucharist'. In *Luther and Melanchthon in the History and Theology of the Reformation*, ed. Vilmos Vajta. Philadelphia: Muhlenberg, 146–64.

Gößner, Andreas (2003). *Die Studenten an der Universität Wittenberg: Studien zur Kulturgeschichte des studentischen Alltags und zum Stipendienwesen in der zweiten Hälfte des 16. Jahrhunderts*. Leipzig: Evangelische Verlagsanstalt.

Gummelt, Volker (1994). *Lex und Evangelium: Untersuchungen zur Jesajavorlesung von Johannes Bugenhagen*. Berlin and New York: de Gruyter.

—— (2009). 'Justus Jonas als Bibelexeget an der Wittenberger Universität'. In *Justus Jonas (1493–1555) und seine Bedeutung für die Wittenberger Reformation*, ed. Irene Dingel. Leipzig: Evangelische Verlagsanstalt, 121–30.

Hamm, Berndt (2010). *Der frühe Luther: Etappe reformatorischer Neuorientierung*. Tübingen: Mohr/Siebeck.

Junghans, Helmar (1984). *Der junge Luther und die Humanisten*. Weimar: Böhlau.

—— (2002). 'Luthers Einfluß auf die Wittenberger Universitätsreform'. In *Die Theologische Fakultät Wittenberg 1502–1602: Beiträge zur 500. Wiederkehr des Gründungsjahres der Leucorea*, ed. Irene Dingel and Günter Wartenberg. Leipzig: Evangelische Verlagsanstalt, 55–70.

—— (2009). 'Justus Jonas und die Erfurter Humanisten'. In *Justus Jonas (1493–1555) und seine Bedeutung für die Wittenberger Reformation*, ed. Irene Dingel. Leipzig: Evangelische Verlagsanstalt, 15–37.

Kawerau, Gustav (ed.) (1964). *Der Briefwechsel des Justus Jonas*, 2 vols. Rpr. Hildesheim: Olms.

Kohnle, Armin (2002). 'Wittenberger Autorität: Die Gemeinschaftsgutachten als Typos'. In *Die Theologische Fakultät Wittenberg 1502–1602: Beiträge zur 500. Wiederkehr des Gründungsjahres der Leucorea*, ed. Irene Dingel and Günter Wartenberg. Leipzig: Evangelische Verlagsanstalt, 189–200.

Kolb, Robert (2009). 'The Theology of Justus Jonas'. In *Justus Jonas (1493–1555) und seine Bedeutung für die Wittenberger Reformation*, ed. Irene Dingel. Leipzig: Evangelische Verlagsanstalt, 103–20.

Kötter, Ralf (1994). *Johannes Bugenhagens Rechtfertigungslehre und der römische Katholizismus*. Göttingen: Vandenhoeck & Ruprecht.

Kruse, Jens-Martin (2002). *Universitätstheologie und Kirchenreform. Die Anfänge der Reformation in Wittenberg 1516–1522*. Mainz: Zabern.

Leder, Hans-Günter (1983). 'Luthers Beziehungen zu seinen Wittenberger Freunden'. In *Leben und Werk Martin Luthers von 1526 bis 1546*, ed. Helmar Junghans. Göttingen: Vandenhoeck & Ruprecht, 1.419–40.

Leder, Hans-Günter and Norbert Buske (1985). *Reform und Ordnung aus dem Wort. Johannes Bugenhagen und die Reformation im Herzogtum Pommern*. Berlin: Evangelische Verlagsanstalt.

Lohrmann, Martin (2008). 'A Newly Discovered Report of Luther's Reformation Breakthrough from Johannes Bugenhagen's 1550 Jonah Commentary: Translation and Commentary'. *Lutheran Quarterly* 22: 324–30.

—— (2010a). 'Bugenhagen's Pastoral Care of Martin Luther'. *Lutheran Quarterly* 24: 125–36.

—— (2010b). 'Johannes Bugenhagen's Commentary on Jonah (1550): Biblical Interpretation as Public Theology in the Reformation'. Ph.D. dissertation, Lutheran Theological Seminary Philadelphia.

Mennecke, Ute (2009). 'Justus Jonas als Übersetzer—Sprache und Theologie. Dargestellt am Beispiel seiner Übersetzung von Luthers Schrift "De servo arbitrio"—"Das der freie wille nichts sey" (1526)'. In *Justus Jonas (1493–1555) und seine Bedeutung für die Wittenberger Reformation*, ed. Irene Dingel. Leipzig: Evangelische Verlagsanstalt, 131–44.

Oberman, Heiko Augustinus (1984). *The Roots of Anti-Semitism in the Age of Renaissance and Reformation*, James Porter (trans.). Philadelphia: Fortress.

Schäfer, Rolf (1997). 'Melanchthon's Interpretation of Romans 5.15: His Departure from the Augustinian Concept of Grace Compared to Luther's'. In Schäfer, *Philip Melanchthon (1497–1560) and the Commentary*. Sheffield: Sheffield Academic Press, 79–104.

Scheible, Heinz (1997). *Melanchthon: Eine Biographie*. Munich: Beck.

—— (2000). 'Luther and Melanchthon'. *Lutheran Quarterly* 4: 317–39.

—— (2009). 'Melanchthon und Justus Jonas'. In *Justus Jonas (1493–1555) und seine Bedeutung für die Wittenberger Reformation*, ed. Irene Dingel. Leipzig: Evangelische Verlagsanstalt, 59–86.

—— (2010) 'Die Reform von Schule und Universität in der Reformationszeit'. In Scheible, *Aufsätze zu Melanchthon*. Tübingen: Mohr/Siebeck, 152–72.

Steinmetz, David C. (1980). *Luther and Staupitz*. Durham: Duke University Press.

Vogt, Otto (ed.) (1888). *Johannes Bugenhagens Briefwechsel*. Stettin: Saunier.

Wengert, Timothy J. (1987). *Philip Melanchthon's 'Annotationes in Johannem' of 1523 in Relation to Its Predecessors and Contemporaries*. Geneva: Droz.

—— (1989). 'Caspar Cruciger (1504–1548): The Case of the Disappearing Reformer'. *Sixteenth Century Journal* 20: 417–41.

—— (1992). 'Caspar Cruciger Sr.'s 1546 "Enarratio" on John's Gospel: An Experiment in Ecclesiological Exegesis'. *Church History* 61: 60–74.

—— (1997). 'Georg Major (1502–1574): Defender of the Wittenberg's Faith and Melanchthonian Exegete'. In *Melanchthon in seinen Schülern*, ed. Heinz Scheible. Wiesbaden: Harrassowitz, 129–56.

—— (1998). *Human Freedom, Christian Righteousness: Philip Melanchthon's Exegetical Dispute with Erasmus of Rotterdam*. New York: Oxford University Press.

—— (1999) 'Luther and Melanchthon—Melanchthon and Luther'. *Lutherjahrbuch* 66: 55–88.

—— (2001). 'Luther and Melanchthon on Consecrated Communion Wine (Eisleben 1542–43)'. *Lutheran Quarterly* 15: 24–42.

—— (2002). 'Certificate of Ordination (1545) for George von Anhalt, Coadjutor Bishop of Merseburg'. *Lutheran Quarterly* 16: 229–33.

—— (2003). 'Philip Melanchthon and a Christian Politics'. *Lutheran Quarterly* 17: 29–62.

—— (2005). 'Georg Major as Exegete of 1 Timothy'. In *Georg Major (1502–1574): Ein Theologe der Wittenberger Reformation*, ed. Irene Dingel and Günter Wartenberg. Leipzig: Evangelische Verlagsanstalt, 69–92.

—— (2007). '"Per mutuum colloquium et consolationem fratrum". Monastische Züge in Luthers ökumenischer Theologie'. In *Luther und das monastische Erbe*, ed. Christoph Bultmann, Volker Leppin and Andreas Lindner. Tübingen: Mohr/Siebeck, 243–68.

—— (2010). *Philip Melanchthon, Speaker of the Reformation: Wittenberg's Other Reformer*. Farnham: Ashgate.

Wolgast, Eike (2009). 'Luther, Jonas und die Wittenberger Kollektivautorität'. In *Justus Jonas (1493–1555) und seine Bedeutung für die Wittenberger Reformation*, ed. Irene Dingel. Leipzig: Evangelische Verlagsanstalt, 87–100.

Zophy, Jonathan (1998). 'Philip Melanchthon as a Family Man and Friend'. *Lutheran Quarterly* 12: 429–44.

CHAPTER 37

....

LUTHER'S ROMAN
CATHOLIC CRITICS

....

†HERIBERT SMOLINKSY

I. The Setting

....

PASTORAL concern and theological conviction moved Martin Luther to attack the Roman Catholic church, but he in no way intended to cause schism. Nonetheless, in the unfolding development of the Reformation ever greater rifts arose. Increasingly harsher and more critical positions emerged, calling into question the traditional form of the church. Though even earlier the unity of the Latin church with its Roman contours seemed threatened, division took place at this time. How could its institutions and practices be defended and rescued; which methods and teachings could attain agreement between the feuding parties and avert a break? Within this framework the 'theology of controversy' of the sixteenth century arose (Dingel 2007). Leading voices within the church, like Erasmus, intervened. Emperor, princes, and ecclesiastical institutions strove for unity with greater or less enthusiasm and became involved in influencing the course of events.

Luther's Ninety-five Theses on indulgences became public knowledge very quickly. In 1518 the Roman proceedings against him initiated a dynamic which led to ever more controversy between adherents of the Roman Catholic church and Protestants of various shades over the opponents' actual or presumed teaching and ways of life. Initially these controversies focused on Luther himself (see Klaiber 1978; Bagchi 1991, for bibliography of primary sources). The Catholic side faced a series of problems. First, the context of controversy let the agenda set by their foes shape the Roman Catholic theologians' refutations without their having to formulate their own ideas. Second, the questions that had been posed treated topics, such as the doctrine of indulgences and the sacrifice of the mass, which had not been thought through in previous theological discussion. Recourse to previously formulated arguments was therefore difficult; new arguments were not easily conceived. Above all, the methodological and doctrinal demand of Luther and most reformers to recognize Holy Scripture as the source of theology led to great difficulties and required the development of a new methodology from the 1530s on. Third, the political and regional commitments bound individual theologians to specific concerns. Rome had different interests than the imperial court; the Bavarian duchies or solidly Catholic ducal Saxony than electoral Saxony or Hesse; governments and theologians in Spain, France, and Italy, than those in England. Many polemical works must thus be viewed in the context of local conditions as well as that of the entire church. Fifteenth-century theology was in no way homogeneous but in flux, with a spectrum from speculative late scholasticism to Erasmian humanism; multi-faceted currents such as the Neoplatonism of the Florentine Academy were at work. The theologians dependent on these currents could not find a unified approach.

Historiographically, attempts have been made to classify Catholic responses and responders to the Reformation according to several foci, in order to create some systematic ordering: theologians of Scripture, who accepted the 'sola Scriptura' principle for their argumentation and perhaps also fundamentally agreed with it; humanistic theologians with their philological and rhetorical methods; pure scholastics; irenic theologians; or those like Thomas Murner, who turned satire against the Reformation, utilizing instruments of literary style to translate their points into a catchy, aggressive literary form. Granting the wisdom of making such distinctions to clarify the movement, it must be said that no convincing typology has emerged from current research. The controversies were too deeply embedded in the larger dialectic between the Reformation, in its continually developing forms, and its critics for easy systematization. Neither the reformers nor their opponents demonstrate consistency apart from their fundamental convictions, e.g., regarding the doctrines of the church, justification, or the sacraments. Forms of argumentation changed as did content; modernity and obsolete sterility coincided in the same person. Experts from the Scholastic tradition, with its strong emphasis on philosophy, the connection between authority and reason, and an analytic method tried at the same time to utilize humanist philology; humanists like Johannes Cochlaeus often argued scholastically. The leading biblical humanist of the time, Erasmus of Rotterdam, knew Scholasticism and late medieval piety better than his critics imagined.

There was no precedent for the impact of recently produced academic theses comparable to the impact of Luther's theses. The printing press gave them a power that had never been previously experienced. Thus, theologians in the resulting controversies from all camps became concerned about the extent to which the public could be successfully reached with appropriate means of communication, attractive content, plausible arguments, and language that made an impact on the public. Alongside public preaching, printing offered a prime tool for communication, not only through texts but also through pictorial propaganda. However, Catholic controversialists lagged decisively behind in the first decades of the Reformation. Only in the second half of the century could the Catholic book production catch up significantly, with systematic works on the academic and popular level, by members of orders, such as the literarily-productive Jesuits. Ecclesiastical and governmental supervision of books increasingly ensured that the process of confessionalization dominated the book market: unsuitable books dare not be sold or read.

II. The Beginning of the Controversies (1517–20)

Luther's Ninety-five Theses initiated the controversy and made two issues of prime importance: first, the function of the church in the mediation of grace; second, the practice of penance, which the Wittenberg Augustinian believed the doctrine of indulgences of the time had seriously distorted. It was not criticism of indulgences as such which lent the Theses their force—they were very inconsistent anyway—for such criticism had long existed. It was rather a highly plausible biblically based theology which shaped the Theses and determined their effectiveness. In early 1518 Luther's *Sermon on Indulgences and Grace* (WA1.243–246) appeared, rejecting the medieval doctrine of satisfaction. A few months later he produced his explanation of the theses on indulgences, dedicated to Pope Leo X, which reflected the exchanges which had begun in the meantime (WA1.525–628; LW31.83–252). The wave of treatises and counter-treatises, typical for the sixteenth century, had begun to roll. Opponents sought no peaceful exchange of ideas but practised their theology in combat. That meant that the two sides shaped each other's message and method of argumentation.

This first phase produced criticism of Luther from two directions. The Dominican Johannes Tetzel, under attack because his proclamation of the indulgence had elicited Luther's theses, defended himself. With the aid of fellow Dominican Konrad Wimpina, professor of theology in Frankfurt an der Oder, he composed counter-theses, which offered a very simple defence of the practice of indulgences (Fabisch and Iserloh 1988/91: 1.369–75). Thus, the Dominican order was involved in the controversy from the very beginning and would continue to be. The second reaction came from Rome. Again, a Dominican, the papal court theologian (Magister sancti Palatii) Sylvester Prierias (Silvestro Mazzolini), issued a *Dialogue on the Power of the Pope* in connection with the legal proceedings against Luther launched in 1518. It took an almost extreme position, insisting on obedience to the papacy, emphasizing the pope's power.

In spring 1518 began Luther's controversy with Johannes Eck, theology professor in Ingolstadt, a versatile, cultivated intellectual, preacher, and ecclesiastical politician, who had actively participated in a reform movement at his university to establish correct, unsullied texts for instruction in philosophy; his interests extended beyond scholastic learning to the Hebrew and Greek languages. From 1518 until his death in 1543 Eck remained one of the most influential and serious opponents of the Reformation.

At first the subject of dispute was the indulgence. Its importance for the religious life of the time dare not be underestimated any more than its financial significance. More comprehensively, the controversy concerned sin and guilt, punishment and forgiveness, and certainty of salvation for people performing penance as well as the fate of the departed in purgatory, with whom relatives felt solidarity, wanting to ease their fate by purchasing indulgences. Finally, the very position of the church stood at the centre of the discussion (Bagchi 1991: 117–80).

In the context of these questions another Dominican theologian rose to prominence: Thomas de Vio, called Cajetan, whose impressive capabilities were widely recognized. Theologically, he was one of the most important Thomists, author of a pioneering commentary on Thomas Aquinas. Since 1508 he had served as General Master of his Order, since 1517 as a cardinal. In 1518 he became archbishop of Palermo and a year later bishop of his birthplace, Gaeta. Cajetan recognized the weaknesses of the theology of indulgences up to that time and in 1517 composed a *Tractatus on Indulgences* (Fabisch and Iserloh 1988/91: 2.142–68), which he expanded in 1518 with another publication, *Quaestio de thesauro indulgentiarum* (Fabisch and Iserloh 1988/91: 2.169–85; Felmberg 1998) on the 'treasury of merits'. Both treatises gave Pope Leo X the decisive ideas for his bull, issued 9 November 1518, which established officially the doctrine of indulgence.

These developments elicited the first important topics of the controversies the participants on both sides would address: the doctrine of the church and its tasks as well as the theological anthropology involved in it, the doctrine of the human being in the light of the revelation of the fall into sin and redemption, as laid down in Holy Scripture and expounded in the theological tradition. Such questions were no purely theological game in an era in which the teaching and practice of the Christian faith served as an essential means of understanding and coping with reality in general. As Cardinal Cajetan questioned Luther in Augsburg in October 1518, he addressed these problems and with his Thomistic theology of the sacraments countered Luther's existentially oriented doctrine of justification, which together with his principle of biblical authority more and more surfaced as the heart of his reformational message. He recognized or at least sensed the significance of this new way of thinking for the institution of the church and its functions in mediating salvation. He concluded in one of his writings that Luther's doctrine would mean 'building a new church' (Cajetan 1611: 111a).

The Leipzig Disputation of June and July 1519 between Eck and Luther and his colleague Andreas Bodenstein von Karlstadt deepened the controversy. The doctrine of the church emerged prominently alongside the topics penance, purgatory, free will, sin, and grace. Prierias had reduced the question to the power of the pope, which was discussed on the basis of the traditional passages cited for the Roman primacy from the New Testament, Matthew 16:18 and John 21:17. Eck raised the issue of papal power in a series of theses, against which Luther published an explanation of counter-theses which he had composed. That work influenced the discussion of the pope and his position in the church into the 1520s: *Resolutio Lutheriana super propositione sua decia tertia de potestate papae* (WA2.183–240). Responses came from Prierias, Cajetan, and Eck; the case was summarized by the Dominican Ambrosius Catharinus, in response to the request of the head of his order. Nonetheless, the number of Catholic publications up to 1520 was small in comparison to the following years, and their content less than theologically profound.

The next phase began in 1520: the topics under discussion grew. The Roman condemnation of Luther (1520), the censures issued by the universities of Leuven (Louvain) and Cologne in 1519, and the condemnation by the theological faculty in Paris (1521) created a new situation, involving immediately Catharinus and others. Cajetan defended the condemnations in print, as did the inquisitor Jacob Hoogsträten of Cologne and the Leuven theologian Jacob Latomus. They did not determine further developments. The weakness of their critiques became clear in the bull which threatened Luther with excommunication. The expansion of the Reformation itself was shaping the arguments and eliciting new opponents.

III. The Diffusion of Controversy (1520–30)

After 1520 the Reformation spread and became diffuse, in the content of its message and in its proponents, as new divisions and new reformers appeared. That altered the theological controversies. Initially Luther's programmatic writings on the doctrine of the church and the papacy, the priesthood of all believers, the doctrine of the sacraments, Scripture and Tradition, law and gospel, and the question of the freedom of the Christian provoked critiques. As dividing lines were drawn, efforts grew to strengthen arguments against the reformer and his adherents.

The agenda of controversy expanded. Conflict over the papacy reached its climax in 1520. The mass became a focus of Catholic controversialists after 1521, repentance and penance between 1521 and 1525; purgatory claimed their attention especially in 1526–30. Baptism became a concern for Catholic writers after 1528. They were served by printers above all in Leipzig and Cologne. Leipzig printers complained about poor sales for these works despite the warm support of Duke George of Saxony.

The nature of the church remained a key point. Even the Catholic authors were not of one mind although all defended the papacy and the hierarchy. Eck's *Enchiridion* (1525) equated the church with the kingdom of heaven and defended its infallibility because it is the bride of Christ, ruled by the Holy Spirit. The Franciscan Minorite Kaspar Schatzgeyer presented a sophisticated if unsystematic concept of the church in *Traductio Sathanae* (1525). The baptized include good and evil people; the elect alone are the true body of Christ. He spoke of the true church in almost Evangelical fashion as invisible. Grace and the Spirit ensure the unity of the church. Its visible institutions need visible leadership. Cardinal Cajetan also emphasized the dogmatic over legal elements of the definition of the church and saw in it the body of Christ, united with Christ, whose members are found in mystical form with each other in a 'communicatio'. In a sermon at the Fifth Lateran Council Cajetan had previously enumerated 'marks of the church': holiness, peace, eternal newness, purity.

The humanist John Fisher, bishop of Rochester, was the first to address the question of council, holding a general council in concert with the pope infallible. Prierias had earlier taken an extreme position on the power of councils which made an approach to Luther's concern more difficult. In *Dialogus de potestate papae* (1518) his defence of the authority of the Roman church and the pope reflected Roman nervousness over conciliarism but potentially offered the impression that they were superior to Scripture.

In the complex discussions over justification and grace, Augustine's authority played a major role, especially in Cajetan's writings. He rejected a doctrine of assurance for individual believers. Original sin and concupiscence also commanded significant interest, for example by Jacob Hoogsträten.

In Leipzig the Franciscan Augustine von Alveldt (Smolinsky 1983) published theologically shallow works on the communion in both kinds, papal power and the sacraments. Hieronymus Emser, humanist and court preacher in Dresden, whose interests and efforts in forming and carrying out the ecclesiastical policies of Duke George of Saxony displayed themselves in his literary campaign against the Reformation ever since the Leipzig Disputation, issued several publications, dealing with the value of the Church Fathers and ecclesiastical tradition, and with the interpretation and clarity of Scripture (Smolinsky 1983). That caused Luther to reflect more deeply on the dialectic of law and gospel, spirit and letter. From 1523 on, Emser, who as a humanist was very interested in the sources, criticized Luther's translation of the New Testament and his explanations (glosses) on it. In 1527 Emser published a kind of purified New Testament, essentially based on Luther's text.

In 1520 the Strasbourg Franciscan Thomas Murner entered the controversy. Murner, versatile and controversial as few others through his satirical critiques of the times, began with moderate but then ever sharper theological criticism. He translated Luther's *Babylonian Captivity* into German; in 1522 he wrote *On the Great Lutheran Fool*, one of the best anti-reformational satires. King Henry VIII of England entered the fray; his *Assertion of the Seven Sacraments against Martin Luther* appeared in London in 1521 (Fraenkel 1992), defending the seven sacraments against Luther's *Babylonian Captivity*. The pope awarded him the title 'Defender of the Faith' (though that did not prevent the king from introducing the Reformation into England in 1534). John Fisher defended the royal treatise. A long series of treatises with varying content against a variety of foes followed.

Not only did the list of topics under discussion expand in the 1520s—e.g. the veneration of the saints and Mary—the first comprehensive critiques of reformational teaching and practice began to appear, heralding many such efforts. One of the pioneers of this literary genre was Schatzgeyer, author of *Scrutinium divinae scripturae pro conciliatione dissidentium dogmatum* (1522). He mentioned no specific writing of Luther's in his unique combination of biblical theology and his own systematic approach as a Catholic controversialist. He chose not to follow the usual pattern of rejecting Luther directly but tried to offer a positive presentation of disputed doctrines, using the method of mostly biblical argumentation.

Further progress developed after Philip Melanchthon's *Loci communes* (1521) introduced the application of the humanists' loci method to theology, grouping reformational teachings topically. Comparable Catholic controversial works appeared although they did not reach Melanchthon's niveau. Johannes Eck was the most successful in this regard. His *Enchiridion locorum communium adversus Lutherum et alios hostes ecclesiae* appeared in 1525; repeatedly revised, it reflected the course of the Reformation (Fraenkel 1979). It was translated into German, French, and Flemish, in at least 121 editions. At the same time the compendium of Bishop Berthold of Chiemsee, *Tewtsche Theologey* (1528), offered an overview of doctrine and strengthened the polemic of the controversialists.

Luther introduced the topic of 'Christian freedom' in 1520, in order to address true Christian, evangelical freedom as Saint Paul presented it, but contemporaries focused immediately on a much-disputed problem: ecclesiastical commands, their merit, and their compelling force. This also revealed the complexity of the controversies, for this was a topic which Erasmus raised, repeatedly eliciting the suspicion of the conservative theologians. His *Epistola de interdicto esu cranium* (1522) called into question the church's laws concerning eating. Erasmus' chief opponents, the theologians of the Sorbonne, including Noel Beda and Petrus Sutor, had sought to associate him with Luther and in the mid-1520s condemned him. Jodocus Clichtoveus held a similar position. Though influenced by humanism and Jacques Lefèvre d'Etaples, he prized monasticism and sought reform of the monasteries and the clergy. Despite his concern for reform he issued his *Anti-Lutherus* (1524) on Christian freedom, focusing on ecclesiastical law and Erasmus' treatise on eating meat. He also criticized Luther's rejection of monastic vows. Others, including Cardinal Jerome Aleander, the papal commissar for the publication of the bull of excommunication against Luther, papal nuncio and a humanist; Albert Pio von Carpi; the Italian canon Augustine Steuchus, and the Spaniard Diego López de Zuñiga (Stunica) followed this practice of grouping Erasmus, Erasmians, and Lutherans together. Their critique also addressed Erasmus' edition of the New Testament, where he, for example, had questioned the interpretation of Ephesians 5:32 which based the sacramental status of marriage on this passage. That had provoked a dispute with the Dominican Johannes Dietenberger, also a critic of Protestant theology. Erasmus' questioning of Dionysius the Areopagite's being a student of the apostles, his plea for inner piety, his view of marriage, and his scepticism over the worth of monastic vows and virginity aroused the wrath of many controversialists, including Eck. Erasmus' conflict with Luther on the free will could not change this view appreciably. He stood between the fronts. His theology would not conform to one of the confessional positions, as became clear later.

Other opponents caught the attention of Catholic controversialists. Karlstadt's radical rejection of the veneration of images elicited critiques from Emser and Eck. Especially the Swiss reformers, Ulrich Zwingli and Johannes Oecolampadius, had to be addressed. Mostly south German theologians addressed them. Also Anabaptists aroused fierce refutations of their theology.

This did not, however, avert attention from the Wittenberg reformers at the end of the 1520s. Emser's successor in Dresden, Johannes Cochlaeus, published a pamphlet, *Sieben Köpffe Martini Luthers vom Hochwirdigen Sacrament des Altars* (1529), to highlight the inner contradictions of Luther's message. He addressed Luther's Wittenberg colleagues Melanchthon and Bugenhagen as well (Keen 1988, 1995). He also pioneered the genre of polemical biography with his account of Luther's life, composed in the 1530s but first published after Luther's death (Keen et al. 2003).

IV. Converts and Colloquies

Although polemic continued in the 1530s, over specific issues and works by Luther (cf., e.g., Volz 1932) and others, that decade gave prominence to two phenomena in Catholic opposition to the Wittenberg Reformation. Some of Luther's adherents returned to the Roman obedience. Some of them contributed to attempts to reconcile the warring camps, often under direction of princes and especially Emperor Charles V. Georg Witzel was one who did both (Henze 1995). His 'apostasy' fired fierce personal criticism among the Wittenberg theologians (Clemen 1920), but he also played a significant role in dialogues dedicated to reconciliation, in negotiations anticipating the imperial colloquy in Hagenau, Worms, and Regensburg (1539–41) (Kuhaupt 1998) and in the colloquy itself. Following its failure to win approval for its formula for rapprochement, the Council of Trent, Luther's death, and the Smalcald War, a new era in Roman Catholic–Protestant relationships developed in other directions.

V. Catholic Critique and Luther's Theology

Without doubt contemporary Roman Catholic critique shaped Luther's theology at points although the main lines of his thinking fell into place on the basis of his engagement with his scholastic and monastic masters more than with his foes. His own experience shaped his rejection of monasticism more than did the objections of his critics (Lohse 1963). His progress towards his view of the papacy as Antichrist certainly was not impeded by Eck and other foes, however (Hendrix 1974). His view of councils also assumed form in dialogue with Catholic critics (Spehr 2010), as did his understanding of the Lord's Supper (Wisløff 1964). In exchanges with individual critics and groups within the Catholic camp Luther also refined his understanding of grace, faith, justification, and related matters of soteriology. He had set questions in place on the basis and in the context of his scholastic and monastic training, but in the actual dialogue with contemporaries his ideas took their public shape.

Although of varying quality and genre, the critiques of his theology by Roman Catholic critics contributed to the precise formulation of Luther's thought. The precise form of their arguments and Luther's specific responses continue to need careful research and analysis. Without the discipline of meeting objects from the heart of the medieval experience, many particulars of his theology would have had another form.

Translated by Theodore J. Hopkins.

References

Bagchi, David V. N. (1991). *Luther's Earliest Opponents, Catholic Controversialists, 1518–1525.* Minneapolis: Fortress.

Cajetan, Thomas de Vio (1611). *Opuscula omnia.* Lyon.

Clemen, Otto (1920). 'Georg Witzel und Justus Jonas'. *Archiv für Reformationsgeschichte* 17: 132–52.

Dingel, Irene (2007). 'Streitkultur und Kontroversschrifttum im späten 16. Jahrhundert. Versuch einer methodischen Standortbestimmung'. In *Kommunikation und Transfer im Christentum der Frühen Neuzeit,* ed. Irene Dingel and Wolf Friedrich Schäufele. Mainz: Zabern, 95–111.

Fabisch, Peter and Erwin Iserloh (eds.) (1988/1991). *Dokumente zur Causa Lutheri (1517–1521).* 2 vols. Münster: Aschendorff.

Felmberg, Bernhard Alfred R. (1998). *Die Ablasstheologie Kardinal Cajetans (1469–1534).* Leiden: Brill.

Fraenkel, Pierre (ed.) (1979). *Johannes Eck. Enchiridion locorum communium adversus Lutherum et alios hostes ecclesiae (1525–1543).* Münster: Aschendorff.

—— (ed.) (1992). *Heinrich VIII. Assertio septem sacramentorum adversus Martinum Lutherum.* Münster: Aschendorff.

Hendrix, Scott H. (1974). *Ecclesia in via. Ecclesiological Developments in the Medieval Psalm Exegesis and the Dictata supra Psalterium (1513–1515) of Martin Luther.* Leiden: Brill.

Henze, Barbara (1995). *Aus Liebe zur Kirche Reform. Die Bemühungen Georg Witzels (1501–1573) um die Kircheneinheit.* Münster: Aschendorff.

Keen, Ralph (1988). *Johannes Cochlaeus. Responsio ad Johannem Bugenhagium Pomeranum.* Niewkoop: de Graaf.

—— (1995). *Johannes Cochlaeus. Philippicae I–VII.* 2 vols. Nieuwkoop: de Graaf.

Keen, Ralph, Elizabeth Vandiver, and Thomas D. Frazel (trans./eds.) (2003). *Luther's Lives: Two Contemporary Accounts of Martin Luther.* Manchester and New York: Manchester University Press.

Klaiber, Wilbirgis (ed.) (1978). *Katholische Kontroverstheologen und Reformer des 16. Jahrhunderts.* Münster: Aschendorff.

Kuhaupt, Georg (1998). *Veröffentlichte Kirchenpolitik. Kirche im publizistischen Streit zur Zeit der Religionsgespräche (1538–1541).* Göttingen: Vandenhoeck & Ruprecht.

Lohse, Bernhard (1963). *Mönchthum und Reformation. Luthers Auseinandersetzung mit dem Mönchsideal des Mittelalters.* Göttingen: Vandenhoeck & Ruprecht.

Smolinsky, Heribert (1983). *Augustin von Alveldt und Hieronymus Emser. Eine Untersuchung zur Kontroverstheologie der fruhen Reformationszeit im Herzogtum Sachsen.* Munster: Aschendorff.

Spehr, Christopher (2010). *Luther und das Konzil.* Tübingen: Mohr/Siebeck.

Volz, Hans (1932). *Drei Schriften Gegen Luthers SchmalkaldischeArtikel von Cochläus, Witzel und Hoffmeister (1538 und 1539).* Münster: Aschendorff.

Wisløff, Carl Fredrik (1964). *The Gift of Communion: Luther's Controversy with Rome on Eucharistic Sacrifice,* trans. Joseph M. Shaw. Minneapolis: Augsburg.

CHAPTER 38

....

LUTHER AND THE
SCHWÄRMER

....

AMY NELSON BURNETT

I. LUTHER AND THE *SCHWÄRMER* IN
TWENTIETH-CENTURY SCHOLARSHIP

....

IN his influential 1922 essay 'Luther und die Schwärmer', Karl Holl contrasted the reformer's religious and social teachings with those of Thomas Müntzer and his successors. Holl portrayed Müntzer as the first to express ideals that would be taken up by other religious radicals, from the Zürich Anabaptists through the English Quaker George Fox. Against an emphasis on the inner word and calls for the transformation of society that characterized the *Schwärmer*, Holl presented Luther's understanding of the relationship between God and human beings and of the roles of church and state in a Christian society (Holl 1928; on Holl, see Stayer 1997).[1]

Holl wrote his essay in conscious opposition to Ernst Troeltsch, who made a fundamental distinction between the sectarian Swiss Anabaptists and the mystics and spiritualists who were Müntzer's spiritual heirs (Troeltsch 1931: 691–807). Mennonite historians, especially Harold S. Bender and his students, followed Troeltsch's lead by rejecting any linkage of the revolutionary teachings of Müntzer with the Swiss Anabaptists. By the 1960s scholars of the Radical Reformation had limited the term

---

[1] There is no satisfactory equivalent for *Schwärmer* in English. The two terms used most often, 'fanatic' or 'enthusiast', no longer have the specific connotations of prophetic frenzy or claims to special revelation that they had in the seventeenth century; *Oxford English Dictionary*, s.v. 'enthusiast', 1, 2b; 'fanatic', 2a. Although the term has a negative connotation in German—not least due to Luther himself—I use it here because those connotations are not so evident in English.

'*Schwärmer*' to Müntzer and other revolutionary radicals, distinguishing them from Anabaptists, Spiritualists, and Antitrinitarians.[2]

Discussions of Luther and the *Schwärmer* since Holl reflect the evolution of research on Reformation radicalism. Written from a systematic perspective and particularly concerned with Luther's pneumatology, the older works of Regin Prenter (1953: 247–305) and Karl Gerhard Steck (1955) did not distinguish among Luther's opponents but used the term *Schwärmer* or 'Enthusiast' in an undifferentiated way. Wilhelm Maurer (1952) moved beyond a concern with the Reformation radicals to give equal treatment to another group that Luther included among the *Schwärmer*—the sacramentarians, those who denied the presence of Christ's body and blood in the Lord's Supper. More recently some restrict the term *Schwärmer* to Müntzer and Andreas Bodenstein von Karlstadt (Gritsch 1976; Haas 1997), while others avoid the term entirely in their examinations of Luther's relations with his evangelical opponents (Edwards 1975; Loewen 1974).

The fact that Luther saw all of these various groups united in their false teaching about Word and sacrament has been obscured by limiting or abandoning the term *Schwärmer*. The reformer coined the term to describe those whose ideas 'swarmed' or flew about like bees. It became a polemical label for all his opponents, but throughout his career he continued to use it especially for those who confused the proper ordering of external and internal.[3] As a consequence of this error, they did not share his understanding of how God works through the oral and written word and through both sacraments as means of grace.

Luther's conflicts with the *Schwärmer* had the greatest impact on the development of his thought through the 1520s and early 1530s. During this period he dealt, in roughly chronological order, with three groups of evangelical opponents whose origins were related but who differed significantly in their concerns. Each contributed to the development of Luther's understanding of Word and sacrament and his formulation of the responsibility of both ministers and magistrates to safeguard true religion. The earliest were those Luther called 'new prophets': the Zwickau prophets, together with Müntzer and Karlstadt. Against them Luther developed his defence of infant baptism and his view of the sacraments more generally. Karlstadt was also the first of the sacramentarians, who disagreed with Luther about the content and purpose of the Lord's Supper. The eucharistic controversy pushed Luther to elaborate his understanding of the Lord's Supper and work out the implications of that understanding for Christology; it also confronted him with the problem of heresy within the evangelical movement. Only at the end of the decade did Luther turn his attention to the Anabaptists, not chiefly to refute their views of baptism since his understanding of the sacraments had already been fully expressed in his works against the 'new prophets' and sacramentarians, but because he saw them as a threat

---

[2] Bender 1953. The distinction between the groups was made at about the same time on both sides of the Atlantic by Fast 1962 and Williams 1992. Williams posited three groups (Anabaptists, spiritualists, and evangelical rationalists) but divided the Anabaptists into evangelical (Zürich), revolutionary (Münster), and contemplative (Denck) branches.

[3] Jacob Grimm et al., *Deutsches Wörterbuch* (Leipzig: Hirzel, 1854–1960), s.v. 'Schwärmer', 1–2, and 'schwärmen', 4a. Mühlpfordt (1986) identified twelve different uses of the term in Luther's writing.

to true doctrine and the political order. In response he made a more explicit link between heresy, blasphemy, and rebellion, elaborated on the office of the ministry, and faced the question of whether and to what extent secular rulers should take action against religious dissent.

II. Luther and the 'New Prophets:' Spirit, Word, and Sacrament

In *The Babylonian Captivity of the Church* (1520), Luther defined the sacraments as God's promises to which signs were attached. With this definition he accepted only baptism and the Lord's Supper as legitimate sacraments. While he stated that baptism had been preserved 'untouched and untainted by human ordinances', he rejected the sacrifice of the mass and the conversion of the elements into Christ's body and blood. He argued that the laity should receive both bread and wine during communion (WA6.526,35–527,8, 502,1–526,34; LW36.57,19–57). Over the next two years, Luther's redefinition of the Lord's Supper generated significant debate, and disagreements over the prescription of liturgical changes contributed to his first public conflict with Karlstadt when Luther returned from the Wartburg (March 1522).

There was little controversy over baptism until the appearance of the Zwickau prophets in Wittenberg at the end of 1521. Originally dismissive of these 'prophets', Luther became more alarmed after meeting several of them in early 1522. He believed that Satan lay behind their claims to receive visions from God and their questioning of infant baptism.[4] Over the next year Luther became aware of others who opposed his teaching, including Müntzer and Karlstadt. Expelled from Saxony in September 1524, Karlstadt published several pamphlets attacking the conservative liturgical reforms in Wittenberg and rejecting Christ's corporeal presence in the sacrament.

The challenge posed by this group, connected by personal as well as theological ties (though Karlstadt rejected Müntzer's call for violence against the godless; Stayer 1993) caused Luther to make more explicit his understanding of Word and sacrament. Luther's earliest discussions of the sacraments had focused especially on the Lord's Supper, but by 1524 his attention was drawn to baptism as well, and especially the justification for baptizing infants.[5] He publicly condemned *Schwärmer* and 'proud spirits' who claimed 'to speak with the Divine Majesty as with a cobbler's apprentice' (WA12.499). Although not identical, there was an affinity between Luther's definition of the sacraments as signs joined to divine promises and his demand that the 'new

---

[4] See his letters, both dated 12 April 1522, to Johann Lang and Georg Spalatin, WABr2.492–495, and his later recollections of meetings with Marcus Stübner, Nicolaus Storch, Thomas Drechsel, and Martin Cellarius, WATR 1.153, §362; 2.206–207, §2060; 3.14–17, §2837a–b; 5.248–9, §5568. Storch asked Luther how 'a handful of water could save anyone'; in Luther's later treatments of baptism he often cited this phrase in order to refute it.

[5] Luther's earliest defence of infant baptism in letters to Melanchthon, 13 January 1522, WABr 2.424–427; LW 48.364–372, and to Spalatin, 29 May 1522, WABr 2.545–547. Luther told Nicolaus Hausmann

prophets' produce a sign to attest to the outpouring of the Spirit: in both cases there had to be some external indication that accompanied God's pronouncement. While God had given such signs in apostolic times, he no longer did so, which undermined the claims of the 'new prophets' to divine revelation (Lectures on Joel [2:30–32] July 1524, WA13.109–114; LW18.107–112; cf. his later description of his meeting with Marcus Stübner, WATR 3.13–17, §2837a–b).

In *Against the Heavenly Prophets* Luther presented his understanding of Word and sacrament most fully (WA18.126–214; LW40.79–223). The treatise, composed in two parts at the turn of 1524/5 in response to Karlstadt's pamphlets on the Lord's Supper, was more than just a defence of Christ's presence in the sacrament. It attacked the views of all the 'new prophets' or *Schwärmer* who erred with regard to the proper ordering of internal faith and external actions. This fundamental summary of Luther's understanding of the relationship between the Spirit, Word, and sacraments served as the foundation for his exchanges with later opponents.

Part I of *Against the Heavenly Prophets* chastised the legalists who taught that obedience to specific commands or prohibitions made one Christian. By emphasizing externals rather than faith, they denied Christian freedom. Luther focused on the removal of images and the abolition of the elevation of the host, but he made the broader point that the 'papists' were also *Schwärmer* since they too destroyed Christian freedom (WA18.111–112; LW40.128–129). Part II condemned those who placed the inspiration of the Holy Spirit before and outside of the external means of Word and sacraments. Against all the 'new prophets' Luther asserted that God gives the Holy Spirit only through these external means. Only after he had established this principle did Luther move on to the issue of Christ's bodily presence in the elements of the Lord's Supper. He rejected Karlstadt's exegesis of Christ's words instituting the Supper, arguing that the simple literal understanding of the words was the most certain. He then provided his own explanation of other New Testament texts on the Lord's Supper and refuted arguments raised by human reason against Christ's bodily presence. He warned readers against all who boasted of possessing the spirit but taught without the proper calling. Over the next several years in his debate with sacramentarians and Anabaptists Luther would elaborate on each of these ideas.

III. LUTHER AND THE SACRAMENTARIANS: THE LORD'S SUPPER, CHRISTOLOGY, AND HERESY

One of the first tangible consequences of Luther's conflict with Karlstadt and the 'new prophets' was the addition of sermons on baptism and the Lord's Supper to the

in March 1524 that he had just finished an excursus on infant baptism for his Lenten postil; he implied that his discussion was a reaction to reports of the 'monstrosities' that Karlstadt was introducing, WABr 3.255–256; cf. WA17,1.72–88. Luther's correspondence over the spring and summer of 1524 contains several other references to Karlstadt and Müntzer.

Wittenberg tradition of preaching on the three parts of the catechism during Lent. (Because it had been the custom to preach on the Lord's Supper during Holy Week, the more significant change was the introduction of regular sermons on baptism beginning in 1525. The closer integration of the two sacraments with the traditional catechetical material bore fruit in the *Large* and *Small Catechisms* of 1529.) In his own preaching and lecturing, Luther also repeated themes he had discussed in *Against the Heavenly Prophets*. Thus in his sermon on Exodus 15:13–21 preached in March, Luther emphasized, 'against our false prophets, sectarian spirits and *Schwärmer*', that God gives material signs—the oral word, baptism, and the Lord's Supper—where he wants to be found (WA16.209,25–29). He insisted on Christ's bodily presence in the elements in his sermon on 1 Corinthians 9:24–10:4 for Septuagesima Sunday, written for his Lenten postil in the autumn of 1525 (WA17,2.125–136). He was clearly concerned with countering the spread of false teaching on the sacraments among his pastoral charges.

Müntzer's execution at the end of May removed one major source of false teaching. Another was eliminated when Karlstadt published a partial retraction and promised to write nothing further as the price of being allowed to return to Saxony. The public debate over the content and meaning of the Lord's Supper did not end with Karlstadt's withdrawal from the public debate, however, for over the course of 1525 Ulrich Zwingli and Johann Oecolampadius published their own works rejecting Christ's corporeal presence in the sacrament.

Although the Swiss reformers distanced themselves from Karlstadt, Luther saw little difference between them. This was not due to any mistaken identification on Luther's part, as has sometimes been claimed. Instead, Luther realized that the Swiss, like Karlstadt, separated internal and external things and downgraded the latter. He perceived little difference between Karlstadt's claim that the Spirit's work preceded reception of the sacraments and the insistence of the Swiss that physical things could not convey spiritual benefit; indeed, all used John 6:63, 'the flesh is of no use', as the basis for their understanding of the Lord's Supper. The Swiss did not accept Karlstadt's exegesis of Christ's words, 'this is my body', but they did agree with his interpretation of all other New Testament passages concerning the Lord's Supper. Finally, in Luther's eyes both the Swiss and Karlstadt allowed human reason rather than God's Word to determine the content and meaning of the sacrament. For these reasons Luther included the Swiss among the *Schwärmer*. When he became aware of Kaspar von Schwenckfeld's views at the end of 1525, he added the Silesians as well.

Luther initially felt that his arguments in *Against the Heavenly Prophets* had not been refuted by any of the sacramentarians, so he did not write against them directly. He did, however, provide prefaces for two different German translations of Johann Brenz's *Swabian Syngramma* (referring in both cases to *Against the Heavenly Prophets*: WA19.457–461, 529–530), and in his German commentaries on Job (WA19.197–198, 206–207; LW19.44, 54–55) and Habakkuk (WA19.390; LW19.192–193), published in early 1526, he emphasized the Word and sacraments as the only sure means by which one knew God and his promises. His position became more widely known as others published his statements about the Lord's Supper: his letter to Reutlingen (early 1526, in print by June, WA19.118–125) and his sermons from Holy Week 1526 (published in autumn as *The Sacrament of the Body and Blood of Christ—Against the Fanatics,* WA19.482–523; LW36.335–361). By late 1526, after what he regarded as the sacramentarians' deliberate attempt to spread their false teaching under the appearance of the Wittenbergers' approval, Luther resolved to write on the Lord's Supper himself. The provocations included Martin Bucer's translation of Bugenhagen's Psalms commentary, which included a sacramentarian presentation of the Lord's Supper, Bucer's translation of Luther's Lenten postil, which Bucer prefaced with an understanding of 1 Corinthians 10:1–4 at variance with Luther's sermon for Septuagesima Sunday, and Leo Jud's pseudonymous publication of a pamphlet that presented both Luther and Erasmus as agreeing with Zwingli's understanding of the Lord's Supper (cf. Luther's letter to Johann Herwagen, WA19:471–473; LW59.163–72).

Luther's delayed entry into the public debate put him in the position of responder rather than initiator. This shaped the content of his two most important treatises on the Lord's Supper, *That These Words of Christ, 'This is my Body,' Still Stand Firm Against the Fanatics* (1527) and *Confession Concerning Christ's Supper* (1528). In *Babylonian Captivity* (WA6.510,16–35; LW36.32–33) he had asserted that it should be enough to cling to Christ's words without inquiring about how Christ's body was present, but he now discussed the various modes of presence and types of union between two substances (on the three types of presence, WA26.326,29–330,28; LW37.214–217 and on identical predication, WA26.437,30–445,17; LW37.294–303) in order to demonstrate that Christ's bodily presence in the elements could be defended rationally though he did not assert that one must accept these rational arguments for his bodily presence. Instead, he introduced them to show that the Swiss could not prove that Christ's body was *not* present. In his catechism sermons from 1528 Luther told his hearers to leave quarrels about how the elements changed to the learned; it was sufficient simply to believe that the bread and wine are Christ's body and blood (WA30,1.54,7–31, 118,2–119,33). Likewise, the insistence of the Swiss that Christ's human body was located at the right hand of the Father led him to consider more deeply the relationship between Christ's divine and human natures and to argue for the ubiquity of Christ's body (*That These Words,* WA23.131–155; LW37.55–70). Luther also adopted arguments advanced earlier by others against the Swiss, e.g. he used the same patristic citations as had Willibald Pirckheimer's critique of Oecolampadius (Burnett 2012).

Just as Luther's discussion of the sacraments shaped his defence of infant baptism in the early 1520s, so his defence of the Lord's Supper against the sacramentarians had implications for his discussion of baptism. His correspondence from 1527 reflects his growing awareness of the threat posed by Anabaptist teachings; in early 1528 he wrote a treatise *Concerning Rebaptism*. There Luther compared the Anabaptists to the Donatists, who also based baptism on human holiness. He repeatedly linked these two groups thereafter; Article VIII of the Augsburg Confession also associates them (WA26.163,15–25; LW40.250; cf. *Confession,* WA26.506,19–29; LW37.366; sermon on John 20:19–23, 30 March 1529, WA29.303,7–11, at Marburg, WA30,3.126,6; LW40.27; BSLK 62; BC 42).

Throughout 1527 and 1528 Luther explained his understanding of Word and both sacraments against all these evangelical opponents. Underlying that understanding was his nominalist conception of a hidden God whose pact with humankind established the sole reliable means by which he could be known (Oberman 1987). Luther argued that God has bound himself to externals and can be grasped surely only through his Word, whether written, preached, or added to water or bread and wine to make a sacrament. In response to the Swiss insistence that the bread and wine were only signs, Luther downplayed his earlier definition of the sacraments as promise and sign. He did not abandon it completely, but he now emphasized the Word joined to the external elements. The sacraments derived their power from God's institution and promise, independent of the faith of either the minister or the recipient (WA23.151,3–24; LW37.68; WA26.285,3–24; LW37.184–185; WA26.164,39–165,33; LW40.252–253; on Zechariah 4:1, WA23.558,13–21; LW20.222–223; on Titus 3:5, WA25.63,26–66,7; LW29.81–85; sermons on baptism, February 1528, WA27.32–38, 41–45, 49–53, 55–60, and the three series of catechism sermons, May, September, and December 1528, WA30,1.18,16–27,24, 50,28–56,20, 109,32–122,21; LW51.182–193). Although he did not consider absolution a sacrament, Luther emphasized the power of God's Word working through the office of the ministry in absolution as well (see especially his sermon on John 20:19–23, 1529, WA29.302–310; cf. the English translation of the expanded version published after Luther's death, WA28.464–479; LW69.349–372; 'Brief Exhortation to Confession in the Large Catechism', BSLK 725–30; BC 476–8). This message would be incorporated into the catechisms and became a staple of Luther's later writings (BSLK 515–21, 691–725; BC 359–63, 456–76; cf. Trigg 2001; Kolb 1999).

Although he responded to his condemnation by the pope in 1520 by calling the pope a heretic, Luther was initially reluctant to use the word 'heresy' against his evangelical opponents (Gensichen 1967). In *Against the Heavenly Prophets*, and in lectures and sermons through 1524, he referred to 'factious spirits', 'desecrators of the sacrament', and other terms of abuse, but he did not call others heretics. His response to the outbreak of the eucharistic controversy was to apply the disciplinary procedure outlined in Scripture to his opponents. In late 1525 he told the Strasbourgers that the sacramentarians had been warned repeatedly against error, and he pronounced all those who argued against Christ's corporeal presence as 'alien to the faith'. At that time he introduced the concept of heresy by comparing the dispute over Christ's presence to the turmoil in the early church caused by the Arians (WABr3.604–611; cf. Wolfgang Capito's report to Zwingli that the Wittenbergers had denounced them as blasphemers, heretics, and rebels, 14 November 1525, Z8.426).

As the eucharistic controversy developed, Luther became more outspoken in identifying his opponents as heretics, particularly as he gave up hope that they would acknowledge their error (WA26.261,6–262,7; LW37.161–162). In *On the Councils and the Church* (1539) he stated that the difference between heretics and those who simply erred was that the former persisted in their error despite admonition (WA50.544,17–545,5; LW41.50), the medieval church's definition of heresy as well.

He was scandalized by Zwingli's understanding of original sin (his response to the Strasbourg pastors, 5 November 1525, WABr3.602, and his lecture on 1 John. 1:6–7, WA20.621,8–19; LW30.229), and he condemned as blasphemous the Zürich reformer's use of alloiosis to explain the relationship between Christ's divine and human natures (WA26.319,14–40, 341,39–342,27; LW37.209–210, 230–231; Cross 1996). In autumn 1527 he began his lectures on 1 John by referring to the sacramentarians as 'our heretics' (WA20.602,19–20; cf. LW30.222). Throughout these lectures he drew a parallel with the Christological heresies of the fifth century, condemned all heretics who attacked the person of Christ, whether in his divinity or his humanity, and asserted that one who denied Christ on one point necessarily denied him everywhere. Citing Titus 3:10, Luther said such heretics should be shunned when admonition was unsuccessful (WA20.667,3–671,39, 681,2–682,29, 685,3–15, 752,19–754,33, 769,23–38; LW30.252, 257–258, 260, 299–300, 309–310; Windhorst 1977). In *On the Councils and the Church* Luther identified Zwingli with the Nestorians although he stated that when he had written against Zwingli earlier, he was still ignorant of Nestorius' Christology (WA50.591,9–21; LW41.105).

Although the Marburg Colloquy (1529) failed to resolve differences over the Lord's Supper, the fifteen articles accepted by both parties dismantled at least some of Luther's suspicions of the Swiss and Strasbourgers. The result was an end to the bitter polemical battle that had raged for four years. Martin Bucer's efforts to bring about concord between the two sides, begun in earnest at the Diet of Augsburg, finally bore fruit with the Wittenberg Concord (1536). The Concord was a statement describing the teaching of the South German churches rather than a consensus reflecting the views of both sides, and its success rested in large part on its ambiguity. Luther was willing to accept the Concord even though it could be interpreted in a way that did not accord fully with his view of the sacrament.

Luther's attitude towards the Swiss hardened after their rejection of the Wittenberg Concord, however. His uncompromising rejection of Zwingli in particular made any kind of agreement impossible, for although Heinrich Bullinger's view of the Lord's Supper was not the same as Zwingli's during the 1520s, he and his Zürich colleagues were compelled to defend the teaching and reputation of the founder of their church (Sanders 1992). In his treatises on the Lord's Supper, Luther was much harsher in his judgement of Zwingli than of Oecolampadius, and he treated the Basler's arguments more seriously (cf. *Confession*, WA26.261,19–22, 379,17–23; LW37.161, 252). In Luther's eyes Zwingli and the other sacramentarians obstinately rejected a doctrine grounded in Scripture and held by the entire church for 1,500 years. Luther saw Zwingli's *Exposition of the Faith*, prepared for the Diet of Augsburg, as a retreat from the positions endorsed at Marburg, and he regarded the Zürich reformer's death, like that of Müntzer, as God's punishment (open letter to Duke Albrecht of Prussia, February 1532, WA30,3.547–553). His *Brief Confession Concerning the Holy Sacrament* (1544) repeated many of the charges he had earlier levelled at the sacramentarians, and he again condemned Karlstadt, Zwingli, Oecolampadius, and Schwenckfeld as heretics (WA54.141–167; LW38.287–319).

IV. LUTHER AND THE ANABAPTISTS: THE LIMITS OF TOLERATION

The sacramentarians may have provoked Luther to consider the nature of heresy, but Müntzer first convinced him that false teaching led to rebellion, a position that influenced his later endorsement of the secular authority's right to take action against the Anabaptists. Through the early 1520s Luther frequently stated that faith could not be compelled and consciences should be left free. In *Temporal Authority: to what Extent it Should be Obeyed* (1523) he argued that secular authorities had no right to intervene in spiritual matters, and ministers could use only God's Word against religious dissent (WA11.247–271; LW45.75–118). If dissenters refused to listen to instruction and admonition, the only other option was to shun them as obstinate heretics. This explains his harsh judgement of the Zürich church after 1538, when hope for concord had ended. He refused to accept a copy of the Zürich Bible from the printer Christoph Froschauer because it was the work of the Zürich pastors, with whom he could not have fellowship (31 August 1543, WABr10.387).

The situation changed, though, if religious dissent threatened the civil order. When Müntzer's followers turned violent, Luther urged the elector to punish them as rebels (*Letter to the Princes of Saxony*, WA15.210–215; LW40.49–59; Bräuer 1980). He also granted rulers the right to take action against blasphemy, and so at the end of 1524 he called on the authorities to abolish private masses, which he regarded as idolatry and an abomination (*Ain Sermon von der höchsten Gottßlesterung*, WA15.764–774, reworked and published as *The Abomination of the Secret Mass* in early 1525, WA18.22–36; LW36.307–328; note the appeal to the authorities at the end of each work). The two issues of rebellion and blasphemy came together in *Against the Robbing and Murdering Hordes of Peasants* (1525), where Luther condemned as blasphemous the claim that the gospel justified the Peasants' Revolt, and he urged Christian rulers to take up the sword against the rebels (WA18.357–361; LW46.45–55). Not content with addressing his own ruler, he concluded *That These Words... Stand Firm Against the Fanatics* by warning the city councillors of Basel, Strasbourg, 'and all who have such sacramentarian sects in your midst' against 'Müntzer's spirit' (WA23.283,4–23; LW37.150). In his letter to Herwagen of 13 September 1526, Luther had condemned Bucer's fall into 'the blasphemy of the sectarian spirit', as attested by his insertions into his translation of the fourth volume of Luther's postil (WA19.47–73; LW59.168–72).

Closer to home, Luther also defended the elector's right to safeguard true religion. In his preface to the *Instruction for the Visitors of Parish Pastors* (1528), he stated that the elector should prevent sects and rebellion among his subjects, just as Emperor Constantine had supported the Council of Nicaea in order to keep the Arians from causing division among Christians (WA26.195–201; LW40.269–273; appeal to the elector at the end of the preface). Thus the elector could prohibit the sale of sacramentarian works, and his subjects could be compelled to attend sermons, so that they at least learned 'the external work of obedience' (letter to Joseph Metzsch, 26 August 1529, WABr5.136–137; on the prohibition of books in Wittenberg, Oecolampadius to Zwingli, 9 April 1526, Z8.559). In effect, Luther continued to uphold freedom of conscience, but he did not extend freedom of expression or of worship to those who rejected true doctrine. The tensions inherent in such a policy are evident in the case of Karlstadt, who continued to reject Luther's understanding of the Lord's Supper (cf. Luther's advice to the elector about his former colleague, 24 September 1528, WABr4.568–571).

A controversy in Nuremberg over the right of the secular authority to act against religious dissenters prompted Luther to address the question at greater length in his commentary on Psalm 82 (spring 1530). There he stated that rulers had the right to punish not only seditious heretics, but also those who taught doctrines contradicting Scripture and the common faith of Christendom and so were guilty of blasphemy. He also asserted that when religious dissent disturbed the peace of a parish or political unit, the magistrate had the right to silence the party that lacked scriptural support. Finally, he stated that unauthorized preaching and private ceremonies were not to be tolerated because they undermined public tranquillity. Only pastors had the properly constituted call and office that authorized them to preach, teach, and administer the sacraments (WA31,1.207–213; LW13.61–67). Luther had emphasized the importance of the call to pastoral office already in his sermon on John 20:19–23 in 1529 (WA29.306–308; cf. WA28.471–476; LW69.360–366). Luther sharpened this point even further in *Infiltrating and Clandestine Preachers* (1532). Those who preached without a call were emissaries of the Devil, destroyers of the parish system that was ordained by God (WA30,3.518–527; LW40.383–394).

In his commentary on Psalm 82 Luther did not specify what the appropriate punishment for heretics should be. As Anabaptists began to infiltrate Saxony, it was Melanchthon rather than Luther who played the leading role in shaping the elector's policy towards them.[6] In 1531 and 1536 Melanchthon drafted memoranda that prescribed the execution of Anabaptist leaders and those who refused to recant, according to the provisions of imperial law. Luther signed both memoranda, but he added a postscript to each indicating that he was uneasy about their contents. In 1531 he stated that although it seemed cruel to punish Anabaptists with the sword, it was even crueller that they condemned the ministry of the Word and suppressed true doctrine. Five years later he noted that the advice in the memorandum was the common rule, but one could also proceed with mercy as circumstances allowed (1531: CR 4.737–740; WABr 6.223; 1536: WA50.8–15). Luther was reluctant to approve the execution of religious dissenters, but he agreed with the policy when other alternatives proved ineffective.

∗∗∗

---

[6] In *Concerning Rebaptism*, Luther had admitted that because the Anabaptists had not caused problems in Saxony, he was not familiar with their teaching, WA26.145–146; LW40.230. The groups that were strongest in Saxony and neighbouring Hesse were those influenced by Hans Hut and Melchior Rink; Oyer 1964: 46–74.

It has been observed that in his attacks on the *Schwärmer*, Luther did not carefully distinguish between the positions of his various opponents. To modern readers it often seems like he made little effort to understand their theological principles and religious priorities (Köhler 1924: 1.495–96; Oyer 1964: 123; Edwards 1975: 201). From Luther's perspective, however, the distinctions between the individuals and groups he attacked were not relevant. Far more important was the fact that they all rejected God's ordering, which placed the Word at the centre of his self-revelation to humans and then added the sacraments and the ministry as external means to assure Christians of his gracious will. Luther's chief concern was to defend the proper relationship of external and internal established by God, and so while he attacked the various positions of his opponents, he did not consider it important to distinguish between them (Oberman 1989: 226–45).

Moreover, behind the *Schwärmers'* common devaluation of Word and sacrament Luther saw the work of Satan (Edwards 1975: 58–9, 200–1). In his first publication against Müntzer, he used 1 Corinthians 11:19 ('there must be factions among you') to explain why Satan was able to 'make himself a nest in Allstedt' (*Letter to the Princes of Saxony*, WA15.211,13–14; LW40.50). In one of his last sermons, on the parable of the wheat and the tares, he stated that 'wherever God establishes a fine, pure church, the devil immediately builds a chapel next door' (WA51.173–196; LW58.442–459). The Devil was always present among God's children, and so it was inevitable that he would stir up sects (on Titus 3:10, WA25.67; LW29.87; preface to Justus Menius' *Der Wiedertäufer Lehre* [1530], WA30,2.211; cf. Gensichen 1967: 61–79). Through the *Schwärmer* Satan attacked the gospel now being proclaimed in its purity, and it was the responsibility of ministers to oppose them. Luther therefore responded with harsh denunciations and by giving a more prominent place to Word and sacrament in his preaching and teaching.

This essay has focused especially on the later 1520s and early 1530s as the period in which a key element of Luther's theology was shaped by his conflicts with his evangelical opponents. Research on the last fifteen years of the reformer's life, focusing particularly on his lectures and sermons, could add additional details to the picture sketched here. Perhaps the most important consideration for future research, however, is that any discussion of the reformer's attitude towards other evangelical groups must take account of his understanding of Word, sacraments, and the ministry as a whole. Especially in the light of newer linguistic discussions of 'performative speech', we may gain new insights into the criticism of Luther from the range of opponents discussed here and his response as well as its vehemence.

REFERENCES

Bender, Harold S. (1953). 'The Zwickau Prophets, Thomas Müntzer, and the Anabaptists'. *Mennonite Quarterly Review* 27: 3–16.

Bräuer, Siegfried (1980). 'Die Vorgeschichte von Luthers "Ein Brief an die Fürsten zu Sachsen von dem aufrührerischen Geist"'. *Lutherjahrbuch* 47: 40–70.

Burnett, Amy Nelson (2012). ' "According to the Oldest Authorities": The Use of the Fathers in the Early Eucharistic Controversy'. In *The Reformation as Christianization: Essays on Scott Hendrix's Christianization Thesis*, ed. Anna M. Johnson and John A. Maxfield. Tübingen: Mohr/Siebeck.

Cross, Richard (1996). "Alloiosis" in the Christology of Zwingli'. *Journal of Theological Studies* n.s. 47: 105–22.

Edwards, Mark U. (1975). *Luther and the False Brethren*. Stanford: Stanford University Press.

Fast, Heinold (ed.) (1962). *Der Linke Flügel der Reformation: Glaubenszeugnisse der Täufer, Spiritualisten, Schwärmer und Antitrinitarier*. Bremen: Schünemann.

Gensichen, Hans-Werner (1967). *We Condemn: How Luther and Sixteenth Century Lutheranism Condemned False Doctrine*, trans. Herbert J. A. Bouman. Saint Louis: Concordia.

Gritsch, Eric (1976). 'Luther und die Schwärmer'. *Luther* 47: 105–21.

Haas, Alois M. (1997). *Der Kampf um den Heiligen Geist: Luther und die Schwärmer*. Fribourg: Universitätsverlag.

Holl, Karl (1928). 'Luther und die Schwärmer'. In Holl, *Gesammelte Aufsätze zur Kirchengeschichte*. Tübingen: Mohr/Siebeck, 420–67.

Köhler, Walther (1924/53). *Zwingli und Luther: Ihre Streit über das Abendmahl nach seinen politischen und religiösen Beziehungen*. Gütersloh: Bertelsmann.

Kolb, Robert (1999). ' "Was sollt' ein Handvoll Wassers der Seelen helfen?" Luthers Predigten über die Taufe in den Jahren 1528–1539'. *Lutherische Theologie und Kirche* 23: 126–49.

Loewen, Harry (1974). *Luther and the Radicals: Another Look at some Aspects of the Struggle between Luther and the Radical Reformers*. Waterloo: Wilfred Laurier University Press.

Maurer, Wilhelm (1952). 'Luther und die Schwärmer'. In Maurer et al., *Luther und die Schwärmer*. Berlin: Lutherisches Verlaghaus, 7–37.

Mühlpfordt, Günter (1986). 'Luther und die "Linken". Eine Untersuchung seiner Schwärmerterminologie'. In Günter Vogler (ed.), *Martin Luther. Leben—Werk—Wirkung*. Berlin: Akademie, 325–45.

Oberman, Heiko A. (1987). ' "Via Antiqua" and "Via Moderna": Late Medieval Prolegomena to Early Reformation Thought'. *Journal of the History of Ideas* 48: 23–40.

—— (1989). *Luther: Man between God and the Devil*. New Haven: Yale University Press.

Oyer, John S. (1964). *Lutheran Reformers Against Anabaptists: Luther, Melanchthon and Menius and the Anabaptists of Central Germany*. The Hague: Nijhoff.

Prenter, Regin (1953). *Spiritus Creator*, trans. John M. Jensen. Philadelphia: Muhlenberg.

Sanders, Paul (1992). 'Heinrich Bullinger et le "zwinglianisme Tardif" aux lendemains du "Consensus Tigurinus" '. In *Reformiertes Erbe. Festschrift für Gottfried W. Locher zu seinem 80. Geburtstag*, ed. Heiko A. Oberman, et al. Zürich: Theologischer Verlag, 307–23.

Stayer, James M. (1993). 'Saxon Radicalism and Swiss Anabaptism: The Return of the Repressed'. *Mennonite Quarterly Review* 67: 5–30.

Steck, Karl Gerhard (1955). *Luther und die Schwärmer*. Zollikon- Zürich: Evangelischer Verlag.

Trigg, Jonathan D. (2001). *Baptism in the Theology of Martin Luther*. Leiden: Brill.

Troeltsch, Ernst (1931, German 1912). *The Social Teaching of the Christian Churches*, trans. Olive Wyon. New York: Macmillan.

Williams, George Huntston (1992, 1st edn., 1962). *The Radical Reformation*. Kirksville: Sixteenth Century Journal.

Windhorst, Christof (1997). 'Luthers Kampf gegen die "Schwärmer": ihre theologische Beurteilung in der Vorlesung über den 1. Johannesbrief (1527)'. *Wort und Dienst* NF 14: 67–87.

SUGGESTED READING

Barge, Hermann (1968). *Andreas Bodenstein von Karlstadt*, 2. vols., 2nd edn. Niewkoop: de Graaf.

Bizer, Ernst (1962, 1940). *Studien zur Geschichte des Abendmahlsstreits im 16. Jahrhundert*. Darmstadt: Wissenschaftliche Buchgesellschaft.

Bornkamm, Heinrich (1983). *Luther in Mid-Career, 1521–1530*. Philadelphia: Fortress.

Brecht, Martin (1983). 'Luthers Beziehungen zu den Oberdeutschen und Schweizern von 1530/31 bis 1546'. In *Leben und Werk Martin Luthers von 1526 bis 1546. Festgabe zu seinem 500. Geburtstag*, ed. Helmer Junghans. Göttingen: Vandenhoeck & Ruprecht, 497–517, 891–4.

—— (1990). *Martin Luther*. Vol. 2: *Shaping and Defining the Reformation, 1521–1532*, trans. James L. Schaaf. Philadelphia: Fortress.

Burnett, Amy Nelson. (2011). *Karlstadt and the Origins of the Eucharistic Controversy: A Study in the Circulation of Ideas*. New York: Oxford University Press.

Cargill Thompson, W. D. J. (1984). *The Political Thought of Martin Luther*. Totowa: Barnes and Noble.

Edwards, Mark U. (1975). *Luther and the False Brethren*. Stanford: Stanford University Press.

Estes, James M. (2005). *Peace, Order and the Glory of God: Secular Authority and the Church in the Thought of Luther and Melanchthon 1518–1559*. Leiden: Brill.

Fischer, Norbert and Marion Kobelt-Groch (eds.) (1997). *Außenseiter zwischen Mittelalter und Neuzeit. Festschrift für Hans-Jürgen Goertz*. Leiden: Brill.

Friesen, Abraham (1977). 'Social Revolution or Religious Reform? Some Salient Aspects of Anabaptist Historiography'. In *Umstrittenes Täufertum, 1525–1975*, ed. Hans-Jürgen Goertz. Göttingen: Vandenhoeck & Ruprecht, 223–43.

Gäbler, Ulrich (1983). 'Luthers Beziehung zu den Schweizern und Oberdeutschen von 1526 bis 1530/31'. In *Leben und Werk Martin Luthers von 1526 bis 1546. Festgabe zu seinem 500. Geburtstag*, ed. Helmer Junghans. Göttingen: Vandenhoeck & Ruprecht, 481–96, 885–91.

Goertz, Hans-Jürgen (2007). 'Karlstadt, Müntzer and the Reformation of the Commoners, 1521–1525'. In *A Companion to Anabaptism and Spiritualism, 1521–1700*, ed. John D. Roth and James M. Stayer. Leiden: Brill, 1–44.

Junghans, Helmer (eds.) (1983). *Leben und Werk Martin Luthers von 1526 bis 1546. Festgabe zu seinem 500. Geburtstag*. Göttingen: Vandenhoeck & Ruprecht.

Köhler, Walther (1924/53). *Zwingli und Luther: Ihr Streit über das Abendmahl nach seinen politischen und religiösen Beziehungen*. Gütersloh: Bertelsmann.

Kühn, Ulrich (1983). 'Luthers Zeugnis vom Abendmahl in Unterweisung, Vermahnung und Beratung'. In *Leben und Werk Martin Luthers von 1526 bis 1546. Festgabe zu seinem 500. Geburtstag*, ed. Helmer Junghans. Göttingen: Vandenhoeck & Ruprecht, 139–52, 771–4.

Lecler, Joseph (1965). *Toleration and the Reformation*, trans. T. L. Westow, 2 vols. New York: Association Press.

Lienhard, Marc (1997). 'Die Grenzen der Toleranz. Martin Luther und die Dissidenten seiner Zeit'. In *Außenseiter zwischen Mittelalter und Neuzeit. Festschrift für Hans-Jürgen Goertz*, ed. Norbert Fischer and Marion Kobelt-Groch. Leiden: Brill, 127–34.

Lohse, Bernhard (1969). 'Die Stellung der "Schwärmer" und "Täufer" in der Reformationsgeschichte'. *Archiv für Reformationsgeschichte* 60: 5–26.

McLaughlin, R. Emmet (1983). 'The Genesis of Schwenckfeld's Eucharistic Doctrine'. *Archiv für Reformationsgeschichte* 74: 94–121.

—— (1986). *Caspar Schwenckfeld, Reluctant Radical: His Life to 1540*. New Haven: Yale University Press.

Maron, Gottfried (1973/4). 'Thomas Müntzer in der Sicht Martin Luthers'. *Theologia Viatorum* 12: 71–85.

Mühlen, Karl-Heinz zur (1983). 'Luthers Tauflehre und seine Stellung zu den Täufern'. In *Leben und Werk Martin Luthers von 1526 bis 1546. Festgabe zu seinem 500. Geburtstag*, ed. Helmer Junghans. Göttingen: Vandenhoeck & Ruprecht, 119–38, 765–70.

Sasse, Hermann (1959). *This is my Body: Luther's Contention for the Real Presence in the Sacrament of the Altar*. Minneapolis: Augsburg.

Seebaß, Gottfried (1997). 'Luthers Stellung zur Verfolgung der Täufer und ihre Bedeutung für den deutschen Protestantismus'. In Gottfried Seebaß, *Die Reformation und ihre Außenseiter: Gesammelte Aufsätze und Vorträge*, ed. Irene Dingel. Göttingen: Vandenhoeck & Ruprecht, 267–82.

Stayer, James M. (1997). '"Luther und die Schwärmer": Karl Holl und das abenteuerliche Leben eines Textes'. In *Außenseiter zwischen Mittelalter und Neuzeit. Festschrift für Hans-Jürgen Goertz*, ed. Norbert Fischer and Marion Kobelt-Groch. Leiden: Brill, 169–88.

—— (1990). 'Thomas Müntzer in 1989: A Review Article'. *Sixteenth Century Journal* 21: 655–70.

Steinmetz, Max (1971). *Das Müntzerbild von Martin Luther bis Friedrich Engels*. Berlin: Verlag der Wissenschaften.

CHAPTER 39

LUTHER'S AUTHORITY IN THE LATE REFORMATION AND PROTESTANT ORTHODOXY

IRENE DINGEL

I. THE STRUGGLE OVER THE THEOLOGICAL LEGACY OF MARTIN LUTHER IN THE LATE REFORMATION

THE outstanding protagonists of the several streams of reform that arose in sixteenth-century Europe, e.g. in Wittenberg, Zurich, and Geneva, placed their stamp on their movements in various ways. These figures gained even more respect as authorities as a result of their impact on circles of disciples and students, who worked with them for the cause of reformation and aided in its spread. In Wittenberg such a group of reformers formed around Martin Luther, above all, Philip Melanchthon, but also Johannes Bugenhagen, Justus Jonas, Nikolaus von Amsdorf, Georg Rörer, Georg Major, and Paul Eber. However, after Luther's death in 1546, a struggle over his theological legacy began, dividing the Wittenberg Reformation over the years. While Luther lived, he succeeded in holding together the various divergent accents in teaching among his followers, including those which distinguished him from Melanchthon, and in integrating them in the promotion of their common cause. However, after his death endeavours to establish clear positions, formulations of doctrinal content that could not be misunderstood, began, seeking the clear demarcation of Luther's thought from all views that were regarded as irreconcilable with his original theological positions.

The Augsburg Interim of 1548 initiated this process of clarification. With this law on religious policy Emperor Charles V attempted to restore religious unity in the Holy Roman Empire of the German nation that had been lost through the divisions which the Reformation provoked. The Interim permitted clerical marriage and communion in both kinds but apart from that made medieval doctrine and ceremonies binding. The fact that, contrary to original intentions, it finally applied only to the Evangelical estates of the Empire aggravated the situation since that meant abandonment of efforts to reach consensus between Roman Catholics and Evangelicals. Instead, from the Evangelical perspective, the only question was, to what extent one would yield to the coercive introduction of the principles of the Interim or whether one would go into exile.

Many territories and cities considered alternative models or other ways to obviate the Interim's regulations. Elector Moritz of Saxony, whose territorial and dynastic interests had moved him to ally himself with the emperor, tried to mitigate the situation for his lands by formulating an alternative policy to the Augsburg Interim. It was to be presented for consideration to the territorial diet in Leipzig. The draft of this policy tried to offer a compromise by retaining reformational teaching and merely altering some rites and ceremonies. It was not accepted by the diet. But Matthias Flacius Illyricus and Nikolaus Gallus, two students of Luther and Melanchthon, had it printed with their polemical commentary, and thus made its text public. They dubbed it the 'Leipzig Interim' and disparaged all who had worked on it in order to warn the public of a development which they regarded as an agreement between 'Christ and Belial', i.e. an irresponsible compromise between good and evil, right and wrong. They thought it called into question the entire tradition of the Wittenberg Reformation.

Among the authors of Moritz's proposal was, alongside Georg von Anhalt, Wittenberg professors Johannes Bugenhagen the elder, Paul Eber, Georg Major, and the Leipzig superintendent Johannes Pfeffinger, Melanchthon himself. With this criticism of the Augsburg Interim and especially the Leipzig Proposal a process of differentiation within Protestantism began which took form in the organization of different groups and in theological variation and doctrinal demarcation. For the evangelical doctrine contained in the Leipzig Proposal bore the hand of Melanchthon and contained statements which, more than previously, appeared to diverge from Luther. They concerned particularly the role of the free will in the justification of sinners, the proper place of good works, and the role of the law in the Christian life. Later, questions regarding the Lord's Supper and Christology came under discussion as well. Disputes also arose over questions of the reintroduction of medieval rites and ceremonies as adiaphora, practices regarded as neutral and thus permitted, and of resistance against unchristian governmental authority.

The controversies begun in 1548 extended over several decades. They occurred in a vacuum of authority that arose not only because of Luther's death but also because Melanchthon and the entire Wittenberg faculty were discredited as 'Adiaphorists'. The debates kindled by specific theological positions revolved implicitly around the question of who could correctly represent Luther's theological legacy and which theology preserved his views most faithfully. Their disciples began to differentiate Luther's and

Melanchthon's theologies from each other, distinguishing their own positions in order to guarantee that the churches would follow Luther's teaching as the most authentic reformational doctrine. Martin Luther was simply the guarantor of that doctrine. Theological authority was ascribed to him alone, not to Melanchthon or the other members of the Wittenberg circle of reformers, as influential as they individually might have been.

Above all, the creation of an edition of Luther's writings served to establish Luther's authority. The edition gave the reformer a lasting voice, even after his death, at the same time paving the way for different approaches to appropriating his theology and authority. His writings were cited in order to decide disputed questions, to solve theological problems, and especially to legitimate one's own position in critical situations, theological, legal, and political. Already in 1539 the Wittenberg edition of Luther's works began, under the leadership of Georg Major, Georg Rörer, and Johannes Aurifaber. It was completed in 1559 (Wolgast 1968, 1980; Schilling 1991). Since this edition placed Luther's writings in a thematic, not chronological, order, it made it easier to find Luther's utterances on specific topics. Thus, one could quickly assemble his opinions on various theological questions and critical problems. Especially the Wittenberg theologians gathered around Melanchthon after Luther's death, who shared the former's theological sentiments, preferred citing the Wittenberg edition, to prove their agreement with Luther's Reformation. The layout of the edition permitted placing positions of the 'young Luther' over against his opinions when older, ascribing mostly to the former a greater historical significance. Increasingly, the positions of the theologically mature, later Luther could be regarded as opinions of an ever more impatient older man.

Soon the Wittenberg edition found a rival in the Jena edition. Ernstine Saxony compensated for the loss of the electoral title and lands around Wittenberg to the Albertine branch of the ruling Wettin family by founding a new institution of higher learning at Jena. It attained university status and was intended to continue Luther's reformational legacy, so as not to abandon it to those remaining in Wittenberg. The Wittenberg edition was now regarded as the possession of Melanchthon and his Wittenberg colleagues. In 1555 Georg Rörer left Wittenberg to join the project of creating the Jena edition.

Jena aspired to be seen as the centre of Lutheran theology; the theological faculty there, Matthias Flacius (1557–61 in Jena), Simon Musaeus (1559–61), Johannes Wigand (1560–1, 1568–73), Matthäus Judex (1560–1), Johann Friedrich Coelestin (1560–1, 1568–72), Tilemann Heshusius (1569–73), and Timotheus Kirchner (1571–3), all claimed to continue Luther's theology in pure form, free from all alien influences. Scholars have designated this group as 'Gnesio-Lutherans', although they did not always represent the same theological argumentation. In contrast to the Wittenberg edition of Luther's works, the Jena edition was arranged chronologically, a conception advanced by Weimar court preacher Johannes Stoltz (Scheible 2004: 1747) to prevent historically unjustifiable interpretations of Luther. This was to enable consideration of how Luther's early reformational concerns became more precise and developed further, also in exchanges with opposing positions. That meant that Luther's later theological developments, even when they permitted no compromise, assumed the higher authority.

Opponents of the Lutheran Reformation rejected the Lutheran claims of prophetic authority and pure teaching for Luther. Johannes Cochlaeus launched the genre of polemical biography with the publication of his *Commentary on Martin Luther's Deeds and Writings* (1546; cf. Vandiver, Keen, and Frazel 2003; cf. Herte 1935), a tradition continued to other Roman Catholics and rebutted by Lutheran authors (Kolb 1999: 75–101) beginning with Ludwig Rabus, Johannes Mathesius (Volz 1929), and Cyriakus Spangenberg (Herrmann 1934/35).

The attempts to claim Luther's authority as their own which typified the process of forming different theological directions within the Wittenberg circle after Luther's death contributed to the strengthening of his reformational authority. Citations from his letters and his 'prophecies' were published to reinforce specific theological positions with similar utterances from the departed reformer. In this way the estimate of Luther's person and his authority also became the subject of controversy.

II. The Designation of Luther as a Prophet of the End Times

Luther himself had given a decisive impulse for his designation as an authority beyond the bounds of his own age to provide direction for the church. Even before his death, his understanding of himself, recorded in his own writings, contributed decisively to the estimate of his person and his significance among his contemporaries and the spread of these estimates in popular publications. During his lifetime and particularly after his death this led to ascribing to him the role of a prophet and winning him corresponding respect.

Luther's prophetic self-consciousness was closely connected to his understanding of history and others' perception and interpretation of it. His rediscovery of the gospel and the message of a God who loves human beings and frees them from the necessity of justifying themselves gained great importance for the society of the time and with it a lasting impact. This sprang largely from his own and his contemporaries' conviction that this perception of his actions was anchored in the flow of history that was moving toward an apocalyptic end. Luther himself saw this reformational awakening as a sign of the end of time, and he viewed it as a part of God's all-embracing plan, in which he himself was functioning as God's instrument. He took the stage not only as a conveyor of a new orientation for religion but also, like the Old Testament prophets, called for repentance and change. His reformational rediscovery of the gospel of the justification of sinners *sola gratia* and *sola fide* and his proclamation of the message with exceptional power in both its use of language and its content, made him in fact a dynamic personality, whose counsel was sought and whose words provided orientation for many, also societal leaders. His roles, on the one hand as a prophet of doom, and on the other as a proclaimer of salvation and deliverance, like the apostles, constituted the two sides of

Luther's understanding of himself. In this perception traditions from the Old and the New Testaments merged and were incorporated into the historical circumstances of the early sixteenth century.

The self-designation as a 'prophet' or 'the German prophet' occurs already in Luther's early writings. Even if it appears superficial, it was intended to be less a claim for a particular honour and respect, more a reflection of Luther's conviction that he must carry out an assignment from God. This self-designation expresses not an unrealistic arrogance but a consciousness of a special call to execute a demanding, dangerous task in the End Times. From Luther's viewpoint God had commissioned him as part of his plan for human salvation as the rediscoverer of the gospel, making Luther his servant and instrument in order to bring to light once again the saving truth of faith that had been submerged in the Middle Ages. On the basis of his belief in his divine commission Luther categorically rejected similar claims by others, e.g. the dissenters of the Reformation, and rebuffed the reproach that the Wittenberg Reformation had remained stalled half the way to true reform.

Luther's proclamation of the gospel also bears elements of this understanding of his role in the flow of history in the End Times. Frequently his sermons referred to the threat of catastrophe and the advent of doom if people continued to ignore God's gospel. Luther's apostolic proclamation therefore always contained admonition, announcing divine judgement, following Old Testament models with their threat of divine punishment should the people disregard and show contempt for God's grace, now so publicly proclaimed. This stance was strengthened by the reformer's daily experiences. He viewed himself surrounded by indifference to God's commands, particularly the first table of the Decalogue, which commanded proper worship of God. But also the behaviour of the people in regard to its second table, which was to regulate human coexistence in a peaceful, just life in society and the home, left much to be desired. Therefore, Luther neglected no opportunity to call to remembrance God's punishments, which condemned such indifference. His behaviour and action fit the picture of Elijah, the prophet expected at the end of time, whose divine commission before the Last Day the prophet Malachi (3:23) had foretold. Indeed, Luther rejected an interpretation of this passage that applied to the concrete present and the return of Elijah bodily, but he could view his action as analogous to the conduct of the Old Testament prophet. Luther's prophetic self-consciousness was uncontested, accepted and assumed by his contemporaries. To be a 'prophet' or 'Germany's prophet' did not remain only his own comment about himself. Others used this description as well. His contemporaries recognized in the reformer a second Elijah, who, following the first, Old Testament, Elijah, preached against false teaching and superstitious ritual, and announced God's wrath over all the unrepentant.

An identification of Luther with the prophet Elijah appeared in the early Reformation, placing him in a succession with John the Baptist, seen as the second Elijah, In line with late medieval conceptions of the Antichrist, the reformer then fell into place as the third Elijah. Surprisingly, it was probably Hudrych Zwingli who, under the impression made by the Leipzig debate of 1519, first expressed the conviction that the Wittenberg reformer was Elijah returning at the end of time. Whether he can be regarded as the originator of this thought is not completely clear; he may have borrowed it from Erasmus. Luther's friend and colleague Philip Melanchthon made similar statements, which continued to be used in the second generation of reformers. In the context of Late Reformation controversies Nikolaus Selnecker, a co-author of the Formula of Concord (1577), who worked on the composition of the *Apology of the Book of Concord*, stated that Melanchthon referred to Luther as Father, Preceptor, and the Elijah of the last times (Hasse 1995). This served to counter the claim by the opponents of the Formula of Concord that Melanchthon was on their side. The exaltation of Luther as second or third Elijah or the prophet of the Last Times also found its place in popular writings, pamphlets, and songs, which not only spread this idea among the public but also offered ground for cultivating the idea further (Dingel 1996).

This also had an impact on how one used Luther's oral and written statements after his death. By the end of the 1540s, beginning of the 1550s, countless collections, e.g. of his 'prophecies' appeared, often intentionally assembled in order to strengthen and legitimate positions in the theological controversies and efforts toward doctrinal concord or to cultivate theological orientation and contemporary applications of this thought on the popular level (Kolb 1999). Frequent reprints demonstrate the success of such efforts, not only in learned circles. In 1557, for example, the Dresden preacher Peter Glaser edited a collection of *One Hundred Twenty Prophecies* of Luther, which he republished in an expanded edition (*Two Hundred Prophecies*) in 1574, available in a reasonably priced octavo format. The first edition, according to the later preface, had been completely sold out. At least two other editions (1592, 1628) became available. In 1578, immediately after the adoption of the Formula of Concord, Johannes Lapaeus produced another volume of Luther's prophecies, designating him as the Third Elijah. Lapaeus, pastor in Nordhausen, gathered so-called 'prophecies' from Luther's writings under the title *True Prophecies of the Precious Prophet and Holy Man of God, Dr. Martin Luther* and arranged them topically in six chapters. The popular impact of this compendium of '*dicta Lutheri*' should not be underestimated. It aimed to convey an apocalyptic interpretation of the times and strengthened the conviction 'that indeed the true divine prophetic spirit, which spoke through the holy prophets, also has spoken in these last times through the blessed Dr. Martin Luther' (cited from Koch 1986: 105–6).

Luther's contemporaries and the next generation gave prophetic authority not only to his call for repentance and his announcement of divine punishment; they also accorded it to his statements in questions of doctrine and public confession. As the reformational changes were interpreted, he had indeed led the church out of its 'Babylonian captivity' under the papacy as God's elect instrument. In 1575, in the midst of negotiations leading to the Formula of Concord, a collection of Luther's writings on the question of interpreting the Lord's Supper appeared under the title, *The Most Important and Best Writings of the Highly-Enlightened and Spiritually-Endowed Man of God, Dr. Martin Luther*. In the context of the ongoing disputes over the Lord's Supper and Christology, which had led to the fall of the so-called Crypto-Calvinists—better labelled Crypto-Philippists—this publication was designed to legitimize and provide authority for the doctrine of Luther that would be adopted in the Formula of Concord. This collection's goal was to make these writings of Luther, 'the true Elijah of the last times', accessible again. It is therefore not surprising that even the authors of the Formula of Concord appear to have used this volume when they cited Luther and his writings as the guarantor of this doctrine (Koch 1992: 128–59).

III. Various Appropriations of the Authority and Teaching of Luther in the Second Generation of Reformers

That Luther was regarded as the prophet who was to appear at the end of time and that prophetic authority was ascribed to his theology did not only serve to cultivate his memory and appreciation of his contribution to the reform of Christendom. By appropriating his theological statements to legitimate their own positions in public confession and teaching, the second generation of reformers claimed him as an authority for their teaching. This combined both aspects of the office bestowed on Luther as 'German prophet' or 'Elijah of the last days': his role as prophet of doom and his role as rediscoverer of the gospel and evangelical truth. All groups with the stamp of Wittenberg on them which took shape, especially after 1548, appropriated Luther's authority in one way or another, even if with differing emphases.

That became clear already as the group of Luther's disciples assembled around Flacius and Gallus after 1548 formulated judgements on the so-called adiaphora, that is, against the labelling of rites and ceremonies as permissible neutral practices which neither promote nor distract from human salvation. The group called Gnesio-Lutherans opposed the possibility of the reintroduction of medieval ceremonies as a religious and political compromise of electoral Saxony with the imperial policies which were intended to use the Augsburg Interim to force a consistent re-catholicization of the evangelical territories in doctrine and ritual (with the exception of clerical marriage and communion in both kinds). The alternative proposal, the so-called 'Leipzig Interim' (1548), aimed at guaranteeing the retention of evangelical teaching and saw room for negotiation in the realm of rites and ceremonies. Flacius saw in the Leipzig proposal a 'compromise between Christ and Belial': that is, the attempt to reconcile God and the devil. His comrade Joachim Westphal, pastor in Hamburg, supported this position with the help of a collection of citations from Luther (*The Position on Adiaphora of the Honourable and Precious Man, the Blessed Dr. Martin Luther* (Latin 1549, German 1550). He thereby constructed, in his own words, an 'armory' which was to be used as a powerful arsenal against opponents, and that in a time in which clearly many thought they could simply move beyond the reformer's authority (Dingel 2005). In Westphal's eyes the confusion that had set in was nothing else than a divine punishment for the weariness people were exhibiting toward the evangelical truth which Luther had rediscovered. Westphal intentionally sought passages from Luther's writings to counter this way of thinking. Luther's 'dicta' could and should serve to prove the propriety of Westphal's own contrary position. These citations strengthened the Gnesio-Lutherans in their confession of the faith without any compromise. Luther's authority took hold through his teaching and his clear positions in regard to disputed questions.

But those disciples of Matthias Flacius who separated from the other Gnesio-Lutherans on the doctrine of original sin, the so-called Flacians, also appealed to Luther and did so gladly and frequently (Dingel 2000). They preferred especially the prophet of doom and disaster. They cited his theological interpretation of history and his observations which they counted as prophecies for explaining their own situations and fate. That included Luther's conviction that the word of the gospel would continue to be obscured from time to time and that a time of darkness and disaster would break in and divide the church through controversy. The Flacians related these 'prophecies of doom' to the efforts of Jacob Andreae toward achieving an all-embracing agreement and to the conclusion of that long process in the much-disputed Formula of Concord (1577); its first article decisively rejected and condemned Flacius' position that original sin is the substance of the fallen human creature. The Flacians for their part regarded the teaching of the Formula on original sin as an intolerable diminution of the effective presence of original sin, which thoroughly corrupts human beings and affirms their absolute dependence on God's grace. The Flacians regarded the teaching of the Formula, which indeed disallowed the opposing position of Viktorin Strigel (original sin is merely an [Aristotelian] accident and adheres to a person only loosely), as an insupportable compromise which opened the door for error and false teachers. Confession of true teaching without compromise could, according to the Flacians, take place only by withdrawing from the majority group and its communion, to form a persecuted 'tiny flock' for the sake of the truth. It emphasized therefore that Luther's prophetic description of the situation at the end of time applied to their own situation. Both their like-minded Gnesio-Lutheran comrades, with whom they were one in other theological questions, and the political authorities, had distanced themselves from the Flacians, and that drove them even deeper into isolation. Luther's prophecies concerning history and his theology of history served them as a consolation in their frequent exiles, a legitimization for their refusal to compromise and a proof for the truth of their teaching. As 'exiles of Christ' they knew at the end of the day that they were one with Martin Luther in their resolute stance in behalf of evangelical truth (Dingel 1996: 467–541).

But the theologians of the Formula of Concord, who strove for formulations that would integrate elements decidedly Luther's own and also the concerns of Melanchthon in an all-embracing unity of the Protestants of the Augsburg Confession, cited Luther as the guarantor of proper teaching and the proper understanding of Holy Scripture. This served the goal of firmly establishing Luther's authority and that of the Augsburg Confession, for its authors understood the Formula of Concord to be a direct explication of that Confession. For those authors it was indisputable that Luther had always acted as God's chosen instrument and his writings reflected the message of the gospel without any falsification. God himself had 'brought the truth of his Word into the light out of the abominable darkness of the papacy through the faithful service the precious man of God, Dr. Luther' (BSLK 834,44–385,2; BC 527). This teaching had found its appropriate and purest expression in the Augsburg Confession presented to the emperor at the imperial diet in Augsburg in 1530.

The Augsburg Confession was not only appropriated for Luther's theology but also vice versa, the authority of the reformer was transferred to the authority of the Confession. Alongside Luther's own writings the Augsburg Confession in its unaltered version took its place as the inheritance bestowed by the Reformation and a timeless expression of the authority of the reformer. Its frequent reprinting in the framework of various editions of Luther's collected writings, both the Wittenberg and the Jena, provides clear evidence for this. Volumes 6 and 9 of the Wittenberg edition (1557) integrate the *Confessio Augustana invariata* in German of 1531 and the first revision of 1533, in which the article on the Lord's Supper was unchanged. Volume 6 of the Jena edition also published the *Confessio Augustana invariata* of 1531 (Neuser 1987: 72 (§40, 41), 75 (§46), 92 (§67), 113 (§93), 115 (§95), 130 (§§114, 115); cf. 76 (§47) and 119 (§101) for the Latin editions). In his *Historia der Augsburgischen Confession* (1576) David Chytraeus presented Luther not only as the decisive initiator of the Reformation but also as the major player in constructing the confessional documents of the Reformation. He designated Luther as the heroic confessor and real originator of the Augsburg Confession while emphasizing his peaceable intentions and his great pastoral service (Dingel forthcoming). Against this background Luther's doctrinal and controversial writings along with the Augsburg Confession, interpreted according to Luther's theology, served as a correct interpretation of Holy Scripture, the authority of which for faith and teaching obviously stood over that of Luther.

That the Wittenberg reformer functioned as guarantor of the true understanding of Holy Scripture and that Luther's writings held the status of additional witness for a proper and clear understanding of the truth which was to be confessed became clear in the Formula of Concord as well as the *Apology of the Book of Concord* (Dingel 1996: 603–85). The authors of the Formula regarded Luther as 'the most outstanding teacher of the Augsburg Confession' (BSLK 984,36; BC 600). Against reproach from the Calvinists, especially Zacharias Ursinus, that the Lutheran theologians exaggerated the authority of the Wittenberg reformer and attributed to him characteristics unfitting for any human creature, making his authority absolute, the authors of the *Apology of the Book of Concord*, Timothy Kirchner, Nikolaus Selnecker, and Martin Chemnitz replied that no appeal was being made to Luther or the Augsburg Confession for their own sake. Decisive was their clear foundation on the content of the Holy Scripture, the truth and relevance of which were emphasized for the first time in Luther's writings and sermons and in the articles of the Augsburg Confession and thus were adequately conveyed to the people (Dingel 1994, 1996: 141–55).

The context for this change in Luther's stature as a secondary authority had begun to develop with the composition of the *Corpus doctrinae Philippicum* (1560). Gradually this and similar collections of confessional documents assumed the function of setting public standards for theology. This led to a kind of hierarchical ranking in the question of ecclesiastical authority (Dingel 2012). Among these *Corpora doctrinae* was the Book of Concord (1580), which declared as its goal the restoration of the clarity of teaching and confession in the midst of the existing differences. Luther served from this point as an authority only in so far as his teaching clarified the statements of the Augsburg Confession, which in turn was regarded as a timeless confessional summary of the highest authority of Holy Scripture. In its unaltered version the Confession stood at the centre of all *Corpora doctrinae* within the Lutheran sphere. Those who accepted the Augsburg Confession as their prime secondary authority defined Luther's authority on the basis of his proper understanding of biblical statements. His writings were accorded authority because, faithful to Scripture, they voiced the position of the Augsburg Confession. As the Wittenberg Reformation's foundational confession, it had also assumed the highest political and legal significance for its 'adherents' as the basis of their legal toleration since the Religious Peace of Augsburg (1555). The authority of Luther's person found a rival in the growing authority of the Confession and began to be placed under the confessional documents.

Recourse to Luther's authority, as seen in the Lutheranism of the Formula of Concord, had not concentrated so much on reverence for Luther's person. It served rather, above all, to reinforce the doctrine of the Lord's Supper held by the Lutherans in view of the success of Calvinism and Calvinistic tendencies within the Empire. The doctrine of the Lord's Supper, together with his Christology of Christ's two natures, stood as the divisive issues between the Calvinist and Lutheran confessions. Calling on Luther's authority supported the literal interpretation of the words of institution, Christ's statement that his body and his blood are really present in and under the sacramental elements of bread and wine. This interpretation was seen as that of the tenth article of the Augsburg Confession. By citing Luther's writings in the sacramental controversy with Zwingli, his students demonstrated the usefulness of the unfolding of his Christological foundations, especially in his *Confession on the Supper of Christ* (1528) as a further, although only secondary, argument for Christ's real presence in the sacrament. There Luther had set forth the concept of the communication of divine characteristics to Christ's human nature, grounded in the personal union of Godhood and humanity in Christ's person and exhibited in his exaltation to the right hand of God, that is, to divine omnipotence. Originally only a supplementary support used to reinforce the exegetical argument, under the theological influence of Johannes Brenz, who taught a complete omnipresence of Christ's humanity, and of Martin Chemnitz, who developed a doctrine of the 'multivolipresence' of Christ, this Christological issue developed into another indicator of confessional differences. Calvinist opponents immediately attacked the argument as an intolerable 'doctrine of ubiquity'.

This bitter, persistent discussion of the Lord's Supper and Christology did not spare the question of the authority ascribed to Luther. It became still another controversial issue. It is striking that for the Lutheran side in this context the prophetic authority of the reformer hardly played any role at all. It retreated behind the doctrinal authority of the confessional documents to which pastors subscribed. In rejecting Calvinist attacks, the authors of the *Apology of the Book of Concord* conceded to their opponents, 'It is true that Luther initially wrote much on indulgences, the pope, purgatory, and similar topics that he later retracted, and it is true that he did not have prophetic authority, but it does not follow from that that he erred in his doctrine of the Lord's Supper, as our opponents want to argue, and that his doctrine on the Lord's Supper should be retracted... We do not bind ourselves or others to Luther's writings as a rule of faith or say that he could not err. [We bind ourselves] to that which he taught and demonstrated on the basis of clear, lucid passages from the prophetic and apostolic writings and we do not doubt but are certain that he did so in the doctrine of the Holy Supper' (Kirchner, Selnecker, and Chemnitz 1583: 276b–7a).

This position presents the criterion that was decisive for the Lutheranism of the Formula of Concord regarding the Wittenberg reformer and what marked him in their eyes as superior to all the other leading figures of the Reformation: his authority was based not only on his rediscovery of the gospel but especially on his interpretation that uncovered abuses and freed the church from them and expressed convincingly the potential of God's Word to lead people to the centre, Christ. From this perspective Nikolaus Selnecker could postulate that the Lutherans were not merely some confessional sect but that they simply represent Christian teaching as 'the Christians': 'We are Christians... and nothing else but... we have Christ's name. Because we know that through Luther's ministry we were brought back to the truth of the gospel, we confess that we believe with Luther concerning teaching and are not papists, not Calvinist, not Anabaptists, or other sectarians, but we who are called Lutherans, that is Christian, retain Christ's word to which Luther led us back' (Selnecker 1581: 264).

IV. Dealing with Luther's Authority in the Seventeenth Century

The developments described here continued in the seventeenth century. Contributing to this was the continuing perception of being in a flow of history that was moving toward an apocalyptic end. In this context authority was therefore ascribed to Luther less as an individual person or an outstanding personality but rather to the extent that he played a special role in the context of the history of salvation. That he accomplished as a proclaimer of the gospel and an instrument of God (Zeeden 1950–2: 1.78). The *Apology of the Book of Concord* had established that Luther was not simply to be equated with the prophets of the Old Testament and the apostles of the New and could not claim prophetic authority to the same extent (even if he still qualified for the designations 'prophet', 'apostle', or 'Evangelist' and continued to be named the 'third Elijah'). His authority was not understood as grounded in and arising from his unusual personality but as an authority derived from its faithfulness to Scripture. His conformity to Scripture as he proclaimed God's Word as God's instrument is that which established his authority. That Lutherans after the Formula of Concord shared the Formula's view that Luther's proclamation presented an understanding of Scripture which conveyed its truth reinforced this appreciation of the reformer. His authority arose, therefore, from his office and his commission. They were subordinate to the authority of Holy Scripture, on the one hand, but on the other functioned as a guarantee that the theology taken from Scripture and the confession which summarized the content of Scripture could claim to be true and valid. With this Luther's catechisms and the Smalcald Articles became ever more prominent as standards for teaching. These documents made Luther's voice and his positions on decisive theological questions present even after his death. They served, particularly in the doctrine of the Lord's Supper, to ensure the proper understanding of the formulations of the *Confessio Augustana invariata* and lent the Wittenberg Concord of 1536 a Lutheran reading.

In the seventeenth century Luther's person and reputation remained a topic for dispute among the confessional groups, above all with the Jesuits (Herte 1943: 91–332). The opposing interpretations both relativized and reinforced Luther's peculiar authority equally. Designating Luther as the fifth evangelist, as happened in the sixteenth century, waned. The epithets 'prophet' and 'apostle' were used more carefully. At the same time Luther's authority became a standard in Lutheran dogmatics. Johann Gerhard emphasized, for example, the coincidence of 'a properly ordered ecclesiastical call and the extraordinary gifts' which marked Luther (Zeeden 1950–2: 1.90–1). This had distinguished him in the eyes especially of other contemporaries. Gerhard viewed in Luther's extraordinary gifts, abilities, and character traits the foundation for his unique status and that which enabled him to perform his great work of reformation. In line with this Gerhard drew up a catalogue of these extraordinary gifts.

Even if the gifts were perverted into their opposite in the Catholic controversial literature of the time—Luther had not been called in orderly fashion; he had not been called and sent by God at all (Herte 1943; Zeeden 1950–2: 1.90–1)—Lutheran 'Orthodoxy' stood steadfast in its reverence for Luther. Foundational for seventeenth-century Lutheran theology was the conviction that the content of Luther's teaching agreed with the message of God's Word and the propositions of Holy Scripture were faithfully reproduced in Luther's utterances. What Luther had taught was regarded as key to understanding the Reformation; the seventeenth-century Lutheran theologians believed that they were in continuity with that teaching. The all-embracing renewal of the church and the revelation of the Antichrist and his corrupting effects were the great accomplishments that constituted Luther's impact. In that impact the Lutheran theologians, like their predecessors, saw God at work. 'Because public teaching is God's Word, the Reformation is a divine activity. Analogously: because the unveiling and overthrow of the Antichrist could only be a divine activity, the Reformation, through which both were set in motion, is *also* a divine activity' (Zeeden 1950–2: 2.103, emphasis Zeeden's).

The concern for the preservation of the 'orthodoxy' of teaching, which arose through its agreement with the teaching of the reformer, offered the perspective from which

Luther was viewed. The concern was always his teaching, that is, his impact. Therefore, his individual personal characteristics were subordinated to what he proclaimed, also in presentations of the reformer at this time. Even the Luther 'biographies', which increased in number compared to the sixteenth century (though the tradition begun by Rabus, Mathesius, and Spangenberg, in concert with Roman Catholic counter-biographies, did produce some already then: Kolb 1999: 86–101), concentrated less on his person and much more on his impact and the teaching connected to it. Johannes Müller's *Luther Defended* (1645) stated: 'Now we know from God's Word that we should not focus on the person of the teacher but consider the teaching in itself, whether it conforms to God's Word or not;…a great and good person cannot make a teaching good which is false; a lowly or bad person cannot make a teaching that is correct bad and false. Thus, we would not be obligated to be concerned about Dr. Luther's person and to reply to criticisms against his person because his teaching is correct and corresponds to that of Holy Scripture…we take seriously what he taught from God's Word and do not pay attention to his person' (cited in Zeeden 1950–2: 2.110).

Thus, Luther's authority was not that of an individual; it was theological authority arising from his teaching. The attacks lodged by Catholic controversial theologians on the personal, individual weaknesses of Luther did not need to be refuted for this reason. In the eyes of the Orthodox theologians they missed the essential and actually important point. For what lent Luther in their eyes his uniqueness and authority was his interpretation of the gospel and the delivery of the true understanding of the gospel which had taken place through him. For this reason the chief court preacher in Dresden Matthias Hoe von Hoenegg could designate Luther—as had his sixteenth-century comrades in the faith—as an elect instrument of God, whose teaching had been exposed to the devil's persecution, which 'papists and other heretics and Schwärmer' had stirred up against him. But God placed him in his protection and so directed the unfolding events 'that the angel (Luther) with the gospel flew through the heavens (Revelation 14) and rescued one hundred thousand souls from papal darkness with the clarity of pure divine teaching and brought them the light…No less than a real Samson he tore down the two supporting columns of the Antichrist's empire (Preface to Erasmus Willich, *Sontantia Luther*, cited by Zeeden 1950–2: 2.99). As a figure in the history of salvation, with his place at the apocalyptic end of the flow of history, Luther appeared as the one who proclaimed divine teaching as the apocalyptic angel of Revelation 14. The teaching for which Luther served as God's instrument and with which he judged the Antichrist, is identical with God's Word itself.

With this stance toward Luther, Orthodox Lutheranism in the seventeenth century revealed that it was the heir of its Late Reformation predecessors. As the authentic interpreter of God's Word, Luther enjoyed the highest authority, which was naturally subordinated to the Holy Scripture as a direct witness of God's Word. It was the eighteenth century that discovered the person 'Luther', that is, his religious personality and the character traits of the individual so important for practical piety.

REFERENCES

Dingel, Irene (1994). 'Ablehnung und Aneignung, Die Bewertung der Autorität Martin Luthers in den Auseinandersetzungen um die Konkordienformel'. *Zeitschrift für Kirchengeschichte* 105: 35–57.

—— (1996). *Concordia controversa. Die öffentlichen Diskussionen um das lutherische Konkordienwerk am Ende des 16. Jahrhunderts.* Gütersloh: Gütersloher Verlagshaus.

—— (2000). 'Flacius als Schüler Luthers und Melanchthons'. In *Vestigia pietatis: Studien zur Geschichte der Frömmigkeit in Thüringen und Sachsen. Festschrift für Ernst Koch*, ed. Gerhard Graf, Hans-Peter Hasse et al. Leipzig: Evangelische Verlagsanstalt, 77–93.

—— (2005). 'Strukturen der Lutherrezeption am Beispiel einer Lutherzitatensammlung von Joachim Westphal'. In *Kommunikationsstrukturen im europäischen Luthertum der Frühen Neuzeit*, ed. Wolfgang Sommer. Gütersloh: Gütersloher Verlagshaus, 32–50.

—— (2012). 'Melanchthon and the Establishment of Confessional Norms'. In Irene Dingel, Robert Kolb, Nicole Kuropka, and Timothy J. Wengert, *Philip Melanchthon: Theologian in Classroom, Confession, and Controversy.* Göttingen: Vandenhoeck & Ruprecht, 141–60.

—— (forthcoming). 'Das Bild Luthers und Melanchthons in den Historiae der Augsburgischen Konfession'. In *Die Aufnahme Luthers und Melanchthons in der Schülergeneration. Memoria— theologische Synthese—Autoritätenkonflikte*, ed. Irene Dingel. Göttingen: Vandenhoeck & Ruprecht.

Hasse, Hans Peter (1995). 'Die Lutherbiographie von Nikolaus Selnecker. Selneckers Berufung auf die Autorität Luthers im Normenstreit der Konfessionalisierung in Kursachsen'. *Archiv für Reformationsgeschichte* 86: 91–123.

Herrmann, Wolfgang (1934/1935). 'Die Lutherpredigten des Cyriacus Spangenberg'. *Mansfelder Blätter* 39: 7–95.

Herte, Adolf (1935). *Die Lutherkommentare des Johannes Cochlaeus.* Münster: Aschendorff.

—— (1943). *Das katholische Lutherbild im Bann der Lutherkommentare des Cochlaeus*, 3 vols. Münster: Aschendorff.

Koch, Ernst (1986). 'Lutherflorilegien zwischen 1550 und 1600. Zum Lutherbild der ersten nachreformatorischen Generation'. *Theologische Versuche* 16: 105–17.

—— (1992). 'Auseinandersetzungen um die Autorität von Philipp Melanchthon und Martin Luther in Kursachsen im Vorfeld der Konkordienformel von 1577'. *Lutherjahrbuch* 59: 128–59.

Kirchner, Timotheus, Nikolaus Selnecker, and Martin Chemnitz (1583). *Apologia, oder Verantwortung deß Christlichen Concordien Buchs...* Heidelberg: Spies.

Kolb, Robert (1999). *Martin Luther as Prophet, Teacher, and Hero: Images of the Reformer, 1520–1620.* Grand Rapids: Baker.

Neuser, Wilhelm H. (1987). *Bibliographie der Confessio Augustana und Apologie 1530–1580.* Nieuwkoop: De Graaf.

Schilling, Johannes (1991). 'Lutherausgaben'. In *Theologische Realenzyklopädie* 21: 594–9.

Scheible, Heinz (2004). 'Art. Stoltz, Johann'. In *Religion in Geschichte und Gegenwart*, ed. Hans Dieter Betz. Tübingen: Mohr/Siebeck, 1998-2007, 7: 1747.

Selnecker, Nikolaus (1581). *Recitationes aliqvot...4. De avtoritate Lvtheri et Philippi...* Leipzig: Defner.

Vandiver, Elizabeth, Ralph Keen, and Thomas D. Frazel (ed. and trans.) (2003). *Luther's Lives: Two Contemporary Accounts of Martin Luther.* Manchester: Manchester University Press.

Volz, Hans (1929). *Die Lutherpredigten des Johannes Mathesius. Kritische Untersuchung zur Geschichtsschreibung im Zeitalter der Reformation*. Halle: Waisenhaus.

Wolgast, Eike (1968). 'Der Streit um die Werke Luthers im 16. Jahrhundert'. *Archiv für Reformationsgeschichte* 59: 177–202.

—— (1980). 'Geschichte der Luther-Ausgaben vom 16. bis zum 19. Jahrhundert'. In WA 60, 431–60.

—— (1993). 'Biographie als Autoritätsstiftung. Die ersten evangelischen Lutherbiographien'. In *Biographie zwischen Renaissance und Barock. Zwölf Studien*, ed. Walter Berschin. Heidelberg: Mattes, 41–71.

Zeeden, Ernst Walter (1950–2). *Martin Luther und die Reformation im Urteil des deutschen Luthertums*, 2 vols. Freiburg im Breisgau: Herder.

CHAPTER 40

....

THE USE OF LUTHER'S THOUGHT IN PIETISM AND THE ENLIGHTENMENT

....

PAUL R. HINLICKY

I. THE FOUNDATIONALIST ERA

....

THE Cartesian epoch might better be designated the Foundationalist Era than 'the' Enlightenment, i.e., it was the project of grounding knowledge on rationally indubitable foundations, whether empirical or intellectual. In the young Spinoza's words the task was '(1) to put aside all prejudice, (2) to discover the foundations on which everything should be built, (3) to uncover the cause of error, (4) to understand everything clearly and distinctly' (Spinoza 1998: 7). This was an agenda shared also by 'empiricists', who demurred from Descartes' intellectualism; unlike the 'rationalists', who pursued a strategy of intellectual intuition to found knowledge, empiricists looked to rock-bottom sense experience of the external world. In either case, however, the attempt is to know how we know by making time, as it were, stand still. The belief is that we can transcend somehow to see ourselves seeing (or, as in Kantian transcendentalism, to deduce the unconditioned conditions for the possibility of our cognition) and thereby ascertain the universally valid criteria for knowledge as such. So equipped, we would no longer have to 'test the spirits' in the vicissitudes of historical existence nor patiently to work at hermeneutical understanding of others since we would already know in principle what can and cannot be claimed as knowledge. We would be the very Tribunal of Reason (Kant 1979).

It is little wonder, then, that modern scholarship experiences vertigo in trying to define and evaluate this epoch of the pietists and the rationalists with its paradigmatic possibilities for 'continuing' Luther's reformation (Weigelt 1970; Ward 1993; Strom 2002). The early modern age was characterized by the peculiar polarization between an affective 'theology of the heart' (Campbell 1991: 2–3) over against the rationalistic theology of the inerrant Bible in Protestant Scholasticism, increasingly giving way to a rationalistic philosophical theology within the limits of reason alone, what Kant finally named 'ontotheology' (1978: 37–9). The question that arose and dominated research was not, as presently hinted, whether and how these alternatives framed new appropriations of Luther. Rather, assuming the incorrigibility of the foundationalist endeavour, research asked whether and in what way pietism or rationalism arose from Luther. Which is Luther's true legacy? Albrecht Ritschl's late nineteenth-century study of pietism sought to delegitimize its Lutheran credentials (1972: 76; cf. Tillich 1967: 3.241–3, for a critique). Ever since, our topic has been subject to widely varying interpretations, as pietist or rationalist played surrogate in a convoluted debate about who truly inherits Luther's mantle. Generally speaking, these rivals have been seen on one side to represent real alternatives to one another, as in Ritschl's disciple, Ernst Troeltsch, who disparaged a compromised, reactionary 'church pietism' in favour of the ethical idealism of neo-Protestantism (Troeltsch 1912–25: 4.488–531; see the trenchant criticism of Troeltsch's artificial schematization by Yeide 1997: 25–7). On the other side, these two apparent rivals have also been seen as siblings, kindred expressions of the same fundamental impulse, as in Karl Barth, who detected the same titanism of 'modern man' at work in both (Barth 1959: 44). Broadly speaking, Barth had the deeper insight (Busch 2004: 269–75). It is imperative to grasp this deeper unity of a shared foundationalism in the age of pietism and the Enlightenment in terms of which rival theologies of the heart and of the head appropriated Luther for their own purposes, even if in either case they drew lines of continuity from Luther as well.

II. Changed Horizons

The desire to ground Christian faith in the *experienced* reality of the New Birth may thus be seen as a kind of empiricist foundationalism within the more rationalistic milieu of the Continent, also, if not especially, in Lutheranism (Frank 2003). Philip Jacob Spener (1635–1705) posited it in his manifesto: 'Hence it is not enough that we hear the Word with the outward ear, but we must let it penetrate to our heart, so that we may hear the Holy Spirit speak there, that is, with vibrant emotion and comfort feel the sealing of the Spirit and the power of the Word' (Spener 1964: 117). Luther can readily be quoted to the same effect, and Spener did so—copiously. But the motives subtly diverge. R. W. Meyer called attention to this difference between Luther and Spener's disciple, August Hermann Francke (1663–1727): 'There is little in common between Francke's and Luther's experience of the religious crisis' (Meyer 1952: 76. Stoeffler 1973: 7–23 and Brown 1996 give a sympathetic account of Francke's Lutheranism; cf. sources in translation, Lund 2002: chapter 8). Luther sought assurance of grace as a troubled penitent. Francke, as an orthodox

Lutheran, affirmed this doctrine of grace. 'But Francke had lost the immediate and personal experience of this love. Leibniz on the other hand believes that with the aid of "the light" of science he does possess this experience' (Meyer 1952: 76). Study of Francke's account of his conversion makes it clear that his 'religious dilemma becomes identical with an intellectual dilemma unknown to Luther'. What was this new dilemma brought by a changed horizon? When, in his spiritual anguish, Francke turned to the Bible, it occurred to him 'to wonder whether the Scriptures are truly the Word of God. Do not the Turks make this claim on behalf of their Koran, and the Jews on behalf of the Talmud? And who shall say who is right?' (Meyer 1952: 76). The early modern pietist worries as much about historical relativism as about finding a gracious God. Francke's resolution of this worry is not cognitive; the rational objection is simply overwhelmed by the experience of the New Birth:

> So great was his fatherly love that he wished to take me finally, after such doubts and unrest of my heart, so that I might be more convinced that he could satisfy me well, and that my erring reason might be tamed, so as not to move against his power and faithfulness. He immediately heard me. My doubt vanished... I was assured in my heart... Reason stood away; victory was torn from its hands, for the power of God had made it subservient to faith. ('Autobiography', in Erb 1983: 105)

Meyer's parenthetic allusion to Gottfried Leibniz (1646–1716) by way of contrast to Francke is glib; Leibniz did not claim for 'natural theology' what Meyer assumes.[1] But a corresponding rationalist foundationalism certainly can be uncovered in early Lutheranism, indeed among Leibniz's contemporaries. Inspired by Hobbes, the motives are in the first place political. Writing in the fictional voice of Monzambano, an Italian observer and interpreter of all things German, Samuel Pufendorf (1632–94) retold the story of 'the Reformation' as a purely secular contest of powers, beginning with 'the inconsiderate rashness and haste of Leo X'. The demystification continued:

> For some contemptible [miselli] Monks [were] contending with one another, one Party of which was very zealous for Religion, and the other Party no less concern'd for their Profit; and at first both of them had the Papal Power in great esteem, [as Sacred]... [But] when Martin Luther saw he could have no Justice done to him [at the Pope's Tribunal], he began to court the Grace and good Opinion of the Laity, and soon after, he positively refused to submit to the Judgment of the Pope... [and] he began to teach, That the Care of the Church belonged to Secular Princes... And they again reflecting, That the great Revenues their Ancestors had given to pious uses,

---

[1] On Leibniz's apologetic genre, see Antognazza 2007 and Hinlicky 2009: especially chapter 5, 'General Pneumatology: The Sublimation of the Spirit into Progressive Christian Culture', 177–222.

were spent in [nourishing the] Sloth and Luxury [of the clergy], [quickly embraced the opportunity of turning these lazy fat Cattel to Grass].

> (Pufendorf, 2007: 126–7; in quoting the early Bohun translation, the modern editors have placed in brackets language added by Bohun for pleonasm, periphrasis, and elaboration)

Pufendorf's witty demythologizing of Lutheranism's sacred narrative of 'the Reformation' concluded with Manzambano's caustic description of its outcome in Lutheran Orthodoxy's Caesaro-papism:

> The People [*plebi*] are taught by them to reverence their Magistrates [and Princes], as [the Ministers of God], and [finally] that all the good works expected of them, is to do the Duties of Good men: Nor [am I displeased], that they have retained [so much of the Ceremonial Part and the Pomp of Religion, which serves] to divert [guide] the minds of the [simple] People, who have not sense enough to contemplate [the Beauty of] simple, undress'd Piety…So that it is not possible to imagine a Religion that can be more serviceable and useful to the Princes of Germany, [than that of the Lutherans,] we may from hence conclude, that this is [generally] the best [suited] for a Monarchy than any in the World. (Pufendorf 2007: 226)

The appearance of early rationalism in Lutheran Germany took this form of political philosophy in a project of secularizing natural law under the auspices of enlightened reason in the aftermath of decades of religious warfare. But as John Witte has shown, the reformation of jurisprudence in the sixteenth century had taken place under the aegis of a dogma of revealed theology: the creation of humankind in the image and likeness of God, on account of which the natural law of God was indelibly inscribed on the human heart (Witte 2002). For the Reformation that meant that law was to be 'secularized' in the sense of removing it from the jurisdiction of the clergy, as in traditional canon law. But it was not at all 'secularized' in the sense of removing the divine-human vocation (Gen. 1:26–28) as the *ratio ultima* of human rights and duties and indeed the basis of criminal justice with its penalties (Gen. 9:4). The political was not abandoned to the Devil; rather, it was to be reformed and renewed. Similarly in this connection Joshua Mitchell has shown how Luther had 're-enchanted' the secular by regarding it as the holy time in which service of God and neighbour takes place (Mitchell 1992). But with Pufendorf, this original Reformation-theological basis for a holy secularity came under attack in the name and for the sake of emergent secular*ism*.

Pufendorf's champion at Leipzig was Christian Thomasius (1655–1728, Leibniz' contemporary there, though Leibniz opposed his and Pufendorf's legal positivism) (see Leibniz' 'Opinion on the Principles of Pufendorf', Riley 2001: 64–75; cf. Riley 1996). Thomasius 'endorsed Pufendorf's secularized political absolutism. In making social peace the goal of politics and the source of its norms, Pufendorf had sought to exclude the church from the political arena…' (Thomasius 2007: xi). In Thomasius' own words, 'the right in religious affairs belongs to the prince as such, not to him as a member of the church' (Thomasius 2007: 84, a critical reference to Luther's rationale for the emergency custodianship of the church by the secular princes; cf. *To the Christian Nobility*, WA6.404–469; LW44.115–217)—exactly *not* the rationale Luther had given for the duty of the nobility as lay leaders to reform the church in the emergency situation of apostate bishops. In Thomasius the same motif hinted at in Pufendorf emerges: the 'encouragement of a non-doctrinal inward Protestantism...a style of piety that was sceptical of the "visible" church with its creeds, sacraments and rituals; mute regarding the afterlife; and focused on the achievement of inner peace through a calming of the passions and desires'. The parallel with the contemporaneous emergence of the 'religion of the heart' is unmistakable.[2] Thomasius likewise anticipated the pietist repudiation of disputational theology with the same parody as in Pufendorf:

> [B]y means of Platonic, and then Aristotelian arts of disputation ... [it] was thought that if the denunciation of heretics did not proceed apace, then the professors would have nothing to dispute about at the universities. Polemical theology would thus fall by the wayside, and the cost of maintaining theology professors would be in vain. This restless and factious theology served to perpetuate the quarrel between the two Protestant churches.
>
> (Thomasius 2007: 40)[3]

First for the political philosophers of the early Enlightenment, then increasingly for their pietist cohorts, Luther's reform as a result no longer consisted in Luther's doctrine, but in his example. The pan-Protestant political example of reform that he was said to provide is separation from the papacy in all its works and ways and the corresponding restoration of authority to reason and the secular sovereign. 'The disciples of Luther should follow his example, not defend his deeds and his sayings and confuse consciences' (Thomasius 2007: 121–3). Thomasius may thus be said to foreshadow the cultural synthesis of Halle pietism and Prussian absolutism in the eighteenth century.[4]

Apparently polarizing theologies of the heart and of the head may thus collaborate, then, even synthesize in a cultural truce according to a certain division of labour. This tenuous

---

[2] Thomasius 2007: 40 recalls Luther's republication of Tauler's *Theologia deutsch*. He repeats Pufendorf's analysis verbatim in discounting the historical dispute between Luther and Zwingli as a quarrel over (Christological!) non-essentials, a scandalous obstacle to a pan-Protestant alliance against the pope under the leadership of the secular prince (60). But the ubiquity of Christ's glorified body is the basis for Luther's assertion of religious authority.

[3] In a fictional dialogue between an Orthodox and a Christian, Luther is made to redefine heresy as factionalism (180), and thus the true Christian is able to rebuke the Orthodox, 'you have converted the faith of the heart into a thing of the intellect' when in truth you are the true heretic, 'a man full of hatred for dissenters' (183).

[4] Thomasius 2007: 104. On the Halle–Prussia synthesis, see Gritsch 2002: 149–50, 171. Israel 2001: 654 notes Thomasius' criticisms of the more radical, more consistent Spinozist, Theodor Ludwig Lau (1670–1740). Likewise, Gritsch 2002: 142 underscores Spener's functional agreement with Thomasius when he reports how Spener at first 'supported orthodox laws compelling attendance of Sunday worship and catechetical instruction. But he was soon convinced that legal force would never instill the kind of piety that Arndt had advocated.'

alliance is possible because of the underlying unity in foundationalism. The rival designa-tions—'empiricist', 'rationalist', 'pietist', '*Aufklärer*'—obscure what unites all these rivals in the quest for foundations after the trauma of confessional warfare and in face of the rise of modern science, including historical science and its application to Scripture, and the concomitant discovery by European colonialism of the world religions. Such rivalries in foundationalism had to render Luther into a man who misunderstood himself, remain-ing half-way tangled in papist error, failing to complete what he had begun. Only so could both pietist and rationalist employ Luther in their service, each claiming to complete his work. With no little textual justification pietism appropriated Luther in service of a theol-ogy of the affects; but rationalists too could appeal to Luther's way of distinguishing theol-ogy from philosophy to constrict faith to the realm of interiority for the sake of secularist politics under the sole dominion of enlightened Reason. Yet this dualism of the head and the heart is a new Platonism. Such appropriations of Luther could be made only at the cost of re-Platonizing (or, Cartesianizing, or Kantianizing) Luther's Pauline–Johannine apoca-lyptic battle of the Spirit by the Word against the flesh with its vain imaginations.[5]

What pietist and rationalist indisputably shared was a changed historical horizon over against Luther. The historical Luther's horizon, as Heiko Oberman demonstrated (1969), was an apocalyptic eschatology, requiring church and theology to keep 'the gospel afloat in the world's last, ravaged hour' (Oberman 1984: 122). But pietist and rationalist think quite otherwise about human prospects. The world has not ended; nature is opening up to scientific investigations. Commerce is bringing home the discovery of new peoples in new lands. After the Thirty Years religious war had ceased there was new hope in this world for this world, whether it be Spener's 'better times for the church' ('Spener correctly sensed that the times had changed. The ministry of his day did not have to deal with peo-ple who wanted to be blessed from good works but with people who regarded them as unnecessary and impossible', Brown 1996: 107) or Kant's dream of the maturation of the enlightened human race progressing onward towards perpetual peace. Accordingly, our epoch thinks in terms of 'completing' the reformation of religion which Luther began with a reformation of life. When we bear in mind this shift in historical horizon, at least one aspect of the scholarly ferment about claims to Luther's mantle can be clarified.

III. THE SCHOLARLY QUANDARY

As mentioned above, Albrecht Ritschl influentially portrayed spiritually egoistic, 'world-denying' pietism as a foreign development on the soil of Luther's Reformation,

---

[5] Luther thought that this exegetical discovery had liberated him from traditions which obscured the Spirit's vital role in bringing the *Verbum externum*. See Luther's *On Bound Choice*, WA18.735,20–736,5, 742,3–21, 756,24–761,37, 765,2–766,7, 780,18–781,3, 781,29–782,11, LW33.215, 224–225, 246–254, 259–261, 283–284, 285–286.

a recrudescence of the medieval ascetic and mystical spirituality of 'monastics who live a life free from cares' by flight from the world and mystical ascent to God. How different for the socially responsible 'protestant Christians who remain within the midst of their secular conditions of life and who must stand the test of their faith within the inescapable cares of those conditions[!]' (Ritschl 1972: 105). But Oberman, who has done so much to relocate Luther in the context of late medieval Catholicism (2000), argued that the medieval 'mystical' legacy is integral to Luther's 'chief' doctrine:

> If future research confirms my suggestions that Luther's concept 'extra nos' [outside the self] is related to [mystical] *raptus* [rapture], one of the major arguments for a forensic interpretation of Luther's doctrine of justification has been preempted. Though we have no claim to the *iustitia Christi* which is not our 'property' (*proprietas*), it is granted to us as a present possession (*possessio*). *Extra nos* and *raptus* indicate that the *iustitia Christi*—and not our own powers—is the source and resource for *our* righteousness. Epithets such as 'external' and 'forensic' righteousness cannot do justice to Luther's doctrine of justification. (Oberman 1986: 150–1)

Oberman's claim here has been extended in recent years by the Finnish scholar, Tuomo Mannerma (1989) and his students, though others have independently made the same kind of critique of the Ritschl paradigm (Lotz 1974; Bielfeldt et al. 2008).

One effect of Oberman's historiography is to lend credence to the reclaiming of medieval spiritual theology by Johann Arndt (1555–1621) at the wellspring of Lutheran pietism, on the model of Luther's own publication of the 1516 *Theologia deutsch*. What Arndt appropriated, as Luther before him, and Spener afterwards ('Resignation', in Erb 1983: 83–7), is the theme of resignation, the Gethsemane of the soul, the *theologia crucis*: 'a pure simple suffering of the divine will; man allows God to work all things in him and does not hinder God with his own will or strive against God' (Arndt 1979: 30–1). Thus, as Oberman commented, 'Albrecht Ritschl was not completely wrong in tracing Arndt's lineage back to medieval and mystical traditions; it is the value judgment that went with Ritschl's work that deserves reconsideration...the learned theology of the schools was [to be] complemented by an affective theology accessible as well to the simple and unlettered.' Indeed, Oberman claims, Arndt proves in this 'to be a true disciple of Luther', a 'second Luther, Luther *redivivus*', in articulating the paradox of the *simul iustus et peccator* precisely by means of the 'mystical' rapture of encounter with the Christ who comes to unite with the self from outside of the self, as in Luther's celebrated 'joyful exchange' (Oberman's preface to Arndt 1979: xvi). Gritsch (2002: 145) concurs: 'Spener cited numerous texts from Luther and orthodox theologians that true theology could not be based on natural, rational power but only on the gift of the Holy Spirit.' Luther's own theology of 'true faith, that gift of the Holy Spirit' (WA39,1.44,4; LW34.109) and of justification correspondingly as a 'joyful exchange' at a wedding feast (WABr1.35,15–36–45; LW48.12–13), then, are indisputable sources of pietism's Bridegroom of the Soul. The latter for its part, to be sure, is not an unproblematic development of these resources.

In an influential article in the 1957 *Lutherjahrbuch* Martin Schmidt did not reject, but sharply qualified, the continuity which Oberman detects from medieval spiritual theologians like Tauler and Bernard, whom Luther knew and drew upon, on through Arndt to Spener and Francke. He patiently dissected the relationship of justification and regeneration in Spener in terms of the latter's new, more optimistic eschatology. On this basis Schmidt developed a sympathetic and convincing sketch of Spener's theological innovation over against Luther (Schmidt 1957). Sanctification, in short, became the programme of optimistic living in this world after and on the basis of justification. Justification here becomes a past event, the believer's secured possession. God's free grace becomes a presupposition for what truly matters existentially, the believer's new life progressing forward. For the historical Luther, by contrast, the movement in Christian life remains the triune God's, the Spirit by the Word apocalyptically breaking into the closed system of this world to justify the ungodly, who remain *simul iustus et peccator* until the eschaton completes the coming of the Beloved Community.

Schmidt's analysis, however, produces a quandary for theology in Luther's tradition. How could one ever adjudicate such a shift in horizon? Perhaps a deeper self-examination among those claiming Luther's mantle is required. F. Ernst Stoeffler was right to raise the important question about impulses from Puritanism and Dutch Calvinism in the formation of Spener's programme (1965: 231–2; others, e.g., Max Weber 2002: 83–9, have rightly stressed the differences between Reformed and Lutheran pietism) while at the same time documenting an indigenous Lutheran reform party bridging the time between Arndt and Spener (Stoeffler 1965: 187–228). More importantly, Stoeffler pointed out that with Spener 'the reform party within seventeenth century Lutheranism had moved from sincere but indiscriminate criticism to a plan of action' (1965: 235). The programmatic action announced in *Pia Desideria* was the provocation that ignited conflict since it implied that Luther's Reformation itself needed reform. While Arndtian reform literature had been theologically challenged by Lutheran Orthodoxy from the beginning regarding its understanding of the relation of imputative justification to regeneration, it was acting on the Arndtian understanding of regeneration that threatened the hegemony of confessionalized Lutheran Orthodoxy. Bible study threatened the dogmatic method; small groups of laity gathered for prayer and edification threatened the rule of the clergy; and optimistic eschatology threatened its closed-ranks battlefield mentality. For such reasons, Stoeffler observes, 'the printed announcement of [Spener's] platform, which today seems so eminently sane, sensible and moderate, became the center of one of the most bitter theological debates in the history of Protestantism' (1965: 235). In some ways the battle has never ceased. Stoeffler himself, however, wondered whether there was a Lutheran contradiction, so to say, at the root of the bitter incomprehension that arose between Orthodox and Pietist. He suggested that it was the doctrine of baptismal regeneration, quite in tension with Luther's notion of living, active, justifying faith. The inner contradiction virtually required an eventual parting of the ways (Stoeffler 1965: 242). There is indeed a 'Lutheran contradiction' at the root of things, but Stoeffler's suggestion here does not quite lay it bare.

IV. The Lutheran Contradiction and Its (Possible) Postmodern Resolution

Baptismal regeneration is not an unintelligible assertion of magic when regeneration is understood as the social event of adoption into the family of God, not an invisible miracle supposedly instantaneously transforming an infant's interior (Hinlicky 1999). Here, too, the work of the Spirit proceeds from the outside according to Luther's teaching on the *Verbum externum*. Yet Lutheran Orthodoxy, in its confused reaction against Osiander's teaching of infused divine righteousness, contradicted the Augsburg Confession's teaching that justifying faith, *fiducia ex corde*, is the regenerating work of the Spirit *per Verbum* (cf. FC, SD III:19 to Ap IV:12, 45–8, 62–8, 72, 110, 114–18, cf. Hinlicky 2012), i.e., that justification by faith *is* regeneration, that faith *is* the Spirit's gift and sanctification, because it is *God's* movement *into* the world, not the believer's movement out of it. Pietism was not wrong to insist on *fiducia ex corde*; it went wrong in viewing this gift as a private event within the safe ghetto of modern interiority, a 'new birth' there over against the public and external, the audible and sacramental. Here it became the secured property of the believer as its datable past event rather than Oberman's ever-renewed 'rapture' of faith in Luther's encounter with Christ by the joyful exchange in Word and sacrament.

Something in parallel may be said regarding faith and reason. We have learned since the passing of 'the' Enlightenment of the profound historicity of reason. There is no Reason transcending time and able therefore to impose order on the flux of becoming once and for all. The conceit of this supposition has been made manifest in exposing Reason's rationalizations (i.e., Luther's 'whoredom' [Dragseth 2011]) of the imperialism of post-Christian Euro-American political sovereignty in all its various forms: fascism, communism and also capitalism/colonialism. May it be then that Luther's (not Kant's) critique of reason finally comes into its own in our 'postmodern' times? For Luther, the reasons of the heart are also reason's reasons since human creatures are psychosomatic wholes created for the Beloved Community, not coalitions of parts to be organized hierarchically from above or magically from within. What matters to such somatic selves both intellectually and affectively is *which* light it is in which they are to be enlightened. There are no foundations, but there are events of light shining in the darkness which for good or for ill capture hearts and illumine minds and demand loyalty. Paul and John understood this, and Luther did after them, as today do some from surprising quarters (Badiou 2003; Agamben 2005; and Hinlicky 2013). But theology in their train must test the spirits.

References

Adkins, Brent and Paul R. Hinlicky (2013). *Rethinking Philosophy and Theology with Deleuze: A New Cartography*. London: Continuum.

Agamben, Giorgio (2005). *The Time That Remains: A Commentary on the Letter to the Romans*, trans. Patricia Dailey. Stanford: Stanford University Press.

Antognazza, Maria Rosa (2007). *Leibniz on the Trinity and the Incarnation: Reason and Revelation in the Seventeenth Century*, trans. G. Parks. New Haven: Yale University Press.

Arndt, Johann (1979). *True Christianity*, trans. Peter Erb. New York: Paulist.

Badiou, Alain (2003). *Saint Paul: The Foundation of Universalism*, trans. R. Brassier. Stanford: Stanford University Press.

Barth, Karl (1959). *Protestant Thought From Rousseau to Ritschl*, trans. Brian Cozens. London: SCM.

Bielfeldt, Dennis, Mickey Mattox, and Paul R. Hinlicky (2008). *The Substance of the Faith: Luther's Doctrinal Theology for Today*. Minneapolis: Fortress.

Brown, Dale W. (1996). *Understanding Pietism*, rev. edn. Nappanes, IN: Evangel.

Busch, Eberhard (2004). *Karl Barth and the Pietists: The Young Karl Barth's Critique of Pietism and Its Response*, trans. Donald W. Bloesch. Downer's Grove: Intervarsity.

Campbell, Ted A. (1991). *The Religion of the Heart: A Study of European Religious Life in the Seventeenth and Eighteenth Centuries*. Columbia: University of South Carolina Press.

Dragseth, Jennifer Hockenberry (ed.) (2011). *The Devil's Whore: Reason and Philosophy in the Lutheran Tradition*. Minneapolis: Fortress.

Erb, Peter (1983). *Pietists: Selected Writings*. New York: Paulist.

Frank, Günther (2003). *Die Vernunft des Gottesgedankens. Religionsphilosophische Studien zur frühen Neuzeit*. Stuttgart-Cannstatt: Frommann-Holzboog.

Gritsch, Eric W. (2002). *A History of Lutheranism*. Minneapolis: Fortress.

Hinlicky, Paul R. (1999). 'The Doctrine of the New Birth: From Bullinger to Edwards'. *Missio Apostolica* 7: 102–19.

—— (2009). *Paths Not Taken: Theology from Luther through Leibniz*. Grand Rapids, MI: Eerdmans.

—— (2012). 'Staying Lutheran in the Changing Church(es)'. Afterword in Mickey L. Mattox and Gregg Roeber, *Changing Churches*. Grand Rapids, MI: Eerdmans.

Israel, Jonathan I. (2001). *Radical Enlightenment: Philosophy and the Making of Modernity 1650–1750*. Oxford: Oxford University Press.

Kant, Immanuel (1978). *Lectures on Philosophical Theology*, trans. A. W. Wood and G. M. Clark. Ithaca: Cornell University Press.

—— (1979). *The Conflict of the Faculties*, trans. Mary J. Gregor. New York: Abaris.

Lotz, David (1974). *Luther and Ritschl: A Fresh Perspective on Albrecht Ritschl's Theology in the Light of His Luther Study*. Nashville: Abingdon.

Lund, Eric (ed.) (2002). *Documents from the History of Lutheranism 1517–1750*. Minneapolis: Fortress.

Mannermaa, Tuomo (1989). *Der im Glauben Gegenwärtige Christus. Rechtfertigung und Vergottung Zum ökumenischen Dialog*. Hannover: Lutherisches Verlagshaus.

Meyer, R. W. (1952). *Leibniz and the Seventeenth Century Revolution*, trans. J. P. Stern. Cambridge: Bowes and Bowes.

Mitchell, Joshua (1992). 'Protestant Thought and Republican Spirit: How Luther Enchanted the World'. *The American Political Science Review* 86: 688–95.

Oberman, Heiko (1984). *The Roots of Anti-Semitism in the Age of Renaissance and Reformation*, trans. J. I. Porter. Philadelphia: Fortress.

—— (1986). 'Luther and Mysticism'. In Oberman, *The Dawn of the Reformation: Essays in Late Medieval and Early Reformation Thought*. Edinburgh: T&T Clark.

Oberman, Heiko (1989). *Luther: Man between God and the Devil*, trans. Eileen Walliser-Schwarzbart. New Haven: Yale University Press.

—— (2000). *The Harvest of Medieval Theology: Gabriel Biel and Late Medieval Nominalism*. Grand Rapids, MI: Baker.

Pufendorf, Samuel (2007). *The Present State of Germany*, trans. Edmund Bohun, ed. M. J. Seidler. Original 1696. Indianapolis: Liberty Fund.

Riley, Patrick (1996). *Leibniz' Universal Jurisprudence: Justice as the Charity of the Wise*. Cambridge, MA: Harvard University Press.

—— (ed.) (2001). *Leibniz: Political Writings*, 2nd edn. Cambridge: Cambridge University Press.

Ritschl, Albrecht (1972). *Three Essays: Theology and Metaphysics, Prolegomena to The History of Pietism, Instruction in the Christian Religion*, trans. Philip Hefner. Philadelphia: Fortress.

Schmidt, Martin (1957). 'Spener und Luther: Noch zum 250. Todestag Philipp Jakob Speners am 5. Februar 1955'. *Lutherjahrbuch* 24: 102–29.

Spener, Philip Jacob (1964). *Pia Desideria*, trans. Theodore Tappert. Philadelphia: Fortress.

Spinoza, Baruch (1998). *Principles of Cartesian Philosophy with Metaphysical Thoughts*, trans. Samuel Shirley. Indianapolis: Hackett.

Stoeffler, F. Ernst (1965). *The Rise of Evangelical Pietism*. Leiden: Brill.

—— (1973). *German Pietism during the Eighteenth Century*. Leiden: Brill.

Strom, Jonathan (2002). 'Problems and Promises of Pietism Research'. *Church History* 71: 536–54.

Thomasius, Christian (2007). *Essays on Church, State, and Politics*, ed. and trans. I. Hunter, T. Ahnert, and F. Grunert. Indianapolis: Liberty Fund.

Tillich, Paul (1967). *Systematic Theology*. 3 vols. Chicago: University of Chicago Press.

Troeltsch, Ernst (1912–25). 'Leibniz und die Anfänge des Pietismus'. In *Gesammelte Schriften*. 4 vols. Vol. 4: *Aufsätze zur Geistesgeschichte und Religionssoziologie*. Tubingen: Mohr/Siebeck, 488–531.

Ward, W. R. (1993). 'German Pietism: 1670–1750'. *Journal of Ecclesiastical History* 44: 476–505.

Weber, Max (2002). *The Protestant Ethic and the Spirit of Capitalism*, trans. S. Kalberg. Los Angeles: Roxbury.

Weigelt, Horst (1970). 'Interpretations of Pietism in the Research of Contemporary German Church Historians'. *Church History* 39: 236–41.

Witte, John, Jr. (2002). *Law and Protestantism: The Legal Teachings of the Lutheran Reformation*. Cambridge: Cambridge University Press.

Yeide, Harry, Jr. (1997). *Studies in Classical Pietism: The Flowering of the Ecclesiola*. New York and Frankfurt am Main: Lang.

CHAPTER 41

THE USE OF LUTHER'S THOUGHT IN THE NINETEENTH CENTURY AND THE LUTHER RENAISSANCE

HEINRICH ASSEL

I. Presuppositions and Main Foci

I.1. 'The Use of Luther's Thought'

When we ask about the use of Luther's thought in the nineteenth century, we should distinguish between (a) the reception of *topical doctrinal contents* (e.g. justification and God's righteousness, the Christology of the *communicatio idiomatum*), (b) the reception of characteristic structural *rhetorical and dialectical figures of thought* (e.g. synecdoche as rhetorical metaphor and dialectical structure), and (c) the embedding of both in specific genres of Luther's writings.

I.2. An Overview of Main Foci

When we define the use of Luther's *thought* in the epoch of German Idealism before 1848, we have to recognize that this use often intended to critically expand the then-dominant concept of theological *doctrine* and scholarly or historical *reflection*, by means of an appeal to Luther himself. The use of Luther's thought assumed a principally philosophical status. Prominent examples include Hamann's meta-criticism of Kant's critique of pure reason, aiming at an expanded sense of the rationality of language; Hegel's dialectic of the living spirit (*Geist*); and finally Feuerbach. The early Marxist use of 'Luther' as a cipher and a medium for the critique of bourgeois religion and society presumes this status.

Adolf von Harnack's thesis regarding the *historicity* of Luther as a 'demonic personality' of *post-dogmatic Christendom* is symptomatic for the tectonic shift of reception in the age of historicism (Ranke, Treitschke, Dilthey). Harnack moved, though not for the first time, the historical-theological question of the relationship between Luther's thinking and his ambiguous *personality* into the centre. Doctrine, or thought, is an expression of the historical-theological self-conception in a specific vocation (*Beruf*) and in the moral-political crises of the modern world. Luther's demonic personality offers an example of this.

Symptoms of a new move in the status of the question of Luther's thought are visible in the work of Ernst Troeltsch and Karl Holl and their critical attitude toward historicism. Troeltsch interprets Luther's religion of certitude and individuality as a functional social teaching of Protestantism. He judges its potential for a theory of church and society in modernity with scepticism. Simultaneously, Troeltsch believes, Luther's thought contains the origin of a new idea of God, which, in religious-philosophical terms, is typically modern because it implies the question of an historical and developmental concept of the absolute. Holl opposes Troeltsch with his thesis of Luther's existential religion of conscience, in the context of historical-political crises; for Holl, this religion of conscience also contains a proper understanding of the *Volkskirche* and a typically German cultural synthesis and social theory applicable to modernity. Thus, the so-called Luther Renaissance begins.

Holl and Troeltsch are turning points in the historicist reception of Luther. The dilemmas they pose become new starting points, which between 1926 and 1945 develop in the Luther Renaissance (and in the so-called Dialectical Theology) into distinctive traditions and paradigms of debate.

I.3. The History of the Reception and the Impact of Luther

Today, the study of the history of reception of Luther 'in the mirror of German intellectual history' (Bornkamm 1970) must include theoretical perspectives regarding modernity, society, and science. Simultaneously, it demands concrete evidence as to which writings and genre of Luther were known and used at a given time and which doctrinal and structural typologies were derived from them. Preliminary studies have been undertaken in a number of cases (e.g. on Hamann, Herder, Feuerbach, Ranke, Ritschl, the so-called Erlangen school of theology, Nietzsche)—some of them with methodological constraints—, while in regard to other figures they do not yet exist (e.g. Hegel, Schelling).

Luther's impact is conveyed historically in its selectivity and with its discontinuity, from the period of Protestant confessionalism and its public doctrine up to Hamann. A more sophisticated history of this impact is needed. For example, as one problematic focal point a (yet unwritten) history of Luther's impact on F. D. E. Schleiermacher (or, e.g. F. C. Baur and Martin Kähler) can be mentioned. Schleiermacher's explicit reception of Luther's writings is meagre, because his dogmatic work focuses on the Protestant confessions and the respective doctrinal principle of a specific period and not on Luther as an individual theologian. Nonetheless, at the same time, Schleiermacher occupies a distinctive turning point in the history of Luther's impact, from an increasing marginalization of Luther in Protestant theology to an ongoing discussion of his theological reception. In addition to these complex, indirect, and mediated forms of impact, the 'impact' in a narrower sense of the term comes into play when one claims one's own philosophical or theological programme as a contemporary impact of Luther's concerns. However, such a claim cannot be verified in terms of reception history. 'Luther' (and expressly not Calvin or Melanchthon) then becomes a cipher of what is regarded as reformational.

In part, measured by today's standards, but also by the critical reception at the time—e.g. by Herder (compared with Hamann's standards), such claims of a 'reception' of Luther are questionable. In part, this claim of a 'reception' is not simply wrong. Hegel provides a test case. He could not have known essential documents from Luther's early theology of the cross (Romans commentary, *Operationes in Psalmos*, 'Anti-Latomus'), but his early writings and his *Phänomenologie des Geistes* present dialectical models (e.g. the reconciliation through Jesus' crucifixion and the ontology of the person of the crucified) which objectively, and properly, claim to be a legacy of Luther's theology.

I.4. Luther's Thinking and the 'Demonic Person'

Alongside Luther's impact on doctrinal contents, structural expressions, and certain literary genres, the usage of Luther's historical person and vocation also demands consideration: In particular, the transformation of the idea of his 'eschatological' office as 'reformer' into his mission as a 'demonic person' within the history of emancipation and freedom (cf. I.2).

The prophetic or eschatological office of a reformer becomes the idea of a genius who shaped history (Herder) and later a 'demonic personality' (Harnack). The 'demonic' characterizes the alleged irreconcilable contradictions in Luther's history-shaping genius, the vigour of paradox, which defies ethical or doctrinal rationalization. The attempt to integrate the ambivalences of Luther's influence into his image is the reason why Luther changed around 1890 from 'genius in the history of emancipation' into 'demonic personality'.

The emancipatory figure of Luther was already open for a certain national-religious interpretation for Herder. It became ever more linked with national religion and culture—an ideological variation on the theme of the 'demonic' Luther.

The historical Luther reception among Catholics in the nineteenth century, in contrast, provides historical arguments for interpreting this alleged 'demonic' factor critically. It consistently connects criticism of Luther's doctrine with questions regarding the opaque development of his personality as a reformer.

The great critics of the leading cultural and religious concept of modernity (Kierkegaard, Nietzsche) and the stylization of Luther in terms of historical genius and emancipation highlight influences of Luther which are viewed as critical. In such cases, Luther becomes, above all, a cipher of a constructive reformatory intention, which now is critical of the 'Modern'.

This provides the background for the various stages of the reception of Luther's thesis of the unfree will and his treatise *De servo arbitrio* (J. G. Herder, F. W. J. Schelling, Theodosius Harnack, Karl Holl, Emanuel Hirsch, H. J. Iwand) in Protestant theology. Rather than a simply affirmative or a simply critical reception of Luther's *De servo arbitrio* attempt to interpret it in more sensitive fashion. In his treatise Luther anticipated possible crises and even the unavoidable breakdown of Christian freedom in actual, existential situations. The experience of being justified in the conscience opens a freedom in faith that is realizable only through crises and 'judgements' and ultimately is real only in a trans-historical sense.

II. Starting Positions: J. G. Hamann and J. G. Herder

1. J. G. Hamann's (1730–88) affinity for Luther is based on a series of original insights and impulses which he received chiefly in 1759–65 and 1780–8. Hamann's crisis in London (in early 1758) reveals a theology of Trinitarian condescension even *before* he read Luther. In this framework his initial reception of Luther could take place in 1759, expressed in a figural and typological view of the world and history, as a biblical overall view of creation and redemption. In engaging Paul, Hamann discovered elements of the theology of justification and the Christology of divine–human exchange and recognized them in Luther as well. In this context he appraised Luther: 'What a power in rhetorical expression—what a spirit of interpretation—what a prophet!' (Hamann 1955: 294, 11–12). From April 1762 (his reading of Luther's Heidelberg Theses) Hamann called himself a '*philologus crucis*', confirming and expanding this in 1765 with the catchphrase '*Scheblimini*', from Luther's interpretation of Psalm 110:1, referring to Jesus' exaltation and status as God's Son. It is seen as an emblem of Lutheranism. In April 1780 Hamann renewed his study of Luther, impelled by reading Kant's *Critique of Pure Reason* before its publication. Luther became the essential bastion of his (uncompleted) meta-criticism in the draft of his *Fliegender Brief*.

Hamann's early theology of condescension is not primarily soteriological but a philosophy of revelation that aims at a typological phenomenology of revelation, which describes the concrete closeness of God to the world and to human beings. God's Word is what constitutes reality, expanded by means of a philosophy of language in view of materially arbitrary, conventional linguistic signs. Luther's doctrine of the communication of attributes, expressing his philosophy of language, stood at the centre of Hamann's meta-critique of Kant and is extended beyond the context of Christology and the Lord's Supper. The Christological meaning of the doctrine concerns the exchange of attributes of the divine and human natures, but Hamann applied it to the connection between sensibility and reason which continually takes place in ordinary language (Hamann 1955: 287, 17–19). This formulation formed the centre of Hamann's understanding of language: language is analogous to a sacrament.

2. J. G. Herder's (1744–1803) lifelong reception of Luther treated a broad range of topics and was closest to Luther's thesis regarding the unfree will in the years 1771–6 (in Bückeburg). Yet it was not the reception of a particular doctrinal topic but the application of the *genuinely historical* personality of Luther, arising from Herder's philosophy of history, which anticipated an innovative methodological use of Luther's thought. The topic of the unfree will and the instrumentality of the elect became an expression of Luther's understanding of himself in his historical context. Herder's historical-theological interpretation of Luther's work as a cultural synthesis that is creative as well as caught in crisis at the turning point of two epochs set forth important patterns for the Luther reception in the nineteenth and early twentieth centuries. Following Lessing, Herder's application of the concept of genius to Luther defined Luther's religious, linguistic-cultural, and political-legal influence as liberating, due to his historical individuality and his unifying of contradictory elements. 'It is he who awakened and unchained the German language, a sleeping giant...through his Reformation he stimulated an entire nation to think and feel' (Herder 1985: 381, 16–17 [367–540]). His reception of *De servo arbitrio* in his Bückeburg years transformed Luther's thesis into a self-interpretation that Herder attributed to Luther. Luther's insight into the instrumentality of the elect was seen as being based upon a deeper consciousness of freedom impacting history. 'The deeper the consciousness of freedom, which he could and should have, the more he feels like a slave, when all shallow, superficial heads feel like gods' ('Vom Erkennen und Empfinden, Entwurf', Herder 1892: 308).

In Herder's later writings, a new motif arose: Luther's reformational Christendom was seen as 'national religion in the narrowest sense of the word, i.e. *conscientiousness* and *conviction*', that is, an emphasis on the cultural particularity of Christianity as that which becomes truly universal only as nationally and personally individualized religion.

III. Experience and a Dialectical Concept of Justification: Kant and Idealism

1. Immanuel Kant's (1724–1804) explicit reception of Luther is marginal and limited, presumably, to the Small Catechism. Yet for later receptions of Luther the reference to Kant as well as the criticism of his ideas is far-reaching. Kant's anti-metaphysical concept of

the dialectic of reason and his foundation of experience in the *a priori* act of the synthesis of apperception, which opens the way for experience, in many ways prepared the framework for theories of reality in which Luther's thinking was understood (rival concepts of 'dialectic', transcendental personalism vs Ontology) and in which his doctrinal topics were read (e.g. justification as synthetic or analytic divine judgement [Albrecht Ritschl]). Simultaneously, Kant's idea of freedom as autonomy and self-determination formulated problems on the basis of which Luther's *libertas christiana* was interpreted in various ways—including contradictory or seemingly better models. Still, Kant's idea of freedom is shaped by his individualistic as well as contractualistic theory of possessions and personal rights. Perspectives on Luther's *libertas christiana* shaped by Kant's concept of autonomy elicited new types of criticism of Luther, motivated by social theory (Feuerbach, Marx, Troeltsch, Holl). The rationalization of Protestant doctrinal formulations in Kant's religious writings (e.g. sin as radical evil, the church and God's kingdom as ethical commonwealth), that is, the foundation of biblical and dogmatic theology on a critical philosophy of religion, triggered the foundational debate regarding the principles of a theology that appealed to Luther (the Word of God and/or a religion of Reason?).

2. J. G. Fichte's (1762–1814) selective and highly constructive reception of some of Luther's doctrinal expressions offers the first example of a new situation for the reception of Luther: theocentric piety and an (impersonal) inwardness defined by love—typifying the relationship with God—are elements in Fichte's philosophy of religion, which claims to supersede and, at the same time, complete Luther's thinking ('justification' in the genuine sense). A tradition of reception entitled 'Fichte and Luther' begins (cf. Emanuel Hirsch).

This is also true of F. D. E. Schleiermacher (1768–1834), whose '*Glaubenslehre*' focuses on the formation of Protestant confessional thinking, not on Luther. But since he seeks to take into account the emerging problems of Protestant theology after Kant (and the various forms of the Enlightenment), contemporary attempts to reconcile 'Schleiermacher and Luther' in the context of various topics (e.g. piety and certitude, election and the bondage of the will) are integral aspects of Luther's influence in the framework of the history of nineteenth-century theology.

3. In particular, it was G. W. F. Hegel (1770–1831) who thought through the genuine problem with the history of Luther's influence, the understanding of Luther's influences based on the subject matter of theology and *in that context* on the reformer's person. To what extent, Hegel asked, did the spirit (*Geist*) of Christianity, as the absolute spirit, take a decisive historical step in Luther, experienced as contingent but understood as necessary? Hegel concentrates on Luther's *theology*, in such a way that he distinguishes the subjective *experience* of the spirit in Luther's experience of justification and the *concept of the self-emptying Geist* appropriate to this historical experience. In this framework he selectively uses topics from Luther: justification as experience and as concept of liberated freedom; repentance and asceticism as mortification and the abandonment of the *sensus proprius*; faith as mystical union; the consumption of the sacramental 'visible' presence of Christ with the synecdochal rhetoric of the words of institution; the priesthood of the baptized; and the

theological distinctions of Luther's political theology. In his *Phänomenologie des Geistes* (1807) Hegel repeats basic insights from Luther's developing and mature reformational theology, but this reception is difficult to pinpoint accurately. He focuses on the emptying of the spirit manifest in the event 'Luther' as the *experience* of the historic subject and as the speculative *concept* of truth. A key question in the interpretation of Hegel's philosophy is whether a complete suspension of the faith experience, for which the designation 'Martin Luther' stands, took place between Hegel's early and later writings.

Implicit references to Luther's early *theologia crucis* appear in Hegel's early writings (1798–1807), e.g. in the much-debated expression 'speculative Good Friday' and in the rhetorical topic of 'the death of God'. In the *Phänomenologie des Geistes* (1807) this expression is developed in the chapters on the *'unhappy consciousness'* (alluding to Luther's experience of repentance) and *revealed religion* most extensively as the conscience's 'direct' experience of reconciliation and justification: the transition from the 'unhappy' to the liberated consciousness rests in the continuing externality of the Crucified One as the absolute emptying of God and as reconciliation for immediate faith, the absolute knowledge of which does not set aside the revelation of the spirit in Jesus' cross but preserves it. According to Hegel, the reconciliation which Luther experienced and conceptualized in his theology of the cross is interpreted in the doctrinal expressions of the Lutheran tradition in the sense of a political-theological conceptualization of self-determined freedom. Hegel sees the realization of such a freedom as the continuing task of the Reformation and especially of his own time. The religiously liberated conscience is to find its substantial truth in the national-religious language of a single book of the German people, Luther's translation of the Bible. The creation of the state finds its truth in its formulation of law, in which 'the norms and innermost foundation of religion itself and of the state [are joined] into a genuine and true peace' (Hegel's address at the festive tricentennial celebration of the presentation of the Augsburg Confession at the Royal Friedrich-Wilhelms University, Berlin, 25 June 1830; Schuffenhauer and Steiner, 1983: 344–7). This is a political-theological glorification of the reality and the law of the Prussian state at the time. In Hegel's *Vorrede der Rechtsphilosophie*, such a glorification explicitly refers to Luther as a forerunner but dismisses and distorts the eschatology inherent in the *theologia crucis*.

4. F. W. J. Schelling's (1775–1854) middle and late *'Philosophie der Offenbarung'*, beginning with the *Philosophische Untersuchungen über das Wesen der menschlichen Freiheit und die damit zusammenhängenden Gegenstände* (1809), formulates a criticism of Hegel that remains within the framework of the idealist subjectivity of reason. This paves the way for the post-idealist definition of the will as a counterforce opposed to reason. In a central passage, Schelling refers to Luther's *On the Unfree Will* (Schelling 1860: 386). Kant's doctrine of radical evil as an intelligible act is sharpened by means of Luther's expression of the necessary immutability of divine freedom: every form of freedom of choice is obsolete. Instead, the genuine concept of freedom is appropriate: human freedom, comprehended as real and active, is 'the capacity for good and evil'; this establishes Evil as reality, and 'to integrate the Evil into the eternal substance or the original will,

which entirely destroys the concept of the most perfect essence' becomes unavoidable (Schelling 1860: 352).

Luther's theological idea of predestination is here mediated with the idea of human self-determination and the constitution of character, countering the suspicion of determinism: 'we also maintain predestination, but in a totally different sense: human beings act here as they have acted from eternity and already at the beginning of creation. Their actions do not become, as their moral essence does not develop but by nature eternally is' (Schelling 1860: 387–8). Schelling uses this expression 'bewusstlose Wille zum Wollen'—differently than Nietzsche—to reconcile will and reason as spirit in the revelation that is experienced immemorially (*Weltalter-Philosophie*, 1811/1813).

5. Ludwig Feuerbach's (1804–72) reception of Luther, concentrated between 1841/1842 and 1845, was, as Feuerbach himself claimed, the catalyst that permitted him to overcome his Hegelianizing criticism of religion in favour of a sensual-materialist 'I-thou' philosophy (Feuerbach 1846: XIII). Moreover, it falls into the short phase of attraction and rejection between Feuerbach and Karl Marx (1818–83) between August 1844 and April 1845. In their correspondence in August 1844, both men dubbed *Das Wesen des Glaubens im Sinne Luthers: Ein Beitrag zum 'Wesen des Christentums'* as 'communist' but, in doing so, interpreted it differently, as a theory of intersubjectivity (Feuerbach) and of society (Marx, cf. his famous 'Feuerbach Theses' as a result). This demonstrates that the position Feuerbach reached through his criticism of Luther was not free from misunderstanding, either by Feuerbach himself or by others. In this important transitional stage the reception of Luther's Christology accelerated his self-understanding but simultaneously retarded it, because he integrates his idealistic-subjectivistic philosophical expressions *nolens volens* into his superseding criticism of Luther's Christology.

In *Grundsätze der Philosophie der Zukunft* Feuerbach sets forth poignant theses of a confessional-political nature on Luther's Christology against Protestant critics (J. Müller): '§1. The task of this age was to make God real and human—the transformation and dissolution of theology into anthropology. §2. The religious or practical way of attaining this humanization was Protestantism. The God who is human, the human God, Christ—he alone is the God of Protestantism. Protestantism is no longer concerned, as is Catholicism, about what God is in Himself, but only about what He is for human beings' (Feuerbach 1982: 265 [264–341]). Feuerbach seeks to demonstrate that this Protestant *'pro me'* was the principle that transformed theology into anthropology. The idea of universal reconciliation sensualizes and individualizes itself intersubjectively between 'Thou' and 'I': 'In life the "thou" is the God of the "I," in faith God is the "thou" of the human being. God is the essence of the human, but as an essence different from him, that is, as an objective essence' (Feuerbach 1982: 407 [353–412], *Das Wesen des Glaubens im Sinne Luthers*). The transformation of Luther's expressions regarding justification into the anthropological dialectic of individual and species (*Gattung*) becomes a theory of humanizing practice, in which the loving subject finds itself, its immanent end, and its dignity. This practice of philanthropy is the point of Feuerbach's transformation of Luther. One must note critically that this does not comprehend the interpersonal event of faith and love which respects the otherness of God's Word and the neighbour. Feuerbach's thinking remained within the frame of an abstract philanthropy. Marx noted this point, from his own standpoint, in his letter to Feuerbach from 11 August 1844: 'in these works (*Grundsätze* and *Das Wesen des Glaubens*) you have—intentionally?—given socialism a philosophical foundation, and the communists have immediately understood this effort in this way. The unity of the human being with the human being, which is based on the real difference among human beings, the concept of the human species pulled down from the heaven of abstraction to the real earth, this is nothing other but the concept of *society*' (Marx and Engels 1961–83: 27: 425 [425–8]).

6. Opposing Voices of Romanticism: Novalis's (1772–1801) programmatic address '(Christianity or) Europe', 1799 (published 1826), projects a counter-image to the emancipatory and national-historical perspective from the Reformation to the (French) Revolution and envisions a 'kairos' in European-German history. He contrasts the previous perspective with the unified Christian culture of the Middle Ages as an ideal youthful era, for which the world was not yet ready. The occurrence of this 'kairos' makes possible a new post-confessional Christianity of the spirit as a European culture. Thus, the Reformation was only the ferment at the origin of 'true anarchy' for the 'element which generates religion' (Novalis 2008: 463 [452–71]). It arose out of the decline of the ideal medieval unified Christian culture as a protest, and in this regard legitimately, but it declined into a partition of European Christendom guided by political interests and into an arbitrary treatment of religion by Luther. Precisely Luther's Biblicism misjudged the spirit of Christianity and established the domination of the letter and of philology, which 'infinitely' impedes 'the revival, penetration, and revelation' of the Holy Spirit (Novalis 2008: 458).

Fichte offered a similar evaluation. It highlights what distinguishes Ranke's appreciation of Luther's 'foundation' *sola Scriptura*, which had been inspired by Fichte but interpreted historically, from Novalis's Christendom as religion of the spirit. Since the Reformation, Christendom no longer exists. There are only confessions (denominations). In contrast, Novalis offers an early Romantic vision of a spiritually Christian Europe, of Romantic art and scholarship (natural philosophy). Closely related is Friedrich Schlegel's (1772–1829) critical view of Luther. He turns the view of Luther as demonic person into a criticism of modernity, through which Luther becomes an emblem of antagonisms: 'Throughout his (Luther's) writings, there seems to be a battle between light and darkness...between God and Luther himself' (lecture in Vienna, 1812, 'History of Ancient and Contemporary Literature', Schlegel 1846: 179). This prepares the way for the critical turning of Luther into an emblem exclusively related to cultural and national history and the refusal to discuss theological questions. A further dimension of this constriction leads from early Romanticism to E. M. Arndt (1769–1860), who attaches Luther to stereotypes from the 'wars of liberation' and thereafter to National Protestantism.

IV. Historicism: Reformation History, National History, Modern Worldviews

IV.1. Early Historicism

Leopold Ranke's (1795–1886) *Luther-Fragment von 1817* (Ranke: 1973: 329–465) formulates specific presuppositions for a radically new historicization of Luther and Ranke's early understanding of history, within the context of an extensive study of sources for a biography of Luther he never completed. The fragment was integrated into Ranke's *Deutsche Geschichte im Zeitalter der Reformation* (1839–47) (Ranke 1925), though modified and distinct in character—Ranke no longer uses a biographical approach but rather composes a history of institutions and national states. At the centre of the early *Fragment* stands the idea, shaped by Fichte, of a divine–historical life, which manifests itself both in great individuals and in the distinctiveness of larger units (epochs, states) at the climactic points of history, and is comprehended most clearly at its *origin*. This is the significance of the *initia Lutheri* in the Reformation era although Ranke's concept is not yet supported by a study of Luther's early exegesis: 'nothing would have sustained him if not the power of his secret, inner life. What he said and did streamed from an innermost fountain; he could have given up the battle he fought only with his whole internal and external life' (Ranke 1973: 362). In his presentation of Luther's beginnings (1839) his early idea, shaped by Fichte, was still influential: 'It was the longing of the creature for the Creator's purity, to which it felt related in the foundations of its being, at the same time feeling itself alienated from that purity by an infinite chasm: a feeling which Luther nourished with his incessant solitary brooding... Yet does it not belong to the laws of the world's eternal order that such a genuine need for the God-seeking soul be satisfied by an overflowing of conviction?' (Ranke 1925: 1.212–13). The new factor here is the comprehensive execution within a history of the Reformation in terms of politics and the national historical state, in which Luther becomes the instrument of overarching tendencies. The assessment of the relationship of the doctrine of justification to the scriptural principle is also new, compared to Fichte. While Luther formulated his individual breakthrough in terms of justification (the *Fragment* of 1817 labels this Luther's *opinion*), his criticism of authority in his scholarly Biblicism was the truly history-shaping factor (the *Fragment* calls this Luther's *principle*). Thus, Ranke assigns a particular functional role to the Reformation's Scripture principle: the latter preserves the continuity of western Christendom in continuing the conservative authority of Scripture (Ranke's assessment of Luther in the controversy over the Lord's Supper is similar).

IV.2. Metamorphoses of Historicism: National Protestantism and the Transformation of *Weltanschauung*

Heinrich von Treitschke and Wilhelm Dilthey represent the metamorphosis of the historical interpretation of Luther's person and theology in the generation after Ranke.

With his address on the occasion of Luther's 400th birthday on 7 November 1883 (Treitschke 1929: 233–49), von Treitschke (1834–96), Ranke's successor in Berlin, represents the broad tendency of a national-political interpretation of Luther's person. The 'whole' Luther was being recognized again, first and foremost, in historicism. He is the ideal image of the 'German essence and German faith'. Luther embodied the moral-historical ethos of free scholarship, recognized the mature state as God's order, liberated the Roman Empire from ecclesiastical domination, created the national language, overcame the medieval hierarchical order by teaching that each estate (including the estate of defence, i.e. secular government) has direct access to God, opened a new understanding of woman over against Marian piety, and inspired the enduring musical, sentiment-laden national culture. The new factor in these stereotypes is that Treitschke now defines the conditions for understanding the demonic figure of Luther, with his inherent tensions, in national-cultural, latently anti-French, terms. 'We Germans find in all of this no puzzle; we simply say: this is blood from our blood. From the deep eyes of this earthy German peasant's son blazed the old heroic courage of the ancient Germans, which does not flee the world but tries to master it through the power of the moral will' (Treitschke 1929: 246). In association with the demand for a dominant Protestant culture in Germany, such a claim was open for racialist appropriations.

Wilhelm Dilthey (1833–1911), biographer and heir of Schleiermacher's hermeneutic and theorist of history, interpreted Luther as a 'religious genius' and an exponent of the transformation of worldviews in the fifteenth and sixteenth centuries, on the way to the system of humanities of the seventeenth century. Luther's experience of justification expressed itself in a form of doctrine which essentially lived from presuppositions of older worldviews (original sin and Augustinianism, sacrifice and Paulinism, the medieval doctrine of the Lord's Supper). These presuppositions, together with their doctrinal framework, were obsolete, while the experience of justification—according to the rule: interpret no longer from the text but from life, in order to understand an author better than he understood himself—was to be interpreted in the light of those aspects that point to the future. The experience of justification includes the transition to the German religion of spirit, to modern Idealism, and to the new, religious-social-ethical ideal of a faith-formed, secular, social way of life. Simultaneously, Dilthey unmistakably poses the question of the relationship of Luther's worldview to Erasmus's 'religiously universalist theism'. It was Zwingli's combination of the two worldviews which had rendered the idea of the new secular-political way of life influential for all of Europe. Dilthey does not ask, however, why Zwingli and Calvin agreed with Luther's anti-Erasmian doctrine of election and his thesis of the unfree will. Already in 1892 Dilthey's congenial scholarly correspondent Graf P. Yorck von Wartenburg (1835–97) identified this paradox: allegedly obsolete aspects of the worldview of the experience of justification actually accurately express the latter and contain in themselves the dynamic of modernity. This insight anticipated Max Weber's analysis of the origins of capitalism from the spirit of predestinarian Protestantism (1906).

V. THE LIBERAL 'TRUE' AND THE CONFESSIONAL 'WHOLE' LUTHER

V.1. Theological Liberalism

Albrecht Ritschl (1822–89), *spiritus rector* of liberal Luther scholars such as Adolf von Harnack, Friedrich Kattenbusch, and Friedrich Loofs, supports his theology of reconciliation by critical appeals to Luther and specifically by detecting an entanglement of metaphysical and theological (based on revelation) insights regarding God (cf. *Geschichtliche Studien zur christlichen Lehre von Gott* [1865/8]; Ritschl 1895: 25–176) in Luther's exchange with Erasmus. This entanglement, a form of naturalism, burdens the whole of Lutheran theology. Ritschl's own doctrine of God contrasts this view, in anti-metaphysical fashion, with a principle designated as 'value judgement': God is love. Ritschl thus falls back on R. H. Lotze's practical concept of 'value' as subjective appropriateness of an objective phenomenon. In Ritschl's foundation of his dogmatic system this was to create a space for religion as the object of theological doctrine, which especially his doctrine of religious and moral calling (*Beruf*) as the genuine Christian practice of freedom was to fill. Ritschl's doctrine of calling was seen as a reception of Luther's concept of calling, determined by Calvinism, in the bourgeois context (the rise of bourgeois professions). This stands in tension with other interpretations of the practice of the freedom of faith, which Harnack and Holl set forth, with critical reference to Ritschl. Ritschl distinguishes between calling and the work of calling, a distinction which opens the goal of life religiously, beyond the specific goals of the work of calling themselves.

Adolf von Harnack's (1851–1930) wide-ranging influence on scholarship and educational policy effectively concentrates on the fundamental elements of Luther's theology and, even more, on his demonic personality. Harnack's thesis of the undogmatic or post-dogmatic 'essence of Christianity' is founded on the thesis that for Luther faith is the genuine *practice* of Christian freedom: the reformer liberated Christian freedom from the necessity of a theonomous foundation and redefined it as an ideal of Christian perfection.

Harnack analyses the perfection of Christian freedom by defining the present place of the calling as being inevitably conflict-laden—in distinction from older Liberalism and Culture-Protestantism. With Luther the history of dogma came to a halt. The reformer continued to exercise influence not through his doctrine but through his demonic personality, in which the 'power of the gospel' (Harnack 1901: 91) was realized through conflicts of universal historical significance. Through these conflicts, even catastrophes, the power of Christian freedom takes as its standard a Jesus-like self-sacrifice, not moral autonomy and integrity. For Harnack, as a scholar-politician active in government, Christian freedom and the individual personality—including the risk of failure—are the place where justification is to be understood (only religiously, not morally) as otherworldly certitude of the transition to God's kingdom. The appeal to Luther's otherworldly certitude, beyond the activities of political responsibility, here becomes, in the form of a Prussian-Lutheran bourgeois religion, a kind of ultimate assurance or 'over-assurance' against the risks of political failure—thus revealing an aporia of this liberal appropriation of Luther. The Luther-Renaissance will refine the task of a 'post-dogmatic' concept of Luther's religion and theology, by decisively focusing it in Karl Holl's thesis of Luther's religion of conscience, critically examining it (R. Hermann, H. J. Iwand, D. Bonhoeffer), and sharpening its aporia (E. Hirsch).

V.2. Confessionalism

Within the framework of the Neo-Lutheran revival, the theological faculty in Erlangen provided the university context for the emerging historical research on Luther although it was not connected with the Erlangen edition of Luther's works (1826–86, the first historical edition of its kind). Adolf von Harleß, called to a professor's position in 1833, formulated this theology, which was represented in Erlangen until the death of F. H. R. von Frank (1894). This programme intended to demonstrate the certitude of rebirth as an experience, as it was expressed by the Lutheran confessions, which were understood as the summary of the entire Scripture.

The results of Erlangen theology for the reception of Luther can be seen in two different ways, depending on how one relates its various parts. The biblical hermeneutics expounded by J. C. K. von Hofmann and his student Ch. E. Luthardt exhibits an understanding of the Bible as a document of *Heilsgeschichte*, which embraces the whole of church history; this idea provoked sharp debates regarding the understanding of Lutheran ecclesiology and exposed the difference between Luther and Lutheran Orthodoxy (cf. the polemical controversy surrounding Hofmann's doctrine of reconciliation in the 1850s). G. Thomasius and von Frank seek to maintain the Formula of Concord as an adequate doctrinal statement regarding the experience of rebirth: von Frank distinguishes an immanent (anthropology) and a transcendent (God) object of faith, while Thomasius contrasts Lutheran doctrine with Luther's 'inner movement through life'; this contrast stimulated historical Luther research, which was further developed by Theodosius Harnack. The contextual analysis of confessionalism in Erlangen and Leipzig (Ch. E. Luthardt, L. Ihmels) is indispensable for the prehistory of the contested political-theological topic of the 'two kingdoms (or spheres) doctrine' (1921).

Theodosius Harnack (1817–89), practical theologian in Dorpat (Tartu) and father of Adolf von Harnack, taught in Erlangen between 1853 and 1866. In his *Luthers Theologie* (two volumes, 1862, 1886) he moves the doctrine of reconciliation, which was controversial among his 'confessionalist' contemporaries, to the centre. He differentiates between the doctrines themselves and their historical development. The latter he pursues particularly in regard to Luther's doctrine of predestination. His positive estimation of *De servo arbitrio* is characteristic of his general position, compared to Ritschl's almost contemporaneous critical judgement, and it leads Harnack to emphasize the idea that God's wrath is incommensurable with his grace. In 1927 this specific point, along with a metaphysical Christology and doctrine of reconciliation, finally gained importance, as Harnack's presentation of Luther was re-edited by representatives of dialectical theology. The irreducibility of wrath and grace in Luther was now adopted, just as it was in the Luther Renaissance, but it was seen as paradigmatic of the dialectic of human existence before God and thus developed within an altered hermeneutical framework. Harnack rejected the viewpoint of the history of dogma of his son Adolf because of the conflict over the Apostles Creed.

VI. Opposing Voices: Roman Catholic Luther Interpretation, Nietzsche, Kierkegaard

Ranke's history of the Reformation and its national-Protestant adaptations aroused opposing voices in Roman Catholic accounts of the Reformation. The latter collect a reservoir of critical excerpts of sources and historical counter-stereotypes. Critical spirits like Friedrich Nietzsche (and earlier J. Burckhardt) turn to this reservoir to break the spell of Luther as an emblematic figure of bourgeois-religious, nation-state-related, and national-cultural emancipation. Their sharpest opponent is Kierkegaard although the latter also directs his critique of church and Christendom in his later works against certain aspects of Luther's theology and piety. A few decades later K. Holl and the Luther-Renaissance (E. Hirsch, D. Bonhoeffer) will use this criticism for a post-confessionalist, post-liberal understanding of Luther.

VI.1. The Roman-Catholic Picture Puzzle of the Historical Luther

In 1832–5 controversy broke out between two prominent Tübingen historians of church and dogma, the Catholic J. A. Möhler (1796–1838) and the Protestant F. C. Baur (1792–1860). The debate did not directly concern Luther but rather the distinguishing principle of Catholicism and Protestantism. It highlights the distinctive relationship of doctrine and ecclesiastical office, or doctrine and the internalization of the subjectivity of faith, as the basic confessional difference, historically exemplified at the time in the question whether Luther claimed the office of a reformer legitimately or not.

The Munich church historian Ignaz (von) Döllinger (1799–1890) altered his view of Luther strikingly in the course of his critique of Vatican I and its dogma of papal infallibility. His history of the Reformation (1846–8) (*Die Reformation, ihre inneren Entwicklungen und Wirkungen*) adopts Ranke's new historical standard but endeavours to demonstrate Luther's historical guilt for destroying the unity of western Christendom and dividing the church. It assembles Luther's disparaging remarks about the German nation, which contradict the idealizations of National-Protestantism, and problematizes his pre-Reformation development, especially the failure of monastic asceticism for him, attributing it to a character deficiency ('the inability to find comfort'). For the first time, a gap in the historical picture of Luther becomes visible—the problem of the sources for Luther's development up to 1518. While Döllinger thoroughly revised this view in the 1870s, Johannes Janssen's (1829–91) eight volumes of *Geschichte des deutschen Volkes seit dem Ausgang des Mittelalters* (1876–1894) contrast Luther's development with a flourishing Late Middle Ages, presented in culturally and socially varied terms. Against this background the Reformation appears as a period of degeneration or, at least, retardation and loss of future possibilities on the way to modernity. Beyond the confessional controversial stereotypes, Janssen's work provided a reservoir for interpreting Luther's demonic person as being critical of modernity. H. Grisar, S.J. (1845–1932) and H. S. Denifle, O.P. (1844–1905) further highlighted these tendencies in Luther's biography and the need to address the problem of the sources for the development of the early Luther. The editions of Luther's early lectures on Romans and Hebrews met this need.

VI.2. Friedrich Nietzsche

Friedrich Nietzsche (1844–1900) was among Janssen's readers. Under Janssen's influence, his picture puzzle of Luther—based on the sparsest knowledge of the sources— bemoaned Luther's obstruction of the influence of the Renaissance, his antipathy against asceticism, and the Reformation's deceleration of the inevitable disintegration of Christendom. At the same time, what Janssen regarded as Luther's lack of character and desire for domination Nietzsche interpreted as his supra-moral will for power, paired with moral mendacity and the courage to be sensual. His philosophy of language led Nietzsche to genuinely admire Luther's Bible translation for its rhythm and prose.

VI.3. Søren Kierkegaard

Kierkegaard's late criticism of contemporary Christendom and of Denmark's liberal-bourgeois Lutheranism, which was a state-church, took shape after 1847 while he was intensively reading Luther, especially his postils. To interpret them is one of the chief tasks of the study of the history of Luther's impact. Simultaneously, Kierkegaard formulated a fundamental criticism of particular doctrinal arguments of Luther by using central dialectical expressions borrowed from him. Thus, for Kierkegaard, Luther's '*pro me*' posits the demand for existential appropriation, but simultaneously it poses the question of the relationship of existential faith and the reconciliation accomplished in Christ. Kierkegaard exposed the problem of the understanding of grace and simultaneity with Jesus Christ in a way which remained significant until the twentieth century because the rediscovery and fresh appropriation of Luther's long-forgotten thesis *simul justus et peccator* gives an answer to this problem. His anti-quietistic transformational dialectic of law and gospel, gospel and law takes up topics of the early *theologia crucis*. This is, however, transformed into a 'late modern' ethical-religious subjectivity, bound with a provocative criticism of the loss of asceticism. Finally, with his refusal to regard contemporary Christendom as being capable of reform, Kierkegaard sensitizes anew to the differences between early Christianity, the Reformation, and the present age and to the question what it really means to call Luther a 'reformer'.

VII. Historicist Aporia and Competing Cultural Syntheses: Luther's Controversial Modernity

Ernst Troeltsch's (1865–1923) *Luther und die moderne Welt* (1908; Troeltsch 2001: 59–97) is closely related to his overall historical viewpoint in *Bedeutung des Protestantismus für die Entstehung der modern Welt* (1906/11, Troeltsch 2001: 199–316) and in the broader context of his *Soziallehren* (1912, Troeltsch 1994, planned in Troeltsch 2001: 9/1–2). These writings criticize Ranke, the thesis of Luther's specific German modernity, and Ritschl's and Wilhelm Herrmann's synthesis of the Reformation's ethos of vocation/calling with a liberal work ethic. The central theme of Troeltsch's interpretation of Luther is not the *initia Lutheri* but its necessary (*kausalgeschichtliche*) development and the evaluation of Protestantism's effect on 'the rise of modern culture, including its religious elements' (Troeltsch 2001: 314–15), in the context of a Weberian theory of modernity.

Troeltsch's *Soziallehren* give priority to the pre-institutional, cultic-religious form of the Christian ethos. How does the power of the otherworldly kingdom of God translate into a liturgical and ethical system 'of continuing ethical values'? The 'institutional blooming' as church, sect, or mysticism and its relationship to the social spheres of family, state, etc., finally pose the question: which ideal for society belongs to which church? Modernity is defined as the development from a culture of authority in the institutional church of a *corpus christianum*—still conceived as a unity, operating according to natural law, with its partly outward-looking, partly inward-looking asceticism—into a culture of autonomy and individualization of religion. In its actual centre, religious thinking, and feeling, this development has the effect of retardation, in the name of reformation, as well as (moderate and defensive) modernization. In this context, Troeltsch (like Dilthey) asks how Luther's religiosity can be understood in terms of modern religiosity.

In *Luther und die moderne Welt* Troeltsch finds, according to his own estimation, far clearer formulations. Proceeding from the question of conscience, Luther's religion is characterized in four points as: (1) a religion of faith and knowledge, critical of the sacraments; (2) religious individualism, which overcomes dogma and hierarchical authority; (3) a practice of faith based on an ethics of conviction, transforming eschatology into a doctrine of the necessary emergence of the ultimate destiny of the person according to the soul's religious and ethical character; and (4) openness towards the world in the form of an 'inner-worldly asceticism'. This finally was based—surprisingly—on Luther's unique concept of God: 'The essential relationship of God and creature is originally an internal unity of the living element of divine grace, which exalts the finite creature to itself and sanctifies it for itself, not arbitrarily but essentially, not super-naturally but with human nature essentially destined for its own self-realization' (Troeltsch 2001: 79). The idea of an ethical unity of will and life with God—an idea of absoluteness *avant la lettre*—makes the modern historical-theological idea of development possible. Troeltsch argues that Luther's Christology of condescension (*Luther und die moderne Welt*, 1908: 90–1) prepared the way for this even though it was contaminated by mythical (original state of humanity and the fall) and supernatural (God's wrath) content as well as an authoritarian Biblicism. In Luther's concept of the church his rational, religious-idealistic individualism and his authoritative-dogmatic concept of doctrine remained in tension, thus pointing to the Neo-Protestant future.

VIII. SEARCHING FOR ANSWERS: THE LUTHER RENAISSANCE

1. The decisive initiator of the Luther Renaissance, Berlin church historian Karl Holl (1866–1926), was the first to focus on Luther's lectures on Romans (1515/16). Holl's idea of Luther's 'religion of conscience' explained Luther's experience of justification in a manner that turns theology into a doctrine of the dialectics of existence. This replaced, at least in principle, the previously dominant foundational understanding of justification as the basis of a *Weltanschauung* (Dilthey) or a synthetic value judgement (Ritschl). One example of the attempt to define a new doctrinal form of Luther's thinking by demarcating it from others is Holl's thesis regarding the status of God's verdict of justification: the young Luther did not regard it as a Christologically 'synthetic' but as a theologically 'analytic' verdict because it acknowledges the faith of the sinner as righteousness in the moment of temptation, on the basis of the eternal fulfilment which God guarantees. If God's eternal judgement determines the 'justification from above', the 'justification from below' unfolds in terms of a dialectic of conscience: faith experiences stages of ethical-religious conflicts of conscience, which, under the impact of

God's effective predestination and the aporia of God's holy, loving will alongside his wrath against unexplainable evil, can lead to the final conflict: the resistance against or the surrender unto divine rejection (*resignatio ad infernum*). In the conflict engendered by election, the conscience, which continues to exist but surrenders its right to exist, recognizes God as God and experiences the full paradox of the justification of the godless, the 'eternal moment'. The foundation of this two-sided—theocentric and existential—analysis of justification is also recognizable in the other representations of the Luther Renaissance; indeed, all its adherents try to articulate them as consistently as possible. Holl's view became particularly influential in its radical shape under the influence of the German defeat of 1918. According to Holl, Luther's religion of conscience contains the power of sacrificial love and the genuine principle of the community as each person takes the other's place, combining the doctrines of *Stellvertretung* [vicarious representative action] and the priesthood of all baptized believers. On this basis the *Volkskirche* and the national culture could be constructed anew after 1918. The institutions of society, based upon the *Volk* as 'order of creation', communicates the experience of justification as the power of self-sacrifice and *Stellvertretung*. The centre of this ethic of conscience is the invisible community of conscience derived from 'Luther's concept of the church', the kingdom of God. After 1918 this (allegedly) Lutheran social type of God's kingdom as a 'community of conscience' was contrasted confessionally with the (supposedly) Anglo-Saxon social type of God's kingdom as *empire*. The attempt to construct a normative theory of culture based on Luther's historical religion of conscience and the aporia of this attempt make Holl a contemporary of Troeltsch and Weber.

2. The Luther Renaissance is a theological, ecclesial, and cultural reform movement between 1910 and 1935, which, according to its self-understanding as well as its impact, can be understood as a second renewal movement in Protestantism after 1918 alongside 'dialectical theology' (Assel 1994). In Germany it included, alongside Holl, Carl Stange (1870–1959), Emanuel Hirsch (1888–1972), Paul Althaus (1888–1966), Rudolf Hermann (1887–1962), Georg Wehrung (1880–1959), Hans Joachim Iwand (1899–1960), and Dietrich Bonhoeffer (1906–45). The international importance becomes evident by well-known theologians from Northern Europe, Gustaf Aulén (1879–1977), Anders Nygren (1890–1978), Torsten Bohlin (1889–1950), Eduard Geismar (1871–1939), and Gustaf Wingren (1910–2000). The Luther Renaissance distinguished itself from Liberalism, the *Religionsgeschichtliche Schule*, and 'dialectical theology' in terms of philosophy of religion, theories of the *Volkskirche*, and political theory. It intended to make clear the foundational status of the experience of justification in terms of the philosophy of religion. Contemporary neo-idealistic and neo-Kantian philosophies of religion set the horizon for interpreting justification as a foundational as well as orientational religious experience in the 'crisis of modernity' after 1918. This took place in different ways, with increasingly contradictory results. After 1933 the Luther Renaissance disintegrated because of contradictory theological and ecclesial positions. It lost its international nature by the end of the 1930s, due to the divergent interpretation of the role of Lutheran ecumenical relationships for the churches under National Socialism.

3. Emanuel Hirsch was, as Holl's disciple, the representative of a Luther Renaissance transformed into a specific political theology. He explicated justification as 'an experience of certitude' in Fichte's, and later Kierkegaard's, framework. According to Hirsch, historical-political subjectivity exists in the dialectic of absoluteness and facticity and should be formulated in the context of a doctrine of intersubjectivity which integrated 'völkische', ethical-religious, and Christian dimensions. Hirsch's political theology took up Holl's thesis that Luther's concept of the church and his ideal of society were to be defined by the community of conscience shaped by its consciousness of being an instrument of God and the idea of *Stellvertretung*. As an example of the personalistic social ontology of his times, Hirsch's thinking conceptualized social-political intersubjectivity as conflictual alienation. After 1926 he interpreted this basic situation of historical-political subjects before God as being under the *law*. He radicalized his views between 1926 and 1931 (Hirsch edited Luther's lectures on Hebrews, 1929) into a theology of the law, which postulates the necessity of the individual's collapse of subjectivity (that is, the co-origin of creation and sin) as the precondition of the transformation of existence by the gospel (the experience of justification).

Hirsch's heterodoxy, according to which the historical 'hour of National Socialism' is to be understood as a divine–historical call to decide to sacrifice oneself (e.g. the 'Volksnomos' as 'hidden sovereign', the 'Führer' as 'revealed sovereign'), claimed to enrich Holl's programme with a political-theological concept of the law and a new Christology. In this sense, he saw himself as a legitimate heir of Luther (Hirsch 1933, 1954/89, 1954). In fact, however, he transformed the topics of 'Volk', sacrifice, and freedom vs bondage and thus arrived at strongly modified interpretations of law and gospel, conscience and Word.

4. Rudolf Hermann comes from the milieu of so-called 'positive theology'. Within the context of his critical engagement with Schleiermacher's theory of piety and Ernst Cassirer's theory of symbolic forms, he develops his concept of the experience of justification from the interplay of the rhetoric of *promissio* and *assertio* and the dialectic of the temporal-individual 'being a person in faith'. This leads to his chief work, *Luthers These 'Gerecht und Sünder zugleich'* (1930/60). Its centre is a dialogical and historical-eschatological concept of the person of the believer, determined *simultaneously* by God's promise of righteousness and the reality of human sinfulness. The person of the believer is understood as being-in-transition, in two related regards (e.g. *homo carnalis/homo spiritualis*) and related to their symbolic forms of expression (e.g. the various forms of Christian prayer). The doctrine of justification here has the logic of a conversation between God and human beings (instead of a justification from above and from below). This is the non-paradoxical sense of the often paradoxical distinctions attributed to the expression *simul iustus et peccator*. Similar to the concurrent analysis of Martin Heidegger, Hermann showed how this formula opens the sources of the self (again) and expresses a life of freedom in communion with God, determined by temporality and language. Believers understand themselves, their actions, and therein their bondage *in the present* precisely *in* their moral and political autonomy, as the location of the *adventus* of the liberation in faith. In turn, the promise of liberating autonomy at

the location of the liberated conscience entails the individualization of life-time within individual biography and communitarian practices. Hermann's political ethics, though not democratic, did not fall captive to the totalitarian streamlining ('*Gleichschaltung*') of Nazi ideology but confronted it critically. He supported the argument of his central thesis particularly with linguistic-theological reflections of Luther's *Anti-Latomus* (1521) on the truth and reality of the biblical term 'justification' (metaphor), alongside the lectures on Romans (1515/16) discovered in 1908.

5. Whereas Hermann interpreted the *Anti-Latomus*, Hans Joachim Iwand concentrated on Luther's debate with Erasmus (and his scepticism), especially in *De servo arbitrio*. The title of Iwand's chief work, *Glaubensgerechtigkeit nach Luthers Lehre*, contains the concept 'doctrine' (already formulated in 1939 in *Rechtfertigungslehre und Christusglaube*). Luther's *assertions* are dialectical doctrinal statements, i.e. not direct, psychologically experienced statements, but statements which open up experience with experiences, thus, an experience of the second order hidden under its opposite: the statement on the unfree will does not articulate experiences of liberation directly, i.e. psychologically. Rather, on the basis of reconciliation, which the Christian believer confesses in regard to the saving work of Jesus on the cross, it acknowledges its own bondage, and, hidden in it, its own freedom, which is understood strictly as a liberation from bondage. Faith in liberation, hidden in its opposite, bondage, and moral faith in autonomous freedom are open to each other, precisely because they are foreign to each other (Iwand 1936, 1941/91). Eventually, the *assertions* of the doctrine of justification have the first commandment as their subject, and the first commandment's claim to life is verified in Jesus Christ, but only indirectly, hidden in the cross. The justification of the sinner before God, which reaches its goal in the confession, 'I am godless', correlates with this indirect verification of God in the Crucified One. In this way Iwand's correlative concept of righteousness uses Holl's dialectic of conscience and Hermann's thesis of the '*simul*', interpreting them through the fundamental distinction of law and gospel and the *unity* of God's Word, being directed explicitly against Hirsch's political theology of the law. Despite many points of contact, Iwand did not simply endorse Karl Barth's 'theology of the Word of God' and its criticism of the political theology of the law. He continually worked on Luther's *theologia crucis* as a critical, political-ethical practice of life and on the task of the publicly, politically proclaimed law. A central question was how the liberation conveyed through the gospel can have an impact on Germany's post-war society. Iwand's support for a new order of the Evangelical Churches in Germany (EKD), built on a concept of confession of faith based not on confessional-legal statutes but on the contemporary relevance of confessional traditions, and his striving for political reconciliation with Eastern Europe prior to the famous EKD memorandum on this topic (1965) were results of his theology of justification and the cross.

6. A programme for the reform of the *Volkskirche* and of society stood at the beginning of the Luther Renaissance. It was particularly Dietrich Bonhoeffer (Bethge 2000) who produced a systematic theory of the church and a political ethics. Bonhoeffer's dissertation *Sanctorum communio* (1926, the year of Holl's death) is 'a dogmatic investigation of the sociology of the church' (Bonhoeffer 1986; Green 1999), which takes up

and develops Holl's thesis regarding Luther's concept of the church as a fellowship of *Stellvertretung*, combined with Troeltsch's demand for a sociological clarification of the idea of modernity in Lutheran social teaching.

Bonhoeffer regards the spiritual community, which Holl had in mind with his reform programme for the life of the *Volk*, as an essential mark of the *church*. He develops it in social-philosophical terms on the basis of the 'I-Thou' encounter (in which ethical claims construct a person's identity) and in dogmatic terms through the distinction of sin and revelation as objective spirit and as Holy Spirit.

Dependent on the social philosophy of Ferdinand Tönnies and influenced by the philosophy of religion of Hegelianism, this concept of the church as a 'collective person' allows the realization of the vision of 'Christ existing as community'. In this way, the concept of person has both a dialogical and an eschatological character, though in a social-ontological framework. Bonhoeffer's theory of the church precipitates for the life of society consequences in the concept of personal communities, in which the realities of *Stellvertretung* are ethically recognizable when they are formulated as God's concrete commands. A few decades later, Gerhard Ebeling (who was Bonhoeffer's student for a while) recognized this aspect of Bonhoeffer's theology as an original interpretation of Luther.

References

Assel, Heinrich (1994). *Der andere Aufbruch. Die Lutherrenaissance—Ursprünge, Aporien und Wege: Karl Holl, Emanuel Hirsch, Rudolf Hermann (1910–1935)*. Göttingen: Vandenhoeck & Ruprecht.

Bethge, Eberhard (2000). *Dietrich Bonhoeffer: A Biography*, trans. Eric Mosbacher et al. Minneapolis: Fortress.

Bonhoeffer, Dietrich (1986). *Sanctorum Communio. Eine dogmatische Untersuchung zur Soziologie der Kirche*. In Joachim von Soosten (ed.), *Dietrich Bonhoeffers Werke 1*. Munich Kaiser. English translation: *Sanctorum Communio: A Theological Study of the Sociology of the Church*, trans. Reinhard Kraus and Nancy Lukens. Minneapolis: Fortress, 1998.

Bornkamm, Heinrich (1970). *Luther im Spiegel der deutschen Geistesgeschichte: Mit ausgewählten Texten von Lessing bis zur Gegenwart*. Göttingen: Vandenhoeck & Ruprecht.

Feuerbach, Ludwig (1982). *Gesammelte Werke*, ed. Werner Schuffenhauer. Berlin: Akademie-Verlag.

—— (1846). *Sämtliche Werke*. Leipzig: Wigand.

Green, Clifford J. (1999). *Bonhoeffer: A Theology of Sociality*. Grand Rapids: Eerdmans.

Hamann, J. G. (1955). *Briefwechsel*, ed. W. Ziesmer and A. Henkel. Wiesbaden: Insel.

Harnack, Adolf von (1901). *Das Wesen des Christentums: Sechzehn Vorlesungen vor Studierenden aller Facultäten im Wintersemester 1899/1900 an der Universität Berlin gehalten*. Leipzig: Reichert.

Hegel, G. W. F. ([1807] 1980). 'Phänomenologie des Geistes', in W. Bonsiepen and R. Heede (eds), *Gesammelte Werke*, Bd. 9. Hamburg.

—— (1969–71). *Werke in 20 Bänden. Auf der Grundlage der Werke von 1832 bis 1845*, ed. von E. Moldenhauer and K. M. Michel. Frankfurt/M.: Suhrkamp, 601–20.

Herder, J. G. (1985). *Werke in zehn Bänden*, ed. J. Brummack and M. Bollacher. Frankfurt am Main: Klassiker-Verlag.

Herder, J. G., with Hirsch, I., Ranke, T. (1892). *Sämmtliche Werke*, ed. B. Suphan. Berlin: Weidman.

Hermann, Rudolf (1930/60). *Luthers These, 'Gerecht und Sünder zugleich'.* Gütersloh: Bertelsmann; 2nd edn, Darmstadt: Wissenschaftliche Buchgesellschaft.

Hirsch, Emanuel (1933). 'Vom verborgenen Suverän'. *Glaube und Volk* 2: 4–13.

—— (1954). *Lutherstudien*, 2 vols. Gütersloh: Bertelsmann.

—— (1954/89). *Christliche Rechenschaft*, vols I–II, ed. Hayo Gerdes and Hans Hirsch. Tübingen: Katzmann.

Holl, Karl (1921). *Gesammelte Aufsätze zur Kirchengeschichte*, ed. I. Luther, (Tübingen; 2nd and 3rd edn 1923; 7th edn 1948).

Iwand, Hans-Joachim (1941/91). *Glaubensgerechtigkeit: Lutherstudien*, ed. Gerhard Sauter. Munich: Kaiser.

—— (1930). *Rechtfertigungslehre und Christusglaube. Eine Untersuchung zur Systematik der Rechtfertigungslehre Luthers in ihren Anfängen.* Leipzig: Hinrichs.

Marx, Karl and Friedrich Engels (1961–83). *Werke*, ed. Manfred Kliem et al. Berlin: Dietz.

Novalis (2008). *Gesammelte Werke*, ed. H. J. Balmes. Frankfurt: M. Fischer.

Ranke, Ludwig (1925). *Deutsche Geschichte im Zeitalter der Reformation*, ed. Paul Joachimsen, 6 vols. Munich: Drei-Masken-Verlag.

—— (1973). *Frühe Schriften, Aus Werk und Nachlaß*, ed. W. P. Fuchs. Munich: Oldenbourg.

Ritschl, Albrecht (1893, 1896). *Gesammelte Aufsätze*, ed. Otto Ritschl, 2 vols. Tübingen: Mohr/Siebeck.

Schelling, F. W. J. (1860). *Sämmtliche Werke*, ed. K. F. A. Schelling. Stuttgart and Augsburg: Cotta.

Schleiermacher, F. (1980) 'Der christliche Glaube nach den Grundsätzen der evangelischen Kirche im Zusammenhang dargestellt (1821/22)', in H. Peiter (ed.), *Kritische Gesamtausgabe* I, 7.1. Berlin/New York: de Gruyter.

Schlegel, Friedrich von (1846). *Sämmtliche Werke.* Vienna: Klang.

Schuffenhauer, Werner and Klaus-Michael Steiner (1983). *Martin Luther in der deutschen bürgerlichen Philosophie 1517–1845: Eine Textsammlung.* Berlin: Akademie-Verlag.

Treitschke, Heinrich von (1929). *Aufsätze, Reden und Briefe*, ed. K. M. Schiller. Meersburg: Hendel.

Troeltsch, Ernst (1994). *Die Soziallehren der christlichen Kirchen und Gruppen* (1912) (*Gesammelte Schriften I*), rpt. Tübingen: Mohr/Siebeck.

—— (2001). *Kritische Gesamtausgabe*, ed. Trutz Rendtorff and Stefan Pautler. Berlin: de Gruyter.

CHAPTER 42

....

MARXIST EVALUATIONS OF
LUTHER'S THOUGHT

....

THOMAS A. BRADY, JR.

I. Introduction: Martin Luther in Marxist Thought

MARXIST ideas on Martin Luther's person, deeds, and ideas began with the Young Hegelians in the years following Hegel's death in 1831. They developed in four phases, each of which produced its image of the reformer:

(1) Luther as intellectual/spiritual revolutionary—from Hegel's death (1831) to the Revolution of 1848;
(2) Luther as class traitor to the common people—from 1850 to the Great War;
(3) Luther as reactionary antagonist to Thomas Müntzer—the interwar era; and
(4) Luther as forerunner of a democratic German culture—German Democratic Republic (GDR), 1945–89.

Today, by contrast, Marxist thought evinces little interest in Martin Luther.[1]

II. Karl Marx's Luther

Young Karl Marx (1818–83) knew Luther from the Young Hegelians, radical philosophers who attacked bourgeois politics and religion. In his introduction to the *Critique of Hegel's Philosophy of Right* (1843), Marx adopted Ludwig Feuerbach's (1809–72)

---

[1] See the afterword to this contribution. My thanks go to Katherine G. Brady for her critical eye and her suggestions.

argument that religion is 'an *inverted consciousness*...the *fantastic realization* of the human essence since the *human essence* has not [yet] acquired any true reality' (Marx 1970: 132). To relieve the world present and future from its past dependence on religion, 'the criticism of Heaven' must be brought down to 'the criticism of Earth' (Marx 1970: 132). In Germany this meant beginning with Martin Luther. 'Germany's revolutionary past', Marx wrote, 'is precisely theoretical, it is the Reformation. As at that time it was a monk, so now it is the philosopher [Feuerbach? Marx himself?] in whose brain the revolution begins' (Marx 1970: 137–8). Whereas Protestantism transformed German laymen into priests, he added, 'the philosophical transformation of priestly Germans into men will emancipate the *people*'. Marx contributed two essential points to what became the official narrative of Marxist history: first, Luther liberated the Germans from the feudal, reactionary Catholic church; second, Luther bound men to the power of state and society.

III. Luther as Class Traitor—Engels and Kautsky

Friedrich Engels (1820–95), Marx's collaborator, created the classic Marxist image of Luther as a class traitor who led the movement against Rome and then betrayed the emerging bourgeoisie and the common people in Germany. Thereby Engels aimed to console disheartened German revolutionaries after the failed insurrection of 1848 by defining a German revolutionary heritage. Plundering his facts entirely from predecessors, Engels argued that during the Peasants' War of 1525, Luther had betrayed his spiritual children and delivered them up for slaughter by the German princes' armies. The genuine revolutionary hero was not Luther but Thomas Müntzer (d. 1525), the radical priest who had actually organized and led armed rebels, given them a revolutionary vision rooted in their own experience of oppression, and led them in battle at the cost of his own life.

Engels cast the Reformation and the Peasants' War as Europe's earliest bourgeois revolution, which purposed an overthrow of the political order of German and European feudal society, beginning with its capstone, the Roman Catholic church. The revolution was doomed by not Luther's treachery but a German economic development too feeble to launch the Germans on the path of capitalist development within a national state comparable to those of France and England. Germany's revolutionary inadequacy around 1500 meant that the possibility of any connection between the German Reformation and Peasants' War and modern revolution depended on the figure not of Luther but of Thomas Müntzer. All subsequent efforts to connect Reformation and Peasants' War to modern socialist revolutions depended on arguments for his utopian theology as an anticipatory vision.

Engels created much of the modern vocabulary of anti-Luther invective: 'princes' lackey', 'cowardly parasite of the absolute monarch', 'betrayer of the peasants' (Lehmann 2004a: 501). Yet he also saw the flaw in casting the German Peasants' War as a prologue to socialist revolution. 'The revolution of 1525 was a local German affair', he judged, whereas 'the revolution of 1848 was...one phase of a great European movement', in which the main theatres were 'not confined to the narrow limits of one individual country, nor even to the limits of one-quarter of the globe...This is why the revolution of 1848–50 could not end in the way that the revolution of 1525 ended' (Engels 1956: 157). The future does not recapitulate, it overcomes the past. German Marxists held to this idea until European communism came to its end.

Karl Kautsky (1854–1938), Engels' principal disciple, fixed Marxism's canonical interpretation of Martin Luther and the Reformation. In his *Forerunners of Modern Socialism* (1921 [1895]) Kautsky allotted but a few short passages to Luther, 'the man who was alleged to have sent sparks into the power keg, from which erupted the monstrous firestorm', but who in truth owed his place at the centre of the movement 'not to superior insight and sharp intelligence, for on this score many of his contemporaries were ahead of him' (Kautsky 1921: 257). The entire conflict began as merely 'a monkish quarrel' about money more than about ideas, and it escalated only because of papal intervention and pressure exerted on Luther by both friends and foes. At Worms in 1521 Luther defied the emperor's order to recant only because 'submission posed to him a greater threat than resistance did'. While he mocked Luther's cowardice, Kautsky nonetheless acknowledged the reformer's 'rare gift...of simultaneously moving the masses and impressing the ruling classes' (Kautsky 1921: 259–61).

In Kautsky's views as in Engels', Luther's Reformation altered merely the manner, not the fact, of the Germans' bondage to the feudal order. Not Luther but Thomas Müntzer stood at 'the center of the entire communist movement in Germany...in the first years of the Reformation' (Kautsky 1921: 276). Kautsky, who despised all living forms of Christianity, compressed the Reformation into a prologue to the Peasants' War, of which Luther was a mere herald. The reformer's subsequent apotheosis as a liberator from the Middle Ages was but a cunning fraud, cunning because it so long held centre stage, fraudulent because it obscured the true harbinger of the socialist future—Thomas Müntzer's utopian communism.

Kautsky's portrait of Luther as a failure became a set piece of German Marxist historiography. The journalist Franz Mehring (1846–1919) summed up this view: Luther 'declared every form of resistance, even to rulers godless and without conscience, to be sins against God. He interpreted literally demands for servile obedience he found in the New Testament' (Bornkamm 1970: 369, from Mehring 1960–7: 5.250–1). Harsh words, but worse was said of Luther by ordinary socialists, among whom Luther became the paragon of a class traitor.

Non-German socialists did not always adopt the Engels–Kautsky picture of Luther. The French socialist Jean Jaurès (1859–1914) 'detected the germ of socialist ideas at every point in the history of German idealism, beginning with Martin Luther. The idea of Christian equality paved the way for that of civic equality; fighting against the tyranny of Rome, Luther taught his countrymen to fight tyranny of every kind' (Kołakowski 1978: 2.133). Many European socialists agreed that Luther had fought on the side of human progress. Others, notably the communists, agreed with the Irishman who called Luther 'the pampered son of an iron-foundry owner' and 'a pacifist-Fascist fraud' (quoted by Roy 1961: 38, from a brother of the Irish writer Liam O'Flaherty).

IV. MARXISM, REFORMATION, AND REVOLUTION—ERNST BLOCH AND LEO KOFLER

The coming of the Great War fractured European Marxism, and the Russian Revolution of 1917 broke it further into factions for or against Lenin's version of Marxism. In the 1920s emerged in Central and Western Europe the movement called 'Western Marxism', the adherents of which rejected the Leninist and later the Stalinist orthodoxy. Unable to restore the pre-1914 coordination between Marxist theory and socialist practice, it devoted its main energies to exploring theory, philosophy, and bourgeois culture. With several significant exceptions Western Marxism had no use for Martin Luther.

The outstanding exception to Western Marxist indifference was the German philosopher Ernst Bloch (1885–1977), who turned from present revolutions to explore Jewish and Christian intimations of messianic communism and their implications for a future utopia conceived not as 'nowhere' but as 'not yet'. Bloch's central work, *The Principle of Hope*, which he composed in the United States, aimed to provide a comprehensive account of human propensities and premonitions of a future improved both technologically and socially and rid of all exploitation of humanity by humanity. He searched the past for clues to the future.

Bloch confronted Luther in his second book, *Thomas Münzer als Theologe der Revolution* (1921), in which his searching of the Reformation for signs of a revolutionary future reflected both the victorious Russian and the defeated German revolutions of 1917–18 (the following quotations are collected by Kruttschnitt 1993: 235–9). Unlike Engels and Kautsky, Bloch did not dismiss theology out of hand, and, like Marx, he retained a certain admiration for the early Martin Luther. In the Peasants' War, however, Bloch's Luther becomes the dark rival to Münzer the child of light, in whom he finds the final and greatest figure of the heretical Christian messianism that descended from the proletarian communism of the early Christians. Luther became an 'ideologue of the tyrants', who greeted the rebels with a 'lukewarm position of compromise' that soon degenerated into 'a labored renegadism'. Münzer and Luther together enacted a dialectical confrontation of two forces, revolutionary engagement in the name of the future vs. treacherous compromise with the powers that be.

Bloch's juxtaposition of Luther and Münzer reflects his dialectical concept of history, which arose less from social development and class struggle than from recurring conflicts between belief in the human future and compromise with the human present. At once psychological, philosophical, moral, and ultimately philosophical-theological, the conflicts recapitulated the past in ways that altered present understanding of the future but did not change the perennial hope for human freedom. For Bloch, the wars and revolutions of 1914–19 disempowered the claims of evolutionary historicism and encouraged an apocalypticism in which dreams once broken—Reformation and Peasants' War—could reappear transfigured as the future's face. 'In Germany the class of the princes and the army, to which Luther surrendered all the power of his demonic nature and all the perversion of his paradoxical concept of freedom and faith, has now at last collapsed', and 'the final earthly revolution is being born' (Bloch 1963: 126).

Ernst Bloch's utopian prophecy did not displace the Engels–Kautsky picture of Luther the class traitor. His major contribution was to recast the drama of the German Reformation. While Luther retained, of course, his role as a renegade from the revolution, his position derived less from personal ambition than from his theology. And if Müntzer were to be taken as a plausible rival of and (ultimately) victor over his rival, his ideas, too, must be recognized as a Christian theology comparable to Luther's. Günter Vogler, today's foremost interpreter of Müntzer, puts this point in the clearest possible way: 'Müntzer, whose theological ideas led to revolutionary action, thus united theology and revolution. He was *the* theologian of the Revolution' (Vogler 2003: 174). To Ernst Bloch is owed this recovery of the common discourse of Reformation and Peasants' War, which he cast in the still intelligible language of Judaeo-Christian messianic theology.

The Western Marxists turned away from both Kautsky's evolutionary materialism and Lenin's dictatorship of the proletariat to find answers to the most pressing question— why was there no revolution in Western Europe? Their vision was less German than European, and if they noticed Martin Luther at all, they acknowledged his Reformation's basis in the German masses as the forerunner of the German nation and its status as a turning point in Western civilization. 'Luther and the Reformation', wrote the Italian Communist Antonio Gramsci (1897–1937), 'stand at the beginning of all modern philosophy and civilization' (Gramsci 1994: 1.365). The Viennese Marxist Franz Borkenau (1900–57), by contrast, held that 'by his rejection of everything earthly as "carnal", Luther conceives state and society as simply products of sin...so that the religiously based harmony of the Catholic worldview is rent asunder and the state is relegated to evil and justified by religion' (Borkenau 1971: 104–5). Marxist or not, in this kind of intellectual history there was no place at all for a Thomas Müntzer.

One Western Marxist did take a lesson from Luther and his Reformation. Leo Kofler (1907–95), born to a Jewish family in eastern Galicia, was reared in Vienna, whence he fled in 1938 to Basel. There he drafted his early masterpiece, *On the History of Bourgeois Society: An Explanatory Interpretation of the Modern Age* (1948). Driven by the need to know why bourgeois culture had migrated from humanistic rationalism to irrationalism and fascism, Kofler turned from the rigid economism of Engels and Kautsky to 'the best representatives of bourgeois learning', Max Weber (1864–1920) and Ernst Troeltsch (1865–1923). It hardly surprises, therefore, that Kofler addressed the subject of religious history, which he found both important and puzzling. In the advanced cities of Renaissance Italy, he discovered, scepticism and free thought flourished among the educated classes, while the common people remained 'caught in a strict religiosity'. Discovery of this gulf diminished, of course, the possibility of a general Christian reform à la Luther because the still medieval conservatism behind his apparent radicalism fitted his own social milieu very well. 'Lutheranism', Kofler wrote, 'is nothing more—something few historians have realized—than a movement for compromise, which initially arose as an alliance with popular forces and their sectarianism. This movement corresponded to the unripe character of the social relations that mediated between feudalism and humanism.' This outcome Kofler named 'the Lutheran compromise' (Kofler 1971: 13, 203–4, 274–5).

Kofler found nothing unexpected in Germany's failure to become the vanguard of bourgeois development in Europe, and he saw in Müntzer's coupling of theology and revolution but a noble dream. Luther was a man of his time; Müntzer was a man of no time before the end of time. Even Troeltsch, whom Kofler honoured as 'among the most dialectically literate, deep-thinking, and clear-sighted of the bourgeois historians, could not master the chaotic picture of the German Reformation', in which he was forced to recognize 'a most complicated subject' (Kofler 1971: 280).

It is hardly surprising that Kofler found a favourable milieu neither in the German Democratic Republic, where he was attacked as a 'Trotskyist' and stripped of his history professorship at Halle, nor among the well-travelled stars of Western Marxism. Leo Kofler was and remains the 'invisible man' of Marxist historical writing.

V. Martin Luther from Class Traitor to German Forefather

Of the immediate post-war Marxist treatments of the German Reformation, easily the most important came from the Soviet historian M. M. Smirin (1895–1975), whose book of 1947 (German translation 1952) set a stamp of approval on Engels' highly negative judgement of Martin Luther even before the German Democratic Republic was founded (1949) (Bräuer 1983: 3). Martin Luther entered the new republic's public life in the hateful guise of a class traitor; eleven years later began his transformation into 'one of the greatest sons of the German people' (Honecker 1980: 11). With these words Erich Honecker, chairman of the State Council of the GDR, approved a joint state–church committee to prepare the official celebration on 10 November 1983 of Martin Luther's five-hundredth birthday. Luther's rehabilitation continued apace until the GDR dissolved itself in October 1990.

In the entire world of post-1945 Marxism, only in the German communist state did conditions exist for a Marxist treatment of Luther. The Cold War rivalry between the two German states practically assured that, once the state and the ruling party of the GDR decided to compete for the mantle of progressive German national history, Martin Luther and his Reformation would not be left mouldering in the political and historical shadows. Fortunately, Engels had opened a door to revising his condemnation of Luther when he linked Reformation *and* Peasants' War as the earliest actions of a rising German bourgeoisie. The hour for revision struck in 1960, when the Leipzig historian Max Steinmetz (1912–90) called Reformation *and* Peasants' War 'the most significant revolutionary mass movement of the German people until the November Revolution of 1918' (Steinmetz 1979: 9). By then the process of revision was well underway, marked by official observances of anniversaries: Reformation (1967), Peasants' War (1975), and Luther's five-hundredth birthday (1983). Each contributed to an understanding of German history that emphasized continuity and development rather than rupture and revolution.

In 1960 Steinmetz revamped Engels' story: a rising line of class conflict from the Hussites to Luther, a peak in the mid-1520s, and a decline from 1531 to 1536 ending with 'the final victory of the Princes' Reformation' (Steinmetz 1979: 9–10). He also called for a methodologically up-to-date picture of the economic and social structures and forces that shaped Reformation and Peasants' War as an early bourgeois revolution. A practical order of collaboration was worked out. The Marxist historians concentrated on social history, the church historians on Luther studies. In time the division of labour became more flexible and the sense of opposition softened. Gerhard Zschäbitz (1920–70), a Steinmetz student who supplied the official biography of Luther for the Reformation jubilee of 1967, respected the original division of labour. Yet he approached the reformer as a man of his time, who had not only attacked abuses and teachings within the church, but had also condemned more general social abuses and economic oppression. Placed in historical context, Zschäbitz concluded, Luther's achievement was simply enormous.

Under these conditions the rehabilitation of Luther in the GDR moved rapidly forward. In 1971 the project gained formal approval from the ruling party's congress, which placed 'the refurbishment of the cultural heritage' on the agenda for the struggle to claim the GDR's place as 'the real Germany' (cited by Laube 1983: 137 from a speech given 27 January 1981 by Bishop Albrecht Schönherr (1911–2009), president of the Association of Protestant Churches in the GDR)—democratic, peace-loving, and modern. The first general history of Reformation and Peasants' War as an early bourgeois revolution appeared in 1974 (Laube et al. 1974); three years later the Protestant churches proposed to host the International Luther Congress in 1983, Luther's five-hundredth birthday; and in 1980 the state assumed sponsorship of a celebration (*Verehrung*) of Martin Luther and his 'humanistic legacy' to the German Democratic Republic. It did so, one official stated, based on the broad conviction 'that Martin Luther and his fellow rebels belong together in the ranks of those great figures who have greatly influenced the course of the history of our people and of humanity, and from whom issued significant impulses for the progress of history' (Götting 1982: 8). State and party, churches and theologians, and the historians united to prepare the celebrations of the jubilee. Their peak came in the International Luther Congress that assembled at Erfurt on 14–20 August 1983.

The cultural shift that lay behind Luther's rehabilitation in his own land could be read from the biography Gerhard Brendler (1932–) composed for the jubilee. Whereas Zschäbitz had limited his volume of 1967 to Luther's biography, Brendler's subtitle—*Theology and Revolution*—announced a more ambitious goal (Brendler 1983, 1991). It elicited strong approval from leading Luther scholars. The American Scott Hendrix judged it a 'sympathetic and open-minded appreciation of Luther' despite the skimpy treatment of the late medieval background and Luther's later years (Hendrix 1992: 601–2). Today many historians of the German Reformation would agree with Brendler's judgement: 'Both the Reformation from above and that from below are elements of the early bourgeois revolution... The Luther–Müntzer opposition was thus not a trivial friend–foe relationship but a genuinely historical dialectic' (Brendler 1983: 322). These words echoed the views of Ernst Bloch, who, once denounced in the GDR for 'ideological subversion' and now rehabilitated as an advocate of 'humanism', lay six years in his grave.

At the end of the GDR in 1990, what one observer has called 'graveyard silence' descended over the concept of Reformation and Peasants' War as an early bourgeois revolution (Lehmann 2004b). Still, the rehabilitation of Martin Luther in the GDR had raised the 'princes' lackey' and 'class traitor' to a complex figure on which most parties could agree: Martin Luther was a mighty but deeply flawed figure, partly a humanistic liberator of the human spirit and partly a reactionary enemy of the common people (and, not incidentally, the Jews). In late May 1945 Thomas Mann (1875–1955), speaking at the American Library of Congress, confessed of Luther, 'I do not love him', for 'Germanism in its unalloyed state, the Separatist, Anti-Roman, Anti-European shocks me and frightens me, even when it appears in the guise of evangelical freedom and spiritual emancipation'. Yet Luther's contradiction of creativity and destruction made him 'great in the most German manner, great and German even his duality as a liberating and at once reactionary force, a conservative revolutionary... He was a liberating hero—but in the German style, for he knew nothing of liberty' (Mann 1963: 52–3).

Mann, at his most radical no socialist, attested to the place Martin Luther, the anti-revolutionary revolutionist, had assumed in German culture. Luther survived his encounter with communism, but his greatness could not be disembedded from the contradictions of his own Germany in his own time. Today, when communism has collapsed and Christianity slides into decline in Europe, and when Marxists and Christians discuss how to defeat the global conditions of poverty, oppression, and injustice and the global power of capitalism, Luther's voice rarely if ever joins in the conversation.

VI. AFTERWORD: MARXISM, LUTHER, AND THE REFORMATION TODAY

The original idea for this chapter included the topic of Marxist evaluations of Luther in liberation theology today. Although there is no connected discussion of Luther or the

Reformation in contemporary Marxism, sporadic and sometimes interesting forays in their direction can be found, for example, in the writings of the Slovene Marxist Slavoj Žižek (Boer 2009: ch. 7). Neither he nor older Western Marxist writers, such as Theodor Adorno (1903–69), are primarily interested in Luther, somewhat more in Protestantism as a whole. Boer's treatment of Žižek and other Marxists expresses a belief that 'given the crucial role of the Bible and theology in their work, we ignore those elements at our peril' (2009: xii). This is perfectly appropriate, for contemporary discussions of Marxism and Christianity, both in- and outside of the realm of liberation theology, are grounded in biblical theology and early Christian history, and the Reformation is introduced almost exclusively from the Christian, not the Marxist, side (e.g., Dahling-Sander 2003).

This is not to say that Luther's specific tradition yields nothing of value for seekers of Christian liberation today. 'For Luther's theological heirs', writes the Brazilian theologian Walter Altmann, 'the essential point of reference is that of the "little ones," the weaker ones…share-croppers, small farmers, employees, the unemployed, factory workers, immigrants, refugees, people of color, native peoples, women, children. If these "little ones" do not form the reference point for the church, then the church is not of Christ…' (Altmann 2000: 145). Still, Altmann goes no further towards proposing Christian means of change than the 'preference for the poor' taught by the much better known and more universalizing figures of Catholic liberation theology. They, too, however, stumble at the barrier of revolutionary violence, on which issue Altmann holds that Luther's *theologia crucis* renounces 'the road to power; only the path of weakness counts' (Altmann 2000: 144).

On the other side of this issue stands the British philosopher Andrew Collier, who proposes to 'make Lenin and Althusser meet Augustine and Luther' by using 'their roots…in scholasticism' as a dialectical conception of Christian philosophy (Collier 2001: 1, 3). To him Luther represents but one step, if a major one, towards an erasure of the boundaries between sacrality and secularity, the developed stage of which appeared with the radical sects, such as the Ranters. Yet the issue of violence posed a conundrum—the conundrum of deploying power on behalf of the 'wretched of the earth', which neither Luther nor the sects could resolve. Collier advocates the classic view that 'so long as human authority exists, it should as far as possible be organised so that the greatest power serves the least powerful with all its might'. This he holds to be the 'the ideal of Davidic kingship, the defender of the poor', the modern form of which is called 'the dictatorship of the proletariat' (Collier 2001: 122). And here rests the discussion between post-European Christianity and post-Stalinist Marxism.

References

Altmann, Walter (2000). *Luther and Liberation: A Latin American Perspective*, trans. Mary M. Solberg. Eugene, OR: Wipf & Stock.
Bloch, Ernst (1963). *Thomas Münzer als Theologe der Revolution*. Frankfurt/Main: Suhrkamp.
Boer, Roland (2009). *Criticism of Heaven: On Marxism and Theology*. Chicago: Haymarket.

Borkenau, Franz (1972). *Der Übergang vom feudalen zum bürgerlichen Weltbild. Studien zur Geschichte der Philosophie der Manufakturperiode.* Darmstadt: Wissenschaftliche Buchgesellschaft.

Bornkamm, Heinrich (ed.) (1970). *Luther im Spiegel der deutschen Geistgeschichte,* 2nd edn. Göttingen: Vandenhoeck & Ruprecht.

Bräuer, Siegfried (1983). *Martin Luther in marxistischer Sichte von 1945 bis zum Beginn der achtziger Jahre.* Berlin: Evangelische Verlagsanstalt.

Brendler, Gerhard (1983). *Martin Luther, Theologie und Revolution: eine marxistische Darstellung.* Berlin: Deutsche Verlag der Wissenschaft; Cologne: Pahl-Rugenstein.

—— (1991). *Martin Luther: Theology and Revolution,* trans. Claude R. Foster, Jr. New York and Oxford: Oxford University Press.

Collier, Andrew (2001). *Christianity and Marxism: A Philosophical Contribution to their Reconciliation.* London and New York: Routledge.

Dahling-Sander, Christoph (2003). *Zur Freiheit Befreit. Das theologische Verständnis von Freiheit und Befreiung nach Martin Luther, Huldrych Zwingli, James H. Cone und Gustavo Gutiérrez.* Frankfurt/Main: Lembeck.

Engels, Friedrich (1956). *The Peasant War in Germany,* trans. Moissaye J. Olgin. Moscow: International Publishers.

Götting, Gerald (1982). 'Sozialismus vollendet das humanistische Vermächtnis'. In *Martin-Luther-Ehrung 1983. Bewahrung und Pflege des progressiven Erbes in der Deutchen Demokratischen Republik.* Berlin: Aufbau.

Gramsci, Antonio (1994). *Letters from Prison,* trans. R. Rosenthal, ed. F. Rosengarten. 2 vols. New York: Columbia University Press.

Hendrix, Scott H. (1992). Review of Brendler (1991), in *The Sixteenth Century Journal* 23: 601–2.

Honecker, Erich (1980). 'Unsere Zeit verlangt Parteinahme für Fortschritt, Vernunft und Menschlichkeit'. In *Martin Luther und unsere Zeit. Konstituierung des Martin-Luther-Komitees der DDR am 13. Juni 1980 in Berlin.* Berlin/Weimar: Aufbau-Verlag.

Kautsky, Karl (1921). *Vorläufer des neueren Sozialismus,* 2nd edn., ed. Hans-Jürgen Mende. Berlin: Vorwärts.

Kofler, Leo (1971). *Zur Geschichte der bürgerlichen Gesellschaft. Versuch einer verstehenden Deutung der Neuzeit,* 4th edn. Neuwied/Berlin: Luchterhand.

Kołakowski, Leszek (1978). *Main Currents of Marxism: Its Rise, Growth, and Dissolution,* trans. P. S. Falla. 3 vols. Oxford: Clarendon Press.

Kruttschnitt, Elke (1993). *Ernst Bloch und das Christentum: der geschichtliche Prozess und der philosophische Begriff der 'Religion des Exodus und des Reiches'.* Mainz: Grünewald.

Laube, Adolf (1983). 'Martin Luther in der Erbe- und Traditionsauffassung der Deutschen Demokratischen Republik'. In *Luther und die Folgen. Beiträge zur sozialgeschichtlichen Bedeutung der lutherischen Reformation,* ed. Hartmut Löwe and Claus-Jürgen Roepke. Munich: Kaiser.

Laube, Adolf, Max Steinmetz, and Günter Vogler (eds.) (1974). *Illustrierte Geschichte der deutschen frühbürgerlichen Revolution.* Berlin: Dietz.

Lehmann, Hartmut (2004a). 'Das marxistische Lutherbild von Engels bis Honecker'. In *Luther zwischen den Kulturen. Zeitgenossenschaft—Weltwirkung,* ed. Hans Medick and Peer Schmidt. Göttingen: Vandenhoeck & Ruprecht, 500–16.

—— (2004b). 'The Rehabilitation of Martin Luther in the GDR, or Why Thomas Müntzer Failed to Stabilise the Moorings of Socialist Ideology'. In *Religion and the Cold War,* ed. Dianne Kirby. New York: Vandenhoeck & Ruprecht, 200–10.

Mann, Thomas (1963). ' Germany and the Germans'. In *Thomas Mann's Addresses Delivered at the Library of Congress, 1942–1949*. Washington, DC: Library of Congress, 45–66.

Marx, Karl (1970). *Critique of Hegel's Philosophy of Right. Introduction*, ed. Joseph O'Malley, trans. Annette Jolin and Joseph O'Malley. Cambridge: Cambridge University Press.

Mehring, Franz (1960–7). *Gesammelte Schriften*. Berlin: Dietz.

Roy, Ralph Lord (1961). *Communism and the Churches*. New York: Harcourt Brace.

Steinmetz, Max (1979). 'Theses on the Early Bourgeois Revolution in Germany, 1476–1535'. In *The German Peasant War of 1525: New Viewpoints*, ed. Bob Scribner and Gerhard Benecke. London: Unwin, 9–22.

Vogler, Günter (2003). 'Ernst Bloch und Thomas Müntzer. Historie und Gegenwart in der Müntzer-Interpretation eines Philosophen'. In *Thomas Müntzer und die Gesellschaft seiner Zeit*, ed. Günter Vogler. Mühlhausen: Thomas-Müntzer-Gesellschaft, 174–92.

SUGGESTED READING

Bartel, Horst and Walter Schmidt (1984). 'Das Historisch-materialistische Lutherbild in Geschichte und Gegenwart'. *Zeitschrift für Geschichtswissenschaft* 32: 291–301.

Kautsky, Karl (1897). *Communism in Central Europe in the Time of the Reformation*, trans. J. L. Mulliken and E. G. Mulliken. London: Unwin.

—— (1991). *Vorläufer des Neueren Sozialismus*. Vol. I: *Von Plato bis zu den Wiedertäufern*, 2nd edn., ed. Hans-Jürgen Mende. Berlin: 1991. First edition, Stuttgart, 1895.

Walinski-Kiehl, Robert (2004). 'Reformation History and Political Mythology in the German Democratic Republic, 1949–1989'. *European History Quarterly* 34: 43–67.

CHAPTER 43

....

ROMAN CATHOLIC LUTHER RESEARCH IN THE TWENTIETH CENTURY

From Rejection to Rehabilitation

....

THEO M. M. A. C. BELL

I. UNDER THE BAN OF COCHLAEUS

....

IN the middle of the Second World War Adolf Herte (1887–1970), professor in Paderborn, published a three-volume work *Das katholische Lutherbild im Bann der Lutherkommentare des Cochläus* (1943). Herte had dedicated his whole academic career up to that point to Cochlaeus, but this monumental work was the apotheosis. He had researched an enormous amount of material in several languages to conclude that almost all Catholic (generally 'Catholic' in this essay is understood as 'Roman Catholic') Luther biographies till the twentieth century had derived their judgements and opinions from a book by Johannes Cochlaeus which was published three years after Luther's death and which was called *De actis et scriptis Martini Lutheri* (1549). The humanist priest Cochlaeus (Johann Dobneck) initially sympathized with Luther, but very soon he turned out to be a fierce opponent. He wrote his *Commentaria* with the intention to cure Catholics of the idea that Luther had been an honest and pious man. On the contrary Luther had been a monster, a child of the Devil, a drunkard, and violator of nuns. He had loved women and wine, had been a liar, a cowardly and a quarrelsome person. Herte wrote his work 'to seek understanding, to depoison the confessional atmosphere and to heal old wounds' (Herte 1943: 1.XXII). When he wrote his opus magnum, Roman Catholic Luther research already was in full swing. The twentieth century has not only been the age of a Protestant Luther renaissance, but also the age of the Catholic discovery of Martin Luther. This did not happen without a struggle; the road very often was bumpy and winding.

To start at the beginning: in 1904 the Dominican friar Heinrich Suso Denifle (1844–1905) wrote a voluminous work, *Luther und Luthertum in der ersten Entwickelung*. The sub-librarian of the Bibliotheca Vaticana was a renowned specialist in the study of the Middle Ages, but the image he gave of Luther was completely in line with Cochlaeus: full of blind hatred, but presented under the cover of scholarly objectivity. Luther had been a morally reprehensible person who had used the Reformation as an excuse to give up his monastic vows and to cover up his immorality and sexual desires. Moreover, he had been theologically incompetent and a 'half-knower' (*Halbwisser*). Educated in the *Schola Moderna* of Ockham and in nominalism, he had had no knowledge of the golden age of high Scholasticism. The harsh tone of Denifle not only aroused indignation with Protestant historians and theologians, but also some Catholic scholars thought the tone of his work was improper and too harsh. It must be said to his credit that he had extensive knowledge of the medieval sources. Nevertheless he applied his knowledge with negative intentions. However, he forced Protestant scholars to get themselves more involved with Scholastic theology and with Luther as a biblical theologian.

After Denifle the Jesuite Hartmann Grisar (1845–1932) followed with a three-volume study (Grisar 1911–2). While Denifle criticizes the reformer furiously, the statements of Grisar are more ambivalent and subtle. The tenor seems more objective, but Grisar took a psychological perspective. Luther had been a psychopath and a neurasthenic; in his psychic suffering Grisar found the key to understanding Luther. He did not restrict his definition of Luther's desires to the sexual, but treated them as all-embracing: the ego that turns itself against God. Luther was a sinner, one who fell victim to his egoism, pride, and sensuality. Like Denifle, Grisar did not have the intention to write a biography of Luther. He only wanted to show that Luther and Lutheranism had advanced the process of decay which had started in the medieval church and to demonstrate how the doctrine of justification and the autonomy of the individual created a new historical situation in the sixteenth century (Schnabel 1931: 323).

In the first decades of the twentieth century Catholic Luther studies inside as well as outside of Germany were strongly influenced by the writings of Denifle and Grisar, at first in France, where Jules Paquier soon translated the first volume of Denifle. Also in the Anglo-Saxon world the influence of Denifle and Grisar could be noticed soon and lasted for a long time, e.g., in the extensive article of Henry George Ganss (1855–1912) in *The Catholic Encyclopedia* (1910). He brought 'the views of Denifle to the English speaking world' (Atkinson 1983: 323). Also Philip Hughes had a significant influence through his compilation of the critical views of Grisar and Paquier in the third volume of *A History of the Church*, but he passed by the massive accusations of Denifle (Hughes 1947). He showed a certain respect for the person of Luther but at the same time criticized his doctrine.

II. THE DAWN OF A NEW APPRAISAL

The tone of Denifle's criticisms went too far for some Catholic scholars; it was viewed as a relapse to the controversy theology of the sixteenth and seventeenth centuries. It was Franz Xaver Kiefl (1869–1928), a theology professor at Würzburg, who was the first to promote a more objective approach. In the Catholic journal *Hochland* (1917) he broke with the views of Denifle and Grisar. According to Kiefl, Luther's actions can only be interpreted on the basis of theological motives. Luther was seized by the biblical thought of God's omnipotence. He also discussed Luther's deep religiosity, his untameable will, and his extraordinary literary talents. Twelve years later an anthology was published with two remarkable contributions, one by Sebastian Merkle and one by Anton Fischer (von Martin 1929). Fischer emphasized that Luther as a man of prayer has something to say to the whole of Christianity. Merkle set forth the conditions that the Catholic historical research had to fulfil. According to Merkle the religious motives behind Luther's actions had to be acknowledged: he had been anything but a free-thinker or a revolutionary.

Thus, the years between 1920 and 1940 can be seen as a transitional phase. Leaving behind a polemical approach, research moved in the direction of trying to do historical justice to Luther. Joseph Lortz (1887–1975) must receive credit for writing the first comprehensive study. With his two-volume work *Die Reformation in Deutschland* he managed to evoke interest in Catholic and Protestant circles alike (Lortz 1939–40). Later he would compile his views in smaller works for the sake of the ecumenical dialogue, among others *Wie kam es zu Reformation?*, which was also translated into English (Lortz 1950). Lortz's works attracted much attention because of their irenical tenor. Along with John Henry Newman (1801–90), he contended that the Roman Catholic Church was implicated in the schism of the sixteenth century because of the sharp decline of the church. For Lortz Luther is a '*homo religiosus*', whose life and work can only be explained from a theological perspective. In spite of the positive approach Lortz was also critical. Luther has not been a 'Vollhörer' (full hearer) of the Word of God. He had explained it in a simplified and abbreviated way. How was that possible? The reason was that Luther did not comprehend the full significance of Scripture due to his education in the school of Ockham. Clearly for Lortz, Thomism is the correct orthodox theology, and Ockhamism a 'Fremdkörper' within Catholic theology. So Luther overcame in himself a Catholicism that was not 'full-catholic'. That means that a misunderstanding caused the Reformation.

Furthermore, Lortz held that Luther has not comprehended revelation in the full sense because his personal needs guided his thinking. He became guilty of subjectivism. His explanation of the biblical text was driven by his concern about personal salvation, and therefore he has not been able to grasp the Bible as a whole. His conscience captured his theologizing, and he was no longer able to listen to the teaching authority of the Church. It may be clear that Lortz's view did not do full justice to Luther, but still he considered Luther as a genuine *homo religiosus*. The ban of Cochlaeus had been broken.

Lortz's views prevailed very decisively after the Second World War. His monumental work *Die Reformation in Deutschland* appeared in its third edition in 1948. Lortz had many students, also because of his position as director of the Institut für Europäische Geschichte at Mainz (Abteilung für Religionsgeschichte). Even internationally his views were getting attention. For the wider reception of this Catholic image of Luther it was important that it found its way into handbooks and lexicons which were part of university instruction. Lortz contributed the article 'Reformation' to the *Lexikon für Theologie und Kirche* (1963) and *Sacramentum Mundi* (1969), a lexicon which was published in five languages at the same time.

Erwin Iserloh (1915–96), Lortz's one-time student and assistant, followed in his footsteps and was responsible for several treatments in Catholic handbooks. He wrote articles about Luther and the German Reformation for the fourth volume of the *Handbuch der Kirchengeschichte* (1979³), edited by Hubert Jedin (1900–80). In the early 1960s he had created a sensation in Lutheran Germany with his publications on Luther's Ninety-five Theses (Iserloh 1966). Iserloh maintained that Luther had never posted them on the Castle Church door in Wittenberg, but had sent them to some bishops. Until today the posting of the theses as a historical fact has remained controversial.

Apart from approval Lortz also won criticism. Already in 1947 the philosopher Johannes Hessen (1889–1971) rejected Lortz's view that the subjectivism of Luther had been the main cause of his errors. Luther was not a subjectivist or an individualist. For Luther man is not the measure of all things (Hessen 1947: 12–24). Luther should be viewed as a much needed prophet within the universal church in the line of the Old Testament prophets. He called for conversion and had only one goal in mind, namely to uncover the pure gospel, from which the Roman Church had turned itself away. We will not deal with the content of Hessen's book; going a step beyond Lortz, he advanced the search for ecumenical agreements.

Also in the Francophone world new developments could be viewed. So Paul Vignaux (1904–87), professor at the Sorbonne, felt challenged to research Luther's theological sources. He was especially interested in his Ockhamist roots. Also Philip Böhmer was considerably more positive about Ockhamism than Lortz. The works of the Jesuit Yves Congar (1904–95) were of great ecumenical importance; he saw the Reformation as a purely religious movement which had the intention to renew the religious life from the sources. Alongside Congar, Louis Bouyer (1913–2004) and Georges Tavard (1922–2007) should be mentioned. Both assessed the positive aspects of the Reformation principles as genuinely Catholic. Tavard was the author of the popular booklet *Le protestantisme*, meant for a broad readership, which was also translated into English (Tavard 1958).

The USA already had a long (Protestant) tradition of Luther research, but the renewal of the Roman Catholic Luther research began later. For a long time the views of Denifle and Grisar lived on. George H. Tavard's *The Catholic Approach to Protestantism* provided a new starting point (Tavard 1955). Tavard had emigrated from France to the USA in 1952, where he acquired a reputation as an expert on Protestantism. He was an ecumenist like Hans Küng, but not a Luther scholar in the strict sense. His views strongly agreed with Lortz. Alongside Tavard the names of Thomas McDonough, F. M. Quealey, and Leonard Swidler should be mentioned.

In Great Britain Luther has received little attention through the ages. Gordon Rupp (1910–86) noticed in his important book *The Righteousness of God* (1953), 'For good and ill, moreover, no single person dominates the English sixteenth century scene as does Luther in Germany' (Rupp 1951: 28). He concluded: 'We have some leeway to make up in our study of the Continental Reformation, and particularly in awareness of the intricate field known as "Luther Research" ' (Rupp 1951: ix). Rupp has inspired many Luther scholars, among others the Catholic convert John M. Todd (1918–93) who wrote two popular Luther biographies (Todd 1964, 1982). Building on the achievements of Rupp and Lortz, Todd sketches a well-balanced image of Luther. To him is it clear that Luther wanted to be a reformer of the Church in service of the one Church. Todd also deserves credit for publishing the standard work of Lortz for the English-speaking world (Lortz 1939–40).

III. The Golden Years of Catholic Luther Research

The continuing study of Luther's life and person certainly were profitable because they brought about a change in Catholic thinking about Luther. However, these historical studies had their limitations insofar as they did not treat Luther's theology and its significance for today. That would change in the late 1950s. A new generation of Catholic Luther scholars searched for an open dialogue with Luther and his theology. A number of doctoral students, not only in Germany, but also in Rome and Paris, found in Luther the subject for their dissertations. They wanted to take Luther's theology seriously, research it open-mindedly and without designating Luther as a subjectivist or not fully-catholic. The Catholic scholars focused on particular aspects of his theology and mainly turned to the young Luther. Without trying to give a complete enumeration we mention here just a few names: Jan Aarts, Johannes Brosseder, George Chantraine, August Hasler, Harry McSorley, Wolfgang Schwab, Joseph Vercruysse, Reinhold Weier, and Jared Wicks.

The open ecumenical atmosphere of the second Vatican Council (1962–5) definitely contributed to the fact that Catholics started to look across the borders of their own church. According to some scholars Luther had now found his council (Brandenburg 1969: 64) pointing to the central position of the Scriptures, the spoken word, liturgy in the vernacular, and the ministry understood as service. In fairness one should notice that Luther is nowhere mentioned in the conciliar documents. But the climate had been changed, and Catholic Luther research went on. When in 1967 the posting of the Ninety-five Theses was commemorated, the celebrations were defined in part by the contributions of Catholic Luther scholars.

Albert Brandenburg (1908–78) deserves special attention. He can be considered as the beginning of the new Catholic Luther research. In 1960 he wrote a book about young Luther's theology. It was clearly inspired by Gerhard Ebeling's existentialist Luther interpretation, its argument that Luther's theology was mainly a new hermeneutics (Brandenburg 1960). The centre of his theology in his first Commentary on the Psalms (1513–15) could be found in the notions of '*deus absconditus*' (the Hidden God) and '*iudicium*' (judgement), culminating in '*fides*' (faith). Luther described the existential unity between the objective act of Christ and the subjective understanding of it by human beings. The saving act of God becomes reality in the Word as it is received and realized by human beings in faith. It is because of this existentialist character of Luther's theology, Brandenburg declared, that the reformer is a '*Lutherus praesens*' for all Christians—an interpretation that did not find unanimous agreement. But Brandenburg insisted on the Catholic integration of Luther's theology. In *Die Zukunft des Martin Luther* (1977: 41, 65, 81) he calls the reformer the 'first evangelical theologian in the Church', a person who must get 'his deserved place in the Church' and from whom alone Catholicism and Protestantism can expect a 'renewal of Christianity'. The views of Brandenburg have caused an inner-Catholic tension between the older 'historical' school (J. Lortz, H. Jedin, E. Iserloh, P. Manns) and the younger 'systematical' school (A. Brandenburg, S. Pfürtner, H. Fries, O. H. Pesch). The Lortz School sharply rejected the efforts of Brandenburg. Lortz and his followers attributed an underevaluation of the objective and the sacramental in the young Luther to the Brandenburg School. They emphasized Luther's sacramental thinking, which means that he had remained committed principally to the meaning of the traditional view of the dogma. To a decisive degree Luther was an ontological thinker (Lortz, Preface to *Reformation in Deutschland*[4]: viii).

The more systematically orientated scholars criticized the historical school on three points: (1) the historians presumed that the Catholic dogma is not to be disputed; (2) they saw Luther's doctrine of God's sovereign action in salvation, an action that excludes cooperation on the side of the recipient, as irreconcilable with Catholic teaching; (3) most of them were not ready to learn anything from Luther (Heinz 1988: 259). The most outstanding representative of the new approach, Otto Hermann Pesch (1931–), a pupil of Heinrich Fries in Munich, advanced this threefold criticism.

From the third International Luther Congress in Järvenpää (1966), to which for the first time also Roman Catholic Luther scholars were invited, the discussion was continued by Lortz's former assistant Peter Manns (1923–91) and Otto-Hermann Pesch (Manns 1967). According to Pesch, there was no doubt that the traditional historical way to study Luther was definitely passé. He wanted to discuss the legitimacy of the content of reformatory statements precisely by abandoning their historical and biographical genesis (Pesch 1966: 401, 397).

Pesch even spoke of a trans-historical approach. This approach, which he prefers for Catholic Luther research, is essentially different from one of the Lortz School. It no longer aims to distinguish the Catholic and the heretical in Luther, but to consider Luther a challenge to treat his theology as a genuinely Catholic possibility for theological thinking and living, notwithstanding some critical points one may have (Pesch 1966: 406).

The Dominican friar Pesch wanted to show this on the basis of the doctrine of justification of Thomas Aquinas and Martin Luther. In a very comprehensive dissertation he tried to put them in dialogue showing theological compatibility between them (Pesch 1967). A few years earlier his fellow friar Stephan Pfürtner (1922–2012) had already published a booklet which deals with the specific topic of assurance of salvation in Thomas and Luther (Pfürtner 1964: 40). Pesch's 1967 thesis was subtitled: 'An attempt for a systematic-theological dialogue'. Pesch believes that there are only formal differences, but no substantial ones, between the two theologians. He characterizes Luther's theology as existential and Aquinas' theology as sapiential. But they do not differ in significant points regarding justification, and therefore there is no reason for condemning one or the other. Pesch further points out that the polemics between Protestants and Catholics for five hundred years have perhaps been only a huge misunderstanding. In a shorter treatise in 1982 he elaborates similarities and differences in the doctrine of justification and tries to smooth the way for mutual understanding. In spite of some differences which he observes, Pesch is convinced that according to the present understanding of many Lutheran and Catholic theologians these differences no longer divide the churches (Pesch 1982a: 48).

Anniversary years always give rise to a flow of publications. In 1980 the occasion of the 450th anniversary of the Augsburg Confession occasioned ecumenical discussions on Vinzenz Pfnür's (1937–) proposal to reach an agreement on the basis of this Confession. The thought behind this proposal was that it might be easier to talk with the 'systematic' Melanchthon than with the 'unsystematic' Luther (Pfnür 1970). Though the discussions were vivid and clarifying, they had no effect on Roman Catholic authorities. The Luther commemoration of 1983 (his 500th birthday) again elicited quite a number of Catholic publications. Perhaps most eye-catching was the richly illustrated biography of Peter Manns. He depicted Luther's cloister years in an extensive and positive way and refuted the idea of any pathological trait in Luther's character. He underlined the normality of Luther's monastic crisis and the profound theological character of the Reformation (Manns and Loose 1982: 52). This biography is still worth reading though it may be deplored that the author did not supply any references to the sources. In the same year another interesting book written by Pesch appeared entitled *Hinführung zu Luther* (Pesch 1983). It is a kind of general introduction to Luther's theology in an ecumenical perspective. In sixteen chapters the author opens up the main subjects and presents the actual state of affairs. Many statements are—if well understood—not church-dividing any longer.

IV. The Roman Catholic Hierarchy and Luther Research

Walter Kasper (1933–) and Hans Küng (1928–), both once professors in Tübingen, have suggested that, on the one hand, the Catholic understanding of Luther's person and theology has made enormous progress in the last few decades, while on the other hand, the Catholic hierarchy has failed to keep in step with this progress (Kasper and Küng 1976: 473). This dissension still continues. It is not easy to point out to what extent the Catholic authorities have recognized the developments in Catholic Luther research. It is a fact that ecumenical dialogues which began after the Second World War strongly intensified after the second Vatican Council. In Germany, particularly in the 'Ökumenische Arbeitskreis' of Lutheran and Catholic theologians, in the United States in 'Lutherans and Catholics in Dialogue', and on world level in the 'Joint Lutheran–Roman Catholic Study Commission' important results have been achieved, for instance, a document on mutual recognition of Baptism. Most discussions on church, ministry, and sacraments still continue for the time being. In the important statement of 1983, *Martin Luther—Witness to Jesus Christ*, the Joint Commission declared: 'He [Martin Luther] is beginning to be honored in common as a witness to the gospel, a teacher in the faith and a herald of spiritual renewal' (*Martin Luther-Witness*: I.4). These words referred to the speech of Cardinal Johannes Willebrands (1909–2006) on the occasion of the fifth Assembly of the Lutheran World Federation gathered in Evian (1970). Willebrands, at that time President of the Secretariat for Promoting Christian Unity, spoke of Luther in terms that Catholic theologians usually reserve for Thomas Aquinas by calling him a 'doctor communis'. This title indicates that Luther should be respected by all theological schools of the Catholic Church. Speaking about the doctrine of justification, Willebrands applied this title to Luther. 'In a session whose theme is *Sent to the World*, it is good to reflect upon a man for whom the doctrine of justification was the turning point of the enduring Church. He can be our common master in this field, as he states that God must continuously remain the Lord and our most essential human response must be an absolute confidence in and worship of God' (Willebrands 1970: 766). When he returned to Rome, it appeared that his words had not met with a favourable reception by all (Hasler 1976: 524). This was remarkable, as one should notice that Willebrands did not actually go beyond Lortz's opinion in 1939. For Willebrands as for Lortz Luther was 'a profoundly religious personality who sought the message of the Gospel honestly and with abnegation'. But did this mean a full acknowledgement of Luther and his theology?

On occasion of the Luther-year 1983 Pope John Paul II adopted Willebrands' reference to Luther's 'profoundly religious personality'. He added to this that the rupture in the church could be reduced neither to only a lack of understanding by the pastors of the Catholic Church nor to a defective understanding of the true Catholicism on Luther's side. The crucial decisions reached deeper because fundamental questions of the right explanation and appropriation of the Christian faith were at stake. The attentive listener is reminded of Lortz's opinion (Vercruysse 1996: 123). One must conclude that Luther-reception in the Catholic Church takes place on different levels and at different speeds at the same time (Pesch 1982a: 137). Although one might get the impression that much has happened and that the Catholic Church eventually received Luther, on second thought one must acknowledge that only a thin upper layer of Catholic Christians, those interested in ecumenical dialogue, knows about the developments described here. In addition, it has to be admitted that still everywhere prejudices, resentments, clichés, and lack of reliable information live on, and it will still take a long time before these will be all removed. Especially the Roman hierarchy remains reserved. The French Luther scholar Daniel Olivier (1927–2005) has the following explanation: The bureaucracy of the Roman Catholic Church did not look at the theology of Luther on its own merits but more from the context of organizational preservation. Thus, in the Council of Trent, the Roman Catholic Church defined itself dogmatically in a way that contributed to the further split within Christianity. Thus, the Church focused its energies on trying to maintain authority and outward unity, and in the process, refused to see the good in much of Luther's theology and reforms. Therefore for the time being even the abolition of the papal ban as a symbolic act will still be a bridge too far.

V. Another Face of Catholic Luther Research

In spite of all progress, one can acknowledge with Karl Lehmann (1936–) 'that the new Catholic image of Luther is still far from being received yet' (Lehmann 1983: 560). Thus the old controversy has reared its head in the writings of Paul Hacker (1913–79) and Remigius Bäumer (1918–98). In his book *Das Ich im Glauben bei Martin Luther* Hacker, an Indologist and a convert, strove to interpret the Tower-experience and the reformatory breakthrough as a discovery of subjective faith (Hacker 1966). The faith and all its statements were completely reduced to human subjectivity. This 'reflexive faith' collides radically with the whole pre-Lutheran tradition concerning the Christian faith. In this way the '*pro me*', in which the acts of salvation are existentially accepted by the believer, becomes for Hacker the downfall of Lutheran theology. Moreover Hacker picks up opinions of Denifle, so that Pesch calls him a 'resurrected Denifle'.

Also in line with the old polemic is church historian Remigius Bäumer. He had published earlier on Luther's relation to the papacy, seeking to rehabilitate Luther-polemicist Cochlaeus and had chosen Melanchthon and the Diet of Augsburg as interlocutor rather than Luther. In his controversial contribution to the *Kleine Deutsche Kirchengeschichte* he contended that Luther had not become a reformer unintentionally, but as a self-appointed reformer, had risked splitting the church. Also Bäumer shows his affinity to Denifle by taking up an old polemical point; Luther's theology and reformatory acting can be traced back to traits of his character which are to be qualified as morally negative (Bäumer 1980: 68). Theobald Beer (1902–2000), a pastor in the German Democratic Republic, strove to show in a voluminous study that Luther's theology from the very beginning broke with the theological tradition (Beer 1980). Beer believed he had discovered in Luther's theology 'a doubling of realities', which may not be synthesized (Pesch 1982a: 144–6). According to him Luther's theology was heavily influenced by the medieval Neoplatonist Pseudo-Hermes Trismegistos, whose ideas were totally unbiblical. They had nothing to do with Augustine, Peter Lombard, Thomas Aquinas, William of Ockham, and Gabriel Biel but rather originated from Gnosticism and Neoplatonism. Close examination reveals that Beer's work is filled with inaccurate readings and unsound interpretations of Luther's views of the Incarnation, redemption, faith, and justification (Wicks 1978, 1982). His strongly deviating opinions and statements did not affect the mainstream of Luther research.

VI. Catholic Luther Research Today

After the Vatican Council and the flourishing period of Catholic Luther research a changing of the guards has been taking place. The first generations of post-war pioneers have retired or have passed away. Jos Vercruysse (1931–) states: 'It has become quiet around the dramatized battle of methods. Further it seems as if the term "catholic Luther research" no longer—if it ever did so—covers a uniform content' (Vercruysse 1996: 124) The situation now seems to be much more complicated. The ecumenical breakthrough has certainly not produced an unambiguous image of Luther and his theology. Surveying the international spectrum, one perceives a series of divergent Luther-images.

Also it has to be concluded that Catholic attention to Luther in particular has decreased (Vercruysse 2004). The latest peak of Catholic Luther research occurred in 1983, Luther's 500th birthday when Lutheran professor Gottfried Maron stated that 'the interest of Catholic theology in Luther... will be the most important characteristic of the thinking of this half millennium' (Maron 1982: 5). The enthusiasm for Luther seems often to have changed into 'Luther oblivion'. In many Catholic faculties of theology interest in ecumenical issues has diminished. There seems to be a certain ecumenical tiredness or weariness together with an attention more directed to internal ecclesiastical perspectives. Nevertheless Catholic Luther studies are still appearing today (Posset 2011). Surely one can question: what is specifically Catholic in these studies? Maybe it is better not to talk of Catholic Luther research as if it could be defined in method and in content. That is no longer the case. Luther research has been highly deconfessionalized. Rather it is the case that Luther scholars of various confessions find each other in their study of Luther and the Reformation, whereas Luther's Reformation is seen more and more in the broad perspective of sixteenth-century reform movements. Different methods, interests, and intentions play a role in it, and scholars find each other across confessional boundaries. Two examples are the circle of Reformation scholars around Kenneth Hagen at Marquette University and the interconfessional Working Group for Luther Research in the Netherlands, which gave rise to the foundation of the *Luther Bulletin* in 1991.

Also the selection of subjects is not defined confessionally, but one finds connection to questions which instigate further study. Jürgen Lutz's work about the relation between justification and the understanding of the church (Lutz 1990), Hubertus Blaumeiser's study of the theology of the Cross in the *Operationes in Psalmos* (Blaumeiser 1995), and the thesis of Theodorus Akerboom (1947–) on the (un)free will in Luther and Erasmus

(Akerboom 1995), all illustrate this point. Already in the Protestant Luther research of the 1930s Luther's relation to Bernard of Clairvaux had received some attention, drawing an image of this medieval theologian that depicted him on the one hand as a mystical theologian, on the other hand the embodiment of a monastic ideal which was radically rejected by Luther. New attention to Luther as an heir of monastic theology which had found its peak in the person of Bernard of Clairvaux, came from Catholic church historians like Peter Manns and Erich Kleineidam and Protestant church historians like Reinhard Schwarz and Ulrich Köpf (Ruhbach and Schmidt-Clausen 1985). On the Catholic side, Luther scholars Theo Bell (1945–) and Franz Posset (1945–), independently from each other, studied extensively the position of Bernard in Luther's works (Bell 1993; Posset 1999). They stated that Luther had had a great and lifelong appreciation for Bernard as an interpreter of Holy Scripture and as a preacher of the incarnate Christ. There also was an amazing congeniality between Luther and Bernard. A further exploration of monastic theology could make it clear that Luther had not only turned against Scholastic theology from the very beginning, but that he had been able to draw from a rich monastic-theological tradition (centred in Scripture and the Church Fathers), in which he could develop his views on penitence, faith, humility, and justification. Along with Johann von Staupitz, Bernard belonged to those who directly inspired Luther's biblically humanistic theology. A further study of Luther's monastic-patristic tradition will enable us to place him in the wider perspective of his Augustinian order with its endeavours for reform of theology and spirituality (Posset 2003, 2011).

The radically reversed Roman Catholic understanding of the person, work, and continuing relevance of Luther has led to an attitude and a conviction which consider Luther as part of a common heritage. It has been a long way from a Luther under the ban of Cochlaeus to a more positive picture of the reformer. What are the prospects for Catholic Luther research in the twenty-first century? It is hard to predict. Probably Luther will be again in the centre of attention in 2017, when the 500th anniversary of the beginnings of the Reformation will be commemorated. Possibly it will give rise to some new initiatives. Furthermore there are still some fundamental questions which have not been answered sufficiently. One of the most important is: can Luther find his place in the Roman Catholic Church as a *doctor communis*? This question can only be answered in a positive way if the Roman Catholic teaching authority is willing to acknowledge the churches proceeding from the Reformation as churches in the full sense. Only then can there also be a rehabilitation of Luther in a full sense. Not until then will O.-H. Pesch be put in the right with his thesis: 'In spite of some necessary criticism, Luther and his thought can today be perceived as another possibility of theological thinking and Christian existence which has its correct place in the Catholic Church' (Pesch 1972: 42).

REFERENCES

Akerboom, Theodorus (1995). *Vrije wil en/of genade. Een theologie-historisch onderzoek naar het disputt tussen Erasmus en Luther over de (on)vrijheid van het menselijk willen.* Nijmegen: Akerboom.

Atkinson, James (1983). *Martin Luther: Prophet to the Church Catholic.* Exeter: Paternoster.

Bäumer, Remigius (1980). 'Das Zeitalter der Glaubensspaltung'. In *Kleine Deutsche Kirchengeschichte*, ed. Bernhard Kötting. Freiburg/Br.: Herder, 53–79.

Beer, Theobald (1974). *Der fröhliche Wechsel und Streit. Grundzüge der Theologie Martin Luthers.* Leipzig: St.-Benno-Verlag. 2nd rev. edn.: Einsiedeln: Johannes-Verlag, 1980.

Bell, Theo (1993). *Divus Bernhardus. Bernhard von Clairvaux in Martin Luthers Schriften.* Mainz: Zabern.

Blaumeiser, Hubertus (1995). *Martin Luthers Kreuzestheologie. Eine Untersuchung anhand der Operationes in Psalmos (1519–1521).* Paderborn: Bonifatius.

Brandenburg, Albert (1960). *Gericht und Evangelium. Zur Worttheologie in Luthers erster Psalmenvorlesung.* Witten/Paderborn: Bonifatius.

—— (1969). *Martin Luther gegenwärtig.* Munich/Paderborn/Wien: Schöningh.

—— (1977). *Die Zukunft des Martin Luther.* Münster: Aschendorff.

Ganss, Henry George (1910). 'Martin Luther'. In *The Catholic Encyclopedia*, vol. IX. New York: Appleton, 438–59.

Grisar, Hartmann (1911–12). *Luther*, 3 vols. Freiburg/Br.: Herder. English translation in 6 vols.: London: Kegan/Paul/Trench.

Hacker, Paul (1966). *Das Ich im Glauben bei Martin Luther.* Graz: Styria.

Hasler, August (1976). 'Luther in der katholischen Schultheologie'. *Concilium* 12: 522–5.

Heinz, Johann (1988). 'Martin Luther and his Theology in German Catholic Interpretation before and after Vatican II'. *Andrews University Seminary Studies* 26: 253–65.

Herte, Adolf (1943). *Das katholische Lutherbild im Bann der Lutherkommentare des Cochläus*, 2 vols. Münster: Aschendorff.

Hessen, Johannes (1947). *Luther in katholischer Sicht.* Bonn: Röhrscheid.

Hughes, Philip (1947). *History of the Church*, vol. III. London: Sheed and Ward (2nd edn. 1960).

Iserloh, Erwin (1966). *Luther zwischen Reform und Reformation. Der Thesenanschlag fand nicht statt.* Münster: Aschendorff. English translation: *The Theses Were Not Posted: Luther between Reform and Reformation.* Toronto: Saunders, 1966; Boston: Beacon, 1968.

Jedin, Hubert (ed.) (1979³). *Handbuch der Kirchengeschichte.* Freiburg/Br.: Herder.

Kasper, Walter and Hans Küng (1976). 'Verständigung über Luther?' *Concilium* 12: 473.

Lehmann, Karl (1983). 'Worüber jetzt zu sprechen wäre: Luther und die Einheit der Kirchen heute'. *Herder-Korrespondenz* 37: 555–61.

Lortz, J. (1939–40). *Die Reformation in Deutschland.* Freiburg/B.: Herder, 4th. edn., 1964. English translation: *The Reformation in Germany.* London: Darton, Longman & Todd; New York: Herder, 1968.

Lortz, J., with Oliver, D., Pesch, O. H., Posset, F., Tavard, G. H., Todd, J. M., and Vercruysse, J. (1950). *Wie kam es zur Reformation?* Einsiedeln: Johannes Verlag. English translation: *The Reformation: A Problem for To-Day.* Westminster, MD: Newman, 1969.

Lutz, Jürgen (1990). *Unio und Communio. Zum Verhältnis von Rechtfertigungslehre und Kirchenverständnis bei Martin Luther. Eine Untersuchung zu ekklesiologisch relevanten Texten der Jahre 1519–1528.* Paderborn: Bonifatius.

Manns, Peter (1967). *Lutherforschung heute: Krise und Aufbruch.* Wiesbaden: Steiner.

Manns, Peter and Helmuth Nills Loose (1982). *Martin Luther*. Freiburg/Br./Basel/Vienna: Herder.

Maron, Gottfried (1982). *Das katholische Lutherbild der Gegenwart*, Bensheimer Hefte 58. Göttingen: Vandenhoeck & Ruprecht.

Martin, Alfred von (ed.) (1929). *Luther in ökumenischer Sicht*. Stuttgart: Fromann.

Oliver, Daniel (1971). *The Trial of Luther*, trans. John Tonkin. London: Mowbrays.

—— (1978). *Luther's Faith. The Cause of the Gospel in the Church*, trans. John Tonkin. Saint Louis: Concordia.

Pesch, Otto Hermann (1966). 'Zwanzig Jahre katholische Lutherforschung'. *Lutherische Rundschau* 16: 392–406.

—— (1967). *Die Theologie der Rechtfertigung bei Martin Luther und Thomas von Aquin. Versuch eines systematisch-theologisches Dialogs*. Mainz: Matthias-Grünewald.

—— (1972). *Ketzerfürst und Kirchenlehrer. Wege katholischer Begegnung mit Martin Luther*. Stuttgart: Calwer Verlag.

—— (1982a). *Gerechtfertigt aus Glauben. Luthers Fragen an die Kirche*. Freiburg/Br.: Herder.

—— (1982b). '"Ketzerfürst" und "Vater im Glauben". Die seltsamen Wege katholischer "Lutherrezeption"'. In *Weder Ketzer noch Heiliger. Luthers Bedeutung für den ökumenischen Dialog*, ed. Hans Friedrich Geisser. Regensburg: Pustet, 123–74.

—— (1983). *Hinführung zu Luther*. Mainz: Matthias-Grünewald.

Pfnür, Vinzenz (1970). *Einig in der Rechtfertigungslehre? Die Rechtfertigungslehre der Confessio Augustana (1530) und die Stellungnahme der katholischen Kontroverstheologie zwischen 1530 und 1535*. Wiesbaden: Steiner.

Pfürtner, Stephan (1964). *Luther und Thomas im Gespräch*. Heidelberg: Kerle. English translation: *Luther and Aquinas: A Conversation*. London: Darton, Longman & Todd, 1964.

Posset, Franz (1999). *Pater Bernhardus: Martin Luther and Bernard of Clairvaux*. Kalamazoo: Cistercian.

—— (2003). *The Front-Runner of the Catholic Reformation: The Life and Works of Johann von Staupitz*. Aldershot: Ashgate.

—— (2011). *The Real Luther, A Friar at Erfurt and Wittenberg: Exploring Luther's Life with Melanchthon as Guide*. Saint Louis: Concordia.

Ruhbach, Gerhard and Kurt Schmidt-Clausen (eds.) (1985). *Kloster Amelungsborn 1135–1985*. Hannover: Kloster Amelungsborn. Essays by Ulrich Köpf, 'Martin Luthers Lebensgang als Mönch' (187–208), and Reinhold Schwarz, 'Luther unveräusserte Erbschaft an der monastischen Theologie' (209–32). English translation: 'Luther's Inalienable Inheritance of Monastic Theology'. *Australian Biblical Review* 39 (1988): 430–50.

Rupp, Ernest Gordon (1953). *The Righteousness of God: Luther Studies*. London: Hodder & Stoughton.

Schnabel, Franz (1931). *Deutschlands geschichtliche Quellen und Darstellungen in der Neuzeit*, Teil 1: *Das Zeitalter der Reformation 1500–1550*. Berlin: Teubner; repr. Darmstadt: Wissenschaftliche Buchgesellschaft, 1972.

Tavard, George H. (1955). *The Catholic Approach to Protestantism*. New York: Harper & Row. English translation of *A la rencontre du protestantisme*. Paris: Centurion, 1954.

—— (1958). *Le protestantisme*. Paris: Fayard. English translation: *Protestantism*. New York: Burns & Oates, 1959.

Todd, John M. (1964). *Martin Luther: A Biographical Study*. London: Paulist.

—— (1982). *Luther: A Life*. New York: Hamilton.

Vercruysse, Joseph (1996). 'Luther in der römisch-katholischen Theologie und Kirche'. *Lutherjahrbuch* 63: 103–28.

—— (2004). 'Katholische Lutherforschung im 20. Jahrhundert'. In *Katholische Lutherforschung im 20. Jahrhundert, Rückblick—Bilanz—Ausblick*, ed. Rainer Vinke. Mainz: Zabern.

Wicks, Jared (1978). Review of Beer, *Fröhliche Wechsel*. *Theologische Revue* 78: 1–12.

—— (1982). Review of Beer, *Fröhliche Wechsel*. *Gregorianum* 63: 162–4.

Willebrands, Johannes (1970). 'Lecture to the 5th Assembly of the Lutheran World Federation, on July 15, 1970', *La Documentation Catholique*, 6 September: 766.

CHAPTER 44

LUTHER'S ABIDING SIGNIFICANCE FOR WORLD PROTESTANTISM

KENNETH G. APPOLD

Assessing Luther's legacy and continued significance for World Protestantism involves two considerable challenges: identifying that legacy, and defining 'World Protestantism'. Neither of the two terms is static; both are dynamic and evolving. This essay addresses those challenges as concisely and responsibly as space allows, while tracing both Luther's influence on recent Protestant theology and his importance for the larger historical processes that shape contemporary Protestant church life globally. The most straight-forward and conventional way of determining Luther's significance for contemporary Protestantism begins with an empirical accounting of how and where the reformer's theology figures in modern-day Protestant thought. Taking such an approach is unsatis-fying but remains an interesting and useful place to start.

A survey of contemporary Protestant theology reveals a landscape largely void of Luther's overt influence. Less than 10 per cent of those articles published in the *Zeitschrift für Theologie und Kirche* between 2001 and 2011 deal directly with Martin Luther. That number would be far lower if it were limited to papers which primarily focused on a constructive engagement with the reformer's thought. If one broadens the survey to include journals from other traditions and contexts, the number dwindles even further. Of the nearly 150 articles published in the English-language quarterly *Modern Theology*[1] between 2007 and 2012, for example, only one deals with Luther, comparing him with Dionysius the Areopagite (Malysz 2008). Of the nearly 250 books reviewed by the same journal during that timespan, only one concerned Luther, Michael Root's (2011) review of Oswald Bayer's overview of Luther's theology (2007/8). As of this writing,

---

[1] Though broadly ecumenical, not strictly 'Protestant', it yields helpful insights into contemporary theological culture, particularly, though not exclusively, in the English-speaking world.

Modern Theology has not published an article specifically on Luther's thought since 2002 (Helmer 2002).

Luther's lack of visibility continues even at venues where one would expect him to be more conspicuous, those devoted directly to scholarship of the Reformation. At the 2011 convention of the Sixteenth Century Studies Conference, for example, less than five of the 189 scheduled sessions, and less than 15 of roughly 500 presentations mentioned Luther in their titles.[2] Especially curious is the low profile given Luther by many celebrations planned for 2017, the 500th anniversary of Luther's 'Ninety-five Theses'. While the very decision to celebrate 2017 implies a willingness to regard the 'Ninety-five Theses' as the 'beginning of the Reformation', an astonishing number of scholars and celebrants seem reluctant to connect Luther with that event. One of the largest international groups of such academics, organized under an umbrella named 'Refo500', serves as a good example. Dedicated to celebrating 500 years of 'the Reformation', the organization barely mentions Luther in its promotional literature, stated goals, formal vision, and mission statement, or, as of this writing, its academic programmes. Even its definition of 'the Reformation' makes no mention of Luther.[3]

Such examples do not signal an overall decline in Luther research, however. The annual *Lutherjahrbuch* bibliography of Luther-related works regularly lists close to one thousand titles. Even if a relatively modest number of those works deals with Luther's thought, one cannot claim that interest in Luther has vanished, or that Luther's theological influence has ceased. The disparity in numbers between the *Lutherjahrbuch*'s annual bibliography and the appearance of such works in major theological publications reveals something else. Luther research, while evidently still prolific, occupies a specific niche within an increasingly pluriform landscape of theological discourse. Publications such as the *Lutherjahrbuch* and its sister journal, *Luther*, as well as the English-language *Lutheran Quarterly* and *Lutheran Forum*, provide rich platforms for disseminating work on Luther but remain anchored in a largely Lutheran subculture. Similarly, it is unsurprising that—important exceptions notwithstanding—much contemporary engagement with Luther's theology takes place in the academies and churches of Finland, Germany, and the United States. The fact that additional centres of Lutheran theological discourse are emerging in other parts of the globe is exciting but underscores rather than contradicts that pattern unless these new centres begin to resonate more broadly.

Such trends towards parochialism are not as inexorable as they may seem. The Reformation itself had a remarkably pluriform character, yet virtually all of its protagonists, from major reformers to semi-literate peasants, were familiar with some of Luther's thoughts and frequently took them as a point of departure. The recognition by contemporary scholars that the Reformation's diversity has too often been ignored in the past should not give rise to the opposite error, overlooking Luther's vital significance for those admittedly diverse developments. While one may argue over whether it is better

---

[2] The Sixteenth Century Studies Conference programme, Fort Worth, Texas, 27–30 October 2011.

[3] <http://www.refo500.nl/en/pages/131/what-is-the-reformation.html>. Retrieved 29 January 2012.

to speak of 'Reformation' in the singular or 'Reformations' in the plural, without Luther one would likely speak of neither. Luther's current scarcity in Reformation-historical academic discussions is unlikely to continue indefinitely.

Lutheran theology's recent retreat into confessionally specific niches is also fuelled in part by inner-Lutheran dynamics which are neither necessary nor irreversible. True, the great unifying voices that focused Protestant discourse and proved a universal reference for theological discourse beyond their disciplines and confessional communities in bygone days (such as Karl Barth in systematic theology or Gerhard Ebeling in the realm of Luther interpretation) belong to the past. But such observations in no way legitimate the lack of effort made by many contemporary Lutheran theologians to communicate beyond their immediate cultural and intellectual confines. Such trends are particularly lamentable in large, formerly dominant Lutheran contexts which remain astonishingly oblivious to any development elsewhere—and to any text not written in their own native language. If one only preaches to the choir, one need not be surprised when everyone else stops listening.

Surveying recent publications on Luther's theology, another pattern also emerges. A marked number of works make overt—but, judging by their proliferation, not entirely successful—attempts to be normative and definitive. There are 'handbooks' on Luther, new Luther biographies, new editions of Luther's works in translation, additions to existing editions, and new introductions to Luther's thought. A remarkable number of shorter publications strive to 'make a case for Luther', arguing for Luther's continued significance. On the other hand, there have been comparatively few recent works that offer constructive theological engagements with Luther, or even fundamental reassessments of Luther's historical significance.[4] There seems to be more map-making than exploration. As a response to the dynamics of pluralism, that may be understandable though one hopes it marks a period of preparation for future creativity rather than long-term retreat.

Both the pluriform nature of contemporary global Protestantism and the home-grown parochial tendencies in much recent Lutheran theology make it challenging to assess Luther's significance for modern-day Protestant thought. The reformer's influences are too scattered to be readily apparent and are not always acknowledged by those without an in-house interest in doing so. Nevertheless, Luther's influences are present in contemporary Protestant theology to a considerable degree.

The most obvious examples of Luther's continued influence on Protestant thought come in explicitly Lutheran dogmatic theology. (That may seem like a truism, but has not always been the case historically.) Some, such as Oswald Bayer in his *Martin Luthers Theologie. Eine Vergegenwärtigung*, hew so close to Luther that the line between historical exegesis and constructive theology is often blurred; this is a 'contemporary interpretation' in the true sense of the term. The task of interpreting Luther is taken up as

---

[4] Finnish Lutheran scholars continue to produce some of the most notable exceptions. Cf. the overview in Vainio 2010.

well by proponents of the 'Finnish school' founded by Tuomo Mannermaa, often with highly stimulating results. More far-ranging in their engagement with historical voices and much looser in their attachment to Luther are the multi-volume systematic theologies of Wolfhart Pannenberg (1988–93) and Robert Jenson (1997–9). Neither project aims at a direct 'interpretation' of Luther, but instead places Luther within the larger context of the historical Christian tradition, which these works seek to continue. While recognizably 'Lutheran' in their doctrinal positions, they also go well beyond Luther on topics treated less copiously by the reformer himself, for example, in Jenson's theological explorations of the Trinity, and in entering into dialogue with other traditions, including Luther's erstwhile opponents.

Identifying Luther's influence in works written by non-Lutheran Protestants is more difficult since that influence is typically far less overt. Three fairly recent examples illustrate the point. All represent theological 'systems' from different non-Lutheran Protestant traditions (conservative evangelical, Anabaptist, and Pentecostal), two written by theologians working in North America, a context distinctive both for its high degree of Protestant pluralism and its large number of Protestant educational institutions. Both of these factors are conducive to the production of systematic theology.

Norman Geisler's four-volume *Systematic Theology* (2002) shows very little direct engagement with Luther or any other theologian of the Lutheran tradition. That is especially remarkable since Geisler borrows his structure almost directly from the *ordo analyticus* pioneered by seventeenth-century Lutheran Orthodoxy, beginning with prolegomena, including an extensive section on Scripture, continuing with a doctrine of God and an anthropology, and culminating in a soteriology. Like many early Lutherans, Geisler then adds appendix-like sections on eschatology and the church. Some of his methodological assumptions, including a robust theism and a commitment to Scripture's verbal inerrancy, evoke the spirit of the seventeenth century as well although Geisler employs a much less intricate philosophical substructure than those favoured by his baroque predecessors. Though he does not acknowledge it, and instead engages mainly Calvinist and Wesleyan interlocutors, his soteriology also borrows heavily from the Lutheran tradition. Lutherans might take issue with Geisler's readiness to speak of 'synergism' when describing a person's need for 'accepting' God's offer of grace in faith (Geisler 2002: III.191–4), but many other components, such as his explication of 'resistible' grace, are close to Luther—closer than to Calvin (Geisler 2002: III. 376–7). Such clear Lutheran influence, along with the fact that it remains almost entirely unacknowledged by the conservative evangelical Geisler, points to an interesting and probably typical phenomenon. Luther's theological positions—particularly the so-called 'solas': *sola Scriptura, sola gratia, solus Christus,* and *sola fide*—are so deeply foundational to much of Protestant thought that they are accepted by many theologians as general truths, with little consideration of their historical origins.

James William McClendon's three-volume *Systematic Theology* (1986–2002) remains one of the most stimulating projects of this kind to emerge in recent decades. McClendon describes his perspective as 'baptist', deliberately lower-case in order to distinguish it from the more specific 'Baptist' denomination and to align it with what others might call the 'Anabaptist' tradition. In doing so, McClendon certainly claims a Reformation legacy, but that of the Radical Reformation rather than of magisterial Lutheranism. Structurally, too, McClendon's system has little in common with classic Lutheran models, and begins with a volume on 'Ethics'. A closer look, however, reveals deeper affinities. McClendon's 'Ethics' has less to do with explicating a traditional ethical system (or with grounding his system in 'the Law') than with developing a vision for the life of the church: 'how the church must live if the church was to be the church' (McClendon 1994: II.[7]). Throughout the work McClendon remains guided by a powerful concern for the 'here and now', and for the church's dynamic relationship to 'the world'. Clearly, a Radical-Reformation legacy is at work here. On the other hand, his perspective takes up key concerns of the magisterial reformers as well and could plausibly figure in a broader stream of Lutheran discussion on proper discipleship. Indeed, one of McClendon's inspirations is Dietrich Bonhoeffer, whom he engages liberally and far more deeply than any historical Anabaptist thinker. The author's willingness and ability to make creative use of key parts of the Lutheran heritage testify to that tradition's enduring viability at least as powerfully as do some of the more overt—and predictable—'interpretations' by confessional Lutherans.

British theologian Keith Warrington's *Pentecostal Theology* (2008) shows even fewer points of direct contact with Luther than does McClendon's system. That is as much a function of Warrington's style as of his theology. The work is more descriptive than propositional, focusing to a greater degree on describing what (and how) contemporary Pentecostals believe than on defining doctrine normatively. As a consequence, Warrington makes little effort explicitly to relate *Pentecostal Theology* to the historical Christian dogmatic tradition, and one finds very few references to any pre-Pentecostal theologian at all. J. Rodman Williams' earlier *Renewal Theology: Systematic Theology from a Charismatic Perspective* (1988–92), for example, is both more traditionally thetic in structure and much more conversant with historical theology, engaging an enormous range of interlocutors and antecedents (including Luther). On the other hand, Williams' project is perhaps less useful for our present purposes since it more closely resembles classic Protestant theological systems in other ways as well.

Warrington, for his part, strives to make a clean break with that tradition. His descriptive approach is based on an appreciation of Pentecostalism's experiential focus: 'Pentecostals do not simply affirm a list of biblical beliefs; they have encountered them experientially' (Warrington 2008: 22). Warrington aims to describe how that happens. The result is a kind of biblical pragmatism, a hermeneutics concerned with *applying* biblical and dogmatic insights—though Warrington admittedly spends more time describing how that application works than in suggesting first-order applications himself. Such an approach makes it difficult to trace individual doctrines in Warrington's book; doctrine functions differently in his project than it does in more traditionally propositional works. When discussing various understandings of predestination, for example, Warrington is less concerned with taking a particular dogmatic position than with assessing the doctrine's consequences for the spiritual life (Warrington 2008: 38–40). It is therefore challenging to locate precise examples of Lutheran influence at a dogmatic level. However, Warrington's approach itself owes much to the Reformation's legacy. Both his biblicism and his pragmatism, reading scriptural insights in light of their *pro nobis* applicability, show a strong kinship with Luther's own biblical and soteriological emphases. Even Warrington's desire to break with traditional patterns of doing theology has an antecedent in Luther's impatience with Scholasticism. Both represent reforming impulses, an attempt to re-ground theology's project in a more immediate, more spiritually relevant substratum. As Pentecostals like Warrington turn to notions of 'encounter' for aid in such projects, they make use—whether consciously or not—of a patently Lutheran prototype: Luther's own theological reflection on his 'Reformation breakthrough', along with its components of *Anfechtung* and experienced grace, is nothing if not a theology of encounter. There is, therefore, much in Warrington's *Pentecostal Theology* that resonates with the Lutheran tradition—more, certainly, than meets the eye upon an initial reading.

These three examples suggest different ways in which Luther's legacy influences contemporary non-Lutheran Protestant theology. Surveying these examples reveals a basic pattern. Overt references to Luther are rare in these works. They corroborate the earlier observation that explicit engagement with Luther has been relegated to confessional niches. On the other hand, Luther's unacknowledged influence is pervasive. A more thorough examination of the works in question would easily strengthen this point. Luther's theology of Scripture, his doctrine of *sola gratia* justification, his Christocentric soteriology, and his specific understanding of theology as a 'practical' science all contribute foundationally to contemporary Protestant thought across the spectrum. Inner-Protestant diversity tends to obscure these commonalities. However, while all Protestant theologians arguably owe *something* to Luther, they tend to emphasize different parts of Luther's legacy. One would be hard-pressed to identify a single heir to Luther in today's theological landscape. In fact, those who seem least 'Lutheran' often reveal particularly invigorating adaptations of the reformer's thought. Still, in nearly all of these cases, Luther's influence is far greater than acknowledged. Such observations undermine the notion of Luther niches and suggest the need for a more nuanced account of Luther's apparent retreat from the forefront of Protestant discourse.

In working towards a more adequate account of Luther's seeming disappearance from large parts of Protestant discourse, one could begin with a broader observation: academic theology itself has in several ways become a niche phenomenon. First, theology's ability to influence the language of church communities has declined markedly in the last fifty years. Protestants nearly everywhere lament a perceived disconnect between academic theology and 'the life of the church'. To appreciate this highly complex point, one need only compare the impact made by twentieth-century theologians such as Karl Barth or Rudolf Bultmann on preaching, Bible reading, catechesis, and the general discourse of their churches with that of any academic theologian today, or the theological weight of the Barmen Declaration with recent nearly a-theological proclamations issued by Protestant church bodies. While in the past theology provided a foundation for the church's language, it appears at present to have become a specialized discourse confined to a small circle of authors and readers.

Part of that decline stems from the disappearance of unifying, normative voices within the ongoing globalization of theological discourse. This points to a second way in which theology has become a niche phenomenon. Any list of the most influential theologians of the twentieth century is likely to be dominated by German (and Swiss) names. Building upon a centuries-old academic tradition distinguished by rigorous educational standards, dedication to research, and high expectations of theological literacy, German-language theology set the tone for much of Protestant thought globally. That has changed significantly in recent decades as the theological 'marketplace' has become globalized and other cultural traditions have gained confidence. Whether intentionally or not, German theologians today write primarily for German audiences. The same largely holds true for writers in other languages. Even where English has emerged as a new international standard, authors are now likely to be confined by denominational boundaries: Finnish Lutherans may publish works in English, but that does not mean that American Baptists are any more likely to read them. Pluralization and globalization have fragmented the field and created further niches of influence, many of which have become mutually incomprehensible.

These observations are important for assessing Luther's significance for contemporary Protestantism. The very notion of 'World Protestantism' is highly problematic and requires further qualification in order to be workable at all. Furthermore, the thought that World Protestantism—or even any of its denominational subsets—may be defined only by its theology appears no longer tenable. Pluralization of denominational and cultural contexts along with the marginalization of dogmatic theology in virtually all of those contexts have created a situation in which those who are capable of reading and writing theology constitute little more than a niche within a niche. Because of that, one will have to look beyond the field of theological publication in order to measure Luther's abiding significance for global Protestantism.

Both globalization and pluralization have contributed to the decline of academic theology's significance, as has the phenomenon of *secularization*. Defined by historians and sociologists in various ways, the term may refer broadly to a decrease in organized public religiosity. Because that decrease involves a depreciation of the institutions in which religiosity is organized publicly—churches—secularization also plays a role in theology's marginalization. Theology's traditional connection to the church is undermined whenever notions of what constitutes 'church' become unclear. Theology's natural field of reference becomes porous and indistinct, particularly as theologians themselves disagree over ecclesiological definitions. Because that lack of clarity is not only seen by theologians, but in fact experienced by religious constituencies unable to identify themselves corporately, the audience of those who feel addressed by theology disintegrates as well.

Paradoxically, Luther himself is frequently held responsible for the dynamic of secularization. If true, this would suggest that Luther may have set in motion his own path to obsolescence. It would also mean that Luther's abiding significance for World Protestantism may lie in its ultimate demise—or at least in its transformation from a corporate entity to a mode of private religiosity.

The term 'secularization' is used in several ways and often refers to different phenomena. Sociologist José Casanova argues that

> what usually passes for a single theory of secularization is actually made up of three very different, uneven and unintegrated propositions: secularization as differentiation of the secular spheres from religious institutions and norms, secularization as decline of religious beliefs and practices, and secularization as marginalization of religion to a privatized sphere. (Casanova 1994: 211)

In popular usage, the second of Casanova's three meanings is probably most widespread—and the most obviously problematic. Those who speak of a general 'decline of religious beliefs and practices' typically have the very low rates of church participation in Western Europe in mind and have taken that situation to be the global norm. As thinkers such as Peter L. Berger (1999) and David Martin (2005) have pointed out, however, Western European religiosity more likely constitutes an exception to global patterns. Religious expression—and even church attendance—in most other parts of the world have not only not declined during the twentieth century; they have often risen.

Furthermore, touching on Casanova's third proposition, a decline of *public* religious expression even in Western Europe does not mean that religious beliefs and practices in general have ceased there; they may simply have become more *private*. That process of privatization has also attracted considerable scholarly attention. The notion of 'privacy' also remains problematic since the phenomena to which it is applied are complex and varied. For one thing, 'private' does not necessarily mean 'individualistic'. Clearly, one observes many people who do not attend church services but still consider themselves 'religious' or 'spiritual'. Often, they can identify beliefs and practices that make them so. Frequently, they do express their religiosity 'in private', i.e., without involving others. At other times, however, such persons move their religious practice outside the established churches and into new forms of spiritual community. Those forms are typically less firmly institutionalized, but nonetheless recognizably communal. The most obvious example is Pentecostalism, particularly in North America, where it has mostly emerged from pre-existing church structures. Tellingly, many Pentecostals (and evangelicals) describe themselves as 'non-denominational', thereby underscoring both their rejection of confessional and denominational institutions as well as their acceptance of at least some form of corporate life and practice. That in many parts of the world such non-denominational Christians not only seek some outwardly recognizable pattern of the common life, but participate publicly as such in their context's political arena, has even fuelled talk of a trend of 'de-privatization'.

Casanova and many other sociologists emphasize the first use of the term 'secularization' most strongly: a process of social differentiation in which secular entities assume functions previously exercised by churches. The legal separation of church and state is a fitting symbol (and also a symptom) of this form of secularization. Far more than a legal construct, however, it exhibits a comprehensive embrace on entire cultures. Whereas in previous eras, Western churches took responsibility for educating the young and administering charity; saw their church calendars structure public rhythms of work, holiday, and religious observation; participated directly in government; and took the lead in propagating moral and ethical norms; they only do so in a very limited way in most Western societies today. The trajectory seems headed in one direction only. Here, too, of course, there is considerable variety, ranging from the remarkably vigilant separation of church and state in multi-religious France, for example, to the more cooperative relationships in relatively homogeneous Scandinavia. Churches have rarely accepted this process passively and in many settings continue to counteract such trends by seeking out new models of social engagement and cultural influence.

How is secularization related to the Reformation and Luther's legacy? Some sociologists contend that all of the above-mentioned forms of secularization (social differentiation, reduced religiosity, and privatization) are most conspicuous in Protestant countries. While such claims are not entirely tenable (Catholic France, for example, is arguably more 'secularized' in at least two of the three ways than are Anglican England or Lutheran Norway), they nonetheless give rise to interesting attempts at historical explanation. Most of these draw in some way on the 'father' of modern sociology of religion: Max Weber.

Several aspects of Weber's thought continue to influence academic discussion of the Reformation's long-term legacy. Most famous is Weber's connection of the rise of capitalism with Calvinist theology, arguing that anxiety caused by Calvinist teachings on predestination fuelled an obsession with securing material 'proofs' of God's approval—and one's election (Weber 1934). Coupled with an ethos of self-denial and forged in the crucible of seventeenth-century Puritanism, that dynamic laid the foundation for the remarkable economic ascendancy of Dutch, English, and finally American commercial and capitalist cultures (Weber). The fact that the results had little to do with Calvin's and even less with Luther's Reformation vision, and indeed flatly contradicted many of their values, does not diminish, in the eyes of some observers, their connection to the Reformation's legacy. In that vein historian Brad S. Gregory has recently spoken of an 'unintended Reformation', identifying, among other things, the unbridled and avaricious consumerism of contemporary capitalist cultures as a reality made possible by the Reformation to a particular feature of its theology (Gregory 2012: 235–97).

Because Weber also regarded the rise of capitalism as a feature of modernity and linked its success to the progressive ability of empirical science to explain—and subjugate—the workings of nature, historians often raise notions of 'modernization' and 'disenchantment' (*Entzauberung*) when describing secularization in Weberian terms. Broadly speaking, the Reformation is said to have instigated these dynamics by opposing superstition and 'magical' understandings of religion, particularly with respect to the sacraments. The reformers thereby launched a process of 'rationalization' of religion that, after a decisive boost by the Enlightenment, continues to the present.

While all of these notions are controversial and hotly debated by contemporary scholars, one cannot deny them an element of plausibility. If Weber's theses were not so powerfully suggestive, they would not continue to fuel discussion. Furthermore, it is incontrovertible that Western society is thoroughly capitalistic; it has, at least among its educated members, adopted a view of nature more 'scientific' than 'magical'; and its religiosity reflects those developments in both belief and practice. That does not, however, make those facts necessary outcomes of Luther's theology.

As has already been observed, Luther's connection to the rise of capitalism has typically been thought less direct than that of Calvin. According to Weber, Luther's primary contribution to that process came through his ethos of vocation (*Beruf*). Luther sought to emphasize the spiritual value of non-religious vocations, arguing that one did not need to be a monk or nun in order to live a life dedicated to serving God. Every vocation, according to Luther, can be God-pleasing if it is exercised in obedience to God's call and in a spirit of honest Christian service. In Weber's view Luther's characterization of secular work as something ordained by God was easily harnessed to the machinery of emerging capitalism, especially when melded with Calvin's later contributions. Weber is less interested, however, in pursuing the trajectory of Luther's ethic of vocation in its distinctively *Lutheran* cultural contexts—because the history of early modern and modern Germany and Scandinavia is less suited to documenting the rise of liberal capitalism. In fact, those societies are better known for their cultivation of state-sponsored social welfare, which more than a few historians have associated with Luther's legacy. In that model Luther's *Berufsethos* and efforts at social reform, such as his support of centralized poor relief, his educational initiatives (extending to women as well as men), and comprehensive civic reform, further developed by the large-scale charity work of Lutheran pietism, laid the spiritual and institutional foundation for the modern social-welfare states of Germany and Scandinavia. It is certainly plausible that, in those contexts, Luther's expansion of *Beruf* was *not* instrumentalized by an emergent capitalism, but instead undergirded a social vision built with collective Christian charity.

Luther's contribution to the dynamic of 'disenchantment' is also unclear. With respect to the sacraments, Luther was far less 'rationalistic' than Zwingli and even Calvin, and more than willing to attribute to baptism and the eucharist a degree of mystery that transcends human reason. On the other hand, Luther rigorously opposed many aspects of medieval religiosity, such as the cult of saints—though his rationale typically owed as much to inherently theological commitments as it did to a critique of superstition (Cameron 2010). A more plausible agent of disenchantment may lie in the university reforms and curricular changes that began in Luther's time and continued into the seventeenth and eighteenth centuries, changes that saw the establishment of modern natural sciences, a revolution in academic medicine, and incorporated the era's celebrated paradigm shifts in astronomy. These, too, were 'Lutheran' in spirit and had an enormous impact on Lutheran theology and biblical exegesis, but it would be hard to see in them a programme of disenchantment originating with the reformer himself.

Luther's role in establishing 'state churches' is easier to identify. While he does not appear to have envisioned this as a long-term solution, it is clear that Luther lobbied the German princes to take responsibility for the churches in their territories, thereby detaching those churches from the episcopal supervision administered by Rome. By

1555 the Lutheran princes were declared *summus episcopus* (highest bishop) of 'their' respective churches, creating the state churches that existed in Germany until 1918, and, though by a different historical process, in some Scandinavian countries to the present day.

Secularization theories make the point that contemporary Protestant societies are no longer shaped by that kind of state-church institution. In fact, secularization—in almost every sense of the word—describes, at least in part, the dismantling of those institutions and the cultural legacies of the *Volkskirchen* they supported. Luther's contribution to such processes, however, is far from clear. It is especially conflicted with respect to the social differentiation exhibited by church–state separation. On the one hand, Luther's own social ethos and reform programme led to an expansion of the state's jurisdiction over religious matters and to the absorption of some church functions by the state, argu-ably facilitating a long-term dynamic of differentiation. On the other hand, Luther's vision for church and society clearly aimed at a more integrative model—the state exercised its custodial duties as *part* of the church, not from outside or above it.[5] While Luther entertained the theoretical possibility of having the church administered by a non-Christian prince, he certainly did not expect this to apply to his own case. Instead, he assumed that church and state authorities would be working towards the same ultimate goals that could be defined in Christian terms. From the context of his own biography, Luther would have had greater sympathy for the ideal of a state-supported *Volkskirche* than for that of differentiation and denominational pluralism.

Denominational pluralism is, however, the face of contemporary Protestantism. Paradoxically, Protestantism, especially in its Pentecostal variant, is flourishing most vibrantly in situations where state-churches do not exist and where denominational structures are pluriform and weak. Assessing Luther's legacy for that reality depends in part on whether one sees it as a regrettable outcome of secularization (and as a symptom of decline), or as an opportunity for a new and vital form of Christianity. Put another way: is 'Lutheranism' linked inextricably with *Volkskirchen* and state-church structures, or has that linkage come as the result of accidental historical contingencies whose dis-appearance may liberate Luther's legacy to be rediscovered by a new, post-secularized Protestantism?

For the latter to happen, several conditions will have to be met. Most importantly, Luther's legacy will need to be redefined in non-denominational terms. Doing so would be historically appropriate since Luther did not aim to launch a 'Lutheran' church, but composed his reforming theology for what he took to be a universal, 'catholic' audi-ence. Ecumenical dialogue, such as recent efforts involving Lutherans and Pentecostals, indicates that Luther's theology can offer a profoundly applicable resource and witness beyond denominational Lutheranism. The implicit and typically unacknowledged

---

[5] One example of Luther's integrative approach is his conception of society as being comprised of 'three estates' (domestic, political, and ecclesial), which supplants the oft-misunderstood language of 'two kingdoms' in his later writings.

influence of Luther on non-Lutheran theologies (see above) is further suggestive. Luther's legacy *already* extends beyond Lutheranism; but it needs to be identified more clearly so that it can play a more fruitful and/or critical role.

Second, Luther's legacy needs to be reconceived in a truly global perspective. While all may well rejoice over Luther's contributions to the German language and to German culture, Luther's significance will remain parochial unless it resonates more broadly, and specifically in the non-Western cultures where Protestantism has expanded most rapidly. Clearly, that will depend in large part on the ability (and desire) of voices from Asia, Africa, and Latin America not only to claim Luther in their own terms, but to make themselves heard globally. Fortunately, that process is already well under way.

Finally, the history of the Reformation itself awaits rediscovery and re-evaluation. Reformation master narratives have long been dominated by the imposition of a faulty *terminus ad quem*: they culminate, implicitly or explicitly, in the establishment of Western Europe's state-supported confessions. Since those structures are now passé, or fast disappearing, attention may move to the crafting of Reformation narratives for a contemporary age. In particular, long-neglected studies of Luther's relationship to the Radical Reformation, to the so-called 'enthusiasts', and to the rise of both capitalism and its religiously motivated alternatives appear pertinent. In that way, much of Luther's legacy may yet await discovery, just as it has only in recent decades become possible for many to view the ordination of women as a proper part of Lutheranism (on new roles for women in early Lutheran ministry, cf. Appold 2006).

One part of Luther's institutional legacy remains indispensable to the flourishing of World Protestantism: academic education. Luther promoted educational institutions of all levels, ranging from the broad-based schooling of children to the nurturing of advanced and elite scholarship. They were central to his Reformation vision. Today, too, institutionally safeguarded spaces for sustained, rigorous, and disciplined reflection on all aspects of Christian truth remain essential to the survival of Protestantism in any context. Only in this way will we continue to make sure that the Jesus of our personal encounters bears some resemblance to the Christ of Scripture.

REFERENCES

Appold, Kenneth G. (2006). 'Frauen im frühneuzeitlichen Luthertum. Kirchliche Ämter und die Frage der Ordination'. *Zeitschrift für Theologie und Kirche* 103: 253–79.

Bayer, Oswald (2007/8). *Martin Luthers Theologie. Eine Vergegenwärtigung*, 3rd edn. Tübingen: Mohr/Siebeck. English translation: *Martin Luther's Theology: A Contemporary Interpretation*, trans. Thomas H. Trapp. Grand Rapids, MI: Eerdmans.

Berger, Peter L. (1999). *The Desecularization of the World: Resurgent Religion and World Politics*. Grand Rapids, MI: Eerdmans.

Cameron, Euan (2010). *Enchanted Europe: Superstition, Reason, and Religion, 1250–1750*. Oxford: Oxford University Press.

Casanova, José (1994). *Public Religions in the Modern World*. Chicago: University of Chicago Press.

Geisler, Norman (2002). *Systematic Theology*, 4 vols. Minneapolis: Bethany.

Gregory, Brad S. (2012). *The Unintended Reformation: How a Religious Revolution Secularized Society*. Cambridge, MA: Harvard University Press.

Helmer, Christine (2002). 'Luther's Trinitarian Hermeneutics and the Old Testament'. *Modern Theology* 18: 49–73.

Jenson, Robert W. (1997–9). *Systematic Theology*, 2 vols. Oxford: Oxford University Press.

McClendon, James William, Jr. (1986–2002). *Systematic Theology*. Vol. I: *Ethics*; *Systematic Theology*. Vol. II: *Doctrine*; *Systematic Theology*. Vol. III: *Witness*. Nashville: Abingdon.

Malysz, Piotr J. (2008). 'Luther and Dionysius: Beyond Mere Negations'. *Modern Theology* 24: 679–92.

Martin, David (2005). *On Secularization: Towards a Revised General Theory*. Aldershot: Ashgate.

Pannenberg, Wolfhart (1988–93). *Systematische Theologie*, 3 vols. Göttingen: Vandenhoeck & Ruprecht.

Root, Michael (2011). Review of Oswald Bayer, *Martin Luther's Theology: A Contemporary Interpretation*. *Modern Theology* 27: 200–2.

Vainio, Olli-Pekka (2010). *Engaging Luther: A (New) Theological Assessment*. Eugene, OR: Cascade.

Warrington, Keith (2008). *Pentecostal Theology: A Theology of Encounter*. London: Clark.

Weber, Max (1934 [1904–5]). *Die Protestantische Ethik und der Geist des Kapitalismus*. Tübingen: Mohr/Siebeck.

Williams, J. Rodman (1988–92). *Renewal Theology: Systematic Theology from a Charismatic Perspective*, 3 vols. Grand Rapids, MI: Academie Books.

CHAPTER 45

....

LUTHER AND ASIA

....

PILGRIM W. K. LO

THERE is no evidence that Roman Catholic missionaries introduced Martin Luther to Asia after the Reformation. But even apart from his theology, Luther was known as a great man of the Reformation who changed the history of the West among some Asian intellectuals. His name had been mentioned in publications before the arrival of Lutheran missionaries in Asia. Nevertheless, Asians learned about the person, works, and thought of Martin Luther as Lutheran missions introduced him.

I. THE BEGINNINGS

....

The first Lutheran missionaries in Asia, Bartholomäus Ziegenbalg (1682–1719) and Heinrich Plütschau (1677–1746), were sent by the Dänisch-Hallesche Mission. On 9 July 1706 they arrived from Germany in the Danish colony Tranquebar on the south-east coast of India. Although early in 1715 Ziegenbalg had published the Tamil translation of Luther's Small Catechism, he concentrated on evangelization. Similarly, Karl R. A. Gützlaff (1803–51), who initiated the second Asian Lutheran mission in China, translated the *Small Catechism* into Chinese in 1843, twelve years after landing in China, yet he had no intention to promote Luther or initiate Luther studies in China.

Many Protestant missions came to Asia in the imperialistic colonial era; Lutheran churches developed like others under the protection of colonial powers. Lutheran mission achieved much in evangelization as well as in medical and educational ministries. However, for over a century local Christians were not allowed to assume leadership in the church. Particularly in India, China, and Indonesia, where Lutheran missions began relatively early, Luther was introduced through the eyes of the missionaries, and church life followed European or North American patterns.

Lutheran missions began in the countries of Asia at different times. The outcomes of their ministries vary due to diverse political situations and distinct cultures. Thus, the reception of Luther varies in its development from country to country although Lutherans generally regard him as the father of the faith and his teaching is regarded as standard Christian doctrine.

II. THE EARLY DEVELOPMENT

Lutheran history in Asia is short, indigenous Luther study in Asia much shorter. Few writings of Luther were translated into Asian languages before 1945. Only some of his very significant publications were available in native languages, such as the *Small Catechism* (1715 in Tamil, 1843 in Chinese, 1939 in Japanese), *On Christian Freedom* (1911 in Tamil and in Japanese, 1932 Chinese), *The Smalcald Articles* (1872/1880 in Tamil, 1939 Japanese) and *The Ninety-Five Theses* (1927 in Chinese).

Significant was the establishment of Lutheran theological seminaries, such as in China the Lilang Cunzhen College (1864) in Canton and the Lutheran Theological Seminary (1913) in Hubei, the Japan Lutheran Theological Seminary (originally Lutheran School of Theology, 1909) in Kumamoto, Japan, and the United Lutheran Theological College (1931) in Madras (now Chennai), India. Rajah B. Manikam emphasized in the first Asia Lutheran Conference held at Gurukul College, Madras, South India in 1956, that 'the Asian churches are seen as "pale imitations" of Western churches, [and] they are too Western in their theology' (Scherer 1976/7: 337). The missionaries who founded these seminaries employed curriculum and teaching methods from the West. Luther and the Lutheran doctrine were taught from the Western perspective. Nevertheless, this new start was vital for the future of Luther studies and the development of the Lutheran churches. Without theological education there could be no church growth. Theological education by Lutheran seminaries is the foundation for nurturing local Lutheran theologians.

Differing conditions and situations in the Asian societies and scarcity of information make it difficult to build a detailed or a general picture of Luther study in Asia immediately after the Second World War. Two remarkable examples do deserve attention, however. The leading Lutheran seminary in China, Lutheran Theological Seminary (now in Hong Kong), played a most influential role in Luther study in Chinese society. The leadership of various Lutheran missions from North America, Norway, and Finland shaped its development for many years, until 1971 when the first Chinese president was appointed. For over one hundred years almost no Chinese were involved in scholarly study of Luther or participated in the translation of writings on and of Luther (P. Lo 2006: 144–50). Although the first Lutheran mission arrived in Japan sixty-one years later, in marked contrast to China, the Japanese initiated Luther research much earlier, even before the Second World War (e.g., Shigehiko Satô's *Luther's Fundamental Thought as seen in his Commentary on the Epistle to the Romans* [1933]). In particular, soon after the Second World War, the topic of freedom and emancipation became a relevant concern. Publications like Katsuya Sano's *The Reformation and the Spirit of the Modern Times* (1946), Hisao Otsuka's *The Reformation and the Modern Society* (1950), and Kazô Kitamori's *Luther—His Meaning for Our Own Day* (1951) demonstrate the self-reliance of Luther study in Japan (Masuda 1962: 227–8).

III. Contributions of the Lutheran World Federation

By origin Asian Lutheran churches are all 'Lutheran', yet distinct from one another since the mission societies had different resources, interests, and agendas for their ministry. Thus, Lutheran churches in Asia have received Luther in differing ways. After the founding of the Lutheran World Federation (LWF) Lutheran churches in Asia have shown enthusiasm for Lutheran cooperation and have had a stronger sense of belonging to the Lutheran family. Although the LWF held the First Asia Lutheran Conference early in 1956 at Gurukul, the real concern for the development of Lutheranism in Asia emerged in the 1970s. An Asian Programme for Advanced Studies (since 2003 Asian Programme for the Enhancement of Lay Training) was established in 1974, designed 'to foster renewal of theological understanding in Lutheran churches in Asia and to further their witness to the gospel in various life situations, encouraging indigenous creative theological thinking, expression and production'. Research on the regional level was to focus on 'Luther studies in an ecumenical, Asian context, including study, evaluation, translation, adaptation and application to the Asian setting' (Sitompul and Rajaratnam 1978: 6, 4). Consultations, conferences, and seminars sponsored by the LWF were held on a regular basis for over two decades, focused on concerns regarding Lutheran identity, the significance of Luther's thought, theological education, Lutheran mission, etc. Although only a few Luther scholars from Asia participated in these conferences, the LWF did make the young Lutheran churches aware of the significance of Luther and his teachings for their churches and encourage young theologians to engage in Luther research.

During this period Luther's writings were published rapidly in Asian languages: the Japanese edition of Luther's *Works*, 36 volumes (about half published by Seibunsha, Tokyo); the Korean edition of Luther's Works, 12 volumes (completed 1989, two additional volumes published later by Concordia, Seoul); and the publication of a Luther Series by the Taosheng Publishing House, Hong Kong. Unlike initial translation of the Bible in Asia, all by Western scholars, the Asian scholars assumed the task of translating Luther. It is also noteworthy that Luther research at this stage involved an exchange between East and West, rather than education by the West. Speakers taking part in conferences are mostly local scholars, not missionaries. Increasingly, Asian theologians are writing on Luther.

IV. THE ASIAN AGENDA

In comparison with Western Luther study from the Luther Renaissance to the new 'Finnish' interpretation of Luther, Luther studies in Asia lag behind. Although Lei Yutian, the director of the China Luther Study Centre, sees a 'Luther Renaissance' in China in the 1980s (Lei 2002: 116–19), and Won Jong Ji, the general editor of the *Korean Luther Works*, published an article entitled 'Luther Renaissance in East Asia' (Ji 1999: 292–4), these point merely to interest in Luther. The phenomenon as such, however, has not resulted in pronounced development of scholarly studies of Luther. Nonetheless, the future of Luther study in Asia is promising.

Distinct contexts from place to place in Asia create a variety of interests in Luther. In some countries like Thailand and the Philippines, Luther research has not yet really begun. In China and South Korea Luther is more highly regarded. Luther's theology as an integral part of Western culture receives more and more serious attention. Nevertheless, scholarly Luther studies in China (Ruokanen 2008: 171), as well as in Korea, have for the most part not yet attained Western standards. While Luther research in Japan has followed German models more closely, Indian theologians are much more interested in the contextualization of Luther's theology. In order to give a general, though not comprehensive, picture of Luther study in Asia, this essay focuses on two areas: the development of Lutheran identity and the contextualization of Luther's theology.

Questions regarding Lutheran identity in Asia preoccupied Asian Lutherans from the end of the Second World War through to the 1970s. Their shared concern for 'Lutheran solidarity' (Sormin 1976: 173), namely the acknowledgement of the historical origin and the continuity of the Lutheran tradition in Asia in cooperation with LWF, was the centre of attention. The same question arose again in the globalization process at the end of the last century as Lutherans faced both various kinds of religious resurgence in Asia (*Asian Lutheran News* 38, 2008: 4), and ecumenical challenges. The word used to designate 'Lutheran' in Chinese combines the concepts of 'faith' and 'righteousness' rather than an expression associated with Luther (Choong 2000: 154).

Asian scholars today are pursuing Luther studies by translating Luther's works, introducing and interpreting Luther's faith, teaching Luther's theology, and writing monographs on Lutheran doctrine, in order to rediscover and retain Lutheran identity. Challenges also come from outside Lutheran circles. The movement of theological reconstruction in the Chinese church led by Bishop K. H. Ting of the Protestant Church in China, begun some ten years ago, holds that the doctrine of justification by faith generates Christian hostility towards non-Christians, causing serious problems for church development in China. This doctrine caused a rift between believers and unbelievers by claiming that the majority of humankind is bound for hell regardless of their morality, just because they are unbelievers. He proposed therefore a reconstruction of Chinese theology by tempering the doctrine of justification by faith and stressing justification by love instead (P. Lo 2004a: 297–80). The *Joint Declaration on the Doctrine of Justification* of the LWF and the Roman Catholic church has raised another problem since many Asian Protestant churches regard the Roman Catholic church as heretical. The *Joint Declaration* creates difficulties for fellowship with non-Lutherans (W. Lo 1999: 216–17).

In contrast to doctrinal theology, theologians in Asia care more about context. There is one Asia, and the phrase 'Asian culture' is commonly used; however, Asian countries are not uniform in culture. Asia is arguably the most pluralistic of all continents religiously and ideologically (Choong 2000: 156; Kang 2000: 158). Since 'theology is dead' if it pays no attention to context, Luther's theology has no future in Asia if it merely imports sixteenth-century reformational doctrine without paying attention to different Asian contexts. Questions for Luther study are focusing on the significance of Luther's theology for Asians and how relevant his teaching is for different contexts of Asian society. Since the Dalits comprise about 80 per cent of the Indian church, many Indian theologians, including Lutherans, share many concerns for these oppressed people. Although he teaches at a Lutheran seminary (Gurukul Lutheran Theological College and Research Institute) as a Dalit theologian, V. Devasahayam is strongly critical of Luther's '*sola* doctrine'. He contends that Luther's doctrine of the bondage of the will, which emphasized the total depravity of humans in need of a saviour from outside, will lead to enslavement and prevents a new liberated psycho-social identity (Devasahayam 1997: 48). In opposition to Devasahayam, Santhosh Sahayadoss argues that Luther's response to social and political issues in his time is relevant and meaningful for Indian society. With his teaching of the two realms Luther emphasized the active participation of Christians in society which is in consonance with Indian theologians who are concerned to build a society of justice and peace (Sahayadoss 2006).

Inter-religious dialogue poses special challenges for Luther study in Asia. Luther's soteriology, grounded on his *sola* doctrine, provokes considerable religious controversy. Moreover, in regard to religious knowledge Luther's *Wortmonopolismus* is of primary significance for Lutheran theology, yet other religious leaders often regard it as a stumbling block for dialogue.

Some Asian theologians, like Japanese Luther scholar Yoshikazu Tokuzen, regard Luther's attitude towards other religions as a good model for religious dialogue as he made efforts to obtain more knowledge about other religions and attempted to understand religions in the light of the gospel (Tokuzen 1986: 83). Yet Luther's criticism of particular religions, such as Islam, is surely a formidable obstacle between Lutherans and Muslims in view of his placing the Turks together with the Jews, papists, and fanatics in the same category (cf., e.g., WA30,2.122,16–24; LW 46.177). However, Luther's theology in a specific area could offer common ground for religious dialogue with particular religions in Asia, for example his *theologia crucis*. Paul Chung, a Korean Luther scholar (now teaching in the United States) attempts to address Luther's understanding of divine suffering in relation to the Buddhist idea of *dukkha* [suffering] (Chung 2002: xix). Chung is convinced that 'a common basis for inter-religious dialogue between Luther and Buddhism lies in the interpretation of *dukkha*, in which an attempt is made to construct a theological aesthetics of divine suffering and human suffering' (Chung 2002: xviii). Luther's *theologia crucis* is unquestionably thought of as fundamental for Luther study in the West, as well as in Asia (cf. Ji 1998). Sixty-five years ago, immediately after the Second World War, Kazoh Kitamori, a Japanese Lutheran theologian, attempted to develop a Japanese theology in his book *The Theology of the Pain of God* (1946) by criticizing the theological tradition of divine impassability of the West. He echoed Luther's *theologia crucis*: 'The essence of God can be comprehended only from the word of the cross. The pain of God is his essence' (Kitamori 1966: 47). In his view the heart of Japanese tragedy in the war corresponds most closely to the pain of God (Kitamori 1966: 148). However, the theology of the pain of God for him plays a significant role in producing positive moral actions through human existence. Human pain should only be considered as service to God's pain. Therefore he postulated that 'the pain of God brings unity to the divisions existing between him and the world ... In order to have true peace, the divisions between God and the world must be united' (Kitamori 1966: 11–12).

An attempt of Jhamak Neeraj Ekka, an Indian theologian, also focuses on Luther's theology of the cross, yet with concerns for the pluralistic context of India. He argues for the uncompromising claim of Luther's theology of the cross that Jesus Christ is the final revelation of God on the cross. It should be the foundation for openness towards other faiths and commitment to the other. For him Christian faith could address the problems of poverty, oppression, and injustice adequately within the framework of the *theologia crucis*. Thus Luther's theology of the cross is a viable resource for contextual theology in India (Ekka 2007).

The theology of the cross as the core of Luther's theology has not yet been contextualized in Chinese Luther study. However, the significance of Luther's theology of the cross has received considerable recognition by Chinese theologians. Papers from a conference sponsored by the LWF at China Lutheran Seminary in Taiwan in 1990 and 1992 appeared as *A Look at the Theology of the Cross*. The conference sought to define the correct understanding of Luther's *theologia crucis* from different perspectives and to explore its theological significance. The editor concluded that Luther's theology of the cross can foster understanding of God, provide assurance of salvation, and aid carrying out ministry and facing suffering (Yu 1997: 6).

For Luther study in Asia translation is another main concern. For many Asian countries, translation of Luther's writings plays a very crucial role. Some Lutheran scholars have been aware of the necessity of accurate translation of Luther's theology and tried to clarify or amend existing translations which have been used for a long time. For instance Won Jong Ji has a critical concern for the translation of the word 'reformation'. 'Reformation' is translated into Korean as '*Jong-gyo* (religious) *gaehyuk* (reform)'. Ji is of the opinion that the concept of *Jong-gyo gaehyuk* used for 'reformation' will lose its original meaning in all aspects of life which the word 'reformation' can reach. In order to avoid such loss, he suggests restoring the original meaning of reformation by a thorough study of cultural, intellectual, social, and political aspects for the translation (Choi 2010: 268). Another noteworthy example is the translation of 'justification by faith' into Chinese. The words used in the Union Version Chinese Bible, the most authoritative Chinese Bible, are '*Yīn Xìn Chēng Yì*', which means literally 'designated to be righteous because of belief'. This translation is regrettably not precise enough to express Luther's theological understanding of justification by faith (P. Lo 2003: 36).

V. The Future of Luther Study in Asia

Paul Chung attempts to make concrete suggestions for the theological agenda of Luther study in Asia, such as 'Justification and a Theology of Divine Suffering', 'Theology of Two Kingdoms', and 'Ecclesiology in Word and Sacraments' (Chung 2003: 62–4). Certainly, many important, meaningful, and interesting topics should be included in Asian Luther study.

What is undeniable is the so-called Luther Renaissance in East Asia: the increasing interest in Luther and his theology in the countries of East Asia. Four fundamental and decisive elements are needed to facilitate the advancement of Luther study: scholars, study materials, theological concerns arising from the context, and theological discourse among theologians. It is too early to say what contribution the Asian Lutheran theologians have made to Lutheranism, but Luther's theological ideas have challenged Asian Christians and non-Christians alike in facing their own problems or difficulties with Christian ministry and society.

Scholarship depends on the development of good scholars. Fostering more Asians as Luther scholars is the primary task. They should be able to read both original sources and scholarly publications on Luther in German and in English. The original writings and the fruitful results of Luther study of the West are essential for Asian Luther study. But the Weimar edition of Luther's *Works* is available in only a few places in Asia (Japan, Hong Kong, Taiwan). Luther's *Works* published in the native languages of Asian countries are mainly translated from the American edition of Luther's *Works*. Lack of significant parts of the literature on Luther and his theology poses a serious difficulty, which must be overcome for the advancement of Luther study in Asia.

Other than linguistic ability, scholarship, and materials, reflections on the problems of context and integration of Luther's theology with Asian life here and now are significant for making Luther's theology alive through contextualization of sixteenth-century insights. Last but not least, the sharing and exchange of ideas about and results of Luther study between Asia and the West is vital. Looking back over the past fifty years, apart from the conferences sponsored by LWF held in Asia and for Asian Lutherans, the participation of Lutheran theologians from Asia in international conferences on Luther has been rather limited and largely passive. The number of scholars who participated in the International Congress for Luther Research is very small. Luther study in Asia as such is rightly regarded as at an elementary level but is developing and promising. Improvement of the above-mentioned decisive elements in the particular Asian context can enrich understanding of Luther's theology and make Luther study more fruitful.

References

Choi, Joo-Hoon (2010). 'Lutherische Kirche in Korea und Luther-Studien'. In *Glaube und Denken—Mission, Dialog & friedliche Koexistenz*. Frankfurt am Main: Lang, 261–274.

Choong, Chee Pang (2000). 'Lutheran Identity in a Pluralistic context: An Outline'. In *Asian Lutheranism: Which Way?* ed. Paul Rajashekar. Chicago: Asian Lutheran International Conference.

Chung, Paul (2002). *Martin Luther and Buddhism: Aesthetics of Suffering*. Eugene, OR: Wipf & Stock.

—— (2003). 'The Future of Martin Luther in an Asian Context'. *Dialog* 42: 62–74.

Devasahayam, V. (1997). *Frontiers of Dalit Theology*. Gurukul: ISPCK.

Ekka, Jhakmak Neeraj (2007). *Christ as Sacrament and Example: Luther's Theology of the Cross and its Relevance for South Asia*. Minneapolis: Lutheran University Press.

Ji, Won Yong (1998). 'Luther's Theology of the Cross and Eastern Thought'. *Concordia Journal* 24: 130–7.

—— (1999). 'Luther Renaissance in East Asia'. *Concordia Journal* 25: 25–35.

Kang, Wi Jo (2000). 'Response to Lutheran Identity in a Pluralistic Context: A Response'. In *Asian Lutheranism: Which Way?* ed. Paul Rajashekar. Chicago: Asian Lutheran International Conference, 157–60.

Kitamori, Kazoh (1966). *The Theology of the Pain of God*. London: SCM.

Lei, Yutian (2002). 'China's Luther Research and the Project of a Chinese Edition of Luther's Work'. *Theology and Life* 25: 116–19.

Lo, Pilgrim W. K. (2003). '(DJJD) Reception in the Chinese Context of Hong Kong'. In *The Doctrine of Justification: Its Reception and Meaning Today*, ed. Karen Bloomquist and W. Greive. Geneva: Lutheran World Federation, 35–8.

—— (2004a). 'From "Justification by Faith" to "Justification by Love"? A Reflection on Theological Reconstruction'. In *Glaube und Denken: Die Bedeutung der Theologie für die Gesellschaft, Festschrift für Hans Schwarz zum 65 Geburtstag*, ed. Anna M. Madsen. Frankfurt am Main: Lang, 277–87.

—— (2006). 'Lutherrezeption in China'. *Lutherjahrbuch* 73: 139–70.

Lo, Wingkwong (1999). 'Eine theologische Überlegung über die Stellungnahme der HK Kirchen zur *Gemeinsame Erklärung zur Rechtfertigungslehre*'. In *Glaube und Denken—Theologie zu Beginn des 3. Jahrtausends im globalen Kontext*, ed. David C. Ratke. Frankfurt am Main: Lang, 211–25.

Masuda, Kenji (1962). 'Luther Studies in Japan'. *Church History* 31: 227–30.

Rajashekar, Paul (ed.) (2000). *Asian Lutheranism: Which Way?* Chicago: Asian Lutheran International Conference.

Ruokanen, Miikka (2008). 'Luther and China'. *Dialog* 47: 167–71.

Sahayadoss, Santhosh (2006). *Martin Luther on Social and Political Issues: His Relevance for the Church and Society in India*. Frankfurt am Main: Lang.

Sitompul, Adelbert Augustin and K. Rajaratnam (eds.) (1978). *Equipping God's People in Asia, Reports and Minutes of the [APATS] Biannual Meeting in Hong Kong 1978*. Geneva: Lutheran World Federation.

Sormin, P. (1976). 'Lutheranism in the Context of Ecumenism in Asia'. *Third All Asia Lutheran Conference—Singapore, 29 Nov.–4 Dec.* Geneva: Lutheran World Federation, 135–44.

Tokuzen, Yoshikazu (1986). 'Tradition in Dialogue: The Case of Luther and Lutheranism'. In *Theology in Dialogue: Theology in the Context of Religious and Cultural Plurality in Asia*, ed. Paul Rajashekar and Satoru Kishii. Geneva: Lutheran World Federation, 74–84.

Yu, Thomas (ed.) (1997). *A Look at the Theology of the Cross* [in Chinese]. Xinzhu: China Lutheran Seminary.

SUGGESTED READING

Aageson, James W. (2007). *The Future of Lutheranism in a Global Context.* Minneapolis: Fortress.
APATS *Luther Studies Symposia, Reports 1980–1984 (I, II, and III) of Luther Studies Symposia* (1985). Geneva: Lutheran World Federation.
The Augsburg Confession in Asia Today: Relevance and Challenge for Mission and Ecumenism. Report of the First Luther Studies Symposium held 1–6 December 1980 in Hong Kong (1983). Geneva: Lutheran World Federation.
Chung, Paul (2005). 'Discovering the Relevance of Martin Luther for Asian Theology'. *Dialog* 44: 38–49.
Eastborn, S. (1961). *Luther/Lutheranism in the Indian Church: Some Essays on Luther and Lutheran Confessions in their Relation to Indian Christendom.* Madras: Diocesan.
Eom, Jin-Seop (2003). 'Luther Reception in Korea'. *Lutherjahrbuch* 70: 149–72.
—— (2006) 'The Lutheran Confessions in Korea'. *Dialog* 45: 138–42.
The Gospel and Asian Traditions: APATS Luther Studies Workshop, Hong Kong, March 1979. Lectures, reports, minutes (1979). Geneva: Lutheran World Federation.
Huddle, Benjamin P. (1958). *History of the Lutheran Church in Japan.* New York: United Lutheran Church in America.
Ji, Won Yong (1988). *A History of Lutheranism in Korea: A Personal Account.* Saint Louis: Concordia Seminary Press.
—— (1993). 'Luther in Asia'. *Concordia Journal* 19: 6–8.
—— (1994). 'Luther in East Asia'. *Concordia Journal* 20: 33–8.
—— (2000). 'Luther's Works and the Lutheran Confessions: Toward Indigenization of the Christian Faith'. *Concordia Journal* 26: 24–35.
Johnson, Jonas (1972). *Lutheran Missions in a Time of Revolution: The China Experience, 1944–1951.* Uppsala: Tvåväga.
Knudten, Arthur C. (1984). *The Forgotten Years and Beyond: Sketches in History, the Japan Evangelical Lutheran Church, 1942–1972.* N.p.: n.p.
Kuramatso, Isao (2002). 'Japanische Lutherbibliographie 1986–2000'. *Lutherjahrbuch* 69: 119–30.
Lo, Pilgrim W. K. (2004b). 'Die Bedeutung von Luthers Theologie für das 21. Jahrhundert'. *Lutherjahrbuch* 71: 61–4.
Lo, Wingkwong (2006). 'A Lutheran Reflection on the Understanding of Episcopé in a Pluralistic Society—Hong Kong as Example'. *Journal of the Asian Theological Society* 1: 49–57.
LWF Seminar on Dialogue in Life, Medan, Indonesia, 27–30 June 2006 (2007). Geneva: Lutheran World Federation.
Michalson, Carl (1962). 'Theology of Luther in Japan'. *Lutheran Quarterly* o.s. 14: 68–71.
Papers Presented at the Luther Studies Symposium II, Bangkok, Thailand, December 1–6, 1982 (1983). Geneva: Lutheran World Federation.
Rajashekar, Paul and Satoru Kishii (eds.) (1987). *Theology in Dialogue: Theology in the Context of Religious and Cultural Plurality in Asia.* Geneva: Lutheran World Federation.
Scherer, James (1976/7). 'Growth Toward Selfhood and Maturity: Africa, Asia, and Australasia'. In *The Lutheran Church, Past and Present,* ed. Vilmos Vajta. Minneapolis: Augsburg, 330–51.

Sitompul, Adelbert Augustin and K. Rajaratnam (eds.) (1977). *Current Asian Theological Thinking—Progress Reports and Papers from Seminars*. Geneva: Lutheran World Federation.

Syrdal, Rolf A. (1958). *Mission in Japan: Studies in the Beginning and Development of the Indigenous Lutheran Church in Japan*. Minneapolis: Augsburg.

Theology and Life (2002). Special Issue: *Luther in Asian Context*. Hong Kong: Lutheran Theological Seminary.

Third All Asia Lutheran Conference, Singapore, 29th November to 4th December 1976 (1976). Geneva: Lutheran World Federation.

Tokuzen, Yoshikazu (1979). 'Luther Studies in Asia'. In *The Gospel & Asian Traditions*. Geneva: Lutheran World Federation, 88–93.

Vajta, Vilmos (ed.) (1977). *The Lutheran Church, Past and Present*. Minneapolis: Augsburg.

Yu, Ke (1999). 'Lutherstudien in China'. *Luther* 70: 42–4.

CHAPTER 46

··

LUTHER IN AFRICA

··

TOM JOSEPH OMOLO

ACCORDING to the statistics released by the Lutheran World Federation (LWF) a decade ago, Africa occupies second place, after Europe, in terms of Lutheran demographics. But the two continents may soon swap positions given the high rate of church growth in Africa and the steady secularization of Europe. Despite such strength in the membership index, the Lutheran Church in Africa still has a long way to go in theological scholarship in general and Luther scholarship in particular. Danish missionaries brought the gospel in Luther's tradition to the West African coast in the mid-seventeenth century, and nineteenth- and twentieth-century mission efforts from several countries gave birth to Lutheran churches in thirty African nations, but a tradition of Luther research did not develop. Specifically, although Lutheran leaders, such as Manas Buthelezi, have sought ways of expressing Lutheran identity in a suitable way, Lutheran theologians and those from other traditions in Africa have done relatively little on Luther and his significance for the continent although exceptions prove the value of his thought for the African context (Maimela 1983, 1990; Yri 1998; Palmer 2005; Isaak 2008; Katabaro 2009). His five-hundredth birthday evoked some reflection (Kibira 1983; Hofmeyr 1983; as well as a special issue of the *Africa Theological Journal*, volume 12); missionaries from the north or South Africans of European ancestry have reflected occasionally on their experience with Luther's thought while in Africa (Lambert 1983; Nuernberger 1983, 2005; Borchardt 1984; Buys 1984; Fowler 1984; Carter 1991); and one survey of Luther's relationship with Africa through missionary activity has appeared (Rüther 2004).

How then is Luther relevant to the African context in the twenty-first century? What are some of his theological principles that may be applicable to the African way of life today within the framework of the Lutheran theological heritage and the wider biblical faith tradition? These are some of the questions that the Lutheran church in Africa has to address if it is to remain faithful in its theological identity and creatively African in its contextual particularity.

There have been attempts to employ the spirit and letter of certain articles of faith as articulated by Luther to address particular situations in Africa. One example is the address by the South African bishop Simon Maimela, at the time professor of system-atic theology at the University of Pretoria, to the International Congress for Luther Research in Oslo in 1988. Maimela endeavoured to show how the material substance of the Lutheran theology, justification by faith alone, could meaningfully be applied to apartheid-ridden South Africa. In accordance with his introductory disclaimer not to delve deeply into technical explication of the doctrine of justification, he tries to 'appropriate and interpret' the article in a manner that renders it relevant and applica-ble to the South African situation (Maimela 1990: 147). The gist of Maimela's submis-sion is that the racial segregation rampant in South Africa is irreconcilable with the letter and the spirit of the doctrine of justification as outlined by Luther and Lutheran theology. His understanding is that justification is not only a juridical matter, but it is also 'a divine transformative act which creates and regenerates the sinner, thus creat-ing a new person with new attitudes and behaviour pattern' (Maimela 1990: 156). This interpretation, reached in the context of racial segregation, casts aspersion on any claim of justification of anyone who practises or endorses racism in whatever form. Maimela's perspective somehow bears the yeast of liberation theology, which may eclipse the significant theological distinctions typical of the Lutheran theology such as the two realms, the two kinds of righteousness, and similar fundamental tenets. He says, for instance:

> because a person is declared by political law either justified or unjustified to enjoy certain privileges and rights, life of quality and security in South Africa has come to be seen not as a gift from God but as a reward of what individuals have earned on the basis of this or that natural worthiness such as one's race, culture, and economic status. (Maimela 1990: 153–4)

In this context the meaning of 'life' and 'justification' can be deepened and clarified by explaining that for Luther justification has theological, indeed existential, significance that goes beyond dealing with civil or political elitism and dominance to the worth of individual human beings and groups of human beings. Maimela's certainly legitimate concern does raise an important question about the connection between righteousness *coram Deo* which comes gratuitously *extra nos*, and the righteousness *coram mundo*, which is the direct effect of the former. That is, one's relationship with God affects one's relationship with fellow human beings and other creatures. Without watering down the theological meaning of 'justification' with interpretations limited to socio-political significance, the same aim of condemning racism is achievable by looking at how, in Luther's theology, the justified sinners are expected to live with one another. On the basis of our justification, we are not expected to consciously and deliberately per-petrate systematic or structural sin of any kind against God's creation. In this regard Luther remains relevant to Africa, a continent which has suffered much socio-political injustice.

A few examples will suffice to demonstrate how Luther's theology would be useful in Luther scholarship and for Christian living in Africa today. It has been argued that one of the basic presuppositions underlying Luther's theology and how he envisioned its being lived out focuses on the relational identity of the human person (Kolb and Arand 2008: 12). Such an identity is tied to how we relate to the Creator and to one's fellow creatures. In the Lutheran theological parlance, this falls under the category of the two kinds of righteousness. That is to say, 'to be a human being as God created us to be, a perfect human specimen, involves being totally passive, as a newborn child of God, and totally active, as a responsible neighbour to other people and to the whole of God's world' (Kolb and Arand: 2008: 30). Such an anthropological framework would perhaps be more applicable to African socio-religious life than to any other continent in the twenty-first century.

Africans are very religious people if John Mbiti's sentiment is truly indicative:

> Because traditional religions permeate all departments of life, there is no formal distinction between the sacred and the secular, between the religious and non-religious, between the spiritual and the material areas of life. Wherever the African is, there is his religion: he carries it to the fields where he is sowing seeds or harvesting a new crop; he takes it with him to the beer party or to attend a funeral ceremony; and if he is educated, he takes religion with him to the examination room at school or in the university; if he is a politician he takes it to the house of parliament. (Mbiti 1969: 83)

Such sentiment implies that Africans are deeply engrossed in religious endeavours of all sorts in order to satisfy, and hence rightly relate with, their 'god(s)'. Their understandings of how to 'attain' the right relationship with 'god' parallel somewhat certain aspects of the late medieval theology against which Luther revolted. Such understandings are based on what we can, or rather should, do in order to please 'god' and thereby be rightly related with him or, in other words, be righteous before him. This is what has been termed works-righteousness. Such a conception of the righteousness of God which is rife in Africa, and which is often transposed into African Christian theology and practice, calls for Luther's theological thought pattern, if Africans are to know the peace of God. Luther, in his evangelical discovery, came to realize that he could not storm heaven by good works but that he could only enter paradise through the gate which is open on account of Christ's work. Thus, Luther's view of the righteousness of God which comes by faith on account of Christ is very much relevant to the African context, where traditional religions have held sway with an emphasis on achieving righteousness before 'god' by human actions of one sort or another.

The genius of Luther's approach to theologizing is that he mastered the art of holding paradoxes in tension. Most of his theological axioms have other 'sides of the coin' which must be held in tension and accounted for. In this respect, the righteousness of God which comes by faith on account of Christ, passive righteousness, is indissolubly connected to the active righteousness according to which the justified are by God's design bound to rightly relate with fellow human beings and other non-human entities in creation. This active righteousness may be said to be the other side of Luther's two spheres of human existence which form our identity and which must be taken into account. If our core identity as human beings, as we saw above, is based on the passive righteousness that comes by faith, the other side of that identity, the active righteousness, flows from that core identity out into the world.

This is another front in which Luther would dialogue meaningfully with Africans. The ideal African life is one which defines human identity in terms of individuals' relation with the larger community. The I-me-and-myself lifestyle that characterizes day-to-day existence for many in the individualistic West does not belong in African social life, at least ideally. Africans know that they live for one another and that each individual has a duty to the entire community. Laurenti Magesa captures this when he states that 'just as one is nothing without belonging to a community, the community disintegrates some-what without the membership and contribution of everyone' (Magesa 1997: 96). Luther can therefore engage Africans in conversation to show how the two kinds of righteous-ness relate to each other in the Christian calling by the gospel to membership in the household of God. Luther would be useful for Africans in clarifying the proper distinc-tions between their standing before the Creator and their standing and responsibility before one another. Like Paul when speaking to the Athenians (Acts 17:22–31), Luther's writings can be used to draw from the people's experience and point them to the true righteousness of God that comes by faith in God's promise in the gospel. Luther's way of thinking explains how such righteousness before God, *coram Deo*, positively affects their life with one another and with the rest of God's creation. Luther's theology of the two kinds of righteousness therefore remains relevant to Africa today.

Another area in which Luther's theological acumen remains relevant and construc-tive in Africa today is the emphasis on biblical literacy and the knowledge of the basics of the Christian faith. His writings help identify those things which are necessary to know for salvation from the labyrinth of the scriptural message. Luther's Catechisms resulted from what he found in the visits he made in the parishes: the revelation, to his dismay, that both the clergy and the laity out there lacked basic biblical knowledge. He writes in the preface to the *Small Catechism*, 'The deplorable, wretched deprivation that I recently encountered while I was a visitor has constrained and compelled me to pre-pare this catechism' (BSLK 501; BC 347). He therefore wrote the Catechism, which he says 'contains what every Christian should know'. He further charges that 'Anyone who does not know it should not be numbered among Christians or admitted to any sacra-ment, just as artisans who do not know the rules and practices of their craft should be rejected and considered incompetent' (BSLK 553–4; BC 383). Many people in Africa are not knowledgeable in the content of the Bible. Some people try to read Scripture and master the major stories but lack the larger picture to help them piece together a jigsaw puzzle or draw a map to help them move through the landscape of biblical revelation. It is here that Luther becomes significant as he puts in place a summary of the biblical truth that we need to know for our salvation. It is also noteworthy that Africa still has a significant number of people who cannot read. Such people can thus benefit from the rote learning of the Catechism. Their situation is indeed similar to that of Luther's time when there were great masses of unlearned peasants.

Besides the level of complexity, Luther's Catechism is also important to Africa with regard to its content. For instance, the framework laid in the first commandment for our relationship with God bears three chief elements by which man becomes *Gottesmacher*, maker of God. These are fear, love, and trust. Luther taught that whatever you fear, love, and trust more than God the Creator becomes a god for you. Thus, we can *make* as many gods as the things we fear, love, and trust above our Creator and Saviour. This is a universal problem with humanity. The only difference is that it wears different colours depending on the context. In many parts of Africa, for example, relationship with the departed members of the community is characterized by activities and rituals of a religious nature. People fear, love, and trust the departed spirits not only alongside but evidently above the Creator and Saviour God, the Father of our Lord Jesus Christ. In such a context Luther's Catechism can help the people of Africa to understand how they would live out their Trinitarian-monotheistic faith without syncretistic tendencies.

These few examples serve the purpose of showing how Luther remains relevant and thus significant for Christian theological reflection and life in Africa. In this regard, serious Luther scholarship is required to bring Luther into dialogue with Africans in different areas of Christian theology and life.

References

Borchardt, C. F. A. (1984). 'Die relevansie van Luther se beroep op die Skrif alleen in Afrika-konteks'. In *New Faces of Africa*, ed. J. W. Hofmeyr and W. S. Vorster. Pretoria: University of South Africa, 1–13.

Buys, P. W. (1984). 'Luther, the Reformation and Us'. In *Our Reformational Tradition*. Potchefstroom: Institute for Reformational Studies, 86–97.

Carter, Richard (1991). 'A Lutheran Doctrine of Vocation in the Ibibio Context'. Ph.D. dissertation, Luther Seminary, Saint Paul.

Fowler, S. (1984). 'Faith and Reason in the Period of the Reformation' and 'Martin Luther: Faith beyond Reason'. In *Our Reformational Tradition*. Potchefstroom: Institute for Reformational Studies, 61–85, 98–112.

Hofmeyr, J. W. (ed.) (1983). *Martin Luther Lives*. Pretoria: University of South Africa.

Isaak, Paul John (2008). 'Spirituality and Social Activism: Insights from Luther'. In *Lutherans Respond to Pentecostalism*, ed. Karen Bloomquist. Minneapolis: Lutheran University Press, 129–38.

Katabaro, Brighton Mufuruki (2009). *Pfingstcharismatische Lehre und Praktiken als Herausforderung für die Lutherische Rechtfertigungslehre in Tansania*. Göttingen: Cuvillier.

Kibira, Josiah M. (1983). 'Has Luther Reached Africa? The Testimony of a Confused Lutheran'. *Africa Theological Journal* 12: 6–15.

Kolb, Robert and Charles P. Arand (2008). *The Genius of Luther's Theology*. Grand Rapids, MI: Baker Academic.

Lambert, J. (1983). 'Luther in the Historical Context of Late Medieval Thought'. In *Martin Luther Lives*, ed. J. W. Hofmeyr. Pretoria: University of South Africa, 1–17.

Magesa, Laurenti (1997). *African Religion: The Moral Traditions of Abundant Life*. Maryknoll, NY: Orbis.

Maimela, Simon (1983). 'Luther's Doctrine of Justification by Faith Alone and its Continuing Relevance for South Africa'. In *Martin Luther Lives*, ed. J. W. Hofmeyr. Pretoria: University of South Africa, 58–63.

—— (1990). 'Responsibility for the World: Luther's Intentions and the Effects from a South African Perspective'. *Lutherjahrbuch* 57: 147–62.

Mbiti, John S. (1969). *African Religions and Philosophy*. New York: Praeger.

Nuernberger, Klaus (1983). 'Luther as Reformer of the Church'. In *Martin Luther Lives*, ed. J. W. Hofmeyr. Pretoria: University of South Africa, 72–90.

—— (2005). *Martin Luther's Message for Us Today: A Perspective from the South*. Pietermaritzburg: Cluster.

Palmer, Timothy P. (2005). 'Luther's Theology of the Cross, and Africa'. *Africa Journal of Evangelical Theology* 24: 129–37.

Rüther, Kirsten (2004). 'Kannte Luther Africa? Afrika kennt Luther'. In *Luther zwischen den Kulturen: Zeitgenossenschaft—Weltwirkung*, ed. Hans Medick and Peer Schmidt. Göttingen: Vandenhoeck & Ruprecht, 337–72.

Yri, Norvald (1998). 'Luther Speaks to Africa: The Question of Salvation'. In *Issues in African Christian Theology*, ed. Samuel Ngewa, Mark Shaw, and Tiet Tienou. Nairobi: East African Educational Publishers, 186–91.

CHAPTER 47

LUTHER STUDIES IN LATIN AMERICA

NESTOR LUIZ JOÃO BECK

I. INTRODUCTION

SPAIN and Portugal colonized Latin America in the spirit of the Counter-Reformation. In this context Luther's name was eclipsed or, if mentioned at all, referred to as a heretic and enemy of the church. After independence some governments promoted immigration from Protestant territories. Lutheran immigrants brought Luther to Latin America, especially to Brazil and Argentina. This chapter therefore focuses on these two countries that received significant numbers of German immigrants.

II. HISTORY

German immigration to Argentina and Brazil resulted in the organization of Lutheran church bodies and the establishment of Lutheran seminaries. In the case of Brazil the Protestant immigrants formed the Evangelical Church of Lutheran Confession in Brazil, known as IECLB (*Igreja Evangélica de Confissão Luterana no Brasil*, <http://www.ieclb.org.br>; Prien 1985, 1989). It maintains the EST (*Escola Superior de Teologia*, <http:www.est.edu.br>). Since 1961 the school has published a theological journal, *Estudos Teológicos*. It is an institution of higher learning that offers undergraduate and graduate programmes in theology in São Leopoldo, the city that throughout the nineteenth century received large numbers of German immigrants who spread out, initially along the rivers, in the state of Rio Grande do Sul.

While IECLB was organized with the support of German church organizations, the Evangelical Lutheran Church of Brazil, commonly referred to as IELB (*Igreja Evangélica*

Luterana do Brasil, <http://www.ielb.org.br>), was organized with leadership from the Lutheran Church—Missouri Synod/USA (Rehfeldt 2003). It maintains the *Seminário Concórdia* that offers a master's programme and undergraduate studies in theology (<http://www.seminarioconcordia.com.br>). Since 1940 the seminary has published *Igreja Luterana: Revista Semestral de Teologia.* Its undergraduate programme is offered in cooperation with ULBRA (*Universidade Luterana do Brasil,* <http://www.ulbra.br>). The university was organized with Luther's education philosophy prominently in view (CELSP 1987; Beck 1988); since 2001 it has published *Theophilus: Revista de Teologia e Filosofia.*

In Argentina as well the immigrants and their descendants organized Lutheran church bodies and created theological seminaries in Buenos Aires, namely ISEDET (*Instituto Superior de Estudos Teológicos,* <http://www.isedet.edu.ar>; Held 1998), since 1971 the publisher of *Cuadernos de Teologia,* and *Seminário Concórdia* (<http://www.seminarioconcordia.com.ar>), publisher of *Revista Teológica* since 1977 and *Suplemento de Teología* since 1997.

III. RESOURCES

Lutheran families traditionally owned and read copies of Luther's translation of the Bible. These also served to record data of family history. Many families also owned and treasured Johann Friedrich Starck's prayer book, a product of eighteenth-century Lutheran pietism. Lutheran congregations instructed children in Luther's Catechism, at first in German and later on in translations. Liturgical services followed Luther's *Deutsche Messe* in abbreviated form; his hymns were sung in church, school, and home. The immigrants, abandoned by governments that had enticed them with magnificent promises, established elementary schools with their own scant resources, in Luther's spirit. These schools flourished until prohibited and dismantled by nationalistic governments during the Second World War. Some managed to recover and were expanded into high schools and colleges. Luther's presence was felt in church, school, and family in much the same way as in the original communities in Europe. During the first half of the twentieth century the Saint Louis edition of Luther's works, also known as 'Walch II', was commonly acquired and used by IELB pastors. Other German editions were used in the IECLB. Thereafter, some pastors acquired single volumes of the American edition of *Luther's Works.*

Since the new generations were no longer fluent in German or English, it became necessary to provide Spanish and Portuguese translations. A selection of Luther's works in ten volumes was published in Argentina under the sponsorship of Publicaciones El Escudo, New York (Luther 1967). The liturgical renaissance found expression in the publication of *El Culto Cristiano* by Publicaciones El Escudo (1964).

In Brazil a joint effort by the Lutheran churches with support from German and American organizations resulted in the publication of the *Book of Concord,* including

Luther's catechisms and his Smalcald Articles (*Livro de Concórdia* 1981). A special volume of selected Luther's works was published in commemoration of Luther's 500th anniversary (Luther 1983). A special committee created by the churches set up a plan for the translation and publication of selected Luther works. So far eleven volumes have been published (Luther 1987–).

IV. Theological Reflection

In spite of persistent effort for close to two centuries, Luther's theology has not made a significant impact on Latin American societies, not even in Brazil. Even though church leaders were familiar with Luther's so-called doctrine of the two kingdoms, they had difficulties in coping with totalitarian regimes during the Second World War. Some pastors aligned themselves with Nazi rhetoric; others were imprisoned for ministering to people in their own (German) language. Most churches, Chile's being an exception, failed to take a firm, critical stance towards the violation of human rights by national dictatorships in the 1960s and 1970s that resulted in the imprisonment and 'disappearance' of hundreds of citizens (Dreher 2003). The fact remains that democratic constitutions of Latin American countries show no traces of Luther's presence and impact. It still remains to be investigated whether his thinking contributed to the definition and establishment of human rights in contemporary democratic constitutions. This should not surprise us since Luther's name is not even mentioned in an English handbook on politics published recently in Portuguese translation (MacKenzie 2011). The churches were in the process of creating themselves in their new environment until and even during the second half of the twentieth century; the number of people with doctoral degrees in theology was very small because the degree had to be earned in a foreign country. In the case of IELB, for instance, the first Th.D. degrees were received only in November 1973 (Beck 1973, Warth 1973).

IV.1. Theological Production

Nearly a quarter of a century ago Vítor Westhelle sketched the particular challenges of bringing Luther's thought into the Latin American context (1990). Latin American Lutherans and others have paid some attention to Luther's thought, with original contributions and translations of works in German or English (see the surveys of Fischer 1983; Brakemeier 2009). A number of theological leaders have cultivated dialogue with the theology of liberation and presented new insights on Luther's work and stance, chief among them being Walter Altmann and Martin Dreher (see esp. Dreher 1984). Altmann presented his ideas in a book-length study (1994) and addressed the 1993 Luther Congress on Luther's concept of freedom in that context (1995). Dreher's work also addressed societal issues in Luther, such as relationships between the church and governmental authorities (e.g., 2004), as does Ricardo Rieth's study of Luther's under-standing of greed (1996).

Nestor Beck brought Luther's and Melanchthon's concept of faith and justification by faith into dialogue with twentieth-century ecumenical statements on the subject in his assessment of the Augsburg Confession's definition of *doctrina fidei*. In contrast to many who place the Wittenberg doctrine of faith alongside other doctrines, Beck dem-onstrated that for Melanchthon, *doctrina fidei* is the whole cluster of teachings that both evoked and justified the Reformation (Beck 1973, 1985, 1987; cf. Warth 2003). In addition to studies focused on Luther (e.g., 2004, 2005), and working largely in a North American environment, the Brazilian Westhelle's systematic reflection shows the influence of his engagement with the Wittenberg reformer even when Luther's texts are not the focus of his analysis (e.g., 2007). Also noteworthy is the study of Luther's sacramental theology by Clovis Prunzel (2004).

Catholic research on Luther has not yet put down roots in Latin America despite engagement with his thought by both sharp critics (Segundo 1975; Echegaray 1981) and more favourable readings (Boff 1986).

Since 1983 Brazilian Lutheran theologians have participated regularly in the International Luther Congress. This Congress met at the Lutheran University in Canoas, Brazil, in 2007. Latin American works on Luther have been carefully recorded in the bib-liographies of the *Lutherjahrbuch*.

IV.2. Perspectives

Since the second half of the twentieth century many institutions of higher learning have acquired the status of universities that requires consistent research and graduate programmes.

In Brazil, for instance, there are: two Methodist universities (<http://www.unimep.br> and <http://www.metodista.br>; complete listing at <http://www.cogeime.org.br>), a Presbyterian university (<http://www.mackenzie.br>), and a Lutheran university. There are also over a hundred Protestant university centres, colleges, and seminaries. Having regard for Luther, their disciplines and programmes in theology, history, edu-cation, and law will certainly provoke studies on Luther's work (<http://www.ibict.br>; <http://www.bdtd.ibict.br>). Catholic universities also are known to have promoted studies on Luther. State universities, unlike those of the United States, do not provide 'Renaissance and Reformation' studies, and yet have sponsored theses and dissertations on Luther (e.g., Barbosa 2007).

The future will show whether the academic production of these institutions of higher learning will be of sufficient quality and relevance to impact society. The answer depends very much on whether international Luther scholars will continue cultivating their limited academic gardens or whether they will regard and use Luther as a source from which to extract solutions or at the least suggestions for helping solve identified human and global problems.

Some years ago a German publication asked whether Luther had reached us (Knuth and Krause 1983). Significantly perhaps, it contained no report from Latin America. Recalling Gadamer's concept of *Wirkungsgeschichte* (1975: 275), one may assume that students, lawyers, and politicians will study Luther only inasmuch as they have been impacted by his work. So far he appears to be a prisoner of the churches that call themselves Lutheran. In Latin America Luther has yet to become *patrimonium societatis*.

REFERENCES

Altmann, Walter (1994). *Lutero e Libertação. Releitura de Lutero em Perspectiva Latino-Americana*. São Leopoldo and São Paulo: Sinodal and Ática. English translation: *Luther and Liberation: A Latin American Perspective*, trans. Mary M. Solberg. Minneapolis: Fortress, 1992.

—— (1995). 'The Reception of Luther's Concept of Freedom in Latin American Liberation Theology'. *Lutherjahrbuch* 62: 167–84.

Barbosa, Luciane Muniz Ribeiro (2007). 'Igreja, estado e educação em Martinho Lutero. Uma análise das origens do direito à educação' [Church, State and Education in Martin Luther: An Analysis of the Origin of the Right to Education]. Master's thesis, Universidade de São Paulo. Available at <http://www.teses.usp.br/teses/disponiveis/48/48134/tde-11122007-085529/pt-br.php>.

Beck, Nestor L. J. (1973). 'Faith and Works: A Study of Articles IV–VI and XX of the Augsburg Confession'. Th.D. dissertation, Concordia Seminary, Saint Louis.

—— (1985). 'Christian Righteousness in the Augsburg Confession and Contemporary Ecumenical Documents'. Typescript available at Concordia Seminary Library, Saint Louis, Missouri.

—— (1988). 'Caracterização da Universidade Luterana do Brasil'. In Beck, *Igreja, Sociedade & Educação. Estudos em torno de Lutero*. Porto Alegre: Concórdia, 129–43.

—— (1987/2005). *The Doctrine of Faith: A Study of the Augsburg Confession and Contemporary Ecumenical Documents*, trans. Érico Sexauer. Saint Louis: Concordia. Spanish translation: *La Doctrina acerca de La Fe en la Confesión de Augsburgo y Documentos Ecumenicos*, trans. Érico Sexauer. Canoas: ULBRA.

Boff, Leonardo (1986). 'A significação de Lutero para a libertação dos oprimidos'. In Boff, *E a igreja se fez povo, eclesiogênese*, 3rd edn. Petrópolis: Vozes. English translation: 'Luther, the Reformation, and Liberation'. In *Faith Born in the Struggle for Life*, ed. Dow Kirkpatrick, trans. Lewstine McCoy. Grand Rapids, MI: Eerdmans, 1988.

Brakemeier, Gottfried (2009). 'Luthers Auftrag in Brasilien heute'. *Lutherjahrbuch* 76: 9–18.

CELSP—Comunidade Evangélica Luterana São Paulo (1987). *Projeto de Criação pela Via da Autorização da Universidade Luterana do Brasil*. Canoas: ULBRA.

Dreher, Martin (ed.) (1984). *Reflexões em torno de Lutero*, 3 vols. São Leopoldo: Editorial Sinodal.

—— (2003). *Igreja e Germanidade. Estudo Crítico da IECLB*, 2nd edn. São Leopoldo: EST.

—— (2004). 'Obrigkeit und kirchliche Ordnung beim späten Luther'. *Lutherjahrbuch* 71: 73–101.

Echegaray, Hugo (1981). 'Lutero y Münzer. Dos conceptiones antitéticas de la liberation'. In Echegaray, *Anunciar el reino*. Lima: Centro de Estudios y Publicaciones.

El Culto Cristiano (1964). Buenos Aires: Publicaciones El Escudo.

Fischer, Joachim (1983). 'Luther in Brasilien'. *Lutherjahrbuch* 50: 150–66.

Gadamer, Hans Georg (1975). *Wahrheit und Methode. Grundzüge einer philosophischen Hermeneutik*, 4th edn. Tübingen: Mohr/Siebeck.

Held, Heinz-Joachim (1998). 'Béla Léski. Um pastor migrante en un mundo en migración'. *Cuadernos de Teologia* 17: 7–34.

Knuth, Hans Christian and Christian Krause (1983). *Hat Luther uns erreicht? Antworten aus fünf Kontinenten*. Hanover: Lutherisches Verlagshaus.

Livro de Concórdia. As Confissões da Igreja Evangélica Luterana, 2nd edn. Porto Alegre: Concórdia; São Leopoldo: Sinodal.

Luther, Martin (1967). *Obras de Martin Lutero*, vols. I–X. Buenos Aires: Editorial Paidós; Ediciones La Aurora.

—— (1983). *Pelo Evangelho de Cristo. Obras Selecionadas de Momentos Decisivos da Reforma*. Porto Alegre: Concórdia; São Leopoldo: Editorial Sinodal.

—— (1987–). *Obras Selecionadas*, vols. I–XI. São Leopoldo: Editorial Sinodal; Porto Alegre: Concórdia.

MacKenzie, Iain (2011). *Política. Conceitos-Chave em Filosofia*, trans. Nestor L. J. Beck. Porto Alegre: Artmed. Orig. *Politics: Key Concepts in Philosophy*. London: Continuum, 2009.

Prien, Hans-Jürgen (1985). *La Historia del Cristianismo en America Latina*. Salamanca: Sígueme; São Leopoldo: Sinodal.

—— (1989). *Evangelische Kirchwerdung in Brasilien: Von den deutsch-evangelischen Einwanderergemeinden zur Evangelischen Kirche Lutherischen Bekenntnisses in Brasilien*. Gütersloh: Mohn.

Prunzel, Clóvis Jair (2004). *A Exortação de Lutero à Santa Ceia. A Retórica a serviço da Ética Cristã*. Porto Alegre: Concórdia; Canoas: ULBRA.

Rehfeldt, Mario L. (2003). *Um Grão de Mostarda. A História da Igreja Evangélica Luterana do Brasil*, Vol. I. Porto Alegre: Concórdia.

Rieth, Ricardo (1996). *'Habsucht' bei Martin Luther. Ökumensiches und theologisches Denken, Tradition und soziale Wirklichkeit im Zeitalter der Reformation*. Weimar: Böhlau.

Segundo, Juan Luis (1975). *Liberación de la teologia*. Buenos Aires: Lohlé. English translation: *The Liberation of Theology*, trans. John Drury. Maryknoll: Orbis, 1988.

Warth, Martim Carlos (1973). 'Existential Faith in a Secular World: A Comparative Study of Francis Pieper and Gerhard Ebeling on the Nature and Function of Faith'. Ph.D. dissertation, Concordia Seminary, Saint Louis.

—— (2003). *Fé Existencial num Mundo Secular*. Porto Alegre: Concórdia; Canoas: Ulbra.

Westhelle, Vitor (1990). 'Thinking about Luther in a Submersed Reality'. *Lutherjahrbuch* 57: 163–73.

—— (2004). 'The Dark Room, the Labyrinth, and the Mirror: On Interpreting Luther's Thought on Justification and Justice'. In *By Faith Alone: Essays on Justification in Honor of Gerhard O. Forde*, ed. Joseph A. Burgess and Marc Kolden. Grand Rapids, MI: Eerdmans, 316–31.

—— (2005). 'Luther on the Authority of Scriptures'. *Lutheram Quarterly* 19: 373–91.

—— (2007). *The Scandalous God: The Use and Abuse of the Cross*. Minneapolis: Fortress.

CONCLUSION

Venturing into the Study of Luther

L'UBOMÍR BATKA, IRENE DINGEL,
AND ROBERT KOLB

IN conclusion, the editors will not attempt to offer a comprehensive summary of Luther's way of thinking or its significance. The essays in this volume demonstrate the impossibility of such a brief synthetic synopsis. At best, concluding words can only point to tools and ideas that can aid further study.

Luther's theological challenge to the church of his day changed the agenda of Western Christian discussion quite radically; his ecclesiastical call for reform provided upheaval in the institutions of church and society. Beyond that, his cultural impact contributed to significant developments in language and literature within the German lands and to new ways of spreading ideas that shaped their formulation as well as their distribution. Both his actions and his thinking affected political and legal theory and practice within the German empire. Though his place in the formation of early modern European public life should not be exaggerated, he looms large over the societal landscape of many lands and cultures in the period. His influence endured, particularly through his publications, and that influence has continued to this day and has not been confined to Western Europe.

Luther's writings contain a vast array of insights and angles from which to assess reality and daily life. The sheer quantity of what his pen produced overwhelms some who consider a venture into his thought. Not only does Luther's thinking, as complex and as simple as the everyday challenges and dilemmas people find in different circumstances around the world, sometimes seem intimidating. The literature accumulated by the beginning decade of the twenty-first century that has explored and exploited his words certainly seems no less daunting. Nonetheless, individual readers and researchers, from the streets of São Paulo and San Francisco to the jungles of Togo and Tamil Nadu, have been attracted by his way of thinking. Scholars and students from schools in Adelaide and Aarhus to libraries in Beijing and Berlin, continue to turn to Luther for ideas for forming fresh perspectives on questions and problems that beset them in their contexts.

Luther's medieval German environment stands in contrast to many elements in every culture around the globe today. His view of life, its framework and its functions, arose in strikingly different circumstances from the surroundings of all those who delve into his work today. Despite this fact, his parsing of the human condition rings true and seems translatable in the widest spectrum of societal settings in this 'post-modern' world. Chinese educational reformers in the nineteenth century and Indian and South African social critics in the twentieth found inspiration and initiatives in his work for proceeding with their own tasks. The agenda he set for theological discussions of who God is and what it means to be human has occupied the Christian church's thinkers until this day. His conceptions of humanity and reality have influenced many of the shapers of modern thought, from Ludwig Feuerbach to Martin Heidegger.

How can new students of the Wittenberg reformer reach back five hundred years to sort out these conceptions of human life and truth? Honest and helpful engagement with his writings requires some grasp of the historical cultural and social environment that created the framework for his thought. This setting included the life of the church and the pious, the university and its thinkers, the political structures and societal crises of sixteenth-century Europe at the cusp of early modern Western ways of thinking and organizing society. Such historical context can be gained through a variety of studies of specific aspects of late medieval and early modern Europe. This concluding postscript presents some of the basic editions of the source material from Luther's own pen, some tools for studying these texts, and some of useful surveys of this thought, from which new students can gain a foothold in the exploration and application of his way of thinking to their own lives. This literature is vast; here are mentioned tools aimed largely at those working in an English-language environment but that will prove helpful to those in other environments as well.

Luther's writings began to be published in a 'collected works' in 1518. Two decades later his oeuvre had grown considerably, and his Wittenberg colleagues resolved to publish a new 'complete' works, the so-called 'Wittenberg edition' (after its place of publication) (1539–59). Within the troubled landscape of controversy over the interpretation of elements of Luther's legacy that followed his death and the Smalcald War, a rival 'Jena edition' (1555–8) soon appeared and became the edition of choice for several generations. One of Luther's student editors, Johann Aurifaber, provided supplements to these editions in the 'Eisleben edition' (1564–5); an edition of Luther's letters (1565); and a collection of his words at the supper table in the Augustinian cloister, where he and his family hosted students, colleagues, and guests, the 'Tischreden' (Table Talks, Eisleben, 1566).

A century passed before need was found to issue a new edition of Luther's collected writings, the Altenburg edition (1661/4), and its material was supplemented in the one-volume 'Halle edition' (1702). The 'Leipzig edition' of 1729/34 was followed quickly by a German translation of Latin writings and an updating of the language in the German writings, edited by Jena professor Johann Georg Walch (Halle, 1740–53); it was adapted and expanded by A. F. Hoppe in the 'Saint Louis' edition (1880–1910).

By the time this edition for North American German-reading pastors began to appear, the first edition of Luther's works composed according to the developing critical standards of modern editing appeared in the 'Erlangen' edition (1826–57), updated in its second edition (Frankfurt/M and Erlangen 1862–85). By the time its final volumes appeared, a new era had begun with the appearance of the first volumes of what now serves as the standard edition of Luther's works.

The monumental 'Weimar edition' serves scholars today as the most complete, extensive modern critical edition of what Luther put on paper, divided into sections presenting his general works of all genre (73 volumes), his work on the German Bible translation (12 volumes), his correspondence (18 volumes), and his Table Talks (6 volumes): *D. Martin Luthers Werke* (Weimar: Böhlau, 1883–1993). During the 110 years of its production nearly all leading German Luther scholars contributed. A number of other 'study' editions have appeared over the past century. The most significant of these are *Martin Luther. Studienausgabe*, edited by Hans-Ulrich Delius (Berlin and Leipzig: Evangelische Verlagsanstalt, 1979/1999, 6 volumes), *Martin Luther. Lateinisch-Deutsche Studienausgabe*, edited by Wilfried Härle, Johannes Schilling, and Günther Wartenberg (Leipzig: Evangelische Verlagsanstalt, 2006–9), and *Martin Luther. Deutsch-Deutsche Studienausgabe*, edited by Johannes Schilling (Leipzig: Evangelische Verlagsanstalt, 2012–).

Multi-volume collections of selected works of Luther may be found in libraries under his name, in a number of languages, including Japanese, Chinese, Korean, Spanish, Portuguese, and English. In English much of Luther's oeuvre appeared in *Luther's Works*, edited by Helmut T. Lehmann, Hilton C. Oswald, and Jaroslav Pelikan (Saint Louis and Philadelphia: Concordia/Fortress, 1958–86). A twenty-volume supplement has begun to make additional materials available in English, edited by Christopher Boyd Brown (2009–). For English-only readers access to Luther's printed sermons on the appointed lessons for Sundays and festivals is possible through the reprint of the *Sermons of Martin Luther: The Church Postils*, edited by John Nicholas Lenker (Minneapolis, 1905–9; Grand Rapids: Baker, 1983/95) and freshly translated *Sermons of Martin Luther: The House Postils*, edited by Eugene F. A. Klug (Grand Rapids: Baker, 1996).

Luther did not work alone. Particularly his colleague Philip Melanchthon supported him and in fact stimulated and expanded his thinking. Luther studies lead those who read the older reformer's works inevitably into contact with his younger comrade in arms. Melanchthon's works were edited already in the sixteenth century. The first modern edition that approaches complete coverage of his writings was published between 1834 and 1860, the *Corpus Reformatorum [1–25]. Philippi Melanthonis Opera quae supersunt omnia*, edited by C. G. Bretschneider and H. E. Bindweil (Halle and Braunschweig: Schwetschke). Improved editions of selected writings may be found in the seven volumes of *Melanchthons Werke in Auswahl [Studienausgabe]* edited by Robert Stupperich (Gütersloh: Mohn, 1951–75) and *Melanchthons Briefwechsel*, edited by Heinz Scheible et al. (Stuttgart-Bad Cannstatt: fromann-holzbog, 1977–).

The reading of Luther's and Melanchthon's texts may well be facilitated for scholars around the world by reading translations in their own languages, but engaging Luther on his own turf demands perusing the texts in early modern high German

(*Frühneuhochdeutsch*) or Latin. To aid the process of working one's way into the former, the authoritative dictionary of the German language launched by the brothers Grimm, Jakob Ludwig Carl and Wilhelm Carl, in 1854 serves as a reference for the language of the sixteenth century as well (*Deutsches Wörterbuch* [²Leipzig: Herzel, 1965–]). For most questions regarding sixteenth-century vocabulary Alfred Götze's *Frühneuhochdeutsches Glossar* (⁷Berlin: de Gruyter, 1967) suffices, supplemented by Robert R. Anderson, Ulrich Goebel, Oskar Reichmann, and Anja Lobenstein-Reichmann (eds.), *Frühneuhochdeutsches Wörterbuch* (Berlin: de Gruyter, 1986–) and Matthias Lexer, *Mittelhochdeutsches Taschenwörterbuch* (³⁸Stuttgart: Hirzel, 1992). For support from modern usage readers may consult the *Oxford Duden German–English Dictionary* (²Oxford: Clarendon Press/Mannheim: Brockhaus, 1997).

The lexicographical work of Charles du Fresne Du Cange, a seventeenth-century French historian and philologist, *Glossarium mediae et insimiae latinitatis* (Niort: Favre, 1883–7) remains the most complete guide to the Latin of Luther's time. J. F. Niemeyr's *Mediae Latinitatis Lexicon Minus* (Leiden: Brill, 1984) and—despite its geographical focus on Great Britain—the *Dictionary of Medieval Latin from British Sources* (London: Oxford University Press, 1975–) are also helpful. The *Oxford Latin Dictionary* (Oxford: Clarendon Press, 1968/2012) provides the standard classical vocabulary.

An extensive bibliography of such aids is found in Hans-Otto Schneider, 'Bibliographische Hinweise zur sprachlichen Erschließung der frühneuhochdeutschen Texte in unserer Ausgabe', in Irene Dingel (ed.), *Controversia et Confessio. Theologische Kontroversen 1548–1577/80, Kritische Auswahledition. 1. Reaktionen auf Das Augsburger Interim, Der Interimische Streit (1548–1549)* (Göttingen: Vandenhoeck & Ruprecht, 2010), 35–9.

Identification of Latin geographical references to towns and other places is facilitated by use of *Orbus Latinus* (Braunschweig: Klinkhardt & Biermann, 1971). The ecclesiastical calendar often determined the dates given for events in sixteenth-century Germany; to find on what day and month 'the Friday before the second Sunday after Trinity' or 'the eve of Saint Agatha's day' fell, readers can turn to Hermann Grotefend, *Taschenbuch der Zeitrechnung* (¹⁴Hannover: Hahn, 2007).

A host of biographies of Luther can help the reader to understand the course of Luther's career and something of his surroundings. The most detailed of these in English remains Martin Brecht's three-volume study, *Martin Luther. [1] His Road to Reformation, 1483–1521; [2] Shaping and Defining the Reformation, 1521–1532; [3] The Preservation of the Church* (Philadelphia: Fortress, 1985–1993), translated by James Schaaf from *Martin Luther, [1] Sein Weg zur Reformation 1483–1521; [2] Ordnung und Abgrenzung der Reformation 1521–1532; [3] Die Erhaltung der Kirche 1532–1546* (Stuttgart: Calwer Verlag, 1981–7). Two more recent biographies deserve intention: Volker Leppin, *Martin Luther* (Darmstadt: Primus, 2006), and Heinz Schilling, *Martin Luther: Rebell in einer Zeit des Umbruchs* (Munich: Beck, 2012).

Those who wish to explore Luther's theology may proceed from this volume to grasp an overview of his thought through a number of one-volume surveys. Those that have guided readers in the past half century include Paul Althaus, *The Theology of Martin Luther*, translated by Robert C. Schultz (Philadelphia: Fortress, 1966) from *Die Theologie Martin Luthers* (Gütersloh: Gütersloher Verlagshaus, 1962). Althaus's accompanying *The Ethics of Martin Luther* was also translated by Robert C. Schultz (Philadelphia: Fortress, 1972) from *Die Ethik Martin Luthers* (Gütersloh: Gütersloher Verlagshaus, 1965).

Gerhard Ebeling produced more of a hermeneutic to Luther's theology in his *Luther: An Introduction to His Thought*, translated by R. A. Wilson (Minneapolis: Fortress, 1970) from *Luther: Einführung in sein Denken* (⁵Stuttgart: Mohr/Siebeck, 2006). Bernhard Lohse's *Martin Luther's Theology, its Historical and Systematic Theology* was translated by Roy A. Harrisville (Minneapolis: Fortress, 1999) from *Luthers Theologie in ihrer historischen Entwicklung und in ihrem systematischen Zusammenhang* (Göttingen: Vandenhoeck & Ruprecht, 1995). Oswald Bayer's *Martin Luther's Theology: A Contemporary Interpretation* was translated by Thomas H. Trapp (Grand Rapids: Eerdmans, 2008) from *Martin Luthers Theologie: eine Vergegenwärtigung* (Tübingen: Mohr/Siebeck, 2004). Hans-Martin Barth's *The Theology of Martin Luther: A Critical Assessment* (Minneapolis: Fortress, 2012) was translated by Linda M. Maloney from *Die Theologie Martin Luthers, eine kritische Würdigung* (Gütersloh: Gütersloher Verlagshaus, 2009). Robert Kolb wrote *Martin Luther, Confessor of Faith* (Christian Theology in Context; Oxford: Oxford University Press, 2009).

Some people in many parts of the world find late medieval and early modern European history a fascinating theatre for viewing human life. Larger numbers find Martin Luther's way of thinking of significance for their own situations. However, the meaningful rendering of his insights into any contemporary cultural and social context demands sensitivity to the dynamics of Western European life in his time. Dynamic translations of historical texts, for instance those from Luther's pen, become possible through creative but disciplined readings. Translators of ways of thinking must have some sensitivity to the thought patterns and political, social, economic, institutional, and intellectual factors which impacted those thought patterns in another age and place. The illocutionary thrust of Luther's thinking must guide the reading of what he wrote, and its perlocutionary force can aid in assessing how he was understood in his day. From such readings of texts readers gain the ability to derive insights from him that can be of use in their own context.

Not all the problems which Luther addressed have parallels in twenty-first-century situations, of course, and not all twenty-first-century questions will find direct or even near equivalents in his time and in his thinking. Nonetheless, his concerns and insights did model an approach to the challenges of everyday life in his context that can broaden and deepen perceptions of our own situations. Readers of this volume will find in it a variety of models for imaginative and creative engagement with questions regarding the person and modus operandi of God, what it means to be human, and what gives human beings dignity and hope today as they seek orientation in fast-changing cultures and societies of various kinds.

Glossary

Active righteousness: According to Luther, the righteousness or identity within the relationships among human beings and in the care of creation, which is practised through obedience to God's commands and the various activities which concretize his love. Passive righteousness creates this active righteousness.

Alien righteousness: In Latin, *iustitia aliena*, better translated 'righteousness bestowed from outside the person'. Luther used it as a synonym for 'passive righteousness', the identity God gives believers out of unconditional grace and mercy.

Alien work of God: Luther's term for God's work of condemning sinners through the law, which he viewed as intended to bring them to repentance.

Allegorical method: A method of biblical interpretation (and the interpretation of other literary works), introduced in the context of Graeco-Roman culture and literary principles, particularly promoted by the third-century Alexandrian theologians Clement of Alexandria and Origen. It aimed to find spiritual significance behind the literal text. More broadly, the term is applied to a 'four-fold' interpretation, which sought to find meaning on the basis of the level of the literal wording of a text on three other levels, generally labelled (following John Cassian, 360–430/435) allegorical (a doctrinal concept, pointing to Christ, the sacraments, or the church), tropological (moral application to human life), and anagogical (pointing toward the mysteries of heaven). In Luther's view allegories were to be sought only to serve as a rhetorical means of repeating an idea firmly anchored in a literal text within the Scriptures.

Alloiosis: A Greek term meaning 'exchange'; used in rhetorical theories for metaphorical expressions. Zwingli labelled the communication of attributes between the divine and human natures of Christ a rhetorical device to express the unity of Christ's two natures in one person and not to signify an actual exchange of the properties between the two natures as such.

Anfechtung/tentatio: Luther's designation for spiritual struggles against temptations of all kinds, particularly against doubt and despair of God's love. He used the concept as the third of the triad which forms the proper study of Scripture, including *oratio* (prayer) and *meditatio* (meditation).

Anthropology: Doctrine or teaching concerning what it means to be human.

Apocalypticism: Derived from the Greek word for 'revelation' and in Greek the title of the final book of the New Testament, the word assumed early in church history the meaning of a particularly dramatic unfolding of the last day or days of the earth's existence, before and including the return of Christ to judge sinners. The term is used in the twenty-first century for a wide variety of cataclysmic events; this usage can obscure its sixteenth-century usage.

Calling/vocation: In Luther's terminology, not based on specific biblical usage of Hebrew or Greek equivalents, 'calling' refers to the call or placement by God of people in specific societal responsibilities. Christians, according to Luther, realize that their 'offices' (*Ämter*) or responsibilities in life are exercised in response to God's calling them to these responsibilities.

Canon law: The legal system developed within the church, which brought together into one code the decisions of bishops and councils which governed life in the church and much of society. The fundamental text of these laws was edited by Gratian, in his *Decretum* of 1140; with supplements it provided the foundation for a discipline taught at universities. Luther harshly criticized canon law for imposing above and beyond biblical revelation rules that were enforced in the lives of the Christian populace.

***Causa(e)*:** Aristotle developed (and his later followers further developed) a system of explaining the reality of all things, comprehended in four fundamental *causae*, better translated 'factors' rather than 'cause' in the strict sense. These four fundamental factors—the *formal*, which gives the design of a thing; the *effective*, which in the strict sense causes the thing to exist; the *material*, the stuff of which the thing consists; and the *final*, the goal or purpose of the thing— were subdivided to aid logical analysis. Luther and particularly Melanchthon often made use of this system of analysis.

Chalcedon, Council of: The fourth ecumenical council, held in Chalcedon, near Constantinople, in 451, formulated a settlement of the controversy over the teaching of Eutychus, that Christ's divine nature absorbs his human nature, a 'monophysite' view. The council formulated the doctrine of the communication of attributes of Christ's divine and human natures, that the two natures share their characteristics and are 'not blended together, not changed, not divided, not separated'. This phrase was variously interpreted by various sixteenth-century reformers.

Christology: The doctrine of the person of Christ, treating the relationship of the personal or 'hypostatic' union, his person, to his divine and human natures.

***Communicatio idiomatum*/communication of attributes:** The teaching of the Council of Chalcedon that the divine and human natures 'communicate their attributes' to each other, as they share the unique characteristics of each nature with the other. The Council taught that Christ's divine and human natures united in one person or 'hypostasis' and are 'not blended together, not changed, not divided, not separated'. Luther interpreted the communication of attributes as a potential argument in favour of his understanding of the true presence of Christ's body and blood as present in the Lord's Supper. He suggested that —by virtue of the two natures' sharing their characteristics, including the ability to be where God wills in more than one place at the same time, a property of the divine nature which is "communicated" to the human nature, —Christ's body and blood could be present in the Lord's Supper. Luther held that while in no way actually assuming the characteristics of the other nature as its own, each could exercise these characteristics.

Conciliarism: The belief that supported a strong role for and significant power of councils in the life of the church, particularly important in solving the great Schism of the fourteenth and early fifteenth centuries, in which finally three rival popes claimed power over Western Christendom. The position of the conciliarists was largely repudiated during the course of the fifteenth century, but their ideas were sufficiently widespread to permit Luther to appeal to the council as an authoritative voice which could decide his case.

Concupiscence: Desire, particularly desire to sin. Late medieval theologians debated over whether concupiscence was actually sinful or only the 'tinder' from which sins sprang. Luther held that concupiscence itself demonstrated a failure to fear, love, and trust in God above all things and thus violated the first commandment.

Consubstantiation: A view which held that in the Lord's Supper the substance, as understood in Aristotelian physics, of both Christ's body and the bread, his blood and the wine, existed on the altar at consecration and in the reception of the elements. Certain late medieval theologians held out the possibility that this view could have been true had the church not decided on the doctrine of transubstantiation at the fourth Lateran Council in 1215. Although this position is sometimes attributed to Luther, he sharply rejected it, regarding all attempts to explain the mystery of Christ's presence in the Supper as human reason's presumption.

Deus absconditus/revelatus: Luther's distinguished 'God hidden' (either by his simple majesty, which no creature, to say nothing of sinner, could grasp fully, or by human sinfulness that creates images of God that are false because they are based only on human imagination) and 'God revealed' (as Jesus of Nazareth in the incarnation and in the words of Scripture, as they are conveyed in oral, written, and sacramental forms). Luther also taught that the revealed God hides himself in crib and cross, by taking form in humble ways that human reason finds unworthy of the Divine.

Devotio moderna: A lay movement originating in the Netherlands in the fourteenth century in the writings of Gerhard Groote (1340–84), spread particularly by the Brethren of the Common Life. The Christocentric piety of the movement attracted many lay people into its congregations that cultivated a life of prayer and service within the community. In his schooling in Magdeburg and Eisenach Luther was exposed to the piety of this movement.

Diet: The designation of the assembly of the ruling 'estates' of the German empire and of the nobles and towns in individual German lands.

Disputation: A form of instruction and testing in the medieval university, begun in Western schools, building on an ancient tradition, in the twelfth and thirteenth centuries. Disputations were formal argumentative exchanges designed to assess students' abilities in logic and rhetoric or to give instructors the field on which to discuss their ideas and exchange points of view. Disputations took as their subject matter theses, short thetical statements, penned either by professors or by the student under professorial supervision.

Docetism: The ancient Christian heresy that denied that Christ, the second person of the Trinity, had actually assumed a human nature but instead claimed that his human appearance only 'seemed' (from the Greek *dokein*) to exist.

Donum Dei: Literally, 'God's gift,' which Luther distinguished from God's *favor*, his favour or grace. The latter designates his attitude and relationship toward human creatures; his gift(s) include all tangible, visible, and audible things human beings receive from him, especially their capabilities, opportunities, and efforts for service in the world.

Ecclesia: Literally, 'church', one of the three 'hierarchies' or 'estates' in medieval social theory, the situations or walks of life into which God places all human creatures, with responsibilities for the well-being of others through service in this area of life.

Ecclesiology: The doctrine of the church, embracing all aspects of the church's existence and life.

Election: The doctrine of God's gracious and unconditional choice of those who are brought to faith by the Holy Spirit to be his children. Luther held that believers can attribute their salvation ultimately to God's choosing them although he rejected the idea that God also predestines those who do not believe to damnation. He held these two seemingly contradictory theses in tension through his distinction of law and gospel. The law places the burden of responsibility upon the human creature; the gospel as it is delivered in oral, written, and sacramental forms acknowledges the Creator's responsibility for salvation. God's choice of the believer is a matter that can only be used to convey the gospel. Beyond that, no one should try to fathom the mystery of God's choosing his own.

Empire, Holy Roman: The political organization which brought together most German-speaking lands, founded by Charlemagne at the beginning of the ninth century. Its emperor was elected by seven 'electors', the princes of Brandenburg, the Palatinate, and Saxony, the archbishops of Mainz, Cologne, and Trier, and the king of Bohemia, a system set in place by the Golden Bull of 1356.

Eschatology: The doctrine of 'last things', including the final judgement by Christ at his return, the struggle between God and Satan, and the death of human beings. Luther's entire theology was permeated by the eschatological convictions that every human being stands every day in the judging and forgiving presence of God and that Satan battles against God throughout human history. He also expected the world to end within his lifetime or shortly thereafter, reflecting his acceptance of much medieval eschatological speculation, although he refused to assign a specific date to Christ's return to judge.

Estate(s) as German institutions: The political entities that constituted the governing assembly of the Holy Roman Empire under the emperor's leadership. The estates of the Empire embraced secular princes (dukes, counts, etc.), and princes of the church (archbishops, bishops, abbots). Free or imperial knights and free or imperial cities also took part in the diets of the empire but with fewer rights and voice in decision-making.

Estate(s) in medieval society: According to medieval social theory, the situations or walks of life into which God places all his human creatures, three in number, the household, which embraced both familial life and economic activities; society, particularly secular governance; and the church.

Ex opere operato: Literally, 'accomplished by [external] performance [of a task]'. This phrase was used to describe the validity of the performance of the sacraments. Although Roman Catholic theologians protested that it was a misunderstanding of the intent of the phrase, designed originally to base the validity of the sacraments only in the validity of the divine words that established them, the reformers all argued that in popular belief the phrase was understood to guarantee spiritual benefits from outward participation in sacramental acts, even apart from trust in Christ. All the Protestant reformers vehemently criticized this view. It ran afoul of Luther's insistence that God's Word bestows forgiveness and his grace only upon those who are moved to trust in him.

Experience: Experience played a significant role, according to Luther, in the development of the faith of Christians. In the cauldron of experiences of spiritual struggle and trial God bestows and strengthens trust in him, Luther taught, and he also highlighted the joy and peace which believers experience in the gospel of forgiveness and life through the work of Christ.

Faith: Under the influence of linguistic studies, particularly of the New Testament word *pistis*, by Erasmus and Melanchthon, Luther abandoned his late medieval view of faith as *fides*, a belief in the factuality of something, and taught instead that faith is *fiducia*, reliance, trust, dependence on the object of faith.

Favor Dei: Luther's explanation of the term 'grace', meaning that God gives his favour in his love to those whom he has chosen to be his and brought to faith. The *favor Dei* points to his attitude of steadfast mercy and love toward his people and to his relationship of love and faithfulness which he establishes with them on the basis of his Word of promise and the trust that responds to it.

Forensic justification: The justification of sinners on the basis of God's pronouncement of forgiveness for the sake of the death and resurrection of Jesus Christ. Seen by some as a 'legal fiction' because it uses the language of imputation, affirming the way God 'regards' sinners, it is in Luther's view a parallel to the way in which God created reality at creation, by speaking. Luther held that God's regard and his pronouncement of forgiveness create an unshakeable reality even if the mysterious presence of sin and evil in believers' lives persists. Forensic justification also focuses in some scholars' work on the courtroom metaphor of pronouncing innocent. Luther's usage, based on his understanding of God's Word, was broader though it embraced that metaphor as well.

Frömmigkeitstheologie: A twentieth-century designation for the theological development of approaches to cultivating piety, particularly in the late medieval period, that provided bridges into Luther's new reading of Scripture and into the openness of the populace to his ideas.

Hermeneutics: The study of interpretation, its methods, underlying assumptions, and goals.

Humanism: A movement of educational and cultural reform, arising in Italy in the fourteenth century and spreading north of the Alps rapidly at the end of the fifteenth century. It called for a reform of method, emphasizing the importance of effective communication of ideas through good rhetoric while not abandoning effective training in logic, and cultivating the ancient languages, classical Latin, Greek, and Hebrew in order to mine the sources. Its adherents criticized the scholastic secondary treatments and translations used at their time. Humanism influenced instruction at the University of Erfurt while Luther studied there and had attracted interest at the University of Wittenberg during his first years there. He used materials prepared by the Hebrew scholar Johannes Reuchlin and the Greek scholar Desiderius Erasmus before the arrival of Melanchthon in Wittenberg, but it was Melanchthon's presence that enhanced the role of humanism in Wittenberg instruction and made the university a centre of its spread throughout Germany and beyond.

Hussites/Hussitism: The followers and belief system of the Bohemian reformer Jan Hus (c.1369–1415), who was burned at the stake for heresy at the Council of Constance, particularly for his teaching that the church should be defined as the elect children of God, not the hierarchy, and for his insistence that the chalice should be given to the laity.

Imitatio Christi: The way of life cultivated especially by the Brethren of the Common Life which accentuated the simple, devout following of Christ's example. This concept was spread above all through writings such as the *Imitatio Christi* of Thomas à Kempis (1380–1471).

Incurvatus in se: Literally, 'curved in upon oneself', a definition for sin that Luther used frequently, indicating that sinners are self-seeking and self-centred, finding a substitute for God in their own persons.

Indulgence: An act or document granting the complete or partial remission of the temporal punishments attached to sins forgiven in the sacrament of penance by the priest. Indulgences were popularly understood in the Late Middle Ages as pardon of eternal guilt itself. The doctrine and rules for the practice of dispensing indulgences had not yet been developed at Luther's time. Therefore, his call for further discussion of both the doctrine and practice of indulgences in his Ninety-five Theses was in fact a normal academic exercise. He objected to the abuses associated with the sale of indulgences associated with the campaign of Archbishop Albrecht of Mainz to use this source of income to pay the papacy for his assuming more than one ecclesiastical office at an age when he was not yet qualified to assume such offices.

Joyous exchange: In German, *'fröhlicher Wechsel'*, in Latin, *'commercium admirabile'*, Luther's expression for the saving activity of Christ with the metaphor of the exchange of property executed according to Germanic common law in a marriage. The bridegroom, Christ, takes possession of the sins of the sinner, and the bride, the sinner, receives the righteousness and innocence of Christ.

Justification: Literally, to make righteous, the doctrine of the restoration of the human being's righteousness and proper relationship with God, accomplished on the basis of the work of Christ, and effected through the word of forgiveness which comes in oral, written, and sacramental forms, according to Luther.

Larva Dei/**mask of God**: Luther's phrase for Christians as they exercise their callings in carrying out love and service for other people and the rest of creation. He viewed the actions of believers in performing their responsibilities in the various situations of human life as tools of God's providential care.

Loci communes **as literary genre**: Melanchthon issued the first edition of his handbook for organizing teaching of the faith under the title *Loci communes Rerum Theologicorum* in 1521. It reflected particularly Luther's distinction of law and gospel. Highly praised by Luther, the work appeared in two later editions (1535, 1543), fully restructured. This work provided the foundation for later Lutheran dogmatic teaching.

Loci communes **as method**: Literally, 'common places', a method for learning and teaching in all academic disciplines cultivated by humanists. It rested on Aristotle's use of *'topoi'*, topics, which became a standard part of rhetorical theory as a tool for the organization of ideas gleaned from other writers. Melanchthon adapted new developments in the use of the *loci communes* by Rudolf Agricola and Erasmus and in his 1521 *Loci communes Rerum Theologicorum* established this method as a key to theological study.

Marvellous duel: *'Duellum mirabile'*, Luther's metaphor for the conflict between Christ and Satan, in which Christ defeats the Devil, death, and human sinfulness through his resurrection. This concept is well expressed in Luther's explanation of the second article of the Apostles' Creed in the *Large Catechism* and in his hymn, 'Christ Jesus Lay in Death's Strong Bands'.

Masks of God: See *Larva Dei*

Means of grace: A medieval term which Luther relatively seldom used, but which by the end of the sixteenth century had become a fundamental element of Lutheran dogmatic terminology. It refers to the tools or instruments with which the Holy Spirit delivers and works with God's Word in the gospel of Christ in oral (preaching, absolution, conversation of Christians with one another), written (Scripture, as the authoritative source of all uses of God's Word, and other forms of Christian literature), and sacramental (baptism and the Lord's Supper) forms.

Modalism: A term for the ancient Christological heresy that denied the distinct existence of three persons within the Godhead, teaching instead that God appears in three different modes, as Father, Son, and Holy Spirit. Modalism is also labelled Sabellianism, after one of its alleged advocates, or 'monarchianism'.

Monastic vows: The vows made as one becomes a monk or a nun, pledging oneself to lifelong poverty, chastity, and obedience. Luther criticized the imposition of such vows upon the young and the popular belief that taking these vows provided a more certain, even if more difficult, path to heaven.

Mysticism: A term used in so many different ways that readers must carefully ascertain what individuals authors mean with it. In the Middle Ages it includes views ranging from (1) the belief represented in the Pseudo-Dionysian corpus (writings attributed to the Athenian convert of Saint Paul, Acts 17:34, but written in the fifth or sixth century), which taught a Neoplatonic view of the union of the human creature with God, furthered in a somewhat similar form by the Dominican Meister Eckhart (*c*.1260–1328), to (2) popular devotional piety which emphasized emotional nearness to God and faithful service to him.

Natures of Christ: The doctrine that Jesus Christ is the incarnate second person of the Trinity, who unites in the 'hypostatic' or 'personal' union the second person of the Trinity and the human creature, born of the Virgin Mary, Jesus of Nazareth. Disputes over the exact relationship of the two natures plagued the early church, especially in the fourth and fifth centuries, and also figured in Reformation-era debates in connection with the Lord's Supper. See 'Chalcedon, Council of' and '*communicatio idiomatum*'.

Neoplatonism: A philosophical system originating in third-century Alexandria, propagated above all by Plotinus, Prophyry, and Proclus, continuing and expanding on critical elements of Plato's thought, and emphasizing the original and ultimate unity of all things in an impersonal spiritual essence, and the descent of various planes of existence ever downwards into the material. Luther rejected the Neoplatonism found in the tradition and in its revival in Renaissance circles in the fifteenth century.

Nominalism: A philosophical system, opposed to 'realism', which taught that human language and conceptualization emerges from encounters with individual things that produce in the mind generalizations which are codified as words and concepts; these 'universals' have no real existence in and of themselves. In scholarly literature it is often associated with the thought of William of Ockham, but the simple equation of nominalism, Ockham's own thought, and the 'Ockhamism' which allegedly stems from him has become problematic for scholars in recent years.

Ockhamism: The term used to designate a large, influential group of thinkers that emerged in the wake of the teaching of William of Ockham (*c*.1285–1347), reflecting a nominalistic view of reality, emphasizing the almighty, sovereign power of God as Creator, holding that God makes a pact or covenant with human creatures which requires them to do their best (*facere quod in se est*) in order to win the grace that enables them to do the good works required for salvation. Luther adopted much of Ockham's understanding of God's power but sharply rejected his understanding of the way of salvation. Recently some scholars have questioned whether all those who employed elements of Ockham's thought can actually be considered to constitute a single 'school'.

Oeconomia: Literally, 'household', one of the three 'hierarchies' or 'estates' in medieval social theory, the situations or walks of life into which God places all human creatures, with given responsibilities for the well-being of others through service in this area of life. The household embraced both family life and economic activities.

Original sin: The original rejection of God, by Adam and Eve in the Garden of Eden, that is passed from parents to children. The medieval focus on the inherited and inherent nature of sin in every human being became a part of Luther's teaching, but his emphasis fell upon this 'original sin' as the 'root' of all other sins in every individual because both in Genesis 3 and in every human life it consisted of the doubt of God's Word and the rejection of God as Lord, or, as he wrote in the *Small Catechism*'s explanation of the first commandment, the failure to 'fear, love, and trust in God above all things'.

Passive righteousness: According to Luther the righteousness or identity in God's sight which God bestows through forgiveness of sins, unconditionally out of his grace. Out of passive righteousness proceeds active righteousness, the performance of God's commands.

Pelagianism: The teaching that human beings have the potential with little or no aid from God, apart from grace, to please God and be saved. Named after the early fifth-century British monk, Pelagius, who debated Augustine over grace and free will, Pelagianism became a designation for a variety of views that minimized God's grace and emphasized the ability of human beings on the strength of their own free will to meet God's standards for righteousness.

Penance: The sacrament of repentance, which in medieval theology included (1) contrition, variously defined by theologians as genuine sorrow over sin for the sake of the love of God, or as mere terror, also for less worthy reasons, in the face of God's judgement (labelled *attritio*), (2) oral confession of sins to a priest and reception of absolution of eternal guilt, and (3) satisfactions to alleviate the temporal punishment which sin also imposes, either through good works assigned by the priest or, in the late medieval practice, the purchase of an indulgence. Luther taught that repentance permeates the Christian life, as he applied law and gospel to believers on a daily basis, and that individuals should confess their sins to one another, and especially to their pastors, and receive from their confessor the pronouncement of the forgiveness of sins.

Pietism: A movement beginning in the seventeenth century, with foreshadowings in the writings of the sixteenth-century reformers, which emphasized the practice of Christian piety, in Bible reading and prayer, with strict adherence to God's commands. Scholars dispute its origins, assigning the origin to early seventeenth-century devotional writers within Lutheran churches or to Philipp Jakob Spener (1635–1705) later in the century.

Pneumatology: The doctrine of the Holy Spirit, his person and his work.

Politia: Literally, 'community', one of the three 'hierarchies' or 'estates' in medieval social theory, the situations or walks of life into which God places all human creatures, with given responsibilities for the well-being of others through service in this area of life. Luther followed medieval usage in defining the *politia* most often as governmental authorities, but he also included the responsibilities of citizens and subjects in relationship to those authorities and to each other within society as part of the situation of the *politia*.

Postil: A literary genre, a collection of sermons on biblical texts, by the time of the Reformation specifically on the assigned lessons (pericopes) for the Sundays and festivals of the church year. Postils appeared first in the High Middle Ages (e.g., the widely influential commentary on Scripture by Nikolaus of Lyra [1270/5–1349], which Luther used extensively). Luther wrote sermons for Advent and Christmas, his 'Wartburg Postil' at the Wartburg in 1521/2. Certain of Luther's students edited selected sermons into his *Church Postil* in the 1520s and again in the 1540s and also in the 1540s into the *House Postil*.

Preached/unpreached God: Luther's paraphrase of his distinction between *Deus revelatus* (God revealed) and *Deus absconditus* (God hidden). In his semi-literate society the chief means by which the revelation of God in Christ and in Scripture came to the people was through the sermon.

Predestination, See Election

Presence of Christ: Luther accentuated God's presence and most of all the presence of Christ, in the various forms of his Word. He saw a unique form of Christ's presence in the presence of his body and blood in the mystery of the Lord's Supper, in which he believed God gives recipients in an unexplainable fashion 'the forgiveness of sins, life, and salvation' through the true presence of the body and blood sacrificed and risen for the salvation of his people.

Prevenient grace: The term in medieval theology that accentuated the temporal priority and theological necessity of God's grace coming before all human efforts at reconciliation with God.

Promise: Luther emphasized the nature of God's Word of gospel as his promise of forgiveness of sins, life, and salvation through Christ's work. The nature of a promise is that it cannot be proven by rational analysis but simply must be trusted. Thus, it is the appropriate way in which the Creator communicates with creatures who are to depend on him without condition.

Proper righteousness: In Latin, *iustitia propria*, better translated 'righteousness performed by the person'. Luther used it as a synonym for 'active righteousness', the performance of God's commands both in relationship to God and in relationship to other human beings and the entire created order.

Proper work of God: Luther's term for God's work of forgiving sins and bestowing life and salvation upon sinners, as he brings them his gospel through the Word in oral, written, and sacramental forms.

Quadrivium: In the medieval curriculum, following ancient educational models, the four disciplines that built on the *trivium* and completed the foundational studies required in the school. The quadrivium consisted of arithmetic, geometry, astronomy, and music.

Rationalism: The philosophical teaching that emphasized the primacy of human reason. The term is applied to the movement that stands at the centre of the late seventeenth- and eighteenth-century Enlightenment.

Realism: A philosophical system, opposed to 'nominalism'; according to the realist view generalizations or universals stem from eternal forms, for some, in the mind of God, and that these forms determine what exists in individual instances, in Plato's system, for instance, as 'shadows' of the eternal forms.

Sacrament: For Luther, a form of God's Word, in which his promise is expressed in oral language accompanied by an external 'sign' or physical elements. Luther defined as 'sacrament' those forms of conveying the gospel that Christ commissioned himself in Scripture that convey the forgiveness of sins according to his promise, and that have the external elements. He rejected the medieval rites of ordination, marriage, confirmation, and extreme unction as sacraments. At times he labelled confession and absolution a sacrament, at other times he saw it as a renewal and continuation of baptism. Baptism and the Lord's Supper remained for him as sacraments because they convey 'forgiveness of sins, life, and salvation'.

Schwärmer(ei): Luther's terms, meaning 'raver' and 'raving' for those who looked for an inner illumination from the Holy Spirit apart from the external forms of God's Word.

Seelsorge: Literally, 'care of souls'. Luther's theology arose out of the exchange between the revelation of God's truth in his Word and proper spiritual care of believers through the call to repent for those caught in sin and the Word of deliverance through Christ for the repentant.

Simul justus et peccator: Literally, 'at the same time a righteous person and a sinner'. Luther recognized the mystery of the continuation of sin and evil in the lives of those who through God's word of forgiveness have become totally righteous in his sight. This relatively seldom-used phrase but ever-present concept in his writings emphasized that believers are totally righteous by God's creating the reality of their righteousness through his Word but remain totally afflicted by sin until deliverance through death and resurrection.

Soteriology: The doctrine of salvation, including all aspects of the work of Christ and its application to human lives.

Sub contrario/sub contraria specie: Literally, 'under the contrary form', often translated 'under the appearance of opposites', Luther's phrase describing God's mysterious way of dealing with sinners, in which his wrath or his seeming abandonment of the individual functions as a call to repentance. Luther refused to find explanations for God's 'appearance as the Devil' in people's lives in all cases.

Subordinationism: A Christological heresy arising in the second and third centuries out of a Neoplatonic framework which held that Jesus Christ was a divine person but of a lower level of divinity and subordinate to the Father. Arius is the most prominent representative of this view.

Theologia crucis/**Theology of the cross:** Luther's designation for a hermeneutical framework that accentuated the distinction of the hidden and revealed God, the necessity of trust rather than human reason as the means of relating to God, the sacrificial death and resurrection of Christ as the basis of salvation, the continuing suffering of the church and individual believers in the battle between Christ and Satan, and the call of believers to carry the burdens of others in love for the neighbour. The phrase originated in the context of his Heidelberg Theses of 1518, which focused on the first two of the elements just listed; all elements of the theology of the cross continued to guide Luther's thinking throughout his life.

Theosis: The soteriological teaching that salvation comes to human beings through their 'divinization', prominent in strains of Eastern Orthodox theology, proceeding from the works of Gregory of Palamas (1296–1358). The concept has been introduced into Luther studies as an interpretation of Luther's doctrine of justification in recent years.

Theses: The brief propositions put forth for debate in a medieval disputation.

Transubstantiation: A view which held that in the Lord's Supper the substances, as understood in Aristotelian physics, of the physical elements, bread and wine, disappear and are replaced in the consecration of the sacrament by the substances of Christ's body and his blood. Luther rejected this view as an attempt to explain in rational terms the mystery of the true presence of Christ's body and blood in the Lord's Supper.

Trivium: In the medieval curriculum, following ancient educational models, the foundational basis of education, consisting of grammar, rhetoric, and logic.

Two kingdoms: A phrase used by Luther in at least three different ways: (1) seldom, as designation for the institutions of church and secular governmental authority; (2) the domains of God and Satan and their respective ways of exercising power, locked in unceasing conflict; and (3) the spheres of the human relationship with God and of the human relationship with all other creatures, especially human beings.

Two realms or regiments: A phrase used by Luther for the third type of 'kingdoms' listed above, the two spheres of human relationship, with God and with other creatures. Also labelled by Luther God's 'heavenly or eternal' realm and God's 'earthly or temporal' realm, the two spheres of human life integrated the various aspects of daily living for Luther.

Typology, typological interpretation: A method of interpretation which views specific Old Testament individuals, rites, and events as foreshadowings of the New Testament unfolding of God's plan of salvation in Christ. Typological interpretation permeated Luther's treatment of the Old Testament,

Usury: For Luther and much of the medieval tradition, usury, or the taking of interest for money loaned, was sinful, a failure to share temporal goods willingly and freely with others.

Via antiqua: Literally, 'the old way', a designation in the late medieval university for the realist school of thought.

Via moderna: Literally, 'the new or modern way', a designation in the late medieval university for the nominalist school of thought.

Vocation, see Calling

Vulgate, Vulgata: The Latin translation of the Bible, the work of Jerome (c.347–419/420) and others on the basis of earlier translations and Hebrew and Greek manuscripts. It was passed down through the Middle Ages with various adaptations. The Vulgate was regarded as the official text of Scripture and was officially made so by the Council of Trent.

Will, human, bound and free: Luther regarded the human will, the organ for decision-making, as bound in its ability to commit itself to trust in and love for God. Sin has bound the will to decide always to adhere to other gods. In the sphere of human relationships on earth and actions within the created order Luther acknowledged the ability to make decisions even though also in this realm sin had limited this ability.

Wittenberg Articles: A document drawn up by Melanchthon on the Lord's Supper in 1536, which led to agreement between Luther and his Wittenberg supporters, on the one hand, and, on the other, Martin Bucer of Strasbourg and his followers.

Wittenberg circle: The group of colleagues, students, and other adherents around Luther, both resident in Wittenberg and also active in many other locations, who aided him in carrying out his Reformation, assuming a wide variety of tasks in the work of reform.

Word of God: Luther viewed God's Word as his creative instrument, whereby he brought the entire creation into existence (Gen. 1), and through which he effected his will among human beings throughout human history. He distinguished in Scripture, the authoritative source of God's communication with his human creatures, the 'law' as the expression of God's will for human performance from the 'gospel' as the message of life and salvation in Christ. He used in limited fashion the designation of Jesus Christ as the 'Word made flesh' (John 1:14) and regarded God's Word, especially the gospel, in oral, written, and sacramental forms as active, effective instruments through which God carries out his will.

Worms, diet of: The assembly of the German empire in the city of Worms in 1521, at which Emperor Charles V condemned Luther as an outlaw. Luther stood before the emperor and refused to recant. Sources for the final words of the quotation ascribed to him, 'here I stand, I cannot do otherwise', are relatively late.

Index

Printed in the USA
CPSIA information can be obtained
at www.ICGtesting.com
CBHW041357280923
1178CB00009B/310

9 780198 766476